1900

Monroe County, Kentucky
CENSUS

Pansy Page Allison

Heritage Books
2025

HERITAGE BOOKS

AN IMPRINT OF HERITAGE BOOKS, INC.

Books, CDs, and more—Worldwide

For our listing of thousands of titles see our website
at
www.HeritageBooks.com

A Facsimile Reprint
Published 2025 by
HERITAGE BOOKS, INC.
Publishing Division
5810 Ruatan Street
Berwyn Heights, MD 20740

Mountain Press
Signal Mountain, Tennessee
1999

International Standard Book Number
Paperbound: 978-0-7884-9503-8

MONROE COUNTY KENTUCKY
1900 CENSUS

Transcribed and Indexed by
Pansy Page Allison
1999

PRECINCTS

GUM	1- 69
TURNER	70-123
BRUSH	132-182
MARTINSBURGH	183-214a
CENTER POINT	214b-256
TOMPKINSVILLE TOWN	257-261
TOMPKINSVILLE EAST	262-330
TOMPKINSVILLE WEST	331-405
UNION	406-448
GAMALIEL	449-508

EXPLANATORY NOTES

1. Enumerators often spelled names the way they sounded. It is helpful to sound out the name yourself to be sure you have seen all the listings. Some enumerators couldn't spell at all! And some were not very neat!
2. AGES are given according to the Federal instructions: Name of every person whose place of abode on JUNE 1, 1900 was with this family.

TWELFTH CENSUS OF THE UNITED STATES 1900
— P. 1 —

STATE - KENTUCKY
COUNTY - MONROE
Township or other division GUM
Enumerator THOMAS R. EVANS

Supervisor's Dist. No. _102_ Sheet No.
Enumeration Dist. No. _80_ _1_

No. of Family	No. of Dwelling	NAME	Relation	Color	Sex	Date of Birth Mon/Yr	Age	Marital Status	# Years married	Mother of how many children	# of these children living	Place of birth	Father	Mother	Occupation	Months not employed	Attended school	Can read	Can write	Speak English	Owned/Rent	Farm	# farm schedule
1	1	AGERS, JAMES J	HEAD	W	M	Jul 1877	22	M	6			KY	TN	KY	FARMER	0		✓	X	✓	R	F	1
		ANNA	wife	W	F	May 1878	22	M	6	4	4	KY	TN	TN				✓	✓	✓			
		MATHEW A	Son	W	M	May 1895	5	S				KY	KY	KY									
		JOHN	Son	W	M	Jan 1897	3	S				KY	KY	KY									
		(L-?)(S-?)SIE	Dau	W	F	Mar 1898	2	S				KY	KY	KY									
		JAMES J	Son	W	M	Oct 1899	7/12	S				KY	KY	KY									
2	2	GREEN, NATHAN W	HEAD	W	M	Dec 1847	37	M	8			KY	—	—	FARMER	0		✓	✓	✓	R	F	2
		SUSIE (C.?)	wife	W	F	Mar 1847	—	M	8	4	4	KY	TN	KY									
		WILLIE H.	Son	W	M	Apr 1892	8	S				KY	KY	KY									
		FANNIE M.	Dau	W	F	Feb 1894	6	S				KY	KY	KY									
		PEARLY	Dau	W	F	Nov 1895	4	S				KY	KY	KY									
		EDDIE	Dau	W	F	Dec 1897	2	S				KY	KY	KY									
3	3	SHORT, WILLIAM	HEAD	W	M	Mar 1833	67	Wd				KY	NC	NC	FARMER	0		✓	X	✓	Own	F	3
		MARY A	Dau	W	F	Aug 1863	36	S				KY	KY	KY				✓	✓	✓			
		JOSEPH B	Son	W	M	Oct 1865	34	S				KY	KY	KY				✓	✓	✓			
		CARVER, KIT	LODGER	B	M	May 1845	55	S				KY	KY	KY	SERVANT	0		X	X	✓			
4	4	?COBY, JOHN J.	HEAD	W	M	Apr 1864	36	M	13			KY	TN	TN	FARMER	0		✓	✓	✓	R	F	4
		DRUSILA	wife	W	F	May 1864	36	M	13	7	5	TN	TN	TN				✓	✓	✓			
		WILLIAM S.	Son	W	M	Jan 1888	12	S				KY	KY	TN	FARM LABORER	0	2	✓	✓	✓			
		(?) SERNIE (L.?)	Son	W	M	Sept 1889	10	S				KY	KY	TN	" "	0	2	✓	✓	✓			
		FLORA M.	Dau	W	F	Apr 1892	8	S				TX	KY	TN		0		✓	X	✓			
		(?) TESSA G.	Son	W	M	Aug 1897	2	S				KY	KY	TN									
		ELNORA	Dau	W	M	Oct 1899	7/12	S				KY	KY	TN									
5	5	TEMPLE, CAMILA	HEAD	W	F	Oct 1871	28	Wd		5	3	KY	KY	KY	FARMER	0 3		X	X	✓	R	F	4
		BERTHA J.	Dau	W	F	July 1890	9	S				KY	KY	KY									
		THOMAS H.	Son	W	M	Oct 1892	7	S				KY	KY	KY									

STATE - KENTUCKY
COUNTY - MONROE
Township or other division GUM

Enumerator THOMAS R. EVANS

Supervisor's Dist. No. 102 Sheet No.
Enumeration Dist. No. 80 1

No. of Family	No. of Dwelling	NAME	Relation	Color	Sex	DATE OF BIRTH Mon/Yr	Age at last birthday	Marital Status	# Years married	Mother of how many children?	# of these children living	Place of birth (this person)	Father of this person	Mother of this person	Year of immigr.	# years in U.S.	Naturalization	OCCUPATION 10 years +	Months not employed	Attended school in month	Can read	Can write	Speak English	Owned or Rent	Owned - no mortgage	Farm or house	# of farm schedule
		TEMPLE, MARY D	Dau	W	F	Jan 1895	4	S				KY	KY	KY													
		" MINNIE	Step Dau	W	F	July 1882	17	S				KY	KY	KY						0	✓	✓					
		" VIRGIE	"	W	F	Oct 1884	15	S				KY	KY	KY						4	✓	✓	✓				
		" (?) ELIZA	"	W	F	Mar 1888	12	S				KY	KY	KY						4	✓	✓	✓				
6	6	VAUGHN, WILLIAM H	HEAD	W	M	Dec 1843	56	M	35			KY	TN	KY				FARMER	0		✓	✓	✓	OWN		F	5
		" FRANCIS (A or C)	Wife	W	F	May 1841	59	M	35	7	6	KY	KY	NC							X	X	✓				
		" NEWTON	Son	W	M	Dec 1874	25	S				KY	KY	KY				FARM LABORER	0		X	X	✓				
		" MARTHA B	Dau	W	F	Dec 1876	23	S				KY	KY	KY							✓	✓	✓				
		SINNA F.	Dau	W	F	May 1883	17	S				KY	KY	KY						0	✓	✓	✓				
7	7	CREEK, ELI B.	HEAD	W	M	Feb 1857	43	M	16			KY	KY	KY				FARMER	0		X	X	✓	Own		FF	6
		" ARCENIA P	Wife	W	F	Apr 1866	34	M	16	8	5	KY	KY	KY							✓	✓	✓				
		" THOMAS (?) C.	Son	W	M	Apr 1887	13	S				KY	KY	KY				FARM LABORER	0	3½	✓	✓	✓				
		" ELIGHA G.	Son	W	M	Jun 1889	10	S				KY	KY	KY				" "	0	5	✓	✓	✓				
		" ANNA B.	Dau	W	F	Feb 1893	7	S				KY	KY	KY						5	X	X	✓				
		" EZRA S.	Son	W	M	Aug 1895	4	S				KY	KY	KY													
		" GEO. I	Son	W	M	Mar 1900	3/12	S				KY	KY	KY													
8	8	CREEK, ISAAC S.	HEAD	W	M	Mar 1856	44	S				KY	KY	KY				FARMER	0		✓	✓	✓	Own		FF	7
		" MARY A.	Mother	W	F	Dec 1826	72	Wd				KY	KY	NC							X	X	✓				
		" MARGARET E.	Sister	W	F	Nov 1862	—	S				KY	KY	KY							X	X	✓				
		" JOHN S.	Nephew	W	M	Aug 1888	11	S				KY	KY	KY				FARM LABORER			X	X	✓				
9	9	BRANDON, WILLIAM	HEAD	W	M	Apr 1867	33	M	12			KY	KY	KY				FARMER	0		✓	✓	✓	R		F	8
		" MARY	Wife	W	F	Aug 1868	31	M	12	4	4	KY	KY	KY							✓	X	✓				
		" S— (?)(LOIS?)	Dau	W	F	Aug 1889	10	S				KY	KY	KY						3	✓	✓	✓				
		" BERLY (?) H.	Son	W	M	Jul 1890	9	S				KY	KY	KY						5	✓	✓	✓				
		" ANNA	Dau	W	F	Jul 1892	7	S				KY	KY	KY							✓	✓	✓				
		" HENRY	Son	W	M	Aug 1899	10/12	S				KY	KY	KY													

STATE - KENTUCKY
COUNTY - MONROE
Township or other division GUM   Enumerator T.R. Evans

Supervisor's Dist. No. 102   Sheet No.
Enumeration Dist. No. 80

No. of Family	No. of Dwelling	NAME	Relation	Color	Sex	DATE OF BIRTH Mon/Yr	Age at last birthday	Marital Status	# Years married	Mother of how many children?	# of these children living	Place of birth (this person)	Father of this person	Mother of this person	Year of immigr.	# years in U.S.	Naturalization	OCCUPATION 10 years +	Months not employed	Attended school in months	Can read	Can write	Speak English	Owned or Rent	Owned -no mortgage	Farm or house	# of farm schedule	
10	10	BRANDON, JONATHAN	HEAD	W	M	Oct 1862	37	M	16			KY	KY	KY				FARMER	0		✓	✓	✓	R		F	9	
		SARAH C	Wife	W	F	Apr 1865	35	M	16	7	6	TN	TN	TN						—	X	✓					
		MARY B.	Dau	W	F	—? 1894	15	S				KY	KY	TN						✓	✓	✓					Jan or June
		PEARL C	Dau	W	F	—? 1887	12	S				KY	KY	TN						✓	✓	✓					? Jan or Jun
		KATE	Dau	W	F	Dec 1889	10	S				KY	KY	TN						✓	X	✓					
		SAMUEL	Son	W	M	Oct 1893	6	S				KY	KY	TN													
		TIMMIE D	Son	W	M	Oct 1896	3	S				KY	KY	TN													
		NANNIE M	Dau	W	F	Nov 1899	6/12	S				KY	KY	TN													
11	11	BRANDON, MARTHA	HEAD	W	F	Mar 1831	69	Wd				KY	SC	PA						X	X	✓	OWN		FH		
		ELIZABETH	Dau	W	F	June 1858	41	Wd				KY	KY	KY						✓	✓	✓					
		VICTORIA	GrDau	W	F	June 1889	10	S				KY	TN	KY						3	✓	✓	✓				
12	12	BRANDON, GEORGE W.	HEAD	W	M	Mar 1872	28	M	7			KY	KY	KY				FARMER	0		✓	✓	✓	R		F	10	
		LIZA	WIFE	W	F	Feb 1879	21	M	7	2		KY	TN	KY							✓	✓	✓					
		MARY (E.?)	Dau	W	F	July 1894	5	S				KY	KY	KY													
		IVA P.	Dau	W	F	Feb —	9/12	S				KY	KY	KY													
13	13	BRANDON, ARTHUR	HEAD	W	M	Oct 1869	30	M	4			KY	KY	KY				FARMER	0		✓	✓	✓	R		F	11	
		PRISCILLA	Wife	W	F	Dec 1873	26	M	4	4		KY	TN	KY							✓	✓	✓					
		LAURA J.	Dau	W	F	Nov 1892	7	S				KY	KY	KY													
		ALLICE M.	Dau	W	F	Feb 1896	4	S				KY	KY	KY													
		ANNA M.	Dau	W	F	Apr 189—	2	S				KY	KY	KY													
		MARY M.	Dau	W	F	Aug 1899	9/12	S				KY	KY	KY													
14	14	SHOCKLY, BENJ.	HEAD	W	M	Feb 1875	25	M	6			KY	KY	KY				FARMER	0		✓	✓	✓	OWN		F	12	
		MANDY	wife	W	F	May 1873	27	M	6	3	2	TN	TN	TN							✓	✓	✓					
		SANFORD T.	Son	W	M	Nov 1894	5	S				KY	KY	TN													
		BO—?	Son	W	M	Sept 1898	1	S				KY	KY	TN													
15	15	BRYANT, GEO. H	HEAD	W	M	Nov 1874	25	M	3			KY	TN	KY				FARMER	0		✓	✓	✓	R		F	13	

STATE - KENTUCKY
COUNTY - MONROE
Township or other division: **GUM**
Enumerator: **T. R. EVANS**

Supervisor's Dist. No. **102** Sheet No. ____
Enumeration Dist. No. **80** ____

No. of Family	No. of Dwelling	NAME	Relation	Color	Sex	Date of Birth Mon/Yr	Age at last birthday	Marital Status	# Years married	Mother of how many children?	# of these children living	Place of birth (this person)	Father of this person	Mother of this person	OCCUPATION 10 years +	Months not employed	Attended school in months	Can read	Can write	Speak English	Owned or Rent	Owned -no mortgage	Farm or house	# of farm schedule
		BRYANT, LILIE H.	Wife	W	F	Jul 1879	20	M	3	1	0	KY	KY	KY				✓	✓	✓				
16	16	KEY, HENRY	HEAD	W	M	Nov 1866	33	M	12			KY	KY	KY	FARMER	0		X	X	✓	R		F	14
		SARAH J.	Wife	W	F	Sept 1866	33	M	12	7	4	KY	KY	KY				✓	✓	✓				
		BEN H	Son	W	M	Dec 1889	10	S				KY	KY	KY			5	✓	X	✓				
		MAGGIE	Dau	W	F	Dec 1891	8	S				KY	KY	KY										
		MOLLIE	Dau	W	F	Sept 1895	4	S				KY	KY	KY										
		CLAUDE W	Son	W	M	Mar 1898	2	S				KY	KY	KY										
17	17	MARSH, HENRY	HEAD	W	M	May 18	35	M	13			TN	TN	TN	FARMER	0		X	X	✓	R		F	15
		NANCY	Wife	W	F	May 1866	34	M	13	4	3	KY	KY	KY				✓	✓	✓				
		Benj. H.	Son	W	M	Jun 1889	10	S				KY	T	KY			0	✓	X	✓				
		JOHN (W. or M)	Son	W	M	Feb 1893	7	S				KY	TN	KY										
		ALICE	Dau	W	F	May 1900	1/12	S				KY	TN	KY										
18	18	KING, JOHN H.	HEAD	W	M	Oct 1834	35	M	11			KY	TN	KY	FARMER	0		✓	✓	✓	R		F	16
		MARY (C. or E)	Wife	W	F	Dec 1872	27	M	11	4	2	TN	TN	TN				X	X	✓				
		MINNIE S.	Dau	W	F	Dec 1889	10	S				KY	KY	TN				X	X	✓				
		MARTHA A.	Dau	W	F	Aug 1892	7	S				KY	KY	TN										
		MARSH, JOHN W.	Bro-in Law	W	M	Mar 1874	26	S				TN	TN	TN	FARMER	0		X	X	✓	R		F	17
19	19	SADLER, ELICK	HEAD	W	M	July 1855	44	M	15			TN	TN	TN	FARMER	0		✓	✓	✓	O	F	F	18
		MARY C.	Wife	W	F	Sept 1864	35	M	15	6	6	KY	KY	KY				✓	✓	✓				
		JOHN	Son	W	M	Aug 1880	19	S				KY	TN	KY	Farm Laborer			✓	X	✓				
		MARK (?)	Son	W	M	Apr 1883	17	S				KY	TN	KY	Farm Laborer	0		✓	✓	✓				
		MARY M.	Dau	W	F	Jan 1886	14	S				KY	TN	KY			4	✓	✓	✓				
		SALLIE F.	Dau	W	F	June 1888	11	S				KY	TN	KY			4	✓	✓	✓				
		LUCINDA J.	Dau	W	F	June 1890	9	S				KY	TN	KY			4							
		HOMER	Son	W	M	Aug 1892	7	S				KY	TN	KY										
		(?) BEREY A.	Dau	W	F	Dec 1894	5	S				KY	TN	KY										

STATE - KENTUCKY
COUNTY - MONROE
Township or other division — GUM
Enumerator — T.R. EVANS

Supervisor's Dist. No. 102 Sheet No.
Enumeration Dist. No. 80

No. of Family	No. of Dwelling	NAME	Relation	Color	Sex	DATE OF BIRTH Mon/Yr	Age at last birthday	Marital Status	# Years married	Mother of how many children?	# of these children living	Place of birth (this person)	Father of this person	Mother of this person	Year of immigr.	# years in U.S.	Naturalization	OCCUPATION 10 years +	Months not employed	Attended school in months	Can read	Can write	Speak English	Owned or Rent	Owned -no mortage	Farm or house	# of farm schedule
		SADLER, ALEXANDER P.	Son	W	M	Jun 1897	2	S				KY	TN	KY													
20	20	BROWN, JOE N.	HEAD	W	M	Jun 1868	31	M	7			KY	TN	TN				FARMER	0		X	X	✓	R		F	19
		" MARTHA A.	wife	W	F	Oct 1874	25	M	7	3	3	KY	KY	KY							✓	✓	✓				
		" ORIEN	Son	W	M	Jul 1893	6	S				TN	KY	KY													
		" VIDA	Dau	W	F	Sept 1895	4	S				KY	KY	KY													
		" GEORGE	Son	W	M	Dec 1897	2	S				KY	KY	KY													
21	21	McPEAK, ALBERT W.	HEAD	W	M	Oct 1871	28	M	6			KY	KY	KY				FARMER			✓	X	✓	?	?	F	20
		" MILLY J.	WIFE	W	F	May 1876	24	M	6	3	3	KY	KY	KY							✓	✓	✓				
		" OMER C.	Son	W	M	Feb 1895	5	S				KY	KY	KY													
		" MARY	Dau	W	F	Feb 1897	3	S				KY	KY	KY													
		" WILLIAM	Son	W	M	Nov 1899	6/12	S				KY	KY	KY													
22	22	LEWIS, JOSEPH	HEAD	W	M	Nov 1849	50	M	23			KY	KY	KY				FARMER	0		X	X	✓	R		F	21
		" MARTHA	WIFE	W	F	May 184-	51	M	23	2	1	TN	KY	TN							X	X	✓				
	23	GREEN, MARSHAL F.	HEAD	W	M	Feb 1878	22	M	1			KY	KY	KY				FARMER	0		✓	✓	✓	R		F	22
		" MARY D(?)	wife	W	F	Mar 1883	17	M	1	1	1	KY	KY	TN							✓	✓	✓				
		" JOEL, E.(?)	Son	W	M	— 1900	1/12	S				KY	KY	KY													
23	24	LEE, HARVEY J.	HEAD	W	M	Apr 1851	49	M	15			KY	KY	TN				FARMER	0		✓	✓	✓	R		F	23
		" CATHERINE E?	wife	W	F	Feb ?	?	M	15	3	3	KY	KY	NC				Farm LaborER	9		✓	✓	✓				
		" EDWARD F.	Son	W	M	Jun 1882	17	S				KY	KY	KY													
		" MERTIE	Dau	W	F	Jul 1887	12	S				KY	KY	KY						3	✓	X	✓				
		" HENRY B.	Son	W	M	Jan 1889	11	S				KY	KY	KY						3	✓	X	✓				
		" NANNIE G.	Dau	W	F	Oct 1895	4	S				KY	KY	KY													
24	25	LANCASTER, WILLIAM	HEAD	W	M	Jan 1844	46	M	20			KY	KY	KY				FARMER	0		✓	✓	✓	O		F	24
		" MARY C	wife	W	F	Apr 1860	40	M	20	12	6	KY	KY	TN							X	X	✓				
		" WILLIAM	Son	W	M	Aug 1886	13	S				KY	KY	KY				Farm Laborer	0		X	X	✓				
		" ELIZABETH	Dau	W	F	Sept 1887	12	S				KY	KY	KY							X	X	✓				

STATE - KENTUCKY
COUNTY - MONROE
Township or other division — GUM

Enumerator — THOMAS B. EVANS

Supervisor's Dist. No. _102_ Sheet No. ___
Enumeration Dist. No. _80_ ___

No. of Family	No. of Dwelling	NAME	Relation	Color	Sex	DATE OF BIRTH Mon/Yr	Age at last birthday	Marital Status	# Years married	Mother of how many children?	# of these children living	Place of birth (this person)	Father of this person	Mother of this person	Year of immigr.	# years in U.S.	Naturalization	OCCUPATION 10 years +	Months not employed	Attended school in months	Can read	Can write	Speak English	Owned or Rent	Owned - no mortgage	Farm or house	# of farm schedule
		LANCASTER, LUEZA (?)	Dau	W	F	Sept 1888	11	S				KY	KY	KY						0	X	X	✓				
		" MARY D.	Dau	W	F	Oct 1891	8	S				KY	KY	KY						0	X	X	✓				
		" JOHN (?)	Son	W	M	Mar 1892	8	S				TN	KY	KY							X	X	✓				
		" MAY (?)	Dau	W	F	Jan 1897	3	S				KY	KY	KY													
25	26	DISMAN, THOMAS F.	HEAD	W	M	Jul 1877	22	M	9			KY	TN	TN							X	X	✓	R		F	25
		" ELZIRA	wife	W	F	Jul 1876	23	M	9	3	3	TN	TN	KY							X	X	✓				
		" HENRY	Son	W	M	Jun 1893	6	S				KY	KY	TN													
		" EDWARD N.	Son	W	M	May 1896	4	S				KY	KY	TN													
		" MARTHA F.	Dau	W	F	May 1899	1	S				KY	KY	TN													
		" NEAL S.	Lodger	W	M	May 1850	50	S				TN	NC	TN				FARM LABORER	0		X	X	✓				
26	27	TURNER, ROBERT E.	HEAD	W	M	Apr 1838	62	M	40			KY	VA	VA				FARMER	0		X	X	✓	O	F	F	26
		" ELIZABETH	wife	W	F	Oct 1839	60	M	40	9	5	TN	TN	TN							✓	✓	✓				
27	28	COLLINS, JESSE	HEAD	W	M	Sept 1880	21	M	1			TN	TN	TN				FARMER	0		✓	✓	✓	R		F	27
		" FANNY L.	wife	W	F	Feb 1880	3	M	1	1	1	KY	TN	TN							✓	✓	✓				
		" HESTER E.	Dau	W	F	Nov 1899	6/12	S				KY	TN	TN													
28	29	DISMAN, JAMES R.	HEAD	W	M	Mar 1859	41	M	19			KY	KY	ALA				FARMER	0		✓	✓	✓	R		F	28
		" FANNY	wife	W	F	Dec 1863	36	M	19	8	5	KY	KY	KY						0	✓	✓	✓				
		" NANCY (?)	Dau	W	F	Mar 188-	16	S				KY	TN	KY							✓	✓	✓				
		" FRANK	Son	W	M	Oct 188-	—	S				KY	TN	KY				FARM LABORER	0	6	✓	✓	✓				
		" MELIA	Dau	W	F	Aug 1894	5	S				KY	TN	KY						0							
		" BESSIE	Dau	W	F	Nov 1896	3	S				KY	KY	KY													
		" CHRISLINE	Mother	W	F	Mar 1815	85	Wd		1	1	Ala	Ala	NC							X	X	✓				
29	30	WILLIAMS, JOHN W.	HEAD	W	M	Jul 1854	45	M	27			TN	TN	TN				FARMER	0		X	X	✓	R		F	29
		" NANCY A.	wife	W	F	Feb 1852	48	M	27	2	2	TN	KY	Ala							X	X	✓				
		" MALISSA M.	Dau	W	F	Nov 1978	21	S				KY	TN	TN							✓	✓	✓				
		" JANE H.	Aunt	W	F	Apr 1814	86	S				TN	NC	NC							X	X	✓				

STATE - KENTUCKY
COUNTY - MONROE
Township or other division GUM

Enumerator THOMAS R. EVANS

Supervisor's Dist. No. 102 Sheet No.
Enumeration Dist. No. 80

No. of Family	No. of Dwelling	Name	Relation	Color	Sex	Date of Birth Mon/Yr	Age at last birthday	Marital Status	# Years married	Mother of how many children?	# of these children living	Place of birth	Father	Mother	Occupation	Months not employed	Attended school	Can read	Can write	Speak English	Owned or Rent	Farm or house	# of farm schedule
30	31	COLLINS, OSIAS D.	Head	W	M	Oct 1844	55	M	20			TN	TN	TN	FARMER	0		X X	✓		R	F	30
		CARA J.	Wife	W	F	May 1854	46	M	20	8	8	TN	TN	TN				X X	✓				
		CLORA	Dau	W	F	Apr 1880	20	S				KY	TN	TN			6	✓	✓				
		CREDE C.	Son	W	M	Dec 1882	17	S				KY	TN	TN	FARM LABORER	0		✓	X	✓			
		MILDRED	Dau	W	F	June 1886	13	S				KY	TN	TN			3	✓	✓				
		SANFORD	Son	W	M	Apr 1890	10	S				KY	TN	TN	FARM LABORER	0	0	X X	✓				
		MARY A.	Dau	W	F	Jun 1893	7	S				KY	TN	TN									
		G——²	Dau	W	F	Jan 1897	3	S				KY	TN	TN									
		ONIA D.	Dau	W	F	Dec 1899	5/12	S				KY	TN	TN									
31	32	GREEN, EDMOND	Head	W	M	Sept 1846	53	Wd				TN	VA	VA	FARMER			✓	✓	✓	O	F F	31
		MAUD	Dau	W	F	May 1882	18	S				KY	TN	TN			2	✓	✓	✓			
		BENJ H.	Gr. Son	W	M	June —	10	S				KY	KY	KY			5	✓	X	✓			
		MERTIE J.	Gr. Dau	W	F	June —	6	S				KY	KY	KY									
		DAVIS, LUISA R.	Lodger	W	F	July 1877	22	Wd		1	1	KY	KY	KY				✓	X	✓			
		OMER C.	Lodger	W	M	Apr 1899	1	S				KY	KY	KY									
32	33	FRANKLIN, MILTON	Head	B	M	Mar 1876	24	M	1			KY	KY	TN	TANNER	0		✓	✓	✓	R	F	32
		ADA	Wife	B	F	Jan 1880	20	M	1			TN	TN	TN				✓	✓	✓	M	F	33
33	34	FRANKLIN, JOHN E.	Head	B	M	Apr 1856	44	M(3?)				KY	TN	KY	FARMER	0		✓	✓	✓	O	M F	33
		AMANDA J.	Wife	B	F	Dec 1849	50	M(3?)		10	9	TN	TN	TN				✓	X	✓			
		MARY A.	Dau	B	F	Jan 1879	21	S				KY	KY	TN				✓	✓	✓			
		HUBERT	Son	B	M	Jan 1882	18	S				KY	KY	TN	FARM LABORER	6		✓	✓	✓			
		BUD B.	Son	B	M	Jul 1885	14	S				KY	KY	TN	FARM LABORER		4	✓	✓	✓			
		HENRY C.	Son	B	M	Sept 1887	12	S				KY	KY	TN	FARM LABORER		4	✓	✓	✓			
		MAGGIE	Dau	B	F	May 1891	9	S				KY	KY	TN									
		CLORA B.	Dau	B	F	Nov 1895	4	S				KY	KY	TN									
34	35	GILLENWATERS, GEORGE W.	Head	B	M	Feb 1867	33	M	4			KY	VA	TN	FARMER	0		✓	✓	✓	R	F	34

STATE - KENTUCKY
COUNTY - MONROE
Township or other division: GUM
Enumerator: THOMAS R. EVANS

Supervisor's Dist. No. 102 Sheet No.
Enumeration Dist. No. 80

No. of Family	No. of Dwelling	NAME	Relation	Color	Sex	Date of Birth Mon/Yr	Age at last birthday	Marital Status	# Years married	Mother of how many children?	# of these children living	Place of birth (this person)	Father of this person	Mother of this person	Year of immigr.	# years in U.S.	Naturalization	Occupation 10 years +	Months not employed	Attended school in months	Can read	Can write	Speak English	Owned or Rent	Owned -no mortgage	Farm or house	# of farm schedule
		GILLENWATERS, SARAH S.	Wife	B	F	Nov 1872	27	M	4	3		TN	TN	TN							✓	✓	✓				
		" NORA B.	Dau	B	F	Sep 1896	3	S				KY	TN	TN													
		" WILLIAM E.	Son	B	M	Sep 1897	2	S				KY	KY	TN													
		" LUTHER	Son	B	M	Jan 1899	1	S				KY	KY	TN													
		" MARY	Mother	B	F	Jan 1844	56	Wd				TN	TN	TN							X	X	✓				
35	36	BROWN, GEORGE	Head	B	M	Dec 1860	39	M	16			KY	KY	TN				FARMER	O		✓	X	✓	R		F	35
		" MOLLIE	Wife	B	F	June 1863	37	M	16	8	7	KY	KY	KY							✓	✓	✓				
		" CECIL	Son	B	M	Apr 1879	21	S				KY	KY	KY				Farm Laborer	4	4	✓	✓	✓				
		" OLLIE	Son	B	M	Feb 1888	12	S				KY	KY	KY						3	3	✓	X	✓				
		" ROBERT E.	Son	B	M	Jul 1891	8	S				KY	KY	KY													
		" THOMAS E.	Son	B	M	May 1894	6	S				KY	KY	KY													
		" HOWARD H.	Son	B	M	Nov 1896	3	S				KY	KY	KY													
		" MITCHEL	Son	B	M	Dec 1898	1	S				KY	KY	KY													
		KINSLOW, DELLA	Neice	B	F	Jan 1883	17	S				KY	KY	TN						5	✓	✓	✓				
36	37	CHISM, GEORGE B.	Head	B	M	Nov 1858	41	M	15			KY	KY	KY				FARMER	O		✓	✓	✓	O		F	36
		" CAMILLA J.	Wife	B	F	Aug 1867	32	M	15	5	5	KY	KY	KY							X	X	✓				
		" WILHILMA	Dau	B	F	Sep 1885	14	S				KY	KY	KY			3				✓	X	✓				
		" ULYSSES	Son	B	M	May 1888	12	S				KY	KY	KY			4				✓	X	✓				
		" HARRISON	Son	B	M	Oct 1889	10	S				KY	KY	KY				Farm Laborer	O	4	✓	X	✓				
		" MARY	Dau	B	F	Feb 1892	8	S				KY	KY	KY													
		" DON DEMETRIS	Son	B	M	Aug 1893	6	S				KY	KY	KY													
37	38	TAYLOR, NEWTON J.	Head	B	M	Mar 1836	64	M	36			TN	TN	TN				FARMER	O		X	X	✓	R		F	37
		" POLLY A.	Wife	B	F	Jun 1854	45	M	36	0	0	TN	TN	TN							X	X	✓				
38	39	FRANKLIN, JAMES T.	Head	B	M	Mar 1873	27	M				KY	KY	TN				FARMER	O		✓	✓	✓	O		M F	38
		" LIZZIE E.	Wife	B	F	May 1885	15	M		0		KY	KY	KY							✓	✓	✓				
39	40	SAMPSON, JOHN J.	Head	W	M	Jan 1862	38	M	7			TN	TN	TN				FARMER	O		✓	X	✓	R		F	39

STATE - KENTUCKY
COUNTY - MONROE
Township or other division   GUM

Enumerator   THOMAS R. Evans

Supervisor's Dist. No. 102   Sheet No.
Enumeration Dist. No. 80

No. of Family	No. of Dwelling	NAME	Relation	Color	Sex	Date of Birth Mon/Yr	Age at last birthday	Marital Status	# Years married	Mother of how many children?	# of these children living	Place of birth [this person]	Father of this person	Mother of this person	Year of immigr.	# years in U.S.	Naturalization	Occupation 10 years +	Months not employed	Attended school in months	Can read	Can write	Speak English	Owned or Rent	Owned - no mortage	Farm or house	# of farm schedule
		SAMPSON, MARYETTA	Wife	W	F	Sep 1872	27	M	7	3	3	KY	KY	KY							✓	✓	✓				
		" WILLIAM F	Son	W	M	Apr 1893	7	S				KY	TN	KY													
		" JOHN H.	Son	W	M	May 1895	5	S				KY	TN	KY													
		" EARNEY E.	Son	W	M	Feb 1898	2	S				KY	TN	KY													
40	41	DEWEESE, FRANCIS M.	Head	W	M	Aug 1852	47	M	22			TN	NC	TN				FARMER	0		✓	X	✓	R		F	40
		" NANCY E.	Wife	W	F	Nov 1849	50	M	22	3	2	KY	VA	TN							✓	✓	✓				
		" CHARLES G.	Son	W	M	Aug 1878	21	S				KY	TN	KY				FARM LABORER	0								
		" LEN I	Son	W	M	Aug 1890	9	S				KY	TN	KY													
41	42	PENDGRASS, JETTIE	Head	W	M	May 1851	49	M	22			TN	TN	TN				FARMER	0		X	X	✓	R		F	41
		" SARAH M.	Wife	W	F	June 1862	37	M	22	7	5	KY	KY	KY							✓	✓	✓				
		" RICHARD W.	Son	W	M	Aug 1886	13	S				KY	TN	KY				Farm Laborer	0	0	X	X	✓				
		" ROSA	Dau	W	F	Apr 1890	10	S				KY	TN	KY						0	X	X	✓				
		" JESSE W.	Son	W	M	Aug 1898	1	S				KY	TN	KY													
		STINSON, ETTA	Dau	W	F	Aug 1873	16	Wd				KY	TN	KY						0	X	X	✓	R		F	
42	43	MARCUM, JAMES B.	Head	W	M	Jan 1848	52	M	33			TN	TN	TN				FARMER	0		✓	✓	✓	R		F	42
		" MARY	Wife	W	F	Feb 1847	53	M	33	8	7	TN	NC	TN							X	X	✓				
		" IDA B.	Dau	W	F	Dec 1877	22	S				KY	TN	TN							✓	✓	✓				
		" WILLIAM J	Son	W	M	June 1879	20	S				KY	TN	TN				Farm Laborer	0		✓	✓	✓				
		" ALLIE C	Dau	W	F	June 1881	18	S				KY	TN	TN						0	✓	✓	✓				
43	44	EVANS, JOHN W.	Head	W	M	Mar 1839	61	M	39			KY	SC	KY				FARMER	0		✓	✓	✓	O		F	43
		" JULIA E.	Wife	W	F	Nov 1843	56	M	39	12	8	KY	KY	KY							✓	X	✓				
		" MARGERY E.	Dau	W	F	June 1882	17	S				KY	KY	KY							✓	X	✓				
		" JESSE T.	Son	W	M	Oct 1885	14	S				KY	KY	KY				Farm Laborer	0	2	✓	✓	✓				
44	45	BRANDON, CATHERINE	Head	W	F	May 1835	65	S				KY	SC	SC				FARMER	0		✓	✓	✓	R		F	44
		" MARGARET	Sister	W	F	Oct 1841	58	S				KY	SC	SC				Farm Laborer	0		✓	✓	✓				
45	46	GREEN, JAMES O.	Head	W	M	Mar 1875	25	M	1			KY	TN	KY				TANNER	1		✓	✓	✓	R		F	45

STATE - KENTUCKY
COUNTY - MONROE
Township or other division   GUM

Enumerator THOMAS R. EVANS

Supervisor's Dist. No. 102 Sheet No.
Enumeration Dist. No. 80

No. of Family	No. of Dwelling	NAME	Relation	Color	Sex	Date of Birth Mon/Yr	Age at last birthday	Marital Status	# Years married	Mother of how many children?	# of these children living	Place of birth (this person)	Father of this person	Mother of this person	Year of immigr.	# years in U.S.	Naturalization	Occupation 10 years +	Months not employed	Attended school in months	Can read	Can write	Speak English	Owned or Rent	Owned - no mortgage	Farm or house	# of farm schedule
		EVANS, MARGARET A.	wife	W	F	Nov 1842	57	M	33			KY	ILL	KY							✓	X	✓				
		" MATTIE A	Dau	W	F	Jun 1873	26	S				KY	KY	KY							✓	✓	✓				
		GENTRY, THOMAS	Lodger	W	M	Jul 1887	12	S				KY	KY	KY				FARM LABORER	0	0	X	X	✓				
47	48	HALE, GUSTAVUS A.	HEAD	W	M	Sep 1858	41	M				TN	TN	TN				FARMER	0	0							
		" NANCY R	wife	W	F	Oct 1866	33	M		5	5	KY	KY	KY							✓	✓	✓	R		F	47
		" LUTHER S	Son	W	M	Dec 1885	14	S				KY	TN	KY				FARM LABORER	0	4	✓	✓	✓				
		" JAMES F.	Son	W	M	Sept 1887	12	S				KY	TN	KY				FARM LABORER	0	4	✓	✓	✓				
		" JESSE S	Son	W	M	June 1890	9	S				KY	TN	KY													
		" ELTON	Son	W	M	Apr 1893	7	S				KY	TN	KY													
		" GERTIE F.	Dau	W	F	Nov 1895	4	S				KY	TN	KY													
48	49	HALE, MATHIAS K.	HEAD	W	M	June 1831	68	M				TN	TN	TN				FARMER	0		✓	✓	✓	O		F	48
		" MARY	Dau	W	F	Sept 1858	41	S				TN	TN	TN							✓	✓	✓				
		" MARTHA E.	Dau	W	F	Apr 1866	34	S				TN	TN	TN							✓	✓	✓				
		ARTERBURN, SALLIE	Dau	W	F	Jun 1870	29	Wd				KY	TN	TN							✓	✓	✓				
		" IVA A.	GrDau	W	F	Apr 1891	9	S				KY	KY	KY													
49	50	NEAL, THOMAS B.	HEAD	W	M	May 1830	70	M	15			TN	KY	TN				FARMER	0		✓	✓	✓	O		F	48
		" REBECA J.	wife	W	F	Sept 1848	57	M	15			TN	TN	TN							✓	X	✓				
		" WILLIAM H.	Son	W	M	Oct 1853	46	S				KY	TN	TN				FARM LABORER	0		✓	✓	✓				
		" LUEZA	Boarder	W	F	Dec 1823	76	Wd				VA	VA	VA							✓	X	✓				
50	51	VANCE, WILLIAM J.	HEAD	W	M	May 1852	48	M	25			KY	KY	KY				FARMER	0		✓	✓	✓	O		F	49
		" DEBORAH C.	WIFE	W	F	Jul 1855	44	M	25	3	3	KY	TN	KY							✓	✓	✓				
		" IZORA	DAU	W	F	Nov 1879	20	S				KY	KY	KY							✓	✓	✓				
		" CONNZA(?)	Son	W	M	Oct 1883	16	S				KY	KY	KY				FARM LABORER		1	✓	✓	✓				
51	52	PINCKLEY, ANDREW C.	HEAD	W	M	Aug 1863	36	M	15			TN	TN	KY				FARMER	0		✓	✓	✓	O		F	50
		" LETTIE B	wife	W	F	May 1665	35	M	15	7	5	KY	KY	KY							✓	✓	✓				
		" JENNIE F.	Dau	W	F	Aug 1885	14	S				KY	TN	KY						5	✓	✓	✓				

TWELFTH CENSUS OF THE UNITED STATES 1900

STATE - KENTUCKY
COUNTY - MONROE
Township or other division **GUM**

Enumerator **THOMAS R. EVANS**

Supervisor's Dist. No. **107** Sheet No.
Enumeration Dist. No. **80**

No. of Family	No. of Dwelling	NAME	Relation	Color	Sex	DATE OF BIRTH Mon/Yr	Age at last birthday	Marital Status	# Years married	Mother of how many children?	# of these children living	Place of birth (this person)	Father of this person	Mother of this person	Year of immigr.	# years in U.S.	Naturalization	OCCUPATION 10 years +	Months not employed	Attended school in months	Can read	Can write	Speak English	Owned or Rent	Owned - no mortgage	Farm or house	# of farm schedule
		PINCKLEY, BESSIE	Dau	W	F	Feb 1888	12	S				KY	TN	KY						5	✓	✓	✓				
		" ISAAC F.	Son	W	M	Dec 1891	8	S				KY	TN	KY													
		" WILLIAM H.	Son	W	M	Nov 1894	5	S				KY	TN	KY													
		" ANNA	Dau	W	F	Aug 1896	3	S				KY	TN	KY													
52	52	BROWN, (FRANK?) T.	HEAD	W	M	Sept 1863	36	S				KY	KY	KY				FARMER	0		X	X	✓	R		F	51
		" PERNIE	SISTER	W	F	Nov 1865	34	S				KY	KY	KY							✓	X	✓				
		" ULYSUS H.	BRO	W	M	MAY 1870	30	S				KY	KY	KY				FARM LABORER			✓	X	✓				
		" MOLLIE	SIS.	W	F	SEPT 1872	27	S				KY	KY	KY							✓	✓	✓				
		" CONWAY B.	BRO	W	M	June 1874	25	S				KY	KY	KY				FARM LABORER	0		✓	✓	✓				
		" NEAL P.	BRO	W	M	MAR 1877	23	S				KY	KY	KY				FARM LABORER	0		✓	✓	✓				
53	54	FLOWERS, LEWIS B.	HEAD	W	M	MAY 1865	35	M	12			KY	KY	KY				FARMER	0		✓	✓	✓	O		F	F	52
		" MARY J.	Wife	W	F	Oct 1866	33	M	12	0	0	KY	KY	KY							✓	✓	✓				
		DENHAM, AMANDA M.	MOTHER-IN-LAW	W	F	Apr 1835	65	Wd		1	1	KY	VA	KY				FARMER	0		✓	✓	✓	O		F	F	53
54	55	FRAIM, GEORGE T.	HEAD	W	M	Feb 1841	59	M	35			KY	TN	KY				FARMER	0		✓	✓	✓	O		F	F	54
		" CATHERINE H.	Wife	W	F	Apr 1844	56	M	35	9	9	KY	KY	KY							✓	✓	✓				
		" MELIA A.	Dau	W	F	Feb 1874	26	S				KY	KY	KY							✓	✓	✓				
		" ABSOLOM C.	Son	W	M	Sept 1876	23	S				KY	KY	KY				FARM LABORER	0		✓	✓	✓				
		" DEMETRI O.	Son	W	M	Mar 1879	21	S				KY	KY	KY				FARM LABORER	0		✓	✓	✓				
		" THOMAS C.	Son	W	M	Feb 188-	19	S				KY	KY	KY						3	✓	✓	✓				
		^ IVA A.	Dau	W	F	Oct 188-	14	S				KY	KY	KY						5	✓	✓	✓				
		BROWN, JOSEPH	Lodger	W	M	Mar 1879	21	S				KY	KY	TN				FARM LABORER	2		✓	✓	✓				
55	56	FLIPPIN, TABITHA	HEAD	W	F	Apr 1838	62	Wd		2	2	TN	VA	VA				FARMER	0		✓	✓	✓	O		F	F	55
		" GENNIE C.	Dau	W	F	Mar 1867	33	S				KY	KY	TN							✓	✓	✓				
		" VINNIE V.	Dau	W	F	Nov 1878	21	S				KY	KY	TN							✓	✓	✓				
56	57	JOHNSON, DAVID S.	HEAD	W	M	Oct 1868	31	M	11			KY	KY	KY				FARMER	0		✓	✓	✓	O		F		56
		" LUCY B.	Wife	W	F	Feb 1872	28	M	11	6	4	KY	KY	KY							✓	✓	✓				

STATE - KENTUCKY
COUNTY - MONROE
Township or other division GUM

Enumerator THOMAS R. EVANS

Supervisor's Dist. No. 102 Sheet No.
Enumeration Dist. No. 80

Location (No. of Family / No. of Dwelling)	NAME	Relation	Color	Sex	DATE OF BIRTH Mon/Yr	Age at last birthday	Marital Status	# Years married	Mother of how many children?	# of these children living	Place of birth (this person)	Father of this person	Mother of this person	Year of immigr.	# years in U.S.	Naturalization	OCCUPATION 10 years +	Months not employed	Attended school in months	Can read	Can write	Speak English	Owned or Rent	Owned -no mortage	Farm or house	# of farm schedule
	JOHNSON, NONA C.	Dau	W	F	Nov 1889	10	S				KY	KY	KY				AT SCHOOL		5	✓	✓					
	" (GERNUS)?	Dau	W	F	Sept 1891	8	S				KY	KY	KY													
	" DEMETRIS	Son	W	M	Sept 1895	4	S				KY	KY	KY													
	" ALVIS C.	Son	W	M	Feb 1897	2	S				KY	KY	KY													
57 58	SILCOX, RICHARD	HEAD	W	M	May 1841	59	M	13			TN	VA	TN							X	X	✓	R		H	
	" SARAH	WIFE	W	F	Jan 1848	52	M	13	10	8	KY	KY	KY							X	X	✓				
	" SUSAN E.	Dau	W	F	Jan 1876	24	S				KY	TN	KY							X	X	✓				
	" ROSINA	Dau	W	F	Jul 1877	22	S				KY	TN	KY							X	X	✓				
	" CALVIN S.	Son	W	M	Oct 1878	21	S				TN	IN	KY				DAY LABORER			X	X	✓				
	" RICHARD	Son	W	M	Nov 1881	18	S				TN	TN	KY				DAY LABORER		5	X	X	✓				
	STRONG, ROXIE	Dau	W	F	June 1883	16	Wd				TN	TN	KY							X	X	✓				
	SILCOX, JASPER N.	Son	W	M	June 1885	14	S				TN	TN	KY				DAY LABORER	0		X	X	✓				
	" DAISY A.	Dau	W	F	Apr 1889	11	S				TN	TN	KY					0		X	X	✓				
	" MAGGIE J.	Dau	W	F	Jan 1891	9	S				TN	TN	KY													
	" WILLIAM	GR-SON	W	M	May 1898	2	S				TN	TN	TN													
58 59	GILLENWATERS, JAMES N.	HEAD	W	M	Sept 1870	27	M	7			KY	TN	KY				MERCH. DRY GOODS	0		✓	✓	✓	O	F	H	
	" BETTIE	WIFE	W	F	May 1879	21	M	7	2	2	KY	KY	KY							✓	✓	✓				
	" EDDIE	Dau	W	F	Jan 1895	5					KY	KY	KY													
	" WILLIAM P.	SON	W	M	Aug 1899	9/12					KY	KY	KY													
59 60	STALLINGS, JAMES B.	HEAD	W	M	Oct 1833	66	M				TN	NC	TN				CABINET WORKMAN	0		✓	✓	✓	R	F		57
	" LUIZA	WIFE	W	F	June 1863	36	M	7	1	1	TN	TN	TN							✓	✓	✓				
	" FLORENCE	Dau	W	F	MAR 1894	6					TN	TN	TN													
60 61	DOLLIN, CHARLES M.	HEAD	W	M	Apr 1867	33	M	2			KY	KY	KY				CABINET WORKMAN	0		✓	✓	✓	R	F		58
	" EFFIE L.	WIFE	W	F	May 1876	24	M	2	1	1	KY	TN	KY							✓	✓	✓				
	" MILLIE P.	Dau	W	F	Jul 1899	10/12	S				KY	KY	KY													
61 62	GILLENWATERS, EDWARD E.	HEAD	W	M	Sept 1868	31	M	2			KY	TN	KY				FARMER	0		✓	✓	✓	O	F	F	59

STATE - KENTUCKY
COUNTY - MONROE
Township or other division GUM   Enumerator THOMAS R. EVANS

Supervisor's Dist. No. 102 Sheet No.
Enumeration Dist. No. 80

No. of Family	No. of Dwelling	NAME	Relation	Color	Sex	Date of Birth Mon/Yr	Age at last birthday	Marital Status	# Years married	Mother of how many children?	# of these children living	Place of birth (this person)	Father of this person	Mother of this person	Year of immigr.	# years in U.S.	Naturalization	Occupation 10 years +	Months not employed	Attended school in months	Can read	Can write	Speak English	Owned or Rent	Owned -no morage	Farm or house	# of farm schedule
		GILLENWATERS, LUCY	Wife	W	F	Dec 1872	27	M	2			KY	KY	KY							✓	✓	✓				
62	63	DOSSEY, KITCHEN D.	Head	W	M	Oct 1854	45	M	24			KY	KY	KY				FARMER	0		✓	✓	✓	0		F	60
		" AMANDA J	Wife	W	F	Mar 1854	46	M	24	9	7	KY	KY	KY							✓	✓	✓				
		" (TIRAS)? H.	Son	W	M	Feb 1876	24	S				KY	KY	KY				FARM LABORER	0		✓	✓	✓				
		" ARRIE	Dau	W	F	May 1880	20	S				KY	KY	KY							✓	✓	✓				
		" NETTIE	Dau	W	F	Sept 1882	17	S				KY	KY	KY				AT SCHOOL		3	✓	✓	✓				
		" BARNEY	Son	W	M	Sept 1885	14	S				KY	KY	KY				FARM LABORER	0	1	✓	✓	✓				
		" ELLEN B	Dau	W	F	Apr 1887	1	S				KY	KY	KY				AT SCHOOL		5	✓	✓	✓				
		" TRUMAN	Son	W	M	Aug 1893	6	S				KY	KY	KY													
		" ALVA (S or L)	Dau	W	F	Jul 1896	3	S				KY	KY	KY													
63	64	SIMMONS, JOHN W	Head	W	M	Sept 1868	31	M	11			KY	KY	KY				FARMER	0		✓	✓	✓	0		F	61
		" MOLLIE	Wife	W	F	July 1869	30	M	11	1	1	KY	KY	KY							✓	✓	✓				
		" MINNIE	Dau	W	F	Apr 1890	10					KY	KY	KY				AT SCHOOL		3	✓	X	✓				
64	65	BUTTON, FRANCIS M.	Head	W	M	Feb 1845	53	Wd				KY	KY	KY				MERCH. DRY GOODS			✓	✓	✓	0	F	F	62
		" HALIE	Dau	W	F	Nov 1883	16	S				KY	KY	KY						2	✓	✓	✓				
		" THOMAS G.	Son	W	M	May 1887	13	S				KY	KY	KY				FARM LABORER	0	5	✓	✓	✓				
		" FRANCIS (S or L)	Son	W	M	Apr 1891	9	S				KY	KY	KY													
		SHIPLEY, BLANCHE	Servant	W	F	Jul 1848	51	S				KY	TN	KY				SERVANT		2	✓	✓	✓				
		JONES, JOEL B.	Boarder	W	M	Nov 1876	23	S				KY	KY	KY				SALESMAN - DRY GOODS			✓	✓	✓				
65	66	BURNETT, JOSEPH (H?)	Head	W	M	Apr 1872	28	M	7			KY	KY	KY				FARMER	0		✓	✓	✓	0	M	F	63
		" ADA C	Wife	W	F	Mar 1877	23	M	7	3	3	KY	KY	KY							✓	✓	✓				
		" WILLIAM (S or L)	Son	W	M	Oct 1894	5	S				KY	KY	KY													
		" ALVA E.	Son	W	M	Jul 1895	4	S				KY	KY	KY													
		" CAROL E.	Son	W	M	Jan 1899	1	S				KY	KY	KY				MERCH. DRY GOODS	0		✓	✓	✓	0	F	F	64
66	67	SHORT, JOHN B.	Head	W	M	Jul 1866	33	M	2			KY	KY	KY													
		" HATTIE	Wife	W	F	Jun 1877	22	M	2	1	1	KY	KY	KY							✓	✓	✓				

STATE - KENTUCKY
COUNTY - MONROE
Township or other division — GUM

Enumerator — THOMAS R. Evans

Supervisor's Dist. No. 102 Sheet No.
Enumeration Dist. No. 80

No. of Family / No. of Dwelling	NAME	Relation	Color	Sex	DATE OF BIRTH Mon/Yr	Age at last birthday	Marital Status	# Years married	Mother of how many children?	# of these children living	Place of birth [this person]	Father of this person	Mother of this person	Year of immigr.	# years in U.S.	Naturalization	OCCUPATION 10 years +	Months not employed	Attended school in months	Can read	Can write	Speak English	Owned or Rent	Owned-no mortage	Farm or house	# of farm schedule
	SHORT, ELVA	Son	W	M	May 1899	1	S				KY	KY	KY													
67/68	JORDAN, WILLIAM	HEAD	W	M	Apr 1866	34	M	13			KY	KY	KY				FARMER	0		✓	✓	✓	0		F	65
	" JENNIE G.	WIFE	W	F	Dec 1870	29	M	13	4	3	KY	KY	KY							✓	✓					
	" JACOB B.	Son	W	M	Oct 1888	11	S				KY	KY	KY				FARM LABORER	0		✓	✓	✓				
	" FINLEY D.	Son	W	M	Nov 1894	5	S				KY	KY	KY													
	" ROBERT	Son	W	M	Oct 1897	2	S				KY	KY	KY													
68/69	GILLENWATERS, JOE T.	HEAD	W	M	Mar 1867	33	M	5			KY	TN	KY				FARMER			✓	✓	✓	0	F	F	66
	" GERTRUDE (D or G)	WIFE	W	F	Dec 1874	25	M	5	3	3	KY	TN	KY							✓	✓					
	" MILLIE	Dau	W	F	Jul 1895	4	S				KY	KY	KY													
	" LIND—?	Son	W	M	Feb 1897	3	S				KY	KY	KY													
	" JOEL	Son	W	M	June 1899	11/12	S				KY	KY	KY													
69/70	STEWART, ELIZABETH	HEAD	W	F	Nov 1832	67	Wd				TN	TN	TN							✓	✓		0	F	H	
	" ANNA M.	Dau	W	F	Dec 1857	42	D?				KY	TN	TN							✓	✓	✓				
70/71	QUINN, JANE	HEAD	W	F	Nov 1842	57	S				KY	KY	KY							✓	✓	✓	O	M	H	
71/72	PURCELL, ELIGHA	HEAD	W	M	May 1835	65	M	39			TN	VA	TN				CAPALIST ?			✓	✓	✓	O	F	H	
	" JOSIE	WIFE	W	F	Feb 1844	56	M	39			KY	TN	KY							✓	✓	✓				
	NEAL, ARORA P.	NEPHEW	W	M	Aug 1873	26	S				KY	KY	KY				CAPALIST ?			✓	✓	✓				
72/73	BEALS, CATHERINE	HEAD	W	F	Jul 1836	63	W				TN	TN	TN				FARMER	0		✓	✓	✓	0	F	F	67
	" AVO	Dau	W	F	Jun 1879	20	S				KY	KY	TN							✓	✓	✓				
	" REBECCA (SISTER IN LAW)		W	F	May 1841	59	S				KY	TN	TN							✓	✓	✓				
73/74	PINCKLEY, THOMAS A.	HEAD	W	M	May 1865	35	M	10			KY	TN	KY				FARMER	0		✓	✓	✓	0	M	F	68
	" BRITANA	WIFE	W	F	Aug 1869	30	M	10	4	3	KY	KY	TN							✓	✓	✓				
	" ALVA C.	Son	W	M	Oct 1890	9	S				KY	KY	KY				AT SCHOOL		5	✓	✓	✓				
	" CALIE D.	Dau	W	F	Aug 1892	7	S				KY	KY	KY							✓	✓	✓				
	" MARION H.	Son	W	M	Jul 1899	1/12	S				KY	KY	KY													
74/75	OGDEN, JAMES T.	HEAD	W	M	Nov 1867	32	M	0			KY	KY	KY				FARMER	0		✓	✓	✓	0	F	F	69

STATE - KENTUCKY
COUNTY - MONROE
Township or other division — GUM — Enumerator THOMAS R. EVANS

Supervisor's Dist. No. _102_ Sheet No.
Enumeration Dist. No. _80_

No. of Family	No. of Dwelling	NAME	Relation	Color	Sex	DATE OF BIRTH Mon/Yr	Age at last birthday	Marital Status	# Years married	Mother of how many children?	# of these children living	Place of birth (this person)	Father of this person	Mother of this person	Year of immigr.	# years in U.S.	Naturalization	OCCUPATION 10 years +	Months not employed	Attended school in months	Can read	Can write	Speak English	Owned or Rent	Owned - no mortage	Farm or house	# of farm schedule
		OGDEN, SARAH S.	WIFE	W	F	Aug 1869	30	M	0	4	4	KY	TN	KY							✓	✓	✓				
		" JOHN R.	SON	W	M	June 1892	7	S				KY	KY	KY													
		" EFFIE (Sor L)	DAU	W	F	Nov 1894	5	S				KY	KY	KY													
		" ARORA T.	SON	W	M	June 1896	3	S				KY	KY	KY													
		McWERTER, CASSA C.	STEP DAU	W	F	Dec 1892	7	S				KY	KY	KY													
75	76	MEADOR, ISAAC P.	HEAD	W	M	Dec 1853	46	M	20			TN	TN	TN				DENTIST	0		✓	✓	✓	R	H		
		" LOVENIA	WIFE	W	F	Sept 1862	37	M	20	7	6	TN	TN	TN							✓	✓	✓				
		" LULA E	DAU	W	F	Feb 1881	19	S				TN	TN	TN				AT SCHOOL		10	✓	✓	✓				
		" SAMUEL A.	SON	W	M	Jan 1885	15	S				TEXAS	TN	TN				AT SCHOOL		5	✓	✓	✓				
		" CAM	DAU	W	F	June 1888	11	S				TN	TN	TN				AT SCHOOL		5	✓	✓	✓				
		" THOMAS	SON	W	M	Feb 1891	9	S				KY	TN	TN													
		" CLEMIS	DAU	W	F	Feb 1894	6	S				KY	TN	TN													
		" CLIFTON	SON	W	M	Dec 1897	2	S				KY	TN	TN													
76	77	RIGDON, GEORGE W.	HEAD	W	M	Feb 1833	67	M	13			TN	NC	VA				CAPALIST	0		X	X	✓	O	EH		
		" EMALINE	WIFE	W	F	Jan 1852	48	M	13	0	0	KY	TN	TN							✓	✓	✓				
77	78	FISH, MALISE	HEAD	W	F	Nov 1861	38	Wd		2	2	KY	KY	KY							✓	✓	✓	R	H		
		" VIRGIL	SON	W	M	Oct 1885	14	S				KY	TN	KY				DAY LABORER	0		✓	✓	✓				
		" OLLIE H	SON	W	M	Sept 1890	9	S				KY	TN	KY							✓	✓	✓	O	EH		
78	79	GILLENWATERS, MARGARET	HEAD	W	F	Dec 1838	61	Wd				KY	KY	KY							✓	✓	✓	O	EH		
		" ELIZABETH	DAU	W	F	Apr 1862	38	S				KY	KY	KY							✓	✓	✓				
79	80	SMITH, JOHN A.	HEAD	W	M	Mar 1848	52	M	31			TN	TN	TN				FARMER	0		✓	✓	✓	O	FF	70	
		" NANCY W.	WIFE	W	F	Dec 1845	54	M	31	8	8	TN	TN	TN							✓	✓	✓				
		" JANE C	DAU	W	F	Oct 1878	21	S				TN	TN	TN							✓	X	✓				
		" JOHN W.	SON	W	M	Apr 1884	16	S				KY	TN	TN				FARM LABORER	10		X	X	✓				
		" JAMES A.	SON	W	M	Oct 1886	13	S				KY	TN	TN				FARM LABORER	0		X	X	✓				
		TURNER, JOSEPH C.	LABORER	W	M	Apr 1898	2	S				KY	KY	KY													

STATE - KENTUCKY
COUNTY - MONROE
Township or other division **GUM**
Enumerator **THOMAS R. EVANS**

Supervisor's Dist. No. _102_ Sheet No.
Enumeration Dist. No. _80_

No. of Family	No. of Dwelling	NAME	Relation	Color	Sex	Date of Birth Mon/Yr	Age at last birthday	Marital Status	# Years married	Mother of how many children?	# of these children living	Place of birth (this person)	Father of this person	Mother of this person	Year of immigr.	# years in U.S.	Naturalization	Occupation 10 years +	Months not employed	Attended school in months	Can read	Can write	Speak English	Owned or Rent	Owned - no mortage	Farm or house	# of farm schedule
80	81	SHORT, JOHN C.	HEAD	W	M	DEC 1849	50	M	31			KY	KY	KY				FARMER	0		Y	X	✓	R		F	71
		KETURAH	WIFE	W	F	MAR 1849	51	M	31	6	4	TN	TN	TN							✓	✓	✓				
		JOHN H.	SON	W	M	JUL 1877	22	S				KY	KY	TN				FARM LABORER			✓	✓	✓				
		THOMAS N.	SON	W	M	APR 1881	19	S				KY	KY	TN				FARM LABORER	8		X	X	✓				
		VADIA K.	Dau	W	F	AUG 1888	11	S				KY	KY	TN				AT SCHOOL		1	✓	✓	✓				
81	82	KEY, CALVIN	HEAD	W	M	MAY 1873	27	M				TN	TN	TN				FARM LABORER	3		✓	✓	✓	R		F	72
		FRANCIS A.	Wife	W	F	NOV 1871	28	M	9	4	4	KY	KY	TN							✓	X	✓				
		PEARL E.	Dau	W	F	MAY 1892	8	S				KY	TN	KY													
		NORA J.	Dau	W	F	MAR 1894	6	S				KY	TN	KY													
		HERMIE E.	Dau	W	F	OCT 1896	3	S				KY	TN	KY													
		EARLY	SON	W	M	MAY 1899	1	S				KY	TN	KY													
		JACKSON	BROTHER	W	M	MAY 1875	25	S				TN	TN	TN				FARMER	0		X	X	✓	R		F	73
82	83	CREEK, JOHN S.	HEAD	W	M	FEB 1856	44	M	19			KY	KY	KY				OPERATES FLOUR AND GRIST MILL			✓	✓	✓				
		MARTHA A.	WIFE	W	F	MAR 1853	47	M	19	7	5	KY	KY	KY							✓	X	✓				
		JAMES W.	SON	W	M	OCT 1881	18	S				KY	KY	KY				FARM LABORER	0		✓	X	✓				
		LILIE M.	Dau	W	F	JAN 1884	16	S				KY	KY	KY							✓	X	✓				
		LICCIE J.	Dau	W	F	JUN 1889	10	S				KY	KY	KY				AT SCHOOL		2	✓	X	✓				
		DELBERT B.	SON	W	M	FEB 1891	9	S				KY	KY	KY				AT SCHOOL		2	X	X	✓				
		MAGGIE L.	DAU	W	F	MAY 1897	3	S				KY	KY	KY													
83	84	DUNN, JACKSON	HEAD	W	M	DEC 1849	50	Wd				KY	KY	KY				FARMER	0		X	X	✓	R		F	74
		LIZZIE	DAU	W	F	DEC 1872	27	S				KY	KY	KY							✓	✓	✓				
		NANNIE	DAU	W	F	NOV 1876	23	S				KY	KY	KY							✓	✓	✓				
		JOHN S	SON	W	M	SEPT 1881	18	S				KY	KY	KY							✓	✓	✓				
		CARSON	SON	W	M	DEC 1886	13	S				KY	KY	KY						0	X	X	✓				
		JENNIE H.	Dau	B	F	DEC 1889	11	S				KY	KY	KY						0	X	X	✓				
		SANFORD C.	SON	B	M	FEB 1892	8	S				KY	KY	KY													

TWELFTH CENSUS OF THE UNITED STATES 1900

STATE - KENTUCKY
COUNTY - MONROE
Township or other division GUM   Enumerator THOMAS R. EVANS

Supervisor's Dist. No. 102 Sheet No.
Enumeration Dist. No. 80

No. of Family	No. of Dwelling	NAME	Relation	Color	Sex	DATE OF BIRTH Mon/Yr	Age at last birthday	Marital Status	# Years married	Mother of how many children?	# of these children living	Place of birth (this person)	Father of this person	Mother of this person	Year of immigr.	# years in U.S.	Naturalization	OCCUPATION 10 years +	Months not employed	Attended school in months	Can read	Can write	Speak English	Owned or Rent	Owned-no mortgage	Farm or house	# of farm schedule
		LIGHTFOOT, MARY E.	GR DAU	B	F	Jan 1895	5	S				KY	KY	KY													
		DUNN, LILLIE M.	GR DAU	B	F	Apr 1898	2	S				KY	KY	KY													
		", MAMMIE C.	GR DAU	B	F	Mar 1897	3	S				KY	KY	KY													
		GEE, CLIDE	LODGER	B	M	May 1875	25	S				KY	KY	KY				FARM LABORER	3		X	✓	✓				
84	85	GRAVES, LETTIE	HEAD	W	F	June 1828	71	Wd				KY	NC	KY							✓	✓	✓	O		F H	
		PATTERSON, LUISA	LODGER	W	F	Apr 1835	65	S				TN	ALA	TN							X	X					
	86	COLLINS, SMITH	HEAD	W	M	Oct 1869	30	M	9			KY	TN	KY				FARMER	0		✓	✓	✓	R		F 75	
		" DELIA E.	WIFE	W	F	May 1871	29	M	9	3	3	KY	KY	KY							✓	✓	✓				
		" N— C.	SON	W	M	Nov 1891	8	S				KY	KY	KY													
		" WILLIAM H.	SON	W	M	June 1895	4	S				KY	KY	KY													
		" HATTIE B.	DAU	W	F	Aug 1898	1	S				KY	KY	KY				FARMER			✓	✓	✓	O		F F 76	
85	87	SHORT, MANCHER	HEAD	W	M	—	—	M	0			KY	KY	KY				FARMER	0		✓	✓	✓				
		" VIRGIE H.	WIFE	W	F	Jan 1873	27	M	0	0	0	KY	KY	KY							✓	✓	✓				
86	88	HOWARD, MIKE C.	HEAD	W	M	Aug 1842	57	Wd				KY	KY	KY				FARMER	0		✓	✓	✓	O		F F 77	
		" MINNIE M.	DAU	W	F	Mar 1875	25	S				KY	KY	KY							✓	✓	✓				
		" THOMAS M.	SON	W	M	Aug 1881	18	S				KY	KY	KY							✓	✓	✓				
		" MERTIE B.	DAU	W	F	Sept 1884	15	S				KY	KY	KY				AT SCHOOL		5	✓	✓	✓				
		" IRVINE	LODGER	W	M	Aug 1883	16	S				KY	KY	KY				FARM LABORER	0	0	✓	✓	✓	O		E F 78	
67	89	YOKELEY, JOHN D.	HEAD	W	M	Feb 1835	65	M	39			KY	KY	KY			?	FARMER	0		✓	X	✓				
		" MARY C.	WIFE	W	F	Aug 1845	54	M	39	11	11	KY	KY	KY				FARM LABORER	0		✓	X	X				
		" W—BERTA(?) B.	SON	W	M	Dec 1870	29	M	0			KY	KY	KY				FARM LABORER	0		✓	✓	✓				
		" JOSEPH T.	SON	W	M	Feb 1872	28	S				KY	KY	KY				FARM LABORER	0		✓	✓	✓				
		" JOHN S.	SON	W	M	Jul 1876	23	S				KY	KY	KY				FARM LABORER	0		✓	✓	✓				
		" MARY L.	DAU	W	F	May 1878	22	S				KY	KY	KY							✓	✓	✓				
		" LIGE H.	SON	W	M	Mar 1881	19	S				KY	KY	KY				FARM LABORER	0	3	✓	✓	✓				
		" MAGGIE	DAU	W	F	Dec 1882	17	S											0		✓	✓	✓				

STATE - KENTUCKY
COUNTY - MONROE
Township or other division GUM

Enumerator THOMAS R. EVANS

Supervisor's Dist. No. _102_ Sheet No.
Enumeration Dist. No. _80_

No. of Family	No. of Dwelling	NAME	Relation	Color	Sex	Date of Birth Mon/Yr	Age at last birthday	Marital Status	# Years married	Mother of how many children?	# of these children living	Place of birth (this person)	Father of this person	Mother of this person	Year of immigr.	# years in U.S.	Naturalization	Occupation 10 years +	Months not employed	Attended school in months	Can read	Can write	Speak English	Owned or Rent	Owned – no mortgage	Farm or house	# of farm schedule
		YOKELEY, ANNA B.	Dau	W	F	Mar 1885	15	S				KY	KY	KY							✓	✓	✓				
		" DAISY E.	Dau-in-law	W	F	May 1877	23	M	0	0	0	KY	KY	KY							✓	✓	✓				
88	90	WHEELER, MARSHALL E.	Head	W	M	Dec 1873	26	M	0			KY	KY	KY				FARMER	0		✓	✓	✓	R		F	79
		" FEBA(?) E.	Wife	W	F	Apr 1871	29	M	0			KY	KY	KY							✓	✓	✓				
89	91	WHEELER, MARCELUS A.	Head	W	M	Feb 1851	49	M	28			KY	VA	KY				FARMER			X	X	✓	O		F	80
		" GEORGE A.	Wife	W	F	Oct 1855	44	M	28	8	7	KY	KY	KY							✓	X	✓				
		" SCHYLER	Son	W	M	Dec 1876	23	M	0			KY	KY	KY				DAY LABORER			✓	✓	✓				
		" TOY	Dau	W	F	Mar 1887	13	S				KY	KY	KY				AT SCHOOL		5	✓	✓	✓				
		" WORTHY	Son	W	M	Jul 1890	9	S				KY	KY	KY				AT SCHOOL		5	✓	✓	✓				
		" WORTTY	Son	W	M	Apr 1893	7	S				KY	KY	KY													
		" ELZY	Son	W	M	Nov 1897	2	S				KY	KY	KY													
90	92	ROWLAND, JAMES C.	Head	W	M	Sept 1830	69	M	42			KY	KY	KY				FARMER	0		✓	✓	✓	O	F	F	81
		" MARY E.	Wife	W	F	Mar 1831	69	M	42	7	4	KY	VA	VA							X	X	✓				
		" GEORGE H.	Son	W	M	Jan 1869	31	S				KY	KY	KY				FARM LABORER	0		✓	✓	✓				
91	93	ROWLAND, JAMES T.	Head	W	M	Aug 1873	26	M	4			KY	KY	KY				FARMER	0		✓	✓	✓	O	F	F	82
		" MARY L.	Wife	W	F	Dec 1877	22	M	4	1	1	KY	KY	KY							✓	✓	✓				
		" CLARENCE F.	Son	W	M	Apr 1898	2	S				KY	KY	KY													
92	94	ROBINSON, JANE	Head	W	F	Nov 1859	40	Wd		6	6	KY	KY	KY							✓	✓	✓	R		H	
		" OLLIE G.	Son	W	M	May 1885	15	S				KY	KY	KY				DAY LABORER	0	8	✓	X	✓				
		" WILLIE C.	Son	W	M	Oct 1886	13	S				KY	KY	KY				DAY LABORER	2		✓	✓	✓				
		" BERTIE	Son	W	M	Jan 1889	11	S				KY	KY	KY				DAY LABORER		5	✓	X	✓				
		" McTHOMAS	Son	W	M	Aug 1892	7	S				KY	KY	KY													
		" VIVIAN	Dau	W	M	Jul 1895	4	S				KY	KY	KY													
93	95	DOWNING, BETTIE T.	Head	W	F	Jan 1861	39	Wd		2	2	KY	NC	KY				FARMER	0		✓	✓	✓	R		F	83
		" CLIFTON	Son	W	M	Mar 1882	18	S				KY	KY	KY				FARM LABORER	0		✓	✓	✓				
		" GEORGE T	Son	W	M	Oct 1889	10	S				KY	KY	KY				FARM LABORER	0	2	✓	✓	✓				

STATE - KENTUCKY
COUNTY - MONROE
Township or other division: GUM
Enumerator: THOMAS R. EVANS

Supervisor's Dist. No. 102 Sheet No.
Enumeration Dist. No. 80

No. of Family	No. of Dwelling	NAME	Relation	Color	Sex	DATE OF BIRTH Mon/Yr	Age at last birthday	Marital Status	# Years married	Mother of how many children?	# of these children living	Place of birth (this person)	Father of this person	Mother of this person	Year of immigr.	# years in U.S.	Naturalization	OCCUPATION 10 years +	Months not employed	Attended school in months	Can read	Can write	Speak English	Owned or Rent	Owned -no mortage	Farm or house	# of farm schedule
94	96	ARTERBURN, ELBERT P.	HEAD	W	M	Nov 1841	58	M	39			KY	TN	TN				FARMER	0		✓	✓	✓	O		F F	84
		" JULIA A	WIFE	W	F	May 1842	58	M	39	2	2	KY	TN	TN							✓	✓	✓				
95	97	HUGHES, HENRY H.	HEAD	W	M	Sept 1869	30	S				KY	KY	KY				FARMER	0		✓	✓	✓	O		M F	85
		" WILLIAM B.	BRO	W	M	Aug 1871	28	S				KY	KY	KY				FARM LABORER	0		✓	✓	✓				
		" RODA A.	SIS	W	F	Dec 1875	24	S				KY	KY	KY							✓	✓	✓				
96	98	BROWN, WILLIAM A.	HEAD	W	M	Sept 1847	52	M	18			KY	KY	KY				FARMER			✓	✓	✓	O		F F	86
		" MELIA E.	WIFE	W	F	Dec 1863	36	M	18	5	5	KY	KY	KY							✓	✓	✓				
		" WATSON D.	SON	W	M	Oct 1883	16	S				KY	KY	KY				FARM LABORER	0	0	✓	✓	✓				
		" (?) HUBERTA B.	SON	W	M	July 1887	12	S				TN	KY	KY				FARM LABORER		3	✓	✓	✓				
		" NEAL B.	SON	W	M	Dec 1891	8	S				KY	KY	KY													
		" BETTIE C.	DAU	W	F	Apr 1896	4	S				KY	KY	KY													
		" ROBERT C.	SON	W	M	May 1899	1	S				KY	KY	KY													
97	99	HOWARD, WILLIAM H.	HEAD	W	M	Mar 1873	27	M	0			KY	KY	KY				FARMER	0		✓	✓	✓	R		F	87
		" SARAH J.	WIFE	W	F	Jan 1880	20	M	0	0	0	KY	KY	KY							✓	✓	✓				
98	100	LANDRUM, ROBERT S.	HEAD	W	M	Apr 1827	73	Wd				KY	VA	VA				FARMER			✓	✓	✓	O		F F	88
		" ROBERT B.	SON	W	M	Aug 1872	27	S				KY	KY	KY				TEACHER IN COMMON SCHOOLS			✓	✓	✓				
		" VIRGIL C.	SON	W	M	Jun 1875	24	S				KY	KY	KY				TEACHER IN COMMON SCHOOLS			✓	✓	✓				
		" OMER C.	GRAND-SON	W	M	Mar 1885	15	S				KY	KY	KY				FARM LABORER	0		✓	✓	✓				
99	101	LOYD, ABLE N.	HEAD	W	M	Jul 1872	27	M	8			KY	KY	KY				FARMER	0		✓	✓	✓	R		F	89
		" LIZA	WIFE	W	F	Feb 1874	26	M	8	4	4	KY	KY	KY							✓	X	✓				
		" AVERY H.	SON	W	M	Aug 1892	7	S				KY	KY	KY													
		" VERNIE M.	DAU	W	F	Jan 1894	6	S				TN	KY	KY													
		" VIRGIL P.	SON	W	M	Apr 1896	4	S				TN	KY	KY													
		" JOSEPH W.	SON	W	M	Feb 1898	2	S				KY	KY	KY													
100	102	FLOWERS, (LIBBRUM?) P.	HEAD	W	M	Apr 1837	63	Wd				KY	VA	VA				FARMER	0		✓	✓	✓	O		F F	90
		" ELLA S.	DAU	W	F	Sept 1875	24	S				KY	KY	KY				TEACHER OF COMMON SCHOOLS		4	✓	✓	✓				

STATE - KENTUCKY
COUNTY - MONROE
Township or other division: GUM

Enumerator: THOMAS B. EVANS

Supervisor's Dist. No. 102 Sheet No.
Enumeration Dist. No. 80

Location (No. of Family / No. of Dwelling)	NAME	Relation	Color	Sex	DATE OF BIRTH Mon/Yr	Age at last birthday	Marital Status	# Years married	Mother of how many children?	# of these children living	Place of birth (this person)	Father of this person	Mother of this person	Year of immigr.	# years in U.S.	Naturalization	OCCUPATION 10 years +	Months not employed	Attended school in months	Can read	Can write	Speak English	Owned or Rent	Owned –no mortgage	Farm or house	# of farm schedule
	FLOWERS, BASSIE C.	Dau	W	F	Jul 1879	20	S				KY	KY	KY							✓	✓	✓				
	" JOHN L.	Son	W	M	May 1885	15	S				KY	KY	KY				FARM LABORER	0		✓	✓	✓				
101/103	FLIPPIN, PRIMUS	HEAD	B	M	–	–	–													–	–	–				
102/104	LOYD, JOHN W	HEAD	W	M	Jan 1868	32	M	11			KY	KY	KY				FARMER	0		✓	✓		R		F	91
	" , ELLER B.	Wife	W	F	Mar 1873	27	M	11	4	4	KY	TN	KY							✓	✓	✓				
	" HECTOR A.	Son	W	M	Apr 1890	10	S				KY	KY	KY							✓	✓	✓				
	" , LUISA N.	Dau	W	F	Jul 1892	7	S				KY	KY	KY							✓	✓	✓				
	" FREDERICK L.	Son	W	M	Jan 1896	4	S				ILL	KY	KY													
	" ALTA	Dau	W	F	Dec 1898	1	S				KY	KY	KY													
103/105	RIGGS, JESSE A.	HEAD	W	M	Jul 1864	35	M	6			ILL	TN	TN				FARMER	0		✓	✓	✓	R		F	92
	" SARAH B	WIFE	W	F	Mar 1866	34	M	6	4	4	KY	KY	KY							✓	✓	✓				
*	MONTI H	DAU	W	F	Apr 1896	4	S				KY	IL	KY													
	LILLIAN E.	DAU	W	F	Aug 1897	2	S				KY	IL	KY													
*	GILBERT	Son	W	M	Apr 1895	5	S				KY	IL	KY									✓				
	GOLFEL(?)	Son	W	M	Feb 1899	1	S				KY	IL	KY													
104/106	WARD, HUSTON G	HEAD	W	M	Jun 1863	36	M	12			KY	TN	TN				FARMER	0		✓	X	✓	O		F	93
	" LUCY A.	Wife	W	F	Mar 1870	30	M	12	5	5	KY	KY	KY							✓	X	✓				
	" BITTIE C.	Dau	W	F	Nov 1889	10	S				KY	KY	KY						4½	✓	✓	✓				
	" TILDA B.	Dau	W	F	Feb 1892	8	S				KY	KY	KY													
	" HENRY C.	Son	W	M	Apr 1894	6	S				KY	KY	KY													
	" MAUDIE E.	DAU	W	F	Aug 1896	3	S				KY	KY	KY													
	" MARTHA E.	DAU	W	F	Jan 1899	1	S				KY	KY	KY													
105/107	TAYLOR, LORETTA A.	HEAD	W	F	May 1869	31	Wd				BY	KY	KY							✓	✓	✓	O		F	H
	ISENBERG, JAMES S.	Son	W	M	Aug 1884	16	S				KY	KY	KY				FARM LABORER	0	8	X	X	✓				
	" TILDA J.	DAU	W	F	Jul 1886	13	S				KY	KY	KY							X	X	✓				
	" EFFIE A	DAU	W	F	Sept 1888	11	S				KY	KY	KY							X	X	✓				

STATE - KENTUCKY
COUNTY - MONROE
Township or other division GUM

Enumerator THOMAS B. EVANS

Supervisor's Dist. No. 102 Sheet No.
Enumeration Dist. No. 80

Location No. of Family / No. of Dwelling	NAME	Relation	Color	Sex	DATE OF BIRTH Mon/Yr	Age at last birthday	Marital Status	# Years married	Mother of how many children?	# of these children living	NATIVITY Place of birth [this person]	Father of this person	Mother of this person	CITIZENSHIP Year of immigr. / # years in U.S. / Naturalization	OCCUPATION 10 years +	Months not employed	Attended school in months	Can read	Can write	Speak English	OWNERSHIP Owned or Rent	Owned -no mortage	Farm or house	# of farm schedule
	ISENBERG, WILLIAM T	Son	W	M	MAY 1891	9	S				KY	KY	KY											
	" FRANK	Son	W	M	DEC 1897	2	S				KY	KY	KY											
	TAYLOR, LOLA B.	Dau	W	F	FEB 1900	3/12	S				KY	KY	KY											
	CROSS, WILLIAM C.	Lodger	W	M	FEB 1877	23	S				KY	TN	KY					✓	✓	✓				
	" DARTHELA	Lodger	W	F	Sep 1874	25	S				KY	TN	KY					X	X	✓				
	KIRBY, VERA M.	Lodger	W	F	MAY 1881	19	S				KY	TN	KY					✓	✓	✓				
	" OLLIE T.	Lodger	W	M	NOV 1896	3	S				KY	KY	KY											
	" HERBERT J.	Lodger	W	M	Jun 1899	11/12	S				KY	TN	KY											
106/108	McCUE, ELIZABETH	HEAD	W	F	Oct 1830	69	W		1	1	TN	TN	TN		FARMER	O		✓	✓	✓	O	F	F	94
	" HATTIE V.	DAU	W	F	MAR 1876	24	S				KY	VA	TN					✓	✓	✓				
107/109	CARVER, HENRY	HEAD	W	M	APR 1847	53	M	10			TN	KY	TN		FARMER			✓	✓	✓	R		F	95
	" MOLLIE	WIFE	W	F	MAY 1871	29	M	10	4	3	KY	KY	KY					X	X	✓				
	" JOHN	SON	W	M	OCT 1887	12	S				KY	TN	KY		AT SCHOOL		3	✓	✓	✓				
	" PEARL	DAU	W	F	MAR 1893	7	S				KY	TN	KY											
	" WILLIAM	SON	W	M	JUL 1895	5	S				KY	TN	KY											
	" HAYSEY	DAU	W	F	JUN 1899	1	S				KY	TN	KY											
108/110	JOHNSON, HENRY C.	HEAD	W	M	SEP 1873	26	M	1			KY	KY	KY		FARMER	O		✓	✓	✓	O		F	96
	" ORIEN	WIFE	W	F	OCT 1880	19	M	1			KY	KY	KY											
109/111	HAYNES, WILLIAM T.	HEAD	W	M	JAN 1848	52	S				TN	TN	TN		FARMER	O		✓	✓	✓	O	F	F	97
110/112	FORD, JAMES	HEAD	W	M	DEC 1851	48	M	20			KY	KY	TN		FARMER	O		✓	✓	✓	R		F	98
	" PEARLINA W.	WIFE	W	F	SEP 1853	46	M	20			TN	TN	TN					✓	✓	✓				
111/113	GOAD, JOSEPH	HEAD	W	M	AUG 1868	31	M	3			KY	KY	TN		DAY LABORER	5		✓	✓	✓	R		H	
	" LAURA	WIFE	W	F	JUL 1877	22	M	3	3	3	KY	KY	KY					X	X	✓				
	" ELBERT	SON	W	M	APR 1896	4	S				KY	KY	KY											
	" WILLIAM	SON	W	M	FEB 1898	2	S				KY	KY	KY											
	" FRANK	SON	W	M	FEB 1900	3/12	S				KY	KY	KY											

STATE - KENTUCKY
COUNTY - MONROE
Township or other division   GUM

Enumerator THOMAS R. EVANS

Supervisor's Dist. No. _102_ Sheet No.
Enumeration Dist. No. _80_

No. of Family	No. of Dwelling	NAME	Relation	Color	Sex	DATE OF BIRTH Mon/Yr	Age at last birthday	Marital Status	# Years married	Mother of how many children?	# of these children living	Place of birth [this person]	Father of this person	Mother of this person	Year of immigr.	# years in U.S.	Naturalization	OCCUPATION 10 years +	Months not employed	Attended school in months	Can read	Can write	Speak English	Owned or Rent	Owned -no mortgage	Farm or house	# of farm schedule
112	114	JONES, CORNELIUS W	HEAD	W	M	FEB 1867	33	M				KY	KY	KY				MERCHANT DRY GOODS	1		✓	✓	✓	O	F	F	99
		" SUELA(?)	WIFE	W	F	MAY 1875	25	M	8	3	3	KY	KY	KY							✓	✓	✓				
		" GIRTIE E.	DAU	W	F	DEC 1892	7	S				KY	KY	KY													
		" NEOMA	DAU	W	F	JAN 1896	4	S				KY	KY	KY													
		" JD	SON	W	M	FEB 1898	2	S				KY	KY	KY													
113	115	McCUE, ELIGH	HEAD	W	M	FEB 1862	38	M	10			KY	VA	KY				FARMER	0		✓	✓	✓	O	M	F	100
		" SARAH A.	WIFE	W	F	JUN 1869	30	M	10	3	2	KY	KY	KY							✓	✓	✓				
		" CHARLES G.	SON	W	M	NOV 1891	9	S				KY	KY	KY													
		" WERTIE	SON	W	M	JAN 1895	5	S				KY	KY	KY													
		BROOKS, ENVIRA H.	BOARDER	W	F	MAY 1864	36	Wd				KY	VA	KY							✓	✓	✓				
114	116	PARSLEY, ANDREW C.	HEAD	W	M	FEB 1856	44	M	16			KY	TN	KY				FARMER	0		X	X	✓	O	F	F	101
		" ELIZABETH	WIFE	W	F	AUG 1863	36	M	16	5	3	KY	KY	KY							X	X	✓				
		" JAMES W.	SON	W	M	OCT 1885	14	S				KY	KY	KY				FARM LABORER	5		✓	X	✓				
		" CHARLES B	SON	W	M	JAN 1888	12	S				KY	KY	KY				FARM LABORER	5		✓	X	✓				
		" MARY B.	DAU	W	F	AUG 1890	9	S				KY	KY	KY													
115	117	TAYLOR, CORNELIUS W.	HEAD	W	M	MAR 1878	22	M	6			KY	NC	TN				TEAMSTER	2		✓	X	✓	O	F	H	
		" CORA G.	WIFE	W	F	DEC 1876	23	M	6	3	3	KY	KY	KY							✓	✓	✓				
		" OMA	STEP-DAU	W	F	MAY 1891	9	S				KY	KY	KY													
		" MOLLIE E.	DAU	W	F	JUL 1895	4	S				KY	KY	KY													
		" DONNA T.	DAU	W	F	NOV 1897	2	S				KY	KY	KY													
116	118	TAYLOR, CORNELIUS, SR	HEAD	W	M	OCT 1821	78	M	26			KY	TN	TN				FARMER	0		✓	X	✓	O	F	H	
		" SARAH J.	WIFE	W	F	JUL 1840	59	M	26	2	2	TN	KY	KY							✓	✓	✓				
117	119	ROBINSON, Mc	HEAD	W	M	MAY 1865	35	M				KY	TN	TN										R		F	102
		" AMANDA C.	WIFE	W	F	SEPT 1862	37	M	13	5	5	KY	KY	KY							✓	✓	✓				
		" JEROME	SON	W	M	JUN 1888	11	S				KY	KY	KY				FARM LABORER	2		✓	X	✓				
		" GEORGE H.	SON	W	M	DEC 1890	9	S				KY	KY	KY						2							

STATE - KENTUCKY
COUNTY - MONROE
Township or other division GUM
Enumerator THOMAS R. EVANS

Supervisor's Dist. No. 102 Sheet No. ___
Enumeration Dist. No. 80 ___

No. of Family	No. of Dwelling	NAME	Relation	Color	Sex	DATE OF BIRTH Mon/Yr	Age at last birthday	Marital Status	# Years married	Mother of how many children?	# of these children living	Place of birth (this person)	Father of this person	Mother of this person	Year of immigr.	# years in U.S.	Naturalization	OCCUPATION 10 years +	Months not employed	Attended school in month	Can read	Can write	Speak English	Owned or Rent	Owned -no mortage	Farm or house	# of farm schedule
		ROBINSON, NORA M.	Dau	W	F	DEC 1892	7	S				KY	KY	KY													
		" SIMON(?) R.	Son	W	M	Jan 1895	5	S				KY	KY	KY													
		" LOLES(?) E.	Dau	W	F	Sept 1898	1	S				KY	KY	KY													
118	120	WILKERSON, JOHN W.	HEAD	W	M	Jun 1865	34	M	10			IOWA	KY	KY				FARMER	0		✔	✔	✔	R		F	103
		" SARAH E.	WIFE	W	F	Jun 1870	29	M	10	4	3	KY	KY	KY							✔	✔	✔				
		" NACY J.	Son	W	M	Sept 1890	9	S				KY	IOWA	KY													
		" NELLY M.	DAU	W	F	Sept 1894	5	S				KY	IOWA	KY													
		" NAOMA	DAU	W	F	MAR 1898	2	S				KY	IOWA	KY							✔	✔	✔				
		HAGAN, FIDLIA E.	Sister in law	W	F	Nov 1866	33	Wd				KY	KY	KY							✔	X	✔				
	S10	" JENNIE B.	(Nephew?)	W	F	Sept 1893	6	S				KY	KY	KY													
		" SARAH E.	NEICE	W	F	Sept 1895	4	S				KY	KY	KY													
119	121	WARD, JOHN	HEAD	W	M	Aug 1879	20	M	1			KY	TN	KY				FARMER	0		✔	X	✔	O		F	104
		" MAGGIE	WIFE	W	F	MAR 1883	17	M	1			KY	KY	KY							✔	✔	✔				
120	122	JOHNSON, ANDREW J.	HEAD	W	M	Jun 1873	26	M	4			TN	TN	TN				FARMER	0		✔	✔	✔	R		F	105
		" RACHEL F.	WIFE	W	F	Oct 1876	23	M	4	2	1	TN	TN	TN							✔	✔	✔				
		" EFFIE J.	DAU	W	F	Jul 1897	2	S				KY	TN	TN													
		" LIDA B.	DAU	W	F	DEC 1898	1	S				KY	TN	TN													
121	123	WARD, HENRY C.	HEAD	W	M	MAR 1858	42	M	21			KY	TN	TN				FARMER	0		✔	✔	✔	O		M F	106
		" MARY E.	WIFE	W	F	FEB 1855	45	M	21	2	2	KY	TN	TN							✔	✔	✔				
		" HATTIE E.	DAU	W	F	SEPT 1883	16	S				KY	KY	KY							✔	✔	✔				
		" JAMES T.	SON	W	M	MAY 1889	11	S				KY	KY	KY				FARM LABORER			✔	X	✔				
122	124	GOAD, WILLIAM H.	HEAD	W	M	FEB 1845	55	M	34			KY	TN	TN				FARMER	0		✔	✔	✔	O		F F	107
		" SARAH J.	WIFE	W	F	MAY 1839	61	M	34	6	4	TN	TN	TN							✔	✔	✔				
		" IDA B.	GR.DAU	W	F	Apr 1893	7	S				KY	KY	KY													
123	125	BRITT, GRANT	HEAD	W	M	— —	—	Wd				KY	—	—												H	
124	126	DUNN, WILLIAM M.	HEAD	B	M	Oct 1869	30	M	6			KY	KY	KY				FARM LABORER	5		✔	✔	✔	R		H	

STATE - KENTUCKY
COUNTY - MONROE
Township or other division: GUM
Enumerator: THOMAS R. EVANS
Supervisor's Dist. No. 102 Sheet No.
Enumeration Dist. No. 80

No. of Family / No. of Dwelling	NAME	Relation	Color	Sex	Date of Birth Mon/Yr	Age at last birthday	Marital Status	# Years married	Mother of how many children?	# of these children living	Place of birth (this person)	Father of this person	Mother of this person	Occupation	Months not employed	Attended school in months	Can read	Can write	Speak English	Owned or Rent	Owned - no mortgage / Farm or house	# of farm schedule
	DUNN, LIZA J.	WIFE	B	F	Oct 1878	21	M	6	3	3	KY	KY	KY				✓	X	✓			
	" LUCY C.	DAU	B	F	May 1895	5	S				KY	KY	KY									
	" WILLIAM S.	SON	B	M	Apr 1897	4	S				KY	KY	KY									
	" ANNA L.	DAU	B	F	May 1899	1	S				KY	KY	KY									
	SIMMONS, ADA	LODGER	B	F	Jul 1883	16	S				KY	KY	KY				✓	✓	✓			
	" BERTHA B.	LODGER	B	F	Aug 1899 9/12		S				KY	KY	KY									
	WHITNEY, HICKMAN	LODGER	B	M	Jun 1891	8	S				KY	KY	KY									
125/127	DOWNING, BERT C.	HEAD	W	M	Feb 1872	28	M	4			KY	KY	KY	FARMER	0		✓	✓	✓	O	M F	108
	" LELA F.	WIFE	W	F	Sept 1876	23	M	4	2	2	KY	KY	KY				✓	✓	✓			
	" WILLIAM G.	SON	W	M	Jan 1897	3	S				KY	KY	KY									
	" RADFORD	SON	W	M	Apr 1899	1	S				KY	KY	KY									
	BROOKS, WAYNIE C.	BRO-IN-LAW	W	M	Feb 1895	5	S				KY	KY	KY									
126/128	CROSS, ABRAHAM	HEAD	W	M	Dec 1841	58	M	24			TN	TN	TN	FARMER	0		✓	✓	✓	O	F F	109
	" REBECCA A.	WIFE	W	F	Dec 1850	49	M	24	6	4	KY	TN	TN				✓	✓	✓			
	" MARY E.	DAU	W	F	Apr 1874	26	S				KY	TN	KY				✓	✓	✓			
	" RUSA A.	DAU	W	F	Apr 1877	23	S				KY	TN	KY				✓	✓	✓			
	" WILLIAM J.	SON	W	M	Mar 1879	21	S				KY	TN	KY				✓	✓	✓			
	" WILLIAM A.	GR. SON	W	M	Apr 1893	7	S				KY	KY	KY									
127/129	BRYANT, GEORGE B(?)	HEAD	W	M	Sept 1872	27	M	7			KY	KY	KY	FARMER	0		✓	X	✓	R	F	110
	" LIZA	WIFE	W	F	Dec 1868	31	M	7	2	2	KY	KY	KY				✓	✓	✓			
	" BERTA E.	DAU	W	F	Sept 1896	3	S				KY	KY	KY									
	" HESLARD(?) B	SON	W	M	Mar 1899	1	S				KY	KY	KY				✓					
128/130	COLLEY, ABEL G.	HEAD	W	M	Feb 1833	67	M	42			TN	VA	VA	FARMER	0		✓	✓	✓	O	F F	111
	" ELIZABETH	WIFE	W	F	Mar 1837	63	M	42	6	6	TN	TN	TN				X	X	✓			
	" ABEL H.	RELATIVE	W	M	Sept 1888	11	S				KY	KY	KY	AT SCHOOL		5	✓	✓	✓			
129/131	ROBBINSON, ANDREW	HEAD	W	M	Jul 1874	25	M	2			KY	TN	TN	FARMER			✓	✓	✓	R	F F	112

TWELFTH CENSUS OF THE UNITED STATES 1900

– 25 –

STATE - KENTUCKY
COUNTY - MONROE
Township or other division: GUM

Enumerator: THOMAS R. EVANS

Supervisor's Dist. No. 102 Sheet No. ____
Enumeration Dist. No. 80 ____

No. of Family	No. of Dwelling	NAME	Relation	Color	Sex	Date of Birth Mon/Yr	Age at last birthday	Marital Status	# Years married	Mother of how many children?	# of these children living	Place of birth (this person)	Father of this person	Mother of this person	Year of immigr.	# years in U.S.	Naturalization	Occupation 10 years +	Months not employed	Attended school in months	Can read	Can write	Speak English	Owned or Rent	Owned – no mortgage	Farm or house	# of farm schedule	
		ROBBINSON, MINNIE B	Wife	W	F	Mar 1873	27	M	2	1	1	KY	KY	KY							✓	✓	✓					
		" NETTIE J.	Dau	W	F	Aug 1898	1					KY	KY	KY														
129	132	HENLEY, FRANK	Head	W	M	Mar 1851	49	M	27			TN	TN	TN				FARMER	0		✓	✓		R		F	113	
		" SARAH J.	Wife	W	F	Sept. 1851	48	M	27	3	3	GA	NC	GA							✓	✓	✓					
		" WILLIS	Son	W	M	Feb 1875	25	S				TN	TN	GA				FARM LABORER	0	8	✓	✓	✓					
130	133	MORROW, JAMES G.	Head	W	M	Feb 1843	57	M				KY	TN	VA				FARMER	0		✓	✓	✓	O		F	114	
		" LUCIAN	Son	W	M	Apr 1873	27	S				KY	KY	KY				FARMER	0		✓	✓	✓	R		F	115	
		" KITTIE	Sister	W	F	Oct 1848	51	S				KY	TN	VA							X	X	✓					
131	134	PARSLEY, AHASURUS(?)	Head	W	M	Jan 1853	47	M	18			TN	TN	KY				FARMER	0		✓	✓	✓	Q	M	F	116	
		" ELIZABETH	Wife	W	F	May 1860	40	M	18	8	8	TN	TN	TN							X	X	✓					
		" FOUNTAIN J.	Son	W	M	Sept 1883	16	S				KY	TN	TN				FARM LABORER	0		✓	✓						
		" BENJAMIN F.	Son	W	M	Aug 1885	14	S				KY	TN	TN				FARM LABORER	0		X	X	✓					
		" MARY J.	Dau	W	F	Oct 1887	12	S				KY	TN	TN						0	X	X	✓					
		" MARTHA A.	Dau	W	F	Jan 1889	11	S				KY	TN	TN							X	X	✓					
		" JOHN W.	Son	W	M	Feb 1892	8	S				KY	TN	TN							X	X	✓					
		" PEARALEE	Dau	W	F	Oct 1894	5	S				KY	TN	TN							X	X	✓					
		" NANCY C.	Dau	W	F	Sept 1896	3	S				KY	TN	TN														
		" JAMES H.	Son	W	M	Oct 1899	7/12	S				KY	TN	TN														
132	135	HENLEY, JAMES	Head	W	M	Dec 1878	21	M				KY	TN	KY				FARMER	0		✓	✓	✓	O		E	117	
		" REBECCA M.	Wife	W	F	Jan 1883	17	M				KY	KY	KY							✓	✓	✓					
133	136	HENLEY, WILLIAM M.	Head	W	M	Jan 1847	53	M	30			TN	TN	TN				FARMER	0		✓	✓	✓	O		F	117	SIC
		" SARAH	Wife	W	F	Aug 1854	45	M	30	8	5	KY	TN	TN							✓	✓	✓					
		" LEN(?) S.	Son	W	M	Jan 1887	13	S				KY	TN	KY				FARM LABORER	0	4½	✓	✓						
		" BERLIN H.	Son	W	M	May 1896	4	S				KY	TN	KY														
134	137	MURPHY, WILLIAM N.	Head	W	M	Apr 1853	47	M	15			KY	NC	KY				FARMER	0		✓	✓	✓	O	M	F	118	
		" SARAH J.	Wife	W	F	Oct 1860	39	M	15	3	3	KY	KY	KY							✓	✓	✓					

TWELFTH CENSUS OF THE UNITED STATES 1900

STATE - KENTUCKY
COUNTY - MONROE
Township or other division — GUM

Enumerator — THOMAS R. EVANS

Supervisor's Dist. No. 102   Sheet No.
Enumeration Dist. No. 80

No. of Family	No. of Dwelling	NAME	Relation	Color	Sex	Date of Birth Mon/Yr	Age at last birthday	Marital Status	# Years married	Mother of how many children	# of these children living	Place of birth (this person)	Father of this person	Mother of this person	Year of immigr.	# years in U.S.	Naturalization	Occupation 10 years +	Months not employed	Attended school in months	Can read	Can write	Speak English	Owned or Rent	Owned - no mortage	Farm or house	# of farm schedule
		MURPHY, JETTE D.	Dau	W	F	Jan 1886	14	S				KY	KY	KY				AT SCHOOL		5	✓	✓	✓				
		" OMER C.	Son	W	M	Oct 1887	12	S				KY	KY	KY				FARM LABORER	O	5	✓	✓	✓				
		" ALLEN B.	Son	W	M	Oct 1889	10	S				KY	KY	KY				FARM LABORER	O	5	✓	✓	✓				
134	138	FERMALL, JOSEPH	Head	W	M	Nov 1852	47	M	23			KY	TN	KY				FARMER	O		✓	✓	✓	O	F	F	119
		" CATHERINE	Wife	W	F	Aug 1847	53	M	23	5	3	KY	NC	TN							✓	✓	✓				
		" LUCY	Dau	W	F	Jun 1882	17	S				KY	KY	KY				AT SCHOOL		2	✓	✓	✓				
		" ELDRIDGE G.	Son	W	M	Aug 1885	14	S				KY	KY	KY				FARM LABORER	O	4	✓	✓	✓				
		" ROBERT G.	Son	W	M	Jul 1887	12	S				KY	KY	KY				FARM LABORER	O	4	✓	✓	✓				
135	139	WOODS, ANDREW J.	Head	W	M	Apr 1866	34	M	7			KY	KY	KY				FARMER	O		✓	✓	✓	R		F	120
		" SARAH E.	Wife	W	F	Jan 1876	24	M	7	2	2	KY	KY	KY							✓	✓	✓				
		" WILLIAM E.	Son	W	M	Sept 1893	6	S				KY	KY	KY													
		" MARY J.	Dau	W	F	Jan 1896	4	S				KY	KY	KY													
136	140	BRUCE, JASPER	Head	W	M	Feb 1824	76	M	38			NEW HAMPSHIRE	VT	NEW HAMPSHIRE				FARMER	O		✓	✓	✓	O	F	F	121
		" AMANDA (?)	Wife	W	F	Mar 1830	70	M	38	1	1	ILL	ILL	NEW HAMPSHIRE							X	X	✓				
137	141	SLAUGHTER, JENNIE A.	Head	W	F	Jul 1845	54	Wd		1	1	TN	KY	KY							X	X	✓	R		H	
		" THOMAS	Son	W	M	Aug 1889	10	S				KY	TN	TN													
138	142	LAWRENCE(?), ORIEN	Head	W	M	Jun 1876	23	M	6			KY	TN	KY				FARMER	O		✓	✓	✓	O	F	F	122
		" SARAH J.	Wife	W	F	May 1871	29	M	6	2	2	KY	TN	KY							✓	✓	✓				
		OLEY, BENJAMIN	Step-son	W	M	Oct 1889	10	S				KY	KY	KY				FARM LABORER	O	3	✓	✓	✓				
		" BETTIE	Step-dau	W	F	Jan 1892	8	S				KY	KY	KY													
		GOAD, JOHN	Boarder	W	M	Dec 1811	88	Wd				TN	VA	VA							X	X	✓				
		RODGERS, BUFORD	Boarder	W	M	Oct 1876	23	S				KY	KY	KY				FARM LABORER	O	3	✓	X	✓				
139	143	ROBINSON, LUISA	Head	W	F	Nov 1849	50	Wd		2	2	KY	TN	TN							✓	X	✓	O	F	F	123
		" THOMAS J.	Son	W	M	Sept 1883	16	S				KY	IND	KY				FARM LABORER	O	2	✓	✓	✓				
		" SAMUEL G.	Son	W	M	Sept 1886	13	S				KY	IND	KY				FARM LABORER	O	2	✓	✓	✓				
140	144	TAYLOR, MARTHA	Head	W	F	Mar 1851	49	Wd		0	0	KY	KY	KY							✓	✓	✓	R		H	

TWELFTH CENSUS OF THE UNITED STATES 1900

— 27 —

STATE - KENTUCKY
COUNTY - MONROE
Township or other division — GUM

Enumerator THOMAS R. EVANS

Supervisor's Dist. No. 102 Sheet No.
Enumeration Dist. No. 80

No. of Family	No. of Dwelling	NAME	Relation	Color	Sex	Date of Birth Mon/Yr	Age at last birthday	Marital Status	# Years married	Mother of how many children?	# of these children living	Place of birth (this person)	Father of this person	Mother of this person	Year of immigr.	# years in U.S.	Naturalization	Occupation 10 years +	Months not employed	Attended school in months	Can read	Can write	Speak English	Owned or Rent	Owned - no mortage	Farm or house	# of farm schedule
		RODGERS, ELIZABETH	MOTHER IN LAW	W	F	Jun 1823	76	W		1	0	VA	VA	VA							✓	X	✓				
141	145	WARD, MARY A	HEAD	W	F	Aug 1851	48	W		1	1	KY	TN	NC				FARMER	0		✓	X	✓	O	F	F	124
		" HARISON	SON	W	M	Jun 1892	7	S				KY	KY	KY													
		TEMPLES, MARTHA B	MOTHER	W	F	Oct 1816	83	Wd		1	1	NC	NC	NC							X	X	✓				
142	146	DOSSEY, KINTCHIN	HEAD	W	M	Dec 1834	65	M	32			KY	KY	TN				FARMER	0		✓	✓	✓	O	M	F	125
		" ELIZA J.	WIFE	W	F	Oct 1848	51	M	32	14	12	KY	KY	KY							X	X	✓				
		" RILEY	SON	W	M	May 1883	17	S				KY	KY	KY				FARM LABORER			X	X	✓				
		" EFFIE J.	DAU	W	F	Jul 1885	14	S				KY	KY	KY				AT SCHOOL		2	✓	✓	✓				
		" CLAUDE	SON	W	M	Jan 1889	11	S				KY	KY	KY				FARM LABORER	0	2	✓	X	✓				
		" MAUDE	DAU	W	F	Jan 1889	11	S				KY	KY	KY				AT SCHOOL		2	✓	X	✓				
		" OLLIE W.	DAU	W	F	Apr 1892	8	S				KY	KY	KY				AT SCHOOL		2	✓	X	✓				
143	147	LEE, RILDA	HEAD	B	F	May 1842	58	Wd				KY	KY	KY				FARMER	0		X	X	✓	O	F	F	126
		" DANIEL	SON	B	M	Jun 1883	26	S				KY	KY	KY				FARM LABORER	0		✓	✓	✓				
		" KITTIE A.	DAU	B	F	May 1880	20	S				KY	KY	KY							✓	✓	✓				
144	148	GROOM, ANN	HEAD	B	F	May 1853	47	Wd		5	5	KY	KY	VA				FARMER	0		X	X	✓	O	F	F	127
		" BETTIE	DAU	B	F	Oct 1873	26	M	1	1	1	KY	KY	KY							✓	✓	✓				
		GROOMS, SALLIE	DAU	B	F	Jan 1875	25	S				KY	KY	KY							✓	✓	✓				
		" JESSE	SON	B	M	Jan 1878	22	S				KY	KY	KY				FARM LABORER	0		✓	✓	✓				
		" JAMES	SON	B	M	Sept 1883	16	S				KY	KY	KY				FARM LABORER	0		✓	✓	✓				
		" ELIGAH	SON	B	M	Jul 1886	13	S				KY	KY	KY				FARM LABORER	0		✓	✓	✓				
		LEE, MARY S.	GDAU	B	F	May 1894	6	S				KY	KY	KY													
		YOUNG, SALLY	MOTHER	B	F	May 1825	75	Wd				VA	VA	VA							X	X	✓				
		WHITNEY, ANNA	NEICE	B	F	Sept 1894	5	S				KY	KY	KY							X	X	✓				
145	144	WOOD, ORA	HEAD	W	F	Oct 1880	19	S				KY	VA	KY							✓	✓	✓	R		H	
		" SALLIE E.	DAU	W	F	Apr 1898	2	S				KY	KY	KY													
		" MAGNOLIA	DAU	W	F	May 1900	1/12	S				KY	KY	KY													

STATE - KENTUCKY
COUNTY - MONROE
Township or other division **GUM**

Enumerator THOMAS R. EVANS

Supervisor's Dist. No. _102_ Sheet No.
Enumeration Dist. No. _80_

No. of Family	No. of Dwelling	NAME	Relation	Color	Sex	DATE OF BIRTH Mon/Yr	Age at last birthday	Marital Status	# Years married	Mother of how many children?	# of these children living	NATIVITY Place of birth [this person]	Father of this person	Mother of this person	CITIZENSHIP Year of immigr.	# years in U.S.	Naturalization	OCCUPATION 10 years +	Months not employed	EDUCATION Attended school in months	Can read	Can write	Speak English	OWNERSHIP Owned or Rent	Owned -no mortage	Farm or house	# of farm schedule
		ISENBERG, TILDA J.	Lodger	W	F	Apr 1886	14	S				KY	KY	KY							X	X	✓				
146	150	GILLENWATERS, LUCIAN B	HEAD	W	M	May 1840	60	M	8			TN	TN	TN							✓	X	✓	O		F F	128
		" KITTIE H.	WIFE	W	F	Mar 1864	36	M	8	2	0	KY	KY	KY							✓	✓	✓				
		BENJAMIN H.	Son	W	M	Feb 1888	12	S				KY	TN	KY				FARM LABORER		5	✓	✓	✓				
		BARLOW, CHARLES P.	Lodger	W	M	July 1829	70	Wd				KY	VA	TN							✓	✓	✓				
147	151	WOODS, JESSE	HEAD	W	M	Aug 1843	56	M	23			KY	TN	TN				FARMER			✓	✓	✓	O		F F	129
		" NANCY A.	WIFE	W	F	Dec 1834	65	M	23	3	2	KY	KY	KY							✓	✓	✓				
		" MARY E.	DAU	W	F	Oct 1877	22	S				KY	KY	KY								✓	✓				
		" ISAAC J.	Son	W	M	Oct 1882	17	S				KY	KY	KY				FARM LABORER			✓	✓	✓				
		EMMIT, CHARLES	Lodger	W	M	July 1875	24	S				KY	KY	KY				FARM LABORER			✓	✓	✓				
148	152	BRITT, GEORGE W.	HEAD	W	M	Feb 1866	34	M	17			TN	KY	TN				FARMER			✓	X	✓	O		M F	130
		" SARAH	WIFE	W	F	Dec 1860	39	M	17	4	2	TN	TN	TN							✓	X	✓				
		" WILLIAM V.	Son	W	M	Sept 1882	17	S				KY	TN	TN				FARM LABORER			✓		✓ ✓				
		" LUTHER R.	Son	W	M	Oct 1891	8	S				KY	TN	TN													
149	153	RODGERS, WILLIAM J.	HEAD	W	M	Feb 1851	49	M	26			KY	KY	VA				FARMER			✓	X	✓	R		F	131
		" AMANDA	WIFE	W	F	Apr 1845	45	M	26	14	6	KY	TN	KY							X	X	✓				
		" EMILY	DAU	W	F	Aug 1875	24	S				KY	KY	KY							✓	X	✓				
		" CHARLES B.	Son	W	M	Nov 1877	22	S				KY	KY	KY				FARM LABORER			✓	✓	✓				
		" JERRY H.	Son	W	M	Oct 1888	11	S				KY	KY	KY				FARM LABORER	2	2	✓	X	✓				
		" VIRGIL	Son	W	M	Jul 18—	12	S				KY	KY	KY				FARM LABORER	2		✓	✓	✓				
		" CHRISTOPHER	Son	W	M	May 1892	8	S				KY	KY	KY													
		" MAY C.	DAU	W	F	Apr 1896	4	S				KY	KY	KY													
150	154	DOSSEY, WILLIAM J.	HEAD	W	M	May 1833	67	M	45			KY	VA	NC				FARMER			✓	✓	✓	O		F F	132
		" CATHERINE C.	WIFE	W	F	Jan 1835	65	M	45	14	10	KY	NC	KY							✓	✓	✓				
		" HENRY B.	Son	W	M	Aug 1879	21	S				KY	KY	KY							✓	✓	✓				
151	155	GUM, LIDDIE	HEAD	W	F	Mar 1835	65	Wd		1	1	KY	TN	TN							✓	X	✓	O		F F	133

STATE - KENTUCKY
COUNTY - MONROE
Township or other division GUM

Enumerator THOMAS R. EVANS

Supervisor's Dist. No. 102 Sheet No.
Enumeration Dist. No. 80

Location (No. of Family / No. of Dwelling)	NAME	Relation	Color	Sex	DATE OF BIRTH Mon/Yr	Age at last birthday	Marital Status	# Years married	Mother of how many children?	# of these children living	NATIVITY Place of birth [this person]	Father of this person	Mother of this person	CITIZENSHIP Year of immigr. / # years in U.S. / Naturalization	OCCUPATION 10 years +	Months not employed	Attended school in months	Can read	Can write	Speak English	Owned or Rent	Owned - no mortgage	Farm or house	# of farm schedule
	GUM, GILBERT G.	Son	W	M	Jan 1872	28	M				KY	KY	KY		FARMER			✓	✓	✓				
	" KITTIE A	Dau-in-law	W	F	Feb 1882	18	M				KY	KY	KY					✓	✓	✓				
152 156	ROBINSON, LEMUN	Head	W	M	May 1872	28	M	4			KY	TN	KY		FARMER			✓	✓	✓	R		F	134
	" ELLEN, N.	Wife	W	F	Oct 1876	23	M	4	2	2	KY	KY	KY					✓	✓	✓				
	" LACL(?) O.	Son	W	M	Jul 1896	3	S				KY	KY	KY											
	" PEARL S.	Dau	W	F	Sep 1898	1	S				KY	KY	KY											
153 157	LEWIS, THEODORE W.	Head	W	M	Jan 1820	80	M	11			TN	VA	TN		CAPALIST			✓	X	✓	O		F	H
	" ELIZABETH J.	Wife	W	F	Apr 1843	57	M	11			TN	VA	TN					✓	✓	✓				
154 158	GUM, JOHN	Head	W	M	May 1866	34	M	2			KY	KY	KY		FARMER			✓	✓	✓	O		F	135
	" MARY B.	Wife	W	F	Feb 1867	33	M	2	2	1	KY	KY	KY					✓	✓	✓				
	" PEARNIE W	Dau	W	F	Dec 1894	5	S				KY	KY	KY											
155 159	MILLER, ALEXANDER	Head	W	M	Jan 1846	54	M	2			KY	TN	KY		FARM LABORER			X	X	✓	R			H
	" , ANGLINE	Wife	W	F	Apr 1875	25	M	2			KY	KY	TN					X	X	✓				
156 160	GOAD, HARVEY	Head	W	M	Jul 1825	74	M	23			KY	KY	KY		FARMER			✓	✓	✓	O		F	136
	" SENSILDA(?)	Wife	W	F	Sep 1841	58	M	23	3	3	KY	KY	KY					X	X	✓				
	" MARY M.	Dau	W	F	Aug 1877	22	S				KY	KY	KY					✓	✓	✓				
	" WILLIAM T.	Son	W	M	Jul 1874	20	S				KY	KY	KY		FARM LABORER		3	✓	✓	✓				
	" HENRY T.	Son	W	M	Jul 1882	17	S				KY	KY	KY		FARM LABORER			✓	✓	✓				
157 161	PAYNE, MILARD F.	Head	W	M	Dec 1862	37	M	13			KY	KY	KY		FARMER			✓	✓	✓	O		F	137
	" , MARY	Wife	W	F	Feb 1860	40	M	13	3	3	KY	KY	KY					✓	✓	✓				
	" MAUD	Dau	W	F	Jul 1887	12	S				KY	KY	KY		AT SCHOOL		5	✓	✓	✓				
	" CHARLES	Son	W	M	Mar 1890	10	S				KY	KY	KY		FARM LABORER		5	✓	✓	✓				
	" CORA	Dau	W	F	May 1892	8	S				KY	KY	KY											
158 162	BRYANT, HUEL	Head	W	M	Jan 1840	60	M	14			KY	VA	KY		FARMER			✓	X	✓	O		F	138
	" JANE	Wife	W	F	Jan 1843	57	M	14	4	3	KY	TN	VA					✓	✓	✓				
	" ARTHUR	Son	W	M	Apr 1877	23	S				KY	KY	KY					✓	✓	✓				

STATE - KENTUCKY
COUNTY - MONROE
Township or other division   GUM

Enumerator THOMAS R. EVANS

Supervisor's Dist. No. 102 Sheet No.
Enumeration Dist. No. 80

No. of Family	No. of Dwelling	NAME	Relation	Color	Sex	DATE OF BIRTH Mon/Yr	Age at last birthday	Marital Status	# Years married	Mother of how many children?	# of these children living	Place of birth [this person]	Father of this person	Mother of this person	Year of immigr.	# years in U.S.	Naturalization	OCCUPATION 10 years +	Months not employed	Attended school in months	Can read	Can write	Speak English	Owned or Rent	Owned –no mortgage	Farm or house	# of farm schedule	
		BRYANT, ELLEN B	DAU	W	F	Aug 1883	16	S				KY	KY	KY							✓	✓	✓					
159	163	MURPHY, JOSEPH	HEAD	W	M	Oct 1845	54	M	45			KY	KY	KY				FARMER			✓	X	✓	O	F	H	139	
		" MARTHA J.	wife	W	F	Jul 1836	63	M	45	5	2	KY	TN	TN							✓	✓						
		" WILLIAM B.	Son	W	M	Dec 1872	27	S				KY	KY	KY				FARMER			✓	✓	✓					
160	164	FRANCE, EDWARD S.	HEAD	W	M	Feb 1866	34	M	8			KY	KY	KY				FARMER			X	X	✓	R		F	140	
		" WILLIE B.	wife	W	F	May 1878	22	M	8	3	3	KY	KY	KY							✓	✓	✓					
		" ARTHUR C.	Son	W	M	Aug 1893	6	S				KY	KY	KY														
		" MAIMIE E.	DAU	W	F	Jun 1896	3	S				KY	KY	KY														
		" BRYAN	Son	W	M	Mar 1899	1	S				KY	KY	KY														
161	165	ISENLANG(?), MARY	HEAD	W	F	Apr 1857	43	Wd				TN	TN	TN							✓	✓	✓	O		FH		
	166	MURPHY, PERNELIA A.	HEAD	W	F	Nov 1838	61	S				KY	NC	KY							✓	✓	✓	O		FH		
		" MARY J.	Sister	W	F	Feb 1844	56	S				KY	NC	KY							✓	✓	✓					
		MARGARET A.	Sister	W	F	Feb 1951	49	S				KY	NC	KY							✓	✓	✓					
		GILLENWATERS, MINNIE	LODGER	W	F	Mar 1878	22	S				KY	TN	KY							✓	✓	✓					
	167	FERMALL, GEORGE W.	HEAD	W	M	Feb 1859	41	M	15			KY	TN	KY				FARMER			✓	✓	✓	R		F	141	
		" JULIA A.	wife	W	F	Dec 1848	51	M	15	3	3	KY	NC	KY							✓	✓	✓					
		" BERTON(?)	Son	W	M	Sept 1885	14	S				KY	KY	KY				FARM LABORER			✓	✓	✓					
		" NORA E.	DAU	W	F	Jan 1889	11	S				KY	KY	KY				AT SCHOOL		5	✓	✓	✓					
		" MAUD J.	DAU	W	F	May 1890	10	S				KY	KY	KY				AT SCHOOL		5	✓	X	✓					
162	168	FERMALL, ANDREW H.	HEAD	W	M	Jan 1825	75	M	49			TN	TN	TN				FARMER	O		X	X	✓	O		FE	142	
		" LUCINDA	wife	W	F	Mar 1836	64	M	49	12	4	KY	VA	KY							✓	X	✓					
	169	FERMALL, PATRICK	HEAD	W	M	Feb 1875	25	M	7			KY	TN	KY				FARMER	O		✓	✓	✓	R		F	142	sic
		" ELLER	wife	W	F	Jan 1879	21	M	7	2	2	KY	KY	KY							✓	✓	✓					
		" MINNIE C.	DAU	W	F	Oct 1894	5	S				KY	KY	KY														
		" LUCINDA G.	DAU	W	F	Jan 1896	4	S				KY	KY	KY														
163	170	DOSSEY, ARTIS(?) P.	HEAD	W	M	Apr 1858	42	M	19			KY	KY	KY				FARMER	O		✓	✓	✓	O		F	143	

STATE - KENTUCKY
COUNTY - MONROE
Township or other division — GUM

Enumerator — THOMAS R. EVANS

Supervisor's Dist. No. 102 Sheet No.
Enumeration Dist. No. 80

Location (No. of Family / No. of Dwelling)	NAME	Relation	Color	Sex	DATE OF BIRTH Mon/Yr	Age at last birthday	Marital Status	# Years married	Mother of how many children?	# of these children living	Place of birth (this person)	Father of this person	Mother of this person	Year of immigr.	# years in U.S.	Naturalization	OCCUPATION 10 years +	Months not employed	Attended school in months	Can read	Can write	Speak English	Owned or Rent	Owned - no mortage	Farm or house	# of farm schedule
	DOSSEY, MANISA	WIFE	W	F	Apr 1856	44	M	19	7	7	TN	TN	TN							✓	✓	✓				
"	MAGGIE C.	DAU	W	F	Jul 1888	11	S				KY	KY	TN				AT SCHOOL		5	✓	✓	✓				
"	JEFFERSON	SON	W	M	Jan 1883	17	S				KY	KY	TN				FARM LABORER		5	✓	✓	✓				
"	GEORGE C.	SON	W	M	Aug 1884	15	S				KY	KY	TN				FARM LABORER		5	✓	✓	✓				
"	ELLER M.	DAU	W	F	Dec 1885	14	S				KY	KY	TN				AT SCHOOL		5	✓	✓	✓				
"	JOHN	SON	W	M	Dec 1888	11	S				KY	KY	TN				FARM LABORER		5	✓						
"	LECTA	DAU	W	F	Mar 1892	8	S				KY	KY	TN													
"	MARTA	DAU	W	F	Mar 1894	6	S				KY	KY	TN													
164/171	BUSH, MARY E.	HEAD	W	F	Mar 1839	61	W		2	2	KY	KY	VA				FARMER			✓	✓	✓	O	F	F	144
"	GILLAN C.	SON	W	M	Aug 1878	21	S				KY	KY	KY				FARM LABORER			✓	✓	✓				
"	ALMA M.	DAU	W	F	May 1882	18	S				KY	KY	KY				AT SCHOOL		5	✓	✓	✓				
165/172	MORAN(?) JOHN	HEAD	W	M	Aug 1834	65	M	4			KY	VA	KY				FARMER			✓	✓	✓	O	F	F	145
"	KITTIE A.	wife	W	F	Feb 1852	48	M	4	4	3	KY	KY	KY													
"	JAMES	SON	W	M	Fe 1871	29	S				KY	KY	KY				FARMER	0		✓	✓	✓				
"	SALLIE	DAU	W	F	May 1873	27	S				KY	KY	KY							✓	✓	✓				
"	FANNIE	DAU	W	F	Mar 1876	24	S				KY	KY	KY				FARM LABORER		3	✓	X	✓	R		H	
166/173	HARP, JOHN T.	HEAD	W	M	Jan 1867	33	M				KY	TN	TN							✓	X	✓				
"	TENNESSEE	WIFE	W	F	Sep 1857	42	M		1	1	TN	TN	TN							✓	X	✓				
"	MAUD A.	St.Dau	W	F	Jun 1889	10	S				KY	KY	TN				AT SCHOOL		2	✓	X	✓				
167/174	AUSTIN, CHARLES A.	HEAD	W	M	Jun 1853	46	M	25			KY	KY	TN				FARMER						O	F	F	146
"	MATILDA F.	WIFE	W	F	May 1856	44	M	25	10	8	KY	TN	KY							✓	✓	✓				
"	JAMES W.	SON	W	M	Jan 1879	21	S				KY	KY	KY				SALESMAN GROCERIES	0		✓	✓	✓				
"	GEORGE F.	SON	W	M	Nov 1886	13	S				KY	KY	KY				FARM LABORER		5	✓	✓	✓				
"	JOHN M.	SON	W	M	Apr 1889	11	S				KY	KY	KY				FARM LABORER		5	✓	✓	✓				
"	HARRY V.	SON	W	M	Jul 1891	8	S				KY	KY	KY													
"	GLADIUS N.	DAU	W	F	Aug 1894	5	S				KY	KY	KY													

STATE - KENTUCKY
COUNTY - MONROE
Township or other division   GUM

Enumerator THOMAS B. EVANS

Supervisor's Dist. No. 102 Sheet No.
Enumeration Dist. No. 80

No. of Family	No. of Dwelling	NAME	Relation	Color	Sex	DATE OF BIRTH Mon/Yr	Age at last birthday	Marital Status	# Years married	Mother of how many children?	# of these children living	Place of birth (this person)	Father of this person	Mother of this person	Year of immigr.	# years in U.S.	Naturalization	OCCUPATION 10 years +	Months not employed	Attended school in months	Can read	Can write	Speak English	Owned or Rent	Owned-no mortgage	Farm or house	# of farm schedule
		HARP, LIZZIE L.	DAU	W	F	Sep 1897	3	S				KY	KY	KY													
168	175	DOWNING, BARTON W.	HEAD	W	M	Mar 1879	21	M	1			KY	KY	KY				FARMER	0		✓	✓	✓	R		F	147
		" BESSIE M.	WIFE	W	F	Apr 1881	19	M	1			KY	KY	KY							✓	✓	✓				
169	176	SHORT, JEREMIAH B.	HEAD	W	M	Oct 1873	26	S				KY	KY	KY				FARMER	0		✓	✓	✓	O		F	148
		" JAMES H.	BROTHER	W	M	Feb 1876	24	S				KY	KY	KY				SALESMAN- GROCERIES	0		✓	✓	✓				
		" LAURA B.	SISTER	W	F	Mar 1879	21	S				KY	KY	KY							✓	✓	✓				
		" ROBERT	BROTHER	W	M	Mar 1884	16	S				KY	KY	KY				FARM LABORER		5	✓	✓	✓				
		" ORION C.	BROTHER	W	M	Aug 1886	13	S				KY	KY	KY				FARM LABORER		5	✓	✓	✓				
170	177	DOWNING, HARVEY	HEAD	B	M	Jan 1867	33	M	6			KY	KY	KY				FARMER	0		✓	✓	✓	R		F	149
		" ROSA E	WIFE	B	F	Oct 1876	23	M	6	1	1	KY	KY	KY							✓	✓	✓				
		" ALLIE	DAU	B	F	Dec 1896	3	S				KY	KY	KY													
171	178	PATTERSON, JOHN	HEAD	W	M	Oct 1857	43	M	22			KY	TN	TN				FARMER	0		✓	✓	✓	O		F	150
		" MARSELLA P.	WIFE	W	F	Jan 1860	40	M	22	6	6	KY	KY	KY							✓	✓	✓				
		" CORNELIUS P.	SON	W	M	Jul 1881	19	S				KY	KY	KY				AT SCHOOL		5	✓	✓	✓				
		" KITTIE	DAU	W	F	Oct 1882	17	S				KY	KY	KY				AT SCHOOL		4	✓	✓	✓				
		" ELIZABETH	DAU	W	F	Jan 1885	15	S				KY	KY	KY				AT SCHOOL		4	✓	✓	✓				
		" JAMES C.	SON	W	M	Dec 1888	11	S				KY	KY	KY				AT SCHOOL		5	✓	✓	✓				
		" MARY E.	DAU	W	F	Nov 1892	7	S				KY	KY	KY													
		" EMILY A.	DAU	W	F	Feb 1897	3	S				KY	KY	KY													
172	179	JONES, JAMES M. H.	HEAD	W	M	Jan 1859	41	M	22			KY	KY	KY				FARMER	0		✓	✓	✓	O		F	151
		" MARY A.	WIFE	W	F	May 1857	43	M	22	6	5	KY	KY	KY							✓	✓	✓				
		" EFFIE	DAU	W	F	Oct 1883	16	S				KY	KY	KY							✓	✓	✓				
		" MAUD	DAU	W	F	Feb 1887	13	S				KY	KY	KY							✓	✓	✓				
		" JAMES B.	SON	W	M	Feb 1899	1	S				KY	KY	KY													
173	180	SIMMONS, JAMES W.	HEAD	W	M	Dec 1860	39	Wd				KY	KY	KY							X	X	✓	O		F	152
		" IDA	DAU	W	F	Apr 1881	19	S				KY	KY	KY							X	X	✓				

STATE - KENTUCKY
COUNTY - MONROE
Township or other division — GUM

Enumerator THOMAS R. EVANS

Supervisor's Dist. No. 102 Sheet No.
Enumeration Dist. No. 80

No. of Family	No. of Dwelling	NAME	Relation	Color	Sex	DATE OF BIRTH Mon/Yr	Age at last birthday	Marital Status	# Years married	Mother of how many children?	# of these children living	Place of birth [this person]	Father of this person	Mother of this person	Year of immigr.	# years in U.S.	Naturalization	OCCUPATION 10 years +	Months not employed	Attended school in months	Can read	Can write	Speak English	Owned or Rent	Owned -no mortage	Farm or house	# of farm schedule
		SIMMONS, WILLIAM A.	Son	W	M	MAR 1884	16	S				KY	KY	KY				FARM LABORER	0		X	X	✓				
		" LUELLA	DAU	W	F	Sept 1885	14	S				KY	KY	KY							X	X	✓				
		" GEORGE F.	SON	W	M	Aug 1888	11	S				KY	KY	KY				FARM LABORER			X	X	✓				
		" JAMES H.	SON	W	M	MAY 1891	9	S				KY	KY	KY									✓				
174	181	EATON, THOMAS	HEAD	W	M	MAR 1871	29	M	8			KY	KY	KY				FARMER	0		X	X	✓	0	F	F	153
		" ALLIE	Wife	W	F	DEC 1866	33	M	8	4	3	KY	KY	KY							X	X	✓				
		" CLAUD A.	SON	W	M	JUL 1894	5	S				KY	KY	KY													
		" WILLIAM T.	SON	W	M	JUL 1895	4	S				KY	KY	KY													
		" LUCY A.	DAU	W	F	Apr 1899	1	S				KY	KY	KY													
175	182	WALLER(?) JAMES D.	HEAD	W	M	MAY 1856	44	M				KY	TN	KY							✓	X	✓	0	F	F	154
		" CORA E.	DAU-IN-LAW	W	F	DEC 1883	16	M				KY	KY	KY							✓	✓	✓				
		" JOSEPH C.	SON	W	M	NOV 1877	22	M				KY	KY	KY				FARM LABORER			✓	✓	✓				
		" ANNA	DAU	W	F	OCT 1891	8	S				KY	KY	KY													
176	183	WALLER, GEORGE	HEAD	W	M	JUL 1875	24	M	6			KY	TN	KY				FARMER			✓	X	✓	R		F	155
		" MARY T. W.	Wife	W	F	JAN 1877	23	M	6	2	2	KY	KY	KY							✓	✓	✓				
		" NOLA L.	DAU	W	F	MAR 1895	5	S				KY	KY	KY													
		" JAMES E.	SON	W	M	MAR 1898	2	S				KY	KY	KY													
	184	WALLER, JAMES A.	HEAD	W	M	AUG 1830	69	M	7			TN	TN	TN							✓	✓	✓	0		H	
		" TILLDA A.	Wife	W	F	MAY 1835	65	M	7	4		KY	KY	TN													
177	185	HAGAN, ROBERT	HEAD	W	M	MAY 1863	37	M	14			KY	KY	VA				FARMER	0		✓	✓	✓	0	F	F	156
		" MAY E.	Wife	W	F	—186(?)	33	M	14	6	6	KY	KY	KY							X	X	✓				
		" ROBERT L.	SON	W	M	MAR 1887	13	S				KY	KY	KY				FARM LABORER	0	3	✓	✓	✓				
		" HERSCHEL T.	SON	W	M	DEC 1888	11	S				KY	KY	KY				FARM LABORER	0	3	✓	X	✓				
		" ROSA (?)	SON	W	M	JUNE 1891	8	S				KY	KY	KY													
		" FLORA	DAU	W	F	JUL 1893	6	S				KY	KY	KY													
		" JAMES C	SON	W	M	JUN 1896	3	S				KY	KY	KY													

STATE - KENTUCKY
COUNTY - MONROE
Township or other division   GUM

TWELFTH CENSUS OF THE UNITED STATES 1900
- 34 -
Enumerator   THOMAS R. EVANS

Supervisor's Dist. No. 102   Sheet No.
Enumeration Dist. No. 80

No. of Family	No. of Dwelling	NAME	Relation	Color	Sex	DATE OF BIRTH Mon/Yr	Age at last birthday	Marital Status	# Years married	Mother of how many children?	# of these children living	NATIVITY Place of birth [this person]	Father of this person	Mother of this person	CITIZENSHIP Year of immigr.	# years in U.S.	Naturalization	OCCUPATION 10 years +	Months not employed	Attended school in months	Can read	Can write	Speak English	Owned or Rent	Owned -no mortage	Farm or house	# of farm schedule	
		HAGAN, FLOSSIE(?)	DAU	W	F	JUL 1898	1	S				KY	KY	KY														
178	186	THOMAS, JOE	HEAD	W	M	MAR 1855	45	M	22			KY	KY	KY				FARMER	0		✓	X	✓	0	F	F	157	
		" MARY S.	WIFE	W	F	AUG 1855	44	M	22	5	4	KY	IL	KY							✓	X	✓					
		" WILLIAM G.	SON	W	M	SEP 1884	15	S				KY	KY	KY				FARM LABORER		3	✓	X	✓					
		" HERSCHEL K.	SON	W	M	SEP 1889	10	S				KY	KY	KY				FARM LABORER		3	✓		✓					
		" JAMES L.	SON	W	M	MAY 1898	2	S				KY	KY	KY														
		PAYNE, SARAH	MOTHER IN LAW	W	F	APR 1830	70	Wd				KY	TN	TN							X	X	✓					
179	187	CANADA, GEORGE E.	HEAD	W	M	OCT 1874	25	M	8			KY	KY	KY				FARMER	0		✓	✓	✓	R		F	158	
		" LENA S.	WIFE	W	F	AUG 1875	24	M	8	2	2	KY	KY	KY							✓	✓	✓					
		" VERDA	DAU	W	F	OCT 1894	5	S				KY	KY	KY														
		" CARLAN	SON	W	M	NOV 1896	3	S				KY	KY	KY														
180	188	WALBERT, WILLIAM S.	HEAD	W	M	MAR 1855	45	M	25			KY	KY	KY				FARMER			✓	✓	✓	0	M	F	159	
		" CATHERINE	WIFE	W	F	JAN 1857	43	M	25	12	10	TN	TN	TN							✓	✓	✓					
		" DRUCILLA	DAU	W	F	DEC 1879	20	S				KY	KY	TN							✓	✓	✓					
		" JAMES D.	SON	W	M	DEC 1881	18	S				KY	KY	TN				FARM LABORER	0	0	✓	✓	✓					
		" SCHYLER R.	SON	W	M	DEC 1883	16	S				KY	KY	TN				FARM LABORER	0	0	✓	✓	✓					
		" LUCY E.	DAU	W	F	JUL 1886	13	S				KY	KY	TN				AT SCHOOL		3	✓	✓	✓					
		" WILLIAM R.	SON	W	M	JAN 1888	12	S				KY	KY	TN				FARM LABORER	0		✓	✓	✓					
		" NORA C.	DAU	W	F	JAN 1890	10	S				KY	KY	TN				AT SCHOOL		3	✓	X	✓					
		" ELLA L.	DAU	W	F	MAR 1893	7	S				KY	KY	TN														
		" ANNA C.	DAU	W	F	SEP 1894	5	S				KY	KY	TN														
		" MARY J.	DAU	W	F	FEB 1898	2	S				KY	KY	TN														
		" HUGH W.	FATHER	W	M	FEB 1825	75	Wd				KY	NC	KY				CAPALIST	0		✓	✓	✓					
181	189	COOK, ENOCH	HEAD	W	M	AUG 1869	30	M	9			TN	TN	TN				FARMER	0		✓	✓	✓	0	F	F	160	
		" VIRGIE B.	WIFE	W	F	NOV 1872	27	M	9	2	2	KY	KY	KY							✓	✓	✓					
		" WILLIAM H.	SON	W	M	MAR 1892	8	S				KY	TN	KY														

STATE - KENTUCKY
COUNTY - MONROE
Township or other division — GUM
Enumerator THOMAS R. EVANS

Supervisor's Dist. No. 102 Sheet No.
Enumeration Dist. No. 80

No. of Family	No. of Dwelling	NAME	Relation	Color	Sex	Date of Birth Mon/Yr	Age at last birthday	Marital Status	# Years married	Mother of how many children?	# of these children living	Place of birth (this person)	Father of this person	Mother of this person	Year of immigr.	# years in U.S.	Naturalization	Occupation 10 years +	Months not employed	Attended school in months	Can read	Can write	Speak English	Owned or Rent	Owned - no mortage	Farm or house	# of farm schedule
		COOK, MAMMIE B.	DAU	W	F	Feb 1895	5	S				KY	TN	KY													
182	190	WALBERT, DAVID S.	HEAD	W	M	Apr 1849	51	M	27			KY	KY	KY					0		✓	✓	✓	0	F	F	161
		" JULIA A.	WIFE	W	F	Jun 1854	45	M	27	5	3	KY	TN	KY							✓	✓	✓				
		" NANNY	DAU	W	F	Dec 1886	13	S				KY	KY	KY				AT SCHOOL		4	✓	✓	✓				
183	191	CARPENTER, GEORGE	HEAD	B	M	Aug 1858	41	Wd				KY	KY	KY				FARMER			✓	✓	✓	0	F	F	162
		" CLAY	SON	B	M	Aug 1881	18	S				KY	KY	KY				FARM LABORER	0		✓	✓	✓				
		" HALL (?) M.	DAU	B	F	Dec 1883	16	S				KY	KY	KY				AT SCHOOL		2	✓	✓	✓				
		" ADA	DAU	B	F	Aug 1887	13	S				KY	KY	KY				AT SCHOOL		2	✓	✓	✓				
		" EDWARD	SON	B	M	Aug 1889	10	S				KY	KY	KY				AT SCHOOL			✓	X	✓				
		" ROSA D.	DAU	B	F	Mar 1891	9	S				KY	KY	KY													
		" LUCY B.	DAU	B	F	Jul 1896	3	S				KY	KY	KY													
184	192	FRANKLIN, GILBERT	HEAD	B	M	Oct 1865	34	M	12			KY	KY	KY				FARMER	0		X	X	✓	R		F	163
		" LUTISIA	WIFE	B	F	Jun 1875	24	M	12	6	3	KY	KY	KY							✓	✓	✓				
		" MERTIE	DAU	B	F	Jun 1889	10	S				KY	KY	KY				AT SCHOOL		3	✓	✓	✓				
		" FOREST	SON	B	M	Mar 1892	8	S				KY	KY	KY													
		" LETHA	DAU	B	F	Feb 1896	4	S				KY	KY	KY													
185	193	FRANKLIN, BETTIE	HEAD	B	F	Jun 1866	33	Wd		5	5	KY	KY	KY							X	X	✓	R		H	
		" MOLLIE E.	DAU	B	F	Sep 1883	16	S				KY	KY	KY							X	X	✓				
		" WILLIAM J.	SON	B	M	Jul 1888	11	S				KY	KY	KY				FARM LABORER		6	X	X	✓				
		" PEARLY	DAU	B	F	Jul 1891	8	S				KY	KY	KY													
		" JOHN E.	SON	B	M	Mar 1894	6	S				KY	KY	KY													
		" BERTON	SON	B	M	Mar 1899	1	S				KY	KY	KY													
		HOWARD, RODA	MOTHER	B	F	Jun 1829	70	Wd				KY	KY	KY													
186	194	GOAD, MILTON B.	HEAD	W	M	Apr 1875	25	M	3			KY	TN	KY				SALES - DRY GOODS	0		✓	✓	✓	0		H	
		" ALMA	WIFE	W	F	Apr 1877	23	M	3	2	2	KY	KY	KY							✓	✓	✓				
		" MAUD E.	DAU	W	F	Dec 1897	2	S				KY	KY	KY													

STATE - KENTUCKY
COUNTY - MONROE
Township or other division **GUM**

Enumerator THOMAS R. EVANS

Supervisor's Dist. No. **102** Sheet No.
Enumeration Dist. No. **88**

No. of Family	No. of Dwelling	NAME	Relation	Color	Sex	Date of Birth Mon/Yr	Age at last birthday	Marital Status	# Years married	Mother of how many children?	# of these children living	Place of birth (this person)	Father of this person	Mother of this person	Year of immigr.	# years in U.S.	Naturalization	Occupation 10 years +	Months not employed	Attended school in months	Can read	Can write	Speak English	Owned or Rent	Owned—no mortage	Farm or house	# of farm schedule
		GOAD, ALLEEN	DAU	W	F	Apr 1899	1	S				KY	KY	KY													
187	195	FRANKLIN, BENJAMIN	HEAD	W	M	Nov 1861	38	M	18			KY	KY	KY				SALES MAN - DRY GOODS	0		✓	✓	✓	O		H	
		" LULA	WIFE	W	F	Mar 1864	36	M	18	4	4	TN	TN	TN							✓	✓	✓				
		" ELIZABETH C.	DAU	W	F	Nov 1883	16	S				KY	KY	TN				AT SCHOOL		5	✓	✓	✓				
		" (C-AI-?)	SON	W	M	Jun 1885	14	S				KY	KY	TN				AT SCHOOL		5	✓	✓	✓				
		" EULA	DAU	W	F	Feb 1887	13	S				KY	KY	TN				AT SCHOOL		5	✓	✓	✓				
		" LUCIUS (?)	SON	W	M	Jul 1892	7	S				KY	KY	TN													
188	196	HARRIS, WILLIAM H.	HEAD	W	M	May 1866	34	M	10			KY	VA	TN				PHYSICIAN	0		✓	✓	✓	O		F	164
		" LUCY	WIFE	W	F	Apr 1874	26	M	10	3	3	KY	KY	KY							✓	✓	✓				
		" MILLIE N.	DAU	W	F	May 1891	9	S				KY	KY	KY													
		" JAMES H.	SON	W	M	May 1893	7	S				KY	KY	KY													
		" GEORGE W.	SON	W	M	Jul 1895	4	S				KY	KY	KY													
189	197	AUSTIN, CHARLES Z.	HEAD	W	M	Jul 1870	29	M	4			KY	KY	KY							✓	✓	✓	O		H	
		" ELLEN S.	WIFE	W	F	Oct 1873	26	M	4			KY	KY	KY							✓	✓	✓				
190	198	COOK, WILLIAM G.	HEAD	W	M	Feb 1854	46	M	1			KY	KY	TN							✓	✓	✓	R		F	165
		" SALLY	WIFE	W	F	Nov 1861	38	M	1			KY	TN	TN							✓	✓	✓				
		" ROSA E.	DAU	W	F	Mar 1884	16	S				KY	KY	KY				AT SCHOOL		2	✓	✓	✓				
		" JAMES C.	SON	W	M	Aug 1885	14	S				KY	KY	KY				FARM LABORER	0	3	✓	✓	✓				
		" NANNIE M.	DAU	W	F	Nov 1889	10	S				KY	KY	KY				AT SCHOOL		5	✓	✓	✓				
		GOODMAN, NANCY	MOTHER IN LAW	W	F	Feb 1827	83	Wd				KY	NC	NC							✓	✓	✓				
191	199	GENTRY, ANDREW H.	HEAD	W	M	Aug 1845	54	M	31			TN	TN	TN				FARMER	0		✓	✓	✓	O		F	166
		" ELIZABETH	WIFE	W	F	Mar 1849	51	M	31	6	5	KY	KY	KY							✓	✓	✓				
		" ELLEN	DAU	W	F	Sept 1869	30	S				KY	TN	KY							✓	✓	✓				
		" THOMAS G.	SON	W	M	May 1871	29	M				KY	TN	KY				FARMER	0		✓	✓	✓	R		F	167
		" LOLA	DAU	W	F	Aug 1873	26	S				KY	TN	KY							✓	✓	✓				
		" FLORENCE	DAU	W	F	Feb 1877	23	S				KY	TN	KY				TEACHER			✓	✓	✓				

TWELFTH CENSUS OF THE UNITED STATES 1900

- 37 -

STATE - KENTUCKY
COUNTY - MONROE
Township or other division — GUM

Enumerator THOMAS R. EVANS

Supervisor's Dist. No. 162   Sheet No. ___
Enumeration Dist. No. 80   ___

Location No. of Family	No. of Dwelling	NAME	Relation	Color	Sex	DATE OF BIRTH Mon/Yr	Age at last birthday	Marital Status	# Years married	Mother of how many children?	# of these children living	Place of birth [this person]	Father of this person	Mother of this person	Year of immigr.	# years in U.S.	Naturalization	OCCUPATION 10 years +	Months not employed	Attended school in months	Can read	Can write	Speak English	Owned or Rent	Owned -no mortage	Farm or house	# of farm schedule	
		GENTRY, BURNSFORD	SON	W	M	JUL 1879	20	S				KY	TN	KY				FARM LABORER	0		✓	✓	✓					
		" GERTRUDE	DAU N LAW	W	F	JAN 1876	24	M				KY	TN	KY							✓	✓	✓					
192	200	FRANKLIN, HENRY C.	HEAD	W	M	MAR 1835	65	M	44			KY	VA	KY				DRUGIST (?)			✓	✓	✓	O	F	H		
		" MATILDA H.	WIFE	W	F	SEP 1837	62	M	44	5	4	KY	KY	KY							✓	✓	✓					
193	201	STONE, FRANCIS M.	HEAD	W	M	FEB 1836	64	M	36			TN	KY	KY				PHYSICIAN			✓	✓	✓	O	F	H		
		" MARTHA E.	WIFE	W	F	JUN 1843	56	M	36			KY	VA	KY							✓	✓	✓					
		CRANTZ, FRANCIS A.	LODGER	W	M	OCT 1869	30	—				KY	TN	TN				FARMER			✓	✓	✓	O		F	168	
194	202	HARLIN, WILLIAM J.	HEAD	W	M	DEC 1863	37	M	12			KY	TN	TN							✓	✓	✓	O	M	H		
		" SALLIE B.	WIFE	W	F	JUL 1871	28	M	12	1	1	KY	KY	KY							✓	✓	✓					
		" VERA L.	DAU	W	F	SEP 1888	11	S				KY	KY	KY				AT SCHOOL		5	✓	✓	✓					
		COMER, A. BUD (?)	BOARDER	W	M	MAR 1867	33	M	9			KY	KY	KY				MERCHANT - DRY GOODS	0		✓	✓	✓					
		" MATTIE G.	BOARDER	W	F	DEC 1872	27	M	9			KY	KY	KY							✓	✓	✓					
195	203	HARLIN, GEORGE W.	HEAD	W	M	APR 1848	52	M				KY	SC	SC				MERCHANT - DRY GOODS			✓	✓	✓	O	F	F	169	
		" FRANCIS N.	WIFE	W	F	NOV 1857	42	M				KY	KY	KY							✓	✓	✓					
196	204	NEAL, JAMES M.	HEAD	W	M	NOV 1827	72	M	50			TN	KY	VA				FARMER	0		✓	✓	✓	O	F	F		
		" MARGARET	WIFE	W	F	FEB 1830	70	M	50	10	5	KY	KY	KY							✓	✓	✓					
		TURNER, MARTHA J.	SERVANT	W	F	JUN 1866	33	Wd				KY	KY	KY				SERVANT			✓	✓	✓					
		" ROSA	LODGER	W	F	JUL 1885	14	S				KY	KY	KY							✓	✓	✓					
197	205	GIBBS, EUCLID W.	HEAD	W	M	DEC 1874	25	M	6			KY	TN	VA				FARMER	0		✓	✓	✓	O	F	F	170	
		" JENNIE	WIFE	W	F	MAY 1879	21	M	6	3	3	KY	KY	KY							✓	✓	✓					
		" RAY J.	SON	W	M	NOV 1895	4	S				KY	KY	KY														
		" REX J.	SON	W	M	JAN 1897	3	S				KY	KY	KY														
		" FRANK	SON	W	M	OCT 1899	7/12	S				KY	KY	KY														
198	206	COOK, EDGAR	HEAD	W	M	JUN 1878	21	M	1			KY	KY	KY				FARMER	0		✓	✓	✓	R		F	171	
		" ALLIE	WIFE	W	F	JUN 1881	18	M	1			KY	TN	KY							✓	✓	✓					
199	207	SEAY, WILLIAM H.	HEAD	W	M	AUG 1843	57	M	24			KY	VA	VA				PHYSICIAN	0		✓	✓	✓	O	T	H		

STATE - KENTUCKY
COUNTY - MONROE
Township or other division GUM

Enumerator THOMAS R. EVANS

Supervisor's Dist. No. 102 Sheet No.
Enumeration Dist. No. 80

No. of Family	No. of Dwelling	NAME	Relation	Color	Sex	DATE OF BIRTH Mon/Yr	Age at last birthday	Marital Status	# Years married	Mother of how many children?	# of these children living	Place of birth [this person]	Father of this person	Mother of this person	Year of immigr.	# years in U.S.	Naturalization	OCCUPATION 10 years +	Months not employed	Attended school in months	Can read	Can write	Speak English	Owned or Rent	Owned –no mortage	Farm or house	# of farm schedule
		SEAY, ZILLIA	WIFE	W	F	Jul 1857	42	M	24	9	6	TN	NC	TN							✓	✓	✓				
		" EMMET	Son	W	M	Nov 1876	23	S				KY	KY	TN				TEACHER OF COMMON SCHOOLS	6		✓	✓	✓				
		" MARY S.	DAU	W	F	Oct 1878	21	S				KY	KY	TN				TEACHER OF COMMON SCHOOLS	6		✓	✓	✓				
		" FLORA D.	DAU	W	F	Jul 1886	13	S				KY	KY	TN				A.T. SCHOOL		5	✓	✓	✓				
		" CECIL	DAU	W	F	Jun 1891	8	S				KY	KY	TN													
		" JOSEPH H.	Son	W	M	Dec 1894	5	S				KY	KY	TN													
		" BLANCHE	DAU	W	F	Jul 1899	10/12	S				KY	KY	TN													
200	208	HARLIN, JOHN H.	HEAD	W	M	Aug 1873	26	M	3			KY	KY	TN				MERCHANT– GROCERIES	0		✓	✓	✓	O	F	H	
		" SARAH M.	WIFE	W	F	Feb 1880	20	M	3	1	1	KY	NC	KY							✓	✓	✓				
		" SEWELL C.	Son	W	M	Oct 1899	7/12	S				KY	KY	KY													
201	209	GOAD, MILTON	HEAD	W	M	Feb 1837	63	M	31			TN	TN	TN				FARMER	0		✓	✓	✓	O	F	F	172
		" MARTHA E.	WIFE	W	F	Aug 1847	52	M	31	12	6	KY	KY	KY							✓	✓	✓				
		" BASCOM C.	Son	W	M	Nov 1871	28	S				KY	TN	KY				FARM LABORER	0		✓	✓	✓				
		" ADA M.	DAU	W	F	May 1882	18	S				KY	TN	KY				A.T. SCHOOL		4	✓	✓	✓		?		
		" DORA L.	DAU	W	F	Oct 1885	14	S				KY	TN	KY				A.T. SCHOOL		4	✓	✓	✓				
		" CAROL B.	Son	W	M	Nov 1888	11	S				KY	TN	KY				FARM LABORER		4	✓	✓	✓				
202	210	WILLIAMS, WILLIAM M.	HEAD	W	M	Dec 1844	55	M	32			TN	TN	VA				UNDERTAKER	0		✓	✓	✓	O	F	H	
		" CHARLOTTE	WIFE	W	F	Mar 1846	54	M	32			KY	VA	VA							✓	✓	✓				
		" IMOGENE	DAU	W	F	Dec 1872	27	S				KY	TN	KY							✓	✓	✓				
		" FRANK P.	Son	W	M	Dec 1879	20	S				KY	TN	KY							✓	✓	✓				
		" FANNIE	DAU	W	F	Apr 1884	16	S				KY	TN	KY				A.T. SCHOOL		5	✓	✓	✓				
203	211	LANE, JOHN B.	HEAD	W	M	Mar 1863	37	M	10			KY	KY	KY				BLACKSMITH			✓	✓	✓	R		H	
		" ANNA M.	WIFE	W	F	Oct 1872	27	M	10	3	3	KY	KY	KY							✓	✓	✓				
		" LURA M.	DAU	W	F	Sep 1890	9	S				KY	KY	KY							✓	✓	✓				
		" ROY J.	Son	W	M	Sep 1894	5	S				KY	KY	KY													
		" THOMAS R.	Son	W	M	Jul 1897	2	S				KY	KY	KY													

STATE - KENTUCKY
COUNTY - MONROE
Township or other division — GUM

Enumerator — THOMAS R. EVANS

Supervisor's Dist. No. 102 Sheet No.
Enumeration Dist. No. 80

No. of Family	No. of Dwelling	NAME	Relation	Color	Sex	Date of Birth Mon/Yr	Age at last birthday	Marital Status	# Years married	Mother of how many children?	# of these children living	Place of birth [this person]	Father of this person	Mother of this person	Year of immigr.	# years in U.S.	Naturalization	Occupation 10 years +	Months not employed	Attended school in months	Can read	Can write	Speak English	Owned or Rent	Owned -no mortage	Farm or house	# of farm schedule
204	212	FAULKNER, JAMES	HEAD	W	M	Jul 1831	68	M	44			KY	VA	KY				CARPENTER	0		✓	✓	✓	0		H	
		" THUSA J.	WIFE	W	F	Oct 1835	64	M	44	7	5	TN	TN	TN							✓	✓	✓				
		" JAMES H.	SON	W	M	Sep 1859	40	S				TN	KY	TN				CARPENTER	0		✓	✓	✓				
205	213	GROOMS, EDWARD	HEAD	W	M	Jul 1856	43	M	14			KY	VA	KY							✓	✓	✓	0	F	F	173
		" HALLIE	WIFE	W	F	Dec 1866	33	M	14	7	5	KY	TN	TN							✓	✓	✓				
		" LERA M.	DAU	W	F	Apr 1887	13	S				KY	KY	KY				AT SCHOOL		7	✓	✓	✓				
		" HUGH	SON	W	M	Oct 1889	10	S				KY	KY	KY				AT SCHOOL		7	✓	✓	✓				
		" WALTER B	SON	W	M	Oct 1891	8	S				KY	KY	KY													
		" RALPH B.	SON	W	M	Dec 1894	5	S				KY	KY	KY													
		" FRED	SON	W	M	Apr 1897	3	S				KY	KY	KY													
		FISHER, MINNIE	SERVANT	W	F	Nov 1880	19	S				KY	KY	KY				SERVANT			—	—	✓				
206	214	CARUTH, LUKE	HEAD	B	M	Mar 1848	52	M	25			KY	SC	TN				FARMER			X	X	✓	0	F	F	174
		" CELIE	WIFE	B	F	Feb 1859	41	M	25	4	4	KY	KY	KY							X	X	✓				
		" HENRY	SON	B	M	Nov 1875	24	S				KY	KY	KY				FARM LABORER		4	✓	✓	✓				
		" ISAAC	SON	B	M	Feb 1880	20	S				KY	KY	KY				FARM LABORER			✓	✓	✓				
		" ELLA	DAU	B	F	Oct 1883	16	S				KY	KY	KY				AT SCHOOL		1	✓	✓	✓				
		" EMERY	SON	B	M	Feb 1894	6	S				KY	KY	KY													
207	215	BASS, JAMES T.	HEAD	W	M	Feb 1839	61	M	39			TN	NC	VA				MILLER	3		✓	✓	✓	0	F	H	
		" JENNIE	WIFE	W	F	Jan 1845	55	M	39	10	7	TN	TN	TN				MILLINERY			✓	✓	✓				
		" BULAH	DAU	W	F	Nov 1884	16	S				KY	TN	TN				AT SCHOOL		3	✓	✓	✓				
		" LATON	DAU	W	F	Feb 1885	15	S				KY	TN	TN				AT SCHOOL		5	✓	✓	✓				
		" PAUL	SON	W	M	Oct 1890	9	S				KY	TN	TN							✓	✓	✓				
208	216	STONE, BARTON W.	HEAD	W	M	Feb 1830	70	M	49			TN	KY	TN				PHYSICIAN			✓	✓	✓	0	F	H	
		" MARTHA	WIFE	W	F	May 1830	70	M	49	3	0	KY	KY	TN							✓	✓	✓				
		BLYSE, NELLIE	SERVANT	B	F	Apr 1860	40	S				KY	KY	TN				SERVANT			✓	X	✓				
209	217	GOODMAN, JACOB	HEAD	W	M	Jan 1825	75	M	38			KY	NC	KY				HOTEL KEEPER	0		✓	✓	✓	0	F	F	175

TWELFTH CENSUS OF THE UNITED STATES 1900

STATE - KENTUCKY
COUNTY - MONROE
Township or other division — GUM

— 40 —

Enumerator THOMAS R. EVANS

No. of Family	No. of Dwelling	NAME	Relation	Color	Sex	Date of Birth Mon/Yr	Age at last birthday	Marital Status	Years married	Mother of how many children?	# of these children living	Place of birth (this person)	Father of this person	Mother of this person	Year of immigr.	# years in U.S.	Naturalization	Occupation	Months not employed	Attended school in months	Can read	Can write	Speak English	Owned or Rent	Owned - no mortgage	Farm or house	# of farm schedule
		GOODMAN, CATHERINE	Wife	W	F	Jul 1835	64	M	38			TN	VA	VA							✓	✓	✓				
		THOMAS, LAURA	Lodger	W	F	Feb 1882	18	S				KY	KY	KY							✓	✓	✓				
		SMITH, FANNY	Gr-Dau	W	F	Aug 1874	25	M	1			KY	KY	KY							✓	✓	✓				
		AUSTIN, WALTER	Gr-Son	W	M	Jan 1879	21	S				KY	KY	KY				SALESMAN DRY GOODS	0		✓	✓	✓				
210	218	STEEN, SARAH A.	Head	W	F	Mar 1826	74	Wd				KY	KY	KY							X	X	✓	O		FH	
		", JORINE(?)	Sister	W	F	Apr 1835	65	S				KY	KY	KY							X	X	✓				
211	219	GOODMAN, JACOB	Head	W	M	Oct 1867	32	M	8			KY	KY	KY				FARMER			✓	✓	✓	O		FF	176
		" ANNA G.	Wife	W	F	Jul 1873	26	M	8	2	1	KY	KY	KY							✓	✓	✓				
		" WALTER R.	Son	W	M	Aug 1899	10/12	S				KY	KY	KY													
212	220	HAGAN, JAMES R.	Head	W	M	Dec 1869	30	M	4			KY	KY	VA				FARMER	0		✓	✓	✓	R		F	177
		" ANNA F.	Wife	W	F	Mar 1881	19	M	4	1	1	KY	KY	KY							✓	✓	✓				
		" WILLIAM B.	Son	W	M	Mar 1896	4	S				KY	KY	KY													
213	221	FAULKNER, JOHN M.	Head	W	M	Aug 1869	30	M	12			KY	KY	VA				FARMER			✓	✓	✓	O		FF	178
		" IDA B.	Wife	W	F	Sept 1873	26	M	12	5	5	KY	KY	KY							✓	✓	✓				
		" NOLAN	Dau	W	F	Jun 1890	9	S				KY	KY	KY													
		" SNADA(?)	Son	W	M	Jun 1892	7	S				KY	KY	KY													
		" ROBERT A.	Son	W	M	Jun 1896	4	S				KY	KY	KY													
		" AMADALE	Dau	W	F	Apr 1897	3	S				KY	KY	KY													
		" ALDRICK	Son	W	M	Jul 1899	11/12	S				KY	KY	KY													
214	222	SHIVES, JAMES	Head	W	M	Apr 1839	61	M	32			KY	KY	KY				MILLER			✓	✓	✓	O		FH	
		" MOLLIE D.	Wife	W	F	Oct 1845	54	M	32	1	1	TN	TN	TN				FARMER			✓	✓					
215	223	GOODMAN, WILLIAM T.	Head	W	M	Apr 1869	31	M	10			KY	KY	KY				FARMER			✓	✓	✓				179
		" ANN T.	Wife	W	F	Jul 1869	30	M	10	4	4	KY	KY	KY							✓	✓	✓				
		" (MILLS I-?)	Son	W	M	Sep 1891	8	S				KY	KY	KY													
		" MARVIN	Son	W	M	May 1894	6	S				KY	KY	KY													
		" BITTUE(?)	Dau	W	F	Nov 1897	2	S				KY	KY	KY													

STATE - KENTUCKY
COUNTY - MONROE
Township or other division — 41 — GUM

Enumerator THOMAS R. EVANS

Supervisor's Dist. No. 102 Sheet No.
Enumeration Dist. No. 80

No. of Family	No. of Dwelling	NAME	Relation	Color	Sex	DATE OF BIRTH Mon/Yr	Age at last birthday	Marital Status	# Years married	Mother of how many children?	# of these children living	Place of birth [this person]	Father of this person	Mother of this person	Year of immigr.	# years in U.S.	Naturalization	OCCUPATION 10 years +	Months not employed	Attended school in months	Can read	Can write	Speak English	Owned or Rent	Owned -no mortgage	Farm or house	# of farm schedule
		GOODMAN, ERBIE	Son	W	M	Nov 1899	6/12	S				KY	KY	KY													
216	224	GENTRY, SIMON	Head	W	M	Jul 1854	45	M	18			TN	KY	KY				FARMER			✓	✓	✓	O		F	180
		" SARAH S	Wife	W	F	Nov 1866	33	M	18	1	1	KY	TN	KY							✓	✓					
		" EDWARD	Son	W	M	May 1886	14	S				KY	KY	KY				FARM LABORER	O		✓	✓					
		" KITTIE W.	Dau	W	F	Aug 1882	17	S				KY	KY	KY							✓	✓	✓				
217	225	SPILMAN, ROBERT H.	Head	W	M	May 1846	54	M	26			KY	IL	KY				MINISTER	O		✓	✓	✓	O		FH	
		" M. FANNY	Wife	W	F	June 1846	53	M	26			KY	KY	VA							✓	✓	✓				
218	226	DUNN, THOMAS C.	Head	W	M	Mar 1861	39	M	12			KY	KY	KY				PHYSICIAN	O		✓	✓	✓	O		FF	
		" BETTIE C.	Wife	W	F	Feb 1868	32	M	12	1	1	KY	KY	KY							✓	✓	✓				
		" JACK C.	Son	W	M	Apr 1892	8	S				KY	KY	KY								✓	✓				
219	227	WILLIAMSON, JAMES	Head	W	M	Feb 1850	50	M	23			TN	TN	TN				FARMER			✓	✓	✓	O		F	181
		" NANCY	Wife	W	F	Oct 1850	49	M	23			KY	KY	KY							✓	✓	✓				
		" WILLIAM O.	Son	W	M	Jun 1881	18	S				KY	TN	KY							✓	✓	✓				
		" EMERY J.	Son	W	M	Oct 1884	15	S				KY	TN	KY							✓	✓	✓				
		" BRUTON	Son	W	M	Jul 1891	8	S				KY	TN	KY													
220	228	GIBBS, JOHN A.	Head	W	M	Dec 1852	47	M	27			TN	NC	TN				SADLER (?)			✓	✓	✓	O		F	182
		" CALADONIA	Wife	W	F	Feb 1850	50	M	27	9	8	VA	VA	VA							✓	✓	✓				
		" Ka (?)	Son	W	M	Feb 1884	16	S				KY	TN	VA				FARMER			✓	✓	✓				
		" FANNY	Dau	W	F	May 1886	14	S				KY	TN	VA				AT SCHOOL		5	✓	✓	✓				
		" MEREDITH	Son	W	M	Sept 1889	10	S				KY	TN	VA				FARM LABORER		5	✓	✓	✓				
		" JUAY (?)	Son	W	M	Feb 1892	8	S				KY	TN	VA							✓	✓	✓				
		" MAUD	Dau	W	F	May 1878	22	S				KY	TN	VA							✓	✓	✓				
221	229	FAULKNER, ROSCOE R.	Head	W	M	Oct 1858	41	M	12			KY	KY	KY				CARPENTER			✓	✓	✓	O		FH	
		" EFFIE, J	Wife	W	F	Nov 1872	27	M	12	6	4	TN	TN	TN							✓	✓	✓				
		" LENA	Dau	W	F	Feb 1892	8	S				TN	KY	TN													
		" ALBERT C.	Son	W	M	Jul 1894	5	S				TN	KY	TN													

STATE - KENTUCKY
COUNTY - MONROE
Township or other division: GUM
Enumerator THOMAS R. EVANS

Supervisor's Dist. No. 102 Sheet No.
Enumeration Dist. No. 80

No. of Family	No. of Dwelling	Name	Relation	Color	Sex	Date of Birth Mon/Yr	Age	Marital Status	# Yrs married	Mother of how many children	# living	Place of birth	Father	Mother	Occupation	Months not employed	Attended school	Can read	Can write	Speak English	Owned/Rent	Farm/house	# farm sched.
		FAULKNER, ALTA	DAU	W	F	Feb 1897	3	S				TN	KY	TN									
		" WILLIE M.	DAU	W	F	Mar 1899	1	S				TN	KY	TN									
222	230	GOODMAN, JAMES	HEAD	W	M	Oct 1847	52	M	30			KY	NC	TN	FARMER	0		✓	✓	✓	0	F	183
		" DARTHULA H.	wife	W	F	Aug 1849	50	M	30	4	3	KY	KY	TN				✓	✓				
		" MINNIE M	DAU	W	F	Sep 1872	27	S				KY	KY	KY	MILLINERY	0		✓	✓				
223	231	GOAD, PAULINE P.	HEAD	W	F	May 1842	58	Wd				TN	TN	TN				✓	✓		0	FH	
224	232	ROARK, SALLIE	HEAD	W	F	Jun 1866	33	Wd		5	5	KY	KY	KY				✓	✓		0	FH	
		" LIZZIE	DAU	W	F	Dec 1882	17	S				KY	KY	KY	AT SCHOOL		4	✓	✓				
		" ALLIE B.	DAU	W	F	Jan 1885	15	S				KY	KY	KY	AT SCHOOL		2½	✓	✓				
		" ELLER D.	DAU	W	F	Oct 1890	9	S				KY	KY	KY									
		" AUGUSTINE N.	SON	W	M	Jan 1894	6	S				KY	KY	KY									
		" SCOTT	SON	W	M	Apr 1896	4	S				KY	KY	KY									
		NEAL, ELIZABETH	MOTHER	W	F	Mar 1840	60	Wd				KY	KY	KY				✓	✓				
225	233	DOWNING, BEN	HEAD	W	M	Nov 1849	50	Wd				KY	KY	VA	FARMER	0		✓	✓	✓	0	F F	184
	234	DOWNING, GEORGE W.	HEAD	W	M	Nov 1868	31	M	8			KY	KY	KY	TRADER	0		✓	✓	✓	R	H	
		" K P	wife	W	F	Jan 1874	26	M	8	4	2	KY	KY	KY				✓	✓	✓			
		" RUDOLPH	SON	W	M	Jun 1893	6	S				KY	KY	KY									
		" RUTH	DAU	W	F	May 1897	3	S				KY	KY	KY									
226	235	FERGUSON, HENRIETTA	HEAD	B	F	May 1866	34	Wd		5	5	KY	KY	KY	DAY WASHER WOMAN	0		X	X	✓	R	H	
		" MARS	SON	B	M	Nov 1881	18	S				KY	KY	KY	DAY LABORER	0		✓	X	✓			
		" HALLE B.	DAU	B	F	Jun 1883	16	S				KY	KY	KY	AT SCHOOL		3	✓	✓	✓			
		" JAMES T.	SON	B	M	May 1888	12	S				KY	KY	KY	AT SCHOOL		3	✓	X	✓			
		" HENRY W.H.	SON	B	M	Mar 1890	10	S				KY	KY	KY	AT SCHOOL		3	✓	X	✓			
		" FRED D.	SON	B	M	Jun 1893	6	S				KY	KY	KY									
227	236	DEMPSY, WILLIAM K.	HEAD	W	M	Apr 1851	49	M	19			KY	VA	KY	PAINTER			✓	✓	✓	R	H	
		" CAROLINE	WIFE	W	F	Mar 1856	44	M	19	6	3	KY	KY	KY				✓	✓	✓			

STATE - KENTUCKY
COUNTY - MONROE
Township or other division: GUM
Enumerator: THOMAS R. EVANS

Supervisor's Dist. No. 102 Sheet No.
Enumeration Dist. No. 80

No. of Family	No. of Dwelling	NAME	Relation	Color	Sex	DATE OF BIRTH Mon/Yr	Age at last birthday	Marital Status	# Years married	Mother of how many children?	# of these children living	Place of birth [this person]	Father of this person	Mother of this person	Year of immigr.	# years in U.S.	Naturalization	OCCUPATION 10 years +	Months not employed	Attended school in months	Can read	Can write	Speak English	Owned or Rent	Owned - no mortgage	Farm or house	# of farm schedule
		DEMPSY, ANNA E.	DAU	W	F	Apr 1885	15	S				KY	KY	KY				At School		5	✓	✓	✓				
		" FLORENCE E.	DAU	W	F	Sep 1888	11	S				KY	KY	KY				AT SCHOOL		5	✓	✓	✓				
		JACKSON, BENJAMIN	BOARDER	W	M	MAY 1840	60	Wd				KY	KY	KY				CARPENTER			✓	✓	✓				
228	237	LANE, JAMES M.	HEAD	W	M	OCT 1865	34	M	13			KY	KY	KY				BLACKSMITH	0		✓	✓		R		H	
		" MOLLIE	WIFE	W	F	Sep 1870	29	M	13	4	4	KY	KY	KY							✓	✓					
		" JOHN H.	SON	W	M	Nov 1887	12	S				KY	KY	KY				AT SCHOOL		9	✓	✓					
		" BERTHA M.	DAU	W	F	MAR 1889	11	S				KY	KY	KY				AT SCHOOL		9	✓	✓					
		" OLLIE L.	DAU	W	F	JUN 1891	8	S				KY	KY	KY													
		" OMER J.	DAU	W	F	MAY 1893	7	S				KY	KY	KY													
		" MARTHA	MOTHER	W	F	MAY 1840	60	Wd			2	KY	KY	KY							✓	✓	✓				
		" MARCELLA	SISTER	W	F	JAN 1872	28	S				KY	KY	KY							✓	✓	✓				
229	238	STEVENS, JAMES T.	HEAD	W	M	JUL 1857	42	M	12			KY	KY	KY				FARMER	0		✓	✓	✓	R		F	185
		" NANNIE	WIFE	W	F	Nov 1862	37	M	12	2	2	KY	KY	KY							✓	✓	✓				
		" WILLIAM T.	SON	W	M	Aug 1888	11	S				KY	KY	KY													
		" CORA D.	DAU	W	F	DEC 1892	7	S				KY	KY	KY													
		GILLAM, JOHN D.	BOARDER	W	M	JUL 1842	57	Wd				KY	KY	KY				MINISTER			✓	✓	✓				
230	239	SEAY, JOHN W.	HEAD	W	M	Nov 1831	68	Wd				VA	VA	VA				FARMER			✓	✓	✓		O	F	186
231	240	FRAIM, JAMES M.	HEAD	W	M	SEP 1848	51	M	22			KY	TN	KY				FARMER			✓	✓	✓		O	F	187
		" KITTIE A.	WIFE	W	F	Apr 1853	47	M	22	9	8	KY	KY	KY							✓	✓	✓				
		" WILLIAM W.	SON	W	M	MAY 1879	21	S				KY	KY	KY				FARM LABORER			✓	✓	✓				
		" LUCY N.	DAU	W	F	Sept 1880	19	S				KY	KY	KY							✓	✓	✓				
		" LILY M.	DAU	W	F	JUL 1882	17	S				KY	KY	KY							✓	✓	✓				
		" JOHN P.	SON	W	M	JUN 1884	15	S				KY	KY	KY				FARM LABORER		4	✓	✓	✓				
		" JILEY(?) B.	SON	W	M	OCT 1886	13	6				KY	KY	KY				FARM LABORER		4	✓	✓	✓				
		" MARK C.	SON	W	M	DEC 1888	11	S				KY	KY	KY				FARM LABORER		4	✓	✓	✓				
		" MONNA	DAU	W	F	JUN 1891	8	S				KY	KY	KY													

STATE - KENTUCKY
COUNTY - MONROE
Township or other division

TWELFTH CENSUS OF THE UNITED STATES 1900

— 44 —

GUM

Enumerator THOMAS R. EVANS

Supervisor's Dist. No. 102 Sheet No.
Enumeration Dist. No. 80

No. of Family	No. of Dwelling	NAME	Relation	Color	Sex	DATE OF BIRTH Mon/Yr	Age at last birthday	Marital Status	# Years married	Mother of how many children?	# of these children living	Place of birth [this person]	Father of this person	Mother of this person	Year of immigr.	# years in U.S.	Naturalization	OCCUPATION 10 years +	Months not employed	Attended school in months	Can read	Can write	Speak English	Owned or Rent	Owned -no mortgage	Farm or house	# of farm schedule	
		FRAIM, ROBERT	Son	W	M	Nov 1893	6	S				KY	KY	KY														
		HUGHES, JOHN P.	Nephew	W	M	Jun 1897	2	S				KY	KY	KY														
232	241	TEMPLE, WILLIAM	Head	W	M	Jul 1847	52	M	15			TN	TN	NC				FARMER			X	X	✓	O	F	F	188	
		" EFFIE E.	Wife	W	F	Mar 1855	45	M	15	2	2	TN	TN	TN							X	X	✓					
		" JOHN R.	Son	W	M	Apr 1876	24	S				KY	TN	TN				DAY LABORER	6		X	X	✓					
		" MARY E.	Dau	W	F	Aug 1878	21	S				TN	TN	TN							X	X	✓					
		" WILLIAM J.	Son	W	M	Oct 1879	20	S				KY	TN	TN				DAY LABORER	6		X	X	✓					
		" DORRIS	Son	W	M	Nov 1884	15	S				KY	TN	TN				FARM LABORER			X	X	✓					
		" HARISON	Son	W	M	May 1889	11	S				KY	TN	TN				FARM LABORER			X	X	✓					
		" HENRY	Son	W	M	Jan 1891	9	S				KY	TN	TN														
233	242	WILLIAMS, TIMOTHY	Head	W	M	Oct 1875	24	M	9			KY	KY	TN				FARMER	0		✓	X	✓	O	F	F	189	
		" MARY I.	Wife	W	F	May 1874	26	M	9	4	3	KY	KY	KY							✓	✓	✓					
		" BERTHA N.	Dau	W	F	Feb 1892	8	S				KY	KY	KY														
		" JOHN D.	Son	W	M	Aug 1894	5	S				KY	KY	KY														
		" JAMES H.	Son	W	M	Dec 1898	1	S				KY	KY	KY														
234	243	BISHOP, MARY	Head	W	F	Mar 1834	66	Wd				KY	KY	KY							X	X	✓	O		H		
		" HENRY F.	Son	W	M	Mar 1870	30	M	1			KY	KY	KY							✓	✓	✓					
		" FRANCIS	Dau-in-law	B	F	Apr 1874	26	M	1			KY	KY	KY							X	X	✓					
235	244	JONES, ALFRED	Head	W	M	Apr 1875	25	M	6			TN	NC	NC				FARMER	0		✓	✓	✓	R		F	190	
		" MAGGIE M.	Wife	W	F	Mar 1876	24	M	6	3	3	KY	TN	KY							✓	✓	✓					
		" BUFORD E.	Son	W	M	Jan 1895	5	S				KY	TN	KY														
		" JENNIE P.	Dau	W	F	Nov 1896	3	S				KY	TN	KY														
		" BESSIE	Dau	W	F	Jul 1899	10/12	S				KY	TN	KY														
		WALLER, DAVID	Servant	W	M	— —	—					KY	KY	KY				FARM LABORER	4		✓	✓	✓					
236	245	DUNCAN, JOHN G.	Head	W	M	Dec 1858	41	M				TN	TN	VA				FARMER	0		✓	✓	✓	O	F	F	191	
		" NANNIE	Wife	W	F	Apr 1869	31	M				KY	TN	KY							✓	✓	✓					

STATE - KENTUCKY
COUNTY - MONROE
Township or other division — GUM

Enumerator — THOMAS R. EVANS

Supervisor's Dist. No. 102 Sheet No.
Enumeration Dist. No. 80

No. of Family	No. of Dwelling	NAME	Relation	Color	Sex	Date of Birth Mon/Yr	Age at last birthday	Marital Status	# Years married	Mother of how many children?	# of these children living	Place of birth (this person)	Father of this person	Mother of this person	Year of immigr.	# years in U.S.	Naturalization	Occupation 10 years +	Months not employed	Attended school in months	Can read	Can write	Speak English	Owned or Rent	Owned - no mortage	Farm or house	# of farm schedule
		DUNCAN, HERSCHEL	Son	W	M	NOV 1888	11	S				KY	TN	KY				FARM LABORER			✓	✓	✓				
		" CHARLES W.	Son	W	M	MAR 1890	10	S				KY	TN	KY				FARM LABORER			✓	✓	✓				
237	246	BUTRAM, THOMAS	Head	W	M	MAY 1862	38	M	13			KY	KY	KY				FARMER	0		✓	✓	✓	R		F	192
		" DUESSA	Wife	W	F	MAR 1859	41	M	13			KY	TN	TN							✓	✓	✓				
		" JOHN	Son	W	M	JUL 1894	5	S				KY	KY	KY													
		" DOLPHA	Son	W	M	JUN 1897	3	S				KY	KY	KY													
238	247	GREGORY, HENRY E.	Head	W	M	APR 1875	25	M	0			KY	VA	VA				FARM LABORER	2		✓	✓	✓	R		H	
		" ARTIE	Wife	W	F	OCT 1879	20	M	0	1	1	KY	KY	KY							✓	✓	✓				
		" WILLIAM F.	Son	W	M	APR 1899	1	S				KY	KY	KY													
239	248	FRANKLIN, JEFFERSON	Head	B	M	DEC 1829	70	M	32			KY	KY	VA				FARMER	0		X	X	✓	O		F	193
		" MARY L.	Wife	B	F	MAR 1842	58	M	32	5	5	KY	KY	KY							X	X	✓				
		" JOHN	Son	B	M	AUG 1868	31	Wd				KY	KY	KY				DAY LABORER	3		✓	✓	✓				
		" DONNY	Dau	B	F	OCT 1881	18	S				KY	KY	KY							✓	✓	✓				
		" WILLIAM T.	Son	B	M	JUL 1884	15	S				KY	KY	KY				FARM LABORER									
		" FLORA GR-DAU		B	F	SEP 1891	8	S				KY	KY	KY													
		" ALMA GR-DAU		B	F	JUN 1899	11/12	S				KY	KY	KY													
240	249	CRAWFORD, ALFRED	Head	W	M	MAY 1861	39	M	16			KY	KY	KY				FARMER			✓	✓	✓	O	M	F	194
		" ARDELLA B.	Wife	W	F	MAR 1869	31	M	16	7	5	KY	KY	KY							✓	X	✓				
		" MARY E.	Dau	W	F	JAN 1885	15	S				KY	KY	KY				AT SCHOOL		4	✓	✓	✓				
		" JAMES G.	Son	W	M	NOV 1886	13	S				KY	KY	KY				FARM LABORER		4	✓	✓	✓				
		" WILLIAM	Son	W	M	APR 1890	10	S				KY	KY	KY				FARM LABORER		4	✓	✓	✓				
		" CECIL	Dau	W	F	JUN 1893	7	S				KY	KY	KY													
		" TIMOTHY B.	Son	W	M	OCT 1894	5	S				KY	KY	KY													
		" MARTHA O.	Dau	W	F	SEP 1896	3	S				KY	KY	KY													
241	250	GOODMAN, FINIS	Head	W	M	MAR 1854	46	M	23			KY	KY	KY				FARMER	0		✓	X	✓	O		F	195
		" SARAH E.	Wife	W	F	JUN 1858	41	M	23	5	5	KY	KY	KY													

STATE - KENTUCKY
COUNTY - MONROE
Township or other division — GUM

Enumerator THOMAS R. EVANS

Supervisor's Dist. No. _102_ Sheet No.
Enumeration Dist. No. _80_

No. of Family	No. of Dwelling	NAME	Relation	Color	Sex	DATE OF BIRTH Mon/Yr	Age at last birthday	Marital Status	# Years married	Mother of how many children?	# of these children living	Place of birth [this person]	Father of this person	Mother of this person	Year of immigr.	# years in U.S.	Naturalization	OCCUPATION 10 years +	Months not employed	Attended school in months	Can read	Can write	Speak English	Owned or Rent	Owned -no mortgage	Farm or house	# of farm schedule
		GOODMAN, HENRY S.	SON	W	M	Nov 1877	23	S				KY	KY	KY				FARM LABORER	0		✓	✓	✓				
		" WILLIAM S.	SON	W	M	Mar 1882	18	S				KY	KY	KY				FARM LABORER			✓	✓	✓				
		" BENJAMIN	SON	W	M	Jun 1886	13	S				KY	KY	KY				FARM LABORER			✓	✓	✓				
		" RILDA B.	DAU	W	F	May 1889	11	S				KY	KY	KY													
		" BASSIE	DAU	W	F	Aug 1891	8	S				KY	KY	KY													
242	251	BISHOP, JOHN C.	HEAD	W	M	Feb 1861	39	S				KY	KY	KY				DAY LABORER			✓	✓		R		H	
243	252	JONES, JOHN C.	HEAD	W	M	Jan 1878	21	M				KY	KY	KY				FARMER			✓	✓		R		F	196
		" MATTIE E.	WIFE	W	F	Nov 1877	22	M				KY	KY	KY								✓	✓				
244	253	EATON, HENRY W.	HEAD	W	M	Dec 1861	38	M	15			KY	KY	KY				FARMER			✓	✓	✓	O	F	F	197
		" ARENA A.	WIFE	W	F	Feb 1863	37	M	15	8	5	KY	KY	KY								✓	✓				
		" ALLIE A.	DAU	W	F	Dec 1885	14	S				KY	KY	KY				AT SCHOOL		3	✓	X	✓				
		" MAGGIE	DAU	W	F	Apr 1890	10	S				KY	KY	KY				AT SCHOOL		3	✓	✓	✓				
		" MOLLIE B.	DAU	W	F	Mar 1891	9	S				KY	KY	KY													
		" WILLIAM G.	SON	W	M	Oct 1895	4	S				KY	KY	KY													
		" JOHN B.	SON	W	M	Nov 1898	1	S				KY	KY	KY													
245	254	STREET, CHARLES	HEAD	B	M	Mar 1851	49	M	28			GA	GA	GA				FARMER	0		X	X	✓	O	F	F	198
		" SARAH A.	WIFE	B	F	Jan 1852	48	M	28	5	0	TN	TN	TN							✓	✓	✓				
		MATOX, WILLIAM A.	GR-SON	B	M	Mar 1893	7	S				KY	KY	KY													
246	255	HOWARD, JOHN R.	HEAD	B	M	Nov 1839	60	Wd				KY	KY	KY				FARMER	0		✓	X	✓	O	F	F	199
		" THOMAS N.	SON	B	M	Jan 1873	27	S				KY	KY	KY				TEACHER	7		✓	✓	✓				
		" MARY M.	DAU	B	F	Jul 1875	24	S				KY	KY	KY							✓	✓	✓				
		" SAMUEL C.	SON	B	M	Nov 1877	22	S				KY	KY	KY				TEACHER	7		✓	✓	✓				
		" JAMES H.	SON	B	M	Sept 1880	19	S				KY	KY	KY				FARM LABORER			✓	✓	✓				
		" HENRY B.	SON	B	M	Feb 1883	17	S				KY	KY	KY				FARM LABORER			✓	✓	✓				
		" SUELLA	DAU	B	F	Mar 1885	15	S				KY	KY	KY				AT SCHOOL		5	✓	✓	✓				
		" ROBERT B.	SON	B	M	Sept 1887	12	S				KY	KY	KY				FARMER		5	✓	✓	✓				

STATE - KENTUCKY
COUNTY - MONROE GUM
Township or other division

— 47 —

Enumerator THOMAS R. EVANS

Supervisor's Dist. No. 102 Sheet No.
Enumeration Dist. No. 80

No. of Family	No. of Dwelling	NAME	Relation	Color	Sex	Date of Birth Mon/Yr	Age at last birthday	Marital Status	# Years married	Mother of how many children?	# of these children living	Place of birth this person	Father of this person	Mother of this person	Citizenship	Occupation 10 years +	Months not employed	Attended school in months	Can read	Can write	Speak English	Owned or Rent	Owned -no mortgage	Farm or house	# of farm schedule
247	256	STINSON, MAY B.	HEAD	W	F	DEC 1860	39	wd				KY	KY	KY		FARMER			✓	✓	✓	O		FF	200
		" WILLIAM W.	SON	W	M	FEB 1889	11	S				KY	TN	KY		FARM LABORER		5	✓	✓	✓				
		" LEROY	SON	W	M	MAR 1893	7	S				TN	TN	TN											
248	257	HARRIS, HALLIE E.	HEAD	W	F	APR 1847	53	wd				TN	TN	TN					✓	✓	✓	O		FH	
		" MARY G.	STEP DAU	W	F	APR 1858	42	S				KY	KY	KY					X	X	✓				
249	258	COOK, ROBERT N.	HEAD	W	M	JAN 1856	44	M	19			KY	KY	KY		FARMER	O		✓	✓	✓	O		FF	201
		" OLLIE B.	wife	W	F	JAN 1859	41	M	19	10	5	KY	KY	KY					✓	✓	✓				
		" NETTIE E.	DAU	W	F	NOV 1884	15	S				KY	KY	KY		AT SCHOOL		5	✓	✓	✓				
		" AVA	DAU	W	F	JAN 1887	13	S				KY	KY	KY		AT SCHOOL		5	✓	✓	✓				
		" VERA P.	DAU	W	F	FEB 1889	11	S				KY	KY	KY		AT SCHOOL		5	✓	X	✓				
		" CLOYD F.	SON	W	M	OCT 1891	8	S				KY	KY	KY											
		" CLARENCE B.	SON	W	M	AUG 1894	5	S				KY	KY	KY											
250	259	FERMALL, JOHN C.	HEAD	W	M	APR 1862	38	M	8			KY	KY	KY		FARMER	O		✓	✓	✓	O		MF	202
		" LUCY A.	wife	W	F	DEC 1865	34	M	8			KY	KY	KY					✓	✓	✓				
251	260	STARR, WILLIAM A.	HEAD	W	M	JUL 1852	47	M	26			KY	TN	NC		FARMER	O		✓	✓	✓	O		FF	203
		" VIRGINNIE	wife	W	F	JUN 1851	48	M	26	6	4	KY	VA	KY					✓	✓	✓				
		" HATTIE J.	DAU	W	F	JUL 1877	22	S				KY	KY	KY					✓	✓	✓				
		" LOU A.	DAU	W	F	NOV 1879	20	S				KY	KY	KY		SCHOOL TEACHER	7		✓	✓	✓				
		" ROBERT P. E.	SON	W	M	NOV 1881	18	S				KY	KY	KY		AT SCHOOL		9	✓	✓	✓				
		" WILLIAM J.	SON	W	M	NOV 1883	16	S				KY	KY	KY		FARM LABORER			✓	✓	✓				
252	261	LAYNE, JAMES	HEAD	W	M	MAR 1856	44	M	20			KY	KY	KY		FARMER			✓	✓	✓	O		MF	204
		" MILDRED C.	wife	W	F	APR 1857	43	M	20	3	3	KY	KY	KY					✓	✓	✓				
		" UBERT L.	SON	W	M	FEB 1881	19	S				KY	KY	KY		FARM LABORER			✓	✓	✓				
		" HALLIE C.	DAU	W	F	NOV 1884	15	S				KY	KY	KY					✓	✓	✓				
		" NETTIE S.	DAU	W	F	AUG 1888	11	S				KY	KY	KY		AT SCHOOL		5	✓	✓	✓				
253	262	STREET, CHARLES C.	HEAD	B	M	APR 1873	27	M	9			KY	KY	KY		FARMER			✓	X	✓	O		FF	205

STATE - KENTUCKY
COUNTY - MONROE
Township or other division: GUM

Enumerator: THOMAS R. EVANS

Supervisor's Dist. No. 102 Sheet No.
Enumeration Dist. No. 80

Location (No. of Family / No. of Dwelling)	NAME	Relation	Color	Sex	DATE OF BIRTH Mon/Yr	Age at last birthday	Marital Status	# Years married	Mother of how many children?	# of these children living	Place of birth [this person]	Father of this person	Mother of this person	OCCUPATION 10 years +	Attended school in months	Can read	Can write	Speak English	Owned or Rent	Owned - no mortgage	Farm or house	# of farm schedule
	STREET, CAMILA J.	Wife	B	F	Jul 1871	28	M	9	5	5	KY	KY	KY			✓	✓					
	" NOAH	Son	B	M	Jan 1892	8	S				KY	KY	KY									
	" MAY	Dau	B	F	May 1894	6	S				KY	KY	KY									
	" BENTON	Dau	B	F	Mar 1895	5	S				KY	KY	KY									
	" ALLIE	Dau	B	F	Feb 1898	2	S				KY	KY	KY									
	" HUE	Son	B	M	Feb 1900	3/12	S				KY	KY	KY									
	HOWARD, JAMES	Nephew	B	M	Jan 1878	22	S				KY	KY	KY	FARM LABORER 3		✓	✓	✓				
254/263	DIAL, HOUSTON C.	Head	W	M	Aug 1879	20	M	3			KY	KY	KY	FARMER		✓	✓	✓	R		F	206
	" FANNY S.	Wife	W	F	Nov 1881	18	M	3	1	1	KY	KY	KY			✓	✓	✓				
	" CALEB F.	Son	W	M	Nov 1898	1	S				KY	KY	KY									
255/264	EPLIN (EXLIN?) SIDNEY	Head	W	M	Aug 1851	48	M	25			KY	KY	KY	FARMER		✓	✓	✓	O		F	207
	" RILLA E.	Wife	W	F	Jan 1856	44	M	25	6	4	KY	TN	KY			✓	X	✓				
	" JOHN B.	Son	W	M	Apr 1879	21	M	1			KY	KY	KY	FARM LABORER		✓	✓	✓				
	" GEORGE A.	Son	W	M	Mar 1886	14	S				KY	KY	KY	FARM LABORER	1	✓	✓	✓				
	" ADA B.	Dau	W	F	Jan 1888	12	S				KY	KY	KY	AT SCHOOL	4	✓	✓	✓				
	" MAIME B.	Dau	W	F	Jun 1896	4	S				KY	KY	KY									
	" MAY M.	Dau in-law	W	F	Jan 1880	20	M	1			KY	KY	KY			✓	✓	✓				
256/265	GREGORY, ELISHA A.	Head	W	M	Mar 1871	29	M	9			KY	TN	TN	FARMER	0	✓	✓	✓	R		F	208
	" MATILDA	Wife	W	F	May 1864	36	M	9	4	4	KY	KY	KY			✓	✓	✓				
	" HENRY V.	Son	W	M	Jul 1893	6	S				KY	KY	KY									
	" ULINA	Dau	W	F	Jun 1895	4	S				KY	KY	KY									
	" JANE E.	Dau	W	F	Jan 1897	3	S				KY	KY	KY									
	" JEFFERSON C.	Son	W	M	Jan 1899	1	S				KY	KY	KY									
	" LETHA E.	Mother	W	F	Aug 1845	54	Wd				KY	KY	KY			X	X	✓	R		F	209
257/266	KEY, FRANKLIN	Head	W	M	May 1863	37	M	16			KY	KY	KY	FARMER		✓	✓	✓	R		F	209
	" MARY J.	Wife	W	F	Aug 1862	37	M	16	4	4	KY	KY	KY			✓	X	✓				

TWELFTH CENSUS OF THE UNITED STATES 1900

STATE - KENTUCKY
COUNTY - MONROE
Township or other division — GUM

— 49 —

Enumerator — THOMAS R. EVANS

Supervisor's Dist. No. 102 Sheet No.
Enumeration Dist. No. 80

Location No. of Family	No. of Dwelling	NAME	Relation	Color	Sex	DATE OF BIRTH Mon/Yr	Age at last birthday	Marital Status	# Years married	Mother of how many children?	# of these children living	NATIVITY Place of birth (this person)	Father of this person	Mother of this person	CITIZENSHIP Year of immigr.	# years in U.S.	Naturalization	OCCUPATION 10 years +	Months not employed	EDUCATION Attended school in months	Can read	Can write	Speak English	OWNERSHIP Owned or Rent	Owned -no mortgage	Farm or house	# of farm schedule	
		KEY, WILLIAM J.	SON	W	M	JUN 1886	13	S				KY	KY	KY				FARM LABORER	0		✓	X	✓					
		" EMILY J.	DAU	W	F	OCT 1890	9	S				KY	KY	KY														
		" DORA	DAU	W	F	MAR 1893	7	S				KY	KY	KY														
		" (?) BETSY T.	DAU	W	F	AUG 1897	2	S				KY	KY	KY														
258	267	GOODMAN, JAMES A.	HEAD	W	M	MAY 1877	23	M	1			KY	KY	KY				FARMER	0		✓	✓	✓	O		F F	210	
		" IVA	wife	W	F	JUL 1879	20	M	1			KY	KY	KY							✓	✓	✓					
		" JOSEPH L.	BRO	W	M	JAN 1880	20	S				KY	KY	KY				FARM LABORER	0		✓	✓	✓					
259	268	TURNER, ALONZO	HEAD	W	M	JAN 1854	46	Wd				KY	KY	KY				FARMER	0		✓	X	✓	R		F	211	
		" NANCY A.	DAU	W	F	JUL 1883	16	S				KY	KY	KY				HOUSE KEEPER	0		✓	✓	✓					
		" JAMES E.	SON	W	M	DEC 1884	15	S				KY	KY	KY				FARM LABORER	0		✓	X	✓					
		" OTTO W.	SON	W	M	NOV 1886	13	S				KY	KY	KY				FARM LABORER	0		✓	X	✓					
		" SHADRACH	SON	W	M	OCT 1888	11	S				KY	KY	KY				FARM LABORER	0		X	X	✓					
		" HARRY	SON	W	M	FEB 1891	9	S				KY	KY	KY														
		" LATICIA G.	DAU	W	F	JUL 1893	6	S				KY	KY	KY														
		" MARY	DAU	W	F	OCT 1896	3	S				KY	KY	KY														
		" JOHN B	SON	W	M	JUN 1899	11/12	S				KY	KY	KY														
260	269	STINSON, WILLIAM	HEAD	W	M	APR 1870	30	M	3			KY	KY	KY				FARMER	0		X	X	✓	R		F	212	
		" CORNELIA E	wife	W	F	OCT 1878	21	M	3	1	1	KY	KY	KY							✓	X	✓					
		" LUTHER D.	Son	W	M	MAY 1898	2	S				KY	KY	KY														
		" CHARITY M	Mother	W	F	APR 1834	66	Wd		2	2	KY	KY	KY							✓	X	✓					
		" NEALY E	Sister	W	F	MAY 1880	20	S				KY	KY	KY							✓	X	✓					
261	270	ROSS, WILLIAM L.	Head	W	M	DEC 1859	40	M	20			KY	VA	TN				FARMER	0		✓	✓	✓	O		F F	213	
		" MATILDA C.	wife	W	F	NOV 1860	39	M	20	3	3	KY	KY	KY							✓	✓	✓					
		" WILLIAM C.	Son	W	M	DEC 1881	18	S				KY	KY	KY				FARM LABORER	0	4	✓	✓	✓					
		" HOWARD	Son	W	M	DEC 1884	15	S				KY	KY	KY					0		✓	✓	✓					
		" FRANK	Son	W	M	MAR 1888	12	S				KY	KY	KY					0		✓	✓	✓					

TWELFTH CENSUS OF THE UNITED STATES 1900

STATE - KENTUCKY
COUNTY - MONROE
Township or other division

GUM
-50-
Enumerator THOMAS R. EVANS

Supervisor's Dist. No. 102 Sheet No.
Enumeration Dist. No. 80

No. of Family	No. of Dwelling	NAME	Relation	Color	Sex	Date of Birth Mon/Yr	Age at last birthday	Marital Status	# Years married	Mother of how many children?	# of these children living	Place of birth (this person)	Father of this person	Mother of this person	Citizenship	Occupation	Months not employed	Attended school in months	Can read	Can write	Speak English	Owned or Rent	Owned - no mortage	Farm or house	# of farm schedule
262	271	ROSS, LUIZA	HEAD	W	F	DEC 1833	66	Wd				KY	KY	KY				✓	X	✓		O		F H	
263	272	HOWARD, THOMAS H.	HEAD	W	M	Sep 1853	46	M	24			KY	NC	KY		FARMER		✓	✓	✓		O		F F	214
		" MARY A.	Wife	W	F	MAR 1854	46	M	24	11	9	KY	NC	KY				✓	✓	✓					
		" WILLIAM A.	Son	W	M	Nov 1881	18	S				KY	KY	KY		FARM LABORER		✓	✓	✓					
		" NANCY H.	Dau	W	F	Jul 1883	16	S				KY	KY	KY		AT SCHOOL		5	✓	✓					
		" LULA M.	Dau	W	F	Jun 1885	14	S				KY	KY	KY		AT SCHOOL		5	✓	✓					
		" FANNY S.	Dau	W	F	APR 1888	12	S				KY	KY	KY		AT SCHOOL		5	✓	✓					
		" (?)LENIE G.	Son	W	M	Feb 1890	10	S				KY	KY	KY		FARM LABORER		5	✓	✓					
		MARGARET N.	Dau	W	F	Aug 1892	7	S				KY	KY	KY											
		THOMAS H.	Son	W	M	APR 1898	2	S				KY	KY	KY											
		FRANCIS, FANNY H.	Mother in-law	W	F	JAN 1837	63	Wd		1	1	KY	KY	KY				✓	✓	✓					
264	273	HOWARD, JOHN W.	Head	W	M	JAN 1865	35	M	7			KY	KY	KY		FARMER	O	✓	✓	✓		O		F F	215
		" ETHEL H.	Wife	W	F	Oct 1872	27	M	7	2	2	KY	KY	KY				✓	✓	✓					
		" WINNIE	Dau	W	F	Jul 1893	6	S				KY	KY	KY											
		" JOHN T.	Son	W	M	Oct 1896	3	S				KY	KY	KY											
265	274	GHINT, STEVEN	HEAD	W	M	Jul 1863	36	M	11			KY	KY	KY		FARMER	O	X	X	✓		R		F	216
		" SARAH A.	Wife	W	F	MAR 1857	43	M	11	1	1	KY	KY	KY				X	X	✓					
		" WILLIAM O.	Son	W	M	Jul 1892	7	S				KY	KY	KY											
266	275	YOUNG, CHARLES H.	HEAD	W	M	JUN 1875	24	M	8			TN	TN	TN				✓	✓	✓		R		F	217
		" MARY A.	Wife	W	F	JAN 1866	34	M	8	3	3	KY	KY	KY				X	X	✓					
		" LUCY H.	Dau	W	F	Jul 1892	7	S				KY	KY	KY											
		" VIRGIE M.	Dau	W	F	Sept 1895	4	S				KY	KY	KY											
		" JAMES A.	Son	W	M	Sept 1898	1	S				KY	KY	KY											
		" WILLIAM	Father	W	M	— —	—	M	1			TN	KY	KY											
267	276	HOWARD, NANCY	HEAD	W	F	Sept 1835	64	Wd		3	3	KY	KY	KY		FARMER	O	✓	✓	✓		O		F F	218
		" HATTIE A.	Dau	W	F	JAN 1873	27	S				KY	KY	KY				✓	✓	✓					

STATE - KENTUCKY
COUNTY - MONROE
Township or other division — GUM — -51- — Enumerator THOMAS R. EVANS
Supervisor's Dist. No. 102 Sheet No. Enumeration Dist. No. 80

No. of Family	No. of Dwelling	NAME	Relation	Color	Sex	DATE OF BIRTH Mon/Yr	Age at last birthday	Marital Status	# Years married	Mother of how many children	# of these children living	Place of birth (this person)	Father of this person	Mother of this person	OCCUPATION 10 years +	Months not employed	Attended school in months	Can read	Can write	Speak English	Owned or Rent	Owned –no mortgage	Farm or house	# of farm schedule	
		GILLENWATERS, MARY D.	DAU	W	M	JUL 1868	31	Wd				KY	KY	KY				✓	✓	✓					
		HAYS, CHRISTOPHER	GR-SON	W	M	DEC 1878	21	S				KY	KY	KY	FARM LABORER	0		✓	✓	✓					
268	277	NEAL, JOHN	HEAD	W	M	AUG 1869	30	M	9			KY	KY	KY	FARMER			✓	✓	✓	R		F	376	7
		" JULIA	WIFE	W	F	SEP 1863	36	M	9	6	5	IL	NEW HAMP	GA				✓	✓	✓					
		" DOLLA B.	DAU	W	F	MAY 1892	8	S				KY	KY	IL											
		" MALISSA M.	DAU	W	F	NOV 1894	5	S				KY	KY	IL											
		" JOHN M.N.	SON	W	M	MAY 1896	4	S				KY	KY	IL											
		" JULIA B.	DAU	W	F	DEC 1897	2	S				KY	KY	IL											
		" GEORGE T.	SON	W	M	MAY 1899	1	S				KY	KY	IL											
269	278	STINSON, JOSEPH	HEAD	W	M	JUL 1862	38	M	18			KY	KY	KY	FARMER	0		✓	✓	✓	R		F	219	
		" MARY F.	WIFE	W	F	DEC 1852	47	M	18	4	4	KY	KY	KY				✓	✓	✓					
		" EVA L.	DAU	W	F	SEP 1883	16	S				KY	KY	KY				X	X	✓					
		" MAGGIE E.	DAU	W	F	FEB 1885	15	S				KY	KY	KY				✓	✓	✓					
		" CHARLES C.	SON	W	M	MAR 1886	14	S				KY	KY	KY				✓	✓	✓					
		" JENNIE C.	DAU	W	F	NOV 1888	11	S				KY	KY	KY				✓	✓	✓					
270	279	REGISTER, EUDORA E.	HEAD	W	F	MAR 1861	39	Wd				TX	KY	KY				✓	✓	✓	R		H		
		" MAUD E.	DAU	W	F	MAR 1882	18	S				KY	KY	TX				✓	✓	✓					
		" WILLIAM T.	SON	W	M	AUG 1883	16	S				KY	KY	TX	FARM LABORER	0		✓	✓	✓					
		" ABCH F.	SON	W	M	APR 1885	15	S				KY	KY	TX	FARM LABORER	6		✓	✓	✓					
		" JOHN	SON	W	M	OCT 1886	13	S				KY	KY	TX	FARM LABORER	8		✓	✓	✓					
		" SARAH J.	DAU	W	F	SEPT 1888	11	S				KY	KY	TX	AT SCHOOL			✓	✓	✓					
		" NELLIE C.	DAU	W	F	MAY 1890	10	S				KY	KY	TX				✓	✓	✓					
		" IVA P.	DAU	W	F	FEB 1894	6	S				KY	KY	TX											
		" NANNIE B.	DAU	W	F	DEC 1897	2	S				KY	KY	TX											
271	280	PEDIGO, JAMES B.	HEAD	W	M	SEPT 1866	33	M				KY	KY	KY	FARMER	0		X	X	✓	R		F	220	
		" MAGGIE	WIFE	W	F	SEPT 1867	32	M		5	4	KY	KY	KY				✓	✓	✓					

TWELFTH CENSUS OF THE UNITED STATES 1900

STATE - KENTUCKY
COUNTY - MONROE
Township or other division — GUM — 52 —
Enumerator THOMAS R. EVANS

Supervisor's Dist. No. 102   Sheet No.
Enumeration Dist. No. 80

No. of Family / No. of Dwelling	NAME	Relation	Color	Sex	Date of Birth Mon/Yr	Age at last birthday	Marital Status	# Years married	Mother of how many children?	# of these children living	Place of birth (this person)	Father of this person	Mother of this person	Occupation	Months not employed	Attended school in months	Can read	Can write	Speak English	Owned or Rent	Owned-no mortgage	Farm or house	# of farm schedule
	PEDIGO, THOMAS R.	Son	W	M	Aug 1887	12	S				KY	KY	KY	Farm Laborer	0		✓	✓	✓				
	" JAMES A.	Son	W	M	Aug 1890	9	S				KY	KY	KY	Farm Laborer	0		X	X	✓				
	" ELLER C.	Dau	W	F	Mar 1892	8	S				KY	KY	KY										
	" CAMIE M.	Dau	W	F	May 1895	5	S				KY	KY	KY										
272 281	WHEAT, MATTHEW W.	Head	W	M	Aug 1875	24	M				KY	KY	KY	Farmer	0		✓	✓	✓	R		F	221
	" NANNIE B.	Wife	W	F	Jun 1877	22	M				KY	KY	KY				✓	✓	✓				
	THOMAS, ELZY T.	Boarder	W	M	Sep 1862	37	S				KY	KY	KY	Farmer	0		✓	✓	✓	O	M	F	222
273 282	ROBINSON, CHARLES H.	Head	W	M	Apr 1844	56	M	15			TN	TN	TN	Farmer			X	✓	✓	O	F	F	223
	" SARAH	Wife	W	F	Oct 1847	52	M	15	2	1	TN	TN	TN				✓	✓	✓				
	" LILIA A.	Dau	W	F	Dec 1885	14	S				KY	TN	TN	At School		4	✓	✓	✓				
274 283	BRAY, SAMUEL	Head	W	M	Dec 1862	37	M	2			TN	TN	KY	Farmer	0		✓	✓	✓	O	F	F	224
	" GEORGIA	Wife	W	F	Sep 1873	26	M	2			KY	KY	KY				✓	✓					
	" ELKA	Dau	W	F	Feb 1899	1	S				KY	KY	KY										
275 284	DAWSON, FRANKLIN	Head	B	M	Nov 1862	37	M	18			KY	KY	KY	Farmer			✓	✓	✓	R		F	225
	" SARAH A.	Wife	B	F	Apr 1866	34	M	18	13	8	KY	KY	KY				✓	✓	✓				
	" NOVELLA	Dau	B	F	Nov 1882	17	S				KY	KY	KY	At School		5	✓	✓	✓				
	" WILLIAM	Son	B	M	Jun 1884	15	S				KY	KY	KY	Farm Laborer		5	✓	✓	✓				
	" GARNET	Son	B	M	Mar 1886	14	S				KY	KY	KY	Farm Laborer		5	✓	✓	✓				
	" THOMAS	Son	B	M	Aug 1887	13	S				KY	KY	KY	Farm Laborer		5	✓	✓	✓				
	" EDWARD	Son	B	M	Mar 1889	11	S				KY	KY	KY	Farm Laborer		5	✓	✓	✓				
	" HOWARD	Son	B	M	Feb 1891	9	S				KY	KY	KY										
	" VINSON	Son	B	M	Nov 1892	7	S				KY	KY	KY										
	" FANNY	Dau	B	F	Apr 1897	3	S				KY	KY	KY										
276 285	DUMA(?) HENRY	Head	W	M	Feb 1824	76	M	22			KY	MD	KY	Farmer	0		✓	✓	✓	O	F	F	226
	" MARGARET	Wife	W	F	Dec 1827	72	M	22			KY	KY	KY				✓	✓	✓				
277 286	WHEAT, ROBERT R.	Head	W	M	Sep 1859	40	M	19			KY	VA	VA	Farmer	0		✓	X	✓	R		F	227

STATE - KENTUCKY
COUNTY - MONROE
Township or other division GUM

Enumerator THOMAS R. EVANS

Supervisor's Dist. No. 102 Sheet No.
Enumeration Dist. No. 80

Location No. of Family	No. of Dwelling	NAME	Relation	Color	Sex	DATE OF BIRTH Mon/Yr	Age at last birthday	Marital Status	# Years married	Mother of how many children?	# of these children living	Place of birth (this person)	Father of this person	Mother of this person	Year of immigr.	# years in U.S.	Naturalization	OCCUPATION 10 years +	Months not employed	Attended school in months	Can read	Can write	Speak English	Owned or Rent	Owned -no mortage	Farm or house	# of farm schedule	
		WHEAT, SURILDA J.	Wife	W	F	Sept 1865	34	M	19			KY	KY	KY							✓	✓	✓					
		" HIBBERT T.	Son	W	M	Apr 1882	18	S				KY	KY	KY				FARM LABORER	0		X	X	✓					
		" LEONA	Dau	W	F	Apr 1888	12	S				KY	KY	KY							X	X	✓					
		" ANDIE H.	Son	W	M	Jul 1890	9	S				KY	KY	KY														
		DONNA P.	Dau	W	F	Jun 1893	7	S				KY	KY	KY														
287 287	SHAW, JAMES C.		Head	W	M	Nov 1823	76	M	30	14	5	TN	NC	NC				MILLER	0		✓	✓	✓	R		H		
		" AMANDA	Wife	W	F	Jan 1832	68	M	30	14	5	KY	VA	VA							X	X	✓					
	288	SHAW, GEORGE E.	Head	W	M	Nov 1878	21	M	2			KY	TN	KY				FARMER	0		✓	✓	✓	R		F	228	
		" DOLLA	Wife	W	F	Jun 1879	20	M	2	1	1	KY	KY	KY							✓	✓	✓					
		PERNA E.	Dau	W	F	Jan 1899	1	S				KY	KY	KY														
279 289	PROFFITT, WILLIAM T.		Head	W	M	Aug 1841	58	M	29			KY	TN	TN				FARMER	0		✓	✓	✓	O		F F		
		" MARY E.	Wife	W	F	Jul 1856	43	M	29	2	1	KY	KY	KY							✓	✓	✓					
		SHAW, JOHN	Father in-law	W	M	Nov 1827	72	Wd				KY	NC	NC							✓	✓	✓					
280 290	HAGAN, JAMES W.		Head	W	M	Jun 1872	27	M	1			KY	KY	KY				FARMER	0		✓	✓	✓	O	M	F	229	
		" ALLIE D	Wife	W	F	Dec 1876		M	1			KY	KY	KY							✓	✓						
		" MARY C	Dau	W	F	Apr 1900	1/12	S				KY	KY	KY														
281 291	LAYNE, JAMES H.		Head	W	M	Jun 1828	71	Wd				KY	VA	NC				FARMER	0		X	X	✓	O		F F	230	
		" MATILDA E	Sister	W	F	Sept 1838	61	S				KY	VA	NC							X	X	✓					
		GLURES(?) WILLIAM	Lodger	W	M	Mar 1888	12	S				KY	KY	KY				FARM LABORER	0		X	X	✓					
282 292	BRAY, CHARLES W.		Head	W	M	May 1870	30	M	1			KY	TN	KY				MILLER			✓	✓	✓	O		H		
		" MARY B.	Wife	W	F	Aug 1875	24	M	1	1	1	KY	KY	KY							✓	✓	✓					
		" MONA	Dau	W	F	Jan 1900	4/12	S				KY	KY	KY														
293 293	JONES, WILLIAM N.		Head	W	M	Nov 1861	38	M	18			KY	TN	TN				FARMER	0		✓	✓	✓	O	M	F	231	
		" LUELLA	Wife	W	F	Mar 1866	34	M	18	5	5	KY	KY	KY							✓	✓	✓					
		" WILLIAM G.	Son	W	M	Mar 1883	17	S				KY	KY	KY				FARM LABORER			X	X	✓					
		" LUMADA(?)	Dau	W	F	Apr 1885	15	S				KY	KY	KY				AT SCHOOL		3	✓	X	✓					

TWELFTH CENSUS OF THE UNITED STATES 1900

STATE - KENTUCKY
COUNTY - MONROE
Township or other division — GUM   — 54 —   Enumerator THOMAS R. EVANS

Supervisor's Dist. No. 102   Sheet No.
Enumeration Dist. No. 80

No. of Family	No. of Dwelling	NAME	Relation	Color	Sex	Date of Birth Mon/Yr	Age at last birthday	Marital Status	# Years married	Mother of how many children	# of these children living	Place of birth	Father of this person	Mother of this person	Occupation	Months not employed	Attended school in months	Can read	Can write	Speak English	Owned or Rent	Owned no mortgage	Farm or house	# of farm schedule
		JONES, GENETTA	DAU	W	F	May 1889	11	S				KY	KY	KY			3	X	X	✓				
		" NOAH A.	DAU	W	F	Jul 1891	8	S				KY	KY	KY										
		" ERMA E.	DAU	W	F	Jul 1897	2	S				KY	KY	KY										
294	294	HUTSON, JOHN	HEAD	W	M	Sep 1859	40	M	15			TN	TN	TN	FARMER	0		✓	✓	✓	R		F	232
		" SARAH J.	wife	W	F	Nov 1857	42	M	15	8	7	KY	KY	KY				✓	✓	✓				
		" LUNETTIE	DAU	W	F	Oct 1885	14	S				KY	TN	KY	AT SCHOOL		5	✓	✓	✓				
		" EDWARD H.	SON	W	M	Jan 1887	13	S				KY	TN	KY	FARM LABORER	0		✓	✓	✓				
		" LOMA	DAU	W	F	Mar 1889	11	S				KY	TN	KY	AT SCHOOL		5	✓	X	✓				
		" WILLIAM R.	SON	W	M	Nov 1891	9	S				KY	TN	KY										
		" LALBERT C.	SON	W	M	Oct 1892	7	S				KY	TN	KY										
		" IDA V.	DAU	W	F	Nov 1896	3	S				KY	TN	KY										
		" JOSEPH C.	SON	W	M	May 1899	1	S				KY	TN	KY										
295	295	BRAY, JOHN T.	HEAD	W	M	Jun 1868	31	M	9			KY	KY	KY	DRUMMER			✓	✓	✓	O		FH	
		" NEALY A.	wife	W	F	Apr 1874	26	M	9	3	3	KY	TN	KY				✓	✓	✓				
		" BERTHA E.	DAU	W	F	Nov 1892	7	S				KY	KY	KY										
		" LINNIE D.	DAU	W	F	Feb 1896	4	S				KY	KY	KY										
		" JAMES L.	SON	W	M	Jun 1899	11/12	S				KY	KY	KY										
296	296	BROOKS, ENOCH	HEAD	W	M	Oct 1876	23	M	2			KY	KY	TN	BLACKSMITH	0		✓	✓	✓	R		H	
		" CELIE C.	wife	W	F	Feb 1879	21	M	2	1	0	KY	TN	TN				✓	✓	✓				
297	297	BRAUNER, JAMES	HEAD	W	M	Aug 1857	42	M	4			TN	TN	TN	FARMER	0		✓	✓	✓	O		F	233
		" MARTHA J.	wife	W	F	Feb 1870	30	M	4	3	3	KY	KY	KY				✓	✓	✓				
		" PORTER O.	SON	W	M	Jun 1896	3	S				KY	KY	KY										
		" DEWEY S.	SON	W	M	Mar 1898	2	S				KY	KY	KY										
		" IVY P.	DAU	W	F	Feb 1900	3/12	S				KY	KY	KY										
		PAYNE, SHERMAN E.	Son	W	M	Aug 1891	8	S				KY	KY	KY										
298	298	PATTERSON, SAMUEL W.	HEAD	W	M	May 1829	71	Wd				TN	KY	NC	CAPALIST			✓	✓	✓	O		FH	

TWELFTH CENSUS OF THE UNITED STATES 1900

STATE - KENTUCKY
COUNTY - MONROE
Township or other division — GUM — -55-

Enumerator THOMAS R. EVANS

Supervisor's Dist. No. 102 Sheet No.
Enumeration Dist. No. 80

Location (No. of Family / No. of Dwelling)	NAME	Relation	Color	Sex	DATE OF BIRTH Mon/Yr	Age at last birthday	Marital Status	# Years married	Mother of how many children?	# of these children living	NATIVITY Place of birth [this person]	Father of this person	Mother of this person	CITIZENSHIP Year of immigr.	# years in U.S.	Naturalization	OCCUPATION 10 years +	Months not employed	Attended school in months	Can read	Can write	Speak English	OWNERSHIP Owned or Rent	Owned –no mortgage	Farm or house	# of farm schedule	
	PATTERSON, MARGARET E.	GRAND DAU	W	F	Nov 1853	46	S				KY	TN	KY							✓	✓	✓					
	" CHARLES B.	Son	W	M	Jun 1898	1	S				KY	KY	KY														
	COUNTS, SARAH	DAU	W	F	Nov 1857	42	Wd				KY	KY	KY							✓	✓						
289 299	LEE, THOMAS H.	HEAD	W	M	Apr 1844	56	M	28			KY	NC	KY				FARMER	0		✓	✓	✓	R		F	234	
	" CATHERINE	wife	W	F	Feb 1843	57	M	28	8	5	KY	KY	KY														
	" LORETTA	DAU	W	F	Aug 1881	18	S				KY	KY	KY														
	" CORA C.	DAU	W	F	Feb 1885	15	S				KY	KY	KY														
290 300	HOLLAND, JAMES T.	HEAD	W	M	Oct 1867	32	M	10			KY	KY	KY				FARMER	0		✓	✓	✓	R		F	235	
	" MITTIE	wife	W	F	Aug 1869	30	M	10	4	3	KY	KY	KY							✓	✓						
	" LEONA	DAU	W	F	Nov 1891	8	S				KY	KY	KY														
	" BERLY	Son	W	M	Jan 1893	7	S				KY	KY	KY														
	" HARISON	Son	W	M	Sep 1898	1	S				KY	KY	KY														
291 301	CRABTREE, JOSEPH A.	HEAD	W	M	Nov 1842	57	M				TN	TN	IND.				PHYSICIAN	0		✓	✓	✓	0		F	236	
	" MARY B.	wife	W	F	Jan 1860	40	M	24	8	7	TN	TN	TN							✓	✓	✓					
	" ARTHUR	Son	W	M	Aug 1884	15	S				KY	TN	TN				FARM LABORER			✓	✓	✓					
	HENRY W.	Son	W	M	Apr 1886	14	S				KY	TN	TN				FARM LABORER			✓	✓	✓					
	LOUIS R.	Son	W	M	Jun 1890	9	S				KY	TN	TN														
	CHRISTOPHER C.	Son	W	M	Jan 1893	6	S				KY	TN	TN														
	HUSFORD	Son	W	M	Jul 1897	2	S				KY	TN	TN														
	BULEY, MARTHA	Servant	W	F	Apr 1869	31	S				KY	KY	VA				SERVANT			X	X	✓					
292 302	CRABTREE, GARFIELD	HEAD	W	M	Jan 1881	19	M				KY	TN	TN				FARMER	0		✓	✓		R		F	237	
	" LIDDIE	wife	W	F	Nov 1883	16	M				KY	TN	TN							✓	✓	✓					
293 303	CARTER, JAMES	HEAD	W	M	Oct 1870	29	M	8			KY	KY	KY				FARMER	0		✓	✓	✓	R		F	238	
	" FRANCIS	wife	W	F	Jul 1871	28	M	8	4	4	KY	KY	KY							✓	✓						
	" SAMUEL	Son	W	M	Aug 1892	7	S				KY	KY	KY														
	" JESSE	Son	W	M	Aug 1895	4	S				KY	KY	KY														

STATE - KENTUCKY
COUNTY - MONROE
Township or other division — GUM

Enumerator — THOMAS R. EVANS

Supervisor's Dist. No. 102   Sheet No.
Enumeration Dist. No. 80

No. of Family	No. of Dwelling	NAME	Relation	Color	Sex	DATE OF BIRTH Mon/Yr	Age at last birthday	Marital Status	# Years married	Mother of how many children?	# of these children living	Place of birth (this person)	Father of this person	Mother of this person	Year of immigr.	# years in U.S.	Naturalization	OCCUPATION 10 years +	Months not employed	Attended school in months	Can read	Can write	Speak English	Owned or Rent	Owned –no mortage	Farm or house	# of farm schedule
		CARTER, STACY F.	DAU	W	F	OCT 1897	2	S				KY	KY	KY													
		" ADA A.	DAU	W	F	MAR 1899	1	S				KY	KY	KY													
294	304	JOHNSON, YANCY L.	HEAD	W	M	JUN 1862	37	M	15			KY	KY	NC				FARMER	0		✓	✓	✓	0	F	F	239
		" LUTISIA T.	wife	W	F	NOV 1865	34	M	15	8	7	KY	TN	KY							✓	✓	✓				
		" LON W.	Son	W	M	JAN 1887	13	S				KY	KY	KY				FARM LABORER	0		✓	✓	✓				
		" MARY D.	DAU	W	F	AUG 1888	11	S				KY	KY	KY				AT SCHOOL		5	✓	X	✓				
		" LUCY J.	DAU	W	F	JAN 1891	9	S				KY	KY	KY													
		" ROXY E.	DAU	W	F	DEC 1892	7	S				KY	KY	KY													
		" LUTHER O.	Son	W	M	Sep 1894	5	S				KY	KY	KY													
		" STELLA M.	DAU	W	F	JUN 1897	2	S				KY	KY	KY													
		" ELIZABETH	DAU	W	F	APR 1900	1/12	S				KY	KY	KY													
295	305	MEADOR, BLUFORD R.	HEAD	W	M	Feb 1828	72	M	48			TN	VA	VA				CAPISLIST	0		✓	✓	✓	0	F	H	
		" SARAH A.	wife	W	F	MAY 1832	68	M	48			KY	KY	KY							✓	✓	✓				
		BRAY, EDWARD B.	NEPHEW	W	M	NOV 1863	36	S				KY	KY	KY				MERCHANT	0		✓	✓	✓				
296	306	YORK, KINDRED J.	HEAD	W	M	JAN 1858	42	M				TN	TN	TN				CARPENTER	0		✓	✓	✓	0	F	H	
		" ROBERTA	wife	W	F	NOV 18—1	—	M				KY	TN	TN							✓	✓	✓				
297	307	YORK, LEROY C.	HEAD	W	M	JAN 1863	37	M				TN	TN	TN				CARPENTER	0		✓	✓	✓				
		" CORA G.	wife	W	F	JAN 1870	30	M	14	6	5	KY	TN	KY							✓	✓	✓				
		" CLATON E.	Son	W	M	Sept 1886	13	S				KY	KY	KY				AT SCHOOL		5	✓	✓	✓				
		" FREDERICK O.	Son	W	M	JAN 1889	11	S				KY	KY	KY				AT SCHOOL		5	✓	✓	✓				
		" JAMES D.	Son	W	M	JAN 1891	9	S				KY	KY	KY													
		" JESSE D.	Son	W	M	NOV 1894	6	S				KY	KY	KY													
		" NORMA G.	DAU	W	F	JAN 1900	4/12	S				KY	KY	KY													
298	308	SMALLING, JAMES H.	HEAD	W	M	OCT 1858	41	M	17			KY	TN	KY				FARMER	0		✓	✓		0	M	F	240
		" FRANCIS A.	wife	W	F	OCT 1860	39	M	17	6	5	MISSOURI	KY	KY							✓	✓	✓				
		" MEREDITH	Son	W	M	JUL 1883	16	S				KY	KY	MO				FARM LABORER	0		✓	✓	✓				

STATE - KENTUCKY
COUNTY - MONROE
Township or other division — GUM

Enumerator — THOMAS R. EVANS

Supervisor's Dist. No. _102_ Sheet No. _____
Enumeration Dist. No. _80_ _____

No. of Family	No. of Dwelling	NAME	Relation	Color	Sex	DATE OF BIRTH Mon/Yr	Age at last birthday	Marital Status	# Years married	Mother of how many children?	# of these children living	Place of birth (this person)	Father of this person	Mother of this person	Year of immigr.	# years in U.S.	Naturalization	OCCUPATION 10 years +	Months not employed	Attended school in months	Can read	Can write	Speak English	Owned or Rent	Owned -no mortgage	Farm or house	# of farm schedule
		SMALLING, WILLIAM K.	SON	W	M	MAR 1886	14	S				KY	KY	MO				FARM LABORER	0		✓	✓	✓				
		" THOMAS G.	(DAU?)	W	F(?)	APR 1892	8	S				KY	KY	MO													
		" PEARL A.	DAU	W	F	MAY 1894	6	S				KY	KY	MO													
		" EDWARD H.	SON	W	M	APR 1898	2	S				KY	KY	MO													
299	309	BRAUNER, SAMUEL O.	HEAD	W	M	NOV 1868	31	S				TN	TN	TN				FARMER	0		✓	✓	✓	O	F	F	241
		" MELVINA S.	Mother	W	F	APR 1828	72	Wd				TN	VA	GA							✓	X	✓				
		" MARY E.	Sister	W	F	– –	45	S				KY	TN	TN							✓	✓					
300	310	CELSOR, SAMUEL	HEAD	W	M	DEC 1868	31	M	6			KY	KY	KY				FARMER	0		✓	✓	✓	O	F	F	242
		" ALMA	WIFE	W	F	AUG 1877	22	M	6	2	2	KY	KY	KY							✓	✓	✓				
		" RASBERY F.	SON	W	M	APR 1896	4	S				KY	KY	KY													
		" RAMOND L.	SON	W	M	JUN 1897	3	S				KY	KY	KY													
301	311	JOHNSON, FRANKLIN	HEAD	W	M	JAN 1855	45	M	22			KY	KY	KY				FARMER	0		✓	✓	✓	O	F	F	243
		" NANCY E.	wife	W	F	Sept 1859	40	M	22	3	1	KY	KY	KY							✓	✓	✓				
		" ———	Mother	W	F	Aug 1824	75	Wd			1	KY	KY	KY													
302	312	LEWIS, GEORGE F.	Head	W	M	JAN 1867	33	M	12			KY	KY	KY				FARMER	0		✓	X	✓	R		F	244
		" HENNIE	Wife	W	F	MAY 1873	27	M	12	5	5	KY	TN	KY							✓	✓	✓				
		" NED O.	SON	W	M	JAN 1889	11	S				KY	KY	KY				FARM LABORER	0		✓	X	✓				
		" BESSIE B.	DAU	W	F	NOV 1892	7	S				KY	KY	KY													
		" ELIZABETH P.	DAU	W	F	JAN 1895	5	S				KY	KY	KY													
		" NELLIE A.	DAU	W	F	JUL 1897	2	S				KY	KY	KY													
		" MARY	DAU	W	F	Sep 1899	8/12	S				KY	KY	KY													
303	313	WILSON, MARTHA	HEAD	W	F	Jan 1856	44	Wd				TN	TN	TN				FARMER	0		✓	✓	✓	O	M	F	245
		" FRANKLIN	SON	W	M	NOV 1884	15	S				KY	KY	TN				FARM LABORER	0		✓	✓	✓				
		" LUCY J.	DAU	W	F	Jun 1887	12	S				KY	KY	TN				AT SCHOOL		5	✓	✓	✓				
		" LINDSEY R.	SON	W	M	Jun 1890	9	S				KY	KY	TN				AT SCHOOL		5	✓	✓	✓				
		" JOHN D.	SON	W	M	Aug 1893	6	S				KY	KY	TN													

STATE - KENTUCKY
COUNTY - MONROE GUM
Township or other division

Enumerator THOMAS R. EVANS

Supervisor's Dist. No. 102 Sheet No.
Enumeration Dist. No. 80

Location No. of Family / No. of Dwelling	NAME	Relation	Color	Sex	DATE OF BIRTH Mon/Yr	Age at last birthday	Marital Status	# Years married	Mother of how many children?	# of these children living	Place of birth [this person]	Father of this person	Mother of this person	Year of immigr.	# years in U.S.	Naturalization	OCCUPATION 10 years +	Months not employed	Attended school in months	Can read	Can write	Speak English	Owned or Rent	Owned -no mortgage	Farm or house	# of farm schedule
304 314	COOK, HENDERSON H.	HEAD	W	M	Apr 1867	33	M	13			KY	KY	KY				FARMER	0		✔	X	✔	R		F	246
"	HANNAH A.	Wife	W	F	Dec 1866	33	M	13	6	6	TN	VA	TN							✔	X	✔				
"	ROBERT B.	Son	W	M	Dec 1887	12	S				KY	KY	TN				FARM LABORER	0	3	✔	X	✔				
"	CLISSIE S.	Son	W	M	Aug 1890	9	S				TN	KY	TN													
"	MARY E.	DAU	W	F	May 1892	8	S				KY	KY	TN													
"	SEREY E.	DAU	W	F	Feb 1894	6	S				KY	KY	TN													
"	WILLIAM H.	SON	W	M	Mar 1897	3	S				KY	KY	TN													
"	NANNIE M.	DAU	W	F	Jan 1899	1	S				KY	KY	TN													
305 315	GAULDEN, JAMES C.	HEAD	W	M	Aug 1827	72	M	51			VA	PA	VA				CAPALIST			✔	X	✔	O	M	H	
"	MARY A.	Wife	W	F	May 1836	64	M	51	13	9	TN	GA	NC							X	X	✔				
"	MARTHA W.	DAU	W	F	Sept 1864	35	S				TN	VA	TN							X	X	✔				
"	TULA E.	GR DAU	W	F	Oct 1887	12	S				KY	TN	TN				AT SCHOOL		2	✔	✔	✔				
"	EFFIE M.	GR DAU	W	F	Jul 1892	7	S				KY	KY	TN						*							
306 316	GAULDEN, CHARLES A.	HEAD	W	M	Feb 1877	23	M				TN	VA	TN				FARMER	0		✔	✔	✔	O		F	247
"	BERTHA A.	Wife	W	F	Jul 1868	31	M	2	5	4	NC	NC	NC							✔	✔	✔				
"	MARY B.	DAU	W	F	Dec 1899	1	S				KY	TN	NC													
	WELCH, GROVER R.	STEP SON	W	M	Jul 1890	9	S				KY	TN	NC													
"	MINNIE	STEP DAU	W	F	Aug 1893	6	S				KY	TN	NC													
	FARLEY, EFFIE M.	STEP DAU	W	F	Nov 1895	4	S				KY	TN	NC													
307 317	ISAAC, JOHN	HEAD	W	M	Jul 1876	23	M				NC	NC	NC				FARMER	0		✔	✔	✔	R		F	247 (?)
"	DORA	WIFE	W	F	Mar 1880	20	M	1	1	1	TN	TN	TN							✔	✔	✔				
317 318	JONES, ZACHARAH	HEAD	W	M	Mar 1845	55	M	22			TN	TN	TN				FARMER	0		X	X	✔	O		F	248
"	PHANEY	WIFE	W	F	Nov 1857	42	M	22	10	9	KY	VA	KY							✔	✔	✔				
"	DOVEY	DAU	W	F	Jan 1880	20	S				KY	TN	KY							✔	✔	✔				
"	YETMAN(?)	SON	W	M	Oct 1883	16	S				KY	TN	KY				FARM LABORER			✔	X	✔				
"	JOHN R.	SON	W	M	Oct 1885	14	S				KY	TN	KY				FARM LABORER			✔	X	✔				

STATE - KENTUCKY
COUNTY - MONROE GUM
Township or other division

Enumerator Thomas R. Evans

Supervisor's Dist. No. _102_ Sheet No.
Enumeration Dist. No. _80_

Location No. of Family / No. of Dwelling	NAME	Relation	Color	Sex	DATE OF BIRTH Mon/Yr	Age at last birthday	Marital Status	# Years married	Mother of how many children?	# of these children living	Place of birth [this person]	Father of this person	Mother of this person	Year of immigr.	# years in U.S.	Naturalization	OCCUPATION 10 years +	Months not employed	Attended school in months	Can read	Can write	Speak English	Owned or Rent	Owned -no mortage	Farm or house	# of farm schedule	
	JONES, WIRT	Son	W	M	Dec 1887	12	S				KY	TN	KY				FARM LABORER			✓	X	✓					
"	WICK	Son	W	M	Jan 1892	8	S				KY	TN	KY														
"	LIBIE (?)	Son	W	M	Oct 1894	5	S				KY	TN	KY														
"	MARY	Dau	W	F	Oct 1894	5	S				KY	TN	KY														
"	CLORA A.	Dau	W	F	Dec 1897	2	S				KY	TN	KY														
318 319 FRANKLIN, JOHN H.	HEAD	W	M	Jul 1838	61	M	34			KY	VA	TN				DAY LABORER	5		✓	✓		R		H		
" MARGARET	Wife	W	F	Sep 1848	51	M	34	13	11	TN	TN	TN							✓	✓						
" MATTIE E.	Dau	W	F	Jun 1883	16	S				KY	KY	TN														
" KATTIE	Dau	W	F	Apr 1885	15	S				KY	KY	TN														
" RUBY	Son	W	M	Jan 1887	12	S				KY	KY	TN														
" WILLIAM	Son	W	M	Jun 1889	10	S				KY	KY	TN				FARMER	0		✓	✓		O	M	F	249	
319 320 JONES, NATHAN E.	HEAD	W	M	Mar 1859	41	M	19			KY	TN	TN				FARMER	0		✓	✓		O	M	F	249	
" LUCRITTY(?)	Wife	W	F	Jul 1864	35	M	19	5	5	KY	TN	TN							✓	✓					?	
" ADA D.	Dau	W	F	May 1883	17	S				KY	KY	TN				AT SCHOOL		4	✓	✓	✓					
" ETTA	Dau	W	F	Oct 1884	15	S				KY	KY	TN				AT SCHOOL		2	✓	✓	✓					
" CLAUDE	Son	W	M	Nov 1885	14	S				KY	KY	TN				FARM LABORER			✓	✓	✓					
" BRON	Son	W	M	Jan 1888	12	S				KY	KY	TN				FARM LABORER			✓	✓	✓					
" PATTIE M.	Dau	W	F	Oct 1890	9	S				KY	KY	KY							✓	✓	✓					
STONE, RICHARD	Lodger	W	M	Feb 1879	21	S				KY	TN	TN				FARMER	0		✓	✓	✓	R		F	249(?)	
" VOLL	Lodger	W	M	Mar 1878	22	S				KY	TN	TN				LABORER - MILL	0		✓	✓	✓					
320 321 BRAUNER, GEORGE W.	HEAD	W	M	Sep 1866	33	M	12			KY	TN	TN				FARMER	0		✓	✓	✓	O	F	F	→	
" FERNIBY(?)	Wife	W	F	Jun 1871	28	M	12			KY	KY	KY							✓	✓	✓					
" HERBIT(?) O.	Son	W	M	Dec 1890	9	S				KY	KY	KY														
" ANNIE M.	Dau	W	F	— 1893	6	S				KY	KY	KY														
322 ROARK, WILLIAM J.	HEAD	W	M	Feb 1841	59	M	31			MO	KY	KY				FARMER	0		✓	X	✓	O	F	F	250	
" MILIE A.	Wife	W	F	Apr 1839	61	M	31	6	4	TN	VA	VA							X	X	✓					

STATE - KENTUCKY
COUNTY - MONROE
Township or other division — GUM

– 60 –

Enumerator THOMAS R. EVANS

Supervisor's Dist. No. 10? Sheet No. _____
Enumeration Dist. No. 80 _____

No. of Family	No. of Dwelling	NAME	Relation	Color	Sex	Date of Birth Mon/Yr	Age at last birthday	Marital Status	# Years married	Mother of how many children?	# of these children living	Place of birth (this person)	Father of this person	Mother of this person	Occupation 10 years +	Months not employed	Attended school in months	Can read	Can write	Speak English	Owned or Rent	Owned-no mortgage	Farm or house	# of farm schedule
		ROARK, WILLIAM H.	Son	W	M	Jul 1874	25	S				KY	MO	TN	Farm Laborer	0		✓	✓	✓				
312	323	PAYNE, JAMES K.	Head	W	M	May 1849	51	M	23			TN	TN	TN	Farmer	0		✓	X	✓	O	M	F	251
		" SUSAN	Wife	W	F	May 1856	44	M	23	7	4	TN	TN	TN				✓	✓	✓				
		" ALLISE	Dau	W	F	Jun 1877	22	S				TN	TN	TN				✓	✓	✓				
		" SARAH E.	Dau	W	F	Feb 1879	21	S				TN	TN	TN				✓	✓	✓				
		" DORA B.	Dau	W	F	Dec 1892	7	S				KY	TN	TN										
		" IDA D.	Dau	W	F	May 1896	4	S				KY	TN	TN										
313	324	WILLSON, EDGAR G.	Head	W	M	Jun 1873	26	M				TN	TN	TN	Farmer	0		✓	✓	✓	O	F	F	252
		" SARAH J.	Wife	W	F	Feb 1878	22	M				KY	KY	KY					✓	✓				
314	325	COMBS, JAMES	Head	W	M	Jun 1879	20	M				KY	KY	KY				✓	X	✓	R		F	253
		" MAIZE	Wife	W	F	Sep 1881	18	M				KY	KY	TN				✓	✓	✓				
315	326	GUM, JOSIE	Head	W	F	Jun 1860	40	W				KY	KY	TN				✓	✓	✓	R		H	
		" ELZA B	Son	W	M	Jan 1886	14	S				KY	KY	KY	Farm Laborer	3		✓	✓	✓				
		" BERTA	Dau	W	F	Jun 1888	12	S				KY	KY	KY	At School		5	✓	✓	✓				
		" BUMION (?)	Son	W	M	Feb 1890	10	S				KY	KY	KY	Farm Laborer	0		✓	✓					
		" ZULA	Dau	W	F	Oct 1892	7	S				KY	KY	KY										
316	327	HOWSER, STEPHEN	Head	W	M	Mar 1846	54	M	30			KY	KY	KY	Farmer			✓	X	✓	O	F	F	254
		" MELVINA	Wife	W	F	Aug 1853	46	M	30	3	3	TN	TN	TN				X	X	✓				
		" JOSEPH D	Son	W	M	Feb 1879	21	S				TN	KY	TN	Farm Laborer			✓	✓	✓				
317	328	CARTER, SIDNEY	Head	W	M	Mar 1874	26	M	5			IN	IN	IN	Farmer			✓	X	✓	R		F	255
		" SARAH H.	Wife	W	F	Sep 1875	24	M	5	2	2	KY	KY	TN				✓	✓	✓				
		" IDA M	Dau	W	F	Nov 1896	3	S				KY	TN	KY										
		WHYLEY D	Son	W	M	Jan 1900	3/12	S				KY	TN	KY										
318	329	HALE, PINCKNEY M.C.	Head	W	M	Jun 1828	71	M	21			TN	TN	TN	Farmer	0		✓	✓	✓	O	F	F	256
		" MATILDA	Wife	W	F	Jan 1844	56	M	21	2	1	KY	KY	KY				✓	X	✓				
		" FRANCIS	Son	W	M	Feb 1882	18	S				KY	TN	KY	Farm Laborer			✓	✓	✓				

STATE − KENTUCKY
COUNTY − MONROE
Township or other division   GUM   Enumerator THOMAS R. EVANS

Supervisor's Dist. No. 102   Sheet No.
Enumeration Dist. No. 80

No. of Family	No. of Dwelling	NAME	Relation	Color	Sex	DATE OF BIRTH Mon/Yr	Age at last birthday	Marital Status	# Years married	Mother of how many children?	# of these children living	Place of birth [this person]	Father of this person	Mother of this person	Year of immigr.	# years in U.S.	Naturalization	OCCUPATION 10 years +	Months not employed	Attended school in months	Can read	Can write	Speak English	Owned or Rent	Owned –no mortgage	Farm or house	# of farm schedule
314	330	DOSS, BERRY M	HEAD	W	M	DEC 1877	22	M	2			TN	TN	TN				FARMER	0		✓	✓	✓	R		F	257
		" MAUD	wife	W	F	FEB 1880	20	M	2	1	1	KY	TN	TN							✓	✓	✓				
		" BERRY J.	Son	W	M	DEC 1898	1	S				TN	TN	KY													
		FARLEY, HOUSER	Boarder	W	M	Sep 1874	25	S				KY	KY	KY				FARMER			✓	✓	✓		0	F	F	258
		" RUE	Boarder	W	M	Oct 1875	24	S				KY	KY	KY				FARMER			✓	✓	✓				
320	331	AGERS, WILLIAM	HEAD	W	M	MAR 1843	57	W				KY	TN	KY				DAY LABORER			X	X	✓	R		H	
		" HANNAH	DAU	W	F	DEC 1878	21	S				KY	KY	KY				SERVANT		5	X	X	✓				
		" MARGARET	DAU	W	F	MAR 1884	16	S				KY	KY	KY							X	X	✓				
		" DARTHULA(?)	DAU	W	F	MAY 1887	13	S				KY	KY	KY							X	X	✓				
		" JAMES	Son	W	M	NOV 1888	11	S				KY	KY	KY							X	X					
		" NELLIE	DAU	W	F	MAY 1893	7	S				KY	KY	KY													
321	332	ALLEN, GEORGE W.	HEAD	W	M	DEC 1866	33	M	9			TN	TN	TN				FARMER	0		X	X	✓	R		F	259
		" LYDIA E.	WIFE	W	F	NOV 1870	29	M	9	4	4	TN	TN	TN							X	X	✓				
		" BELLZONER	DAU	W	F	AUG 1892	7	S				TN	TN	TN													
		" NEWTON A.	Son	W	M	AUG 1894	5	S				KY	TN	TN													
		" ROBERT	Son	W	M	JULY 1896	3	S				KY	TN	TN													
		" RICHARD J	Son	W	M	MAY 1898	2	S				KY	TN	TN													
322	333	DAVIS, RILEY D.	HEAD	W	M	AUG 1844	55	M	38			IL	TN	TN				FARMER	0		X	X	✓	R		F	260
		" CATHERINE	wife	W	F	APR 1845	55	M	38	6	4	KY	TN	TN							X	X	✓				
		DAVIS, JOHN H(?)	HEAD	W	M	MAY 1876	24	M				KY	IL	KY				FARMER			X	X	✓	R		F	261
		" FRANCIS	wife	W	F	MAY 1883	17	M				KY	KY	KY							✓	✓	✓				
		" SAMUEL	Son	W	M	JAN 1897	3	S				KY	KY	KY													
		" SIMON	BROTHER	W	M	Feb 1881	19	Wd				KY	IL	KY				FARMER LABORER			✓	✓	✓				
323	335	CREEK, THOMAS N.	HEAD	W	M	MAR 1845	55	M	17			KY	KY	KY				FARMER			✓	✓	✓		0	F	F	262
		" MARY F.	wife	W	F	June 1863	36	M	17	7	7	KY	KY	KY							✓	✓	✓				
		" MYRTIE D.	DAU	W	F	APR 1884	16	S				KY	KY	KY				AT SCHOOL		3	✓	✓	✓				

STATE - KENTUCKY
COUNTY - MONROE
Township or other division — GUM

Enumerator — THOMAS R. EVANS

Supervisor's Dist. No. 102 Sheet No.
Enumeration Dist. No. 81

Location No. of Family / No. of Dwelling	NAME	Relation	Color	Sex	DATE OF BIRTH Mon/Yr	Age at last birthday	Marital Status	# Years married	Mother of how many children?	# of these children living	Place of birth (this person)	Father of this person	Mother of this person	OCCUPATION 10 years +	Months not employed	Attended school in months	Can read	Can write	Speak English	Owned or Rent	Owned -no mortgage	Farm or house	# of farm schedule
	CREEK, JOHN L.	Son	W	M	Feb 1886	14	S				KY	KY	KY	FARM LABORER	0	3	✓	✓	✓				
	" THURMAN H.	Son	W	M	Jun 1888	11	S				KY	KY	KY	FARM LABORER	0	3	✓	✓	✓				
	" BERTHA B.	Dau	W	F	Aug 1890	9	S				KY	KY	KY										
	" LITCHED(?) M.	Dau	W	F	Jan 1893	7	S				KY	KY	KY										
	" JOSEPH C.	Son	W	M	Jul 1895	4	S				KY	KY	KY										
	" ELZY M.	Son	W	M	Oct 1897	2	S				KY	KY	KY										
324 336	FLIPPIN, ANN R.	Head	W	F	Feb 1846	54	Wd				KY	TN	KY	FARMER	0		✓	✓	✓	O	F	F	263
	" SUMMER (?)	Lodger	W	M	Dec 1880	19	S				KY	KY	TN	FARM LABORER	0		✓	✓	✓				
	FARMER, BENNETT	Lodger	W	M	Oct 1872	28	S				KY	TN	KY				✓	✓	✓				
325 337	FISHER, THOMAS F.	Head	W	M	Apr 1835	65	M				TN	VA	VA	FARMER	0		✓	✓	✓	O	F	F	264
	" LUISA	Wife	W	F	Sep 1839	61	M	34	9	8	TN	NC	TN				✓	✓	✓				
	" NOAH	Son	W	M	Sep 1871	28	S				TN	TN	TN	FARM LABORER	0		✓	✓	✓				
	" JAMES	Son	W	M	Dec 1877	22	S				TN	TN	TN	FARM LABORER	0		✓	✓	✓				
	" LENORE	Dau	W	F	Jul 1879	20	M				TN	TN	TN				✓	✓	✓				
	" DOC M.	Son	W	M	Jul 1882	17	S				TN	TN	TN				✓	✓	✓				
	ADAMS, AMY E.	Step Dau	W	F	Jan 1861	39	S				TN	TN	TN				X	X	✓				
	DRIVER, THOMAS J.	Son-in-law	W	M	Apr 1879	21	M				TN	TN	TN	FARMER			✓	✓				(276)	?
326 338	MEADOR, WILLIAM F	Head	W	M	Feb 1853	47	M	22			TN	VA	TN	FARMER	0		✓	✓	✓	O		F	265
	" LIZZIE	Wife	W	F	Mar 1859	41	M	22	7	6	TN	VA	TN				✓	✓	✓				
	" SIRUS I	Son	W	M	Dec 1878	21	S				TN	TN	TN	FARM LABORER	5		✓	✓	✓	R		F	266
	" HEARLY H.	Son	W	M	Feb 1885	15	S				TN	TN	TN	FARM LABORER	0		✓	✓	✓				
	" CHARLES H.	Son	W	M	Jul 1890	9	S				TN	TN	TN										
	" CAMIE M.	Dau	W	F	Apr 1896	4	S				KY	TN	TN										
	" EARNEST E.	Son	W	M	Sept 1898	1	S				KY	TN	TN										
327 339	CREEK, JACKIE(?)	Head	W	M	Jul 1832	67	M	28			KY	KY	KY	FARMER	0		✓	✓	✓	O	F	F	267
	" ELIZABETH	Wife	W	F	Jun 1849	50	M	28	8	7	KY	KY	KY				✓	✓	✓				

STATE - KENTUCKY
COUNTY - MONROE
Township or other division: GUM

— 63 —

Enumerator: THOMAS R. EVANS

Supervisor's Dist. No. 102 Sheet No.
Enumeration Dist. No. 80

Location: No. of Family	No. of Dwelling	NAME	Relation	Color	Sex	DATE OF BIRTH Mon/Yr	Age at last birthday	Marital Status	# Years married	Mother of how many children?	# of these children living	NATIVITY Place of birth [this person]	Father of this person	Mother of this person	CITIZENSHIP Year of immig.	# years in U.S.	Naturalization	OCCUPATION 10 years +	Months not employed	EDUCATION Attended school in months	Can read	Can write	Speak English	OWNERSHIP Owned or Rent	Owned -no mortgage	Farm or house	# of farm schedule
		CREEK, DEBBIE H.	DAU	W	F	JAN 1874	26	S				KY	KY	KY							✓	✓	✓				
		" BESSIE	DAU	W	F	Sep 1876	23	S				KY	KY	KY							✓	✓	✓				
		" JOSEPH D.	SON	W	M	Nov 1877	22	S				KY	KY	KY				AT SCHOOL		4	✓	✓	✓				
		" COY N.	SON	W	M	OCT 1879	20	S				KY	KY	KY				FARM LABORER		4	✓	✓	✓				
		" CORA P.	DAU	W	F	Feb 1882	18	S				KY	KY	KY				AT SCHOOL		5	✓	✓	✓				
		" NELLIE	DAU	W	F	MAR 1885	15	S				KY	KY	KY				AT SCHOOL		3	✓	✓	✓				
		" BARTON S.	SON	W	M	Sep 1886	13	S				KY	KY	KY				FARM LABORER			✓	✓	✓				
328	340	HALCOMB, WILLIAM	HEAD	W	M	Nov 1869	30	M	8			TN	TN	KY				FARMER	0		✓	✓	✓	O	F	F	268
		" VICTORIA	WIFE	W	F	Nov 1872	27	M	8	2	2	KY	KY	KY							✓	✓	✓				
		" SARAH E.	DAU	W	F	Sept 1894	5	S				KY	TN	KY													
		" ROXIE M.	DAU	W	F	Jan 1897	3	S				KY	TN	KY													
329	341	DYER, FISHER B.	HEAD	W	M	MAR 1866	34	M	18			TN	TN	TN				FARMER	0		✓	✓	✓	O	F	F	269
		" MARY J.	WIFE	W	F	Sep 1861	38	M	18	2	2	TN	TN	TN							✓	✓					
		" JOSEPH	SON	W	M	MAR 1874	16	S				KY	TN	TN							✓	✓					
		" VIOLA M.	DAU	W	F	Sept 1875	14	S				KY	TN	TN							✓	✓					
330	342	CREEK, ELIGAH	HEAD	W	M	Jan 1857	43	M	9			KY	KY	KY							✓	✓		O	M	F	270
		" FRANKEY H.	WIFE	W	F	Sept 1872	27	M	9	3	3	KY	TN	TN							✓	✓					
		" MAIMEY C.	DAU	W	F	Feb 1892	8	S				KY	KY	KY													
		THOMAS C.	SON	W	M	Aug 1894	5	S				KY	KY	KY													
		CLARENCE	SON	W	M	Feb 1898	2	S				KY	KY	KY													
331	343	RHYHERD, SAMUEL	HEAD	W	M	Sept 1869	30	M	4			KY	KY	KY				FARMER	0		✓	✓	✓	R		F	271
		" AMERICA	WIFE	W	F	Sept 1874	25	M	4	2	1	KY	VA	KY							✓	✓					
		SARAH E.	DAU	W	F	MAY 1897	3	S				KY	KY	KY													
332	344	SHOCKLEY, WILLIAM T.	HEAD	W	M	MAR 1854	46	M	24			TN	TN	TN				FARMER			X	X	✓	O	M	F	272
		" NANCY T.	WIFE	W	F	MAY 1848	52	M	24	4	3	TN	TN	TN							✓	✓					
		" WILLIAM T.	SON	W	M	Sept 1879	20	S				TN	TN	TN				FARM LABORER	3		✓	✓	✓				

STATE - KENTUCKY
COUNTY - MONROE
Township or other division — GUM

Enumerator — Thomas R. Evans

Supervisor's Dist. No. 102   Sheet No.
Enumeration Dist. No. 80

Location No. of Family / No. of Dwelling	NAME	Relation	Color	Sex	DATE OF BIRTH Mon/Yr	Age at last birthday	Marital Status	#Years married	Mother of how many children?	# of these children living	NATIVITY Place of birth	Father	Mother	OCCUPATION	Months not employed	Attended school in months	Can read	Can write	Speak English	OWNERSHIP Owned or Rent	Owned-no mortgage	Farm or house	# of farm schedule
	SHOCKLEY, NANCY M.	DAU	W	F	May 1882	18	S				TN	TN	TN				✓	✓	✓				
	" LUELLA T.	DAU	W	F	Jun 1890	9	S				KY	TN	TN										
333 345	HOLLAND, SAMUEL	HEAD	W	M	Mar 1876	24	M	2			KY	VA	KY	FARMER			✓	✓	✓	R		F	273
	" BEDIE A.	WIFE	W	F	Jul 1879	20	M	2	1	1	KY	TN	TN				✓	✓	✓				
	" IDA H.	DAU	W	F	Dec 1898	1	S				TN	KY	KY										
334 346	SCOTT, BISHOP E.	HEAD	W	M	Apr 1839	61	M	31			TN	TN	TN	FARMER			✓	✓		O		F	F 274
	" SARAH J.	WIFE	W	F	Jul 1841	59	M	31	6	4	TN	TN	TN				✓	✓					
	" DOLLIE A.	DAU	W	F	Sept 1875	24	S				TN	TN	TN				✓	✓					
	" MANUEL W.	SON	W	M	Jan 1879	21	S				KY	TN	TN	FARMER			✓	✓					275
	" ALLIE B.	DAU	W	F	Nov 1881	18	S				KY	TN	TN	AT SCHOOL		5	✓	✓					
	" SARAH B.	DAU	W	F	Mar 1883	17	S				KY	TN	TN	AT SCHOOL		5	✓	✓					
335 347	HORN, WESLY	HEAD	W	M	Sep 1846	53	M	33			TN	TN	TN	FARMER	0		✓	✓		O		F	276
	" NESSA J.	WIFE	W	F	Jun 1840	59	M	33	7	7	TN	TN	TN				X	X	✓				
	" FRONEA	DAU	W	F	May 1868	32	S				TN	TN	TN				✓	✓					
	" JOHN W.	SON	W	M	Oct 1882	17	S				TN	TN	TN	FARM LABORER	0		✓	✓					
	" LULA	DAU	W	F	Mar 1887	13	S				TN	TN	TN	AT SCHOOL		3	✓	✓					
	" HARISON	SON	W	M	Jul 1888	11	S				KY	TN	TN	FARM LABORER		3	✓	✓					
	" HASSE	GR-DAU	W	F	Sept 1899	9/12	S				KY	TN	TN										
336 348	HORN, WALTER	HEAD	W	M	May 1876	24	M	3			KY	TN	TN	FARMER	0		✓	✓	✓	R		F	277
	" MATILDA C.	WIFE	W	F	Sep 1876	23	M	3	2	2	TN	TN	TN				✓	✓	✓				
	" McKINLEY	SON	W	M	May 1898	2	S				TN	KY	TN										
	" NETTIE B.	DAU	W	F	Apr 1899	5/12	S				KY	KY	TN										
337 349	HOLLAND, WHYLEY	HEAD	W	M	Apr 1874	26	M	4			KY	VA	KY	FARMER	0		✓	✓	✓	O		F F	278
	" ETTA G.	WIFE	W	F	Jan 1877	23	M	4	3	2	TN	TN	MO				✓	✓	✓				
	" ALTA S.	DAU			May 1896	4	S				KY	KY	TN										
	" LESTER W.	DAU			Mar 1899	1	S				KY	KY	TN										

STATE - KENTUCKY
COUNTY - MONROE   GUM
Township or other division

Enumerator THOMAS R. EVANS

Supervisor's Dist. No. *102*   Sheet No.
Enumeration Dist. No. *80*

Location (No. of Family / No. of Dwelling)	NAME	Relation	Color	Sex	DATE OF BIRTH Mon/Yr	Age at last birthday	Marital Status	# Years married	Mother of how many children?	# of these children living	Place of birth (this person)	Father of this person	Mother of this person	CITIZENSHIP	OCCUPATION 10 years +	Months not employed	Attended school in months	Can read	Can write	Speak English	Owned or Rent	Owned - no mortgage	Farm or house	# of farm schedule
338 350	ADAMS, WILLIAM E.	HEAD	W	M	OCT 1855	44	M	22			TN	TN	TN		FARMER	0		✓	✓	✓	0	F	F	279
"	NANCY J.	WIFE	W	F	NOV 1856	43	M	22	1	0	TN	TN	KY					✓	✓	✓				
339 351	HOLLAND, HARVEY D.	HEAD	W	M	OCT 1864	35	M	16			KY	VA	KY		FARMER			✓	✓	✓	R		F	280
"	SARAH F.	WIFE	W	F	NOV 1866	33	M	16	6	5	KY	KY	KY					✓	✓	✓				
"	JAMES E.	SON	W	M	MAR 1885	15	S				TN	KY	KY		FARM LABORER	0		✓	✓	✓				
"	ELA F.	DAU	W	F	JUN 1888	11	S				KY	KY	KY		AT SCHOOL		2	✓	✓	✓				
"	ROXIE M.	DAU	W	F	DEC 1890	9	S				KY	KY	KY											
"	ALLIE B.	DAU	W	F	AUG 1896	3	S				KY	KY	KY											
"	BERLEY D.	SON	W	M	FEB 1899	1	S				KY	KY	KY											
340 352	EVANS, FRANCIS M.	HEAD	W	M	AUG 1862	37	M	13			KY	KY	KY		FARMER	0		✓	✓	✓	0	F	F	281
"	NANNIE M.	WIFE	W	F	MAY 1863	37	M	13	3	3	KY	KY	KY		FARM LABORER			✓	✓	✓				
"	HARISON E.	SON	W	M	MAR 1888	12	S				KY	KY	KY		FARM LABORER									
"	DELTA G.	DAU	W	F	DEC 1894	5	S				KY	KY	KY											
"	NELLIE A.	DAU	W	F	OCT 1897	2	S				KY	KY	KY											
341 353	GUM, SIMPSON	HEAD	W	M	NOV 1840	59	M				TN	KY	TN		FARMER			✓	✓	✓	0	F	F	282
"	SARAH H.	WIFE	W	F	MAY 1856	44	M	6			KY	KY	KY											
342 354	GUM, WILLIAM B.	HEAD	W	M	OCT 1873	26	M	2			KY	TN	KY		FARMER			✓	✓	✓	0	M	F	283
"	JENNIE	WIFE	W	F	APR 1880	20	M	2			KY	KY	KY					✓	✓	✓				
343 355	BEATON, JOHN T.	HEAD	W	M	MAY 1869	31	M	3			KY	KY	KY		FARMER	0		✓	✓	✓	0	F	F	284
"	CULLI	WIFE	W	F	— — —			3	1	1	KY	KY	KY					✓	✓	✓				
"	DUESA	MOTHER	W	F	SEPT 1833	66	Wd		1	1	KY	KY	KY					✓	✓	✓				
"	MAGGIE M.	DAU	W	F	JUL 1897	2	S				KY	KY	KY											
"	CHRISTOPHER	BRO	W	M	APR 1876	24	S				KY	KY	KY		FARMER	0		✓	✓	✓				
344 356	BRAY, WILLIAM V.	HEAD	W	M	AUG 1872	27	S				KY	KY	KY		FARMER	0		✓	✓	✓	0	F	F	285
	CELSOR, SURILDA F.	SISTER	W	F	SEP 1861	38	Wd		1	1	KY	KY	KY					✓	✓	✓				
	BRAY, HENRY B.	BRO	W	M	OCT 1875	24	S				KY	KY	KY					✓	✓	✓				

STATE - KENTUCKY
COUNTY - MONROE
Township or other division   GUM

Enumerator THOMAS R. EVANS

Supervisor's Dist. No. 102   Sheet No.
Enumeration Dist. No. 80

No. of Family	No. of Dwelling	NAME	Relation	Color	Sex	DATE OF BIRTH Mon/Yr	Age at last birthday	Marital Status	# Years married	Mother of how many children?	# of these children living	Place of birth (this person)	Father of this person	Mother of this person	Year of immigr.	# years in U.S.	Naturalization	OCCUPATION 10 years +	Months not employed	Attended school in months	Can read	Can write	Speak English	Owned or Rent	Owned -no mortage	Farm or house	# of farm schedule
		BRAY, JAMES H.	BRO	W	M	APR 1881	19	S				KY	KY	KY				FARMER	0		✓	✓	✓	0		F	F 286
		" SAMUEL E	BRO	W	M	SEP 1883	16	S				KY	KY	KY				FARM LABORER			✓	✓	✓				
		CELSOR, AIMIE	NEICE	W	F	JUL 1883	16	S				KY	KY	KY				AT SCHOOL		10	✓	✓	✓				
		WOOD(COCK?), ELIZABETH	SERVANT	W	F	MAR 1867	33	Wd				KY	KY	KY				SERVANT			✓	✓	✓				
345	357	CARTER, JOHN	HEAD	W	M	JUN 1865	34	M				KY	KY	KY				FARMER			✓	✓	✓	R		F	287
		" LUDA	Wife	W	F	OCT 1872	27	M	10	5	3	KY	KY	KY							✓	✓	✓				
		" BURTON	SON	W	M	JUL 1890	9	S				KY	KY	KY													
		" HERSCHEL	SON	W	M	NOV 1892	7	S				KY	KY	KY													
		" AUDRIE	SON	W	M	JUL 1898	1	S				KY	KY	KY													
		" ADALINE	MOTHER	W	F	MAR 1838	62	Wd				KY	NC	TN													
346	358	COSBY, BAILEY P.	HEAD	W	M	DEC 1840	59	M	16			TN	GA	NC				MERCHANT			✓	✓	✓	0		F	F 288
		" LUCY A.	Wife	W	F	AUG 1860	39	M	16	9	7	KY	KY	KY							✓	✓	✓				
		" ARTHOR G.	SON	W	M	DEC 1883	16	S				KY	TN	KY				FARM LABORER			✓	✓	✓				
		" MARY E. C.	DAU	W	F	MAR 1885	15	S				KY	TN	KY				AT SCHOOL		5	✓	✓	✓				
		" RODA I	DAU	W	F	DEC 1887	12	S				KY	TN	KY				AT SCHOOL		5	✓	✓	✓				
		" HETTIE V.	DAU	W	F	SEPT 1889	10	S				KY	TN	KY				AT SCHOOL		5	✓	✓	✓				
		" LUTHER E.	SON	W	M	APR 1892	8	S				KY	TN	KY													
		" MALISSA C.	DAU	W	F	OCT 1893	6	S				KY	TN	KY													
		" ORA M.	DAU	W	F	AUG 1895	4	S				KY	TN	KY													
		" ALLIE P.	SON	W	M	JUN 1899	1/12	S				KY	TN	KY													
347	359	PAYNE, JOSIAH	HEAD	W	M	MAY 1849	51	M	29			TN	VA	TN				FARMER			✓	X	✓	R		F	289
		" MARY A.	Wife	W	F	FEB 1853	47	M	29	12	10	KY	TN	TN							X	X	✓				
		ALFRED	SON	W	M	OCT 1874	25	S				TN	TN	KY				DAY LABORER 2			✓	✓	✓	0		F	F 290
		CARTER, SAMANTHA	DAU	W	F	AUG 1876	23	Wd				TN	TN	KY							✓	✓	✓				
		PAYNE, ROBERT M.	SON	W	M	APR 1879	21	S				TN	TN	KY				FARM LABORER 3			✓	✓	✓				
		" TILDA BELL	DAU	W	F	DEC 1880	19	S				TN	TN	KY							✓	✓	✓				

TWELFTH CENSUS OF THE UNITED STATES 1900

STATE - KENTUCKY
COUNTY - MONROE   GUM   – 67 –
Township or other division

Enumerator   THOMAS R. EVANS

Supervisor's Dist. No. 102   Sheet No.
Enumeration Dist. No. 80

No. of Family	No. of Dwelling	NAME	Relation	Color	Sex	DATE OF BIRTH Mon/Yr	Age at last birthday	Marital Status	# Years married	Mother of how many children?	# of these children living	Place of birth	Father of this person	Mother of this person	Year of immigr.	# years in U.S.	Naturalization	OCCUPATION 10 years +	Months not employed	Attended school in months	Can read	Can write	Speak English	Owned or Rent	Owned-no mortgage	Farm or house	# of farm schedule
		PAYNE, RILEY F.	Son	W	M	Oct 1882	17	S				TN	TN	KY				FARM LABORER			✓	X	✓				
		" WILLIAM B.	Son	W	M	Jan 1885	15	S				TN	TN	KY				FARM LABORER			✓	X	✓				
		" AMANDA J.	Dau	W	F	Jun 1891	8	S				TN	TN	KY													
		" DAISEY A.	Dau	W	F	Jul 1893	6	S				KY	TN	KY													
		" JOHN W.	Son	W	M	Apr 1896	4	S				KY	TN	KY													
348	360	MAHANY, JOHN T.	Head	W	M	Sep 1865	34	S				KY	TN	KY				FARMER	0		✓	X	✓	0	M	F	291
		" GEORGE	Bro	W	M	Sep 1867	32	S				KY	TN	KY				FARMER	0		✓	✓	✓				
		SAMUEL J.	Bro	W	M	Sep 1869	30	S				KY	TN	KY				FARM LABORER	0		✓	✓	✓				
		POE, KATIE	Sis	W	F	Sep 1863	36	Wd				KY	TN	KY							✓	✓	✓				
		MARTIN, MARGARET E.	Sis	W	F	Apr 1859	41	Wd		4	4	KY	TN	KY							X	X	✓				
		" GILBERT	Neph.	W	M	Jan 1889	11	S				KY	KY	KY				FARM LABORER	0		X	X	✓				
		" DANIEL W.	Neph.	W	M	Sep 1891	8	S				KY	KY	KY													
		" VIRGIL C.	Neph.	W	M	Aug 1893	6	S				KY	KY	KY													
		" THOMAS B.	Neph.	W	M	Mar 1896	4	S				KY	KY	KY													
		" THOMAS J.	Lodger	W	M	Aug 1884	15	S				KY	KY	KY				FARM LABORER	0		X	X	✓				
349	361	POWEL, W. AKERS	Head	W	M	Jun 1858	41	M	16			KY	KY	KY				FARMER	0		✓	✓	✓	0	F	F	292
		" AGNES E.	Wife	W	F	Jul 1868	32	M	16	8	8	TN	TN	KY							✓	✓	✓				
		" GEORGE D.	Son	W	M	Sep 1885	14	S				KY	KY	TN				FARM LABORER			✓	✓	✓				
		" JAMES B.	Son	W	M	Aug 1887	12	S				KY	KY	TN				FARM LABORER			✓	X	✓				
		" HENRY W.	Son	W	M	Jul 1889	10	S				KY	KY	TN				FARM LABORER			✓	X	✓				
		" JASPER H.	Son	W	M	Apr 1891	9	S				KY	KY	TN													
		" NELLIE	Dau	W	F	Mar 1893	7	S				KY	KY	TN													
		" LESLY B.	Son	W	M	May 1895	5	S				KY	KY	TN													
		" JOHN T.	Son	W	M	Feb 1897	3	S				KY	KY	TN													
		" DUESA	Dau	W	F	Feb 1899	1	S				KY	KY	TN													
350	362	SHAW, JOHN D.	Head	W	M	Mar 1850	50	M	31			MO	KY	KY				BLACKSMITH						0	F	F	293

STATE - KENTUCKY
COUNTY - MONROE
GUM
Township or other division
Enumerator THOMAS R. EVANS
Supervisor's Dist. No. 102 Sheet No.
Enumeration Dist. No. 80

No. of Family	No. of Dwelling	NAME	Relation	Color	Sex	Date of Birth Mon/Yr	Age at last birthday	Marital Status	Years married	Mother of how many children	# of these children living	Place of birth (this person)	Father of this person	Mother of this person	Year of immigr.	# years in U.S.	Naturalization	Occupation	Months not employed	Attended school in months	Can read	Can write	Speak English	Owned or Rent	Owned-no mortgage	Farm or house	# of farm schedule
		SHAW, MILLY F.	Wife	W	F	Jan 1853	47	M	31	4	4	KY	KY	KY							✓	✓	✓				
		" CORA E.	Dau	W	F	Jan 1876	24	S				KY	MO	KY							✓	✓	✓				
		" WILLIAM E	Son	W	M	Nov 1881	18	S				KY	MO	KY							✓	✓	✓				
		" DUESA F.	Dau	W	F	Jan 1890	10	S				KY	MO	KY							✓	✓	✓				
		HUGHES, SUSAN	Step mother	W	F	Apr 1830	70	Wd				KY	KY	KY							X	X	✓				
		", MANERVA	S-in-law	W	F	Dec 1860	39	S				KY	KY	KY							✓	✓	✓				
351	363	HOLDER, OSCAR	Head	W	M	Nov 1867	32	M	2			KY	KY	KY				FARMER	0		✓	✓	✓	O	F	F	294
		" ARMINDA	wife	W	F	Apr 1866	34	M	2	1	1	KY	KY	KY							✓	✓	✓				
		" ESTER	Dau	W	F	Sep 1898	1	S				KY	KY	KY													
352	364	BOYD, JOSEPH	Head	W	M	Sep 1866	33	M	2			KY	KY	KY				FARMER			✓	✓	✓	R		F	
		" TEMPEST F.	wife	W	F	Dec 1877	22	M	2	1	1	KY	KY	KY							✓	X	✓				
		" GRACE G.	Dau	W	F	Sep 1886	13	S				KY	KY	KY							✓	✓	✓				
*	81/82	KEY, JANE	Sister	W	F	Mar 1857	43	S				KY	KY	KY							X	X	✓				
		" WILLIAM	Nephew	W	M	Jan 1889	11	S				KY	KY	KY													
353	365	BACHELDER, DAVID	Head	W	M	Feb 1859	41	M	12			MAINE	MAINE	MAINE				SHOWMAN			✓	✓	✓			H	
		" LIZZIE	wife	W	F	Mar 1870	30	M	12			Can-Eng	Can-Eng	Can-Eng							✓	✓	✓				
		SHAGGS, MACK	Boarder	W	M	Jan 1881	19	S				KY	KY	KY				SHOWMAN			✓	✓	✓				
		HUNT, HENRY H.	Boarder	B	M	Apr 1871	29	M				ALA	ALA	ALA				SHOWMAN			✓	✓					
		ROBERTS, RICHARD	Boarder	B	M	Apr 1876	24	S				KY	KY	KY				SHOWMAN			✓	✓					
354	366	EVANS, THOMAS R.	Head	W	M	Mar 1866	34	M	11			KY	KY	KY				SURVEYOR			✓	✓	✓	O	F	F	295
		" DONNA M.T.	wife	W	F	Jan 1871	29	M	11	5	3	KY	KY	TN							✓	✓	✓				
		" OLA L.	Dau	W	F	Oct 1889	10					KY	KY	KY							✓	✓	✓				
		" JAMES H.	Son	W	M	Sep 1892	7					KY	KY	KY							✓	✓	✓				
		ESTHER	Dau	W	F	Nov 1898	1	S				KY	KY	KY													
		MARGERY J.	Mother	W	F	Jul 1830	69	Wd				KY	TN	VA							✓	✓	✓				

* See next page

TWELFTH CENSUS OF THE UNITED STATES 1900

STATE - KENTUCKY
COUNTY - MONROE
Township or other division — GUM

Enumerator THOMAS R. EVANS

Supervisor's Dist. No. 102 Sheet No.
Enumeration Dist. No. 80

Location		NAME	Relation	Color	Sex	DATE OF BIRTH Mon/Yr	Age at last birthday	Marital Status	# Years married	Mother of how many children?	# of these children living	NATIVITY			CITIZENSHIP			OCCUPATION 10 years +	Months not employed	EDUCATION				OWNERSHIP				
No. of Family	No. of Dwelling											Place of birth [this person]	Father of this person	Mother of this person	Year of immigr.	# years in U.S.	Naturalization			Attended school in months	Can read	Can write	Speak English	Owned or Rent	Owned –no mortage	Farm or house	# of farm schedule	
																		* A FARM 296 SHOULD BE 219.									296	
																		BY MISTAKE IT WAS NOT										
																		NUMBERED. THERE ARE TWO										
																		FARM SCHEDULES (NO?) 48									297	
																		IN ALL										

TWELFTH CENSUS OF THE UNITED STATES 1900

STATE - KENTUCKY
COUNTY - MONROE
Township or other division — TURNER

— 70 —

Enumerator ABIJAH STRICKLER

Supervisor's Dist. No. 102 Sheet No.
Enumeration Dist. No. 81

No. of Family	No. of Dwelling	NAME	Relation	Color	Sex	Date of Birth Mon/Yr	Age at last birthday	Marital Status	# Years married	Mother of how many children?	# of these children living	Place of birth (this person)	Father of this person	Mother of this person	Year of immigr.	# years in U.S.	Naturalization	Occupation	Months not employed	Attended school in months	Can read	Can write	Speak English	Owned or Rent	Owned - no mortgage	Farm or house	# of Farm schedule
1	1	MYRES, DIM —	—	W M		DEC 1863	36	S				KY	NC	—				—			✓	✓	✓	O	F F		1
		— DIM —	SISTER	W F		—	38	—				KY	NC	—													
2	2	EUBANK — DIM —	HEAD	W M		MAR 1822	—	M	52			KY	VA	VA				FARMER	O		✓	✓		O	F F		2
		" NANCY E.	Wife	W F		Sep —	70	M	52	11	7	TN	TN	VA							✓	✓					
		" MACK	Son	W M		Feb 1866	34	M				KY	KY	TN				FARMER	O		✓	✓	✓				
		" MAGNOLIA D-in-law	Wife	W F		Nov 1877	22	M		1	1	KY	KY	KY							✓	✓					
		" BETHEL Gt-Son		W M		Sept 1899 9/12		S				KY	KY	KY													
		QUIGLEY, ELSIRA F. Dau		W F		Feb 1856	44	Wd		5	5	KY	KY	TN							✓	✓	✓				
		" VERLERIA	Son	W M		Aug 1870	29	S				KY	KY	TN				FARMING			✓	✓	✓				
3	3	ENGLAND, WILLIAM J.	Head	W M		Aug 1861	38	M	12			KY	KY	KY				FARMER	O		✓	✓	✓	O	F F		3
		" ELIZA A.	Wife	W F		Jul 1862	37	M	12	4	4	KY	KY	KY							✓	✓	✓				
		" DEWEY B.	Son	W M		Oct 1888	11	S				KY	KY	KY						5	✓	✓	—				
		" HUSHEL	Son	W M		Jun 1890	9	S				KY	KY	KY						5	✓	✓	✓				
		" (?)BLANHEY T.	Dau	W F		Oct 1892	7	S				KY	KY	KY													
		" (?)AROS C.	Son	W M		Jul 1895	5	S				KY	KY	KY													
4	4	ENGLAND, ELLENDER J. (HEAD)(MOTHER)		W F		MAY 1838	62	Wd				KY	KY	KY							✓	X	✓	O	F F		4
5	5	HOWARD, JESSE	HEAD	W M		— 1871	28	M				KY	KY	KY				FARM LABOR	O		✓	✓	✓	R	H		
		" ELIZA J.	Wife	W F		Feb 1871	27	M				KY	KY	KY							✓	✓	✓				
		" ZUENIE	Dau	W F		Feb 1889	11	S				KY	KY	KY						5	✓	✓	✓				
		" CLYDE J.	Son	W M		Jun 1893	6	S				KY	KY	KY													
6	6	WHEAT, WILLIAM H.	HEAD	W M		JAN 1871	29	M	8			KY	KY	KY				FARMER	O		✓	✓		R	H		
		" FRANCES S.	Wife	W F		JAN 1867	33	M		1	1	KY	KY	KY													
		" NOVY S.	Dau	W F		AUG 1893	6	S				KY	KY	KY													
7	7	WHEAT, JAMES T.	Head	W M		Jul 1859	40	M	13			KY	KY	KY				FARMER	O		✓	✓	✓	O	F F		5
		" IVIE A.	Wife	W F		Dec 1869	30		13	3	3	KY	KY	KY							✓	✓	✓				
		" VIRGIL	Son	W M		Sep 1889	10	S				KY	KY	KY							✓	✓	✓				

STATE - KENTUCKY
COUNTY - MONROE
Township or other division — TURNER   Enumerator — ABIJAH STRICKLER

Supervisor's Dist. No. 102 Sheet No. —
Enumeration Dist. No. 81

No. of Family	No. of Dwelling	NAME	Relation	Color	Sex	DATE OF BIRTH Mon/Yr	Age at last birthday	Marital Status	# Years married	Mother of how many children?	# of these children living	Place of birth [this person]	Father of this person	Mother of this person	Year of immigr.	# years in U.S.	Naturalization	OCCUPATION 10 years +	Months not employed	Attended school in months	Can read	Can write	Speak English	Owned or Rent	Owned -no mortage	Farm or house	# of farm schedule	
		WHEAT, QUEATS (?)	Son	W	M	APR 1893	7	S				KY	KY	KY							✓X		✓					
		" HALLIE	Dau	W	F	Nov 1893	6	S	8			KY	KY	KY														
8	8	WHEAT, BIRD	Head	W	M	Feb 1869	31	M	8			KY	KY	KY				FARMER			✓	✓	✓	R		F	6	
		" MAGGA	Wife	W	F	Feb 1870	30	M	8	3	3	KY	KY	KY							✓	✓	✓					
		" ARLEY J.	Son	W	M	OCT 1893	6	S				KY	KY	KY														
		" BERNES D.	Son	W	M	Sept 1896	4	S				KY	KY	KY														
		" ORAL W.	Son	W	M	Oct 1899	7/12	S				KY	KY	KY														
9	9	WHEAT, GREENBERRY J.	Head	W	M	Sep 1862	37	M	11			KY	KY	KY				FARMER			✓	✓	✓	R		F	7	
		" BETTY H.	Wife	W	F	Aug 1860	39	M	11	3	3	KY	KY	KY							✓	-	✓					
		" ALVA	Son	W	M	Sep 1889	10	S				KY	KY	KY						5	✓	✓	✓					
		" ILIE (?)	Son	W	M	Oct 1892	7	S				KY	KY	KY														
		" OLIE	Son	W	M	Jan 1898	2	S				KY	KY	KY														
10	10	WHEAT, JOHN A.	Head	W	M	Jan 1838	62	M	41			KY	VA	VA				FARMER			✓	✓	✓	O		F F	8	
		" (?) MARY A.	Wife	W	F	Apr 1832	68	M	41	12	11	KY	KY	TN								✓	✓					
		" COLIE	Dau	W	F	Feb 1862	36	S				KY	TN	KY									✓					
11	11	DANIEL, JAMES O.	Head	W	M	Dec 1832	67	M	30			KY	TN	KY				FARMER			✓	✓	✓	O		F F	9	
		" MATILDA J.	Wife	W	F	Oct 1845	54	M	30	10	10	KY	KY	KY							✓	-	✓					
		" DEBRAH E.	Dau	W	F	Mar 1875	25	S				KY	KY	KY							✓	✓	✓					
		" JINIA	Dau	W	F	Nov 1876	23	S				KY	KY	KY							✓	✓	✓					
		" JAMES B.	Son	W	M	May 1878	22	S				KY	KY	KY							✓	✓	✓					
		" EVIE F.	Dau	W	F	Mar 1880	20	S				KY	KY	KY							✓	✓	✓					
		" ARIZONA	Dau	W	F	May 1882	18	S				KY	KY	KY				AT SCHOOL		3	✓	✓	✓					
		" GARDLAR	Dau	W	F	May 1884	16	S				KY	KY	KY						3	✓	✓	✓					
		" NANCY D.	Dau	W	F	APR 1887	13	S				KY	KY	KY						3	✓	✓	✓					
12	12	GEARLDS, LOUISA M.	Head	W	F	Jan 1837	63	Wd		10	6	KY	KY	VA				FARMER			✓	X	✓	O		F	10	
		" JAMES B	Son	W	M	Feb 1865	35	Wd				KY	KY	KY				FARMER			✓	✓	✓					

STATE - KENTUCKY
COUNTY - MONROE
Township or other division — TURNER

Enumerator — ABIJAH STRICKLER

Supervisor's Dist. No. *102* Sheet No.
Enumeration Dist. No. *81*

No. of Family	No. of Dwelling	NAME	Relation	Color	Sex	DATE OF BIRTH Mon/Yr	Age at last birthday	Marital Status	# Years married	Mother of how many children?	# of these children living	Place of birth [this person]	Father of this person	Mother of this person	Year of immigr.	# years in U.S.	Naturalization	OCCUPATION 10 years +	Months not employed	Attended school in months	Can read	Can write	Speak English	Owned or Rent	Owned -no mortgage	Farm or house	# of farm schedule
		GEARLDS, GRACY	Gr-Dau	W	F	Aug 1893	6	S				KY	KY	KY							✓	✓	✓				
13	13	THOMAS, WIOT	HEAD	W	M	Aug 1860	39	M	21			KY	KY	KY				FARMER			✓	✓	✓	O		F	11
		" SARAH A.	wife	W	F	Apr 1857	43	M	21	7	7	KY	TN	KY							✓	✓	✓				
		" FLONIA	SON	W	M	May 1882	18	S				KY	KY	KY				FARM LABOR	O	1	✓	✓	✓				
		" BERTHA	DAU	W	F	Apr 188	15	S				KY	KY	KY							✓	✓	✓				
		" SAORA (?)	DAU	W	F	Jul 1885	14	S				KY	KY	KY						2	✓	✓	✓				
		" LUCY N.	DAU	W	F	Jul 1885	14	S				KY	KY	KY						2	✓	✓	✓				
		" LEVY E.	SON	W	M	May 1889	11	S				KY	KY	KY				FARM LABOR	O				✓				
		" HOMER	SON	W	M	Feb 1893	7	S				KY	KY	KY					O								
14	14	THOMAS, WILLIAM	HEAD	W	M	Feb 1830	69	M	48			VA	VA	VA				FARMER			X	X	✓	O		F	12
		" MALINDA H.	wife	W	F	Apr 1832	67	M	48	7	3	TN	TN	VA							✓	X	✓				
		" IVA M.	Gr-Dau	W	F	Sep 1889	10	S				KY	KY	KY				AT SCHOOL		5	✓	✓					
15	15	THOMAS, JOSEPH	HEAD	W	M	Sep 1856	43	M	16			KY	VA	TN				FARMER			✓	✓	✓	O		F	13
		" JOSEY F.	wife	W	F	Jun 1862	37	M	16	6	6	KY	KY	TN							✓	✓	✓				
		" OLIVER J.	SON	W	M	Mar 1886	14	S				KY	KY	KY				FARM LABOR		5	✓	✓	✓				
		" ELVERTA	DAU	W	F	Nov 1891	8	S				KY	KY	KY						5	✓	✓					
		" ALFORD T.	SON	W	M	Jun 1894	5	S				KY	KY	KY													
		" LUTHER D.	SON	W	M	Mar 1897	3	S				KY	KY	KY													
16	16	HOOD, FRANK P.	HEAD	W	M	Jul 1853	46	M	9			KY	KY	KY				FARMER	O		✓	✓	✓	O		F	14
		" HENRY ETTER	wife	W	F	Jan 1857	43	M	9	1	1	KY	KY	KY							✓	✓	✓				
		" VERNON D.	DAU	W	F	Oct 1894	5	S				KY	KY	KY													
		" WILLIAM E.	SON	W	M	Dec 1978	21	S				KY	KY	KY				FARMER	O		✓	✓	✓				
17	17	RICH, SARAH A.	HEAD	W	F	Jan 1823	77	Wd		10	9	VA	VA	VA				FARMER						O		F	15
		TURNER, LUCY	Grand-Dau	W	F	Nov 1881	18	S				KY	KY	KY							✓	✓	✓				
		LEE, — OSS, N.	Grand-son	W	M	Oct 1873	26	S				—	KY	KY							✓	✓	✓				
18	18	TURNER, WILLIAM B.	Head	W	M	Mar 1845	55	M	34			KY	VA	VA				FARMER			✓	✓	✓	O		F	16

STATE - KENTUCKY
COUNTY - MONROE TURNER
Township or other division

Enumerator ABIJAH STRICKLER

Supervisor's Dist. No. 102 Sheet No.
Enumeration Dist. No. 81

No. of Family	No. of Dwelling	NAME	Relation	Color	Sex	DATE OF BIRTH Mon/Yr	Age at last birthday	Marital Status	# Years married	Mother of how many children?	# of these children living	Place of birth [this person]	Father of this person	Mother of this person	Year of immigr.	# years in U.S.	Naturalization	OCCUPATION 10 years +	Months not employed	Attended school in months	Can read	Can write	Speak English	Owned or Rent	Owned -no mortage	Farm or house	# of farm schedule
		TURNER, LUCY E.	Wife	W	F	Apr 1841	59	M	34			KY	VA	VA							✓	✓	✓				
		HOOD, ROBERT B.	Nephew	W	M	Sep 188	17	S				KY	KY	KY													
		", BENJAMIN	Father	W	M	Jan 1812	88	Wd				VA	VA	VA				FARMER	12								
		THOMAS, WILLIAM J.	Lodger	W	M	Aug 1875	24	S				KY	TN	TN				FARM LABOR			✓	✓					
19	19	TURNER, DANIEL W	Head	W	M	Sept 1856	43	M	11			KY	KY	KY				FARMER			✓	✓	✓	0		F F	17
		" MANDY H.	Wife	W	F	Jun 1861	38	M	11	7	5	KY	TN	TN							✓	✓	✓				
		" CLAUDY P.	Son	W	M	MAR 1884	16	S				KY	KY	KY				FARM LABOR	0	0		✓	✓				
		" OLIVER J.	Son	W	M	Jun 1889	10	S				KY	KY	KY				FARM LABOR	0	0		✓	✓				
		" BASSEY E.	Dau	W	F	Jul 1892	7	S				KY	KY	KY													
		" EARLY E.	Son	W	M	Nov 1893	6	S				KY	KY	KY													
		" DEWEY P.	Son	W	M	Aug 1895	4	S				KY	KY	KY													
		" HETTY A.	Dau	W	F	May 1899	1	S				KY	KY	KY				FARMER	0		✓	✓	✓	0		F F	18
20	20	WRICH, WILLIAM J.	HEAD	W	M	Aug 1858	41	M	23			KY	VA	VA							✓	✓	✓				
		" WILLIEAN (?)	Wife	W	F	Jun 1857	42	M	23	10	9	KY	KY	KY							X	X	✓				
		" JOSEY P.	Dau	W	F	OCT 1884	15	S				KY	KY	KY							✓	X	✓				
		" (?) BETY E.	Dau	W	F	May 1886	14	S				KY	KY	KY						3	✓	✓	✓				
		" LUCINDY	Dau	W	F	DEC 1889	10	S				KY	KY	KY						4	✓	X	✓				
		" JIMEY	Son	W	M	Aug 1892	7	S				KY	KY	KY													
		" SARY AN	Dau	W	F	Oct 1894	5	S				KY	KY	KY													
		(?) DAUNEY	Dau	W	F	MAR 1897	3	S				KY	KY	KY													
		" (DAUGHTER) un named		W	F	Feb 1900	4/12	S				KY	KY	KY													
21	21	ENGLAND, JOSEPH F.	HEAD	W	M	Jan 1866	33	M				KY	KY	KY				FARMER			✓	✓	✓				19
		" MARY B.	Wife	W	F	Jun 1861	38	M	15	6	5	KY	VA	VA							X	X	✓				
		" SARAH E.	Dau	W	F	Jun 1886	13	S				KY	KY	KY							✓	✓	✓				
		" WILLIAM C.	Son	W	M	Jul 1890	9	S				KY	KY	KY							X	X	✓				
		" JAMES H.	Son	W	M	Nov 1893	6	S				KY	KY	KY													

TWELFTH CENSUS OF THE UNITED STATES 1900

STATE - KENTUCKY
COUNTY - MONROE
Township or other division: TURNER
Enumerator: ABIJAH STRICKLER

Supervisor's Dist. No. _102_ Sheet No.
Enumeration Dist. No. _81_

No. of Family	No. of Dwelling	NAME	Relation	Color	Sex	DATE OF BIRTH Mon/Yr	Age at last birthday	Marital Status	# Years married	Mother of how many children?	# of these children living	Place of birth [this person]	Father of this person	Mother of this person	Year of immigr.	# years in U.S.	Naturalization	OCCUPATION 10 years +	Months not employed	Attended school in months	Can read	Can write	Speak English	Owned or Rent	Owned –no mortgage	Farm or house	# of farm schedule
		ENGLAND, NETY A.	DAU	W	F	Jul 1895	4	S				KY	KY	KY													
		" LONEY F.	DAU	W	F	Oct 1898	1	S				KY	KY	KY													
22	22	TURNER, JOHN	HEAD	W	M	Jan 1848	52	M	34			KY	VA	VA				FARMER			✓	X	✓			F	20
		" MARY S.	wife	W	F	Mar –	53	M	34	4	2	KY	VA	VA							✓	X	✓				
		" MAHALIA E.	DAU	W	F	Oct 1866	33	Divc		1	1	KY	KY	KY							✓	✓	✓				
		TREVITT, MINIE E.	GR DAU	W	F	Oct 1881	19	S				KY	KY	KY							✓	✓	✓				
		BROWNFIELD, SARAH M.	SISTER	W	F	Aug 1851	48	Wd		4	3	KY	KY	KY							X	X	✓				
23	23	CLARKSON, JOHN S.	HEAD	W	M	Jun 1865	34	M	15			KY	KY	KY				FARMER			✓	✓	✓	O	F	F	21
		" NANCY E.	wife	W	F	Jul 1865	34	M	15	2	2	KY	KY	KY							X	X	✓				
		" SARAH F.	DAU	W	F	Oct 1886	13	S				KY	KY	KY						5	✓	✓	✓				
		" MARY B.	DAU	W	F	Aug 1891	8	S				KY	KY	KY							✓	✓	✓				
24	24	ENGLAND, JOHN W.	Head	W	M	Aug 1868	31	M	11			KY	KY	KY				FARMER			✓	✓	✓	R		F	22
		" JAMES B.(?)	Wife	W	F	Sep 1872	27	M	11	4	4	KY	KY	KY							X	X	✓				
		" ETTY F.	DAU	W	F	Jun 1890	9	S				KY	KY	KY													
		" WILLIAM J.	SON	W	M	Dec 1891	8	S				KY	KY	KY													
		" MARTHY S.	DAU	W	F	Mar 1894	6	S				KY	KY	KY													
		" LEVY J	SON	W	M	Jun 1896	3	S				KY	KY	KY													
25	25	ENGLAND, MARY P.	HEAD	W	F	Feb 1838	62	Wd				KY	VA	VA				FARMER			X	X	✓	O	F	F	23
		RICH, LENZY B.	GR SON	W	M	Mar 1881	19	S				KY	KY	KY				FARM LABOR			✓	✓	✓				
26	26	HOOD, THOMAS J.	Head	W	M	Apr 1843	57	M	2			KY	VA	VA				FARMER			✓	✓	✓	O	F	F	24
		" SARAH E. E.	wife	W	F	Apr 1851	49	M	2			KY	VA	VA							X	X					
27	27	MYERES, CORNELIUS	Head	W	M	Aug 1841	58	M	23			TN	NC	NC				FARMER			✓	✓	✓	O	F	F	25
		" ALLICE	wife	W	F	Aug 1859	40	M	23			TN	TN	TN							✓	✓	✓				
		WAX, ETHEL E.	Lodger	W	M(?)	Apr 1884	16	S				KY	KY	KY													
		WAX, LENIA O.	Lodger	W	F	Jul 1889	10	S				KY	KY	KY													
28	28	CLARKSON, JAMES J.	Head	W	M	Aug 1855	44	M	25			KY	KY	KY				FARMER			X	X	✓	R		F	26

TWELFTH CENSUS OF THE UNITED STATES 1900

STATE - KENTUCKY
COUNTY - MONROE
Township or other division — TURNER — 75 —
Enumerator ABIJAH STRICKLER

Supervisor's Dist. No. 102 Sheet No.
Enumeration Dist. No. 81

No. of Family	No. of Dwelling	NAME	Relation	Color	Sex	DATE OF BIRTH Mon/Yr	Age at last birthday	Marital Status	# Years married	Mother of how many children?	# of these children living	Place of birth (this person)	Father of this person	Mother of this person	Year of immigr.	# years in U.S.	Naturalization	OCCUPATION 10 years +	Months not employed	Attended school in months	Can read	Can write	Speak English	Owned or Rent	Owned -no mortage	Farm or house	# of farm schedule
		CLARKSON, WILLIA	Wife	W	F	Apr 1858	42	M	25	5	3	KY	VA	VA							X	X	✓				
		" IDER E.	Dau	W	F	May 1883	17	S				KY	KY	KY							✓	✓	✓				
		" WYETT	Son	W	M	Sept 1888	11	S				KY	KY	KY							✓	✓	✓				
		" ROBERT E. lodger		W	M	Jun 1874	25	S				KY	KY	KY				FARM LABOR			X	X	✓				
29	29	GENTRY, SANILL (?)	HEAD	W	M	Nov 1858	41	M	17			KY	KY	KY				BLACKSMITH			✓	✓	✓	O	F	F	27
		" MARY M.	wife	W	F	May 1865	34	M	17	5	5	KY	KY	KY							✓	✓	✓				
		" VARNA H.	Son	W	M	Jul 1884	15	S				KY	KY	KY						3	✓	✓	✓				
		" SARAH A.	Dau	W	F	Jan 1886	14	S				KY	KY	KY						5	✓	✓	✓				
		" MAUD E	Dau	W	F	Mar 1888	12	S				KY	KY	KY				AT SCHOOL		5	✓	✓	✓				
		" OMALT H.	Dau	W	F	Jun 1892	7	S				KY	KY	KY						5	✓	✓	✓				
		" OSEY D.	Dau	W	F	Oct 1894	5	S				KY	KY	KY													
30	30	TURNER, ROBERT S.	Head	W	M	Jul 1848	57	M	31			KY	VA	VA				FARMER			X	X	✓	O	F	F	28
		" VIRGENY A	wife	W	F	Jul 185	48	M	31	8	7	KY	VA	VA							X	X	✓				
		" OMA D	Dau	W	F	May 1878	22	S				KY	KY	KY							✓	✓	✓				
		" SANFORD B.	Son	W	M	Nov 1882	17	S				KY	KY	KY				FARM LABOR			✓	✓	✓				
		" ROBERT E.	Son	W	M	May 1887	13	S				KY	KY	KY				FARM LABOR			X	X	✓				
31	31	FOX, HENRY F.	Head	W	M	Nov 1873	26	M	7			KY	KY	KY				FARMING			✓	✓	✓	R		F	29
		" MARY M.	wife	W	F	Dec 1873	26	M	7	4	4	KY	KY	KY							✓	✓	✓				
		" AUDY P.	Son	W	M	May 1892	7	S				KY	KY	KY													
		" ORA V.	Dau	W	F	Nov 1894	5	S				KY	KY	KY													
		" ROXEY B.	Dau	W		Aug 1897	2	S				KY	KY	KY													
		" DAVY A.	Son	W	M	Jul 1899	11/12	S				KY	KY	KY													
32	32	BECKHAN, WILLIAM G	Head	W	M	Aug 1854	45	M	1			KY	KY	KY				PAINTER		5	✓	✓	✓	R		F H	30
		" SARY F.	wife	W	F	Jan 1866	34	M				KY	KY	KY							✓	✓	✓				
		" BESSY	Dau	W	F	Dec 1889	10	S				KY	KY	KY						5	✓	✓	✓				
		" EDGER	Son	W	M	Dec 1891	8	S				KY	KY	KY													

TWELFTH CENSUS OF THE UNITED STATES 1900

STATE - KENTUCKY
COUNTY - MONROE
Township or other division — TURNER — 76 —
Enumerator ABIJAH STRICKLER

Supervisor's Dist. No. _102_ Sheet No. _____
Enumeration Dist. No. _81_

No. of Family	No. of Dwelling	NAME	Relation	Color	Sex	Date of Birth Mon/Yr	Age	Marital Status	#Years married	Mother of how many children?	# living	Place of birth	Father	Mother	Occupation	Months not employed	Attended school	Can read	Can write	Speak English	Ownership		#of Farm schedule
		BECKHAN, CARSON	Son	W	M	Aug 1896	3	S				KY	KY	KY						✓			
		RUSSELL, MARY E.	Servant	W	F	Aug 1879	20	S				KY	KY	KY				✓	✓	✓			
33	33	TURNER, WILLIAM A.	Head	W	M	Feb 1834	66	M	22			KY	VA	VA	Farmer		X	X	✓		R	F	31
		" MARY J.	Wife	W	F	Feb 1852	48	M	22	7	7	KY	KY	TN				✓	✓	✓			
		" AARY C.	Dau	W	F	Jul 1880	19	S				KY	KY	KY				✓	✓	✓			
		" JOHN W.	Son	W	M	Sep 1881	18	S				KY	KY	KY				X	X	✓			
		" MILLIE A.	Dau	W	F	Sep 1885	15	S				KY	KY	KY				X	X	✓			
		" MARY B.	Dau	W	F	Dec 1886	13	S				KY	KY	KY			5	X	X	✓			
		" RACHEL L.	Dau	W	F	Jul 1891	8	S				KY	KY	KY			5	X	X	✓			
		" WILLIAM R.	Son	W	M	Feb 1896	4	S				KY	KY	KY						✓			
		CREEK, WILLIAM	Father-in-law	W	M	Jun 1817	83	M	53			KY	VA	VA				X	X	✓			
		" RACHEL	Mother-in-law	W	F	Oct 1836	63	M	10	1	1	KY	KY	KY				✓	✓	✓			
34	34	TURNER, JAMES A.	Head	W	M	Oct 1877	22	M	6			KY	KY	KY	Farmer	0		—	—	—		R	F	32
		" ABACILL	Wife	W	F	Oct 1875	24	M	6	4	4	KY	KY	KY				✓	✓	✓			
		" ROCKSY M.	Dau	W	F	Jan 1895	5	S				KY	KY	KY									
		" PERL	Dau	W	F	Feb 1896	4	S				KY	KY	KY									
		" ADER B.	Dau	W		Sep 1897	2	S				KY	KY	KY									
		" ODOS F.	Son	W	M	Nov 1899	7/12	S				KY	KY	KY									
35	35	CROW, WILLIAM B.	Head	W	M	Jun 1859	39	M	13			KY	VA	TN	Farmer		X	X	✓		R	F	33
		" LIZIA J.	Wife	W	F	May 1856	44	M	13	3	2	KY	VA	TN				✓	X	✓			
		" LUELLER	Dau	W	F	Jun 1880	19	S				KY	KY	KY				✓	X	✓			
		" LAURA	Dau	W	F	May 1882	18	S				KY	KY	KY				X	X	✓			
		" LIZZY	Dau	W	F	Sep 1883	16	S				KY	KY	KY				X	X	✓			
		" GRANTY	Son	W	M	Jul 1890	9	S				KY	KY	KY				X	X	✓			
		ARCHANY	Dau	W	F	Aug 1892	7	S				KY	KY	KY									
36	36	DEWEESE, HENRY	Head	W	M	Mar 1814	86	M	55			TN	VA	TN	Farmer			✓	✓	✓		O	F	34

TWELFTH CENSUS OF THE UNITED STATES 1900

STATE - KENTUCKY
COUNTY - MONROE
Township or other division — TURNER — -77-
Enumerator ABIJAH STRICKLER

Supervisor's Dist. No. 102 Sheet No.
Enumeration Dist. No. 81

No. of Family	No. of Dwelling	NAME	Relation	Color	Sex	DATE OF BIRTH Mon/Yr	Age at last birthday	Marital Status	# Years married	Mother of how many children	# of these children living	Place of birth	Father of this person	Mother of this person	Year of immigr.	# years in U.S.	Naturalization	OCCUPATION	Months not employed	Attended school in months	Can read	Can write	Speak English	Owned or Rent	Owned - no mortage	Farm or house	# of Farm schedule
		DEWEESE, RACHEL	wife	W	F	Aug 1829	70	M	55			TN	TN	TN							✓	✓	✓				
37	37	DEWEESE, ANDREW J.	Head	W	M	Dec 1855	44	M	21			TN	VA	TN				FARMER			✓	✓	✓	0		F	34
		" LUELLER J.	wife	W	F	Sep 1860	39	M	21	4	4	KY	VA	KY							✓	✓	✓				
		" WILLIAM H.	Son	W	M	Jul 1879	20	S				KY	KY	KY						7	✓	✓	✓				
		" JOHN (G?)	Son	W	M	Nov 1885	14	S				KY	KY	KY						5	✓	✓	✓				
		" ELLEY B.	Dau	W	F	Jul 1890	9	S				KY	KY	KY						5	✓	✓	✓				
38	38	PROFFITT, BENJAMIN	Head	W	M	Apr 1874	26	M				KY	KY	KY				FARMER			✓	✓	✓	0	M	F	35
		" MARY B.	wife	W	F	Jan 1879	21	M				KY	VA	TN							✓	✓	✓				
39	39	THOMAS, JOHN O.	Head	W	M	Sep 1853	44	M	25			KY	VA	TN				FARMER			X	X	✓	0	-	F	36
		" CATHERINE	wife	W	F	Feb 1839	61	M	25	4	4	KY	TN	TN							✓	✓	✓				
		" NORA B.	Dau	W	F	Jun 1887						KY	KY	KY							✓	✓	✓				
		" JAMES W.	Son	W	M	May - INK BLOT						KY	KY	KY				FARM LABORER	4		✓	✓	✓				
40	40	TURNER, WYOTT	Head	W	M	Jan 1865	35	M	10			KY	KY	KY				FARMER			✓	✓	✓	R		F	37
		" NETTY	wife	W	F	Nov 1870	29	M	10	6	6	KY	KY	KY							✓	✓	✓				
		" OSCAR W	Son	W	M	Sept 1890	9	S				KY	KY	KY						5	✓	✓	✓				
		" HERBERT J	Son	W	M	Jun 1892	7	S				KY	KY	KY						5	✓	✓	✓				
		" EARLY H.	Son	W	M	May 1894	6	S				KY	KY	KY													
		" OVY E	Dau	W	F	May 1896	4	S				KY	KY	KY													
		" BERTY C.	Son	W	M	Jul 1898	1	S				KY	KY	KY													
		" IRLEY P	Son	W	M	Apr 1900	½2	S				KY	KY	KY													
		HALL, JOHN A.	FATHER IN LAW	W	M	Mar 1818	82	Wd				TN	VA	VA							✓	✓	✓				
41	41	THOMAS, NELSON A.	Head	W	M	Jan 1858	42	M	17			KY	VA	VA				FARMER			✓	✓	✓	0		F	38
		" ROSINA E.	wife	W	F	Dec 1865	36	M	17	2	2	KY	KY	KY							✓	✓	✓				
		" BERTHA	Dau	W	F	Jan 1886	13	S				KY	KY	KY						5	✓	✓	✓				
		" ADER B	Dau	W	F	Sep 1896	3	S				KY	KY	KY													
42	42	TURNER, THOMAS J	Head	W	M	Jun 1877	23	M	3			KY	KY	KY				FARMER	0		✓	✓	✓			F	

TWELFTH CENSUS OF THE UNITED STATES 1900

STATE - KENTUCKY
COUNTY - MONROE
Township or other division — TURNER

— 78 —

Enumerator ABIJAH STRICKLER

Supervisor's Dist. No. 102 Sheet No.
Enumeration Dist. No. 81

No. of Family	No. of Dwelling	NAME	Relation	Color	Sex	Date of Birth Mon/Yr	Age at last birthday	Marital Status	# Years married	Mother of how many children?	# of these children living	Place of birth (this person)	Father of this person	Mother of this person	Year of immigr.	# years in U.S.	Naturalization	Occupation 10 years +	Months not employed	Attended school in months	Can read	Can write	Speak English	Owned or Rent	Owned -no mortage	Farm or house	# of farm schedule
		TURNER, GILLEY S.	Wife	W	F	Apr 1878	22	M	3	2	2	KY	KY	KY							✓	✓	✓				
		" HARRY D.	Son	W	M	May 1897	3	S				KY	KY	KY													
		" OAKLEY B.	Son	W	M	Feb 1899	1	S				KY	KY	KY													
		GENTRY, JOHN	Lodger	W	M	May 1879	20	S				KY	KY	KY							✓	X	✓				
43	43	TURNER, WILLIAM C.	Head	W	M	Sep 1874	25	M	6			KY	KY	KY				FARMER	0		✓	✓	✓	R		F	39
		" EFFIE	Wife	W	F	Sep 1877	22	M	6	3	2	KY	KY	KY							✓	✓	✓				
		" HILA H.	Son	W	M	Aug 1897	2	S				KY	KY	KY													
		" LONEY T.	Son	W	M	Aug 1898	1	S				KY	KY	KY													
44	44	COUNTS, THOMAS	Head	W	M	Apr 1870	30	M	5			KY	KY	KY				FARMER	0		X	X	✓	R		F	40
		" HARRIET	Wife	W	F	Jan 1863	37	M	5	1	1	KY	KY	KY							✓	✓	✓				
		"(?) NEUMERS S.	Son	W	M	Oct 1898	1	S				KY	KY	KY													
45	45	GENTRY, ISAAC D.	Head	W	M	Oct 1869	30	M	5			KY	KY	KY				FARMER	0		✓	✓	✓	R		F	41
		" ABYGILL	Wife	W	F	Aug 1879	20	M	5	3	3	KY	KY	KY							X	X	✓				
		" VIOLIA	Dau	W	F	Aug 1895	4	S				KY	KY	KY													
		" FLORA A.	Dau	W	F	May 1897	3	S				KY	KY	KY													
		" JOHN F.	Son	W	M	Jul 1899	10/12	S				KY	KY	KY													
46	46	POPE, SIDNEY	Head	W	M	Oct 1873	26	M	4			KY	TN	TN							✓	✓	✓	R		H	
		" MINIA	Wife	W	F	Mar 1877	22	M	4	1	1	KY	KY	KY							✓	✓	✓				
		" CECIL	Son	W	M	Jun 1899	1/12	S				KY	KY	KY													
47	47	SMITH, WILLIAM J.	Head	W	M	May 1858	42	M	3			KY	KY	KY				FARMER			✓	✓	✓	O		F	42
		" LUELLER	Wife	W	F	Apr 1873	27	M	3	1	1	KY		KY							✓	✓	✓				
		" OSCAR	Son	W	M	Jun 1888	12	S				KY	KY	KY						3	X	X	✓				
		" OVA	Dau	W	F	Aug 1889	10	S				KY	KY	KY						3	✓	✓	✓				
		" LENER	Dau	W	F	Nov 1892	7	S				KY	KY	KY													
		" ALLAS	Dau	W	F	Apr 1898	2	S				KY	KY	KY													
48	48	SMITH, GEORGE	Head	W	M	Sep 1824	75	M	35			TN	TN	TN				FARMER			✓	✓	✓	O	F	F	43

TWELFTH CENSUS OF THE UNITED STATES 1900

STATE - KENTUCKY
COUNTY - MONROE   TURNER   —79—   ABIJAH STRICKLER
Township or other division   Enumerator

Supervisor's Dist. No. 102 Sheet No.
Enumeration Dist. No. 81

No. of Family	No. of Dwelling	NAME	Relation	Color	Sex	DATE OF BIRTH Mon/Yr	Age at last birthday	Marital Status	# Years married	Mother of how many children?	# of these children living	Place of birth (this person)	Father of this person	Mother of this person	Year of immigr.	# years in U.S.	Naturalization	OCCUPATION 10 years +	Months not employed	Attended school in months	Can read	Can write	Speak English	Owned or Rent	Owned -no mortage	Farm or house	# of farm schedule
		SMITH, SARAH	Wife	W	F	Jul 1837	62	M	35	2	2	TN	TN	TN													
		" ULISSES	Son	W	M	Dec 1873	26	M	1			KY	KY	KY				FARMER			✓	✓	✓				
		" LUIESEY	Dau-in-law	W	F	Feb 1875	25	M	1	1	1	KY	KY	KY							X	X	✓				
		" LONEY	Gr-son	W	M	Dec 1899 6/12		S				KY	KY	KY													
49	49	TRIVETT, JOHN W.	Head	W	M	Jul 1863	36	M	5			KY	KY	KY				FARMER	0		✓	✓	✓	O	F	F	44
		" PHEBY	Wife	W	F	Mar 1867	33	M	5	2	2	KY	KY	KY							✓	✓	✓				
		" VIOLIA	Dau	W	F	Jan 1894	6	S				KY	KY	KY													
		" IDY M	Dau	W	F	Aug 1895	4	S				KY	KY	KY													
50	50	CLARKSON, WILLIAM J.	Head	W	M	Aug 1856	43	M	19			KY	VA	VA				FARMER			X	X	✓	R		F	45
		" SARAH C	Wife	W	F	Mar 1865	35	M	19	2	2	KY	KY	KY							X	X	✓				
		" BROCKET F	Son	W	M	Jul 1882	17	S				KY	KY	KY						3	✓	✓	✓				
		" JOHN W	Son	W	M	Sep 1892	7	S				KY	KY	KY						3	✓	✓	✓				
51	51	MOORE, JAMES	Head	W	M	Dec 1858	41	M	14			KY	TN	TN				FARMER			✓	✓	✓	O	F	F	46
		" CRATON E.	Wife	W	F	May 1864	36	M	14	4	4	KY	KY	KY							✓	✓	✓				
		" WILLEY	Son	W	M	Jul 1887	12	S				KY	KY	KY			5				✓	✓	✓				
		" EVEY	Dau	W	F	Nov 1889	10	S				KY	KY	KY			4				✓	✓	✓				
		" EFFA	Dau	W	F	Feb 1892	8	S				KY	KY	KY							✓	✓	✓				
		" JAMES M.	Son	W	M	May 1897	3	S				KY	KY	KY													
		THOMAS, CHARLEY	Lodger	W	M	Apr 1877	23	S				KY	KY	KY				FARMER	0		✓	✓					
52	52	HOOD, SAM M.	Head	W	M	Oct 1864	35	S				KY	VA	KY				FARMER			✓	✓	✓	R		F	47
		" SANIEL	Father	W	M	Jun 1819	80	M	51			VA	VA	KY							✓	✓	✓				
		" LIZA J.	Mother	W	F	Mar 1826	74	M	51	6	4	KY	VA	VA							✓	X	✓				
		" HARET E.	Sister	W	F	Oct 1864	35	S				KY	VA	KY							X	X	✓				
53	53	TYREE, NANCY G.	Head	W	F	Dec 1863	36	S				KY	KY	VA				FARMER			X	X	✓	O	F	F	48
		" JONES	Brother	W	M	Mar 1858	42	S				KY	KY	VA				FARMER			X	X	✓				
54	54	TYREE, JOHN S.	Head	W	M	Jun 1860	40	M	17			KY	KY	VA				FARMER			✓	✓	✓	O	M	F	49

STATE - KENTUCKY
COUNTY - MONROE
Township or other division — TURNER

Enumerator — ABIJAH STRICKLER

Supervisor's Dist. No. 102 Sheet No.
Enumeration Dist. No. 81

No. of Family	No. of Dwelling	NAME	Relation	Color	Sex	DATE OF BIRTH Mon/Yr	Age at last birthday	Marital Status	# Years married	Mother of how many children?	# of these children living	Place of birth (this person)	Father of this person	Mother of this person	Year of immigr.	# years in U.S.	Naturalization	OCCUPATION 10 years +	Months not employed	Attended school in months	Can read	Can write	Speak English	Owned or Rent	Owned - no mortage	Farm or house	# of farm schedule
		TYREE, MARTHY J.	Wife	W	F	Sept 1862	37	M	17	5	5	KY	TN	TN							✓	✓	✓				
		" HUBIE D.	Son	W	M	Sept 1883	16	S				KY	KY	KY													
		" THOMAS J.	Son	W	M	Oct 1885	14	S				KY	KY	KY						4	✓	✓	✓				
		" CORAH S.	Dau	W	F	Dec 1887	12	S				KY	KY	KY						5	✓	✓	✓				
		" ELLEN D.	Dau	W	F	Feb 1890	10	S				KY	KY	KY							X	X	✓				
		" NATTY D.	Dau	W	F	Feb 1892	8	S				KY	KY	KY							X	X	✓				
55	55	TYREE, JOSEPH	Head	W	M	Jul 1878	21	M	1			KY	KY	KY				FARMER			✓	✓	✓	R	F	50	
		" DELLER	Wife	W	F	Sept 1878	21	M	1	1	1	KY	TN	KY							✓	✓	✓				
		" NELLIE	Dau	W	F	Feb 1900	3/12	S				KY	KY	KY							✓	✓	✓				
56	56	TYREE, HANER	Head	W	M	May 1845	55	Wd				KY	VA	VA				FARMER			✓	✓	✓	O	F	51	
		" SOL	Son	W	M	May 1874	26	S				KY	KY	KY				DAY LABOR			✓	✓	✓				
		" MARTHY I.	Dau	W	F	Apr 1880	20	S				KY	KY	KY							✓	✓	✓				
		" VIRGIA	Dau	W	F	Oct 1882	17	S				KY	KY	KY							✓	✓	✓				
57	57	TYREE, SOLOMON J.	Head	W	M	Jun 1856	44	M	25			KY	KY	VA				FARMER			✓	✓	✓	O	F	52	
		" MARTHA A.	Wife	W	F	Jul 1848	51	M	25	7	6	KY	KY	KY							✓	✓	✓				
		" MARY J.	Dau	W	F	Sept 1877	22	S				KY	KY	KY							✓	✓	✓				
		" PERNEY B.	Dau	W	F	Oct 1881	18	S				KY	KY	KY							✓	✓	✓				
		" GLOVER C.	Son	W	M	May 1885	15	S				KY	KY	KY							X	X	✓				
		" RILEY T.	Son	W	M	Feb 1887	13	S				KY	KY	KY							X	X	✓				
58	58	BOWLS, CLABE	Head	W	M	May 1854	46	M	24			KY	KY	KY				FARMER			✓	✓	✓	O	F	53	
		" LEVENIA F.	Wife	W	F	Mar 1854	46	M	24	9	7	KY	KY	VA							✓	X	✓				
		" WILLIAM T.	Son	W	M	Nov 1875	24	S				KY	KY	KY							✓	X	✓				
		" LUCY E.	Dau	W	F	Aug 1879	20	S				KY	KY	KY							✓	✓	✓				
		" JAMES N.	Son	W	M	Apr 1881	19	S				KY	KY	KY						2	✓	✓	✓				
		" HANER B.	Dau	W	F	Apr 1885	15	S				KY	KY	KY						2	✓	✓	✓				
		" CLABERT F.	Son	W	M	Jul 1888	11	S				KY	KY	KY						2	X	X	✓				

TWELFTH CENSUS OF THE UNITED STATES 1900

STATE - KENTUCKY
COUNTY - MONROE
Township or other division

TURNER
—81—
ABIJAH STRICKLER
Enumerator

Supervisor's Dist. No. 102 Sheet No.
Enumeration Dist. No. 81

No. of Family	No. of Dwelling	NAME	Relation	Color	Sex	DATE OF BIRTH Mon/Yr	Age at last birthday	Marital Status	# Years married	Mother of how many children?	# of these children living	Place of birth [this person]	Father of this person	Mother of this person	Year of immigr.	# years in U.S.	Naturalization	OCCUPATION 10 years +	Months not employed	Attended school in months	Can read	Can write	Speak English	Owned or Rent	Owned -no mortgage	Farm or house	# of farm schedule	
		BOWLS, HATLEY O.	Son	W	M	Jul 1890	9	S				KY	KY	KY														
		" ELLEY	Dau	W	F	Apr 1895	5	S				KY	KY	KY														
59	59	BLACK, GAMALIEL	Head	W	M	Mar 1840	60	M	37			KY	KY	KY				FARMER	0		X	X	✓	0		F	54	
		" MARTHY	Wife	W	F	Dec 1847	52	M	37	11		KY	KY	KY							X	X	✓					
		" ISABEL	Dau	W	F	Oct 1865	34	S				KY	KY	KY							X	X	✓					
		" LUCY J	Dau	W	F	Jun 1867	32	S				KY	KY	KY							X	X	✓					
		" TISHA	Dau	W	F	Jun 1873	26	S				KY	KY	KY							X	X	✓					
		" JAMES L.	Son	W	M	Feb 1875	24	S				KY	KY	KY							X	X	✓					
		" JARSH	Son	W	M	Nov 1879	20	S				KY	KY	KY							X	X	✓					
		" MARY L.	Dau	W	F	Sep 1881	18	S				KY	KY	KY							X	X	✓					
		" MARTHY	Dau	W	F	Dec 1888	11	S				KY	KY	KY							X	X	✓					
60	60	BLACK, JOHN S.	Head	W	M	Mar 1872	28	M				KY	KY	KY				FARMER			✓	✓	✓	0	M	F	55	
		" EVEY F.	Wife	W	F	Mar 1876	24	M				KY	KY	KY				FARMER			✓	✓	✓					
61	61	FOX, WILLIAM J.	Head	W	M	Oct 1851	48	M	27			KY	VA	VA				FARMER			X	X	✓	0		F	56	
		" MARTLIE	Wife	W	F	Jan 1853	47	M	27	13	3	TN	TN	TN							✓	✓	✓					
		" ISAZORA	Dau	W	F	May 1885	15	S				KY	KY	TN				AT. SCHOOL		3	✓	✓	✓					
		" AUDY P.	Son	W	M	Sep 1887	12	S				KY	KY	TN				FARM LABOR		4	✓	✓	✓					
		" LEONA	Dau	W	F	Sep 1891	8	S				KY	KY	TN						5	✓	X	✓					
		" NEOMA	Dau	W	F	Sep 1891	8	S				KY	KY	TN														
		" FRANK	Son	W	M	Dec 1894	5	S				KY	KY	TN														
		" DANNEY	Dau	W	F	Mar 1898	2	S				KY	KY	TN														
62	62	RUSSEL, ARCHEY	Head	W	M	Nov 1874	25	M	4			KY	KY	TN				FARM LABOR	0		✓	✓	✓	R		H		
		" ROSEY J.	Wife	W	F	Aug 1874	25	M	4			KY	KY	TN							✓	✓	✓					
63	63	ISENBERG, JOHN	Head	W	M	Mar 1869	31	M	10			KY	TN	TN				FARMER			✓	✓	✓	R		F	57	
		" WILLIA A.	Wife	W	F	Jul 1871	28	M	10	3	3	KY	KY	KY							✓	✓	✓					
		" CHESTER B.	Son	W	M	Oct 1890	9	S				KY	KY	KY						4	✓	X	✓					

STATE - KENTUCKY
COUNTY - MONROE
Township or other division — TURNER

TWELFTH CENSUS OF THE UNITED STATES 1900
- 82 -
Enumerator — ABIJAH STRICKLER

Supervisor's Dist. No. 102   Sheet No.
Enumeration Dist. No. 81

No. of Family	No. of Dwelling	NAME	Relation	Color	Sex	DATE OF BIRTH Mon/Yr	Age at last birthday	Marital Status	# Years married	Mother of how many children?	# of these children living	Place of birth [this person]	Father of this person	Mother of this person	Year of immigr.	# years in U.S.	Naturalization	OCCUPATION 10 years +	Months not employed	Attended school in months	Can read	Can write	Speak English	Owned or Rent	Owned -no mortage	Farm or house	# of farm schedule
		ISENBERG, GERVES E.	Son	W	M	Aug 1892	7	S				KY	KY	KY						4	X	X	✓				
		" CLONEY D.	Son	W	M	Apr 1894	6	S				KY	KY	KY							X	X	✓				
64	64	PROFFITT, JAMES M.	Head	W	M	Feb 1839	61	M				KY	TN	TN				FARMER			✓	✓	✓	O	F	F	58
		" BELLVENES	wife	W	F	Jul 1861	38	M	5	2	2	KY	KY	TN							✓	✓	✓				
		" McKINLEY M.	Son	W	M	May 1896	4	S				KY	KY	KY													
		" DEWEY C.	Son	W	M	May 1899	1	S				KY	KY	KY													
		" LAURA E	Dau	W	F	Apr 1876	24	S				KY	KY	KY							✓	✓	✓				
65	65	IRVEN, WILLIAM J.	Head	W	M	Jun 1834	65	M	21			KY	MD	VA				FARMER			✓	✓	✓	O	F	F	59
		" SARAH M	wife	W	F	May 1842	58	M	21			TN	VA	KY							✓	✓	✓				
		" ARCH B.	Son	W	M	Sep 1872	27	S				KY	KY	KY				FARM LABOR			✓	✓	✓				
		ROBINSON, LUCINDA C.	Sister in law	W	F	Sep 1846	55	S				TN	VA	KY							✓	✓	✓				
66	66	ARTERBURN, ELIJAH	Head	W	M	Jan 1850	50	M	16			KY	TN	KY				FARMER			X	X	✓	O	M	E	60
		" ALVINIA S.	wife	W	F	Mar 1855	45	M	16			KY	KY	VA							✓	X	✓				
		" JOHN T	Son	W	M	Jul 1886	13	S				KY	KY	TN						4	✓	✓	✓				
67	67	PROFFITT, NANCY C.	Head	W	F	Jan 1856	44	Wd		3	1	KY	VA	TN				FARMER			✓	✓	✓	O	F	F	61
		" HOMER G.	Son	W	M	May 1886	14	S				KY	KY	KY				FARM LABOR		5	✓	✓	✓				
		" OTTY J.	Son	W	M	Oct 1881	10	S				KY	KY	KY				FARM LABOR		5	✓	✓	✓				
68	68	BRADY, CHARLEY C.	Head	W	M	Oct 1865	34	M	9			TN	TN	TN				FARMER			✓	✓	✓	R	F		62
		" LOUISA	wife	W	F	Sept 1869	30	M	9	4	1	KY	TN	VA							✓	✓	✓				
		" AUTHOR	Son	W	M	Apr 1892	8	S				KY	TN	KY							X	X	✓				
		" LOCKY A	Dau	W	F	July 1894	5	S				KY	TN	KY									✓				
		" OMA	Dau	W	F	May 1899	1	S				KY	TN	KY													
69	69	BURKS, FANEY	Head	W	F	Feb 1830	70	Wd		8	6	TN	VA	VA				FARMER			✓	✓	✓	O	F	F	63
70	70	MYERES, HENRY	Head	W	M	Aug 1843	56	M	22			TN	NC	TN				FARMER			✓	✓	✓	O	F	F	64
		" AMERICA	wife	W	F	Jan 1857	43	M	22	6	4	KY	VA	TN							✓	✓	✓				
		" LOLAR A	Dau	W	F	Oct 1882	17	S				KY	TN	KY				AT SCHOOL		5	✓	✓	✓				

TWELFTH CENSUS OF THE UNITED STATES 1900

STATE - KENTUCKY
COUNTY - MONROE TURNER
Township or other division

— 83 —
ABIJAH STRICKLER — Enumerator

Supervisor's Dist. No. _102_ Sheet No. ____
Enumeration Dist. No. _81_ ____

No. of Family	No. of Dwelling	NAME	Relation	Color	Sex	DATE OF BIRTH Mon/Yr	Age at last birthday	Marital Status	# Years married	Mother of how many children?	# of those children living	Place of birth (this person)	Father of this person	Mother of this person	Year of immigr.	# years in U.S.	Naturalization	OCCUPATION 10 years +	Months not employed	Attended school in months	Can read	Can write	Speak English	Owned or Rent	Owned -no mortgage	Farm or house	# of farm schedule
		MYERES, DONIA	DAU	W	F	Feb 1885	15	S				KY	TN	KY						5	✓	✓					
		" SANIEL B	SON	W	M	Sep 1891	8	S				KY	TN	KY						5	✓	✓					
		" JOHN B.	SON	W	M	Oct 1896	3	S				KY	TN	KY								✓					
71	71	MYERES, JOSEPH B	Head	W	M	Nov 1870	29	M	12			KY	TN	KY				FARMER			X	X	✓	R		H	
		" ELIZABETH	Wife	W	F	Jul 1888	31	M	12	5	4	KY	KY	KY							X	X	✓				
		" WILLIAM B.	Son	W	M	Feb 1889	11	S				KY	KY	KY				FARM LABOR			✓	X	✓				
		" HILLERY F.	Son	W	M	Aug 1894	5	S				KY	KY	KY							✓	X	✓				
		" HERMIN D.	Son	W	M	Aug 1897	2	S				KY	KY	KY													
		" BERTHY C.	DAU	W	F	Feb 1900	4/12	S				KY	KY	KY													
72	72	MYERES, FELIAX	HEAD	W	M	Feb 1840	60	M	36			TN	NC	TN				FARMER	0		✓	✓	✓	O		F	65
		" NANCY J.	Wife	W	F	Jun 1843	56	M	36	9	5	KY	VA	VA							✓	✓	✓				
		" WILLIAM M	Son	W	M	Mar 1883	17	S				KY	VA	KY				FARM LABOR			X	X	✓				
73	73	LOYD, WILL J.	Head	W	M	Feb 1877	23	M	4			KY	KY	KY				FARMER			X	X	✓	R		F	66
		" MARTHY J.	Wife	W	F	May 1879	21	M	4	3	3	KY	KY	KY							✓	✓	✓				
		" ROXEY M	DAU	W	F	Oct 1897	2	S				KY	KY	KY									✓				
		" RAVY W.	DAU	W	F	Oct 1898	1	S				KY	KY	KY													
		" CLARANCE	Son	W	M	May 1900	0/12	S				KY	KY	KY													
74	74	BURKS, JOSEPH B.	HEAD	W	M	Dec 1846	53	M	12			KY	KY	KY				FARMER	0		✓	✓	✓	O		F	67
		" LAUREY E.	Wife	W	F	Aug 1871	28	M	12	0	0	KY	TN	KY							✓	✓	✓				
		" WILLIAM J.	Son	W	M	Mar 1883	17	S				KY	TN	KY				FARM LABOR		2	✓	✓	✓				
		" HARSON G.	Son	W	M	Apr 1885	15	S				KY	TN	KY				FARM LABOR		2	✓	✓	✓				
75	75	MYERES, JESEY J.	HEAD	W	M	Jan 1875	25	M	6			KY	TN	KY				FARMER	0		X	X	✓	O	F	F	68
		" SARAH S.	Wife	W	F	Mar 1874	26	M	6	2	2	KY	KY	KY							X	X	✓				
		" CLARANCE J.	Son	W	M	Jul 1896	3	S				KY	KY	KY													
		" ARLY B.	Son	W	M	Jun 1899	4/12	S				KY	KY	KY													
76	76	WHITEHEAD, WILLIAM J.	Head	W	M	May 1845	55	M	35			KY	VA	VA				FARMER	0		✓	✓	✓	O	F	F	69

STATE - KENTUCKY
COUNTY - MONROE
Township or other division: TURNER
Enumerator: ABIJAH STRICKLER
—84—
Supervisor's Dist. No. 102 Sheet No.
Enumeration Dist. No. 81

No. of Family	No. of Dwelling	Name	Relation	Color	Sex	Date of Birth Mon/Yr	Age	Marital Status	Yrs married	Mother of how many children	# living	Birthplace	Father birthplace	Mother birthplace	Occupation	Attended school (months)	Can read	Can write	Speak English	Owned/Rent	Farm/house	# farm sched.
		WHITEHEAD, HENEY W.	wife	W	F	Feb 1845	55	M	35	5	5	TN	VA	TN			✓	X	✓			
		" JOHN G.	Son	W	M	Oct 1887	12	S				KY	KY	TN		5	✓	X	✓			
		" ANNEY P.	Dau	W	F	Jul 1891	8	S				KY	KY	TN			X	X	✓			
		" PATRICK H.	Son	W	M	Jul 1874	25	M	2			KY	KY	TN			✓	✓	✓	R	F	70
		" NANCY F.	Dau-in-law	W	F	Nov 1878	21	M	2	1	0	KY	KY	TN			✓	✓	✓			
77	77	BURKS, BARY L.	Head	W	M	Aug 1862	37	Wd				KY	VA	TN	FARMER		✓	✓	✓	O	F	71
		" OLLIE	Son	W	M	Apr 1882	8	S				KY	KY	KY					✓			
		" ROSEY	Dau	W	F	Jan 1894	6	S				KY	KY	KY								
		" BENEY C.	Son	W	M	Jan 1897	3	S				KY	KY	KY								
78	78	TURNER, NOAH J.	Head	W	M	Jan 1856	44	M				KY	VA	VA	BLACKSMITH		✓	✓	✓	O	F	72
		" MAGGA R.	wife	W	F	Jul 1879	20	M	1	1	1	KY	TN	KY			✓	✓	✓			
		" EDMON	Son	W	M	May 1880	20	S				KY	KY	KY	FARMER		✓	✓	✓			
		" ELIZA	Dau	W	F	Nov 1887	12	S				KY	KY	KY	AT SCHOOL	3	✓	✓	✓			
		" JAMES	Son	W	M	Nov 1889	10	S				KY	KY	KY	FARM LABOR		X	X	✓			
		" GEORGE	Son	W	M	Feb 1893	7	S				KY	KY	KY			X	X	✓			
		" LUCY	Dau	W	F	Mar 1896	4	S				KY	KY	KY								
		" GRACY	Dau	W	F	Jan 1900	4/12	S				KY	KY	KY								
79	79	WHITEHEAD, WILLIAM T.	Head	W	M	Feb 1874	26	M	7			KY	KY	KY	FARMER	O	✓	✓	✓	O M	F	73
		" MARTINIA	wife	W	F	Jul 1876	23	M	7	4	3	KY	KY	KY			✓	✓				
		" LEE H.	Son	W	M	Oct 1894(?)	5	S				KY	KY	KY					✓			
		" HERMEN	Son	W	M	Jan 1895	5	S				KY	KY	KY					✓			
		" FRANCES C.	Son	W	M	Apr 1897	3	S				KY	KY	KY					✓			
		TURNER, AMERICA C.	Gr-mother	W	F	Dec 1828	71	Wd		1	1	VA	VA	VA			X	X	✓			
80	80	WHITEHEAD, ROBERT	Head	W	M	Jul 1847	52	Wd				KY	KY	KY	FARMER		✓	✓	✓	O	F	74
		" MATTY M.	Dau	W	F	Feb 1885	15	S				KY	TN	TN			✓	✓	✓			
		" JOHNEY P.	Son	W	M	Jul 1889	10	S				KY	TN	KY			X	X	✓			

STATE - KENTUCKY
COUNTY - MONROE
Township or other division: TURNER — 85— ABIJAH STRICKLER Enumerator

Supervisor's Dist. No. 102 Sheet No.
Enumeration Dist. No. 81

No. of Family	No. of Dwelling	NAME	Relation	Color	Sex	DATE OF BIRTH Mon/Yr	Age at last birthday	Marital Status	# Years married	Mother of how many children?	# of these children living	Place of birth [this person]	Father of this person	Mother of this person	Year of immigr.	# years in U.S.	Naturalization	OCCUPATION 10 years +	Months not employed	Attended school in months	Can read	Can write	Speak English	Owned or Rent	Owned -no mortage	Farm or house	# of farm schedule	
81	81	TURNER, MARY	Head	W	F	MAY 1822	79	Wd				KY	TN	TN				FARMER		✓	X	✓		O		F	75	
		BURNETT, MARTHA	?	W	F	APR 1872	27	M				KY	TN	KY							✓	✓							
82	82	TURNER, WILLIAM H.	Head	W	M	NOV 1858	41	M	20			KY	KY	KY				FARMER			✓	✓	✓		O		F	76	
		" KITTY E.	Wife	W	F	NOV 1861	38	M	20	9	8	KY	KY	KY							✓	X	✓						
		" DAVID O.	Son	W	M	OCT 1882	17	S				KY	KY	KY				FARM LABOR			✓	✓	✓						
		" CORA F.	Dau	W	F	Feb 1885	15	S				KY	KY	KY							✓	✓	✓						
		4 AUTHER G.	Son	W	M	OCT 1886	13	S				KY	KY	KY				FARM LABOR			✓	✓	✓						
		" BETTY J.	Dau	W	F	NOV 1888	11	S				KY	KY	KY															
		" WILLIAM J.	Son	W	M	JAN 1891	9	S				KY	KY	KY															
		" LEVIE E.	Son	W	M	OCT 1893	6	S				KY	KY	KY															
		" LILEY P.	Dau	W	F	JAN 1897	3	S				KY	KY	KY															
		" EDWARD F.	Son	W	M	OCT 1899	8/12	S				KY	KY	KY															
83	83	KEES, WILLIAM J.	Head	W	M	?— 1854	46	M	15			TN	KY	TN				FARMER			✓	✓		R		F	77	
		" MARTHY J.	Wife	W	F	NOV 1857	42	M	15	2	1	KY	KY	KY							X	X	✓						
		" LETHIA E.	Dau	W	F	Jul 1889	10	S				KY	KY	KY							X	X	✓						
		" MARY F.	Sis in law	W	F	Jul 1877	22	S				KY	KY	KY							✓	✓	✓						
84	84	THOMAS, JAMES(?)	Head	W	M	Aug 1838	61	M				KY	VA	VA				FARMER			X	X	✓	O		F	F 78	
		" LUCINDY E.	Wife	W	F	OCT 1841	58	M	41	12	12	KY	VA	VA							X	X	✓						
		" JAMES A.	Son	W	M	Feb 1876	24	S				KY	KY	KY				FARMER			✓	✓	✓						
		" FLORA E.	Dau	W	F	— —	13	S				KY	KY	KY							✓	✓	✓						
		TURNER, LOUISA	Mother in law	W	F	Jul 1815	84	Wd		9	6	VA	VA	VA							X	X							
85	85	TURNER, JAMES G.	Head	W	M	Dec 1862	38	M	19			KY	VA	VA							✓	✓	✓	O		F F 79	
		" MARY S.	Wife	W	F	JAN 1867	33	M	19	10	8	KY	KY	TN							X	X	✓						
		" JOSEPH G.	Son	W	M	APR 1882	18	S				KY	KY	KY				FARM LABOR			✓	✓	✓						
		" FELIN N.	Son	W	M	Jul 1888	11	S				KY	KY	KY				FARM LABOR			X	X	✓						
		" PERNEY E.	Dau	W	F	NOV 1890	9	S				KY	KY	KY									✓						

TWELFTH CENSUS OF THE UNITED STATES 1900

STATE - KENTUCKY
COUNTY - MONROE
Township or other division

TURNER -86- ABIJAH STRICKLER

Supervisor's Dist. No. _102_ Sheet No.
Enumeration Dist. No. _81_

Enumerator

No. of Family	No. of Dwelling	NAME	Relation	Color	Sex	DATE OF BIRTH Mon/Yr	Age at last birthday	Marital Status	# Years married	Mother of how many children?	# of these children living	Place of birth [this person]	Father of this person	Mother of this person	Year of immigr.	# years in U.S.	Naturalization	OCCUPATION 10 years +	Months not employed	Attended school in months	Can read	Can write	Speak English	Owned or Rent	Owned -no mortgage	Farm or house	# of farm schedule
		TURNER, HATTIE E.	Dau	W	F	Oct 1892	7	S				KY	KY	KY									✓				
		" LULY	Dau	W	F	May 1894	6	S				KY	KY	KY									✓				
		" NOVEY E.	Dau	W	F	Mar 1895	5	S				KY	KY	KY									✓				
		" BERDY A.	Dau	W	F	Aug 1898	1	S				KY	KY	KY									✓				
		" ALLIS	Dau	W	F	Dec 1899	6/12	S				KY	KY	KY													
86	86	MARRS, WILLIAM L(?)	Head	W	M	Apr 1852	48	M	22			TN	KY	TN				FARMER			✓	✓		O	F	F	80
		" MARY E.	Wife	W	F	Feb 1855	45	M	22			KY	TN	VA							✓	✓					
		" JULY P.	Dau	W	F	Aug 1879	20	S				KY	TN	KY				TEACHER-SCHOOL			✓	✓					
		" JOHN F.	Son	W	M	Oct 1881	19	S				KY	TN	KY				FARM LABOR		5	✓	✓					
		" FRED P.	Son	W	M	May 1882	18	S				KY	TN	KY				FARM LABOR		5	✓	✓					
		" WILLIAM F.	Son	W	M	Jul 1883	16	S				KY	TN	KY				AT SCHOOL		5	✓	✓					
		" LIZZIE M.	Dau	W	F	Feb 1885	15	S				KY	TN	KY						5	✓	✓					
		" MARY A.	Dau	W	F	— 1886	13	S				KY	TN	KY						5	✓	✓					
		" PERNEY G.	Dau	W	F	Aug 1890	9	S				KY	TN	KY						5	✓	✓					
		" HERMAN L.	Son	W	M	Apr 1892	8	S				KY	TN	KY						5	✓	✓	✓				
		" HETTIE E.	Dau	W	F	Apr 1892	8	S				KY	TN	KY						5	✓	✓					
		PAYNE, LOY	Lodger	W	M	Nov 1881	18	S				KY	KY	KY				FARM LABOR		5	✓	✓					
87	87	KINGERY, ——?	Head	W	M	Jul 1854	45	M	16			KY	KY	KY				FARMER			X	X	✓	R		F	81
		" MARTHY JANE	Wife	W	F	Jul 1865	34	M	16	6	6	KY	KY	KY							✓	✓					
		" JACKSON	Son	W	M	Oct 1885	15	S				KY	KY	KY				FARM LABOR			X	X	✓				
		" (?) GENEVA	Dau	W	F	Feb 1887	13	S				KY	KY	KY				AT SCHOOL		3	✓	✓	✓				
		" JOANN	Dau	W	F	Aug 1889	10	S				KY	KY	KY				AT SCHOOL		3	✓	✓	✓				
		" (?) HANSNER	Dau	W	F	Aug 1892	7	S				KY	KY	KY						3	✓	X	✓				
		" VERDY	Dau	W	F	Feb 1895	5	S				KY	KY	KY													
		" RAD	Son	W	M	Dec 1897	2	S				KY	KY	KY													
88	88	EUBANK, JOHN F.	Head	W	M	May 1826	74	M	35			KY	VA	VA				FARMER			✓	✓	✓	O		F	82

STATE - KENTUCKY
COUNTY - MONROE
Township or other division — TURNER — 87 —
Enumerator ABIJAH STRICKLER
Supervisor's Dist. No. 102 Sheet No.
Enumeration Dist. No. 81

| Location | | NAME | Relation | Color | Sex | DATE OF BIRTH Mon/Yr | Age at last birthday | Marital Status | # Years married | Mother of how many children? | # of these children living | NATIVITY | | | CITIZENSHIP | | | OCCUPATION 10 years + | Months not employed | EDUCATION | | | OWNERSHIP | | | |
No. of Family	No. of Dwelling											Place of birth [this person]	Father of this person	Mother of this person	Year of immigr.	# years in U.S.	Naturalization			Attended school in months	Can read	Can write	Speak English	Owned or Rent	Owned -no mortgage	Farm or house	# of farm schedule
		EUBANK, MARY E.	Wife	W	F	Feb 1847	53	M	35	5	1	KY	KY	KY							✓	✓	✓				
		" ETTY V.	Dau	W	F	Mar 1878	22	S				KY	KY	KY							✓	✓	✓				
89	89	TURNER, JOHN H.	Head	W	M	May 1854	46	M	22			KY	VA	VA				FARMER	0		✓	✓	✓	R		F	83
		" LUE T(?)	Wife	W	F	May 1868	32	M	22(?)	8	7	TN	TN	TN							X	X	✓				
		" LONZO M.	Son	W	M	Oct 1885	14	S				KY	KY	TN				FARM LABOR			X	X	✓				
		" LORA A.	Dau	W	F	May 1887	13	S				KY	KY	TN				FARM LABOR			X	X	✓				
		" GLOVER C.	Son	W	M	Oct 1891	8	S				KY	KY	TN							X	X	✓				
		" LUCY J.	Dau	W	F	Oct 1893	6	S				KY	KY	TN							X	X	✓				
		" DAVID F.	Son	W	M	Oct 1895	4	S				KY	KY	TN													
		" WILLIAM V.	Son	W	M	Sep 1898	1	S				KY	KY	TN													
90	90	GEARLD, WILLIAM B.	Head	W	M	Feb 1871	29	M	6			KY	KY	KY				FARMER			✓	✓	✓	R		F	84
		" EVEY	Wife	W	F	Oct 1876	23	M	6	3	3	KY	KY	KY							✓	✓	✓				
		" MAUDY B.	Dau	W	F	Dec 1895	4	S				KY	KY	KY									✓				
		" OLAR	Dau	W	F	Dec 1896	3	S				KY	KY	KY									✓				
		" DORA	Dau	W	F	Oct 1898	1	S				KY	KY	KY									✓				
91	91	TURNER, JAMES R.	Head	W	M	May 1864	36	M	16			KY	VA	KY				FARMER			X	X	✓	R		F	85
		" LUCY M.	Wife	W	F	Mar 1867	33	M	16	7	7	KY	VA	KY							X	X	✓				
		" EMERY L.	Dau	W	F	Sept 1885	14	S				KY	KY	KY							X	X	✓				
		" ABIJAH E.	Son	W	M	Jan 1888	12	S				KY	KY	KY				FARM LABOR			X	X	✓				
		" WILLIAM T.	Son	W	M	Sep 1890	9	S				KY	KY	KY							X	X	✓				
		" JOHNEY T.	Son	W	M	Sep 1893	6	S				KY	KY	KY							X	X	✓				
		" NANCY C.	Dau	W	F	Jan 1896	4	S				KY	KY	KY									✓				
		" ROBERT F.	Son	W	M	Mar 1899	1	S				KY	KY	KY													
92	92	RITTER, JAMES W.	Head	W	M	Jan 1865	35	M	10			KY	TN	TN				FARMER			✓	✓	✓	R		F	86
		" VICTORY A.	Wife	W	F	May 1870	30	M	10	6	4	KY	KY	KY							✓	✓	✓				
		" LIEU (?) E.	Dau	W	F	Mar 1893	7	S				KY	KY	KY							✓	X	✓				

STATE - KENTUCKY
COUNTY - MONROE
Township or other division

TWELFTH CENSUS OF THE UNITED STATES 1900

TURNER   —88—   ABIJAH STRICKLER
Enumerator

Supervisor's Dist. No. 102 Sheet No.
Enumeration Dist. No. 81

No. of Family	No. of Dwelling	NAME	Relation	Color	Sex	DATE OF BIRTH Mon/Yr	Age at last birthday	Marital Status	Years married	Mother of how many children?	# of these children living	Place of birth [this person]	Father of this person	Mother of this person	Year of immigr.	# years in U.S.	Naturalization	OCCUPATION 10 years +	Months not employed	Attended school in months	Can read	Can write	Speak English	Owned or Rent	Owned –no mortage	Farm or house	# of farm schedule	
		RITTER, VERDER L.	Dau	W	F	Aug 1895	4	S				KY	KY	KY									✓					
		" ERNEST W.	Son	W	M	Jul 1898	1	S				KY	KY	KY														
		MEADOW, JOHNEY B.	Step Dau	W	F	Jul 1889	10	S				KY	KY	KY							✓	✓	✓					
93	93	HOOD, JAMES S.	Head	W	M	Jun 1858	41	M				KY	VA	VA				BLACKSMITH	0		✓	✓	✓	O	F	F	87	
		" POLLEY	wife	W	F	May 1877	23	M		3	1	KY	KY	KY							✓	✓	✓					
		" ELIC Z.	Son	W	M	Sep 1880	19	S				KY	KY	KY				FARM LABOR			✓	✓	✓					
		" BRUCE I.	Son	W	M	Feb 1882	18	S				KY	KY	KY				FARM LABOR			✓	X	✓					
		" WILLIAM B.	Son	W	M	Jul 1884	15	S				KY	KY	KY				FARM LABOR			X	X	✓					
		" GEORGE H.	Son	W	M	Jan 1887	13	S				KY	KY	KY				FARM LABOR			✓	✓	✓					
		" JOHN W.	Son	W	M	Oct 1891	8	S				KY	KY	KY							X	X	✓					
		" JAMES T.	Son	W	M	Oct 1895	4	S				KY	KY	KY									✓					
		" DONEY A. S.	Dau	W	F	May 1900	1/12	S				KY	KY	KY														
94	94	SMITH, NATHEN J.	Head	W	M	May 1848	52	M	26			KY	TN	KY				FARMER			X	X	✓	R		F	88	
		" BECKY J.	wife	W	F	Oct 1857	42	M	26	9	9	KY	KY	KY							X	X	✓					
		" JESSEY E.	Son	W	M	May 1884	16	S				KY	KY	KY				FARM LABOR			X	X	✓					
		" WILLIAM T.	Son	W	M	Mar 1887	13	S				KY	KY	KY							X	X	✓					
		" MOLLEY R.	Dau	W	F	Jan 1891	9	S				KY	KY	KY							X	X	✓					
		" ADER	Dau	W	F	Mar 1894	6	S				KY	KY	KY									✓					
		" HAZY A.	Son	W	M	May 1897	3	S				KY	KY	KY									✓					
95	95	COMBS, CHARLES M.	Head	W	M	Mar 1870	30	M				KY	KY	KY				FARMER			✓	✓	✓	R		F	89	
		" JOANN	wife	W	F	Aug 1877	22	M				KY	KY	KY							✓	✓	✓					
96	96	SMITH, JOHN T.	Head	W	M	Aug 1874	25	M	4			KY	KY	KY							X	X	✓	R		H		
		" MARTHY J.	wife	W	F	Apr 1878	22	M	4	2	1	KY	KY	KY							✓	✓	✓					
		LACEY C	Dau	W	F	Nov 1898	1	S				KY	KY	KY														
		EARLES, WILLIAM J.	Lodger	W	M	— —	27	S				KY	KY	KY							X	X	✓					
	97	SMITH, SAMIEL F.	Head	W	M	Feb 1881	19	M				KY	KY	KY							X	X	✓	R		H		

TWELFTH CENSUS OF THE UNITED STATES 1900

STATE - KENTUCKY
COUNTY - MONROE TURNER – 89 – ABIJAH STRICKLER
Township or other division Enumerator

Supervisor's Dist. No. _102_ Sheet No.
Enumeration Dist. No. _81_

No. of Family	No. of Dwelling	NAME	Relation	Color	Sex	DATE OF BIRTH Mon/Yr	Age at last birthday	Marital Status	# Years married	Mother of how many children?	# of these children living	Place of birth [this person]	Father of this person	Mother of this person	Year of immigr.	# years in U.S.	Naturalization	OCCUPATION 10 years +	Months not employed	Attended school in mouths	Can read	Can write	Speak English	Owned or Rent	Owned -no mortage	Farm or house	# of farm schedule
		SMITH, NANCY R	Wife	W	F	MAR 1885	15	M				KY	KY	KY							X	X	✓				
97	98	GEARLD SAMIEL H.	Head	W	M	OCT 1861	38	M	12			KY	TN	KY				FARMER			✓	✓	✓	O	F	F	90
		" ELIZZA	Wife	W	F	AUG 1863	36	M	12	2	2	KY	TN	KY							✓	✓	✓				
		" HATTIE E.	Dau	W	F	JUL 1882	17	S				KY	KY	KY				AT SCHOOL		4	✓	✓	✓				
		" MERTY H.	Dau	W	F	OCT 1883	16	S				KY	KY	KY				AT SCHOOL		4	✓	✓	✓				
		" GROVER	Son	W	M	NOV 1885	14	S				KY	KY	KY				AT SCHOOL		4	✓	✓	✓				
		" HERMAN	Son	W	M	JAN 1892	7	S				KY	KY	KY						4	✓	X	✓				
		" LEVIE	Son	W	M	JAN 1896	4	S				KY	KY	KY													
98	99	BIRG, HENRY	Head	W	M	AUG 1858	41	M	23			KY	KY	KY				FARMER			X	X	✓	R		F	91
		" NANCY	Wife	W	F	SEP 1859	40	M	23	7	7	KY	KY	KY							X	X	✓				
		" MARGARET E.	Dau	W	F	MAY 1879	21	DIV				KY	KY	KY							✓	✓					
		" JOHN O.	Son	W	M	FEB 1882	18	S				KY	KY	KY				FARM LABOR			✓	✓					
		" JAMES H.	Son	W	M	SEP 1884	15	S				KY	KY	KY				FARM LABOR			X	X	✓				
		" WILLIAM T.	Son	W	M	FEB 1887	13	S				KY	KY	KY				FARM LABOR			X	X	✓				
		" LUE M.	Dau	W	F	OCT 1889	10	S				KY	KY	KY							X	X	✓				
		" LOLLER M.	Dau	W	F	MAY 1892	8	S				KY	KY	KY									✓				
99	100	PEDEN, WILLIAM T.	Head	W	M	AUG 1850	49	M	27			KY	KY	KY				FARMER			✓	✓	✓	O	F	F	92
		" SARAH P.	Wife	W	F	JAN 1850	50	M	27	3	2	KY	KY	KY							✓	✓	✓				
		" ORA B.	Son	W	M	DEC 1874	25	S				KY	KY	KY				FARMER			✓	✓	✓				
		" LONEY T.	Son	W	M	OCT 1882	17	S				KY	KY	KY				FARM LABOR			✓	✓					
100	101	NAANEY, GEORGE	Head	W	M	MAY 1862	38	M	17			KY	IN	IN				FARMER			X	X	✓	R		F	93
		" BECKY	Wife	W	F	JUN 1864	36	M	17	2	L	KY	VA	KY							✓	✓	✓				
		" ALBERT	Son	W	M	DEC 1887	12	S				KY	KY	KY				FARM LABOR			X	X	✓				
101	102	TEMPELES, RICHARD	Head	W	M	OCT 1831	68	M	5			KY	TN	TN				FARMER			X	X	✓	R		F	94
		" SARAH A.	Wife	W	F	MAY 1839	61	M	5	2	2	TN	TN	TN							✓	✓					
102	103	RICHARDSON, GEORGE	Head	B	M	JUL 1867	32	M	6			KY	KY	KY				FARMER			✓	X	✓	R		F	

STATE - KENTUCKY
COUNTY - MONROE
Township or other division

TURNER — 90 — ABIJAH STRICKLER
Enumerator

Supervisor's Dist. No. 102 Sheet No.
Enumeration Dist. No. 81

Location (No. of Family / No. of Dwelling)	NAME	Relation	Color	Sex	DATE OF BIRTH Mon/Yr	Age at last birthday	Marital Status	# Years married	Mother of how many children?	# of these children living	Place of birth (this person)	Father of this person	Mother of this person	Occupation 10 years +	Months not employed	Attended school in months	Can read	Can write	Speak English	Owned or Rent	Owned -no mortgage	Farm or house	# of farm schedule
	RICHARDSON, MARY E.	wife	B	F	Feb 1877	23	M	6	4	2	KY	KY	KY				✓	✓	✓				
	" WILLEY D.	Son	B	M	May 1896	6	S				KY	KY	KY						✓				
	" JIMEY O.	Son	B	M	May 1897	3	S				KY	KY	KY						✓				
	MUNCY, ESTA	Lodger	B	F	Aug 1890	9	S				KY	KY	KY				✓	X	✓				
103/104	WALKER, PARKER	Head	B	M	Mar 1843	57	M	22			TN	TN	VA	FARMER			X	X	✓	R		F	95
	" SARA F.	wife	B	F	Jan 1858	42	M	22	3	3	KY	VA	VA				X	X	✓				
	" THOMAS	Son	B	M	Oct 1890	9	S				KY	TN	KY			9	X	X	✓				
104/105	JACKSON, ROBERT	Head	W	M	Dec 1856	43	M	20			KY	KY	KY	FARMER			✓	✓	✓	O		F	96
	" NANCY L.	wife	W	F	Dec 1862	37	M	20	7	5	KY	KY	KY				X	X	✓				
	" BETTY E.	DAU	W	F	Dec 1884	15	S				KY	KY	KY	AT SCHOOL		3	✓	✓	✓				
	" EARNEAST	SON	W	M	May 1886	14	S				KY	KY	KY	FARM LABOR		3	✓	✓	✓				
	" LUCY D.	DAU	W	F	May 1888	12	S				KY	KY	KY	AT SCHOOL		5	✓	✓	✓				
	" EARLY F.	SON	W	M	Mar 1892	8	S				KY	KY	KY	AT SCHOOL		5	✓	X	✓				
	" WILLIAM R.	SON	W	M	Sep 1894	5	S				KY	KY	KY						✓				
105/106	TURNER, WILLIAM B.	Head	W	M	Aug 1871	28	M	9			KY	KY	KY	FARMER			✓	✓	✓	O		F	97
	" MARY E	wife	W	F	Jan 1867	33	M	9	5	3	KY	KY	KY				✓	✓	✓				
	" MYRTY J	DAU	W	F	Sep 1893	7	S				KY	KY	KY			5	✓	X	✓				
	" BERDY E.	DAU	W	F	Aug 1897	2	S				KY	KY	KY						✓				
	" GEORGE M.	Son	W	M	Feb 1900	4/12	S				KY	KY	KY						✓				
106/107	CHISEM, WILLIAM R.	Head	W	M	Nov 1830	69	M	45			KY	KY	KY	FARMER			✓	✓	✓	O		F	98
	" EMLEY V.	wife	W	F	Apr 1837	63	M	45	13	11	KY	KY	KY				✓	✓	✓				
	" KITTY B.	DAU	W	F	Aug 1868	31					KY	KY	KY				✓	✓	✓				
	" FEBY T.	DAU	W	F	Jul 1870	29	S				KY	KY	KY	TEACHER SCHOOL			✓	✓	✓				
	" SAMIEL H.	Son	W	M	Mar 1875	25	S				KY	KY	KY	SCHOOL TEACHER			✓	✓	✓				
	" QUEENIE R.	DAU	W	F	May 1880	20	S				KY	KY	KY	SCHOOL TEACHER			✓	✓	✓				
107/108	COMBS, JOHN B.	Head	W	M	Feb 1860	40	M	17			TN	TN	TN	FARMER			✓	✓	✓	O		F	99

TWELFTH CENSUS OF THE UNITED STATES 1900

STATE - KENTUCKY
COUNTY - MONROE
Township or other division — TURNER — -91- ABIJAH STRICKLER, Enumerator

Supervisor's Dist. No. 102 Sheet No.
Enumeration Dist. No. 81

No. of Family / Dwelling	NAME	Relation	Color	Sex	Date of Birth Mon/Yr	Age	Marital Status	# Yrs married	Mother of # children	# living	Place of birth	Father	Mother	Occupation	Attended school	Can read	Can write	Speak English	Ownership
	COMBS, MAUD E.	wife	W	F	Jan 1868	32	M	17	6	6	KY	KY	KY			✓	✓	✓	
	" AUTHER	Son	W	M	Oct 1886	13	S				KY	TN	KY	Farm Labor		✓	✓	✓	
	" OLEY W.	Son	W	M	May 1889	11	S				KY	TN	KY	Farm Labor		✓	✓	✓	
	" WALTER S.	Son	W	M	Nov 1892	7	S				KY	TN	KY			✓	X	✓	
	" OMY L.	Dau	W	F	Oct 1893	6	S				KY	TN	KY					✓	
	" IVA E.	Dau	W	F	Apr 1896	4	S				KY	TN	KY						
	" ADAER J.	Dau	W	F	Dec 1897	2	S				KY	TN	KY						
108/109	NORMAN, JOHN J.	Head	W	M	May 1844	56	M				KY	KY	KY	Farmer		X	X	✓	O FF 100
	" SARAH L.	wife	W	F	Jun 1859	42	M				KY	KY	KY			X	X	✓	
	BARTLEY, NANCY	Sister-in-law	W	F	May 1860	40	S				KY	KY	KY			✓	X	✓	
109/110	RAY, EDMON	Head	B	M	Jul 1832	67	M	35			KY	KY	KY	Farmer		X	X	✓	O FF 101
	" CAROLINE	Wife	B	F	Mar 1848	52	M	35	2	2	KY	KY	KY			X	X	✓	
	" JOSEY P.	Dau	B	F	May 1884	16	S				KY	KY	KY			✓	✓	✓	
	" JOANN	Dau	B	F	Apr 1886	14	S				KY	KY	KY	Farmer		✓	✓	✓	O FF 102
110/111	WELBORN, DANIEL J.	Head	W	M	Nov 1854	45	M	14			KY	KY	KY			✓	✓	✓	
	" LELAH	wife	W	F	Jul 1868	31	M	14	6	6	KY	TN	TN			✓	✓	✓	
	" MINTIE F.	Dau	W	F	Oct 1887	12	S				KY	KY	KY			✓	✓	✓	
	" MARVIN S.	Son	W	M	Nov 1888	11	S				KY	KY	KY	Farm Laborer		✓	X	✓	
	" FLOSSIE J.	Dau	W	F	May 1891	9	S				KY	KY	KY			✓	X	✓	
	" LOU V.	Dau	W	F	Jun 1892	7	S				KY	KY	KY			✓	X	✓	
	" AUDIE C. V.	Son	W	M	Apr 1895	5	S				KY	KY	KY					✓	
	" LIZZY B.	Dau	W	F	July 1896	3	S				KY	KY	KY					✓	
111/112	HICKS, EDMON D.	Head	B	M	May 1850	50	M	15			NC	GA	GA	Farmer		✓	✓	✓	R F
	" LAURA A.	wife	B	F	May 1850	50	M	15			KY	KY	KY	Farmer		✓	✓	✓	
	" ELONZO	Son	B	M	Dec 1879	20	S				KY	KY	KY			✓	✓	✓	
	GAINES, FLARNCE	Lodger	B	F	Jan 1889	11	S				KY	KY	KY			X	X	✓	

TWELFTH CENSUS OF THE UNITED STATES 1900

STATE - KENTUCKY
COUNTY - MONROE   TURNER   — 92 —   ABIJAH STRICKLER
Township or other division   Enumerator

Supervisor's Dist. No. _102_ Sheet No. _____
Enumeration Dist. No. _81_

Location No. of Family / No. of Dwelling	NAME	Relation	Color	Sex	DATE OF BIRTH Mon/Yr	Age at last birthday	Marital Status	# Years married	Mother of how many children?	# of these children living	NATIVITY Place of birth [this person]	Father of this person	Mother of this person	OCCUPATION 10 years +	Months not employed	Attended school in months	Can read	Can write	Speak English	Owned or Rent	Owned -no mortage	Farm or house	# of farm schedule
112/113	COMBS, MARY D.	Head	W	F	Sep 1856	43	Wd				KY	TN	KY	FARMER			✓	✓	✓	O	F	F	103
	GEARLD, NANCY T	Mother	W	F	Nov 1835	64	Wd	17	5		KY	VA	TN				✓	✓	✓				
"	EDDIE	Sister	W	F	Mar 1870	30	Div				KY	KY	KY				✓	✓	✓				
	EMBERTON, EARNEST H.	Nephew	W	M	Sep 1888	11	S				KY	KY	KY			5	✓	✓	✓				
	LEE, JAMES E.	—	W	M	Dec 1856	43	S				KY	KY	KY	FARMER	0		✓	✓	✓				
113/114	TURNER, WILLIAM J.	Head	W	M	Nov 1868	31	M	5			KY	VA	TN	FARMER	0			✓	✓	R		F	104
"	JUDE M.	Wife	W	F	Jul 1869	30	M	5	1	1	KY	TN	TN					✓	✓				
"	ADER L.	Dau	W	F	Aug 1899	9/12	S				KY	KY	KY										
114/115	PILE, JOHN A.	Head	W	M	Mar 1871	28	M	7			KY	TN	TN	FARMER	0		✓	✓		R	M	F	105
"	MOLEY E.	Wife	W	F	Jul 1873	26	M	7	1	1	KY	TN	KY				✓	✓	✓				
"	EDITH M.	Dau	W	F	Mar 1894	6	S				KY	KY	KY						✓				
115/116	PILE, SAM(?) D.	Head	W	M	Nov 1858	41	M	13			TN	TN	TN	FARMER	0		✓	✓		O	F	F	106
"	ELLON E.	Wife	W	F	Mar 1860	40	M	13	5	4	KY	KY	KY				✓	✓	✓				
"	JOHN E.	Son	W	M	Mar 1882	18	S				KY	TN	KY	FARM LABOR		5	✓	✓	✓				
"	DAISY M.	Dau	W	F	Dec 1883	16	S				KY	KY	KY	AT SCHOOL		4	✓	✓	✓				
"	MAISY N.	Dau	W	F	Aug 1885	14	S				KY	KY	KY	AT SCHOOL		4	✓	✓	✓				
"	PHARIS G.	Son	W	M	May 1888	12	S				KY	KY	KY	FARM LABOR		4							
"	LENNY C.	Son	W	M	May 1890	10	S				KY	KY	KY	Farm Labor		4	✓	✓	✓				
"	DELLA F.	Dau	W	F	Jan 1892	8	S				KY	KY	KY			4							
"	CLARANCE E.	Son	W	M	Dec 1893	6	S				KY	KY	KY						✓				
116/117	GOLDEN, JANE E.	Head	W	F	Oct 1851	48	Wd				KY	KY	KY						✓	R		H	
"	JOSEPH T.	Son	W	M	Mar 1888	12	S				KY	KY	KY	FARM LABOR			✓	✓	✓				
"	MALINDA	Dau	W	F	Dec 1889	10	S				KY	KY	KY				✓	✓	✓				
117/118	PLUMLEE, ROSCOE S.	Head	W	M	Dec 1865	34	M	4			TN	TN	TN	PHYSICIAN			✓	✓	✓	O	F	F	107
"	GRACE M.	Wife	W	F	Apr 1882	18	M	4			KY	KY	TN				✓	✓	✓				
	MITCHEL, NANCY J.	Sis-in-law	W	F	Oct 1845	54	Wd				KY	KY	KY				✓	✓	✓				

STATE - KENTUCKY
COUNTY - MONROE
Township or other division

TURNER   -93-   ABIJAH STRICKLER
Enumerator

Supervisor's Dist. No. 10² Sheet No.
Enumeration Dist. No. 81

No. of Family	No. of Dwelling	NAME	Relation	Color	Sex	DATE OF BIRTH Mon/Yr	Age at last birthday	Marital Status	# Years married	Mother of how many children?	# of these children living	Place of birth [this person]	Father of this person	Mother of this person	Year of immigr.	# years in U.S.	Naturalization	OCCUPATION 10 years +	Months not employed	Attended school in months	Can read	Can write	Speak English	Owned or Rent	Owned -no mortgage	Farm or house	# of farm schedule	
118	119	PLUMLEE, LEO S.	Head	W	M	Jan 1870	30	M				TN	TN	TN				FARMER			✓	✓	✓	R		F	108	
		" MITTIE M.	Wife	W	F	Jun 1885	14	M				KY	KY	TN							✓	✓	✓					
119	120	HARLIN, VERIDA	Head	W	F	Dec 1873	26	S				KY	KY	KY				FARMER			✓	✓	✓	O		F	109	
		PILE, SAMIEL F.	Bro-in-law	W	M	Jan 1869	31	M	10			KY	TN	TN				FARMER			✓	✓	✓					
		" NORA	Sister	W	F	Dec 1871	28	M	10	1	1	KY	KY	KY							✓	✓	✓					
		" ELKIE	Neice	W	F	Apr 1894	6	S				KY	KY	KY				AT SCHOOL		5								
120	121	PILE, JAMES S.	Head	W	M	Jul 1876	23	M	2			KY	TN	TN				FARMER			✓	✓	✓	O		F	110	
		" GILLEY	Wife	W	F	Feb 1881	19	M	2	1	1	KY	KY	KY							✓	✓	✓					
		" VERGEL O.	Son	W	M	Feb 1899	1	S				KY	KY	KY														
121	122	TOOMS, JOHN H.	Head	W	M	Mar 1866	34	M	8			TN	VA	TN				FARMER			✓	✓	✓	O		M	F	111
		" LOU W	Wife	W	F	Jun 1870	29	M	8	2	1	KY	TN	TN							✓	✓	✓					
		" CHARLES H.	Son	W	M	Aug 1899	9/12	S				KY	TN	KY														
		JONES, BECKY	Sis-in-law	W	F	Aug 1861	38	Wd				KY	TN	TN							✓	✓						
122	123	JONES, JOHN K.	Head	W	M	Oct 1824	75	Wd				TN	TN	VA				FARMER			✓	X	✓	O		F	F	112
		" SARAH J.	Dau	W	F	Apr 1855	45	S				TN	TN	VA							✓	✓	✓					
		" JOHN W.	Son	W	M	Mar 1862	38	S				KY	TN	VA				FARMER			✓	✓	✓					
		" MARY F.	Dau	W	F	Jun 1868	31	S				KY	TN	VA							✓	✓	✓					
123	124	LEE, HARSON	Head	W	M	Oct 1844	55	M	29			KY	VA	VA				FARMER			✓	✓	✓	O		F	F	113
		" MARY S.	Wife	W	F	Jun 1852	47	M	29	2	2	KY	VA	VA							✓	X	✓					
		" MINIA A.	Dau	W	F	Mar 1875	25	S				KY	KY	KY							✓		✓					
		" PERRY M.	Son	W	M	Aug 1876	23	S				KY	KY	KY				FARMER			✓	✓	✓					
124	125	DENHAM, WILLIAM J.	Head	W	M	Feb 1866	34	M	12			KY	TN	TN				FARMER			✓	✓	✓	O		F	F	114
		" ELIZZY F.	Wife	W	F	Sep 1855	44	M	12	0	0	KY	VA	VA							✓	X	✓					
		HOOD, DEWEY P.	Step-son	W	M	Jul 1875	24	S				KY	KY	KY				FARMER			✓	✓	✓					
		" WILLIAM E.	Step-son	W	M	Jun 1884	15	S				KY	KY	KY						3	✓	✓	✓					
125	126	COCHRAN, THOMAS	Head	W	M	Sep 1859	40	M	14			TN	TN	TN							✓	✓	✓	R		H		

STATE - KENTUCKY
COUNTY - MONROE
Township or other division

TURNER -94- ABIJAH STRICKLER

Enumerator

Supervisor's Dist. No. 102 Sheet No.
Enumeration Dist. No. 81

Location No. of Family / No. of Dwelling	NAME	Relation	Color	Sex	DATE OF BIRTH Mon/Yr	Age at last birthday	Marital Status	# Years married	Mother of how many children?	# of these children living	NATIVITY Place of birth [this person]	Father of this person	Mother of this person	CITIZENSHIP Year of immigr.	# years in U.S.	Naturalization	OCCUPATION 10 years +	Months not employed	EDUCATION Attended school in month	Can read	Can write	Speak English	OWNERSHIP Owned or Rent	Owned -no mortage	Farm or house	# of farm schedule
	COCHRAN, LUZORIA	Wife	W	F	MAR 1863	37	M	14	6	6	KY	KY	KY							✓	✓	✓				
	" BRIGEY E.	Son	W	M	MAR 1883	17	S				KY	TN	KY							✓	✓	✓				
	" WILLIAM E.	Son	W	M	AUG 1886	13	S				KY	TN	KY							✓	✓	✓				
	" THOMAS E.	Son	W	M	MAR 18	11	S				KY	TN	KY			3				✓	✓					
	" JOHN E.	Son	W	M	Feb 1894	6	S				KY	TN	KY													
	" CARRY B.	Dau	W	F	Sep 1896	3	S				KY	TN	KY													
126/127	SMITH, WILLIAM A.	Head	W	M	JAN 1857	43	M	22			KY	VA	VA				FARMER			✓	✓	✓	O	F	115
	" ELIGA E.	Wife	W	F	Feb 1862	38	M	22	5	5	KY	KY	KY							✓	✓	✓				
	" LILLIE E.	Dau	W	F	Sep 1890	9	S				KY	KY	KY			5										
	" ALLEY D.	Son	W	M	Jul 1894	5	S				KY	KY	KY			1										
	" GRACE B.	Dau	W	F	Oct 1894	3	S				KY	KY	KY													
	" WILLIAM P.	Son	W	M	APR 1900	1/12	S				KY	KY	KY													
127/128	ALLEE, ELEMON	Head	W	M	MAR 1857	43	M	2			KY	KY	KY				FARMER			✓	✓	✓	R	F	116
	" RACHEL	Wife	W	F	MAY 1862	38	M	2	1		KY	KY	KY							✓	✓	✓				
	" OBY	Son	W	M	Dec 1886	13	S				KY	KY	KY							✓	✓	✓				
	" KENT	Son	W	M	MAR 1892	8	S				KY	KY	KY													
128/129	SMITH, WYATT	Head	W	M	MAR 1859	41	M	19			KY	VA	VA				FARMER			✓	✓	✓	O	F	117
	" TULEY B.	Wife	W	F	Sep 1864	35	M	19	5	5	KY	KY	MO							✓	✓	✓				
	" EVEY E.	Dau	W	F	Jul 1881	18	S				KY	KY	KY							✓	✓	✓				
	" JOHN T.	Son	W	M	OCT 1882	17	S				KY	KY	KY							✓	✓	✓				
	" PERRY T.	Son	W	M	JAN 1890	10	S				KY	KY	KY							✓	✓	✓				
	" MARY E.	Dau	W	F	Nov 1893	6	S				KY	KY	KY													
	" WELTHY	Dau	W	F	Feb 1900	3/12	S				KY	KY	KY													
	" ALEXANDER	Father	W	M	DEC 1814	85	Wd				VA	VA	VA				FARMER			✓	✓	✓				
129/130	DENHAM, WATSON	Head	W	M	MAR 1827	73	M	36			KY	VA	VA				FARMER			✓	✓	✓	R	F	
	" PACIENT	Wife	W	F	OCT 1837	62	M	36	1	1	KY	TN	TN							X	X	✓				

STATE - KENTUCKY
COUNTY - MONROE
Township or other division

TURNER - 95 - ABIJAH STRICKLER
Enumerator

Supervisor's Dist. No. _102_ Sheet No.
Enumeration Dist. No. _81_

No. of Family	No. of Dwelling	NAME	Relation	Color	Sex	DATE OF BIRTH Mon/Yr	Age at last birthday	Marital Status	# Years married	Mother of how many children?	# of these children living	Place of birth [this person]	Father of this person	Mother of this person	Year of immigr.	# years in U.S.	Naturalization	OCCUPATION 10 years +	Months not employed	Attended school in months	Can read	Can write	Speak English	Owned or Rent	Owned -no mortgage	Farm or house	# of farm schedule	
		DENHAM, JAMES R.	Son	W	M	OCT 1868	31	S				KY	KY	KY				DAY LABOR	4		X	X	✓					
130	131	EARLS, JOHN N.	Head	W	M	DEC 1864	35	M	11			KY	KY	KY				FARMER			X	X	✓	O		F	118	
		" FRANCES J.B.	Wife	W	F	JAN 1869	31	M	11	4	4	KY	KY	KY							✓	✓	✓					
		" BERTHY	Dau	W	F	Jul 1890	9	S				KY	KY	KY														
		" WILLIAM W	Son	W	M	APR 1893	7	S				KY	KY	KY														
		" EFFEY A.	Dau	W	F	JAN 1896	4	S				KY	KY	KY														
		" HECKEL E.	Son	W	M	OCT 1898	1	S				KY	KY	KY														
131	132	BOYD, ROBERT R.	Head	W	M	DEC 1860	39	M	18			KY	KY	KY				FARMER			✓	✓	✓	R		F	119	
		" SARAH E	Wife	W	F	AUG 1864	35	M	18	8	6	KY	KY	KY							✓	✓	✓					
		" OCIA E	Dau	W	F	APR 1883	17	S				KY	KY	KY				AT SCHOOL		4	✓	✓	✓					
		" OVA E.	Dau	W	F	MAR 1885	15	S				KY	KY	KY				AT SCHOOL		4	✓	✓	✓					
		" GROVER C.	Son	W	M	Jul 1888	11	S				KY	KY	KY				FARM LABOR		4	✓	✓	✓					
		" THIRMON	Son	W	M	NOV 1890	9	S				KY	KY	KY						4	✓	✓	✓					
		" FLOSSIA P.	Dau	W	F	AUG 1896	3	S				KY	KY	KY														
		" OSBY	Son	W	M	APR 1899	1	S				KY	KY	KY														
132	133	WILBORN, HESEY K.	Head	W	M	MAR 1858	42	M	10			KY	KY	KY				FARMER			✓	✓	✓	O		F	120	
		" MARY B.	Wife	W	F	OCT 1866	33	M	10	3	3	KY	KY	KY							✓	✓	✓					
		" HARASS D.	Son	W	M	MAR 1891	9	S				KY	KY	KY							✓	✓	✓					
		" POTER R.	Son	W	M	OCT 1896	3	S				KY	KY	KY														
		" HATTY M.	Dau	W	F	DEC 1898	1	S				KY	KY	KY														
		" FRANCES	Mother	W	F	APR 1838	62	Wd		4	2	KY	KY	KY				FARMER			✓	✓	✓					
133	134	BARLOW, JAMES	Head	W	M	DEC 1873	26	M	1			KY	KY	KY							X	X	✓	R		F		
		" LUE	Wife	W	F	APR 1877	23	M	1	1	1	KY	KY	KY							✓	✓	✓					
		" LILEY	Dau	W	F	DEC 1899	5/12	S				KY	KY	KY														
134	135	HOOD, SANTFORD	Head	W	M	DEC 1844	55	M	15			KY	VA	VA				FARMER			✓	✓	✓	O		F	121	
		" RACHEL A.	Wife	W	F	OCT 1861	38	M	15	5	5	KY	KY	KY							✓	✓	✓					

STATE - KENTUCKY
COUNTY - MONROE   TURNER   -96-   ABIJAH STRICKLER
Township or other division   Enumerator

Location No. of Family / No. of Dwelling	NAME	Relation	Color	Sex	DATE OF BIRTH Mon/Yr	Age at last birthday	Marital Status	# Years married	Mother of how many children?	# of these children living	NATIVITY Place of birth (this person)	Father of this person	Mother of this person	CITIZENSHIP Year of immigr. / # years in U.S. / Naturalization	OCCUPATION 10 years +	Months not employed	Attended school in months	Can read	Can write	Speak English	OWNERSHIP Owned or Rent	Owned -no mortgage	Farm or house	# of farm schedule
	HOOD, GILLBER	Son	W	M	Mar 1888	12	S				KY	KY	KY		FARM LABOR			✓	✓	✓				
	" ESSTER	Dau	W	F	Nov 1891	8	S				KY	KY	KY											
	" ELLA	Dau	W	F	Oct 1893	6	S				KY	KY	KY											
	" EDNEY	Dau	W	F	Mar 1895	5	S				KY	KY	KY											
	" OSCAR	Son	W	M	May 1898	2	S				KY	KY	KY											
135/136	JACKSON, JOHN W.	Head	W	M	Jan 1861	39	M	10			KY	KY	KY		FARMER			X	X	✓	R		F	122
	" MANDY M.	Wife	W	F	May 1873	27	M	10	7	6	KY	TN	KY					✓	X	✓				
	" EARLEY	Son	W	M	Oct 1890	9	S				KY	KY	KY											
	" MACK	Son	W	M	Dec 1891	8	S				KY	KY	KY											
	" JULY B.	Dau	W	E	May 1893	7	S				KY	KY	KY											
	" ANDREW	Son	W	M	Oct 1894	5	S				KY	KY	KY											
	" ANNA	Dau	W	F	Feb 1896	4	S				KY	KY	KY											
	" IVA L.	Dau	W	F	Mar 1899	1	S				KY	KY	KY											
136/137	HAMMETT, CHARLES B.	Head	W	M	Jul 1863	36	M	7			KY	SC	KY		FARMER			✓	✓	✓	O	F	F	123
	" MATTIE	Wife	W	F	Sep 1871	28	M	7	1	1	KY	KY	KY					✓	✓	✓				
	" BRYAN W.	Son	W	M	Oct 1896	3	S				KY	KY	KY											
37/138	MYERS, JAMES K.	Head	W	M	Mar 1845	55	M	18			TN	NC	TN		FARMER			✓	✓	✓	O	F	F	124
	" MANDY K.	Wife	W	F	Mar 1852	48	M	18	5	2	TN	TN	TN					✓	✓	✓				
	" MARY E.	Dau	W	F	Nov 1883	16	S				KY	KY	TN		AT SCHOOL		5	✓	✓	✓				
	" JAMES A.G.	Son	W	M	Jun 1888	12	S				KY	KY	TN		FARM LABOR		5	✓	✓	✓				
138/139	HARLAN, BURFORD	Head	W	M	Mar 1872	28	M				KY	KY	KY					✓	✓	✓	R		F	125
	" DAISY	Wife	W	F	Jun 1879	20	M				KY	KY	KY					✓	✓	✓				
	ADISON, BRINT	→	W	M	Mar 1880	20	S				KY	KY	KY		LOG TEAMSTER			✓	✓	✓				
139/140	LYONS, JOHN T.	Head	W	M	Mar 1854	46	M	10			KY	KY	KY		FARMER			✓	X	✓	O	F	126	
	" CORDELIA	Wife	W	P	Aug 1873	26	M	10			TN	TN	TN											
	" MARY F.	Dau	W	F	May 1880	20	S				KY	KY	KY											

STATE - KENTUCKY
COUNTY - MONROE TURNER -97- ABIJAH STRICKLER
Township or other division / Enumerator

Supervisor's Dist. No. 102 Sheet No.
Enumeration Dist. No. 81

No. of Family	No. of Dwelling	NAME	Relation	Color	Sex	Date of Birth Mon/Yr	Age at last birthday	Marital Status	# Years married	Mother of how many children?	# of these children living	Place of birth (this person)	Father of this person	Mother of this person	Year of immigr.	# years in U.S.	Naturalization	Occupation 10 years +	Months not employed	Attended school in months	Can read	Can write	Speak English	Owned or Rent	Owned - no mortgage	Farm or house	# of farm schedule
140	141	OLIVER, DAVID	Head	W	M	Feb 1842	58	M	38			TN	TN	TN				FARMER	0		X	X	✓	O	F	F	127
		" MARY A.	wife	W	F	Apr 1842	58	M	38	10	10	KY	TN	TN							X	X	✓				
		" WILLIAM W	Son	W	M	May 1881	19	S				KY	KY	TN				FARM LABOR			X	X	✓				
141	142	MARTAIN, JAMES B	Head	W	M	Aug 1836	63	M	11			KY	KY	TN				FARMER			✓	✓	✓	O	F	F	128
		" ANNIE L.	WIFE	W	F	Jun 1861	38	M	11	4	3	KY	KY	TN							✓	✓	✓				
		" ELLER D.	DAU	W	F	Jul 1890	9	S				KY	KY	KY							✓	✓	✓				
		" JOHN T.	Son	W	M	Sep 1892	7	S				KY	KY	KY													
		" EDWARD K.	Son	W	M	Nov 1898	1	S				KY	KY	KY													
142	143	BARLOW, WILLIAM	Head	B	M	May 1881	19	M				KY	KY	KY				FARMER			✓	✓	+	R		H	
		" LUCY D.	Wife	B	F	Dec 1882	17	M				KY	KY	KY							✓	✓	✓				
143	144	SIMMONS, TIVIS C.	Head	W	M	Dec 1847	52	M	27			TN	TN	TN				FARMER			✓	✓	✓	R		F	129
		" NANCY A.	wife	W	F	May 1850	50	M	27	6	3	KY	KY	KY							X	X	✓				
		" MARY J.	DAU	W	F	Dec 1874	25	S				KY	KY	KY							✓	✓	✓				
		" CAMILEA P.	DAU	W	F	Oct 1878	21	S				KY	KY	KY							✓	✓	✓				
		" JAMES W.A.	Son	W	M	Jul 1882	17	S				KY	KY	KY				FARM LABOR			✓	✓	✓				
144	145	ADWELL, JOHN S.	Head	W	M	Aug 1853	46	M	25			KY	TN	TN				FARMER			✓	✓		O	M	F	130
		" SARAH E.	wife	W	F	Aug 1854	45	M	25	7	7	TN	VA	TN							✓	✓					
		" LULAR B.	DAU	W	F	Mar 1885	15	S				KY	KY	TN							✓	✓					
		" MARY P.	DAU	W	F	Dec 1887	12	S				KY	KY	TN				AT SCHOOL		5	✓	✓					
		" JOHN B.	Son	W	M	Jun 1890	9	S				KY	KY	TN						3	X	X					
		" WILLIAM V.	Son	W	M	Sep 1894	5	S				KY	KY	TN													
		ROE, MARY	Mother in-law	W	F	Oct 1827	72	Wd		7	1	TN	TN	TN							✓	✓					
145	146	ADWELL, JESSEY	HEAD	W	M	Mar 1882	18	M				KY	KY	TN				FARMER			✓	✓	✓	R		H	
		" MARY T.	WIFE	W	F	Apr 1882	18	M				KY	TN	TN							✓	✓	✓				
146	147	WALLER, WILLIAM T.	Head	W	M	Sep 1855	44	M	23			KY	TN	TN				FARMER			✓	✓	✓	O	M	F	131
		" MARTHY J.	wife	W	F	Aug 1856	43	M	23	3	2	KY	KY	TN							✓	✓	✓				

STATE - KENTUCKY
COUNTY - MONROE
Township or other division: TURNER — 98 —
Enumerator: ABIJAH STRICKLER

Supervisor's Dist. No. 102   Sheet No.
Enumeration Dist. No. 81

No. of Family	No. of Dwelling	NAME	Relation	Color	Sex	DATE OF BIRTH Mon/Yr	Age at last birthday	Marital Status	# Years married	Mother of how many children?	# of these children living	Place of birth [this person]	Father of this person	Mother of this person	Year of immigr.	# years in U.S.	Naturalization	OCCUPATION 10 years +	Months not employed	Attended school in mouths	Can read	Can write	Speak English	Owned or Rent	Owned - no mortgage	Farm or house	# of farm schedule
		WALLER, WILLIAM F.	Son	W	M	Jul 1885	14	S				KY	KY	KY				FARM LABOR		4	✓	✓					
		" LORANER	Dau	W	F	Ju 1888	11	S				KY	KY	KY						5	✓	✓	✓				
147	148	JONES, JUSTON	Head	W	M	Jun 1869	30	M	7			KY	KY	KY				FARMER	0		✓	✓	✓	R		F	
		" MATTY	Wife	W	F	Mar 1878	22	M	7	2	2	KY	KY	KY							✓	✓	✓				
		" OEL R.	Son	W	M	May 1894	6	S				KY	KY	KY													
		" CALLEY	Dau	W	F	Nov 1896	3	S				KY	KY	KY													
		JEFFERSON, NILEY(?) S-in-Law		W	F	Apr 1876	24	Wd		2	2	KY	KY	KY							✓	✓	✓				
148	149	SHIPLEY, BENJAMIN R.	Head	W	M	Sep 1870	29	M	7			KY	KY	KY				FARMER			✓	✓	✓	R		F	
		" LONY	Wife	W	F	Mar 1878	22	M	7	4	4	KY	TN	KY							X	X	✓				
		" ISAAC	Son	W	M	Apr 1893	7	S				KY	KY	KY													
		" CATHERINE	Dau	W	F	Dec 1894	5	S				KY	KY	KY													
		" ELIGA T	Son	W	M	May 1896	4	S				KY	KY	KY													
		" JAMES D.	Son	W	M	Jul 1897	2	S				KY	KY	KY													
149	150	TURNER, WILLIAM H.	Head	W	M	Jan 1859	41	M	23			KY	KY	KY				FARMER			✓	✓	✓	O	F	F	132
		" SARAH E.	Wife	W	F	Nov 1858	41	M	23	7	5	KY	KY	KY							✓	✓	✓				
		" FLOYD B.	Son	W	M	May 1880	20	S				KY	KY	KY						3	✓	✓	✓				
		" CAUSEY P.	Son	W	M	Mar 1884	16	S				KY	KY	KY				FARM LABOR		3	✓	✓	✓				
		" CLAUD	Son	W	M	Sep 1886	13	S				KY	KY	KY				FARM LABOR		3	✓	✓	✓				
		" MAY	Dau	W	F	Jul 1889	10	S				KY	KY	KY				A.T SCHOOL		3	✓	✓	✓				
		" NINA	Dau	W	F	Oct 1893	6	S				KY	KY	KY													
150	151	GEARLD, SAMUEL W.	Head	W	M	Aug 1868	31	M	9			KY	KY	KY				FARMER			✓	✓	✓	R		F	133
		" BECKY F.	Wife	W	F	Nov 1871	28	M	9	4	4	KY	KY	KY							✓	✓	✓				
		" LEO	Son	W	M	Sep 1891	8	S				KY	KY	KY													
		" OVA	Son	W	M	Jun 1894	5	S				KY	KY	KY													
		" IVY T.	Dau	W	F	Jul 1896	3	S				KY	KY	KY													
		" ERNEST G.	Son	W	M	Jan 1899	1	S				KY	KY	KY													

TWELFTH CENSUS OF THE UNITED STATES 1900

STATE - KENTUCKY
COUNTY - MONROE
Township or other division — TURNER — 99 —
Enumerator — ABIJAH STRICKLER

Supervisor's Dist. No. 102 Sheet No. ___
Enumeration Dist. No. 81 ___

No. of Family	No. of Dwelling	NAME	Relation	Color	Sex	Date of Birth Mon/Yr	Age at last birthday	Marital Status	# Years married	Mother of how many children	# of these children living	Place of birth (this person)	Father of this person	Mother of this person	Year of immig.	# years in U.S.	Naturalization	Occupation 10 years +	Months not employed	Attended school in months	Can read	Can write	Speak English	Owned or Rent	Owned no mortage	Farm or house	# of farm schedule
151	152	TURNER, LEROY	Head	W	M	Oct 1832	67	M	13			KY	VA	—				FARMER			✓	✓	✓	O		F	134
		" SARAH J.	Wife	W	F	May 1847	53	M	13			TN	TN	TN							✓	✓	✓				
152	153	TURNER, HEWEY	Head	W	M	Dec 1879	20	M				KY	KY	KY				FARMER			✓	✓	✓	O		F	135
		" IDA	Wife	W	F	Dec 1881	18	M				KY	KY	KY							✓	✓	✓				
153	154	HUFFMAN, ALBERT A.	Head	W	M	May 1861	39	M	12			IND	KY	VA				DRY GOODS SALESMAN			✓	✓		R		H	
		" REBECKY F.	Wife	W	F	Jun 1868	31	M	12	5	4	KY	KY	KY							✓	✓	✓				
		" SYLVESTER G.	Son	W	M	Aug 1889	10	S				KY	IND	KY				FARM LABOR		5	✓	✓	✓				
		" MINIA F.	Dau	W	F	Oct 1892	7	S				KY	IND	KY													
		" NORA M.	Dau	W	F	Jun 1895	5	S				KY	IND	KY													
		" WILLIAM A.	Son	W	M	Jun 1898	2	S				KY	IND	KY							✓	✓		R		F	136
154	155	TURNER, ISAAC	Head	W	M	Jan 1868	32	M	8			KY	KY	KY				FARMER			✓	✓	✓	R		F	136
		" MATILDA	Wife	W	F	Dec 1869	30	M	8	3	3	KY	KY	KY							✓	✓	✓				
		" MAMIE C.	Dau	W	F	Oct 1892	7	S				KY	KY	KY													
		" EARNEST	Son	W	M	Oct 1896	3	S				KY	KY	KY													
		" GERTRUDE	Dau	W	F	Sep 1899 8/12		S				KY	KY	KY													
155	156	TURNER, JOSEPH F.	Head	W	M	Jun 1842	58	M	33			KY	VA	KY				FARMER			✓	✓	✓	O		F	137
		" MELVINIA	Wife	W	F	Mar 1845	55	M	33	2	2	KY	TN	TN							✓	✓	✓				
		SMITH, WILLIAM H.	Son-in-law	W	M	Oct 1870	29	M				KY	KY	KY				FARMER			✓	✓	✓	R		F	138
		" OVA L.	Dau	W	F	Aug 1884	15	M				KY	KY	KY							✓	✓	✓	R		H	
156	157	VEACH, GEORGE	Head	W	M	Sept 1861	38	M	19			KY	KY	KY				BLACKSMITH			✓	✓	✓	R		H	
		" NANCY E.	Wife	W	F	Nov 1863	36	M	19	9	7	KY	KY	KY							✓	✓	✓				
		" MINIE B.	Dau	W	F	Sep 1881	18	S				KY	KY	KY							✓	✓	✓				
		" JAMES H.	Son	W	M	Feb 1883	17	S				KY	KY	KY				FARM LABOR			✓	✓	✓				
		" CORA E.	Dau	W	F	Aug 1885	14	S				KY	KY	KY				AT SCHOOL		4	✓	✓	✓				
		" CHARLES M.	Son	W	M	Jan 1890	10	S				KY	KY	KY				FARM LABOR			✓	X	✓				
		" ROBBERT R.	Son	W	M	Jan 1892	8	S				KY	KY	KY													

TWELFTH CENSUS OF THE UNITED STATES 1900

STATE - KENTUCKY
COUNTY - MONROE
Township or other division — TURNER — 100 —

Enumerator — ABIJAH STRICKLER

Supervisor's Dist. No. 102 Sheet No.
Enumeration Dist. No. 81

Location No. of Family	No. of Dwelling	NAME	Relation	Color	Sex	DATE OF BIRTH Mon/Yr	Age at last birthday	Marital Status	# Years married	Mother of how many children?	# of these children living	Place of birth [this person]	Father of this person	Mother of this person	Year of immigr.	# years in U.S.	Naturalization	OCCUPATION 10 years +	Months not employed	Attended school in months	Can read	Can write	Speak English	Owned or Rent	Owned –no mortage	Farm or house	# of farm schedule
		VEACH, BETTY B.	Dau	W	F	Nov 1896	3	S				KY	KY	KY													
		" ETTY F.	Dau	W	F	Jan 1899	1	S				KY	KY	KY													
159	158	MARTAIN, JOHN B.	Head	W	M	Nov 1857	42	M	20			KY	KY	TN				FARMER			✓	✓	✓	O	M	F	139
		" JAMES (?) G.	Wife	W	F	Feb 1863	37	M	20	7	5	KY	KY	KY							✓	✓	✓				
		" ANNIE L.	Dau	W	F	Jun 1884	16	S				KY	KY	KY						4	✓	✓	✓				
		" SARAH J. F.	Dau	W	F	Nov 1886	12	S				KY	KY	KY				AT SCHOOL		4	✓	✓	✓				
		" JAMES O.	Son	W	M	Jul 1889	10	S				KY	KY	KY				A.T. SCHOOL		4	✓	✓	✓				
		JOHN B.	Son	W	M	Jul 1893	6	S				KY	KY	KY							✓	✓	✓				
		WILLIAM W.	Son	W	M	Aug 1896	3	S				KY	KY	KY													
		STEEN, CLAY	Lodger	W	M	Feb 1874	26	S				KY	KY	KY				FARM LABOR			✓	✓	✓				
		McCUE, FELIN	Lodger	W	M	Aug 1876	24	S				KY	KY	KY				FARM LABOR			✓	✓	✓				
158	159	ISENBERG, HENY E.	Head	W	F	Aug 1868	31	M	13	5	5	KY	KY	KY							✓	✓	✓	R		H	
		" JOSEPH L.	Son	W	M	AN 1888	12	S				KY	KY	KY				DAY LABOR			✓	✓	✓				
		" HATTY	Dau	W	F	Apr 1891	9	S				KY	KY	KY						5	✓	✓	✓				
		" OLA L.	Dau	W	F	Jan 1892	8	S				KY	KY	KY							✓	X	✓				
		" CLORA	Dau	W	F	Mar 1894	6	S				KY	KY	KY													
		" WILLEY D.	Son	W	M	Jul 1896	3	S				KY	KY	KY													
159	160	RITTER, GEORGE W.	Head	W	M	Dec 1830	69	M	3			TN	—	TN				FARMER			✓	✓	✓	O	F	F	140
		" CATHERINE L.	Wife	W	F	Dec 1853	46	M	3			TN	TN	TN							✓	X	✓				
		" VINEY C.	Dau	W	F	Mar 1871	22	S				KY	TN	TN							✓	✓	✓				
		" MALINDA B.	Dau	W	F	Jan 1874	26	S				KY	TN	TN							X	X	✓				
		MACUNE, POLK	Gr-Son	W	M	Jan 1892	8	S				KY	TN	KY													
		JACKSON, LUCINDY J.	Dau	W	F	Aug 1868	31	M	2	1	1	KY	TN	KY							✓	X	✓				
		" EMLEY B.	Gr-Dau	W	F	May 1899	1	S				KY	TN	KY													
160	161	MASON, MARTAIN M.	Head	W	M	May 1872	28	M	4			TN	TN	TN				DAY LABOR			X	X	✓	R		H	
		" ELIZZA S.	Wife	W	F	Mar 1874	26	M	4	3	2	TN	TN	TN							X	X	✓				

STATE - KENTUCKY
COUNTY - MONROE
Township or other division — TURNER — -101-

Enumerator — ABIJAH STRICKLER

Supervisor's Dist. No. 102 Sheet No.
Enumeration Dist. No. 81

Location No. of Family / No. of Dwelling	NAME	Relation	Color	Sex	DATE OF BIRTH Mon/Yr	Age at last birthday	Marital Status	# Years married	Mother of how many children?	# of these children living	NATIVITY Place of birth [this person]	Father of this person	Mother of this person	CITIZENSHIP Year of immigr. / # years in U.S. / Naturalization	OCCUPATION 10 years +	Months not employed	Attended school in months	Can read	Can write	Speak English	OWNERSHIP Owned or Rent	Owned –no mortgage	Farm or house	# of farm schedule
	MASON, WILLBERN	Son	W	M	Apr 1897	3	S				ALA	TN	TN											
	" WILLIAM	Son	W	M	Apr 1897	3	S				ALA	TN	TN											
161/162	QUINN, ULYSSES	Head	W	M	Apr 1868	32	M	8			KY	KY	KY		FARMER			X	X	✓	R		F	141
	" MAGNORA A.	Wife	W	F	Nov 1868	31	M	8	4	4	KY	KY	KY					✓	✓	✓				
	" FINLEY B.	Son	W	M	May 1893	7	S				KY	KY	KY				5			✓				
	" IVA M.	Dau	W	F	Nov 1894	5	S				KY	KY	KY											
	" PERLEY B.	Dau	W	F	May 1897	3	S				KY	KY	KY											
	" ANNIE F.	Dau	W	F	Jan 1900	3/12	S				KY	KY	KY											
162/163	DOSSEY, HUE	Head	W	M	Mar 1866	34	M	10			KY	KY	KY					X	X	✓	R		H	
	" MANDY J.	Wife	W	F	Jun 1871	28	M	10	4	4	KY	KY	KY					✓	✓	✓				
	" EMLEY E.	Dau	W	F	Jan 1891	9	S				KY	KY	KY				4							
	" ELIZA A.	Dau	W	F	Aug 1893	6					KY	KY	KY				4							
	" MAY L.	Dau	W	F	May 1896	4	S				KY	KY	KY											
	" LAURA B.	Dau	W	F	Dec 1898	1	S				KY	KY	KY											
163/164	KITTER, GEORGE A.	Head	W	M	Dec 1876	23	M				KY	TN	TN		FARMER			X	X	✓	R		F	142
	" MARY L.	Wife	W	F	Apr 1883	17	M				KY	TN	KY					✓	✓	✓				
164/165	JEFFREYS, PAYTON J.	Head	W	M	Sep 1865	34	M	10			KY	TN	KY		FARMER			✓	✓	✓	O	M	F	143
	" MARTHY L.B.	Wife	W	F	Apr 1869	31	M	10	1	1	KY	KY	KY					✓	✓	✓				
	" NOLEY L.A.	Dau	W	F	Oct 1895	4	S				TX	KY	KY											
165/166	LANE, HENRY T.	Head	W	M	Sep 1847	52	M	27			KY	VA	VA					✓	✓	✓	O	F	F	144
	" SARAH L.	Wife	W	F	Mar 1848	52	M	27	8	6	KY	VA	VA					X	X	✓				
	" MARY R.	Dau	W	F	Apr 1873	27	S				KY	KY	KY					✓	X	✓				
	" JOSEPH C.	Son	W	M	Sep 1878	21	S				KY	KY	KY		FARM LABOR			✓	✓	✓				
	" ROBERT J.	Son	W	M	Jul 1882	17	S				KY	KY	KY		FARM LABOR		2	✓	X	✓				
	" RICHARD A.	Son	W	M	Mar 1884	16	S				KY	KY	KY		FARM LABOR			X	X	✓				
	" LASSIMA	Dau	W	F	Jan 1888	12	S				KY	KY	KY		AT SCHOOL		1	X						

STATE - KENTUCKY
COUNTY - MONROE
Township or other division   TURNER   -102-   ABIJAH STRICKLER
Enumerator

Supervisor's Dist. No. _102_ Sheet No.
Enumeration Dist. No. _81_

Location		NAME	Relation	Color	Sex	DATE OF BIRTH Mon/Yr	Age at last birthday	Marital Status	# Years married	Mother of how many children?	# of these children living	NATIVITY Place of birth [this person]	Father of this person	Mother of this person	CITIZENSHIP Year of immigr.	# years in U.S.	Naturalization	OCCUPATION 10 years +	Months not employed	EDUCATION Attended school in months	Can read	Can write	Speak English	OWNERSHIP Owned or Rent	Owned -no mortage	Farm or house	# of farm schedule	
No. of Family	No. of Dwelling																											
		LANE, BACCY C.	DAU	W	F	JAN 1888	12	S				KY	KY	KY														
166	167	LANE, JOHN F.	Head	W	M	MAY 1866	34	M	11			KY	KY	KY				FARMER			✓	✓	✓	O		F	145	
		" KITTY E.	Wife	W	F	OCT 1870	29	M	11	5	5	KY	KY	KY							✓	✓	✓					
		" PERRY F.	Son	W	M	JAN 1890	10	S				KY	KY	KY						3	X	X	✓					
		" ADER M.	DAU	W	F	MAR 1892	8	S				KY	KY	KY						3	X	X	✓					
		" THOMAS B.	Son	W	M	MAY 1894	6	S				KY	KY	KY														
		" JEWEL B.	DAU	W	F	JAN 1897	3	S				KY	KY	KY														
		" VERNEY C.	DAU	W	F	MAY 1899	1	S				KY	KY	KY														
167	168	KEYS, DAVID	Head	W	M	MAR 1862	38	M	18			TN	TN	TN				FARMER			X	X	✓	R		F	146	
		V KITTY A.	Wife	W	F	JAN 1860	40	M	18	3	3	KY	VA	VA							✓	✓	✓					
		" JAMES F.	Son	W	M	JAN 1885	15	S				KY	TN	KY						1	✓	✓	✓					
		" JANE W.	DAU	W	F	Aug 1886	13	S				KY	TN	KY						1	✓	✓	✓					
		" OLLIE	Son	W	M	OCT 1891	8	S				KY	TN	KY									✓					
168	169	LEE, JOHN T.	HEAD	W	M	JUN 1868	31	M	8			KY	KY	KY				FARMER			✓	✓	✓	O		F	147	
		" DELLER	Wife	W	F	JAN 1873	27	M	8	4	4	KY	KY	KY						4	✓	✓	✓					
		" JAZIE B.	DAU	W	F	NOV 1892	7	S				KY	KY	KY														
		" PERNY C.	DAU	W	F	Sep 1894	5	S				KY	KY	KY														
		" JACOB T.	Son	W	M	NOV 1896	3	S				KY	KY	KY														
		" BERTHA A.	DAU	W	F	NOV 1898	1	S				KY	KY	KY														
169	170	JONES, WILLIAM	HEAD	W	M	JUL 1865	34	M	12			KY	TN	TN				FARMER			X	X	✓	R		F	148	
		" SUSEN M.	Wife	W	F	OCT 1874	25	M	12			KY	KY	KY							✓	✓	✓					
		" ALEY	Son	W	M	OCT 1890	9	S				KY	KY	KY							X	X	✓					
		" EFFIE	DAU	W	F	AUG 1892	7	S				KY	KY	KY									✓					
		" JOHN H.	Son	W	M	OCT 1895	4	S				KY	KY	KY														
		" WILLIAM B.	Son	W	M	MAY 1899	1	S				KY	KY	KY														
170	171	LEE, JOHN L.	HEAD	W	M	JUN 1830	69	M				KY	VA	VA				FARMER			✓	✓	✓	O		F	149	

STATE - KENTUCKY
COUNTY - MONROE TURNER - 103 -
Township or other division   Enumerator ABIJAH STRICKLER

Supervisor's Dist. No. 102 Sheet No.
Enumeration Dist. No. 8

No. of Family	No. of Dwelling	NAME	Relation	Color	Sex	DATE OF BIRTH Mon/Yr	Age at last birthday	Marital Status	# Years married	Mother of how many children?	# of these children living	Place of birth [this person]	Father of this person	Mother of this person	Year of immigr.	# years in U.S.	Naturalization	OCCUPATION 10 years +	Months not employed	Attended school in month	Can read	Can write	Speak English	Owned or Rent	Owned -no mortgage	Farm or house	# of farm schedule	
		LEE, MARY A.	Wife	W	F	DEC 1839	60	M	24			TN	VA	TN							✓	✓	✓					
		" GEORGE M.	Son	W	M	Jun 1866	33	M	24	1	0	KY	KY	KY				FARMER			✓	✓	✓					
171	172	ENGLAND, TOBIAS	Head	W	M	MAR 1849	51	M	27			KY	KY	KY				FARMER			✓	✓	✓	O	M	F	150	
		" ELIZABETH J.	Wife	W	F	Jul 1849	50	M	27			KY	VA	KY							✓	✓	✓					
		" JOHN S.	Son	W	M	OCT 1873	26	M				KY	KY	KY				TEAMSTER			✓	✓	✓					
		" SARAH B.	Dau-in-law	W	F	Sep 1880	19	M				KY	KY	KY							✓	✓	✓					
		" HARLOW J.	Gr-son	W	M	May 1899	1	S				KY	KY	KY														
172	173	BURKS, MARY A.	Head	W	F	APR 1822	78	Wd		3	3	KY	VA	CAROLINA				FARMER			✓	X	✓	O		F	151	
173	174	BURKS, JOHN A.	Head	W	M	APR 1847	53	M	34			KY	VA	KY				FARMER			✓	✓	✓	O	M	F	152	
		" CANSADY	Wife	W	F	MAY 1848	52	M	34			KY	KY	VA							X	X	✓					
174	175	WHITEHEAD, JOHN H.	Head	W	M	AUG 1840	59	M	42	7	4	KY	VA	VA				FARMER			✓	✓	✓	R		F	153	
		" NANCY E.	Wife	W	F	AUG 1840	59	M	42			KY	TN	KY							X	X	✓					
175	176	GENTRY, WILLIAM	Head	W	M	Nov 1853	46	M	19			KY	KY	IND.				FARMER			✓	✓	✓	O	M	F	154	
		" MARY D.	Wife	W	F	AUG 1859	40	M	19	7	7	KY	VA	KY							✓	✓	✓					
		" OLIE E.	Son	W	M	Feb 1882	18	S				KY	KY	KY				FARM LABOR		3	✓	✓	✓					
		" ISAAC J.	Son	W	M	OCT 1884	15	S				KY	KY	KY				FARM LABOR		3	✓	✓	✓					
		" VERGY S.	Dau	W	F	Sep 1887	12	S				KY	KY	KY				AT SCHOOL		5	✓	X	✓					
		" MARY E.	Dau	W	F	APR 1891	9	S				KY	KY	KY						5	X	X	✓					
		" NOAH J.	Son	W	M	OCT 1893	6	S				KY	KY	KY						5			✓					
		" OVA E.	Dau	W	F	APR 1895	5	S				KY	KY	KY														
		" HENRY W.	Son	W	M	APR 1897	3	S				KY	KY	KY														
176	177	OGDANE, JAMES H.	Head	W	M	MAR 1856	44	M	6			KY	KY	TN				FARMER			X	X	✓	O	E	E	155	
		" MOLIE S.	Wife	W	F	MAY 1870	30	M	6	3	2	KY	TN	KY							✓	✓	✓					
		" THEA	Son	W	M	Feb 1883	17	S				KY	KY	TN				FARM LABOR			✓	✓	✓					
		" DANNEY E	Dau	W	F	Jul 1884	15	S				—	KY	TN						3	✓	✓	✓					
		" ULA J.	Dau	W	F	Jul 1889	10	S				KY	KY	TN							✓	✓	✓					

TWELFTH CENSUS OF THE UNITED STATES 1900

STATE - KENTUCKY
COUNTY - MONROE
Township or other division

TURNER — 104 — ABIJAH STRICKLER
Enumerator

Supervisor's Dist. No. _102_ Sheet No. ___
Enumeration Dist. No. _81_ ___

No. of Family	No. of Dwelling	NAME	Relation	Color	Sex	DATE OF BIRTH Mon/Yr	Age at last birthday	Marital Status	# Years married	Mother of how many children?	# of these children living	Place of birth [this person]	Father of this person	Mother of this person	Year of immigr.	# years in U.S.	Naturalization	OCCUPATION 10 years +	Months not employed	Attended school in months	Can read	Can write	Speak English	Owned or Rent	Owned –no mortgage	Farm or house	# of farm schedule
		OGDANE, PHEBY T.	Dau	W	F	Jul 1896	3	S				KY	KY	KY													
		" JENEY H.	Dau	W	F	Sep 1898	1	S				KY	KY	KY													
177	178	TURNER, FELIN N.	Head	W	M	May 1827	73	M	54			VA	VA	VA				FARMER		X	X	✓		O	F	F	156
		" MALINDA	Wife	W	F	Apr 1828	72	M	54	7	4	TN	TN	TN						X	X	✓					
		" RODY E.	Dau	W	F	Feb 1865	35	S				KY	VA	TN						✓	X	✓					
178	179	TURNER, JOSEPH B.	Head	W	M	Jun 1854	45	M	23			KY	VA	TN				FARMER		✓	✓	✓		O	F	F	157
		" JOSEY F.	Wife	W	F	May 1851	49	M	22			KY	TN	VA							✓	✓					
179	180	DIAL, JACOB N.	Head	W	M	July 1850	49	M	32			KY	TN	KY				FARMER	12	X	X	✓		O	F	F	158
		" MATILDA A.	Wife	W	F	Oct 1847	52	M	32	8	8	KY	KY	KY							✓	✓	✓				
		" THOMAS E.	Son	W	M	Oct 1873	26	S				KY	KY	KY							✓	✓	✓				
		" AMBER H.	Son	W	M	Oct 1882	17	S				KY	KY	KY				FARM LABOR			✓	✓	✓				
		" MOLEY B.	Dau	W	F	Dec 1884	15	S				KY	KY	KY							✓	✓	✓				
		" MINA F.	Dau	W	F	Apr 1888	12	S				KY	KY	KY							✓	✓	✓				
180	181	SCOTT, SUSAN M.	Head	W	F	May 1846	54	Wd		4	4	KY	KY	TN				FARMER		X	X	✓		O	F	F	159
		" ROBERT	Son	W	M	Sep 1872	27	S				KY	KY	KY				FARMER			✓	✓	✓				
		" HATTA U. J.	Dau	W	F	Oct 1878	21	S				KY	KY	KY							✓	✓	✓				
		" MANDA	Dau	W	F	Dec 1880	19	S				KY	KY	KY							✓	✓	✓				
		MARTAIN, FRANK	—	W	M	Jul 1859	40	S				KY	KY	KY				FARMER			✓	✓	✓				
181	182	WARDE, CHARLES	Head	W	M	Sep 1856	43	M	18			KY	TN	TN				FARMER			✓	✓	✓		O	F	F	160
		" MARY E.	Wife	W	F	Jan 1857	43	M	18	4	2	KY	TN	KY							✓	X	✓				
		" IDA S.	Dau	W	F	Mar 1884	16	S				KY	KY	KY				AT SCHOOL		1	✓	✓	✓				
		VERGA E.	Dau	W	F	Sep 1887	12	S				KY	KY	KY				AT SCHOOL		1	✓	✓	✓				
182	183	PINKLEY, DAVID J.	Head	W	M	Sep 1873	26	M	2			TN	TN	KY				FARMER			✓	✓	✓		R		F	161
		" MAUD C.	Wife	W	F	Feb 1881	19	M	2	1	1	KY	KY	KY							✓	✓	✓				
		" LILLIE M.	Dau	W	F	Jan 1899	1	S				KY	TN	KY													
183	184	HOWARD, JAMES R.	Head	W	M	Dec 1865	34	M	3			KY	KY	KY				FARMER			✓	✓			O	M	F	162

STATE - KENTUCKY
COUNTY - MONROE
Township or other division — TURNER — 105 —

Enumerator — ABIJAH STRICKLER

Supervisor's Dist. No. 102 Sheet No.
Enumeration Dist. No. 81

No. of Family	No. of Dwelling	NAME	Relation	Color	Sex	DATE OF BIRTH Mon/Yr	Age at last birthday	Marital Status	# Years married	Mother of how many children?	# of these children living	Place of birth [this person]	Father of this person	Mother of this person	Year of immigr.	# years in U.S.	Naturalization	OCCUPATION 10 years +	Months not employed	Attended school in months	Can read	Can write	Speak English	Owned or Rent	Owned -no mortgage	Farm or house	# of farm schedule
		HOWARD, MAGGA	Wife	W	F	Jan 1877	22	M	3	1	1	TN	TN	KY							✓	✓	✓				
		" FEDRICK	Son	W	M	Oct 1897	2	S				KY	KY	TN													
184	185	PINKLEY, JULIE	Head	W	F	Jul 1824	72	Wd		4	1	TN	TN	PA				FARMER			✓	✓	✓	O	F	F	163
		" TIPTON	Step Son	W	M	Sep 1859	40	S				TN	TN	KY				FARMER			✓	✓	✓				
185	186	JOHNSON, JAMES B.	Head	W	M	Apr 1857	43	M	17			MO	KY	TN				FARMER			✓	✓	✓	R		F	164
		" ANNIS	Wife	W	F	Oct 1860	39	M	17	6	6	TN	TN	KY							✓	✓	✓				
		" MERTY	Dau	W	F	Apr 1884	16	S				KY	MO	KY				AT SCHOOL		5	✓	✓	✓				
		" DAVID	Son	W	M	Mar 1886	14	S				KY	KY	KY				FARM LABOR		5	✓	✓	✓				
		" BERTHY	Dau	W	F	Sep 1889	10	S				KY	KY	KY				AT SCHOOL		5	✓	✓	✓				
		" LECTAR	Son	W	M	Aug 1891	8	S				KY	KY	KY						5	✓	✓	✓				
		" ANNIE P.	Dau	W	F	Jun 1893	6	S				KY	KY	KY									✓				
		" KITTY	Dau	W	F	May 1898	2	S				KY	KY	KY													
186	187	JONES, JAMES S.	Head	W	M	Jan 1846	54	M	13			KY	KY	VA				FARMER			✓	✓	✓	O	F	F	165
		" SARAH E.	Wife	W	F	Oct 1852	47	M	13	3	3	TN	TN	KY							✓	✓	✓				
		" OZRAS A.	Son	W	M	Sept 1880	19	S				KY	KY	TN				FARMER			✓	✓	✓				
		" MARGY E.	Dau	W	F	Mar 1882	18	S				KY	KY	TN							✓	✓	✓				
		" ONEY B.	Dau	W	F	Feb 1888	12	S				KY	KY	TN				AT SCHOOL		5	✓	✓	✓				
		" WILLIAM H.	Son	W	M	Sep 1890	9	S				KY	KY	TN						5	✓	X	✓				
		" EMA L.	Dau	W	F	Feb 1894	6	S				KY	KY	TN									✓				
187	188	COOK, JAMES K.	Head	W	M	Nov 1843	56	M	19			TN	VA	TN				FARMER			X	X	✓	R		F	166
		" JULY A.	Wife	W	F	Jan 1864	39	M	19	7	7	KY	KY	KY							X	X	✓				
		" JAMES G.	Son	W	M	July 1884	15	S				KY	TN	KY							X	X	✓				
		" JOSEPH F.	Son	W	M	Nov 1886	13	S				KY	TN	KY				FARM LABOR			✓	✓	✓				
		" JOHN L. (?)	Dau	W	F	Jul 1889	10	S				KY	TN	KY									✓				
		" ELIZZA	Dau	W	F	May 1892	8	S				KY	TN	KY													
		" GERTREW	Dau	W	F	Jun 1894	5	S				KY	TN	KY													

STATE - KENTUCKY
COUNTY - MONROE
Township or other division   TURNER — 106 —

Enumerator   ABIJAH STRICKLER

Supervisor's Dist. No. 102   Sheet No.
Enumeration Dist. No. 81

No. of Family	No. of Dwelling	NAME	Relation	Color	Sex	Date of Birth Mon/Yr	Age at last birthday	Marital Status	# Years married	Mother of how many children?	# of these children living	Place of birth [this person]	Father of this person	Mother of this person	Year of immigr.	# years in U.S.	Naturalization	Occupation 10 years +	Months not employed	Attended school in months	Can read	Can write	Speak English	Owned or Rent	Owned -no mortgage	Farm or house	# of Farm schedule
		COOK, MANDY C.	Dau	W	F	Apr 1898	2	S				KY	TN	KY													
188	189	GILLENWATERS, MAY	Head	B	F	May 1864	36	Wd	11	8		KY	KY	KY				Day Labor			X	X	✓	R		H	
		" OSCER C.	Son	B	M	Apr 1881	19	S				KY	KY	KY				Farm Labor			X	X	✓				
		" KITTY M.	Dau	B	F	Aug 1883	16	S				KY	KY	KY							X	X	✓				
		" ELIZZY J.	Dau	B	F	Aug 1891	8	S				KY	KY	KY									✓				
		" VISA V.	Son	B	M	Sep 1886	13	S				KY	KY	KY				Farm Labor					✓				
		BEDFORD	Son	B	M	Apr 1894	6	S				KY	KY	KY													
189	190	JACKSON, WILLIAM	Head	W	M	Mar 1850	50	M	6			KY	KY	KY				Farmer			X	X	✓	R		F	167
		" HENRY E.	Wife	W	F	Oct 1870	29	M	6	3	3	KY	KY	KY							✓	✓	✓				
		" GEORGE H.	Son	W	M	Jun 1882	17	S				KY	KY	KY				Farm Labor			X	X	✓				
		" DESSEY	Dau	W	F	Dec 1893	6	S				KY	KY	KY													
		" VERTY	Dau	W	F	Aug 1895	4	S				KY	KY	KY													
		" OCA	Dau	W	F	Apr 1898	2	S				KY	KY	KY													
		BARTLEY, MARTAIN	Father in law	W	M	Oct 1838	61	Wd				KY	KY	TN				Farmer			X	X	✓				
190	191	SMITH, JAMES	Head	W	M	Jan 1847	53	M	9			KY	TN	KY				Farmer			X	X	✓	R		F	168
		" MOLIE	Wife	W	F	Mar 1876	24	M	9	4	1	KY	TN	TN							X	X	✓				
		" TURNER	Son	W	M	Mar 1885	15	S				KY	KY	KY				Farm Labor			X	X	✓				
		" MENTY B.	Dau	W	F	Oct 1893	6	S				KY	KY	KY													
191	192	SMITH, DOCK	Head	W	M	Feb 1877	23	M				KY	KY	KY				Farmer			X	X	✓	R		F	
		" LIDDY	Wife	W	F	Dec 1883	16	M				KY	KY	KY							X	X	✓				
192	193	FLOWERS, JOHN T.	Head	W	M	Apr 1835	65	M	11			KY	VA	VA				Farmer			✓	✓	✓	O	M	F	169
		" MARY	Wife	W	F	Dec 1860	39	M	11			KY	TN	KY							✓	✓	✓				
193	194	SOARDS, HENRY	Head	W	M	May 1848	52	M				KY	PA	TN				Farmer			✓	✓	✓	O	F	F	170
		" MOLIE B.	Wife	W	F	Nov 1873	26	M		0	0	KY	TN	KY							✓	✓	✓				
		" GEORGE T.	Son	W	M	Jun 1869	30	S				KY	KY	TN				Farmer			✓	✓	✓				
		" VIENA	Dau	W	F	Oct 1885	14	S				KY	KY	TN							✓	✓	✓				

STATE - KENTUCKY
COUNTY - MONROE
Township or other division — TURNER — 107 — Enumerator ABIJAH STRICKLER

Supervisor's Dist. No. 102 Sheet No.
Enumeration Dist. No. 81

Location No. of Family	No. of Dwelling	NAME	Relation	Color	Sex	DATE OF BIRTH Mon/Yr	Age at last birthday	Marital Status	# Years married	Mother of how many children?	# of these children living	Place of birth (this person)	Father of this person	Mother of this person	Year of immigr.	# years in U.S.	Naturalization	OCCUPATION 10 years +	Months not employed	Attended school in months	Can read	Can write	Speak English	Owned or Rent	Owned -no mortage	Farm or house	# of farm schedule
		SOARDS, WILLIAM L.	Son	W	M	Feb 1888	12	S				KY	KY	TN				FARM LABOR	3		✓	X	✓				
194	195	SOARDS, HENRY	Head	W	M	Feb 1879	21	M	1			KY	KY	TN				FARMER			✓	✓	✓	R		F	171
		" MINIE	Wife	W	F	Sep 1883	16	M	1			TN	TN	TN							✓	✓	✓				
		" ETHEL H.	Dau	W	F	Dec 1899	5/12	S		1	1	KY	KY	—													
195	196	LOYD, ABE P.	HEAD	W	M	Aug 1874	25	M	3			KY	KY	KY				FARMER			✓	✓	✓	R		F	172
		" TASIE R.	Wife	W	F	Sep 1877	22	M	3	1	1	KY	KY	KY							✓	✓	✓				
		" CRUMPTY C.	Son	W	M	Apr 1899	1	S				KY	KY	KY													
196	197	ARTERBURN, RHODA M.	HEAD	W	F	Arr 1839	61	Wd		4	4	KY	VA	VA				FARMER			✓	✓	✓	O		F	173
		" WILLIAM J.	Son	W	M	Aug 1873	26	M	5			KY	KY	KY				FARMER			✓	✓	✓				
		" ANNIE	Dau-in-law	W	F	Mar 1880	20	M	5	3	3	KY	KY	KY							✓	✓	✓				
		" LULA [GR]	Dau	W	F	Oct 1895	4	S				KY	KY	KY													
		" OLA E. [GR]	Dau	W	F	Mar 1897	3	S				KY	KY	KY													
		" WALLAS [GR]	Son	W	M	Mar 1899	1	S				KY	KY	KY													
		SMITH, HARSON	Lodger	W	M	May 1883	17	S				KY	KY	KY				FARM LABOR			X	X	✓				
197	198	JONES, JOHN T.	Head	W	M	Jul 1847	52	M	23			KY	VA	VA				FARMER			✓	✓	✓	O	M	F	174
		" ELIZZA B.	Wife	W	F	Aug 1856	43	M	23	6	3	KY	VA	VA							✓	✓	✓				
		" JAMES S.	Son	W	M	Nov 1876	23	S				KY	KY	KY							—	—	—				
		" MAUD C.	Dau	W	F	Feb 1881	19	S				KY	KY	KY							✓	✓	✓				
		" WILLIAM H.	Son	W	M	Feb 1890	10	S				KY	KY	KY				FARM LABOR		5	✓	✓	✓				
198	199	WELCH, SHERMIN	Head	W	M	Aug 1863	36	M	15			KY	KY	KY				FARMER			✓	✓	✓	O		F	175
		" JOANN	Wife	W	F	Aug 1867	32	M	15	2	2	KY	KY	KY							✓	✓	✓				
		" FILLMORE	Son	W	M	Nov 1885	14	S				KY	KY	KY				FARM LABOR		4	✓	✓	✓				
		" VERDA	Dau	W	F	Jan 1891	9	S				KY	KY	KY						4	✓	X	✓				
199	200	WELCH, MILES D.	Head			Jan 1830	70	M	46			KY	KY	KY				MILLER			✓	✓	✓	O		F	176
		" DICY A.	Wife			Aug 1832	67	M	46	9	8	KY	TN	TN							✓	✓	✓				
		" MERTY	Dau			Nov 1875	24	S				KY	KY	KY							✓	✓	✓				

STATE - KENTUCKY
COUNTY - MONROE
Township or other division — TURNER —108—

Enumerator — ABIJAH STRICKLER

Supervisor's Dist. No. _102_ Sheet No. _____
Enumeration Dist. No. _81_ _____

No. of Family	No. of Dwelling	NAME	Relation	Color	Sex	DATE OF BIRTH Mon/Yr	Age at last birthday	Marital Status	# Years married	Mother of how many children?	# of these children living	Place of birth [this person]	Father of this person	Mother of this person	Year of immigr.	# years in U.S.	Naturalization	OCCUPATION 10 years +	Months not employed	Attended school in months	Can read	Can write	Speak English	Owned or Rent	Owned -no mortgage	Farm or house	# of farm schedule
200	201	WELCH, FRANK P.	Head	W	M	Aug 1872	27	M	2			KY	KY	KY				FARMER			✓	✓	✓			F	
		" NELIE C.	Wife	W	F	Apr 1878	22	M	2			KY	KY	KY												F	
201	202	BURNETT, MILLER F.	Head	W	M	Nov 1852	47	M	29			KY	TN	KY							X	X	✓	O	F	F	177
		" MARY E.	Wife	W	F	May 1856	44	M	29	2	2	KY	KY	KY							X	X	✓				
		" AVO	Dau	W	F	Feb 1885	15	S				KY	KY	KY							✓	✓	✓				
202	203	JOHNSON, JOHN T.	Head	W	M	Sep 1852	47	M	24			KY	KY	KY				FARMER			✓	✓	✓	O	F	F	178
		" SARAH L.	Wife	W	F	Dec 1848	51	M	24	6	5	TN	TN	TN								✓	✓				
		" FLORY A.	Dau	W	F	Jan 1876	24	S				KY	KY	TN							✓	✓	✓				
		" JAMES F.	Son	W	M	Jun 1878	21	S				KY	KY	TN							✓	✓	✓				
		" LUTHER	Son	W	M	Nov 1887	12	S				KY	KY	TN				FARM LABOR			✓	✓	✓				
203	204	ENGLAND, ERIE	Head	B	M	Sept 1847	59	M	18			KY	VA	VA				FARMER			X	X	✓	O	F	F	179
		" KIZZY J.	Wife	B	F	Sept 1857	42	M	18			KY	KY	KY							X	X	✓				
		" GEORGE A.	Neice	B	F	Jul 1891	8	S				KY	KY	KY							X	X	✓				
204	205	JOHNSON, NEWTON	Head	B	M	May 1850	50	M	26			KY	TN	TN				FARMER			X	X	✓	R		F	180
		" PARKY	Wife	B	F	Apr 1856	44	M	26	13	6	KY	KY	KY							X	X	✓				
		" NEALEY	Dau	B	F	Aug 1874	25	S				KY	KY	KY							X	X	✓				
		" ELLAR	Dau	B	F	Feb 1885	15	S				KY	KY	KY				AT SCHOOL		5	✓	✓	✓				
		" PORA	Dau	B	F	Jan 1887	13	S				KY	KY	KY				AT SCHOOL		5	✓	✓	✓				
		" HALLEY	Dau	B	F	Dec 1888	11	S				KY	KY	KY				AT SCHOOL		5	✓	✓	✓				
		" ORA	Dau	B	F	Apr 1893	7	S				KY	KY	KY				AT SCHOOL		5	X	X	✓				
		" EDMON	Son	B	M	Jun 1897	2	S				KY	KY	KY									✓				
205	206	BARTLEY, WILLIAM	Head	W	M	Nov 1865	34	Wd.				KY	KY	KY				FARMER			✓	✓	✓	O	F	F	181
		" LEVIE	Son	W	M	Jul 1887	12	S				KY	KY	KY				FARM LABOR			✓	✓	✓				
		" DANNIE E.	Dau	W	F	May 1890	10	S				KY	KY	KY							✓	✓	✓				
		" EFFA T.	Dau	W	F	Oct 1892	7	S				KY	KY	KY									✓				
		" ELIZZA B.	Dau	W	F	Dec 1895	4	S				KY	KY	KY													

TWELFTH CENSUS OF THE UNITED STATES 1900

STATE - KENTUCKY
COUNTY - MONROE
Township or other division

TURNER — 109 —

ABIJAH STRICKLER
Enumerator

Supervisor's Dist. No. _102_ Sheet No.
Enumeration Dist. No. _81_

No. of Family	No. of Dwelling	NAME	Relation	Color	Sex	DATE OF BIRTH Mon/Yr	Age at last birthday	Marital Status	# Years married	Mother of how many children?	# of these children living	Place of birth (this person)	Father of this person	Mother of this person	Year of immigr.	# years in U.S.	Naturalization	OCCUPATION 10 years +	Months not employed	Attended school in months	Can read	Can write	Speak English	Owned or Rent	Owned -no mortage	Farm or house	# of farm schedule	
		BARTLEY, JAMES M.	Head	W	M	Oct 1872	27	M				KY	KY	KY				FARMER			✓	✓	✓					
		" MERTY	Sister in Law	W	F	Oct 1882	17	M				KY	KY	KY							✓	✓	✓					
		" JACOB T.	Father	W	M	Jan 1840	60	Wd				KY	KY	KY							✓	✓	✓					
206	207	WILLIAMS, MORGAN	Head	W	M	Jul 1879	20	S				KY	KY	KY				FARMER			✓	✓	✓	O		F	182	
		" ANNIE	Sister	W	F	Mar 1878	22	S				KY	KY	KY								✓	✓					
		" BERDY	Sister	W	F	Sep 1882	17	S				KY	KY	KY								✓	✓					
		" EDIE	Bro	W	M	Jul 1883	16	S				KY	KY	KY				FARM LABOR				✓	✓					
		" TALLIE	Bro	W	M	— 1887	13	S				KY	KY	KY								✓	✓					
		" DORA	Sister	W	F	Aug 1892	7	S				KY	KY	KY								✓	✓					
207	208	REYNOLDS, STANFORD	Head	W	M	Jun 1844	55	M	16			KY	KY	KY				FARMER			✓	✓	✓	O		F	183	
		" MARY J.	Wife	W	F	Mar 1865	35	M	16	1	1	KY	KY	KY							✓	✓	✓					
		" MILES S.	Son	W	M	Mar 1885	15	S				KY	KY	KY				FARM LABOR		5	✓	✓	✓					
208	209	BARLOW, BENJAMIN	Head	B	M	May 1859	41	M	23			KY	KY	KY				FARMER			✓	✓	✓	O	M	F	184	
		" MANDY	Wife	B	F	Apr 1860	40	M	23	12	10	KY	KY	KY							X	X	✓					
		" FLARNCE	Dau	B	F	Sept 1883	16	S				KY	KY	KY							✓	✓	✓					
		" PERNIA	Dau	B	F	Feb 1887	13	S				KY	KY	KY				AT SCHOOL		5	✓	✓	✓					
		" MINIE	Dau	B	F	Mar 1889	11	S				KY	KY	KY				AT SCHOOL		5	✓	✓	✓					
		" ELLER	Dau	B	F	Apr 1893	7	S				KY	KY	KY				AT SCHOOL		5	✓	✓	✓					
		" CARL	Son	B	M	Jul 1894	6	S				KY	KY	KY								✓	✓					
		" KITTY A.	Mother	B	F	Apr 1825	75	Wd		1	1	KY	KY	KY							X	X	✓					
209	210	JOHNSON, JOSEPH B.	Head	W	M	Jan 1862	38	M	11			KY	KY	KY				FARMER			✓	✓	✓	R		F	185	
		" MARTHY J.	Wife	W	F	Jul 1862	37	M	11	3	3	KY	KY	KY							✓	✓	✓					
		" NANIE F.	Dau	W	F	Sep 1884	15	S				KY	KY	KY				AT SCHOOL		3	✓	✓						
		" CHARLES D.	Son	W	M	Jun 1886	13	S				KY	KY	KY				FARM LABOR		3	✓	✓	✓					
		" BESSIE M.	Dau	W	F	May 1891	9	S				KY	KY	KY				AT SCHOOL		3	X	X	✓					
		" HOMER	Son	W	M	Jan 1893	7	S				KY	KY	KY				AT SCHOOL		3	✓	X	✓					

STATE - KENTUCKY
COUNTY - MONROE
Township or other division   TURNER —110—

Enumerator ABIJAH STRICKLER

Supervisor's Dist. No. 102 Sheet No.
Enumeration Dist. No. 81

No. of Family	No. of Dwelling	NAME	Relation	Color	Sex	DATE OF BIRTH Mon/Yr	Age at last birthday	Marital Status	# Years married	Mother of how many children?	# of these children living	Place of birth (this person)	Father of this person	Mother of this person	OCCUPATION 10 years +	Months not employed	Attended school in months	Can read	Can write	Speak English	Owned or Rent	Owned -no mortage	Farm or house	# of Farm schedule
		JOHNSON, JOHNEY	Son	W	M	Aug 1895	4	S				KY	KY	KY						✓				
210	211	DICKERSON, LANDAU	Head	W	M	Oct 1872	27	M	1			KY	KY	KY	FARMER			✓	✓	✓	O	F	F	186
		" BETTY	Wife	W	F	Dec 1882	17	M	1	1	1	KY	KY	KY				✓	✓	✓				
		" WILLIAM C.	Son	W	M	Apr 1900	2/12	S				KY	KY	KY										
211	212	EMBERTON, POLLY A.	Head	W	F	Sep 1827	72	Wd				TN	TN	TN	FARMER			✓	✓	✓	O	F	F	187
		PROFFITT, JAMES W.	Son-in-law	W	M	Feb 1861	39	M	17			KY	TN	TN	FARMER			✓	✓					
		" LIDDIA	Dau	W	F	Apr 1859	41	M	17	8	5	TN	KY	TN				✓	✓					
		" LUTHER R.	Son	W	M	Aug 1887	12	S				KY	KY	KY	FARM LABOR		3	✓	✓					
		" LAMASCUS	Son	W	M	Dec 1890	9	S				KY	KY	KY				✓	✓					
		" MATTIE I.	Dau	W	F	Mar 1894	6	S				KY	KY	KY				✓	✓					
		" WILLIAM R.	Son	W	M	Dec 1895	4	S				KY	KY	KY						✓				
		" EDNA M	Dau	W	F	Apr 1898	2	S				KY	KY	KY						✓				
212	213	FOX, JOSEPH	Head	W	M	Oct 1872	27	M	7			KY	TN	KY	FARMER			✓	✓		R		F	188
		" IDA	Wife	W	F	Sep 1874	25	M	7	3	1	KY	TN	KY				✓	✓					
		" CHARLEY M.	Son	W	M	Jun 1893	6	S				KY	KY	KY										
213	214	BURKS, CAS	Head	W	M	May 1867	33	M	4			KY	KY	KY	FARMER			✓	✓	✓	R		F	189
		" OPHELIA	Wife	W	F	Nov 1868	31	M	4			KY	KY	KY				✓	✓					
214	215	OGDON, JAMES W.	Head	W	M	Oct 1875	24	M	3			KY	KY	TN				✓	✓	✓	R		H	
		" ELLER	Wife	W	F	May 1882	18	M	3	1	1	KY	KY	KY				✓	✓	✓				
		" ANNIE	Dau	W	F	Oct 1898	1	S				KY	KY	KY										
215	216	LAWSON, HENRY T.	Head	W	M	Aug 1878	21	M	1			MO	KS	MO	DAY LABOR			✓	X	✓	R		H	
		" LUCY	Wife	W	F	May 1876	24	M	1	3	3	TN	KY	KY				✓	✓					
		" EESTIE G.	Step Son	W	M	Jul 1892	7	S				KY	KY	TN										
		" JEFERSON G.	Step Son	W	M	Aug 1894	5	S				KY	KY	TN										
		" WILLIAM	Son	W	M	Jul 1899	10/12	S				KY	MO	TN										
216	217	GENTRY, WILLIAM H.	Head	W	M	Apr 1853	47	M	20			TN	TN	NC	FARMER			✓	✓	✓	O	F	F	190

TWELFTH CENSUS OF THE UNITED STATES 1900

STATE - KENTUCKY
COUNTY - MONROE
Township or other division — TURNER — 111 —

Enumerator — ABIJAH STRICKLER

Supervisor's Dist. No. 102 Sheet No.
Enumeration Dist. No. 81

Location (No. of Family / No. of Dwelling)	NAME	Relation	Color	Sex	DATE OF BIRTH Mon/Yr	Age at last birthday	Marital Status	#Years married	Mother of how many children?	# of these children living	NATIVITY (Place of birth this person / Father of this person / Mother of this person)			CITIZENSHIP	OCCUPATION 10 years +	Months not employed	Attended school in months	Can read	Can write	Speak English	OWNERSHIP (Owned or Rent / Owned-no mortage / Farm or house / # of farm schedule)			
	GENTRY, LUELLAR B.	Wife	W	F	Sep 1857	42	M	20	8	8	KY	KY	KY					✓	✓					
"	JAMES P.	Son	W	M	Dec 1880	19	S				KY	TN	KY		FARM LABOR									
"	GROVER C.	Son	W	M	Oct 1884	15	S				KY	TN	KY				3	✓	✓					
"	HURSHEL G.	Son	W	M	Mar 1887	13	S				KY	TN	KY		FARM LABOR		3	✓	✓					
"	JOSEPH C.	Son	W	M	Dec 1889	10	S				KY	TN	KY		FARM LABOR		3	✓	✓					
"	ADER C.	Dau	W	F	Jan 1891	9	S				KY	TN	KY		AT SCHOOL		3	✓	✓	✓				
"	WILLIAM E.	Son	W	M	Aug 1893	6	S				KY	TN	KY											
"	MATTIE G.	Dau	W	F	Oct 1895	4	S				KY	TN	KY											
217 218	HALE, JOHN C.	Head	W	M	Apr 1880	20	M	1			KY	TN	TN		FARMER			✓	✓	✓	R		F	191
"	ANTHONEY	Wife	W	F	Sep 1882	17	M	1	1	1	KY	TN	KY					✓	✓	✓				
"	GOLDMON	Son	W	M	Nov 1899	7/12	S				KY	KY	KY											
218 219	LOVELADY, RADFORD	Head	W	M	Apr 1864	36	M	16			TN	TN	TN		FARMER			✓	✓	✓	R		F	192
"	MOLIE	Wife	W	F	Aug 1867	32	M	16	5	4	TN	TN	TN					✓	✓					
"	BERTHY F.	Dau	W	F	Oct 1889	10	S				TN	TN	TN		AT SCHOOL		3	✓	✓	✓				
"	BUFORD J.	Son	W	M	Sep 1891	8	S				KY	TN	TN		AT SCHOOL		3	✓	✓					
"	BULAH	Dau	W	F	Oct 1893	6	S				KY	TN	TN		AT SCHOOL		3	✓	✓					
"	BERDY D.	Dau	W	F	Jul 1895	4	S				TN	TN	TN											
219 220	LOYD, NATHANIEL	Head	W	M	Jun 1849	50	M	9			TN	TN	TN		FARMER			X	X	✓	O	FF		193
"	LOCKY J.	Wife	W	F	Feb 1866	34	M	9			KY	VA	TN					✓	✓					
220 221	GOODALL, WILLIAM H.	Head	W	M	Jul 1865	34	M	11			TN	KY	TN		FARMER			✓	✓		R		F	194
"	SUSAN A.	Wife	W	F	Jul 1867	32	M	11	4	4	KY	TN	TN					✓	✓					
"	PLUNNEY D.	Dau	W	F	Nov 1890	9	S				TN	TN	KY				2	X	X	✓				
"	ODOS C.	Son	W	M	Sep 1892	7	S				TN	TN	KY				2	X	X	✓				
"	BESSY B.	Dau	W	F	Jan 1894	5	S				KY	TN	KY							✓				
"	MERTY E.	Dau	W	F	Sep 1898	1	S				KY	TN	KY											
221 222	JORDAN, ROBERT	Head	W	M	Apr 1866	34	M	13			KY	KY	KY		FARMER			✓	✓		R		F	195

STATE - KENTUCKY
COUNTY - MONROE
Township or other division

TURNER — 112 —

Enumerator ABIJAH STRICKLER

Supervisor's Dist. No. 102 Sheet No.
Enumeration Dist. No. 81

No. of Family	No. of Dwelling	NAME	Relation	Color	Sex	DATE OF BIRTH Mon/Yr	Age at last birthday	Marital Status	# Years married	Mother of how many children	# of these children living	Place of birth [this person]	Father of this person	Mother of this person	Year of immigr.	# years in U.S.	Naturalization	OCCUPATION 10 years +	Months not employed	Attended school in months	Can read	Can write	Speak English	Owned or Rent	Owned -no mortgage	Farm or house	# of farm schedule	
		JORDAN, MATILDA A.	Wife	W	F	Apr 1866	34	M	13	3	2	KY	KY	KY							✓	✓	✓					
		" MERTY B.	Dau	W	F	Jan 1888	12	S				KY	KY	KY				AT SCHOOL		4	✓	✓	✓					
		" GUI (GUY?)E	Son	W	M	Sep 1895	4	S				KY	KY	KY									✓					
222	223	KIRBY, SAMIEL J.	Head	W	M	Apr 1870	30	M	5			KY	TN	TN				FARMER		6	✓	✓	✓			F		
		" HARRET	Wife	W	F	Apr 1869	31	M	5	3	2	KY	TN	KY							X	X	✓					
		" HALLEY	Step Dau	W	F	Jul 1889	10	S				KY	KY	KY				AT SCHOOL		5	✓	✓	✓					
		" IVA	Dau	W	F	Feb 1896	4	S				KY	KY	KY									✓					
223	224	GOODMON, JAMES D.	Head	W	M	May 1854	46	M	27			KY	KY	KY				FARMER			✓	✓	✓		R	F	196	
		" FRANCES E.	Wife	W	F	May 1856	44	M	27	9	8	KY	KY	TN							✓	✓	✓					
		" ALLAS	Dau	W	F	Oct 1875	24	S				KY	KY	KY							✓	✓	✓					
		" CHARLES A.	Son	W	M	Nov 1883	16	S				KY	KY	KY				FARM LABOR		5	✓	✓						
		" HENRY	Son	W	M	Dec 1884	13	S				KY	KY	KY				FARM LABOR		5	✓	✓	✓					
		" WILLIAM	Son	W	M	Oct 1888	11	S				KY	KY	KY				FARM LABOR		5	✓	✓	✓					
		" KITTY B.	Dau	W	F	Feb 1894	6	S				KY	KY	KY									✓					
		" DERO	Son	W	M	Sep 1896	3	S				KY	KY	KY									✓					
224	225	DIAL, JOSEPH B.	Head	W	M	Oct 1874	23	M	2			KY	KY	KY							✓	✓	✓		R	H		
		" KITTY	Wife	W	F	Sep 1879	20	M	2	1	1	KY	KY	KY						3	✓	✓	✓					
		" LEVEY K.	Son	W	M	Dec 1898	1	S				KY	KY	KY														
225	226	SIMMONS, WILLIAM A.	Head	W	M	May 1841	59	M	28			TN	TN	TN				FARMER			✓	✓			O	F	197	
		" MALISSIE E.	Wife	W	F	Jun 1859	48	M	28	9	9	KY	TN	KY							✓	✓						
		" WILLIAM C.	Son	W	M	Apr 1878	22	S				KY	TN	KY				FARM LABOR										
		" THOMAS M.	Son	W	M	Mar 1880	20	S				KY	TN	KY				FARM LABOR										
		" SALLIE L.	Dau	W	F	Jun 1884	15	S				KY	TN	KY				AT SCHOOL		3	✓	✓	✓					
		" VICKEY M.	Dau	W	F	Feb 1888	12	S				KY	TN	KY				AT SCHOOL		3	✓	X	✓					
		" MITTY A.	Dau	W	F	Aug 1890	9	S				KY	TN	KY						5	✓	✓	✓					
		" BASEL H.	Son	W	M	Feb 1895	5	S				KY	TN	KY														

STATE - KENTUCKY
COUNTY - MONROE
Township or other division: TURNER –113–
Enumerator: ABIJAH STRICKLER

Supervisor's Dist. No. 102 Sheet No. ___
Enumeration Dist. No. 81

No. of Family	No. of Dwelling	NAME	Relation	Color	Sex	DATE OF BIRTH Mon/Yr	Age at last birthday	Marital Status	#Years married	Mother of how many children?	# of these children living	Place of birth [this person]	Father of this person	Mother of this person	Year of immigr.	# years in U.S.	Naturalization	OCCUPATION 10 years +	Months not employed	Attended school in months	Can read	Can write	Speak English	Owned or Rent	Owned –no mortgage	Farm or house	# of farm schedule
226	227	RICH, SHELTON C.	HEAD	W	M	APR 1847	53	M	22			KY	TN	VA				FARMER			✓	✓	✓	O	F	F	198
		" ZIDIE	WIFE	W	F	OCT 1857	42	M	22	11	6	KY	VA	TN							✓	✓					
		" LEE (LEO?) C.	SON	W	M	Jul 1879	20	S				KY	KY	KY				FARMER			✓	✓					
		" OORA M.	DAU	W	F	OCT 1881	18	S				KY	KY	KY				AT SCHOOL		3	✓	✓	✓				
		" MERTY E.	DAU	W	F	DEC 1884	15	S				KY	KY	KY				AT SCHOOL		5	✓	✓	✓				
		" WILLIAM J.	SON	W	M	OCT 1888	11	6				KY	KY	KY				FARM LABOR		5	✓	✓	✓				
		" GRACIE C.	DAU	W	F	Feb 1893	7	S				KY	KY	KY						5			✓				
		" VERAER D.	DAU	W	F	JAN 1897	3	S				KY	KY	KY									✓				
227	228	DENHAM, JAMES	HEAD	W	M	Feb 1847	53	M	6			KY	VA	KY				FARMER – 12			✓	✓	✓	O	F	F	199
		" RACHEL E.	WIFE	W	F	Feb 1863	37	M	6	1	1	KY	TN	TN							✓	✓	✓				
		" FANIE A.	DAU	W	F	NOV 1899	6/12	S				KY	KY	KY													
228	229	BURKS, ARILLIE	HEAD	W	F	NOV 1818	81	Wd		1	1	VA	VA	VA				FARMER			X	X	✓	O	F	F	200
		" SARAH E.	DAU	W	F	SEP 1849	50	S				KY	VA	VA							X	X	✓				
		RUSSELL, NANCY	—	W	F	MAY 1839	61	S				KY	KY	KY							X	X	✓				
229	230	TURNER, JOHN T.	HEAD	W	M	NOV 1860	39	Wd				KY	KY	KY				FARMER			✓	X	✓	R		F	201
		" ELIZZA E.	DAU	W	F	Jul 1884	15	S				KY	KY	KY							✓	✓					
		" ELLER B.	DAU	W	F	DEC 1888	11	S				KY	KY	KY				AT SCHOOL		2	✓	✓	✓	O	F	F	202
230	231	GOOLSBY, HANSFORD	HEAD	W	M	APR 1849	51	M	28			TN	TN	TN				FARMER			✓	✓	✓				
		" SUSAN A.	WIFE	W	F	AUG 1866	33	M	28	8	5	KY	KY	KY							✓	✓					
		" ARAMATHA	SON	W	M	MAR 1884	16	S				KY	TN	KY				FARM LABOR		5	✓	✓	✓				
		" WORIE	SON	W	M	JAN 1888	12	S				KY	TN	KY				FARM LABOR		5	✓	✓	✓				
		" MILES P.	SON	W	M	MAR 1890	10	S				KY	TN	KY				FARM LABOR		5	✓	✓	✓				
		" FIRD	SON	W	M	JAN 1892	8	S				KY	TN	KY						5	✓	✓	✓				
		" JEWEL	SON	W	M	OCT 1893	6	S				KY	TN	KY						5	✓	✓	✓				
231	232	DOWNING, JAMES T.	HEAD	W	M	JAN 1848	52	M	27			KY	KY	KY				FARMER			✓	0	✓	O	F	F	203
		" DARTHULA L.	WIFE	W	F	OCT 1846	53	M	27	2	1	TN	TN	TN							✓	✓	✓				

STATE - KENTUCKY
COUNTY - MONROE
Township or other division: TURNER —114— ABIJAH STRICKLER
Enumerator

Supervisor's Dist. No. *102* Sheet No.
Enumeration Dist. No. *81*

No. of Family	No. of Dwelling	NAME	Relation	Color	Sex	DATE OF BIRTH Mon/Yr	Age at last birthday	Marital Status	# Years married	Mother of how many children?	# of these children living	Place of birth [this person]	Father of this person	Mother of this person	Year of immigr.	# years in U.S.	Naturalization	OCCUPATION 10 years +	Months not employed	Attended school in months	Can read	Can write	Speak English	Owned or Rent	Owned -no mortgage	Farm or house	# of farm schedule
		DOWNING, LILIE H.	DAU	W	F	Jul 1874	25	S				KY	KY	TN							✓	✓	✓				
232	233	NEAL, THOMAS L.	HEAD	W	M	Dec 1853	46	M	22			KY	TN	KY				FARMER			✓	✓	✓	O	F	F	204
	"	SALLIE L.	wife	W	F	Apr 1861	39	M	22	9	8	KY	VA	TN							✓	✓	✓				
	"	GA—?	SON	W	M	Jan 1881	19	S				KY	KY	KY				FARM LABOR		2	✓	✓	✓				
	"	WILLIAM L.	SON	W	M	Jul 1882	17	S				KY	KY	KY				FARM LABOR		2	✓	✓	✓				
	"	ANNIE L.	DAU	W	F	Jan 1885	15	S				KY	KY	KY							✓	✓	✓				
	"	SIDNEY	DAU	W	F	Jun 1885(?)14		S				KY	KY	KY				AT SCHOOL		5	✓	✓	✓				
	"	JURY C.	SON	W	M	Jul 1888	11	S				KY	KY	KY				FARM LABOR		8	X	X	✓				
	"	AVRA	SON	W	M	Jan 1890	10	S				KY	KY	KY				FARM LABOR		5	✓	X	✓				
	"	CHARLES	SON	W	M	Apr 1893	7	S				KY	KY	KY													
	"	FANIE E.	DAU	W	F	Aug 1896	3	S				KY	KY	KY													
	"	NANCY	Mother	W	F	May 1822	78	Wd		1	1	KY	VA	TN							✓	✓	✓				
		WAX, FLORA	Neice	W	F	Jul 1891	8	S				KY	TN	KY							✓	✓	✓				
233	234	DOWNING, WILLIAM B.	HEAD	W	M	Feb 1853	47	M	24			KY	KY	KY				FARMER			✓	✓	✓	O	F	F	205
	"	BASSIE	WIFE	W	F	Oct 1857	42	M	24	9	9	TN	TN	TN							✓	✓	✓				
	"	ELIZZA C.	DAU	W	F	Apr 1879	21	S				KY	KY	TN							✓	✓	✓				
	"	ALVA H.	SON	W	M	Sep 1881	18	S				KY	KY	TN				FARM LABOR		4	✓	✓	✓				
	"	WILLIAM C.	SON	W	M	Nov 1883	16	S				KY	KY	TN						4	✓	✓	✓				
	"	DEWITT T.	SON	W	M	Apr 1886	14	S				KY	KY	TN						4	✓	✓	✓				
	"	DARTHULIA K.	DAU	W	F	Oct 1888	11	S				KY	KY	TN						4	✓	✓	✓				
	"	BENJAMIN E	SON	W	M	Oct 1891	8	S				KY	KY	TN						5	✓	✓	✓				
	"	VICTOR L.	SON	W	M	Dec 1894	5	S				KY	KY	TN													
	"	FRED —	SON	W	M	Dec 1897	2	S				KY	KY	TN													
234	235	BROCKET, ADLINE	HEAD	W	F	Aug 1823	76	Wd				TN	VA	VA							✓	✓	✓		H		
235	236	ORR, RICHARD	HEAD	W	M	Apr 1872	28	M	3			KY	VA	VA						4	X	X	✓	R		F	206
	"	MATILDA J.	wife	W	F	Aug 1868	31	M	3			KY	KY	TN							✓	✓	✓				

TWELFTH CENSUS OF THE UNITED STATES 1900

STATE - KENTUCKY
COUNTY - MONROE
Township or other division

TURNER — 115 —   ABIJAH STRICKLER
Enumerator

No. of Family	No. of Dwelling	NAME	Relation	Color	Sex	DATE OF BIRTH Mon/Yr	Age at last birthday	Marital Status	# Years married	Mother of how many children?	# of these children living	Place of birth [this person]	Father of this person	Mother of this person	Year of immigr.	# years in U.S.	Naturalization	OCCUPATION 10 years +	Months not employed	Attended school in months	Can read	Can write	Speak English	Owned or Rent	Owned -no mortgage	Farm or house	# of farm schedule
236	237	MURPHEY JOHN	HEAD	W	M	Aug 1844	55	Wd				KY	NC	VA							✓	✓	✓	O		F	207
237	238	ISENBERG, WILLIAM	HEAD	W	M	May 1875	25	S				KY	TN	KY				FARMER			✓	✓	✓	R		F	208
		" SHERMAN	BROTHER	W	M	Mar 1879	21	S				KY	TN	KY							✓	✓	✓				
		" NUANIE F.	SISTER	W	F	Nov 1881	18	S				KY	TN	KY							✓	✓	✓				
		GERALD, JAMES A.	BRO-IN-LAW	W	M	Jan 1873	37	M	2			KY	TN	TN							✓	✓	✓				
		" CLARIA B.	SISTER	W	F	Feb 1870	30	M	2	1	1	KY	TN	KY							✓	✓	✓				
		" HALLEY	NEICE	W	F	Mar 1899	1	S				KY	KY	KY													
		TURNER, LAURA B.	LODGER	W	F	Apr 1886	14	S				KY	KY	KY				AT SCHOOL		5	✓	✓	✓				
238	239	KELCER, ABE	HEAD	B	M	Apr 1870	30	M	10			KY	KY	KY							X	X	✓	R		H	
		" ELLON	Wife	B	F	Mar 1869	31	M	10	6	5	KY	KY	KY													
		" MERTY B.	DAU	B	F	Aug 1890	9	S				KY	KY	KY													
		" WORTHY M.	DAU	B	F	Jul 1893	6	S				KY	KY	KY													
		" DOW(?) E.	DAU	B	F	May 1896	4	S				KY	KY	KY													
		" BESSIE M.	DAU	B	F	Apr 1897	3	S				KY	KY	KY													
		" HETTY D.	DAU	B	F	Mar 1899	1	S				KY	KY	KY													
		MARTAIN, MAHALIE	SIS-IN-LAW	B	F	May 1874	26	M				KY	KY	KY							✓	✓	✓				
239	240	STEWART, JAMES E.	HEAD	W	M	Mar 1861	39	M	17			KY	VA	KY							✓	✓	✓	O		F	209
		" MALINDA	WIFE	W	F	Feb 1862	38	M	17	12	9	KY	VA	KY							✓	✓	✓				
		" EFFA J.	DAU	W	F	Oct 1883	16	S				KY	KY	KY				AT SCHOOL		5	✓	✓	✓				
		" OLIE K.	DAU	W	F	May 1885	15	S				KY	KY	KY						3	✓	✓	✓				
		" ODOUS O.	SON	W	M	Dec 1886	13	S				KY	KY	KY						4	✓	X	✓				
		" NELLIE G.	DAU	W	F	Jun 1888	11	S				KY	KY	KY				FARM LABOR		5	✓	✓	✓				
		" JAMES T.	SON	W	M	Oct 1889	10	S				KY	KY	KY				AT SCHOOL		3	✓	X	✓				
		" MALLIE M.	DAU	W	F	Feb 1892	8	S				KY	KY	KY						5	✓	X	✓				
		" JOHNEY B.	DAU?	W	M?	Oct 1893	6	S				KY	KY	KY													
		" PAUL	SON	W	M	Oct 1898	1	S				KY	KY	KY													

STATE - KENTUCKY
COUNTY - MONROE
Township or other division   TURNER -116-   Enumerator ABIJAH STRICKLER

Supervisor's Dist. No. _102_ Sheet No. _____
Enumeration Dist. No. _81_ _____

No. of Family	No. of Dwelling	NAME	Relation	Color	Sex	DATE OF BIRTH Mon/Yr	Age at last birthday	Marital Status	# Years married	Mother of how many children?	# of these children living	Place of birth [this person]	Father of this person	Mother of this person	Year of immigr.	# years in U.S.	Naturalization	OCCUPATION 10 years +	Months not employed	Attended school in months	Can read	Can write	Speak English	Owned or Rent	Owned -no mortage	Farm or house	# of farm schedule
		STEWART, ISAAC H.	Son	W	M	May 1900	1/12	S				KY	KY	KY													
239	241	KIRBY, ARENIA	Head	W	F	Dec 1844	55	Wd	14	11		KY	KY	KY				FARMER		X	X	✓		O	F	F	210
		" ADIE I.	Dau	W	F	May 1879	21	S				KY	TN	KY						✓	✓	✓					
		" WILLIAM C.	Son	W	M	Aug 1880	19	S				KY	TN	KY				FARM LABOR		✓	✓	✓					
		" THEAD O.	Son	W	M	Aug 1883	16	S				KY	TN	KY				FARM LABOR		4	✓	✓					
		" LUCY A.	Dau	W	F	May 1886	14	S				KY	TN	KY						4	✓	✓	✓				
		JENKINS, NANCY	Dau	W	F	Aug 1874	25	Wd				KY	TN	KY						✓	✓	✓					
		" WALTER	Gr-Son	W	M	Feb 1897	3	S				KY	KY	KY													
240	242	ARTERBURN, SAMUEL P.	Head	W	M	Oct 1845	54	M	35			KY	VA	TN				FARMER		✓	✓	✓		O	F	F	211
		" FRANCIS N.	Wife	W	F	Dec 1849	50	M	35	7	6	KY	VA	KY						X	X	✓					
		" JAZZA B.	Dau	W	F	Apr 1874	26	Wd				KY	KY	KY						✓	✓	✓					
		" GUSTA O.	Dau	W	F	Dec 1882	17	S				KY	KY	KY				AT SCHOOL		4	✓	✓	✓				
		" NELLIE G.	Dau	W	F	Sep 1884	15	S				KY	KY	KY				AT SCHOOL		5	✓	✓	✓				
		McCUE, LAURIA	Dau	W	F	Aug 1870	29	Wd				KY	KY	KY						✓	✓	✓					
		" WILLIAM S.	(GR-T) Son	W	M	Sep 1898	1	S				KY	KY	KY													
241	243	SIMMONS, JOHN S.	Head	W	M	Mar 1856	50	M	2			KY	KY	KY				DAY LABOR		X	X	✓		R		H	
		" ELIZZA	Wife	W	F	Dec 1878	21	M	2	1	1	KY	VA	VA						X	X	✓					
		" MAUD C.	Dau	W	F	Sep 1885	14	S				KY	KY	KY				FARM LABOR		5	✓	✓	✓				
		" PERL E.	Dau	W	F	Oct 1888	11	S				KY	KY	KY				FARM LABOR		3	✓	✓	✓				
		" ROBERT G.	Son	W	M	Apr 1900	1/12	S				KY	KY	KY													
242	244	JOHNSON, JEMIEMA	Head	W	F	Dec 1834	65	Wd				KY	NC	KY				FARMER		✓	✓	✓		O	F	F	212
		" JOHNSON (?)	Son	W	M	Aug 1863	36	M	6			KY	TN	KY				FARMER		✓	✓	✓					
		" JOSEY	Dau-in-Law	W	F	Jun 1872	27	M	6	2	2	KY	KY	KY						✓	✓	✓					
		" VERNA A.	Gr-Dau	W	F	Nov 1894	5	S				KY	KY	KY													
		" ROBERT L.	Gr-Son	W	M	May 1899	1	S				KY	KY	KY													
243	245	PARE, FRANCES M.	Head	W	M	Oct 1844	55	M	31			KY	NC	KY				FARMER		✓	✓	✓		O	F	F	213

STATE - KENTUCKY
COUNTY - MONROE   TURNER   -117-   ABIJAH STRICKLER
Township or other division   Enumerator

Supervisor's Dist. No. 102 Sheet No.
Enumeration Dist. No. 81

No. of Family	No. of Dwelling	NAME	Relation	Color	Sex	DATE OF BIRTH Mon/Yr	Age at last birthday	Marital Status	# Years married	Mother of how many children?	# of these children living	Place of birth [this person]	Father of this person	Mother of this person	Year of immigr.	# years in U.S.	Naturalization	OCCUPATION 10 years +	Months not employed	Attended school in months	Can read	Can write	Speak English	Owned or Rent	Owned -no mortage	Farm or house	# of farm schedule	
		PARE, NANCY E.	Wife	W	F	Mar 1854	46	M	31	7	7	KY	KY	KY							✓	✓	✓					
		" MARY L.	Dau	W	F	Jan 1872	28	S				KY	KY	KY							✓	✓	✓					
		" JAMES H.	Son	W	M	Apr 1874	26	S				KY	KY	KY				FARM LABOR			✓	✓	✓					
		" JOHN T.	Son	W	M	Nov 1883	16	S				KY	KY	KY				FARM LABOR		3	✓	✓	✓					
		" HERBERT	Son	W	M	Dec 1889	10	S				KY	KY	KY				FARM LABOR		3	✓	✓	✓					
		MORROW, ELLER B.	Dau	W	F	Jul 1876	23	Wd				KY	KY	KY							✓	✓	✓					
		JOHNSON, CLATON	Dau	W	F	Nov 1878	21	Wd				KY	KY	KY							✓	✓	✓					
244	246	JOHNSON, JOHN N.	Head	W	M	Aug 1853	46	M	24			TN	KY	KY				FARMER			✓	✓	✓	O	F	F	214	
		" MARGRET A.	Wife	W	F	Aug 1856	43	M	24	6	4	KY	KY	KY							✓	✓	✓					
		" JAMES P.	Son	W	M	Feb 1882	18	S				KY	TN	KY				FARM LABOR			✓	✓	✓					
		" HUSHEL	Son	W	M	Sep 1883	16	S				KY	TN	KY				FARM LABOR		5	✓	✓	✓					
		" OLIE	Dau	W	F	Apr 1889	11	S				KY	TN	KY				AT SCHOOL		5	✓	✓	✓					
		" DELLIE M.	Dau	W	F	Aug 1891	8	S				KY	TN	KY						5	✓	✓						
		" EARSKIN	Son	W	M	May 1894	6	S				KY	TN	KY						5	✓	X	✓					
		" WINCEN B	Son	W	M	Jan 1896	4	S				KY	TN	KY														
245	247	SAMPSON, STEAVE	Head	W	M	Aug 1850	49	M	26			TN	TN	TN				FARMER			✓	✓	✓	O	F	F	215	
		" ANJA J.	Wife	W	F	Feb 1857	43	M	26	6	6	KY	KY	VA							✓	✓	✓					
		" TEVIE J.	Son	W	M	May 1894	6	S				KY	TN	KY														
		" JUDY M.	Dau	W	F	Feb 1897	3	S				KY	TN	KY														
	248	SAMPSON, WILLIAM	Head	W	M	May 1877	23	M				KY	TN	KY				FARMER			✓	✓	✓	R		F	216	
		" BERTY F	Wife	W	F	Mar 1881	19	M				KY	KY	KY							✓	✓	✓					
246	249	WARD, JOHN	Head	W	M	Feb 1848	52	M	8			TN	TN	TN				FARMER			✓	✓	✓	O	F	F	217	
		" SUSAN A	Wife	W	F	Aug 1860	39	M	8			KY	KY	KY							✓	✓	✓					
		" MARY V.	Dau	W	F	Jul 1885	14	S				KY	TN	KY				FARMER		2	✓	✓	✓					
		" EDGAR L.	Son	W	M	Nov 1894	5	S				KY	TN	KY														
		" ORA E.	Dau	W	F	Aug 1896	3	S				KY	TN	KY														

STATE - KENTUCKY
COUNTY - MONROE
Township or other division — TURNER — -118-

Enumerator ABIJAH STRICKLER

Supervisor's Dist. No. 102 Sheet No.
Enumeration Dist. No. 81

No. of Family	No. of Dwelling	NAME	Relation	Color	Sex	DATE OF BIRTH Mon/Yr	Age at last birthday	Marital Status	# Years married	Mother of how many children?	# of these children living	NATIVITY Place of birth [this person]	Father of this person	Mother of this person	CITIZENSHIP Year of immigr.	# years in U.S.	Naturalization	OCCUPATION 10 years +	Months not employed	EDUCATION Attended school in month	Can read	Can write	Speak English	OWNERSHIP Owned or Rent	Owned -no mortgage	Farm or house	# of Farm schedule
		WARD, ADER D.	Son	W	M	Aug 1899	9/12	S				KY	TN	KY									✓				
		" SHERMAN	Lodger	W	M	May 1885	15	S				KY	KY	KY				FARMER		X	X	✓				
247	250	JOHNSON, JAMES M.	Head	W	M	Dec 1833	66	M	30			TN	TN	TN				FARMER	12			✓				
		" SUSAN	Wife	W	F	Mar 1829	71	M	30	6	4	TN	NC	VA							X	X	✓				
248	251	TAYLOR, CATHERINE	Head	W	F	Feb 1855	45	Wd				KY	TN	TN							X	X	✓	O	F	F	218
		" OVA L.	Dau	W	F	May 1895	5	S				KY	KY	KY							✓	✓	✓				
		JACKSON, SARAH B.	Dau	W	F	Sep 1882	17	M				KY	KY	KY							✓	✓	✓				
249	252	JONES, CHIN(?) M.	Head	W	M	Aug 1867	32	M	12			KY	TN	TN				FIREMAN		X	X	✓	R		F	219
		" AMERICA	Wife	W	F	Apr 1868	32	M	12	5	4	TN	TN	TN							✓	✓	✓				
		" TAFIE R.	Son	W	M	Sep 1887	12	S				KY	KY	TN							✓	✓	✓				
		" EZRA R.	Son	W	M	Jul 1894	5	S				KY	KY	TN													
		" TRUDY E.	Dau	W	F	Oct 1896	3	S				KY	KY	TN													
		" GEORGE H.	Son	W	M	Apr 1899	1	S				KY	KY	TN													
		TAYLOR, LUKE	Lodger	W	M	Dec 1877	22	S				TN	TN	KY				FARM LABOR		X	X	✓				
250	253	JONES, JAMES M.	Head	W	M	May 1849	51	M	20			TN	TN	TN				FARMER		X	X	✓	R		F	220
		" LIDDY A.	Wife	W	F	Nov 1849	50	M	20			KY	VA	TN							✓	✓	✓				
251	254	GOSNELL, WILLIAM	Head	W	M	Oct 1861	38	M				KY	KY	KY				FARMER		✓	✓	✓	O	F	F	221
		" CORA	Wife	W	F	Jan 1875	25	M				KY	KY	KY							✓	✓	✓				
252	255	GOSNELL, THOMAS G.	Head	W	M	Dec 1835	64	M	42			KY	KY	KY				FARMER		✓	✓	✓	O	F	F	222
		" NANCY J.	Wife	W	F	Dec 1840	59	M	42	9	7	KY	KY	KY							X	X	✓				
		" JUDIA	Dau	W	F	Aug 1874	25	S				KY	KY	KY							✓	✓	✓				
		" JAMES	Son	W	M	Apr 1880	20	S				KY	KY	KY				FARM LABOR		✓	✓	✓				
		WHITEHEAD, AREBELL	Dau	W	F	Apr 1872	28	Wd		1	1	KY	KY	KY							✓	✓	✓				
		" HENRY E.	GrSon	W	M	Aug 1898	1	S				KY	KY	KY													
253	256	LARANCE, HURON	Head	W	M	Oct 1871	28	M				KY	TN	KY				SAWYER		✓	✓	✓			H	
		" MILLIE	Wife	W	F	Feb 1878	22	M				KY	KY	KY							✓	✓	✓				

STATE - KENTUCKY
COUNTY - MONROE
Township or other division   TURNER   -119-   Enumerator ABIJAH STRICKLER

Supervisor's Dist. No. 10 r Sheet No.
Enumeration Dist. No. 81

No. of Family	No. of Dwelling	NAME	Relation	Color	Sex	DATE OF BIRTH Mon/Yr	Age at last birthday	Marital Status	# Years married	Mother of how many children?	# of these children living	Place of birth [this person]	Father of this person	Mother of this person	Year of immigr.	# years in U.S.	Naturalization	OCCUPATION 10 years +	Months not employed	Attended school in months	Can read	Can write	Speak English	Owned or Rent	Owned -no mortgage	Farm or house	# of farm schedule
254	257	QUINN, WILLIAM J.	Head	W	M	AUG 1837	62	M	33			KY	KY	KY				FARMER			✓	✓	✓	O		F	223
		" FRANCES C.	Wife	W	F	JAN 1840	60	M	33	2	2	KY	NC	NC							✓	✓	✓				
255	258	SAMPSON, LESLIE	Head	W	M	OCT 1875	24	M	3			KY	TN	KY				FARMER			✓	✓	✓	R		F	224
		" GERZELLER	Wife	W	F	OCT 1880	19	M	3			KY	KY	KY							✓	✓	✓				
256	259	BELCHER, MARGARET	Head	W	F	Feb 1828	72	Wd		12	5	KY	TN	VA							X	X	✓	O		F	225
		RIGS, EDWARD	Gr Son	W	M	JAN 1881	19	S				KY	KY	KY				DAY LABOR			X	X	✓				
257	260	FAWBUSH, WILLIAM J	Head	W	M	AUG 1867	32	M	11			KY	TN	TN				FARMER			✓	✓	✓	R		F	226
		" SARAH	Wife	W	F	MAY 1867	33	M	11	2	2	KY	KY	KY							✓	✓	✓				
		" WILLIAM W.	Son	W	M	MAY 1891	10	S				KY	KY	KY				FARM LABOR		3	X	X	✓				
		" ALFORD, P.	Son	W	M	FEB 1892	8	S				KY	KY	KY													
258	261	FULTS, HASCAL J.	Head	W	M	MAR 1877	23	M	4			KY	KY	KY				FARMER			✓	✓	✓	O		F	227
		" MANEBVA	Wife	W	F	FEB 1882	18	M	4	2	2	TN	TN	TN							X	X	✓				
		" CANCEL	Son	W	M	JUN 1898	2	S				KY	KY	TN													
		" DANNEY	Dau	W	F	AUG 1899	9/12	S				KY	KY	TN													
		KNIGHT, ANDREW J	Lodger	W	M	APR 1882	18	S				TN	TN	TN							✓	✓	✓				
259	262	JENKINS, CAREL P.	Head	W	M	Feb 1878	22	M	2			TN	TN	TN							✓	✓	✓	R		H	
		" DAISY E.	Wife	W	F	MAR 1882	18	M	2			TN	TN	TN							✓	✓	✓				
260	263	BACON, LOUISA	Head	W	F	JAN 1839	61	Wd		4	3	IN	IN	IN							✓	✓	✓	O		F	228
	264	SHIRLEY, THOMAS B.	Head	W	M	APR 1864	36	S				KY	KY	TN				FARMER			✓	✓	✓	O		F	229
		NANY, ELIE H.	Lodger	W	M	MAY 1855	45	M				KY	TN	IN				FARM LABOR			X	X	✓				
		JACKSON, ELIZZA	Servant	W	F	JUL 1868	31	S				KY	KY	KY				HOUSEKEEPER			✓	✓	✓				
		" FRANK	Son	W	M	MAR 1891	9	S				KY	-	KY													
261	265	MARTAIN, WILLIAM H.	Head	B	M	OCT 1872	27	M	9			KY	KY	KY				O.F.F. BARER (?)			✓	✓	✓	R		H	
		" ELIZZA	Wife	B	F	FEB 1871	29	M	9	5	5	KY	KY	KY													
		" WILLIAM	Son	B	M	JUN 1890	9	S				KY	KY	KY			5										
		" ELLER	Dau	B	F	FEB 1892	8	S				KY	KY	KY			5										

STATE - KENTUCKY
COUNTY - MONROE
Township or other division: TURNER — 120 —

Enumerator: ABIJAH STRICKLER

Supervisor's Dist. No. 102   Sheet No.
Enumeration Dist. No. 81

No. of Family	No. of Dwelling	NAME	Relation	Color	Sex	DATE OF BIRTH Mon/Yr	Age at last birthday	Marital Status	# Years married	Mother of how many children?	# of these children living	Place of birth [this person]	Father of this person	Mother of this person	Year of immigr.	# years in U.S.	Naturalization	OCCUPATION 10 years +	Months not employed	Attended school in months	Can read	Can write	Speak English	Owned or Rent	Owned -no mortage	Farm or house	# of farm schedule	
		MARTAIN, AUTHER	Son	B	M	Mar 1893	7	S				KY	KY	KY														
		" ODOUS	Son	B	M	May 1897	3	S				KY	KY	KY														
		" PONTOUS	Son	B	M	Oct 1899 8/12		S				KY	KY	KY														
262	266	CARTER, JESSEY T.	Head	W	M	Oct 1859	40	M	18			KY	TN	TN				FARMER			✓	✓		O		F	230	
		" IBBIE T	Wife	W	F	Oct 1858	41	M	18	4	4	KY	KY	KY								✓	✓						
		" HAD H.T.	Son	W	M	Jan 1882	18	S				KY	KY	KY				FARM LABOR		5	✓	✓						
		" ELIGA C.	Son	W	M	May 1890	10	S				KY	KY	KY				FARM LABOR		5								
		" MARY B	Dau	W	F	Jul 1892	7	S				KY	KY	KY				AT SCHOOL		5								
		" LIOSA T.	Dau	W	F	Aug 1894	5	S				KY	KY	KY														
		BOLES, ELIGA	Father in law	W	M	Jan 1846	56	M	44			KY	KY	KY				FARMER	12									
263	267	WILLIAMS, MOSS	Head	W	M	Nov 1875	24	M				KY	KY	KY							✓	✓		R		H		
		" PERNIA	Wife	W	F	Apr 1880	20	M				KY	KY	KY							✓	✓						
264	268	BOLES, CLIFF	Head	W	M	Jul 1877	22	M				KY	KY	KY				FARMER			✓	✓				F		
		" JINIE	Wife	W	F	Feb 1879	21	M				KY	KY	KY							✓	✓						
265	269	BOWLS, HESSIA	Head	W	M	Apr 1875	25	S				KY	KY	KY				FARMER			✓	✓		R		F		
		" EMMALINE	Mother	W	F	Aug 1837	62	M	44	8	6	KY	KY	KY							✓	✓						
266	270	KIRKPATRIC, MATILDA	Head	B	F	May 1837	63	Wd		10	1	KY	KY	KY				DAY LABOR			X	X	X(?)	O		H		
267	271	CLARKSON, REUBEN	Head	W	M	Feb 1838	62	M	13			KY	VA	VA				FARMER			✓	✓		O	F	F	231	
		" LIDDY A.	Wife	W	F	Oct 1842	57	M	13			KY	VA	VA							✓	✓						
268	272	TURNER, J.D.	Head	W	M	Mar 1870	30	M	9			KY	KY	KY				FARMER			✓	✓		R		F	232	
		" MARY E.	Wife	W	F	Apr 1876	24	M	9	6	5	KY	KY	KY							✓	✓						
		" MERTY B.	Dau	W	F	Jan 1893	7	S				KY	KY	KY				AT SCHOOL		2	X	X	✓					
		" LULAR M.	Dau	W	F	Sep 1894	5	S				KY	KY	KY														
		" CHARLEY J.	Son	W	M	Feb 1896	4	S				KY	KY	KY														
		" GRACY C.	Dau	W	F	Feb 1898	2	S				KY	KY	KY														
		" HUSHEL B.	Son	W	M	Oct 1899 7/12		S				KY	KY	KY														

STATE - KENTUCKY
COUNTY - MONROE
Township or other division

TURNER — 121 — ABIJAH STRICKLER

Enumerator

Supervisor's Dist. No. 102 Sheet No.
Enumeration Dist. No. 81

Location		NAME	Relation	Color	Sex	DATE OF BIRTH Mon/Yr	Age at last birthday	Marital Status	# Years married	Mother of how many children?	# of these children living	NATIVITY Place of birth [this person]	Father of this person	Mother of this person	CITIZENSHIP Year of immigr.	# years in U.S.	Naturalization	OCCUPATION 10 years +	Months not employed	EDUCATION Attended school in month	Can read	Can write	Speak English	OWNERSHIP Owned or Rent	Owned -no mortage	Farm or house	# of farm schedule	
No. of Family	No. of Dwelling																											
269	273	SIMMONS, JOEL E.	HEAD	W	M	AUG 1860	39	M	17			KY	TN	KY				FARMER			✓	✓	✓	R		F	233	
		" LEONIA	WIFE	W	F	OCT 1861	38	M	17	6	5	KY	KY	KY							✓	✓	✓					
		" OMA	DAU	W	F	JUN 1883	16	S				KY	KY	KY						3	✓	✓	✓					
		" JAMES W.	SON	W	M	MAR 1887	13	S				KY	KY	KY						3	✓	✓	✓					
		" GEORGE P.	SON	W	M	OCT 1893	6	S				KY	KY	KY														
		" CALEY D.	DAU	W	F	SEP 1896	3	S				KY	KY	KY														
270	274	GOODALL, LODOWICK T.	HEAD	W	M	JUL 1826	73	M	19			KY	VA	TN				FARMER			✓	✓	✓	O		F	234	
		" REBECKY J.	WIFE	W	F	APR 1854	46	M	19	2	2	TN	VA	TN							✓	✓	✓					
		" EDGER C.	SON	W	M	JAN 1877	23	S				KY	KY	KY				FARM LABOR			✓	✓	✓					
		" LODOWICK T.	SON	W	M	JUL 1881	18	S				KY	KY	TN				FARM LABOR		2	✓	✓	✓					
		" CERENIA B.	DAU	W	F	MAR 1889	11	S				KY	KY	TN				AT SCHOOL		4	✓	✓	✓					
271	275	KELSO, JOHN	HEAD	B	M	MAR 1866	34	M	6			TN	TN	TN				FARMER			X	X	✓	R		F	235	
		" LENAR H.H.	WIFE	B	F	MAY 1878	32	M	6			TN	KY	KY							✓	✓	✓					
		MARY S.	DAU	B	F	JAN 1886	14	S				KY	TN	TN							✓	✓	✓					
		McMILLEN, HENRY	LODGER	B	M	MAY 1868	32	M				KY	KY	KY				DAY LABOR			X	X	✓					
		NEAL, SALLY	MOTHER	B	F	MAR 1835	65	Wd		5	3	KY	KY	KY							X	X	✓					
272	276	ISENBERG, JAMES S.	HEAD	W	M	JUL 1847	52	M	18			KY	TN	VA				FARMER			X	X	✓	O		F	236	
		" MARY M.	WIFE	W	F	APR 1846	54	M	18			IN	VA	TN							X	X	✓					
273	277	AGERS, JAMES	HEAD	W	M	DEC 1840	59	M	35			TN	TN	TN				FARMER			X	X	✓	O		F	237	
		" SARAH E.	WIFE	W	F	MAR 1842	58	M	35	8	7	KY	VA	VA							X	X	✓					
		" MOSES S.	SON	W	M	APR 1885	15	S				KY	TN	KY				AT SCHOOL		5	✓	✓	✓					
		BROWN, SANFORD N.	LODGER	W	M	AUG 1876	23	S				KY	KY	TN				FARMER			✓	X	✓					
274	278	PROFFITT, WILLIAM J.	HEAD	W	M	SEP 1855	44	M	18			KY	TN	TN				FARMER			✓	✓	✓	O		F	238	
		" FRANCES T.	WIFE	W	F	JUN 1860	39	M	18	9	6	KY	VA	VA							✓	✓	✓					
		" BASCUM C.	SON	W	M	FEB 1888	12	S				KY	KY	KY				AT SCHOOL		5	✓	✓	✓					
		" ALTIA P.	DAU	W	F	DEC 1890	9	S				KY	KY	KY				AT SCHOOL		5	✓	✓	✓					

STATE - KENTUCKY
COUNTY - MONROE
Township or other division

TURNER -122-

Enumerator ABIJAH STRICKLER

Supervisor's Dist. No. 10 2 Sheet No.
Enumeration Dist. No. 8l

No. of Family	No. of Dwelling	NAME	Relation	Color	Sex	DATE OF BIRTH Mon/Yr	Age at last birthday	Marital Status	# Years married	Mother of how many children?	# of these children living	Place of birth [this person]	Father of this person	Mother of this person	Year of immigr. / # years in U.S. / Naturalization	OCCUPATION 10 years +	Months not employed	Attended school in months	Can read	Can write	Speak English	Owned or Rent	Owned -no mortgage	Farm or house	# of farm schedule
		PROFFITT, HILLIS D.	Son	W	M	Jan 1894	6	S				KY	KY	KY		AT SCHOOL		5	✓	✓					
		" MAMIA A.	Dau	W	F	Feb 1896	4	S				KY	KY	KY											
		" EDDIE O.	Son	W	M	Mar 1898	2	S				KY	KY	KY											
		" MALLIE L.	Dau	W	F	Feb 1900	3/12	S				KY	KY	KY											
275	279	SIMMONS, NARCIS	Head	W	F	Sep 1838	61	M	38	7	4	IL	KY	KY		KEEPING BOARDERS			✓	✓		O	F F	239	
		OGDON, ULIE J.	Lodger	W	F	Jul 1890	9	S				KY	KY	TN											
276	280	KIRBY, ELIXANDER R.	Head	W	M	May 1868	32	S				KY	TN	KY		FARMER			✓	✓		O	F F	240	
		" ELIZZA B	Mother	W	F	Jul 1846	52	M		1	1	TN	TN	VA					✓	✓					
		" FRANCES	G-Mother	W	F	Jul 1821	78	Wd		9	4	KY	NC	NC					X	X	✓				
277	281	KIRBY, JAMES R.	Head	W	M	Dec 1875	24	M	3			KY	TN	KY		FARMER	4		✓	✓		R	F	241	
		" CORA S.	Wife	W	F	Nov 1875	24	M	3	2	2	KY	TN	TN					✓	✓					
		" LEO H.	Son	W	M	Oct 1897	2	S				KY	KY	KY											
		" INA N.	Dau	W	F	Dec 1899	5/12	S				KY	KY	KY											
278	282	JACKSON, JAMES M.	Head	W	M	Nov 1852	47	M	23			TN	TN	TN		LAWYER			✓	✓		O	M F	242	
		" SINAH C.	Wife	W	F	Jul 1860	39	M	23			KY	KY	KY					✓	✓					
		" LUCY M.	Dau	W	F	May 1893	7	S				KY	TN	KY				3	✓	X	✓				
		BRANDON, MARY C.	S-in-Law	W	F	Feb 1852	48	S				KY	KY	KY					✓	✓					
279	283	YONG, CYRUS H.	Head	W	M	Apr 1848	52	M	7			TN	VA	TN		PHYSICIAN			✓	✓	✓	O	F	243	
		" SUSAN B.	Wife	W	F	May 1873	27	M	7	1		KY	KY	KY					✓	✓					
		" JAMES M.	Son	W	M	Aug 1880	18	S				KY	TN	KY		CLERK- DRY GOODS			✓	✓	✓				
		THOMASON, LILLIE		W	F	Oct 1878	21	S				KY	KY	KY					✓	✓	✓				
280	284	SIMMONS, ARTHUR B	Head	W	M	Aug 1863	36	M	15			KY	TN	IL		FARMER			✓	✓		O	F F	244	
		" MARILDA	Wife	W	F	Sept 1866	33	M	15	6	5	KY	KY	KY					✓	✓					
		" CLIFTON	Son	W	M	Jan 1886	14	S				KY	KY	KY		FARM LABOR		3	✓	✓	✓				
		" EARNEST	Son	W	M	Jan 1888	12	S				KY	KY	KY		FARM LABOR		3	✓	✓	✓				
		" DANNY	Dau	W	F	Nov 1889	10	S				KY	KY	KY				3	✓	✓	✓				

STATE - KENTUCKY
COUNTY - MONROE
Township or other division

TURNER — 123 —

Enumerator ABIJAH STRICKLER

Supervisor's Dist. No. 102 Sheet No.
Enumeration Dist. No. 81

No. of Family	No. of Dwelling	NAME	Relation	Color	Sex	DATE OF BIRTH Mon/Yr	Age at last birthday	Marital Status	# Years married	Mother of how many children?	# of these children living	Place of birth [this person]	Father of this person	Mother of this person	Year of immigr.	# years in U.S.	Naturalization	OCCUPATION 10 years +	Months not employed	Attended school in months	Can read	Can write	Speak English	Owned or Rent	Owned -no mortgage	Farm or house	# of farm schedule
		SIMMONS, NACE	Son	W	M	Jul 1896	3	S				KY	KY	KY													
		" HARLIN	Son	W	M	Apr 1899	1	S				KY	KY	KY													
		" JOHN W.	Father	W	M	May 1836	64	M	38			TN	TN	TN				FARMER	10		✓	✓	✓				
281	285	CREEK, JAMES B.	Head	W	M	Jan 1842	58	M	28			KY	KY	KY				FARMER			✓	✓	✓	R		F	245
		" SUSAN	Wife	W	F	Sep 1851	48	M	28	10	5	KY	VA	VA						5	X	X	✓				
		" JOHN M.	Son	W	M	Mar 1876	24	S				KY	KY	KY				DAY LABOR			✓	✓	✓				
		" ROBBERT C.	Son	W	M	Sep 1885	14	S				KY	KY	KY				FARM LABOR			X	X	✓				
282	286	LOYD, ANDREW J.	Head	W	M	May 1864	36	M	9			KY	KY	TN				FARMER			X	X	✓	O	F	F	246
		" MARGRET E.	Wife	W	F	Jan 1874	26	M	9	4	4	KY	KY	KY							X	X	✓				
		" MAGGA A.	Dau	W	F	Nov 1893	6	S				KY	KY	KY													
		" LEVEIA	Son	W	M	Jun 1894	5	S				KY	KY	KY													
		" HUEY V.	Son	W	M	Nov 1896	3	S				KY	KY	KY													
		" IDA	Dau	W	F	Aug 1899	7/12	S				KY	KY	KY													
283	287	DOWNING, JOHN M.	Head	W	M	Jul 1861	38	M	17			KY	KY	KY				FARMER			✓	✓	✓	O	F	F	247
		" MINIE A.	Wife	W	F	Sep 1861	38	M	17	7	7	KY	KY	KY							✓	✓	✓				
		" WILLIAM E.	Son	W	M	Oct 1883	16	S				KY	KY	KY				FARM LABOR		4	✓	✓	✓				
		" ORESTA B.	Son	W	M	Jan 1886	14	S				KY	KY	KY				FARM LABOR		4	✓	✓	✓				
		" NORA M.	Dau	W	F	Mar 1888	12	S				KY	KY	KY				A.T. SCHOOL		4	✓	✓	✓				
		" LESTER W.	Son	W	M	Jan 1890	10	S				KY	KY	KY				FARM LABOR		4	✓	✓	✓				
		" HETTIE C.	Dau	W	F	Mar 1892	8	S				KY	KY	KY						4	✓	✓	✓				
		" ELLAR P.	Dau	W	F	Feb 1894	6	S				KY	KY	KY													
		" ALVIS C.	Son	W	M	Jul 1898	1	S				KY	KY	KY													
284	288	EMBERTON, SAMIEL	Head	W	M	Nov 1866	33	M	12			KY	KY	KY				FARMER			X	X	✓	R		F	248
		" MARY E.	Wife	W	F	Feb 1867	33	M	12			KY	KY	KY							✓	✓	✓				
285	289	HOOD, WILLIAM T.	Head	W	M	Aug 1871	28	M	3			KY	KY	KY				FARMER			✓	✓	✓	O	F	F	249
		" LOCKY J.	Wife	W	F	Dec 1877	22	M	3	1	1	KY	KY	KY							✓	✓	✓				

STATE - KENTUCKY
COUNTY - MONROE
Township or other division

TURNER -124-

Enumerator ABIJAH STRICKLER

Supervisor's Dist. No. 107   Sheet No.
Enumeration Dist. No. 81

Location No. of Family / No. of Dwelling	NAME	Relation	Color	Sex	DATE OF BIRTH Mon/Yr	Age at last birthday	Marital Status	# Years married	Mother of how many children?	# of these children living	Nativity: Place of birth (this person)	Father of this person	Mother of this person	Citizenship	Occupation 10 years +	Months not employed	Attended school in months	Can read	Can write	Speak English	Owned or Rent	Owned –no mortgage	Farm or house	# of farm schedule
	HOOD, VERGEL B.	Son	W	M	May 1897	3	S				KY	KY	KY											
286 290	BURKS, JAMES W.	Head	W	M	Mar 1858	42	M	22			KY	VA	TN		FARMER			✓	X	✓	R		F	250
"	ARDELLAR	Wife	W	F	May 1858	42	M	22	7	7	TN	TN	TN					✓	✓	✓				
"	LUCY E.	Dau	W	F	Sep 1881	18	S				KY	KY	TN					✓	✓	✓				
"	SARAH F.	Dau	W	F	Aug 1883	16	S				KY	KY	TN					✓	✓	✓				
"	JOHN C.	Son	W	M	Mar 1887	13	S				KY	KY	TN		FARM LABOR			✓	✓	✓				
"	HERBERT C.	Son	W	M	Sep 1890	9	S				KY	KY	TN				2	✓	X	✓				
"	EARLEY D.	Son	W	M	Aug 1893	6	S				KY	KY	TN											
"	BERTHY	Dau	W	F	Aug 1897	2	S				KY	KY	TN											
287 291	BELCHER, HENRY F.	Head	W	M	May 1844	56	M	26			KY	KY	KY		FARMER			✓	✓	✓	O	F	F	251
"	MARTHEY F.	Wife	W	F	Nov 1852	47	M	26	5	5	KY	TN	VA					✓	✓	✓				
"	ALFORD B.	Son	W	M	Apr 1878	22	S				KY	KY	KY		FARM LABOR			✓	✓	✓				
"	HULIT A.	Son	W	M	Jan 1880	20	S				KY	KY	KY		FARM LABOR									
"	GERTIE E.	Dau	W	F	Apr 1885	15	S				KY	KY	KY				5	✓						
"	WILLIAM F.	Son	W	M	Jan 1889	10	S				KY	KY	KY		FARM LABOR		5	✓	✓	✓				
"	ALLICIA D.	Dau	W	F	Oct 1890	9	S				KY	KY	KY				5							
288 292	PROFFITT, TASVIL B.	Head	W	M	Sep 1860	39	M	19			KY	KY	KY		FARMER			✓	✓	✓	R		F	252
"	JULIA F.	Wife	W	F	Aug 1864	35	M	19	10	8	KY	KY	KY					✓	✓	✓				
"	MAUD D.	Dau	W	F	Oct 1883	16	S				KY	KY	KY				5	✓	✓	✓				
"	MITIE B.	Dau	W	F	Sep 1886	13	S				KY	KY	KY		FARM LABOR		5	✓	✓	✓				
"	BURFORD P.	Son	W	M	Aug 1887	12	S				KY	KY	KY		FARM LABOR		4	✓	✓	✓				
"	ARLEY W.	Son	W	M	Jan 1890	10	S				KY	KY	KY		FARM LABOR		4	✓	✓	✓				
"	MATTIE L.	Dau	W	F	Jan 1892	8	S				KY	KY	KY				5	✓	✓	✓				
"	ORPHY E.	Dau	W	F	Jan 1895	5	S				KY	KY	KY											
"	ODOUS C.	Son	W	M	Sep 1899	8/12	S				KY	KY	KY											
289 293	PROFFITT, BERTY K.	Head	W	M	Jul 1881	18	M				KY	KY	KY					✓	✓	✓	R		F	253

TWELFTH CENSUS OF THE UNITED STATES 1900

STATE - KENTUCKY
COUNTY - MONROE
Township or other division: TURNER —125— ABIJAH STRICKLER
Enumerator

Supervisor's Dist. No. 102 Sheet No.
Enumeration Dist. No. 81

No. of Family	No. of Dwelling	NAME	Relation	Color	Sex	Date of Birth Mon/Yr	Age at last birthday	Marital Status	# Years married	Mother of how many children	# of these children living	Place of birth [this person]	Father of this person	Mother of this person	Citizenship	Occupation 10 years +	Months not employed	Attended school in months	Can read	Can write	Speak English	Owned or Rent	Owned-no mortg.	Farm or house	# of farm schedule
		PROFFITT, MINIE	wife	W	F	Jan 1884	16	M				KY	KY	KY					✓	✓	✓				
290	294	CHISEM, BENJAMIN T.	Head	W	M	Oct 1852	47	S				KY	KY	KY		FARMING			✓	✓	✓	O	F	F	254
		" SARAH T.	Mother	W	F	Jan 1825	75	Wd		12	5	KY	VA	VA						✓	✓				
		CABLE, LYTT	Lodger	W	M	Feb 1874	26	S				KY	KY	TN		FARM LABOR			✓	✓	✓				
		HOOD, HAYDEN K.	Lodger	W	M	Jul 1876	23	S				KY	KY	KY		FARM LABOR			✓	✓	✓				
		GENTRY, JOHN F.	Lodger	B	M	May 1888	12	S				KY	KY	KY		AT SCHOOL		3	✓	✓	✓				
		WEBB, JAMES J.	Boarder	W	M	Feb 1874	26	Wd				KY	KY	TN		LOG TEAMSTER			✓	✓	✓				
291	295	ENGLAND, JEFFERSON F.	Head	W	M	Dec 1869	30	M	14			KY	KY	KY		FARMER			✓	✓	✓	O	F	F	255
		" SUSAN B.	Wife	W	F	Nov 1869	30	M	14	4	4	KY	KY	KY					X	X	✓				
		" MARY D.	Dau	W	F	Oct 1887	12	S				KY	KY	KY		AT SCHOOL		5	✓	✓	✓				
		" EARLY C.	Son	W	M	Apr 1892	8	S				KY	KY	KY				5							
		" BETTY M.	Dau	W	F	May 1894	6	S				KY	KY	KY											
		" IVA L.	Dau	W	F	Mar 1896	4	S				KY	KY	KY											
292	296	THOMAS, NANCY T.	Head	W	F	Sep 1840	59	Wd		6	4	KY	KY	KY					✓	X	✓	O	F	F	256
		" ROLEN G.	Son	W	M	Aug 1870	29	S				KY	KY	KY		FARMER			✓	✓	✓				
		" EMMA G.	Dau	W	F	Sep 1876	23	S				KY	KY	KY											
		" KITTY E.	Dau	W	F	Sep 1873	26	Div.				KY	KY	KY					✓	✓	✓				
		LEE, AUTHER C.	Gr-son	W	M	Dec 1891	8	S				KY	KY	KY				5	✓	✓	✓				
293	297	WEBB, WILL T.	Head	W	M	Aug 1870	29	M	5			KY	VA	VA		FARMER			✓	✓	✓	O	F	F	257
		" DANNIE T.	Wife	W	F	Jan 1874	26	M	5	1	1	KY	KY	MISSISSIPPI					✓	✓	✓				
		" TOL T.	Son	W	M	Feb 1900	3/12	S				KY	KY	KY											
		" SUSAN	Mother	W	F	Apr 1824	76	Wd		5	2	VA	VA	VA					✓	✓	✓				
		" WILLIAM	Nephew	W	M	Aug 1885	15	S				KY	KY	KY		FARMER			✓	✓	✓				
		MYERS, JAMES R.	Lodger	W	M	Mar 1871	29	S				KY	TN	KY		FARM LABOR			✓	✓	✓				
294	298	WEBB, WILLIAM	Head	W	M	Nov 1848	51	M	30			KY	VA	VA		FARMER			✓	✓	✓	O		F	258
		" DEBORAH	Wife	W	F	Aug 1849	50	M	30	6	6	TN	TN	TN					✓	✓	✓				

STATE - KENTUCKY
COUNTY - MONROE
Township or other division: TURNER
Enumerator: ABIJAH STRICKLER

Supervisor's Dist. No. _102_ Sheet No.
Enumeration Dist. No. _81_

No. of Family	No. of Dwelling	NAME	Relation	Color	Sex	DATE OF BIRTH Mon/Yr	Age at last birthday	Marital Status	# Years married	Mother of how many children	# of these children living	Place of birth [this person]	Father of this person	Mother of this person	Year of immigr.	# years in U.S.	Naturalization	OCCUPATION 10 years +	Months not employed	Attended school in months	Can read	Can write	Speak English	Owned or Rent	Owned - no mortgage	Farm or house	# of farm schedule
		WEBB, THOMAS N.	Son	W	M	Jul 1871	28	S				KY	KY	TN				TEAMSTER			✓	✓	✓				
		" ELIZZA B. J.	Dau	W	F	Dec 1882	17	S				KY	KY	TN						8	✓	✓	✓				
		" CHARLES D.	Son	W	M	Sep 1886	13	S				KY	KY	TN						3	✓	✓	✓				
		" MARY P.	Dau	W	F	Feb 1892	8	S				KY	KY	TN						4	✓	✓					
		" EDMON	Son	W	M	Apr 1898	2	S				KY	KY	TN													
298	299	BRADSHAW, SETH	Head	W	M	Jul 1867	32	M	10			KY	KY	KY							✓	✓	✓	R		H	
		" PERNIE	Wife	W	F	Apr 1869	21	M	10	4	4	KY	KY	KY							✓	✓	✓				
		" LIETA	Dau	W	F	Jun 1890	9	S				KY	KY	KY						10							
		" WALTER L.	Son	W	M	Apr 1892	8	S				KY	KY	KY						10							
		" EVA J.	Dau	W	F	Dec 1893	6	S				KY	KY	KY													
		" MAY B.	Dau	W	F	Jul 1897	2	S				KY	KY	KY													
		BROOKS, WILLIAM J.	Boarder	W	M	Mar 1879	21	S				KY	KY	KY				SAWYER			✓	✓	✓				
286	300	JOHNSON, WILLIAM B.	Head	W	M	Jun 1844	56	M	32			KY	TN	INDIANA							✓	✓	✓	O	M	F	259
		" MARTHY E.	Wife	W	F	Dec 1843	59	M	32	8	8	KY	KY	KY							✓	✓	✓				
		" JOHN T.	Son	W	M	May 1871	29	S				KY	KY	KY				TEACHER			✓	✓	✓				
		" WILLIE F.	Son	W	M	Mar 1876	24	S				KY	KY	KY				SAWYER				✓	✓				
		" HARIETT E.	Dau	W	F	Jun 1881	19	S				KY	KY	KY						5	✓	✓	✓				
		" CLAUDY	Son	W	M	Oct 1883	16	S				KY	KY	KY				FARM LABOR		4	✓	✓	✓				
		" MAUDY	Dau	W	F	Oct 1883	16	S				KY	KY	KY						4	✓	✓	✓				
		JONES, JAMES F.	Son-in-law	W	M	Feb 1874	26	M	1			KY	NC	KY				ENGINEER			✓	✓	✓				
		" LOUISA E.	Dau	W	F	Jul 1878	21	M	1			KY	KY	KY													
287	301	SMITH, JOHN D.	Head	W	M	Apr 1847	53	M	30			KY	TN	TN				FARMER			✓	✓	✓	O	F	F	260
		" MARY T.	Wife	W	F	Jul 1850	49	M	30	7	6	KY	KY	KY							✓	✓	✓				
		" HANNER E.	Dau	W	F	Feb 1875	25	S				KY	KY	KY							✓	✓	✓				
		" JAMES T.	Son	W	M	Oct 1876	23	S				KY	KY	KY				FARMER			✓	✓	✓				
		" GEORGE W.	Son	W	M	Oct 1883	16	S				KY	KY	KY				FARM LABOR		4	✓	✓	✓				

TWELFTH CENSUS OF THE UNITED STATES 1900

STATE - KENTUCKY
COUNTY - MONROE   TURNER   —127—
Township or other division   Enumerator ABIJAH STRICKLER

Supervisor's Dist. No. _102_ Sheet No. _____
Enumeration Dist. No. _81_

No. of Family	No. of Dwelling	NAME	Relation	Color	Sex	DATE OF BIRTH Mon/Yr	Age at last birthday	Marital Status	# Years married	Mother of how many children?	# of these children living	Place of birth [this person]	Father of this person	Mother of this person	Year of immigr.	# years in U.S.	Naturalization	OCCUPATION 10 years +	Months not employed	Attended school in months	Can read	Can write	Speak English	Owned or Rent	Owned -no mortgage	Farm or house	# of farm schedule
		SMITH, BENJAMIN C.	SON	W	M	OCT 1887	12	S				KY	KY	KY				FARM LABOR		4	✓	✓	✓				
298	302	McCUE, MARTHY F.	HEAD	W	F	AUG 1852	47	Wd	11	7		KY	VA	TN				FARMER			✓	✓	✓	R		F	261
		" JOHN I.	SON	W	M	AUG 1884	15	S				KY	KY	KY				FARMER			✓	✓	✓				
		" ADER M.	DAU	W	F	NOV 1892	7	S				KY	KY	KY							✓	✓	✓				
		WISDOM, WILLIE F.	SON-IN-LAW	W	M	SEP 1874	25	M	1			KY	KY	KY				FARMER			✓	✓	✓				
		" ELIZZA B.	DAU	W	F	APR 1875	25	M	1	1	1	KY	KY	KY							✓	✓	✓				
		" LUHER C.	GR. SON	W	M	JAN 1900	4/12	S				KY	KY	KY													
299	303	PROFFITT, PLESANT W.	HEAD	W	M	NOV 1836	63	M	42			TN	TN	TN				FARMER			✓	✓	✓	O		F	262
		" SUSAN A.	WIFE	W	F	NOV 1840	59	M	42	10	9	TN	VA	VA							✓	✓	✓				
		" CLAUDUS T.	SON	W	M	JUN 1880	20	S				KY	TN	TN				FARMER			✓	✓	✓				
		" EFFIE I.	DAU	W	F	AUG 1883	16	S				KY	TN	TN							✓	✓	✓				
300	304	ISENBERG, JAMES P.	HEAD	W	M	NOV 1864	35	M	14			KY	TN	TN				BLACKSMITH			✓	✓	✓	O	M	F	263
		" SARAH C.	WIFE	W	F	JUL 1867	32	M	14	6	6	KY	KY	KY							✓	✓	✓				
		" HERBERT	SON	W	M	AUG 1886	13	S				KY	KY	KY				FARM LABOR		3	✓	✓	✓				
		" HARRY J.	SON	W	M	FEB 1890	10	S				KY	KY	KY				FARM LABOR		5	✓	✓					
		" BUFORD	SON	W	M	JUL 1891	8	S				KY	KY	KY						5							
		" CLARANCE	SON	W	M	AUG 1894	5	S				KY	KY	KY													
		" VINIA M.	DAU	W	F	JUL 1897	2	S				KY	KY	KY													
		UN-NAMED SON	SON	W	M	MAY 1900	0	S				KY	KY	KY													
301	305	ISENBERG, HASSEY? D.	HEAD	W	M	APR 1836	64	M	45			TN	VA	VA				FARMER	12		✓	✓	✓	O		F	264
		" SARAH	WIFE	W	F	MAR 1836	64	M	45	6	5	TN	TN	TN							✓	✓	✓				
302	306	ISENBERG, WILLIAM J.	HEAD	W	M	OCT 1876	23	M	3			KY	TN	TN				FARMER			✓	✓	✓	R		F	265
		" EMLA	WIFE	W	F	JAN 1880	20	M	3	1	1	KY	KY	KY							✓	✓	✓				
		" HUSHELL B.	SON	W	M	DEC 1897	2	S				KY	KY	KY													
303	307	THOMAS, BRUCE	HEAD	W	M	OCT 1870	29	M	8									FARMER			✓	✓	✓	R		F	266
		" MARY E.	WIFE	W	F	SEP 1871	28	M	8	1	1										✓	✓	✓				

STATE - KENTUCKY
COUNTY - MONROE
Township or other division — TURNER —128— ABIJAH STRICKLER Enumerator

Supervisor's Dist. No. 102 Sheet No.
Enumeration Dist. No. 81

Fam/Dwel	Name	Relation	Color	Sex	Date of Birth Mon/Yr	Age	Marital Status	Yrs married	Mother # children	# living	Birthplace	Father	Mother	Occupation	Months not empl	Attended school	Can read	Can write	Speak Eng	Own/Rent	Own-no mortg	Farm/house	# farm sched
	THOMAS, VIREAL D.	Son	W	M	Jun 1893	6	S				KY	KY	KY	AT SCHOOL									
304 308	CLARKSON, THOMAS N.	Head	W	M	Oct 1874	25	M	6			KY	KY	KY	FARMER			✓	✓	✓	R		F	267
	" VERNIA C.	Wife	W	F	Dec 1879	20	M	6	4	4	KY	KY	KY				✓	✓	✓				
	" LUCY MAY	Dau	W	F	Dec 1894	5	S				KY	KY	KY										
	" SAMUEL H.	Son	W	M	Sep 1895	4	S				KY	KY	KY										
	" NOLIE	Dau	W	F	Mar 1898	2	S				KY	KY	KY										
	(Dim) THOMAS (?) D.	Son	W	M	Mar 1909 2/12		S				KY	KY	KY										
305 309	FOX, SAMIEL	Head	W	M	May 1849	51	M	28			KY	VA	TN	FARMER			X	X	✓	O		F	268
	" MARY E.	Wife	W	F	Jan 1855	45	M	28	7	5	KY	TN	TN		5		✓	✓	✓				
	" JOHN D.	Son	W	M	Mar 1875	25	S				KY	KY	KY	FARMER			✓	✓	✓				
	" EMMA L.	Dau	W	F	Apr 1878	22	S				KY	KY	KY				✓	✓	✓				
	" BERTHY B.	Dau	W	F	Mar 1880	20	S				KY	KY	KY				✓	✓	✓				
306 310	BAILEY, L. (Dim)	Head	W	M	Jan 1862	38	M	6			KY	VA	VA				X	X	—	—		F	269
	" ELIZA	Wife	W	F	Nov 1873	26	M	6	1	1	KY	KY	KY				✓	✓	✓				
	" VELMAS	Dau	W	F	Feb 1898	2	S				KY	KY	KY										
307 311	MARCUM, DASH	Head	W	M	Dec 1874	25	M	4			KY	KY	KY	SAWYER			✓	✓	✓	R		H	
	" NETTIE	Wife	W	F	Dec 1876	23	M	4	2	2	KY	KY	KY				✓	✓	✓				
	" MARYANY	Dau	W	F	Jul 1896	3	S				KY	KY	KY										
	" JIMMIE C.	Dau	W	F	Oct 1898	1	S				KY	KY	KY										
308 312	WHITEHEAD, STEVEN	Head	W	M	Aug 1837	62	M	45			KY	VA	VA	MILLER			✓	✓	✓	O	F	F	270
	" SARAH E.	Wife	W	F	Sep 1836	63	M	45	6	5	KY	KY	TN				✓	✓	✓				
309 313	LYNES, ZACHRI W.	Head	W	M	Feb 1873	27	M	3			TN	TN	TN	MILLER			✓	✓	✓	R		H	
	" ELIZZA L.	Wife	W	F	Apr 1879	21	M	3	2	1	KY	KY	TN				✓	✓	✓				
	" SADA	Dau	W	F	May 1900 9/12		S				KY	TN	KY										
310 314	LANE, JOHN (W.?)	Head	W	M	Feb 1862	38	M	18			KY	VA	VA	BLACKSMITH			✓	✓	✓	R		H	
	" ELIZA	Wife	W	F	Sep 1856	43	M	18	4	4	KY	KY	KY				✓	X	✓				

STATE - KENTUCKY
COUNTY - MONROE   TURNER   -129-   ABIJAH STRICKLER
Township or other division   Enumerator

Supervisor's Dist. No. 102   Sheet No. _____
Enumeration Dist. No. 81 _____

Location (No. of Family / No. of Dwelling)	NAME	Relation	Color	Sex	DATE OF BIRTH Mon/Yr	Age at last birthday	Marital Status	# Years married	Mother of how many children?	# of these children living	Place of birth (this person)	Father of this person	Mother of this person	Year of immigr.	# years in U.S.	Naturalization	OCCUPATION 10 years +	Months not employed	Attended school in months	Can read	Can write	Speak English	Owned or Rent	Owned -no mortgage	Farm or house	# of farm schedule
	LANE, IDA C.	DAU	W	F	Jul 1883	16	S				KY	KY	KY						5	✓	✓	✓				
	" ADER T.C.	SON	W	M	Oct 1891	8	S				KY	KY	KY						5							
311 315	FLETCHER, LINVEL	HEAD	W	M	Jan 1854	49	M	23			KY	TN	KY				FIREMAN			✓	✓	✓	O	F F		271
	" MARY E.	WIFE	W	F	Jul 1860	39	M	23	5	5	KY	KY	KY							✓	X	✓				
	" HUEY P.	SON	W	M	Nov 1881	18	S				KY	KY	KY						4	✓	✓	✓				
	" WILLIE B.	SON	W	M	Sep 1883	16	S				KY	KY	KY				DAY LABOR		4	✓	✓	✓				
	" PORTER L.	SON	W	M	Sep 1885	14	S				KY	KY	KY				DAY LABOR		4	✓	✓	✓				
	" TINEY E.	DAU	W	F	Jun 1895	5	S				KY	KY	KY							✓	✓	✓				
312 316	FERGURSON, JAMES T.	HEAD	W	M	May 1870	30	M	7			KY	KY	KY				FARMER			✓	✓	✓	O	F F		272
	" KITTY K.	WIFE	W	F	May 1871	29	M	7	3	3	KY	KY	KY							✓	✓	✓				
	" WILLIAM E.	SON	W	M	Oct 1893	6	S				KY	KY	KY													
	" RUTH	DAU	W	F	Dec 1895	4	S				KY	KY	KY													
	" KITTY G.	DAU	W	F	Oct 1899	9/12	S				KY	KY	KY													
313 317	FERGURSON, HENRY E.	HEAD	W	M	Apr 1837	63	M	31			KY	VA	VA				FARMER			✓	✓	✓	O	F F		273
	" MANDIA J.	WIFE	W	F	Jan 1850	50	M	31	14	12	KY	VA	KY							✓	✓	✓				
	" WILLIAM T.	SON	W	M	Oct 1882	17	S				KY	KY	KY				EDGER			✓	✓	✓				
	" LILLIA	DAU	W	F	Feb 1888	12	S				KY	KY	KY						5	✓	✓	✓				
	" JOSEPH C.	SON	W	M	Dec 1890	9	S				KY	KY	KY						4							
	" LULAR P.	DAU	W	F	Oct 1893	6	S				KY	KY	KY													
	WILLIAMS, LESLIE (LODGER?)		W	M	Aug 1879	20	S				KY	KY	KY				FARM LABOR			✓	✓	✓				
314 318	HAME, GEORGE	HEAD	W	M	Dec 1869	30	M	5			KY	TN	KY							✓	✓	✓	R	H		
	" HATTY P.	WIFE	W	F	Jun 1862	36	M	5	2	2	KY	KY	KY							✓	✓	✓				
	" ENDRE D.	DAU	W	F	Jun 1897	3	S				KY	KY	KY													
	" LEROY	SON	W	M	Mar 1900	2/12	S				KY	KY	KY													
	SAUNDERS, FRED	B-IN-LAW	W	M	Dec 1885	14	S				KY	KY	KY				DAY LABOR			✓	✓					
	HAUK, PATRICK	—	W	M	Aug 1880	19	S				KY	KY	KY				BLOCKING			✓	✓					

STATE - KENTUCKY
COUNTY - MONROE
Township or other division **TURNER** — 130 — Enumerator **ABIJAH STRICKLER**

Supervisor's Dist. No. **102** Sheet No.
Enumeration Dist. No. **81**

No. of Dwelling	No. of Family	NAME	Relation	Color	Sex	Date of Birth Mon/Yr	Age at last birthday	Marital Status	# Years married	Mother of how many children?	# of these children living	Place of birth this person	Father of this person	Mother of this person	Occupation	Months not employed	Attended school in months	Can read	Can write	Speak English	Owned or Rent	Owned -no mortgage	Farm or house	# of farm schedule
315	319	CARTER, JAMES R.	HEAD	W	M	Jul 1861	38	M	8			TN	TN	TN				✓	✓	✓	R		H	
		" MANDA S.	WIFE	W	F	Mar 1856	44	M	8	5	5	TN	TN	TN				X	X	✓				
		" BIRTHY	DAU	W	F	Oct 1887	12	S				KY	TN	TN			3	✓	✓	✓				
316	320	SMITH, EMLEY A.	HEAD	W	F	Sep 1834	65	Wd		6	4	TN	TN	KY	FARMER			✓	✓		O		F	274
		" BARTON W.	SON	W	M	Dec 1859	40	S				KY	TN	TN	FARMER			✓	✓					
		" EMMA A.	DAU	W	F	Oct 1871	28	S				KY	TN	TN				✓	✓	✓				
		" MARIENIA	DAU	W	F	Mar 1877	23	S				KY	TN	TN				✓	✓	✓				
		MYERS, CARANCE	G-SON	W	M	Jan 1893	7	S				KY	TN	TN			0							
		" VIRGA	GR-DAU	W	F	Nov 1894	5	S				KY	TN	KY										
		EMBERTON, WALTER	LODGER	W	M	Apr 1883	17	S				KY	KY	KY	FARMER			✓	✓	✓				
317	321	STRICKLER, GEORGE W.	HEAD	W	M	Feb 1856	44	M	9			KY	KY	TN	FARMER			✓	✓	✓	O		F	275
		" SARAH E.	WIFE	W	F	Oct 1873	26	M	9	4	4	KY	KY	TN				✓	✓	✓				
		" FLORA E.	DAU	W	F	Mar 1880	20	S				KY	KY	KY	AT SCHOOL		5	✓	✓	✓				
		" ABIJAH T.	SON	W	M	Jan 1882	18	S				KY	KY	KY	FARM LABOR			✓	✓	✓				
		" STANFORD B.	SON	W	M	Sep 1886	13	S				KY	KY	KY	FARM LABOR			✓	✓	✓				
		" CORA E.	DAU	W	F	Dec 1892	7	S				KY	KY	KY	AT SCHOOL		3							
		" MANERVA B.	DAU	W	F	Mar 1894	6	S				KY	KY	KY										
		" BENJAMIN	SON	W	M	Sep 1895	4	S				KY	KY	KY										
		" JOHN O.	SON	W	M	Nov 1898	1	S				KY	KY	KY										
318	322	BARLOW, CHARLES M.	HEAD	W	M	Nov 1870	29	M	10			KY	KY	KY	FARMER			✓	✓		R		F	276
		" SARAH J.	WIFE	W	F	Dec 1873	26	M	10	4	4	KY	TN	KY				✓	✓	✓				
		" NOLIA	DAU	W	F	May 1891	9	S				KY	KY	KY			5							
		" VIRGIA	DAU	W	F	Feb 1893	7	S				KY	KY	KY			5							
		" HATTIE	DAU	W	F	Apr 1895	5	S				KY	KY	KY										
		" DAISY	DAU	W	F	Mar 1900	3/12	S				KY	KY	KY										
319	323	KEELIN, JAMES T.	HEAD	W	M	Oct 1872	27	M	2			KY	KY	KY	FARMER						R		F	277

TWELFTH CENSUS OF THE UNITED STATES 1900

STATE - KENTUCKY
COUNTY - MONROE
Township or other division   TURNER   Enumerator _ABIJAH STRICKLER_

Supervisor's Dist. No. _102_ Sheet No.
Enumeration Dist. No. _81_

No. of Family	No. of Dwelling	NAME	Relation	Color	Sex	DATE OF BIRTH Mon/Yr	Age at last birthday	Marital Status	# Years married	Mother of how many children?	# of these children living	Place of birth (this person)	Father of this person	Mother of this person	Year of immigr.	# years in U.S.	Naturalization	OCCUPATION 10 years +	Months not employed	Attended school in months	Can read	Can write	Speak English	Owned or Rent	Owned -no mortgage	Farm or house	# of farm schedule
		KEELIN, ESTHER E.	Wife	W	F	MAR 1873	27	M	2	1	1	KY	KY	KY							✓	✓	✓				
		" EMLEY C.	Dau	W	F	APR 1899	1	S				KY	KY	KY													
320	324	BELCHER, ARCHEY P.	HEAD	W	M	OCT 1871	28	M	4			KY	KY	TN				DRY GOODS SALESMAN			✓	✓	✓	R		H	
		" LUISA	WIFE	W	F	NOV 1875	24	M	4	2	2	NEB	VA	MISSOURI							✓	✓					
		" LEO (?)	SON	W	M	MAR 1897	3	S				KY	KY	NEB													
		" WARDER	SON	W	M	FEB 1898	2	S				KY	KY	NEB													
321	325	RICH, LENZY B.	HEAD	W	M	MAR 1881	19	S				KY	KY	KY				FARMER			✓	✓	✓	R		F	278
		STRICKLER, ABIJAH	HEAD	W	M	JAN 1858	42	M	12			KY	TN	TN				FARMER			✓	✓	✓	O	E	F	279
		" MARGERET E	WIFE	W	F	JUL 1869	30	M	12	4	4	KY	TN	TN							✓	✓					
		" AUDIE B.	SON	W	M	DEC 1889	10	S				KY	KY	KY				FARM LABOR		5	✓	✓					
		" GEORGE E.	SON	W	M	OCT 1892	7	S				KY	KY	KY						5							
		" DEWEY	SON	W	M	JUN 1895	4	S				KY	KY	KY													
		" RADFORD	SON	W	M	NOV 1898	1	S				KY	KY	KY													

STATE - KENTUCKY
COUNTY - MONROE
Township or other division

BRUSH

— 132 —

Enumerator S. H. CARTER

Supervisor's Dist. No. _102_ Sheet No.
Enumeration Dist. No. _82_

No. of Family	No. of Dwelling	NAME	Relation	Color	Sex	Date of Birth Mon/Yr	Age at last birthday	Marital Status	# Years married	Mother of how many children?	# of these children living	Place of birth (this person)	Father of this person	Mother of this person	Occupation 10 years +	Attended school in months	Can read	Can write	Speak English	Owned or Rent	Farm or house	# of farm schedule
1	1	SMITH, JAMES (?)	HEAD	W	M	MAR 1868	32	M	7			KY	KY	KY	FARMER		✓	✓	✓	O	F	1
		" SALLIE M	WIFE	W	F	APR 1873	27	M	7	2	2	KY	KY	KY			✓	✓	✓			
		" ETHER (?) VERY DIM	DAU	W	F	AUG 1894	5	S				KY	KY	KY								
		" EMINIA (?)	DAU	W	F	DEC 1897	2	S				KY	KY	KY								
		" MATILDA	MOTHER	W	F	MAR 1847	52	Wd		3	3	KY	KY	KY			✓					
2	2	MILLER, LANDON	HEAD	W	M	FEB 1838	62	M	33			KY	TN	TN	FARMER		✓	✓	✓	O	F	2
		" ELIZA J.	WIFE	W	F	JAN 1844	56	M	33	4	3	KY	VA	KY			✓	✓	✓			
		" JOSEPH	SON	W	M	MAR 1873	27	S				KY	KY	KY	FARM LABORER			✓	✓			
		" GEORGE F.	SON	W	M	AUG 1886	13	S				KY	KY	KY	AT SCHOOL		✓	✓	✓			
3	3	GEARLD, JESSE N.	HEAD	W	M	JUN 1837	62	M	42			TN	TN	TN	FARMER		✓	✓	✓	R	F	3
		" CARLINE M.	WIFE	W	F	MAY 1837	62	M	42	6	6	KY	KY	KY			✓	✓	✓			
		" JOHN L(?)	SON	W	M	FEB 1881	19	S				KY	TN	KY	FARM LABOR		✓	✓	✓			
4	4	BREWINGTON, GEORGE	HEAD	W	M	MAR 1863	36	M	6			TN	TN	TN	TEAMSTER		✓	✓	✓	R	H	
		" SUSAN	WIFE	W	F	JUL 1874	25	M	6	2	2	KY	KY	KY			✓	✓	✓			
		" IDRU	DAU	W	F	FEB 1888	11	S				TN	TN	TN	AT SCHOOL		✓	✓	✓			
		" VALLIE	DAU	W	F	SEP 1890	9	S				TN	TN	TN	AT SCHOOL		✓	✓	✓			
		" JOHN	SON	W	M	AUG 1893	6	S				KY	TN	TN	AT SCHOOL		X	X	✓			
		" HERMAN	SON	W	M	JUL 1895	4	S				KY	TN	KY			X	X	✓			
		" ANNIE	DAU	W	F	JAN 1897	2	S				KY	TN	KY								
5	5	FUGET(?), JASPER	HEAD	W	M	MAY 1843	56	M	4			KY	VA	KY	STONEMASON		✓	✓	✓	R	H	
		" PERMELIA	WIFE	W	F	SEP 1867	32	M	4	3	3	KY	KY	KY			✓	✓	✓			
		" DELLA	DAU	W	F	JUN 1890	9	S				KY	KY	KY					✓			
		" TABITHIA	DAU	W	F	SEP 1892	7	S				KY	KY	KY					✓			
		" MARY	DAU	W	F	MAY 1895	4	S				KY	KY	KY								
6	6	MILLER, J. SIMPSON	HEAD	W	M	JAN 1859	41	M	3			KY	TN	KY	FARMER		✓	✓	✓	O	H	4
		" LOU E.	WIFE	W	F	FEB 1875	25	M	3			KY	KY	KY			✓	✓	✓			

STATE - KENTUCKY
COUNTY - MONROE
BRUSH
Township or other division

Enumerator S. H. CARTER

Supervisor's Dist. No. 102 Sheet No.
Enumeration Dist. No. 82

No. of Family	No. of Dwelling	NAME	Relation	Color	Sex	DATE OF BIRTH Mon/Yr	Age at last birthday	Marital Status	# Years married	Mother of how many children	# of those children living	Place of birth (this person)	Father of this person	Mother of this person	Year of immigr.	# years in U.S.	Naturalization	OCCUPATION 10 years +	Months not employed	Attended school in months	Can read	Can write	Speak English	Owned or Rent	Owned -no mortg.	Farm or house	# of farm schedule
		MILLER, NEVADA	DAU	W	F	DEC 1882	17	S				KY	KY	KY				AT SCHOOL		10	✓	✓	✓				
		" THOMAS	SON	W	M	APR 1885	15	S				KY	KY	KY				AT SCHOOL		4	✓	✓					
		" BESSIE J.	DAU	W	F	MAR 1889	11	S				KY	KY	KY				AT SCHOOL		5	✓	✓					
7	7	RASNER, JOHN	HEAD	W	M	JUL 1872	21	M	5			KY	KY	KY				FARMER			✓	✓	✓	O		F	5
		" FLAUDIE	WIFE	W	F	JUL 1877	22	M	5	3	3	KY	KY	KY							✓	✓	✓				
		" BEATRICE	DAU	W	F	OCT 1895	4	S				KY	KY	KY													
		" BUFORD	SON	W	M	MAR 1898	2	S				KY	KY	KY													
		" WILLIE	SON	W	M	MAR 1899	1	S				KY	KY	KY													
8	8	CARTER, JOSEPH	HEAD	W	M	Feb 1876	24	M	2			KY	KY	KY				FARMER			✓	✓	✓	O	F	F	6
		" OCTAVA	WIFE	W	F	Feb 1880	20	M	2	1	1	KY	KY	KY							✓	✓	✓				
		" IDRU	DAU	W	F	MAR 1899	1	S				KY	KY	KY													
		" JOSEPH S. P.	FATHER	W	M	JAN 1840	60	Wd				KY	VA	KY				FARM LABOR			✓	✓	✓				
		" SAM B.	BROTHER	W	M	MAY 1873	27	S				KY	KY	KY				FARM LABOR			✓	✓	✓				
9	9	HOLIWAY, HULIT	HEAD	W	M	DEC 1846	53	M	1			KY	KY	KY				FARMER			✓	✓	✓	O	F	F	7
		" MARY N.	WIFE	W	F	MAY 1860	40	M	1			KY	KY	KY							✓	✓	✓				
		" SARAH F.	DAU	W	F	MAR 1883	17	S				KY	KY	KY							✓	✓	✓				
		" ELIZABETH	DAU	W	F	JUN 1884	15	S				KY	KY	KY				AT SCHOOL		5	✓	✓					
		" MALICIE	DAU	W	F	JAN 1888	12	S				KY	KY	KY				AT SCHOOL		5	✓	✓					
		" BERTHA S.	DAU	W	F	Feb 1890	10	S				KY	KY	KY				AT SCHOOL		5	✓	✓					
10	10	MILLER, JOHN S.	HEAD	W	M	OCT 1867	32	M	13			KY	KY	KY										R	F		8
		" SUSAN	WIFE	W	F	Sep 1866	33	M	13	1	1	KY	KY	KY													
		" OSIE L.(?)	DAU	W	F	Sep 1895	4	S				KY	KY	KY													
11	11	HOLLOWAY, ABRAHAM	HEAD	W	M	SEP 1854	45	M	22			KY	KY	KY				FARMER			✓	✓		O		F	9
		" NANCY	WIFE	W	F	JAN 1858	42	M	22	6	5	KY	KY	KY							✓	✓	✓				
		" RUTHERFORD S.	SON	W	M	OCT 1878	21	S				KY	KY	KY				SCHOOL TEACHING 2			✓	✓	✓				
		" GEO. F.	SON	W	M	JAN 1880	20	S				KY	KY	KY				SCHOOL TEACHING 2			✓	✓	✓				

STATE - KENTUCKY
COUNTY - MONROE
Township or other division: BRUSH — 134 —
Enumerator: S. H. CARTER

Supervisor's Dist. No. 102   Sheet No.
Enumeration Dist. No. 82

Location		NAME	Relation	Color	Sex	DATE OF BIRTH Mon/Yr	Age at last birthday	Marital Status	# Years married	Mother of how many children?	# of these children living	NATIVITY Place of birth [this person]	Father of this person	Mother of this person	CITIZENSHIP Year of immigr.	# years in U.S.	Naturalization	OCCUPATION 10 years +	Months not employed	EDUCATION Attended school in months	Can read	Can write	Speak English	OWNERSHIP Owned or Rent	Owned -no mortage	Farm or house	# of farm schedule
No. of Family	No. of Dwelling																										
		HOLLOWAY, JAMES R	Son	W	M	Aug 1884	15	S				KY	KY	KY				AT SCHOOL		5	✓	✓	✓				
		" HERROD G.	Son	W	M	Aug 1887	12	S				KY	KY	KY				AT SCHOOL		5	✓	✓	✓				
		" LAURA S.	Dau	W	F	Aug 1889	10	S				KY	KY	KY				AT SCHOOL		5	✓	✓	✓				
12	12	BAZZLE, JOHN	Head	W	M	Oct 1820	79	M	33			TN	TN	TN				FARMER			✓	✓	✓			F	10
		" RHODA	Wife	W	F	Oct 1840	59	M	33	8	8	KY	KY	KY							✓	✓	✓				
		" NANNIE	Dau	W	F	Aug 1867	32	S				KY	TN	KY							✓	✓	✓				
		" TERRY	Son	W	M	Nov 1874	25	S				KY	TN	KY				DAY LABORER			✓	✓	✓				
		" EVA	Dau	W	F	Mar 1881	18	S				KY	TN	KY							✓	✓	✓				
13	13	NORMAN, FRANCIS L.	Head	W	M	Feb 1839	61	Wd				KY	KY	KY				FARMER			✓	✓	✓	R		F	11
		" EVIE F.	Dau	W	F	Jul 1889	10	S				KY	KY	KY							✓	✓	✓				
		" VESTA G.	Dau	W	F	Apr 1893	7	S				KY	KY	KY													
14	14	FANSLER, BENJAMIN	Head	W	M	Jan 1835	65	M	34			TN	NC	TN				FARMER			✓	✓	✓	R		F	12
		" NANCY E.	Wife	W	F	Dec 1845	54	M	34	7	4	KY	KY	KY							✓	✓	✓				
		" MARY F.	Dau	W	F	May 1880	20	S				KY	TN	KY							✓	✓	✓				
15	15	CHAPMAN, ROBERT	Head	W	M	Feb 1872	28	M	9			KY	KY	KY				FARMER			✓	✓	✓	O		F	13
		" GERTRUDE	Wife	W	F	Nov 1874	25	M	9	4	4	KY	KY	KY							✓	✓	✓				
		" INA F.	Dau	W	F	Jan 1892	8	S				KY	KY	KY													
		" LOYEL(?) C.	Dau	W	F	Sep 1894	5	S				KY	KY	KY													
		" GRACIE E.	Dau	W	F	Sep 1897	2	S				KY	KY	KY													
		" BUDFORD	Son	W	M	May 1900	1/12	S				KY	KY	KY													
16	16	FERGUSON, THOMAS	Head	W	M	Feb 1862	38	M	6			KY	KY	KY				FARMER			✓	✓	✓	O		F	14
		" NORA F.(?)	Wife	W	F	Apr 1875	25	M	6	1	1	KY	KY	KY							✓	✓	✓				
		" WILLIAM E.	Son	W	M	Nov 1894	5	S				KY	KY	KY													
17	17	BARTLEY, PHOEBE	Head	W	F	Jun 1859	40	Wd		5	5	KY	KY	KY				FARMER			✓	✓	✓	O		F	15
		" WILLIAM S.	Son	W	M	Jan 1882	18	S				KY	KY	KY							✓	✓	✓				
		" JAMES I.	Son	W	M	Jan 1884	16	S				KY	KY	KY							✓	✓	✓				

TWELFTH CENSUS OF THE UNITED STATES 1900

STATE - KENTUCKY
COUNTY - MONROE   BRUSH   -135-
Township or other division   Enumerator S.H. CARTER

Supervisor's Dist. No. 102   Sheet No.
Enumeration Dist. No. 82

No. of Family	No. of Dwelling	NAME	Relation	Color	Sex	Date of Birth Mon/Yr	Age at last birthday	Marital Status	# Years married	Mother of how many children?	# of these children living	Place of birth [this person]	Father of this person	Mother of this person	Year of immigr.	# years in U.S.	Naturalization	OCCUPATION 10 years +	Months not employed	Attended school in months	Can read	Can write	Speak English	Owned or Rent	Owned -no mortgage	Farm or house	# of farm schedule
		BARTLEY, MAGGIE N.	DAU	W	F	Jan 1887	13	S				KY	KY	KY						✓	✓	✓					
		" JOHN F.	SON	W	M	Jan 1889	11	S				KY	KY	KY						✓	✓	✓					
		" MAUD N.	DAU	W	F	Sep 1891	8	S				KY	KY	KY						✓	✓	✓					
18	18	CLEMONS, SANFORD	HEAD	W	M	Mar 1847	53	M	30			KY	KY	KY				FARMER			✓	✓		O		F	16
		" MANDA	WIFE	W	F	May 1851	49	M	30	8	7	KY	VA	KY								✓					
		" IBIE E.	DAU	W	F	Mar 1881	19	S				KY	KY	KY							✓	✓					
		" MELVIN N.	SON	W	M	Feb 1885	15	S				KY	KY	KY							✓	✓	✓				
		" HARRISON M.	SON	W	M	Jun 1888	11	S				KY	KY	KY							✓	✓	✓				
		" ANCEL S.	SON	W	M	Nov 1890	9	S				KY	KY	KY							✓	✓					
		" ELZIE T.	SON	W	M	Aug 1894	5	S				KY	KY	KY													
19	19	HAGAN, WILLIAM	HEAD	W	M	Jun 1857	42	M	20			KY	KY	KY				FARMER			✓	✓		R		F	17
		" NANCY D.	WIFE	W	F	Jan 1863	37	M	20	3	3	KY	KY	KY							✓	✓					
		" JAMES W.	SON	W	M	Oct 1881	18	S				KY	KY	KY							✓	✓					
		" LILIE C.	DAU	W	F	May 1886	14	S				KY	KY	KY							✓	✓	✓				
		" DAVID M.	SON	W	M	Jul 1890	9	S				KY	KY	KY													
20	20	NORMAN, JAMES W.	HEAD	W	M	Jan 1873	27	M	8			KY	KY	KY				FARMER			✓	✓		O		F	18
		" GENIE	WIFE	W	F	Sep 1869	30	M	8	2	1	KY	KY	KY							✓	✓	✓				
		" VERA	DAU	W	F	Jun 1894	5	S				KY	KY	KY													
21	21	MURPHY, PARKER	HEAD	W	M	Aug 1864	35	M	2			KY	KY	KY				DAY LABORER			✓	✓	✓	R		H	
		" LUCY A.	WIFE	W	F	Jan 1878	22	M	2	1	1	KY	KY	KY							✓	✓					
		" BETTIE(?) J.	DAU	W	F	Jan 1899	1	S				KY	KY	KY													
22	22	VAUTER, JAMES	HEAD	W	M	Jan 1827	73	M	49			KY	KY	KY				MERCHANT			✓	✓		O		F	
		" SUSAN	WIFE	W	F	May 1832	68	M	49	7	5	KY	VA	VA							✓	✓					
		" DORA E.	GR-DAU	W	F	Nov 1878	21	S				KY	KY	KY							✓	✓					
23	23	BOWMAN, STOKES	HEAD	W	M	Oct 1862	37	M	20			KY	KY	IN				FARMER			✓	✓	✓	R		F	19
		" SARAH	WIFE	W	F	May 1857	43	M	20	9	9	KY	KY	KY							✓	✓					

STATE - KENTUCKY
COUNTY - MONROE
Township or other division: BRUSH — 136 —
Enumerator: S.H. CARTER

Supervisor's Dist. No. 10 2   Sheet No.
Enumeration Dist. No. 82

No. of Family	No. of Dwelling	NAME	Relation	Color	Sex	Date of Birth Mon/Yr	Age at last birthday	Marital Status	# Years married	Mother of how many children?	# of these children living	Place of birth (this person)	Father of this person	Mother of this person	Year of immigr.	# years in U.S.	Naturalization	Occupation 10 years +	Months not employed	Attended school in months	Can read	Can write	Speak English	Owned or Rent	Owned -no mortgage	Farm or house	# of farm schedule
		BOWMAN, EFFIE	DAU	W	F	MAY 1880	20	S				KY	KY	KY				SCHOOL TEACHING			✓	✓	✓				
		" WILLIE M.	SON	W	M	DEC 1881	18	S				KY	KY	KY				AT SCHOOL		9	✓	✓	✓				
		" ALPHA	SON	W	M	Sep 1883	16	S				KY	KY	KY				AT SCHOOL		9	✓	✓	✓				
		" EVERT	SON	W	M	APR 1886	14	S				KY	KY	KY				AT SCHOOL		9	✓	✓	✓				
		" HUSTON	SON	W	M	APR 1888	12	S				KY	KY	KY				AT SCHOOL		9	✓	✓	✓				
		" COLLONEL	SON	W	M	Feb 1889	11	S				KY	KY	KY				AT SCHOOL		9	✓	✓	✓				
		" JESSIE	SON	W	M	AUG 1891	8	S				KY	KY	KY													
		" BLISS	SON	W	M	AUG 1893	6	S				KY	KY	KY													
		" FARICE	SON	W	M	DEC 1896	3	S				KY	KY	KY													
24	24	NORMAN, LINDSAY	HEAD	W	M	MAR 1868	32	M	10			KY	KY	KY				FARMER			✓	✓	✓	R		F	20
		" SUSAN M.	WIFE	W	F	JAN 1873	27	M	10	3	3	KY	KY	KY							✓	✓	✓				
		" RALEIGH	SON	W	M	OCT 1890	9	S				KY	KY	KY							✓	✓	✓				
		" AIDA L.(?)	DAU	W	F	Feb 1893	7	S				KY	KY	KY				AT SCHOOL		5			✓				
		" INA C.	DAU	W	F	Feb 1895	5	S				KY	KY	KY				AT SCHOOL					✓				
		" SIMON T.	FATHER	W	M	MAY 1828	72	Wd				KY	VA	VA										O	F	F	21
25	25	BELCHER, JAMES	HEAD	W	M	Feb 1866	34	M	10			KY	KY	KY				FARMER			✓	X	✓	O	F	F	22
		" ELNORA	WIFE	W	F	AUG 1874	25	M	10	3	3	KY	KY	KY							✓	✓	✓				
		" CLONIE(?)S	DAU	W	F	Sep 1890	9	S				KY	KY	KY				AT SCHOOL		5			✓				
		" CLAUDIE J.	DAU	W	F	APR 1892	8	S				KY	KY	KY				AT SCHOOL					✓				
		" FRANK L.	SON	W	M	MAR 1894	6	S				KY	KY	KY													
26	26	HIGH, WILLIAM	HEAD	W	M	DEC 1832	68	M	42			KY	VA	KY				FARMER			✓	X	✓	O	F	F	23
		" MARY	WIFE	W	F	APR 1836	64	M	42	9	4	KY	KY	KY							X	X	✓				
		" SARAH J.	DAU	W	F	OCT 1860	39	S				KY	KY	KY							X	X	✓				
		" THOMAS	SON	W	M	AUG 1876	23	S				KY	KY	KY				DAY LABORER			X	X	✓				
		" GOY(?) T.	GR SON	W	M	APR 1892	8	S				KY	KY	KY													
27	27	STRODE, LINDSAY	HEAD	W	M	APR 1857	43	M	18			KY	KY	KY				FARMER			✓	✓	✓	O	F	F	24

TWELFTH CENSUS OF THE UNITED STATES 1900

STATE - KENTUCKY
COUNTY - MONROE   BRUSH
Township or other division   Enumerator   S. H. CARTER

Supervisor's Dist. No. 10 2   Sheet No.
Enumeration Dist. No. 82

No. of Family	No. of Dwelling	NAME	Relation	Color	Sex	DATE OF BIRTH Mon/Yr	Age at last birthday	Marital Status	#Years married	Mother of how many children?	# of these children living	Place of birth (this person)	Father of this person	Mother of this person	Year of immigr.	# years in U.S.	Naturalization	OCCUPATION 10 years +	Months not employed	Attended school in months	Can read	Can write	Speak English	Owned or Rent	Owned –no mortage	Farm or house	# of farm schedule
		STRODE, MALICCIE	WIFE	W	F	Jun 1859	40	M	18	6	5	MO	KY	KY							✓	✓	✓				
		" BERTHA G.	DAU	W	F	Nov 1882	17	S				MO	KY	MO				AT SCHOOL		5	✓	✓	✓				
		" JAMES (T) C.	SON	W	M	Sept 1884	15	S				KY	KY	MO				AT SCHOOL		5	✓	✓	✓				
		" EVA M.	DAU	W	F	APR 1886	14	S				KY	KY	MO				AT SCHOOL		5	✓	✓	✓				
		" WILLIE L.	SON	W	M	Jul 1889	10	S				KY	KY	MO				AT SCHOOL		5	✓	✓	✓				
		" NELLIE G.	DAU	W	F	AUG 1891	8	S				KY	KY	MO				AT SCHOOL									
28	28	McWHERTER, HENRY	HEAD	W	M	DEC 1858	41	M	12			TN	TN	TN				FARMER			✓	✓	✓	O	F	F	25
		" SARAH E.	WIFE	W	F	MAR 1852	48	M	12	5	4	KY	KY	KY							✓	✓	✓				
		" EVA E.	DAU	W	F	OCT 1883	16	S				KY	TN	KY				AT SCHOOL		5	✓	✓	✓				
		" SARAH L.	DAU	W	F	Sep 1885	14	S				KY	TN	KY				AT SCHOOL		5	✓	✓	✓				
		" JOHN H.	SON	W	M	Feb 1888	12	S				KY	TN	KY				AT SCHOOL		5	✓	✓	✓				
		" JAMES M.	SON	W	M	May 1890	10	S				KY	TN	KY				AT SCHOOL		5	✓	✓	✓				
		" AIDA	DAU	W	F	Jun 1893	6	S				KY	TN	KY													
		" FLOSSIE	DAU	W	F	Feb 1896	4	S				KY	TN	KY													
29	29	WALDEN, JOHN R.	HEAD	W	M	Nov 1842	57	M	30			KY	KY	KY				FARMER			✓	✓	✓	R		F	26
		^ SARAH E.	WIFE	W	F	Nov 1844	55	M	30	3	1	KY	KY	KY							✓	✓	✓				
		" INGRAM	SON	W	M	Nov 1879	20	S				KY	KY	KY				FARM LABOR			✓	✓	✓				
		" JANE E.	MOTHER	W	F	DEC 1820	79	Wd		9	8	KY	KY	KY							✓	✓	✓				
30	30	PALMORE, WILLIAM	HEAD	W	M	Sep 1863	36	M	13			KY	KY	KY				FARMER			✓	✓	✓	O		F	27
		" MATILDA	WIFE	W	F	Jul 1865	34	M	13	5	5	KY	KY	KY							✓	✓	✓				
		" THOMAS B.	SON	W	M	Oct 1887	12	S				KY	KY	KY				AT SCHOOL		5	✓	✓	✓				
		" ROY E.	SON	W	M	AUG 1889	10	S				KY	KY	KY				AT SCHOOL		5	✓	✓	✓				
		" BIRLIE O.	DAU	W	F	Nov 1891	8	S				KY	KY	KY				AT SCHOOL		5							
		" HUBERT L.	SON	W	M	Sep 1894	5	S				KY	KY	KY													
		" DEWEY R.	SON	W	M	APR 1898	2	S				KY	KY	KY													
31	31	FORD, BENJAMIN	HEAD	W	M	Feb 1849	51	M	30			KY	TN	TN				FARMER			✓	✓	✓	R		F	28

STATE – KENTUCKY
COUNTY – MONROE
Township or other division **BRUSH**

Enumerator **S.H. CARTER**

Supervisor's Dist. No. _102_ Sheet No.
Enumeration Dist. No. _82_

No. of Family	No. of Dwelling	NAME	Relation	Color	Sex	DATE OF BIRTH Mon/Yr	Age at last birthday	Marital Status	# Year married	Mother of how many children?	# of these children living	Place of birth (this person)	Father of this person	Mother of this person	Year of immigr.	# years in U.S.	Naturalization	OCCUPATION 10 years +	Months not employed	Attended school in months	Can read	Can write	Speak English	Owned or Rent	Owned -no mortage	Farm or house	# of farm schedule
		FORD, LETHA (?) M	WIFE	W	F	Jun 1851	48	M	30	9	8	KY	KY	KY							✓	✓	✓				
		" GEO. P.	SON	W	M	Sept 1875	24	S				KY	KY	KY				DAY LABORER			✓	✓	✓				
		" SARAH J.	DAU	W	F	Sept 1876	23	S				KY	KY	KY				DRESS MAKER			✓	✓	✓				
		" THOMAS	SON	W	M	Jan 1882	18	S				KY	KY	KY				AT SCHOOL		9	✓	✓	✓				
		" JULIA O.	DAU	W	F	Apr 1886	14	S				KY	KY	KY				AT SCHOOL		7	✓	✓	✓				
		" ARTHUR M.	SON	W	M	Jan 1889	11	S				KY	KY	KY				AT SCHOOL		8	✓	✓	✓				
		" NELA (D?)	DAU	W	F	Feb 1892	8	S				KY	KY	KY								✓	✓				
		" LUTHER H.	SON	W	M	Dec 1893	6	S				KY	KY	KY													
32	32	JACKSON, WILEY (?)	HEAD	W	M	Mar 1873	27	M	8			KY	KY	KY				FARMER			✓	✓	✓	R		F	29
		" NANIE	WIFE	W	F	Mar 1872	28	M	8	4	3	KY	KY	KY							✓	✓	✓				
		" OCIA	SON	W	M	Nov 1891	8	S				KY	KY	KY													
		" LUTHER	SON	W	M	Aug 1895	4	S				KY	KY	KY													
		" VIOLA	DAU	W	F	May 1898	2	S				KY	KY	KY													
33	33	NORMAN, GALASPA	HEAD	W	M	Feb 1853	47	M	18			KY	KY	KY				FARMER			✓	✓		O	F	F	30
		" ELIZABETH W.	WIFE	W	F	Jun 1854	45	M	18	2	2	KY	KY	KY							✓	✓	✓				
		" MAUD (C?)	DAU	W	F	Jun 1888	11	S				KY	KY	KY				AT SCHOOL		5	✓	✓	✓				
		" ELVIE M.	DAU	W	F	Oct 1892	7	S				KY	KY	KY				AT SCHOOL		5	✓	✓	✓				
34	34	STRODE, LORENZO C.	HEAD	W	M	Apr 1874	26	M	4			KY	KY	KY				FARMER			✓	✓	✓	R		F	31
		" MARTHA	WIFE	W	F	Apr 1875	25	M	4	2	2	KY	KY	KY							✓	✓	✓				
		" ALVIS	SON	W	M	Mar 1891	8	S				KY	KY	KY													
		" ROSCO	SON	W	M	Jun 1898	1	S				KY	KY	KY													
35	35	CLEMONS, WILLIAM	HEAD	W	M	Sep 1869	30	M	6			KY	KY	KY				FARMER			✓	✓	✓	R		F	32
		" ELLEN N.	WIFE	W	F	Nov 1875	24	M	6	2	2	KY	KY	KY							✓	✓	✓				
		" WALTER G.	SON	W	M	Aug 1895	4	S				KY	KY	KY													
		" PEARL M.	DAU	W	F	Nov 1897	2	S				KY	KY	KY													
36	36	SYMPSON, JOHN	HEAD	W	M	Apr 1856	44	M	21			KY	KY	KY				FARMER			✓	✓	✓	O	F	F	33

TWELFTH CENSUS OF THE UNITED STATES 1900

STATE - KENTUCKY
COUNTY - MONROE
Township or other division — BRUSH — 139 —
Enumerator — S. H. CARTER

Supervisor's Dist. No. 102 Sheet No.
Enumeration Dist. No. 82

No. of Family	No. of Dwelling	NAME	Relation	Color	Sex	Date of Birth Mon/Yr	Age at last birthday	Marital Status	# Years married	Mother of how many children	# of these children living	Place of birth this person	Father of this person	Mother of this person	Year of immigr.	# years in U.S.	Naturalization	Occupation	Months not employed	Attended school in months	Can read	Can write	Speak English	Owned or Rent	Owned-no mortgage	Farm or house	# of farm schedule
		SYMPSON, TILDA	WIFE	W	F	Nov 1857	42	M	21			KY	KY	KY							✓	✓					
37	37	PICKERAL, JAMES T.	HEAD	W	M	Oct 1855	44	M	18			KY	KY	KY				FARMER			✓	✓		O	F	F	34
		" MARTHA	WIFE	W	F	Mar 1863	37	M	18	6	5	KY	KY	KY							✓	✓					
		* " CARRIE	SON	W	M	May 1882	18	S				KY	KY	KY	*CARY			AT SCHOOL		7	✓	✓	✓				
		" EVA S.	DAU	W	F	Nov 1884	15	S				KY	KY	KY				AT SCHOOL		7	✓	✓					
		" BARLOW B.	SON	W	M	Jul 1886	13	S				KY	KY	KY				AT SCHOOL		7	✓	✓					
		" HUGHIE	SON	W	M	Aug 1894	5	S				KY	KY	KY													
		" ARTHUR	SON	W	M	Jan 1900	4/12	S				KY	KY	KY													
38	38	CHAPMAN, HIRAM	HEAD	W	M	May 1867	33	M	3			KY	KY	KY				FARMER						O	F	F	35
		" IBIE B.	WIFE	W	F	May 1879	21	M	3	2	2	KY	KY	KY													
		" STELLA R.	DAU	W	F	Feb 1898	2	S				KY	KY	KY													
		" J. W.	SON	W	M	Oct 1899	7/12	S				KY	KY	KY													
39	39	COPASS, WILLIAM	HEAD	W	M	Feb 1862	38	M	7			KY	KY	KY				FARMER			✓	✓		R		F	36
		" MARY E.	WIFE	W	F	Jan 1871	29	M	7	2	1	KY	KY	KY							✓	✓					
		" WILLIAM B.	SON	W	M	Jan 1895	4	S				KY	KY	KY													
		" JAMES (L?)	SON	W	M	Aug 1896	3	S				KY	KY	KY													
40	40	PICKERAL, LINDSAY	HEAD	W	M	Aug 1868	32	M	2			KY	KY	KY				TEAMSTER			X	X	✓	R		H	
		" MINNIE	WIFE	W	F	Aug 1875	24	M	2			KY	KY	KY							✓	✓	✓				
41	41	PALMORE, E(LLSWORTH)	HEAD	W	M	Oct 1871	28	M	7			KY	KY	KY				FARMER			✓	✓	✓	O	F	F	37
		" GERTRUDE	WIFE	W	F	Sept 1861	38	M	7	4	4	KY	KY	KY							✓	✓	✓				
		BOWMAN, ARTHUR	STEP-SON	W	M	Feb 1880	20	S				KY	KY	KY				TEACHER			✓	✓	✓				
		" LIZZIE	STEP-DAU	W	F	Apr 1882	18	S				KY	KY	KY				AT SCHOOL		7½	✓	✓	✓				
		PALMORE, REGINALD	SON	W	M	Feb 1895	5	S				KY	KY	KY													
		" CECIL	SON	W	M	Apr 1897	3	S				KY	KY	KY													
42	42	HUME, JOHN D.	HEAD	W	M	Dec 1862	37	M	18			KY	IN	IN				FARMER			X	X	✓	R		F	38
		" JULIE	WIFE	W	F	May 1860	40	M	18	7	5	KY	KY	KY							✓	✓	✓				

TWELFTH CENSUS OF THE UNITED STATES 1900

STATE - KENTUCKY
COUNTY - MONROE
Township or other division   BRUSH   — 140 —
Enumerator   S.H. CARTER

Supervisor's Dist. No. _102_ Sheet No. ____
Enumeration Dist. No. _82_ ____

Location No. of Family / No. of Dwelling	NAME	Relation	Color	Sex	DATE OF BIRTH Mon/Yr	Age at last birthday	Marital Status	#Years married	Mother of how many children?	# of these children living	Place of birth [this person]	Father of this person	Mother of this person	Year of immigr.	# years in U.S.	Naturalization	OCCUPATION 10 years +	Months not employed	Attended school in months	Can read	Can write	Speak English	Owned or Rent	Owned -no mortgage	Farm or house	# of farm schedule
DIM	HUME, (MINNIE?)	DAU	W	F	Jul 1882	18	S				KY	KY	KY				AT SCHOOL			✓	✓					
	" (DONIE?)	DAU	W	F	Jul 1891	8	S				KY	KY	KY													
	" CLAUD D.	SON	W	M	APR 1894	6	S				KY	KY	KY													
	" CLAYTON W	SON	W	M	AUG 1897	2	S				KY	KY	KY													
	CRUSE, DEWEY I	STEP-SON	W	M	AUG 1878	21	Wd				KY	KY	KY				DAY LABORER			✓	✓					
43 43	PENNINGTON, (JOHN?)	HEAD	W	M	JUN 1840	59	M	30			TN	KY	KY				FARMER			✓	✓		R		F	39
	" SARAH	WIFE	W	F	JUL 1844	55	M	30	4	4	KY	NC	KY							✓	✓					
	" TOLBERT G.	SON	W	M	MAY 1877	23	S				KY	TN	KY				FARM LABORER			✓	✓					
SK -- --	STRODE, NELSON	HEAD	W	M	Sep 1874	25	M	8			KY	KY	KY				FARMER			✓	✓		R		F	40
	" NANCY	WIFE	W	F	JUN 1874	25	M	8	2	2	KY	KY	KY							✓	✓					
	" (J—?)	DAU	W	F	AUG 1893	6	S				KY	KY	KY													
	" WILLIAM C.	SON	W	M	Feb 1896	4	S				KY	KY	KY													
44 44	STRODE, JAMES	HEAD	W	M	JUN 1869	30	M	9			KY	KY	KY				FARMER			✓	✓		R		F	41
	" (? SUSAN)	WIFE	W	F	Feb 1870	30	M	9	3	2	KY	KY	KY							✓	✓					
	" LECTA	DAU	W	F	NOV 1892	7	S				KY	KY	KY				AT SCHOOL		5							
	" ETHEL	DAU	W	F	APR 1896	4	S				KY	KY	KY													
	" GERTRUDE	DAU	W	F	MAR 1900 3/12		S				KY	KY	KY													
45 45	STRODE, WILLIAM S.	HEAD	W	M	JUN 1842	57	M	37			KY	KY	KY				FARMER			✓	✓		O		F	42
	" JULIE	WIFE	W	F	AUG 1842	57	M	37			KY	KY	KY							✓	✓					
	" BIRCHIE	GR-DAU	W	F	Sep 1890	9	S				KY	KY	KY													
46 46	CHAPMAN, DE—?	HEAD	W	M	JUN 1866	33	Wd				KY	KY	KY				FARMER			✓	✓		O		F	43
	" WILLIAM I.	SON	W	M	JAN 1883	17	S				KY	KY	KY				FARM LABORER			✓	✓					
	" NANCY M.	DAU	W	F	JUN 1884	15	S				KY	KY	KY				AT SCHOOL		5	✓	✓					
	" EVA A.	DAU	W	F	OCT 1885	14	S				KY	KY	KY				AT SCHOOL		5	✓	✓					
	" REVENA J.	DAU	W	F	NOV 1887	12	S				KY	KY	KY				AT SCHOOL		5	✓	✓					
	" WESLEY L.	SON	W	M	OCT 1889	10	S				KY	KY	KY				AT SCHOOL		5	✓	✓					

TWELFTH CENSUS OF THE UNITED STATES 1900

STATE - KENTUCKY
COUNTY - MONROE
Township or other division: BRUSH

Enumerator: SAMUEL H. CARTER

Supervisor's Dist. No. 102   Sheet No.
Enumeration Dist. No. 82

No. of Family	No. of Dwelling	NAME	Relation	Color	Sex	Date of Birth Mon/Yr	Age at last birthday	Marital Status	# Years married	Mother of how many children?	# of these children living	Place of birth (this person)	Father of this person	Mother of this person	Year of immigr.	# years in U.S.	Naturalization	Occupation 10 years +	Months not employed	Attended school in months	Can read	Can write	Speak English	Owned or Rent	Owned - no mortgage	Farm or house	# of farm schedule
		CHAPMAN, (QUEENIE?) S.	DAU	W	F	MAR 1892	8	S				KY	KY	KY				AT SCHOOL									
		" (LULIE?) E.	DAU	W	F	JUN 1896	3	S				KY	KY	KY													
47	47	WALDEN, DAVID	HEAD	W	M	JUN 1850	49	M	13			KY	KY	KY				FARMER			✓	✓	✓	O	F	F	44
		" MARTHA T.	WIFE	W	F	JAN 1858	42	M	13	6	6	KY	KY	KY							✓	✓	✓				
		" CARY C.	SON	W	M	NOV 1874	25	S				KY	KY	KY				DAY LABORER			✓	✓	✓				
		" ENOCH S.	SON	W	M	DEC 1876	23	S				KY	KY	KY				FARM LABORER			✓	✓	✓				
		" WILLIAM K.	SON	W	M	OCT 1878	21	S				KY	KY	KY				FARM LABORER			✓	✓	✓				
		" LOCKIE	DAU	W	F	FEB 1880	20	S				KY	KY	KY							✓	✓	✓				
		" IDRU	DAU	W	F	OCT 1882	17	S				KY	KY	KY				AT SCHOOL		5	✓	✓	✓				
		" FANUS P.	SON	W	M	APR 1886	14	S				KY	KY	KY				AT SCHOOL		5	✓	✓	✓				
		" EVA	DAU	W	F	JUN 1891	8	S				KY	KY	KY				AT SCHOOL		5	✓	✓	✓				
		" JEFFERSON	SON	W	M	JUN 1893	6	S				KY	KY	KY				AT SCHOOL		5							
		" OMER	SON	W	M	OCT 1894	5	S				KY	KY	KY													
		" LAURA	DAU	W	F	OCT 1897	2	S				KY	KY	KY													
		" ROXIE	DAU	W	F	SEP 1899	9/12	S				KY	KY	KY													
48	48	HAGAN, DAVID	HEAD	W	M	DEC 1860	39	M	17			KY	KY	KY				FARMER			✓	✓	✓	O	F	F	45
		" DILEMMA	WIFE	W	F	JUN 1862	37	M	17	2	1	KY	KY	KY							✓	✓	✓				
		" DEWEY	SON	W	M	SEP 1890	9	S				KY	KY	KY				AT SCHOOL		5							
49	49	HIGH, JAMES	HEAD	W	M	DEC 1863	36	M	12			KY	KY	KY				FARMER			✓	✓	✓	R		F	46
		" LEORA R.	WIFE	W	F	JUN 1869	30	M	12	5	4	KY	KY	KY							✓	✓					
		" ROMOLA	DAU	W	F	SEP 1889	10	S				KY	KY	KY				AT SCHOOL		5	✓	✓					
		" ROY	SON	W	M	JUN 1891	9	S				KY	KY	KY				AT SCHOOL		5							
		" RAY	SON	W	M	MAR 1894	6	S				KY	KY	KY													
		" JOHN F.	SON	W	M	MAR 1899	1	S				KY	KY	KY													
50	50	HARLAN, JOHN	HEAD	W	M	MAY 1842	58	M	32			KY	KY	KY				FARMER			✓	✓	✓	O	F	F	47
		" ELIZABETH	WIFE	W	F	MAR 1846	54	M	32	8	8	KY	KY	KY							✓	✓	✓				

STATE - KENTUCKY
COUNTY - MONROE
Township or other division: BRUSH

Enumerator: SAMUEL H. CARTER

Supervisor's Dist. No. 10✓ Sheet No.
Enumeration Dist. No. 82

No. of Family	No. of Dwelling	NAME	Relation	Color	Sex	DATE OF BIRTH Mon/Yr	Age at last birthday	Marital Status	# Years married	Mother of how many children?	# of these children living	Place of birth [this person]	Father of this person	Mother of this person	Year of immigr.	# years in U.S.	Naturalization	OCCUPATION 10 years +	Months not employed	Attended school in months	Can read	Can write	Speak English	Owned or Rent	Owned –no mortage	Farm or house	# of farm schedule	
		HARLAN, HENRY E.	Son	W	M	Feb 1873	27	S				KY	KY	KY				FARM LABOR			✓	✓						
		" JAKCOB	Son	W	M	Sep 1876	23	S				KY	KY	KY				FARM LABOR			✓	✓						
		" CORDELIA F.	Dau	W	F	Nov 1879	20	S				KY	KY	KY							✓	✓						
		" VIOLA J.	Dau	W	F	Nov 1882	17	S				KY	KY	KY				AT SCHOOL			✓	✓						
		" MYRTIE S.	Dau	W	F	Feb 1887	13	S				KY	KY	KY				AT SCHOOL			✓	✓						
		" EDWARD N.	Son	W	M	May 1890	10	S				KY	KY	KY				AT SCHOOL			✓	✓						
51	51	PALMORE, ANSEL S.	Head	W	M	Mar 1866	34	M	12			KY	KY	KY				SAW MILL MAN			✓	✓		O		FH		
		" JULIE	Wife	W	F	Dec 1871	28	M	12	3	2	KY	KY	KY							✓	✓						
		" EARL	Son	W	M	Sep 1895	4	S				KY	KY	KY														
		" MAY	Dau	W	F	May 1899	1	S				KY	KY	KY														
52	52	VAWTER, JOSEPH	Head	W	M	Mar 1852	48	M	27			KY	KY	KY				FARMER			✓	✓		R		F	48	
		" NANCY O(?)	Wife	W	F	Jan 1850	50	M	27	6	4	KY	KY	KY							✓	✓						
		" JAMES W.	Son	W	M	Oct 1873	27	S				KY	KY	KY				DAY LABOR			✓	✓						
		" EVA (G n L)	Dau	W	F	Aug 1883	16	S				KY	KY	KY				AT SCHOOL		5	✓	✓						
		" JUDIE A.	Dau	W	F	Apr 1887	13	S				KY	KY	KY				AT SCHOOL		5	✓	✓						
53	53	GRIMESLY, WILLIAM	Head	W	M	Dec 1866	33	Wd				KY	KY	KY				FARMER			✓	✓		R		F	49	
		" LEONA	Dau	W	F	Apr 1887	13	S				KY	KY	KY				AT SCHOOL		5	✓	✓						
		" LUTHER H.	Son	W	M	Aug 1890	9	S				KY	KY	KY				AT SCHOOL		5								
54	54	STRODE, WILLIAM C.	Head	W	M	Mar 1866	34	M	13			KY	KY	KY				FARMER			✓	✓	✓	O		FF	50	
		" ELIZABETH Y.	Wife	W	F	Aug 1863	36	M	13	4	3	KY	KY	KY							✓	✓						
		" SUSAN R.	Dau	W	F	Sep 1887	12	S				KY	KY	KY				AT SCHOOL		5								
		" MEDIE M.	Dau	W	F	Oct 1893	7	S				KY	KY	KY														
55	55	MILLER, JOHN S.	Head	W	M	Oct 1858	41	M	16			KY	VA	KY				FARMER			✓	✓		O		FF	51	
		" MARY (F?)	Wife	W	F	Mar 1867	33	M	16	7	6	KY	KY	KY							✓	✓						
		" BERLIE L.	Son	W	M	Oct 1886	13	S				KY	KY	KY				AT SCHOOL		5	✓	✓						
		" ELIZA J.	Dau	W	F	Apr 1889	11	S				KY	KY	KY				AT SCHOOL		5	✓	✓						

TWELFTH CENSUS OF THE UNITED STATES 1900

STATE - KENTUCKY
COUNTY - MONROE
Township or other division — BRUSH

Enumerator — SAMUEL H. CARTER

Supervisor's Dist. No. 102 Sheet No.
Enumeration Dist. No. 82

Location No. of Family	No. of Dwelling	NAME	Relation	Color	Sex	DATE OF BIRTH Mon/Yr	Age at last birthday	Marital Status	# Years married	Mother of how many children?	# of these children living	NATIVITY Place of birth (this person)	Father of this person	Mother of this person	CITIZENSHIP Year of immigr.	# years in U.S.	Naturalization	OCCUPATION 10 years +	Months not employed	EDUCATION Attended school in months	Can read	Can write	Speak English	OWNERSHIP Owned or Rent	Owned - no mortage	Farm or house	# of farm schedule
		MILLER, JOHN	Son	W	M	Jun 1890	9	S				KY	KY	KY				AT SCHOOL		5							
		" WILLIAM M.	Son	W	M	Jun 1892	7	S				KY	KY	KY				AT SCHOOL									
		" ELLA M.	Dau	W	F	Aug 1896	4	S				KY	KY	KY													
		" MARTHA D.	Dau	W	F	Aug 1896	4	S				KY	KY	KY													
56	56	SMITH, ANDREW	Head	W	M	Feb 1857	43	M	21			TN	TN	TN				FARMER			✓	✓	✓	R		F	52
		" MARTHA (T.?)	Wife	W	F	Nov 1855	44	M	21	2	2	KY	KY	KY							✓	✓	✓				
		" FLORA E.	Dau	W	F	Mar 1880	20	S				KY	TN	KY				DRESS MAKER			✓	✓	✓				
		" ELON E.	Son	W	M	Jun 1882	18	S				KY	TN	KY				FARM LABOR			✓	✓	✓				
57	57	HARDIN, BENJAMIN	Head	W	M	Jun 1861	38	M	15			KY	KY	KY				FARMER			✓	✓		O	F	F	53
		" MINTIE	Wife	W	F	Jun 1867	32	M	15	5	5	KY	KY	KY							✓	✓					
		" AIDA	Dau	W	F	May 1886	14	S				KY	KY	KY							✓	✓					
		" DEWEY	Son	W	M	Dec 1887	12	S				KY	KY	KY							✓	✓					
		" EVA	Dau	W	F	Aug 1892	7	S				KY	KY	KY													
		" WILLIE	Dau	W	F	Oct 1894	5	S				KY	KY	KY													
		" RAY	Son	W	M	Jan 1898	2	S				KY	KY	KY													
58	58	HARDIN, JOHN	Head	W	M	Sep 1834	65	M	47			KY	KY	KY				FARMER			✓	✓		O	F	F	54
		" ELIZA	Wife	W	F	Oct 1837	62	M	47	5	5	KY	KY	KY							✓	✓					
		" GEORGE W.	Son	W	M	Sep 1876	23	S				KY	KY	KY				SCHOOL TEACHING			✓	✓					
59	59	DIXON, JOHN	Head	W	M	Oct 1842	57	S				KY	KY	KY				FARMER			✓	✓		O	F	F	55
		" MARY W.	Mother	W	F	Sep 1821	78	Wd		6	2	KY	KY	KY							✓	✓					
60	60	BRADY, JOHN	Head	W	M	Jul 1864	36	M	15			TN	TN	TN				FARMER			✓	✓	✓	R		F	56
		" ELIZA J.	Wife	W	F	May 1864	36		15	4	4	KY	KY	KY													
		" BIRTIE N.	Dau	W	F	May 1889	11	S				KY	TN	KY				AT SCHOOL			✓	✓					
		" DONIE	Dau	W	F	Nov 1890	9	S				KY	TN	KY				AT SCHOOL					✓				
		" ELVA	Dau	W	F	Dec 1894	5	S				KY	TN	KY									✓				
		" LOLLIE (?)	Dau	W	F	May 1897	3	S				KY	TN	KY									✓				

TWELFTH CENSUS OF THE UNITED STATES 1900

STATE - KENTUCKY
COUNTY - MONROE
Township or other division — BRUSH

Enumerator — SAMUEL H. CARTER

Supervisor's Dist. No. 102 Sheet No.
Enumeration Dist. No. 82

No. of Family	No. of Dwelling	NAME	Relation	Color	Sex	DATE OF BIRTH Mon/Yr	Age at last birthday	Marital Status	# Years married	Mother of how many children?	# of these children living	Place of birth [this person]	Father of this person	Mother of this person	Year of immigr.	# years in U.S.	Naturalization	OCCUPATION 10 years +	Months not employed	Attended school in months	Can read	Can write	Speak English	Owned or Rent	Owned -no mortage	Farm or house	# of farm schedule
		BRADY, CHARLES H.	FATHER	W	M	MAY 1825	75	Wd				TN	TN	TN				MILLER			✓	✓	✓				
61	61	BIRCH, MARY	HEAD	W	F	APR 1830	70	Wd				NC	NC	NC				FARMER			X	X	X (?)	O	FF	57	
		" CUTHBERT	GR-SON	W	M	JAN 1876	24	S				KY	KY	KY				FARM LABOR			✓	✓	✓				
62	62	BIRCH, JAMES	HEAD	W	M	APR 1845	55	M	32			KY	NC	NC				FARMER			✓	✓	✓	O	FF	58	
		" MANERVA	WIFE	W	F	Sep 1852	47	M	32	9	7	KY	KY	KY							✓	✓	✓				
		" ROSCO M.	SON	W	M	JAN 1874	26	S				KY	KY	KY				FARM LABORER			✓	✓	✓				
		" WILLIAM	SON	W	M	Sep 1882	17	S				KY	KY	KY				FARM LABORER			✓	✓	✓				
		" CASSIE B.	SON	W	M	Jun 1885	14	S				KY	KY	KY				AT SCHOOL		5	✓	✓					
		" SILVESTER	SON	W	M	Jul 1889	11	S				KY	KY	KY				AT SCHOOL		5	✓	✓					
63	63	CLEMONS, WILLIAM	HEAD	W	M	Aug 1862	37	M	16			KY	KY	KY				FARMER			✓	✓	✓	O	FF	59	
		" MANERVA	WIFE	W	F	Feb 1866	34	M	16	5	5	KY	KY	KY							✓	✓	✓				
		" ROSCO B.	SON	W	M	APR 1886	14	S				KY	KY	KY				AT SCHOOL		5	✓	✓	✓				
		" MYRTIE	DAU	W	F	Feb 1888	12	S				KY	KY	KY				AT SCHOOL		5	✓	✓	✓				
		" HADA F.	DAU	W	F	Feb 1890	10	S				KY	KY	KY				AT SCHOOL		5	✓	✓	✓				
		" ELMAR E.	SON	W	M	JAN 1894	6	S				KY	KY	KY													
		" LOLLIE P.	DAU	W	F	JAN 1899	1	S				KY	KY	KY													
		" THOMAS J.	BRO	W	M	MAY 1870	30	S				KY	KY	KY													
64	64	HOPKINS, JOHN	HEAD	W	M	Nov 1865	35	M	9			KY	KY	KY				FARMER			✓	✓	✓	R	F	60	
		" JOSIE (T?)	WIFE	W	F	OCT 1866	33	M	9	3	3	KY	KY	KY							✓	✓	✓				
		" BESSIE L.	DAU	W	F	Jul 1892	7	S				KY	KY	KY				AT SCHOOL			✓	✓	✓				
		" HUGH W.	SON	W	M	Aug 1894	5	S				KY	KY	KY													
		" SALLIE H.	DAU	W	F	MAR 1898	2	S				KY	KY	KY													
		HARDIN, RANDOLPH	BOARDER	W	M	MAR 1874	26	S				KY	KY	KY				SCHOOL TEACHING			✓	✓	✓				
65	65	BUSHONG, HENRY S.	HEAD	W	M	MAR 1853	47	S				KY	KY	KY				FARMER			✓	✓	✓	O	FF	61	
		" HUDSON K.	NEPHEW	W	M	MAR 1881	19	S				KY	KY	KY				FARMER			✓	✓	✓	O	FF	62	
66	66	BOWMAN, CINDA	HEAD	W	F	Feb 1842	58	Wd		4	4	TN	TN	TN				FARMER			✓	✓	✓	O	FF	63	

TWELFTH CENSUS OF THE UNITED STATES 1900

STATE - KENTUCKY
COUNTY - MONROE
Township or other division

BRUSH

— 145 —

Enumerator SAMUEL H. CARTER

Supervisor's Dist. No. 102   Sheet No.
Enumeration Dist. No. 82

No. of Family	No. of Dwelling	NAME	Relation	Color	Sex	DATE OF BIRTH Mon/Yr	Age at last birthday	Marital Status	# Years married	Mother of how many children	# of these children living	Place of birth (this person)	Father of this person	Mother of this person	Year of immigr.	# years in U.S.	Naturalization	OCCUPATION 10 years +	Months not employed	Attended school in months	Can read	Can write	Speak English	Owned or Rent	Owned - no mortage	Farm or house	# of farm schedule	
		BUSH, JANIE F	DAU	W	F	AUG 1878	22	S				TN	TN	TN							✓	✓	✓					
		BOWMAN, BENDIGO	SON	W	M	JUN 1883	16	S				KY	TN	TN				AT SCHOOL		5	✓	✓	✓					
		" ELIZA A	DAU	W	F	DEC 1884	15	S				KY	TN	TN				AT SCHOOL		5	✓	✓	✓					
		" GEORGE H	SON	W	M	AUG 1887	12	S				KY	TN	TN				AT SCHOOL		5	✓	✓	✓					
67	67	WALKER, WILLIAM	HEAD	W	M	OCT 1867	32	M	8			KY	TN	KY				FARMER			✓	✓	✓	R		F	64	
		" LAURA	WIFE	W	F	AUG 1876	23	M	8	4	3	KY	KY	KY							✓	✓	✓					
		" EZRA	SON	W	M	AUG 1891	8	S				KY	KY	KY														
		" LUTHER	SON	W	M	JUN 1896	3	S				KY	KY	KY														
		" LEANDER	SON	W	M	JAN 1900	4/12	S				KY	KY	KY														
68	68	MILLER, JOHN	HEAD	W	M	DEC 1827	72	M	50			KY	KY	KY				FARMER			✓	✓	✓	O		F	65	
		" ELIZA	WIFE	W	F	SEPT 1830	69	M	50	8	7	KY	KY	KY							✓	✓	✓					
		" LANDON C.	SON	W	M	AUG 1861	38	S				KY	KY	KY				DAY LABOR			✓	✓	✓					
		" ABRAHAM H.	SON	W	M	AUG 1868	31	S				KY	KY	KY				FARM LABORER			✓	✓	✓					
69	69	DUNCAN, RICHARD	HEAD	B	M	OCT 1845	54	Wd				KY	KY	KY				FARMER			✓	✓	✓	O		F	67	SIC
		" JUDGE D.	SON	B	M	SEP 1881	18	S				KY	KY	KY				DAY LABOR			✓	✓	✓					
		" GEORGE M.	SON	B	M	JUL 1884	15	S				KY	KY	KY				DAY LABOR			X	X	X					
70	70	HUME, ROBERT M.	HEAD	W	M	JUN 1866	33	M	7			KY	KY	KY				FARMER			✓	✓	✓	R		F	68	
		" MARTHA S.	WIFE	W	F	APR 1866	34	M	7	5	4	KY	KY	KY							✓	✓	✓					
		" EMMA	STEP-DAU	W	F	MAY 1888	12	S				KY	KY	KY							✓	✓	✓					
		" ISAAC L.	SON	W	M	JAN 1895	5	S				KY	KY	KY														
		" ANNIE L.	DAU	W	F	DEC 1896	3	S				KY	KY	KY														
		" WILLIAM M.	SON	W	M	DEC 1898	1	S				KY	KY	KY														
71	71	WILLIAMS, LORENZA	HEAD	W	M	NOV 1867	32	M	6			KY	KY	KY				FARMER						O		F	69	
		" EDNA B.	WIFE	W	F	JAN 1875	25	M	6			KY	KY	KY							✓	✓	✓					
72	72	HAGAN, JAMES M.	HEAD	W	M	JUN 1854	45	M	22			KY	KY	KY				FARMER			✓	✓	✓	O		F	70	
		" MARY J.	WIFE	W	F	JUL 1858	41	M	22	2	2	KY	KY	KY							✓	✓	✓					

STATE - KENTUCKY
COUNTY - MONROE
Township or other division — BRUSH

Enumerator — SAMUEL H. CARTER

Supervisor's Dist. No. 102 Sheet No.
Enumeration Dist. No. 82

No. of Family	No. of Dwelling	NAME	Relation	Color	Sex	DATE OF BIRTH Mon/Yr	Age at last birthday	Marital Status	# Years married	Mother of how many children?	# of these children living	NATIVITY Place of birth [this person]	Father of this person	Mother of this person	CITIZENSHIP Year of immigr.	# years in U.S.	Naturalization	OCCUPATION 10 years +	Months not employed	EDUCATION Attended school in months	Can read	Can write	Speak English	OWNERSHIP Owned or Rent	Owned -no mortage / Owned or house	Farm or home / # of farm schedule
		HAGAN, VIRGIL V.	SON	W	M	Jul 1881	18	S				KY	KY	KY							✓	✓	✓			
73	73	BAZZLE, JAMES	HEAD	W	M	Oct 1857	42	M	14			KY	KY	KY				FARMER			X	X	✓	R	F	71
		" MARY	WIFE	W	F	Nov 1864	35	M	14	5	5	KY	KY	KY							X	X	✓			
		" NANCY M.	DAU	W	F	Aug 1886	13	S				KY	KY	KY							X	X	✓			
		" GUY	SON	W	M	Sep 1889	10	S				KY	KY	KY							X	X	✓			
		" EFFIE H.	DAU	W	F	Mar 1894	6	S				KY	KY	KY												
		" RUTH	DAU	W	F	Nov 1895	4	S				KY	KY	KY												
		WALTER	SON	W	M	Dec 1898	1	S				KY	KY	KY												
74	74	PICKERAL* RUBY	HEAD	W	M	Jun 1862	37	Wd				KY	KY	KY	*Reuben			FARMER			X	X	✓	R	F	72
		" JOHN	BROTHER	W	M	Jan 1859	41	S				KY	KY	KY				FARM LABORER			X	X	✓			
75	75	BUSHONG, JACOB	HEAD	W	M	Jan 1836	64	M	31			MISS.	KY	KY				FARMER			✓	✓	✓	O	F	73
		" MARY N.	WIFE	W	F	Mar 1847	53	M	31	4	4	KY	TN	TN							✓	✓	✓			
		" WILLIAM P.	SON	W	M	Aug 1874	25	S				KY	MISS.	KY				FARMER			✓	✓	✓	O	F	74
		" NANNIE P.	DAU	W	F	Mar 1877	23	S				KY	MISS.	KY				SCHOOL TEACHING			✓	✓	✓	O	F	75
76	76	BILLINGSLEY, ARTHUR	HEAD	W	M	Feb 1872	28	M	11			KY	KY	KY				FARMER			✓	✓	✓	O	F	75
		" AMERICA I.	WIFE	W	F	Nov 1872	27	M	11	5	5	KY	KY	KY							✓	✓	✓			
		" BETHEL E.	SON	W	M	Dec 1889	10	S				KY	KY	KY				AT SCHOOL			X	X	✓			
		" CLOY J.	SON	W	M	May 1893	6	S				KY	KY	KY												
		" WILLIAM F.	SON	W	M	Feb 1895	4	S				KY	KY	KY												
		" PEARL C.	SON	W	M	Oct 1896	3	S				KY	KY	KY												
		RALPH C.	SON	W	M	Sep 1898	1	S				KY	KY	KY												
77	77	SYMPSON, UNICE	HEAD	W	F	Sept 1842	57	S				KY	KY	KY				FARMER			✓	✓	✓	O	F	76
		" SARAH E.	SISTER	W	F	Sept 1831	68	S				KY	KY	KY							✓	✓	✓			
		" REBECCA A.	SISTER	W	F	Mar 1824	76	S				KY	KY	KY							✓	✓	✓	O	F	77
78	78	MILLER, JOSEPH	HEAD	W	M	Mar 1854	46	M	16			KY	TN	KY				FARMER			✓	✓	✓	O	F	77
		" OMA W.	WIFE	W	F	Dec 1861	38	M	16	7	7	KY	TN	KY							✓	✓	✓			

STATE - KENTUCKY
COUNTY - MONROE
Township or other division — BRUSH — 147 — SAMUEL H. CARTER
Enumerator

Supervisor's Dist. No. 102 Sheet No.
Enumeration Dist. No. 82

No. of Family	No. of Dwelling	NAME	Relation	Color	Sex	DATE OF BIRTH Mon/Yr	Age at last birthday	Marital Status	# Years married	Mother of how many children	# of these children living	Place of birth [this person]	Father of this person	Mother of this person	Year of immigr.	# years in U.S.	Naturalization	OCCUPATION 10 years +	Months not employed	Attended school in months	Can read	Can write	Speak English	Owned or Rent	Owned -no mortgage	Farm or house	# of farm schedule
		MILLER, MELVIN	Son	W	M	Apr 1885	15	S				KY	KY	KY				FARM LABOR			X	X	✓				
		" CLARRA M.	Dau	W	F	May 1887	13	S				KY	KY	KY				AT SCHOOL		5	✓	✓	✓				
		" ELZIE M.	Dau	W	F	Aug 1889	10	S				KY	KY	KY				AT SCHOOL		5	✓	✓	✓				
		" ANNA M.	Dau	W	F	May 1891	9	S				KY	KY	KY				AT SCHOOL		5							
		" DELLA	Dau	W	F	May 1894	6	S				KY	KY	KY													
		" JOHN M.	Son	W	M	Jan 1897	3	S				KY	KY	KY													
		" MARY M.	Dau	W	F	May 1899	1	S				KY	KY	KY													
79	79	BUSHON(G), BENTON S.	Head	W	M	Apr 1880	20	M				KY	KY	KY				FARMER			X	X	✓	R		F	78
		" VICTORIA	Wife	W	F	May 1878	22	M		1	1	KY	KY	KY							X	X	✓				
		" AVERY	Step-Dau	W	F	Mar 1897	3	S				KY	KY	KY													
80	80	KEEN, JOHN R.	Head	W	M	Jul 1844	55	M	32			KY	VA	VA				FARMER			✓	X	✓	O	F	F	79
		" NANCY M.	Wife	W	F	May 1853	47	M	32	10	7	KY	VA	VA							✓	✓	✓				
		" AMANDA G.	Dau	W	F	Oct 1880	19	S				KY	KY	KY							✓	✓	✓				
		" RICHARD S.	Son	W	M	Aug 1885	14	S				KY	KY	KY				AT SCHOOL		5	✓	✓	✓				
		" SARAH M.	Dau	W	F	Feb 1888	12	S				KY	KY	KY				AT SCHOOL		5	✓	✓	✓				
		" LAURIE C.	Dau	W	F	Jan 1890	10	S				KY	KY	KY				AT SCHOOL		5	✓	✓	✓				
		" ALFORD M.	Son	W	M	Apr 1892	8	S				KY	KY	KY				AT SCHOOL									
81	81	HAGAN, DAVID	Head	W	M	May 1831	69	M	48			KY	KY	VA				FARMER			✓	✓	✓	O	F	F	80
		" MARGERT	Wife	W	F	Jul 1835	64	M	48	10	8	KY	VA	VA							✓	✓	✓				
		" NANCY J.	Dau	W	F	Sep 1867	32	S				KY	KY	KY							✓	✓	✓				
		" GEORGE D.	Son	W	M	Nov 1874	25	S				KY	KY	KY							X	X	✓				
82	82	BIRCH, ORLANDER	Head	W	M	Jun 1871	28	M	3			KY	KY	KY				FARMER			✓	✓	✓	R		F	81
		" MARY C.	Wife	W	F	Jul 1878	21	M	3	1	1	KY	KY	KY							✓	✓	✓				
		" MARGRET A.	Dau	W	F	Nov 1897	2	S				KY	KY	KY													
83	83	WILLIAMS, LAFAYETTE F.	Head	W	M	Jul 1838	61	M	39			KY	VA	KY				FARMER			✓	✓	✓	O	F	F	82
		" LUCINDA	Wife	W	F	Apr 1844	56	M	39	4	4	KY	KY	KY							✓	✓	✓				

STATE - KENTUCKY
COUNTY - MONROE
Township or other division   BRUSH

Enumerator SAMUEL H. CARTER

Supervisor's Dist. No. 102 Sheet No.
Enumeration Dist. No. 82

No. of Family	No. of Dwelling	NAME	Relation	Color	Sex	DATE OF BIRTH Mon/Yr	Age at last birthday	Marital Status	# Years married	Mother of how many children	# of these children living	Place of birth [this person]	Father of this person	Mother of this person	Year of immigr.	# years in U.S.	Naturalization	OCCUPATION 10 years +	Months not employed	Attended school in month	Can read	Can write	Speak English	Owned or Rent	Owned -no mortgage	Farm or house	# of farm schedule
		WILLIAMS, HARDIN E.	Son	W	M	Dec 1875	24	S				KY	KY	KY				FARM LABORER			✓	✓	✓				
84	84	PALMORE, TECUMSEH	Head	W	M	Dec 1847	52	M	28			KY	KY	KY				FARMER			✓	✓	✓	O	F	83	
		" LEANA N.	Wife	W	F	Jun 1853	46	M	28	5	5	KY	KY	KY							✓	✓	✓				
		" TIPTON R.	Son	W	M	Feb 1873	27	S				KY	KY	KY				PHOTOGRAPHER			✓	✓	✓				
		" VERTA V.	Dau	W	F	Jan 1876	24	S				KY	KY	KY							✓	✓	✓				
		" EWING L.	Son	W	M	Sep 1879	20	S				KY	KY	KY				FARM LABOR			✓	✓	✓				
		" ELBERT C.	Son	W	M	Dec 1888	12	S				KY	KY	KY				AT SCHOOL		5	✓	✓	✓				
		" NELLIE A.	Dau	W	F	Jun 1891	8	S				KY	KY	KY													
85	85	WRIGHT, SAMUEL D.	Head	W	M	Feb 1872	28	M	1			KY	KY	KY				FARMER			✓	✓	✓	R	F	84	
		" JANE	Wife	W	F	Sep 1877	22	M	1	1	1	KY	KY	KY							✓	✓	✓				
		" DEWEY S.	Son	W	M	Sep 1899	8/12	S				KY	KY	KY													
86	86	WRIGHT, BLEAKY W.	Head	W	M	Aug 1830	69	M	48			KY	VA	SC				FARMER			✓	✓	✓	O	F	85	
		" LUCINDA	Wife	W	F	Oct 1833	67	M	48	8	8	KY	KY	KY							✓	✓	✓				
87	87	PAGE, CALVIN A.	Head	W	M	May 1869	31	M	6			KY	KY	KY				FARMER			✓	✓	✓	R	F	86	
		" RISSA T.	Wife	W	F	Nov 1873	26	M	6	3	0	KY	KY	KY							✓	✓	✓				
88	88	PAGE, JAMES W.	Head	W	M	Oct 1859	40	M	19			KY	KY	KY				FARMER			✓	✓	✓	R	F	87	
		" JINNIE	Wife	W	F	Oct 1860	39	M	19	7	5	KY	KY	KY							✓	✓	✓				
		" EPHREN S.	Son	W	M	Jul 1882	17	S				KY	KY	KY				AT SCHOOL		5	✓	✓	✓				
		" GROVER C.	Son	W	M	Sep 1884	15	S				KY	KY	KY				AT SCHOOL		5	✓	✓	✓				
		" T-NAS T.	Son	W	M	Oct 1891	8	S				KY	KY	KY				AT SCHOOL									
		" BUNIE C.	Dau	W	F	Jun 1894	6	S				KY	KY	KY													
		" LOLLIE T.	Dau	W	F	Dec 1898	1	S				KY	KY	KY													
89	89	CHAPMAN, ALONZO	Head	W	M	Aug 1864	35	M	5			KY	KY	KY				FARMER			✓	✓	✓	R	F	88	
		" NANCY E.	Wife	W	F	Aug 1871	28	M	5	3	2	KY	KY	KY							✓	✓	✓				
		" BARNEY H.	Stepson	W	M	Jul 1891	8	S				KY	KY	KY				AT SCHOOL									
		" FLORENCE	Dau	W	F	Aug 1897	2	S				KY	KY	KY													

TWELFTH CENSUS OF THE UNITED STATES 1900

STATE - KENTUCKY
COUNTY - MONROE
Township or other division: BRUSH — 149 — Enumerator SAMUEL H. CARTER

Supervisor's Dist. No. 102 Sheet No.
Enumeration Dist. No. 82

No. of Family	No. of Dwelling	NAME	Relation	Color	Sex	DATE OF BIRTH Mon/Yr	Age at last birthday	Marital Status	# Years married	Mother of how many children?	# of these children living	Place of birth [this person]	Father of this person	Mother of this person	Year of immigr.	# years in U.S.	Naturalization	OCCUPATION 10 years +	Months not employed	Attended school in months	Can read	Can write	Speak English	Owned or Rent	Owned –no mortgage	Farm or house	# of farm schedule
90	90	PALMORE, NEWTON	Head	W	M	AUG 1839	60	M	39			KY	KY	KY				FARMER			✓	✓	✓	O		F F	89
		" EUPHANY	Wife	W	F	MAY 1843	57	M	39	1	1	KY	KY	KY							✓	✓	✓				
91	91	PALMORE, DORA L.	Head	W	M	MAY 1873	27	M	6			KY	KY	KY				FARMER			✓	✓	✓	R		F	90
		" MARY E.	Wife	W	F	JAN 1873	27	M	6	1	1	KY	KY	KY							✓	✓	✓				
		" YOLA	Dau	W	F	JUN 1894	5	S				KY	KY	KY							✓	✓					
92	92	WRIGHT, LINDY(?)	Head	W	M	OCT 1854	45	M	7			KY	KY	KY				FARMER			✓	✓	✓	O		F F	91
		" MARY E.	Wife	W	F	MAY 1856	44	M	7			KY	KY	KY							✓	✓					
93	93	PALMORE, JAMES	Head	W	M	MAY 1841	59	M	6			KY	KY	KY				FARMER			✓	✓	✓	O		F F	92
		" MANDA	Wife	W	F	SEP 1863	36	M	6	1	0	KY	KY	KY							✓	✓					
		BARTLEY, CRATIE	Servant	N	F	JUN 1882	17	S				KY	KY	KY				HOUSEKEEPER									
94	94	PALMORE, ANDREW	Head	W	M	JUL 1843	56	M	34			KY	KY	VA				FARMER			✓	✓	✓	O		F F	93
		" MARY E.	Wife	W	F	APR 1850	50	M	34	13	10	TN	IND	VA							✓	✓	✓				
		" CAEFFIE A.	Dau	W	F	OCT 1873	26	S				KY	KY	TN				SCHOOL TEACHER 2			✓	✓	✓				
		" RICHARD A.	Son	W	M	JUL 1875	24	S				KY	KY	TN				SCHOOL TEACHER 2			✓	✓	✓				
		" MARY LENA	Dau	W	F	JAN 1878	22	S				KY	KY	TN				SCHOOL TEACHER 2			✓	✓	✓				
		" EFFIE A.	Dau	W	F	JUN 1880	19	S				KY	KY	TN				SCHOOL TEACHER 2			✓	✓	✓				
		" EMMA L.	Dau	W	F	APR 1882	18	S				KY	KY	TN				SCHOOL TEACHER 2			✓	✓	✓				
		" ADDIE B.	Dau	W	F	MAR 1884	16	S				KY	KY	TN				AT SCHOOL		8	✓	✓					
		" HOVEY D.	Son	W	M	DEC 1886	13	S				KY	KY	TN				AT SCHOOL		5	✓	✓	✓				
		" JOHN S.	Son	W	M	MAR 1888	12	S				KY	KY	TN				AT SCHOOL		5	✓	✓					
		" EDNA H.	Dau	W	F	DEC 1890	9	S				KY	KY	TN				AT SCHOOL									
95	95	SMITH, (H___) D.	Head	W	M	JAN 1860	40	M	11			TN	TN	TN				GROCERY MAN			✓	✓	✓	O		F H	
		" VALERIE A.	Wife	W	F	DEC 1867	32	M	11	1	1	KY	KY	KY							✓	✓	✓				
		" CLAUD E.	Son	W	M	DEC 1890	9	S				KY	TN	KY				AT SCHOOL									
96	96	ISENBERG, THOMAS B.	Head	W	M	NOV 1865	34	M	13			KY	TN	TN				FARMER			✓	✓	✓	O		F F	94
		" JELLA	Dau	W	F	DEC 1888	11	S				KY	KY	KY				AT SCHOOL		5	✓	✓	✓				
		" JEVA M.	Dau	W	F	DEC 1890	9	S				KY	KY	KY				AT SCHOOL		5							

STATE - KENTUCKY
COUNTY - MONROE
Township or other division: BRUSH — 150 —
Enumerator: SAMUEL H. CARTER
Supervisor's Dist. No. 102   Sheet No.
Enumeration Dist. No. 82

No. of Family / No. of Dwelling	Name	Relation	Color	Sex	Date of Birth Mon/Yr	Age at last birthday	Marital Status	# Years married	Mother of how many children?	# of these children living	Place of birth (this person)	Father of this person	Mother of this person	Occupation	Months not employed	Attended school in months	Can read	Can write	Speak English	Owned or Rent	Owned -no mortage	Farm or house	# of farm schedule
	ISENBERG, ORA B.	DAU	W	F	APR 1894	6	S				KY	KY	KY		AT SCHOOL	5							
	" LECTTA H.	DAU	W	F	DEC 1896	3	S				KY	KY	KY										
97/97	SMITH, CALVIN	HEAD	W	M	JULY 1836	63	M	45			TN	TN	TN	FARMER			✓	✓	✓	O		F	95
	" SARAH	WIFE	W	F	APR 1830	70	M	45	4	3	TN	TN	TN				X	X	✓				
98/98	WALDEN, CATHERINE	HEAD	W	F	MAY 1837	63	Wd		5	5	KY	VA	KY	FARMER			✓	✓	✓	O		F	96
	" CLARK M.	DAU	W	F	OCT 1870	29	S				KY	KY	KY	DRESSMAKER			✓	✓		O		F	
	" GENINE	DAU	W	F	Sep 1876	23	S				KY	KY	KY				✓	✓					
99/99	HOLLOWAY, JOHN F.	HEAD	W	M	Nov 1872	27	M	4			KY	KY	KY				✓	✓		R		F	97
	" BUNIE	WIFE	W	F	Jun 1674	25	M	4	2	2	KY	KY	KY				✓	✓					
	" WILLIAM H.	SON	W	M	MAR 1897	3	S				KY	KY	KY										
	" ULYSSES H.	SON	W	M	NOV 1898	1	S				KY	KY	KY	FARMER			✓	✓	✓	O		F	98
100/100	WALDEN, SAMUEL T.	HEAD	W	M	Nov 1864	35	M	17			KY	KY	KY				✓	✓	✓				
	" VICTORIA M.	WIFE	W	F	APR 1862	38	M	17	6	6	KY	KY	KY				✓	✓	✓				
	" WILLIAM H.	SON	W	M	DEC 1883	16	S				KY	KY	KY	AT SCHOOL	5	✓	✓	✓					
	" MARY E.	DAU	W	F	Jan 1885	15	S				KY	KY	KY	AT SCHOOL	5	✓	✓						
	" JOHN S.	SON	W	M	DEC 1886	13	S				KY	KY	KY	AT SCHOOL	5	✓	✓						
	" HATTIE M.	DAU	W	F	OCT 1888	11	S				KY	KY	KY	AT SCHOOL	5	✓	✓						
	" IDRU J.	DAU	W	F	Jul 1891	8	S				KY	KY	KY	AT SCHOOL									
	" ADA L.	DAU	W	F	Jul 1891	8	S				KY	KY	KY	AT SCHOOL									
	" MALINDA R.	MOTHER	W	F	AUG 1829	70	Wd		4	2	KY	VA	KY				✓	✓	✓	R		F	99
101/101	JONES, MARTHA E.	HEAD	W	F	Sep 1864	35	Wd		6	6	KY	KY	KY	FARMER			✓	✓	✓	R		F	99
	" NORMA E.	DAU	W	F	DEC 1887	12	S				KY	KY	KY	AT SCHOOL	5	✓	✓						
	" NOVA B.	DAU	W	F	Feb 1890	10	S				KY	KY	KY	AT SCHOOL	5	✓							
	" SALLIE E.	DAU	W	F	Nov 1891	8	S				KY	KY	KY	AT SCHOOL	5								
	" NANCY A.	DAU	W	F	OCT 1893	6	S				KY	KY	KY										
	" LENA E.	DAU	W	F	Nov 1895	4	S				KY	KY	KY										

TWELFTH CENSUS OF THE UNITED STATES 1900

STATE - KENTUCKY
COUNTY - MONROE
Township or other division: BRUSH

Enumerator: SAMUEL H. CARTER

Supervisor's Dist. No. 107 Sheet No.
Enumeration Dist. No. 82

Location		NAME	Relation	Color	Sex	DATE OF BIRTH Mon/Yr	Age at last birthday	Marital Status	# Years married	Mother of how many children?	# of these children living	Place of birth [this person]	Father of this person	Mother of this person	CITIZENSHIP Year of immigr.	# years in U.S.	Naturalization	OCCUPATION 10 years +	Months not employed	Attended school in month	Can read	Can write	Speak English	Owned or Rent	Owned –no mortgage	Farm or house	# of farm schedule
No. of Family	No. of Dwelling																											
		JONES, EDNA T.	DAU	W	F	Feb 1898	2	S				KY	KY	KY														
102	102	NORMAN, JEAN? W.	HEAD	W	M	DEC 1843	56	W				KY	KY	KY				FARMER			✓	✓		R		F	100
103	103	NORMAN, HENRY N.	HEAD	W	M	AUG 1850	50	M	28			KY	KY	KY				FARMER			✓	✓		R		F	101
		" MARY B.	WIFE	W	F	OCT 1854	45	M	28	13	9	KY	KY	KY							X	X	✓				
		" SUSIE E.	DAU	W	F	JUN 1878	21	S				KY	KY	KY							✓	✓					
		" JOHN W.	SON	W	M	OCT 1885	15	S				KY	KY	KY				AT SCHOOL		5	✓	✓	✓				
		" VERNIE	DAU	W	F	OCT 1888	11	S				KY	KY	KY				AT SCHOOL		5	✓	✓	✓				
		" ADOLPHUS M.	SON	W	M	JUL 1890	9	S				KY	KY	KY				AT SCHOOL		5							
		" OVA R.	SON	W	M	MAY 1894	6	S				KY	KY	KY													
		" HOMER T.	SON	W	M	DEC 1896	3	S				KY	KY	KY													
104	104	BARTLEY, JAMES W.	HEAD	W	M	Feb 1879	21	M	1			KY	KY	KY				FARMER			✓	✓	✓	R		F	102
		" MINNIE T.	WIFE	W	F	MAR 1877	23	M	1	1	1	KY	KY	KY							✓	✓	✓				
105	105	WALLING, HARVEY J.	HEAD	B	M	JUN 1872	28	S				KY	KY	KY				FARMER			✓	✓		O		F	103
		" GILBERT	BROTHER	B	M	MAY 1877	23	S				KY	KY	KY				DAY LABORER			✓	✓					
		" ALLIE	NEICE	B	F	AUG 1881	18	S		1	1	KY	KY	KY				HOUSEKEEPER			X	X	✓				
		" OLIVER	NEPHEW	B	M	OCT 1893	6	S				KY	KY	KY													
106	106	MURPHY, PARKER M.	HEAD	W	M	AUG 1836	63	M	44			KY	KY	KY				FARMER			✓	✓		R		F	104
		" LONLIE E.	WIFE	W	F	OCT 1834	65	M	44	1	1	KY	VA	KY							X	X	X				
107	107	FERGUSON, THOMAS S.	HEAD	W	M	OCT 1873	26	M	1			KY	KY	KY				FARMER			✓	✓	✓	O		F	105
		" CARRIE L.	WIFE	W	F	OCT 1881	18	M	1	1	1	KY	KY	KY							✓	✓	✓				
		" DOYL R.	SON	W	M	DEC 1899	5/12	S				KY	KY	KY													
108	108	FERGUSON, MOLLIE	HEAD	W	F	APR 1845	45	S(?)		10	7	KY	KY	KY				FARMER			✓	✓	✓	O		F	106
		" ESAW	SON	W	M	NOV 1886	13	S				KY	KY	KY							✓	✓					
		" JACOB	SON	W	M	NOV 1886	13	S				KY	KY	KY							✓	✓	✓				
		" GRACIE	DAU	W	F	MAR 1894	6	S				KY	KY	KY													
		" FLORA	DAU	W	F	NOV 1897	2	S				KY	KY	KY													

TWELFTH CENSUS OF THE UNITED STATES 1900

STATE - KENTUCKY
COUNTY - MONROE
Township or other division: BRUSH

Enumerator: SAMUEL H. CARTER

Supervisor's Dist. No. 107   Sheet No.
Enumeration Dist. No. 82

- 152 -

No. of Family	No. of Dwelling	NAME	Relation	Color	Sex	DATE OF BIRTH Mon/Yr	Age at last birthday	Marital Status	# Years married	Mother of how many children?	# of these children living	Nativity: Place of birth this person	Father of this person	Mother of this person	Year of immigr.	# years in U.S.	Naturalization	OCCUPATION 10 years +	Months not employed	Attended school in months	Can read	Can write	Speak English	Owned or Rent	Owned-no mortgage	Farm or house	# of farm schedule
		FERGUSON, FLOYD	DAU	W	F	Nov 1897	2	S				KY	KY	KY													
		FERGUSON, RICHARD	BOARDER	W	M	Jan 1845	55	Wd				KY	KY	KY				PHYSICIAN			✓	✓					
109	109	FERGUSON, WILLIAM S.	HEAD	W	M	Feb 1870	30	M	4			KY	KY	KY				FARMER			✓	✓	✓	O	F	F	107
		" IDRU M.	WIFE	W	F	Apr 1877	23	M	4	2	2	KY	KY	KY							✓	✓	✓				
		" EARNEST C.	SON	W	M	Jun 1897	3	S				KY	KY	KY													
		" GEORGE E.	SON	W	M	Nov 1899	7/12	S				KY	KY	KY													
110	110	PAGE, CALVIN R.	HEAD	W	M	Jul 1827	72	M	53			KY	TN	KY				FARMER			✓	✓	✓	O	F	F	108
		" PRUDIE J.	WIFE	W	F	Feb 1831	69	M	53	7	6	KY	VA	KY							✓	✓					
		" BRONNIE	GRANDSON	W	M	Feb 1890	10	S				KY	KY	KY				AT SCHOOL		5	✓	✓	✓				
111	111	PELOR, HENRY D.	HEAD	W	M	Mar 1846	54	M	26			KY	KY	KY				FARMER			✓	✓	✓	O	F	F	109
		" MARY D.	WIFE	W	F	Apr 1847	53	M	26	4	3	KY	KY	KY							✓	✓					
		" RACHEL M.	DAU	W	F	Sep 1877	22	S				KY	KY	KY							✓	✓	✓				
112	112	CARTER, RACHEL C.	HEAD	W	F	Nov 1841	58	S				KY	VA	KY				FARMER			✓	✓	✓	O	F	F	110
		" LOUCINDA S.	SISTER	W	F	Nov 1843	56	S				KY	VA	KY				INVALID			✓	✓					
		WHITE, LAURA A.	NEICE	W	F	Apr 1892	8	S				KY	KY	KY				AT SCHOOL									
		RUSSELL, MARTHA	SERVANT	W	F	Nov 1859	40	S				KY	KY	KY				HOUSEKEEPER			X	X	✓				
113	113	CARTER, JOHN S.	HEAD	W	M	Apr 1848	52	M	12			KY	VA	KY				FARMER			✓	✓	✓	R		F	111
		" ALTA M.	WIFE	W	F	Aug 1864	35	M	12	2	2	KY	KY	KY							✓	✓	✓				
		" JOSEPH H.	SON	W	M	Nov 1888	11	S				KY	KY	KY				AT SCHOOL		5	✓	✓	✓				
		" BENTON E.	SON	W	M	Apr 1893	7	S				KY	KY	KY				AT SCHOOL		5							
114	114	HUME, JOSEPH N.	HEAD	W	M	Nov 1872	27	M	5			KY	KY	KY				FARMER			✓	✓	✓	R		F	112
		" RACHEL M.	WIFE	W	F	Nov 1875	24	M	5	1	1	KY	KY	KY							✓	✓					
		" WILLIAM I.	SON	W	M	Sep 1895	4	S				KY	KY	KY													
115	115	BEDFORD, SARAH J.	HEAD	B	F	May 1848	52	S		5	5	KY	KY	KY				DAY LABORER			X	X	✓	O		H	
		" LOU F.	DAU	B	F	Apr 1873	27	S		2	2	KY	KY	KY				DAY LABORER			✓	✓	✓				
		" MINNIE	DAU	B	F	Apr 1884	16	S				KY	KY	KY				AT SCHOOL		5	✓	✓	✓				

TWELFTH CENSUS OF THE UNITED STATES 1900

STATE - KENTUCKY
COUNTY - MONROE
Township or other division — BRUSH — 153 —

Enumerator — SAMUEL H. CARTER

Supervisor's Dist. No. 102   Sheet No.
Enumeration Dist. No. 82

No. of Family	No. of Dwelling	NAME	Relation	Color	Sex	DATE OF BIRTH Mon/Yr	Age at last birthday	Marital Status	# Years married	Mother of how many children?	# of these children living	Place of birth [this person]	Father of this person	Mother of this person	Year of immigr.	# years in U.S.	Naturalization	OCCUPATION 10 years +	Months not employed	Attended school in months	Can read	Can write	Speak English	Owned or Rent	Owned -no mortage	Farm or house	# of farm schedule
		BEDFORD, IDRU NEICE		B	F	MAY 1888	12	S				KY	KY	KY				AT SCHOOL		5	✓	✓	✓				
		" GALLIE NEICE		B	F	MAR 1890	10	S				KY	KY	KY				AT SCHOOL		5	X	X					
		" ROBERT NEPHEW		B	M	Sep 1893	2	S				KY	KY	KY													
		" LOU E. MOTHER		B	F	— UNKNOWN		W				VA	VA	VA							X	X	✓				
116	116	HUME, JOSEPH N. HEAD		W	M	MAR 1844	56	M	33			TN	TN	TN				FARMER			✓	✓	✓	O	F	F	113
		" MARY A. WIFE		W	F	MAY 1842	58	M	33	3	3	KY	KY	KY							X	X	✓				
		CARTER, WILLIAM A. NEPHEW		W	M	OCT 1881	18	S				KY	TN	KY													
		HUME, ISAAC NEPHEW		W	M	NOV 1890	9	S				KY	KY	KY													
117	117	BOWMAN, CYNTHIA HEAD		W	F	MAR 1856	44	Wd		1	1	KY	KY	KY				FARMER			✓	✓	✓	O	F	F	114
		HAGAN, AMMIE D. DAU		W	F	NOV 1886	13	S				KY	KY	KY				AT SCHOOL		5	✓	✓	✓				
118	118	MILLER, JAMES F. HEAD		W	M	MAR 1856	44	M	6			KY	KY	KY				FARMER			✓	✓	✓	O	F	F	115
		" MARY E. WIFE		W	F	DEC 1868	31	M	6	4	3	KY	KY	KY							✓	✓	✓				
		" WILLIAM SON		W	M	APR 1895	5	S				KY	KY	KY													
		" JOSEPH F. SON		W	M	JUL 1896	3	S				KY	KY	KY													
		" RUTHIE C. J. DAU		W	F	MAR 1899	1	S				KY	KY	KY													
		WHITE, RUTHIE E. MOTH-IN-LAW		W	F	OCT 1844	55	Wd		8	7	KY	KY	KY							✓	✓	✓				
		" LOU SIS-IN-LAW		W	F	MAR 1885	15	S				KY	KY	KY							✓	✓	✓				
119	119	MILLER, WILLIAM T. HEAD		W	M	JUN 1850	49	M	14			KY	KY	KY				FARMER			✓	✓	✓	O	F	F	116
		" MARTHA A. WIFE		W	F	JUL 1860	39	M	14	3	3	KY	KY	KY							✓	✓	✓				
		" LAURA P. DAU		W	F	DEC 1882	17	S				KY	KY	KY				AT SCHOOL		5	✓	✓	✓				
		" AIDA B. DAU		W	F	NOV 1889	10	S				KY	KY	KY				AT SCHOOL		5	✓	✓	✓				
		" MARY S. DAU		W	F	JUN 1892	7	S				KY	KY	KY				AT SCHOOL									
		" ELIZZA DAU		W	F	JUN 1894	5	S				KY	KY	KY													
120	120	STRODE, JAMES W. HEAD		W	M	JAN 1833	67	M	43			KY	N.C	ALABAMA				FARMER			✓	✓	✓	O	F	F	117
		" GENETTA WIFE		W	F	JAN 1838	62	M	43	3	3	KY	VA	VA							✓	✓	✓				
		BELCHER, PRUDENCE M. SISTER		W	F	Sep 1840	60	Wd		7	5	KY	NC	ALABAMA							X	X	✓				

STATE - KENTUCKY
COUNTY - MONROE
Township or other division: BRUSH

— 154 —

Enumerator: SAMUEL H. CARTER

Supervisor's Dist. No. 107 Sheet No.
Enumeration Dist. No. 82

No. of Family	No. of Dwelling	NAME	Relation	Color	Sex	DATE OF BIRTH Mon/Yr	Age at last birthday	Marital Status	# Years married	Mother of how many children?	# of these children living	Place of birth [this person]	Father of this person	Mother of this person	Year of immigr.	# years in U.S.	Naturalization	OCCUPATION 10 years +	Months not employed	Attended school in months	Can read	Can write	Speak English	Owned or Rent	Owned —no mortgage	Farm or house	# of farm schedule
121	121	BAZZLE, CHARLES	Head	W	M	Mar 1847	53	M	12			TN	VA	VA				FARMER			X	X	✓	O	F	F	118
		" MARGRET	Wife	W	F	Feb 1876	24	M	12	5	5	KY	KY	KY							✓	✓	✓				
		" JEAMES H.	Son	W	M	Feb 1884	16	S				TN	TN	TN				DAY LABOR			✓	✓	✓				
		" DANIEL	Son	W	M	May 1890	10	S				TN	TN	KY				AT SCHOOL		5							
		" TILDA L.	Dau	W	F	May 1893	7	S				TN	TN	KY				AT SCHOOL		5							
		" WINDFIELD	Son	W	M	Mar 1894	6	S				TN	TN	KY													
		" RHODA M.	Dau	W	F	Aug 1896	3	S				TN	TN	KY													
		" LILLIE	Dau	W	F	Feb 1900	4/12	S				KY	KY	KY													
122	122	CRUZE, LINDSAY	Head	W	M	Aug 1864	35	M	9			KY	KY	KY				DAY LABORER			X	X		R		H	
		" EVA H.	Wife	W	F	Jul 1875	24	M	9	3	2	KY	KY	KY							X	X					
		" TROY S.	Son	W	M	Jul 1892	7	S				KY	KY	KY				AT SCHOOL		5							
		" LAURA	Dau	W	F	Aug 1898	1	S				KY	KY	KY													
123	123	STRODE, BERTIE L.	Head	W	M	May 1880	20	M	2			KY	KY	KY				DAY LABORER			X	X		R		H	
		" CYNTHA	Wife	W	F	May 1876	24	M	2	2	2	KY	KY	KY							✓	✓	✓				
		" DONIE	Step Dau	W	F	Mar 1897	3	S				KY	KY	KY													
		" ARLIE	Son	W	M	Feb 1899	1	S				KY	KY	KY													
124	124	CURTIS, JESSEE M.	Head	W	M	Apr 1860	40	M	21			KY	KY	KY				DAY LABORER			X	X	✓			H	
		" ELLA M.	Wife	W	F	May 1855	45	M	21	9	9	KY	KY	KY							✓	✓	✓				
		" VENIE	Dau	W	F	Apr 1881	19	S				KY	KY	KY				AT SCHOOL		5	✓	✓	✓				
		" JOHN W.	Son	W	M	Jul 1882	17	S				KY	KY	KY				AT SCHOOL		5	✓	✓	✓				
		" SARAH M.	Dau	W	F	Aug 1884	15	S				KY	KY	KY				AT SCHOOL		5	✓	✓	✓				
		" LABORN	Son	W	M	Feb 1886	14	S				KY	KY	KY				AT SCHOOL		5	✓	✓	✓				
		" RUTHIE C.	Dau	W	F	Mar 1888	12	S				KY	KY	KY				AT SCHOOL		5	✓	✓	✓				
		" THOMAS	Son	W	M	Mar 1891	9	S				KY	KY	KY				AT SCHOOL		5							
		" ELVIRA	Dau	W	F	Apr 1893	7	S				KY	KY	KY													
		" MASIE	Dau	W	F	May 1895	5	S				KY	KY	KY													

STATE - KENTUCKY
COUNTY - MONROE — BRUSH
Township or other division

Enumerator SAMUEL H. CARTER

Supervisor's Dist. No. 102   Sheet No.
Enumeration Dist. No. 82

Location No. of Family	No. of Dwelling	NAME	Relation	Color	Sex	DATE OF BIRTH Mon/Yr	Age at last birthday	Marital Status	# Years married	Mother of how many children?	# of these children living	Place of birth [this person]	Father of this person	Mother of this person	Year of immigr.	# years in U.S.	Naturalization	OCCUPATION 10 years +	Months not employed	Attended school in months	Can read	Can write	Speak English	Owned or Rent	Owned - no mortage	Farm or house	# of farm schedule
		CURTIS, CALVIN	Son	W	M	Jun 1899	11/12	S				KY	KY	KY													
125	125	CLEMONS, JAMES S.	Head	W	M	Feb 1866	34	M	13			KY	KY	KY				FARMER			✓	✓	✓	O	F	F	119
		" ENER T.	Wife	W	F	May 1869	31	M	13	6	5	KY	KY	KY							✓	✓	✓				
		" CHARLIE C.	Son	W	M	May 1889	11	S				KY	KY	KY				AT SCHOOL		5	✓	✓	✓				
		" FIDELL F.	Dau	W	F	Apr 1892	8	S				KY	KY	KY				AT SCHOOL		5							
		" GOMER G.	Son	W	M	Sept 1894	5	S				KY	KY	KY													
		" MAY B.	Dau	W	F	May 1897	3	S				KY	KY	KY													
		" WILLARD W.	Son	W	M	Jan 1899	1	S				KY	KY	KY													
126	126	DUBREE, WILLIAM	Head	W	M	Jan 1862	38	M	17			KY	KY	KY				FARMER			X	X	✓	O	F	F	120
		" IBIE T.	Wife	W	F	Mar 1868	32	M	17	7	7	KY	KY	KY							X	X	✓				
		" LINDSAY V.	Son	W	M	Aug 1883	16	S				KY	KY	KY				AT SCHOOL		5	✓	✓					
		" JOHN B.	Son	W	M	Aug 1886	13	S				KY	KY	KY				AT SCHOOL		5	✓	✓					
		" WILLIAM T.	Son	W	M	Nov 1888	11	S				KY	KY	KY				AT SCHOOL		5	X	✓					
		" INGRAM T.	Son	W	M	Aug 1892	8	S				KY	KY	KY				AT SCHOOL		5	✓	✓					
		" PRINTUS	Son	W	M	Nov 1893	6	S				KY	KY	KY													
		" VADA	Dau	W	F	Feb 1895	5	S				KY	KY	KY													
		" LISSIA P.	Dau	W	F	Sept 1898	1	S				KY	KY	KY													
127	127	DUBREE, JOHN F.	Head	W	M	Dec 1865	34	M	12			KY	KY	KY				FARMER			✓	✓	✓	O	F	F	121
		" MANERVIA	Wife	W	F	Aug 1867	32	M	12			KY	KY	KY							✓	✓	✓				
128	128	WRIGHT, SMITH B.	Head	W	M	Jan 1858	42	M	18			KY	KY	KY				FARMER			✓	✓	✓	O	F	F	122
		" FANNIE T.	Wife	W	F	Jun 1865	34	M	18	6	6	KY	KY	KY							✓	✓	✓				
		" ROXIE	Dau	W	F	Jun 1883	17	S				KY	KY	KY				AT SCHOOL		5	✓	✓	✓				
		" LOCKIE E.	Dau	W	F	Oct 1884	14	S				KY	KY	KY				AT SCHOOL		5	✓	✓	✓				
		" ALLICE H.	Dau	W	F	Apr 1891	9	S				KY	KY	KY				AT SCHOOL		5							
		" HERBERT E.	Son	W	M	Sep 1893	6	S				KY	KY	KY													
		" RICHARD O.	Son	W	M	Apr 1897	3	S				KY	KY	KY													

STATE - KENTUCKY
COUNTY - MONROE

BRUSH
Township or other division

Enumerator SAMUEL H. CARTER

Supervisor's Dist. No. 107 Sheet No.
Enumeration Dist. No. 82

Location		NAME	Relation	Color	Sex	DATE OF BIRTH Mon/Yr	Age at last birthday	Marital Status	# Years married	Mother of how many children?	# of these children living	NATIVITY Place of birth [this person]	Father of this person	Mother of this person	CITIZENSHIP Year of immigr.	# years in U.S.	Naturalization	OCCUPATION 10 years +	Months not employed	EDUCATION Attended school in months	Can read	Can write	Speak English	OWNERSHIP Owned or Rent	Owned -no mortage	Farm or house	# of farm schedule	
No. of Family	No. of Dwelling																											
		WRIGHT, GEO. C.	SON	W	M	JAN 1900	4/12	S				KY	KY	KY														
		" WILLIAM W.	UNCLE	W	M	APR 1834	66	M	34			KY	KY	KY				CAN'T READ IT			✓	✓	✓					
		" DARCUS S.	AUNT	W	F	NOV 1834	65	M	34			KY	KY	KY							✓	✓	✓					
129	129	HALE, ARCH	HEAD	W	M	JUL 1635	64	M	17			KY	TN	TN				FARMER			✓	✓	✓	R		F	123	
		" MARY T.	WIFE	W	F	JUL 1845	54	M	17	4	4	KY	KY	KY							✓	✓	✓					
		" ROSIE B.	DAU	W	F	APR 1864	16	S				KY	KY	KY				AT SCHOOL				✓	✓					
		" JOHN W.	SON	W	M	JUN 1885	15	S				KY	KY	KY				AT SCHOOL			✓	✓	✓					
		" BESSIE A.	DAU	W	F	MAY 1888	12	S				KY	KY	KY				AT SCHOOL			✓	✓	✓					
		" MINTIE B.	DAU	W	F	APR 1890	10	S				KY	KY	KY				AT SCHOOL			✓	✓	✓					
130	130	FANSLER, THOMAS A.	HEAD	W	M	JAN 1869	31	M	6			KY	KY	KY				FARMER			✓	✓	✓	O	F	F	124	
		" SARAH	WIFE	W	F	AUG 1874	25	M	6			KY	KY	KY							✓	✓	✓					
131	131	FERGUSON, WILLIAM	HEAD	W	M	MAY 1854	46	M	22			KY	KY	KY				FARMER			✓	✓	✓	O	M	F	125	
		" MARY J.	WIFE	W	F	OCT 1855	44	M	22	9	7	KY	KY	KY							✓	✓	✓					
		" DELMA L.	DAU	W	F	SEP 1878	21	S				KY	KY	KY							✓	✓	✓					
		" TOLLIE E.	SON	W	M	OCT 1883	16	S				KY	KY	KY				AT SCHOOL		5	✓	✓	✓					
		" BIRTIE D.	SON	W	M	APR 1886	14	S				KY	KY	KY				AT SCHOOL		5	✓	✓	✓					
		" HORRICE	SON	W	M	JUN 1888	11	S				KY	KY	KY				AT SCHOOL		5	✓	✓	✓					
		" SARAH E.	DAU	W	F	OCT 1890	9	S				KY	KY	KY				AT SCHOOL		5	✓	✓	✓					
		" EDNA L.	DAU	W	F	FEB 1893	7	S				KY	KY	KY							✓	✓	✓					
132	132	FRANKLIN, JAMES	HEAD	W	M	OCT 1865	34	M	10			KY	KY	KY				FARMER			✓	✓	✓	R		F	126	
		" ORA L.	WIFE	W	F	OCT 1876	23	M	10	1	1	KY	KY	KY							✓	✓	✓					
		" HERMAN T.	SON	W	M	MAY 1896	4	S				KN	KY	KY														
133	133	BARTLEY, JAMES	HEAD	W	M	APR 1852	48	M	32			KY	KY	KY				FARMER			✓	✓	✓	O	F	F	127	
		" REBECCA	WIFE	W	F	OCT 1846	53	M	32	3	3	KY	KY	KY							✓	✓	✓					
		" JOHN W.	SON	N	M	MAR 1870	30	S				KY	KY	KY							✓	✓	✓					
134	134	HAGAN, SAMUEL	HEAD	W	M	JAN 1858	42	M	23			KY	KY	KY				FARMER			X	X	✓	O	F	F	128	

STATE - KENTUCKY
COUNTY - MONROE   BRUSH
Township or other division   Enumerator SAMUEL H. CARTER

Supervisor's Dist. No. 10 ? Sheet No.
Enumeration Dist. No. 82

No. of Family	No. of Dwelling	NAME	Relation	Color	Sex	DATE OF BIRTH Mon/Yr	Age at last birthday	Marital Status	# Years married	Mother of how many children?	# of these children living	Place of birth [this person]	Father of this person	Mother of this person	Year of immigr.	# years in U.S.	Naturalization	OCCUPATION 10 years +	Months not employed	Attended school in months	Can read	Can write	Speak English	Owned or Rent	Owned –no mortage	Farm or house	# of farm schedule	
		HAGAN, MARTHA	WIFE	W	F	MAY 1858	42	M	23	9	9	KY	KY	KY							✓	✓	✓					
		" TOLLIE J.	SON	W	M	MAY 1877	23	S				KY	KY	KY				FARM LABORER			✓	✓	✓					
		" LICCIE J.	DAU	W	F	OCT 1880	19	S				KY	KY	KY							✗	✗	✓					
		" LOUIS L.	SON	W	M	AUG 1883	16	S				KY	KY	KY				AT SCHOOL		5	✓	✓	✓					
		" WILLIAM B.	SON	W	M	SEP 1885	14	S				KY	KY	KY				AT SCHOOL		5	✓	✓	✓					
		" EVA L.	DAU	W	F	JAN 1888	12	S				KY	KY	KY				AT SCHOOL		5	✓	✓	✓					
		" CHARLIE C.	SON	W	M	SEP 1894	5	S				KY	KY	KY														
		" HARLIE F.	SON	W	M	SEP 1894	5	S				KY	KY	KY														
		" CAELIE E.	DAU	W	F	DEC 1896	3	S				KY	KY	KY														
		" IDRU Q.	DAU	W	F	MAY 1899	1	S				KY	KY	KY														
135	135	WHITE, GEO. W	HEAD	W	M	JUN 1861	38	M	4			KY	KY	KY				FARMER			✓	✓	✓	O	F	F	129	
		" MARY E.	WIFE	W	F	JUN 1871	28	M	4	4	4	KY	KY	KY							✓	✓	✓					
		" JA V.	SON	W	M	NOV 1886	13	S				KY	KY	KY				AT SCHOOL		5	✓	✓	✓					
		" CHARLIE L.	SON	W	M	OCT 1888	11	S				KY	KY	KY				AT SCHOOL		5	✓	✓	✓					
		" ROXIE	DAU	W	F	APR 1894	6	S				KY	KY	KY														
		" ELLICE L.	SON	W	M	DEC 1896	3	S				KY	KY	KY														
		" CARRIE D.	SISTER	W	F	JUN 1883	16	S				KY	KY	KY				AT SCHOOL		5	✓	✓	✓					
136	136	CHAPMAN, NICKLDS	HEAD	W	M	JUL 1852	47	M	11			KY	KY	KY				FARMER			✓	✓		O	M	F	130	
		" SARAH K.	WIFE	W	F	AUG 1863	36	M	11	4	3	KY	KY	KY							✓	✓	✓					
		" CLAUD E.	SON	W	M	MAY 1892	8	S				KY	KY	KY				AT SCHOOL		5								
		" ROY B.	SON	W	M	DEC 1893	6	S				KY	KY	KY														
		" WILLIARD	SON	W	M	MAR 1896	4	S				KY	KY	KY														
		" MANERVIA D.	SISTER	W	F	JUL 1843	56	S				KY	KY	KY							✗	✗	✗					
137	137	HARLAN, ALLICE(?)	HEAD	W	F	APR 1866	34	Wd		5	5	KY	KY	KY				FARMER			✓	✓	✓	O	F	F	131	
		" GALLIE F.	DAU	W	F	MAY 1882	18	S				KY	KY	KY				AT SCHOOL		5	✓	✓	✓					
		" CAUDUS(?) B.	SON	W	M	OCT 1886	13	S				KY	KY	KY				AT SCHOOL		5	✓	✓	✓					

STATE - KENTUCKY
COUNTY - MONROE
Township or other division   BRUSH
Enumerator   SAMUEL H. CARTER

Supervisor's Dist. No. 107   Sheet No.
Enumeration Dist. No. 81

No. of Family	No. of Dwelling	NAME	Relation	Color	Sex	DATE OF BIRTH Mon/Yr	Age at last birthday	Marital Status	#Years married	Mother of how many children?	# of these children living	Place of birth [this person]	Father of this person	Mother of this person	Year of immigr.	# years in U.S.	Naturalization	OCCUPATION 10 years +	Months not employed	Attended school in months	Can read	Can write	Speak English	Owned or Rent	Owned -no mortage	Farm or house	# of farm schedule
		HARLAN, WARREN B.	Son	W	M	Apr 1888	12	S				KY	KY	KY				AT SCHOOL		5	✓	✓	✓				
		" LEO S	Son	W	M	Aug 1892	7	S				KY	KY	KY													
		" CECIL O.	Son	W	M	Aug 1897	2	S				KY	KY	KY													
138	138	DENHAM, ALLEN	HEAD	W	M	Nov 1855	44	M	19			KY	KY	KY				FARMER			✓	✓	✓	R		F	132
		" MARY J.	WIFE	W	F	Oct 1861	38	M	19	5	3	KY	KY	KY							✓	✓	✓				
		" GEDIE H.	Son	W	M	Jul 1884	15	S				KY	KY	KY				AT SCHOOL		5	✓	✓	✓				
		" BERTHA M.	Dau	W	F	Feb 1886	14	S				KY	KY	KY				AT SCHOOL		5	✓	✓	✓				
		" HOBERT M.	Son	W	M	Oct 1896	3	S				KY	KY	KY													
139	139	BARTLEY, JOHN W.	HEAD	W	M	Feb 1864	36	M	18			KY	KY	KY				FARMER			✓	✓	✓	R		F	133
		" POLLIE A.	WIFE	W	F	Jul 1865	34	M	18	7	7	KY	KY	KY							✓	✓	✓				
		" ELZIE F.	Son	W	M	Aug 1883	16	S				KY	KY	KY				FARM LABORER			✓	✓	✓				
		" NANNIE E.	Dau	W	F	Dec 1885	14	S				KY	KY	KY				AT SCHOOL		5	✓	✓	✓				
		" MATILDA	Dau	W	F	Nov 1886	13	S				KY	KY	KY				AT SCHOOL		5		✓	✓				
		" FLORA E.	Dau	W	F	Jun 1888	12	S				KY	KY	KY				AT SCHOOL		5	✓	✓	✓				
		" ORA D.	Dau	W	F	Mar 1893	7	S				KY	KY	KY													
		" ARLEY	Son	W	M	Aug 1895	4	S				KY	KY	KY													
		" EARLEY	Dau	W	F	Aug 1898	1	S				KY	KY	KY													
140	140	BARTLEY, WILLIAM H.	HEAD	W	M	Mar 1836	64	M	40			KY	KY	KY				FARMER			✓	✓	✓	O		F	F 134
		" EDA J.	WIFE	W	F	Apr 1843	57	M	40	4	3	KY	KY	KY							✓	✓	✓				
		" WILLSON H.	SON	W	M	Jun 1862	37	Wd				KY	KY	KY				DAY LABORER			✓	✓	✓				
141	141	BUSHONG, WILLIAM	HEAD	W	M	May 1853	47	M	18			KY	KY	KY				FARMER			✓	✓	✓	O		F	F 135
		" MARTHA E.	WIFE	W	F	Oct 1860	39	M	18	5	3	KY	KY	KY							✓	✓					
		" PERNIE	Dau	W	F	Jun 1882	17	S				KY	KY	KY				AT SCHOOL		5	✓	✓	✓				
		" FRANLIN	Son	W	M	Jun 1884	15	S				KY	KY	KY				AT SCHOOL		5	✓	✓	✓				
		" SALLIE	Dau	W	F	Aug 1887	12	S				KY	KY	KY				AT SCHOOL		5	✓	✓	✓				
142	142	HUTCHEONS, (JOHN?)	HEAD	W	M	Aug 1837	62	M	41			KY	KY	KY				FARMER			✓	✓	✓	O		F	F 136

TWELFTH CENSUS OF THE UNITED STATES 1900

STATE - KENTUCKY
COUNTY - MONROE   BRUSH
Township or other division   Enumerator SAMUEL H. CARTER

Supervisor's Dist. No. _102_ Sheet No.
Enumeration Dist. No. _82_

Location No. of Family	No. of Dwelling	NAME	Relation	Color	Sex	DATE OF BIRTH Mon/Yr	Age at last birthday	Marital Status	# Years married	Mother of how many children?	# of these children living	Place of birth [this person]	Father of this person	Mother of this person	Year of immigr.	# years in U.S.	Naturalization	OCCUPATION 10 years +	Months not employed	Attended school in months	Can read	Can write	Speak English	Owned or Rent	Owned -no mortgage	Farm or house	# of farm schedule
		HUTCHEONS, MARGRET	WIFE	W	F	Jul 1837	62	M	41	5	3	KY	KY	KY							✓	✓	✓				
		" SYLVESTER H.	GRANSON	W M		DEC 1881	18	S				KY	KY	KY				AT SCHOOL			✓	✓	✓				
143	143	SYMPSON, JOSEPH	HEAD	W M		OCT 1858	41	M	20			KY	KY	KY				FARMER			✓	✓	✓	O	F	F	137
		" AMANDA	WIFE	W	F	May 1862	38	M	20	2	1	KY	KY	KY							✓	✓	✓				
		" INGRAM	SON	W M		May 1881	19	S				KY	KY	KY				FARM LABORER			✓	✓	✓				
		HARDIN, LUCY M.	HIRELING	W	F	APR 1877	23	S				KY	KY	KY				HOUSEKEEPER			✓	✓	✓				
144	144	WASHAM, JOHN	HEAD	W M		May 1870	30	M	6			KY	KY	KY				FARMER			✓	✓	✓	R		F	138
		" SALLIE E.	WIFE	W	F	DEC 1872	27	M	6	2	1	KY	KY	KY							✓	✓	✓				
		" BERTHA	DAU	W	F	Sept 1895	5	S				KY	KY	KY													
145	145	CHAPMAN, JAMES	HEAD	W M		Jun 1835	64	Wd				KY	KY	VA				FARMER			✓	✓	✓	O	F	F	139
		" JAMES H.	SON	W M		APR 1859	41	S				KY	KY	KY				INVALID			✓	✓	✓				
		" PARTHENIA	DAU	W	F	OCT 1847	32	S				KY	KY	KY							✓	✓	✓				
146	146	BUSHONG, WILLIAM G.	HEAD	W M		Jun 1847	52	Wd				KY	KY	KY				FARMER			✓	✓	✓	R		F	140
		" NANCY C.	DAU	W	F	AUG 1872	27	S				KY	KY	KY				DRESSMAKER			✓	✓	✓				
		" RISSIE	DAU	W	F	JAN 1876	24	S				KY	KY	KY				DRESSMAKER			=	=	-				
		" JONES	SON	W M		JAN 1878	22	S				KY	KY	KY				FARM LABORER			✓	✓	✓				
		" JOHN S.	SON	W M		JAN 1880	20	S				KY	KY	KY				FARM LABORER			✓	✓	✓				
		" VERNON	SON	W M		DEC 1883	16	S				KY	KY	KY				FARM LABORER			=	=	-				
		" ENNER	DAU	W	F	NOV 1885	14	S				KY	KY	KY				AT SCHOOL		5	✓	✓	✓				
		" LOTT L.	SON	W M		MAY 1887	13	S				KY	KY	KY				AT SCHOOL		5	✓	✓	✓				
		" AIDER B.	DAU	W	F	Jul 1889	10	S				KY	KY	KY				AT SCHOOL		5	✓	✓	✓				
147	147	SIMS, WILLIAM	HEAD	W M		NOV 1858	41	M	18			KY	KY	KY				FARMER			✓	✓	✓	O	F	F	141
		" NANCY E.	WIFE	W	F	Feb 1859	41	M	18			KY	KY	KY							✓	✓	✓				
148	148	FERGUSON, JOHN R.	HEAD	W M		DEC 1873	26	M	8			KY	KY	KY				FARMER			✓	✓	✓	R		F	142
		" DELA S.	WIFE	W	F	OCT 1874	25	M	8	4	4	KY	KY	KY							X	X					
		" ZORA J.	DAU	W	F	AUG 1892	7	S				KY	KY	KY													

STATE - KENTUCKY
COUNTY - MONROE
Township or other division: BRUSH
—160—
Enumerator: SAMUEL H. CARTER
Supervisor's Dist. No. 102 Sheet No.
Enumeration Dist. No. 82

No. of Family	No. of Dwelling	NAME	Relation	Color	Sex	Date of Birth Mon/Yr	Age at last birthday	Marital Status	# Years married	Mother of how many children	# of these children living	Place of birth (this person)	Father	Mother	Occupation	Attended school in months	Can read	Can write	Speak English	Owned or Rent	Farm or house	# of farm schedule
		FERGUSON, WALTER G	SON	W	M	Jul 1895	4	S				KY	KY	KY								
		" ARABELL	DAU	W	F	Mar 1898	2	S				KY	KY	KY								
		" MANERVIA	DAU	W	F	May 1900	1/300	S				KY	KY	KY								
149	149	BUSHONG, JOSEPH C	HEAD	W	M	Jul 1860	39	M	13			KY	KY	KY	FARMER		✓	✓		R	F	143
		" RUTHA H	WIFE	W	F	Sep 1865	34	M	13	5	3	KY	KY	KY			✓	✓				
		" CLAY D	SON	W	M	Nov 1891	8	S				KY	KY	KY	AT SCHOOL	5						
		" LABIN G	SON	W	M	Feb 1893	7	S				KY	KY	KY								
		" JOHN H	SON	W	M	May 1899	1	S				KY	KY	KY								
150	150	HARLAN, WILLICE	HEAD	W	M	May 1874	26	M	1			KY	KY	KY	FARMER		✓	✓		R	F	144
		" MARTHA J	WIFE	W	F	Aug 1874	25	M	1	1	1	KY	KY	KY			✓	✓				
		" DEWEY E	SON	W	M	Apr 1900	4/300	S				KY	KY	KY								
151	151	HARLAN, FRANCIS	HEAD	W	M	Jul 1819	80	M	14			KY	KY	KY	FARMER		✓	✓		R	F	145
		" SARAH J	WIFE	W	F	Nov 1844	55	M	14			KY	KY	KY			X	✓				
152	152	CREWS, JAMES	HEAD	W	M	Dec 1830	69	M	42			KY	KY	KY	FARMER		X	X		O	F	146
		" NARCISSUS	WIFE	W	F	Mar 1837	62	M	42	2	2	KY	KY	KY			X	X				
		" JOHN W	SON	W	M	Jun 1866	33	M	4			KY	KY	KY	FARMER		✓	✓		O	F	147
		" LOUCINDA	DAU	W	F	Oct 1878	21	M	4			KY	KY	KY			✓	✓				
153	153	CREWS, WILLIAM	HEAD	W	M	Mar 1870	30	M	6			KY	KY	KY	FARMER		✓	✓		O	F	148
		" LAURA S	WIFE	W	F	Nov 1876	23	M	6	2	1	KY	KY	KY			✓	✓				
		" JOHN F	SON	W	M	May 1897	3	S				KY	KY	KY			✓	✓	SIC			
154	154	BUSHONG, SAM H	HEAD	W	M	Feb 1864	36	M	1			KY	KY	KY	FARMER		✓	X	✓	R	F	149
		" IBBIE	WIFE	W	F	Apr 1874	26	M	1	1	1	KY	KY	KY			✓	✓				
		" WILLIAM P	SON	W	M	Apr 1899	1	S				KY	KY	KY								
155	155	WALKER, ROBERT B	HEAD	W	M	Oct 1861	38	M	9			KY	KY	KY	FARMER		✓	✓		R	F	150
		" TILDA J	WIFE				Jul 1867	32	M	9	5	4	KY	KY	KY			✓	✓				
		" WILSON H	SON				Feb 1892	8	S				KY	KY	KY	AT SCHOOL	5						

TWELFTH CENSUS OF THE UNITED STATES 1900

STATE - KENTUCKY
COUNTY - MONROE
Township or other division **BRUSH**

Enumerator **SAMUEL H. CARTER**

Supervisor's Dist. No. **102** Sheet No.
Enumeration Dist. No. **82**

No. of Family	No. of Dwelling	NAME	Relation	Color	Sex	DATE OF BIRTH Mon/Yr	Age at last birthday	Marital Status	# Years married	Mother of how many children?	# of these children living	Place of birth (this person)	Father of this person	Mother of this person	Year of immigr.	# years in U.S.	Naturalization	OCCUPATION 10 years +	Months not employed	Attended school in months	Can read	Can write	Speak English	Owned or Rent	Owned -no mortgage	Farm or house	# of farm schedule
		WALKER, WILLIAM H.	Son	W	M	Dec 1895	4	S				KY	KY	KY													
		" GEORGE H.	Son	W	M	Jan 1898	2	S				KY	KY	KY													
		" NANCY E.	Dau	W	F	May 1900	1/12	S				KY	KY	KY													
156	156	CARTER, JOHN B.	Head	W	M	Jun 1862	37	M	13			KY	KY	KY				FARMER			✓	✓	✓	O	F	F	[5]
		" LOU E.	Wife	W	F	Feb 1875	25	M	13	4	4	KY	KY	KY						4		✓	✓					
		" MAY B.	Dau	W	F	Feb 1889	11	S				KY	KY	KY				AT SCHOOL		5	✓	✓	✓				
		" HARRISON	Son	W	M	Mar 1892	8	S				KY	KY	KY				AT SCHOOL		5	✓	✓	✓				
		" HUGH	Son	W	M	Jul 1894	5	S				KY	KY	KY													
		" IDRU	Dau	W	F	Jul 1896	3	S				KY	KY	KY													
		" CHARLOTTIE	Sister	W	F	May 1860	40	S				KY	KY	KY				DRESSMAKER			✓	✓	✓				
		COPASS, NANCY	Step-Mother	W	F	Apr 1828	72	Wd				KY	KY	KY							✓	✓	✓				
157	157	KEEN, AMANDA	Head	W	F	Jan 1873	27	Wd		3	2	KY	KY	KY				DRESSMAKER			✓	✓	✓	R		H	
		" GENETTA M.	Dau	W	F	Oct 1892	7	S				KY	KY	KY													
		" LECTA H.	Dau	W	F	Dec 1895	4	S				KY	KY	KY													
158	158	SILVEY, MALLINDA	Head	W	F	Dec 1871	28	Wd		4	4	KY	KY	KY				FARMER			✓	✓	✓	R		F	152
		" OVA E.	Dau	W	F	Oct 1889	11	S				KY	KY	KY				AT SCHOOL		5	✓	✓	✓				
		" AGNES	Dau	W	F	May 1892	8	S				KY	KY	KY				AT SCHOOL		5							
		" CARL B.	Son	W	M	Apr 1894	6	S				KY	KY	KY													
		" CLAUD J.	Son	W	M	Aug 1896	3	S				KY	KY	KY													
159	159	RASNER ADISON A.	Head	W	M	Oct 1854	45	S				KY	KY	KY				FARMER			✓	✓		O	M	F	153
		" ELIZABET	Mother	W	F	Jun 1824	75	Wd		5	2	KY	KY	KY							X	X					
		" ROSA E.	Neice	W	F	Feb 1886	14	S				KY	KY	KY				HOUSEKEEPER			X	X					
160	160	FERGUSON, JAMES	Head	W	M	May 1848	52	M	27			KY	KY	KY				FARMER			✓	✓	✓	O	M	F	154
		" MARY M.	Wife	W	F	May 1858	42	M	27	8	7	KY	KY	KY							✓	✓	✓				
		" INGRAM C.	Son	W	M	Sep 1879	20	S				KY	KY	KY				FARM LABORER			✓	✓	✓				
		" SMITH	Son	W	M	Feb 1882	18	S				KY	KY	KY				DAY LABORER			✓	✓	✓				

STATE - KENTUCKY
COUNTY - MONROE
Township or other division — BRUSH

— 162 —

Enumerator SAMUEL H. CARTER

Location		NAME	Relation	Color	Sex	DATE OF BIRTH Mon/Yr	Age at last birthday	Marital Status	# Years married	Mother of how many children	# of these children living	Place of birth (this person)	Father of this person	Mother of this person	Year of immigr.	# years in U.S.	Naturalization	OCCUPATION 10 years +	Months not employed	Attended school in months	Can read	Can write	Speak English	Owned or Rent	Owned –no mortage	Farm or house	# of Farm schedule
No. of Family	No. of Dwelling																										
		FERGUSON, CEBEI	Son	W	M	Sep 1884	15	S				KY	KY	KY				INVALID			✓	✓	✓				
		" BASSIE	Dau	W	F	May 1888	12	S				KY	KY	KY				AT SCHOOL		5	✓	✓	✓				
		" VIRGIE	Dau	W	F	Nov 1890	9	S				KY	KY	KY				AT SCHOOL		5	✓	✓	✓				
		" FOYD	Son	W	M	Jun 1894	5	S				KY	KY	KY													
161	61	WILEY, JOHN H.	HEAD	W	M	May 1868	32	M	13			KY	KY	KY				FARMER			✓	✓	✓	R	F	155	
		" JULIE	WIFE	W	F	Mar 1861	39	M	13	9	7	KY	KY	KY							✓	✓	✓				
		" JOHN E.	Son	W	M	Mar 1888	12	S				KY	KY	KY				AT SCHOOL		5	✓	✓	✓				
		" JESSEE E.	Son	W	M	Jul 1889	10	S				KY	KY	KY				AT SCHOOL		5	✓	✓	✓				
		" HIRAM F.	Son	W	M	Jan 1891	9	S				KY	KY	KY				AT SCHOOL		5	✓	✓	✓				
		" MARY F.	Dau	W	F	Nov 1892	7	S				KY	KY	KY													
		" JOSEPH W.	Son	W	M	Mar 1894	6	S				KY	KY	KY													
		" DELLA M.	Dau	W	F	Jun 1897	2	S				KY	KY	KY													
		" WILLIAM L.	Son	W	M	Jun 1899	1/12	S				KY	KY	KY													
162	62	WILEY, JOHN W.	HEAD	W	M	May 1840	60	M	37			KY	KY	KY				FARMER			✓	✓	✓	O	F	156	
		" DELA H.	WIFE	W	F	Sept 1844	55	M	37			KY	KY	KY							X	X	✓				
	163	WILEY, JAMES J.	Head	W	M	May 1870	30	M	3			KY	KY	KY							✓	✓	✓	O	F	157	
		" ELIZABETH A	Wife	W	F	May 1877	23	M	3	1	1	KY	KY	KY							✓	✓	✓				
		" MIRLIE	Dau	W	F	Mar 1898	2	S				KY	KY	KY													
163	64	FERGUSON, JOHN C.	HEAD	W	M	Jul 1856	43	M	21			KY	KY	KY				FARMER			✓	✓	✓	O	F	158	
		" MARGRET	WIFE	W	F	May 1864	36	M	21	9	8	KY	KY	KY							✓	✓	✓				
		" DELLA E.	DAU	W	F	Feb 1880	20	S				KY	KY	KY							✓	✓	✓				
		" NANCY M.	DAU	W	F	Sep 1881	18	S				KY	KY	KY							✓	✓	✓				
		" IZORA	DAU	W	F	Dec 1883	16	S				KY	KY	KY							✓	✓	✓				
		" WILLIAM J.	SON	W	M	Nov 1887	12	S				KY	KY	KY				AT SCHOOL		5	✓	✓	✓				
		" DONIE B.	DAU	W	F	Sep 1889	10	S				KY	KY	KY				AT SCHOOL		5	✓	✓	✓				
		" LEONA M.	DAU	W	F	Jun 1893	6	S				KY	KY	KY													

STATE - KENTUCKY
COUNTY - MONROE
Township or other division — BRUSH

Enumerator SAMUEL H. CARTER

Supervisor's Dist. No. 107   Sheet No.
Enumeration Dist. No. 82

Location		NAME	Relation	Color	Sex	DATE OF BIRTH Mon/Yr	Age at last birthday	Marital Status	# Years married	Mother of how many children?	# of these children living	NATIVITY Place of birth	Father of this person	Mother of this person	CITIZENSHIP Year of immigr.	# years in U.S.	Naturalization	OCCUPATION 10 years +	Months not employed	EDUCATION Attended school in months	Can read	Can write	Speak English	OWNERSHIP Owned or Rent	Owned -no mortgage	Farm or house	# of farm schedule
		FERGUSON, OLLETHA	DAU	W	F	JUN 1896	3	S				KY	KY	KY													
		" EVA	DAU	W	F	DEC 1897	2	S				KY	KY	KY													
164	165	WILSON, ROBERT K.(?)	HEAD	W M		MAY 1875	25	M	4			KY	KY	KY				FARMER			✓	✓	✓	R		F	159
		" LUDIE A.	WIFE	W	F	JUN 1879	20	M	4	2	1	KY	KY	KY							✓	✓					
		" DOAL P.	SON	W M		DEC 1898	1	S				KY	KY	KY													
165	166	BILLINGSLEY, SAM.M	HEAD	W M		DEC 1837	62	M	42			KY	KY	KY				FARMER			✓	✓		O	F	F	160
		" MARY E.	WIFE	W	F	JUN 1842	57	M	42	10	10	KY	KY	KY							✓	✓					
		" LOU C.	DAU	W	F	DEC 1881	18	S				KY	KY	KY							✓	✓					
		" WILLIAM R.	SON	W M		APR 1886	14	S				KY	KY	KY				AT SCHOOL		5	✓	✓					
166	167	BILLINGSLEY, LUTHER L.	HEAD	W M		MAR 1876	24	M	6			KY	KY	KY							✓	✓		R		F	161
		" MARY E.	WIFE	W	F	JUN 1872	27	M	6	3	2	KY	KY	KY							✓	✓					
		" OLLIE G.	SON	W M		APR 1898	2	S				KY	KY	KY													
		" FRED M.	SON	W M		AUG 1899 8/12		S				KY	KY	KY													
167	168	PROFFIT, DANIEL S.	HEAD	W M		AUG 1868	31	M	7			KY	KY	KY				FARMER			✓	✓	✓	R		F	162
		" MERICA	WIFE	W	F	DEC 1871	28	M	7	2	2	KY	KY	KY													
		" ARVEY A.	SON	W M		JAN 1894	6	S				KY	KY	KY													
		" LANARY	DAU	W	F	OCT 1896	3	S				KY	KY	KY													
168	169	MILLER, JOSEPH S.	HEAD	W M		JAN 1857	43	M	20			KY	KY	KY				FARMER			✓	✓	✓	O	F	F	163
		" ALVIRA	WIFE	W	F	DEC 1862	37	M	20	6	6	KY	KY	KY							✓	✓	✓				
*_		" ENGHLISH P.	SON	W M		MAY 1881	19	S				KY	KY	KY				FARM LABORER			✓	✓	✓				
		" ARIZONA	DAU	W	F	AUG 1884	15	S				KY	KY	KY							✓	✓	✓				
		" CINDA	DAU	W	F	APR 1886	14	S				KY	KY	KY				AT SCHOOL			✓	✓	✓				
		" MOLLIE E.	DAU	W	F	MAY 1892	8	S				KY	KY	KY				AT SCHOOL			✓	✓	✓				
		" CLAYTON F.	SON	W M		SEP 1896	3	S				KY	KY	KY													
*		" MALINDA	DAU	W	F	MAR 1883	17	S				KY	KY	KY							✓	✓	✓				
169	170	McGUIRE, JOHN R.	HEAD	W M		NOV 1845	54	M	36			KY	KY	KY				FARMER			✓	✓	✓	O	F	F	164

TWELFTH CENSUS OF THE UNITED STATES 1900

STATE - KENTUCKY
COUNTY - MONROE
Township or other division — BRUSH

Enumerator — SAMUEL H. CARTER

Supervisor's Dist. No. 102 Sheet No. _____
Enumeration Dist. No. 82 _____

No. of Family	No. of Dwelling	NAME	Relation	Color	Sex	DATE OF BIRTH Mon/Yr	Age at last birthday	Marital Status	# Years married	Mother of how many children?	# of these children living	Place of birth (this person)	Father of this person	Mother of this person	Year of immigr.	# years in U.S.	Naturalization	OCCUPATION 10 years +	Months not employed	Attended school in months	Can read	Can write	Speak English	Owned or Rent	Owned – no mortgage	Farm or house	# of farm schedule
		McGUIRE, ELLEN	WIFE	W	F	Sep 1838	61	M	36	2	1	KY	KY	KY							✓	✓	✓				
170	171	McGUIRE, SAMUEL	HEAD	W	M	Sep 1873	26	M	9			KY	KY	KY				FARMER			✓	✓	✓	R		F	165
		" LUCRESSA	WIFE	W	F	Jan 1877	23	M	9	6	5	KY	KY	KY							✓	✓	✓				
		" OLLIE R.	SON	W	M	Sep 1892	7	S				KY	KY	KY													
		" JOEL	SON	W	M	Jan 1894	6	S				KY	KY	KY													
		" ALONZO	SON	W	M	Sep 1896	3	S				KY	KY	KY													
		" CARL	SON	W	M	Apr 1898	2	S				KY	KY	KY													
		" MAY L.	DAU	W	F	Mar 1900	2/12	S				KY	KY	KY													
171	172	EMBERTON, HARMON C.	HEAD	W	M	Jun 1853	46	M	8			KY	KY	KY				FARMER			✓	✓	✓	R		F	166
		" EURETHA	WIFE	W	F	May 1874	26	M	8	3	3	KY	KY	KY							✓	✓	✓				
		" VIRGINIA	DAU	W	F	Nov 1885	14	S				KY	KY	KY							✓	✓	✓				
		" WILLIAM H.	SON	W	M	Feb 1887	13	S				KY	KY	KY				AT SCHOOL			✓	✓	✓				
		" NEVADA E	DAU	W	F	Jun 1894	5	S				KY	KY	KY													
		" ANNIE A.	DAU	W	F	Jun 1896	3	S				KY	KY	KY													
		" PEARL F	DAU	W	F	Aug 1898	1	S				KY	KY	KY													
172	173	MILLER, ABRAHAM	HEAD	W	M	Mar 1846	54	M	22			KY	KY	KY				FARMER			✓	✓	✓	O		F	167
		" LON S.	WIFE	W	F	Nov 1858	41	M	22	6	6	KY	KY	KY							✓	✓	✓				
		" JOSEPH E.	SON	W	M	Oct 1879	20	S				KY	KY	KY				FARM LABORER			✓	✓	✓				
		" JOHN	SON	W	M	Apr 1887	13	S				KY	KY	KY				AT SCHOOL		5	✓	✓	✓				
		" IBBIE P	DAU	W	F	Sep 1888	11	S				KY	KY	KY				AT SCHOOL		5	✓	✓	✓				
		" PRISCILLA E	DAU	W	F	Feb 1892	8	S				KY	KY	KY													
		" TILDA A.	DAU	W	F	Mar 1894	6	S				KY	KY	KY													
		" WILLIAM M.	SON	W	M	Jul 1898	1	S				KY	KY	KY													
173	174	KINGERY, HARMON	HEAD	W	M	Oct 1873	26	M	2			KY	KY	KY				FARMER			✓	✓	✓	R		F	168
		" LOU F.	WIFE	W	F	Apr 1880	20	M	2	1	1	KY	KY	KY							✓	✓	✓				
		" ORVAL	SON	W	M	Jul 1899	11/12	S				KY	KY	KY													

TWELFTH CENSUS OF THE UNITED STATES 1900

STATE - KENTUCKY
COUNTY - MONROE
Township or other division — BRUSH

Enumerator SAMUEL H. CARTER

Supervisor's Dist. No. 107   Sheet No.
Enumeration Dist. No. 82

No. of Family	No. of Dwelling	NAME	Relation	Color	Sex	DATE OF BIRTH Mon/Yr	Age at last birthday	Marital Status	# Years married	Mother of how many children?	# of these children living	Place of birth [this person]	Father of this person	Mother of this person	Year of immigr.	# years in U.S.	Naturalization	OCCUPATION 10 years +	Months not employed	Attended school in months	Can read	Can write	Speak English	Owned or Rent	Owned -no mortage	Farm or house	# of farm schedule	
174	175	STRODE, LINDSAY	Head	W	M	Sep 1869	30	M	10			KY	KY	KY				FARMER			✓	✓	✓	O		F	169	
		" PRUDIE	Wife	W	F	Jul 1871	28	M	10	4	4	KY	KY	KY							✓	✓	✓					
		" WALTER A.	Son	W	M	Dec 1890	9	S				KY	KY	KY														
		" ELIZA D.	Dau	W	F	Jul 1891	8	S				KY	KY	KY														
		" OLLIE G.	Son	W	M	Jul 1894	5	S				KY	KY	KY														
		" CLOE J.	Dau	W	F	Nov 1896	3	S				KY	KY	KY														
175	176	HAGAN, JOHN	Head	W	M	Nov 1861	28	Wd				KY	KY	KY				FARMER			✓	✓	✓	R		F	170	
		" WILLIAM R.	Son	W	M	Oct 1885	14	S				KY	KY	KY				AT SCHOOL		5	✓	✓	✓					
		" MAUD	Dau	W	F	Dec 1890	9	S				KY	KY	KY				AT SCHOOL		5								
		" MANDALA	Dau	W	F	Oct 1892	7	S				KY	KY	KY														
		" OLLIE M.	Dau	W	F	May 1899	1	S				KY	KY	KY														
176	177	MAXEY, GILBERT	Head	B	M	May 1836	64	Wd				KY	VA	KY				FARMER			✓	✓		O		F	171	
		" ROXIE	Dau	B	F	Jun 1873	26	S				KY	KY	KY				SCHOOL TEACHING 2			✓	✓	✓					
		" TEMPLE	Dau	B	F	Feb 1876	24	S				KY	KY	KY				SCHOOL TEACHING 5T			✓	✓	✓					
		" GILBERT L.	Grand Son	B	M	May 1886	14	S				KY	KY	KY				AT SCHOOL		5	✓	✓	✓					
		" OSCAR	Grand Son	B	M	Feb 1892	8	S				KY	KY	KY				AT SCHOOL		5	✓	✓	✓					
177	178	DENHAM, CHARLES D.	Head	W	M	May 1851	49	M	21			TN	TN	TN				FARMER			✓	✓	✓	O		F	172	
		" MARY	Wife	W	F	July 1857	42	M	21	1	0	KY	KY	KY							✓	✓	✓					
178	179	BARTLEY, WILSON	Head	W	M	Aug 1841	58	M	33			KY	KY	KY				FARMER			✓	X	✓	O		F	173	
		" AMERICA W.	Wife	W	F	Jan 1851	49	M	33	6	6	KY	KY	KY							✓	✓	✓					
		" NANCY W.	Dau	W	F	May 1874	26	S				KY	KY	KY							✓	✓	✓					
		" ISERAH H.	Son	W	M	May 1877	23	S				KY	KY	KY				FARM LABORER			✓	✓	✓					
		" DORA B.	Dau	W	F	Apr 1882	18	S				KY	KY	KY							✓	✓	✓					
		" EDNA V.	Dau	W	F	May 1885	15	S				KY	KY	KY							✓	✓	✓					
179	180	PITCOCK, ELIJAH	Head	W	M	Mar 1864	36	M	14			KY	KY	KY				FARMER			✓	✓	✓	O		F	174	
		" GILLIE F.	Wife	W	F	Jan 1862	38	M	14	3	3	KY	KY	KY							✓	✓	✓					

STATE - KENTUCKY
COUNTY - MONROE
Township or other division — BRUSH

Enumerator — SAMUEL H. CARTER

Supervisor's Dist. No. *102*   Sheet No.
Enumeration Dist. No. *82*

No. of Family	No. of Dwelling	NAME	Relation	Color	Sex	Date of Birth Mon/Yr	Age at last birthday	Marital Status	# Years married	Mother of how many children?	# of these children living	Place of birth (this person)	Father of this person	Mother of this person	Year of immigr.	# years in U.S.	Naturalization	Occupation 10 years +	Months not employed	Attended school in months	Can read	Can write	Speak English	Owned or Rent	Owned –no mortgage	Farm or house	# of farm schedule
		PITCOCK, WALTER P.	Son	W	M	Feb 1887	13	S				KY	KY	KY				AT SCHOOL		5	✓	✓					
		" PEARL	Dau	W	F	Jun 1894	5	S				KY	KY	KY													
		" FRANCIS R.	Son	W	M	Dec 1896	3	S				KY	KY	KY													
180	181	SMITH, ANDREW J.	Head	W	M	Aug 1865	34	M	8			KY	KY	KY				FARMER			✓	✓	✓	O	F	F	175
		" MATTIE	Wife	W	F	Aug 1868	31	M	8	4	4	KY	KY	KY							✓	✓	✓				
		" HERBERT C.	Son	W	M	Aug 1893	6	S				KY	KY	KY													
		" ERSIE	Dau	W	F	Feb 1896	4	S				KY	KY	KY													
		" NELLIE	Dau	W	F	Nov 1897	2	S				KY	KY	KY													
		" MALLA	Dau	W	F	Jan 1900	4/12	S				KY	KY	KY													
181	182	GEARLDS, JAMES	Head	W	M	May 1866	34	M	1			KY	KY	KY				FARMER			✓	✓	✓	R		F	176
		" CORA	Wife	W	F	Jul 1870	29	M	1	1	1	KY	KY	KY							✓	✓					
		" PAUL L.	Son	W	M	Aug 1899	9/12	S				KY	KY	KY													
182	183	EMBERTON, JAMES F.	Head	W	M	May 1864	36	M	9			KY	KY	KY				FARMER			✓	✓	✓	O	F	F	177
		" LAURA E	Wife	W	F	Oct 1876	23	M	9	4	1	KY	KY	KY							X	X	✓				
		" NANCY A.	Dau	W	F	Feb 1896	4	S				KY	KY	KY													
183	184	FERGUSON, SAMUEL	Head	W	M	Jan 1864	36	M	16			KY	KY	KY				FARMER			✓	✓	✓	O	F	F	178
		" LOU E.	Wife	W	F	Mar 1867	33	M	16	5	5	KY	KY	KY							✓	✓	✓				
		" MAUD	Dau	W	F	Apr 1886	14	S				KY	KY	KY				AT SCHOOL		5	✓	✓	✓				
		" BUFORD	Son	W	M	May 1888	12	S				KY	KY	KY				AT SCHOOL		5	✓	✓	✓				
		" MILLIARD	Son	W	M	Jun 1891	8	S				KY	KY	KY													
		" CLARANCE	Son	W	M	Aug 1893	6	S				KY	KY	KY													
		" ANNIE	Dau	W	F	Nov 1895	4	S				KY	KY	KY													
184	185	PALMORE, IVY	Head	W	F	Nov 1835	64	Wd		9	5	KY	VA	KY				FARMER			✓	✓	✓	O		F	179
185	186	CARTER, JOSEPH R.	Head	W	M	Sep 1848	51	M	24			KY	KY	KY				FARMER			✓	✓	✓	R		F	180
		" AMERICA J.	Wife	W	F	Jun 1858	41	M	24	9	9	KY	KY	KY							✓	✓	✓				
		" GEORGE W.	Son	W	M	Oct 1881	18	S				KY	KY	KY				FARM LABORER			✓	✓	✓				

TWELFTH CENSUS OF THE UNITED STATES 1900

STATE - KENTUCKY
COUNTY - MONROE
Township or other division — BRUSH

Enumerator SAMUEL H. CARTER

Supervisor's Dist. No. 102   Sheet No.
Enumeration Dist. No. 82

Location (No. of Family / No. of Dwelling)	NAME	Relation	Color	Sex	DATE OF BIRTH Mon/Yr	Age at last birthday	Marital Status	# Years married	Mother of how many children	# of these children living	Place of birth [this person]	Father of this person	Mother of this person	Year of immigr.	# years in U.S.	Naturalization	OCCUPATION 10 years +	Months not employed	Attended school in months	Can read	Can write	Speak English	Owned or Rent	Owned-no mortgage	Farm or house	# of farm schedule
	CARTER, GUY B.	Son	W	M	Apr 1884	16	S				KY	KY	KY				FARM LABORER			✓	✓	✓				
	" ELIZABETH A.	Dau	W	F	Feb 1887	13	S				KY	KY	KY				AT SCHOOL		5	✓	✓	✓				
	" LOU B.	Dau	W	F	Apr 1890	10	S				KY	KY	KY				AT SCHOOL		5	✓	✓	✓				
	" DONIE L.	Dau	W	F	Aug 1893	6	S				KY	KY	KY													
	" IDRU E.	Dau	W	F	Jun 1896	3	S				KY	KY	KY													
	" BROCKIE M.	Dau	W	F	Aug 1897	2	S				KY	KY	KY													
	HARLAN, WINNIE	Boarder	W	F	Jun 1828	71	Wd		2	0	KY	KY	VA				INCOME (?)			X	X	✓				
186/187	STRODE, JOHN M.	Head	W	M	Oct 1877	22	M	2			KY	KY	KY				FARMER			✓	✓	✓	R		F	181
	" ISABELL S.	Wife	W	F	Oct 1877	22	M	2	2	2	KY	KY	KY							✓	✓	✓				
	" LESLIE	Son	W	M	Mar 1897	3	S				KY	KY	KY													
	" FLORENCE E.	Dau	W	F	Aug 1898	1	S				KY	KY	KY													
187/188	BUSHONG, HENRY C.	Head	W	M	Nov 1835	64	M	40			KY	KY	KY				FARMER			✓	✓	✓	R		F	182
	" LUCY S.	Wife	W	F	Jul 1840	59	M	40	10	8	KY	KY	KY							X	X					
	" GEO. S.	Son	W	M	Nov 1874	25	S				KY	KY	KY				FARM LABORER			✓	✓	✓				
	" OSCAR G.	Grand-son	W	M	Apr 1887	13	S				KY	KY	KY				FARM LABORER			✓	✓	✓				
	" WILLIAM A.	Grand-son	W	M	Jul 1893	6	S				KY	KY	KY							✓	✓	✓				
188/189	BOCKMAN, SIDNEY	Head	W	M	Jan 1863	37	M	9			KY	KY	KY				SAWYER			✓	✓	✓	R		H	
	" MOLLIE H.	Wife	W	F	May 1872	28	M	9	2	1	KY	KY	KY							✓	✓	✓				
	" FLOY	Son	W	M	Apr 1893	7	S				KY	KY	KY													
189/190	DOCKRY, WILLIAM	Head	W	M	Oct 1871	28	M	10			TN	TN	TN				DAY LABORER			X	X	✓	R		H	
	" MAGIE	Wife	W	F	Oct 1873	26	M	10	4	4	TN	TN	TN							X	X	✓				
	" SYDNEY L.	Son	W	M	Nov 1892	7	S				TN	TN	TN													
	" JAMES R.	Son	W	M	Dec 1893	6	S				TN	TN	TN													
	" SUSIE E.	Dau	W	F	Jan 1897	3	S				TN	TN	TN													
	" JESSEE E.	Son	W	M	Apr 1900	1/12	S				TN	TN	TN													
	WOLF, GILLEM	Boarder	W	M	Apr 1880	20	S				TN	TN	TN				DAY LABORER			X	X	✓				

TWELFTH CENSUS OF THE UNITED STATES 1900

STATE - KENTUCKY
COUNTY - MONROE
Township or other division: BRUSH
Enumerator: SAMUEL H. CARTER

Supervisor's Dist. No. 10? Sheet No.
Enumeration Dist. No. 82

No. of Family	No. of Dwelling	NAME	Relation	Color	Sex	Date of Birth Mon/Yr	Age at last birthday	Marital Status	# Years married	Mother of how many children	# of these children living	Place of birth (this person)	Father of this person	Mother of this person	Occupation	Months not employed	Attended school in months	Can read	Can write	Speak English	Owned or Rent	Farm or house	# of farm schedule
190	191	LEMONS, WILLIAM J.	HEAD	W	M	MAY 1855	45	M	18			TN	TN	TN				✓	✓	✓	R	H	
		" REBECCA E.	WIFE	W	F	Nov 1861	38	M	18	1	1	TN	TN	TN				X	X	✓			
191	192	HAGAN, LABAN G.	HEAD	W	M	Sep 1856	43	M	11			KY	KY	KY	DAY LABORER	2		X	X	✓	R	H	
		" BETTIE A.	WIFE	W	F	MAY 1867	33	M	11	6	4	KY	KY	KY				✓	✓	✓			
		" THOMAS A.	SON	W	M	DEC 1889	10	S				KY	KY	KY				X	X	✓			
		" FLOY	DAU	W	F	JAN 1893	7	S				KY	KY	KY									
		" JEAMES R.	SON	W	M	MAR 1895	5	S				KY	KY	KY									
		" JACOB M.	SON	W	M	JAN 1897	3	S				KY	KY	KY									
192	193	GRIDER, CYRUS W.	HEAD	W	M	JUN 1854	45	M	25			KY	KY	KY	FARMER			✓	✓	✓	R	F	183
		" MAY L.	WIFE	W	F	MAR 1854	46	M	25	9	9	KY	KY	KY				✓	✓	✓			
		" LILLEY J.	DAU	W	F	MAY 1880	20	S				KY	KY	KY	AT SCHOOL			✓	✓	✓			
		" HATTIE M.	DAU	W	F	APR 1884	16	S				KY	KY	KY	AT SCHOOL		5	✓	✓	✓			
		" LULIE	DAU	W	F	JAN 1886	14	S				KY	KY	KY	AT SCHOOL		5	✓	✓	✓			
		" BENJAMIN H.	SON	W	M	Feb 1888	12	S				KY	KY	KY	AT SCHOOL		5						
		" VICTOR H.	SON	W	M	Feb 1892	8	S				KY	KY	KY									
		" CYBEL	DAU	W	F	Feb 1894	6	S				KY	KY	KY									
193	194	CURTIS, CAIRL	HEAD	W	M	APR 1874	26	S				KY	KY	KY	FARMER			✓	✓	✓	R	F	184
		" CATHERINA	MOTHER	W	F	APR 1838	62	Wd		5	4	KY	KY	KY				X	X	✓			
194	195	POLAND, RUTHIE	HEAD	W	F	Sep 1858	41	Wd		7	6	KY	KY	KY	FARMER			✓	✓	✓	O	F	185
		" TURNER	SON	W	M	AUG 1882	17	S				KY	KY	KY	FARM LABORER			✓	✓	✓			
		" JOHN E.	SON	W	M	MAR 1885	15	S				KY	KY	KY	FARM LABORER			✓	✓	✓			
		" RACHEL C.	DAU	W	F	Sep 1887	12	S				KY	KY	KY	AT SCHOOL		5	✓	✓	✓			
		" WILLIAM M.	SON	W	M	APR 1890	10	S				KY	KY	KY	AT SCHOOL		5	✓	✓	✓			
		" NANCY H.	DAU	W	F	OCT 1893	6	S				KY	KY	KY									
		" CALVIN F.	SON	W	M	MAR 1895	5	S				KY	KY	KY									
195	196	PICKERAL, SANFORD	HEAD	W	M	APR 1871	29	M	12			KY	KY	KY	FARMER			X	X	✓	O	F	186

STATE - KENTUCKY
COUNTY - MONROE   BRUSH
Township or other division   Enumerator SAMUEL H. CARTER

Supervisor's Dist. No. 10² Sheet No.
Enumeration Dist. No. 82

No. of Family	No. of Dwelling	NAME	Relation	Color	Sex	DATE OF BIRTH Mon/Yr	Age at last birthday	Marital Status	# Years married	Mother of how many children?	# of these children living	Place of birth (this person)	Father of this person	Mother of this person	Year of immigr.	# years in U.S.	Naturalization	OCCUPATION 10 years +	Months not employed	Attended school in months	Can read	Can write	Speak English	Owned or Rent	Owned - no mortgage	Farm or house	# of farm schedule
		PICKERAL, MACKIE J.	WIFE	W	F	APR 1872	28	M	12	4	4	KY	KY	KY							✓	✓	✓				
		" LUCY M.	DAU	W	F	AUG 1890	10	S				KY	KY	KY				AT SCHOOL		5	X	X	✓				
		" WILLIAM H.	SON	W	M	OCT 1893	6	S				KY	KY	KY													
		" BASSIE	SON	W	M	APR 1896	4	S				KY	KY	KY													
		" LULIE V.	DAU	W	F	DEC 1897	2	S				KY	KY	KY													
196	197	PAULL, JOHN R.	HEAD	W	M	FEB 1864	36	M	17			KY	KY	KY				FARMER			X	X	✓	R		F	187
		" MELVINA	WIFE	W	F	APR 1865	35	M	17	7	6	KY	KY	KY							✓	✓	✓				
		" VIRGIL G.	SON	W	M	APR 1885	15	S				KY	KY	KY				FARM LABORER			✓	✓	✓				
		" DONIE M.	DAU	W	F	MAY 1887	13	S				KY	KY	KY				AT SCHOOL		5	K	✓	✓				
		" ARVIL L.	SON	W	M	MAY 1889	11	S				KY	KY	KY				AT SCHOOL		5	✓	✓	✓				
		" ROBERT M.	SON	W	M	APR 1890	10	S				KY	KY	KY				AT SCHOOL		5	✓	X	✓				
		" LILLIE M.	DAU	W	F	MAY 1893	7	S				KY	KY	KY													
		" ETHEL P.	DAU	W	F	OCT 1898	1	S				KY	KY	KY													
197	198	BAZZLE, HENRY W.	HEAD	W	M	MAR 1866	34	M	11			KY	TN	TN				FARMER			X	X	✓	R		F	188
		" SARAH C.	WIFE	W	F	Sep 1871	28	M	11	5	4	N.C.	N.C.	N.C.							X	X	✓				
		" CATHARINA	DAU	W	F	May 1890	10	S				NC	KY	NC				AT SCHOOL			X	X	✓				
		" CHARLIE	SON	W	M	Sep 1893	6	S				NC	KY	NC													
		" ORIS S.	SON	W	M	MAR 1899	1	S				NC	KY	NC													
198	199	BUSHONG, JOHN M.	Head	W	M	MAR 1855	45	M	20			KY	IND	KY				FARMER			X	X	✓	R		F	189
		" MARGRET B.	Wife	W	F	APR 1860	40	M	20	5	5	TN	TN	TN							✓	✓	✓				
		" NANCY M.	DAU	W	F	JAN 1881	19	S				KY	KY	TN							✓	✓	✓				
		" ELIZA J.	DAU	W	F	DEC 1882	17	S				KY	KY	TN							✓	✓	✓				
		" ROXIE A.	DAU	W	F	FEB 1886	14	S				KY	KY	TN				AT SCHOOL			✓	✓	✓				
		" WILLIE W.	DAU	W	F	MAR 1891	9	S				KY	KY	TN													
		" JOHN A.	SON	W	M	MAR 1896	4	S				KY	KY	TN													
		" JOHN W.	FATHER	W	M	MAY 1834	66	Wd				IND	KY	KY													

STATE - KENTUCKY
COUNTY - MONROE   BRUSH
Township or other division   Enumerator SAMUEL H. CARTER

Supervisor's Dist. No. 102 Sheet No.
Enumeration Dist. No. 82

No. of Family	No. of Dwelling	NAME	Relation	Color	Sex	DATE OF BIRTH Mon/Yr	Age at last birthday	Marital Status	# Years married	Mother of how many children?	# of these children living	Place of birth [this person]	Father of this person	Mother of this person	Year of immigr.	# years in U.S.	Naturalization	OCCUPATION 10 years +	Months not employed	Attended school in months	Can read	Can write	Speak English	Owned or Rent	Owned -no mortgage	Farm or house	# of farm schedule	
199	200	WALDEN, JAMES C.	Head	W	M	DEC 1848	51	M	30			KY	KY	KY				FARMER			✓	✓	✓	O	F	F	190	
		" MAHALA A.	Wife	W	F	FEB 1851	48	M	30	14	10	VA	VA	VA							✓	✓	✓					
		" GARFIELD	Son	W	M	OCT 1881	18	S				KY	KY	VA				DAY LABORER			✓	✓	✓					
		" JOE ANN	Dau	W	F	FEB 1886	14	S				KY	KY	VA				AT SCHOOL		5	✓	✓	✓					
		" WESLEY S.	Son	W	M	APR 1888	12	S				KY	KY	VA				AT SCHOOL		5	✓	✓	✓					
		" ADDA C.	Dau	W	F	MAY 1890	10	S				KY	KY	VA				AT SCHOOL		5	✓	✓	✓					
		" RUFUS E.	Son	W	M	DEC 1891	8	S				KY	KY	VA														
		" NELLA V.	Dau	W	F	MAR 1894	6	S				KY	KY	VA														
		" WANDA P.	Dau	W	F	JAN 1897	3	S				KY	KY	VA														
200	201	STRODE, WILLIAM	Head	W	M	OCT 1821	78	M	8			KY	KY	KY				FARMER			✓	✓	✓	O	F	F	191	
		" NANCY	Wife	W	F	MAR 1845	55	M	8			KY	KY	KY							✓	✓	✓					
201	202	FRAISURE, JESSEE	Head	W	M	MAR 1856	44	M	8			KY	KY	KY				FARMER			✓	X	✓	R		F	192	
		" MARY A.	Wife	W	F	JUN 1866	33	M	8	2	2	KY	KY	KY							✓	✓	✓					
		" LAURA B.	Dau	W	F	NOV 1894	5	S				KY	KY	KY														
		" LINDSAY G.	Son	W	M	NOV 1897	2	S				KY	KY	KY														
202	203	CREWS, GEO.	Head	W	M	NOV 1845	55	M	13			KY	KY	KY				FARMER			✓	✓	✓	R		F	193	
		" CAMILINE	Wife	W	F	JUN 1854	45	M	13	3	2	KY	TN	TN							✓	✓	✓					
		" VIRGIL	Son	W	M	NOV 1887	12	S				KY	KY	KY				AT SCHOOL		5	✓	✓	✓					
		" LECTA M.	Dau	W	F	Feb 1898	2	S				KY	KY	KY														
		" LUCY A.	Mother	W	F	NOV 1825	74	Wd		5	2	KY	VA	VA														
203	204	HARLAN, JAMES	Head	W	M	JAN 1846	54	M	30			KY	KY	KY				FARMER			✓	✓	✓	O	F	F	194	
		" PELINA J.	Wife	W	F	OCT 1825	74	M	30	1	0	KY	KY	KY							X	X						
204	205	PROPES, WILSON	Head	W	M	OCT 1844	55	M	19			KY	VA	VA				FARMER			✓	✓	✓	O	F	F	195	
		" MINTIE T.	Wife	W	F	FEB 1846	54	M	19	2	2	KY	KY	KY							✓	✓	✓					
		" SALLIE A.	Dau	W	F	Jul 1882	17	S				KY	KY	KY				AT SCHOOL		5	✓	✓	✓					
		" JOHN R.	Son	W	M	Sep 1886	13	S				KY	KY	KY				AT SCHOOL		5	✓	✓	✓					

STATE - KENTUCKY
COUNTY - MONROE
Township or other division — BRUSH

— 171 —

Enumerator SAMUEL H. CARTER

Supervisor's Dist. No. 107   Sheet No.
Enumeration Dist. No. 82

No. of Family	No. of Dwelling	NAME	Relation	Color	Sex	DATE OF BIRTH Mon/Yr	Age at last birthday	Marital Status	# Years married	Mother of how many children?	# of these children living	Place of birth (this person)	Father of this person	Mother of this person	Year of immigr.	# years in U.S.	Naturalization	OCCUPATION 10 years +	Months not employed	Attended school in months	Can read	Can write	Speak English	Owned or Rent	Owned –no mortage	Farm or house	# of farm schedule
-		BECK, MARY A. MOTHER IN LAW	W	F	AUG 1826	73	Wd		7	2		VA	VA	VA				INVALID									
205	206	PAGE, SARAH J. HEAD	W	F	DEC 1842	57	Wd		11	10		KY	KY	KY				FARMER			✓	✓	✓	O	F	F	196
"		MARY V. DAU	W	F	JAN 1866	34	S					KY	KY	KY				DRESS MAKER			✓	✓	✓				
"		JOHNIE E. SON	W	M	MAR 1874	26	S					KY	KY	KY				FARM LABORER			✓	✓	✓				
"		ELVIN A. SON	W	M	FEB 1876	24	M	1				KY	KY	KY				FARM LABORER			✓	✓	✓				
"		DORA H. DAU IN LAW	W	F	OCT 1875	24	M	1	1	1		KY	KY	KY							✓	✓	✓				
"		IDRU L. NEICE	W	F	MAY 1899	1	S					KY	KY	KY													
"		SUSAN E. DAU	W	F	FEB 1884	16	S					KY	KY	KY				AT SCHOOL		5	✓	✓	✓				
206	207	KNUCKLES, WILLIAM H. Head	W	M	AUG 1858	41	M	16				KY	KY	KY				FARMER			✓	✓	✓	R		F	197
"		MARTHA C. Wife	W	F	JAN 1861	39	M	16	8	6		KY	KY	KY							X	X	X				
"		JAMES A. SON	W	M	DEC 1886	13	S					KY	KY	KY				AT SCHOOL		5	✓	✓	✓				
"		HESSIE W. SON	W	M	DEC 1888	11	S					KY	KY	KY				AT SCHOOL		5	✓	✓	✓				
"		ELVIN K. SON	W	M	FEB 1891	9	S					KY	KY	KY													
"		ETHEL D. DAU	W	F	MAY 1893	7	S					KY	KY	KY													
"		WILLIE J. SON	W	M	JUN 1895	4	S					KY	KY	KY													
"		ROY E. SON	W	M	APR 1897	3	S					KY	KY	KY													
207	208	HARLAN, WILLIS H. HEAD	W	M	FEB 1852	48	M	22				KY	KY	KY				FARMER			✓	X	✓	R		F	198
"		JANE P. WIFE	W	F	MAR 1860	40	M	22	4	3		KY	KY	KY							✓	✓	✓				
"		ISAAC B. SON	W	M	SEP 1884	15	S					KY	KY	KY				FARM LABORER			✓	✓	✓				
"		HIRAM R. SON	W	M	JUN 1887	12	S					KY	KY	KY				AT SCHOOL			✓	✓	✓				
"		FRANCIS A. SON	W	M	JUL 1893	6	S					KY	KY	KY													
208	209	LEASTER, WODFORD HEAD	W	M	DEC 1857	42	Wd					KY	KY	KY				FARMER			X	X	✓	O	F	F	199
"		GEO. H. SON	W	M	MAY 1881	19	S					KY	KY	KY				FARM LABORER			✓	✓	✓				
"		LOUELLA A. DAU	W	F	NOV 1885	14	S					KY	KY	KY				AT SCHOOL		5	✓	X	✓				
"		ORA R. SON	W	M	NOV 1889	10	S					KY	KY	KY													
"		ELNORA B. DAU	W	F	NOV 1892	7	S					KY	KY	KY													

STATE - KENTUCKY
COUNTY - MONROE
Township or other division

BRUSH

−172−

Enumerator SAMUEL H. CARTER

Supervisor's Dist. No. _102_ Sheet No.
Enumeration Dist. No. _82_

No. of Family	No. of Dwelling	NAME	Relation	Color	Sex	DATE OF BIRTH Mon/Yr	Age at last birthday	Marital Status	#Years married	Mother of how many children?	# of these children living	Place of birth [this person]	Father of this person	Mother of this person	Year of immigr.	# years in U.S.	Naturalization	OCCUPATION 10 years +	Months not employed	Attended school in months	Can read	Can write	Speak English	Owned or Rent	Owned –no mortage	Farm or house	# of farm schedule
		LEASTER, POLLIE	MOTHER	W	F	Nov 1819	80	Wd		2	2	KY	KY	KY				INVALID			X	X	✓				
		" MANERVIA	Sister	W	F	Apr 1836	64	S				KY	KY	KY				HOUSEKEEPER			X	X	✓				
209	210	HARLAN, JACOB M.	HEAD	W	M	Dec 1857	42	M	13			KY	KY	KY				FARMER			X	X	✓	O	F	F	200
		" MARTHA E.	WIFE	W	F	Jan 1857	43	M	13	6	6	KY	KY	KY							X	X	X				
		" HATTIE S.	DAU	W	F	Sep 1887	12	S				KY	KY	KY				AT SCHOOL		5	✓	✓	✓				
		" LOULIE A.	DAU	W	F	Jan 1889	11	S				KY	KY	KY				AT SCHOOL		5	✓	✓	✓				
		" JAMES W.	SON	W	M	May 1891	9	S				KY	KY	KY													
		" PEARLY B.	DAU	W	F	Oct 1893	6	S				KY	KY	KY													
		" MAY J.	DAU	W	F	Sep 1895	4	S				KY	KY	KY													
		" FLORIDA D.	DAU	W	F	Feb 1898	2	S				KY	KY	KY													
210	211	HARPER, TURNER B.	Head	W	M	Oct 1872	27	M	1			KY	KY	KY				FARMER			X	X	✓	I	R	F	201
		" DORA M.	Wife	W	M	Dec 1874	25	M	1	2	2	KY	KY	KY							✓	✓	✓				
		" REBA J.	Dau	W	F	Aug 1892	7	S				KY	KY	KY													
		" JOHN O.	Son	W	M	Nov 1899	7/12	S				KY	KY	KY													
211	212	HARPER, JESSEE C.	Head	W	M	Jan 1871	29	M	5			KY	KY	KY				FARMER			X	X	✓		R	F	202
		" LOUCINDA	WIFE	W	F	Oct 1878	21	M	5	2	2	KY	KY	KY							✓	✓	✓				
		" LERA J.	DAU	W	F	Nov 1895	4	S				KY	KY	KY													
212	213	HARPER, WILLIAM M.	Head	W	M	Feb 1839	61	M	33			KY	KY	KY				FARMER			✓	✓	✓	O	F	F	203
		" AMELIA	Wife	W	F	Jul 1845	54	M	33	4	3	KY	KY	KY							✓	✓	✓				
		" MARY E	DAU	W	F	Nov 1866	33	Wd		1	1	KY	KY	KY				HOUSEKEEPER			✓	✓	✓				
		" OSCAR H.	Grandson	W	M	Dec 1888	11	S				KY	KY	KY				AT SCHOOL		5	✓	X	✓				
213	214	WILSON, LOUCINDA	Head	W	F	Jan 1847	53	Wd				KY	KY	KY				INCOME (?)			✓	✓	✓		R	H	
		PITCOCK, ORVAL	Lodger	W	M	Nov 1885	14	S				KY	KY	KY				FARM LABORER			✓	✓	✓				
214	215	DAVIS, CLAYBORN E.	Head	W	M	Nov 1832	67	M	19			KY	KY	KY				FARMER			✓	X	✓	O	F	F	204
		" ELIZABETH	wife	W	F	Mar 1843	57	M	19	4	2	KY	KY	KY							X	X	X				
		" MARY E	DAU	W	F	Mar 1876	24	S				KY	KY	KY							✓	✓	✓				

STATE - KENTUCKY
COUNTY - MONROE
Township or other division — BRUSH

Enumerator SAMUEL H. CARTER

Supervisor's Dist. No. 107 Sheet No.
Enumeration Dist. No. 82

No. of Family	No. of Dwelling	NAME	Relation	Color	Sex	DATE OF BIRTH Mon/Yr	Age at last birthday	Marital Status	# Years married	Mother of how many children?	# of these children living	Place of birth (this person)	Father of this person	Mother of this person	Year of immigr.	# years in U.S.	Naturalization	OCCUPATION 10 years +	Months not employed	Attended school in months	Can read	Can write	Speak English	Owned or Rent	Owned - no mortgage	Farm or house	# of farm schedule
		DAVIS, NANCY	DAU	W	F	July 1880	19	S				KY	KY	KY							✓	✓					
		" JUDGE I.	SON	W	M	Aug 1882	17	S				KY	KY	KY				DAY LABORER			✓	✓	✓				
		" EVA C.	DAU	W	F	Jan 1887	13	S				KY	KY	KY				AT SCHOOL		5	✓	✓	✓				
		" JULIE V.	GRAND-DAU	W	F	Mar 1899	1	S				KY	KY	KY													
		" MAUD	GRAND-DAU	W	F	Apr 1899	1	S				KY	KY	KY													
215	216	McDONALD, JERRY R.	HEAD	W	M	Aug 1872	27	M	1			KY	KY	KY				FARMER			✓	✓	✓		R	F	205
		" BELL M.	WIFE	W	F	Jan 1880	20	M	1	1	1	KY	KY	KY							✓	✓	✓				
		" WILLIAM I.	SON	W	M	Dec 1899	7/12	S				KY	KY	KY													
216	217	PARKS, NANCY E.	HEAD	W	F	Mar 1853	47	S				KY	KY	KY				DAY LABORER		5	✓	✓			R	H	
		" MARTHA A.	DAU	W	F	May 1875	25	S				KY	KY	KY				DAY LABORER		5	✓	✓					
		" THOMAS N.	SON	W	M	Apr 1879	21	S				KY	KY	KY				DAY LABORER									
		" KIMMONS R.	SON	W	M	Nov 1884	15	S				KY	KY	KY				DAY LABORER			✓	✓	✓				
		ADDA L.	DAU	W	F	Dec 1887	12	S				KY	KY	KY				AT SCHOOL									
		ANNA L.	DAU	W	F	May 1892	8	S				KY	KY	KY													
217	218	AMYX, LUIS M.	HEAD	W	M	Dec 1854	46	S				KY	KY	KY				DAY LABORER			X	X	X		R	H	
		" ROY H.	SON	W	M	Dec 1889	10	S				KY	KY	KY													
		" HUGH E.	SON	W	M	Jun 1891	8	S				KY	KY	KY													
		" ETHEL P.	DAU	W	F	Apr 1894	6	S				KY	KY	KY													
		" SUSAN A.	DAU	W	F	Aug 1897	2	S				KY	KY	KY													
218	219	HOOD, WILLIAM	Head	W	M	Feb 1850	50	M	7			KY	KY	KY				FARMER			✓	✓	✓		O	F	F 206
		" MALICCE J.	Wife	W	F	Jul 1865	35	M	7			KY	KY	KY							✓	✓	✓				
		" SALLIE	DAU	W	F	Mar 1884	16	S				KY	KY	KY				A.T. SCHOOL		5	✓	✓	✓				
		" MAGGIE A.	DAU	W	F	Dec 1885	14	S				KY	KY	KY				A.T. SCHOOL		5	✓	✓	✓				
		" GENNIE L.	DAU	W	F	June 1891	8	S				KY	KY	KY				A.T. SCHOOL		5							
219	220	WHITE, GEO. (T or F)	HEAD	W	M	Jan 1867	33	M	10			KY	KY	KY				FARMER			✓	✓	✓		O	F	F 207
		" AGNES	WIFE	W	F	Apr 1875	25	M	10	7	5	KY	KY	KY							✓	✓					

STATE - KENTUCKY
COUNTY - MONROE   BRUSH
Township or other division   Enumerator SAMUEL H. CARTER

Supervisor's Dist. No. 102 Sheet No.
Enumeration Dist. No. 82

No. of Family	No. of Dwelling	NAME	Relation	Color	Sex	DATE OF BIRTH Mon/Yr	Age at last birthday	Marital Status	# Years married	Mother of how many children	# of these children living	Place of birth [this person]	Father of this person	Mother of this person	Year of immigr.	# years in U.S.	Naturalization	OCCUPATION 10 years +	Months not employed	Attended school in months	Can read	Can write	Speak English	Owned or Rent	Owned-no mortage	Farm or house	# of farm schedule
		WHITE, OMA A.	Dau	W	F	Sep 1891	8	S				KY	KY	KY				AT SCHOOL		5	✓	✓					
		" ORA E.	Dau	W	F	May 1896	4	S				KY	KY	KY													
		" DESSA O.	Dau	W	F	Dec 1897	2	S				KY	KY	KY													
		" ARPHA M.	Dau	W	F	Feb 1899	1	S				KY	KY	KY													
		" WENDAL D.	Son	W	M	May 1900	1/12	S				KY	KY	KY													
220	221	HARLAN, JOHN S.	Head	W	M	Aug 1847	52	M	10			KY	KY	KY				FARMER			✓	✓	✓	O	M	F	208
		" HANNAH E.	wife	W	F	Oct 1866	33	M	10	4	3	KY	KY	KY							X	X	✓				
		WHEAT, SAMIEL P.	Step-Son	W	M	Apr 1883	17	S				TN	KY	KY				DAY LABORER	2		✓	✓	✓				
		" PHILLIP T.	Step-Son	W	M	Jan 1886	14	S				KY	KY	KY				DAY LABORER	2		✓	✓	✓				
		HARLAN, HARRIET E.	Dau	W	F	Apr 1891	9	S				KY	KY	KY				AT SCHOOL		5	✓	✓	✓				
221	222	HUFFMAN, JESSEE	HEAD	W	M	Jun 1838	61	M	41			KY	KY	KY				FARMER			✓	✓	✓	R		F	209
		" LOU E.	WIFE	W	F	Dec 1833	66	M	41	1	1	KY	KY	KY							✓	✓	✓				
		" ALLIE	Dau	W	F	Jul 1863	36	S				KY	KY	KY				INVALID			✓	✓	✓				
222	223	HARLAN, WILLIAM A.	Head	W	M	Jul 1862	37	M	10			KY	KY	KY				FARMER			✓	✓	✓	O	F	F	210
		" FANNIE	wife	W	F	Oct 1861	38	M	10			KY	KY	KY							✓	✓	✓				
		FERGUSON, VIRGINIA	Sister in-law	W	F	Jun 1867	32	S				KY	KY	KY				DRESS MAKER			✓	✓	✓				
223	224	HAGAN, NANCY	HEAD	W	F	May 1860	40	Wd		5	4	KY	KY	KY				FARMER			✓	✓	✓	O	F	F	211
		" DOVIE E.	Dau	W	F	Jul 1886	13	S				KY	KY	KY				AT SCHOOL		5	✓	✓	✓				
		" PRUDIE E.	Dau	W	F	Jul 1890	9	S				KY	KY	KY				AT SCHOOL									
224	225	JACKSON, GEO. S.	HEAD	W	M	Oct 1855	44	M	23			KY	KY	KY				FARMER			✓	✓	✓	O	M	F	212
		" TOMIE E.	WIFE	W	F	Mar 1860	40	M	23	3	2	KY	KY	KY							✓	✓	✓				
		" EARIE	Son	W	M	Jan 1880	20	S				KY	KY	KY				FARM LABORER			✓	✓	✓				
		" ARTHELA	Dau	W	F	Sep 1881	18	S				KY	KY	KY							✓	✓	✓				
225	226	BUSHONG, SIMEON	HEAD	W	M	Feb 1866	32	M	7			KY	KY	KY				FARMER			✓	✓	✓	O	F	F	213
		" IDA E.	WIFE	W	F	May 1875	25	M	7	1	1	KY	KY	KY							✓	✓	✓				
		" HETTIE E.	Dau	W	F	Mar 1895	5	S				KY	KY	KY													

STATE - KENTUCKY
COUNTY - MONROE   BRUSH
Township or other division   Enumerator SAMUEL H. CARTER

Supervisor's Dist. No. 102 Sheet No.
Enumeration Dist. No. 82

No. of Family	No. of Dwelling	NAME	Relation	Color	Sex	Date of Birth Mon/Yr	Age at last birthday	Marital Status	# Years married	Mother of how many children?	# of these children living	Place of birth [this person]	Father of this person	Mother of this person	Year of immigr.	# years in U.S.	Naturalization	Occupation 10 years +	Months not employed	Attended school in months	Can read	Can write	Speak English	Owned or Rent	Owned - no mortage	Farm or house	# of farm schedule
226	227	JACKSON, WILLIAM L.	HEAD	W	M	OCT 1861	38	M	18			KY	KY	KY				FARMER			X	X	✓	O	F	F	214
		" PARTHENIA	WIFE	W	F	MAY 1863	37	M	18	7	7	KY	KY	KY							X	X	✓				
		" DEWEY O.	SON	W	M	JUN 1883	16	S				KY	KY	KY				DAY LABORER			✓	✓	✓				
		" ROMA C.	SON	W	M	JAN 1885	15	S				KY	KY	KY				AT SCHOOL		5	✓	✓	✓				
		" ELIJAH	SON	W	M	APR 1887	13	S				KY	KY	KY				AT SCHOOL		5	✓	✓	✓				
		" THOMAS H.	SON	W	M	AUG 1889	10	S				KY	KY	KY				AT SCHOOL		5	✓	✓	✓				
		" ANNA B.	DAU	W	F	APR 1892	8	S				KY	KY	KY				AT SCHOOL		5							
		" JOSEPH A.	SON	W	M	APR 1895	5	S				KY	KY	KY													
		" JESSEE M.	SON	W	M	MAY 1897	3	S				KY	KY	KY													
227	228	HALE, HENRY J.	HEAD	W	M	MAR 1848	52	Wd				KY	KY	KY				FARMER		5	✓	✓	✓	O	F	F	215
		" HATTIE P.	DAU	W	F	APR 1884	16	S				KY	KY	KY				AT SCHOOL		5	✓	✓	✓				
		" GEO. F.	SON	W	M	OCT 1886	13	S				KY	KY	KY				AT SCHOOL		5	✓	✓	✓				
		" THOMAS M.	SON	W	M	OCT 1889	10	S				KY	KY	KY				AT SCHOOL			✓	✓	✓				
228	229	HODGES, WILLIARD	HEAD	W	M	JUN 1869	30	M	11			KY	KY	KY				FARMER			✓	✓	✓	O	F	F	216
		" SUSAN	WIFE	W	F	MAR 1855	45	M	11			KY	KY	KY							✓	✓	✓				
229	230	MILLER, JOHN S.	HEAD	W	M	MAY 1852	48	M	21			KY	TN	KY				FARMER			✓	✓	✓	O	F	F	217
		" MELISSA	WIFE	W	F	JUL 1859	40	M	21	5	5	KY	KY	KY							✓	✓	✓				
		" VERA	DAU	W	F	MAY 1880	20	S				KY	KY	KY				SCHOOL TEACHING 2			✓	✓	✓				
		" VASCO	SON	W	M	MAR 1883	17	S				KY	KY	KY				FARM LABORER			✓	✓	✓				
		" MARY C.	DAU	W	F	OCT 1886	13	S				KY	KY	KY				AT SCHOOL		5	✓	✓	✓				
		" HARLIN R.	SON	W	M	NOV 1889	10	S				KY	KY	KY				AT SCHOOL		5	✓	✓	✓				
		" FRANK W.	SON	W	M	OCT 1894	5	S				KY	KY	KY													
230	231	MILLER, NANCY	HEAD	W	F	MAR 1826	74	Wd				TN	TN	TN				INCOME ?			X	X	✓	R		H	
231	232	PEDIGO, JAMES E.	HEAD	W	M	MAY 1849	51	M	2			KY	TN	KY				SAW MILL MAN			✓	✓	✓	R		H	
		" JULIE E.	WIFE	W	F	MAR 1877	23	M	2	1	1	KY	KY	KY							✓	✓	✓				
		" BURTON E.	SON	W	M	OCT 1897	2	S				KY	KY	KY													

TWELFTH CENSUS OF THE UNITED STATES 1900

STATE - KENTUCKY
COUNTY - MONROE
Township or other division — BRUSH — -176- — Enumerator SAMUEL H. CARTER

Supervisor's Dist. No. 102 Sheet No.
Enumeration Dist. No. 82

No. of Family	No. of Dwelling	NAME	Relation	Color	Sex	Date of Birth Mon/Yr	Age	Marital Status	# Years married	Mother of how many children	# living	Place of birth	Father	Mother	Occupation	Attended school	Can read	Can write	Speak English	Owned or Rent	Farm	# of farm schedule
232	233	MILLER, SUSAN	HEAD	W	F	Feb 1830	70	S				TN	TN	TN	FARMER		✓	✓	✓	O	F F	218
233	234	CARTER, WILLIAM B.	HEAD	W	M	Jul 1841	58	S				KY	VA	KY	FARMER		✓	✓	✓	O	F F	219
		" VIRGINIA P.	SISTER	W	F	Jul 1840	59	S				KY	VA	KY			X	X	✓			
		" CALISTA M.	SISTER	W	F	Nov 1844	55	S				KY	VA	KY			X	X	✓			
		" ELIZABETH A.	SISTER	W	F	Nov 1846	53	S				KY	VA	KY			X	X	✓			
234	235	BRAY, JASPER E.	HEAD	W	M	Aug 1831	68	M	40			KY	SC	KY	FARMER		✓	✓	✓	O	F F	220
		" ISABELL	WIFE	W	F	Nov 1840	59	M	40	9	8	KY	KY	KY			✓	✓	✓			
		" JASPER H.	SON	W	M	Jul 1880	19	S				KY	KY	KY	FARM LABORER		✓	✓	✓			
235	236	FORD, MARY C.	HEAD	W	F	Jul 1835	64	Wd		12	8	KY	KY	KY	FARMER		X	X	✓	R	F	221
		JACKSON, MAY J.	DAU	W	F	Dec 1874	25	Wd		4	3	KY	KY	KY			✓	✓				
		CARTER, VIRGIL E.	GR SON	W	M	Dec 1891	8	S				KY	KY	KY	AT SCHOOL	5						
		" MILTON A.	GR SON	W	M	Dec 1893	6	S				KY	KY	KY								
		" WUTIE	GR SON	W	M	Feb 1895	5	S				KY	KY	KY								
236	237	RASNER, URIAH	HEAD	W	M	Mar 1834	66	M	15			KY	KY	KY	FARMER		X	X	✓	O	F F	222
		" AMERICA	WIFE	W	F	Aug 1856	43	M	15	4	2	KY	KY	KY			✓	✓	✓			
		" BENJAMIN	SON	W	M	Aug 1878	21	S				KY	KY	KY	DAY LABORER		✓	✓	✓			
		" ALBERT H.	SON	W	M	Sep 1890	9	S				KY	KY	KY	AT SCHOOL	5						
		" ELIZA E.	DAU	W	F	Mar 1893	7	S				KY	KY	KY								
237	238	PAGE, CALVIN R.	Head	W	M	Sep 1864	35	M	11			KY	KY	KY	FARMER		✓	✓	✓	R	F	223
		" MARY A.	wife	W	F	Feb 1867	33	M	11	4	4	KY	KY	KY			✓	✓	✓			
		" ESTA	SON	W	M	May 1894	6	S				KY	KY	KY								
		" ELBERT	SON	W	M	Jan 1896	4	S				KY	KY	KY								
		" ARPHA F.	DAU	W	F	Jan 1899	1	S				KY	KY	KY								
238	239	BRAY, DERASTUS R.	Head	W	M	Mar 1842	58	M	16			KY	NC	KY	FARMER		✓	✓	✓	O	F F	224
		" SALLIE E.	WIFE	W	F	Sep 1852	47	M	16	6	6	KY	KY	VA			✓	✓	✓			
		" CLARANCE A.	SON	W	M	Nov 1886	13	S				KY	KY	KY	AT SCHOOL	5	✓	✓	✓			

STATE - KENTUCKY
COUNTY - MONROE BRUSH
Township or other division   Enumerator SAMUEL H. CARTER

Supervisor's Dist. No. 102 Sheet No.
Enumeration Dist. No. 82

No. of Family	No. of Dwelling	NAME	Relation	Color	Sex	DATE OF BIRTH Mon/Yr	Age at last birthday	Marital Status	# Years married	Mother of how many children?	# of these children living	Place of birth (this person)	Father of this person	Mother of this person	Year of immigr.	# years in U.S.	Naturalization	OCCUPATION 10 years +	Months not employed	Attended school in months	Can read	Can write	Speak English	Owned or Rent	Owned -no mortgage	Farm or house	# of farm schedule
		BRAY, JULIE E.	DAU	W	F	MAR 1887	12	S				KY	KY	KY				AT SCHOOL		5	✓	✓	✓				
		" CARRIE	DAU	W	F	JAN 1890	10	S				KY	KY	KY				AT SCHOOL		5	✓	✓	✓				
		" WALTON D.	SON	W	M	MAR 1891	9	S				KY	KY	KY													
		" RAYMOND O.	SON	W	M	DEC 1893	6	S				KY	KY	KY													
239	240	WALKER, JAMES W.	Head	W	M	DEC 1863	36	M	8			KY	TN	TN				FARMER			✓	✓	✓	R		F	225
		" LON R.	wife	W	F	APR 1864	36	M	8	2	1	KY	VA	KY							✓	✓	✓				
		" NELLIE A.	Dau	W	F	AUG 1898	1	S				KY	KY	KY													
		" IBBIE	MOTHER	W	F	JAN 1824	76	Wd		13	9	TN	TN	TN							X	X	✓				
240	241	WALKER, THOMAS J.	Head	W	M	AUG 1873	27	M	3			KY	KY	KY							✓	✓	✓	O		F	226
		" SUSAN J	wife	W	F	JAN 1876	24	M	3	1	1	KY	KY	KY							✓	✓	✓				
		" CLARANCE E.	SON	W	M	OCT 1897	2	S				KY	KY	KY													
241	242	BRANSTETTER, JAMES H.	Head	W	M	JUL 1872	27	M	5			KY	KY	KY				CARPENTER			✓	✓	✓	R		H	
		" MALLIE B	wife	W	F	Sep 1874	25	M	5			KY	KY	KY							✓	✓	✓				
242	243	BRAY, EDWARD	HEAD	W	M	MAR 1827	73	M	45			KY	NC	KY				FARMER			✓	✓	✓	O		F	227
		" REBECCA	WIFE	W	F	APR 1836	64	M	45	10	3	KY	NC	TN							✓	✓	✓				
		" UNICE	DAU	W	F	JUL 1870	29	S				KY	KY	KY				DRESSMAKER			✓	✓	✓				
243	244	DICKERSON, JAMES	HEAD	W	M	JUL 1860	39	M	20			KY	KY	KY				FARMER			✓	✓	✓	O		F	228
		" JENNIE S.	WIFE	W	F	NOV 1860	39	M	20	2	2	KY	KY	KY							✓	✓	✓				
		" WILLIAM E.	SON	W	M	July 1881	18	S				KY	KY	KY				DAY LABORER			✓	✓	✓				
		" RUIE M.	DAU	W	F	MAY 1892	8	S				KY	KY	KY													
244	245	GRIDER, THOMAS F.	Head	W	M	NOV 1870	29	M	11			KY	KY	NC				CABINET MAKER			✓	✓	✓	R		H	
		" ARENIE B.	wife	W	F	MAR 1867	33	M	11	2	1	KY	KY	KY							✓	✓	✓				
		" BERTHA B.	DAU	W	F	NOV 1894	5	S				KY	KY	KY													
245	246	GRIMESLEY, SAMUEL	HEAD	W	M	Feb 1863	37	M	10			KY	KY	KY				BLACKSMITH			X	✓	X	?		H	
		" MOLLIE	WIFE	W	F	Feb 1875	25	M	10			KY	KY	KY							✓	✓	✓			H	
246	247	BELCHER, GEO. F.	HEAD	W	M	MAR 1868	32	M	12			KY	KY	KY				DAY LABORER			X	X	✓			H	

STATE - KENTUCKY
COUNTY - MONROE   BRUSH
Township or other division   Enumerator SAMUEL H. CARTER

Supervisor's Dist. No. 10? Sheet No.
Enumeration Dist. No. 82

Location		NAME	Relation	Color	Sex	DATE OF BIRTH Mon/Yr	Age at last birthday	Marital Status	# Years married	Mother of how many children?	# of these children living	Place of birth [this person]	Father of this person	Mother of this person	Year of immigr.	# years in U.S.	Naturalization	OCCUPATION 10 years +	Months not employed	Attended school in months	Can read	Can write	Speak English	Owned or Rent	Owned - no mortgage	Farm or house	# of farm schedule		
No. of Family	No. of Dwelling																												
		BELCHER, SARAH J.	Wife	W	F	MAR 1870	30	M	12	4	4	KY	KY	KY							X	X	✓						
		" OLLIE	Dau	W	F	OCT 1888	11	S				KY	KY	KY				AT SCHOOL		5		✓	✓						
		" WILLIAM H.	Son	W	M	Sep 1891	8	S				KY	KY	KY				AT SCHOOL			✓	✓	✓						
		" CLARANCE B.	Son	W	M	Jun 1894	5	S				KY	KY	KY															
		" AIDA M.	Dau	W	F	Nov 1897	2	S				KY	KY	KY															
247	248	BUSHONG, ANDREW	Head	W	M	AUG 1823	76	M	55			KY	KY	KY				FARMER			✓	✓	✓		O	F F	229		
		" NANCY	Wife	W	F	JAN 1826	74	M	55	7	2	KY	KY	KY							✓	✓	✓						
		JACKSON, WARNER	Lodger	W	M	APR 1865	35	S				KY	KY	KY				FARM LABORER				✓	✓						
248	249	HARRIS, FRANCIS	HEAD	W	M	APR 1832	68	M	35			KY	KY	KY				FARMER			✓	✓	✓		O	F F	230		
		" AMANDA	WIFE	W	F	JAN 1843	57	M	35	4	2	TN	VA	SC							✓	✓	✓						
249	250	HARIS, HIRAM W.	HEAD	W	M	Sep 1866	33	M	10			KY	KY	KY				FARMER			✓	✓	✓		O	F F	231		
		" SARAH T.	WIFE	W	F	May 1871	29	M	10	7	4	KY	KY	KY															
		" NOVA J.	DAU	W	F	Feb 1892	8	S				KY	KY	KY															
		" WALTER R.	SON	W	M	Feb 1894	6	S				KY	KY	KY															
		" ALLICE C.	DAU	W	F	DEC 1895	4	S				KY	KY	KY															
		" HUGH W.	SON	W	M	AUG 1898	1	S				KY	KY	KY															
250	251	RASNER, LORENZA	HEAD	W	M	OCT 1864	35	M	3			KY	KY	KY				FARMER			✓	✓	✓		O	F F	282		
		" ELIZA J.	WIFE	W	F	AUG 1858	41	M	3	4	3	KY	KY	KY							✓	✓	✓						
		" EVA E.	STEP DAU	W	F	NOV 1880	19	S				KY	KY	KY							✓	✓	✓						
		" WILLIAM E.	STEP SON	W	M	May 1883	17	S				KY	KY	KY				FARM LABORER			✓	✓	✓						
		" LINDSEY B.	STEP SON	W	M	MAR 1885	15	S				KY	KY	KY				FARM LABORER			✓	✓	✓						
251	252	BOWMAN, OZIAS	HEAD	W	M	APR 1842	58	M	21			KY	KY	KY				FARMER			✓	✓	✓		O	F F	233		
		" LUCINDA S.	WIFE	W	F	DEC 1851	48	M	21	7	6	KY	KY	KY					2		✓	✓	✓						
		" SALLIE J.	DAU	W	F	AUG 1877	22	S				KY	KY	KY				SCHOOL TEACHING			✓	✓	✓						
		" ARPHA P.	DAU	W	F	APR 1880	20	S				KY	KY	KY				SCHOOL TEACHING 2			✓	✓	✓						
		" EVA L.	DAU	W	F	Sep 1881	18	S				KY	KY	KY				AT SCHOOL		5	✓	✓	✓						

STATE - KENTUCKY
COUNTY - MONROE   BRUSH
Township or other division

Enumerator SAMUEL H. CARTER

Supervisor's Dist. No. _102_ Sheet No. ____
Enumeration Dist. No. _82_ _____

No. of Family	No. of Dwelling	NAME	Relation	Color	Sex	DATE OF BIRTH Mon/Yr	Age at last birthday	Marital Status	# Years married	Mother of how many children	# of these children living	Place of birth (this person)	Father of this person	Mother of this person	Year of immigr.	# years in U.S.	Naturalization	OCCUPATION 10 years +	Months not employed	Attended school in months	Can read	Can write	Speak English	Owned or Rent	Owned - no mortage	Farm or house	# of farm schedule
		BOWMAN, SAMUEL M.	Son	W	M	Sep 1882	17	S				KY	KY	KY				AT SCHOOL			✓	✓	✓				
		" CALVIN I.	Son	W	M	Jun 1883	16	S				KY	KY	KY				AT SCHOOL			✓	✓	✓				
		" ALBERT T.	Son	W	M	May 1888	12	S				KY	KY	KY				AT SCHOOL			✓	✓	✓				
		" OZIAS B.	Son	W	M	Oct 1892	7	S				KY	KY	KY				AT SCHOOL			✓	✓	✓				
252	253	CARTER, WILLIAM A.	Head	W	M	Jun 1871	28	M	3			KY	KY	KY				FARMER			✓	✓	✓	O	F	F	234
		" PHOEBE	Wife	W	F	Jun 1877	22	M	3	1	1	KY	KY	KY							✓	✓	✓				
		" EARL R.	Son	W	M	Apr 1898	2	S				KY	KY	KY													
253	254	BOWLS, FLEM C.	Head	W	M	Sep 1866	33	M				KY	KY	KY				FARMER			✓	✓	✓	O	F	F	235
		" SARAH B.	Wife	W	F	Feb 1866	34	M				KY	KY	KY							✓	✓	✓				
		" EARNEY J.	Son	W	M	Sep 1893	6	S				KY	KY	KY													
254	255	STRODE, JAMES K.	Head	W	M	Jan 1845	55	M	4			KY	KY	KY				FARMER			✓	✓	✓	O	F	F	236
		" MARY	Wife	W	F	Jan 1845	55	M	4	2	1	KY	KY	KY							✓	✓	✓				
		" MARTHA S.	Dau	W	F	Jun 1873	26	S				KY	KY	KY				DRESS MAKER			✓	✓	✓				
255	256	BIGGERS, MARTHA	Head	W	F	Apr 1840	60	Wd		11		KY	KY	KY				FARMER			✓	✓	✓	O	F	F	237
		" MARY	Dau	W	F	Aug 1855	45	S				KY	KY	KY				INVALID			✓	✓	✓				
		" WILLIAM T	Son	W	M	Oct 1867	32	S				KY	KY	KY				FARM LABORER			✓	✓	✓				
		" BIRTIE	Son	W	M	Aug 1877	22	S				KY	KY	KY				TEAMSTER			X	X	✓				
		" FRATIE	Son	W	M	Aug 1880	19	S				KY	KY	KY				DAY LABORER	2		✓	✓	✓				
		" MARTHA J.	Gr-Dau	W	F	Sep 1889	10	S				KY	KY	KY							X	X	✓				
256	257	HARLAN, WILLIAM R.	Head	W	M	Jan 1834	66	M				KY	KY	KY				FARMER			✓	✓	✓	O	F	F	238
		" MATILDA	Wife	W	F	Nov 1854	45	M		3	3	KY	KY	KY							✓	✓	✓				
		" POLLIE T.	Dau	W	F	Feb 1883	17	S				KY	KY	KY							✓	✓	✓				
257	258	CLEMONS, WILLIAM	Head	W	M	Mar 1853	47	S				KY	KY	KY				FARM LABORER			✓	✓	✓	R		H	
258	259	HUTCHENS, JOSEPH	Head	W	M	Oct 1864	35	M	17			KY	KY	KY				FARMER			✓	✓	✓	O	F	F	239
		" VICTORIA	Wife	W	F	Jun 1861	38	M	17	3	3	KY	KY	KY							✓	✓	✓				
		" DORA M.	Dau	W	F	Nov 1888	11	S				KY	KY	KY				AT SCHOOL		5	✓	✓	✓				

STATE - KENTUCKY
COUNTY - MONROE
Township or other division: BRUSH

Enumerator: SAMUEL H. CARTER

Supervisor's Dist. No. 102 Sheet No.
Enumeration Dist. No. 82

No. of Family	No. of Dwelling	NAME	Relation	Color	Sex	DATE OF BIRTH Mon/Yr	Age at last birthday	Marital Status	# Years married	Mother of how many children?	# of these children living	Place of birth [this person]	Father of this person	Mother of this person	Year of immigr.	# years in U.S.	Naturalization	OCCUPATION 10 years +	Months not employed	Attended school in months	Can read	Can write	Speak English	Owned or Rent	Owned -no mortage	Farm or house	# of farm schedule
		HUTCHENS, MILLIARD	Son	W	M	Jan 1894	6	S				KY	KY	KY													
		" WILLIARD	Son	W	M	Feb 1900 3/12		S				KY	KY	KY													
259	260	BELCHER, WILLIAM H.	Head	W	M	Nov 1859	40	S				KY	KY	KY				FARMER		X	X	✓		O	F	F	240
		" MOSSES	Brother	W	M	Nov 1863	36	S				KY	KY	KY				FARM LABORER			✓	✓	✓				
		" JAMES R.	Brother	W	M	Oct 1853	46	S				KY	KY	KY				DAY LABORER		X	X	✓					
		" ELIZABETH	Mother	W	F	Nov 1833	66	Wd		8	8	KY	KY	KY						X	X	✓					
		PICKEREL, ORBAN	Nephew	W	M	Oct 1888	11	S				KY	KY	KY				AT SCHOOL		✓	X	✓					
260	261	VIBERT, CHARLES B.	Head	W	M	Dec 1854	45	M	20			KY	KY	KY				BLACKSMITH		✓	✓	✓		R	F	241
		" LAURA C.	Wife	W	F	Apr 1861	39	M	20	8	7	KY	KY	KY						✓	✓	✓				
		" JOHN H.	Son	W	M	Aug 1884	15	S				KY	KY	KY				FARM LABOR		✓	✓	✓				
		" SARAH C.	Dau	W	F	Jun 1887	12	S				KY	KY	KY						X	X	✓				
		" LINDSAY F.	Son	W	M	Nov 1891	8	S				KY	KY	KY												
		" WILLIAM H.	Son	W	M	Oct 1893	6	S				KY	KY	KY												
		" ANNIE L.	Dau	W	F	Jul 1895	4	S				KY	KY	KY												
		" LOLA P.	Dau	W	F	Jun 1898	1	S				KY	KY	KY												
261	262	EMBERTON, SARAH	Head	W	F	— —		Wd	—			KY	KY	KY				FARMER		✓	✓	✓		O	F	F	242
		" BARLOW	Gr-Son	W	M	Oct 1881	18	S				KY	KY	KY				FARM LABOR		✓	✓	✓				
262	263	BUSHONG, JOHN	Head	W	M	May 1866	34	M	8			KY	KY	KY				DAY LABORER		✓	✓	✓		R		H
		" NANCY H.	Wife	W	F	Apr 1875	25	M	8	3	2	KY	KY	KY												
		" LEANUS C.	Son	W	M	Sep 1895	4	S				KY	KY	KY												
		" MILAN B.	Dau	W	F	Mar 1900 3/12		S				KY	KY	KY												
263	264	CHAPMAN, ROBERT L.	Head	W	M	May 1843	57	M	38			KY	KY	KY				FARMER		X	X	✓		O	F	F	243
		" DICEY K.	Wife	W	F	Nov 1841	58	M	38	7	6	KY	KY	KY												
		" PINKEY	Dau	W	F	Sep 1863	36	Wd		2	2	KY	KY	KY												
		" ROBERT L.	Son	W	M	Mar 1877	23	S				KY	KY	KY				FARM LABOR		✓	✓	✓				
		" MAGGIE	Gr-Dau	W	F	Jul 1885	14	S				KY	KY	KY						X	X	X				

TWELFTH CENSUS OF THE UNITED STATES 1900

STATE - KENTUCKY
COUNTY - MONROE   BRUSH   SAMUEL H. CARTER

Township or other division   Enumerator

Supervisor's Dist. No. 107 Sheet No.
Enumeration Dist. No. 82

Location No. of Family / No. of Dwelling	NAME	Relation	Color	Sex	DATE OF BIRTH Mon/Yr	Age at last birthday	Marital Status	# Years married	Mother of how many children?	# of these children living	Place of birth [this person]	Father of this person	Mother of this person	Year of immigr.	# years in U.S.	Naturalization	OCCUPATION 10 years +	Months not employed	Attended school in months	Can read	Can write	Speak English	Owned or Rent	Owned -no mortage	Farm or house	# of farm schedule
	FERGUSON, CALVIN	GR-SON	W	M	MAY 1885	15	S				KY	KY	KY				AT SCHOOL		5	✓	✓	✓				
	" FLORA J.	GR-DAU	W	F	NOV 1887	12	S				KY	KY	KY				AT SCHOOL		5	✓	✓	✓				
264 265	PAGE, SAMUEL J.	HEAD	W	M	MAY 1838	62	Wd				KY	KY	KY				FARMER			✓	✓	✓	O	F	F	244
	" DUGLAS	SON	W	M	AUG 1862	37	S				KY	KY	KY				TEAMSTER			✓	✓					
	" VIRGINIA	DAU	W	F	APR 1866	34	S				KY	KY	KY				DRESS MAKER				✓	✓				
	" MARGRET M.	DAU	W	F	NOV 1868	31	S				KY	KY	KY							✓	✓	✓				
	" ALLICE T.	DAU	W	F	Feb 1871	29	S				KY	KY	KY				SCHOOL TEACHING 2			✓	✓	✓				
	" ARTHUR B.	SON	W	M	Feb 1874	26	S				KY	KY	KY				SCHOOL TEACHING			✓	✓	✓				
	" ROXIE D.	DAU	W	F	MAY 1877	23	S				KY	KY	KY				SCHOOL TEACHING 2			✓	✓	✓				
265 266	MILLER, WILLIAM A.	Head	W	M	NOV 1855	44	M	9			KY	KY	KY				FARMER			✓	✓	✓	O	F	F	245
	" NANCY E.	wife	W	F	AUG 1868	31	M	9	5	5	KY	KY	KY							✓	✓	✓				
	" JOHN G.	SON	W	M	Jul 1891	8	S				KY	KY	KY				AT SCHOOL		5	✓	✓	✓				
	" ANNA B.	DAU	W	F	OCT 1892	7	S				KY	KY	KY				AT SCHOOL									
	" CYRUS F.	SON	W	M	DEC 1893	6	S				KY	KY	KY													
	" MARY E.	DAU	W	F	OCT 1895	4	S				KY	KY	KY													
	" CLARANCE	SON	W	M	APR 1900	2/12	S				KY	KY	KY													
266 267	NORMAN, SUSAN	HEAD	W	F	Jul 1859	40	Wd		5	5	KY	IN	IN				FARMER			✓	✓	✓	R	F	246	
	" AVERY	SON	W	M	JAN 1884	16	S				KY	KY	KY				FARM LABORER			✓	✓	✓				
	" WILLIAM Y.	SON	W	M	MAR 1889	11	S				KY	KY	KY				AT SCHOOL		5	✓	✓	✓				
	" MYRTIE J.	DAU	W	F	Sep 1891	8	S				KY	KY	KY				AT SCHOOL		5	✓	✓	✓				
	" JOHN M.	SON	W	M	Jul 1893	6	S				KY	KY	KY													
	" AIDA M.	DAU	W	F	DEC 1895	4	S				KY	KY	KY													
267 268	EMMERT, MARY	HEAD	W	F	APR 1826	74	Wd		4	4	KY	KY	KY				FARMER			✓	✓	✓	O	F	F	247
268 269	PAGE, ALVIN	HEAD	W	M	MAY 1869	31	M	5			KY	KY	KY				FARMER			✓	✓	✓	R	F	248	
	" IBBIE L (?)	WIFE	W	F	JUN 1867	32	M	5			KY	KY	KY							✓	✓	✓				
	FISH, ETHEL	LODGER	W	F	MAR 1887	13	S				KY	KY	KY							✓	✓	✓				

STATE - KENTUCKY
COUNTY - MONROE   BRUSH
Township or other division   Enumerator SAMUEL H. CARTER

Supervisor's Dist. No. 102 Sheet No.
Enumeration Dist. No. 82

Location (No. of Family / No. of Dwelling)	NAME	Relation	Color	Sex	DATE OF BIRTH Mon/Yr	Age at last birthday	Marital Status	# Years married	Mother of how many children?	# of these children living	NATIVITY Place of birth [this person]	Father of this person	Mother of this person	CITIZENSHIP Year of immigr. / # years in U.S. / Naturalization	OCCUPATION 10 years +	Months not employed	Attended school in months	Can read	Can write	Speak English	Owned or Rent	Owned –no mortage	Farm or house	# of farm schedule
269 270	FERGUSON, JAMES G.	HEAD	W	M	Jan 1867	33	M	4			KY	KY	KY		FARMER			✓	✓	✓	R		F	249
"	EVA	WIFE	W	F	Mar 1880	20	M	4	1	1	KY	KY	KY					✓	✓	✓				
"	HERMAN	SON	W	M	Jul 1898	1	S				KY	KY	KY											
270 271	WILLIAMS, ALONZO	HEAD	W	M	May 1861	39	Wd				KY	KY	KY		FARMER			✓	✓	✓	O		F	250
"	JAMES	SON	W	M	Oct 1887	12	S				KY	KY	KY		AT SCHOOL		5	✓	✓	✓				
"	CARRIE	DAU	W	F	Mar 1889	11	S				KY	KY	KY		AT SCHOOL		5	✓	✓	✓				
"	LAURANCE	SON	W	M	Sep 1891	8	S				KY	KY	KY		AT SCHOOL		5							
"	LANKFORD	SON	W	M	Jan 1893	7	S				KY	KY	KY											
"	LOUIS R.	SON	W	M	Sep 1895	4	S				KY	KY	KY											
"	MARTHA	DAU	W	F	Dec 1899	5/12	S				KY	KY	KY											
271 272	WILLIAMS, MARY	HEAD	W	F	Feb —	66	Wd		5	4	KY	KY	KY		INCOME			✓	✓	✓	O		H	
272 273	CARTER, SAMUEL H.	Head	W	M	Aug 1868	31	M	1			KY	KY	KY		MERCHANT			✓	✓	✓	R		H	
"	LOLA C.	Wife	W	F	Apr 1872	28	M	1	1	1	KY	KY	KY					✓	✓	✓				
"	MAUD	DAU	W	F	Jan 1899	1	S				KY	KY	KY											
273 274	SHEET 3, LINE 17, OMITTED NUMBER FOR WHICH 2203 IS PROVIDED													[?]										

STATE - KENTUCKY
COUNTY - MONROE MARTINSBURGH
Township or other division Enumerator JAMES T. WHITE

Supervisor's Dist. No. 102 Sheet No.
Enumeration Dist. No. 83

No. of Family	No. of Dwelling	NAME	Relation	Color	Sex	DATE OF BIRTH Mon/Yr	Age at last birthday	Marital Status	# Years married	Mother of how many children	# of these children living	Place of birth [this person]	Father of this person	Mother of this person	Year of immigr.	# years in U.S.	Naturalization	OCCUPATION 10 years +	Months not employed	Attended school in months	Can read	Can write	Speak English	Owned or Rent	Owned -no mortgage	Farm or house	# of farm schedule	
1	1	McCLERRAN, JAMES	Head	W	M	Jan 1857	43	M	9			KY	TN	KY				FARMER			✓	✓	✓	O		F	1	
		" ROSETTY	Wife	W	F	Oct 1878	21	M	9	(?)2	2	KY	KY	KY							✓	✓	✓					
		" MAGNOLIA	Dau	W	F	Jan 1893	7	S				KY	KY	KY														
		" ARNOLD	Son	W	M	Mar 1895	5	S				KY	KY	—														
2	2	HESTAND, MARY	Head	W	F	Mar 1807	93	Wd		10	10	KY	KY	KY				NONE	12		✓	✓	✓	R		H		
		" LUDDIE	Dau	W	F	May 184-	UNK	Wd		6	6	KY	KY	KY				NONE	12		✓	✓	✓					
		" LISSIE	Dau	W	F	Nov 1861	33	S				KY	KY	KY				NONE	12		✓	✓	✓					
3	3	GRISSOM, WILLIAM	Head	W	M	Jun 1868	32	M	14			KY	KY	KY				FARMER	0		✓	✓	✓	O		F	2	
		" RETTIE	Wife	W	F	Aug 1863	36	M	14	5	5	KY	KY	KY							✓	✓	✓					
		" FRANK	Son	W	M	Sep 1886	13	S				KY	KY	KY				AT SCHOOL		5	✓	✓	✓					
		" HUSTIAL(?)	Son	W	M	Apr 1888	12	S				KY	KY	KY				AT SCHOOL		5	✓	✓	✓					
		" OVA	Dau	W	F	Oct 1890	9	S				KY	KY	KY				AT SCHOOL		5	✓	✓	✓					
		" EDWARD	Son	W	M	Oct 1892	7	S				KY	KY	KY														
		" CORA	Dau	W	F	Nov 1894	5	S				KY	KY	KY														
4	4	SHAW, CHA—?	Head	W	M	Jan 1853	46	M	25			KY	KY	KY				FARMER			✓	✓	✓	O		F	3	
		" LETTIE	Wife	W	F	Dec 1864	33	M	25	(?)6	6	KY	KY	KY							✓	X	✓					
		" DOW	Son	W	M	Apr 1884	16	S				KY	KY	KY				AT SCHOOL		1	✓	✓	✓					
		" WILLIAM	Son	W	M	Jan 1890	10	S				KY	KY	KY				AT SCHOOL		5	X	X	✓					
		" JOHN T.	Son	W	M	Aug 1892	8	S				KY	KY	KY														
		" MARGARET J.	Dau	W	F	Feb 1894	6	S				KY	KY	KY														
		" JESSIE B.	Son	W	M	Dec 1897	2	S				KY	KY	KY														
		" SARY L.	Dau	W	F	Mar 1898	1	S				KY	KY	KY														
5	5	WATSON, SMITH	Head	W	M	Jun 1857	42	M	12			KY	KY	KY				FARMER			✓	✓	✓	O		F	4	
		" JENNIE	Wife	W	F	May 1865	35	M	12	4	3	KY	KY	KY							✓	✓	✓					
		" JAMES T.	Son	W	M	Jul 1895	5	S				KY	KY	KY														
		" LUALIE	Dau	W	F	Aug 1897	3	S				KY	KY	KY														

TWELFTH CENSUS OF THE UNITED STATES 1900

STATE - KENTUCKY
COUNTY - MONROE
Township or other division **MARTINSBURGH**   Enumerator **JAMES T. WHITE**

Supervisor's Dist. No. **102** Sheet No.
Enumeration Dist. No. **83**

No. of Family	No. of Dwelling	NAME	Relation	Color	Sex	Date of Birth Mon/Yr	Age at last birthday	Marital Status	# Years married	Mother of how many children?	# of these children living	Place of birth (this person)	Father of this person	Mother of this person	Occupation 10 years +	Months not employed	Attended school in months	Can read	Can write	Speak English	Owned or Rent	Owned -no mortage	Farm or house	# of farm schedule
		WATSON, HIRAM S.	Son	W	M	Feb 1899	1	S				KY	KY	KY										
6	6	SHAW, JAMES	Head	W	M	Sep 1875	24	M	3			KY	KY	KY	FARMER			✓	✓	✓	R		F	5
		" MAY	Wife	W	F	May 1880	20	M	3	1	1	KY	KY	KY				✓	✓	✓				
		" MARY B.	Dau	W	F	Jul 1899	10/12	S				KY	KY	KY										
7	7	DYER, ISAAC	Head	W	M	Apr 1860	40	M	9			KY	KY	KY	FARMER			✓	✓	✓	O	F	F	6
		" JOSIE	Wife	W	F	Apr 1867	33	M	9	4	4	KY	KY	KY				✓	✓	✓				
		" LEE A.	Dau	W	F	Sep 1892	7	S				KY	KY	KY										
		" GEORGE A.	Son	W	M	Nov 1894	5	S				KY	KY	KY										
		" DOROTHY	Dau	W	F	Oct 1896	3	S				KY	KY	KY										
		" HAMILTON R.	Son	W	M	Mar 1899	1	S				KY	KY	KY										
8	8	—(UNREADABLE)—	Head	W	F	May 1855	45	Wd		5	3	KY	KY	KY	FARMER			X	X	✓	O	F	F	7
		MAGGIE	Dau	W	F	Mar 1880	20	S				KY	KY	KY	SERVANT			✓	✓	✓				
		DOUGLAS	Son	W	M	Aug 1881	18	S				KY	KY	KY	DAY LABOR			✓	✓	✓				
		BARLOW	Son	W	M	Jan 1884	16	S				KY	KY	KY	DAY LABOR			✓	✓	✓				
9	9	WOOD, ISAM	Head	W	M	Feb 1849	51	M	23			KY	KY	KY	FARMER			✓	✓	✓	O	F	F	8
		" MARY C.	Wife	W	F	Mar 1855	45	M	23	12	12	KY	KY	KY				✓	✓	✓				
		" OLIVER Y.	Son	W	M	Aug 1872	27	S				KY	KY	KY	CLERK			✓	✓	✓				
		" SAVANNAH	Dau	W	F	Dec 1878	21	S				KY	KY	KY	AT SCHOOL		10	✓	✓	✓				
		" EVERT	Son	W	M	Jan 1881	19	S				KY	KY	KY	AT SCHOOL		4	✓	✓					
		" AVRY	Son	W	M	Feb 1883	17	S				KY	KY	KY	AT SCHOOL		4	✓	✓	✓				
		" EZRA	Son	W	M	Feb 1885	15	S				KY	KY	KY	AT SCHOOL		1	✓	✓	✓				
		" BIRTHY	Dau	W	F	Jan 1887	13	S				KY	KY	KY	AT SCHOOL		5	✓	✓	✓				
		" ELMER	Son	W	M	Aug 1889	10	S				KY	KY	KY	AT SCHOOL		5	✓	✓	✓				
		" ADOS	Son	W	M	May 1892	8	S				KY	KY	KY										
		" ESLEI (?)	Son	W	M	Oct 1894	5	S				KY	KY	KY										
		" WUIE (?)	Son	W	M	Aug 1898	1	S				KY	KY	KY										

STATE - KENTUCKY
COUNTY - MONROE
Township or other division MARTINSBURGH   Enumerator JAMES T. WHITE

Supervisor's Dist. No. 102 Sheet No.
Enumeration Dist. No. 83

No. of Family	No. of Dwelling	NAME	Relation	Color	Sex	Date of Birth Mon/Yr	Age at last birthday	Marital Status	# Years married	Mother of how many children?	# of these children living	Place of birth	Father of this person	Mother of this person	Year of immigr.	# years in U.S.	Naturalization	Occupation	Months not employed	Attended school in months	Can read	Can write	Speak English	Owned or Rent	Owned -no mortgage	Farm or house	# of farm schedule
10	10	SIMS, JOHN	Head	W	M	OCT 1841	59	M	31			KY	KY	KY				FARMER			✓	✓	✓	O	F	F	9
		" ELIZA	wife	W	F	DEC 1847	52	M	31	7	5	TN	TN	TN							✓	✓	✓				
		" JOSEPH	Son	W	M	APR 1883	17	S				KY	KY	TN				AT SCHOOL		5	✓	✓	✓				
		" MERTIE M.	Dau	W	F	APR 1889	11	S				KY	KY	TN				AT SCHOOL		5	✓	✓	✓				
11	11	WHITTY (Unreadable), RENEAU	Head	W	M	MAY 1856	44	M	18			KY	KY	KY				FARMER			✓	✓	✓	O	F	F	10
		" MALISSIA	WIFE	W	F	JUN 1862	37	M	18	4	3	KY	TN	KY							✓	✓	✓				
		" LEADIA	DAU	W	F	OCT 1883	16	S				KY	KY	KY				AT SCHOOL		4	✓	✓	✓				
		" GEORGE D.	SON	W	M	APR 1890	10	S				KY	KY	KY				AT SCHOOL		4	✓	✓	✓				
		" WILLIAM Mc.	SON	W	M	NOV 1896	3	S				KY	KY	KY													
12	12	BOON, GEORGE	HEAD	W	M	OCT 1857	42	M	17			TN	TN	TN				FARMER		X	X	✓		O	F	F	11
		" SARA C	WIFE	W	F	MAR 1865	35	M	17	6	6	KY	TN	TN							✓	✓	✓				
		" SIDNEY	Son	W	M	MAY 1882	18	S				TN	TN	TN				DAY LABOR			✓	✓	✓				
		" JOHN T.	Son	W	M	APR 1886	14	S				KY	TN	TN				DAY LABOR			✓	✓	✓				
		" RINDA	DAU	W	F	Feb 1889	11	S				KY	TN	TN				AT SCHOOL		4	✓	✓	✓				
		" LOVIE	DAU	W	F	OCT 1891	8	S				KY	TN	TN							✓	✓	✓				
		" TAB	DAU	W	F	NOV 1894	5	S				KY	TN	TN													
13	13	DICKENS, ALEN	HEAD	W	M	NOV 1837	63	M	34			KY	—	KY				FARMER		X	X	✓		R	F	12	
		" LUANN	WIFE	W	F	MAR 1850	50	M	34	10	8	KY	KY	KY							✓	✓	✓				
		" NANCY E.	DAU	W	F	Jul 1880	19	S				KY	KY	KY				AT SCHOOL		1	✓	✓	✓				
		" JULIA A.	DAU	W	F	AUG 1882	17	S				KY	KY	KY				AT SCHOOL		8	✓	✓	✓				
		" SADIA	DAU	W	F	MAR 1885	15	S				KY	KY	KY				AT SCHOOL		8	✓	✓	✓				
		" WALTER J.	SON	W	M	MAR 1888	12	S				KY	KY	KY				AT SCHOOL		5	✓	✓	✓				
		" WILLIAM J.	SON	W	M	MAR 1875	25	M	2			KY	KY	KY				FARM LABOR			✓	✓	✓				
		" EFFIE	DAU-IN-LAW	W	F	AUG 1881	19	M	2	1	1	KY	KY	KY							✓	✓	✓				
		" WALTER C.	GR-SON	W	M	APR 1900	1/12					KY	KY	KY													
14	14	WATSON, JAMES	HEAD	W	M	OCT 1848	52	M	17			TN	VA	TN				FARMER		X	X	✓		R	F	13	

TWELFTH CENSUS OF THE UNITED STATES 1900

STATE - KENTUCKY
COUNTY - MONROE
Township or other division **MARTINSBURGH**   Enumerator **JAMES T. WHITE**

Supervisor's Dist. No. *102* Sheet No.
Enumeration Dist. No. *83*

No. of Family	No. of Dwelling	NAME	Relation	Color	Sex	DATE OF BIRTH Mon/Yr	Age at last birthday	Marital Status	# Years married	Mother of how many children?	# of these children living	Place of birth (this person)	Father of this person	Mother of this person	Year of immigr.	# years in U.S.	Naturalization	OCCUPATION 10 years +	Months not employed	Attended school in months	Can read	Can write	Speak English	Owned or Rent	Owned -no mortage	Farm or house	# of farm schedule
		WATSON, LOIS	Wife	W	F	Nov 1844	56	M	17	21	1	KY	KY	TN							X	X	✓				
		" EST ?	Son	W	M	May 1875	25	M	6			KY	TN	KY							✓	✓	✓				
		" ELIZA	Dau-in-law	W	F	Jun 1879	21	M	6	2	2	KY	KY	KY							✓	✓	✓				
		" LIZZIE	Gr-Dau	W	F	Dec 1894	5	S				KY	KY	KY													
		" CURTISS ?	Gr-son	W	M	Aug 1897	2	S				TN	KY	KY													
15	15	(UNREADABLE), JAMES	Head	W	M	Dec 1855	44	M	26			TN	TN	TN				FARMER			X	X	✓	R		F	14
		" REBECCA I.	Wife	W	F	Oct 1855	44	M	26	10	7	KY	TN	KY							X	X	✓				
		" ELIZZIEBETH	Dau	W	F	Mar 1877	22	S				KY	TN	KY				DRESS MAKER			✓	✓	✓				
		" SARA M.	Dau	W	F	Mar 1892	18	S				TN	TN	KY				AT SCHOOL		5	✓	✓					
		" THOMAS C.	Son	W	M	Oct 1887	13	S				TN	TN	KY				AT SCHOOL		5	✓	✓					
		" LENOR M.	Dau	W	F	Aug 1891	8	S				KY	TN	KY													
		" MINNIE	Dau	W	F	Dec 1893	6	S				KY	KY	KY													
16	16	STEPHENS, (?)	Head	W	M	Nov 1849	50	M	22			TN	VA	TN				FARMER			✓	✓	✓	O		F	15
		" SARAH B.	Wife	W	F	Mar 1856	44	M	22	11	9	KY	TN	KY							✓	✓	✓				
		" REE	Dau	W	F	Jan 1883	17	S				KY	TN	KY				AT SCHOOL		10	✓	✓	✓				
		" BENNIE	Son	W	M	Dec 1884	15	S				KY	TN	KY				AT SCHOOL		9	✓	✓	✓				
		" LEE	Son	W	M	Dec 1886	13	S				KY	TN	KY				AT SCHOOL		9	✓	✓	✓				
		" ALICE	Dau	W	F	Apr 1889	11	S				KY	TN	KY				AT SCHOOL		9	✓	✓	✓				
		" NOVIA	Dau	W	F	Jan 1890	9	S				KY	TN	KY													
		" SAVAGE	Son	W	M	Sep 1892	7	S				KY	TN	KY													
		" TIM	Son	W	M	Sep 1895	5	S				KY	TN	KY													
		" JESSIE H.	Son	W	M	Sep 1896	3	S				KY	TN	KY													
17	17	RICHARDSON, ELBRIDGE	Head	W	M	May 1858	42	M	9			TN	TN	TN				FARMER			✓	✓	✓	O		F	16
		" MINNIE	Wife	W	F	Jun 1868	31	M	9	4	4	TN	TN	TN							✓	✓	✓				
		" OBIA	Son	W	M	Feb 1892	8	S				KY	TN	TN													
		" ETHEL	Dau	W	F	Jun 1894	6					KY	TN	TN													

STATE - KENTUCKY
COUNTY - MONROE
Township or other division MARTINSBURGH Enumerator JAMES I. WHITE
Supervisor's Dist. No. 102 Sheet No.
Enumeration Dist. No. 83

No. of Family	No. of Dwelling	NAME	Relation	Color	Sex	Date of Birth Mon/Yr	Age at last birthday	Marital Status	# Years married	Mother of how many children	# of these children living	Place of birth	Father	Mother	Occupation	Months not employed	Attended school	Can read	Can write	Speak English	Owned or Rent	Farm or house	# of farm schedule
		RICHARDSON, BASE (?)	Son	W	M	Dec 1895	4	S				KY	TN	TN									
		" BESSIE	Dau	W	F	May 1898	2	S				KY	TN	TN									
18	18	GOOLSBEY, JOHN	Head	W	M	Jan 1855	45	M	12			TN	TN	TN	FARMER			✓	✓	✓	R	F	17
		" ALICE M.	Wife	W	F	Jul 1872	27	M	12	7	5	TN	TN	TN				✓	✓	✓			
		" BENTON	Son	W	M	Jan 1892	8	S				TN	TN	TN									
		" LEONO	Dau	W	F	Feb 1894	6	S				TN	TN	TN									
		" RAZZIE	Son	W	M	Sep 1895	4	S				TN	TN	TN									
		" VIANNE	Dau	W	F	Oct 1896	3	S				TN	TN	TN									
		" JERRY	Son	W	M	— 1899	3/12	S				TN	TN	TN									
19	19	RAINS, SID	Head	W	M	Jul 1875	24	M	3			TN	TN	TN	FARMER			✓	✓		R	F	18
		" ANNIE	Wife	W	F	May 1879	21	M	3	2	2	TN	KY	TN				X	X	✓			
		" ROY	Son	W	M	May 1897	3	S				TN	TN	TN									
		" RAY	Son	W	M	Feb 1900	3/12	S				TN	TN	TN									
20	20	SIMS, PARISH	Head	W	M	Sep 1850	49	M	18			KY	KY	KY	FARMER			✓	✓	✓	O	F F	19
		" PERMELY E.	Wife	W	F	Sep 1850	49	M	18	1		TN	TN	TN				✓	✓	✓			
		WADDLE, HENRY	Boarder	W	M	Sep 1883	16	S				TN	TN	TN	DAY LABOR			✓	✓	✓			
21	21	CRABTREE, HUTON	Head	W	M	Dec 1853	47	M	20			TN	TN	TN	FARMER			✓	✓	✓	O	F F	20
		" CASSIE	Wife	W	F	Dec 1859	40	M	20	3	3	TN	NY	NY				✓	✓	✓			
		" OTIS W.	Son	W	M	Sep 1881	18	S				TN	TN	TN	AT SCHOOL		10	✓	✓	✓			
		" BERLIE	Son	W	M	Dec 1886	13	S				TN	TN	TN	AT SCHOOL		8	✓	✓	✓			
		" FREDDIE	Son	W	M	Mar 1894	6	S				KY	TN	TN									
22	22	ARTERBERRY, CATHRON	Head	W	F	May 1842	58	Wd		7	7	KY	TN	NC	FARMER			✓	✓	✓	O	F F	21
		" MARY	Dau	W	F	May 1862	38	S				KY	TN	KY	SEAMSTRESS			✓	✓	✓			
		STOCTON, WALTER	Boarder	W	M	Apr 1878	22	S				TN	TN	TN	FARMER			✓	✓	✓	R	F	22
23	23	RICHARDSON, JOHN	Head	W	M	Sep 1856	43	M	22			TN	TN	TN	FARMER			✓	✓	✓	O	F F	23
		" NANCY R.	Wife	W	F	Aug 1852	47	M	22	4	3	IL	TN	TN				X	X	✓			

STATE - KENTUCKY
COUNTY - MONROE
Township or other division MARTINSBURGH   Enumerator JAMES I. WHITE

Supervisor's Dist. No. _103_ Sheet No.
Enumeration Dist. No. _83_

No. of Family / No. of Dwelling	NAME	Relation	Color	Sex	Date of Birth Mon/Yr	Age at last birthday	Marital Status	# Years married	Mother of how many children?	# of these children living	Place of birth (this person)	Father of this person	Mother of this person	Year of immigr.	# years in U.S.	Naturalization	OCCUPATION 10 years +	Months not employed	Attended school in months	Can read	Can write	Speak English	Owned or Rent	Owned - no mortage	Farm or house	# of farm schedule
	RICHARDSON, AUTHOR	Son	W	M	Sep 1885	14	S				KY	TN	IL				AT SCHOOL	7		✓	✓	✓				
	" VIRGIL	Son	W	M	May 1887	13	S				KY	TN	IL				AT SCHOOL	8		✓	✓	✓				
	" BROADUS	Son	W	M	APR 1890	10	S				KY	TN	IL				AT SCHOOL	5		✓	✓	✓				
24 24	POOR, AM—?	Head	W	M	May 1871	29	M	10			KY	TN	TN				FARMER			✓	✓	✓	R		F	24
	" MARY	Wife	W	F	Dec 1870	29	M	10	2	2	KY	TN	TN							✓	✓	✓				
	" ALVIS L.	Son	W	M	Jul 1891	8	S				TN	KY	KY													
	" TESSIE E.	Dau	W	F	APR 1892	8	S				TN	KY	KY													
25 25	ARTERBERRY, JOHN	Head	W	M	Nov 1860	39	M	14			KY	KY	KY				FARMER			✓	✓	✓	O		F	25
	" VIRTURE	Wife	W	F	Jul 1868	31	M	14	7	7	KY	KY	KY							✓	✓	✓				
	" HUGH T.	Son	W	M	Aug 1886	13	S				KY	KY	KY				AT SCHOOL	8		✓	✓	✓				
	" HERMAN L.	Son	W	M	Aug 1888	11	S				KY	KY	KY				AT SCHOOL	8		✓	✓	✓				
	" HANDLEY D.	Son	W	M	Dec 1890	9	S				KY	KY	KY				AT SCHOOL	8		✓	✓	✓				
	" HARLAN M.	Son	W	M	Jan 1892	7	S				KY	KY	KY								✓					
	" MAMIE C.	Dau	W	F	Aug 1895	4	S				KY	KY	KY													
	" BESSIE	Dau	W	F	Oct 1897	2	S				KY	KY	KY													
	" BABY	Dau	W	F	APR 1900	2/12	S				KY	KY	KY													
26 26	CASTEEL, LANDON	Head	W	M	Jul 1854	45	M	24			TN	NC	TN				FARMER			✓	✓	✓	O		F	26
	" BERNETTIE	Wife	W	F	Feb 184-58		M	24	5	2	TN	TN	TN							X	X	✓				
	" FERBY	Dau	W	F	APR 1878	22					KY	TN	TN				SEAMSTRESS			✓	✓	✓				
	CABLE, ISAAC(?)	Boarder	W	M	Jan 1880	20					KY	KY	KY				FARMER			X	X	✓	R		F	27
27 27	CASTEEL, JOHN	Head	W	M	Mar 1866	34	M	11			TN	TN	TN				FARMER			X	X	✓	R		F	28
	" ROSSY	Wife	W	F	Sep 1872	27	M	11	4	2	TN	TN	TN							✓	✓	✓				
	" THOMAS L.	Son	W	M	Dec 1889	10	S				KY	TN	TN				AT SCHOOL	3		X	X	✓				
	" PEARL A.	Dau	W	F	APR 1892	8	S				KY	TN	TN													
28 28	SPROWLS, COLMAN	Head	W	M	Sep 1866	33	M	12			KY	KY	KY				FARMER			✓	✓	✓	R		F	29
	" BELLE S.	Wife	W	F	Jan 1869	31	M	12	5	5	TN	TN	TN							✓	✓	✓				

TWELFTH CENSUS OF THE UNITED STATES 1900

STATE - KENTUCKY
COUNTY - MONROE
Township or other division MARTINSBURGH
Enumerator JAMES T. WHITE

Supervisor's Dist. No. 102 Sheet No.
Enumeration Dist. No. 83

No. of Family	No. of Dwelling	NAME	Relation	Color	Sex	DATE OF BIRTH Mon/Yr	Age at last birthday	Marital Status	# Years married	Mother of how many children?	# of these children living	NATIVITY Place of birth [this person]	Father of this person	Mother of this person	CITIZENSHIP Year of immigr. / # years in U.S. / Naturalization	OCCUPATION 10 years +	Months not employed	Attended school in months	Can read	Can write	Speak English	Owned or Rent	Owned - no mortage	Farm or house	# of farm schedule
		SPROWLS, ODIS W.	Son	W	M	Jun 1891	9	S				TX	KY	TN											
		" JOHN T.	Son	W	M	Jan 1893	7	S				KY	KY	TN											
		" MARTHA C.	Dau	W	F	Sep 1895	5	S				KY	KY	TN											
		" PHILLIP W.	Son	W	M	Mar 1896	4	S				KY	KY	TN											
		" FRANK S.	Son	W	M	Aug 1898	1	S				KY	KY	TN											
29	29	SPROWLS, WILLIAM	Head	W	M	Aug 1834	65	M	44			KY	TN	KY		FARMER			✓	✓	✓	O	F	F	30
		" CATHRINE	Wife	W	F	May 1836	64	M	44	8	4	KY	KY	KY					X	✓	✓				
30	30	POLAND, SAM	Head	W	M	Sep 1860	39	M	13			KY	TN	KY		FARMER			X	X	✓	R		F	31
		" AMY F.	Wife	W	F	Nov 1869	30	M	13	6	5	KY	KY	KY					✓	✓	✓				
		" MARY E.	Dau	W	F	Oct 1887	12	S				KY	KY	KY		AT SCHOOL		4	✓	✓	✓				
		" WILLIAM T.	Son	W	M	Mar 1889	11	S				KY	KY	KY		AT SCHOOL		4	✓	✓	✓				
		" WOLFORD T.	Son	W	M	Jul 1891	8	S				KY	KY	KY											
		" DICY C.	Dau	W	F	Mar 1898	2	S				KY	KY	KY											
		" TURNER J.	Son	W	M	Jan 1900	5/12	S				KY	KY	KY											
31	31	BAILEY, MARTIN	Head	W	M	Jan 1858	42	M	20			KY	KY	KY		FARMER			✓	✓	✓	O	M	F	32
		" LELA (?)	Wife	W	F	Oct 1861	38	M	20	11	5	IL	KY	IL					X	X	✓				
		" JOHN T.	Son	W	M	Mar 1885	15	S				KY	KY	IL		AT SCHOOL		5	✓	✓	✓				
		" BRAH	Dau	W	F	Aug 1886	13	S				KY	KY	IL		AT SCHOOL		5	✓	✓	✓				
		" HARISON L.	Son	W	M	Jan 1889	11	S				KY	KY	IL		AT SCHOOL		5	✓	✓	✓				
		" HATTIE G.	Dau	W	F	Oct 1895	4	S				KY	KY	IL											
		" TAYLOR A.	Son	W	M	Nov 1899	7/12	S				KY	KY	IL											
32	32	BLARE, JOHN	Head	W	M	Jun 1876	23	M	2			KY	KY	KY		FARMER			X	X	✓	R		F	33
		" CORDELA	Wife	W	F	Jun 1877	22	M	2	1	1	IN	ENGLAND	VA					✓	✓	✓				
		" FRANKLIN	Son	W	M	May 1899	1	S				KY	KY	IN											
		SIKES, ANN	Mother-in-law	W	F	Jan 1850	50	Wd		5	5	ENG	ENG	ENG		SEAMSTRESS			✓	X	✓				
		" THOMAS (?)	Boarder	W	M	Feb 1881	19	S				KY	ENG	ENG		DAY LABOR			X	X	✓				

STATE - KENTUCKY
COUNTY - MONROE
Township or other division MARTINSBURGH   Enumerator JAMES T. WHITE

Supervisor's Dist. No. _102_ Sheet No. _____
Enumeration Dist. No. _83_ _____

Location (No. of Family / No. of Dwelling)	NAME	Relation	Color	Sex	DATE OF BIRTH Mon/Yr	Age at last birthday	Marital Status	# Years married	Mother of how many children?	# of these children living	Place of birth (this person)	Father of this person	Mother of this person	Year of immigr.	# years in U.S.	Naturalization	OCCUPATION 10 years +	Months not employed	Attended school in months	Can read	Can write	Speak English	Owned or Rent	Owned -no mortgage	Farm or house	# of farm schedule
	SIKES, LUCINDA	Boarder	W	F	MAR 1886	14	S				KY	ENG	ENG				BASKET MAKER			✓	✓	✓				
33 33	BOON, SAM	HEAD	W	M	DEC 1846	53	Wd				TN	TN	TN				FARMER			✓	✓	✓	O		F	34
"	PEARL	DAU	W	F	JAN 1884	16	S				KY	TN	TN				AT SCHOOL		5	✓	✓	✓				
"	MERTIE	DAU	W	F	APR 1887	13	S				KY	TN	TN				AT SCHOOL		5	✓	✓	✓				
"	EDGAR	SON	W	M	JUN 1894	5	S				KY	TN	TN													
"	BESSIE F.	DAU	W	F	NOV 1898	1	S				KY	TN	TN													
34 34	BOON, MARY	HEAD	W	F	JAN 1807	93	Wd		9	2	TN	TN	TN				HOUSEWORK			✓	✓	✓			H	
"	JESSIE F.	GR-SON	W	M	MAY 1892	8	S				KY	TN	KY													
35 35	DAVIS, JAMES	HEAD	W	M	MAY 1880	20	M	1			KY	KY	KY				DAY LABOR			✓	X	✓			H	
"	ARMINTIE	Wife	W	F	JUL 1880	19	M	1	1	1	KY	KY	KY							✓	✓	✓				
"	THOMAS	SON	W	M	MAR 1900	2/12	S				KY	KY	KY													
36 36	ASHLOCK, GEORGE	HEAD	W	M	MAR 1845	55	M	28			KY	TN	TN				FARMER			X	X	✓	O		F	35
"	NANCY J.	WIFE	W	F	JUL 1855	44	M	28	12	12	KY	KY	TN							✓	✓	✓				
"	BIDDIE	DAU	W	F	JUN 1874	25	S				KY	KY	KY				SCHOOL TEACHER			✓	✓	✓				
"	ISAIAH M.	SON	W	M	MAY 1877	23	S				KY	KY	KY				FARMER			✓	✓	✓	R		F	36
"	TABITHIA E.	DAU	W	F	OCT 1880	20	S				KY	KY	KY				AT SCHOOL		10	✓	✓	✓				
"	EDWARD	SON	W	M	SEP 1882	17	S				KY	KY	KY				AT SCHOOL		5	✓	✓	✓				
"	MAUDIE B.	DAU	W	F	JUL 1884	15	S				KY	KY	KY				AT SCHOOL		10	✓	✓	✓				
"	ZORA J.	DAU	W	F	APR 1887	13	S				KY	KY	KY				AT SCHOOL		10	✓	✓	✓				
"	CASSIE C.	DAU	W	F	FEB 1888	12	S				KY	KY	KY				AT SCHOOL		10	✓	✓	✓				
"	JULIA R.	DAU	W	F	JUN 1890	9	S				KY	KY	KY													
"	EZRA J.	SON	W	M	OCT 1891	8	S				KY	KY	KY													
"	INA T.	DAU	W	F	FEB 1894	6	S				KY	KY	KY													
"	SIDNEY B.	SON	W	M	AUG 1895	4	S				KY	KY	KY													
36 37	JONSON, PORTER J.	HEAD	W	M	AUG 1857	42	M	20			TN	TN	TN				FARMER			✓	X	✓	O		F	37
"	MARY J.	WIFE	W	F	OCT 1861	38	M	20	9	8	TN	TN	TN							✓	✓	✓				

STATE - KENTUCKY
COUNTY - MONROE
Township or other division MARTINSBURGH   Enumerator JAMES T. WHITE

Supervisor's Dist. No. _102_ Sheet No. ___
Enumeration Dist. No. _83_ ___

Location (No. of Family / No. of Dwelling)	NAME	Relation	Color	Sex	DATE OF BIRTH Mon/Yr	Age at last birthday	Marital Status	# Years married	Mother of how many children?	# of these children living	Place of birth (this person)	Father of this person	Mother of this person	Year of immigr.	# years in U.S.	Naturalization	OCCUPATION 10 years +	Months not employed	Attended school in months	Can read	Can write	Speak English	Owned or Rent	Owned – no mortgage	Farm or house	# of farm schedule
	JONSON, LINNIE (?)	DAU	W	F	Jun 1881	18	S				TN	TN	TN				AT SCHOOL		8	✓	✓	✓				
	" WAYMON	SON	W	M	Feb 1884	16	S				KY	TN	TN				AT SCHOOL		8	✓	✓					
	" ROBERT L.	SON	W	M	Feb 1889	11	S				TN	TN	TN				AT SCHOOL		8	✓	✓	✓				
	" (UNREADABLE)	SON	W	M	Feb 1887	13	S				TN	TN	TN				AT SCHOOL		8	✓		✓				
	" MARY	DAU	W	F	Feb 1887	13	S				TN	TN	TN				AT SCHOOL		8	✓	✓					
	" CALLIE	DAU	W	F	Jan 1893	7	S				TN	TN	TN													
	" QUINTON	SON	W	M	Mar 1895	5	S				TN	TN	TN													
	" CHARLIE	SON	W	M	Sep 1897	2	S				TN	TN	TN													
	" BABIE	SON	W	M	Mar 1900	3/12	S				TN	TN	TN													
37 38	BOON, WARNEY	HEAD	W	M	May 1880	20	M	2			KY	TN	TN				FARMER			✓	✓	✓	R		F	38
	" NANCY	WIFE	W	F	Sep 1880	19	M	2	1	1	KY	KY	KY							✓	✓					
	" (?) LENVER J.	DAU	W	F	Apr 1900	7/12	S				KY	KY	KY													
38 39	BOON, SIDNEY	HEAD	W	M	Nov 1877	22	M	2			KY	TN	TN				FARMER			✓	✓	✓	R		F	39
	" ERNEST	WIFE	W	F	Sep 1880	19	M	2	1	1	KY	TN	TN							✓	✓	✓				
	" NOVA L	DAU	W	F	May 1898	2	S				KY	KY	KY													
39 40	DICKEN, JOSEPH	HEAD	W	M	Dec 1855	44	M	10			KY	KY	KY				FARMER			✓	✓	✓	O	M	F	40
	" NORA	WIFE	W	F	May 1865	35	M	10	5	5	KY	KY	KY							✓	✓					
	" ERNEST	DAU	W	F	Nov 1891	9	S				KY	KY	KY													
	" VERAH B.	DAU	W	F	Mar 1893	7	S				KY	KY	KY													
	" ISHAM S.	SON	W	M	Jul 1894	5	S				KY	KY	KY													
	" JEFFERSON	SON	W	M	Jan 1897	3	S				KY	KY	KY													
	" EFFHAM (?)	SON	W	M	Jul 1899	1½2	S				KY	KY	KY													
40 41	BOLES, ULYSSES	HEAD	W	M	Jun 1876	23	M	3			TN	TN	KY				FARMER			✓	✓	✓	R		F	41
	" LEANN	WIFE	W	F	Feb 1875	25	M	3	1	1	KY	KY	KY							✓	✓	✓				
	" HERMAN H.	SON	W	M	May 1898	2	S				KY	TN	KY													
	BOLES, MILTON	FATHER	W	M	Jan 1837	63	Wd				TN	NC	KY				FARMER			✓	✓	✓	R		F	42

STATE - KENTUCKY
COUNTY - MONROE
Township or other division MARTINSBURG14   Enumerator JAMES T. WHITE

Supervisor's Dist. No. 102 Sheet No.
Enumeration Dist. No. 83

No. of Family	No. of Dwelling	NAME	Relation	Color	Sex	DATE OF BIRTH Mon/Yr	Age at last birthday	Marital Status	# Years married	Mother of how many children?	# of these children living	Place of birth (this person)	Father of this person	Mother of this person	Year of immigr. to U.S.	# years in U.S.	Naturalization	OCCUPATION 10 years +	Months not employed	Attended school in months	Can read	Can write	Speak English	Owned or Rent	Owned –no mortage	Farm or house	# of farm schedule
41	42	BROWN, JAMES W.	Head	W	M	APR 1864	36	M	16			KY	KY	KY				TEAMSTER			✓	✓	✓	R		H	
		" ANIE B.	Wife	W	F	AUG 1873	26	M	16	5	5	TN	KY	TN							✓	✓	✓			H	
		" LEE W.	Son	W	M	NOV 1885	14	S				KY	KY	TN				DAY LABOR			✓	✓	✓				
		" MAY	Dau	W	F	MAR 1891	9	S				TN	KY	TN													
		" CARRY	Dau	W	F	Sep 1892	7	S				TN	KY	TN													
		" SALENER	Dau	W	F	Sep 1894	5	S				TN	KY	TN													
		" NELLIE B.	Dau	W	F	MAR 1898	2	S				TN	KY	TN													
42	43	MINICK, EDGAR	Head	W	M	APR 1877	23	M	6			TN	TN	TN				(UNREADABLE)			✓	✓	✓	R		H	
		" MARY	Wife	W	F	JUN 1875	24	M	6	2	2	KY	KY	KY								✓	✓				
		" AGNES	Dau	W	F	JUN 1895	4	S				KY	TN	KY													
		" A—? F.	Son	W	M	AUG 1898	1	S				KY	TN	KY													
43	44	BRIDGES, ELIC	Head	W	M	AUG 1862	37	M	4			KY	KY	KY				FARMER			X	X	✓	R		F	43
		" MARGARET	Wife	W	F	JUN 1866	33	M	4	5	4	KY	VA	TN							X	X	✓				
		" NIMROD	Son	W	M	JUN 1886	14	S				KY	KY	KY				AT SCHOOL		5	X	X	✓				
		" ROBERT	Son	W	M	APR 1890	10	S				KY	KY	KY				AT SCHOOL		5	X	X	✓				
		" AYE	Son	W	M	AUG 1894	5	S				KY	KY	KY													
		" EVVIE A.	Dau	W	F	Sep 1898	1	S				KY	KY	KY													
44	45	BAILEY JOSEPH	Head	W	M	AUG 1870	29	M	9			KY	KY	KY				FARMER			✓	✓	✓	R		F	44
		" ANNIE E.	Wife	W	F	NOV 1873	26	M	9	6	3	KY	KY	KY							✓	X	✓				
		" FANNIE P.	Dau	W	F	OCT 1892	7	S				KY	KY	KY													
		" TESSIE A.	Dau	W	F	APR 1896	4	S				KY	KY	KY													
		" -BABY-	Dau	W	F	APR 1900	1/12	S				KY	KY	KY													
45	46	BAILEY, CABEL	Head	W	M	OCT 1827	72	M	50			KY	SC	SC				FARMER			✓	✓	✓	O	M	F	45
		" PARADENE	Wife	W	F	Jul 1829	70	M	50	2	2	KY	TN	KY							✓	X	✓				
		" GRANVILE L.	Son	W	M	NOV 1864	35	S				KY	KY	KY				FARMER			✓	✓	✓	R		F	46
		" RADFORD	Son	W	M	AUG 1867	32	S				KY	KY	KY				FARMER			✓	✓	✓	R		F	47

TWELFTH CENSUS OF THE UNITED STATES 1900

STATE - KENTUCKY
COUNTY - MONROE
Township or other division MARTINSBURGH

Enumerator JAMES T. WHITE

Supervisor's Dist. No. 102 Sheet No.
Enumeration Dist. No. 83

No. of Family	No. of Dwelling	NAME	Relation	Color	Sex	Date of Birth Mon/Yr	Age at last birthday	Marital Status	# Years married	Mother of how many children?	# of these children living	Place of birth [this person]	Father of this person	Mother of this person	Occupation 10 years +	Attended school in months	Can read	Can write	Speak English	Owned or Rent	Owned-no mortgage	Farm or house	# of farm schedule
		SPROWLS, NANCY E.	Boarder	W	F	DEC 1859	40	S				KY	KY	KY	SERVANT		✓	✓	✓				
46	47	DIRE, STEVENS D.	Head	W	M	AUG 1863	30	M	10			TN	TN	TN	FARMER		X	X	✓	R		F	48
		" REBECCA	Wife	W	F	DEC 1875	24	M	10	3	3	KY	KY	KY			✓	✓	✓				
		" MAY	Dau	W	F	OCT 1891	8	S				KY	KY	KY									
		" LENA	Dau	W	F	DEC 1894	5	S				KY	TN	KY									
		" LARY B.	Dau	W	F	OCT 1899	1	S				KY	TN	KY									
		YATES, SARAH L.	Boarder	W	F	MAY 1876	24	Wd				KY	TN	TN			✓	✓	✓				
		" , BURTIE	Boarder	W	F	DEC 1897	2	S				KY	KY	KY									
47	48	BASKET, JOHN	Head	W	M	MAY 1850	50	M	30			TN	TN	TN	FARMER		X	X	✓	R		F	49
		" MARY A.	Wife	W	F	FEB 1857	43	M	30	10	10	KY	KY	KY			✓	✓	✓				
		" TOMAS C.	Son	W	M	OCT 1879	20	S				KY	TN	KY	DAY LABOR		✓	✓	✓				
		" ELONZO	Son	W	M	JUN 1882	17	S				KY	TN	KY	DAY LABOR		✓	✓	✓				
		" MARY E.	Dau	W	F	FEB 1886	14	S				KY	TN	KY			✓	✓	✓				
		" MARTHA E.	Dau	W	F	DEC 1888	11	S				KY	TN	KY			X	X	✓				
		" FRANK T.	Son	W	M	Jul 1891	8	S				KY	TN	KY									
		" FLORY L.	Dau	W	F	DEC 1895	4	S				KY	TN	KY									
48	49	BROWN, SMITH	Head	W	M	Jul 1875	24	M	1			KY	KY	KY	FARMER		✓	✓	✓	R		F	50
		" LIZZIE	Wife	W	F	Aug 1878	21	M	1	1	1	KY	KY	KY			✓	✓	✓				
		" OLIE	Dau	W	F	MAY 1899	1	S				KY	KY	KY									
		" PARKES	Boarder	W	M	— 1893	7	S				KY	KY	KY									
49	50	DIRE, WILLIAM	Head	W	M	MAR 1874	26	M	7			TN	TN	TN	FARMER		X	X	✓	R		F	51
		" ELIZZIEBETH	Wife	W	F	MAY 1877	23	M	7	3	3	KY	KY	KY			✓	✓	✓				
		" CESAL R.	Son	W	M	JUN 1893	6	S				KY	TN	KY									
		" GEORGE R.	Son	W	M	DEC 1897	2	S				KY	TN	KY									
		" ZELMA L.	Dau	W	F	Sep 1899	9/12	S				KY	TN	KY									
50	51	SHORT, GEORG	Head	W	M	MAR 1852	48	M	27			KY	KY	KY	FARMER		X	X	✓	O	M	F	52

STATE - KENTUCKY
COUNTY - MONROE
Township or other division MARTINSBURGH Enumerator JAMES T. WHITE

Supervisor's Dist. No. 102 Sheet No.
Enumeration Dist. No. 83

No. of Family	No. of Dwelling	NAME	Relation	Color	Sex	DATE OF BIRTH Mon/Yr	Age at last birthday	Marital Status	# Years married	Mother of how many children?	# of these children living	Place of birth [this person]	Father of this person	Mother of this person	Year of immigr.	# years in U.S.	Naturalization	OCCUPATION 10 years +	Months not employed	Attended school in months	Can read	Can write	Speak English	Owned or Rent	Owned -no mortage	Farm or house	# of farm schedule
		SHORT, MARTHIE A	WIFE	W	F	AUG 1852	47	M	27	4	3	KY	KY	KY							✓	✓	✓				
51	52	PRUETT, GEORGE	HEAD	W	M	OCT 1873	26	M	5			KY	KY	KY				FARMER			✓	✓	✓	R	F	53	
		" LARRY E.	WIFE	W	F	OCT 1880	19	M	5	2	2	KY	KY	KY							✓	✓				
		" LYSIE A.	DAU	W	F	OCT 1896	3	S				KY	KY	KY													
		" GEORGE A.	SON	W	M	Feb 1900	3/12	S				KY	KY	KY													
52	53	ANDERSON, WILLIAM	HEAD	W	M	Nov 1845	54	M	20			KY	KY	KY				FARMER			X	X	✓	O	F	F	54
		" JANE	WIFE	W	F	May 1860	40	M	20	9	9	KY	KY	KY							X	X	✓				
		" LUELER	DAU	W	F	Jan 1879	21	S				KY	KY	KY							✓	✓	✓				
		" RUBEN	SON	W	M	AUG 1880	19	S				KY	KY	KY				DAY LABOR			X	X	✓				
		" BANEY	SON	W	M	Jul 1883	16	S				KY	KY	KY							X	X	✓				
		" BELLE	DAU	W	F	Jul 1883	16	S				KY	KY	KY							X	X	✓				
		" MARIE	DAU	W	F	Sep 1886	13	S				KY	KY	KY							X	X	✓				
		" DOCIA	DAU	W	F	MAR 1889	11	S				KY	KY	KY							X	X	✓				
		" BETSY	DAU	W	F	OCT 1890	9	S				KY	KY	KY													
		" LESSIE	DAU	W	F	Jul 1891	8	S				KY	KY	KY													
		" DORY	DAU	W	F	MAR 1895	5	S				KY	KY	KY													
		" CREED	SON	W	M	JAN 1897	3	S				KY	KY	KY													
53	54	PRUETT, ANDREW J.	Head	W	M	Feb 1846	54	M	23			KY	VA	KY				FARMER			✓	✓	✓	O	F	F	55
		" MATILDA P.	Wife	W	F	DEC 1854	45	M	23	1	1	KY	TN	KY							✓	✓	✓				
		" SUSIE J.	Dau	W	F	AUG 1887	12	S				KY	KY	KY				AT SCHOOL		10	✓	✓	✓				
54	55	PRUETT, GEORGE H.	Head	W	M	MAY 1852	48	Wd				KY	KY	KY				FARMER			✓	✓	✓	O	F	F	56
		" FRANKLIN J.	SON	W	M	AUG 1884	15	S				KY	KY	KY				FARM LABOR			✓	✓	✓				
		" JOHN A.	SON	W	M	MAY 1887	13	S				KY	KY	KY				FARM LABOR			X	X	✓				
		" FLORNCE M.	DAU	W	F	JAN 1889	11	S				KY	KY	KY							X	X	✓				
		" BRANSFORD R.	SON	W	M	Sep 1890	9	S				KY	KY	KY													
		" JESSIE V.	SON	W	M	AUG 1892	7	S				KY	KY	KY													

TWELFTH CENSUS OF THE UNITED STATES 1900

—195—

STATE - KENTUCKY
COUNTY - MONROE
Township or other division: MARTINSBURGH Enumerator: JAMES T. WHITE

Supervisor's Dist. No. 102 Sheet No. ___
Enumeration Dist. No. 83

No. of Family	No. of Dwelling	NAME	Relation	Color	Sex	Date of Birth Mon/Yr	Age at last birthday	Marital Status	# Years married	Mother of how many children?	# of these children living	Place of birth (this person)	Father of this person	Mother of this person	Year of immigr.	# years in U.S.	Naturalization	Occupation 10 years +	Months not employed	Attended school in months	Can read	Can write	Speak English	Owned or Rent	Owned-no mortage	Farm or house	# of farm schedule
		PRUETT, ETHEL	DAU	W	F	OCT 1893	6	S				KY	KY	KY													
		" HATTIE	DAU	W	F	OCT 1895	4	S				KY	KY	KY													
		" BEDFORD	SON	W	M	MAY 1897	3	S				KY	KY	KY													
		" DOW	SON	W	M	JAN 1899	1	S				KY	KY	KY													
		SHORT, PATSY	MOTHER-IN-LAW	W	F	APR 1840	60	Wd		6	6	KY	KY	KY						X	X	✓					
		" DORA	DAU	W	F	MAR 1878	22	M	2	1	1	KY	KY	KY							✓	✓	✓				
		SCOT, LEE	SON-IN-LAW	W	M	JUL 1878	21	M	2			KY	KY	KY				DAY LABOR			✓	✓	✓				
		" LOVIE	GR-DAU	W	F	JUL 1899	10/12	S				KY	KY	KY													
55	56	SCOT, JAMES P.	HEAD	W	M	MAY 1863	37	M	10			IND	KY	TN				FARMER			✓	✓	✓	R	F	57	
		" MARY W.	WIFE	W	F	MAY 1863	37	M	10	5	3	KY	KY	IL						X	X	✓				
		" ALFORD B.	SON	W	M	MAR 1891	9	S				KY	IND	KY													
(?)		" AMBUSE D.	SON	W	M	MAR 1896	4	S				KY	IND	KY													
		" WILLIAM L.	SON	W	M	FEB 1899	1	S				TN	IND	KY													
56	57	CANE, MAYRENE (?)	HEAD	W	M	JAN 1870	30	M	5			KY	KY	KY				FARMER			X	X	✓	R	F	58	
		" ABBYGILL	WIFE	W	F	MAR 1878	22	M	5	2	2	KY	KY	KY							✓	✓	✓				
		" FANNIE B.	DAU	W	F	JUN 1896	3	S				KY	KY	KY													
		" WILLIAM J.	SON	W	M	AUG 1899	7/12	S				KY	KY	KY													
		SCOT, MIGGIE	SISTER-IN-LAW	W	F	AUG 1874	25	Wd		3	1	KY	KY	KY				SEAMSTRESS			✓	✓	✓				
		" JAMES Y.	SON	W	M	NOV 1899	7/12	S				KY	KY	KY													
57	58	(HEI?) SOLOMON	HEAD	W	M	NOV 1859	40	M	14			TN	TN	TN				FARMER			✓	✓	✓	O	F	59	
		EMMA J.	WIFE	W	F	MAR 1865	35	M	14	5	5	OHIO	N.J.	OHIO							✓	✓	✓				
		DORTHA E.	DAU	W	F	MAY 1887	13	S				TN	TN	OHIO				AT SCHOOL		6	✓	✓	✓				
		HALL B.	SON	W	M	JAN 1889	11	S				KY	TN	OHIO				AT SCHOOL		7	✓	✓	✓				
		PEARL A.	DAU	W	F	FEB 1891	9	S				TN	TN	OHIO													
		CLORA L.	DAU	W	F	MAR 1893	7	S				TN	TN	OHIO													
		BRYAN P.	SON	W	M	JUL 1897	2	S				TN	TN	OHIO													

STATE - KENTUCKY
COUNTY - MONROE
Township or other division MARTINSBURGH   Enumerator JAMES T. WHITE

Supervisor's Dist. No. 102 Sheet No.
Enumeration Dist. No. 83

No. of Family	No. of Dwelling	NAME	Relation	Color	Sex	DATE OF BIRTH Mon/Yr	Age at last birthday	Marital Status	# Years married	Mother of how many children	# of these children living	Place of birth (this person)	Father of this person	Mother of this person	Year of immigr.	# years in U.S.	Naturalization	OCCUPATION 10 years +	Months not employed	Attended school in months	Can read	Can write	Speak English	Owned or Rent	Owned - no mortage	Farm or house	# of farm schedule
58	59	ANDERSON, ( )	HEAD	W	M	Sep 1869	30	M	3			KY	KY	KY				FARMER		X	X		✓	O	F	F	60
		" MALINDA E.	WIFE	W	F	Jan 1878	22	M	3	2	2	KY	KY	KY													
		" MARY C	DAU	W	F	Dec 1897	2	S				KY	KY	KY													
		" ABYAILL (?) L.	DAU	W	F	Jan 1900	5/12	S				KY	KY	KY													
59	60	PRUETT, E C.	HEAD	W	M	Dec 1868	31	M	12			KY	KY	KY				DAY LABOR	7		✓	✓		R		H	
		" WINNIE A	WIFE	W	F	Jan 1871	29	M	12	5	4	KY	KY	KY							✓	✓					
		" JOHN T.	SON	W	M	Jan 1890	10	S				TN	KY	KY				AT SCHOOL		4	✓	✓					
		" MAMY L.	DAU	W	F	Dec 1892	7	S				TN	KY	KY													
		" WILLIAM B.	SON	W	M	Jul 1894	5	S				KY	KY	KY													
		" REED W.	SON	W	M	Nov 1898	1	S				KY	KY	KY													
60	61	GRAY, TOMAS J.	Head	W	M	Feb 1861	39	M	9			TN	TN	KY				FARMER			✓	✓	✓	R		F	61
		" SALLIE M.	wife	W	F	Apr 1872	28	M	9	4	3	KY	KY	KY							✓	✓					
		" IVAH	DAU	W	F	Jul 1892	7	S				KY	TN	KY													
		" AVOS	DAU	W	F	Feb 1894	6	S				OREGON	TN	KY													
		" BESSIE	DAU	W	F	Dec 1898	1	S				KY	TN	KY													
		GRAY, NEBRASKA	SISTER	W	F	Jul 1854	45	S				TN	TN	TN							✓	✓					
		" WILLARD	NEPHEW	W	M	Apr (?) 1888	20	S				TN	TN	TN				DAY LABOR			✓	✓					
61	62	HALE, JOHN H(?)	HEAD	W	M	Jan 1875	25	M	3			TN	TN	TN				FARMER			✓	✓		O	F	F	62
		" ANNIE L.	WIFE	W	F	Apr 1874	26	M	3	2	2	KY	KY	TN							✓	✓					
		" PEARL L.	DAU	W	F	Apr 1898	2	S				KY	KY	TN													
		" LESTER E.	SON	W	M	— 1899	9/12	S				KY	KY	TN													
62	63	SPEAR, MARINETA	HEAD	W	F	May 1846	54	Wd				KY	KY	KY				FARMER			✓	✓		O	F	F	63
		" LUTHER H.	SON	W	M	May 1878	22	S				KY	KY	KY				AT SCHOOL		5	✓	✓	✓				
		" LOU C.	DAU	W	F	Dec 1882	17	S				KY	KY	KY				A.T. SCHOOL			✓	✓	✓				
		" HUBERT K.	SON	W	M	Dec 1884	15	S				KY	KY	KY				A.T. SCHOOL		5	✓	✓	✓				
		" RAMOND C.	SON	W	M	Jun 1888	11	S				KY	KY	KY				AT SCHOOL		5	✓	✓	✓				

STATE - KENTUCKY
COUNTY - MONROE
Township or other division MARTINSBURGH

Enumerator JAMES T. WHITE

Supervisor's Dist. No. 102 Sheet No.
Enumeration Dist. No. 83

No. of Family	No. of Dwelling	NAME	Relation	Color	Sex	DATE OF BIRTH Mon/Yr	Age at last birthday	Marital Status	# Years married	Mother of how many children?	# of these children living	Place of birth [this person]	Father of this person	Mother of this person	Year of immigr.	# years in U.S.	Naturalization	OCCUPATION 10 years +	Months not employed	Attended school in months	Can read	Can write	Speak English	Owned or Rent	Owned -no mortage	Farm or house	# of farm schedule
		SPEAR, BEATRICE M.	DAU	W	F	Sep 1892	7	S				KY	KY	KY													
63	64	HENSON, WADE	HEAD	W	M	Apr 1858	42	M	8			KY	TN	TN				FARMER			✓	✓	✓	R		F	64
		" MARY E.	WIFE	W	F	Jan 1857	43	M	8	2	2	TN	KY	TN							X	X	✓				
		" AVA	DAU	W	F	Feb 1885	15	S				KY	KY	TN				AT SCHOOL		2	✓	✓	✓				
		" DONA	DAU	W	F	Jul 1889	10	S				KY	KY	TN							✓	X	✓				
		" LUCY	DAU	W	F	Jul 1891	8	S				KY	KY	TN													
		" SMITH L.	SON	W	M	Mar 1893	7	S				KY	KY	TN													
64	65	GOOLSBY, BIRD	HEAD	W	M	Sep 1858	41	M				TN	TN	TN				FARMER			✓	✓		R		F	65
		" SOPHA L.	WIFE	W	F	Apr 1866	34	M		4	4	TN	TN	TN							✓	X	✓				
		" HATTIE L.	DAU	W	F	Jun 1882	17	S				TN	TN	TN				AT SCHOOL		10	✓	✓	✓				
		" ELLA A.	DAU	W	F	Sep 1884	15	S				TN	TN	TN				AT SCHOOL		6	✓	✓	✓				
		" FANNIE L.	DAU	W	F	Sep 1888	11	S				TN	TN	TN				AT SCHOOL		10	✓	✓					
		" ALBERT H.	SON	W	M	Mar 1890	10	S				TN	TN	TN				AT SCHOOL		10	✓	✓	✓				
		" MILORD F.	SON	W	M	Apr 1895	5	S				TN	TN	TN													
		" LIZZIE M.	DAU	W	F	Apr 1897	3	S				TN	TN	TN													
65	66	DENHAM, BENJAMIN	HEAD	W	M	Jan 1862	38	M	12			TN	TN	TN				SCHOOL TEACHER	2		✓	✓	✓				
		" MARGARET C	WIFE	W	F	Jan 1862	38	M	12	4	2	KY	TN	TN							✓	✓	✓				
		" HOMER J.	SON	W	M	Nov 1894	5	S				KY	TN	KY													
		" TOMMY E.	DAU	W	F	Jun 1897	3	S				KY	TN	KY													
		" ELIZZBETH	MOTHER	W	F	Aug 1825	74	Wd				TN	TN	TN							✓	✓	✓				
		GIT, TOLL	BOARDER	W	M	Aug 1873	26	S				TN	TN	TN				MERCHANT			✓	✓	✓				
66	67	WHITESIDES JAMES	HEAD	W	M	Sep 1842	58	M	26			KY	KY	KY				FARMER			✓	✓	✓	O		F	67
		" SARAH I.	WIFE	W	F	Jan 1851	49	M	26	1	1	TN	TN	TN							✓	✓	✓				
		" FOWLER G.	SON	W	M	Feb 1875	25	S				KY	KY	TN				AT SCHOOL		8	✓	✓	✓				
		FOWLER, WILLIE B.	NEPHEW	W	M	Jul 1887	12	S				TN	TN	KY				AT SCHOOL		5	✓	✓	✓				
67	68	HALLCELL, ROBERT	HEAD	W	M	Aug 1857	42	M	19			KY	KY	KY				FARMER			✓	✓	✓	R		F	68

STATE - KENTUCKY
COUNTY - MONROE
Township or other division **MARTINSBURGH**   Enumerator **JAMES T. WHITE**

Supervisor's Dist. No. **102** Sheet No. ___
Enumeration Dist. No. **83** ___

No. of Family	No. of Dwelling	NAME	Relation	Color	Sex	DATE OF BIRTH Mon/Yr	Age at last birthday	Marital Status	# Years married	Mother of how many children?	# of these children living	Place of birth [this person]	Father of this person	Mother of this person	Year of immigr.	# years in U.S.	Naturalization	OCCUPATION 10 years +	Months not employed	Attended school in months	Can read	Can write	Speak English	Owned or Rent	Owned –no mortgage	Farm or house	# of farm schedule
		HALLCELL, RUTH A.	WIFE	W	F	MAY 1863	37	M	17	8	5	KY	KY	KY													
		" BENNIE F.	SON	W	M	JUN 1885	14	S				TN	TN	TN				AT SCHOOL		8	✓	✓	✓				
		" LURA V.	DAU	W	F	DEC 1887	12	S				KY	KY	TN				AT SCHOOL		5	✓	✓	✓				
		" BASLAE(?)	SON	W	M	JAN 1893	7	S				KY	KY	TN													
		" BONNIE	DAU	W	F	FEB 1895	5	S				KY	KY	TN													
		" WALTER R.	SON	W	M	APR 1899	1	S				KY	KY	TN													
		" JOHN T.	SON	W	M	JAN 1900	4/12	S				KY	KY	TN													
68	69	COE, MARTHA	HEAD	W	F	JUL 1834	65	Wd		3	1	KY	TN	TN				FARMER			✓	✓	✓	O	F	F	69
		" EDWARD	GR-SON	W	M	SEP 1883	16	S				KY	TN	KY				FARMER			✓	✓	✓	R		F	70
		" CASSIE	GR-DAU	W	F	FEB 1888	12	S				KY	KY	KY				AT SCHOOL		10	✓	✓	✓				
69	70	BOON, OLIVER	HEAD	W	M	APR 1882	18	M	0			KY	KY	TN				DAY LABOR			✓	✓	✓	R		H	
		" LARRY S.	WIFE	W	F	OCT 1878	21	M	0			TN	TN	TN							✓	✓	✓				
70	71	GARRETT, GEORGE	HEAD	W	M	MAR 1840	60	M	32			TN	VA	NC				FARMER			✓	✓	✓	R		F	72
		" SARAH	WIFE	W	F	OCT 1849	50	M	32	10	7	TN	TN	TN							✓	✓	✓				
		" GEORGE T.	SON	W	M	MAR 1884	16	S				TN	TN	TN				AT SCHOOL		3	✓	✓	✓				
		" EDMON H.	SON	W	M	OCT 1887	12	S				TN	TN	TN				AT SCHOOL		3	✓	✓	✓				
		" JOSEPH B.	SON	W	M	JAN 1891	9	S				TN	TN	TN													
		LARRY G.(?)	DAU	W	F	DEC 1894	5	S				TN	TN	TN													
71	72	HIX, JOHN T.	HEAD	W	M	APR 1871	29	M	11			TN	TN	TN				FARM LABOR			✓	✓	✓	R		H	
		" MARY F.	WIFE	W	F	SEP? 1872	27	M	11	5	5	TN	TN	TN							✓	✓	✓				
		" BENTON C.	SON	W	M	AUG 1890	9	S				TN	TN	TN													
		" JAMES L.	SON	W	M	JUL 1893	6	S				TN	TN	TN													
		" SARAH P.	DAU	W	F	JUN 1895	4	S				TN	TN	TN													
		" FLORA	DAU	W	F	DEC 1897	2	S				TN	TN	TN													
		" GEORGE L.	SON	W	M	FEB 1900	4/12	S				TN	TN	TN													
72	73	POOR, EMAN	Head	W	F	JUL 1865	34	Wd		3	3	TN	TN	TN				FARMER			✓	✓	✓	O	F	F	73

STATE - KENTUCKY
COUNTY - MONROE
Township or other division MARTINSBURGH   Enumerator JAMES T. WHITE

Supervisor's Dist. No. 102 Sheet No.
Enumeration Dist. No. 83

No. of Family	No. of Dwelling	NAME	Relation	Color	Sex	Mon/Yr	Age at last birthday	Marital Status	# Years married	Mother of how many children?	# of these children living	Place of birth [this person]	Father of this person	Mother of this person	Year of immigr.	# years in U.S.	Naturalization	OCCUPATION 10 years +	Months not employed	Attended school in months	Can read	Can write	Speak English	Owned or Rent	Owned -no mortage	Farm or house	# of farm schedule
		POOR, MARY B.	DAU	W	F	Jan 1887	13	S				KY	TN	TN				AT SCHOOL		6	✓	✓	✓				
		" ADOS B.	SON	W	M	Jan 1890	10	S				KY	TN	TN				AT SCHOOL		3	X	X	✓				
		" LOIS M.	DAU	W	F	Oct 1891	8	S				KY	TN	TN													
		" PERSILLA	MOTHER	W	F	Sep 1842	57	Wd				TN	TN	TN							✓	✓	✓	O	F	F	74
73	74	CAPS, JOHN R.	HEAD	W	M	Jun 1850	49	M	23			KY	KY	TN				FARMER			✓	✓	✓	R		F	75
		" MARY	Wife	W	F	Jan 1865	35	M	23	10	9	KY	KY	KY							X	X	✓				
		" ANDREW J.	SON	W	M	Jun 1877	22	S				KY	KY	KY				DAY LABOR			X	X	✓				
		" WILLIAM R.	SON	W	M	Oct 1882	17	S				KY	KY	KY				DAY LABOR			X	X	✓				
		" SARAH	DAU	W	F	Sep 1884	15	S				KY	KY	KY							X	X	✓				
		" NANCY P.	DAU	W	F	Dec 1887	13	S				KY	KY	KY							X	X	✓				
		" RIGHT	SON	W	M	Jul 1889	10	S				KY	KY	KY							X	X	✓				
		" ELIZZIE V.	DAU	W	F	Jan 1892	8	S				KY	KY	KY													
		" TE (?)	SON	W	M	Jan 1894	6	S				KY	KY	KY													
		" GEORGE B.	SON	W	M	Nov 1896	4	S				KY	KY	KY													
		" MARY L.	DAU	W	F	May 1898	2	S				KY	KY	KY													
74	75	SHORT, JAMES	Head	W	M	Jan 1850	50	M	18			KY	KY	KY				FARMER			X	X	✓	O	M	F	76
		" BELLE E.	Wife	W	F	Jun 1865	34	M	18	6	6	KY	KY	KY							✓	✓					
		" SAM T.	SON	W	M	Jan 1884	16	S				KY	KY	KY				AT SCHOOL		6	✓	✓	✓				
		" JAMES R.	SON	W	M	Apr 1885	15	S				KY	KY	KY				AT SCHOOL		7	✓	✓	✓				
		" JOHN F.	SON	W	M	Aug 1888	11	S				KY	KY	KY				AT SCHOOL		6	✓	✓	✓				
		" LUTHER B.	SON	W	M	Feb 1890	10	S				KY	KY	KY				AT SCHOOL		6	✓	✓	✓				
		" LELER	DAU	W	F	Apr 1892	8	S				KY	KY	KY													
		" NORA E.	DAU	W	F	Oct 1894	5	S				KY	KY	KY													
75	76	CARTER, JOSEPH	HEAD	W	M	Jan 1870	30	M	7			KY	TN	TN				FARMER			✓	✓	✓				
		" NANCY C.	WIFE	W	F	Sep 1871	28	M	7	4	4	TN	TX	TN							✓	✓	✓	R		F	77
		" CLARNCE U.	SON	W	M	Apr 1894	6	S				TN	KY	TN													

STATE - KENTUCKY
COUNTY - MONROE
Township or other division **MARTINSBURGH**   Enumerator **JAMES I. WHITE**

Supervisor's Dist. No. **10✓** Sheet No.
Enumeration Dist. No. **83**

No. of Family	No. of Dwelling	NAME	Relation	Color	Sex	Date of Birth Mon/Yr	Age at last birthday	Marital Status	# Years married	Mother of how many children?	# of these children living	Place of birth (this person)	Father of this person	Mother of this person	Year of immigr.	# years in U.S.	Naturalization	Occupation 10 years +	Months not employed	Attended school in months	Can read	Can write	Speak English	Owned or Rent	Owned –no mortgage	Farm or house	# of farm schedule
		CARTER, PEARL A.	DAU	W	F	APR 1896	4	S				TN	KY	TN													
		" WILLIAM R. D.	SON	W	M	APR 1897	3	S				TN	KY	TN													
		" JAMES H. L.	SON	W	M	MAY 1899	1	S				TN	KY	TN													
76	77	HAMPTON, GEORGE	HEAD	W	M	MAR 1875	25	M	4			TN	KY	TN				DAY LABOR			✓	✓	✓	R		H	
		" MARTHA	WIFE	W	F	MAY 1882	18	M	4			TN	TN	TN							✓	✓	✓				
77	78	STEPHENS, GEORGE	HEAD	W	M	DEC 1834	65	M	31			TN	TN	TN				FARMER			✓	✓	✓	O	F	F	78
		" JULIA C.	WIFE	W	F	Sep 1851	48	M	31	3	3	KY	TN	KY							✓	✓	✓				
		" GEORGE F.	DAU	W	F	MAY 1879	21	S				TN	TN	KY							✓	✓	✓				
		" JULIA H.	DAU	W	F	OCT 1882	17	S				TN	TN	KY				AT SCHOOL		10	✓	✓	✓				
		" MARY E.	DAU	W	F	AUG 1885	14	S				TN	TN	KY				AT SCHOOL		10	✓	✓	✓				
		WILLIAMS, FRANK	Boarder	W	M	JAN 1875	25	S				TN	TN	TN				DAY LABOR			✓	✓	✓				
78	79	HESS, JAMES F.	HEAD	W	M	Feb 1858	42	M	20			KY	KY	KY				FARMER			✓	✓	✓	R	F	F	79
		" FLORNCE S.	WIFE	W	F	Sep 1865	34	M	20	7	7	KY	KY	KY							✓	✓	✓				
		" STELLA B.	DAU	W	F	Jul 1881	18	S				KY	KY	KY				AT SCHOOL		9	✓	✓	✓				
		" BERTIE B.	SON	W	M	OCT 1884	15	S				KY	KY	KY				AT SCHOOL		5	✓	✓	✓				
		" MAY G.	DAU	W	F	APR 1887	13	S				KY	KY	KY				AT SCHOOL		5	✓	✓	✓				
		" SALLIE V.	DAU	W	F	Jan 1890	10	S				KY	KY	KY				AT SCHOOL		4	✓	✓	✓				
		" TESSIE E.	DAU	W	F	DEC 1891	8	S				KY	KY	KY													
		" WILLIAM B.	SON	W	M	JUN 1894	5	S				KY	KY	KY													
		" LYDIA A.	DAU	W	F	MAY 1896	4	S				KY	KY	KY													
		BOON, JOHN	BOARDER	W	M	APR 1885	15	S				KY	KY	KY				DAY LABOR			✓	✓	✓				
79	80	TINSLEY, LOUIS	HEAD	W	M	JAN 1875	25	M	6			TN	KY	TN				FARMER			✓	✓	✓	O		F	80
		" ELLEN	WIFE	W	F	Sep 1879	21	M	6	1	1	TN	TN	TN							✓	✓	✓				
		" RUBIE M.	DAU	W	F	DEC 1894	5	S				TN	TN	TN													
		GROGAN, CHEATON	Boarder	W	M	Sep 1877	22	S				KY	TN	TN				FARM LABOR			X	X	✓				
80	81	FARISE, LURIS	HEAD	W	M	MAR 1869	31	M	14			TN	TN	TN				FARMER						R		F	82 SIC

STATE - KENTUCKY
COUNTY - MONROE
Township or other division MARTINSBURGH   Enumerator JAMES T. WHITE

Supervisor's Dist. No. 102 Sheet No.
Enumeration Dist. No. 83

No. of Family	No. of Dwelling	NAME	Relation	Color	Sex	DATE OF BIRTH Mon/Yr	Age at last birthday	Marital Status	# Years married	Mother of how many children?	# of these children living	Place of birth [this person]	Father of this person	Mother of this person	Year of immigr.	# years in U.S.	Naturalization	OCCUPATION 10 years +	Months not employed	Attended school in months	Can read	Can write	Speak English	Owned or Rent	Owned - no mortgage	Farm or house	# of farm schedule	
		FARISE, MOLLIE J.	Wife	W	F	Feb 1867	33	M	14	7	6	KY	KY	KY							✓	✓	✓					
		" BENTON L.	Son	W	M	Mar 1888	12	S				KY	TN	KY				AT SCHOOL		4	X	X	✓					
		" NORMA G.	Dau	W	F	Aug 1889	10	S				KY	TN	KY				AT SCHOOL		5	✓	✓	✓					
		" MERTIE G.	Dau	W	F	Dec 1892	7	S				TN	TN	KY														
		" LATEN H.	Son	W	M	May 1894	6	S				TN	TN	KY														
		" MARY E.	Dau	W	F	Jul 1897	2	S				TN	TN	KY														
		" ADA F.	Dau	W	F	May 1899	1	S				KY	TN	KY														
81	82	LAUHERN, AMBER T.	Head	W	M	Oct 1849	50	M	20			KY	VA	KY				FARMER			✓	✓	✓	R		F	83	
		" BERNETTIE	Wife	W	F	Feb 1862	38	M	20	6	4	TN	VA	TN							✓	✓	✓					
		" ANNA M.	Dau	W	F	Jul 1884	15	S				TN	KY	TN								✓	✓					
		" WALTER G.	Son	W	M	Nov 1887	12	S				TN	KY	TN							X	X	✓					
		" LUCIE R.	Son	W	M	Aug 1890	9	S				TN	KY	TN														
		" BIRDIE S.	Son	W	M	Apr 1895	5	S				TN	KY	TN														
82	83	(Unreadable) M.	Head	W	M	Jul 1873	26	M	6			KY	KY	TN				DAY LABOR			X	X	✓	R		H		
		" MARY E.	Wife	W	F	May 1889	21	M	6	2	2	KY	KY	KY							✓	✓	✓					
		" WILLIAM T.	Son	W	M	Jan 1896	4	S				KY	KY	KY														
		" FANNIE R.E.	Dau	W	F	Oct 1898	1	S				KY	KY	KY														
83	84	GRAY, ALVIN	Head	W	M	Jan 1866	34	M	10			TN	TN	TN				FARMER			✓	✓	✓	R		F	84	
		" LUCIE J.	Wife	W	F	Feb 1872	28	M	10	5	5	KY	KY	KY							✓	✓	✓					
		" JAMES E.	Son	W	M	Oct 1890	9	S				KY	TN	KY														
		" ?—ENOW G.	Dau	W	F	Aug 1892	7	S				KY	TN	KY														
		" CORCY L.	Son	W	M	Sep 1895	4	S				KY	TN	KY														
		" CLORSEY V.	Dau	W	F	Sep 1895	4	S				KY	TN	KY														
		" LORA M.	Dau	W	F	Feb 1897	3	S				KY	TN	KY														
		HALLCELL, ELIZZIEBETH	Mother-in-law	W	F	Sep 1832	67	Wd		1	1	KY	TN	TN				FARMER			✓	✓	✓	O		FF	85	
84	85	HALLCELL, TUSS (?)	Head		W	M	Dec 1854	45	M	23		KY	KY	KY				FARMER			✓	✓	✓	R		F	86	

STATE - KENTUCKY
COUNTY - MONROE
Township or other division MARTINSBURGH   Enumerator JAMES T. WHITE

Supervisor's Dist. No. 10 2 Sheet No.
Enumeration Dist. No. 83

No. of Family	No. of Dwelling	NAME	Relation	Color	Sex	DATE OF BIRTH Mon/Yr	Age at last birthday	Marital Status	# Years married	Mother of how many children?	# of these children living	Place of birth [this person]	Father of this person	Mother of this person	Year of immigr.	# years in U.S.	Naturalization	OCCUPATION 10 years +	Months not employed	Attended school in months	Can read	Can write	Speak English	Owned or Rent	Owned - no mortage	Farm or house	# of farm schedule	
		HALLCELL, SARAH A.	WIFE	W	F	APR 1854	46	M	23	6	6	KY	KY	KY							✓		✓					
		" MAGGA B.	DAU	W	F	AUG 1880	19	S				KY	KY	KY				AT SCHOOL		5	✓	✓	✓					
		" MARY E.	DAU	W	F	AUG 1882	17	S				KY	KY	KY				AT SCHOOL		5	✓	✓	✓					
		" MAUD	DAU	W	F	JAN 1885	15	S				KY	KY	KY				AT SCHOOL		5	✓	✓	✓					
		" SARAH S.	DAU	W	F	AUG 1886	13	S				KY	KY	KY				AT SCHOOL		3	✓	✓	✓					
		" JAMES B.	SON	W	M	AUG 1895	4	S				KY	KY	KY														
		DECK, THOMAS A.	Boarder	W	M	Sep 1876	23	S				TN	TN	KY				FARMER			✓	✓		R		F	87	
85	86	SIMS, PATRIC	Head	W	M	MAR 1818	82	M	53			KY	VA	NC				FARMER			✓	✓		O		F	89	SIC
		" MATILDA	wife	W	F	OCT 1819	80	M	53	8	7	KY	VA	VA							✓	X	✓					
		" JULIA	DAU	W	F	Jul 1848	51	S				KY	KY	KY							✓	✓	✓					
		" WELCOM P.	SON	W	M	Sep 1856	44	S				KY	KY	KY				FARMER			✓	✓		O		F	90	
86	87	SIMS, JOSEPH H.	HEAD	W	M	APR 1856	44	M	12			KY	KY	KY				FARMER			✓	✓		R		F	91	
		" DELLA G.	WIFE	W	F	Sep 1866	33	M	12	4	3	KY	KY	KY							✓	✓						
		" OSCAR R.	SON	W	M	Jun 1889	10	S				TX	KY	KY				AT SCHOOL		4	✓	✓						
		" NAVADA E.	DAU	W	F	DEC 1891	8	S				TX	KY	KY								✓						
		" MAY E.	DAU	W	F	Jun 1894	5	S				TX	KY	KY														
87	88	POINDEXTER, JOHN	HEAD	W	M	Nov 1857	42	M	23			KY	KY	KY				FARMER			✓	✓		O	M	F	92	
		" NANCY J.	WIFE	W	F	Jun 1862	37	M	23	8	6	KY	KY	KY							✓	✓						
		" DOLLIE H.	DAU	W	F	MAR 1882	18	S				KY	KY	KY				AT SCHOOL		10	✓	✓						
		" FANNIE J.	DAU	W	F	MAR 1885	15	S				KY	KY	KY				AT SCHOOL		10	✓	✓	✓					
		" HERSCHALL	G. SON	W	M	Nov 1888	11	S				KY	KY	KY				AT SCHOOL		10	✓	✓	✓					
		" FRANK S.	SON	W	M	Feb 1891	9	S				KY	KY	KY														
		" MARY S.	DAU	W	F	Jun 1893	6	S				KY	KY	KY														
		HALLCELL, JOHN	Boarder	B	M	May 1889	21	S				KY	KY	KY				DAY LABOR			✓	✓						
88	89	GEE, JOHN B.	Head	W	M	Nov 1837	62	M	36			KY	KY	KY				FARMER			✓	✓		O		F	93	
		" MARY L.	wife	W	F	Feb 1848	52	M	36	9	7	KY	SC	TN							✓	✓						

STATE - KENTUCKY
COUNTY - MONROE
Township or other division MARTINSBURGH Enumerator JAMES T. WHITE

Supervisor's Dist. No. 107 Sheet No.
Enumeration Dist. No. 83

Location (No. of Family / No. of Dwelling)	NAME	Relation	Color	Sex	DATE OF BIRTH Mon/Yr	Age at last birthday	Marital Status	# Years married	Mother of how many children?	# of these children living	Place of birth (this person)	Father of this person	Mother of this person	Year of immigr.	# years in U.S.	Naturalization	OCCUPATION 10 years +	Months not employed	Attended school in months	Can read	Can write	Speak English	Owned or Rent	Owned - no mortgage	Farm or house	# of farm schedule
	GEE, BARLOW	Son	W	M	May 1877	23	S				KY	KY	KY				DAY LABOR			✓	✓					
	" HEBER (T?)	Son	W	M	Dec 1878	21	S				KY	KY	KY				AT SCHOOL		4	✓	✓					
	" DELBERT E.	Son	W	M	May 1881	19	S				KY	KY	KY				FARMER			✓	✓				F	94
	" WOODRULL M.	Son	W	M	Sep 1873	26	M				KY	KY	KY				FARMER			✓	✓		R		F	93
	" VICTORIA	Dau-in-law	W	F	Dec 1881	18	M				TN	TN	TN													
89 90	HALL, WESLEY	Head	B	M	Jan 1845	55	M	24			KY	VA	VA				DAY LABOR			X	X	✓	R		H	
	" ELIZZEBETH	Wife	B	F	Jan 1840	60	M	24	12	3	KY	KY	VA							X	X	✓				
	" JOSEPH	Gr-son	B	M	Feb 1885	15	S				KY	KY	KY				DAY LABOR			✓	✓	✓				
	" ELLA	Gr-dau	B	F	Aug 1883	17	S		1	1	KY	KY	KY							✓	✓	✓				
	" LULOR	Dau	B	F	Feb 1900	3/12	S				KY	KY	KY													
90 91	HALL, JAMES	Head	B	M	Jan 1877	27	M	1			KY	KY	KY				DAY LABOR			X	X	✓	R		H	
	" JULIA	Wife	B	F	Mar 1874	26	M	1			KY	KY	KY							X	X	✓				
91 92	STEPHENS, EDGAR T.	Head	W	M	Feb 1875	25	Wd				KY	TN	TN				FARMER			✓	✓	✓	O		FF	96
	" BENJAMIN F.	Brother	W	M	Mar 1877	23	S				KY	TN	KY				BANK CLERK			✓	✓	✓				
	" LUCIE J.	Gr-mother	W	F	Feb 1824	76	Wd				KY									✓	✓	✓				
	" MARY	Boarder	W	F	Sep 1879	20	S				KY									✓	✓	✓				
92 93	WILLIAMS, WILLIAM	Head	W	M	Feb 1856	44	M	22									FARMER			✓	✓	✓	O		FF	97
	" BELLE	Wife	W	F	Oct 1858	41	M	22	3	3										✓	✓	✓				
	" WILLIAM C.	Son	W	M	Mar 1879	21	S										FARMER			✓	✓	✓	R		F	98
	" DINNIS E.	Son	W	M	May 1881	19	S										FARMER			✓	✓	✓	R		F	99
	" EARL	Son	W	M	May 1885	15	S										AT SCHOOL		8	✓	✓	✓				
	EARNEST WILLIAM	Boarder	B	M	May 1884	16	S				KY	KY	KY				SERVANT									
93 94	COE, DELLA	Head	W	F	Sep 1872	27	Wd		3	2	KY	TN	KY				SEAMSTRESS			✓	✓	✓	R		H	
	" CECIL	Son	W	M	Nov 1891	8	S				KY	KY	KY													
	" ALICE	Dau	W	F	Dec 1897	2	S				KY	KY	KY									✓				
	ATCHLEY, LIZZIE	Boarder	W	F	Jul 1887	13	S				KY	KY	KY				SERVANT			X	X	✓				

STATE - KENTUCKY
COUNTY - MONROE
Township or other division MARTINSBURGH

Enumerator JAMES T. WHITE

Supervisor's Dist. No. 107 Sheet No.
Enumeration Dist. No. 83

No. of Family	No. of Dwelling	NAME	Relation	Color	Sex	DATE OF BIRTH Mon/Yr	Age at last birthday	Marital Status	# Years married	Mother of how many children?	# of these children living	Place of birth (this person)	Father of this person	Mother of this person	Year of immigr.	# years in U.S.	Naturalization	OCCUPATION 10 years +	Months not employed	Attended school in months	Can read	Can write	Speak English	Owned or Rent	Owned -no mortage	Farm or house	# of farm schedule
94	95	COE, JOHN J.	Head	W	M	MAR 1838	62	M	39			KY	TN	KY				FARMER			✓	✓	✓	O	F	F	100
		" MATILDA	Wife	W	F	Sep 1845	54	M	39	6	3	TN	TN	NC							✓	✓	✓				
		" FANNIE B.	Dau	W	F	MAR 1883	17	S				KY	KY	TN				AT SCHOOL		10	✓	✓	✓				
		" VICTORIA E.	Dau	W	F	OCT 1870	29	Wd			1	KY	KY	TN				SEAMSTRESS			✓	✓	✓				
		" MURRAY H.	Gr-son	W	M	Jun 1898	2	S				KY	KY	KY													
		HALLCELL FRANCES	Boarder	B	F	NOV 1876	23	S				KY	KY	KY				SERVANT			✓	✓	✓				
95	96	COE, JESSE F.	Head	W	M	Sep 1862	37	M	12			KY	KY	KY				MERCHANT			✓	✓	✓	O	F	F	101
		" ZORA	Wife	W	F	AUG 1868	31	M	12			KY	KY	KY							✓	✓	✓				
96	97	SHORT, CHARLES	Head	W	M	AUG 1868	31	M	12			KY	KY	KY				FARMER			✓	✓	✓	R		F	102
		" SARAH F.	Wife	W	F	JAN 1874	26	M	12	6	5	TN	TN	KY							X	X	✓				
		" RICE G.	Son	W	M	Jul 1888	11	S				KY	KY	TN				AT SCHOOL		5	X	X	✓				
		" ANNIE	Dau	W	F	OCT 1890	9	S				KY	KY	TN													
		" MAUDY	Dau	W	F	DEC 1894	5	S				KY	KY	TN													
		" FRANK	Son	W	M	DEC 1896	3	S				KY	KY	TN													
		" BABY	Dau	W	F	JAN 1900	4/12	S				KY	KY	TN													
97	98	YOUNG, WILLIAM B.	Head	W	M	JAN 1865	35	M	9			ALA	TN	ALA				BLACKSMITH			✓	✓	✓	R		F	103
		" LULAR J.	Wife	W	F	NOV 1864	35	M	9	4	3	KY	KY	KY							✓	✓	✓				
		GOODNIGHT	Son	W	M	JAN 1892	8	S				TN	ALA	KY													
		VAUGHN, MEGGIE	Boarder	W	F	JAN 1887	13	S				KY	KY	KY				SERVANT			X	X	✓				
98	99	COE, BENJAMIN	Head	W	M	APR 1846	54	M	26			KY	KY	KY				FARMER			✓	✓	✓	O	F	F	104
		" MARTHA M.	Wife	W	F	Jul 1851	49	M	26	9	8	KY	TN	TN							✓	✓	✓				
		" HATTIE B.	Dau	W	F	NOV 1877	22	S				KY	KY	KY				AT SCHOOL		5	✓	✓	✓				
		" JENNIE G.	Dau	W	F	MAR 1880	20	S				KY	KY	KY				AT SCHOOL		4	✓	✓	✓				
		" JOHN H.	Son	W	M	MAY 1882	18	S				KY	KY	KY				AT SCHOOL		7	✓	✓	✓				
		" CHARLIE E.	Son	W	M	AUG 1884	15	S				KY	KY	KY				AT SCHOOL		7	✓	✓	✓				
		" TIMOTHY E.	Son	W	M	NOV 1886	13	S				KY	KY	KY				AT SCHOOL		4	✓	✓	✓				

STATE - KENTUCKY
COUNTY - MONROE
Township or other division MARTINSBURGH   Enumerator JAMES T. WHITE

Supervisor's Dist. No. 102   Sheet No.
Enumeration Dist. No. 83

No. of Family	No. of Dwelling	NAME	Relation	Color	Sex	DATE OF BIRTH Mon/Yr	Age at last birthday	Marital Status	# Years married	Mother of how many children?	# of these children living	Place of birth (this person)	Father of this person	Mother of this person	Year of immigr.	# years in U.S.	Naturalization	OCCUPATION 10 years +	Months not employed	Attended school in months	Can read	Can write	Speak English	Owned or Rent	Owned - no mortage	Farm or house	# of farm schedule
		COE, CHAWNING V.	DAU	W	F	AUG 1889	10	S				KY	KY	KY				AT SCHOOL		3	✓	✓	✓				
		" OLLIE B.	DAU	W	F	JUL 1892	7	S				KY	KY	KY													
99	100	SHORT, LUFORD	Head	W	M	MAR 1838	62	M	37			KY	KY	KY				FARMER			✓	✓	✓	O	F	F	105
		" MARGARET	Wife	W	F	MAR 1840	60	M	37	4	4	KY	KY	KY							✓	✓	✓				
		" MATTIE	DAU	W	F	APR 1865	35	Wd		2	2	KY	KY	KY							✓	✓	✓				
		" WHEELER J.	Son	W	M	JUL 1870	29	S				KY	KY	KY				FARMER			✓	✓	✓	R		F	106
		" JOHN F.	Son	W	M	JAN 1873	27	S				KY	KY	KY				MERCHANT			✓	✓	✓				
		OOTIN, BELLE	BOARDER	W	F	MAY 1882	18	S				KY	KY	KY				SERVANT			✓	✓	✓				
100	101	RICH, JAMES	HEAD	W	M	OCT 1866	33	M	7			KY	VA	VA				FARMER			✓	✓	✓	O	F	F	107
		" CARRIE C.	WIFE	W	F	APR 1866	34	M	7	3	3	KY	KY	KY							✓	✓	✓				
		" BESSIE	DAU	W	F	OCT 1894	5	S				KY	KY	KY													
		" RUBIE	DAU	W	F	NOV 1897	2	S				KY	KY	KY													
		" BENETT	SON	W	M	OCT 1898	1	S				KY	KY	KY													
101	102	SMITH, MILTON C.	HEAD	W	M	FEB 1872	28	S				KY	KY	KY				FARMER			✓	✓	✓	R		F	108
		BARKESELL, ISAAC	Boarder	B	M	MAR 1872	28	M	4			TN	TN	TN				DAY LABOR			X	X	✓				
		" MARTHA	Boarder	B	M	JAN 1875	25	M	4	2	2	TN	TN	TN				SERVANT			X	X	✓				
		" WILLIE	Boarder	B	M	MAY 1896	4	S				TN	TN	TN													
		FANNIE	Boarder	B	F	AUG 1899	9/12	S				TN	TN	TN													
		MURLEY, WILLIAM	Boarder	W	M	JAN 1877	23	S				KY	KY	KY				DAY LABOR			X	X	✓				
102	103	SMITH, LOT	Head	B	M	JAN 1875	25	S				KY	KY	KY				DAY LABOR			✓	✓	✓			H	
		BARKESELL, MARY	Boarder	B	F	MAR 1875	25	S		5	5	KY	KY	KY							X	X	✓				
		" MATTIE	DAU	B	F	MAY 1890	10	S				KY	KY	KY							X	X	✓				
		" MARVIN	SON	B	M	JAN 1892	8	S				KY	KY	KY													
		" MERTIE	DAU	B	F	MAR 1894	6	S				KY	KY	KY													
		" MICHEL	SON	B	M	JAN 1895	5	S				KY	KY	KY													
		" BABY	SON	B	M	JAN 1900	5/12	S				KY	KY	KY													

TWELFTH CENSUS OF THE UNITED STATES 1900

STATE - KENTUCKY
COUNTY - MONROE
Township or other division MARTINSBURGH   Enumerator JAMES T. WHITE

Supervisor's Dist. No. _102_ Sheet No.
Enumeration Dist. No. _83_

No. of Family / No. of Dwelling	NAME	Relation	Color	Sex	Date of Birth Mon/Yr	Age at last birthday	Marital Status	# Years married	Mother of how many children?	# of these children living	Place of birth (this person)	Father of this person	Mother of this person	Occupation 10 years +	Attended school in months	Can read	Can write	Speak English	Owned or Rent	Farm or house	# of farm schedule
103/104	POE, SIDNEY M.	HEAD	W	M	May 1874	26	M	3			KY	KY	KY	FARMER		✓	✓	✓	R	F	109
	" LOVVIE	WIFE	W	F	Nov 1877	22	M	3	2	1	KY	TN	KY			✓	✓	✓			
	" ANNIE P.	DAU	W	F	Mar 1899	1	S				KY	KY	KY								
104/105	HOLDMAN, M___	Head	B	M	Jan 1864	36	M	11			KY	KY	KY	FARMER		✓	✓		R	F	110
	" MARY J.	WIFE	B	F	Mar 1873	27	M	11	7	7	KY	KY	KY			✓	✓				
	" MARY B.	DAU	B	F	Feb 1890	10	S				KY	KY	KY			✓	✓				
	" HENRY D.	SON	B	M	Apr 1892	8	S				KY	KY	KY								
	" LUCILLE L.	DAU	B	F	Jan 1894	6	S				KY	KY	KY								
	" JOSEPH E.	SON	B	M	Feb 1895	5	S				KY	KY	KY								
	" CALVIN A. H.	SON	B	M	Feb 1897	3	S				KY	KY	KY								
	" OSCAR	SON	B	M	Jan 1898	2	S				KY	KY	KY								
	" JAMES	SON	B	M	Feb 1899	1	S				KY	KY	KY								
105/106	MOODY, JASPER	Head	B	M	May 1873	27	M	7			KY	KY	KY	FARMER		✓	✓	✓	R	F	111
	" TENNESSEE	wife	B	F	Jan 1875	25	M	7	4	3	KY	KY	KY			✓	X	✓			
	" LARRY	DAU	B	F	Sep 1890	9	S				KY	KY	KY								
	" FRED	SON	B	M	May 1893	7	S				KY	KY	KY								
	" NANNIE B.	DAU	B	F	Jan 1896	4	S				KY	KY	KY								
106/107	MURLEY, SURILDA	Head	W	F	Oct 1857	42	Wd	25	5	5	KY	KY	KY	FARMER		✓	✓	✓	O	MF	112
	" WILLIAM T.	SON	W	M	Jun 1879	20	S				KY	KY	KY	FARM LABOR		✓	✓	✓			
	" JAMES L.	SON	W	M	Aug 1882	17	S				KY	KY	KY	AT SCHOOL	3	✓	✓	✓			
	" FANNIE	DAU	W	F	Jul 1887	12	S				KY	KY	KY	AT SCHOOL	5	✓	✓	✓			
	" MALLIE J.	DAU	W	F	Jan 1892	8	S				KY	KY	KY								
107/108	SMITH, SARAH	HEAD	W	F	Jun 1844	55	Wd		4	3	KY	KY	KY	FARMER		✓	✓	✓	O	FF	113
	" DALCHY T.	SON	N	M	Sep 1876	23	S				KY	KY	KY			✓	✓	✓			
	" SAM C.	SON	W	M	Jul 1867	32	M	10			KY	KY	KY	FARMER		✓	✓	✓	R	F	114
	" ALICE L.	WIFE	W	F	Oct 1865	34	M	10	2	2	KY	KY	KY			✓	✓	✓			

TWELFTH CENSUS OF THE UNITED STATES 1900

STATE - KENTUCKY
COUNTY - MONROE
Township or other division **MARTINSBURGH**   Enumerator **JAMES T. WHITE**

Supervisor's Dist. No. **10 ✔** Sheet No.
Enumeration Dist. No. **83**

No. of Family	No. of Dwelling	NAME	Relation	Color	Sex	DATE OF BIRTH Mon/Yr	Age at last birthday	Marital Status	# Years married	Mother of how many children?	# of these children living	Place of birth [this person]	Father of this person	Mother of this person	Year of immigr.	# years in U.S.	Naturalization	OCCUPATION 10 years +	Months not employed	Attended school in months	Can read	Can write	Speak English	Owned or Rent	Owned -no mortage	Farm or house	# of farm schedule
		SMITH, BEDFORD H.	Son	W	M	Jul 1890	9	S				KY	KY	KY													
		" FRED M.	Son	W	M	May 1892	8	S				KY	KY	KY													
108	109	STONE, NELLIE	Head	B	F	Jan 1888 72		Wd		1	1	TN	TN	TN							X	X	✓			H	
		" ELIZIA	Dau	B	F	Feb 1848	52	Wd		8	7	TN	TN	TN							X	X	✓				
		" TOMAS	Gr-Son	B	M	Mar 1878	22	S				KY	TN	TN				DAY LABOR			✓	✓					
		" GEORGE	Gr-Son	B	M	Feb 1881	19	S				KY	TN	TN				DAY LABOR			✓	✓					
		" ELONZO	Gr-Son	B	M	Jan 1884	16	S				KY	TN	TN				DAY LABOR			✓	✓					
		" SARAH P.	Dau	B	F	Mar 1887	13	S				KY	TN	TN				AT SCHOOL		5	✓	✓					
109	110	BARKSTELL, WILLIAM	Head	B	M	Feb 1865	35	M	15			KY	TN	TN				FARMER			✓	✓	✓	O	F	F	115
		" MARTHY	Wife	B	F	Jan 1873	27	M	15	2	2	KY	KY	TN							✓	✓	✓				
		" OLLIE	Dau	B	F	Mar 1889	11	S				KY	KY	KY				AT SCHOOL		5	✓	✓	✓				
		" EDWARD	Son	B	M	Jan 1892	8	S				KY	KY	KY													
110	111	MURLEY, MILTON	Head	W	M	Jan 1874	26	M	9			KY	KY	KY				FARMER			✓	✓	✓	R		F	116
		" JULIA A.	Wife	W	F	Apr 1871	29	M	9	3	3	TN	TN	TN							X	X	✓				
		" WILLIAM T.	Son	W	M	Apr 1892	8	S				KY	KY	TN													
		" MILTON B.	Son	W	M	May 1895	5	S				TN	KY	TN													
		" RAMON C.	Son	W	M	Aug 1897	2	S				KY	KY	KY													
		" RODO	Sister	W	F	Jan 1880	20	S				KY	KY	KY							X	X	✓				
		" LOVY(?)	Brother	W	M	Jan 1886	14	S				KY	KY	KY				AT SCHOOL		4	✓	✓	✓				
111	112	COE, PETER	Head	W	M	Sep 1848	51	M	27			KY	KY	KY				FARMER			✓	✓	✓	O		F	117
		" ELLEN T	Wife	W	F	Sep 1851	48	M	27	5	2	KY	TN	KY							✓	✓	✓				
		" JOHN G.	Son	W	M	Mar 1876	24	S				KY	KY	KY				MERCHANT			✓	✓	✓				
		PRUETT, MAGGIE	Servant	W	F	Jan 1892	8	S				KY	KY	KY							X	X	✓				
		MURLEY, FERBY	Boarder	W	F	Jan 1825	75	Wd				KY	KY	KY													
112	113	LONG, ISAAC	Head	W	M	Apr 1849	51	M	26			TN	VA	VA				FARMER			✓	✓	✓	R		F	118
		" OLLIE	Wife	W	F	Jun 1856	47	M	26	9	7	TN	NC	TN							✓	✓	✓				

TWELFTH CENSUS OF THE UNITED STATES 1900

STATE - KENTUCKY
COUNTY - MONROE
Township or other division **MARTINSBURGH**   Enumerator **JAMES I. WHITE**

— 208 —

Supervisor's Dist. No. **102** Sheet No.
Enumeration Dist. No. **83**

No. of Family	No. of Dwelling	NAME	Relation	Color	Sex	DATE OF BIRTH Mon/Yr	Age at last birthday	Marital Status	# Years married	Mother of how many children?	# of these children living	Place of birth [this person]	Father of this person	Mother of this person	Year of immigr.	# years in U.S.	Naturalization	OCCUPATION 10 years +	Months not employed	Attended school in months	Can read	Can write	Speak English	Owned or Rent	Owned -no mortgage	Farm or house	# of farm schedule
		LONG, ASENO J.	DAU	W	F	MAR 1873	27	S				TN	TN	TN				SEAMSTRESS			✓	✓	✓				
		" THOMAS	SON	W	M	JAN 1875	25	S				TN	TN	TN				FARM LABOR			✓	✓	✓				
		" SARAH A.	DAU	W	F	MAR 1879	23	S				TN	TN	TN				SEAMSTRESS			✓	✓	✓				
		" MARGARET	DAU	W	F	JUL 1880	19	S				TN	TN	TN				SEAMSTRESS			✓	✓	✓				
		" MARTHA E.	DAU	W	F	FEB 1884	16	S				TN	TN	TN				AT SCHOOL		2	✓	✓					
		" WILLIAM J.	SON	W	M	DEC 1887	12	S				TN	TN	TN				AT SCHOOL		2	✓	✓					
		" JOHN	SON	W	M	NOV 1894	5	S				TN	TN	TN													
113	114	SMITH, PERMELY	Head	W	F	MAR 1849	51	Wd		6	3	KY	TN	TN				FARMER			✓	✓		O	F	F	119
		" CHARLIE	SON	W	M	JAN 1882	18	S				KY	KY	KY				AT SCHOOL		5	✓	✓					
		" WILLARD	SON	W	M	OCT 1885	14	S				KY	KY	KY				AT SCHOOL		5	✓	✓					
		" BENNIE J.	SON	W	M	MAR 1888	12	S				KY	KY	KY				AT SCHOOL		5	✓	✓					
		NIVENS, ELLA	SERVANT	W	F	JUL 1883	16	S				TN	TN	TN				SERVANT			✓	✓	✓				
114	115	SHORT, ABNER	HEAD	W	M	JAN 1834	66	M	40			KY	KY	KY				FARMER			✓	✓	✓	O	F	F	120
		" JANE	WIFE	W	F	NOV 1833	66	M	40	11	10	TN	KY	KY							✓	✓	✓				
		" ISIAH	SON	W	M	JUN 1867	32	S				KY	KY	KY				FARMER			✓	✓	✓	R		F	121
115	116	SHORT, JAKE A.	HEAD	W	M	FEB 1865	35	M	8			KY	KY	KY				FARMER			X	X	✓	R		F	122
		" MARTHA	WIFE	W	F	JAN 1868	32	M	8	5	5	KY	KY	KY							✓	✓	✓				
		" PEARL	DAU	W	F	JAN 1893	7	S				KY	KY	KY													
		" FANNIE	DAU	W	F	FEB 1895	5	S				KY	KY	KY													
		" OLIVA	DAU	W	F	MAR 1896	4	S				KY	KY	KY													
		" ANNIE T.	DAU	W	F	MAR 1897	3	S				KY	KY	KY													
		" BEDFORD	SON	W	M	MAR 1898	2	S				KY	KY	KY													
116	117	PRUETT, WILLIAM	Head	W	M	JAN 1876	24	M	4			KY	KY	KY				FARMER			✓	✓	✓	R		F	123
		" LUCY	wife	W	F	FEB 1878	22	M	4	2	2	KY	KY	KY							X	X	✓				
		" CLURA	DAU	W	F	MAR 1897	3	S				KY	KY	KY													
		" BABY	DAU	W	F	FEB 1900	3/12	S				KY	KY	KY													

STATE - KENTUCKY
COUNTY - MONROE
Township or other division MARTINSBURGH   Enumerator JAMES T. WHITE

Supervisor's Dist. No. 102 Sheet No.
Enumeration Dist. No. 83

No. of Family	No. of Dwelling	NAME	Relation	Color	Sex	Date of Birth Mon/Yr	Age at last birthday	Marital Status	# Years married	Mother of how many children?	# of these children living	Place of birth (this person)	Father of this person	Mother of this person	Year of immigr.	# years in U.S.	Naturalization	OCCUPATION 10 years +	Months not employed	Attended school in months	Can read	Can write	Speak English	Owned or Rent	Owned-no mortgage	Farm or house	# of farm schedule
17	18	SHORT, ARCHA	Head	W	M	Jul 1877	22	M	2			KY	KY	KY				FARMER			✓	✓	✓	R		F	124
		" NANCY	Wife	W	F	Jan 1880	20	M	2	2	2	KY	KY	KY							✓	✓	✓				
		" MILTIE	Son	W	M	Jan 1898	1	S				KY	KY	KY													
		" JINNIE	Dau	W	F	Jan 1900	5/12	S				KY	KY	KY													
18	19	HALLCELL, NELL (?)	Head	B	F	May 1825	75	Wd		4	4	KY	KY	KY							X	X	✓	R		H	
		" ANN	Dau	B	F	Jan 1870	30	S		5	5	KY	KY	KY				WASHING CLOTHES			X	X	✓				
		" WILLIAM	Son	B	M	Jun 1889	12	S				KY	KY	KY				AT SCHOOL		5	✓	✓	✓				
		" AND(REW?)	Son	B	M	Jan 1890	10	S				KY	KY	KY				AT SCHOOL		4	X	X	✓				
		" LUCIE	Dau	B	F	Feb 1892	8	S				KY	KY	KY													
		" FRANK	Son	B	M	Jan 1894	6	S				KY	KY	KY													
		" MASAS (?)	Son	B	M	Apr 1900	3/12	S				KY	KY	KY													
		" PEARL	Dau	B	F	Jan 1872	28	S		1	1	KY	KY	KY				WASHING CLOTHING									
		" JOHN C.	Son	B	M	Feb 1899	1	S				KY	KY	KY							X	X	✓				
		" CASSIE	Dau	B	F	Jan 1874	26	S				KY	KY	KY				WASHING CLOTHING			X	X	✓				
		" WILLIAM	Son	B	M	Jun 1876	23	S				KY	KY	KY				DAY LABOR			✓	✓	✓				
		SIMS, WILLIAM Boarder		B	M	Oct 1863	36	S				KY	KY	KY				DAY LABOR			✓	✓	✓	O		F	125
19	20	LIKESTON, EDWARD	Head	W	M	Jan 1860	40	M	15			KY	KY	TN				FARMER			✓	✓	✓				
		" JANE	Wife	W	F	Apr 1864	36	M	15	6	6	KY	TN	TN							✓	✓	✓				
		" MARY J.	Dau	W	F	Jan 1886	14	S				KY	KY	KY				AT SCHOOL		5	✓	✓	✓				
		" MAGGIE	Dau	W	F	Mar 1888	12	S				KY	KY	KY				AT SCHOOL		5	✓	✓	✓				
		" CARRIE C.	Dau	W	F	Jan 1891	9	S				KY	KY	KY													
		" JOHN J.	Son	W	M	Jun 1894	5	S				KY	KY	KY													
		" JAMES T.	Son	W	M	Jan 1897	3	S				KY	KY	KY													
		" SARAH	Dau	W	F	May 1900	1/12	S				KY	KY	KY													
20	21	POINDEXTER, JESSE R.	Head	W	M	Oct 1866	33	M	15			KY	KY	KY				FARMER			X	X	✓	R		F	126
		" REBECCA T.	Wife	W	F	May 1862	38	M	15	8	8	KY	KY	KY							✓	✓	✓				

STATE - KENTUCKY
COUNTY - MONROE
Township or other division MARTINSBURGH Enumerator JAMES. T. WHITE

— 210 —

Supervisor's Dist. No. 107 Sheet No.
Enumeration Dist. No. 83

No. of Family	No. of Dwelling	NAME	Relation	Color	Sex	DATE OF BIRTH Mon/Yr	Age at last birthday	Marital Status	# Years married	Mother of how many children?	# of these children living	Place of birth (this person)	Father of this person	Mother of this person	Year of immigr.	# years in U.S.	Naturalization	OCCUPATION 10 years +	Months not employed	Attended school in months	Can read	Can write	Speak English	Owned or Rent	Owned -no mortage	Farm or house	# of farm schedule
		POINDEXTER, JESSE R.	Son	W	M	Sept 1885	14	S				KY	KY	KY				AT SCHOOL		3	✓	✓					
		" CHARLEY	Son	W	M	Aug 1886	13	S				KY	KY	KY				AT SCHOOL									
		" DOLLY H.	DAU	W	F	Jan 1891	9	S				KY	KY	KY													
		" WILLIAM	Son	W	M	DEC 1892	7	S				KY	KY	KY													
		" ROBERT	Son	W	M	Jun 1895	4	S				KY	KY	KY													
		" ALICE	DAU	W	F	May 1897	3	S				KY	KY	KY													
		" RUTH J.	DAU	W	F	JAN 1898	2	S				KY	KY	KY													
		" BABY	Son	W	M	Feb 1900	4/12	S				KY	KY	KY													
121	122	SCOT, JAMES M.	Head	W	M	APR 1848	52	M	26			KY	KY	KY						✓	X	✓		R		H	
		" POLLY C.	Wife	W	F	APR 1850	50	M	26	6	5	KY	KY	KY							X	X	✓					
		" LUCY B.	DAU	W	F	Jun 1874	25	S				KY	KY	KY							✓	✓	✓					
		" ELLA	DAU	W	F	Sep 1879	20	S				KY	KY	KY							✓	✓	✓					
		" ISAIH E.	Son	W	M	Jan 1882	18	S				KY	KY	KY				DAY LABOR			✓	✓	✓					
		" WILLIAM T.	Son	W	M	AUG 1886	13	S				KY	KY	KY				AT SCHOOL		3	✓	✓	✓					
		" JESSIE F.	Son	W	M	DEC 1887	12	S				KY	KY	KY				AT SCHOOL		3	✓	✓	✓					
122	123	HALLCELL, SYRUS	Head	B	M	MAR 1854	46	Wd				KY	KY	KY				FARMER			✓	✓	✓		R		F	127
		" AUSTEN	Son	B	M	OCT 1879	20	S				KY	KY	KY				DAY LABOR			✓	✓	✓					
		" JESSE	Son	B	M	Feb 1883	17	S				KY	KY	KY				AT SCHOOL		5	✓	✓	✓					
		" COE	Son	B	M	DEC 1887	12	S				KY	KY	KY				AT SCHOOL		5	✓	✓	✓					
		" CLARENCE	Son	B	M	MAY 1890	10	S				KY	KY	KY				AT SCHOOL		5	✓	✓	✓					
		" BENNIE	Son	B	M	JUNE 1894	5	S				KY	KY	KY													
		" BESSIE	DAU	B	F	MAY 1896	4	S				KY	KY	KY													
		" LOVVIE	DAU	B	F	MAR 1898	2	S				KY	KY	KY													
		WILLIAMS, VINA	Boarder	B	F	JUN 1858	41	Wd		4	4	KY	KY	KY							✓	X	✓					
		" HANCE (?)	Son	B	M	Sep 1879	20	S				KY	KY	KY				DAY LABOR			✓	✓	✓					
		" WILLET	DAU	B	F	Feb 1882	18	S				KY	KY	KY				AT SCHOOL		5	✓	✓	✓					

TWELFTH CENSUS OF THE UNITED STATES 1900

STATE - KENTUCKY
COUNTY - MONROE
Township or other division MARTINSBURGH   Enumerator JAMES T. WHITE

Supervisor's Dist. No. 102 Sheet No.
Enumeration Dist. No. 83

Location (No. of Family / No. of Dwelling)	NAME	Relation	Color	Sex	DATE OF BIRTH Mon/Yr	Age at last birthday	Marital Status	# Years married	Mother of how many children?	# of these children living	Place of birth [this person]	Father of this person	Mother of this person	Year of immigr.	# years in U.S.	Naturalization	OCCUPATION 10 years +	Months not employed	Attended school in months	Can read	Can write	Speak English	Owned or Rent	Owned - no mortgage	Farm or house	# of farm schedule
	WILLIAMS, ETHEL	DAU	B	F	Jul 1887	12	S				KY	KY	KY				AT SCHOOL		5	✓	✓	✓				
	" CURTES	SON	B	M	Sep 1890	9	S				KY	KY	KY													
123/124	DODSON, RINE	Head	W	M	Oct 1858	41	M	13			KY	KY	KY				FARMER			✓	✓		O F F			128
	" BELLE	Wife	W	F	Jun 18	38	M	13	6	5	KY	KY	KY							X	X					
	" C RLE	SON	W	M	DEC 1887	12	S				KY	KY	KY				AT SCHOOL		4	✓	✓					
	" FRANK	SON	W	M	AUG 1889	10	S				KY	KY	KY				AT SCHOOL			✓	✓	✓				
	" FLORNCE	DAU	W	F	JAN 1893	7	S				KY	KY	KY													
	" HUNTER	SON	W	M	JAN 1895	5	S				KY	KY	KY													
	" TIM	SON	W	M	Sep 1898	1	S				KY	KY	KY													
	" REDFORD	SON	W	M	AUG 1899	9/12	S				KY	KY	KY												H	
124/125	McMILAND, F	Head	B	M	JAN 1865	35	M	15			KY	KY	KY				DAY LABORER			✓	✓	✓				
	" SARAH	WIFE	B	F	APR 1867	33	M	15	9	6	KY	KY	TN							✓	✓	✓				
	" BENTON	SON	B	M	AUG 1885	14	S				KY	KY	KY				AT SCHOOL		5	✓	✓	✓				
	" ELIZZIEBETH	DAU	B	F	APR 1887	13	S				KY	KY	KY				AT SCHOOL		5	✓	✓	✓				
	" LARRY	DAU	B	F	Feb 1889	11	S				KY	KY	KY				AT SCHOOL		5	✓	✓	✓				
	" EMMA	DAU	B	F	JAN 1892	8	S				KY	KY	KY													
	" ADOS	DAU	B	F	APR 1894	6	S				KY	KY	KY													
	" OVA	DAU	B	F	OCT 1897	2	S				KY	KY	KY													
125/126	DODSON, CARREL	HEAD	W	M	MAR 1860	40	M	11			KY	KY	KY				FARMER			✓	✓		O F F			129
	" NANCY C.	WIFE	W	F	Nov 1869	30	M	11	6	6	KY	KY	KY							✓	✓	✓				
	" LULAR B.	DAU	W	F	Feb 1890	10	S				KY	KY	KY				AT SCHOOL		4	✓	✓	✓				
	" MAUD A.	DAU	W	F	Feb 1892	8	S				KY	KY	KY													
	" ADA	DAU	W	F	MAY 183	7	S				KY	KY	KY													
	" MILARD V.	SON	W	M	MAY 1895	5	S				KY	KY	KY													
	" RUBIE L.	SON	W	M	OCT 1897	2	S				KY	KY	KY													
	" ROSE C.	DAU	W	F	— 1900	6/12	S				KY	KY	KY													

STATE - KENTUCKY
COUNTY - MONROE
Township or other division MARTINSBURGH   Enumerator JAMES T. WHITE

Supervisor's Dist. No. _10 7_ Sheet No. _____
Enumeration Dist. No. _83_

No. of Family	No. of Dwelling	NAME	Relation	Color	Sex	DATE OF BIRTH Mon/Yr	Age at last birthday	Marital Status	# Years married	Mother of how many children?	# of these children living	Place of birth (this person)	Father of this person	Mother of this person	Year of immigr.	# years in U.S.	Naturalization	OCCUPATION 10 years +	Months not employed	Attended school in months	Can read	Can write	Speak English	Owned or Rent	Owned –no mortage	Farm or house	# of farm schedule
126	27	ARMS, JEFF	HEAD	W	M	OCT 1865	36	M	8			TN	TN	TN				FARMER			✓	✓	✓	R		F	130
		" JANE	WIFE	W	F	NOV 1865	36	M	8	4	4	KY	KY	KY							✓	✓	✓				
		" ALVIN C.	SON	W	M	MAR 1892	7	S				TN	TN	KY													
		" BERS(?) M.	SON	W	M	FEB 1895	5	S				TN	TN	KY													
		" CLARNCE C	SON	W	M	OCT 1896	3	S				TN	TN	KY													
		THOMAS S.	SON	W	M	MAR 1900	2/12	S				TN	TN	KY													
127	28	LOLLAR, PORTIE(?)	HEAD	W	M	MAY 1856	44	M	17			KY	KY	KY				FARMER			✓	✓	✓	O		F	131
		" CARLINE	WIFE	W	F	SEP 1861	38	M	17	6	5	MO	TN	TN							✓	✓	✓				
		" GIRTRUDE	DAU	W	F	SEP 1881	18	S				KY	KY	MO				AT SCHOOL		4	✓	✓					
		" MIRTIE	DAU	W	F	SEP 1885	14	S				KY	KY	MO				AT SCHOOL		6	✓	✓					
		" TERRIE	DAU	W	F	OCT 1889	10	S				KY	KY	MO				AT SCHOOL		5	✓	✓					
		" BESSE	DAU	W	F	OCT 1892	7	S				KY	KY	MO													
		" TIM	SON	W	M	OCT 1898	1	S				KY	KY	MO													
128	29	BRUINGTON, GILLA(?)	HEAD	W	M	JAN 1864	36	M	15			KY	KY	KY				FARMER			✓	✓	✓	O		F	132
		" JINNIE	WIFE	W	F	FEB 1866	34	M	15	5	4	KY	KY	KY							✓	✓	✓				
		" MARVIN L.	SON	W	M	JUL 1886	13	S				KY	KY	KY				AT SCHOOL		4	✓	✓	✓				
		" CHARLEY	SON	W	M	OCT 1888	11	S				KY	KY	KY				AT SCHOOL		4	✓	✓	✓				
		" FRANK	SON	W	M	JUN 1897	2	S				KY	KY	KY													
		" EMER F.	DAU	W	F	DEC 1899	5/12	S				KY	KY	KY													
29	130	MILLIR, MATHEW	HEAD	W	M	JAN 1871	29	M	7			KY	KY	KY				FARMER			✓	✓	✓	R		F	133
		" EMMER	WIFE	W	F	AUG 1874	25	M	7	3	3	KY	KY	KY							✓	✓	✓				
		" CORDELIA	DAU	W	F	MAR 1894	6	S				KY	KY	KY													
		" TRAVIS E	SON	W	M	SEP 1895	4	S				KY	KY	KY													
		" RUTHA E	DAU	W	F	AUG 1899	9/12	S				KY	KY	KY													
30	31	RILEY, MARTIN	HEAD	W	M	JAN 1867	33	M	14			KY	KY	KY				FARMER			X	X	✓	O		F	134
		" MARY E.	WIFE	W	F	DEC 1862	37	M	14	7	7	KY	KY	KY							✓	✓	✓				

STATE - KENTUCKY
COUNTY - MONROE
Township or other division MARTINSBURGH   Enumerator JAMES T. WHITE

Supervisor's Dist. No. 102   Sheet No.
Enumeration Dist. No. 83

Location No. of Family / No. of Dwelling	NAME	Relation	Color	Sex	DATE OF BIRTH Mon/Yr	Age at last birthday	Marital Status	# Years married	Mother of how many children?	# of these children living	Place of birth (this person)	Father of this person	Mother of this person	Year of immigr.	# years in U.S.	Naturalization	OCCUPATION 10 years +	Months not employed	Attended school in months	Can read	Can write	Speak English	Owned or Rent	Owned - no mortage	Farm or house	# of farm schedule	
	RILEY, PEARL A.	DAU	W	F	Jul 1888	11	S				KY	KY	KY							X	X	✓					
"	VINEY B.	DAU	W	F	Feb 1890	10	S				KY	KY	KY							X	X	✓					
"	AZORA F.	DAU	W	F	Jan 1891	9	S				KY	KY	KY														
"	DELA	DAU	W	F	Nov 1892	7	S				KY	KY	KY														
"	JOHN T.	SON	W	M	Jan 1895	5	S				KY	KY	KY														
"	MATTIE	DAU	W	F	Feb 1897	3	S				KY	KY	KY														
"	WILLIAM Mc	SON	W	M	Mar 1899	1	S				KY	KY	KY														
131 132	ATCHLEY, EDWARD	Head	W	M	Jan 1846	54	M	8			KY	KY	KY				FARMER			X	X	✓	R		F	135	
"	SARAH A.	Wife	W	F	May 1862	38	M	8	1	1	KY	KY	KY							✓	✓	✓					
"	HNARD (?)	Son	W	M	Jan 1893	7	S				KY	KY	KY														
132 133	JONES, JOHN	Head	W	M	Mar 1855	45	M	21			KY	KY	KY				FARMER			✓	✓	✓	O		F	136	
"	FANNIE	Wife	W	F	Jan 1860	40	M	21	7	7	KY	KY	KY							✓	✓	✓					
"	MARVIN	Son	W	M	Apr 1880	20	S				KY	KY	KY				AT SCHOOL		9	✓	✓	✓					
"	IRVIN	Son	W	M	Feb 1882	18	S				KY	KY	KY				AT SCHOOL		10	✓	✓	✓					
"	PEARL	DAU	W	F	Jun 1884	16	S				KY	KY	KY				AT SCHOOL		6	✓	✓	✓					
"	OCTAVA	DAU	W	F	Mar 1891	9	S				KY	KY	KY														
"	EDWARD	Son	W	M	Nov 1887	12	S				KY	KY	KY				AT SCHOOL		5	✓	✓	✓					
"	AZELMA	DAU	W	F	Mar 1893	7	S				KY	KY	KY														
"	JOHN	Son	W	M	Feb 1900	3/12	S				KY	KY	KY														
	CRAFFORD, JOHN	Boarder	W	M	Nov 1877	23	S				KY	KY	KY				DAY LABOR			✓	✓	✓					
133 134	SHIELDS, JAMES	HEAD	B	M	Jun 1864	35	M	12			TN	TN	TN				FARMER			✓	✓	✓	R		F	137	
"	LUCIE	WIFE	B	F	Jan 1867	33	M	12	5	4	TN	TN	TN							✓	X	✓					
"	MARY	DAU	B	F	Nov 1886	13	S				KY	TN	TN				AT SCHOOL		4	✓	✓	✓					
"	CIRK	DAU	B	F	Apr 1893	7	S				KY	TN	TN														
"	FANNIE	DAU	B	F	Oct 1894	5	S				KY	TN	TN														
"	ANNIE	DAU	B	F	Sep 1899	1	S				KY	TN	TN														

STATE - KENTUCKY
COUNTY - MONROE
Township or other division MARTINSBURGH   Enumerator JAMES T. WHITE

Supervisor's Dist. No. 102 Sheet No.
Enumeration Dist. No. 83

Location No. of Family / No. of Dwelling	NAME	Relation	Color	Sex	DATE OF BIRTH Mon/Yr	Age at last birthday	Marital Status	# Years married	Mother of how many children?	# of these children living	NATIVITY Place of birth (this person)	Father of this person	Mother of this person	CITIZENSHIP Year of immigr. / # years in U.S. / Naturalization	OCCUPATION 10 years +	Months not employed	EDUCATION Attended school in months	Can read	Can write	Speak English	OWNERSHIP Owned or Rent	Owned -no mortage	Farm or house	# of farm schedule
134 135	HILL, BEDFORD	HEAD	W	M	MAY 1864	36	M	6			KY	KY	KY		FARMER			✓	✓	✓	O	F	F	138
	" CORA	WIFE	W	F	AUG 1876	23	M	6	3	2	KY	KY	KY					✓	✓	✓				
	" GEORGE	SON	W	M	JUN 1897	2	S				KY	KY	KY											
	" MAMIE	DAU	W	F	MAR 1900	7/12	S				KY	KY	KY											
135 136	HILL, WILLIAM	HEAD	W	M	JAN 1823	77	Wd				KY	VA	KY		FARMER			✓	✓	✓	O	F	F	139
	" RUSSELAH	DAU	W	F	JUN 1860	39	S				KY	KY	KY					✓	✓	✓				
	" MATTIE	DAU	W	F	NOV 1865	34	S				KY	KY	KY					✓	✓	✓				
	GRAVES, BEDFORD	BOARDER	W	M	JAN 1872	28	S				KY	KY	KY		DAY LABOR			✓	✓	✓				
								CENTER POINT																
136 137	GEE, ALFORD B.	HEAD	W	M	JULY 1846	53	M	22			KY	KY	KY		FARMER			✓	✓	✓	R		F	140
	" SARAH E.	WIFE	W	F	JULY 1855	44	M	22	7	7	KY	KY	KY					✓	✓	✓				
	" MARY E.	DAU	W	F	SEP 1879	20	S				KY	KY	KY		AT SCHOOL		5	✓	✓	✓				
	" JAMES T.	SON	W	M	AUG 1881	18	S				KY	KY	KY		FARM LABOR			✓	✓	✓				
	" DOLLIE E.	DAU	W	F	AUG 1883	16	S				KY	KY	KY		AT SCHOOL		5	✓	✓	✓				
	" CARRY A.	DAU	W	F	FEB 1886	14	S				KY	KY	KY		AT SCHOOL		5	✓	✓	✓				
	" WILLIAM N.	SON	W	M	FEB 1889	11	S				KY	KY	KY		AT SCHOOL		5	✓	✓	✓				
	" EDNER W.	DAU	W	F	OCT 1891	8	S				KY	KY	KY											
	" BYROM F.	SON	W	M	JAN 1894	6	S				KY	KY	KY											
137 138	KUR(?), WILLIAM	HEAD	W	M	SEP 1824	75	Wd				TN	NC	NC		FARMER			✓	✓	✓	O	F	F	141
138 139	HURD(?) SHEB	HEAD	W	M	JUL 1864	35	M	6			KY	TN	TN		FARMER			✓	✓	✓	O	M	F	142
	" LELA	WIFE	W	F	JUL 1874	25	M	6	2	2	KY	KY	KY					✓	✓	✓				
	" COMER	SON	W	M	JUN 1896	3	S				KY	KY	KY											
139 140	COE, JESSE T.	HEAD	W	M	MAY 1854	46	M	20			KY	KY	KY		FARMER			X	X	✓	R		F	143
	" MARY C.	WIFE	W	F	APR 1857	42	M	20	11	9	KY	KY	KY					X	X	✓				

STATE - KENTUCKY
COUNTY - MONROE
Township or other division — CENTER POINT

Enumerator — JAMES T. WHITE

Supervisor's Dist. No. 102 Sheet No.
Enumeration Dist. No. 83

No. of Family	No. of Dwelling	NAME	Relation	Color	Sex	DATE OF BIRTH Mon/Yr	Age at last birthday	Marital Status	# Years married	Mother of how many children?	# of these children living	Place of birth [this person]	Father of this person	Mother of this person	Year of immigr.	# years in U.S.	Naturalization	OCCUPATION 10 years +	Months not employed	Attended school in months	Can read	Can write	Speak English	Owned or Rent	Owned -no mortage	Farm or house	# of farm schedule
		COE, MOLLY Y.	DAU	W	F	JAN 1884	16	S				KY	KY	KY				AT SCHOOL		5	✓	✓					
		" LUCIE B.	DAU	W	F	JAN 1887	13	S				KY	KY	KY				AT SCHOOL		5	✓	✓					
		" FRED B.	SON	W	M	Feb 1893	7	S				KY	KY	KY							✓	✓					
		" TIM E.	SON	W	M	Feb 1895	5	S				KY	KY	KY							✓	✓					
		LONG, JOHN F.	Boarder	W	M	AUG 1881	18	S				KY	KY	KY				DAY LABOR			✓	✓					
140	141	DODSON, WILLIAM	HEAD	W	M	AUG 1845	54	M	29			KY	KY	KY				FARMER			✓	✓		O	F	F	145
		" PHEBY M.	WIFE	W	F	Feb 1855	45	M	29	8	8	KY	KY	KY							✓	X					
		" JAMES F.	SON	W	M	AUG 1876	23	S				KY	KY	KY				FARMER			✓	✓		R		F	146
		" WASHINGTON	SON	W	M	JAN 1878	22	S				KY	KY	KY				DAY LABOR			✓	✓					
		" OLVER	SON	W	M	JAN 1878	22	S				KY	KY	KY				DAY LABOR			✓	✓					
		" LIDDY A.	DAU	W	F	JAN 1879	21	S				KY	KY	KY				AT SCHOOL			✓	✓					
		" NATHAIRE (?)	SON	W	M	Feb 1880	20	S				KY	KY	KY				FARMER			✓	✓		R		F	147
		" DOLLIE	DAU	W	F	Jun 1881	19	S				KY	KY	KY				AT SCHOOL		5	✓	✓					
		" CLORA J.	DAU	W	F	May 1882	18	S				KY	KY	KY				AT SCHOOL		6	✓	✓					
		" CASSIE L.	DAU	W	F	APR 1883	17	S				KY	KY	KY				AT SCHOOL		6	✓	✓					
141	142	THERMAN, CALA	HEAD	W	M	Jun 1875	23	M	2			TN	TN	TN				FARMER			✓	✓		R		F	148
		" LUCIE G.	WIFE	W	F	MAR 1882	18	M	2			KY	KY	KY							✓	✓					
		" BIGGERSTAFF	SON	W	M	MAR 1899	1	S				KY	TN	KY													
142	143	BIGGERSTAFE, HALL	Head	W	M	DEC 1871	29	M	5			KY	KY	KY				FARMER			✓	✓		R		F	149
		" DOLLIE	Wife	W	F	OCT 1873	26	M	5	4	4	KY	KY	KY							✓	✓					
		" CORA H.	DAU	W	F	DEC 1896	3	S				KY	KY	KY													
		" WILLARD	SON	W	M	Jul 1898	1	S				KY	KY	KY													
		" MAMY T.	DAU	W	F	JAN 1900	4/12	S				KY	KY	KY													
		BASKETT, LOSSTAN	Boarder	W	M	JAN 1884	16	S				KY	KY	KY				FARMER			✓	✓	✓	R		F	150
143	144	WHITE, JOHN	Head	W	M	MAR 1876	24	M	3			KY	KY	TN				FARMER			✓	✓	✓	O	F	F	151
		" DEALY	Wife	W	F	Sep 1870	29	M	3	1	1	KY	TN	KY							✓	✓					

TWELFTH CENSUS OF THE UNITED STATES 1900

— 216 —

STATE - KENTUCKY
COUNTY - MONROE
Township or other division — CENTER POINT — Enumerator JAMES T. WHITE

Supervisor's Dist. No. 102 Sheet No. ___
Enumeration Dist. No. 83 ___

No. of Family	No. of Dwelling	NAME	Relation	Color	Sex	Date of Birth Mon/Yr	Age	Marital Status	Yrs married	Mother how many children	# living	Place of birth	Father	Mother	Occupation	Months not employed	Attended school	Can read	Can write	Speak English	Owned/Rent	Owned no mortg.	Farm/house	# farm schedule
		WHITE, RABBY	Dau	W	F	Jun 1898	1	S				KY	KY	KY										
		" TURNER	Sis	W	F	Mar 1885	15	S				KY	KY	TN	At School		5	✓	✓	✓				
44	45	HEARD, WILLIAM C.	Head	W	M	Nov 1839	60	M	30			KY	TN	TN	Farmer			✓	✓	✓	O	F	F	152
		" MARY	Wife	W	F	Jan 1840	60	M	30	4	5	KY	KY	KY				X	X	✓				
45	146	PERDUE, TAT— ?	Head	W	M	Jan 1848	52	Wd				KY	KY	TN	Farmer			✓	✓	✓	O	F	F	153
		" ARCH	Son	W	M	Jun 1881	18	S				KY	KY	KY	Farm Labor		5	✓	✓	✓				
		" ELA	Dau	W	F	Feb 1886	14	S				KY	KY	KY	At School		5	✓	✓	✓				
		" CASSIE P.	Dau	W	F	May 1888	12	S				KY	KY	KY	At School		2	✓	✓	✓				
146	147	BIGGERSTAFF, PERRY	Head	W	M	Nov 1836	63	M	25			KY	KY	TN	Farmer			✓	✓	✓	O	F	F	154
		" NANCY	Wife	W	F	Jun 1843	56	M	25	7	4	KY	KY	KY				✓	✓	✓				
		PROPES, BIRT	Boarder	W	M	Jan 1880	20	S				KY	KY	KY	Farmer			✓	✓	✓	R		F	155
147	148	WILLIAMS, JOHN	Head	W	M	May 1839	61	Wd				KY	KY	KY	Farmer			✓	✓	✓	O	F	F	156
		" EL— A.	Son	W	M	Feb 1876	24	M	5			KY	KY	KY	Farmer			✓	✓	✓	O	F	F	157
		" LARRY L.	Wife	W	F	Mar 1876	24	M	5	1	1	KY	KY	TN				✓	✓	✓				
		" BESSIE E.	Dau	W	F	Jun 1896	3	S				KY	KY	TN										
48	49	FINLEY, JAMES	Head	W	M	May 1861	39	M	12			KY	TN	TN	Farmer			✓	✓	✓	O	M	F	158
		" ALICE	Wife	W	F	Jul 1868	31	M	12	5	5	KY	KY	KY				✓	✓	✓				
		" ROSCO C.	Son	W	M	Feb 1889	11	S				KY	KY	KY	At School		5	✓	✓	✓				
		" BAZEL R.	Son	W	M	Sep 1890	9	S				KY	KY	KY										
		" EFFY	Dau	W	F	Jun 1892	8	S				KY	KY	KY										
		" EBBIE	Dau	W	F	Mar 1894	6	S				KY	KY	KY										
		" THOMAS	Son	W	M	Jul 1895	4	S				KY	KY	KY										
149	150	POINDEXTER, ARCH	Head	W	M	Mar 1837	63	M	18			TN	KY	KY	Farmer			✓	✓	✓	R		F	159
		" MARIE	Wife	W	F	Oct 1857	42	M	18	8	8	TN	KY	KY				X	X	✓				
		" WILLIAM	Son	W	M	May 1882	18	S				KY	TN	TN	Day Labor		7	✓	✓	✓				
		" ELIZZIEBETH	Dau	W	F	Feb 1884	16	S				KY	TN	TN	At School		5	✓	✓	✓				

TWELFTH CENSUS OF THE UNITED STATES 1900

STATE - KENTUCKY
COUNTY - MONROE
Township or other division — CENTER POINT — Enumerator JAMES T. WHITE

Supervisor's Dist. No. 102 Sheet No.
Enumeration Dist. No. 83

Location (No. of Family / No. of Dwelling)	NAME	Relation	Color	Sex	DATE OF BIRTH Mon/Yr	Age at last birthday	Marital Status	# Years married	Mother of how many children	# of these children living	NATIVITY Place of birth (this person)	Father of this person	Mother of this person	CITIZENSHIP Year of immigr. / # years in U.S. / Naturalization	OCCUPATION 10 years +	Months not employed	EDUCATION Attended school in months	Can read	Can write	Speak English	OWNERSHIP Owned or Rent	Owned - no mortgage	Farm or house	# of farm schedule
	POINDEXTER, JOHN B.	Son	W	M	Jul 1885	14	S				KY	TN	TN		AT SCHOOL		5	✓	✓	✓				
	" GEORGE T.	Son	W	M	Mar 1888	12	S				KY	TN	TN		AT SCHOOL		5	✓	✓	✓				
	" BULIE E.	Dau	W	F	May 1890	10	S				KY	TN	TN		AT SCHOOL			X	X	✓				
	" CARRIE M.	Dau	W	F	Jan 1892	8	S				KY	TN	TN											
	" RALF R.	Son	W	M	Jan 1894	6	S				KY	TN	TN											
	" LESLY	Son	W	M	Jul 1898	1	S				KY	TN	TN											
150 151	SHORT, ISAAC	Head	W	M	Aug 1869	30	M	10			KY	KY	KY		FARMER			✓	✓	✓	O	F	F	160
	" POLLY C.	Wife	W	F	Apr 1867	33	M	10	4	3	KY	KY	KY					✓	✓	✓				
	" MARY J.	Dau	W	F	Dec 1891	8	S				KY	KY	KY											
	" MINNIE	Dau	W	F	Aug 1896	3	S				KY	KY	KY											
	" MILTY F.	Son	W	M	Jan 1899	1	S				KY	KY	KY											
	SHORT, JANE	Mother	W	F	Mar 1828	72	Wd				KY	TN	TN					✓	X	✓				
151 152	BAILEY, WINSTON	Head	W	M	May 1847	53	M	17			KY	SC	KY		FARMER			✓	✓	✓	O	F	F	161
	" ANN T.	Wife	W	F	Apr 1848	52	M	17			KY	KY	KY		SEAMSTRESS			✓	✓	✓				
	BOYLES, (ROXIE?)	Neice	W	F	Jan 1878	22	S				KY	TN	KY		SEAMSTRESS			✓	✓	✓				
	" JOHN	Nephew	W	M	Jun 1881	19	S				KY	TN	KY		AT SCHOOL		2	✓	✓	✓				
	" NONA	Neice	W	F	Jan 1883	17	S				KY	TN	KY					✓	✓	✓				
152 153	BASKET, (THOMAS?)	Head	W	M	Feb 18	862	M	40			TN	TN	TN		FARMER			✓	✓	✓	R	F	162	
	" SARAH J.	Wife	W	F	Mar 1844	56	M	40	12	7	TN	TN	TN					✓	✓	✓				
	" JAMES L.	Son	W	M	Jul 1869	30	S				KY	TN	TN		DAY LABOR		7	✓	✓	✓				
	" RUBEN B.	Son	W	M	Oct 1871	28	S				KY	TN	TN		FARMER			✓	✓	✓	R	F	163	
	" (DAVE?) S.	Son	W	M	Apr 1874	26	S				KY	TN	TN		FARM LABOR			✓	✓	✓				
	" JOHN H.	Son	W	M	Apr 1878	22	S				KY	TN	TN		FARMER			✓	✓	✓	R	F	164	
	" ADER L.	Dau	W	F	Jan 1885	15	S				KY	TN	TN		AT SCHOOL		4	✓	✓	✓				
	" LARRY T.	Dau	W	F	Feb 1887	13	S				KY	TN	TN		AT SCHOOL		4	✓	✓	✓				
153 154	MAXEY, LEE A.	Head	W	F	Apr 1863	37	Wd				KY	KY	KY		WASHING CLOTHES			✓	✓	✓			H	

STATE - KENTUCKY
COUNTY - MONROE
Township or other division   CENTER POINT   Enumerator   JAMES T. WHITE

Supervisor's Dist. No. _102_ Sheet No.
Enumeration Dist. No. _83_

No. of Family	No. of Dwelling	NAME	Relation	Color	Sex	DATE OF BIRTH Mon/Yr	Age at last birthday	Marital Status	# Years married	Mother of how many children?	# of these children living	Place of birth [this person]	Father of this person	Mother of this person	Year of immigr.	# years in U.S.	Naturalization	OCCUPATION 10 years +	Months not employed	Attended school in months	Can read	Can write	Speak English	Owned or Rent	Owned -no mortage	Farm or house	# of farm schedule	
		MAXEY, LUE (?)	DAU	B	F	JAN 1884	16	S				KY	KY	KY				AT SCHOOL		5	✓	✓	✓					
		" ERNERT (?)	DAU	B	F	AUG 1887	12	S				KY	KY	KY				AT SCHOOL		5	✓	✓	✓					
		" EVERT (?)	SON	B	M	— 1891	9	S				KY	KY	KY														
		" ATIE (?)	DAU	B	F	Feb 1892	8	S				KY	KY	KY														
		" HENRY C.	SON	B	M	MAR 1895	5	S				KY	KY	KY														
		" VIRGEL	SON	B	M	JUL 1897	3	S				KY	KY	KY														
154	155	YOUNG, WILLIAM	Head	W	M	JAN 1833	67	S				KY	KY	VA				FARMER			✓	✓	✓	R		F	165	
		" LILLY	Sister	W	F	JAN 1830	70	S				KY	KY	VA							X	X						
		" MARTHA	Sister	W	F	JAN 1860	40	S				KY	KY	VA							X	X						
155	156	RICHARDSON —	Head	W	M	— —	72	M	24			TN	VA	VA				FARMER			✓	✓	✓	O	F	F	167	s/c
		" MARTHA	Wife	W	F	AUG —	56	M	24	6	5	TN	KY	KY							✓	✓	✓					
		" PARISH W.	Son	W	M	Sep 1887	22	S				KY	TN	TN				FARMER			✓	✓	✓	R		F	168	
		" CORA	Dau	W	F	May 1880	20	S				KY	TN	TN				SEAMSTRESS			✓	✓	✓					
		" JULIA	Dau	W	F	Feb 1883	17	S				KY	TN	TN				AT SCHOOL		10	✓	✓	✓			?		
		" BUG C.	Son	W	M	Nov 1887	14	S				KY	TN	TN				AT SCHOOL		5	✓	✓	✓					
		" ZORA	Dau	W	F	OCT 1888	12	S				KY	TN	TN														
156	157	BE—, MAXEY	HEAD	W	F	AUG 1863	36	Wd				KY	KY	KY				FARMER			✓	✓	✓	O	M	F	169	
		" BETSY L.	DAU	W	F	JUN 1887	12	S				KY	KY	KY				AT SCHOOL			✓	✓	✓					
		" FRANKLIN S.	Son	W	M	MAR 1891	9	S				KY	KY	KY														
		" ELIZA E	DAU	W	F	JUN 1895	5	S				KY	KY	KY														
		GRIMSLEY, JESSE W.	BRO	W	M	JUN 1872	27	S				IND	KY	KY				FARMER			✓	✓	✓	R		F	170	
157	158	DIRE, LARNCE	Head	W	M	JAN 1866	34	M	7			TN	KY	TN				FARMER			✓	X	✓	R		F	171	
		" FLORNCE F.	Wife	W	F	Feb 1875	25	M	7	5	3	KY	KY	KY							✓	✓	✓					
		" DASSE	Dau	W	F	DEC 1895	4	S				KY	TN	KY														
		" WILLIAM L.	Son	W	M	JAN 1897	3	S				KY	TN	KY														
		" MARTHA E.	DAU	W	F	MAR 1899	1	S				KY	TN	KY														

STATE - KENTUCKY
COUNTY - MONROE
Township or other division CENTER POINT Enumerator JAMES T. WHITE

Supervisor's Dist. No. 102 Sheet No.
Enumeration Dist. No. 83

No. of Family	No. of Dwelling	NAME	Relation	Color	Sex	DATE OF BIRTH Mon/Yr	Age at last birthday	Marital Status	# Years married	Mother of how many children?	# of these children living	Place of birth [this person]	Father of this person	Mother of this person	Year of immigr.	# years in U.S.	Naturalization	OCCUPATION 10 years +	Months not employed	Attended school in months	Can read	Can write	Speak English	Owned or Rent	Owned -no mortage	Farm or house	# of farm schedule
158	159	HARIS, ANDREW J.	Head	W	M	Sep 1865	34	M	15			TN	VA	VA				FARMER			✓	✓	✓	R		F	172
		MARGARET	Wife	W	F	May 1866	34	M	15	6	5	KY	KY	KY							✓	X	✓				
		ELMORE	Son	W	M	Oct 1886	13	S				TN	TN	KY				AT SCHOOL		5	X	X	✓				
		SARAH B.	Dau	W	F	Mar 1888	12	S				KY	TN	KY				AT SCHOOL		5	✓	✓	✓				
		WILLIAM A.	Son	W	M	Mar 1889	11	S				KY	TN	KY				AT SCHOOL		5	X	X	✓				
		JOHN T.	Son	W	M	Feb 1892	8	S				TN	TN	KY													
		TIM C.	Son	W	M	Apr 1898	2	S				KY	TN	KY													
159	160	MAXEY, EMLEY (M or W)	Head	W	F	Mar 1840	60	Wd		12	12	TN	TN	TN				FARMER			✓	✓	✓	O		F	173
		TOLBERT	Son	W	M	Oct 1859	40	S				KY	KY	TN				FARMER			✓	✓	✓	O		M F	174
		MAGGIE	Dau	W	F	Jul 1878	21	S				KY	KY	TN				SEAMSTRESS			✓	✓	✓				
		FANNIE	Dau	W	F	Aug 1880	19	S				KY	KY	TN							✓	✓	✓				
		HARDEN W.	Son	W	M	Sep 1884	15	S				KY	KY	TN				AT SCHOOL		4	✓	✓	✓				
160	161	HEARD, WILSON	Head	W	M	Sep 1862	37	M	14			KY	KY	KY				FARMER			✓	✓	✓	O		F	175
		MARTHA	Wife	W	F	Jun 1864	35	M	14	7	6	KY	KY	KY							✓	✓	✓				
		VERNIE	Dau	W	F	Dec 1886	13	S				KY	KY	KY				AT SCHOOL		5	✓	✓	✓				
		TIP	Son	W	M	Feb 1889	11	S				KY	KY	KY				AT SCHOOL		5	✓	✓	✓				
		LIVIA	Dau	W	F	Feb 1891	9	S				KY	KY	KY													
		JESSIE	Son	W	M	Apr 1895	5	S				KY	KY	KY													
		HERMAN	Son	W	M	Apr 1897	3	S				KY	KY	KY													
		FLONCE	Dau	W	F	Jan 1900	1/12	S				KY	KY	KY													
161	162	MAXEY, ALBERT	Head	B	M	Jan 1865	35	M	15			KY	KY	KY				FARMER			X	X	✓	R		F	176
		LENOR	Wife	B	F	Jan 1873	27	M	15	8	8	KY	KY	KY							X	X	✓				
		EARVO ?	Dau	B	F	Jun 1885	14	S				KY	KY	KY				AT SCHOOL		5	✓	✓	✓				
		BENJAMIN	Son	B	M	Feb 1889	11	S				KY	KY	KY				AT SCHOOL		5	✓	✓	✓				
		LEMMA ?	Dau	B	F	Jan 1893	7	S				KY	KY	KY													
		FREDRICK	Son	B	M	Feb 1895	5	S				KY	KY	KY													

STATE - KENTUCKY
COUNTY - MONROE
Township or other division   CENTER POINT   Enumerator   JAMES T. WHITE

Supervisor's Dist. No. _102_ Sheet No.
Enumeration Dist. No. _83_

Location No. of Family / No. of Dwelling	NAME	Relation	Color	Sex	DATE OF BIRTH Mon/Yr	Age at last birthday	Marital Status	# Years married	Mother of how many children?	# of these children living	Place of birth (this person)	Father of this person	Mother of this person	Year of immigr.	# years in U.S.	Naturalization	OCCUPATION 10 years +	Months not employed	Attended school in months	Can read	Can write	Speak English	Owned or Rent	Owned-no mortage	Farm or house	# of farm schedule	
	MAXEY, LUCIE	DAU	B	F	Feb 1895	5	S				KY	KY	KY														
	" FANNIE	DAU	B	F	Mar 1896	4	S				KY	KY	KY														
	" LUCIE	DAU	B	F	Jan 1898	2	S				KY	KY	KY														
	MAXEY, FAMOS	Nephew	B	M	Jan 1885	15	S				KY	KY	KY				AT SCHOOL		5	✓	✓	✓					
	" JAMES	Nephew	B	M	Jan 1896	4	S				KY	KY	KY														
	" FANNIE	Neice	B	F	Apr 1893	7	S				KY	KY	KY														
162/163	CHAPLE, THOMAS M.	Head	W	M	May —	26	M	10			KY	MO	KY				FARMER			✓	✓	✓	R		F	177	
	" DELLA	Wife	W	F	Feb 1877	23	M	10			KY	KY	KY							✓	✓	✓					
	KIRK, WALKER	Boarder	B	M	Jan 1860	40	Wd				KY	KY	KY				DAY LABOR			✓	✓	✓					
163/164	VANCE, EZRA	Head	W	M	Sep 1875	24	M	3			KY	KY	KY				FARMER			✓	✓		R		F	179	SIC
	" NORA	Wife	W	F	Sep 1874	25	M	3	1	1	KY	KY	KY							✓	✓						
	" WERT	Son	W	M	Nov 1899	1	S				KY	KY	KY														
164/165	HUTCHENS, OLIVER	Head	W	M	Aug 1853	46	M	26			KY	KY	KY				FARMER			✓	✓		O	M	F	180	
	" LUCETTIE	Wife	W	F	Nov 1853	46	M	26	9	8	MO	KY	TN							✓	✓						
	" LIZZIE L.	DAU	W	F	Jun 1876	23	S				KY	KY	MO							✓	✓						
	" KATE L.	DAU	W	F	Oct 1880	19	S				KY	KY	MO				AT SCHOOL		5	✓	✓						
	" WILLELLA	DAU	W	F	Jan 1883	17	S				KY	KY	MO				AT SCHOOL		5	✓	✓						
	" SID T.	Son	W	M	Jan 1889	11	S				KY	KY	MO				AT SCHOOL		5	✓	✓						
	" OLIVER S.	Son	W	M	Nov 1892	8	S				KY	KY	MO														
	" GEORGY	DAU	W	F	Oct 1899	7/12	S				KY	KY	MO														
	HUTCHENS, ELLIZZIEBETH	Mother	W	F	Jan 1824	74	W				KY	KY	KY				FARMER			✓	X	✓	O		F	181	
	KIRKPATRICK, HUE	Boarder	B	M	Jan 1878	22	M				KY	KY	KY				DAY LABOR			✓	✓	✓					
	" KATE	Boarder	B	F	Jan 1878	22	M				KY	KY	KY				SERVANT			X	X	✓					
165/166	BEDFORD, THOMAS	HEAD	W	M	Dec 1845	54	M	18			KY	KY	KY				PHYSICIAN			✓	✓		O		F	182	
	" ELIZZIEBETH	WIFE	W	F	Dec 1862	39	M	14	4	4	KY	KY	KY							✓	✓						
	" GEORGE R.	Son	W	M	Jun 1888	11	S				KY	KY	KY				AT SCHOOL		6	✓	✓	✓					

STATE - KENTUCKY
COUNTY - MONROE
Township or other division CENTER POINT Enumerator JAMES T. WHITE

Supervisor's Dist. No. _102_ Sheet No.
Enumeration Dist. No. _83_

No. of Family	No. of Dwelling	NAME	Relation	Color	Sex	DATE OF BIRTH Mon/Yr	Age at last birthday	Marital Status	# Years married	Mother of how many children?	# of these children living	Place of birth [this person]	Father of this person	Mother of this person	Year of immigr.	# years in U.S.	Naturalization	OCCUPATION 10 years +	Months not employed	Attended school in months	Can read	Can write	Speak English	Owned or Rent	Owned-no mortgage	Farm or farm house	# of farm schedule	
		BEDFORD, FRANK G.	Son	W	M	AUG 1891	8	S				KY	KY	KY														
		" OLLIE M.	Dau	W	F	Nov 1894	5	S				KY	KY	KY														
		" ERNEST	Dau	W	F	OCT 1898	1	S				KY	KY	KY														
		MONDAY, ELISON B.	Boarder	W	M	JAN 1876	24	S				KY	KY	KY				DAY LABOR			✓	✓	✓				
166	167	McMILLAND, MARY S.	Head	W	F	JAN 1848	52	Wd	29	2	2	KY	KY	KY				FARMER			✓	✓	✓	O	F	F	183
		" MARY A.	Boarder	W	F	MAR 1836	64	S				KY	KY	KY				FARMER			✓	✓	✓	O	F	F	184
167	168	COPAS, DOCK J.	Head	W	M	JAN 1858	42	M	16			KY	KY	KY				FARMER			✓	✓	✓	R		F	185
		" MARGARET	Wife	W	F	MAR 1867	33	M	16			KY	KY	KY							✓	✓	✓				
		" HULET H.	Son	W	M	JUN 1886	14	S				KY	KY	KY				AT SCHOOL		5	✓	✓	✓				
		" DOLLIE B.	Dau	W	F	Jul 1888	11	S				KY	KY	KY				AT SCHOOL		5	✓	✓	✓				
		" OSCAR F.	Son	W	M	AUG 1891	8	S				KY	KY	KY							✓	✓	✓				
		" BAZZLE R.	Son	W	M	Jul 1894	5	S				KY	KY	KY							✓	✓	✓				
		" MOSE C.	Son	W	M	Jul 1896	3	S				KY	KY	KY													
168	169	DODSON, RICHARD	Head	W	M	JAN 1871	29	M				KY	KY	KY				FARMER			✓	✓	✓	R		F	186
		" ELLIZZIEBETH	Wife	W	F	Feb 1878	22	M				KY	KY	KY							✓	✓	✓				
		BROWN, SUSAN	Mother-in-law	W	F	MAR 1843	57	Wd		10	5	KY	KY	TN							✓	✓	✓	O	F	F	187
169	170	BEDFORD, PENDY G.	Head	W	M	AUG 1853	46	M	19			KY	KY	KY				FARMER			✓	✓	✓	O	F	F	188
		" FRANCIS	Wife	W	F	MAR 1860	40	M	19	3	2	KY	TN	KY							✓	✓	✓				
		" BENJAMIN L.	Son	W	M	DEC 1881	18	S				TX	KY	KY				AT SCHOOL		5	✓	✓	✓				
		" ANNIE L.	Dau	W	F	JAN 1896	4	S				KY	KY	KY													
		MAXEY, HULET	Boarder	B	M	JAN 1884	16	S				KY	KY	KY				DAY LABOR			X	X	✓				
170	171	ANDREWS, WILLIE	Head	W	M	Jul 1852	47	M	23			KY	KY	KY				FARMER			✓	✓	✓	O	F	F	189
		" NARSISS C.	Wife	W	F	MAR 1853	47	M	23	6	4	KY	VA	TN							✓	✓	✓				
		" NIEL (?)	Son	W	M	AUG 1879	20	S				KY	KY	KY							✓	✓	✓				
		" MARTIE	Dau	W	F	DEC 1882	17	S				KY	KY	KY				AT SCHOOL		9	✓	✓	✓				
		" VERA	Dau	W	F	Feb 1892	8	S				KY	KY	KY													

TWELFTH CENSUS OF THE UNITED STATES 1900

STATE - KENTUCKY
COUNTY - MONROE
Township or other division CENTER POINT Enumerator JAMES T. WHITE

Supervisor's Dist. No. 102 Sheet No.
Enumeration Dist. No. 83

No. of Family	No. of Dwelling	NAME	Relation	Color	Sex	DATE OF BIRTH Mon/Yr	Age at last birthday	Marital Status	# Years married	Mother of how many children?	# of these children living	Place of birth (this person)	Father of this person	Mother of this person	Year of immigr.	# years in U.S.	Naturalization	OCCUPATION 10 years +	Months not employed	Attended school in months	Can read	Can write	Speak English	Owned or Rent	Owned -no mortage	Farm or house	# of farm schedule	
		ANDREWS, CLINT	Son	W	M	Oct 1894	5	S				KY	KY	KY							✓	✓	✓					
		RICH, EDLEY	Boarder	W	M	Nov 1879	20	S				KY	KY	KY				DAY LABOR			✓	✓	✓					
171	172	ANDREWS, VARNY F.	Head	W	M	Nov 1817	81	M	53			KY	KY	KY				FARMER			✓	✓	✓	O	F	F	190	
		" CATHERINE	Wife			Dec 1824	75	M	53	2	2	KY	KY	KY							✓	✓	✓					
		ALLEN, WILLIAMS	Boarder	W	M	Dec 1873	26	S				KY	KY	KY				DAY LABOR		7	✓	✓	✓					
		BEDFORD, ELIZZA	Dau	W	F	Apr 1855	45	M	26	1	1	KY	KY	KY				FARMER			✓	✓	✓	O	F	F	191	
172	173	WHITESIDES, ELIZA	Head	B	F	May 1880	20	S				KY	KY	KY				WASHING CLOTHES			X	X	✓	R		H		
		" JOHN	Bro	B	M	Feb 1882	18	S				KY	KY	KY				DAY LABOR		5	✓	✓	✓					
		" WILLIAM	Bro	B	M	Jan 1885	15	S				KY	KY	KY				DAY LABOR		3	X	X	✓					
		" EDWARD	Bro	B	M	Mar 1887	13	S				KY	KY	KY				DAY LABOR		8	X	X	✓					
		" FRANK	Bro	B	M	Jan 1891	9	S				KY	KY	KY							X	X	✓					
		" GEORGE	Bro	B	M	May 1896	4	S				KY	KY	KY														
		" MARY	Sister	B	F	May 1897	3	S				KY	KY	KY														
173	174	BEDFORD, HUE	Head	W	M	Feb 1843	57	M				KY	KY	KY				FARMER			✓	✓	✓	O	F	F	192	
		" HUE K.	Son	W	M	Sep 1875	24	S				KY	KY	KY				FARMER			✓	✓	✓	R		F	193	
174	175	GRAVES, ROBERT	Head	B	M	Jan 1855	45	M	25			KY	KY	KY				FARMER			✓	✓	✓	O	F	F	194	
		" HELAND	Wife	B	F	May 1860	40	M	25	14	9	KY	KY	KY							X	X	✓					
		" LILA A.	Dau	B	F	Jan 1880	20	S				KY	KY	KY							✓	X	✓					
		" TENNESSEE	Dau	B	F	May 1882	18	S				KY	KY	KY				AT SCHOOL			✓	✓	✓					
		" LANK	Son	B	M	Jan 1886	14	S				KY	KY	KY				AT SCHOOL			X	X	✓					
		" BELLE	Dau	B	F	Apr 1888	12	S				KY	KY	KY				AT SCHOOL			X	X	✓					
		" HARET	Dau	B	F	Jul 1894	5	S				KY	KY	KY														
		" JOHN	Son	B	M	Jun 1899	11/12	S				KY	KY	KY														
175	176	PETERMAN, ISAAC	Head	W	M	Dec 1823	76	Wd				KY	GA	KY				FARMER			✓	✓	✓	O	F	F	195	
		" MARY H.	Dau	W	F	Jan 1861	39	S				MO	KY	KY							✓	✓	✓					
		" ANNIE M.	Dau	W	F	Mar 1876	24	S				KY	KY	KY							✓	✓	✓					

STATE - KENTUCKY
COUNTY - MONROE
Township or other division CENTER POINT Enumerator JAMES T. WHITE

Supervisor's Dist. No. 102 Sheet No.
Enumeration Dist. No. 83

Location (No. of Family / No. of Dwelling)	NAME	Relation	Color	Sex	DATE OF BIRTH Mon/Yr	Age at last birthday	Marital Status	# Years married	Mother of how many children?	# of these children living	Place of birth [this person]	Father of this person	Mother of this person	Year of immigr. / # years in U.S. / Naturalization	OCCUPATION 10 years +	Months not employed	Attended school in months	Can read	Can write	Speak English	Owned or Rent	Owned –no mortgage / Farm or house	# of farm schedule
	BIGGERSTAFF, JOHN M.	Boarder	W	M	Sep 1872	27	S				KY	KY	KY		FARMER			✓	✓	✓	R	F	196
176 177	GEE, ELHORTON (?)	Head	W	M	Dec 1842	57	Wd				KY	KY	KY		FARMER			✓	✓	✓	O	F F	197
	" ANNIE	Dau	W	F	Nov 1889	10	S				KY	KY	KY		AT SCHOOL		5	✓	✓	✓			
	" MARY A. R.	Sister	W	F	Jun 1830	69	Wd				KY	KY	KY		FARMER			✓	✓	✓	O	F F	198
	" ALMIRINDA A.	Sister	W	F	Nov 1836	63	S				KY	KY	KY		FARMER			✓	✓	✓	O	F F	199
	HARDEN, KERTES	Boarder	W	M	May 1883	17	S				KY	KY	KY		DAY LABOR	8		✓	✓	✓			
177 178	RUSH, HADEN	Head	W	M	Dec 1879	20	M	1			KY	KY	KY		FARMER			✓	✓	✓	R	F	200
	" SALLIE	Wife	W	F	Dec 1879	20	M	1			KY	KY	KY					✓	✓	✓			
	" ELVIN	Brother	W	M	Nov 1875	24	S				KY	KY	KY		FARMER			✓	✓	✓	R	F	201
178 179	MAXEY, HARRET	Head	B	F	Jan 1840	60	Wd		10	8	KY	KY	KY		WASHING CLOTHES			X	X	✓		H	
	" LEANN	Dau	B	F	Feb 1880	20	S				KY	KY	KY		AT SCHOOL		5	✓	✓	✓			
	" ADDA	Dau	B	F	Apr 1882	18	S				KY	KY	KY		AT SCHOOL		5	X	X	✓			
	" CHARLEY	Son	B	M	May 1884	16	S				KY	KY	KY		AT SCHOOL		5	✓	✓	✓			
	" HULET	Son	B	M	Mar 1886	14	S				KY	KY	KY		AT SCHOOL		5	✓	✓	✓			
	" HENRY	Son	B	M	Jun 1887	13	S				KY	KY	KY		AT SCHOOL		5	X	X	✓			
	" SAM	Son	B	M	Jun 1892	7	S				KY	KY	KY										
	" RUTHA	Dau	B	F	Mar 1894	6	S				KY	KY	KY										
	" JANE	Dau	B	F	Feb 1896	4	S				KY	KY	KY										
179 180	BEDFORD, JAMES	Head	W	M	Nov 1855	44	M	12			KY	KY	KY		FARMER			✓	✓	✓	O	F F	202
	" BETTIE	Wife	W	F	Aug 1862	37	M	12	1	1	KY	KY	KY					✓	✓				
	" DELLA	Dau	W	F	Aug 1889	10	S				KY	KY	KY		AT SCHOOL			✓	✓	✓			
180 181	JANSON, WILLSUN E	Head	W	M	Nov 1874	25	M	5			TN	TN	KY		FARMER			✓	✓	✓	R	F	203
	" ELIZZIEBETH	Wife	W	F	Jan 1875	25	M	5	4	2	KY	VA	KY					✓	✓	✓			
	" CHARLEY	Son	W	M	Oct 1897	2	S				KY	TN	KY										
	" CARVIN (?)	Son	W	M	Feb 1900	4/12	S				KY	TN	KY										
	" COLUMBUS	Brother	W	M	Jan 1882	18	S				TN	KY	TN		FARM LABOR			✓	✓	✓			

STATE - KENTUCKY
COUNTY - MONROE
Township or other division **CENTER POINT** Enumerator **JAMES J. WHITE**

Supervisor's Dist. No. **102** Sheet No.
Enumeration Dist. No. **83**

Location No. of Family	No. of Dwelling	NAME	Relation	Color	Sex	DATE OF BIRTH Mon/Yr	Age at last birthday	Marital Status	# Years married	Mother of how many children?	# of these children living	NATIVITY Place of birth [this person]	Father of this person	Mother of this person	CITIZENSHIP Year of immigr.	# years in U.S.	Naturalization	OCCUPATION 10 years +	Months not employed	EDUCATION Attended school in months	Can read	Can write	Speak English	OWNERSHIP Owned or Rent	Owned -no mortgage	Farm or house	# of farm schedule
181	182	TOOLEY, JAMES	Head	W	M	Feb 1859	41	M	9			KY	KY	KY				FARMER			✓	✓		R		F	204
		" JULIA	Wife	W	F	Jun 1865	34	M	9	3	2	KY	KY	KY							✓	✓					
		" CLATON	Son	W	M	Jul 1893	6	S				KY	KY	KY													
		" CLINT	Son	W	M	Jun 1894	5	S				KY	KY	KY													
182	183	HOLLAND, LOGGAN	Head	W	M	Jan 1868	32	M	7			KY	KY	KY				FARMER			✓	✓		O		F	205
		" RANDIE	Wife	W	F	May 1873	27	M	7	2	2	KY	KY	KY							✓	✓					
		" MITSEY	Dau	W	F	— 1895	5	S				KY	KY	KY													
		" HARRY (?)	Son	W	M	May 1897	3	S				KY	KY	KY													
183	184	TOOLEY, JOSEPH	Head	W	M	Sep 1861	38	M	17			KY	KY	KY				FARMER			✓	✓		R		F	206
		" LUANN	Wife	W	F	Dec 1865	34	M	17	8	7	KY	KY	KY							✓	✓	✓				
		" ROSCO	Son	W	M	Apr 1884	16	S				KY	KY	KY				AT SCHOOL		5	✓	✓	✓				
		" BALLIE (?)	Dau	W	F	Jun 1886	14	S				KY	KY	KY				AT SCHOOL		5	✓	✓					
		" DONA	Dau	W	F	Jun 1888	11	S				KY	KY	KY				AT SCHOOL		5	✓	✓	✓				
		" BESSIE	Dau	W	F	Jun 1895	5	S				KY	KY	KY									✓				
		" WILLIAM	Son	W	M	Nov 1897	3	S				KY	KY	KY													
		BEDE	Son	W	M	May 1899	1	S				KY	KY	KY													
184	185	MURRY, JOHN A.	Head	W	M	Aug 1835	64	M	42			VA	VA	VA				FARMER			✓	✓		R		F	207
		" MARY J.	Wife	W	F	Feb 1836	64	M	42	8	6	VA	VA	VA							✓	✓					
		" CHARLES	Son	W	M	Jun 1868	31	S				VA	VA	VA				FARM LABOR									
		" JAMES A.	Son	W	M	Aug 1875	24	S				KY	VA	VA				FARM LABOR									
		BROWN, BLISS	Boarder	W	M	Mar 1882	18	S				KY	KY	KY				DAY LABOR									
185	186	MURRY, JOHN H.	Head	W	M	Aug 1859	40	M	10			VA	VA	VA				FARMER			✓	✓		R		F	208
		" LUCY A.	Wife	W	F	Sep 1871	28	M	10	4	4	KY	KY	KY							✓	✓					
		" DELLA C.	Dau	W	F	Jun 1890	9	S				KY	VA	KY													
		" JOHN H.	Son	W	M	Oct 1893	6	S				KY	VA	KY													
		" HULET H.	Son	W	M	Nov 1896	3	S				KY	VA	KY													

STATE - KENTUCKY
COUNTY - MONROE
Township or other division CENTER POINT Enumerator JAMES T. WHITE

Supervisor's Dist. No. 102 Sheet No.
Enumeration Dist. No. 83

No. of Family	No. of Dwelling	NAME	Relation	Color	Sex	DATE OF BIRTH Mon/Yr	Age at last birthday	Marital Status	# Years married	Mother of how many children?	# of these children living	Place of birth (this person)	Father of this person	Mother of this person	Year of immigr.	# years in U.S.	Naturalization	OCCUPATION 10 years +	Months not employed	Attended school in months	Can read	Can write	Speak English	Owned or Rent	Owned –no mortgage	Farm or house	# of farm schedule
		MURRY, MARY B.	Dau	W	F	Nov 1899	8/12	S				KY	VA	KY													
166	167	TURNER, WILLIAM C.	Head	W	M	Mar 1831	69	M	37			KY	VA	VA				FARMER			✓	✓	✓	R		F	209
		" NANCY	Wife	W	F	Oct 1848	51	M	37	10	8	KY	KY	KY							✓	✓	✓				
		" JERY M.	Son	W	M	Feb 1869	31	S				KY	KY	KY				FARMER			✓	✓	✓	R		F	210
		" LOUIS R.	Son	W	M	Sep 1878	21	S				KY	KY	KY				FARMER			✓	✓	✓	R		F	211
		" CHESTER F.	Son	W	M	Aug 1883	16	S				KY	KY	KY				AT SCHOOL		5	✓	✓	✓				
		" MARY S.	Dau	W	F	Mar 1886	14	S				KY	KY	KY				AT SCHOOL		5	✓	✓	✓				
		" BEDFORD	Son	W	M	Jan 1892	8	S				KY	KY	KY							X	X	✓				
		WHITE, SALLIE	Mother in law	W	F	Jan 1827	74	Wd		4	4	KY	KY	KY							X	X	✓				
		" EDMON	Son	W	M	Jan 1874	26	S				KY	KY	KY				SCHOOL TEACHING			✓	✓	✓				
187	188	MILUM, ELIZA	Head	W	F	Dec 1861	38	Wd		3	3	TN	TN	KY				FARMER			✓	X	✓	R		F	212
		" WALTER	Son	W	M	Aug 1882	17	S				KY	KY	TN				AT SCHOOL		5	✓	✓	✓				
		" STEVENS	Son	W	M	May 1884	14	S				KY	KY	TN				AT SCHOOL		5	✓	✓	✓				
		" WILLIE	Son	W	M	Dec 1887	12	S				KY	KY	TN				AT SCHOOL		5	✓	✓	✓				
188	189	GEARLDS WILLIAM	Head	W	M	Dec 1854	45	M	18			TN	TN	TN				FARMER			✓	✓	✓	R		F	213
		" RESECA	Wife	W	F	Sep 1857	42	M	18	6	6	KY	KY	KY							✓	✓	✓				
		" DELLA	Dau	W	F	Oct 1882	17	S				KY	KY	KY							✓	✓	✓				
		" LARRY E.	Dau	W	F	Jun 1884	15	S				KY	KY	KY				AT SCHOOL		4	✓	✓	✓				
		" HARMON L.	Son	W	M	Jun 1886	13	S				KY	KY	KY				AT SCHOOL		2	✓	✓	✓				
		" LEANY B.	Dau	W	F	Mar 1888	12	S				KY	KY	KY				AT SCHOOL		3	✓	X	✓				
		" ELISHA	Son	W	M	May 1890	10	S				KY	KY	KY				AT SCHOOL		3	✓	✓	✓				
		" ANNIE T.	Dau	W	F	May 1892	8	S				KY	KY	KY													
189	190	KIRKPATRICK, JOHN	Head	W	M	Oct 1846	53	M	29			KY	KY	KY				FARMER			✓	✓	✓	O	F	F	214
		" MARY E.	Wife	W	F	Mar 1851	49	M	29	11	10	KY	KY	KY							✓	✓	✓				
		" JAMES D.	Son	W	M	Sep 1872	27	S				KY	KY	KY				BLACKSMITH			✓	✓	✓				
		" ROBBERT	Son	W	M	Mar 1874	26	S				KY	KY	KY				MERCHANT			✓	✓	✓				

STATE - KENTUCKY
COUNTY - MONROE
Township or other division: CENTER POINT Enumerator: JAMES I. WHITE

Supervisor's Dist. No. 102 Sheet No.
Enumeration Dist. No. 83

No. of Family	No. of Dwelling	NAME	Relation	Color	Sex	Date of Birth Mon/Yr	Age at last birthday	Marital Status	# Years married	Mother of how many children?	# of these children living	Place of birth (this person)	Father of this person	Mother of this person	Occupation	Attended school in months	Can read	Can write	Speak English	Owned or Rent	Farm or house	# of farm schedule
		KIRKPATRICK, PRICE	Son	W	M	Feb 1876	24	S				KY	KY	KY	SAWMILL MAN		✓	✓	✓			
		" MOSES	Son	W	M	Oct 1879	20	S				KY	KY	KY	WORKS AT MILL		✓	✓	✓			
		" ELIZA J.	Dau	W	F	Jul 1886	13	S				KY	KY	KY	AT SCHOOL	5	✓	✓	✓			
		" CASS	Son	W	M	Aug 1888	11	S				KY	KY	KY	AT SCHOOL	5	✓	✓	✓			
		" SALLIE G.	Dau	W	F	Aug 1890	9	S				KY	KY	KY								
		" MAYBELLE	Dau	W	F	May 1893	7	S				KY	KY	KY								
190	191	MURPHY, HILLRY	Head	W	M	Oct 1872	27	M	3			KY	KY	KY	FARMER		✓	✓	✓	R	F	215
		" ALLIE L.	Wife	W	F	Jan 1878	22	M	3	1	1	KY	KY	KY			✓	✓	✓			
		" BEULA M.	Dau	W	F	Jul 1898	1	S				KY	KY	KY								
191	192	PHILPOTT, JAMES B	Head	W	M	Jan 1852	48	S				KY	KY	KY	FARMER		✓	✓	✓	R	F	216
192	193	KIRKPATRICK, WILLIAM	Head	W	M	Jun 1881	19	M				KY	KY	KY	FARMER		✓	✓	✓	R	F	217
		" LORA	Wife	W	F	Jan 1877	23	M	1	1	1	KY	KY	KY			✓	✓	✓			
		" BUFORD	Son	W	M	Jan 1900	4/12	S				KY	KY	KY								
193	194	MILUM, HADEN	Head	W	M	Feb 1877	23	M	2			KY	KY	KY	FARMER		✓	✓	✓	R	F	218
		" MINNIE B.	Wife	W	F	Mar 1880	20	M	2	1	1	KY	KY	KY			✓	✓	✓			
		" JOHN B.	Son	W	M	Dec 1898	1	S				KY	KY	KY								
194	195	GEARLDS, KENDRIC	Head	W	M	Mar 1828	72	M	48			TN	TN	TN	FARMER		✓	✓	✓	R	F	219
		" SARAH E.	Wife	W	F	Jun 1830	69	M	48	1	1	TN	TN	TN			X	X	✓			
		" MARY O (or D.)	Dau	W	F	Nov 1863	36	S				KY	TN	TN			X	X	✓			
		" THOMAS	Grandson	W	M	Mar 1889	11	S				KY	KY	KY	AT SCHOOL	5	✓	✓	✓			
195	196	KIRKPATRICK (HUNAY?)	Head	B	F	May 1855	45	Wd	7	4					WASHING		X	X	✓		H	
		" MATILDY	Dau	B	F	Aug 1874	25	S	2	1					WASHING		✓	✓	✓			
		" MAY R.	Dau	B	F	Jun 1879	20	S	2	2					WASHING		✓	✓	✓			
		" MILLA	Dau	B	F	Jan 1886	14	S							AT SCHOOL	5	✓	✓	✓			
		" BERNETTIE	Dau	B	F	Mar 1888	12	S							AT SCHOOL	5	✓	✓	✓			
		" SUSIE	Gr-Dau	B	F	Jan 1896	4	S														

TWELFTH CENSUS OF THE UNITED STATES 1900

STATE - KENTUCKY
COUNTY - MONROE
Township or other division CENTER POINT   Enumerator JAMES T. WHITE

Supervisor's Dist. No. 10 ? Sheet No. _____
Enumeration Dist. No. 83 _____

No. of Family	No. of Dwelling	NAME	Relation	Color	Sex	DATE OF BIRTH Mon/Yr	Age at last birthday	Marital Status	# Years married	Mother of how many children?	# of these children living	Place of birth [this person]	Father of this person	Mother of this person	Year of immigr.	# years in U.S.	Naturalization	OCCUPATION 10 years +	Months not employed	Attended school in months	Can read	Can write	Speak English	Owned or Rent	Owned - no mortage	Farm or house	# of farm schedule	
		KIRKPATRICK, FRANK	Gr-Son	B	M	MAY 1896	4	S				KY	KY	KY														
		" JANE	Gr-Dau	B	F	MAY 1898	2	S				KY	KY	KY														
196	197	KIRKPATRICK, JAMES	Head	B	M	MAY 1860	40	M	26			KY	KY	KY				DAY LABOR			✓	✓				H		
		" MAY R	Wife	B	F	JUN 1850	50	M	26	1	1	KY	KY	KY							X	X	✓					
197	198	PETETT, JACKSON	Head	W	M	NOV 1830	69	Wd				KY	NC	VA				FARMER			✓	X	✓	R		F	220	
		" SARILDO E.	Dau	W	F	DEC 1863	36	S				KY	KY	KY							✓	✓	✓					
		" GEORGE	Son	W	M	OCT 1864	35	Wd				KY	KY	KY				FARM LABOR			X	✓	✓					
		" PEARL	Gr-Dau	W	F	Sep 1885	14	S				KY	KY	KY				AT SCHOOL		8	✓	✓	✓					
		" JINNIE	Gr-Dau	W	F	MAR 1887	13	S				KY	KY	KY				AT SCHOOL		8	✓	✓	✓					
		HICKSON, GEORGE	Boarder	W	M	JAN 1860	40	S				KY	KY	KY				FARMER			X	X	✓	R		F	221	
198	199	PETETT, LARKIN	Head	W	M	APR 1867	33	M	1			KY	KY	KY				FARMER			✓	✓	✓	R		F	222	
		" LUCIE	Wife	W	F	Feb 1880	20	M	1	1	0	KY	KY	KY							✓	✓	✓					
199	200	GETTINGS, JOHN L	Head	W	M	OCT 1854	45	M	22			KY	KY	KY				FARMER			✓	✓	✓	R		F	223	
		" SUSAN	Wife	W	F	Sep 1856	43	M	22	7	7	KY	KY	KY							✓	✓	✓					
		" MARY E.	Dau	W	F	Aug 1878	21	S				KY	KY	KY							✓	✓	✓					
		" JOHN H.	Son	W	M	Nov 1882	17	S				KY	KY	KY				FARM LABOR			✓	✓						
		" LUIS W.	Son	W	M	Nov 1884	15	S				KY	KY	KY							✓	✓						
		" BURLESS(?) C.	Son	W	M	Sep 1886	13	S				KY	KY	KY				AT SCHOOL			✓	✓						
		" SAMUEL B.	Son	W	M	Dec 1889	10	S				KY	KY	KY				AT SCHOOL			✓	✓						
		" HATTIE M.	Dau	W	F	Jan 189	9	S				KY	KY	KY							✓	✓						
200	201	PITCOCK, SUSAN	Head	W	F	Nov 1846	53	Wd		13	10	KY	KY	KY				FARMER			✓	✓	✓	O		F	224	
		" MARY E.	Dau	W	F	Jun 1868	32	S				KY	KY	KY							X	X	✓					
		" VIRGIL	Son	W	M	MAY 1871	29	S				KY	KY	KY				FARMER			✓	✓	✓	R		F	225	
		" ONA	Dau	W	F	MAR 1881	19	S				KY	KY	KY							✓	✓	✓					
		" JOHN B.	Son	W	M	OCT 1882	17	S				KY	KY	KY				AT SCHOOL		3	✓	✓	✓					
		" VERDIA L.	Son	W	M	Nov 1884	15	S				KY	KY	KY				AT SCHOOL		4	✓	✓	✓					

STATE - KENTUCKY
COUNTY - MONROE
Township or other division **CENTER POINT** Enumerator **JAMES T. WHITE**

Supervisor's Dist. No. **102** Sheet No.
Enumeration Dist. No. **83**

No. of Family	No. of Dwelling	NAME	Relation	Color	Sex	DATE OF BIRTH Mon/Yr	Age at last birthday	Marital Status	# Years married	Mother of how many children?	# of these children living	Place of birth [this person]	Father of this person	Mother of this person	Year of immigr.	# years in U.S.	Naturalization	OCCUPATION 10 years +	Months not employed	Attended school in months	Can read	Can write	Speak English	Owned or Rent	Owned -no mortage	Farm or house	# of farm schedule
		PITCOCK, ORVEL	SON	W	M	Feb 1886	14	S				KY	KY	KY				AT SCHOOL		4	✓	✓					
		" JAMES L	SON	W	M	DEC 1889	10	S				KY	KY	KY				AT SCHOOL		6	✓	✓					
		" MAGGIE L.	DAU in-law	W	F	Nov 1881	19	M	1			KY	KY	KY							✓	✓	✓				
201	202	PITCOCK, LAFATE	Head	W	M	Sep 1870	29	M	3			KY	KY	KY				FARMER			✓	✓	✓	R		F	226
		" SARAH E	Wife	W	F	MAR 1880	20	M	3	2	1	KY	KY	KY							✓	✓					
		" —BABY—	SON	W	M	May 1900	1/12	S				KY	KY	KY							✓	✓					
202	203	PITCOCK, WILLIAM	Head	W	M	Oct 1866	33	M	5			KY	KY	KY				FARMER			✓	✓	✓	R		F	227
		" MARTHA	Wife	W	F	Oct 1878	21	M	5	1	1	KY	KY	KY							X	X	✓				
		" MARGARET	DAU	W	F	Sep 1889	10	S				KY	KY	KY				AT SCHOOL		5	✓	✓	✓				
		" INGRAM	SON	W	M	APR 1892	8	S				KY	KY	KY							✓	✓	✓				
		" IONA (?)	DAU	W	F	Jun 1896	4	S				KY	KY	KY													
203	204	PITCOCK, JOSEPH	HEAD	W	M	Sep 1874	25	M	3			KY	KY	KY				FARMER			✓	✓	✓	R		F	228
		" NANCY	Wife	W	F	MAR 1874	26	M	3	3	3	KY	KY	KY							✓	✓	✓				
		" FOWLER	SON	W	M	Jul 1897	2	S				KY	KY	KY													
		" OLIE	DAU	W	F	Feb 1899	1	S				KY	KY	KY													
		" CHALMOS	SON	W	M	Feb 1900	3/12	S				KY	KY	KY													
204	205	MURLEY, JOHN	Head	W	M	Jan 1847	53	M	26			KY	KY	KY							✓	✓	✓	R		H	
		" MARY	Wife	W	F	APR 1855	45	M	26	13	13	KY	KY	KY							✓	✓	✓				
		" MALISSE	DAU	W	F	Feb 1882	18	S				KY	KY	KY				AT SCHOOL		5	✓	✓	✓				
		" LORETTIE	DAU	W	F	May 1884	16	S				KY	KY	KY				AT SCHOOL		5	✓	✓					
		" MARY	DAU	W	F	Feb 1886	14	S				KY	KY	KY				AT SCHOOL		5	✓	✓	✓				
		" BESSIE	DAU	W	F	MAR 1882	12	S				KY	KY	KY				AT SCHOOL		5	✓	✓	✓				
		" SALLIE	DAU	W	F	APR 1890	10	S				KY	KY	KY				AT SCHOOL		5	X	X	✓				
		" JOHN W	SON	W	M	Jun 1892	8	S				KY	KY	KY													
		" SAMUEL L.	SON	W	M	May 1894	6	S				KY	KY	KY													
		" CORA L.	DAU	W	F	Jul 1896	3	S				KY	KY	KY													

TWELFTH CENSUS OF THE UNITED STATES 1900

STATE - KENTUCKY
COUNTY - MONROE
Township or other division: CENTER POINT
Enumerator: JAMES T. WHITE

—229—

Supervisor's Dist. No. 102 Sheet No.
Enumeration Dist. No. 83

Fam/Dwel	Name	Relation	Color	Sex	Date of Birth	Age	Marital	Yrs mar	Children born	Children living	Birthplace	Father	Mother	Occupation	School	Read	Write	Speak Eng	Ownership
	MURLEY, LURA M.	Dau	W	F	Jun 1899	11/12	S				KY	KY	KY						
205 206	ROSS, MARTHA	Head	W	F	Jan 1852	48	Wd		9	7	KY	KY	KY	Farmer		✓	✓	✓	O FF 229
	" DORA	Dau	W	F	Mar 1878	22	S				KY	KY	KY	At School	5	✓	✓	✓	
	" BELLE	Dau	W	F	Apr 1880	20	S				KY	KY	KY	At School	5	✓	✓	✓	
	" JEFFERSON	Son	W	M	Apr 1884	16	S				KY	KY	KY	At School	5	✓	✓	✓	
	JOSEPH	Son	W	M	Apr 1884	16	S				KY	KY	KY	At School	5	✓	✓	✓	
	FLIPPIN, MARY R.	Dau	W	F	Jan 1872	28	Wd		1	1	KY	KY	KY	Seamstress		✓	✓	✓	
	" THELMA	Dau	W	F	Aug 1898	1	S				KY	KY	KY						
206 207	HOLANDWORTH, JAMES	Head	W	M	Apr 1857	43	M	14			KY	KY	KY	Farmer		✓	✓	✓	O FF 230
	" MARY	Wife	W	F	Jun 1864	35	M	14	3	3	KY	KY	KY			✓	✓	✓	
	" CECIL L.	Dau	W	F	Feb 1887	13	S				KY	KY	KY	At School	5	✓	✓	✓	
	" MAUD L.	Dau	W	F	Mar 1891	9	S				KY	KY	KY						
	" JOSEPH	Son	W	M	May 1899	1	S				KY	KY	KY						
	" JOEL	Brother	W	M	Jan 1874	26	S				KY	KY	KY	Farmer		✓	✓		R F 231
207 208	PITCOCK, LABORN	Head	W	M	Dec 1871	38	M	15			KY	KY	KY	Farmer		✓	✓		R F 232
	" MANDE	Wife	W	F	Sep 1871	38	M	15	3	2	KY	KY	KY			✓	✓		
	" ANER	Dau	W	F	Aug 1887	12	S				KY	KY	KY	At School	8	✓	✓		
	" THOMAS	Son	W	M	Sep 1889	10	S				KY	KY	KY	At School	8	✓	✓		
208 209	TOOLEY, MANDERSON	Head	W	M	Mar 1870	30	M	10			KY	KY	KY	Farmer		✓	✓		R F 233
	" MARY	Wife	W	F	Jun 1872	28	M	10	4	4	KY	KY	KY			✓	✓		
	" LEE	Son	W	M	Oct 1891	8	S				KY	KY	KY						
	" CORDA	Dau	W	F	Aug 1892	7	S				KY	KY	KY						
	" ORPHY	Dau	W	F	Jan 1895	5	S				KY	KY	KY						
	" BERTS? L.	Son	W	M	Sep 1898	1	S				KY	KY	KY						
209 210	PAGE, FRANK	Head	W	M	Jan 1878	22	S				KY	KY	KY	Day Labor		✓	✓	✓	R H
210 211	HOLANDWORTH, SAM	Head	W	M	Jun 1872	28	M	9			KY	KY	KY			✓	✓		R F 234

STATE - KENTUCKY
COUNTY - MONROE
Township or other division CENTER POINT Enumerator JAMES T. WHITE

Supervisor's Dist. No. _102_ Sheet No.
Enumeration Dist. No. _83_

No. of Family	No. of Dwelling	NAME	Relation	Color	Sex	DATE OF BIRTH Mon/Yr	Age at last birthday	Marital Status	# Years married	Mother of how many children?	# of these children living	Place of birth (this person)	Father of this person	Mother of this person	Year of immigr.	# years in U.S.	Naturalization	OCCUPATION 10 years +	Months not employed	Attended school in months	Can read	Can write	Speak English	Owned or Rent	Owned –no mortgage	Farm or house	# of farm schedule	
		HOLANDWORTH, MARY E.	Wife	W	F	Jan 1876	24	M	9	4	4	KY	KY	KY							✓	✓	✓					
		" EDNA H.	Dau	W	F	Dec 1891	8	S				KY	KY	KY														
		" ALLEN J.	Son	W	M	Jan 1894	6	S				KY	KY	KY														
		" OSCAR	Son	W	M	Apr 1896	4	S				KY	KY	KY														
		" FRED	Son	W	M	Jun 1898	1	S				KY	KY	KY														
211	212	TOOLEY, THEODORIC	Head	W	M	Oct 1836	63	M	42			KY	VA	VA				FARMER			✓	✓	✓	O	F	F	235	
		" DILEMMA	Wife	W	F	May 1842	58	M	42	4	4	KY	KY	KY							✓	✓	✓					
		" AMANDA	Dau	W	F	Jun 1876	24	S				KY	KY	KY							✓	✓	✓					
		" JAMES E.	Son	W	M	Aug 1882	18	S				KY	KY	KY				FARM LABOR			✓	✓	✓					
		" HUE(?) B.	Son	W	M	Aug 1889	11	S				KY	KY	KY				AT SCHOOL		5	✓	✓	✓					
		" JOHN C.	Son	W	M	Nov 1890	9	S				KY	KY	KY							✓	✓	✓					
212	213	TOOLEY, RUTHY	Head	W	F	Nov 1835	64	Wd		2	2	KY	TN	KY				FARMER			✓	✓	✓	O	F	F	236	
		" ALBERT	Son	W	M	Feb 1868	32	M	11			KY	KY	KY				FARMER			✓	✓		R		F	237	
		" ALICE	Wife	W	F	May 1873	27	M	11	6	6	KY	KY	KY							✓	✓	✓					
		" ELLA	Dau	W	F	Mar 1890	10	S				KY	KY	KY				AT SCHOOL		4	✓	✓	✓					
		" WILLIE	Dau	W	F	Jan 1892	8	S				KY	KY	KY														
		" HOLLBERT	Son	W	M	Jan 1894	6	S				KY	KY	KY														
		" MARY	Dau	W	F	Jan 1896	4	S				KY	KY	KY														
		" THEODORE	Son	W	M	Feb 1898	2	S				KY	KY	KY														
		" FRANK	Son	W	M	Jan 1900	3/12	S				KY	KY	KY														
		RANIAN, CHARLEY	Boarder	W	M	Jan 1886	14	S				KY	KY	KY				AT SCHOOL		5	✓	✓	✓					
213	214	TOOLEY, MAGAR	Head	B	M	Mar 1848	52	M	32			KY	KY	KY				FARMER			X	X	✓	R		F	238	
		" CINDA	Wife	B	F	Jan 1841	59	M	32	3	3	KY	KY	KY							X	X	✓					
		" JEFF	Son	B	M	Jan 1866	34	S				KY	KY	KY				DAY LABOR			X	X	✓					
		" WOLFORD	Son	B	M	Jun 1884	16	S				KY	KY	KY				AT SCHOOL		5	✓	✓	✓					
		KIRKPATRICK, POLLY	Boarder	B	F	Jan 1830	70	Wd		1	0	KY	KY	KY							X	X	✓					

STATE - KENTUCKY
COUNTY - MONROE
Township or other division — CENTER POINT — Enumerator — JAMES I. WHITE

Supervisor's Dist. No. 107 Sheet No.
Enumeration Dist. No. 83

No. of Family	No. of Dwelling	NAME	Relation	Color	Sex	Date of Birth Mon/Yr	Age at last birthday	Marital Status	# Years married	Mother of how many children?	# of these children living	Place of birth (this person)	Father of this person	Mother of this person	Occupation 10 years +	Attended school in months	Can read	Can write	Speak English	Owned or Rent	Owned-no mortage / Farm or house	# of farm schedule
214	215	TOOLEY, FRANKLIN	Head	B	M	Mar 1876	24	M	7			KY	KY	KY	FARMER		✓	✓	✓	R	F	239
		" ELIZA	wife	B	F	Jan 1879	21	M	7	3	3	KY	KY	KY			✓	✓	✓			
		" ROBERT	Son	B	M	Dec 1893	6	S				KY	KY	KY								
		" MARY E	Dau	B	F	Jan 1897	3	S				KY	KY	KY								
		" ALBERT	Son	B	M	Jun 1899	11/12	S				KY	KY	KY								
215	216	GRAVES, SIMON	Head	B	M	Jan 1874	26	M	6			KY	KY	KY	DAY LABOR		✓	X	✓	R	H	
		" NANCY E.	wife	B	F	Jun 1880	19	M	6	3	2	KY	KY	KY			✓	✓	✓			
		" RADFORD	Son	B	M	Jan 1895	5	S				KY	KY	KY								
		" LILA J.	Dau	B	F	May 1897	3	S				KY	KY	KY								
216	217	BROWN, SARAH	Head	W	F	Oct 1864	35	Wd		5	4	KY	KY	KY	SEAMSTRESS		✓	✓		R	H	
		" LENNER	Dau	W	F	Aug 1884	15	S				KY	KY	KY	AT SCHOOL	5	✓	✓	✓			
		" OLIVER	Son	W	M	Apr 1886	14	S				KY	KY	KY	AT SCHOOL	5	✓	✓	✓			
		" REDFORD	Son	W	M	Mar 1891	9	S				KY	KY	KY								
		" EDA	Dau	W	F	Jun 1893	6	S				KY	KY	KY								
217	218	ANDERS, FRANK	Head	B	M	Jan 1876	24	M	2			KY	KY	KY	FARMER		X	X	✓	O	F	240
		" SARAH R.	wife	B	F	May 1878	22	M	2			KY	KY	KY			✓	✓	✓			
218	219	BLAIR, JOHN F.	HEAD	W	M	Aug 1854	46	M	25			KY	KY	KY	FARMER		✓	✓	✓	R	F	241
		" JANE	WIFE	W	F	Jun 1853	47	M	25	11	11	KY	KY	KY			X	X	✓			
		" MARY E.	Dau	W	F	Oct 1875	24	S				KY	KY	KY			X	X	✓			
		" ROBERT N.	Son	W	M	Apr 1879	21	S				KY	KY	KY	DAY LABOR		X	X	✓			
		" JAMES M.	Son	W	M	Feb 1881	19	S				KY	KY	KY	DAY LABOR		X	X	✓			
		" CATHERINE D.	Dau	W	F	Jul 1883	16	S				KY	KY	KY			X	X	✓			
		" GROVER C.	Son	W	M	Apr 1885	15	S				KY	KY	KY			X	X	✓			
		" MARTHA J.	Dau	W	F	Jan 1887	13	S				KY	KY	KY			X	X	✓			
		" HUE B.	Son	W	M	Oct 1889	10	S				KY	KY	KY			X	X	✓			
		" WALIUS S.	Son	W	M	Jan 1893	7	S				KY	KY	KY								

STATE - KENTUCKY
COUNTY - MONROE
Township or other division **CENTER POINT** Enumerator **JAMES T. WHITE**

Supervisor's Dist. No. **102** Sheet No.
Enumeration Dist. No. **83**

No. of Family	No. of Dwelling	NAME	Relation	Color	Sex	Date of Birth Mon/Yr	Age at last birthday	Marital Status	# Years married	Mother of how many children?	# of these children living	Place of birth (this person)	Father of this person	Mother of this person	Occupation	Months not employed	Attended school in months	Can read	Can write	Speak English	Owned or Rent	Owned-no mortgage	Farm or house	# of farm schedule
		BLAIR, HAWOOD	Son	W	M	Feb 1895	5	S				KY	KY	KY										
219	220	ANDERS, MORT	Head	B	M	Jan 1838	62	M	40			KY	KY	KY	FARMER			X	X	✓	O	F	F	242
		" CLARK	Wife	B	F	Jan 1845	55	M	40	7	7	KY	KY	KY				X	X	✓				
		" JOHN	Son	B	M	Feb 1863	37	S				KY	KY	KY	DAY LABOR			X	X	✓				
		" WOODFORD	Son	B	M	May 1873	27	S				KY	KY	KY	DAY LABOR			X	X	✓				
		" THE——(?)	Son	B	M	Jan 1875	25	S				KY	KY	KY	DAY LABOR			X	X	✓				
		" MARSHEL	Son	B	M	Jun 1881	19	S				KY	KY	KY	DAY LABOR			X	X	✓				
		" CLOIR (?)	Son	B	M	Feb 1884	16	S				KY	KY	KY	DAY LABOR			✓	✓	✓				
		" KATE	Dau	B	F	Jan 1889	11	S				KY	KY	KY	AT SCHOOL		5	✓	✓	✓				
		" HATTIE	Dau	B	F	Jan 1890	10	S				KY	KY	KY	AT SCHOOL		5	✓	✓	✓				
		" JOHN	GR-Son	B	M	May 1888	12	S				KY	TN	KY	AT SCHOOL		5	✓	✓	✓				
		" GEORGE M.	GR-Son	B	M	Apr 1891	9	S				KY	TN	KY										
220	221	GRIDER HARRIET	Head	W	F	Oct 1819	80	Wd		11	11	KY	KY	KY	FARMER			✓	✓	✓	O	F	F	243
		" NANCY	Dau	W	F	Nov 1859	40	S				KY	TN	KY				✓	✓	✓				
		" MARY	Dau	W	F	Jan 1862	38	S				KY	KY	KY				✓	✓	✓				
		" MATILDA	Dau	W	F	Jan 1864	36	S				KY	TN	KY				✓	✓	✓				
		" HARRIET	Dau	W	F	Jan 1863	37	S				KY	TN	KY				✓	✓	✓				
221	222	WALDON, JOSEPH A.	Head	W	M	Mar 1850	50	M	23			KY	VA	VA	FARMER			✓	✓	✓	R		F	244
		" ELLA (?)	Wife	W	F	Jan 1860	40	M	23	3	2	KY	TN	KY				✓	✓	✓				
		" FLORENCE	Dau	W	F	May 1884	16	S				KY	KY	KY	AT SCHOOL		7	✓	✓	✓				
222	223	HAMMER, MILTON	Head	W	M	Dec 1845	54	M	16			KY	KY	KY	FARMER			✓	✓	✓	R		F	245
		" PERMELA	Wife	W	F	Jan 1847	53	M	16	7	7	KY	KY	TN				✓	✓	✓				
		" FRANK	Son	W	M	Jan 1885	15	S				KY	KY	KY	AT SCHOOL		6	✓	✓	✓				
		" ANNIE	Dau	W	F	Feb 1886	14	S				KY	KY	KY	AT SCHOOL		9	✓	✓	✓				
		" LEE A.	Son	W	M	Feb 1888	12	S				KY	KY	KY	AT SCHOOL		9	✓	✓	✓				
		" MOLLY T.	Dau	W	F	Feb 1989	11	S				KY	KY	KY	AT SCHOOL		9	✓	✓	✓				

STATE - KENTUCKY
COUNTY - MONROE
Township or other division: CENTER POINT   Enumerator: JAMES T. WHITE

Supervisor's Dist. No. 102   Sheet No.
Enumeration Dist. No. 83

No. of Family	No. of Dwelling	NAME	Relation	Color	Sex	DATE OF BIRTH Mon/Yr	Age at last birthday	Marital Status	# Years married	Mother of how many children?	# of these children living	Place of birth (this person)	Father of this person	Mother of this person	Year of immigr.	# years in U.S.	Naturalization	OCCUPATION 10 years +	Months not employed	Attended school in months	Can read	Can write	Speak English	Owned or Rent	Owned - no mortage	Farm or house	# of farm schedule
		HAMMER, ALIE	Dau	W	F	Apr 1891	9	S				KY	KY	KY													
		" FRED P	Son	W	M	May 1893	7	S				KY	KY	KY													
		" JOE K.	Son	W	M	Jan 1895	5	S				KY	KY	KY													
223	224	(KELS?), JOSEPH	Head	W	M	Mar 1861	39	M	9			KY	TN	TN				FARMER			✓	✓	✓	O	F	F	246
		" SALLIE	Wife	W	F	Jun 1873	27	M	9	3	3	KY	KY	KY							✓	✓	✓				
		" LEON J.	Son	W	M	Jun 1892	7	S				KY	KY	KY													
		" KATE C.	Dau	W	F	Jan 1894	6	S				KY	KY	KY													
		" WILLIAM T.	Son	W	M	Feb 1897	3	S				KY	KY	KY													
224	225	KIDWELL, SAMUEL	Head	W	M	May 1861	39	M	18			KY	KY	KY				FARMER			✓	✓	✓	R	F		247
		" LUCY	Wife	W	F	Dec 1859	40	M	18	3	3	TN	KY	TN							✓	✓	✓				
		" TIP	Son	W	M	Dec 1883	16	S				KY	KY	TN				AT SCHOOL		4	✓	✓	✓				
		" HADE	Son	W	M	Jun 1886	14	S				KY	KY	TN				AT SCHOOL		5	✓	✓	✓				
		" KATE	Dau	W	F	May 1889	11	S				KY	KY	TN				AT SCHOOL		5	✓	✓	✓				
225	226	WILLIAMS, JOHN	Head	W	M	Oct 1862	57	M	16			KY	KY	KY				FARMER			✓	✓	✓	R	F		248
		" SALLIE	Wife	W	F	Jan 1863	57	M	16	6	6	KY	KY	KY							✓	✓	✓				
		" RUBY	Dau	W	F	Jan 1887	13	S				KY	KY	KY				AT SCHOOL		8	✓	✓					
		" WILLIAM	Son	W	M	Apr 1889	11	S				KY	KY	KY				AT SCHOOL		8	✓	✓	✓				
		" JOHN M.	Son	W	M	Jan 1892	8	S				KY	KY	KY													
		" VINCE B.	Son	W	M	May 1894	6	S				KY	KY	KY													
		" JOE A.	Son	W	M	Mar 1896	4	S				KY	KY	KY													
		" ALLIE L.	Dau	W	F	Jan 1898	2	S				KY	KY	KY													
226	227	GRAY, ALBERT	Head	W	M	May 1874	26	M	1			KY	KY	TN				FARMER			✓	✓	✓	O	F	F	249
		" LIDDIA	Wife	W	F	Jan 1878	22	M	1			KY	KY	KY							✓	✓	✓				
		" LILY	Mother	W	F	May 1854	46	Wd		3	3	TN	TN	TN							✓	✓	✓				
		" EMMA	Sister	W	F	Jun 1880	19	S				KY	KY	TN							✓	✓	✓				
		" EUNICE	Sister	W	F	Jan 1888	12	S				KY	KY	TN				AT SCHOOL		5	✓	✓	✓				

STATE - KENTUCKY
COUNTY - MONROE
Township or other division CENTER POINT Enumerator JAMES T. WHITE

Supervisor's Dist. No. 102 Sheet No.
Enumeration Dist. No. 83

No. of Family	No. of Dwelling	NAME	Relation	Color	Sex	DATE OF BIRTH Mon/Yr	Age at last birthday	Marital Status	# Years married	Mother of how many children?	# of these children living	Place of birth (this person)	Father of this person	Mother of this person	Year of immigr.	# years in U.S.	Naturalization	OCCUPATION 10 years +	Months not employed	Attended school in months	Can read	Can write	Speak English	Owned or Rent	Owned - no mortage	Farm or house	# of farm schedule	
		MONDAY, WILLIAM	WORK HAND	W	M	Jun 1865	35	S				KY	KY	TN				DAY LABOR		X	X		✓					
227	228	GRAY, GEORGE	HEAD	W	M	Jun 1849	51	M	26			KY	TN	TN				FARMER			✓	✓	✓	O	F	F	250	
		" LUCIE	WIFE	W	F	Mar 1850	50	M	26			KY	TN	KY							✓	✓	✓					
228	229	VANEVER, HELAND	Head	W	F	May 1831	69	Wd				KY	KY	VA							✓	✓	✓	O	F	H		
		WATSON, ZORA(?)	Servant	W	F	Jan 1878	22	S				KY	KY	KY				SERVANT			✓	✓	✓					
229	230	ALONZO, RICHARD	Head	W	M	May 1855	45	M	11			KY	KY	KY				MERCHANT			✓	✓	✓	O	F	F	251	
		" MARY E.	Wife	W	F	Mar 1869	31	M	11	6	5	KY	KY	KY							✓	✓	✓					
		" BERA	Dau	W	F	Jul 1889	10	S				KY	KY	KY				AT SCHOOL		7	✓	✓	✓					
		" RALF	Son	W	M	Jan 1892	8	S				KY	KY	KY														
		" HERMAN	Son	W	M	Nov 1893	6	S				KY	KY	KY														
		" WILLIAM	Son	W	M	May 1896	4	S				KY	KY	KY														
		" CLINT	Son	W	M	Jan 1900	4/12	S				KY	KY	KY														
230	231	HEAD, JOHN R.	HEAD	W	M	Jan 1850	50	Wd				KY	TN	TN				FARMER			✓	✓	✓	R	F	252	
		" MARY	Dau	W	F	Jun 1881	18	S				KY	KY	TN				AT SCHOOL		6	✓	✓	✓					
		" WILLIAM J.	Son	W	M	Mar 1885	15	S				KY	KY	TN				AT SCHOOL		3	✓	✓	✓					
		" ROXIE	Dau	W	F	Oct 1889	10	S				KY	KY	TN				AT SCHOOL		5	X	X	✓					
		" MIRTLE	Dau	W	F	Jan 1892	8	0				KY	KY	TN														
231	232	WILLIAMS, ALBERT	HEAD	W	M	Jan 1838	62	M	34			IND	VA	VA				FARMER			✓	✓	✓	O	F	F	253	
		" MARY	WIFE	W	F	May 1839	61	M	34	6	5	VA	VA	VA							✓	✓	✓					
		" REFIA (?)	Dau	W	F	Dec 1867	32	S				VA	IND	VA				POSTMISTRESS			✓	✓	✓					
		" WINSTON	Son	W	M	Jul 1872	27	S				VA	IND	VA				MERCHANT			✓	✓	✓					
		" MAGGIE	Dau	W	F	Aug 1877	22	S				KY	IND	VA				SEAMSTRESS			✓	✓	✓					
232	233	CRAFFORD, WILLIAM	Head	W	M	Jan 1864	36	M	14			KY	KY	KY				DAY LABOR			✓	✓	✓	R	H		
		" DORA	Wife	W	F	Aug 1861	38	M	14	6	6	KY	KY	KY							✓	✓	✓					
		" WALTER V.	Son	W	M	Jan 1887	13	S				KY	KY	KY				AT SCHOOL		3	✓	✓	✓					
		" NANNIE B.	Dau	W	F	May 1889	11	S				KY	KY	KY				AT SCHOOL		5	✓	✓	✓					

STATE - KENTUCKY
COUNTY - MONROE
Township or other division CENTER POINT Enumerator JAMES T. WHITE

Supervisor's Dist. No. 102 Sheet No.
Enumeration Dist. No. 83

No. of Family	No. of Dwelling	NAME	Relation	Color	Sex	Date of Birth Mon/Yr	Age at last birthday	Marital Status	# Years married	Mother of how many children?	# of these children living	Place of birth (this person)	Father of this person	Mother of this person	Year of immigr.	# years in U.S.	Naturalization	Occupation 10 years +	Months not employed	Attended school in months	Can read	Can write	Speak English	Owned or Rent	Owned -no mortage	Farm or house	# of farm schedule
		CRAFFORD, CLERNCE	Son	W	M	Apr 1891	9	S				KY	KY	KY													
		" FRED	Son	W	M	Jun 1893	7	S				KY	KY	KY													
		" EVA	Dau	W	F	Jun 1895	5	S				KY	KY	KY													
		" KATE	Dau	W	F	Mar 1897	3	S				KY	KY	KY													
233	234	CARY, PERRY	Head	W	M	Jan 1870	30	M	3			KY	KY	KY				FARMER			✓	✓	✓	R		F	254
		" DOLLA A.	Wife	W	F	Mar 1876	24	M	3	1	1	KY	KY	TN							✓	✓	✓				
		" CORA	Dau	W	F	Dec 1898		S				KY	KY	KY													
234	235	RICHARDSON, WILLIAM	Head	W	M	Oct 1849	50	M	9			KY	KY	KY				PHYSICIAN			✓	✓	✓	O		F	255
		" MARTHA	Wife	W	F	Feb 1869	31	M	9	5	5	KY	KY	KY							✓	✓	✓				
		" FRANK	Son	W	M	Sep 1891	8	S				KY	KY	KY													
		" TABITHA	Dau	W	F	Oct 1893	7	S				KY	KY	KY													
		" MINNIE	Dau	W	F	May 1894	6	S				KY	KY	KY													
		" LOVVIE	Dau	W	F	Oct 1894	5	S				KY	KY	KY													
		" MARY	Dau	W	F	Jun 1899	1	S				KY	KY	KY													
235	236	MONDAY, JANE	Head	W	F	Mar 1840	60	Wd				KY	KY	KY				WASHING			✓	✓	✓	R		H	
236	237	PAGE, JOHN	Head	W	M	Feb 1880	20	M	1			KY	KY	KY				CARPENTER		8	✓	✓	✓	R		H	
		" FANNIE	Wife	W	F	Dec 1880	19	M	1			TN	TN	TN							✓	✓	✓				
237	238	DODSON, STOCKLON?	Head	W	M	Jan 1827	73	M	46			KY	KY	KY				FARMER			✓	✓	✓	O		F	256
		" MARTHA	Wife	W	F	Aug 1831	68	M	46	11	8	KY	KY	KY							✓	✓	✓				
		" MARY	Dau	W	F	Feb 1867	33	S				KY	KY	KY							✓	✓	✓				
		" ELEN I. A.	Dau	W	F	Feb 1871	29	S				KY	KY	KY							✓	✓	✓				
		" CLARK F.	Son	W	M	Nov 1874	25	S				KY	KY	KY				FARMER			✓	✓	✓	R		F	257
238	239	DODSON, SU—	Head	W	M	Dec 1861	38	S				KY	KY	KY				CARPENTER		6	✓	✓	✓	R		H	
239	240	McMILLAND, JAMES	Head	W	M	Jan 1870	30	M	5			KY	KY	KY				DAY LABOR			X	X	✓	R		H	
		" ELIZA	Wife	W	F	Jun 1875	24	M	5			KY	KY	KY							✓	✓	✓				
240	241	WILLIAMS, HA—	Head	B	M	Jul 1868	31	M	8			KY	TN	TN				DAY LABOR		7	✓	✓	✓	O		H	

TWELFTH CENSUS OF THE UNITED STATES 1900

STATE - KENTUCKY
COUNTY - MONROE
Township or other division — CENTER POINT — Enumerator JAMES T. WHITE

Supervisor's Dist. No. 102   Sheet No.
Enumeration Dist. No. 83

No. of Family	No. of Dwelling	Name	Relation	Color	Sex	Date of Birth Mon/Yr	Age at last birthday	Marital Status	# Years married	Mother of how many children?	# of these children living	Place of birth (this person)	Father of this person	Mother of this person	Occupation	Attended school	Can read	Can write	Speak English	Owned or Rent	Farm or house	# of farm schedule
		WILLIAMS, MARY	Wife	B	F	Mar 1870	30	M	8	3	3	KY	KY	TN		X	X		✓			
		" JOHN M.	Son	B	M	Jan 1894	6	S				KY	KY	KY								
		" JAMES R.	Son	B	M	Jun 1897	3	S				KY	KY	KY								
		" MARK	Son	B	M	Feb 1899	1	S				KY	KY	KY								
241	242	LOGAN, SQUIRE D.	Head	W	M	Jan 1863	37	M	4			KY	KY	KY	FARMER	✓	✓	✓		R	F	258
		" LUCIE	Wife	W	F	Aug 1877	22	M	4	3	2	KY	KY	KY		✓	✓	✓				
		" FRED	Son	W	M	Mar 1897	3	S				KY	KY	KY								
		" FRANK	Son	W	M	Apr 1900	2/12	S				KY	KY	KY								
		HALLCELL, PEARL	Servant	B	F	Sep 1878	21	S				KY	KY	KY			✓	✓	✓			
242	243	MOSS, MARION	Head	W	M	Oct 1872	27	M	3			TN	TN	TN	DAY LABOR 6		✓	✓	✓	R	H	
		" ADDA	Wife	W	F	Jan 1879	21	M	3	2	2	KY	TN	TN			✓	✓	✓			
		" CONNIA J.	Dau	W	F	Jun 1895	5	S				KY	TN	KY								
		" GEORGE F.	Son	W	M	Aug 1899	1	S				KY	TN	KY								
243	244	CROW, ROBBERT	Head	W	M	May 1845	55	M	30			TN	TN	TN	FARMER		✓	✓	✓	O	F	259
		" MARGARET	Wife	W	F	May 1845	55	M	30			TN	TN	TN			✓	✓	✓			
		HARIS, LANDONA	Sister	W	F	Aug 1852	48	Wd		3	1	TN	TN	TN			✓	✓	✓			
		HOFFMAN, MARY	Mother-in-law	W	F	Nov 1825	74	Wd		5	4	TN	VA	VA			✓	✓	✓			
		" GEORGE	Nephew	W	M	Jun 1878	21	S				TN	TN	TN	SCHOOL TEACHER		✓	✓	✓			
		" JESSE	Nephew	W	M	Oct 1883	16	S				KY	TN	TN	At School 8	✓	✓	✓				
		HARIS, JOHN M.	Nephew	W	M	Sep 1877	22	S				KY	TN	TN	FARMER		✓	✓	✓	R	F	260
244	245	FITZGEARLS, THOMAS	Head	W	M	Jul 1867	32	M	9			KY	KY	KY	FARMER		X	X	✓	R	F	261
		" ELLIZZIKBETH	Wife	W	F	Jan 1873	27	M	9	1	1	KY	TN	TN			X	X	✓			
245	246	VIBERT, HARVEY	Head	W	M	Jan 1869	31	M	6			KY	KY	KY	FARMER		X	X	✓	R	F	262
		" MINNIE	Wife	W	F	May 1870	30	M	6	2	1	KY	KY	TN			✓	✓	✓			
		" MARTHA	Dau	W	F	Jan 1896	4	S				TN	KY	KY								
246	247	CORRO, BUREL	Head	W	M	Jan 1876	24	M	10?			TN	TN	TN	FARMER		✓	✓	✓	O	F	263

TWELFTH CENSUS OF THE UNITED STATES 1900

— 237 —

STATE - KENTUCKY
COUNTY - MONROE
Township or other division — CENTER POINT Enumerator — JAMES T. WHITE

Supervisor's Dist. No. 102 Sheet No.
Enumeration Dist. No. 83

No. of Family	No. of Dwelling	NAME	Relation	Color	Sex	DATE OF BIRTH Mon/Yr	Age at last birthday	Marital Status	# Years married	Mother of how many children?	# of these children living	Place of birth (this person)	Father of this person	Mother of this person	Year of immigr.	# years in U.S.	Naturalization	OCCUPATION 10 years +	Months not employed	Attended school in months	Can read	Can write	Speak English	Owned or Rent	Owned -no mortage	Farm or house	# of farm schedule
		CORRO, LUCIE A.	Wife	W	F	APR 1874	26	M	10	4	4	KY	KY	KY							✓	✓	✓				
		" NANNIE	Dau	W	F	Feb 1891	9	S				KY	TN	KY													
		" ELIZZIEBETH	Dau	W	F	AUG 1893	6	S				KY	TN	KY													
		" JOHN	Son	W	M	Feb 1896	4	S				KY	TN	KY													
		" MATTIE	Dau	W	F	MAR 1899	1	S				KY	TN	KY													
		FITZGEARLS, MARY	Mother in law	W	F	Sep 1830	69	Wd				KY	KY	KY				FARMER			✓	✓		O	E	F	264
		" HICE	Bro-in-law	W	M	JAN 1878	22	S				KY	KY	KY				DAY LABOR			✓	✓					
		MUSE, FRANK	Workhand	W	M	Jul 1887	12	S				KY	TN	KY				DAY LABOR			✓	X	✓				
247	248	GRAY, ROBERT	HEAD	W	M	JAN 1860	40	M	19			TN	TN	TN				FARMER			✓	✓		R		F	265
		" THURSEY	Wife	W	F	MAY 1868	32	M	19	6	5	TN	TN	TN							✓	✓					
		" SHELLEY	Son	W	M	DEC 1883	17	S				TN	TN	TN				AT SCHOOL		4	✓	✓					
		" MINNIE	Dau	W	F	DEC 1888	11	S				OREGON	TN	TN				AT SCHOOL		4	✓	✓					
		" FRANK	Son	W	M	NOV 1890	9	S				OREGON	TN	TN													
		" HUBERT	Son	W	M	JUN 1895	4	S				TN	TN	TN													
		" CLURA	Son	W	M	Jul 1896	3	S				TN	TN	TN													
248	249	FITZGEARLDS, LEE	HEAD	W	M	NOV 1872	27	M	5			KY	KY	KY				FARM LABOR			✓	✓		R		H	
		" MARSY L.	WIFE	W	F	Jul 1877	23	M	5	2	1	KY	KY	KY							✓	✓					
		" LUIS D.	Son	W	M	Aug 1895	4					KY	KY	KY													
249	250	GEARLDS, JOHN	Head	W	M	APR 1860	40	M	12			KY	KY	KY				FARMER			✓	✓		R		F	264
		" MARY	Wife	W	F	APR 1868	32	M	12	6	5	TN	TN	TN							✓	✓					
		" NANNIE B.	Dau	W	F	Jun 1889	11	S				KY	KY	TN				AT SCHOOL		5	✓	✓	✓				
		" JAMES O.	Son	W	M	APR 1890	10	S				KY	KY	TN				AT SCHOOL		5	✓	✓	✓				
		" BETTIE	Dau	W	F	Sep 1894	5	S				KY	KY	TN													
		" BRYAN	Son	W	M	Nov 1896	3	S				KY	KY	TN													
		" AMIE	Dau	W	F	APR 1899	1	S				KY	KY	TN													
250	251	MURPHY, THOMAS	Head	W	M	APR 1875	25	M				KY	KY	KY				FARMER			✓	✓	✓	R		F	267

STATE - KENTUCKY
COUNTY - MONROE
Township or other division: CENTER POINT   Enumerator: JAMES T. WHITE

Supervisor's Dist. No. 102 Sheet No.
Enumeration Dist. No. 83

No. of Family	No. of Dwelling	NAME	Relation	Color	Sex	DATE OF BIRTH Mon/Yr	Age at last birthday	Marital Status	# Years married	Mother of how many children?	# of these children living	Place of birth (this person)	Father of this person	Mother of this person	Year of immigr. / # years in U.S. / Naturalization	OCCUPATION 10 years +	Months not employed	Attended school in months	Can read	Can write	Speak English	Owned or Rent	Owned -no mortgage	Farm or house	# of farm schedule
		MURPHY, AMERICA	Wife	W	F	Jan 1882	18	M		1	1	KY	NC	KY					✓	✓	✓				
		" BABY	Dau	W	F	May 1900	1/12	S				KY	KY	KY											
251	252	BIGGERSTAFF, PORTER	Head	W	M	Dec 1872	27	M	2			KY	KY	KY		FARMER			✓ X ✓			R		F	268
		" LARRY	Wife	W	F	Aug 1879	20	M	2	1	1	KY	KY	KY					✓	✓	✓				
		" ARPHY	Dau	W	F	Aug 1898	1	S				KY	KY	KY											
		WHITE, WALTER	Boarder	W	M	Jan 1882	18	S				KY	KY	KY		DAY LABOR			✓	✓	✓				
252	253	WHITE, PERRY D.	Head	W	M	Oct 1857	42	M	23			KY	KY	KY		FARMER			✓	✓	✓	R		F	269
		" WANDA	Wife	W	F	Jan 1865	35	M	23	8	8	KY	KY	KY					X X ✓						
		" MARTHA M.	Dau	W	F	Jun 18_4	15	S				KY	KY	KY					✓	✓	✓				
		" NANCY A.	Dau	W	F	Aug 1886	13	S				KY	KY	KY		AT SCHOOL		3	✓	✓	✓				
		" ELBERT P.	Son	W	M	Aug 1888	11	S				KY	KY	KY		AT SCHOOL		3	✓	✓	✓				
		" BESSE E.	Dau	W	F	Feb 1893	7	S				KY	KY	KY											
		" JAMES D.	Son	W	M	Dec 1895	4	S				KY	KY	KY											
		" LUCY	Dau	W	F	May 1897	3	S				KY	KY	KY											
		" WILLIAM	Son	W	M	May 1899	1	S				KY	KY	KY											
253	254	HEAD, GEORGE B.	Head	W	M	Mar 1869	31	M	12			KY	KY	KY		FARMER			✓	✓		R		F	270
		" MARGARET 1	Wife	W	F	Jan 1870	30	M	12	3	3	KY	KY	KY					✓	✓					
		" VIRGIL	Son	W	M	May 1889	11	S				KY	KY	KY		AT SCHOOL		4	✓	✓					
		" NEUMAN	Son	W	M	Jan 1893	7	S				KY	KY	KY											
		" ADER E.	Dau	W	F	Jan 1898	2	S				KY	KY	KY											
254	255	McCOY, JAMES P.	Head	W	M	Jun 1645	54	M	27			NC	NC	NC		FARMER			✓	✓	✓	O	F	F	271
		" MARTHA F.	Wife	W	F	May 1854	46	M	27	7	5	KY	TN	KY					✓	✓	✓				
		" JOHN T.	Son	W	M	Sep 1886	13	S				KY	NC	KY		AT SCHOOL		4	✓	✓	✓				
		" ROBERT L.	Son	W	M	Oct 1887	12	S				KY	NC	KY		AT SCHOOL		4	X X ✓						
		" MIRTTIE B.	Dau	W	F	Dec 1891	8	S				KY	NC	KY											
255	256	STRODE, FERD N.	Head	W	M	Jul 1848	51	M	16			KY	KY	KY		FARMER			✓	✓		O	F	F	272

TWELFTH CENSUS OF THE UNITED STATES 1900

STATE - KENTUCKY
COUNTY - MONROE
Township or other division CENTER POINT   Enumerator JAMES T. WHITE

Supervisor's Dist. No. 102 Sheet No.
Enumeration Dist. No. 83

No. of Family	No. of Dwelling	NAME	Relation	Color	Sex	DATE OF BIRTH Mon/Yr	Age at last birthday	Marital Status	# Years married	Mother of how many children?	# of these children living	Place of birth [this person]	Father of this person	Mother of this person	Year of immigr.	# years in U.S.	Naturalization	OCCUPATION 10 years +	Months not employed	Attended school in months	Can read	Can write	Speak English	Owned or Rent	Owned -no mortgage	Farm or house	# of farm schedule
		STRODE, MARY E.	Wife	W	F	Jun 1856	43	M	16	3	2	KY	KY	KY							✓	✓	✓				
		" JOE B.	Son	W	M	Jul 1890	9	S				KY	KY	KY								✓	✓				
		" JESSE T.	Son	W	M	Sep 1892	7	S				KY	KY	KY													
256	257	CLOYD, MORE (?)	Head	W	M	Mar 1872	28	M	4			KY	KY	KY				FARMER			✓	✓		R		F	273
		" DAPPIE	Wife	W	F	Jan 1873	27	M	4	2	1	KY	KY	MC							✓	✓					
		" CLARNCE	Son	W	M	Aug 1897	2	S				KY	KY	KY													
257	258	BIGGERSTAFF, SARAH	Head	W	F	Jan 1844	56	Wd		5	4	KY	KY	KY				FARMER			✓	✓		O		F	274
		" JEROME D.	Son	W	M	Sep 1863	36	S				KY	KY	KY				FARMER			✓	✓		O		F	275
		" DANIEL W.	Son	W	M	Oct 1869	30	S				KY	KY	KY				FARM LABOR			✓	✓					
258	259	LANEY, POKE D.	Head	W	M	Oct 1875	24	M	1			KY	KY	KY				FARMER			✓	✓		R		F	276
		" BETTIE	Wife	W	F	Aug 1873	26	M	1	2	2	KY	KY	KY							✓	✓	✓				
		" REDFORD	Son	W	M	Mar 1900	2/12	S				KY	KY	KY													
		" -BABY-	Dau	W	F	Mar 1900	2/12	S				KY	KY	KY													
		COLMAN, JAMES	Workhand	W	M	Mar 1879	21	S				KY	KY	KY				DAY LABOR			X	X	✓				
259	260	WHITE, SAMUEL M.	Head	W	M	Jun 1851	48	M	23			KY	KY	KY				FARMER			X	X	✓	O		F	277
		" SARAH F.	Wife	W	F	Oct 1852	47	M	23	6	6	KY	KY	KY							X	X	✓				
		" LARRY J.	Dau	W	F	Apr 1876	24	S				KY	KY	KY							✓	✓					
		" MARTHA B.	Dau	W	F	Oct 1877	22	S				KY	KY	KY							✓	✓	✓				
		" ALFORD C.	Son	W	M	Sep 1881	18	S				KY	KY	KY				AT SCHOOL		5	✓	✓	✓				
		" WILLIAM S.	Son	W	M	Jan 1882	17	S				KY	KY	KY				AT SCHOOL		3	✓	✓	✓				
		" ROBBERT E.	Son	W	M	Nov 1890	9	S				KY	KY	KY													
		MORE, GEORGE	Workhand	W	M	Jan 1880	20	S				KY	KY	KY				DAY LABOR			✓	✓	✓				
260	261	COLMAN, PORTER	Head	W	M	Jan 1866	34	M	12	1	1	TN	TN	TN				FARMER			X	X	✓	R		F	278
		" NANCY	Wife	W	F	Jun 1872	28	M	12			KY	KY	KY							X	X	✓				
		" FLORNCE	Dau	W	F	Aug 1889	10	S				KY	TN	KY				AT SCHOOL		5	✓	✓	✓				
261	262	KIRK, ANDREW	Head	B	M	Jan 1848	52	M	30			KY	KY	KY				FARMER			X	X	✓	O		F	279

STATE - KENTUCKY
COUNTY - MONROE
Township or other division CENTER POINT Enumerator JAMES T. WHITE

Supervisor's Dist. No. 102 Sheet No. _____
Enumeration Dist. No. 83 _____

No. of Family / No. of Dwelling	NAME	Relation	Color	Sex	Date of Birth Mon/Yr	Age at last birthday	Marital Status	# Years married	Mother of how many children?	# of these children living	Place of birth (this person)	Father of this person	Mother of this person	Year of immigr.	# years in U.S.	Naturalization	OCCUPATION 10 years +	Months not employed	Attended school in months	Can read	Can write	Speak English	Owned or Rent	Owned -no mortage	Farm or house	# of farm schedule
	KIRK, LUCINDA	wife	B	F	Jan 1850	50	M	30	12	3	KY	KY	KY							X	X	✓				
	" SALLIE	Dau	B	F	Sep 1877	22	S				KY	KY	KY							✓	✓	✓				
262 263	SHORT, JOHN	Head	W	M	Aug 1845	54	M	30			KY	TN	KY				FARMER			✓	✓	✓	R		F	280
	" SUSAN A.	wife	W	F	Mar 1844	56	M	30	4	4	TN	TN	TN							✓	✓	✓				
	" WILLIAM L.	Son	W	M	Nov 1878	21	S				KY	KY	TN				FARM LABOR			✓	✓	✓				
	" GLATHE	Dau	W	F	Feb 1880	20	S				KY	KY	TN				AT SCHOOL		1	✓	✓	✓				
	" ROBERT	Son	W	M	Jan 1883	17	S				KY	KY	TN				AT SCHOOL		7	✓	✓	✓				
	" JOHN F.	Son	W	M	Oct 1885	14	S				KY	KY	TN				AT SCHOOL		7	✓	✓	✓				
263 264	GEARLDS, LUIS F.	Head	W	M	Apr 1672	28	M	3			KY	KY	KY				FARMER			✓	✓	✓	R		F	281
	" VICTORIA	Wife	W	F	Apr 1874	26	M	3	2	1	TN	KY	TN							X	X	✓				
	" DULCY	Dau	W	F	Sep 18--	--	S				KY	TN	KY													
264 265	PEDIT, EDNON F.	Head	W	M	Apr 1856	44	M	19			KY	TN	KY				FARMER			✓	✓	✓	O	M	F	282
	" LUCY L.	Wife	W	F	Feb 1860	40	M	19	8	8	KY	KY	KY							X	X	✓				
	" ENER	Dau	W	F	Dec 1881	18	S				KY	KY	KY				AT SCHOOL		5	✓	✓	✓				
	" WILLIAM C	Son	W	M	Nov 1884	15	S				KY	KY	KY				AT SCHOOL		2	✓	✓	✓				
	" RILDA	Dau	W	F	Jul 1886	13	S				KY	KY	KY				AT SCHOOL		5	✓	✓	✓				
	" MARY M	Dau	W	F	Oct 1888	11	S				KY	KY	KY				AT SCHOOL		5	✓	✓	✓				
	" LEANN	Dau	W	F	Jul 1889	10	S				KY	KY	KY				AT SCHOOL		8	✓	✓	✓				
	" JOE C.	Son	W	M	Nov 1891	8	S				KY	KY	KY													
	" CORA C.	Dau	W	F	Jan 1896	4	S				KY	KY	KY													
	" DOTIA O.	Dau	W	F	Aug 1898	1	S				KY	KY	KY													
265 266	MUSE, JOHN W.	Head	W	M	Apr 1853	47	M	25			KY	KY	KY				DAY LABOR	4		✓	✓	✓	R		H	
	" MARY	wife	W	F	Mar 1853	47	M	25	4	4	KY	KY	KY							✓	✓	✓				
	" CHING	Dau	W	F	Aug 1879	20	S				KY	KY	KY							✓	✓	✓				
	" MERTLE	Dau	W	F	Sep 1881	18	S				KY	KY	KY							✓	✓	✓				
	" FRANK	Son	W	M	Jul 1885	14	S				KY	KY	KY				DAY LABOR			X	X	✓				

TWELFTH CENSUS OF THE UNITED STATES 1900

STATE - KENTUCKY
COUNTY - MONROE
Township or other division CENTER POINT   Enumerator JAMES T. WHITE

Supervisor's Dist. No. _102_ Sheet No. _____
Enumeration Dist. No. _83_ _____

No. of Family	No. of Dwelling	NAME	Relation	Color	Sex	Date of Birth Mon/Yr	Age at last birthday	Marital Status	# Years married	Mother of how many children?	# of these children living	Birthplace (this person)	Father of this person	Mother of this person	Year of immigr.	# years in U.S.	Naturalization	Occupation 10 years +	Months not employed	Attended school in months	Can read	Can write	Speak English	Owned or Rent	Owned – no mortgage	Farm or house	# of farm schedule
		MUSE, LEE	Son	W	M	Mar 1889	11	S				KY	KY	KY				At School		2	X	X	✓				
266	267	MOORE, AMBER	Head	W	M	Jan 1872	28	M	1			KY	KY	KY				Farmer			X	X	✓	O	F	F	283
		" MARY	Wife	W	F	Sep 1881	18	M	1	1	1	KY	KY	KY							X	✓	✓				
		" ADA	Dau	W	F	Dec 1899	1	S				KY	KY	KY													
267	268	MONDAY, JOHN A.	Head	W	M	Sep 1855	44	M	25			KY	KY	KY				Farmer			✓	✓	✓	O	F	F	284
		" HITTIE	Wife	W	F	May 1860	40	M	25	13	11	KY	KY	KY							✓	X	✓				
		" ELESON	Son	W	M	May 1876	24	S				KY	KY	KY				Day Labor			✓	✓	✓				
		" ISAM	Son	W	M	Jan 1880	20	S				KY	KY	KY				Farmer			✓	✓	✓	R		F	285
		" WILLIAM	Son	W	M	Apr 1882	18	S				KY	KY	KY				Day Labor			✓	X	✓				
		" SARAH	Dau	W	F	Apr 1884	16	S				KY	KY	KY				At School		5	✓	✓	✓				
		" ELIGA	Son	W	M	Jan 1886	14	S				KY	KY	KY				At School		5	✓	X	✓				
		" PEARL	Dau	W	F	May 1888	12	S				KY	KY	KY				At School		5	✓	✓	✓				
		" LONA B.	Dau	W	F	Jun 1890	10	S				KY	KY	KY				At School		5	✓	X	✓				
		" MAUDY	Dau	W	F	Jun 1891	8	S				KY	KY	KY													
		" THOMAS	Son	W	M	May 1894	6	S				KY	KY	KY													
		" JOHN	Son	W	M	Mar 1897	3	S				KY	KY	KY													
		" LARRY	Dau	W	F	Aug 1899	10/12	S				KY	KY	KY													
268	269	BAYSE, THOMAS C.	Head	W	M	Jan 1838	62	M	36			KY	KY	KY							✓	✓		R		H	
		" MARY A.	Wife	W	F	Jan 1839	61	M	36	4	4	MO	KY	KY							✓	✓					
		" WILLIAM H.	Son	W	M	Jul 1862	37	S				KY	KY	MO				Day Labor			✓	✓					
		" VIRGINIA C.	Dau	W	F	Dec 1874	25	S				KY	KY	MO				Seamstress			✓	✓	✓				
		" ELZADA	Dau	W	F	Jan 1878	22	S				KY	KY	MO				At School		7	✓	✓	✓				
269	270	GENTRY, WILLIAM	Head	W	M	May 1847	53	M	30			KY	TN	KY				Farmer			✓	✓	✓	O	F	F	286
		" HELEN	Wife	W	F	Sep 1841	58	M	30	11	7	KY	KY	KY							✓	✓	✓				
		" CORA	Dau	W	F	Jul 1877	22	S				KY	KY	KY							✓	✓	✓				
		" DAISY	Dau	W	F	Dec 1881	18	S				KY	KY	KY				At School		3	✓	✓	✓				

STATE - KENTUCKY
COUNTY - MONROE
Township or other division CENTER POINT Enumerator JAMES T. WHITE

Supervisor's Dist. No. 10Y Sheet No.
Enumeration Dist. No. 83

No. of Family	No. of Dwelling	NAME	Relation	Color	Sex	DATE OF BIRTH Mon/Yr	Age at last birthday	Marital Status	# Years married	Mother of how many children?	# of these children living	Place of birth (this person)	Father of this person	Mother of this person	Year of immigr.	# years in U.S.	Naturalization	OCCUPATION 10 years +	Months not employed	Attended school in months	Can read	Can write	Speak English	Owned or Rent	Owned -no mortage	Farm or house	# of farm schedule
		GENTRY, WALTER	Son	W	M	Mar 1884	16	S				KY	KY	KY				AT SCHOOL		3	✓	✓	✓				
		" CLYDE	Son	W	M	Feb 1886	14	S				KY	KY	KY				AT SCHOOL		9	✓	✓	✓				
		MURPHY, LUCY	Neice	W	F	Sep 1883	16	S				KY	KY	KY				AT SCHOOL		9	✓	✓	✓				
		" PENDA (?)	Nephew	W	M	Jun 1877	22	S				KY	KY	KY				AT SCHOOL		5	✓	✓	✓				
270	271	RICHARDSON, ROBERT	Head	W	M	Jun 1862	37	M	8			KY	TN	KY				FARMER			✓	✓	✓	O	F	F	287
		" LUCIE	Wife	W	F	Jan 1871	29	M	8			KY	KY	KY							✓	✓	✓				
		" JULIA A.	Mother	W	F	Sep 1826	73	Wd		15	7	KY	KY	KY							✓	✓	✓				
		" THOMAS	Brother	W	M	Oct 1868	31	S				KY	KY	KY				MERCHANT			✓	✓	✓	O	F	F	288
		HUDDLESTON, RILDA	Boarder	W	F	Mar 1881	19	S				KY	KY	KY				SERVANT			✓	✓	✓				
		BOLTON, OSCAR	Workhand	W	M	Mar 1880	20	S				KY	KY	KY				DAY LABOR			✓	✓	✓				
271	272	SCOTT, WILLIAM	Head	W	M	Nov 1875	26	M	6			KY	KY	KY				DAY LABOR			✓	✓	✓	R		H	
		" BELLE	Wife	W	F	Jul 1876	23	M	6	3	3	KY	KY	KY							✓	✓	✓				
		" SARAH	Dau	W	F	Jul 1894	5	S				KY	KY	KY													
		" BUROS (?)	Dau	W	F	May 1896	4	S				KY	KY	KY													
		" JOHN W.	Son	W	M	Dec 1899	6/12	S				KY	KY	KY													
272	273	MILUM, WILLIAM B.	Head	W	M	Jul 1845	54	Wd				KY	KY	KY				FARMER			✓	✓	✓	O	M	F	289
		" WILLIAM H.	Son	W	M	Feb 1876	24	M	1			KY	KY	KY				FARM LABOR			✓	✓	✓				
		" DADE	Wife	W	F	May 1876	24	M	1	1	1	KY	KY	KY							✓	✓	✓				
		" NANCY B.	Dau	W	F	Aug 1898	1	S				KY	KY	KY													
273	274	COE, NANCY	Head	W	F	Dec 1842	58	Wd		11	10	KY	KY	KY				FARMER			X	X	✓	R		F	290
		" WALTER	Son	W	M	Nov 1882	17	S				KY	KY	KY				AT SCHOOL		4	✓	✓	✓				
		" JESSE	Son	W	M	Jan 1885	15	S				KY	KY	KY				AT SCHOOL		4	✓	✓	✓				
		" WILLIAM	Son	W	M	Nov 1882	17	S				KY	KY	KY				AT SCHOOL		4	✓	✓	✓				
274	275	CRAFFORD, PETE	Head	W	M	Mar 1856	44	M	21			KY	KY	KY				FARMER			X	X	✓	R		F	291
		" MARTHA J.	Wife	W	F	Mar 1856	44	M	21	4	4	KY	KY	KY							✓	✓	✓				
		" MAGGIE G.	Dau	W	F	Apr 1880	20	S				KY	KY	KY							✓	✓	✓				

STATE - KENTUCKY
COUNTY - MONROE
Township or other division CENTER POINT Enumerator JAMES T. WHITE

Supervisor's Dist. No. _102_ Sheet No. _____
Enumeration Dist. No. _83_

No. of Family	No. of Dwelling	NAME	Relation	Color	Sex	DATE OF BIRTH Mon/Yr	Age at last birthday	Marital Status	# Years married	Mother of how many children?	# of these children living	Place of birth (this person)	Father of this person	Mother of this person	Year of immigr.	# years in U.S.	Naturalization	OCCUPATION 10 years +	Months not employed	Attended school in months	Can read	Can write	Speak English	Owned or Rent	Owned – no mortage	Farm or house	# of farm schedule
		CRAFFORD, WILLIAM O.	Son	W	M	Aug 1883	16	S				KY	KY	KY				FARM LABOR			X	X	✓				
		" HENRYETTA	Dau	W	F	Jan 1886	14	S				KY	KY	KY				AT SCHOOL		2	✓	✓					
		" NANCY E.	Dau	W	F	Apr 1884	16	M				KY	KY	KY							✓	✓					
		HARIS, WILLIAM R.	Son-in-law	W	M	Mar 1880	20	M				KY	KY	KY				DAY LABOR			✓	✓					
276	276	CANNON, JOE	Head	W	M	Mar 1852	48	M	18			KY	KY	KY				DAY LABORER	0		✓	✓		R		H	
		" NANCY	Wife	W	F	Apr 1851	49	M	18	7	7	KY	KY	KY							X	X	✓				
		" MIBERY (?) L.	Dau	W	F	Apr 1885	15	S				KY	KY	KY				AT SCHOOL		1	X	X	✓				
		" NANCY	Dau	W	F	Dec 1888	11	S				KY	KY	KY				AT SCHOOL		2	X	X	✓				
		" JAMES	Son	W	M	Jun 1891	9	S				KY	KY	KY													
		" ROBERT H.	Son	W	M	Oct 1892	7	S				KY	KY	KY													
		" GEORGE	Son	W	M	Sep 1893	6	S				KY	KY	KY													
276	277	COE, JOHN F.	Head	W	M	Apr 1870	30	M	3			KY	KY	KY				FARMER			✓	✓	✓	R		F	292
		" LUCIE	Wife	W	F	Jan 1879	21	M	3	2	2	KY	KY	KY							✓	✓	✓				
		" FLORNCE	Dau	W	F	Jan 1898	2	S				KY	KY	KY							✓	✓	✓				
		" SALLIE	Dau	W	F	Apr 1900	7/12	S				KY	KY	KY							✓	✓	✓				
		GEARLD, HICE	work hand	W	M	Jan 1878	22	S				KY	KY	KY				DAY LABOR	6		✓	✓					
277	278	BALL, SARAH	Head	W	F	Aug 1826	73	Wd		8	4	TN	NC	TN				FARMER			✓	X	✓		O	F	293
		BIGGERSTAFF, MAY	Gr-dau	W	F	Sep 1881	18	S				KY	KY	KY				AT SCHOOL		5	✓	✓					
		HUDDLESTON, JAMES	workhand	W	M	Aug 1875	24	S				KY	KY	KY				WORKHAND	4		✓	✓					
278	279	GEARLDS, WAYN (F.)	Head	W	M	Jan 1860	40	M	10			KY	KY	KY				FARMER			✓	X	✓	R		F	294
		" MARY J.	Wife	W	F	Jan 1866	34	M	10	4	3	KY	KY	KY							✓	✓	✓				
		" WILLIAM	Son	W	M	Jul 1891	9	S				KY	KY	KY													
		" THOMAS	Son	W	M	Jul 1893	6	S				KY	KY	KY													
		" BEDFORD	Son	W	M	Dec 1896	3	S				KY	KY	KY													
279	280	SHEARLY, TURNER	Head	W	M	Nov 1856	43	M	19			KY	KY	KY				FARMER			✓	✓	✓	R		F	295
		" SARAH	Wife	W	F	Dec 1861	38	M	19	11	11	KY	KY	KY							✓	✓	✓				

STATE - KENTUCKY
COUNTY - MONROE
Township or other division CENTER POINT Enumerator JAMES T. WHITE

Supervisor's Dist. No. 102 Sheet No.
Enumeration Dist. No. 83

No. of Family	No. of Dwelling	NAME	Relation	Color	Sex	DATE OF BIRTH Mon/Yr	Age at last birthday	Marital Status	# Years married	Mother of how many children?	# of these children living	Place of birth [this person]	Father of this person	Mother of this person	Year of immigr.	# years in U.S.	Naturalization	OCCUPATION 10 years +	Months not employed	Attended school in months	Can read	Can write	Speak English	Owned or Rent	Owned -no mortage	Farm or house	# of farm schedule	
		SHEARLY, MAUD	DAU	W	F	DEC 1880	19	S				KY	KY	KY				AT SCHOOL		9	✓	✓	✓					
		" WALTER	SON	W	M	MAR 1882	18	S				KY	KY	KY				AT SCHOOL		2	✓	✓	✓					
		" MERTIE	DAU	W	F	Sep 1883	16	S				KY	KY	KY				AT SCHOOL		4	✓	✓	✓					
		" BENTON	SON	W	M	JUN 188	14	S				KY	KY	KY				AT SCHOOL		2	✓	✓						
		" CLARA	DAU	W	F	Feb 1897	13	S				KY	KY	KY				AT SCHOOL		3	✓	✓	✓					
		" BETTIE	DAU	W	F	OCT 1888	11	S				KY	KY	KY				AT SCHOOL		3	✓	✓	✓					
		" GIRTRUE (?)	DAU	W	F	JUN 1891	9	S				KY	KY	KY														
		" KATE	DAU	W	F	Sep 1892	7	S				KY	KY	KY														
		" MINNIE	DAU	W	F	MAR 1894	6	S				KY	KY	KY														
		" FRED	SON	W	M	OCT 1895	4	S				KY	KY	KY														
		" BELLE	DAU	W	F	JAN 1899	1	S				KY	KY	KY														
280	281	GEARLDS, GEORGE F.	HEAD	W	M	NOV 1863	36	M	16			KY	TN	TN				FARMER			✓	✓	✓	R		F	296	
		" SALLIE	Wife	W	F	APR 1866	34	M	16	5	5	KY	TN	TN							X	X	✓					
		" ELMORE	Son	W	M	MAY 1885	15	S				KY	TN	KY				AT SCHOOL		3	✓	✓	✓					
		" JESSE R.	Son	W	M	JAN 1886	13	S				KY	KY	KY				AT SCHOOL		3	✓	✓	✓					
		" HVA(?)B.	Son	W	M	MAR 1888	12	S				KY	KY	KY				AT SCHOOL		3	X	X	✓					
		" ANNIE B.	Dau	W	F	Sep 1892	7	S				KY	KY	KY														
		" LUCIE E.	Dau	W	F	Sep 1895	4	S				KY	KY	KY														
		GULLEY, MARY	Servant	W	F	MAR 1877	23	S				KY	KY	KY				SERVANT			X	X	✓					
281	282	MOORE, SANFORD	HEAD	W	M	NOV 1865	34	M	14			KY	KY	KY							X	X	✓	R		F	297	
		" ALVINA	WIFE	W	F	JAN 1864	36	M	14			KY	KY	KY							✓	✓	✓					
282	283	HALL, JAMES M.	HEAD	W	M	AUG 1852	48	M	19			MO	KY	TN				FARMER			✓	✓	✓	R		F	298	
		" JOSAFFINA	WIFE	W	F	JUN 1859	40	M	19	6	6	TN	TN	TN							✓	✓	✓					
		" ELMORE	SON	W	M	Feb 1882	18	S				KY	MO	TN				AT SCHOOL		4	✓	✓	✓					
		" OSIA R.	SON	W	M	JAN 1885	15	S				KY	MO	TN				AT SCHOOL		6	✓	✓	✓					
		" ELLIE G.	DAU	W	F	JUL 1887	12	S				KY	MO	TN				AT SCHOOL		6	✓	✓	✓					

STATE - KENTUCKY
COUNTY - MONROE
Township or other division: CENTER POINT Enumerator: JAMES T. WHITE

Supervisor's Dist. No. 107 Sheet No.
Enumeration Dist. No. 83

No. of Family	No. of Dwelling	NAME	Relation	Color	Sex	Date of Birth Mon/Yr	Age at last birthday	Marital Status	# Years married	Mother of how many children?	# of these children living	Place of birth (this person)	Father of this person	Mother of this person	Year of immigr.	# years in U.S.	Naturalization	Occupation	Months not employed	Attended school in months	Can read	Can write	Speak English	Owned or Rent	Owned – no mortage	Farm or house	# of farm schedule
		HALL, ARPHA	Dau	W	F	Jun 1889	10	S				KY	MO	TN				At School		6	✓	✓					
		" CECIL	Son	W	M	Nov 1892	7	S				KY	MO	TN													
		" REA	Dau	W	F	Mar 1896	4	S				KY	MO	TN													
283	284	HOFFMAN, JOHN M.	Head	W	M	Jun 1848	52	M	14			TN	TN	TN				Farmer			✓	✓		O	M	F	299
		" NANCY	Wife	W	F	Jan 1856	44	M	14	6	6	KY	KY	KY							X	X	✓				
		" WILLIAM	Son	W	M	Oct 1885	14	S				KY	KY	KY				At School		10	✓	✓	✓				
		" OLIVER	Son	W	M	Aug 1889	10	S				KY	TN	KY				At School		10	✓	✓	✓				
		" GERTRUDE	Dau	W	F	Feb 1892	8	S				KY	TN	KY													
		" OLISON	Son	W	M	Jul 1894	5	S				KY	TN	KY													
		" FRANK	Son	W	M	Dec 1896	3	S				KY	TN	KY													
		" OLIE	Dau	W	F	Jan 1899	1	S				KY	TN	KY													
284	285	PRUETT, GRAND(?)	Head	W	M	Jan 1860	40	M	15			KY	KY	KY				Farmer			X	X	✓	R		F	300
		" MARY	Wife	W	F	Feb 1870	30	M	15	9	6	KY	KY	KY							X	X	✓				
		" LILY A.	Dau	W	F	Jan 1886	14	S				KY	KY	KY				At School		5	✓	✓	✓				
		" BASIL(?)	Son	W	M	Jan 1890	10	S				KY	KY	KY				At School		5	X	X	✓				
		" WILLIAM	Son	W	M	May 1893	7	S				KY	KY	KY													
		" ROBERT	Son	W	M	Jan 1895	5	S				KY	KY	KY													
		" LUCIE	Dau	W	F	Jan 1897	3	S				KY	KY	KY													
		" MARY H.	Dau	W	F	May 1898	1	S				KY	KY	KY													
285	286	MILIUM, NANCY	Head	W	F	Aug —?—?		Wd		1	1	KY	KY	KY							✓	✓	✓	O		H	
		" ELA	Dau	W	F	Mar 1879	21	S		1	1	KY	KY	KY							✓	✓					
		" GID	Son	W	M	Dec 1898	1	S				KY	KY	KY													
286	287	GIDONS, H ?	Head	W	F	Oct 1824	75	Wd		3	2	KY	VA	KY				Farmer			✓	✓	✓	O	F	F	301
		" MARY	Dau	W	F	Sep 1852	47	S				KY	TN	KY				Seamstress			✓	✓	✓				
287	288	CARTER, JOE M.	Head	W	M	Jan 1866	34	M	2(?)			KY	KY	KY													
		" RUTH	Wife	W	F	Feb 1864	36	M	2(?)	6	6	KY	KY	KY													

STATE - KENTUCKY
COUNTY - MONROE
Township or other division CENTER POINT Enumerator JAMES T. WHITE

Supervisor's Dist. No. 102 Sheet No.
Enumeration Dist. No. 83

No. of Family	No. of Dwelling	NAME	Relation	Color	Sex	Date of Birth Mon/Yr	Age at last birthday	Marital Status	# Years married	Mother of how many children?	# of these children living	Place of birth (this person)	Father of this person	Mother of this person	Year of immigr.	# years in U.S.	Naturalization	Occupation 10 years +	Months not employed	Attended school in months	Can read	Can write	Speak English	Owned or Rent	Owned – no mortage	Farm or house	# of farm schedule	
		CARTER, OSCAR	Son	W	M	Jun 1885	14	S				KY	KY	KY				AT SCHOOL		5	✓	✓						
		" BRAMLETE	Son	W	M	Jan 1889	11	S				KY	KY	KY				AT SCHOOL		5	✓	✓						
		" LUVENIA	Dau	W	F	Apr 1893	7	S				KY	KY	KY														
		" TRAMES (?)	Dau	W	F	Apr 1896	4	S				KY	KY	KY														
		" WILLIAM B	Son	W	M	Feb 1898	2	S				KY	KY	KY														
		" HERMAN H.	Son	W	M	Feb 1899	1	S				KY	KY	KY														
288	289	MUSE, GEORGE	Head	W	M	Jun 1849	30	M	15	?		KY	KY	KY				FARMER			X	X	X	O	F	F	303	
		" LIZA	Wife	W	F	Jun 1875	24	M	15	6	5	KY	KY	KY							✓	✓	✓					
		" LITTLE S.	Son	W	M	Feb 1888	16	S				KY	KY	KY				AT SCHOOL		5	✓	✓	✓					
		" DELLA M.	Dau	W	F	Jan 1890	10	S				KY	KY	KY				AT SCHOOL		5	✓	✓	✓					
		" NANCY C.	Dau	W	F	— —	8	S	INK BLOT			KY	KY	KY														
		" THOMAS B.	Son	W	M	Jun 1897	2	S				KY	KY	KY														
		" OLIE	Dau	W	F	Feb 1899	1	S				KY	KY	KY														
289	290	MUSE, SIM	Head	W	M	Dec 1851	48	M	18			KY	KY	KY				FARMER			X	✓	✓	O	F	F	304	
		" JANE C.	Wife	W	F	May 1862	38	M	18	1	1	KY	KY	KY							X	X	✓					
		" HELEN	Dau	W	F	Jun 1889	11	S				KY	KY	KY				AT SCHOOL		3	X	X	✓					
290	291	MUSE, FRANKLIN	Head	W	M	Jun 1820	80	M	52			KY	KY	KY				—			✓	✓	✓	O		H		
		" NANCY C.	Wife	W	F	Jan 1830	70	M	52	10	7	KY	KY	KY							✓	X	✓					
291	292	MUSE, LEE	Head	W	M	Jun 1850	50	M	14			KY	KY	KY				FARMER			✓	✓	✓	R		F	305	
		" NANCY E.	Wife	W	F	Feb 1859	31	M	14	6	5	KY	KY	KY							X	X	✓					
		" ELLA	Dau	W	F	Jan 1888	12	S				KY	KY	KY				AT SCHOOL		2	✓	✓	✓					
		" JULIA	Dau	W	F	Nov 1889	10	S				KY	KY	KY				AT SCHOOL		2	✓	✓	✓					
		" CLEVELAND	Son	W	M	Jan 1891	9	S				KY	KY	KY														
		" VIOLA	Dau	W	F	Sep 1895	4	S				KY	KY	KY														
		" DASIE	Dau	W	F	Sep 1898	1	S				KY	KY	KY														
292	293	MUSE, SAMUEL	Head	W	M	Aug 1869	30	M	10			KY	KY	KY				FARMER			✓	✓	✓	R		F	306	

TWELFTH CENSUS OF THE UNITED STATES 1900

STATE - KENTUCKY
COUNTY - MONROE
Township or other division CENTER POINT   Enumerator JAMES T. WHITE

Supervisor's Dist. No. 102 Sheet No.
Enumeration Dist. No. 83

No. of Family	No. of Dwelling	NAME	Relation	Color	Sex	DATE OF BIRTH Mon/Yr	Age at last birthday	Marital Status	# Years married	Mother of how many children?	# of these children living	Place of birth [this person]	Father of this person	Mother of this person	Year of immigr.	# years in U.S.	Naturalization	OCCUPATION 10 years +	Months not employed	Attended school in months	Can read	Can write	Speak English	Owned or Rent	Owned -no mortage	Farm or house	# of farm schedule	
		MUSE, FLUDILLA	WIFE	W	F	JAN 1875	25	M	10	4	4	KY	KY	KY							✓	✓	✓					
		" NANCY	DAU	W	F	JUN 1891	8	S				KY	KY	KY														
		" LUCIE	DAU	W	F	OCT 1894	5	S				KY	KY	KY														
		" HURSHEL	SON	W	M	Feb 1898	2	S				KY	KY	KY														
		THOMAS	SON	W	M	Aug 1899	10/12	S				KY	KY	KY														
		BIGHT, LUCIE	NEICE	W	F	JUL 1876	23	S				KY	KY	KY				SERVANT			✓	✓	✓					
293	294	BROWN, JAMES	HEAD	W	M	Feb 1861	39	M	19			KY	KY	KY				FARMER			✓	✓	✓	R		F	307	
		" FRANCES	WIFE	W	F	JAN 1859	41	M	19	5	5	KY	KY	KY							✓	✓	✓					
		" IDA P.	DAU	W	F	AUG 1883	16	S				KY	KY	KY				AT SCHOOL		4	✓	✓	✓					
		" IVA T.	DAU	W	F	JUL 1885	14	S				KY	KY	KY				AT SCHOOL		4	✓	✓	✓					
		" THOMAS H.	SON	W	M	Feb 1886	14	S				KY	BY	KY				AT SCHOOL		4	✓	✓	✓					
		" MORSE E.	SON	W	M	JAN 1898	12					KY	KY	KY				AT SCHOOL		4	✓	✓	✓					
		" JOHN E.	SON	W	M	JUN 1890	10	S				KY	KY	KY				AT SCHOOL		4	X	X	✓					
		" OLIA M.	DAU	W	F	MAY 1899	1	S				KY	KY	KY							X	X	✓					
294	295	BUFUORT, DAVID	Head	W	M	JUL 1859	40	M				TN	TN	TN				FARMER			X	X	✓	R		E	308	
		" NANCY E.	wife	W	F	JAN 1876	24	M				TN	KY	TN							X	X	✓					
		" BURL	SON	W	M	OCT 1880	19	S				KY	TN	KY				AT SCHOOL		2	✓	✓	✓					
	(?)	" C—LLWELL	SON	W	M	OCT 1880	19	S				KY	TN	KY				AT SCHOOL		2	✓	✓	✓					
		" BERTHA A.	DAU	W	F	— 1884	16	S				KY	TN	KY				AT SCHOOL		5	✓	✓	✓					
		" JULIA	DAU	W	F	Sep 1892	7	S				KY	TN	KY														
		" GEORGE W.	SON	W	M	MAR 1895	5	S				KY	TN	KY														
		" CARLO	SON	W	M	JAN 1896	4	S				KY	TN	KY														
	(?)	" HILIE	SON	W	M	MAY 1898	2	S				KY	TN	KY														
		" LUCIE	DAU	W	F	MAY 1909	1/12	S				KY	TN	KY														
		CARTER, EFRAM	Workhand	W	M	JAN 1878	22	S				KY	KY	KY				WORKHAND			X	X	✓					
		MUSE, JOHN	Workhand	W	M	JAN 1860	40	Wd				KY	KY	KY				WORKHAND			✓	✓	✓					

STATE - KENTUCKY
COUNTY - MONROE
Township or other division CENTERPOINT Enumerator JAMES T. WHITE

Supervisor's Dist. No. _____ Sheet No. _____
Enumeration Dist. No. _____ _____

No. of Family	No. of Dwelling	NAME	Relation	Color	Sex	Date of Birth Mon/Yr	Age at last birthday	Marital Status	# Years married	Mother of how many children?	# of these children living	Place of birth (this person)	Father of this person	Mother of this person	Year of immigr.	# years in U.S.	Naturalization	OCCUPATION 10 years +	Months not employed	Attended school in month	Can read	Can write	Speak English	Owned or Rent	Owned—no mortage	Farm or house	# of farm schedule
295	296	WILLIAMS, WILLIAM	Head	W	M	Oct 1862	37	M	12			KY	KY	KY				FARMER			✓	✓	✓	O	F	F	309
		" NANCY S.	Wife	W	F	Dec 1861	38	M	12	5	5	KY	KY	KY							✓	✓	✓				
		" PEARL	Dau	W	F	Aug 1888	11	S				KY	KY	KY				AT SCHOOL		6	✓	✓	✓				
		" ORVAL C.	Son	W	M	Dec 1889	10	S				KY	KY	KY				AT SCHOOL		6	✓	✓					
		" CLINT H.	Son	W	M	Sep 1892	7	S				KY	KY	KY													
		" MITT	Son	W	M	Nov 1895	4	S				KY	KY	KY													
		" IVY	Dau	W	F	Nov 1898	1	S				KY	KY	KY													
		PAGE, JOE	Workhand	W	M	Jan 1878	22	S				KY	KY	KY				DAY LABOR			✓	✓	✓				
296	297	CARTER, ALFORD	Head	W	M	Jun 1871	29	M	2			KY	KY	KY				FARMER			✓	✓	✓	R		F	310
		" LARRY	Wife	W	F	May 1881	19	M	2			KY	KY	KY							✓	✓	✓				
297	298	CLOID, DAVID T.	Head	W	M	Jan 1841	59	M	41			KY	VA	VA				FARMER			✓	✓	✓	O	F	F	311
		" AMERICK	Wife	W	F	Jan 1844	55	M	41	11	9	KY	KY	KY							X	X	✓				
		" MARY H.	Dau	W	F	Jan 1863	37	S				KY	KY	KY							✓	✓	✓				
		" OLISON K.	Son	W	M	Jan 1880	20	S				KY	KY	KY				AT SCHOOL		8	✓	✓	✓				
		" FLORNCE A.	Dau	W	F	Jul 1882	17	S				KY	KY	KY				AT SCHOOL		8	✓	✓					
		" FRANK H.	Son	W	M	Dec 1887	12	S				KY	KY	KY				AT SCHOOL		8	✓	✓	✓				
298	299	CLOID, JOSEPH	Head	W	M	Jun 1877	23	M	1			KY	KY	KY				DAY LABOR			✓	✓	✓	R		H	
		" OLVIL(?)	Wife	W	F	Sep 1877	22	M	1			KY	KY	KY							✓	✓	✓				
299	300	CAID, HIRAM B.	Head	W	M	Oct 1874	25	M	6			KY	KY	KY				FARMER			✓	✓	✓	O	F	F	312
		" TASY	Wife	W	F	Aug 1877	22	M	6	3	2	KY	KY	KY							✓	✓	✓				
		" CLUR J.	Son	W	M	Jul 1894	5	S				KY	KY	KY													
		" EDNA F.	Dau	W	F	Jun 1899	11/12	S				KY	KY	KY													
		HUFF, JERRY	Boarder	W	M	Jan 1877	23	S				KY	KY	KY				DAY LABOR		5	✓	✓	✓				
300	301	WILSON, TALOR E.	Head	W	M	Sep 1858	41	M	20			KY	TN	TN				FARMER			X	X	✓	R		F	313
		" SARAH	Wife	W	F	Sep 1856	43	M	20			KY	KY	KY							✓	✓	✓				
		" MARGARET	Dau	W	F	Jun 1882	18	S				KY	KY	KY				AT SCHOOL		5	✓	✓	✓				

TWELFTH CENSUS OF THE UNITED STATES 1900

STATE - KENTUCKY
COUNTY - MONROE
Township or other division   CENTER POINT   Enumerator JAMES T. WHITE

Supervisor's Dist. No. 102   Sheet No.
Enumeration Dist. No. 83

No. of Family	No. of Dwelling	NAME	Relation	Color	Sex	DATE OF BIRTH Mon/Yr	Age at last birthday	Marital Status	#Years married	Mother of how many children?	# of these children living	Place of birth [this person]	Father of this person	Mother of this person	Year of immigr.	# years in U.S.	Naturalization	OCCUPATION 10 years +	Months not employed	Attended school in months	Can read	Can write	Speak English	Owned or Rent	Owned -no mortage	Farm or house	# of farm schedule
		WILSON, FLORA	Dau	W	F	Jan 1884	16	S				KY	KY	KY				AT SCHOOL		5	✓	✓	✓				
		" MAYRN ?	Son	W	M	Feb 1888	12	S				KY	KY	KY				AT SCHOOL		5	✓	✓	✓				
		" LENA	Dau	W	F	Jan 1891	9	S				KY	KY	KY							✓	✓	✓				
		" WADE	Son	W	M	Jun 1893	7	S				KY	KY	KY													
		" MOSE	Son	W	M	Jan 1896	4	S				KY	KY	KY													
301	302	WRIGHT, JAMES	Head	W	M	Oct 1848	51	M	28			TN	TN	TN				FARMER			✓	✓	✓	R		F	314
		" NANCY	Wife	W	F	Sep 1847	52	M	28	4	4	TN	TN	TN							X	X	✓				
		" BENTON J.	Son	W	M	Feb 1876	24	S				KY	TN	TN				DAY LABOR			✓	✓	✓				
		" GIRTRUE	Dau	W	F	Jan 1878	22	S				KY	TN	TN							✓	✓	✓				
		" DORA	Dau	W	F	Sept 1891	18					KY	TN	TN							✓	✓	✓				
		" MANERVA	Dau	W	F	May 1884	16					KY	TN	TN				AT SCHOOL		5	✓	✓	✓				
		OWINS, MANERVA	Mother in law	W	F	Jan 1826	75	Wd		6	5	TN	TN	TN							X	X	✓				
302	303	AUTRY, RUFUS	Head	W	M	Feb 1855	45	M	17			KY	KY	TN				FARMER			✓	✓	✓	R		F	315
		" RISSA	Wife	W	F	Aug 1855	44	M	17	1	1	KY	KY	KY							✓	✓	✓				
		" JAMES E.	Son	W	M	Feb 1884	16	S				KY	KY	KY				AT SCHOOL		4	✓	✓	✓				
303	304	BALARD, WILLIAM	Head	W	M	Apr 1826	74	M				KY	KY	KY				FARMER			X	X	✓	O		F	316
		" ADA A.	Wife	W	F	Mar 1835	65	M	30	6	2	TN	TN	TN							X	X	✓				
		" MARY E.	Dau	W	F	Aug 1864	35	S				KY	KY	TN							✓	✓	✓				
304	305	WILLSON, MINNIE	Head	W	F	Apr 1843	57	W		1	1	TN	TN	TN				FARMER			X	X	✓	O		F	317
		" EVIE	Dau	W	F	Jan 1880	20	S				KY	KY	KY				AT SCHOOL		5	✓	✓	✓				
305	306	KIDWELL, JAMES	Head	W	M	Dec 1860	39	M	16			KY	KY	KY				FARMER			X	X	✓	R		F	318
		" MARTHA	Wife	W	F	Jan 1855	45	M	16	1	1	KY	KY	KY							✓	X	✓				
		" BENTON	Son	W	M	Oct 1885	14	S				KY	KY	KY				AT SCHOOL		5	✓	✓	✓				
306	307	BROWN, THOMAS	Head	W	M	Mar 1844	56	M	37			KY	TN	KY				FARMER			✓	✓	✓	O		F	319
		" NANCY O.	Wife	W	F	Jul 1846	53	M	37	4	4	KY	ALA	KY							✓	✓	✓				
		" MARTHA E.	Dau	W	F	Feb 1866	34	S				KY	KY	KY							✓	✓	✓				

STATE - KENTUCKY
COUNTY - MONROE
Township or other division CENTER POINT   Enumerator JAMES T. WHITE

Supervisor's Dist. No. 10 ? Sheet No.
Enumeration Dist. No. 83

No. of Family	No. of Dwelling	NAME	Relation	Color	Sex	Date of Birth Mon/Yr	Age at last birthday	Marital Status	# Years married	Mother of how many children?	# of these children living	Place of birth this person	Father of this person	Mother of this person	Year of immigr.	# years in U.S.	Naturalization	OCCUPATION 10 years +	Months not employed	Attended school in months	Can read	Can write	Speak English	Owned or Rent	Owned -no mortgage	Farm or house	# of farm schedule
		BROWN, SMITH B.	Son	W	M	Sep 1877	22	S				KY	KY	KY				FARMER			✓	✓	✓	R		F	320
307	308	VIBBERT, WILLIAM	Head	W	M	Sep 1854	45	M	20			KY	KY	KY				FARMER			✓	✓	✓	O	F	F	321
		" SARAH E.	Wife	W	F	Apr 1860	40	M	20	7	6	KY	KY	KY							X	X	✓				
		" MARTHA M.	Dau	W	F	Jan 1886	14	S				KY	KY	KY				AT SCHOOL		2	✓	✓	✓				
		" HARRISON	Son	W	M	Oct 1888	11	S				KY	KY	KY				AT SCHOOL		2	X	X	✓				
		" ANNIE	Dau	W	F	Jun 1891	8	S				KY	KY	KY													
		" JULIA A.	Dau	W	F	May 1894	6	S				KY	KY	KY													
		" WILLIAM	Son	W	M	May 1898	2	S				KY	KY	KY													
308	309	VIBBERT, JAMES B.	Head	W	M	Nov 1870	29	M				KY	KY	KY				FARMER			✓	X	✓	O	F	F	322
		" MARTHA	Wife	W	F	Dec 1858	31	M				KY	KY	KY							✓	✓	✓				
		" MARY J.	Dau	W	F	Jun 1886	16	S				KY	KY	KY				AT SCHOOL		2	✓	X	✓				
		" JAMES M.	Son	W	M	Apr 1887	13	S				KY	KY	KY				AT SCHOOL		5	✓	✓	✓				
		" JOHN T.	Son	W	M	Sep 1889	10	S				KY	KY	KY				AT SCHOOL		3	X	X	✓				
		" FRED A.	Son	W	M	May 1896	4	S				KY	KY	KY													
309	310	BUSHONN, JAMES H.	Head	W	M	Nov 1870	29	M				KY	KY	KY				FARMER			X	X	✓	R		F	323
		" SARAH S.	Wife	W	F	Aug 1882	17	S				KY	KY	KY							✓	✓	✓				
		" SAM	Father	W	M	Jan 1835	65	Wd				KY	KY	KY							✓	X	✓				
310	311	GENTRY, MILTON	Head	W	M	Jan 1860	40	M	20			KY	KY	KY				FARMER			✓	✓	✓	O	F	F	324
		" MARY	Wife	W	F	Mar 1861	39	M	20	5	5	KY	KY	KY							X	X	✓				
		" MATTIE	Dau	W	F	Jan 1882	18	S				KY	KY	KY				AT SCHOOL		4	✓	✓	✓				
		" JOHN J.	Son	W	M	Jun 1884	16	S				KY	KY	KY				AT SCHOOL		2	✓	✓	✓				
		" JAMES G.	Son	W	M	May 1888	12	S				KY	KY	KY				AT SCHOOL		2	X	X	✓				
		" WILLIAM	Son	W	M	Feb 1891	9	S				KY	KY	KY													
		" SMITH	Son	W	M	Mar 1897	3	S				KY	KY	KY													
311	312	McPEAK, WILLIAM	Head	W	M	Mar 1850	50	Wd				KY	KY	KY				FARMER			X	X	✓	O	F	F	325
312	313	VIBBERT, HENRY	Head	W	M	Mar 1860	40	M	5			KY	KY	KY				FARMER			X	X	✓	R		F	326

STATE - KENTUCKY
COUNTY - MONROE
Township or other division   CENTER POINT   Enumerator JAMES T. WHITE

Supervisor's Dist. No. 102 Sheet No.
Enumeration Dist. No. 83

No. of Family	No. of Dwelling	NAME	Relation	Color	Sex	Date of Birth Mon/Yr	Age at last birthday	Marital Status	# Years married	Mother of how many children?	# of these children living	Place of birth [this person]	Father of this person	Mother of this person	Year of immigr.	# years in U.S.	Naturalization	Occupation 10 years +	Months not employed	Attended school in months	Can read	Can write	Speak English	Owned or Rent	Owned -no mortgage	Farm or house	# of farm schedule
		VIBBERT, HETTIE	Wife	W	F	Jan 1875	25	M	5	2	2	KY	KY	KY							X	X	✓				
		" WILLIAM	Son	W	M	Jun 1896	4					KY	KY	KY													
		" CHARLEY	Son	W	M	Jan 1898	2					KY	KY	KY													
313	314	VIBBERT, JAMES	Head	W	M	Jan 1865	35	M	16			KY	KY	KY				FARMER			X	X	✓	O	F	F	327
		" NANCY	Wife	W	F	Apr 1877	23	M	16	6	6	KY	KY	KY							X	X	✓				
		" NANCY	Dau	W	F	Jan 1886	14	S				KY	KY	KY							X	X	✓				
		" ROBERT	Son	W	M	Jan 1891	9	S				KY	KY	KY													
		" WILLIE	Son	W	M	Jun 1893	6	S				KY	KY	KY													
		" THOMAS	Son	W	M	May 1895	5	S				KY	KY	KY													
		" SINDA	Dau	W	F	Mar 1898	2	S				KY	KY	KY													
		" ALLIE	Dau	W	F	Jan 1900	3/12	S				KY	KY	KY													
314	315	VIBBERT, BART	Head	W	M	Feb 1868	32	S				KY	KY	KY				FARMER			X	X	✓	R		F	328
		" CHARLES	Nephew	W	M	Dec 1881	18	S				KY	KY	KY				DAY LABOR			✓	✓	✓				
315	316	ELMORE, CHARLEY	Head	W	M	Jul 1869	30	M	1			KY	KY	KY				WHISKEY MERCHANT			✓	✓	✓	R		H	
		" VERCHIE	Wife	W	F	Dec 1882	17	M	1	1	1	KY	KY	KY							✓	✓	✓				
		" CASHIUS	Son	W	M	Nov 1899	6/12	S				KY	KY	KY													
316	317	HUNTER, SAMUEL	Head	W	M	May 1860	40	M	16			KY	KY	KY				FARMER			✓	✓	✓	O	F	F	329
		" SUSAN	Wife	W	F	Nov 1865	34	M	16	6	5	KY	KY	KY							✓	✓	✓				
		" WILLIE	Son	W	M	Jan 1887	13	S				KY	KY	KY				AT SCHOOL		3	✓	✓	✓				
		" LENA	Dau	W	F	Sep 1888	11	S				KY	KY	KY				AT SCHOOL		3	✓	✓	✓				
		" VELA	Dau	W	F	Sep 1890	9	S				KY	KY	KY													
		" LEON	Son	W	M	Mar 1895	5	S				KY	KY	KY													
		" GUY	Son	W	M	Sep 1899	8/12	S				KY	KY	KY													
317	318	HUNTER, CATHARAN	Head	W	F	Mar 1833	67	Wd		13	6	KY	KY	KY							X	X	✓	O		H	
		" MARTHA A.	Dau	W	F	Feb 1857	43	Divc.		1	1	KY	KY	KY							X	X	✓				
		HAGAN, ANN	Gr-Dau	W	F	Mar 1882	18	S				KY	KY	KY				AT SCHOOL		5	✓	✓	✓				

STATE - KENTUCKY
COUNTY - MONROE
Township or other division: CENTER POINT Enumerator: JAMES T. WHITE

Supervisor's Dist. No. 102 Sheet No.
Enumeration Dist. No. 83

No. of Family	No. of Dwelling	NAME	Relation	Color	Sex	Date of Birth Mon/Yr	Age at last birthday	Marital Status	# Years married	Mother of how many children?	# of these children living	Place of birth (this person)	Father of this person	Mother of this person	Occupation	Attended school in months	Can read	Can write	Speak English	Owned or Rent	Owned-no mortgage	Farm or house	# of farm schedule
318	319	CARTER, GEORGE	Head	W	M	May 1861	39	M	4			KY	KY	KY	FARMER		✓	✓	✓	O		F F	330
		" SARAH B.	Wife	W	F	Jun 1876	23	M	4	3	3	KY	KY	KY			✓	✓	✓				
		" LESLY B.	Son	W	M	Aug 1896	3	S				KY	KY	KY									
		" JOSEPH B.	Son	W	M	Aug 1898	1	S				KY	KY	KY									
		" BULA M.	Dau	W	F	Jan 1900	5/12	S				KY	KY	KY									
319	320	CARTER, JANE	Head	W	F	Jan 1825	75	Wd		1	1	VA	VA	VA	FARMER		✓	✓		O		F F	331
		" MANDA (or WANDA G)	Dau	W	F	Nov 1869	30	S				KY	VA	VA			✓	✓	✓				
380	321	TURNER, JOHN	Head	W	M	Jan 1868	32	M	12			KY	KY	KY	FARMER		X	X	✓	R		F	332
		" MATTIE	Wife	W	F	Jan 1875	25	M	12	3	3	KY	KY	KY									
		" SARAH	Dau	W	F	May 1889	11	S				KY	KY	KY	AT SCHOOL								
		" ELIZABETH	Dau	W	F	May 1896	4	S				KY	KY	KY									
		" WILLIAM E.	Son	W	M	Dec 1898	1	S				KY	KY	KY									
321	322	MILLER, ULYSSES	Head	W	M	Apr 1865	35	M	11			KY	TN	KY	FARMER		✓	✓	✓	O	M	F	333
		" IBBA	Wife	W	F	Mar 1867	33	M	11	2	2	KY	KY	KY			✓	✓	✓				
		" BERCHIE	Dau	W	F	Nov 1889	10	S				KY	KY	KY	AT SCHOOL	5	✓	✓	✓				
		" GEORGE B.	Son	W	M	Aug 1896	3	S				KY	KY	KY									
322	323	TOOLEY, JOHN F.	Head	W	M	Sep 1863	30	S				KY	KY	KY	FARMER		✓	✓	✓	O		F F	334
		" MARTHA	Mother	W	F	Jun 1843	56	Wd		1	1	KY	KY	KY			✓	✓	✓				
313	324	MURLEY, THOMAS	Head	W	M	Aug 1873	26	M	7			KY	KY	KY	DAY LABOR		✓	✓	✓	R		H	
		" NANCY	Wife	W	F	Apr 1867	33	M	7	4	2	KY	KY	KY			✓	✓	✓				
		" CLARNCE	Dau	W	F	May 1894	6	S				KY	KY	KY									
		" SALLY	Dau	W	F	Mar 1899	1	S				KY	KY	KY									
324	325	TOOLEY, ALVAES	Head	W	M	Aug 1867	32	M	11			KY	KY	KY	FARMER		✓	✓	✓	O		F F	335
		" LUE J.	Wife	W	F	Feb 1869	31	M	11	6	6	KY	KY	KY			✓	✓	✓				
		" ARIE	Dau	W	F	Jan 1891	9	S				KY	KY	KY									
		" PERMELIA E.	Dau	W	F	Aug 1892	7	S				KY	KY	KY									

STATE - KENTUCKY
COUNTY - MONROE
Township or other division CENTER POINT Enumerator JAMES T. WHITE

Supervisor's Dist. No. 102 Sheet No.
Enumeration Dist. No. 83

Location (No. of Family / No. of Dwelling)	NAME	Relation	Color	Sex	DATE OF BIRTH (Mon/Yr)	Age at last birthday	Marital Status	# Years married	Mother of how many children?	# of these children living	Place of birth [this person]	Father of this person	Mother of this person	Year of immigr.	# years in U.S.	Naturalization	OCCUPATION 10 years +	Months not employed	Attended school in months	Can read	Can write	Speak English	Owned or Rent	Owned - no mortage	Farm or house	# of farm schedule
	TOOLEY, WILLIAM F.	Son	W	M	Mar 1894	6	S				KY	KY	KY													
	" VIVIAN	Dau	W	F	Aug 1895	4	S				KY	KY	KY													
	" JOHN	Son	W	M	Feb 1897	3	S				KY	KY	KY													
	" ODES K.	Son	W	M	Mar 1899	1	S				KY	KY	KY													
325 326	COPAS, JAMES H.	Head	W	M	Apr 1859	41	M	23			KY	KY	KY				FARMER			✓	✓		R		F	336
	" JANE	Wife	W	F	Mar 1858	42	M	23	7	6	KY	KY	KY							X	X	✓				
	" JOHN(?) H.	Son	W	M	Dec 1878	21	S				KY	KY	KY				DAY LABOR 3			✓	✓					
	" EVERT L.	Son	W	M	Jan 1885	15	S				KY	KY	KY				AT SCHOOL		4	✓	✓	✓				
	" ANNIE B.	Dau	W	F	Jun 1888	11	S				KY	KY	KY				AT SCHOOL		4	✓	X	✓				
	" CORA A.	Dau	W	F	Jan 1891	9	S				KY	KY	KY													
	" ROSS J.	Son	W	M	May 1893	7	S				KY	KY	KY													
	" ROBBERT	Son	W	M	Apr 1896	4	S				KY	KY	KY													
	" GLADIS	Dau	W	F	Jan 1899	1	S				KY	KY	KY													
326 327	PITCOCK, JOHN	Head	W	M	Mar 1872	28	M	9			KY	KY	KY				FARMER			✓	✓	✓	R		F	337
	" ELIZZIEBETH	Wife	W	F	Apr 1872	28	M	9	2	2	KY	KY	KY							✓	✓	✓				
	" TAYABELL (?)	Son	W	M	Jun 1893	7	S				KY	KY	KY													
	" LEMMA	Dau	W	F	May 1894	6	S				KY	KY	KY													
	ROSS, WILLIAM	Boarder	W	M	Apr 1867	33	S				KY	VA	KY				FARMER			✓	✓	✓	O		F	338
327 328	TOOLEY, MARY	Head	W	F	Jun 1837	63	Wd		3	3	KY	IND	MO				FARMER			✓	✓	✓	O		F	339
	" SAMUEL	Son	W	M	May 1872	28	S				KY	KY	KY				TEACHER 2			✓	✓	✓				
	" ALVA	Son	W	M	May 1873	27	S				KY	KY	KY				DAY LABOR 4			✓	✓	✓				
	" LUCIE	Dau	W	F	Aug 1877	22	S				KY	KY	KY							✓	✓	✓				
328 329	TOOLEY, ROBBERT	Head	W	M	Oct 1863	36	M	13			KY	KY	KY				FARMER			✓	✓	✓	O		F	340
	" MARY	Wife	W	F	Mar 1869	31	M	13	2	2	KY	KY	KY							✓	✓	✓				
	" LABON	Son	W	M	Jun 1889	10	S				KY	KY	KY				AT SCHOOL		5	✓	✓	✓				
	" THEE	Son	W	M	May 1893	7	S				KY	KY	KY													

STATE - KENTUCKY
COUNTY - MONROE
Township or other division **CENTERPOINT** Enumerator **JAMES T. WHITE**

Supervisor's Dist. No. _102_ Sheet No.
Enumeration Dist. No. _83_

No. of Family	No. of Dwelling	NAME	Relation	Color	Sex	DATE OF BIRTH Mon/Yr	Age at last birthday	Marital Status	# Years married	Mother of how many children?	# of these children living	Place of birth (this person)	Father of this person	Mother of this person	OCCUPATION 10 years +	Months not employed	Attended school in months	Can read	Can write	Speak English	Owned or Rent	Owned –no mortgage	Farm or house	# of farm schedule
329	330	TOOLEY, THEODORE	Head	W	M	Jan 1870	30	M	1			KY	KY	KY	FARMER			✓	✓	✓		O	F	341
		" MARY C.	Wife	W	F	Mar 1871	29	M	1			KY	KY	KY				✓	✓	✓				
330	331	LUIS(?) C. ROSS	Head	W	M	Mar 1851	49	M	30			KY	VA	VA	FARMER			✓	✓	✓		O	F	342
		" MARY A.	Wife	W	F	Sep 1851	48	M	30	8	8	KY	KY	KY				✓	✓	✓				
		" ROBERT M.	Son	W	M	Feb 1872	28	S				KY	KY	KY	FARMER			✓	✓	✓		O	F	343
		" JOSEPH J.	Son	W	M	Jun 1874	25	S				KY	KY	KY	PHYSICIAN			✓	✓	✓				
		" AMANDA B.	Dau	W	F	Nov 1879	20	S				KY	KY	KY	SCHOOL TEACHER	7		✓	✓	✓				
		" DICKEN R.	Son	W	M	Apr 1883	17	S				KY	KY	KY	AT SCHOOL		5	✓	✓	✓				
		" SAMUEL J.	Son	W	M	Sep 1888	11	S				KY	KY	KY	AT SCHOOL		5	✓	✓	✓				
		" HATTIE M.	Dau	W	F	Nov 1890	9	S				KY	KY	KY				✓						
		" ALBINA D.	Dau	W	F	Jun 1893	7	S				KY	KY	KY										
331	332	MOORE, JOHN	Head	W	M	Sep 1860	39	M	18			KY	KY	KY	FARMER			X	X	✓	R		F	344
		" MARTHA	Wife	W	F	Apr 1852	48	M	18	4	4	KY	TN	KY				✓	✓	✓				
		" LILLIE	Dau	W	F	Dec 1873	26	S				KY	KY	VA	SEAMSTRESS			✓	✓	✓				
		" FRANK	Son	W	M	Mar 1882	18	S				KY	KY	KY	DAY LABOR	5		✓	✓	✓				
		" JOHN B.	Son	W	M	Mar 1886	14	S				KY	KY	KY	AT SCHOOL		5	✓	✓	✓				
		" BELLE	Dau	W	F	Jan 1888	12	S				KY	KY	KY	AT SCHOOL		5	✓	✓	✓				
332	333	PITCOCK, FRANCES	Head	W	F	Jan 1842	58	Wd		8	4	KY	KY	KY	FARMER			✓	✓	✓		O	F	345
		" ELIZZIEBETH L.	Dau	W	F	Jul 1875	24	S				KY	TN	KY				✓	✓	✓				
333	334	SPEAR, LEVI	Head	W	M	May 1855	45	M	20			KY	KY	VA	FARMER			✓	✓	✓		O	F	346
		" MAGGIE	Wife	W	F	Jan 1860	40	M	20	9	9	TN	TN	TN				✓	✓	✓				
		" EVERT	Son	W	M	Mar 1881	19	S				KY	KY	TN	AT SCHOOL		5	✓	✓	✓				
		" AVRY	Son	W	M	Oct 1872	17	S				KY	KY	TN	AT SCHOOL		4	✓	✓	✓				
		" ADA	Dau	W	F	Dec 1884	15	S				KY	KY	TN	AT SCHOOL		4	✓	✓	✓				
		" EDWARD	Son	W	M	Dec 1886	13	S				KY	KY	TN	AT SCHOOL		2	✓	✓	✓				
		" VERNIA	Dau	W	F	Jan 1889	11	S				KY	KY	TN	AT SCHOOL		8	✓	✓	✓				

STATE - KENTUCKY
COUNTY - MONROE
Township or other division CENTER POINT   Enumerator JAMES T. WHITE

Supervisor's Dist. No. 102   Sheet No.
Enumeration Dist. No. 83

No. of Family	No. of Dwelling	NAME	Relation	Color	Sex	DATE OF BIRTH Mon/Yr	Age at last birthday	Marital Status	# Years married	Mother of how many children?	# of these children living	Place of birth [this person]	Father of this person	Mother of this person	Year of immigr.	# years in U.S.	Naturalization	OCCUPATION 10 years +	Months not employed	Attended school in months	Can read	Can write	Speak English	Owned or Rent	Owned -no mortage	Farm or house	# of farm schedule
		SPEAR, FRED	SON	W	M	MAY 1891	9	S				KY	KY	TN													
		" OVA M	DAU	W	F	APR 1893	7	S				KY	KY	TN													
		" CLIDE	SON	W	M	Feb 1895	5	S				KY	KY	TN													
		" WILLIAM C	SON	W	M	JAN 1897	3	S				KY	KY	TN													
		BEDFORD, MAYRN	WORK HAND	W	M	Jul 1873	26	S				KY	KY	KY				DAY LABOR			✓	✓	✓				
		REDFORD, LUTHER	WORK HAND	W	M	MAY 1882	18	S				KY	KY	KY				DAY LABOR			✓	✓	✓				
334	335	DICKENS, THOMAS	Head	W	M	Nov 1871	22	M				KY	KY	KY				DAY LABOR			✓	✓	✓	R		H	
		" DORA	WIFE	W	F	JAN 1882	18	M				KY	KY	TN													
335	336	BURS(?), THOMAS	HEAD	W	M	MAY 1874	26	M	4			MO(?)	TN	TN				DAY LABOR			✓	✓	✓	R		H	
		" MARY	WIFE	W	F	MAR 1868	32	M	4	3	3	TN	TN	TN				SCHOOL TEACHER			✓	✓	✓				
		" MARGERY J	DAU	W	F	Sep 1896	3	S				TN	TN	TN													
		" HERMAN J.	SON	W	M	Nov 1897	2	S				KY	TN	TN													
		" WILLIAM F.	SON	W	M	Jul 1899	11/12	S				KY	TN	TN													
336	337	WHITESIDES, SAMUEL B	Head	W	M	Nov 1867	32	Div?				KY	KY	TN				FARMER			✓	✓	✓	O	FF		347
337	338	ANDERSON, MARANDA	HEAD	W	F	MAY 1854	46	Wd	8	4		KY	KY	KY							✓	✓	✓	O	F	H	
		" SAMUEL	SON	W	M	MAY 1879	21	S				KY	TN	KY				DAY LABOR			✓	✓	✓				
		" MURLIE	DAU	W	F	JAN 1889	11	S				KY	TN	KY				A.T SCHOOL		4	✓	✓	✓				
		" BENNIE	SON	W	M	JUN 1891	8	S				KY	TN	KY													
		" THOMAS E	SON	W	M	MAR 1894	6	S				KY	TN	KY													
338	339	FERGUSON, MARY	Head	W	F	JAN 1864	36	Wd	4	3		KY	KY	TN				DAY LABOR			X	X	✓	R		H	
		" JAMES M.	SON	W	M	MAR 1884	16	S				KY	KY	KY				AT SCHOOL		5	✓	✓	✓				
		" ENGRAM	SON	W	M	MAY 1888	12	S				KY	KY	KY				A.T. SCHOOL		6	✓	✓	✓				
		" ALLIE	DAU	W	F	Nov 1890	9	S				KY	KY	KY													
339	340	WADDLE, MARY	HEAD	W	F	JAN 1856	44	Wd	7	7		KY	KY	KY				WEAVER			X	X	✓	O		H	
		" SALLIE	DAU	W	F	JUN 1880	19	S				KY	KY	KY				AT SCHOOL		4	✓	✓	✓				
		" FANNIE	DAU	W	F	MAY 1884	16	S				KY	KY	KY				AT SCHOOL		5	✓	✓	✓				

STATE - KENTUCKY
COUNTY - MONROE
Township or other division   CENTER POINT   Enumerator   JAMES T. WHITE

Supervisor's Dist. No. _102_ Sheet No.
Enumeration Dist. No. _83_____

Location		NAME	Relation	Color	Sex	DATE OF BIRTH Mon/Yr	Age at last birthday	Marital Status	# Years married	Mother of how many children?	# of these children living	NATIVITY			CITIZENSHIP			OCCUPATION 10 years +	Months not employed	EDUCATION				OWNERSHIP			
No. of Family	No. of Dwelling											Place of birth [this person]	Father of this person	Mother of this person	Year of immigr.	# years in U.S.	Naturalization			Attended school in months	Can read	Can write	Speak English	Owned or Rent	Owned –no mortgage	Farm or house	# of farm schedule
—		WADDLE, ANNIE	DAU	W	F	JAN 1888	12	S				KY	KY	KY				AT SCHOOL		5	✓	✓					
		" JASPER H.	SON	W	M	MAR 1891	9	S				KY	KY	KY													
		" JOHN J.	SON	W	M	DEC 1893	6	S				KY	KY	KY													
		" MAUD	DAU	W	F	APR 1896	4	S				KY	KY	KY													

END OF CENTER POINT

STATE - KENTUCKY
COUNTY - MONROE
Township or other division **Tompkinsville Town** Enumerator **E. R. Baxter**

Supervisor's Dist. No. **102** Sheet No.
Enumeration Dist. No. **84**

No. of Family	No. of Dwelling	NAME	Relation	Color	Sex	DATE OF BIRTH Mon/Yr	Age at last birthday	Marital Status	# Years married	Mother of how many children?	# of these children living	Place of birth (this person)	Father of this person	Mother of this person	Year of immigr.	# years in U.S.	Naturalization	OCCUPATION 10 years +	Months not employed	Attended school in months	Can read	Can write	Speak English	Owned or Rent	Owned –no mortgage	Farm or house	# of farm schedule
1	1	MOODY, CHARLES	Head	W	M	Aug 1836	63	M	39			KY	KY	KY				FARMER			✓	✓	✓	O	P	H	
		" EUNICE	Wife	W	F	Feb 1840	60	M	39	4	4	KY	TN	NC							✓	✓	✓				
2	2	EVANS, RADFORD	Head	W	M	Jul 1866	33	M	6			KY	KY	KY				MERCHANT			✓	✓	✓	O	F	H	
		" LIZZIE	Wife	W	F	May 1873	27	M	6	2	2	KY	KY	KY							✓	✓	✓				
		MARIE	Dau	W	F	Feb 1895	5	S				KY	KY	KY									✓				
		NELLIE B.	Dau	W	F	Jun 1898	2	S				KY	KY	KY									✓				
3	3	PHILPOT, BUD	Head	W	M	Jan 1865	35	M	9			KY	KY	KY				LIVERYMAN			✓	✓	✓	O	F	H	
		" NANNIE	Wife	W	F	Oct 1870	29	M	9	2	2	KY	KY	TN							✓	✓	✓				
		" LOUIS E.	Son	W	M	Apr 1893	6	S				KY	KY	KY							X	X	✓				
		" DORA M.	Dau	W	F	May 1896	4	S				KY	KY	KY							X	X	✓				
4	4	WHITE, WILLIAM	Head	W	M	Jan 1867	33	M	10			KY	KY	TN				DEPUTY SHERIFF			✓	✓	✓	R		H	
		" CORA E.	Wife	W	F	Apr 1871	30	M	10	2	2	KY	KY	TN							✓	✓	✓				
		" ERNEST L.	Son	W	M	Jun 1891	8	S				KY	KY	KY						5	✓	✓	✓				
		" KATE	Dau	W	F	Apr 1893	7	S				KY	KY	KY						5	✓	✓	✓				
		THOMAS, WILLIE E.	Boarder	W	M	May 1876	24	S				KY	KY	KY				MINISTER			✓	✓	✓	O	E	H	
5	5	FLIPPIN, JOE A.	Head	W	M	Aug 1843	56	M	21			KY	KY	KY				PHYSICIAN			✓	✓	✓	O	F	F	2
		" SALLIE E.	Wife	W	F	May 1862	38	M	21			KY	KY	KY							✓	✓	✓				
		" RADFORD M	Nephew	W	M	Apr 1885	15	S				KY	KY	KY						5	✓	✓	✓				
		" BESSIE	Niece	W	F	Jun 1879	20	S				KY	KY	KY				TEACHER	10	10	✓	✓	✓				
		PITCOCK, CARRIE	Boarder	W	F	Jun 1875	25	S				KY	KY	KY				POSTAL CLERK			✓	✓	✓				
6	6	GRAVIN, JAMES	Head	W	M	Oct 1872	27	M	8			KY	KY	KY				DAY LABOR			✓	✓	✓	R		H	
		" FANNIE	Wife	W	F	Sep 1877	22	M	8	2	2	KY	KY	KY							✓	✓	✓				
		" WINNIE	Dau	W	F	Oct 1895	4	S				KY	KY	KY									✓				
		" HALLIE	Dau	W	F	Dec 1897	2	S				KY	KY	KY													
		BRYANT, TOMIE	Bro-in-Law	W	M	Jan 1876	24	S				KY	KY	KY				DAY LABOR			✓	✓	✓				
	7	CONKIN, GRAINGER		W	M	Nov 1866	33	M	2			KY	KY	KY				DEP. TOWN MARSHALL			✓	✓	✓	R		H	

STATE - KENTUCKY
COUNTY - MONROE
Township or other division TOMPKINSVILLE TOWN Enumerator E. R. BAXTER

Supervisor's Dist. No. 102 Sheet No.
Enumeration Dist. No. 84

No. of Family	No. of Dwelling	NAME	Relation	Color	Sex	DATE OF BIRTH Mon/Yr	Age at last birthday	Marital Status	# Years married	Mother of how many children?	# of these children living	Place of birth (this person)	Father of this person	Mother of this person	OCCUPATION 10 years +	Attended school in months	Can read	Can write	Speak English	Owned or Rent	Owned –no mortage	Farm or house	# of farm schedule	
		CONKIN, TILDA	Wife	W	F	MAR 1869	31	M	2			KY	KY	KY			✓	✓						
	8	CONKIN, FERRY	Head	W	M	Sep 1869	30	M	7			KY	KY	KY	LIVERYMAN		✓	✓		R		H		
		" LIZZIE	Wife	W	F	Oct 1872	27	M	7	3	3	KY	KY	KY			✓	✓	✓					
		" CLARA	Dau	W	F	Jul 1895	4	S				KY	KY	KY				✓						
		" WILLIAM	Son	W	M	Jan 1897	3	S				KY	KY	KY				✓						
		" OLLIE	Dau	W	F	Jul 1899	1	S				KY	KY	KY										
	9	GRAVEN, VIRGIL	Boarder	W	M	Dec 1879	20	S				KY	KY	KY	DAY LABOR		✓	✓						
		PERCELL, ELIZABETH	Head	W	F	May 1834	66	Wd		5	5	KY	KY	KY	SEWING		✓	✓		R		H		
		HARLAN, ANGIE	Sister	W	F	DEC 1844	55	Wd				KY	KY	KY	SEWING, QUILTING		✓	✓						
8	10	CULLENS, MATTIE	HEAD	W	F	Nov 1857	42	Wd				TN	NC	TN						O	F	F	3	
		PEDIGO, LUELLA	Servant	W	F	Jan 1882	18	S				KY	KY	KY	SERVANT		✓	✓						
	11	PITCOCK, EDGAR	Head	W	M	Nov 1871	28	M	5			KY	KY	KY	MILLER		✓	✓	✓	R		F	3	sic
		" LIDIA	Wife	W	F	MAY 1866	34	M	5			KY	KY	KY			✓	✓	✓					
9	12	KIRK, MARY	Head	B	F	MAR 1856	44	Wd		7	3	KY	KY	KY	WASHING		X	X	✓	R		H		
		" ELLEN	Dau	B	F	APR 1880	20	S				KY	KY	KY	WASHING		✓	✓	✓					
		" GHERTRUDE	Dau	B	F	MAY 1885	15	S				KY	KY	KY	AT SCHOOL	5	✓	✓						
		" TENISE	Dau	B	F	Feb 1887	13	S				KY	KY	KY	AT SCHOOL	5	✓	✓						
10	13	FORD, ALBERT	HEAD	W	M	Sep 1872	27	M	8			KY	KY	KY	FARMER		✓	✓		R		H		
		" NANCY J.	Wife	W	F	Jun 1873	26	M	8	1	1	KY	TN	TN			✓	✓						
		" BEDFORD	Son	W	M	APR 1893	7	S				KY	KY	KY		3	✓	✓						
11	14	HARLAN, JAMES	Head	W	M	AUG 1826	72	M	52			KY	KY	KY			✓	✓		O		H		
		" SARAH	WIFE	W	F	AUG 1825	73	M	52	12	9	KY	KY	KY			✓	✓						
		GREENE, MATTIE	Servant	W	F	AUG 1857	42	Wd		7	6	TN	TN	KY	HOUSEWORK		✓	✓						
12	15	GLAZEBROOK, WILLIAM	Head	W	M	OCT 1847	52	S				KY	KY	KY			✓	✓		O	F	F	4	
13	16	CARTER, JOE A.	Head	W	M	July 1859	40	M	19			KY	VA	VA	CARPENTER		✓	✓		R		H		
		" LETTITIA	Wife	W	F	Jun 1860	39	M	19	9	8	NC	NC	SC			✓	✓						

TWELFTH CENSUS OF THE UNITED STATES 1900

-259-

STATE - KENTUCKY
COUNTY - MONROE
Township or other division: TOMPKINSVILLE TOWN — Enumerator: E. R. BAXTER

Supervisor's Dist. No. 102 Sheet No. ___
Enumeration Dist. No. 84

Fam.	Dwell.	NAME	Relation	Color	Sex	Date of Birth Mon/Yr	Age	Marital Status	Yrs married	Mother of how many	Children living	Birthplace	Father	Mother	Occupation	Mo. not empl.	School mo.	Read	Write	Speak Eng.	Own/Rent	Own no mtg	Farm/house	Farm sched.
		CARTER, LOUIS	Son	W	M	Aug 1881	18	S				TN	KY	NC	APPRENTICE		5	✓	✓					
		" LENORA	Dau	W	F	Sep 1882	17	S				KY	KY	NC			10	✓	✓	✓				
		" VERNA	Dau	W	F	May 1886	14	S				KY	KY	NC			10	✓	✓					
		" TONE	Dau	W	F	Apr 1888	12	S				TN	KY	NC			10	✓	✓					
		" MAC	Son	W	M	Oct 1889	10	S				TN	KY	NC			10	✓	✓	✓				
		" FANNIE	Dau	W	F	Apr 1893	7	S				KY	KY	NC			10	✓	✓					
		" MARCUS J.	Dau	W	F	Sep 1896	3	S				KY	KY	NC		?	10	✓	✓					
		" GEORGIA E.	Dau	W	F	Jan 1900	5/12	S				KY	KY	NC		?	10	✓	✓					
14	17	CLANCY, JASPER	Head	W	M	Feb 1846	54	M	25			TN	IN	TN	HOTEL KEEPER			✓	✓		O	F	F	11 ?
		" NANCY A.	Wife	W	F	Nov 1862	37	M	25			KY	KY	KY				✓	✓	✓				
		REDFORD, FLORA	Niece	W	F	Aug 1884	15	S				KY	KY	KY	HOUSEWORK	5	5	✓	✓					
		HAGAN, SAMUEL T.	Boarder	W	M	Aug 1876	23	S				KY	KY	KY	MILLER			✓	✓	✓				
		MANES, FRANK	Boarder	W	M	Jun 1874	24	S				KY	KY	KY	DAY LABOR			✓	✓	✓				
15	18	RODY, MACK	Head	W	M	Jan 1878	22	M	1			TN	TN	TN	FARMER			✓	✓	✓	R		F	5
		" HANNA	Wife	W	F	Feb 1882	18	M	1	2	2	KY	KY	KY				✓	✓	✓				
		" BRENDON	Son	W	M	Apr 1898	2	S				KY	TN	KY										
		" EUNICE	Dau	W	F	Jul 1899	10/12	S				KY	TN	KY										
16	19	EMBERTON, MAXEY H.	Head	W	M	Oct 1826	74	M	15			KY	KY	KY	DAY LABOR			✓	✓		O		F	H
		REBECCA J.	Wife	W	F	Aug 1851	48	M	15			KY	KY	KY				✓	✓	✓	O		F	H
17	20	LESLIE, JOHN E.	Head	W	M	Mar 1867	33	M	8			KY	KY	KY	STATE REPRESENTATIVE			✓	✓	✓	O		M	H
		" PATTIE	Wife	W	F	Dec 1873	26	M	8			KY	KY	KY				✓	✓	✓				
18	21	BIGGERSTAFF, SYLVESTER	Head	W	M	Aug 1859	40	S				KY	KY	KY	FARMER			✓	✓	✓	R		F	6
		" BETTIE	Sister	W	F	Dec 1852	47	S				KY	KY	KY	HOUSEWORK			✓	✓	✓				
19	22	CRAFFORD, CLEBENA	Head	W	F	Sep 1826	73	Wd		1	1	TN	VA	TN	HOUSEWORK			✓	✓	✓	O		F	7
		" ENIS	—	B	F	(UNKNOWN)	—	S		10	4	TN	TN	TN	WASHING CLOTHES			X	X	X				
		" BIG	Enis' son	B	M	Jan 1882	18	S				KY	IN	TN	DAY LABOR			✓	✓	✓				

STATE - KENTUCKY
COUNTY - MONROE
Township or other division TOMPKINSVILLE TOWN   Enumerator E. R. BAXTER

Supervisor's Dist. No. _102_ Sheet No. ____
Enumeration Dist. No. _84_ ____

No. of Family	No. of Dwelling	NAME	Relation	Color	Sex	DATE OF BIRTH Mon/Yr	Age at last birthday	Marital Status	# Years married	Mother of how many children?	# of these children living	Place of birth (this person)	Father of this person	Mother of this person	Year of immigr.	# years in U.S.	Naturalization	OCCUPATION 10 years +	Months not employed	Attended school in months	Can read	Can write	Speak English	Owned or Rent	Owned –no mortgage	Farm or house	# of farm schedule
		CRAFFORD, LITTLE	–	B	M	Jan 1882	18	S				KY	TN	TN				DAY LABOR			✓	✓	✓				
		TURNER, BRANSFORD	–	B	M	Mar 1877	23	S				KY	KY	KY				WOOD CUTTING 12			X	X	X				
		CRAFFORD, HATTIE	–	B	F	Mar 1889	11	S				KY	KY	KY				AT SCHOOL		5	✓	✓	✓				
		" MAUD	–	B	F	Jun 1892	8	S				KY	KY	KY				AT SCHOOL		5	✓	X	✓				
		" CLARENCE	–	B	M	Apr 1892	8	S				KY	KY	KY				AT SCHOOL		5	✓	X	✓				
20	23	SPEAR, SHERMAN	Head	W	M	Jul 1867	32	M	8			KY	NC	TN				LAWYER			✓	✓	✓	O	M	F	8
		" ETTA M.	Wife	W	F	Apr 1866	33	M	8			KY	KY	KY							✓	✓	✓				
		" LUCY	Sister	W	F	Jan 1876	24	S				KY	NC	TN				DRESS MAKER			✓	✓	✓				
21	24	COUNTS, SARAH D.	Head	W	F	Aug 1839	60	Wd		5	3	KY	VA	KY				HOTEL KEEPER			✓	✓	✓	O	F	F	9
		" LAURA	Dau	W	F	Nov 1866	33	S				KY	KY	KY				MILLINERY			✓	✓	✓				
		" ABIJA	Son	W	M	Dec 1875	24	S				KY	KY	KY				DRUGGIST			✓	✓	✓				
		" HENRY	Son	W	M	Mar 1880	20	S				KY	KY	KY				DRY GOOD CLERK			✓	✓	✓				
		LOUIS, CHARLIE	Boarder	W	M	Mar 1883	17	S				TN	TN	TN				DRUG CLERK			✓	✓	✓				
		GRAVES, JOHN T.	Boarder	W	M	Mar 1856	44	S				KY	KY	KY				DRUGGIST			✓	✓	✓	O	F	F	10
		DIXION, SAM J.	Boarder	W	M	UNK		Wd				TN	TN	TN				STONE MASON			X	X	✓			H	
22	25	RICHARDSON, HENRY	Head	W	M	May 1847	53	M				KY	TN	KY				MERCHANT D.G.			✓	✓	✓			H	
		" MOLLIE	Wife	W	F	Dec 1871	28	M				KY	KY	KY							✓	✓	✓				
		" MICHEL	Son	W	M	Jul 1879	20	S				KY	KY	KY				BANK CLERK			✓	✓	✓				
		" LUCY	Dau	W	F	Nov 1885	14	S				KY	KY	KY				AT SCHOOL		8	✓	✓	✓				
		" KATE	Dau	W	F	Aug 1888	11	S				KY	KY	KY				AT SCHOOL		8	✓	✓	✓				
		" FOWLER	Son	W	M	Oct 1894	5	S				KY	KY	KY				AT SCHOOL		4	✓	✓	✓				
		LEVI, WILLIAM J.	Boarder	W	M	UNKNOWN		S				KY	KY	KY				MINISTER			✓	✓	✓				
23	26	DAVIS, RICE	Head	W	M	Sep 1870	29	M	8			KY	TN	KY				DAY LABOR			✓	✓	✓	R		H	
		" DOLLIE	Wife	W	F	May 1872	28	M	8	3	2	KY	KY	KY				HOUSEWORK			✓	✓	✓				
		" WILLIAM B.	Son	W	M	Jun 1893	6	S				KY	KY	KY				AT SCHOOL		5	✓	✓	✓				
		" JOHN R.	Son	W	M	Jul 1898	1	S				KY	KY	KY							X	X	✓				

STATE - KENTUCKY
COUNTY - MONROE
Township or other division TOMPKINSVILLE TOWN Enumerator E. R. BAXTER

Supervisor's Dist. No. 102 Sheet No.
Enumeration Dist. No. 84

No. of Family	No. of Dwelling	NAME	Relation	Color	Sex	DATE OF BIRTH Mon/Yr	Age at last birthday	Marital Status	# Years married	Mother of how many children?	# of these children living	Place of birth (this person)	Father of this person	Mother of this person	Year of immigr.	# years in U.S.	Naturalization	OCCUPATION 10 years +	Months not employed	Attended school in months	Can read	Can write	Speak English	Owned or Rent	Owned –no mortage	Farm or house	# of farm schedule	
24	27	SYMPSON, WILLIAM A	Head	W	M	MAY 1866	34	M	10			KY	KY	KY				PHYSICIAN			✓	✓	✓	O		F	12	
		" LOTTIE	Wife	W	F	JAN 1873	27	M	10	5	5	KY	KY	KY				HOUSEWORK			✓	✓	✓					
		" BERTIS	Dau	W	F	AUG 1890	9	S				KY	KY	KY				AT SCHOOL		5	✓	✓	✓					
		" MAY	Dau	W	F	MAY 1893	7	S				KY	KY	KY				AT SCHOOL		5	✓	✓	✓					
		" FLOE	Dau	W	F	MAY 1895	5	S				KY	KY	KY				AT SCHOOL		5	✓	✓	✓					
		" CLOE	Dau	W	F	AUG 1897	2	S				KY	KY	KY							X	X	X					
		" LOUCRECIE	Dau	W	F	OCT 1899 7/12		S				KY	KY	KY							X	X	X					
25	28	NEWMAN, JAMES H	Head	W	M	DEC 1866	33	M	10			KY	KY	KY				COLLECTOR OF ITR			✓	✓	✓	O		F	H	
		" KIRK	Wife	W	F	MAR 1869	31	M	10	2	2	TX	KY	KY				HOUSE WORK			✓	✓						
		" ADA	Dau	W	F	Feb 1892	8	S				KY	KY	TX				AT SCHOOL		5	✓	✓						
		" DAISY	Dau	W	F	MAR 1895	5	S				KY	KY	TX				AT SCHOOL		5	✓	✓						
26	29	MAXEY, WILLIAM H	Head	W	M	Sep 1847	52	M	11			KY	KY	KY				TOWN MARTIAL			✓	✓	✓	R		F	15	SIS
		" CRISSIE G	Wife	W	F	OCT 1859	40	M	11	5	3	KY	TN	TN				HOUSEWORK			✓	✓	✓					
		" DALFORD	Son	W	M	JAN 1890	10	S				KY	KY	KY				AT SCHOOL		8	✓	✓	✓					
		" JAMES H.	Son	W	M	AUG 1892	7	S				KY	KY	KY				AT SCHOOL		8	✓	✓	✓					
		" LOUIE	Son	W	M	MAY 1897	3	S				KY	KY	KY							X	X	✓					

HERE ENDS ENUMERATION OF THE TOWN OF TOMPKINSVILLE

TWELFTH CENSUS OF THE UNITED STATES 1900

STATE - KENTUCKY
COUNTY - MONROE — *EAST* —
Township or other division *TOMPKINSVILLE*

—262—

Enumerator *ERASTUS R. BAXTER*

Supervisor's Dist. No. *102* Sheet No.
Enumeration Dist. No. *84*

Location (No. of Family / No. of Dwelling)	NAME	Relation	Color	Sex	DATE OF BIRTH Mon/Yr	Age at last birthday	Marital Status	# Years married	Mother of how many children?	# of these children living	NATIVITY Place of birth [this person]	NATIVITY Father of this person	NATIVITY Mother of this person	CITIZENSHIP Year of immigr.	# years in U.S.	Naturalization	OCCUPATION 10 years +	Months not employed	Attended school in months	Can read	Can write	Speak English	Owned or Rent	Owned –no mortgage	Farm or house	# of farm schedule
27 30	GARRETT, SARAH	Head	W	F	May 1822	78	Wd		1	0	TN	KY	TN							✓	✓	✓	O	F	F	
31	PAGE, FINIS	Head	W	M	Jun 1858	41	M	7			KY	KY	KY				FARMER			✓	✓	✓	R		F	16
"	JENNIE	Wife	W	F	Oct 1873	26	M	7	2	2	TN	TN	TN				HOUSEWORK			✓	✓	✓				
"	GLEN E.	Son	W	M	Jun 1894	6	S				KY	KY	TN				AT SCHOOL		5	X	X	✓				
"	CHARLIE S.	Son	W	M	Jul 1899	10/12	S				KY	KY	TN							X	X	X				
	READOR, POLLY	Mother in law	W	F	—	@58	S		1	1	TN	NC	VA				HOUSEWORK			✓	✓	✓				
28 32	EMBERTON, ROB	Head	W	M	Oct 1852	47	M	25			KY	KY	KY				GUNSMITH			✓	✓	✓	R		F	17
"	ENNLEE (?) M.	Wife	W	F	Aug 1853	46	M	25	6	4	NC	NC	NC				HOUSEWORK			X	X	✓				
"	ORVIL	Son	W	M	Aug 1880	19	S				KY	KY	NC				DAY LABOR			✓	✓	✓				
"	ANNIE B	Dau	W	F	Jan 1888	12	S				KY	KY	NC				AT SCHOOL		5	✓	✓	✓				
"	ALVIN N.	Son	W	M	Jul 1895	4	S				KY	KY	NC							X	X	✓				
33	BRUCE, JORDAN	Head	W	M	Aug 1861	38	M	3			GA	NC	NC				DAY LABOR			✓	✓	✓	R		H	
"	MARY	Wife	W	F	Nov 1863	36	M	3	1	1	KY	KY	KY				HOUSEWORK			✓	✓	✓				
"	JAMES E.	Son	W	M	Mar 1898	2	S				KY	GA	KY							X	X	X				
"	ELLEN	Mother	W	F	Jun 1832	67	Wd		8	4	NC	NC	NC							X	X	✓				
29 34	YOKELY, SAN B.	Head	W	M	Jan 1875	25	M				KY	NC	KY				FARMER			✓	✓	✓	R		F	18
"	FLORA	Wife	W	F	Apr 1878	22	M				KY	KY	KY				HOUSEWORK			✓	✓	✓				
	SPEAKMAN, —	Hand	W	M	UNKNOWN		M	1			KY	KY	KY				DAY LABOR			✓	✓	✓				
30 35	NORMAN, FRANK	Head	W	M	Sep 1873	26	M	7			KY	KY	KY				FARMER			✓	✓	✓	R		F	19
"	NANNIE	Wife	W	F	Sep 1871	28	M	7			KY	TN	TN				HOUSEWORK			✓	✓	✓				
31 36	HENSON, WILLIAM	Head	W	M	Jan 1862	38	M	5			KY	TN	TN				FARMER			✓	✓	✓	R		F	20
"	SARAH	Wife	W	F	Jun 1865	35	M	5	2	2	KY	TN	KY				HOUSEWORK			✓	✓	✓				
"	HUGH	Son	W	M	Sep 1884	15	S				KY	KY	KY				AT SCHOOL		5	✓	✓	✓				
"	ETTA	Dau	W	F	Jan 1887	13	S				KY	KY	KY				AT SCHOOL		5	✓	✓	✓				
"	FLEMING	Son	W	M	Feb 1890	10	S				KY	KY	KY				AT SCHOOL		4	X	X	✓				
32 37	BAXTER, HAMILTON S)	Head	W	M	Nov 1843	56	M	34			KY	KY	KY				MILLER and FARMER			✓	✓	✓	O	F	F	21

STATE - KENTUCKY
COUNTY - MONROE
Township or other division: EAST TOMPKINSVILLE

Enumerator: ERASTUS R. BAXTER

Supervisor's Dist. No. 102   Sheet No.
Enumeration Dist. No. 84

Location (No. of Family / No. of Dwelling)	NAME	Relation	Color	Sex	DATE OF BIRTH Mon/Yr	Age at last birthday	Marital Status	# Years married	Mother of how many children?	# of these children living	NATIVITY Place of birth [this person]	Father of this person	Mother of this person	CITIZENSHIP (Year of immigr. / # years in U.S. / Naturalization)	OCCUPATION 10 years +	Months not employed	Attended school in months	Can read	Can write	Speak English	Owned or Rent	Owned -no mortgage	Farm or house	# of farm schedule
	BAXTER, MARTHA E.	Wife	W	F	MAR 1850	50	M	34	9	8	KY	KY	KY		HOUSEWORK			✓	✓	✓				
	" ALONZO	Son	W	M	AUG 1867	32	S				KY	KY	KY		FARMING			✓	✓	✓	O	F	F	22
	" BARLOW	Son	W	M	Sep 1876	23	S				KY	KY	KY		FARMING			✓	✓	✓	R		F	23
	" JOSHUA	Son	W	M	NOV 1878	21	S				KY	KY	KY		FARMING	4		✓	✓	✓	R		F	24
	" GROVER C.	Son	W	M	Feb 1884	16	S				KY	KY	KY		AT SCHOOL		5	✓	✓	✓				
	" SIDNEY	Son	W	M	MAR 1886	14	S				KY	KY	KY		AT SCHOOL		5	✓	✓	✓				
	" MATTIE	Dau	W	F	AUG 1888	12	S				KY	KY	KY		AT SCHOOL		5	✓	✓	✓				
33 38	DISHMAN, HAYWOOD	Head	W	M	NOV 1868	31	M	5			TN	TN	TN		FARMER		—	✓	✓		R		F	25
	" JOSIE	Wife	W	F	@	25	M	5	4	4	TN	TN	TN		HOUSEWORK			✓	✓	✓				
	" BIRDIE	Dau	W	F	Sep 1895	4	S				KY	TN	TN					X	X	✓				
	" ETHEL	Dau	W	F	Jan 1897	3	S				KY	TN	TN					X	X	✓				
	" WILLIE	Dau	W	F	MAR 1898	2	S				KY	TN	TN					X	X	X				
	" GOBLE	Son	W	M	Jul 1899 10/12		S				KY	TN	TN					X	X	X				
34 39	PHILLIPS, WILLIAM S.	Head	W	M	Aug 1864	35	M	8			TN	TN	TN		FARMER			✓	✓	✓	R		F	26
	" LILLIE BELL	Wife	W	F	DEC 1875	24	M	8	3	3	TN	TN	TN		HOUSEWORK			X	X	✓				
	" LIZZIE	Dau	W	F	OCT 1892	7	S				TN	TN	TN					X	X	✓				
	" CLARA A.	Dau	W	F	Jul 1896	3	S				TN	TN	TN					X	X	X				
	" CLORA M.	Dau	W	F	Feb 1898	2	S				TN	TN	TN					X	X					
35 40	SPEAR, JAMES M.	Head	W	M	Jun 1866	34	M	7			KY	KY	KY		FARMER-BLACKSMITH			✓	✓	✓	R		F	27
	" LUCY	Wife	W	F	Sep 1876	23	M	7	3	3	KY	KY	KY		HOUSEWORK			✓	✓	✓				
	" CEPHAS	Son	W	M	Sep 1893	6	S				KY	KY	KY					X	X	✓				
	" FANNIE B.	Dau	W	F	Jul 1898	3	S				KY	KY	KY					X	X	X				
	" GEORGE E.	Son	W	M	Jul 1899 10/12		S				KY	KY	KY					X	X	✓				
	" NARCISSUS	Mother	W	F	May 1836	64	Wd		9	8	KY	KY	KY					X	X	✓				
36 41	WHITE, WILLIAM D.	Head	W	M	MAR 1874	26	M	4			KY	KY	KY		FARM HAND	4		✓	✓	✓	R		H	
	" NANNIE	Wife	W	F	Jul 1872	27	M	4	0	0	KY	TN	KY		HOUSEWORK	4		✓	✓	✓				

STATE - KENTUCKY
COUNTY - MONROE — EAST TOMPKINSVILLE
Township or other division — Enumerator E. R. BAXTER

Supervisor's Dist. No. 102 Sheet No.
Enumeration Dist. No. 84

Location — No. of Family	No. of Dwelling	NAME	Relation	Color	Sex	DATE OF BIRTH Mon/Yr	Age at last birthday	Marital Status	# Years married	Mother of how many children?	# of these children living	NATIVITY Place of birth [this person]	Father of this person	Mother of this person	CITIZENSHIP Year of immigr.	# years in U.S.	Naturalization	OCCUPATION 10 years +	Months not employed	Attended school in months	Can read	Can write	Speak English	OWNERSHIP Owned or Rent	Owned –no mortage	Farm or house	# of farm schedule
		WHITE, LAURA	Dau	W	F	Apr 1893	7	S				KY	KY	KY				AT SCHOOL		5	✓	✓					
37	42	COMBS, JAMES B.	Head	W	M	May 1845	55	M	22			KY	KY	KY				FARMER			✓	✓	✓	O	F	H	28
		" KITTIE	Wife	W	F	Jul 1857	42	M	22	7	7	KY	TN	TN				HOUSEWORK			✓	✓	✓				
		" TOMIE	Son	W	M	Nov 1878	21	S				KY	KY	KY				FARMER			✓	✓	✓	R		F	29
		" LINDY	Dau	W	F	Sep 1880	19	S				KY	KY	KY				HOUSEWORK			✓	✓	✓				
		" MANDY	Dau	W	F	Jan 1883	17	S				KY	KY	KY				HOUSEWORK			✓	✓	✓				
		" DANIEL H.	Son	W	M	Sep 1885	14	S				KY	KY	KY				FARM WORK		4	✓	✓	✓				
		" JOSHUA W.	Son	W	M	Oct 1889	10	S				KY	KY	KY				FARM WORK		4	✓	✓	✓				
		MARY M.	Dau	W	F	Oct 1891	7	S				KY	KY	KY				AT SCHOOL		4	✓	✓	✓				
		SARAH E.	Dau	W	F	Aug 1896	4	S				KY	KY	KY							X	X					
		WOOD, DANIEL	Boarder	W	M	Sep 1871	28	S				KY	KY	KY			U.S.	STORE KEEP - GAGER			✓	✓	✓	O	F	H	
38	43	RUSH, RANDOLPH	Head	W	M	Jun 1873	27	M				KY	KY	KY				TEACHER		4	✓	✓	✓	O	E	E	30
		" LENA D.	Wife	W	F	Feb 1883	17	M				KY	KY	KY				HOUSEWORK			✓	✓					
		" LEVESTA J.	Mother	W	F	Feb 1852	48	Divc.		4	3	KY	KY	KY				HOUSEWORK			✓	✓	✓				
		MARSHAL, NANNIE	Sister	W	F	Apr 1878	22	M				KY	KY	KY				HOUSEWORK			✓	✓	✓	R		F	31
39	44	BASKET, ISHAM	Head	W	M	Oct 1877	22	M	1			KY	KY	KY				FARMER			✓	✓	✓				
		" ALICE	Wife	W	F	Dec 1877	21	M	1	1	1	KY	KY	KY				HOUSEWORK			✓	✓	✓				
		" BIRDIE	Dau	W	F	Sep 1899	8/12	S				KY	KY	KY							X	X	X				
		HARLAN, JOHN W.	Boarder	W	M	Jan 1867	33	S				TN	KY	KY				FARMING			✓	✓	✓	O	M	E	32
40	45	COPAS, WESLEY	Head	W	M	Sep 1867	32	M	14			KY	KY	KY				FARMER	2		✓	✓	✓	R		F	33
		" ELLA	Wife	W	F	Feb 1869	31	M	14	5	5	KY	KY	KY				HOUSEWORK	2		✓	✓	✓				
		" MARGARET	Dau	W	F	Feb 1887	13	S				KY	KY	KY				AT SCHOOL		5	✓	✓	✓				
		" LENAN (?)	Dau	W	F	Jan 1889	11	S				KY	KY	KY				AT SCHOOL		5	✓	✓	✓				
		" WILLIE	Son	W	M	Mar 1891	9	S				KY	KY	KY				AT SCHOOL		5	✓	✓	✓				
		" BETTIE	Dau	W	F	May 1893	7	S				KY	KY	KY				AT SCHOOL		5	X	X	✓				
		" HESTER	Dau	W	F	Jun 1899	1	S				KY	KY	KY							X	X	✓				

STATE - KENTUCKY
COUNTY - MONROE
Township or other division: EAST TOMPKINSVILLE
Enumerator: E.R. BAXTER
Supervisor's Dist. No. 102 Sheet No.
Enumeration Dist. No. 84

No. of Family	No. of Dwelling	NAME	Relation	Color	Sex	Date of Birth (Mon/Yr)	Age at last birthday	Marital Status	# Years married	Mother of how many children?	# of these children living	Place of birth (this person)	Father of this person	Mother of this person	Year of immigr.	# years in U.S.	Naturalization	Occupation	Months not employed	Attended school in months	Can read	Can write	Speak English	Owned or Rent	Owned - no mortgage	Farm or house	# of farm schedule	
41	46	COPAS, EDWARD	HEAD	W	M	Mar 1874	26	M	8			KY	KY	KY				FARM HAND	2	2	✓	✓	✓	R		H		
		" SALLIE	WIFE	W	F	Mar 1862	28	M	8	2	2	KY	unk	unk				HOUSEWORK	2		✓	✓	✓					
		" NANCY M.	DAU	W	F	Jan 1897	3	S				KY	KY	KY							X	X	X					
		" MILLAR(D?) F.	SON	W	M	Jan 1899	1	S				KY	KY	KY							X	X	X					
42	47	SLAUGHTER, DEE	Head	W	M	Aug 1875	24	M	5			KY	KY	KY				FARMER	4		✓	✓	✓	R		F	34	
		" FANNIE	Wife	W	F	Oct 1870	29	M	5	2	1	KY	KY	KY				HOUSEWORK	2		✓	✓	✓					
		" HERBERT	Son	W	M	Oct 1895	4	S				KY	KY	KY							X	X	✓					
43	48	GRIMSLEY, MARY E	Head	W	F	- @ 70 -		W		8	5	TN	TN	TN							X	X	✓	O		F		
		" JOHN	Son	W	M	- @ 43 -		S				KY	TN	TN				FARMER	2		✓	✓	✓	R		F	35	
		" JANE	Dau	W	F	- @ 52 -		S		1	1	KY	TN	TN				HOUSEWORK	2		✓	✓	✓					
		" LUTHER	GR-SON	W	M	- 1876	24	S				KY	KY	KY				FACTORY HAND	3		✓	✓	✓					
44	49	GRIMSLEY, PRICE	Head	W	M	- @ 39		M	5			KY	TN	TN				FARMER	3		X	X	✓	R		F	35	?
		" (?)SEASTRATHA A.	Wife	W	F	- @ 30		M	5			KY	TN	TN				HOUSEWORK	3		✓	✓	✓					
45	50	THURMAN, MILARD	Head	W	M	Feb 1878	22	M	3			TN	TN	TN				FARMING	3		✓	✓	✓	R		F	36	
		" ADA	WIFE	W	F	Sep 1877	23	M	3	2	0	KY	KY	KY				HOUSEWORK	3		✓	✓	✓					
46	51	CARTER, WILLIAM	Head	W	M	Nov 1851	48	M	28			TN	TN	KY				FARMER	2		✓	✓	✓	O		F	37	
		" POLLY	Wife	W	F	Aug 1847	52	M	28	7	4	KY	KY	KY				HOUSEWORK	2		✓	✓	✓					
		" CARLOS	Son	W	M	Mar 1883	16	S				KY	TN	KY				FARM WORK	2	5	✓	✓	✓					
	52	CARTER, MONTEHEM(?)	Head	W	M	Mar 1874	26	M				TN	TN	KY				FARMING	2		✓	✓	✓	R		F	38	
		" MAGGIE	WIFE	W	F	Dec 1878	21	M				KY	TN	TN														
47	53	GRIMSLEY, BENNIE	Head	W	M	Jan 1860	40	M	15			KY	TN	TN				FARMER	2		✓	✓	✓	O		F	39	
		" NANCY J.	Wife	W	F	Mar 1856	44	M	15	1	0	KY	TN	TN				HOUSEWORK	2		✓	✓	✓					
48	54	ELDRIDGE, ROBERT	HEAD	W	M	Feb 1868	42	M	21			KY	KY	KY				FARMER			X	X	✓	R		F	40	
		" MARY A.	WIFE	W	F	Mar 1868	42	M	21	10	7	KY	KY	KY				HOUSEWORK			X	X	✓					
		" SARAH C.	DAU	W	F	Nov 1878	21	S				KY	KY	KY				SERVANT			✓	✓	✓					
		" MARY M.	DAU	W	F	Nov 1886	14	S				KY	KY	KY				AT SCHOOL		5	✓	✓	✓					

STATE - KENTUCKY
COUNTY - MONROE
Township or other division EAST TOMPKINSVILLE Enumerator E. R. BAXTER

Supervisor's Dist. No. 102 Sheet No.
Enumeration Dist. No. 84

No. of Family	No. of Dwelling	NAME	Relation	Color	Sex	Date of Birth Mon/Yr	Age at last birthday	Marital Status	# Years married	Mother of how many children?	# of these children living	Place of birth [this person]	Father of this person	Mother of this person	Year of immigr.	# years in U.S.	Naturalization	Occupation 10 years +	Months not employed	Attended school in months	Can read	Can write	Speak English	Owned or Rent	Owned –no mortage	Farm or house	# of farm schedule
		ELDRIDGE, CHRISTINE S.	Dau	W	F	Dec 1887	12	S				KY	KY	KY				AT SCHOOL		4	✓	✓					
		" ARIE F.	Dau	W	F	Apr 1889	11	S				KY	KY	KY				AT SCHOOL		4	✓	✓					
		" MARTHA J.	Dau	W	F	Feb 1891	9	S				KY	KY	KY				AT SCHOOL		4	XX	✓					
		" GEORGE E.	Son	W	M	Mar 1894	6	S				KY	KY	KY							XX	✓					
		" CLURA V.	Son	W	M	Feb 1897	3	S				KY	KY	KY							XX	X					
49	55	BRYANT WILLIE F.	Head	W	M	Mar 1856	44	M	3			KY	TN	TN				MILLING - FARMER			✓	✓		O	M	F	41
		" FLORIDA D.	Wife	W	F	Mar 1877	23	M	3	1	1	KY	KY	KY				HOUSEWORK			✓	✓					
		" CASSIE G.	Dau	W	F	Aug 1898	1	S				KY	KY	KY							XX	X					
		" NANCY D.	Sister in law	W	F	Dec 1865	34	Wd		7	7	TN	TN	KY							✓	✓					
		" ROBERT E.	Nephew	W	M	Jul 1886	13	S				KY	TN	TN				AT SCHOOL		3	✓	✓					
		" MYRTIE B.	Niece	W	F	- UNKNOWN -		S				KY	TN	TN				AT SCHOOL		3	✓	✓					
		" MOLLIE	Niece	W	F	- UNKNOWN -		S				KY	TN	TN													
		" LAURA B.	Niece	W	F	- UNKNOWN -		S				KY	TN	TN													
		" ADA	Niece	W	F	- UNKNOWN -		S				KY	TN	TN													
50	56	WOOD, JAMES T.	Head	W	M	Oct 1858	41	M	17			KY	KY	TN				FARMER			✓	✓		O	F	F	42
		" MELISSA A.	Wife	W	F	Oct 1862	37	M	17	8	8	TN	TN	TN							✓	✓					
		" BERTHA	Dau	W	F	Mar 1884	16	S				KY	KY	TN				AT SCHOOL		5	✓	✓					
		" STANFORD	Son	W	M	Aug 1885	14	S				KY	KY	TN				AT SCHOOL		5	✓	✓					
		" LENA	Dau	W	F	Dec 1887	12	S				KY	KY	TN				AT SCHOOL		5	✓	✓					
		" BEDFORD	Son	W	M	Sep 1889	10	S				KY	KY	TN				AT SCHOOL		5	✓	✓					
		" MARY	Dau	W	F	May 1890	9	S				KY	KY	TN				AT SCHOOL		5	✓	✓					
		" WILLIAM R.	Son	W	M	Apr 1893	7	S				KY	KY	TN				AT SCHOOL		5	X	X					
		" EDGAR F.	Son	W	M	Sep 1895	4	S				KY	KY	TN							X	X					
		" WALTER	Son	W	M	Oct 1898	1	S				KY	KY	TN													
51	57	SMITH, SCOTT W.	Head	W	M	Nov 1861	38	M	14			KY	KY	KY				COUNTY JUDGE			✓	✓		O	F	F	43
		" MINNIE	Wife	W	F	May 1867	33	M	14	5	5	KY	KY	KY							✓	✓					

TWELFTH CENSUS OF THE UNITED STATES 1900

STATE - KENTUCKY
COUNTY - MONROE
Township or other division EAST TOMPKINSVILLE Enumerator E. R. BAXTER

Supervisor's Dist. No. 102 Sheet No.
Enumeration Dist. No. 84

No. of Family	No. of Dwelling	NAME	Relation	Color	Sex	DATE OF BIRTH Mon/Yr	Age at last birthday	Marital Status	# Years married	Mother of how many children?	# of these children living	Place of birth [this person]	Father of this person	Mother of this person	Year of immigr.	# years in U.S.	Naturalization	OCCUPATION 10 years +	Months not employed	Attended school in months	Can read	Can write	Speak English	Owned or Rent	Owned -no mortgage	Farm or house	# of farm schedule
		SMITH, EARNEST H.	Son	W	M	Aug 1887	12	S				KY	KY	KY				AT SCHOOL		5	✓	✓	✓				
		" CASUES C.	Son	W	M	Dec 1890	9	S				KY	KY	KY				AT SCHOOL		5	✓	✓	✓				
		" MARY	Dau	W	F	May 1894	5	S				KY	KY	KY									✓				
		" ANNE	Dau	W	F	Dec 1896	4	S				KY	KY	KY									✓				
		" TOM R.	Son	W	M	Aug 1898	1	S				KY	KY	KY													
52	58	THOMPSON, JAMES I	Head	W	M	Jul 1870	29	M	9			KY	KY	KY				FARMER			✓	✓	✓	O	FF		44
		" IDA B.	Wife	W	F	Oct 1871	28	M	9	2	2	KY	KY	KY							✓	✓	✓				
		" RAY	Son	W	M	Nov 1892	7	S				KY	KY	KY				AT SCHOOL		4	X	X	✓				
		" ANDRA	Dau	W	F	Dec 1894	5	S				KY	KY	KY							X	X	✓				
53	59	HARLIN, WILLIAM	Head	W	M	Jul 1869	30	M	4			KY	KY	KY				FARMER			✓	✓	✓	O	FF		45
		" KATE	Wife	W	F	Mar 1872	28	M	4	1	1	KY	KY	KY							✓	✓	✓				
		" MARY	Dau	W	F	Jul 1897	2	S				KY	KY	KY							X	X	✓				
54	60	HAMMER, GEE	Head	W	M	Feb 1852	48	M	20			KY	KY	KY				FARMER			✓	✓	✓	O	FF		46
		" REBECCA	Wife	W	F	Feb 1859	41	M	20	4	3	KY	KY	KY							✓	✓	✓				
		" WILLIAM E	Son	W	M	Aug 1880	19	S				KY	KY	KY				FARM LABOR		4	✓	✓	✓				
		" LIZZIE	Dau	W	F	Jul 1883	16	S				KY	KY	KY				AT SCHOOL		5	✓	✓	✓				
		" HERMAN B.	Son	W	M	Nov 1889	10	S				KY	KY	KY				AT SCHOOL		5	✓	✓	✓				
55	61	DAVIS, WILLIAM	Head	W	M	May 1858	42	M	19			KY	KY	KY				FARMER			✓	✓	✓	O	FF		47
		" LAURA	Wife	W	F	Feb 1861	39	M	19	2	1	KY	KY	KY							✓	✓	✓				
		" LESLIE	Son	W	M	Oct 1881	18	M	?			KY	KY	KY							✓	✓					
		FLETCHER, MARY B.	NONE	W	F	Apr 1886	14	S				KY	KY	KY						5	✓	✓	✓				
56	62	HAMMER, JOHN T	Head	W	M	Mar 1856	44	M	18			KY	KY	KY				FARMING			✓	✓	✓	O	FF		48
		" MARGARET E	Wife	W	F	Oct 1858	41	M	18	7	6	KY	KY	KY							✓	✓	✓				
		" JOHN H.	Son	W	M	Aug 1884	15	S				KY	KY	KY				AT SCHOOL		4	✓	✓	✓				
		" ELLEN	Dau	W	F	Dec 1886	13	S				KY	KY	KY				AT SCHOOL		4	✓	✓	✓				
		" MAGGIE P.	Dau	W	F	Sep 1889	10	S				KY	KY	KY				AT SCHOOL		4	✓	✓	✓				

STATE - KENTUCKY
COUNTY - MONROE
Township or other division EAST TOMPKINSVILLE   Enumerator E.R. BAXTER

Supervisor's Dist. No. 102 Sheet No.
Enumeration Dist. No. 84

No. of Family	No. of Dwelling	NAME	Relation	Color	Sex	Date of Birth Mon/Yr	Age at last birthday	Marital Status	# Years married	Mother of how many children?	# of these children living	Place of birth (this person)	Father of this person	Mother of this person	Year of immigr.	# years in U.S.	Naturalization	Occupation 10 years +	Months not employed	Attended school in months	Can read	Can write	Speak English	Owned or Rent	Owned -no mortgage	Farm or house	# of farm schedule	
		HAMMER, MAGGIE P.	Dau	W	F	Sep 1889	10	S				KY	KY	KY				AT SCHOOL		4	✓	✓	✓					
		" BILLY L.	Son	W	M	Oct 1891	8	S				KY	KY	KY														
		" JOSEPH A.	Son	W	M	Aug 1893	6	S				KY	KY	KY														
		" BRUCE E.	Son	W	M	Aug 1895	4	S				KY	KY	KY														
57	63	MARSHAL, ANDA J.	Head	W	M	Nov 1846	53	Wd				TN	TN	TN				FARMER			✓	✓		O	F	F	49	
		" LOU	Dau	W	F	Nov 1873	26	S				KY	TN	KY							✓	✓	✓					
		" LUCY	Dau	W	F	Oct 1875	24	S				KY	TN	KY							✓	✓	✓					
		" IVY	Dau	W	F	Apr 1888	14	S				KY	TN	KY						5	✓	✓	✓					
58	64	MARSHAL, WILLIE	Head	W	M	Jul 1878	22	M				KY	TN	KY							✓	✓	✓	O	F	F	50	
		" ALICE	Wife	W	F	Jul 1878	22	M				KY	TN	KY							✓	✓	✓					
		HESTER	Grandmother	W	F	Jul 1820	79	Wd				KY	TN	TN							✓	✓	✓					
59	65	WILLIAMS, MARCUS	Head	W	M	Jun 1848	51	M	31			NC	NC	NC							✓	✓	✓	O	F	F	51	
		" LAURA	Wife	W	F	Jul 1849	50	M	31	8	5	TN	PA	AL							✓	✓	✓					
		" EMERT	Son	W	M	Jul 1875	24	S				TN	NC	TN							✓	✓	✓					
		" EARNEST	Dau	W	F	Feb 1878	21	S				KY	NC	TN							✓	✓	✓					
		" EFFIE	Dau	W	F	Nov 1885	14	S				KY	NC	TN							✓	✓	✓					
		" ESCOE	Son	W	M	Mar 1890	10	S				KY	NC	TN							✓	✓	✓	O	F	F	52	
60	66	MARS, SAM J.	Head	W	M	Aug 1842	57	M	27			KY	VA	KY				FARMER			✓	✓	✓	O	F	F	52	
		" MARGARET E.	Wife	W	F	Jul 1851	48	M	27	1	1	KY	TN	TN							✓	✓	✓					
		RUSH, HARRIET	None	W	F	Apr 1884	15	S				KY	KY	KY				AT SCHOOL		5	✓	✓	✓					
	67	CARLOCK, WILLIE	Head	W	M	Nov 1874	25	M	5			TN	TN	TN				FARMER			✓	✓	✓	R		F	52	SIC
		" CASSIE	Wife	W	F	Feb 1874	26	M	5	3	2	KY	KY	KY							✓	✓						
		" THOMAS C.	Son	W	M	May 1896	4	S				KY	TN	KY														
		" NELLIE	Dau	W	F	Jan 1899	1	S				KY	TN	KY														
61	68	YOKLEY, EMILY J.	Head	W	F	Sep 1839	60	Wd				KY	SC	VA							X	X	✓	O	F	F	53	
		HIGH, MARTHA	Sister	W	F	Mar 1844	55	S				KY	SC	VA							X	X	✓					

STATE - KENTUCKY
COUNTY - MONROE
Township or other division EAST TOMPKINSVILLE
Enumerator E. R. BAXTER

Supervisor's Dist. No. 102 Sheet No.
Enumeration Dist. No. 84

Location No. of Family	No. of Dwelling	NAME	Relation	Color	Sex	DATE OF BIRTH Mon/Yr	Age at last birthday	Marital Status	# Years married	Mother of how many children?	# of these children living	NATIVITY Place of birth [this person]	Father of this person	Mother of this person	CITIZENSHIP	OCCUPATION 10 years +	Months not employed	Attended school in months	Can read	Can write	Speak English	Owned or Rent	Owned -no mortgage	Farm or house	# of farm schedule	
62	69	POLAND, WILLIAM	Head	W	M	Feb 1827	73	M	30			TN	TN	TN					X	X	✓	R		F	54	
		" MELINDA	Wife	W	F	- @ 55 -		M	30	11	5	TN	TN	TN					X	X	✓					
63	70	POLAND, CARTER	Head	W	M	Jul 1872	27	M	1			KY	TN	TN		FARMER			✓	✓	✓	O	F	F	55	
		" MARGARET	Wife	W	F	Sep 1868	31	M	1	3	2	KY	TN	TN					X	X	✓	O	F	F	55	?
		" MOLIE D.	Dau	W	F	Apr 1895	5	S				KY	KY	KY												
		" IDER McKINLEY	Dau	W	F	Nov 1896	3	S				KY	KY	KY												
64	71	STEWART, WILLIAM	Head	W	M	Mar 1830	70	M	17			TN	TN	TN		FARMER			X	X	✓	R		F	56	
		" ELIZZIE BETH J	Wife	W	F	May 1869	40	M	17	7	7	TN	TN	TN					X	X	✓					
		" DORA B.	Dau	W	F	Oct 1884	15	S				KY	TN	TN		AT SCHOOL		4	✓	✓	✓					
		" MARGARET A.	Dau	W	F	Apr 1886	14	S				KY	TN	TN		AT SCHOOL		4	✓	✓	✓					
		" JOHN B. H.	Son	W	M	Oct 1888	11	S				KY	TN	TN		AT SCHOOL		4	X	X	✓					
		" WILLIAM B.	Son	W	M	Nov 1890	9	S				KY	TN	TN												
		" DELLA M.	Dau	W	F	Oct 1891	8	S				KY	TN	TN												
		" OCEA C.	Dau	W	F	May 1894	6	S				KY	TN	TN												
		" HENRY	? Dau	W	-	Oct 1897	2	S				KY	TN	TN												
65	72	YOKELY, MARCUS	Head	W	M	Mar 1853	47	Wd				KY	TN	TN		FARMER			✓	X	✓	R		F	57	
		" WILLIAM C.	Son	W	M	Dec 1880	19	S				KY	KY	KY		AT SCHOOL		4	✓	✓	✓					
		" WILY	Son	W	M	Sep 1883	16	S				KY	KY	KY		AT SCHOOL		4	✓	✓	✓					
66	73	TOOLEY, WILLIAM	Head	W	M	- 1851	49	M	32			KY	KY	TN		TEAMSTER			✓	✓	✓	R		F	58	
		" EUNICE	Wife	W	F	Dec 1844	55	M	32	10	10	KY	TN	KY					✓	✓	✓					
		" EVIE	Dau	W	F	Feb 1876	24	S				KY	KY	KY					✓	✓	✓					
		" ESTELLA	Dau	W	F	Oct 1877	22	S				KY	KY	KY					✓	✓	✓					
		" LIDDIE	Dau	W	F	Aug 1879	20	S				KY	KY	KY					✓	✓	✓					
		" CHARLES	Son	W	M	Oct 1881	18	S				KY	KY	KY		AT SCHOOL		5	✓	✓	✓					
		" BITTIE	Dau	W	F	Oct 1883	16	S				KY	KY	KY		AT SCHOOL		5	✓	✓	✓					
		" JOHNIE	Son	W	M	Oct 1885	14	S				KY	KY	KY		AT SCHOOL		5	✓	✓	✓					

STATE - KENTUCKY
COUNTY - MONROE
Township or other division **EAST TOMPKINSVILLE**
Enumerator **E. B. BAXTER**

Supervisor's Dist. No. **102** Sheet No.
Enumeration Dist. No. **84**

No. of Family	No. of Dwelling	NAME	Relation	Color	Sex	DATE OF BIRTH Mon/Yr	Age at last birthday	Marital Status	# Years married	Mother of how many children?	# of these children living	Place of birth (this person)	Father of this person	Mother of this person	Year of immigr.	# years in U.S.	Naturalization	OCCUPATION 10 years +	Months not employed	Attended school in months	Can read	Can write	Speak English	Owned or Rent	Owned – no mortgage	Farm or house	# of farm schedule
		TOOLEY, FLORENCE	Dau	W	F	Oct 1888	11	S				KY	KY	KY				AT SCHOOL		5	✓	✓	✓				
67	74	TOOLEY, JOHN	Head	W	M	Jun 1865	45	M	23			KY	KY	KY				TEAMSTER			✓	✓	✓	O	M	F	59
		" LIDDIE A.	Wife	W	F	Oct 1858	41	M	23	9	8	KY	TN	KY							✓	✓	✓				
		" LUCY	Dau	W	F	Aug 1880	19	S				KY	KY	KY				AT SCHOOL		5							
		" MARTHA	Dau	W	F	Feb 1883	17	S				KY	KY	KY				AT SCHOOL		5							
		" JOSEPH	Son	W	M	Oct 1885	14	S				KY	KY	KY				AT SCHOOL		5							
		" PEARL	Dau	W	F	Jan 1889	11	S				KY	KY	KY				AT SCHOOL		5							
		" DAISY	Dau	W	F	Jun 1891	9	S				KY	KY	KY							✓	✓	✓				
		" JAYRET(?)	Son	W	M	Jul 1895	4	S				KY	KY	KY													
		" LOTTIE	Dau	W	F	Feb 1898	2	S				KY	KY	KY													
		ORVE, JOHN	Hand	W	M	Feb 1875	25	S				TN	UNKNOWN					TEAMSTER			✓	✓	✓				
		GARRETT, JAMES	Hand	W	M	— UNKNOWN —		M	1			TN	UNKNOWN					TEAMSTER			✓	✓	✓				
		DUNCAN, DUG	Hand	B	M	Feb 1876	24	S				KY	UNKNOWN					DAY LABOR			✓	✓	✓				
	75	PALMORE, POTTER	Head	W	M	Dec 1872	27	M	7			KY	KY	KY				MILL HAND			✓	✓	✓			H	
		" ALICE	Wife	W	F	May 1877	23	M	7	4	3	KY	KY	KY							✓	✓	✓				
		" GRACE	Dau	W	F	Aug 1894	5	S				KY	KY	KY													
		" WORT	Son	W	M	Nov 1896	3	S				KY	KY	KY													
		" ELECTIE	Dau	W	F	Dec 1899	4/12	S				KY	KY	KY													
68	76	FRIER, WILLIAM	Head	W	M	Jan 1829	72	M	14			TN	TN	TN				FARMING			✓	✓	✓	O	F	F	60
		" LIZZIE	Wife	W	F	Mar 1867	33	M	14	1	1	IND	IND	KY							✓	✓	✓				
		" MARY T.	Dau	W	F	Nov 1887	12	S				KY	TN	IND				AT SCHOOL		5	✓	✓	✓				
69	77	YOKELY, BROCK	Head	W	M	Aug 1860	39	M	20			KY	KY	KY				DAY LABOR			X	X	✓	R	F	61	
		" MARY	Wife	W	F	Mar 1862	38	M	20	3	3	KY	KY	KY							X	X	✓				
		" LEMIE J.	Dau	W	F	Dec 1882	17	S				KY	KY	KY							✓	✓	✓				
		" WILLIAM L.	Son	W	M	Aug 1886	13	S				KY	KY	KY				AT SCHOOL		4	✓	✓	✓				
		" HUGH	Son	W	M	Jan 1890	10	S				KY	KY	KY				AT SCHOOL		4	✓	✓	✓				

STATE - KENTUCKY
COUNTY - MONROE
Township or other division — EAST TOMPKINSVILLE
Enumerator — E. R. BAXTER

—271—

Supervisor's Dist. No. 102 Sheet No. ___
Enumeration Dist. No. 84

No. of Family	No. of Dwelling	NAME	Relation	Color	Sex	Date of Birth Mon/Yr	Age at last birthday	Marital Status	# years married	Mother of how many children?	# of these children living	Place of birth (this person)	Father of this person	Mother of this person	Year of immigr.	# years in U.S.	Naturalization	Occupation 10 years +	Months not employed	Attended school in months	Can read	Can write	Speak English	Owned or Rent	Owned-no mortage	Farm or house	# of farm schedule
76	78	GRAVENS, JOHNIE	Head	W	M	Dec 1878	21	M	2			KY	KY	KY				FARMER			✓	✓	✓	O	F	F	62
		" LUCY	wife	W	F	Feb 1884	16	M	2	1	1	KY	KY	KY							✓	✓	✓				
		" NELLIE M.	Dau	W	F	Jul 1899	10/12	S				KY	KY	KY													
71	79	HOWARD, JAMES A.	Head	W	M	Sep 1871	28	M	2			TN	NC	TN				FARMER			✓	✓	✓	R		F	63
		" CORA	wife	W	F	Aug 1878	21	M	2	2	1	KY	KY	KY								✓	✓				
		" ABBIE L	Dau	W	F	May 1900	1/12	S				KY	TN	KY													
72	80	YOKLEY, JOHN W.	Head	W	M	Jan 1876	24	M	2			KY	KY	KY							✓	✓	✓	R		F	64
		" MARY A.	Wife	W	F	Dec 1872	27	M	2	1	1	TN	TN	TN							✓	✓	✓				
		" FINLEY M.	Son	W	M	Oct 1898	1	S				KY	KY	TN													
73	81	SPEAR, PRESTON	Head	W	M	Apr 1870	30	M	11			KY	KY	KY				FARMER			✓	✓	✓	R		F	65
		" ANNIE	Wife	W	F	Jun 1871	30	M	11	4	4	KY	KY	KY							✓	✓	✓				
		" CARMIN	Son	W	M	Apr 1890	10	S				KY	KY	KY				AT School		5	X	X	✓				
		" NEONA	Dau	W	F	Oct 1892	7	S				KY	KY	KY													
		" ORA	Dau	W	F	Apr 1894	6	S				KY	KY	KY													
		" DORA	Dau	W	F	Dec 1896	3	S				KY	KY	KY													
74	82	PEDIGO, CALVIN	Head	W	M	Apr 1853	48	M	5			KY	VA	VA				FARMER			✓	✓	✓	O	M	F	66
		" ANNIE	Wife	W	F	Mar 1861	39	M	5	5		TN	NC	NC							X	X	✓				
		" CHARLIE	Son	W	M	Mar 1885	15	S				KY	TN	KY				AT School		5	✓	✓	✓				
		" MAY	Dau	W	F	Apr 1886	14	S				KY	TN	KY				AT School		5	✓	✓	✓				
		" MARNE	Dau	W	F	Jul 1887	13	S				KY	TN	KY				AT School		5	✓	✓	✓				
		" LAWRENCE	Son	W	M	Jan 1890	10	S				KY	TN	KY				AT School		5	✓	✓	✓				
		" CORBIT	Son	W	M	Feb 1896	4	S				KY	TN	KY													
75	83	RUSH, WILLIAM	Head	W	M	Apr 1853	47	M	1			KY	KY	KY				FARMER			✓	✓	✓	R		F	67
		" KIRK M.	wife	W	F	Dec 1874	25	M	1	2	2	KY	KY	KY							✓	✓	✓				
		" CECIL	Son	W	M	Apr 1897	3	S				KY	KY	KY													
		" (INFANT)	Son	W	M	May 1900	—	S				KY	KY	KY													

STATE - KENTUCKY
COUNTY - MONROE
Township or other division   EAST TOMPKINSVILLE   Enumerator   E. R. BAXTER

Supervisor's Dist. No. 102   Sheet No.
Enumeration Dist. No. 84

No. of Family	No. of Dwelling	NAME	Relation	Color	Sex	DATE OF BIRTH Mon/Yr	Age at last birthday	Marital Status	# Years married	Mother of how many children?	# of these children living	Place of birth (this person)	Father of this person	Mother of this person	Year of immigr.	# years in U.S.	Naturalization	OCCUPATION 10 years +	Months not employed	Attended school in months	Can read	Can write	Speak English	Owned or Rent	Owned -no mortgage	Farm or house	# of farm schedule
76	84	BAILEY, WOLFORD	Head	B	M	Jun 1863	37	M	21			KY	KY	KY				FARMER			✓	✓	✓	R		F	68
		" ANN	Wife	B	F	—	37	M	21	10	8	TN	TN	TN							✓	✓	✓				
		" CORA (?) B.S.	Dau	B	F	APR 1886	17	S				KY	KY	TN				AT SCHOOL		4	✓	✓	✓				
		" FRANK	Son	B	M	APR 1889	11	S				KY	KY	TN				AT SCHOOL		4	✓	✓	✓				
		" HURSHEL G.	Son	B	M	AUG 1889?	10	S				KY	KY	TN				AT SCHOOL		2	X	X	✓				
		" CHARLIE	Son	B	M	Sep 1892	8	S				KY	KY	TN													
		" WESLEY	Son	B	M	AUG 1893	7	S				KY	KY	TN													
		" LEE	Son	B	M	Sep 1894	6	S				KY	KY	TN													
		" ORA	Son	B	M	Feb 1896	4	S				KY	KY	TN													
		" MAXEY	Son	B	M	APR 1899	1	S				KY	KY	TN													
77	85	BARNES, THOMAS N.	Head	W	M	Jun 1844	56	M	32			KY	TN	KY				FARMING	12		✓	✓	✓	R		F	69
		" MARY J.	Wife	W	F	MAR 1852	48	M	32	11	6	KY	KY	KY							✓	✓	✓				
		" JAMES A.	Son	W	M	Jun 1872	27	S				KY	KY	KY				FARMING			✓	✓	✓				
		" WILLIAM J.	Son	W	M	DEC 1873	26	S				KY	KY	KY				FARMING			✓	✓	✓				
		" MELVIN	Son	W	M	MAR 1876	24	S				KY	KY	KY					12		X	X	✓				
		" JOSEPH H.	Son	W	M	Nov 1878	21	S				KY	KY	KY				FARMING			✓	✓	✓				
		" NANCY C.	Dau	W	F	May 1885	15	S				KY	KY	KY				AT SCHOOL		4	✓	✓	✓				
		" KIRBY	Son	W	M	APR 1889	11	S				KY	KY	KY				AT SCHOOL		5	✓	X	✓				
78	86	BROWN, WILLIAM	Head	W	M	Feb 1850	50	M	7			KY	KY	KY				FARMER			✓	✓	✓	O	F	F	70
		" REBECCA	Wife	W	F	OCT 1858	41	M	7			TN	TN	TN							✓	✓	✓				
79	87	YOUNG, JAMES	Head	W	M	— UNKNOWN —		M	19			KY	ALA	VA				FARMER			X	X	✓	R		F	71
		" LIZA A.	Wife	W	F	Jul 1861	37	M	19	3	3	TN	ALA	VA							X	X	✓				
		" EVAN A.	Son	W	M	OCT 1881	18	S				KY	KY	TN				FARM HAND			X	X	✓				
		" WILLIAM B.	Son	W	M	Nov 1883	16	S				KY	KY	TN				FARM HAND			✓	✓	✓				
		" JOHN H.	Son	W	M	Jul 1886	13	S				KY	KY	TN				FARM HAND			X	X	✓				
80	88	HAGAN, THOMAS R.	Head	W	M	DEC 1839	60	M	29			KY	KY	KY				FARMER	4		✓	✓	✓	O	F	F	72

STATE - KENTUCKY
COUNTY - MONROE
Township or other division — EAST TOMPKINSVILLE — Enumerator E.R. BAXTER

Supervisor's Dist. No. 102 Sheet No.
Enumeration Dist. No. 84

No. of Family	No. of Dwelling	NAME	Relation	Color	Sex	DATE OF BIRTH Mon/Yr	Age at last birthday	Marital Status	# Years married	Mother of how many children?	# of these children living	Place of birth (this person)	Father of this person	Mother of this person	Year of immigr.	# years in U.S.	Naturalization	OCCUPATION 10 years +	Months not employed	Attended school in months	Can read	Can write	Speak English	Owned or Rent	Owned -no mortgage	Farm or house	# of farm schedule
		HAGAN, NANCY M.	Wife	W	F	-UNKNOWN-		M	29	6	4	KY	KY	KY						4	X	X	✓				
		" JOHN W	Son	W	M	APR 1878	22	S				KY	KY	KY				FARMING	2		✓	✓	✓				
		" EVIE	Dau	W	F	APR 1882	18	S				KY	KY	KY							✓	✓	✓				
81	89	PAGE, MARTHA J.	Head	W	F	OCT 1837	62	Wd		5	5	KY	KY	KY							X	X	✓	O	F	F	73
		" REBECCA	Dau	W	F	Sep 1860	39	S				KY	KY	KY							✓	✓	✓				
		" CHARLES T.	Son	W	M	Feb 1864	36	S				KY	KY	KY				FARMING			✓	✓	✓				
		" ALICE	Dau	W	F	Sep 1875	24	S				KY	KY	KY				FARMING									
82	90	PITCOCK, THOMAS	HEAD	W	M	JAN 1833	67	M	44			KY	TN	TN				FARMING			X	X	✓	O	F	F	74
		" LUCY J	WIFE	W	F	JUN 1829	71	M	44			KY	KY	KY							X	X	✓				
	91	MARTIN, JOHNIE	Head	W	M	APR 1874	26	M	6			KY	KY	KY				BLACKSMITH			✓	✓	✓	R	F	75	
		" MARY L.	Wife	W	F	MAR 1875	25	M	6	2	2	KY	KY	KY							✓	✓	✓				
		" OSCAR	Son	W	M	APR 1895	5	S				KY	KY	KY													
		" ROSCOE	Son	W	M	MAR 1897	2	S				KY	KY	KY													
83	92	TAYLOR, WILLIAM	Head	W	M	JAN 1844	56	M	34			KY	KY	KY				FARMING 4			✓	✓	✓	O	F	F	76
		" JANE M	Wife	W	F	JAN 1844	56	M	34	7	5	TN	TN	TN				FARMING			✓	✓	✓				
		" JOHN	Son	W	M	MAR 1876	24	S				KY	KY	TN				FARMING			✓	✓	✓				
		" JONAS L.	Son	W	M	JAN 1881	19	S				KY	KY	TN				FARMING			✓	✓	✓				
		" BENTON	Son	W	M	NOV 1883	16	S				KY	KY	TN				FARMING + SCHOOL	4		✓	✓	✓				
84	93	SARTAN, EARNEST	Head	W	M	JUN 1879	20	M	1			KY	KY	KY				FARMING			✓	✓	✓	O	F	F	77
		" EVIE	WIFE	W	F	JUL 1880	19	M	1			KY	KY	KY							✓	✓	✓				
85	94	PILAND, JOHN S.	Head	W	M	APR 1851	49	M	21			KY	KY	KY				FARMING			✓	✓	✓	R	F	78	
		" MANDA	Wife	W	F	DEC 1853	45	M	21	8	7	KY	KY	KY							✓	✓	✓				
		" JOE T.	Son	W	M	Feb 1882	18	S				KY	KY	KY							✓	✓	✓				
		" PEARL	Dau	W	F	APR 1884	16	S				KY	KY	KY				AT SCHOOL		4	✓	✓	✓				
		" JAMES	Son	W	M	APR 1886	14	S				KY	KY	KY				AT SCHOOL		4	✓	✓	✓				
		" KITTIE	Dau	W	F	JAN 1889	11	S				KY	KY	KY				AT SCHOOL		4	✓	✓	✓				

STATE - KENTUCKY
COUNTY - MONROE
Township or other division: EAST TOMPKINSVILLE
Enumerator: E.R. BAXTER
Supervisor's Dist. No. 102   Sheet No.
Enumeration Dist. No. 84

No. of Family	No. of Dwelling	NAME	Relation	Color	Sex	Date of Birth Mon/Yr	Age at last birthday	Marital Status	# Years married	Mother of how many children	# of these children living	Place of birth (this person)	Father of this person	Mother of this person	Year of immigr.	# years in U.S.	Naturalization	Occupation	Months not employed	Attended school in months	Can read	Can write	Speak English	Owned or Rent	Owned - no mortgage	Farm or house	# of farm schedule
		PILAND, HOMER	Son	W	M	Mar 1891	9	S				KY	KY	KY													
		" SHAFER	Son	W	M	Oct 1892	7	S				KY	KY	KY													
86	95	COPAS, IRA	Head	W	M	May 1862	38	M	18			KY	TN	KY				FARMING		4	X	X	✓	R		F	79
		" SARAH	Wife	W	F	— 1860	40	M	18	7	5	KY	TN	TN							X	X	✓				
		" AVERY	Son	W	M	Jun 1885	14	S				KY	KY	KY						4	X	X	✓				
		" DAISY L.	Dau	W	F	Jun 1887	12	S				KY	KY	KY							X	X	✓				
		" SUSIE	Dau	W	F	Jul 1892	7	S				KY	KY	KY													
		" EDGAR	Son	W	M	Oct 1894	3	S				KY	KY	KY													
		" LUCY	Dau	W	F	Oct 1897	2	S				KY	KY	KY													
87	96	BROWN, JAMES	Head	W	M	Feb 1813	87	M	22			KY	KY	KY				FARMER			✓	✓	✓	O		F	80
		" MARY	Wife	W	F	Oct 1836	63	M	22	0	0	KY	KY	KY							X	X	✓				
		" MARY B.	Dau	W	F	Oct 1864	35	S				KY	KY	KY							X	X	✓				
88	97	VANCE, STEVEN	Head	W	M	Feb 1857	42	M	3			KY	VA	KY				FARMING			✓	✓	✓	O		F	81
		" EVIE	Wife	W	F	Nov 1877	22	M	3	2	2	KY	KY	KY							✓	✓	✓				
		" JOHN T.	Son	W	M	Mar 1898	2	S				KY	KY	KY													
		" DENIS C.	Son	W	M	Oct 1899	1	S				KY	KY	KY													
		REDFORD, WILBUR	Nephew	W	M	Dec 1888	12	S				KY	KY	KY				AT SCHOOL		4	✓	✓	✓				
89	98	BRENTS, JACKSON	Head	W	M	Jan 1844	56	M	13			KY	KY	KY				FARMER			✓	✓	✓	R		F	82
		" ALICE N.	Wife	W	F	Jan 1864	36	M	13	6	6	KY	KY	KY							✓	✓	✓				
		" NORA D.	Dau	W	F	Aug 1887	12	S				KY	KY	KY						5	✓	✓	✓				
		" MAUD E.	Dau	W	F	Feb 1889	10	S				KY	KY	KY						5	✓	✓	✓				
		" SALLIE G.	Dau	W	F	Apr 1891	7	S				KY	KY	KY													
		" EDUIE (?)	Dau	W	F	Jun 1894	6	S				KY	KY	KY													
		" NANCY E.	Dau	W	F	Apr 1896	4	S				KY	KY	KY													
		" BETTIE E.	Dau	W	F	Jul 1898	1	S				KY	KY	KY													
90	99	STRODE, HULIT	Head	W	M	Jul 1852	47	S				KY	KY	KY							✓	✓	✓	O		F	84 S10

TWELFTH CENSUS OF THE UNITED STATES 1900

— 275 —

STATE - KENTUCKY
COUNTY - MONROE
Township or other division: EAST TOMPKINSVILLE
Enumerator: E. K. BAXTER

Supervisor's Dist. No. 102   Sheet No.
Enumeration Dist. No. 84

No. of Family	No. of Dwelling	NAME	Relation	Color	Sex	Date of Birth Mon/Yr	Age at last birthday	Marital Status	# Years married	Mother of how many children?	# of these children living	Place of birth (this person)	Father of this person	Mother of this person	Year of immigr.	# years in U.S.	Naturalization	Occupation	Months not employed	Attended school in months	Can read	Can write	Speak English	Owned or Rent	Owned – no mortgage	Farm or house	# of Farm schedule
		STRODE, GEORGE	Brother	W	M	Jun 1858	42	S				KY	KY	KY							✓	✓	✓				
91	100	BARTLEY ELMORE	Head	W	M	Aug 1866	33	M	9			KY	KY	KY				FARMING			✓	✓	✓	O	F	F	85
		" CORDELA	Wife	W	F	Nov 1871	28	M	9	5	5	KY	KY	KY							✓	✓	✓				
		" MARY B.	Dau	W	F	May 1891	9	S				KY	KY	KY													
		" ABRUS(?) L	Son	W	M	May 1893	7	S				KY	KY	KY													
		" LEMUEL H.	Son	W	M	Mar 1895	5	S				KY	KY	KY													
		" BERTHA D.	Dau	W	F	Jun 1897	3	S				KY	KY	KY													
		" BUNA M.	Dau	W	F	Oct 1899	8/12	S				KY	KY	KY													
92	101	BARTLEY MARCUS M	Head	W	M	Jan 1860	40	M	19			KY	KY	KY				FARMING			✓	✓	✓	O	F	F	86
		" PRISSILLA	Wife	W	F	Jan 1861	39	M	19	9	7	KY	KY	KY							✓	✓	✓				
		" SMITH	Son	W	M	Oct 1881	18	S				KY	KY	TN				AT SCHOOL		3	✓	✓	✓				
		" JENNIE P.	Dau	W	F	Aug 1883	16	S				KY	KY	TN				AT SCHOOL		2	✓	✓	✓				
		" JULIA E.	Dau	W	F	Oct 1885	15	S				KY	KY	TN				AT SCHOOL		2	✓	✓	✓				
		" ROXIE L.	Dau	W	F	Apr 1888	12	S				KY	KY	TN				AT SCHOOL		4	✓	✓					
		" EMMA	Dau	W	F	Feb 1892	8	S				KY	KY	TN													
		" EXTES	Son	W	M	Jun 1894	6	S				KY	KY	TN													
		" LUCY F.	Dau	W	F	Feb 1897	3	S				KY	KY	TN													
93	102	BROWN ALEXANDER	Head	W	M	Apr 1872	28	M	12			KY	KY	KY				FARMING	5		✓	✓	✓	O	F	F	87
		" LOUISA A.	Wife	W	F	Jan 1873	27	M	12	5	5	KY	KY	KY							X	X	✓				
		" MAUD	Dau	W	F	May 1890	10	S				KY	KY	KY				AT SCHOOL		5	X	X	✓				
		" FRANK J.	Son	W	M	Sep 1891	8	S				KY	KY	KY													
		" BETHEL	Son	W	M	Jan 1894	6	S				KY	KY	KY													
		" BEDFORD	Son	W	M	Apr 1896	4	S				KY	KY	KY													
		" LUCY	Dau	W	F	Sep 1899	8/12	S				KY	KY	KY					4		X	X	✓	O	F	F	88
94	103	BROWN, MARY	Head	W	F	– UNKNOWN –		Wd		5	5	KY	KY	KY							X	X	✓				
		" HARMON	Son	W	M	– UNKNOWN –		S				KY	KY	KY				FARMING	6		✓	✓	✓				

STATE - KENTUCKY
COUNTY - MONROE
Township or other division

Enumerator E. R. BAXTER

Supervisor's Dist. No. 102 Sheet No. _____
Enumeration Dist. No. 84 _____

No. of Family / No. of Dwelling	NAME	Relation	Color	Sex	DATE OF BIRTH Mon/Yr	Age at last birthday	Marital Status	# Years married	Mother of how many children?	# of these children living	Place of birth (this person)	Father of this person	Mother of this person	Year of immigr.	# years in U.S.	Naturalization	OCCUPATION 10 years +	Months not employed	Attended school in months	Can read	Can write	Speak English	Owned or Rent	Owned -no mortage	Farm or house	# of farm schedule
	BROWN, ALICE	Dau	W	F	Nov 1875	24	S				KY	KY	KY							✓	✓	✓				
95/104	HUFF, JAMES	Head	W	M	Dec 1842	57	M	23			TN	TN	TN				FARMING	6		X	X	✓	O		F	89
"	SARAH E.	Wife	W	F	Mar 1850	50	M	23	6	4	TN	TN	TN							X	X	✓				
"	JERYMIAH	Son	W	M	Jan 1868	22	S				KY	TN	TN							✓	✓	✓				
"	JOHNIE	Son	W	M	May 1881	19	S				KY	TN	TN							✓	✓	✓				
"	MARY A.	Dau	W	F	Sep 1882	17	S				KY	TN	TN							✓	✓	✓				
"	MARTHA B.	Dau	W	F	Nov 1891	9	S				KY	TN	TN							✓	✓	✓				
96/105	WILLIAMS, WILLETT	Head	W	M	Jun 1879	21	M				KY	KY	KY							✓	✓	✓	R		F	90
"	EVIE	Wife	W	F	Mar 1880	19	M				KY	KY	KY							✓	✓	✓				
97/106	JONSON, MARGARET	Head	W	F	Feb 1851	49	Wd		8	6	TN	TN	TN							X	X	✓			H	
"	MARY E.	Dau	W	F	Oct 1873	27	S				KY	TN	TN							✓	✓	✓				
"	WILLIAM H.	Son	W	M	Jun 1877	23	S				KY	TN	TN							✓	✓	✓	O		F	91
"	FRANKLIN A.	Son	W	M	Jun 1879	20	S				KY	TN	TN							✓	✓	✓				
"	MANERVIE A.	Dau	W	F	Jun 1879	20	S				KY	TN	TN							✓	✓	✓				
"	LULA F.	Dau	W	F	Apr 1882	18	S				KY	TN	TN							✓	✓	✓				
"	MINNIE E.	Dau	W	F	Dec 1887	12	S				KY	TN	TN				AT SCHOOL		5	✓	✓	✓				
98/107	BARTLEY, TURNER	Head	W	M	Jul 1861	38	M	19			KY	KY	KY				FARMING			✓	✓	✓	O		F	92
"	ELLEN	Wife	W	F	Jul 1857	43	M	19	8	8	KY	KY	KY							✓	✓	✓				
"	JAMES	Son	W	M	Jan 1882	18	S				KY	KY	KY				FARM HAND			✓	✓	✓				
"	JULIA	Dau	W	F	May 1884	16	S				KY	KY	KY				AT SCHOOL		5	✓	✓	✓				
"	GEORGE	Son	W	M	Feb 1886	14	S				KY	KY	KY				AT SCHOOL		5	✓	✓	✓				
"	SUSAN	Dau	W	F	Jan 1888	12	S				KY	KY	KY				AT SCHOOL		5	✓	✓	✓				
"	BENTON	Son	W	M	Jun 1890	9	S				KY	KY	KY				AT SCHOOL		5	✓	✓	✓				
"	EDGAR	Son	W	M	Jan 1891	8	S				KY	KY	KY													
"	OSCAR	Son	W	M	Aug 1893	6	S				KY	KY	KY													
"	BEDFORD	Son	W	M	May 1895	5	S				KY	KY	KY													

STATE - KENTUCKY
COUNTY - MONROE
Township or other division — EAST TOMPKINSVILLE
Enumerator — E.R. BAXTER

Supervisor's Dist. No. _102_ Sheet No.
Enumeration Dist. No. _84_

Location No. of Family	No. of Dwelling	NAME	Relation	Color	Sex	DATE OF BIRTH Mon/Yr	Age at last birthday	Marital Status	# Years married	Mother of how many children?	# of these children living	Place of birth [this person]	Father of this person	Mother of this person	Year of immigr.	# years in U.S.	Naturalization	OCCUPATION 10 years +	Months not employed	Attended school in months	Can read	Can write	Speak English	Owned or Rent	Owned –no mortage	Farm or house	# of farm schedule	
99	08	BIGGERSTAFF, SAM	HEAD	W	M	MAR 1843	57	M	24			KY	KY	KY				FARMER			✓	✓		O		F	93	
		" ANNIE	WIFE	W	F	APR 1854	46	M	24	6	4	KY	KY	KY							✓	✓	✓					
		" HIRAM	SON	W	M	FEB 1882	18	S				KY	KY	KY				AT SCHOOL		5		✓						
		" SUSAN	DAU	W	F	SEP 1883	16	S				KY	KY	KY				AT SCHOOL		5	✓	✓	✓					
		" LIZZIE	DAU	W	F	AUG 1886	13	S				KY	KY	KY				AT SCHOOL		5	✓	✓	✓					
100	09	BIGGERSTAFF, ALLEN	HEAD	W	M	JUL 1843	56	M	30			KY	KY	KY				FARMER			✓	✓	✓	O		F	94	
		" ELIZZIEBETH	WIFE	W	F	DEC 1851	48	M	30	12	9	KY	KY	KY							✓	✓	✓					
		" JOE	SON	W	M	SEP 1872	27	S				KY	KY	KY				FARMING			✓	✓	✓					
		" SUSAN	DAU	W	F	FEB 1877	23	S				KY	KY	KY							✓	✓	✓					
		" ALICE	DAU	W	F	MAR 1879	20	S				KY	KY	KY							✓	✓	✓					
		" BENNIE	SON	W	M	AUG 1881	18	S				KY	KY	KY				FARMING			✓	✓	✓					
		" MARTHA	DAU	W	F	MAR 1887	13	S				KY	KY	KY						5	✓	✓	✓					
		" MOLLIE	DAU	W	F	AUG 1889	10	S				KY	KY	KY						5	✓	✓	✓					
		" LENA	DAU	W	F	MAR 1894	6	S				KY	KY	KY														
		" HAYDEN	SON	W	M	NOV 1895	4	S				KY	KY	KY							X	X	✓	R		H		
101	10	HALSELL, CYRUS	HEAD	B	M	JUL 1875	25	M	2			KY	KY	KY							✓	✓	✓					
		" RENDY	WIFE	B	F	JAN 1880	20	M	2	2	2	KY	KY	KY							✓	✓						
		" FRANKLIN	SON	B	M	JAN 1895	5	S				KY	KY	KY														
		" BYRNESS	SON	B	M	JUN 1898	2	S				KY	KY	KY														
102	11	MEADOW, GEORGE	HEAD	W	M	MAY 1860	40	M	13			KY	KY	KY				FARMING			✓	✓	✓	O		F	95	
		" MARY	WIFE	W	F	MAY 1866	34	M	13	6	6	KY	KY	KY							✓	✓	✓					
		" DONNIE	DAU	W	F	NOV 1888	11	S				KY	KY	KY				AT SCHOOL		4	✓	✓						
		" DOLLIE	DAU	W	F	SEP 1890	9	S				KY	KY	KY														
		" LUTHER L.	SON	W	M	NOV 1893	6	S				KY	KY	KY														
		" MAUD J.	DAU	W	F	NOV 1895	4	S				KY	KY	KY														
		" MILLARD T.	SON	W	M	NOV 1897	2	S				KY	KY	KY														

STATE - KENTUCKY
COUNTY - MONROE
Township or other division **EAST TOMPKINSVILLE** Enumerator **E. R. BAXTER**

Supervisor's Dist. No. _102_ Sheet No.
Enumeration Dist. No. _84_

No. of Family	No. of Dwelling	NAME	Relation	Color	Sex	DATE OF BIRTH Mon/Yr	Age at last birthday	Marital Status	# Years married	Mother of how many children?	# of these children living	Place of birth (this person)	Father of this person	Mother of this person	Year of immigr.	# years in U.S.	Naturalization	OCCUPATION 10 years +	Months not employed	Attended school in months	Can read	Can write	Speak English	Owned or Rent	Owned - no mortage	Farm or house	# of farm schedule
		MEADOW, HUBERT C	Son	W	M	Dec 1899	5/12	S				KY	KY	KY							✓						
103	112	SPEAR, WILLIAM B.	Head	W	M	Jan 1866	34	M	5			KY	KY	KY				FARMING			✓	✓	✓	R		F	96
		" SARAH J.	Wife	W	F	Sep 1872	27	M	5	2	2	KY	KY	KY							✓	✓	✓				
		" LAWRENCE	Son	W	M	Sep 1895	4	S				KY	KY	KY								✓					
		" SALA BELL	Dau	W	F	Jul 1897	2	S				KY	KY	KY													
104	113	CLOYD, JOHN T.	Head	W	M	Sep 1854	45	M	17			KY	KY	KY				FARMING			✓	✓	✓	R		F	97
		" CANSADA	Wife	W	F	Feb 1861	39	M	17	6	6	KY	KY	KY													
		" LUCY	Dau	W	F	Jul 1883	16	S				KY	KY	KY				AT SCHOOL		4	✓	✓	✓				
		" EMMA	Dau	W	F	Nov 1884	15	S				KY	KY	KY				AT SCHOOL		4	✓	✓	✓				
		" EDGAR	Son	W	M	Mar 1887	13	S				KY	KY	KY				AT SCHOOL		4	✓	✓	✓				
		" MYRTLE	Dau	W	F	Feb 1889	11	S				KY	KY	KY				AT SCHOOL		4	✓	✓	✓				
		" CLINTON	Son	W	M	Apr 1892	8	S				KY	KY	KY													
		" CORA	Dau	W	F	Nov 1898	1	S				KY	KY	KY													
105	114	BOON, WILLIAM	Head	W	M	Jan 1873	27	M	8			KY	KY	KY				FARMING			✓	✓	✓	R		F	98
		" MALLIE	Wife	W	F	Oct 1877	22	M	8	2	2	KY	KY	KY							✓	✓	✓				
		" HURSHUL A.	Son	W	M	Jul 1893	6	S				KY	KY	KY													
		" HERBERT	Son	W	M	May 1898	2	S				KY	KY	KY													
106	115	FOX, MUISON	Head	W	M	Nov 1881	18	M				KY	KY	KY				FARMING HAND			✓	✓	✓	R		H	
		" DORA	Wife	W	F	Nov 1880	19	M		1	1	KY	KY	KY													
		" LELER	Dau	W	F	Jun 1896	3	S				KY	KY	KY													
107	116	BROWN, LISHA	Head	W	M	UNKNOWN	-	M	16			KY	KY	KY				FARMING			✓	✓	✓	R		H	
		" DESSIE	Wife	W	F	Aug 1868	31	M	16	6	5	KY	KY	KY							X	X	✓				
		" LILLIE	Dau	W	F	May 1890	10	S				KY	KY	KY													
		" FLAUDIE(?)	Dau	W	F	Aug 1894	5	S				TN	KY	KY													
		" MARY S.	Dau	W	F	Jun 1892	7	S				TN	KY	KY													
		" JOHN W	Son	W	M	Nov 1896	3	S				TN	KY	KY													

STATE - KENTUCKY
COUNTY - MONROE
Township or other division — EAST TOMPKINSVILLE — Enumerator E. R. BAXTER

— 279 —

Supervisor's Dist. No. 102 Sheet No.
Enumeration Dist. No. 84

No. of Family	No. of Dwelling	NAME	Relation	Color	Sex	DATE OF BIRTH Mon/Yr	Age at last birthday	Marital Status	# years married	Mother of how many children?	# of these children living	Place of birth (this person)	Father of this person	Mother of this person	Year of immigr.	# years in U.S.	Naturalization	OCCUPATION 10 years +	Months not employed	Attended school in months	Can read	Can write	Speak English	Owned or Rent	Owned - no mortgage	Farm or house	# of farm schedule
		BROWN, TROY	SON	W	M	NOV 1899	4/12	S				TN	KY	KY													
108	117	BROWN, SUSAN	HEAD	W	F	MAR 1843	57	Wd		10	5	KY	KY	KY							✓	✓	✓	O	F	F	99
		CABLER, THOMAS	SON-IN-LAW	W	M	Sep 1870	30	M	12			KY	KY	KY				FARMING			X	X	✓	R	F	F	99
	"	MARTHA C.	WIFE	W	F	JUN 1873	26	M	12	4	4	KY	KY	KY							✓	✓	✓				
	"	ROMA	SON	W	M	APR 1890	10	S				KY	KY	KY													
	"	LUCY	DAU	W	F	Sep 1892	7	S				KY	KY	KY													
	"	MARY	DAU	W	F	Feb 1895	5	S				KY	KY	KY													
	"	WILLIE R.	SON	W	M	Sep 1897	2	S				KY	KY	KY													
	"	PATTIE	GR-DAU	W	F	Nov 1896	4	S				KY	KY	KY													
		BROWN, DELLA	GR-DAU	W	F	Feb 1897	3	S				KY	KY	KY													
109	118	LYON, THOMAS	HEAD	W	M	MAR 1853	47	M	12			KY	KY	KY				FARMING			✓	✓	✓	O	F	F	100
	"	LIZZIE	WIFE	W	F	OCT 1870	30	M	12	4	4	KY	KY	KY							✓	✓	✓				
	"	MINNIE	DAU	W	F	APR 1890	10	S				KY	KY	KY													
	"	HOVA	SON	W	M	AUG 1892	7	S				KY	KY	KY													
	"	DANIEL	SON	W	M	AUG 1895	4	S				KY	KY	KY													
	"	ALVIN	SON	W	M	AUG 1898	1	S				KY	KY	KY													
		FOX, EVERD	BRO-IN-LAW	W	M	MAY 1884	16	S				KY	KY	KY				FARM HAND			X	✓	✓	R	F	F	
110	119	BLAND, MARION	HEAD	W	M	MAR 1861	39	M	16			KY	KY	KY				FARMER	4		X	X	✓	R	F	F	101
	"	RHODA R.	Wife	W	F	MAR 1860	40	M	16	7	6	KY	KY	KY							X	X	✓				
	"	SAM L.	SON	W	F	Sep 1885	14	S				KY	KY	KY				FARM HAND	4		X	X	✓				
	"	JOE T.	SON	W	M	Feb 1888	12	S				KY	KY	KY							X	X	✓				
	"	JOHN W.	SON	W	M	OCT 1890	9	S				KY	KY	KY													
	"	ORSBERN	SON	W	M	Sep 1894	5	S				KY	KY	KY													
	"	MARTHA S.	DAU	W	F	MAR 1893	7	S				KY	KY	KY													
	"	LADY I.	DAU	W	F	APR 1897	3	S				KY	KY	KY													
111	120	LYON, SAM W.	HEAD	W	M	MAY 1865	35	M				KY	TN	TN				FARMING	4		✓	✓	✓	R	F	F	102

TWELFTH CENSUS OF THE UNITED STATES 1900

STATE - KENTUCKY
COUNTY - MONROE
Township or other division **EAST TOMPKINSVILLE** — 280 — Enumerator **E. R. BAXTER**

No. of Family	No. of Dwelling	NAME	Relation	Color	Sex	Date of Birth Mon/Yr	Age at last birthday	Marital Status	# Years married	Mother of how many children?	# of these children living	Place of birth (this person)	Father of this person	Mother of this person	Year of immigr.	# years in U.S.	Naturalization	OCCUPATION 10 years +	Months not employed	Attended school in months	Can read	Can write	Speak English	Owned or Rent	Owned —no mortage	Farm or house	# of farm schedule
		LYON, CATHERINE	Wife	W	F	Jun 1872	28	M				KY	KY	KY							✓	✓	✓				
112	121	BIGGERSTAFF, JAMES A	Head	W	M	Feb 1832	68	M	44			KY	KY	KY				FARMING			✓	✓	✓	O	F	F	103
		" LUCY A	Wife	W	F	May 1846	54	M	44	10		KY	KY	KY							✓	✓	✓				
		" ELZY	Son	W	M	Jan 1874	26	S				KY	KY	KY				FARMING	4		✓	✓	✓	R		F	104
		" BRENTIS	Son	W	M	Dec 1877	23	S				KY	KY	KY				FARMING	4		✓	✓	✓				
		" MAY	Dau	W	F	Sep 1881	18	S				KY	KY	KY				A.T. School		4	✓	✓	✓				
		" ADDIE	Dau	W	F	Feb 1884	16	S				KY	KY	KY				A.T. School		4	✓	✓	✓				
		" ORPHA	Dau	W	F	Feb 1889	12	S				KY	KY	KY				A.T. School		5	✓	✓	✓				
		" OLLIE	Dau	W	F	Jun 1892	8	S				KY	KY	KY													
113	122	BROWN, MILTON	Head	W	M	Aug 1847	52	M	32			KY	VA	KY				FARMING			X	X	✓	O	F	F	105
		" EVA	Wife	W	F	Aug 1850	49	M	32	6	6	KY	—	—							X	X	✓				
		" LISSIE	Dau	W	F	Feb 1875	25	S				KY	KY	KY				HOUSEWORK			✓	✓	✓				
		" CORNELIUS R	Son	W	M	Apr 1869	31	S				KY	KY	KY				FARMING			✓	✓	✓				
		" WESLEY	Son	W	M	Aug 1883	17	S				KY	KY	KY				AT SCHOOL		4	✓	✓	✓				
		" FLIRY(?)	Dau	W	F	Mar 1884	16	S				KY	KY	KY				AT SCHOOL		4	✓	✓	✓				
		" BETHEL	Son	W	M	Feb 1891	9	S				KY	KY	KY													
114	123	WILLIAMS, JOHN	Head	W	M	Jan 1856	44	M	27			KY	KY	KY				FARMING			✓	✓	✓	O	F	F	106
		" MANDA	Wife	W	F	Mar 1852	48	M	27	1	1	KY	KY	KY							X	X	✓				
		" CLOYD	Son	W	M	Jun 1888	12	S				KY	KY	KY				AT SCHOOL		4	✓	✓					
115	124	BROWN, JESSIE	Head	W	M	May 1860	40	M	11			KY	KY	KY				FARMING		4	✓	✓	✓	R		F	107
		" MARTHA F	Wife	W	F	Oct 1860	39	M	11	6	4	KY	KY	KY							✓	✓	✓				
		" JESSIE S.	Son	W	M	Mar 1892	8	S				KY	KY	KY				AT SCHOOL		4	✓	✓	✓				
		" ETHEL Y.	Dau	W	F	Feb 1898	2	S				KY	KY	KY													
116	125	WILLIAMS, EPHRUM D.	Head	W	M	Jul 1859	41	M	22			KY	KY	KY				FARMING			✓	✓	✓	O	F	F	108
		" NANCY E.	Wife	W	F	Sep 1861	38	M	22	7	5	KY	KY	KY							✓	✓	✓				
		" BENNIE	Son	W	M	Nov 1883	16	S				KY	KY	KY				FARMING HAND			✓	✓	✓				

STATE - KENTUCKY
COUNTY - MONROE
Township or other division — EAST TOMPKINSVILLE — Enumerator E. R. BAXTER

Supervisor's Dist. No. _102_ Sheet No. ___
Enumeration Dist. No. _84_ ___

No. of Family	No. of Dwelling	NAME	Relation	Color	Sex	DATE OF BIRTH Mon/Yr	Age at last birthday	Marital Status	# Years married	Mother of how many children?	# of these children living	Place of birth [this person]	Father of this person	Mother of this person	Year of immigr.	# years in U.S.	Naturalization	OCCUPATION 10 years +	Months not employed	Attended school in months	Can read	Can write	Speak English	Owned or Rent	Owned -no mortage	Farm or house	# of farm schedule	
		WILLIAMS, MAY	DAU	W	F	APR 1886	14	S				KY	KY	KY				AT SCHOOL		4	✓	✓	✓					
		" JEFFERSON	SON	W	M	DEC 1894	5	S				KY	KY	KY														
		" ISHAM	SON	W	M	MAY 1898	2	S				KY	KY	KY														
117	126	OLDHAM, JOHN T.	HEAD	W	M	MAR 1846	54	Wd				KY	KY	KY				FARMER AND BLACKSMITH			✓	✓	✓	O	M	F	109	
		" WILLIAM	SON	W	M	SEP 1867	32	S				KY	KY	KY				FARMER			✓	✓	✓					
		" CHARLES A.	SON	W	M	MAY 1877	23	S				KY	KY	KY				FARMER			✓	✓	✓					
		" ORLANDER	SON	W	M	DEC 1878	21	S				KY	KY	KY				FARMER			✓	✓	✓					
		" DOLLIE G.	DAU	W	F	OCT 1880	19	S				KY	KY	KY				AT SCHOOL		4	✓	✓	✓					
		" CLINTON W.	SON	W	M	SEP 1884	15	S				KY	KY	KY				AT SCHOOL		4	✓	✓	✓					
		" LOU E.	DAU	W	F	FEB 1886	14	S				KY	KY	KY				AT SCHOOL		4	✓	✓	✓					
		" THOMAS M.	SON	W	M	SEP 1889	11	S				KY	KY	KY				AT SCHOOL		4	✓	✓	✓					
		" LITTLE H.	SON	W	M	JUN 1890	9	S				KY	KY	KY														
		" EDGAR B.	SON	W	M	APR 1892	8	S				KY	KY	KY														
		" MANDA	DAU	W	F	FEB 1883	17	S				KY	KY	KY				AT SCHOOL		4	✓	✓	✓					
118	127	GEE, REUBEN	Head	W	M	DEC 1859	40	M	18			KY	KY	KY				FARMING			✓	✓	✓	O	M	F	110	
		" MARY H.	Wife	W	F	OCT 1852	47	M	18	—	—	KY	KY	KY							✓	✓	✓					
		" MARY A.	Mother	W	F	AUG 1832	67	Wd		6	6	KY	KY	KY				FARMING	10		✓	✓	✓	O	M	F	110	
		" SUSAN	Sister	W	F	AUG 1867	32	S				KY	KY	KY				HOUSEWORK	4		✓	✓	✓					
119	128	PRUIT, SUSAN	Head	W	F	JUN 1836	64	Wd		3	3	TN	TN	TN				HOUSEWORK			✓	✓	✓	R		F	111	
		" CASTLE	Son	W	M	MAY 1857	43	S				KY	TN	TN										R		F	111	
		" VERNA	GR-DAU	W	F	NOV 1884	15	S				KY	TN	KY				AT SCHOOL		5	✓	✓	✓					
		" CLINT	GR-DAU	W	F	MAR 1886	14	S				KY	TN	KY				AT SCHOOL		5	✓	✓	✓					
		" RUTHA	GR-DAU	W	F	FEB 1888	12	S				KY	TN	KY				AT SCHOOL		5	✓	✓	✓					
120	129	GILLENWATERS, THOMAS	Head	W	M	DEC 1861	38	M	18			KY	KY	KY				FARMING			X	X	✓	R		F	112	
		" LOU S.	WIFE	W	F	DEC 1865	34	M	18	7	5	TN	ALA	ALA							✓	✓	✓					
		" JOHN R.	SON	W	M	DEC 1886	13	S				KY	KY	TN				AT SCHOOL		5	✓	✓	✓					

STATE - KENTUCKY   EAST   Supervisor's Dist. No. _102_ Sheet No.
COUNTY - MONROE
Township or other division   TOMPKINSVILLE   Enumerator E. R. BAXTER   Enumeration Dist. No. _84_

Location No. of Family	No. of Dwelling	NAME	Relation	Color	Sex	DATE OF BIRTH Mon/Yr	Age at last birthday	Marital Status	# Years married	Mother of how many children?	# of these children living	NATIVITY Place of birth [this person]	Father of this person	Mother of this person	CITIZENSHIP Year of immigr.	# years in U.S.	Naturalization	OCCUPATION 10 years +	Months not employed	Attended school in months	Can read	Can write	Speak English	OWNERSHIP Owned or Rent	Owned or-no mortage	Farm or house	# of farm schedule	
		GILLENWATERS, ELVA R.	Son	W	M	MAR 1890	10	S				KY	KY	TN				AT SCHOOL		5	✓	✓						
		" WILLIAM H.	Son	W	M	Jan 1893	7	S				KY	KY	TN														
		" JOE B.	Son	W	M	AUG 1898	1	S				KY	KY	TN														
		" KENT L.	Son	W	M	APR 1900	2/12	S				KY	KY	TN														
121	130	RICH, JOEL B.	HEAD	W	M	MAR 1861	39	M	15			TN	TN	TN				FARMING	12		✓	✓		R		F	113	
		" MARTHA	WIFE	W	F	Jan 1862	38	M	15	1	1	KY	TN	KY							✓	✓						
		SPEAR, AMANDA	Moth in-law	W	F	Feb 1833	67	Wd		1	1	KY	SC	SC							✓	✓						
		GRACE, WILLIAM	HAND	W	M	AUG 1868	31	S				TN	KY	TN				FARM HAND			X	X	✓					
		HESTAND, WILLIAM	HAND	W	M	Jan 1852	48	S				MISS	KY	TN	(MISSISSIPPI)			FARM HAND			X	X	✓					
122	131	WILLIAMS, MARTIN	HEAD	W	M	OCT 1874	25	M	3			KY	KY	KY				FARMING			✓	✓		R		F	114	
		" MARY	WIFE	W	M	DEC 1872	27	M	3	2	2	KY	KY	KY							✓	✓						
		" JOHN F.	Son	W	M	OCT 1897	2	S				KY	KY	KY														
		" RAYMOND T.	Son	W	M	APR 1900	3/12	S				KY	KY	KY														
		" WILLIAM T.	BROTHER	W	M	JUL 1877	22	S				KY	KY	KY				DRY GOODS MERCHANT			✓	✓						
		" FERD	BROTHER	W	M	MAR 1880	20	S				KY	KY	KY				DRY GOODS MERCHANT			✓	✓						
123	132	RUNYON, JOHN	HEAD	W	M	DEC 1863	37	M	17			KY	KY	KY				FACTORY HAND			✓	✓		R		H		
		" SARAH I.	WIFE	W	F	Sep 1867	32	M	17	8	7	KY	KY	KY							✓	✓						
		" CHARLES	Son	W	M	MAR 1885	15	S				KY	KY	KY				AT SCHOOL		3	✓	✓	✓					
		" LUTHER	Son	W	M	APR 1887	12	S				KY	KY	KY				AT SCHOOL		3	X	X	✓					
		" HATTIE	DAU	W	F	OCT 1889	11	S				KY	KY	KY														
		" WALTER	Son	W	M	OCT 1891	9	S				KY	KY	KY														
		" PEARLY	DAU	W	F	Jan 1894	6	S				KY	KY	KY														
		" MANSON	Son	W	M	Jan 1896	4	S				KY	KY	KY														
		" BEDFORD	Son	W	M	Sep 1899	8/12	S				KY	KY	KY														
124	133	EMBERTON, JOE	Head	W	M	Jan 1870	30	M	7			KY	KY	KY				DAY LABOR	4		✓	✓		R		H		
		" MARINDA	WIFE	W	F	Jan 1874	26	M	7	3	3	KY	TN	TN							✓	✓						

STATE - KENTUCKY
COUNTY - MONROE
Township or other division: EAST TOMPKINSVILLE —283—
Enumerator: E. R. BAXTER

Supervisor's Dist. No. 102 Sheet No.
Enumeration Dist. No. 84

No. of Family	No. of Dwelling	NAME	Relation	Color	Sex	Date of Birth Mon/Yr	Age at last birthday	Marital Status	# Years married	Mother of how many children	# of these children living	Place of birth (this person)	Father of this person	Mother of this person	Occupation	Months not employed	Attended school in months	Can read	Can write	Speak English	Owned or Rent	Farm or house	# of farm schedule	
		EMBERTON, FLORA H.	DAU	W	F	May 1894	6	S				KY	KY	KY										
		" WILLIAM M.	SON	W	M	Aug 1896	3	S				KY	KY	KY										
		" EVIE R.	DAU	W	F	Oct 1899	7/12	S				KY	KY	KY										
125	134	WRIGHT, LAFAYETTE	HEAD	W	M	Mar 1841	59	M	35			TN	VA	TN	DAY LABORER 4			✓	✓	✓	R	H		
		" TELITHA	WIFE	W	F	Apr 1846	54	M	35	4	3	KY	KY	KY				✓	✓	✓				
		" LAFAYETTE	SON	W	M	Aug 1876	23	S				KY	TN	KY	DAY LABORER 4			✓	✓	✓				
SIC 125	135	WRIGHT, JOE	HEAD	W	M	Sep 1870	29	M	6			KY	TN	KY	DAY LABOR 4			✓	✓	✓	R	H		
		" VICTORIA	WIFE	W	F	Nov 1874	25	M	6	2	2	KY	KY	KY				✓	✓	✓				
		" IRA	SON	W	M	May 1894	5	S				KY	KY	KY										
		" OLLIE	DAU	W	F	Feb 1900	4/12	S				KY	KY	KY										
126	36	BURIS, WAKE	HEAD	W	M	Dec 1866	33	M				KY	KY	KY	LATHE MAN IN FACTORY 4			✓	✓	✓	R	H		
		" PERTIE	WIFE	W	F	May 1882	18	M				KY	KY	KY				✓	✓	✓				
		" ROBERT	SON	W	M	Jul 1889	10	S				KY	KY	KY										
		" WILLIE	SON	W	M	Sep 1891	8	S				KY	KY	KY										
127	137	GRISSOM, JAMES B.	HEAD	W	M	Jan 1878	22	M	1			KY	KY	KY	FARMING 4			✓	✓	✓	R	F	115	
		" DEE	WIFE	W	F	Jan 1879	21	M	1			KY	KY	KY				✓	✓	✓				
128	138	GRAVES, OLIVER	HEAD	W	M	Jan 1866	34	M	2			KY	KY	KY	FARMING 4			✓	✓	✓	R	F	115	SIC
		" SALLIE	WIFE	W	F	Mar 1879	20	M	2			KY	KY	KY				✓	✓	✓				
		" LEE	SON	W	M	Jun 1899	4/12	S				KY	KY	KY										
		PRUIT, LON	NIECE	W	F	Dec 1887	12	S				KY	KY	KY	AT SCHOOL		4	✓	✓	✓				
129	139	KIDWELL, THOMAS	HEAD	W	M	May 1878	22	M				KY	KY	KY	FARMING			✓	✓	✓	R	F	116	
		" SALLIE	WIFE	W	F	Nov 1878	21	M	—	—		KY	KY	KY				✓	✓	✓				
130	140	KIDWELL, JOHN	HEAD	W	M	Nov 1852	47	M	24			KY	KY	KY	FARMING			✓	✓	✓	O	F	117	
		" MANDA E.	WIFE	W	F	Sep 1860	39	M	24	10	10	KY	KY	KY				✓	✓	✓				
		" ISHAM D.	SON	W	M	Sep 1876	23	S				KY	KY	KY	FARMING			✓	✓	✓				
		" CASS R.	SON	W	M	Apr 1882	18	S				KY	KY	KY	AT SCHOOL		4	✓	✓	✓				

TWELFTH CENSUS OF THE UNITED STATES 1900

STATE - KENTUCKY
COUNTY - MONROE
Township or other division — EAST TOMPKINSVILLE — Enumerator E. R. BAXTER

— 284 —

Supervisor's Dist. No. 102   Sheet No.
Enumeration Dist. No. 84

Location		NAME	Relation	Color	Sex	DATE OF BIRTH Mon/Yr	Age at last birthday	Marital Status	# Years married	Mother of how many children?	# of these children living	NATIVITY Place of birth [this person]	Father of this person	Mother of this person	CITIZENSHIP Year of immigr.	# years in U.S.	Naturalization	OCCUPATION 10 years +	Months not employed	EDUCATION Attended school in months	Can read	Can write	Speak English	OWNERSHIP Owned or Rent	Owned –no mortage	Farm or house	# of farm schedule	
		KIDWELL, ALBINIA	DAU	W	F	Apr 1884	16	S				KY	KY	KY				AT SCHOOL		4	✓	✓	✓					
		" MOLLIE P.	DAU	W	F	Sep 1886	14	S				KY	KY	KY				AT SCHOOL		4	✓	✓	✓					
		" BEDFORD T.	SON	W	M	Feb 1890	10	S				KY	KY	KY				AT SCHOOL		4	✓	✓	✓					
		" NANCY C.	DAU	W	F	Sep 1893	6	S				KY	KY	KY														
		" VIOLIE M.	SON	W	M	Feb 1896	4	S				KY	KY	KY														
		" LEAN C.	DAU	W	F	Sep 1898	1	S				KY	KY	KY														
131	41	MOORE, CIT C.	HEAD	W	M	Jun 1865	35	M	14			KY	KY	TN				FARMING	6		✓	✓	✓	O	F	F	118	
		" PATSY	WIFE	W	F	May 1870	30	M	14	6	6	KY	KY	KY							✓	✓	✓					
		" EDGAR	SON	W	M	Jul 1888	11	S				KY	KY	KY				AT SCHOOL		5	✓	✓	✓					
		" EMMA H.	DAU	W	F	Sep 1890	9	S				KY	KY	KY				AT SCHOOL		5								
		" FLORA W.	DAU	W	F	Feb 1893	7	S				KY	KY	KY														
		" DOVIE I.	DAU	W	F	Mar 1896	4	S				KY	KY	KY														
		" VERGIE E.	DAU	W	F	Jan 1898	2	S				KY	KY	KY														
		" STANFORD	SON	W	M	Dec 1899	5/12	S				KY	KY	KY														
132	42	EMMERT, WILLIAM	Head	W	M	Mar 1828	72	M	44			KY	KY	KY				FARMING			✓	✓	✓	R		F	119	
		" LEVESTA	WIFE	W	F	Mar 1835	65	M	44	10	6	KY	KY	KY							✓	X	✓					
133	43	SCOTT, JOHN	HEAD	W	M	Apr 1848	52	M	36			KY	KY	KY				FARMING	4		✓	✓	✓	O	F	F	120	
		" MARY A.	WIFE	W	F	Jan 1847	53	M	36	8	6	KY	KY	KY							X	X	✓					
		" JAMES O.	SON	W	M	Jan 1875	25	S				KY	KY	KY				FARM HAND	5		X	X	✓					
		" DOLLIE	DAU	W	F	Sep 1880	19	S				KY	KY	KY				HIRED GIRL			X	X	✓					
		" GEORGE W.	SON	W	M	Feb 1882	18	S				KY	KY	KY				FARM HAND			X	X	✓					
134	44	CHERRY, WILLIAM	HEAD	W	M	——	54	M	34			TN	TN	TN				FARMING			X	X	✓	O	F	F	121	
		" EMILY	WIFE	W	F	Mar 1836	64	M	34	3	1	TN	TN	TN							✓	✓	✓					
135	45	FINLEY, CLAYTON	HEAD	W	M	Jun 1868	31	M	12			KY	KY	TN				FARMING			X	X	✓	R		F	122	
		" ELIZZIEBETH	WIFE	W	F	Jun —	29	M	12	5	5	KY	KY	KY							X	X	✓					
		" ORA	DAU	W	F	Jul 1888	11	S				KY	KY	KY				AT SCHOOL		4	✓	✓	✓					

STATE - KENTUCKY
COUNTY - MONROE
Township or other division — EAST TOMPKINSVILLE
Enumerator — E.R. BAXTER

Supervisor's Dist. No. _102_ Sheet No.
Enumeration Dist. No. _84_

No. of Family	No. of Dwelling	NAME	Relation	Color	Sex	DATE OF BIRTH Mon/Yr	Age at last birthday	Marital Status	#Years married	Mother of how many children?	# of these children living	Place of birth (this person)	Father of this person	Mother of this person	Year of immigr.	# years in U.S.	Naturalization	OCCUPATION 10 years +	Months not employed	Attended school in months	Can read	Can write	Speak English	Owned or Rent	Owned –no mortgage	Farm or house	# of farm schedule
		FINLEY, CORA	DAU	W	F	OCT 1890	9	S				KY	KY	KY													
		" SARAH	DAU	W	F	Feb 1893	7	S				KY	KY	KY													
		" ROBERT	SON	W	M	AUG 1896	3	S				KY	KY	KY													
		" (INFANT)	SON	W	M	MAY 1900	1/12	S				KY	KY	KY													
136	46	THOMPSON, JASPER	HEAD	W	M	JUN 1844	56	Wd				KY	KY	KY				FARMER			✓	✓		O	F	F	123
		" ADAM (?)	SON	W	M	Sep 1875	24	S				KY	KY	KY				FARMING			✓	✓					
		" ARLIE	DAU	W	F	Dec 1879	20	S				KY	KY	KY							✓	✓					
		" WOOTEN	SON	W	M	Sep 1881	18	S				KY	KY	KY				FARMING			✓	✓					
		" ROSCO	SON	W	M	APR 1883	17	S				KY	KY	KY				AT SCHOOL		5	✓	✓					
		" ELMIRA E.	DAU	W	F	Feb 1885	15	S				KY	KY	KY				AT SCHOOL		5	✓	✓					
		" JESSIE E.	SON	W	M	Sep 1886	13	S				KY	KY	KY				AT SCHOOL		5	✓	✓					
		" ELSIC N.	SON	W	M	APR 1888	12	S				KY	KY	KY				AT SCHOOL		5	✓	✓					
		" PHEBE H.	DAU	W	F	DEC 1891	8	S				KY	KY	KY													
		" HASSIE	DAU	W	F	OCT 1895	4	S				KY	KY	KY													
137	47	EMMERT, JASPER	HEAD	W	M	Sep 1858	41	M	20			KY	KY	KY				FARMING			✓	✓		O	F	F	124
		" ADVILLE	WIFE	W	F	Jun 1861	38	M	20	8	7	KY	KY	KY							✓	✓					
		" BENTON	SON	W	M	Feb 1884	16	S				KY	KY	KY				AT SCHOOL		5	✓	✓					
		" HURSUL	SON	W	M	Sep 1885	14	S				KY	KY	KY				AT SCHOOL		5	✓	✓					
		" FLORENCE	DAU	W	F	JAN 1888	12	S				KY	KY	KY				AT SCHOOL		5	✓	✓					
		" BERTHA	DAU	W	F	JAN 1889	10	S				KY	KY	KY				AT SCHOOL		5	✓	✓					
		" HERBERT	SON	W	M	Jul 1892	7	S				KY	KY	KY													
		" ROBERT	SON	W	M	Apr 1897	3	S				KY	KY	KY													
138	48	THURMAN, ALEXANDER	HEAD	W	M	JUN 1864	35	M	14			KY	KY	KY				FARMING			X	X	✓	R	F	125	
		" DELIE	WIFE	W	F	OCT 1866	33	M	14	6	3	KY	KY	KY													
		" BALEY H.	SON	W	M	DEC 1888	11	S				KY	KY	KY				AT SCHOOL		4	X	X	✓				
		" ROXIE	DAU	W	F	Jul 1890	9	S				KY	KY	KY													

STATE - KENTUCKY
COUNTY - MONROE
Township or other division EAST TOMPKINSVILLE
Enumerator E. R. BAXTER

Supervisor's Dist. No. 102 Sheet No.
Enumeration Dist. No. 84

No. of Family	No. of Dwelling	NAME	Relation	Color	Sex	DATE OF BIRTH Mon/Yr	Age at last birthday	Marital Status	# Years married	Mother of how many children?	# of these children living	Place of birth (this person)	Father of this person	Mother of this person	Year of immigr.	# years in U.S.	Naturalization	OCCUPATION 10 years +	Months not employed	Attended school in months	Can read	Can write	Speak English	Owned or Rent	Owned - no mortage	Farm or house	# of farm schedule
		THURMAN, EUNICE	DAU	W	F	Dec 1891	8	S				KY	KY	KY													
139	149	McMILLIN, RICHARD	HEAD	W	M	Jan 1848	52	M	34			KY	TN	MD				FARMER			X	X	✓	O	F	F	126
		" MARY E	WIFE	W	F	Jan 1846	54	M	34	12	10	KY	KY	VA				INVALID			✓	X	✓				
		" LUTHER	SON	W	M	Apr 1880	20	S				KY	KY	KY				FARM HAND		3	✓	✓	✓				
		" CLAUDIS	SON	W	M	Feb 1892	18	S				KY	BY	KY				FARM HAND		3	✓	✓	✓				
		" BENTON	SON	W	M	Sep 1884	15	S				KY	KY	KY				FARM HAND		3	X	X	✓				
		" AMOS W.	SON	W	M	Feb 1888	12	S				KY	BY	KY				FARM HAND		4	X	X	✓				
		" ALVIN R.	SON	W	M	Aug 1897	7	S				KY	KY	KY													
		DARVY, JULIA	Servant	W	F	Sep 1880	19	M	2	1	1	KY	KY	KY				SERVANT			X	X	✓				
		" WALTER	SON	W	M	Feb 1898	2	S				KY	KY	KY													
140	150	PROPES, JAMES	HEAD	W	M	Sep 1847	52	M	27			TN	TN	TN				DAY LABOR			✓	✓	✓	R		F	127
		" MARY B.	WIFE	W	F	May 1850	50	M	27	8	8	KY	TN	TN							✓	✓	✓				
		" WILLIAM ?	SON	W	M	May 1875	25	S				KY	TN	KY				DAY LABORER			✓	✓	✓				
		" KATIE	DAU	W	F	May 1883	17	S				KY	TN	KY				AT SCHOOL		6	✓	✓	✓				
		" JAMES H.	SON	W	M	Nov 1887	12	S				KY	TN	KY				AT SCHOOL		10	X	X	✓				
		" JOHN R.	SON	W	M	May 1889	11	S				KY	TN	KY							X	X	✓				
141	151	PERDEW, LOU	HEAD	W	F	Jun 1863	36	Divc.		10	8	KY	TN	KY							✓	✓	✓	O	F	F	
		" FRANKLIN	SON	W	M	Jul 1877	22	S				KY	KY	KY				FARMING			✓	✓	✓				
		" ARCHIBALD	SON	W	M	Nov 1880	19	S				KY	KY	KY				FARMING			✓	✓	✓				
		" LIZZIE	DAU	W	F	Mar 1884	16	S				KY	KY	KY				AT SCHOOL		8	✓	✓	✓				
		" ELLA	DAU	W	F	Feb 1886	14	S				KY	KY	KY				AT SCHOOL		8	✓	✓	✓				
		" CASSIE	DAU	W	F	May 1888	12	S				KY	KY	KY				AT SCHOOL		8	✓	✓	✓				
		" ETHEL	DAU	W	F	Feb 1890	10	S				KY	KY	KY													
		" LAFAYETTE	SON	W	M	Feb 1891	9	S				KY	KY	KY													
		" COLUMBUS	SON	W	M	Mar 1892	8	S				KY	KY	KY													
		" BLACK	Nephew	W	M	Aug 1880	19	S				KY	WVA	KY				FARMING			✓	✓	✓	R		F	128

STATE - KENTUCKY
COUNTY - MONROE EAST
Township or other division TOMPKINSVILLE Enumerator E. R. BAXTER

Supervisor's Dist. No. 102 Sheet No.
Enumeration Dist. No. 84

No. of Family	No. of Dwelling	NAME	Relation	Color	Sex	Date of Birth Mon/Yr	Age at last birthday	Marital Status	# Years married	Mother of how many children?	# of these children living	Place of birth (this person)	Father of this person	Mother of this person	Occupation 10 years +	Months not employed	Attended school in months	Can read	Can write	Speak English	Owned or Rent	Owned -no mortgage	Farm or house	# of farm schedule
		MATHEWS, MILLARD	Nephew	W	M	Apr 1878	22	S				KY	ALA	KY										
142	152	PERDEN, MARTHA	Head	W	F	Oct 1833	66	Wd	44	2	1	KY	KY	KY	HOUSEWORK	3		X	X	✓	R		H	
143	153	EMMERT, ABRAHAM	Head	W	M	Aug 1871	28	M	10			KY	KY	KY	FARMING	3		✓	✓	✓	R		F	129
		" MELLIE	Wife	W	F	May 1871	28	M	10	4	4	KY	KY	KY		3		✓	✓	✓				
		" ORVIL	Son	W	M	Dec 1890	9	S				KY	KY	KY										
		" OLLIVER	Son	W	M	Feb 1894	6	S				KY	KY	KY										
		" ONIE N.	Dau	W	F	Sep 1896	3	S				KY	KY	KY										
		" OTTIE	Son	W	M	Jan 1900	5/12	S				KY	KY	KY										
144	154	THOMPSON, EZEKIAL	Head	W	M	Jan 1847	53	M	15			KY	KY	KY	FARMING	4		✓	✓	✓	O	F	F	130
		" MARY K.	Wife	W	F	May 1853	47	M	15	8	7	KY	KY	TN				✓	✓	✓				
		" MOLLIE	Dau	W	F	Jul 1884	15	S				KY	KY	KY	AT SCHOOL		3	✓	✓	✓				
		" GEORGE	Son	W	M	Jan 1887	12	S				KY	KY	KY	AT SCHOOL		4	X	X					
		" JARRET	Son	W	M	Jun 1888	11	S				KY	KY	KY	AT SCHOOL		2	X	X					
		" JOHNIE H.	Son	W	M	Jun 1890	10	S				KY	KY	KY	AT SCHOOL		2							
		" DOW	Son	W	M	Nov 1892	7	S				KY	KY	KY										
		" MILARD	Son	W	M	Feb 1897	3	S				KY	KY	KY										
		" JAMES I.	Son	W	M	Jul 1900	11/12	S				KY	KY	KY										
145	155	THOMPSON, ISAAC	Head	W	M	Feb 1850	50	M	27			KY	KY	KY	FARMING			✓	✓	✓	O	F	F	131
		" MACK	Wife	W	F	Aug 1846	54	M	27	7	5	KY	KY	TN				✓	✓	✓				
		" SALLIE	Dau	N	F	Jun 1878	21	S				KY	KY	KY				✓	✓	✓				
		" MARY A.	Dau	W	F	Nov 1884	15	S				KY	KY	KY	AT SCHOOL		4	✓	✓	✓				
	156	THOMPSON, EDWARD	Head	W	M	Sep 1876	23	M				KY	KY	KY	FARMING			✓	✓	✓			F	
		" DORA	Wife	W	F	Dec 1881	18	M				KY	KY	KY				✓	✓	✓				
146	157	EMMERT, JOHN	Head	W	M	Jul 1870	29	M	6			KY	KY	KY	MILL MAN			✓	✓	✓	O	F	F	132
		" LOU	Wife	W	F	Sep 1873	26	M	6	4	4	KY	KY	KY				✓	✓	✓				
		" ERASMUS H.	Son	W	M	Nov 1894	5	S				KY	KY	KY										

STATE - KENTUCKY
COUNTY - MONROE
Township or other division EAST TOMPKINSVILLE Enumerator E. R. BAXTER

Supervisor's Dist. No. 102 Sheet No.
Enumeration Dist. No. 84

No. of Family	No. of Dwelling	NAME	Relation	Color	Sex	DATE OF BIRTH Mon/Yr	Age at last birthday	Marital Status	# Years married	Mother of how many children?	# of these children living	Place of birth (this person)	Father of this person	Mother of this person	Year of immigr.	# years in U.S.	Naturalization	OCCUPATION 10 years +	Months not employed	Attended school in months	Can read	Can write	Speak English	Owned or Rent	Owned - no mortage	Farm or house	# of farm schedule
-		EMMERT (?AISSIE) D.	Son	W	M	Mar 1896	4	S				KY	KY	KY													
		" VESTIA	Dau	W	F	Feb 1898	2	S				KY	KY	KY													
		" RAYMOND T.	Son	W	M	Feb 1900	3/12	S				KY	KY	KY													
147	158	GRIMSLEY, MACAGER?	Head	W	M	—	50	M	23			KY	KY	KY				DAY LABORER			X	X	✓	R		F	133
		" VICTORY	Wife	W	F	Apr 1857	43	M	23	10	6	KY	KY	KY							X	X	✓				
		" JOHN	Son	W	M	Dec 1877	22	S				KY	KY	KY				DAY LABOR			X	X	✓				
		" BARLOW	Son	W	M	Aug 1880	19	S				KY	KY	KY				DAY LABOR			X	X	✓				
		" OLIVER	Son	W	M	May 1893	17	S				KY	KY	KY				DAY LABOR			X	X	✓				
		" ERASMUS	Son	W	M	Jul 1891	8	S				KY	KY	KY													
		" MOSSIE	Dau	W	F	May 1895	5	S				KY	KY	KY													
		" FLOSSIE	Dau	W	F	Jan 1898	2	S				KY	KY	KY													
148	159	BEDWELL, JOHN	Head	W	M	Sep 1877	22	S				KY	KY	KY				FARMING			✓	✓	✓	O		F	134
		" LIZA	Gr.Mother	W	F	May 1816	84	Wd		4	3	KY	KY	KY							X	X	✓				
		" SARAH	Mother	W	F	Aug 1849	49	S		1	1	KY	KY	KY				HOUSEWORK			✓	✓	✓				
149	160	MOORE, WILLIAM	Head	W	M	—	—	M	6			KY	KY	KY				HORSE JOCKEY			✓	✓	✓	R		F	135
		" ETTA	Wife	W	F	Oct 1873	26	M	6			KY	KY	KY							X	X	X				
		" EDWARD	Son	W	M	Mar 1879	21	S				KY	KY	KY				HORSE JOCKEY			✓	✓	✓				
		" AVERY	Son	W	M	Sep 1881	18	S				KY	KY	KY				HORSE JOCKEY			✓	✓	✓				
150	161	GRAVENS, ROBERT	Head	W	M	Jan 1834	56	M				KY	KY	KY				FARMER			✓	✓	✓	R		F	136
		" MARGARET	Wife	W	F	Jan 1876	23	M		1	1	KY	KY	KY							X	X	✓				
		" LOU	Dau	W	F	Jan 1897	3	S				KY	KY	KY							—	—	—				
151	162	CARLOCK, ISAAC	Head	W	M	Jul 1849	50	M	26			TX	TN	TN				FARMER			X	X	✓	O	F	F	137
		" PELINA B.	Wife	W	F	Jan 1840	60	M	26	5	4	TN	TN	TN							X	X	✓				
		" MGIE (Maggie?)	Dau	W	F	Dec 1877	22	S		1	1	TN	TX	TN							✓	✓	✓				
		" THOMAS	Son	W	M	Mar 1879	21	S				TN	TX	TN				FARMER			✓	✓	✓				
		" ALBERT	Son	W	M	Jul 1885	14	S				TN	TX	TN				AT SCHOOL		4	✓	✓	✓				

STATE - KENTUCKY
COUNTY - MONROE
Township or other division — EAST TOMPKINSVILLE
Enumerator — E.R. BAXTER

Supervisor's Dist. No. _102_ Sheet No.
Enumeration Dist. No. _84_

Location		NAME	Relation	Color	Sex	DATE OF BIRTH Mon/Yr	Age at last birthday	Marital Status	# Years married	Mother of how many children?	# of these children living	NATIVITY Place of birth [this person]	Father of this person	Mother of this person	CITIZENSHIP Year of immigr.	# years in U.S.	Naturalization	OCCUPATION 10 years +	Months not employed	Attended school in months	Can read	Can write	Speak English	OWNERSHIP Owned or Rent	Owned or -no mortgage	Farm or house	# of farm schedule	
		CARLOCK, FAYETTE (GRSON)		W	M	Sep 1898	1	S				KY	UNK	TN														
152	163	CROFFORD, MACAGER	HEAD	W	M	Dec 1858	41	M	7			TN	TN	TN				FARMING 6			✓	✓	✓	R		F	138	
		" NORA J.	WIFE	W	F	Apr 1874	26	M	7	1	1	KY	KY	KY							✓	✓	✓					
		" LYNN M.	SON	W	M	Apr 1894	6	S				KY	TN	KY														
153	164	RUSH, ELIJAH	Head	W	M	May 1863	37	M	13			KY	KY	KY				FARMING			✓	✓	✓	R		F	139	
		" SARAH	WIFE	W	F	Oct 1869	30	M	13	8	5	KY	KY	KY							✓	✓	✓					
		" EDNA	DAU	W	F	Dec 1890	9	S				KY	KY	KY				AT SCHOOL		3	X	X	✓					
		" EUNICE	DAU	W	F	Dec 1892	7	S				KY	KY	KY														
		" ALMIRA	DAU	W	F	Jun 1896	3	S				KY	KY	KY														
		" HARRY(?)	SON	W	M	Oct 1898	2	S				KY	KY	KY														
		" CORA	DAU	W	F	Feb 1900	3/12	S				KY	KY	KY														
154	165	RUSH, ELIZZIEBETH	HEAD	W	F	Jul 1831	58	Wd		7	6	KY	KY	KY							X	X	✓	O	M	F		
		" BERT	SON	W	M	Sep 1867	32	S				KY	KY	KY				FARMING			✓	✓	✓	R		F	140	
		" JAY H.	SON	W	M	Nov 1858	41	Wd				KY	KY	KY				FARM HAND			✓	✓	✓					
		" ETHRY H.	SON	W	M	Oct 1885	14	S				KY	KY	KY				FARM HAND			X	X	✓					
		" IVY E.	DAU	W	F	May 1888	12	S				KY	KY	KY				AT SCHOOL		8	✓	✓	✓					
		" BRUTIS	SON	W	M	Feb 1891	9	S				KY	KY	KY														
		" CHARLES	SON	W	M	Feb 1893	7	S				KY	KY	KY														
		HUGHES, MARTHA	HIRED	W	F	May 1877	23	S				TN	KY	KY														
155	166	ARNETT, ROBERT J	Head	W	M	Jun 1860	40	M	17			TN	TN	TN				FARMING			✓	✓	✓	O		F	141	
		" MARY	Wife	W	F	Jan 1850	50	M	17	4	2	TN	TN	TN							X	X	✓					
		" OSCOE	SON	W	M	Dec 1884	15	S				KY	TN	TN				AT SCHOOL		4	✓	✓	✓					
		" PERNETTE S.	DAU	W	F	Sep 1890	9	S				KY	TN	TN														
156	167	HAMMER, DANIEL	HEAD	W	M	Mar 1869	31	M				KY	TN	TN				FARMING			✓	✓	✓	O		F	142	
		" LOUIZA	WIFE	W	F	Mar 1860	40	M				KY	TN	TN							✓	✓	✓					
157	168	FORD, WILLARD	HEAD	W	M	Apr 1853	47	M	3			KY	VA	KY				BOSS - AX HANDLE FACTORY 13			✓	✓	✓	R		H		

STATE - KENTUCKY
COUNTY - MONROE
Township or other division — EAST TOMPKINSVILLE
Enumerator — E. R. BAXTER

Supervisor's Dist. No. 102 Sheet No.
Enumeration Dist. No. 84

No. of Family	No. of Dwelling	NAME	Relation	Color	Sex	DATE OF BIRTH Mon/Yr	Age at last birthday	Marital Status	# Years married	Mother of how many children?	# of these children living	Place of birth (this person)	Father of this person	Mother of this person	Year of immigr.	# years in U.S.	Naturalization	OCCUPATION 10 years +	Months not employed	Attended school in months	Can read	Can write	Speak English	Owned or Rent	Owned - no mortgage	Farm or house	# of farm schedule
		FORD, CAMILA	WIFE	W	F	Jan 1870	30	M	3	0	0	KY	KY	KY							✓	✓	✓				
		" COLUMBUS E.	SON	W	M	Jun 1879	22	S				KY	KY	IND				HANDLE FACTORY	3		✓	✓	✓				
		" WILT	SON	W	M	May 1893	7	S				KY	KY	IND							✓	✓	✓	O	F	F	143
158	169	FORD, ERLINE A.	Head	W	F	Jun 1853	46	Wd		8	3	TN	TN	TN												H	
		" JUDSON K.	SON	W	M	Dec 1879	20	S				KY	TN	TN				FARMING			✓	✓	✓				
		" EVERT G.	SON	W	M	Jul 1882	17	S				KY	TN	TN				FARMING			✓	✓	✓				
159	170	SPEAR, AMBROSE	HEAD	W	M	May 1877	23	M	2			KY	KY	KY				FARMING			✓	✓	✓	R		F	144
		" SETTIE	WIFE	W	F	May 1876	24	M	2	1	1	KY	KY	KY							X	X	✓				
		" CECIL	SON	W	M	May 1899	1	S				KY	KY	KY													
160	171	SPEAR, PRINCTON	HEAD	W	M	Nov 1856	43	M	3			TN	TN	KY				FARMING			✓	✓	✓	O	F	F	145
		" LAURA A.	WIFE	W	F	May 1866	34	M	3	1	1	KY	KY	KY							✓	✓	✓				
		" LUTHER P.	SON	W	M	Feb 1886	14	S				KY	TN	KY				AT SCHOOL		4	✓	✓	✓				
		" FINETTIE E.	DAU	W	F	Jul 1898	1	S				KY	TN	KY													
161	172	EMMERT, PHEBE	HEAD	W	F	Dec 1839	60	Wd		3	3	KY	KY	KY							✓	✓	✓	O	F	F	146
		" JERRYMIAH T.	SON	W	M	Apr 1878	22	S				TN	KY	KY				FARMING			✓	✓	✓				
		" ZADIE A.	DAU	W	F	Jun 1880	19	S				KY	KY	KY							✓	✓	✓				
		" MARTHA	DAU	W	F	Apr 1884	16	S				KY	KY	KY				AT SCHOOL		4	✓	✓	✓				
162	173	DAVIS, ROBERT	HEAD	W	M	May −	22	S				KY	KY	KY				FARMING			X	X	✓	O	F	F	147
		" POLLY	MOTHER	W	F	− −	67	Wd		9	5	KY	KY	KY							X	X	✓				
		(? CRANE,) TENNESSEE	NIECE	W	F	Apr 1877	23	Wd		2	1	KY	KY	KY				HOUSEWORK			X	X	✓				
		VAN, THOMAS	BOARDER	W	M	Jan 1867	33	DIVC.				TN	−	−													
		SCOT, CLARENCE H.	NEPHEW	W	M	Oct 1896	3	S				KY	KY	KY													
163	174	SPEAR, THOMAS	Head	W	M	Oct 1866	33	M	13			KY	KY	KY				FARM HAND 6			✓	✓	✓	R		F	148
		" RUTHA E.	Wife	W	F	Mar 1863	37	M	13	7	4	TN	TN	TN							X	X	✓				
		CARNAHAN, WILLIAM	Stepson	W	M	Jun 1884	16	S				TN	TN	TN				DAY LABOR 6			X	X	✓				
		" ROSA	DAU	W	F	Sep 1889	10	S				KY	KY	TN				AT SCHOOL 4			✓	X	✓				

TWELFTH CENSUS OF THE UNITED STATES 1900

-291-

STATE - KENTUCKY
COUNTY - MONROE
Township or other division: EAST TOMPKINSVILLE
Enumerator: E. R. BAXTER
Supervisor's Dist. No. 102 Sheet No.
Enumeration Dist. No. 84

No. of Family	No. of Dwelling	Name	Relation	Color	Sex	Date of Birth Mon/Yr	Age at last birthday	Marital Status	# Years married	Mother of how many children	# of these children living	Place of birth (this person)	Father	Mother	Occupation	Months not employed	Attended school in months	Can read	Can write	Speak English	Owned or Rent	Farm or house	# of farm schedule
		CARNAHAN, ALICE M	DAU	W	F	APR 1893	7	S				KY	KY	KY									
		" NANCY A.	DAU	W	F	May 1895	5	S				KY	KY	KY									
164	175	JAMERSON, WALTER	HEAD	W	M	DEC 1854	45	M	15			ENGLAND			FARMING			X	X	✔	O	F	150
		" RHODA	WIFE	W	F	May 1868	32	M	15	9	8	KY	KY	KY				X	X	✔			
		" MATTIE	DAU	W	F	Feb 1886	14	S				KY	ENG	KY	AT SCHOOL		3	✔	✔	✔			
		" ORVIL	DAU	W	F	MAR 1888	12	S				KY	ENG	KY	AT SCHOOL		3	✔	✔	✔			
		" RHODA	DAU	W	F	Jul 1890	9	S				KY	ENG	KY									
		" FANNIE	DAU	W	F	Sep 1892	7	S				KY	ENG	KY									
		" MARY	DAU	W	F	Sep 1894	5	S				KY	ENG	KY									
		" CINDA	DAU	W	F	May 1896	4	S				KY	ENG	KY									
		" VERDIE	DAU	W	F	May 1897	3	S				KY	ENG	KY									
		" WILLIAM B.	SON	W	M	MAY 1900	1/12	S				KY	ENG	KY									
165	176	TADE, JOHN	HEAD	W	M	AUG 1863	36	M	10			KY	TN	TN	FARMING			✔	✔	✔	O	FF	151
		" LOU A	WIFE	W	F	Jun 1863	36	M	10	5	4	TN	TN	TN				✔	✔	✔			
		" LENA	DAU	W	F	OCT 1890	9	S				KY	KY	TN									
		" GEORGIE	DAU	W	F	Nov 1892	7	S				KY	KY	TN									
		" MARY M	DAU	W	F	OCT 1894	5	S				KY	KY	TN									
		" NORA A.	DAU	W	F	Sep 1896	2	S				KY	KY	TN									
166	177	TADE, MARY	HEAD	W	F	Nov 1852	57	Wd		2	2	TN	TN	TN	HOUSEWORK	6		X	X	✔	O	FF	152
		" ELIJAH R.	SON	W	M	Sep 1877	22	S				KY	TN	TN	FARMING	6		✔	✔	✔			
167	178	HESTAND, WILLIAM T.	HEAD	W	M	MAR 1870	29	M	5			KY	KY	KY	FARMING	6		✔	✔	✔	R	F	153
		" FLORENCE	WIFE	W	F	MAR 1871	28	M	5	4	4	KY	KY	KY				✔	✔	✔			
		" DENTON	SON	W	M	MAR 1896	4	S				KY	KY	KY									
		" ADIE	DAU	W	F	Feb 1898	2	S				KY	KY	KY									
		" RAYMAN	SON	W	M	Feb 1898	2	S				KY	KY	KY									
		" FLORA	DAU	W	F	MAR 1900	3/12	S				KY	KY	KY									

TWELFTH CENSUS OF THE UNITED STATES 1900

STATE - KENTUCKY
COUNTY - MONROE
Township or other division: EAST TOMPKINSVILLE
-292-
Enumerator: E. R. HESTAND

Supervisor's Dist. No. 102   Sheet No.
Enumeration Dist. No. 84

No. of Family	No. of Dwelling	NAME	Relation	Color	Sex	Date of Birth Mon/Yr	Age at last birthday	Marital Status	# Years married	Mother of how many children	# of these children living	Birthplace	Father birthplace	Mother birthplace	Occupation	Months not employed	Attended school	Can read	Can write	Speak English	Owned or Rent	Owned free/mortgage	Farm or house	# of farm schedule
168	179	HESTAND, BARTON	Head	W	M	Aug 1839	61	M	39			KY	KY	KY	FARMING	6		✓	✓	✓	O	F	F	154
		" MARY L.	Wife	W	F	Sep 1844	55	M	38	2	2	KY	KY	MISSISSIPPI				✓	✓	✓				
		" BELLE V.	Dau	W	F	Jan 1879	21	S				KY	KY	KY				✓	✓	✓	O	F	F	155
		BRILLIA	Dau	W	F	Jun 1869	30	S				KY	KY	KY	SCHOOL TEACHING	6		✓	✓	✓	O	F	F	156
169	180	HESTAND, JOHN	Head	W	M	Jan 1874	26	M				KY	KY	KY	FARMING	6		✓	✓	✓	R		F	157
		" JULIA S	Wife	W	F	Jun 1884	16	M				KY	KY	KY					✓	✓				
170	181	PENNINGTON, JOE	Head	W	M	Nov 1852	47	M	23			TN	TN	TN	FARMING	4		X	X	✓	R		F	159 sic
		" ELIZZIEBETH	Wife	W	F	Mar 1856	44	M	23	4	3	TN	TN	TN		4			✓	✓				
		" OSCAR H.	Son	W	M	Jul 1885	14	S				TN	TN	TN	AT SCHOOL		4	✓	✓	✓				
		" VIRGIL E.	Son	W	M	Sep 1887	12	S				TN	TN	TN	AT SCHOOL		4	✓	✓	✓				
171	182	PENNINGTON, SYLVESTER	Head	W	M	Mar 1866	34	M	13			TN	TN	TN	FARMING			✓	✓	✓	R		F	160
		" COATRY(?) A.	Wife	W	F	Oct 1867	32	M	13	4	3	KY	KY	KY				✓	✓	✓				
		" ALVA	Son	W	M	Sep 1888	12	S				KY	TN	KY	AT SCHOOL		4	✓	✓	✓				
		" WELKIE	Son	W	M	Jul 1890	9	S				KY	TN	KY										
		" MINNIE O.	Dau	W	F	Jun 1896	4	S				KY	TN	KY										
172	183	SPROWL, OWEN	Head	W	M	Dec 1859	40	M	18			KY	KY	KY	FARMING	4		✓	✓	✓	O	F	F	161
		" LUCINDA	Wife	W	F	Nov 1863	36	M	18			KY	NC	KY		4		✓	✓	✓				
		" MARY C.	Dau	W	F	Feb 1883	17	S				KY	KY	KY	AT SCHOOL		4	✓	✓	✓				
		" LENORA A.	Dau	W	F	Oct 1885	14	S				KY	KY	KY	AT SCHOOL		4	✓	✓	✓				
		" WILLIAM P.	Son	W	M	Jun 1893	7	S				KY	KY	KY										
		" JOSHUA B.	Son	W	M	Feb 1895	5	S				KY	KY	KY										
		" GEORGE A.	Son	W	M	Jan 1897	3	S				KY	KY	KY										
		" ROY M.	Son	W	M	Oct 1899	8/12	S				KY	KY	KY										
173	184	HESTAND, JOHN	Head	W	M	Aug 1855	44	M	9			KY	KY	K	FARMING			✓	✓	✓	R		F	162
		" IDA E.	Wife	W	F	Aug 1869	30	M	9	2	1	TN	TN	TN				✓	✓	✓				
174	185	BAILEY, HIRAM A.	Head	W	M	May 1838	62	M	39			KY	KY	KY	FARMING			✓	✓	✓	O	F	F	163

STATE - KENTUCKY
COUNTY - MONROE
Township or other division — EAST TOMPKINSVILLE — Enumerator E. R. BAXTER

Supervisor's Dist. No. 102 Sheet No.
Enumeration Dist. No. 84

No. of Family	No. of Dwelling	NAME	Relation	Color	Sex	DATE OF BIRTH Mon/Yr	Age at last birthday	Marital Status	# Years married	Mother of how many children?	# of these children living	Place of birth [this person]	Father of this person	Mother of this person	Year of immigr.	# years in U.S.	Naturalization	OCCUPATION 10 years +	Months not employed	Attended school in months	Can read	Can write	Speak English	Owned or Rent	Owned - no mortage	Farm or house	# of farm schedule
		BAILEY, ALMIRA	Wife	W	F	Feb 1835	65	M	19	9		KY	KY	KY							✓	✓	✓				
		" ELIJAH W	Son	W	M	May 1872	28	S				KY	KY	KY				FARMING			✓	✓	✓	O	F	F	164
		" MELLISSIA	Dau	W	F	Oct 1877	22	S				KY	KY	KY							✓	✓	✓				
175	186	BAILEY TICE W.	Head	W	M	Mar 1874	26	M	3			KY	KY	KY				FARMING			✓	✓	✓	R		F	165
		" SALLIE	Wife	W	F	Apr 1880	20	M	3	1	0	KY	TN	TN							✓	✓	✓				
176	187	MOORE, MARY	Head	B	F	— — —		Wd		3	3	TN	TN	TN				WASHING AND COOKING			X	X	✓	O		F	166
		" HAY—(?)	Son	B	M	— — —		S				KY	TN	TN				FARM HAND			✓	✓	✓				
		" CHMING(?)	Dau	B	F	— — —		S			0	KY	TN	TN							✓	✓	✓				
		" CARY	Son	B	M	— — —		S				KY	TN	TN				FARM HAND			✓	✓	✓				
		" ADA	Gr-Dau	B	F	Apr 1885	15	S				KY	KY	KY							X	X	✓				
		" EDGAR	Ga-Son	B	M	Nov 1886	13	S				KY	KY	KY							X	X	✓				
		" BEDFORD	Ga-Son	B	M	Jun 1893	7	S				KY	KY	KY													
177	188	STRODE, THOMAS	Head	W	M	Aug 1856	43	M	12			KY	KY	KY				FARMING			✓	✓		O		F	167
		" VESTINA E.	Wife	W	F	Apr 1868	32	M	12	7	5	KY	KY	KY							✓	✓					
		" RUSELLA	Dau	W	F	Jun 1888	11	S				KY	KY	KY				AT SCHOOL		4	✓	✓	✓				
		" EFFIE	Dau	W	F	Sep 1892	7	S				KY	KY	KY													
		" ETHEL	Dau	W	F	Sep 1892	7	S				KY	KY	KY													
		" LOLIE B.	Dau	W	F	May 1895	5	S				KY	KY	KY													
		" ELLA	Dau	W	F	May 1897	3	S				KY	KY	KY													
		SCOTT, JAMES	Hand	W	M	Aug 1877	22	S				KY	KY	KY				FARM HAND			✓	✓	✓				
178	189	DICKEN, GABREL	Head	W	M	Mar 1824	76	M	40			KY	VA	VA				FARMING 4			X	X	✓	R		F	168
		" JANE	Wife	W	F	Jan 1840	60	M	40	10	7	KY	KY	VA							X	X	✓				
		" EMILY	Dau	W	F	May 1875	25	S				KY	KY	KY							✓	✓	✓				
		" HOMER	Son	W	M	May 1883	17	S				KY	KY	KY				FARM LABOR			✓	✓	✓				
		MAXEY, ALICE	Neice	W	F	Dec 1880	19	S				KY	KY	KY							✓	✓	✓				
179	190	BAILEY, AUSTIN	Head	W	M	May 1852	48	M	19			KY	KY	TN				FARMING			✓	✓	✓	O		F	169

STATE - KENTUCKY
COUNTY - MONROE
Township or other division: EAST TOMPKINSVILLE
Enumerator: E. R. BAXTER

Supervisor's Dist. No. 102 Sheet No.
Enumeration Dist. No. 84

No. of Family	No. of Dwelling	NAME	Relation	Color	Sex	DATE OF BIRTH Mon/Yr	Age at last birthday	Marital Status	# Years married	Mother of how many children?	# of these children living	NATIVITY Place of birth (this person)	Father of this person	Mother of this person	CITIZENSHIP Year of immigr.	# years in U.S.	Naturalization	OCCUPATION 10 years +	Months not employed	Attended school in months	Can read	Can write	Speak English	Owned or Rent	Owned – no mortgage	Farm or house	# of farm schedule
		BAILEY, NANCY	WIFE	W	F	OCT 1842	37	M	19			KY	TN	KY							✓	✓	✓				
		ROARCH, JENA	ADOPTED SON	W	M	DEC 1884	15	S				KY	—	—				FARM HAND			✓	✓	✓				
		MORGAN, ELIZZIEBETH	SIS-IN-LAW	W	F	MAY 1854	45	Wd		5	1	KY	TN	KY				HOUSEWORK			✓	✓	✓				
		" HERBERT P.	NEPHEW	W	M	JUN 1885	15	S				KY	KY	KY				FARMING			✓	✓	✓				
180	191	CHAPPEL, RUFUS W.	HEAD	W	M	JAN 1841	59	M	30			MO	MO	MO				FARMING			✓	✓	✓	O	F	170
		" NANCY E.	WIFE	W	F	Sep 1838	62	M	30	4	3	KY	KY	KY							✓	✓					
		" BARLOW	SON	W	M	JUN 1881	19	S				KY	MO	KY				MERCHANDISE			✓	✓	✓	R	F	171
		WILLIAMS, BUFORD	Boarder	W	M	NOV 1878	21	S				KY	KY	KY				MERCHANT-DRY GOODS			✓	✓	✓				
		PAGE, WILLIAM S.	HAND	W	M	JAN 1877	23	S				KY	KY	KY				FARM HAND			✓	✓	✓	R	F	172
181	192	WRIGHT, ROBERT	HEAD	W	M	JUL 1874	26	M				KY	TN	TN				DAY LABOR			X	X	✓	R	H	
		" BERTHA	WIFE	W	F	MAY 1884	16	M				KY	KY	KY							✓	✓	✓				
182	193	KELLEY, WILLIAM	Head	W	M	DEC 1848	51	M	14			KY	KY	KY				FARMING	6		✓	✓	✓	O	F	173
		" MARTHA	wife	W	F	MAR 1865	35	M	14	7	7	KY	KY	KY							✓	✓	✓				
		" JULIAS	Son	W	M	JUN 1885	15	S				KY	KY	KY				AT SCHOOL		10	✓	✓	✓				
		" GERGIE E. B.	DAU	W	F	MAR 1887	12	S				KY	KY	KY				AT SCHOOL		4	✓	✓	✓				
		" SARAH A.	DAU	W	F	MAR 1889	10	S				KY	KY	KY							✓	✓	✓				
		" DORA L.	DAU	W	F	Sep 1892	8	S				KY	KY	KY													
		" AUGUSTUS G.	Son	W	M	Feb 1893	7	S				KY	KY	KY													
		" WILLIAM J. B.	Son	W	M	Dec 1895	4	S				KY	KY	KY													
		" JUSTUS G.	Son	W	M	May 1899	3/12	S				KY	KY	KY													
183	194	COFFEE, THOMAS	HEAD	W	M	JUN 1850	49	M	9			KY	KY	KY				MILL HAND			X	X	✓	R	H	
		" ANNIE	WIFE	W	F	JUL 1869	30	M	9	4	3	KY	TN	TN							✓	✓	✓				
		" JANE L	DAU	W	F	JUL 1892	7	S				KY	KY	KY													
		" JAMES	Son	W	M	MAY 1896	4	S				KY	KY	KY													
		" BENJAMIN	Son	W	M	DEC 1898	1	S				TN	KY	KY													
184	195	POINDEXTER, ARCH F.	Head	W	M	AUG 1872	27	M	7			KY	—	—				TEAMSTER			✓	✓	✓	R	H	

TWELFTH CENSUS OF THE UNITED STATES 1900

STATE - KENTUCKY
COUNTY - MONROE
Township or other division — EAST TOMPKINSVILLE
Enumerator E. R. BAXTER

Supervisor's Dist. No. 102 Sheet No.
Enumeration Dist. No. 84

No. of Family	No. of Dwelling	NAME	Relation	Color	Sex	DATE OF BIRTH Mon/Yr	Age at last birthday	Marital Status	# Years married	Mother of how many children?	# of these children living	Place of birth [this person]	Father of this person	Mother of this person	Year of immigr.	# years in U.S.	Naturalization	OCCUPATION 10 years +	Months not employed	Attended school in months	Can read	Can write	Speak English	Owned or Rent	Owned -no mortgage	Farm or house	# of farm schedule
		POINDEXTER, AMERICA L	Wife	W	F	Oct 1876	23	M	7	4	4	KY	KY	KY							✓	✓	✓				
		" FRANCIS	Dau	W	F	Sep 1894	5	S				KY	KY	KY							✓	✓	✓				
		" JESSEE F.	Son	W	M	Oct 1896	3	S				KY	KY	KY													
		" BERTHA M.	Dau	W	F	Apr 1898	2	S				KY	KY	KY													
		" EDGAR	Son	W	M	Apr 1900	3/12	S				KY	KY	KY													
		SHORT, LINZY	Boarder	W	M	May 1875	25	S				KY	KY	KY				DAY LABORER			X	X	✓				
		ODLE, RILEY	Boarder	W	M	Jan 1883	17	S				TN	TN	TN				TEAMSTER									
		STAGLAND, RANZY	Boarder	W	M	Jun 1882	18	S				TN	TN	TN													
185	196	HALL, FRANCIS	Head	W	M	Apr 1865	35	M	12			TN	SC	TN				MILLER			✓	✓	✓	R		H	
		" LAURA F.	Wife	W	F	Sep 1872	27	M	12	5	5	KY	TN	KY							✓	✓	✓				
		" MILLIE	Dau	W	F	Jan 1890	10	S				TN	TN	KY						5	✓	✓	✓				
		" NOLIE	Dau	W	F	Feb 1893	7	S				TN	TN	KY													
		" LEFFIE	Dau	W	F	Mar 1895	5	S				KY	TN	KY													
		" LOVY	Dau	W	F	Nov 1896	3	S				KY	TN	KY													
		" IVORY	Son	W	M	Feb 1899	1	S				KY	TN	KY													
		ATCHLEY, VANAS	Boarder	W	M	Feb 1879	21	S				KY	TN	KY				DAY LABORER	4		✓	✓	✓				
		ATCHLEY, LARENCE	Boarder	W	M	Jan 1885	14	S				KY	TN	KY				DAY LABORER	4		✓	✓	✓				
		LAWSON, SHERMAN	Boarder	W	M	Jan 1881	19	S				TN	—	—							✓	✓	✓				
186	197	HOOD, HUGH(?)	Head	W	M	Jul 1865	34	M	7			TN	—	TN				DAY LABORER	4		X	X	✓			H	
		" MARY	Wife	W	F	Jan 1875	25	M	7	3	2	KY	TN	TN							✓	✓	✓				
		" GEORG P.	Son	W	M	Aug 1892	7	S				TN	TN	KY													
		" MARION C.	Son	W	M	Jul 1899	9/12	S				KY	TN	TN													
		WOOD, SAMANTHA	S-in-law	W	F	Apr 1879	21	S				TN	TN	TN				HOUSEWORK	4		✓	✓	✓				
187	198	BAILEY, MARTIN	Head	W	M	Jul 1858	41	M	17			KY	SC	KY				FARMING			✓	✓	✓	O	M	F	174
		" MARY B.	Wife	W	F	Nov 1858	41	M	17	5	4	KY	KY	KY							✓	✓	✓				
		" EDWARD G.	Son	W	M	Aug 1883	16	S				KY	KY	KY				FARMING			✓	✓	✓				

STATE - KENTUCKY
COUNTY - MONROE   EAST
Township or other division   TOMPKINSVILLE   Enumerator   E. R. BAXTER

Supervisor's Dist. No. *102*   Sheet No.
Enumeration Dist. No. *84*

No. of Family	No. of Dwelling	NAME	Relation	Color	Sex	DATE OF BIRTH Mon/Yr	Age at last birthday	Marital Status	# Years married	Mother of how many children?	# of these children living	Place of birth [this person]	Father of this person	Mother of this person	Year of immigr.	# years in U.S.	Naturalization	OCCUPATION 10 years +	Months not employed	Attended school in months	Can read	Can write	Speak English	Owned or Rent	Owned -no mortage	Farm or house	# of farm schedule
		BAILEY, NANCY E.	DAU	W	F	Feb 1885	15	S				KY	KY	KY				AT SCHOOL		5	✓	✓	✓				
		" WILLIAM B	SON	W	M	May 1887	13	S				KY	KY	KY				AT SCHOOL		5	✓	✓	✓				
		" WAYMAN A.	SON	W	M	Jul 1894	6	S				KY	KY	KY													
		BAILEY EDWARD	BROTHER	W	M	Feb 1854	46	S				KY	SC	KY				FARMING			✓	✓	✓	O	M	F	174
		PARKS, JOHN F.	HAND	W	M	Jan 1874	26	S				ILL	KY	ILL				FARM HAND			✓	✓	✓				
198	199	SPEAR, LORENZO	HEAD	W	M	May 1859	41	M	15			KY	NC	SC				FARMING			✓	✓	✓	R		F	175
		" VIRGINIA	WIFE	W	F	Feb 1866	34	M	15	7	7	KY	KY	KY								✓	✓				
		" EDGAR	SON	W	M	Aug 1886	13	S				KY	KY	KY				AT SCHOOL		5	✓	✓	✓				
		" THOMPSON	SON	W	M	Apr 1888	12	S				KY	KY	KY				AT SCHOOL		5	✓	✓	✓				
		" ALBERT	SON	W	M	Oct 1889	10	S				KY	KY	KY				AT SCHOOL		5	✓	✓	✓				
		" PEARL	DAU	W	F	Aug 1891	8	S				KY	KY	KY													
		" BENTON	SON	W	M	Oct 1893	6	S				KY	KY	KY													
		" McKINLEY	SON	W	M	Jan 1896	4	S				KY	KY	KY													
		" BEECHUM	SON	W	M	Apr 1898	2	S				KY	KY	KY													
		DAVIS, WILLIAM	HAND	W	M	Sep 1872	27	Wd				KY	KY	KY				FARM HAND	5		X	X	✓	R		F	
199	200	BAILEY, AMBROSE	HEAD	W	M	Mar 1869	31	M	9			KY	KY	KY				FARMING	4		✓	✓	✓	R		F	176
		" IDA	WIFE	W	F	Dec 1873	26	M	9	4	4	KY	TN	TN							✓	✓	✓				
		" OLLIE B.	DAU	W	F	Nov 1891	8	S				KY	KY	KY													
		" RAY	SON	W	M	Jan 1893	7	S				KY	KY	KY													
		" VERCHIE	DAU	W	F	Jun 1896	4	S				KY	KY	KY													
		" RESSIE	DAU	W	F	Jul 1898	1	S				KY	KY	KY													
200	201	GRISSOM, FRANCIS R.	HEAD	W	M	Dec 1871	28	M				KY	KY	KY				FARMING			✓	✓	✓	R		F	177
		" ADA	WIFE	W	F	Dec 1871	28	M	5	2	2	TN	TN	TN							✓	✓	✓				
		" ORLIE L.	DAU	W	F	Apr 1895	5	S				TEXAS	KY	TN													
		" OMER C.	SON	W	M	Jul 1897	2	S				(INDIAN TERR.)	KY	TN													
201	202	GRISSOM, LEVI	HEAD	W	M	Mar 1842	58	M	34			TN	TN	TN				FARMING			X	X	✓	O	F	F	178

TWELFTH CENSUS OF THE UNITED STATES 1900

STATE - KENTUCKY
COUNTY - MONROE
Township or other division — EAST TOMPKINSVILLE

Enumerator E. R. BAXTER

- 297 -

Supervisor's Dist. No. 102 Sheet No.
Enumeration Dist. No. 84

No. of Family	No. of Dwelling	NAME	Relation	Color	Sex	Date of Birth Mon/Yr	Age at last birthday	Marital Status	# Years married	Mother of how many children?	# of these children living	Place of birth (this person)	Father of this person	Mother of this person	Year of immigr.	# years in U.S.	Naturalization	OCCUPATION 10 years +	Months not employed	Attended school in months	Can read	Can write	Speak English	Owned or Rent	Owned -no mortgage	Farm or house	# of farm schedule
		GRISSOM, CLARISAL	WIFE	W	F	Sep 1841	58	M	34	6	5	KY	KY	KY							✓	✓	✓				
		" MELISSIA B	DAU	W	F	Sep 1870	29	S				KY	KY	KY				SCHOOL TEACHING			✓	✓	✓				
		" CORA E.	DAU	W	F	Nov 1873	26	S				KY	KY	KY				PHOTOGRAPHER			✓	✓	✓				
192	203	BAILEY, HARRISON	HEAD	W	M	Oct 1861	38	M	10			KY	KY	KY				BLACKSMITHING			X	X	✓	O	F	F	179
		" ALICE	WIFE	W	F	Jul 1870	29	M	10	2	2	KY	KY	KY							✓	✓	✓				
		" HANSFORD	SON	W	M	Feb 1891	9	S				KY	KY	KY													
		" ARIE	DAU	W	F	Dec 1892	7	S				KY	KY	KY							✓	✓	✓				
		BAILEY, ANNIE	GR-Mother	W	F	Oct 1826	73	Wd		1	0	TN	—	—													
193	204	BLACK, JOSEPH	HEAD	W	M	Jul 1866	33	S				KY	KY	KY				FARMING 6			✓	✓	✓	O	F	F	180
		" BETSY	Sister	W	F	Dec 1862	37	S				KY	KY	KY							✓	✓					
		" LON	Sister	W	F	Sep 1864	35	S				KY	KY	KY							✓	✓					
194	205	GRACE, VARNIE	HEAD	W	M	Nov 1833	44	M	22			KY	NC	KY				FARMING 10			✓	✓		R		F	181
		" CRECIE A.	wife	W	F	Feb 1854	46	M	22	1	1	TN	TN	TN													
		" LOUIS F.	Son	W	M	Sep 1879	21	S				KY	KY	TN				FARMING			✓	✓	✓				
195	206	SPEAR, AMERICA	HEAD	W	F	May 1847	53	Wd		10	9	TN	TN	TN				FARMING			✓	✓	✓	O	F	F	182
		" FRANCIS M.	Son	W	M	Jul 1871	28	S				KY	KY	TN				FARM HAND 6			✓	✓	✓				
		" WILLIAM B.	Son	W	M	Jun 1877	23	S				KY	KY	TN				FARM HAND 6			✓	✓	✓				
		" ETTA S.	DAU	W	F	Apr 1879	21	S		1	1	KY	KY	TN				HOUSEWORK			✓	✓	✓				
		" BARLOW G.	Son	W	M	Oct 1880	20	S				KY	KY	TN				FARM HAND			✓	✓	✓				
		" LUCILLE M.	DAU	W	F	Dec 1884	15	S				KY	KY	TN				HOUSEWORK			✓	✓	✓				
		" SARAH N.	DAU	W	F	Dec 1886	13	S				KY	KY	TN													
		" ONA L. V.	GR-DAU	W	F	Jan 1897	3	S				KY	KY	KY													
196	207	SPEAR, POLLY	HEAD	W	F	Feb 1847	53	Wd		6	6	KY	KY	KY				FARM WORK			✓	✓	✓	R		F	183
		" EMMERETTE	DAU	W	F	Sep 1880	19	S				KY	TN	KY				WASHING-IRONING 4			✓	✓	✓				
		" LOU A.	DAU	W	F	Mar 1884	16	S				KY	TN	KY				At SCHOOL		5	✓	✓	✓				
		" MARY E.	DAU	W	F	Jan 1886	14	S				KY	TN	KY							X	X	✓				

STATE - KENTUCKY
COUNTY - MONROE   EAST
Township or other division   TOMPKINSVILLE   Enumerator   E. R. BAXTER

Supervisor's Dist. No. _102_   Sheet No. ___
Enumeration Dist. No. _84_ ___

No. of Family	No. of Dwelling	NAME	Relation	Color	Sex	DATE OF BIRTH Mon/Yr	Age at last birthday	Marital Status	# Years married	Mother of how many children?	# of these children living	Place of birth (this person)	Father of this person	Mother of this person	Year of immigr.	# years in U.S.	Naturalization	OCCUPATION 10 years +	Months not employed	Attended school in months	Can read	Can write	Speak English	Owned or Rent	Owned -no mortgage	Farm or house	# of farm schedule
		SPEAR, GEORGIE	Dau	W	F	Feb 1888	12	S				KY	TN	KY							X	X	✓				
		HESTAND, VASSIE	G-Dau	W	F	Dec 1892	7	S				KY	TN	KY													
		" , NORA	Gr-Dau	W	F	Mar 1895	5	S				KY	TN	KY													
		" , MARGARET	Mother	W	F	Jan 1822	78	Wd	9	4		TN	TN	TN							X	X	✓	O	F	F	183
197	208	SPEAR, BELLE	Head	W	F	Nov 1875	24	S		3	3	KY	TN	KY				DAY LABOR			X	X	✓	R	F	F	184
		" OVY P.	Dau	W	F	Aug 1892	7	S				KY	KY	KY													
		" OTIS L.	Son	W	M	May 1895	5	S				KY	KY	KY													
		" OLLIE	Dau	W	F	Apr 1900	2/12	S				KY	KY	KY													
198	209	CARY, GEORGE	Head	W	M	Oct 1859	40	M				KY	TN	TN				FARMING			X	X	✓	R		F	185
		" PERMELIA (?)	Wife	W	F	Apr 1855	45	M	20	6	6	TN	TN	TN							X	X	✓				
		" RASTUS	Son	W	M	Feb 1881	19	S				KY	KY	TN				FARM HAND			X	X	✓				
		" ETHEL	Dau	W	F	Sep 1883	16	S				KY	KY	TN			A.T SCHOOL		4		✓	✓	✓				
		" ANNIE	Dau	W	F	Jul 1887	13	S				KY	KY	TN			A.T SCHOOL		4		✓	✓	✓				
		" MATTIE B.	Dau	W	F	Jul 1889	10	S				KY	KY	TN							X	X	✓				
		" MALLIE	Dau	W	F	Sep 1892	7	S				KY	KY	TN													
		" JAMES	Son	W	M	— 1895	5	S				KY	KY	TN													
199	210	THOMAS, SMITH	Head	W	M	Apr 1874	26	M	9			KY	KY	TN				FARMING			✓	✓	✓	R		F	186
		" FLORENCE	Wife	W	F	Jan 1875	25	M	9	3	3	KY	KY	KY							✓	✓	✓				
		" JOSEPH	Son	W	M	Dec 1894	7	S				KY	KY	KY													
		" PEARLY	Dau	W	F	Aug 1895	4	S				KY	KY	KY													
		" IVEY (?)	Dau	W	F	May 1898	2	S				KY	KY	KY													
200	211	GOAD, GEORGE	Head	W	M	Jan 1875	25	M	6			KY	KY	KY				FARMING			✓	✓	✓	R		F	187
		" ALICE	Wife	W	F	Feb 1880	20	M	6	3	1	KY	KY	KY							✓	✓	✓				
		" ROXIE	Dau	W	F	Oct 1895	4	S				KY	KY	KY													
201	212	GRISSOM, MOSES	Head	W	M	May 1845	55	M	30			TN	TN	TN				FARMING			✓	✓	✓	R	F	F	188
		" BOLLEY	Wife	W	F	Dec 1841	58	M	30	3	2	KY	KY	KY							✓	✓	✓				

STATE - KENTUCKY
COUNTY - MONROE
Township or other division EAST TOMPKINSVILLE Enumerator E. R. BAXTER

No. of Family	No. of Dwelling	NAME	Relation	Color	Sex	DATE OF BIRTH Mon/Yr	Age at last birthday	Marital Status	# Years married	Mother of how many children?	# of these children living	Place of birth (this person)	Father of this person	Mother of this person	Year of immigr.	# years in U.S.	Naturalization	OCCUPATION 10 years +	Months not employed	Attended school in months	Can read	Can write	Speak English	Owned or Rent	Owned –no mortgage	Farm or house	# of farm schedule
		GOAD, CHARLES J.	Son-in-law	W	M	Dec 1870	30	M	8			IN	TN	TN				FARMING	4		√	√	√				
		", BETTIE	Dau	W	F	Jul 1876	23	M	8	3	2	KY	TN	KY							√	√	√	O	F	F	188
		" CORA P.	Gr-Dau	W	F	Feb 1895	5	S				KY	TN	KY													
		" ANGIE L.	Gr-Dau	W	F	Feb 1898	2	S				KY	TN	KY													
202	213	MAXEY, HENRY	Head	W	M	Mar 1843	57	M	3			KY	KY	KY				FARMING			√	√	√	O	F	F	189
		" EARNEST D.	Wife	W	F	Feb 1864	36	M	3			KY	KY	KY							√	√	√				
		" JOHN A. H.	Nephew	W	M	Dec 1879	20	S				KY	KY	KY				FARMING			√	√	√				
203	214	SPEAR, WILLIAM	Head	W	M	Mar 1856	43	M	22			KY	NC	SC				FARMING			√	√	√	R		F	190
		" VIRGINIA A.	Wife	W	F	Aug 1850	49	M	22	2	1	TN	TN	TN							√	√	√				
		" FLORA	Dau	W	F	Mar 1884	16	S				KY	KY	TN				AT SCHOOL	8		√	√	√				
204	215	PENNINGTON, SYLVESTER	Head	W	M	Jun 1870	30	M				KY	TN	KY				FARM WORK	6		X	X	√	R		F	191
		" DISA B.	Wife	W	F	Sep 1873	26	M	7	3	2	TN	KY	KY													
		" JOSEPH L.	Son	W	M	Mar 1893	7	S				KY	KY	KY													
		" ORVIL G.	Son	W	M	Sep 1895	4	S				KY	KY	KY													
205	216	BOON, STEVEN	Head	W	M	Jul 1866	33	M	7			KY	TN	TN				FARMING	4		√	√	√	O	F	F	192
		" PRISCILLA	Wife	W	F	Jun 1874	26	M	7	5	4	KY	KY	KY													
		" OSCAR	Son	W	M	Jun 1894	6	S				KY	KY	KY													
		" OLLIE	Dau	W	F	Jul 1895	4	S				KY	KY	KY													
		" OVA	Dau	W	F	Oct 1898	2	S				KY	KY	KY													
		" ONA	Dau	W	F	Mar 1900	3/12	S				KY	KY	KY													
		SPEAR, ALEXANDER	Bro-in-law	W	M	Jun 1882	18	M				KY	TN	KY				FARM HAND	4		√	√	√				
		" MATTIE	Dau-in-law	W	F	Nov 1885	14	M				KY	KY	KY							√	√	√				
206	217	HUNT, WILLIAM	Head	W	M	Jan 1851	49	S				KY	VA	KY				FARMING			√	√	√	O	F	F	193
		" NANCY	Step-mother	W	F	Jan 1830	70	Wd				KY	VA	KY							X	X	√				
207	218	SHEFFIELD, WILLIAM	Head	W	M	Sep 1856	43	M	18			KY	KY	KY				FARMING			√	√	√	O	F	F	194
		" MARY	Wife	W	F	Apr 1860	40	M	18	8	7	KY	NC	TN							√	√	√				

STATE - KENTUCKY
COUNTY - MONROE
Township or other division — EAST TOMPKINSVILLE

— 300 —

Enumerator E.R. BAXTER

Supervisor's Dist. No. 102 Sheet No.
Enumeration Dist. No. 84

No. of Family	No. of Dwelling	NAME	Relation	Color	Sex	Date of Birth Mon/Yr	Age at last birthday	Marital Status	# Years married	Mother of how many children?	# of these children living	Place of birth [this person]	Father of this person	Mother of this person	Year of immigr. to U.S.	# years in U.S.	Naturalization	Occupation	Months not employed	Attended school in months	Can read	Can write	Speak English	Owned or Rent	Owned -no mortgage	Farm or house	# of farm schedule
		SHEFFIELD, CECIL I.	Dau	W	F	Aug 1882	17	S				KY	KY	KY				HOUSEWORK			✓	✓	✓				
		" HARRY D.	Son	W	M	Mar 1885	15	S				KY	KY	KY				FARM WORK			✓	✓	✓				
		" WILLIAM H.	Son	W	M	Jul 1887	13	S				KY	KY	KY				FARM WORK			X	X	✓				
		" ARTHUR M.	Son	W	M	May 1889	10	S				KY	KY	KY				FARM WORK			X	X	✓				
		" SARAH E.	Dau	W	F	Apr 1891	8	S				KY	KY	KY													
		" BESSIE M.	Dau	W	F	Dec 1894	5	S				KY	KY	KY													
		" VERNIE E.	Dau	W	F	May 1897	3	S				KY	KY	KY													
206	219	PENNINGTON, JOHN	Head	W	M	Feb 1845	55	M	35			TN	TN	TN				FARMING 4			✓	✓	✓	O	F	F	195
		" BERNETTE	Wife	W	F	Jul 1847	52	M	35	10	8	KY	TN	KY							✓	✓	✓				
		" JEFFERSON	Son	W	M	Oct 1880	19	S				KY	TN	KY				FARM HAND 4			✓	✓	✓				
		" HARVEY	Son	W	M	May 1882	17	S				KY	TN	KY				FARM HAND 4			✓	✓	✓				
		" CARLOS	Son	W	M	Jul 1885	14	S				KY	TN	KY				AT SCHOOL		5	✓	✓	✓				
		" EUPHASIM(?)	Dau	W	F	Oct 1888	11	S				KY	TN	KY				AT SCHOOL		5	✓	✓	✓				
		GRACE, KATIE	Mother in law	W	F	Apr 1818	82	Wd		10	7	KY	TN	KY							X	X	✓				
209	220	NETHERTON, MONROE	Head	W	M	Jan 1870	30	M	11			TN	TN	TN				FARMING			✓	✓	✓	S	O	F	F	196
		" LAURA	Wife	W	F	Jan 1870	30	M	11	6	6	KY	KY	TN							✓	✓	✓				
		" VANAS	Son	W	M	Jan 1890	10	S				KY	TN	KY						4	X	X	✓				
		" DONNA	Dau	W	F	Oct 1891	8	S				KY	TN	KY													
		" DORA	Dau	W	F	Dec 1893	6	S				KY	TN	KY													
		" OCEA	Dau	W	F	Jan 1896	4	S				KY	TN	KY													
		" FOWLER	Son	W	M	Mar 1898	2	S				KY	TN	KY													
		" EMMET	Dau	W	F	Mar 1900	3/12	S				KY	TN	KY													
210	221	FRAZIER, WILLIAM	Head	W	M	Jul 1869	30	M	11			KY	TN	KY				FARMING 4			✓	✓	✓	O	F	F	197
		" CORA	Wife	W	F	Oct 1871	28	M	11	4	4	KY	KY	TN							✓	✓	✓				
		" VIRGINIA	Dau	W	F	Oct 1890	9	S				KY	KY	KY													
		" VIRGIL	Son	W	M	Apr 1892	7	S				KY	KY	KY													

STATE - KENTUCKY
COUNTY - MONROE
Township or other division **EAST TOMPKINSVILLE** Enumerator **E. R. BAXTER**

Supervisor's Dist. No. _102_ Sheet No.
Enumeration Dist. No. _84_

No. of Family	No. of Dwelling	NAME	Relation	Color	Sex	DATE OF BIRTH Mon/Yr	Age at last birthday	Marital Status	# Years married	Mother of how many children?	# of these children living	Place of birth [this person]	Father of this person	Mother of this person	Year of immigr.	# years in U.S.	Naturalization	OCCUPATION 10 years +	Months not employed	Attended school in months	Can read	Can write	Speak English	Owned or Rent	Owned -no mortage	Farm or house	# of farm schedule
		FRAZIER, VERLIE	Son	W	M	Jan 1892	3	S				KY	KY	KY													
		" (BABY)	Dau	W	F	July 1900	4/12	S				KY	KY	KY													
211	222	COMBS, BARTIN	Head	W	M	Feb 1856	44	M	15			KY	KY	TN				FARMING		4	✓	✓		0	F	F	198
		" MARY	Wife	W	F	May 1865	35	M	15	3	3	TN	TN	TN							✓	✓	✓				
		" MARGARET	Dau	W	F	Aug 1886	13	S				KY	KY	TN				AT SCHOOL		5	✓	✓	✓				
		" MARTHA	Dau	W	F	Sep 1889	10	S				KY	KY	TN				AT SCHOOL		5	✓	✓	✓				
		" LURA	Dau	W	F	Aug 1891	8	S				KY	KY	TN								✓	✓				
212	223	SLAUGHTER, OSCAR	Head	W	M	Dec 1877	22	M	1			KY	KY	KY				FARMING			✓	✓	✓	R		F	199
		" ROSALA	Wife	W	F	Feb 1878	22	M	1	1	1	KY	TN	KY								✓	✓	✓			
		" ESMOND	Son	W	M	Oct 1899	8/12	S				KY	KY	KY													
213	224	WALLER, NELSON	Head	W	M	May 1871	29	M	5			KY	TN	KY				FARMING	4		✓	✓	✓	0		F	200
		" FRANCIS	Wife	W	F	Jan 1879	21	M	5	2	2	KY	KY	KY							✓	✓	✓			
		" LUCY	Dau	W	F	Apr 1896	4	S				KY	KY	KY													
		" ESTUS	Son	W	M	Nov 1898	1	S				KY	KY	KY													
		COMBS, ISAIAH	B-in-Law	W	M	Jun 1851	49	S				KY	KY	TN				CABINET MAKER			✓	✓	✓	0	F	F	201
214	225	COMBS, JOHN	Head	W	M	Apr 1872	28	M	8			KY	KY	KY				FARMING			✓	✓	✓	0	M	F	202
		" LILLIE	Wife	W	F	Oct 1871	28	M	8	3	3	KY	KY	KY							✓	✓	✓			
		" ETHEL	Dau	W	F	Mar 1895	5	S				KY	KY	KY													
		" EFFIE	Dau	W	F	Jun 1897	2	S				KY	KY	KY													
		" WILLIE D.	Son	W	M	Apr 1900	2/12	S				KY	KY	KY													
215	226	MAXEY, JAMES	Head	W	M	Apr 1863	37	S				KY	KY	KY				FARMING	6		✓	✓	✓	0	M	F	203
		" LAIMA B	Sister	W	F	Oct 1882	17	S				KY	KY	KY				HOUSEWORK	4								
		TOLL H.	Bro.	W	M	Apr 1891	9	S				KY	KY	KY				AT SCHOOL		8							
		ROBERT C	Bro.	W	M	Jul 1867	32	S				KY	KY	KY				FARMING			✓	✓	✓				
		PENNINGTON, William	Bro-in-Law	W	M	May 1874	26	M	3			KY	KY	KY				FARMING			✓	✓	✓	R		F	204
		" Julia	Sister	W	F	Aug 1876	23		3	1	1	KY	KY	KY				HOUSEWORK			✓	✓	✓				

TWELFTH CENSUS OF THE UNITED STATES 1900

- 302 -

STATE - KENTUCKY
COUNTY - MONROE
Township or other division: EAST TOMPKINSVILLE
Enumerator: E. R. BAXTER

Supervisor's Dist. No. 102 Sheet No.
Enumeration Dist. No. 84

No. of Family	No. of Dwelling	NAME	Relation	Color	Sex	Date of Birth Mon/Yr	Age at last birthday	Marital Status	# Years married	Mother of how many children?	# of these children living	Place of birth (this person)	Father of this person	Mother of this person	Year of immigr.	# years in U.S.	Naturalization	Occupation 10 years +	Months not employed	Attended school in months	Can read	Can write	Speak English	Owned or Rent	Owned -no mortage	Farm or house	# of farm schedule
		PENNINGTON, CLIDE F.	SON	W	M	Jun 1897	1	S				KY	KY	KY													
216	227	JOBE, SAMUEL	HEAD	W	M	Apr 1872	28	M	1			KY	TN	TN				FARMING 4			✓	✓	✓	O	F	F	205
"		VIRGINIA	WIFE	W	F	Aug 1878	31	M	1			KY	TN	TN							✓	✓	✓	O	F	F	205
"		CALEB H.	DAU	W	F	Aug 1893	7	S				KY	KY	KY										O	F	F	205
217	228	GOAD, JOHN T.	HEAD	W	M	Mar 1871	29	M	7			KY	KY	KY				FARMING 4			✓	✓	✓	R		F	206
"		LORA F	WIFE	W	F	Oct 1872	27	M	7	2	2	KY	KY	KY							✓	✓	✓				
"		WILLIAM O.	SON	W	M	Nov 1894	5	S				KY	KY	KY													
"		OSBE H.	SON	W	M	Feb 1899	1	S				KY	KY	KY													
218	229	CHERRY, RANDOLPH	HEAD	W	M	Sep 1869	30	M	11			TN	TN	TN				FARMING 4			✓	✓	✓	R		F	207
"		NANCY	WIFE	W	F	Jan 1870	29	M	11	5	4	TN	TN	TN							✓	✓	✓				
"		HARRISON	SON	W	M	Aug 1890	10	S				KY	TN	TN				A.T. SCHOOL		4	✓	✓	✓				
"		LOSIA	DAU	W	F	Sep 1891	8	S				KY	TN	TN													
"		LILLIE A.	DAU	W	F	Oct 1896	3	S				KY	TN	TN													
"		HUSHUL R.	SON	W	M	Apr 1899	1	S				KY	TN	TN													
219	230	ROUSE, JAMES	HEAD	W	M	Apr 1866	33	M	12			TN	TN	TN				FARMING			✓	✓	✓	O	F	F	210
"		MARY	WIFE	W	F	Mar 1867	32	M	12	2	2	KY	TN	KY							✓	✓	✓				
"		NANCY L.	DAU	W	F	Oct 1888	11	S				KY	TN	KY				A.T. SCHOOL		5	✓	✓	✓				
"		ORAL H.	SON	W	M	Apr 1892	8	S				KY	TN	KY													
220	231	RHOTEN, ELI	HEAD	W	M	Oct 1819	80	M	27			VA	VA	VA				FARMING			X	X	✓	O	F	F	211
"		LIDEAN	WIFE	W	F	Aug 1840	59	M	27	4	4	TN	NC	TN							✓	✓	✓				
		BISHOP, ELVIRA	NEICE	W	F	Aug 1874	25	DIVC?		1	1	TN	TN	TN				HOUSEWORK			✓	✓	✓				
"		CORDELIA	GREAT NEICE	W	F	Aug 1892	7	S				TN	TN	TN													
221	232	POLAND, WILLIAM T.	HEAD	W	M	May 1874	26	M	2			KY	KY	KY				FARMING			X	X	✓	R		F	212
"		MARY	WIFE	W	F	Jan 1871	29	M	2	1	1	KY	TN	KY							✓	✓	✓				
"		OTIS	SON	W	M	Jun 1898	2	S				KY	KY	KY								✓	✓				
"		JAMES	BRO.	W	M	Mar 1878	21	S				KY	KY	KY				FARMING			✓	✓					

STATE - KENTUCKY
COUNTY - MONROE
Township or other division

EAST TOMPKINSVILLE   Enumerator E. R. BAXTER

Supervisor's Dist. No. 102 Sheet No.
Enumeration Dist. No. 84

No. of Family	No. of Dwelling	NAME	Relation	Color	Sex	DATE OF BIRTH Mon/Yr	Age at last birthday	Marital Status	# Years married	Member of how many children?	# of these children living	Place of birth (this person)	Father of this person	Mother of this person	Year of immigr.	# years in U.S.	Naturalization	OCCUPATION 10 years +	Months not employed	Attended school in months	Can read	Can write	Speak English	Owned or Rent	Owned –no mortgage	Farm or house	# of farm schedule
222	233	TINSLEY SAMUEL	HEAD	W	M	Jan 1844	56	M	31			TN	TN	TN				FARMING			✓	✓	✓	O		F	213
		MARTHA	WIFE	W	F	Apr 1844	56	M	31	8	8	TN	TN	TN							✓	✓	✓				
		MAGGIE	DAU	W	F	Feb 1874	26	S				TN	TN	TN							✓	✓	✓				
		LILLIE (?)	DAU	W	F	Sep 1877	23	S				TN	TN	TN													
		LUSETIA (?)	DAU	W	F	Mar 1882	18	S				TN	TN	TN													
		ANNIE	DAU	W	F	May 1883	17	S				TN	TN	TN													
		ADDIE	DAU	W	F	Sep 1886	13	S				TN	TN	TN													
223	234	WHITE, ATLOE	HEAD	W	M	Jun 1874	26	M	5			TN	TN	TN				FARMING			✓	X	✓	R		F	214
		MATTIE	WIFE	W	F	Feb 1879	21	M	5	2	1	TN	TN	TN							✓		✓				
		SAMUEL	SON	W	M	Jan 1898	2	S				KY	TN	TN													
224	235	RHOTEN, JAMES	HEAD	W	M	Jan 1876	24	M	2			KY	KY	KY				FARMING			✓	✓	✓	O		F	215
		VILETTE	WIFE	W	F	Jan 1884	16	M	2			TN	TN	TN							✓	✓					
225	236	NEWBERRY, JACOB	HEAD	W	M	Dec 1847	52	M	35			TN	TN	TN				FARMING			X	X	✓	R		F	216
		JANE	WIFE	W	F	Mar 1847	53	M	35	10	9	TN	TN	TN							X	X	✓				
		WILLIS	SON	W	M	Oct 1876	33	S				TN	TN	TN				FARM HAND			✓	✓	✓				
		JOHN A	SON	W	M	Oct 1879	20	M	1			TN	TN	TN				FARM HAND			✓	✓	✓				
		MILLARD	SON	W	M	Jun 1882	18	S				TN	TN	TN				FARM HAND			X	X	✓				
		SALLY	DAU	W	F	Aug 1884	15	S				TN	TN	TN				AT SCHOOL		4	✓	✓	✓				
		ALBY	DAU	W	F	May 1886	14	S				TN	TN	TN				AT SCHOOL		4	✓	✓	✓				
		CATY	DAU	W	F	Oct 1888	11	S				TN	TN	TN							X	X	✓				
226	237	GRINESTAFF, THOMAS	HEAD	W	M	Mar 18 7	33	M	11			TN	TN	KY				FARMING			✓	✓	✓	O		F	217
		EUNICE	WIFE	W	F	Mar 1874	26	M	11	3	3	KY	TN	KY							✓	✓	✓				
		ZINAS H.	SON	W	M	Nov 1890	9	S				KY	TN	KY													
		VERNIE L.	DAU	W	F	Mar 1893	7	S				KY	TN	KY													
		VIRDIE A.	DAU	W	F	Jan 1900	6/12	S				KY	TN	KY													
227	238	PENNINGTON, THOMAS	HEAD	W	M	Jun 1836	64	M	1			TN	TN	TN				FARMING			✓	✓	✓	R		F	218

STATE - KENTUCKY
COUNTY - MONROE
Township or other division   EAST TOMPKINSVILLE   -304-   Enumerator E. R. BAXTER

Supervisor's Dist. No. _102_ Sheet No.
Enumeration Dist. No. _84_

Location		NAME	Relation	Color	Sex	DATE OF BIRTH Mon/Yr	Age at last birthday	Marital Status	# Years married	Mother of how many children?	# of these children living	NATIVITY Place of birth (this person)	Father of this person	Mother of this person	CITIZENSHIP Year of immigr.	# years in U.S.	Naturalization	OCCUPATION 10 years +	Months not employed	EDUCATION Attended school in months	Can read	Can write	Speak English	OWNERSHIP Owned or Rent	Owned -no mortgage	Farm or house	# of farm schedule	
No. of Family	No. of Dwelling																											
		PENNINGTON, AMANDA E.	WIFE	W	F	Sep 1860	39	M	1	0	0	KY	TN	TN							✓	✓	✓					
		" JOSEPH	SON	W	M	May 1876	24	S				TN	TN	KY				FARMING			X	X	✓					
		" WILLIE	SON	W	M	Jan 1888	11	S				TN	TN	KY														
228	239	ARNETT, THOMAS	HEAD	W	M	APR 1851	49	M	24			TN	TN	TN				FARMING			✓	X	✓		O	F F	219	
		" ELIZZEBETH	WIFE	W	F	Mar 1859	41	M	24	12	11	KY	TN	TN							✓	X	✓					
		" WILLIAM	SON	W	M	Aug 1876	23	S				KY	TN	KY				FARM HAND			✓	✓	✓					
		" ANDREW	Son	W	M	Nov 1879	20	S				KY	TN	KY				FARM HAND			✓	✓	✓					
		" JOHN	Son	W	M	Feb 1881	18	S				KY	TN	KY							✓	✓	✓					
		" GEORGE	Son	W	M	Aug 1883	16	S				KY	TN	KY							✓	✓	✓					
		" JESSIE J.	Son	W	M	Feb 1886	14	S				KY	TN	KY							✓	✓	✓					
		" ISAIAH	Son	W	M	Mar 1888	12	S				KY	TN	KY							✓	✓	✓					
		" MANNIE	DAU	W	F	Feb 1890	10	S				KY	TN	KY						4	✓	✓	✓					
		" LAURA B	DAU	W	F	Sep 1892	7	S				KY	TN	KY									✓					
		" JULIA F	DAU	W	F	Mar 1895	5	S				KY	TN	KY														
		" LUTHIN T.	Son	W	M	Oct 1898	2	S				KY	TN	KY														
		" MOLLE	DAU	W	F	Nov 1899	6/12	S				KY	TN	KY														
229	240	RHOTEN, FRANKLIN	HEAD	W	M	Feb 1839	61	M	30			TN	TN	TN				FARMING	12		X	X	✓		O	F F	220	
		" FERIBA(?)	WIFE	W	F	Jun 1840	60	M	30	3	3	TN	TN	TN							X	X	✓					
		" RADFORD	Son	W	M	Sep 1877	22	S				KY	TN	TN				FARMING			✓	✓	✓		R	F	221	
		" OLIVER	Son	W	M	Mar 1879	20	S				KY	TN	TN				FARMING			✓	✓	✓		R	F	222	
		" ELSHA	Son	W	M	May 1882	18	S				KY	TN	TN				AT SCHOOL	8		✓	✓	✓					
		GRACE, ONA	GR-DAU	W	F	— —	—	S				TN	TN	KY														
		" ELLA	GR-DAU	W	F	— —	—	S				TN	TN	KY														
230	241	HALL, LEONARD	HEAD	W	M	Jan 1869	31	M	6			TN	TN	TN				MACHINIST			✓	✓	✓		O	F F	223	
		" SUSAN	WIFE	W	F	Oct 1875	24	M	6	2	1	KY	TN	TN							✓	✓	✓					
		" CHARLES	SON	W	M	Nov 1899	7/12	S				KY	TN	TN														

STATE - KENTUCKY   EAST   Supervisor's Dist. No. _102_ Sheet No.
COUNTY - MONROE   TOMPKINSVILLE   Enumerator E. R. BAXTER   Enumeration Dist. No. _84_
Township or other division

Location (No. of Family / No. of Dwelling)	NAME	Relation	Color	Sex	DATE OF BIRTH Mon/Yr	Age at last birthday	Marital Status	Years married	Mother of how many children?	# of these children living	Place of birth [this person]	Father of this person	Mother of this person	Year of immigr.	# years in U.S.	Naturalization	OCCUPATION 10 years +	Months not employed	Attended school in months	Can read	Can write	Speak English	Owned or Rent	Owned-no mortgage	Farm or house	# of farm schedule	
(24)	GRACE, BENTON	Nephew	W	M	— —	12	S				TN	TN	KY														
"	OVY	Neice	W	F	— —	8	S				TN	TN	KY														
231 242	PLUMLEE, BARLOW	HEAD	W	M	JAN 1862	38	M	10			TN	TN	TN				MILL HAND			✓	✓	✓	R		H		
"	AQUILLA	WIFE	W	F	MAR 1872	28	M	10	4	4	TN	TN	TN							✓	✓						
"	HERMAN J.	SON	W	M	JUL 1891	8	S				TX	TN	TN														
"	GEORGE H.	SON	W	M	NOV 1893	6	S				TN	TN	TN														
"	HERBERT	SON	W	M	MAR 1896	4	S				KY	TN	TN														
"	HUGH H.	SON	W	M	OCT 1898	2	S				KY	TN	TN														
232 243	COMER, ELIZA J.	HEAD	W	F	APR 1848	52	Wd		6	5	TN	IND	KY				FARM WORK			✓	✓		R		F	124	?
	SHOCKLEY, WILLIS	SON	W	M	OCT 1876	23	S				KY	KY	TN				FARMING			✓	✓						
	COMER, FRANKLIN	SON	W	M	AUG 1887	12	S				KY	KY	TN				AT SCHOOL		8	✓	✓						
233 244	RUSH, JAMES T.	HEAD	W	M	MAR 1854	46	M	10			KY	KY	KY				MERCHANT			✓	✓		O		F F	226	?
"	EUNICE	WIFE	W	F	JUL 1867	32	M	10	2	2	KY	KY	TN							✓	✓						
"	REED F.	SON	W	M	AUG 1890	9	S				KY	KY	KY														
"	RAYMOND E.	SON	W	M	JUL 1891	8	S				KY	KY	KY							✓	✓						
	CRAIGHEAD, DESTIE	HIRED GIRL	W	F	JUN 1881	19	S				TN	TN	TN				SERVANT			✓	✓						
	HIX, VIRGIL	CLERK	W	M	JUL 1879	21	S				KY	KY	KY				CLERK - DRY GOODS			✓	✓						
	DUKE, SAM M.	Boarder	W	M	JAN 1871	28	S				KY	TN	TN				MILL PROPRIETER			✓	✓						
234 245	RUSH, RUTH	HEAD	W	F	OCT 1829	71	Wd		7	3	KY	TN	TN					12		✓	✓		O		F F	227	
	CABLE, SYNTHA A.	SISTER	W	F	JAN 1850	50	Wd				KY	TN	TN							X	X	✓					
	MOORE, MYRTLE	Gt-Dau	W	F	OCT 1886	14	S				KY	KY	KY				AT SCHOOL		5	✓	✓						
"	ARTHUR	Gt-Son	W	M	MAR 1888	12	S				KY	KY	KY				FARM HAND			✓	✓						
235 246	RITTER, JAMES T.	HEAD	W	M	FEB 1861	39	Wd				TN	TN	TN				FARMING	6		✓	✓		O		F F	228	
"	WILLIAM	SON	W	M	MAY 1884	16	S				TN	TN	KY				FARM LABOR										
"	CHARLIE	SON	W	M	APR 1886	14	S				TN	TN	KY				AT SCHOOL		5	✓	✓						
"	LEON	DAU	W	F	JAN 1888	12	S				TN	TN	KY				AT SCHOOL		5	✓	✓						

STATE - KENTUCKY
COUNTY - MONROE
Township or other division — EAST TOMPKINSVILLE — -306-

Enumerator E. R. BAXTER

Supervisor's Dist. No. _102_, Sheet No.
Enumeration Dist. No. _84_

No. of Family	No. of Dwelling	NAME	Relation	Color	Sex	DATE OF BIRTH Mon/Yr	Age at last birthday	Marital Status	# Years married	Mother of how many children?	# of these children living	Place of birth (this person)	Father of this person	Mother of this person	Year of immigr.	# years in U.S.	Naturalization	OCCUPATION 10 years +	Months not employed	Attended school in months	Can read	Can write	Speak English	Owned or Rent	Owned -no mortgage	Farm or house	# of farm schedule	
		RITTER, NATHAN	Son	W	M	Dec 1890	10	S				TN	TN	KY														
		" EVILENA	Dau	W	F	Mar 1893	7	S				KY	TN	KY														
		BRANDON, REBECCA	Mother in law	W	F	Jan 1834	66	Wd		8	7	KY	KY	KY				HOUSEWORK			X	X	✓				
236	247	WOOD, JAMES	Head	W	M	Jul 1869	30	M	9			TN	TN	TN				MERCHANT			✓	✓		R	F	229	
		" MARY A.	Wife	W	F	Nov 1870	29	M	9	4	4	TN	TN	TN							✓	✓	✓				
		" EFFIE	Dau	W	F	May 1892	8	S				KY	TN	TN													
		" THOMAS	Son	W	M	Oct 1894	6	S				KY	TN	TN													
		" CLAUD	Son	W	M	Aug 1895	4	S				KY	TN	TN													
		" EDGAR	Son	W	M	Feb 1898	2	S				KY	TN	TN													
237	248	PAGE, WILLIAM H.	Head	W	M	Jul 1851	48	M	28			KY	KY	KY				FARMING			✓	✓		O	F	F	231	?
		" LULAR ?	(Dau)	W	F	Oct 1879	19	S	28	10	8	KY	KY	KY	PROB. LEFT OUT WIFE'S NAME						✓	✓	✓				
		" ANSEL V.	Son	W	M	Dec 1881	18	S				KY	KY	KY				AT SCHOOL		5	✓	✓	✓				
		" HENRY J.	Dau	W	F	Oct 1884	15	S				KY	KY	KY				AT SCHOOL		5	✓	✓	✓				
		" BRUTIS C.	Son	W	M	May 1887	13	S				KY	KY	KY				AT SCHOOL		5	✓	✓	✓				
		" CLIDE	Son	W	M	Nov 1890	9	S				KY	KY	KY				AT SCHOOL		5	✓	✓	✓				
		" PEARL	Dau	W	F	Apr 1892	8	S				KY	KY	KY													
		" BUFORD	Son	W	M	Dec 1894	5	S				KY	KY	KY													
238	249	CHERRY, BROCK	Head	W	M	May 1867	33	M	7			TN	TN	TN				FARMING			✓	✓		O	F	F	232	
		" RUTHA E	Wife	W	F	May 1889?	21	M	7	3	3	KY	TN	TN							✓	✓	✓				
		" ZONA	Dau	W	F	Mar 1884?	6	S				KY	TN	KY													
		" OSCAR	Son	W	M	Jan 1886?	4	S				KY	TN	KY													
		" VIRGIL	Son	W	M	May 1898	2	S				KY	TN	KY													
239	250	RICH, JAMES	Head	W	M	Sep 1847	52	M	34			TN	TN	TN				FARMING			✓	✓		O	F	F	233	
		" MARY A.	Wife	W	F	Dec 1851	48	M	34	8	5	TN	TN	TN							✓	✓	✓				
		" SARAH E.	Hired	W	F	Dec 1881	18	S				TN	TN	TN				SERVANT			✓	✓	✓				
240	251	RICH, ROBERT J.	Head	W	M	Jan 1874	26	M	4			TN	TN	TN				FARMING			✓	✓	✓	R	F	234	

STATE - KENTUCKY
COUNTY - MONROE — EAST
Township or other division — TOMPKINSVILLE   Enumerator E. R. BAXTER

Supervisor's Dist. No. 102 Sheet No.
Enumeration Dist. No. 84

No. of Family	No. of Dwelling	NAME	Relation	Color	Sex	DATE OF BIRTH Mon/Yr	Age at last birthday	Marital Status	# Years married	Mother of how many children?	# of these children living	Place of birth [this person]	Father of this person	Mother of this person	Year of immigr.	# years in U.S.	Naturalization	OCCUPATION 10 years +	Months not employed	Attended school in months	Can read	Can write	Speak English	Owned or Rent	Owned -no mortgage	Farm or house	# of farm schedule
		RICH, SARAH A.	WIFE	W	F	MAR 1881	19	M	4	2	2	KY	–	–							✓	✓	✓				
		" GRACIE	DAU	W	F	MAY 1897	3	S				KY	TN	KY													
		" LOGAN P.	SON	W	M	AUG 1899	10/12	S				KY	TN	TN													
241	252	RICH, ELISHA	HEAD	W	M	JAN 1874	26	M	2			TN	TN	TN				FARMING			✓	✓	✓	O	F	F	235
		" DOSIA	WIFE	W	F	MAR 1880	20	M	2	1	1	KY	TN	TN							✓	✓	✓				
		" JAMES	SON	W	M	MAY 1899	1	S				KY	TN	KY													
242	253	WOOD, JESSIE	HEAD	W	M	JAN 1871	29	M	7			TN	TN	TN				FARMING			✓	✓	✓	O	F	F	236
		" MATTIE D.	WIFE	W	F	DEC 1877	22	M	7	4	4	TN	TN	TN							✓	✓	✓				
		" YATEMAN	SON	W	M	SEP 1894	5	S				KY	TN	TN													
		" HATTIE	DAU	W	F	MAR 1896	4	S				KY	TN	TN													
		" CHARLES	SON	W	M	AUG 1898	1	S				KY	TN	TN													
		" SARAH	DAU	W	F	APR 1900	1/12	S				KY	TN	TN													
		MOORE, EZRIE	HAND	W	M	SEP 1881	18	S				TN	KY	TN				FARM HAND			✓	✓	✓				
243	254	GRINESTAFF, THOMAS S.	HEAD	W	M	DEC 1865	44	M	10			KY	TN	TN				FARMING			✓	✓	✓	O	F	F	237
		" VESSIE	WIFE	W	F	APR 1874	25	M	10	4	3	KY	KY	KY							✓	✓	✓				
		" ONA	DAU	W	F	APR 1892	8	S				KY	KY	KY													
		" OTIS H.	SON	W	M	MAR 1896	4	S				KY	KY	KY													
		" CORA	DAU	W	F	OCT 1898	1	S				KY	KY	KY													
		" ROSCO D	BRO	W	M	NOV 1870	29	S				KY	TN	TN				FARMING			✓	✓	✓	R		F	238
		" WILLIAM K	BRO	W	M	NOV 1857	42	S				KY	TN	TN				FARMING			✓	✓	✓	R		F	239
244	255	CASTEEL, WILLIAM	HEAD	W	M	AUG 1868	31	M	1			TN	TN	TN				FARMING			X	X	✓	R		F	240
		" SETTIE	WIFE	W	F	AUG 1878	21	M	1	1	1	KY	KY	KY							✓	✓					
		" OCEA E.	DAU	W	F	SEP 1890	9	S				KY	TN	KY													
		" HARRISON	SON	W	M	NOV 1893	6	S				KY	TN	KY													
		" OSCAR	SON	W	M	JAN 1900	5/12	S				KY	TN	KY													
		MAXEY, FRAZIER	HAND	W	M	SEP 1882	17	S				KY	KY	KY				FARM HAND			✓	✓	✓				

STATE - KENTUCKY
COUNTY - MONROE — EAST TOMPKINSVILLE
Township or other division — Enumerator E. R. BAXTER

Supervisor's Dist. No. 102 Sheet No.
Enumeration Dist. No. 84

No. of Family	No. of Dwelling	NAME	Relation	Color	Sex	Date of Birth Mon/Yr	Age at last birthday	Marital Status	# Years married	Mother of how many children?	# of these children living	Place of birth (this person)	Father of this person	Mother of this person	Citizenship	Occupation 10 years +	Months not employed	Attended school in months	Can read	Can write	Speak English	Owned or Rent / Owned-no mortgage / Farm or house / # of farm schedule
245	256	HIX, ISAAC	HEAD	W	M	Jan 1823	76	Wd				TN	TN	TN		FARMING			✓	✓		O F F 241
		MARY E	DAU	W	F	Nov 1844	45	S		2	2	TN	TN	TN					✓	✓	✓	O F F 242
		HUGH V.	GR·SON	W	M	Jun 1885	14	S				KY	TN	TN		AT SCHOOL	8		✓	✓	✓	
		HERBERT	GR·SON	W	M	Jul 1888	11	S				KY	TN	TN		AT SCHOOL	8		✓	✓	✓	
246	257	PENNINGTON, JOSEPH	HEAD	W	M	Mar 1852	48	M	10			KY	KY	KY		FARMING			✓	✓	✓	R F 243
		MELVINA	WIFE	W	F	May 1865	35	M	10	2	2	KY	TN	KY					✓	✓	✓	
		WALTER	SON	W	M	Jan 1892	8	S				TN	KY	KY								
		LUTHER	SON	W	M	Aug 1893	6	S				TN	KY	KY								
247	258	DAVIS, DANIEL	HEAD	W	M	Jun 1854	46	M	14			TN	TN	TN		FARMING			X	X	✓	O F F 244
		CHARLIE L.	SON	W	M	Jul 1887	12	S				KY	TN	KY	MR. BAXTER'S MISTAKE	AT SCHOOL		6	X	X	✓	
		WILLIAM R.	SON	W	M	Feb 1889	11	S				KY	TN	KY					X	X	✓	
		NANCY E.	DAU	W	F	Nov 1890	9	S				KY	TN	KY								
		ALTA J.	DAU	W	F	OCT 1891	8	S				KY	TN	KY								
		HENRY C.	SON	W	M	Mar 1893	7	S				KY	TN	KY								
		MABEL	DAU	W	F	—	6	S				KY	TN	KY								
		HOBERT B.	SON	W	M	—	5	S				KY	TN	KY								
		LOSIA	DAU	W	F	APR 1900	—	S				KY	TN	KY								
		VIRGINIA E.	WIFE	W	F	Feb 1856	44	M	14	8	8	KY	KY	KY								
248	259	ODLE, ALBERT	HEAD	W	M	Jan 1875	25	M				KY	TN	TN		FARMING			X	X	✓	R F 245
		MOURNING (?)	WIFE	W	F	Feb 1870	30	M		0	0	TN	TN	TN					X	X	✓	
		CAPSHAW, GEORGE	SON	W	M	APR 1890	10	S				KY	—	TN								
		WINFORD	SON	W	M	Jun 1892	8	S				KY	—	TN								
		AMBROSE	SON	W	M	Jul 1894	5	S				KY	—	TN								
249	260	WOOD, JOHN	HEAD	W	M	Feb 1858	42	Wd				KY	KY	KY		FARMING			✓	✓	✓	O F F 246
		SINTHA A.	DAU	W	F	Feb 1882	18	S				KY	KY	KY					✓	✓	✓	
		LESTER F.	SON	W	M	MAR 1889	11	S				KY	KY	TN					X	X	✓	

STATE - KENTUCKY
COUNTY - MONROE
Township or other division — EAST TOMPKINSVILLE
Enumerator — E. R. BAXTER

Supervisor's Dist. No. _102_ Sheet No.
Enumeration Dist. No. _84_

No. of Family	No. of Dwelling	NAME	Relation	Color	Sex	DATE OF BIRTH Mon/Yr	Age at last birthday	Marital Status	# Years married	Mother of how many children?	# of these children living	Place of birth [this person]	Father of this person	Mother of this person	Year of immigr.	# years in U.S.	Naturalization	OCCUPATION 10 years +	Months not employed	Attended school in month	Can read	Can write	Speak English	Owned or Rent	Owned –no mortgage	Farm or house	# of farm schedule
		WOOD, WILLIS	NEICE	W	F	Sep 1883	16	S				KY	KY	TN				HOUSEWORK		X	X	✓					
250	261	CAPSHAW, JESSIE	HEAD	W	M	APR 1873	27	M	7			TN	TN	TN				FARMING			✓	✓	✓	O	F	F	247
		" MOSIE (?)	WIFE	W	F	Sep 1876	23	M	7	3	3	TN	TN	TN							✓	✓					
		" HURSHUL	SON	W	M	DEC 1893	6	S				KY	TN	TN													
		" TEXIE	DAU	W	F	Jul 1896	3	S				KY	TN	TN													
		" LECTIE	DAU	W	F	Sep 1898	1	S				KY	TN	TN													
251	262	CARTER, LOUIS	HEAD	W	M	MAR 1872	28	M	8			TN	TN	KY				FARMING			✓	✓	✓	R		F	248
		" ZILPHA A.	WIFE	W	F	Nov 1873	26	M	8	4	4	TN	TN	KY							✓	✓	✓				
		" ORA P.	DAU	W	F	May 1893	7	S				KY	TN	KY													
		" HERMAN M.	SON	W	M	Feb 1895	5	S				TN	TN	KY													
		" OZA M.	DAU	W	F	DEC 1896	3	S				TN	TN	KY													
		" MAINARD	SON	W	M	DEC 1898	1	S				TN	TN	KY													
252	263	CHERRY, JOHN	HEAD	W	M	Sep 1887	22	M				TN	TN	TN				FARMING			✓	✓	✓	R		F	249
		" MACK	WIFE	W	F	APR 1888	22	M				KY	TN	TN									✓				
253	264	COMPTON, MACAGER	HEAD	W	M	Jul 1863	36	M	14			TN	TN	TN				FARMING			✓	✓	✓	O	F	F	250
		" ANNIE B.	WIFE	W	F	APR 1869	31	M	14	6	6	TN	TN	TN							✓	✓	✓				
		" OVY M.	DAU	W	F	Feb 1887	13	S				TN	TN	TN				AT SCHOOL		5	✓	✓	✓				
		" (?)AGY L	SON	W	M	DEC 1888	11	S				TN	TN	TN				AT SCHOOL		5	✓	✓	✓				
		" MARY I.	DAU	W	F	APR 1891	9	S				TN	TN	TN													
		" MAUDIE H.	DAU	W	F	MAR 1893	7	S				TN	TN	TN													
		" HERBY	SON	W	M	Nov 1896	3	S				TN	TN	TN													
		" LENA	DAU	W	F	OCT 1898	1	S				TN	TN	TN													
254	265	JACKSON, HAMPTON	Head	W	M	Jun 1874	25	M				KY	TN	TN				FARMING			✓	✓	✓	R		F	251
		" SARAH	Wife	W	F	Sep 1880	19	M				KY	KY	KY													
255	266	HALE, WILLIAM	HEAD	W	M	Nov 1868	31	M	13			KY	MO	MO				FARMING			✓	✓	✓	O	F	F	252
		" MARGRET	WIFE	W	F	May 1870	30	M	13	6	5	KY	TN	TN							✓	✓	✓				

STATE - KENTUCKY
COUNTY - MONROE
Township or other division

EAST TOMPKINSVILLE — 310 —

Enumerator E. R. BAXTER

Supervisor's Dist. No. 102 Sheet No.
Enumeration Dist. No. 84

Location No. of Family	No. of Dwelling	NAME	Relation	Color	Sex	DATE OF BIRTH Mon/Yr	Age at last birthday	Marital Status	# Years married	Mother of how many children?	# of these children living	NATIVITY Place of birth [this person]	Father of this person	Mother of this person	CITIZENSHIP Year of immigr.	# years in U.S.	Naturalization	OCCUPATION 10 years +	Months not employed	EDUCATION Attended school in months	Can read	Can write	Speak English	OWNERSHIP Owned or Rent	Owned -no mortgage	Farm or house	# of farm schedule
		HALE, MARY S.	DAU	W	F	MAY 1891	9	S				KY	KY	KY													
		" ARTHUR O.	SON	W	M	DEC 1893	6	S				KY	KY	KY													
		" OLIVER W.	SON	W	M	MAR 1895	5	S				KY	KY	KY													
		" ELIZA T.	DAU	W	F	MAY 1897	3	S				KY	KY	KY													
		" WILLIAM L.	SON	W	M	APR 1900	2/12	S				KY	KY	KY													
266	267	JACKSON, JESSIE	HEAD	W	M	Feb 1833	67	M	48			TN	TN	TN				FARMING		X	X	✓		O		F	253
		" NANCY J.	WIFE	W	F	Jan 1837	63	M	48	12	10	TN	TN	TN													
257	268	CROWBOX, JOW(?)	HEAD	W	M	MAR 1863	37	M	16			TN	TN	TN				MILL HAND		✓	✓	✓		R		H	
		" MELVINA	WIFE	W	F	MAR 1866	34	M	16	7	7	TN	TN	TN						X	X	✓					
		" WILLIAM	SON	W	M	JAN 1885	15	S				TN	TN	TN				DAY LABORER		X	X	✓					
		" TABITHA	DAU	W	F	AUG 1886	13	S				KY	TN	TN						X	X	✓					
		" SCOTT F.	SON	W	M	DEC 1888	11	S				KY	TN	TN													
		" SARAH B.	DAU	W	F	MAR 1892	8	S				KY	TN	TN													
		" HURSHUL	SON	W	M	MAY 1894	6	S				KY	TN	TN													
		" MARTHA J.	DAU	W	F	Feb 1897	3	S				KY	TN	TN													
		" HARLAN R.	SON	W	M	MAR 1899	1	S				KY	TN	TN													
258	269	HUNTER, ROBERT J.	Head	W	M	APR 1837	63	M	38			TN	SC	TN				FARMING		✓	✓	✓		O		FF	254
		" MATILDA	Wife	W	F	JAN 1842	58	M	38	5	4	TN	KY	TN						X	X	✓					
		CURTIS, LEAR A.	DAU	W	F	Feb 1866	34	Wd		4	4	TN	TN	TN				HOUSEWORK		✓	✓	✓					
		" HURSHUL	GR-SON	W	M	Jun 1884	16	S				KY	KY	TN				FARM HAND	5	✓	✓	✓					
		" NONA B.	GR-DAU	W	F	JAN 1887	13	S				TN	KY	TN				AT SCHOOL		✓	✓	✓					
		" HATTIE C.	GR-DAU	W	F	Feb 1890	10	S				TN	KY	TN				AT SCHOOL		X	X	✓					
		" SIDNEY	GR-SON	W	M	Feb 1893	7	S				KY	KY	TN													
259	270	COLTER, TOLBERT	HEAD	W	M	APR 1869	30	M	3			KY	—	—				FARMING		✓	✓	✓		O		FF	255
		" ROSY	WIFE	W	F	MAR 1874	26	M	3	1	1	KY	TN	TN						✓	✓	✓					
		" HASCAL	SON	W	M	OCT 1898	1	S				KY	KY	KY													

TWELFTH CENSUS OF THE UNITED STATES 1900

STATE - KENTUCKY
COUNTY - MONROE
Township or other division — EAST TOMPKINSVILLE Enumerator E. R. BAXTER

Supervisor's Dist. No. 102 Sheet No.
Enumeration Dist. No. 84

No. of Family	No. of Dwelling	NAME	Relation	Color	Sex	DATE OF BIRTH Mon/Yr	Age at last birthday	Marital Status	# Years married	Mother of how many children?	# of these children living	Place of birth [this person]	Father of this person	Mother of this person	Year of immigr.	# years in U.S.	Naturalization	OCCUPATION 10 years +	Months not employed	Attended school in months	Can read	Can write	Speak English	Owned or Rent	Owned -no mortgage	Farm or house	# of farm schedule
260	271	COX, WILLIAM	HEAD	W	M	MAR 1858	42	M	24			TN	TN	TN				FARMING		X	X	✓		O		F	256
		" FRANCIS	WIFE	W	F	JAN 1860	40	M	24	11	9	TN	TN	TN							X	✓	✓				
		" ADELINE	DAU	W	F	FEB 1877	23	S				TN	TN	TN							✓	✓	✓				
		" WILLIE	DAU	W	F	Sep 1882	17	S				TN	TN	TN							✓	✓	✓				
		" HARLAN H.	SON	W	M	OCT 1884	15	S				TN	TN	TN				FARM HAND			✓	✓	✓				
		" BURFERD	SON	W	M	APR 1886	14	S				TN	TN	TN				FARM HAND			✓	✓	✓				
		" LESLIE	SON	W	M	DEC 1888	11	S				TN	TN	TN				FARM HAND			✓	✓	✓				
		" WALTER	SON	W	M	DEC 1892	7	S				KY	TN	TN													
		" DILLION	SON	W	M	Feb 1895	5	S				KY	TN	TN													
		" BESSIE	DAU	W	F	AUG 1897	2	S				KY	TN	TN													
261	272	SMITH, POCORORS F.	Head	W	M	MAR 1872	28	M	7			TN	TN	KY				FARMING			✓	✓	✓	R		F	257
		" CLORA B	WIFE	W	F	AUG 1871	28	M	7	6	5	KY	TN	KY							✓	✓	✓				
		" OTTIS	DAU	W	F	DEC 1894	5	S				TN	TN	KY													
		" OLIA	DAU	W	F	MAR 1896	4	S				TN	TN	KY													
		" PEARLY	DAU	W	F	NOV 1897	2	S				KY	TN	KY													
		" EDDIE	SON	W	M	Sep 1899	9/12	S				KY	TN	KY													
		" EULLIE	DAU	W	F	Sep 1899	9/12	S				KY	TN	KY													
262	273	RHOTEN, JARRETT	HEAD	W	M	MAR 1868	31	M	9			KY	TN	TN				FARMING			✓	✓	✓	R		F	258
		" FANY	WIFE	W	F	Feb 1872	28	M	9	4	4	KY	-	-							✓	✓	✓				
		" IDA M	DAU	W	F	Nov 1892	7	S				KY	KY	KY													
		" JASPER	SON	W	M	OCT 1894	5	S				KY	KY	KY													
		" HERMAN	SON	W	M	AUG 1896	3	S				KY	KY	KY													
		" ALVEN	SON	W	M	Feb 1899	1	S				KY	KY	KY													
263	274	POLAND, JACOB	Head	W	M	MAR 1850	50	M	27			KY	NC	TN				FARMING			✓	✓	✓	O		F	259
		" MARGARET	Wife	W	F	APR 1857	43	M	27	10	9	KY	TN	KY							✓	X	✓				
		" SARAH E	Dau	W	F	MAR 1877	23	S				KY	TN	KY							✓	✓	✓				

TWELFTH CENSUS OF THE UNITED STATES 1900

STATE - KENTUCKY
COUNTY - MONROE
Township or other division: **EAST TOMPKINSVILLE** Enumerator **E. R. BAXTER**

Supervisor's Dist. No. **102** Sheet No.
Enumeration Dist. No. **84**

No. of Family	No. of Dwelling	NAME	Relation	Color	Sex	Date of Birth Mon/Yr	Age at last birthday	Marital Status	# Years married	Mother of how many children?	# of these children living	Place of birth (this person)	Father of this person	Mother of this person	Occupation 10 years +	Months not employed	Attended school in months	Can read	Can write	Speak English	Owned or Rent	Owned–no mortgage	Farm or house	# of farm schedule
		POLAND, SILAS	Son	W	M	Jun 1881	19	S				KY	TN	KY				✓	✓	✓				
		" GEORGE O.	Son	W	M	Aug 1883	16	S				KY	TN	KY										
		" MARY M.	Dau	W	F	Apr 1885	15	S				KY	TN	KY										
		" EVIE M.	Dau	W	F	Apr 1887	13	S				KY	TN	KY										
		" OSCAR	Son	W	M	Sep 1891	8	S				KY	TN	KY										
		" VIRGIL	Son	W	M	Mar 1894	6	S				KY	TN	KY										
264	275	FORD, ALEXANDER	Head	W	M	Sep 1857	42	M	17			KY	VA	KY	FARMING			✓	✓		O	FF	260	
		" BETTY	Wife	W	F	Aug 1866	33	M	17	9	9	KY	TN	KY				✓	✓					
		" BENJAMIN	Son	W	M	Sep 1884	15	S				KY	KY	KY	FARM HAND			✓						
		" KISSIAH	Dau	W	F	Jan 1886	14	S				KY	KY	KY	AT SCHOOL		5	✓	✓					
		" LIZZIE	Dau	W	F	Feb 1888	12	S				KY	KY	KY	AT SCHOOL		5	✓	✓	✓				
		" THOMAS	Son	W	M	May 1889	11	S				KY	KY	KY	AT SCHOOL		5	✓	✓	✓				
		" ANDREW J.	Son	W	M	May 1890	10	S				KY	KY	KY										
		" SUSAN B.	Dau	W	F	Jun 1892	8	S				KY	KY	KY										
		" MILLER	Son	W	M	Jan 1894	6	S				KY	KY	KY										
		" HANNA E.	Dau	W	F	May 1896	4	S				KY	KY	KY										
		" JAMES E.	Son	W	M	Mar 1898	2	S				KY	KY	KY										
265	276	NETHERTON, JOHN	Head	W	M	Jul 1853	46	M	21			TN	TN	TN	FARMING			X	X	✓	O	FF	261	
		" MARTHA E.	Wife	W	F	Oct 1852	47	M	21	8	8	TN	TN	KY										
		" AVERY B.	Son	W	M	Oct 1879	20	S				KY	TN	TN	FARMING									
		" ELBERT P.	Son	W	M	Feb 1881	19	S				KY	TN	TN	FARMING			✓	✓	✓				
		" OTHO J.	Son	W	M	May 1885	15	S				KY	TN	TN	AT SCHOOL		5	✓	✓	✓				
		" GURZILLA O.	Dau	W	M	Jun 1886	13	S				KY	TN	TN	AT SCHOOL		5	✓	✓	✓				
		" BLUTHUR	Son	W	M	Feb 1889	11	S				KY	TN	TN	AT SCHOOL		5	✓	✓	✓				
		" OCEA E.	Dau	W	F	Nov 1890	9	S				KY	TN	TN										
		" MILLARD	Dau	W	F	Mar 1894	6	S				KY	TN	TN										

STATE - KENTUCKY
COUNTY - MONROE
Township or other division

EAST TOMPKINSVILLE Enumerator E.R. BAXTER

Supervisor's Dist. No. 102 Sheet No.
Enumeration Dist. No. 84

No. of Family	No. of Dwelling	NAME	Relation	Color	Sex	DATE OF BIRTH Mon/Yr	Age at last birthday	Marital Status	# Years married	Mother of how many children?	# of these children living	Place of birth (this person)	Father of this person	Mother of this person	Year of immigr.	# years in U.S.	Naturalization	OCCUPATION 10 years +	Months not employed	Attended school in months	Can read	Can write	Speak English	Owned or Rent	Owned —no mortage	Farm or house	# of farm schedule
		NETHERTON, ESTUS	Son	W	M	May 1898	2	S				KY	TN	TN													
266	277	MOORE, ABRAHAM	Head	W	M	Nov 1837	62	M	45			TN	TN	TN				FARMING			✓	✓	✓	O	F	F	262
		" ELIZZIEBETH	Wife	W	F	Feb 1836	64	M	45	1	1	KY	TN	KY							X	X	✓				
		" RODDY	Son	W	M	Mar 1874	26	S				KY	TN	KY				FARMING			✓	✓	✓				
267	278	JOBE, GEORGE	Head	W	M	Jul 1867	32	M	5			KY	TN	TN				FARMING	4		X	X	✓	O	F	F	263
		" NANNIE	Wife	W	F	Aug 1863	36	M	5	6	6	KY	TN	TN							✓	✓	✓				
		" SARAH B.	Dau	W	F	Aug 1888	11	S				KY	KY	KY				AT SCHOOL		5	✓	K	✓				
		" LEVADA F.	Dau	W	F	Oct 1889	10	S				KY	KY	KY				AT SCHOOL		5							
		" VIOLA M.	Dau	W	F	Feb 1896	4	S				KY	KY	KY													
		" WILLIE F.	Dau	W	F	Feb 1898	2	S				KY	KY	KY													
		" JAMES E.	Son	W	M	May 1900	½2	S				KY	KY	KY													
268	279	FORD, SAMUEL	Head	W	M	Feb 1847	53	M	25			TN	TN	TN				FARMING			✓	✓	✓	O	F	F	264
		" ELZINA	Wife	W	F	Feb 1840	40	M	25	10	7	KY	—	—							X	X	✓				
		" ABBIE G.	Dau	W	F	Jun 1880	19	S				KY	TN	KY				AT SCHOOL		5	✓	✓	✓				
		" LILLIE E.	Dau	W	F	Feb 1883	17	S				KY	TN	KY				AT SCHOOL		5	✓	✓	✓				
		" CORA B.	Dau	W	F	Apr 1885	15	S				KY	TN	KY				AT SCHOOL		5	✓	✓	✓				
		" CHARLIE	Son	W	M	Oct 1887	12	S				KY	TN	KY				AT SCHOOL		5	✓	✓	✓				
		" WILLIAM D.	Son	W	M	Apr 1890	10	S				KY	TN	KY				AT SCHOOL		5	✓	✓	✓				
		" DALLA	Dau	W	F	Apr 1898	2	S				KY	TN	KY													
		SHEFFIELD, BETSY	Mother in law	W	F	Jun 1831	69	Wd		7	5	KY	TN	KY							X	X	✓				
269	280	JOBE, ARNOW	Head	W	M	Jan 1825	75	M	66			TN	TN	TN				FARMING			X	X	✓	O	F	F	265
		" RHODA	Wife	W	F	Oct 1829	70	M	66	11	8	TN	TN	TN							X	X	✓				
		" MARY E.	Dau	W	F	Sep 1851	48	S				KY	TN	TN							X	X	X				
270	281	FORD, HENRY C.	Head	W	M	Mar 1861	39	M	14			KY	TN	TN							✓	✓	✓	O	F	F	266
		" SARA A.	Wife	W	F	Jan 1870	30	M	14	6	6	KY	TN	TN							✓	✓	✓				
		" ARTHUR C.	Son	W	M	Apr 1888	12	S				KY	KY	KY				AT SCHOOL		5	✓	✓	✓				

STATE - KENTUCKY
COUNTY - MONROE
Township or other division   EAST TOMPKINSVILLE   Enumerator E. R. BAXTER

— 314 —

Supervisor's Dist. No. _102_ Sheet No.
Enumeration Dist. No. _84_

No. of Family	No. of Dwelling	NAME	Relation	Color	Sex	DATE OF BIRTH Mon/Yr	Age at last birthday	Marital Status	# Years married	Mother of how many children?	# of these children living	Place of birth	Father of this person	Mother of this person	Year of immigr.	# years in U.S.	Naturalization	OCCUPATION 10 years +	Months not employed	Attended school in months	Can read	Can write	Speak English	Owned or Rent	Owned –no mortage	Farm or house	# of farm schedule
		FORD, EVIE M.	DAU	W	F	Nov 1889	10	S				KY	KY	KY				AT SCHOOL		5	✓	✓					
		" LOU V.	DAU	W	F	Sep 1891	8	S				KY	KY	KY													
		" LEVESTA	DAU	W	F	Aug 1893	6	S				KY	KY	KY													
		" RUBA E.	DAU	W	F	Jun 1896	4	S				KY	KY	KY													
		" ISAAC	SON	W	M	Jan 1898	2	S				KY	KY	KY													
271	282	JOBE, JOHN H.	Head	W	M	May 1868	32	M	12			KY	TN	TN				FARMING HAND			X	X	✓	R		H	
		" SUSIE	WIFE	W	F	Jan 1873	27	M	12	5	5	KY	KY	KY							✓	✓					
		" VIRGINIA B	DAU	W	F	Jun 1889	11	S				KY	KY	KY				AT SCHOOL		5	✓	✓	✓				
		" ROXIE V	DAU	W	F	Jun 1891	9	S				KY	KY	KY													
		" SAMUEL A.	SON	W	M	Feb 1894	6	S				KY	KY	KY													
		" JESSIE	SON	W	M	Feb 1896	4	S				KY	KY	KY													
		" WILLIAM G.	SON	W	M	Feb 1898	2	S				KY	KY	KY													
272	283	THOMPSON, TAS T.	Head	W	M	Nov 1870	29	M	5			KY	KY	KY				FARMING			✓	✓		R	F		267
		" LAURA B.	WIFE	W	F	Jul 1880	19	M	5	2	2	KY	KY	KY							✓	✓					
		" EFFIE G.	DAU	W	F	Oct 1897	2	S				KY	KY	KY													
		" MAUD B.	DAU	W	F	Jul 1899	11/12	S				KY	KY	KY													
273	284	THOMPSON, ELIJAH R.	Head	W	M	Aug 1846	53	M	30			KY	KY	KY				FARMING			✓	✓		O	F	F	268
		" ROZANNA	WIFE	W	F	Oct 1853	46	M	30	11	10	KY	KY	KY							✓	✓					
		" WILLEY	SON	W	M	May 1872	28	S				KY	KY	KY				FARMING HAND			✓	✓					
		" SAMUEL J.	SON	W	M	Apr 1882	18	S				KY	KY	KY				AT SCHOOL		5	✓	✓					
		" LILLIE B.	DAU	W	F	Jul 1887	13	S				KY	KY	KY				AT SCHOOL		5	✓	✓	✓				
		" CHARLES R.	SON	W	M	Jan 1890	10	S				KY	KY	KY				AT SCHOOL		5	✓	✓					
		" EDWIN D.	SON	W	M	Nov 1891	8	S				KY	KY	KY													
		" SANFORD	SON	W	M	Jun 1897	2	S				KY	KY	KY													
274	285	HAMMER, BOSE	Head	W	M	Jul 1861	38	M	16			KY	KY	KY				FARMING			✓	✓		O	F	F	269
		" ELZINA	WIFE	W	F	May 1878	32	M	16	7	7	KY	KY	KY							✓	✓					

STATE - KENTUCKY
COUNTY - MONROE
Township or other division — EAST TOMPKINSVILLE — Enumerator F. R. BAXTER

Supervisor's Dist. No. 102 Sheet No.
Enumeration Dist. No. 84

No. of Family	No. of Dwelling	NAME	Relation	Color	Sex	DATE OF BIRTH Mon/Yr	Age at last birthday	Marital Status	# Years married	Mother of how many children?	# of these children living	Place of birth [this person]	Father of this person	Mother of this person	Year of immigr.	# years in U.S.	Naturalization	OCCUPATION 10 years +	Months not employed	Attended school in months	Can read	Can write	Speak English	Owned or Rent	Owned –no mortgage	Farm or house	# of farm schedule
		HAMMER, MARY C.	DAU	W	F	Jun 1886	14	S				KY	KY	KY				AT SCHOOL		5	✓	✓					
		" HAYDEN	SON	W	M	Dec 1888	11	S				KY	KY	KY				AT SCHOOL		5	✓	✓					
		" MUSE – (?)	DAU	W	F	Feb 1891	9	S				KY	KY	KY													
		" TURNER	SON	W	M	Apr 1893	7	S				KY	KY	KY													
		" HATTIE	DAU	W	F	Jun 1894	5	S				KY	KY	KY													
		" J. W.	SON	W	M	Aug 1897	2	S				KY	KY	KY													
		" GRANGER	SON	W	M	Dec 1899	6/12	S				KY	KY	KY													
275	286	FORD, MARY E.	HEAD	W	F	Mar 1827	73	Wd		9	7	TN	TN	TN				FARM		X	X	✓		O	F	F	270
		" MARY E.	DAU	W	F	Sep 1849	51	S				TN	TN	TN							✓	✓					
		" SARAH M.	DAU	W	F	—	—	S				KY	TN	TN							✓	✓					
		" JOHN W.	GR-SON	W	M	Jan 1875	25	S				KY	TN	TN				FARMING			✓	✓		R	F	F	271
276	287	FORD, PRICE B.	HEAD	W	M	Dec 1866	33	M	10			KY	TN	TN				FARMING			✓	✓		O	F	F	272
		" LAURA B.	WIFE	W	F	Jan 1865	35	M	10	3	3	KY	TN	TN							✓	✓					
		" OAKLEY H.	SON	W	M	Aug 1895	5	S				KY	KY	KY													
		" WEALTHY G.	DAU	W	F	Oct 1896	3	S				KY	KY	KY													
		" HATTIE E.	DAU	W	F	Jan 1899	1	S				KY	KY	KY													
27	28	FORD, WILLIAM	HEAD	W	M	Oct 1849	50	M	28			TN	TN	TN				FARMING		X	X	✓		O	F	F	273
		" SUSAN	WIFE	W	F	Jun 1853	46	M	28	11	8	TN	TN	TN						X	X	✓					
		" LONZO	SON	W	M	Feb 1873	27	S				KY	TN	TN				FARMING			✓	✓					
		" SYLVANIS	SON	W	M	Feb 1879	21	S				KY	TN	TN							✓	✓					
		" OLLIE	DAU	W	F	Feb 1881	19	S				KY	TN	TN							✓	✓					
		" PEARLY	DAU	W	F	Jul 1887	12	S				KY	TN	TN				AT SCHOOL		5	✓	✓					
		" LISBY M.	SON	W	M	Jun 1891	9	S				KY	TN	TN													
		" LAURA E.	DAU	W	F	Jun 1894	6	S				KY	TN	TN													
276	289	HENSON, MARY	HEAD	W	F	—	—	Wd		1	1	KY	TN	TN				FARMING			✓	✓		O	F	F	274
		" JOE	SON	W	M	Jan 1889	11	S				KY	TN	KY				FARM HAND		X	X	✓					

STATE - KENTUCKY
COUNTY - MONROE
Township or other division: EAST TOMPKINSVILLE
Enumerator: E. R. BAXTER
Supervisor's Dist. No. 102   Sheet No.
Enumeration Dist. No. 84

No. of Family / No. of Dwelling	NAME	Relation	Color	Sex	DATE OF BIRTH Mon/Yr	Age at last birthday	Marital Status	# Years married	Mother of how many children?	# of these children living	Place of birth (this person)	Father of this person	Mother of this person	Year of immigr.	# years in U.S.	Naturalization	OCCUPATION 10 years +	Months not employed	Attended school in months	Can read	Can write	Speak English	Owned or Rent	Owned - no mortgage	Farm or house	# of farm schedule
(289)	MULKEY, BETSY	Boarder	W	F	Feb 1852	48	Wd		1	1	KY	KY	KY							X	X	✓				
279 290	HAMMER, MARTIN	Head	W	M	Feb 1824	76	M	46			KY	PA	NC				FARMING	4		X	X	✓	O	F	F	275
"	NANCY	Wife	W	F	Feb 1834	66	M	46	9	8	TN	TN	TN							X	X	✓				
"	BUD R.	Son	W	M	Jun 1866	34	S				KY	KY	TN				FARMING	4		✓	✓	✓	R		F	276
"	JAMES	Son	W	M	Jan 1875	25	S				KY	KY	TN				FARMING	4		✓	✓	✓	R		F	277
"	WILLIAM	Son	W	M	Apr 1878	22	S				KY	KY	TN				FARMING	4		✓	✓	✓	R		F	278
280 291	HAMMER, PETER	Head	W	M	Nov 1860	40	M	16			KY	KY	TN				FARMING			✓	✓	✓	O	F	F	279
"	DEBORA	Wife	W	F	Feb 1867	33	M	16	6	6	KY	TN	KY							X	✓	✓				
"	WILLIAM M.	Son	W	M	Jan 1885	15	S				KY	KY	KY				FARM HAND	4	5	✓	✓	✓				
"	MARY L.	Dau	W	F	Oct 1887	12	S				KY	KY	KY				AT SCHOOL		5	✓	✓	✓				
"	ELLEN N.	Dau	W	F	May 1891	9	S				KY	KY	KY													
"	RICHARD T.	Son	W	M	Nov 1892	7	S				KY	KY	KY													
"	SARAH M.	Dau	W	F	May 1896	4	S				KY	KY	KY													
"	JAMES E.	Son	W	M	May 1900 3/12		S				KY	KY	KY													
281 292	FORD, BENJAMIN	Head	W	M	Mar 1852	48	M	13			TN	TN	TN				FARMING			X	✓		O	F	F	280
"	TILDA A.	Wife	W	F	Aug 1856	43	M	13	11	10	KY	TN	TN							X	X	✓				
"	REBECCA M.	Dau	W	F	Jun 1880	19	S				KY	TN	KY				HOUSEWORK	4		X	X	✓				
"	ADA B.	Dau	W	F	May 1882	18	S				KY	TN	KY				HOUSEWORK	4		X	X	✓				
"	BERTHA	Dau	W	F	Apr 1884	16	S				KY	TN	KY							X	X	✓				
"	MARY E.	Dau	W	F	Apr 1886	14	S				KY	TN	KY							X	X	✓				
"	LULA F.	Dau	W	F	Jan 1889	11	S				KY	TN	KY							X	X					
"	VIRGIL	Son	W	M	Oct 1892	7	S				KY	TN	KY													
"	JESSIE J.	Son	W	M	Apr 1895	5	S				KY	TN	KY													
"	WALTER G.	Son	W	M	Jul 1897	2	S				KY	TN	KY													
"	BENJAMIN	Son	W	M	Mar 1900 3/12		S				KY	TN	KY													
282 293	FORD, RICHARD	Head	W	M	Dec 1856	43	M	10			KY	TN	TN				FARMING	4		X	X	✓	O	F	F	281

TWELFTH CENSUS OF THE UNITED STATES 1900

STATE - KENTUCKY
COUNTY - MONROE — EAST TOMPKINSVILLE
Township or other division — Enumerator E. R. BAXTER

Supervisor's Dist. No. 102   Sheet No.
Enumeration Dist. No. 84

No. of Family	No. of Dwelling	NAME	Relation	Color	Sex	DATE OF BIRTH Mon/Yr	Age at last birthday	Marital Status	# Years married	Mother of how many children?	# of these children living	Place of birth [this person]	Father of this person	Mother of this person	Year of immigr.	# years in U.S.	Naturalization	OCCUPATION 10 years +	Months not employed	Attended school in months	Can read	Can write	Speak English	Owned or Rent	Owned - no mortage	Farm or house	# of Farm schedule
		FORD, SARAH	WIFE	W	F	MAR 1867	33		10	7	5	KY	KY	TN							✓	✓	✓				
		" HOMER	SON	W	M	JUN 1887	12	S				KY	KY	KY				AT SCHOOL		5	✓	✓	✓				
		" GEORGE W	SON	W	M	OCT 1892	7	S				KY	KY	KY													
		" ROXIE	DAU	W	F	AUG 1896	3	S				KY	KY	KY													
		" MYRTIE	DAU	W	F	Sep 1898	1	S				KY	KY	KY													
283	294	ROUSE, ISAAC	Head	W	M	AUG 1836	63	M	1			TN	—	—				FARMING			✓	✓	✓	O	F F		282
		" LINDY J.	wife	W	F	— —	—	M	1	1	0	TN	TN	TN							X	X	✓				
		COMPTON, MATILDA	GR DAU	W	F	DEC 1889	20	S				KY	KY	TN							✓	✓	✓				
284	295	FORD, MARY	HEAD	W	F	JAN 1824	76	Wd		0	0	TN	TN	TN				DAY LABORER			X	X	✓	O		H	
285	296	MOORE, JOEL	HEAD	W	M	JUN 1864	36	M	15			TN	TN	TN							✓	✓	✓	O	F F		283
		" NELLIE J.	WIFE	W	F	JUN 1864	35	M	15	7	6	KY	KY	KY							✓	✓	✓				
		" EVERT	SON	W	M	JUN 1886	14	S				KY	TN	KY				AT SCHOOL		5	✓	✓	✓				
		" ARIZONA	DAU	W	F	NOV 1888	11	S				KY	TN	KY				AT SCHOOL		5	✓	✓	✓				
		" OFELIE	DAU	W	F	JUL 1891	8	S				KY	TN	KY													
		" GEORGE W.	SON	W	M	Feb 1895	5	S				KY	TN	KY													
		" LOCIA	DAU	W	F	Sep 1896	3	S				KY	TN	KY													
		" ERASTUS	SON	W	M	May 1899	1	S				KY	TN	KY													
286	297	WHITE, MARGARET	Head	W	F	Feb 1844	56	Wd		4	3	KY	TN	TN							X	X	✓	O	F F		284
		SLAUGHTER, JOHNIE	NIECE	W	F	JAN 1878	22	S				KY	KY	KY													
		WHITE, JAMES T	SON	W	M	Sep 1870	30	M	10			KY	KY	KY				FARMING 4			✓	✓	✓	O	F F		284
		" ARIE	DAU-IN-LAW	W	F	Dec 1872	27	M	10	2	2	KY	KY	KY							✓	✓	✓				
		" ALICE	GR-DAU	W	F	DEC 1892	8	S				KY	KY	KY													
		" ETHEL	GR-DAU	W	F	JUL 1894	5	S				KY	KY	KY													
		SLAUGHTER, WILLIAM	Father	W	M	JAN 1812	88	Wd				KY	KY	KY				FARMING			X	X	✓	R	F F		285
287	298	CASTEEL, WILLIAM	HEAD	W	M	JAN 1632	68	M	49			TN	TN	TN				FARMING			X	X	✓	R	F F		285
		" ELIZIEBETH	WIFE	W	F	APR 1834	66	M	49	12	8	TN	TN	TN							X	X	✓				

STATE - KENTUCKY
COUNTY - MONROE
Township or other division — EAST TOMPKINSVILLE
Enumerator E. R. BAXTER

Supervisor's Dist. No. 102 Sheet No.
Enumeration Dist. No. 84

No. of Family	No. of Dwelling	NAME	Relation	Color	Sex	DATE OF BIRTH Mon/Yr	Age at last birthday	Marital Status	# Years married	Mother of how many children?	# of these children living	Place of birth (this person)	Father of this person	Mother of this person	Year of immigr.	# years in U.S.	Naturalization	OCCUPATION 10 years +	Months not employed	Attended school in months	Can read	Can write	Speak English	Owned or Rent	Owned -no mortgage	Farm or house	# of farm schedule
		CASTEEL, NANCY	DAU	W	F	DEC 1860	39	S				TN	TN	TN							X	X	✓				
		" JOSEPH T.	SON	W	M	Jul 1876	23	S				TN	TN	TN				FARM HAND			X	X	✓				
288	289	SPEAR, LON S.	HEAD	W	F	DEC 1859	40	Wd		8	6	TN	TN	TN				DAY LABORER			X	X	✓	O		F	286
		" BELL (T.or F.)?	DAU	W	F	OCT 1884	16	S				KY	TN	TN				AT SCHOOL		4	✓	✓					
		" JOHN	SON	W	M	Nov 1886	13	S				KY	TN	TN				AT SCHOOL		4	✓	✓					
		" FRANK	SON	W	M	Nov 1889	10	S				KY	TN	TN													
		" WILLIE S.	DAU	W	F	JAN 1892	8	S				KY	TN	TN													
		" BIRTHA A.	DAU	W	F	Feb 1894	6	S				KY	TN	TN													
289	300	HUNTER, WILLIAM	Head	W	M	OCT 1869	30	M	9			TN	TN	TN				FARMING			✓	✓	✓	R		F	287
		" ELLEN G.	Wife	W	F	APR 1875	25	M	9			KY	KY	TN							✓	✓	✓				
		" MATTIE B.	Dau	W	F	Sep 1892	7	S				KY	TN	KY													
		" JOSIE M.	Dau	W	F	JAN 1894	6	S				KY	TN	KY													
		" CLURA H.	Son	W	M	Jul 1896	3	S				KY	TN	KY													
		" CARRY	DAU	W	F	Sep 1899 10/17		S				KY	TN	KY													
		THOMAS, WILLIAM	HAND	W	M	Jun 1876	23	S				KY	KY	KY				FARM HAND			✓	✓	✓				
290	301	OWENS, JAMES W.	Head	W	M	AUG 1863	36	M	7			TN	TN	TN				FARMING			✓	✓	✓	O	F	F	288
		" EMY	WIFE	W	F	Sep 1873	26	M	7	3	3	TN	TN	TN							✓	✓	✓				
		" JAMES B.	SON	W	M	DEC 1894	5	S				KY	TN	TN													
		" WILLIAM M.	SON	W	M	Jun 1895	3	S				KY	TN	TN													
		" CLARANCE A.	SON	W	M	Jul 1899 11/17		S				KY	TN	TN													
291	302	WOOD, GEORGE W.	Head	W	M	MAY 1848	52	M	19			TN	TN	KY				FARMING			✓	✓		O	F	F	289
		" ABBIE G.	WIFE	W	F	Jul 1859	41	M	19	11	7	TN	TN	TN							✓	✓					
		" ISAAC D.	SON	W	M	Nov 1883	16	S				KY	TN	TN				AT SCHOOL		5	✓	✓					
		" JAMES L.	SON	W	M	Sep 1885	14	S				KY	TN	TN				AT SCHOOL		5	✓	✓					
		" ELIS B.	SON	W	M	JAN 1887	12	S				KY	TN	TN				AT SCHOOL		5	X	X	✓				
		" NEVADA	DAU	W	F	DEC 1890	9	S				KY	TN	TN													

STATE - KENTUCKY
COUNTY - MONROE
Township or other division: EAST TOMPKINSVILLE
Enumerator: E. R. BAXTER

Supervisor's Dist. No. 102 Sheet No.
Enumeration Dist. No. 84

No. of Family	No. of Dwelling	NAME	Relation	Color	Sex	Date of Birth Mon/Yr	Age at last birthday	Marital Status	# Years married	Mother of how many children?	# of these children living	Place of birth (this person)	Father of this person	Mother of this person	Occupation 10 years+	Attended school in months	Can read	Can write	Speak English	Owned or Rent	Owned -no mortgage	Farm or house	# of farm schedule
		WOOD, OLIVER C.	Son	W	M	Aug 1892	7	S				KY	TN	TN									
		" MELISSIA E.	Dau	W	F	Jan 1896	4	S				KY	TN	TN									
242	303	WOOD, MARTHA J.	Head	W	F	May 1845	55	Wd		13	9	TN	TN	TN	INVALID		✓	✓	✓	O	F	F	290
		" CLEVELAND	Son	W	M	Jul 1885	14	S				KY	TN	TN	FARMING		✓	✓	✓				
		" HARLAN	Son	W	M	Apr 1888	12	S				KY	TN	TN	FARMING		✓	✓	✓				
		STEVENS, EFFIE	Hand	W	F	Sep 1881	18	S				TN	TN	TN	HOUSEWORK		✓	✓	✓				
243	304	BIRDWELL, JOSEPH	Head	W	M	Apr 1877	23	S				TN	TN	TN	FARMING		✓	✓	✓	O	F	F	291
		SMITH, STONE	Partner	W	M	Sep 1879	20	S				TN	TN	KY	FARMING		✓	✓	✓				
244	305	THOMPSON, WALTER	Head	W	M	Aug 1877	22	M	2			KY	TN	KY	FARMING		✓	✓	✓	R		F	292
		" MAY B.	Wife	W	F	May 1880	20	M	2	3	2	TN	TN	TN			✓	✓	✓				
		" VILET	Dau	W	F	Mar 1898	2	S				TN	KY	TN									
		" DAISY	Dau	W	F	Mar 1898	2	S				TN	KY	TN									
245	306	FRAZIER, ALFORD	Head	W	M	Jan 1857	43	M	13			—	—	—	FARMING		✓	✓	✓	O	F	F	293
		" LOUIZA	Wife	W	F	Oct 1868	31	M	13	1	1	TN	TN	TN									
		" SARAH E.	Dau	W	F	Feb 1884	16	S				KY	—	—									
246	307	CHERRY, MARY	Head	W	F	Jan 1820	80	Wd		2	2	KY	TN	TN			X	X	✓			H	
247	308	JACKSON, EMILY	Head	W	F	Jan 1840	60	Wd		7	5	KY	KY	KY			✓	✓	✓	O	F	F	294
		" JOHN I.	Son	W	M	Mar 1866	34	S				KY	KY	KY	FARM HAND		✓	✓	✓				
		" MAGGIE	Dau	W	F	Aug 1874	26	S				KY	KY	KY			✓	✓	✓				
		" BIRDIE E.	Dau	W	F	May 1878	22	S				KY	KY	KY			✓	✓	✓				
248	309	CORNWELL, BENTON	Head	W	M	Aug 1880	20	M	3			TN	TN	TN	FARMING		✓	✓	✓	O	F	F	295
		" CATHARINE	Wife	W	M	Feb 1878	22	M	3	1	1	TN	TN	TN			✓	✓	✓				
		" ALTER	Dau	W	F	Apr 1898	2	S				KY	TN	TN									
249	310	CROFFORD, BENTON	Head	W	M	Jan 1875	25	M	4			TN	TN	TN	FARMING		✓	✓	✓	R		F	296
		" IDA	Wife	W	F	Jan 1875	25	M	4	2	1	KY	TN	TN			✓	✓	✓				
		" HERMAN	Son	W	M	Mar 1899	1	S				TN	TN	KY									

STATE - KENTUCKY
COUNTY - MONROE
Township or other division EAST TOMPKINSVILLE

Enumerator E. R. BAXTER

Supervisor's Dist. No. 102 Sheet No.
Enumeration Dist. No. 84

Location (No. of Family / No. of Dwelling)	NAME	Relation	Color	Sex	DATE OF BIRTH Mon/Yr	Age at last birthday	Marital Status	# Years married	Mother of how many children?	# of these children living	NATIVITY (Place of birth this person / Father of this person / Mother of this person)	CITIZENSHIP (Year of immigr. / # years in U.S. / Naturalization)	OCCUPATION 10 years +	Months not employed	Attended school in months	Can read	Can write	Speak English	OWNERSHIP (Owned or Rent / Owned -no mortage / Farm or house / # of farm schedule)
300 311	GENTRY, ROBERT	HEAD	W	M	— — —		M	6			KY TN TN		FARMING			X	X	✓	R F 297
	" NANCY J.	WIFE	W	F	Jan 1876	24	M	6	3	3	KY TN TN					X	X	✓	
	" SARAH E.	Dau	W	F	Nov 1895	4	S				KY KY KY								
	" WILLIAM H.	Son	W	M	Oct 1897	2	S				KY KY KY								
	" ROBERT B.	Son	W	M	Oct 1899	8/12	S				KY KY KY								
301 312	McNEICE, RUFAS	HEAD	W	M	Feb 1878	22	M	3			— — —		DAY LABORER	4		X	X	✓	R H
	" MARY C.	WIFE	W	F	Sep 1877	21	M	3	1	1	KY — —					X	X	✓	
	" WILLIAM T.	SON	W	M	May 1898	2	S				KY — KY								
	GENTRY, GINNIE	HIRED	W	F	Jan 1886	14	S				KY TN TN		HOUSEWORK			X	X	✓	
302 313	RHOTEN, CLOVIS	HEAD	W	M	Dec 1879	20	M				KY TN TN		FARMER	4		✓	✓	✓	R F 298
	" MARY R.	WIFE	W	F	Nov 1877	22	M				TN TN TN					X	X	✓	
303 314	RHOTEN, WILLEY	Head	W	M	Oct 1854	45	M	23			KY TN TN		FARMING	4		✓	✓	✓	O F F 299
	" CATARINE	Wife	W	F	Sep 1854	45	M	23	11	9	KY TN KY					✓	✓	✓	
	" EVIE S.	Dau	W	F	Sep 1876	23	S				KY KY KY					✓	✓		
	" MARY A.	Dau	W	F	Apr 1882	18	S				KY KY KY					✓	✓		
	" SYNTJATHA	Dau	W	F	Jul 1885	14	S				KY KY KY		AT SCHOOL		5	✓	✓	✓	
	" NANCY G.	Dau	W	F	Oct 1887	12	S				KY KY KY		AT SCHOOL		5	✓	✓	✓	
	" ELISHA J.	Son	W	M	Jan 1890	10	S				KY KY KY		AT SCHOOL		5	✓	✓	✓	
	" AUTHER	Son	W	M	Feb 1893	7	S				KY KY KY								
	" GILLIE B.	Dau	W	F	Jan 1896	4	S				KY KY KY								
304 315	WHEAT, JAMES	HEAD	W	M	— — —		M	10			KY KY KY		FARMING			X	X	✓	R F 300
	" LUCINDA	WIFE	W	F	May 1868	32	M	10	4	4	KY TN TN					X	X	✓	
	" LINDA M.	Dau	W	F	Jun 1889	11	S				KY KY KY		AT SCHOOL		4	✓	✓		
	" GUSTIE E.	Dau	W	F	Feb 1891	9	S				KY KY KY								
	" LEANDER R.	Son	W	M	Mar 1895	5	S				KY KY KY								
	" NETTIE F.	Dau	W	F	Oct 1898	1	S				KY KY KY								

STATE - KENTUCKY
COUNTY - MONROE
Township or other division: EAST TOMPKINSVILLE
Enumerator: E. R. BAXTER
Supervisor's Dist. No. 102
Sheet No.
Enumeration Dist. No. 84

No. of Family	No. of Dwelling	Name	Relation	Color	Sex	Date of Birth Mon/Yr	Age	Marital Status	# Years married	Mother of how many children	# of these children living	Birthplace (this person)	Father	Mother	Citizenship	Occupation	Months not employed	Attended school (months)	Can read	Can write	Speak English	Owned or Rent	Owned-no mortage	Farm or house	# of farm schedule
		WHEAT, ELIZIBETH	Mother-in-law	W	F	Jun 1844	56	Wd		6	5	TN	TN	TN			12		X	X	✓				
305	316	WOOD, JOHN SEN	Head	W	M	Jan 1841	59	Divc.				TN	TN	TN		Farming			✓	✓	✓	O	F	F	301
		" SARAH A.	Dau	W	F	Jan 1880	20	S				TN	TN	TN					✓	✓	✓				
		GILLENWATERS, LINZY	Son-law	W	M	Feb 1874	26	M	2			KY	KY	KY		Farming			✓	✓		R		F	302
		" MARY J.	Dau	W	F	Dec 1874	25	M	2	1	1	TN	TN	TN					✓	✓					
		" LEMMUEL	Gr-son	W	M	Apr 1899	1	S				KY	KY	TN											
306	317	WOOD, DENNIS	Head	W	M	Jul 1874	23	M	2			KY	TN	TN		Farming			✓	✓	✓	O	F	F	303
		" NANCY I.	Wife	W	F	May 1881	19	M	2			KY	TN	KY					✓	✓	✓				
307	318	RICH, JOHN	Head	W	M	Jan 1853	47	M	18			KY	TN	TN		Farming			X	X	✓	O	F	F	304
		" MARY E.	Wife	W	F	Jan 1865	35	M	18	9	7	KY	KY	KY					✓	✓					
		" ZONA	Dau	W	F	May 1886	14	S				KY	KY	KY		At School		5	X	✓	✓				
		" LULA J.	Dau	W	F	Nov 1890	9	S				KY	KY	KY											
		" EZRA	Son	W	M	Dec 1892	7	S				KY	KY	KY											
		" ERNY	Dau	W	F	Mar 1895	5	S				KY	KY	KY											
		" SAMPSON	Son	W	M	Sep 1897	2	S				KY	KY	KY											
		" MYRTLE	Dau	W	F	Nov 1899	5/12	S				KY	KY	KY											
308	319	DAVIS, GEORGE W.	Head	W	M	Aug 1848	51	M				TN	NC	NC		Farming			✓	✓	✓	O	F	F	305
		CONDRA, HERBERT	Son-in-law	W	M	Feb 1880	20	M	2			KY	KY	KY		Farming			✓	✓	✓	R		F	306
		" FANNY	Dau	W	F	Sep 1883	16	M	2	1	1	KY	TN	KY					✓	✓	✓				
		" ATLA	Son	W	M	Jun 1899	1					KY	KY	KY											
309	320	DAVIS, LINZAR	Head	W	M	Jan 1850	50	M	36			TN	TN	TN		Farming			✓	✓		O	F	F	307
		" SUSAN	Wife	W	F	Jan 1850	50	M	36			TN	TN	TN					✓	✓	✓				
		" MARY L.	Dau	W	F	Sep 1866	33	S				KY	TN	TN					✓	✓	✓				
		WOOD, SALLIE	Dau	W	F	Mar 1871	29	Wd		4	3	KY	TN	TN					✓	✓					
		" ESCOE	Gr-son	W	M	Feb 1892	8	S				KY	KY	KY											
		" RAYMON	Gr-son	W	M	Dec 1893	6	S				ARK	KY	KY											

STATE - KENTUCKY
COUNTY - MONROE
Township or other division   EAST TOMPKINSVILLE   Enumerator E.R. BAXTER

Supervisor's Dist. No. 102 Sheet No. _____
Enumeration Dist. No. 84 _____

Location (No. of Family / No. of Dwelling)	NAME	Relation	Color	Sex	DATE OF BIRTH Mon/Yr	Age at last birthday	Marital Status	# Years married	Mother of how many children?	# of these children living	NATIVITY Place of birth (this person)	Father of this person	Mother of this person	CITIZENSHIP Year of immigr. / # years in U.S. / Naturalization	OCCUPATION 10 years +	Months not employed	Attended school in months	Can read	Can write	Speak English	OWNERSHIP Owned or Rent	Owned -no mortage	Farm or house	# of farm schedule
	DAVIS, EULA V.	GR-DAU	W	F	Jan 1896	4	S				KY	KY	KY											
310 321	DAVIS, JOHN C.	HEAD	W	M	May 1866	34	M	10			KY	TN	KY		FARMING			✓	✓	✓	O	F	F	308
"	LIZA J.	WIFE	W	F	Jun 1867	30	M	10			KY	CA	KY					✓	✓	✓				
"	MARY H.	DAU	W	F	Nov 1889	10	S				KY	KY	KY		AT SCHOOL			✓	✓	✓				
"	JOHN H.	SON	W	M	Oct 1896	3	S				KY	KY	KY											
311 322	HALE, JOHN L.	HEAD	W	M	Aug 1877	22	M	5			KY	TN	KY		FARMING			✓	✓	✓	O	F	F	309
"	REBECCA E.	WIFE	W	F	Apr 1880	20	M	5	4	2	KY	TN	KY						✓	✓				
"	VERNA M.	DAU	W	F	Oct 1896	3	S				KY	KY	KY											
"	ANNIE M.	DAU	W	F	Sep 1899	9/12	S				KY	KY	KY											
312 323	EMMERT, DEWEY I.	Head	W	M	Sep 1874	25	M	2			KY	KY	KY		FARMING			✓	✓	✓	R		F	310
"	ELLA	WIFE	W	F	Dec 1873	26	M	2	1	1	KY	TN	KY						✓	✓				
"	MELVA	DAU	W	F	Mar 1899	1	S				KY	KY	KY											
313 324	DAVIS, HARRISON	HEAD	W	M	Feb 1864	36	M	15			KY	TN	KY		FARMING			✓	✓		O	F	F	311
"	MARY J.	WIFE	W	F	Apr 1868	32	M	15	5	5	KY	KY	KY					✓	✓	✓				
"	NORA J.	DAU	W	F	Jan 1887	13	S				KY	KY	KY		AT SCHOOL		5	✓	✓	✓				
"	SARAH A.	DAU	W	F	Feb 1889	11	S				KY	KY	KY		AT SCHOOL		5	X	X	✓				
"	LILLIE M.	DAU	W	F	Jun 1892	8	S				KY	KY	KY											
"	EFFIE E.	DAU	W	F	Jan 1894	6	S				KY	KY	KY											
"	LONA E.	DAU	W	F	Apr 1896	4	S				KY	KY	KY											
314 325	DAVIS, HENRY L.	HEAD	W	M	Mar 1829	71	M	48			TN	TN	SC		FARMING			✓	✓		O	M	F	312
"	NANCY E.	WIFE	W	F	Aug 1830	70	M	48	10	7	TN	TN	TN					X	X	✓				
"	SARAH A.	DAU	W	F	Mar 1858	42	S				TN	TN	TN		HOUSEWORK			✓	✓	✓				
315 326	HARLAN, ALEXANDER	Head	W	M	Aug 1828	71	M	50			KY	KY	VA		FARMING			✓	✓	✓	O	M	F	313
"	MARY A.	wife	W	F	Aug 1833	66	M	50	5	4	TN	TN	TN					✓	✓	✓				
"	SAMUEL	Son	W	M	Oct 1857	42	S				TN	KY	TN		FARMING			✓	✓	✓	O	M	F	313
	DENHAM, LETHE	HIRED	W	F	May 1885	15	S				KY	TN	TN		HOUSEWORK			✓	✓	✓				

TWELFTH CENSUS OF THE UNITED STATES 1900

STATE - KENTUCKY
COUNTY - MONROE
Township or other division — EAST TOMPKINSVILLE — Enumerator E. R. BAXTER

Supervisor's Dist. No. _102_ Sheet No. ___
Enumeration Dist. No. _84_ ___

No. of Family	No. of Dwelling	NAME	Relation	Color	Sex	DATE OF BIRTH Mon/Yr	Age at last birthday	Marital Status	# Years married	Mother of how many children?	# of these children living	Place of birth (this person)	Father of this person	Mother of this person	Year of immigr.	# years in U.S.	Naturalization	OCCUPATION 10 years +	Months not employed	Attended school in months	Can read	Can write	Speak English	Owned or Rent	Owned –no mortage	Farm or house	# of Farm schedule
316	321	BIGGERSTAFF, JOHN H.	HEAD	W	M	Jan 1860	40	M	8			KY	KY	KY				FARMING			✓	✓	✓	O		F	314
		" EFFIE	WIFE	W	F	Jan 1878	22	M	8	2	2	KY	KY	TN							✓	✓	✓				
		" LESTER	SON	W	M	Dec 1892	7	S				KY	KY	KY													
		" CLYD	DAU	W	F	Aug 1895	4	S				KY	KY	KY													
		LANDERS, JOHN	HIBER	W	M	Aug 1879	20	S				ARK	ARK	ARK				FARM HAND			✓	✓					
		PIRAM, ELIZA	AUNT	W	F	Aug 1832	67	Wd		4	1	TN	TN	TN							✓	✓	✓				
317	328	WOOD, JONATHAN	HEAD	W	M	Apr 1868	32	S				TN	TN	TN				FARMING			✓	✓	✓	O		F	315
		" MATILDA	MOTHER	W	F	May 1827	73	Wd		8	4	TN	TN	TN							✓	✓	✓				
318	329	WOOD, CLEMENTS	HEAD	W	M	Jul 1876	23	M				TN	TN	TN				FARMING			✓	✓		R		F	316
		" OLLIE	WIFE	W	F	Jan 1882	18	M				KY	TN	KY							✓	✓					
219	330	JACKSON, THOMAS	HEAD	W	M	Dec 1872	27	M	5			KY	TN	TN				FARMING			✓	✓	✓	R		F	317
		" MARY	WIFE	W	F	Oct 1875	24	M	5	2	2	KY	KY	KY							✓	✓	✓				
		" LOLA M.	DAU	W	F	May 1897	3	S				KY	KY	KY													
		" LOSIE J.	DAU	W	F	May 1900	3/12	S				KY	KY	KY													
320	331	LEE, WILLIAM	HEAD	W	M	Jan 1857	43	M	18			TN	TN	KY				FARMING			✓	✓	✓	R		F	318
		" JULIA A.	WIFE	W	F	Nov 1864	35	M	18	5	5	TN	TN	TN							✓	✓	✓				
		" AREA	DAU	W	F	Feb 1884	16	S				TN	TN	TN				AT SCHOOL		5	✓	✓	✓				
		" JOHN H.	SON	W	M	Feb 1886	14	S				TN	TN	TN				AT SCHOOL		5	✓	✓	✓				
		" ADA	DAU	W	F	Jun 1887	12	S				TN	TN	TN				AT SCHOOL		5	✓	✓					
		" CHARLES	SON	W	M	Jul 1890	9	S				TN	TN	TN													
		" AMOS	SON	W	M	Jul 1895	4	S				TN	TN	TN													
321	332	HIX, DANIEL B.	HEAD	W	M	Dec 1852	47	M	9			TN	TN	KY				FARMING			✓	✓	✓	R		F	319
		" EASTER J.	WIFE	W	F	Apr 1845	55	M	9			KY	KY	TN							✓	✓					
322	333	ROUSE, BELLE I.	HEAD	W	F	May 1857	43	Wd		7	7	TN	TN	TN				FARMING			✓	✓	✓	O		F	320
		" JAMES F.	SON	W	M	Oct 1878	21	S				KY	TN	TN				FARMING			✓	✓	✓				
		" WILLIAM	SON	W	M	Jul 1880	19	S				KY	TN	TN				FARM HAND			✓	✓	✓				

TWELFTH CENSUS OF THE UNITED STATES 1900

STATE - KENTUCKY
COUNTY - MONROE
Township or other division — EAST TOMPKINSVILLE — Enumerator E. R. BAXTER

— 324 —

Supervisor's Dist. No. 102 Sheet No.
Enumeration Dist. No. 84

No. of Family	No. of Dwelling	NAME	Relation	Color	Sex	DATE OF BIRTH Mon/Yr	Age at last birthday	Marital Status	# Years married	Mother of how many children?	# of these children living	Place of birth (this person)	Father of this person	Mother of this person	Year of immigr.	# years in U.S.	Naturalization	OCCUPATION 10 years +	Months not employed	Attended school in months	Can read	Can write	Speak English	Owned or Rent	Owned -no mortage	Farm or house	# of farm schedule
		ROUSE, WOLFORD	Son	W	M	Aug 1882	17	S				KY	TN	TN				FARM HAND		X	X	✓					
		" UJEAN (Eugene)?	Son	W	M	Feb 1886	14	S				KY	TN	TN				FARM HAND		X	X	✓					
		" MELINDA E.	Dau	W	F	Feb 1887	13	S				KY	TN	TN				AT SCHOOL		5	✓	✓					
		" LUTHER	Son	W	M	Apr 1892	8	S				KY	TN	TN													
		" HURSUL	Son	W	M	Dec 1896	3	S				KY	TN	TN													
323	334	BRYANT, JAMES B.	Head	W	M	Nov 1859	40	M	10			KY	TN	TN				FARMING			✓	✓		O	M	F	321
		" MARY A.	Wife	W	F	Sep 1871	28	M	10	3	3	KY	TN	TN							✓	✓					
		" BARLOW	Son	W	M	May 1893	7	S				KY	KY	KY													
		" OSCAR	Son	W	M	Jul 1895	4	S				KY	KY	KY													
		" MINNIE B.	Dau	W	F	May 1897	3	S				KY	KY	KY													
		" JAMES E.	Nephew	W	M	Aug 1884	15	S				KY	KY	KY				AT SCHOOL		5	✓	✓					
		" SARAH G.	Mother	W	F	Nov 1829	70	Wd		8	4	TN	NC	NC							✓	✓					
324	335	WHEAT, JAMES C.	Head	W	M	— —⊗	30	M				KY	KY	KY				DAY LABORER		X	X	✓		R		H	
		" JOSEPH	Son	W	M	Jan 1894	6	S				KY	KY	KY													
325	336	CONKIN, NANCY	Head	W	F	Aug 1848	52	Wd		8	8	ARK	TN	TN				FARMING			✓	✓		O	F	F	322
		" NANCY E.	Dau	W	F	Jun 1883	17	S				KY	TN	ARK				AT SCHOOL		5	✓	✓					
		" MINNIE	Dau	W	F	Jul 1884	15	S				KY	TN	ARK				AT SCHOOL		5	✓	✓					
326	337	CONDRA, LEVI	Head	W	M	Nov 1855	44	M	22			KY	SC	SC				FARMING			✓	✓		R		F	323
		" (3)CAI– D.	Wife	W	F	Nov 1857	42	M	22	8	5	KY	KY	TN							✓	✓					
		" RADFORD	Son	W	M	Apr 1886	14	S				KY	KY	KY				AT SCHOOL		5	✓	✓					
		" KATIE	Dau	W	F	Nov 1888	11	S				KY	KY	KY				AT SCHOOL		5	✓	✓					
		" LUTHUR	Son	W	M	Apr 1892	8	S				KY	KY	KY													
327	338	HANNER, MARY A.	Head	W	F	Aug 1828	72	Wd		9	9	KY	VA	PA							✓	✓		O		F	324
		HURT, BELLE	Dau	W	F	Jan 1850	50	Wd		1	1	KY	KY	KY				HOUSEWORK			✓	✓					
		" MARY A.	Dau	W	F	Feb 1888	12	S				KY	VA	KY				AT SCHOOL		5	✓	✓					
328	339	LESLIE, EMBERSON	Head	W	M	Apr 1827	73	M	3			KY	KY	KY				FARMING			✓	✓		O		F	325

STATE - KENTUCKY
COUNTY - MONROE
Township or other division — EAST TOMPKINSVILLE

Enumerator — E. R. BAXTER

Supervisor's Dist. No. 102 Sheet No.
Enumeration Dist. No. 84

No. of Family	No. of Dwelling	NAME	Relation	Color	Sex	DATE OF BIRTH Mon/Yr	Age at last birthday	Marital Status	# Years married	Mother of how many children?	# of these children living	Place of birth (this person)	Father of this person	Mother of this person	Year of immigr.	# years in U.S.	Naturalization	OCCUPATION 10 years +	Months not employed	Attended school in months	Can read	Can write	Speak English	Owned or Rent	Owned -no mortage	Farm or house	# of farm schedule
		LESLIE, ELLEN	WIFE	W	F	Jul 1867	32	M	3	3	3	KY	KY	KY							✓	✓					
		" GEORGE W.	SON	W	M	Sep 1892	7	S				KY	KY	KY													
329	340	McWHERTER, WILLIAM	HEAD	W	M	Sep 1872	27	M	12			KY	KY	KY				FARMING			✓	✓	✓	R		F	326
		" (?) NASSIA	WIFE	W	F	Jun 1867	32	M	12	4	4	KY	KY	KY								✓					
		" DONA B.	DAU	W	F	Nov 1889	10	S				KY	KY	KY				AT SCHOOL		4	✓	✓					
		" HARRISON	SON	W	M	Jul 1893	6	S				KY	KY	KY													
		" BERTHA	DAU	W	F	Nov 1895	4	S				KY	KY	KY													
		" WILLIAM	SON	W	M	Apr 1898	2	S				KY	KY	KY													
330	341	RODDY, WILLIAM B.	HEAD	W	M	Jul 1834	65	M	15			TN	TN	TN				COUNTY ATTORNEY AT LAW			✓	✓	✓	O	F	F	327
		" EUNICE	WIFE	W	F	Apr 1849	51	M	15	3	3	KY	KY	KY							✓	✓	✓				
		" HURSHAL	SON	W	M	May 1880	20	S				KY	TN	KY				FARM WORK			✓	✓	✓				
		" ADA	DAU	W	F	Oct 1882	17	S				KY	TN	KY				AT SCHOOL		5	✓	✓					
		" EDWARD C.	SON	W	M	Feb 1886	14	S				KY	TN	KY				FARM WORK			✓	✓					327
		" BENTON B.	SON	W	M	Mar 1887	13	S				KY	TN	KY				AT SCHOOL		5	✓	✓					
		" WILLIAM H.	SON	W	M	Sep 1888	11	S				KY	TN	KY				AT SCHOOL		5	✓	✓					
331	342	HAMMER, ELKANAH	HEAD	W	M	Oct 1870	29	M	5			KY	KY	KY				FARMING			✓	✓	✓	R		F	328
		" IDA	WIFE	W	F	Sep 1875	24	M	5	2	2	TN	TN	KY							✓	✓	✓				
		" WINNIE M.	DAU	W	F	Feb 1891	3	S				KY	KY	TN													
		" EDWIN T.	SON	W	M	Sep 1899	8/12	S				KY	KY	TN													
332	343	CHISM, NANCY	HEAD	W	M	Nov 1863	36	S		1	1	KY	KY	KY				FARMING			✓	✓	✓	O	F	F	329
		" CORA	DAU	W	F	Jan 1886	14	S				KY	KY	KY				AT SCHOOL		5	✓	✓	✓				
333	344	GEE, TOLBERT J.	HEAD	W	M	Aug 1854	55	M	19			KY	KY	KY				FARMING			✓	✓	✓	R		F	330
		" GEMIMA	WIFE	W	F	May 1858	42	M	19	3	3	KY	KY	KY							✓	✓	✓				
		" WILLIAM A.	SON	W	M	Jun 1881	18	S				KY	KY	KY				FARMING			✓	✓	✓				
		" DONNIE B.	DAU	W	F	Sep 1883	16	S				KY	KY	KY				FARM WORK			✓	✓	✓				
		" SACK H.	SON	W	M	Apr 1889	12	S				KY	KY	KY				AT SCHOOL			✓	✓	✓				

STATE - KENTUCKY
COUNTY - MONROE — EAST
Township or other division — TOMPKINSVILLE — Enumerator E. R. BAXTER

Supervisor's Dist. No. _102_ Sheet No. ___
Enumeration Dist. No. _84_ ___

No. of Family	No. of Dwelling	NAME	Relation	Color	Sex	DATE OF BIRTH Mon/Yr	Age at last birthday	Marital Status	# Years married	Mother of how many children?	# of these children living	Place of birth [this person]	Father of this person	Mother of this person	Year of immigr.	# years in U.S.	Naturalization	OCCUPATION 10 years +	Months not employed	Attended school in months	Can read	Can write	Speak English	Owned or Rent	Owned -no mortgage	Farm or house	# of farm schedule
334	345	MULKY, JOSEPH	HEAD	W	M	May 1874	26	M	1			KY	KY	KY				FARM HAND			✓	✓	✓	R		H	
		" MELIA	WIFE	W	F	Oct 1875	24	M	1			KY	TN	VA							✓	✓					
		JACKSON, EMERET	BOARDER	W	M	May 1847	53	Wd				KY	TN	TN							✓	✓		O	F	F	331
335	346	FRAZIER, REUBEN	HEAD	W	M	Aug 1843	56	M	33 (PARTED)			TN	TN	TN				FARMING	2		✓	✓		R		F	332
		RICHARDSON, VINA	HOUSEWORK	W	F	Jan 1861	39	S		2	2	TN	TN	TN				HOUSEWORK	3		X	X	✓				
		" BENTON	SON	W	M	Jan 1888	12	S				TN	TN	TN				FARM WORK			X	X	✓				
		" NELLIE B.	DAU	W	F	Jan 1891	9	S				TN	TN	TN													
336	347	WOOD, WILLIAM	HEAD	W	M	Dec 1866	33	M	14			TN	TN	TN				FARMING			✓	✓	✓	R		F	333
		" MARY E.	WIFE	W	F	Jan 1865	34	M	14	7	6	KY	KY	KY													
		" HILDA	DAU	W	F	Dec 1887	12	S				KY	TN	KY				AT SCHOOL		6	✓	✓					
		" MYRTLE	DAU	W	F	Feb 1890	10	S				KY	TN	KY													
		" ALTIA	DAU	W	F	Apr 1891	9	S				KY	TN	KY													
		" MARY J.	DAU	W	F	May 1896	4	S				KY	TN	KY													
		" HOMER	SON	W	M	Mar 1892	8	S				KY	TN	KY													
		" CHARLIE	SON	W	M	Jan 1894	6	S				KY	TN	KY													
		" PEARL	BROTHER	W	M	Nov 1881	18	S				KY	TN	KY				FARM HAND			✓	✓	✓	O	F	F	334
337	348	CHISM, DELBERT	HEAD	W	M	Jul 1847	52	M	27			KY	KY	KY				FARMING			✓	✓		O	F	F	335
		" NANCY E.	WIFE	W	F	Mar 1850	50	M	27	8	6	TN	TN	TN							✓	✓					
		" LOU E.	DAU	W	F	May 1880	20	S				KY	KY	TN							✓	✓					
		" MARCIA B.	DAU	W	F	May 1880	20	S				KY	KY	TN							✓	✓	✓				
		" HIRAM G.	SON	W	M	Aug 1881	18	S				KY	KY	TN				AT SCHOOL		4	✓	✓	✓				
		" WILLIAM R.	SON	W	M	Oct 1884	15	S				KY	KY	TN				AT SCHOOL		4	✓	✓					
		" ALICE F.	DAU	W	F	Oct 1885	14	S				KY	KY	TN				AT SCHOOL		4	✓	✓	✓				
338	349	CHISM, SAMUEL	HEAD	W	M	Apr 1856	44	M	22			KY	KY	KY				FARMING			✓	✓	✓	O	F	F	336
		" DIVINE	WIFE	W	F	Nov 1856	43	M	22	8	7	KY	KY	KY													
		" GEORGE V.	SON	W	M	Dec 1878	20	S				KY	KY	KY				FARM HAND			✓	✓	✓				

TWELFTH CENSUS OF THE UNITED STATES 1900

STATE - KENTUCKY
COUNTY - MONROE
Township or other division **EAST TOMPKINSVILLE** Enumerator **E. R. BAXTER**

-327-

Supervisor's Dist. No. _102_ Sheet No. _____
Enumeration Dist. No. _84_ _____

No. of Family	No. of Dwelling	NAME	Relation	Color	Sex	Date of Birth Mon/Yr	Age at last birthday	Marital Status	# Years married	Mother of how many children?	# of these children living	Place of birth (this person)	Father of this person	Mother of this person	Year of immigr.	# years in U.S.	Naturalization	Occupation 10 years +	Months not employed	Attended school in months	Can read	Can write	Speak English	Owned or Rent	Owned-no mortage	Farm or house	# of Farm schedule
		CHISM, MARTHA E.	DAU	W	F	MAY 1881	19	S				KY	KY	KY							✓	✓					
		" SARAH M.	DAU	W	F	AUG 1886	13	S				KY	KY	KY				AT SCHOOL		4	✓	✓					
		" HANNA	DAU	W	F	JUN 1889	10	S				KY	KY	KY				AT SCHOOL		4	✓	✓					
		" LOU V.	DAU	W	F	SEP 1892	7	S				KY	KY	KY													
		" EMILY A.	DAU	W	F	MAY 1895	5	S				KY	KY	KY													
		CLOYD, MELISSIA	SISTER	W	F	FEB 1846	54	S				KY	KY	KY							✓	✓		O	F	F	337
339	350	CURTIS, HENDERSON	HEAD	W	M	AUG 1849	50	M	26			KY	KY	KY				FARMING			X	X	✓	R		F	338
		" SUSAN	WIFE	W	F	JUL 1855	45	M	26	9	7	KY	KY	KY							X	X	✓				
		" JONES	SON	W	M	MAR 1876	23	S				KY	KY	KY				FARMING			✓	✓					
		" NICKLESS	SON	W	M	OCT 1882	17	S				KY	KY	KY				FARM HAND			✓	✓					
		" CATHERINE	DAU	W	F	NOV 1885	14	S				KY	KY	KY				HOUSEWORK			✓	✓					
		" HETTIE	DAU	W	F	JUL 1889	10	S				KY	KY	KY													
		" BENTON	SON	W	M	APR 1892	8	S				KY	KY	KY													
340	351	YOKELY, JOHN	HEAD	W	M	JUL 1852	47	M	14			KY	KY	VA				FARMING			X	X	✓	R		F	339
		" MARTHA	WIFE	W	F	JAN 1864	36	M	14	6	6	KY	TN	TN							X	X	✓				
		" MARY C.	DAU	W	F	SEP 1887	12	S				KY	KY	KY				AT SCHOOL		5	✓	✓	✓				
		" JOHN W.	SON	W	M	JAN 1890	10	S				KY	KY	KY													
		" JANIE	DAU	W	F	MAR 1892	8	S				KY	KY	KY													
		" SARAH	DAU	W	F	MAY 1894	6	S				KY	KY	KY													
		" CORA	DAU	W	F	FEB 1896	4	S				KY	KY	KY													
		" WILLIAM	SON	W	M	APR 1900	3/12	S				KY	KY	KY													
341	352	CONKIN, LOWRIE	HEAD	W	M	NOV 1866	33	M	9			KY	KY	ARK				FARMING			✓	✓		O		F	340
		" SARAH	WIFE	W	F	JAN 1858	42	M	9	2	2	KY	TN	TN							✓	✓	✓				
		" CLOE	DAU	W	F	JUN 1892	7	S				KY	KY	KY													
		" CLARANCE	SON	W	M	AUG 1896	3	S				KY	KY	KY													
		FRAILEY, LENA	COUSIN	W	F	FEB 1885	15	S				KY	KY	KY				HOUSEWORK			✓	✓	✓				

STATE - KENTUCKY
COUNTY - MONROE
Township or other division — EAST TOMPKINSVILLE — Enumerator E. R. BAXTER

Supervisor's Dist. No. _102_ Sheet No.
Enumeration Dist. No. _84_

No. Family	No. Dwelling	NAME	Relation	Color	Sex	Date of Birth Mon/Yr	Age	Marital Status	Yrs married	Mother of how many children	# living	Place of birth	Father	Mother	Occupation	Attended school	Can read	Can write	Speak English	Owned/Rent	Farm/house	# farm schedule
		PATTERSON, ELIZABETH J.	Mother-in-law	W	F	Jun 1826	73	Wd		4	2	KY	—	—								
342	269	PATTERSON, WILLIAM	HEAD	W	M	Jan 1827	73	M	10			TN	TN	TN	FARM LABOR		✓	✓		O	F	F 341
		" SUSAN M.	WIFE	W	F	Dec 1854	45	M	10	1	1	KY	KY	KY			✓	✓				
		" MARY A.	DAU	W	F	Mar 1892	8	S				KY	KY	KY								
343	354	WHITE, JORDAN	HEAD	W	M	Aug 1830	69	M	40			KY	VA	KY	FARMING		✓	✓		O	F	F 342
		" MARTHA L.	WIFE	W	F	Mar 1834	66	M	40	9	7	KY	KY	KY			✓	✓				
		" EFFIE	DAU	W	F	Jan 1873	27	S				KY	KY	KY			✓	✓				
		" SAMUEL	SON	W	M	Apr 1877	23	S				KY	KY	KY	MINISTER		✓	✓				
344	355	CONKIN, SHERMAN	HEAD	W	M	Oct 1871	28	M	2			KY	KY	KY	FARMING		✓	✓		O	F	F 343
		" VERDIE	WIFE	W	F	Dec 1877	22	M	2			TN	TN	TN			✓	✓				
		" DELMA	DAU	W	F	Mar 1898	2	S				KY	KY	TN								
		" GEMIMA	Mother	W	F	Jan 1842	58	Wd		1	1	KY	—	—								
345	356	COULTER, JEFFERSON	HEAD	W	M	Feb 1868	32	M	10			KY	KY	TN	FARMING		✓	✓		R		F 344
		" CORA	WIFE	W	F	Aug 1868	31	M	10	4	4	IND	IND	IND			✓	✓				
		" TANDY	SON	W	M	Feb 1892	8	S				KY	KY	IND								
		" PEARL	DAU	W	F	Jan 1894	6	S				KY	KY	IND								
		" ALICE	DAU	W	F	May 1895	4	S				KY	KY	IND								
		" HONOR	DAU	W	F	Nov 1898	1	S				KY	KY	IND								
		" CATHERINE	Mother	W	F	- 1638	62	Wd		8	7	KY	KY	KY								
346	357	PATTERSON, THOMAS	HEAD	W	M	May 1862	38	M	17			KY	TN	TN	FARMING		✓	✓		O	F	F 345
		" MISSOURI B.	WIFE	W	F	Nov 1864	35	M	17	7	6	KY	KY	KY			✓	✓				
		" EARNES	SON	W	M	Sep 1884	15	S				KY	KY	KY	AT SCHOOL 5		✓	✓				
		" JOHN W.	SON	W	M	Jan 1887	13	S				KY	KY	KY	AT SCHOOL 5		✓	✓				
		" OLLIE M.	DAU	W	F	Nov 1890	9	S				KY	KY	KY	AT SCHOOL 5		✓	✓				
		" LOU E.	DAU	W	F	Jul 1892	7	S				KY	KY	KY								
		" WILLIAM S.	SON	W	M	Mar 1895	5	S				KY	KY	KY								

STATE - KENTUCKY
COUNTY - MONROE
Township or other division: EAST TOMPKINSVILLE

- 329 -

Enumerator: E. R. BAXTER

Supervisor's Dist. No. 102 Sheet No.
Enumeration Dist. No. 84

No. of Family	No. of Dwelling	NAME	Relation	Color	Sex	DATE OF BIRTH Mon/Yr	Age at last birthday	Marital Status	# Years married	Mother of how many children?	# of these children living	Place of birth [this person]	Father of this person	Mother of this person	Year of immigr.	# years in U.S.	Naturalization	OCCUPATION 10 years +	Months not employed	Attended school in months	Can read	Can write	Speak English	Owned or Rent	Owned –no mortgage	Farm or house	# of farm schedule
		PATTERSON, MARY J.	DAU	W	F	DEC 1898	1	S				KY	KY	KY													
347	358	MULKY, WILLIAM	HEAD	W	M	AUG 1845	55	M				KY	KY	KY				FARMING		✓	✓	✓		R		F	346
		" SARAH E.	WIFE	W	F	OCT 1844	55	M		6	4	KY	BY	KY							✓	✓	✓				
348	359	COULTER, JAMES	HEAD	W	M	OCT 1857	42	M	12			KY	KY	KY				FARMING			✓	✓	✓		O		F	347
		" NANCY E.	WIFE	W	F	JAN 1864	36	M	12	5	5	KY	KY	KY							✓	✓	✓				
		" LIDDIE A.	DAU	W	F	MAY 1887	13	S				KY	KY	KY								✓					
		" JESSIE T.	SON	W	M	JAN 1891	8	S				KY	KY	KY													
		" BESSIE E.	DAU	W	F	MAY 1894	6	S				KY	KY	KY													
		" MARY C.	DAU	W	F	JAN 1897	3	S				KY	KY	KY													
		" JAMES A.	SON	W	M	AUG 1899	10/12	S				KY	KY	KY													
349	360	COMPTON, BEE(?)	HEAD	W	M	OCT 1854	45	M	24			KY	TN	TN				FARMING			X	X	✓		R		F	348
		" BELLE	WIFE	W	F	DEC 1854	45	M	24	13	11	TN	TN	TN							✓	✓	✓				
		" ISAAC R.	SON	W	M	APR 1884	16	S				KY	KY	TN				FARM HAND			X	X	✓				
		" RICE	SON	W	M	APR 1886	14	S				KY	KY	TN				FARM HAND			X	X	✓				
		" LUTHER S.	SON	W	M	JUN 1888	12	S				TN	KY	TN				FARM HAND			X	X	✓				
		" LISSIE M.	DAU	W	F	MAR 1890	10	S				KY	KY	TN													
		" OVY B.	DAU	W	F	JUN 1892	7	S				TN	KY	TN													
		" ONY P.	DAU	W	F	JUN 1892	7	S				TN	KY	TN													
		" REBECCA T.	DAU	W	F	MAR 1895	5	S				KY	KY	TN													
		" ANDREW L.	SON	W	M	OCT 1898	2	S				KY	KY	TN													
350	361	HAMMER, RICHARD	HEAD	W	M	MAY 1873	27	M	8			KY	KY	TN				FARMING			✓	✓	✓		O		F	349
		" JULIA G.	WIFE	W	F	JUN 1875	24	M	8	4	4	KY	TN	KY							✓	✓	✓				
		" MARY A.	DAU	W	F	AUG 1893	6	S				KY	KY	KY													
		" LOU E.	DAU	W	F	MAY 1895	5	S				KY	KY	KY													
		" CLURA N.	SON	W	M	MAY 1897	3	S				KY	KY	KY													
		" RICHARD B.	SON	W	M	MAR 1900	4/12	S				KY	KY	KY													

STATE - KENTUCKY
COUNTY - MONROE
Township or other division — EAST TOMPKINSVILLE — Enumerator E. R. BAXTER

Supervisor's Dist. No. 102 Sheet No.
Enumeration Dist. No. 84

No. of Family	No. of Dwelling	NAME	Relation	Color	Sex	DATE OF BIRTH Mon/Yr	Age at last birthday	Marital Status	# Years married	Mother of how many children?	# of these children living	Place of birth [this person]	Father of this person	Mother of this person	Year of immigr.	# years in U.S.	Naturalization	OCCUPATION 10 years +	Months not employed	Attended school in months	Can read	Can write	Speak English	Owned or Rent	Owned -no mortage	Farm or house	# of farm schedule
351	362	HAMMER, ALFORD M.	HEAD	W	M	Feb 1864	36	M	12			KY	KY	TN				FARMING			✓	✓	✓	O	F	F	350
		" MARY H.	WIFE	W	F	Aug 1867	32	M	12			KY	KY	KY							✓	✓	✓				
		" GUY	NEPHEW	W	M	Feb 1886	14	S				KY	KY	KY				FARM HAND			X	X	✓				
352	363	PENNINGTON, CHRISTOPHER	HEAD	W	M	Jul 1846	53	DIVC.				KY	KY	KY				FARM WORK			X	X	✓	O	F	F	351
353	364	DODSON, LOUIS E.	HEAD	W	M	Dec 1855	44	M	18			KY	KY	KY				FARMING			✓	✓	✓	O	F	F	352
		" SARAH	WIFE	W	F	Dec 1856	43	M	18	6	6	TN	TN	TN							✓	✓	✓				
		" SIDNEY P.	SON	W	M	Mar 1883	17	S				KY	KY	TN				AT SCHOOL		4	✓	✓	✓				
		" FLORENCE A.	DAU	W	F	Nov 1885	15	S				KY	KY	TN				AT SCHOOL		4	✓	✓	✓				
		" VIRGIL H.	SON	W	M	Jun 1888	11	S				KY	KY	TN				AT SCHOOL		4	✓	✓	✓				
		" LARENCE A.	SON	W	M	Jan 1891	9	S				KY	KY	TN													
		" CORA P.	DAU	W	F	Mar 1894	6	S				KY	KY	TN													
		" OLLIE	DAU	W	F	Feb 1898	2	S				KY	KY	TN													
354	365	NORMAN, ORA C.	HEAD	W	M	Jan 1880	20	M				KY	KY	KY				FARMING			X	X	✓	R		F	353
		" SARAH	WIFE	W	F	Nov 1877	22	M				KY	KY	KY							✓	✓	✓				
355	366	BAXTER, ERASTUS R.	HEAD	W	M	Jul 1871	28	Wd				KY	KY	KY				MERCHANT			✓	✓	✓	R		F	354

HERE ENDS THE ENUMERATION OF EAST TOMPKINSVILLE PRECINCT

STATE - KENTUCKY
COUNTY - MONROE
Township or other division: WEST TOMPKINSVILLE
Enumerator: MALIA PAGE

Supervisor's Dist. No. 102 Sheet No.
Enumeration Dist. No. 85

No. of Family	No. of Dwelling	NAME	Relation	Color	Sex	DATE OF BIRTH Mon/Yr	Age at last birthday	Marital Status	# Years married	Mother of how many children?	# of these children living	Place of birth [this person]	Father of this person	Mother of this person	Year of immigr. in U.S.	# years in U.S.	Naturalization	OCCUPATION 10 years +	Months not employed	Attended school in months	Can read	Can write	Speak English	Owned or Rent	Owned -no mortgage	Farm or house	# of farm schedule
1	1	EMBERTON, JOHN	HEAD	W	M	OCT 1844	55	M	8			KY	KY	KY				FARMER			✓	✓	✓	O	F	F	1
		" MARY E.	WIFE	W	F	Feb 1869	31	M	8	4	2	KY	NC	KY					7		✓	✓	✓				
		" ORAL	SON	W	M	Jul 1883	16	S				KY	KY	KY				CLERK- DRY GOODS STORE			✓	✓					
		" VOLA	DAU	W	F	APR 1892	8	S				KY	KY	KY				AT SCHOOL		5	✓	✓					
		" MARY V.	DAU	W	F	JAN 1900	4/12	S				KY	KY	KY													
		YOKLEY, HESTER R.	SIS-in-law	W	F	NOV 1871	28	S				KY	NC	KY				MILLINERY 10			✓	✓	✓				
2	2	HARLAN, MAX B.	HEAD	W	M	JAN 1875	25	M	3			TN	TN	TN				LAWYER			✓	✓	✓	R		H	
		" MAGGIE M.	WIFE	W	F	JAN 1872	28	M	3	1	1	KY	KY	KY							✓	✓	✓				
		" HILDA	DAU	W	F	JUN 1898	1	S				KY	TN	KY													
3	3	BUSHONG, GEO. W.	HEAD	W	M	Jul 1872	27	M	2			KY	MISS	KY (MISSISSIPPI)				DOCTOR			✓	✓		O	F	H	
		" PEARL	WIFE	W	F	DEC 1873	26	M	2	1	1	KY	TN	KY							✓	✓					
		" MARY L.	DAU	W	F	JUN 1899	4/12	S				KY	KY	KY													
		ARMSTRONG, ANNARINTHA	HIRED	W	F	OCT 1853	46	WidK				TN	NY	IND				NURSE			✓	✓	✓				
4	4	DAVIS, GEORGE	HEAD	W	M	MAY 1873	27	M	5			KY	TN	TN				BARBER	1		✓	✓	✓	O	F	H	
		" LAURA B.	WIFE	W	F	Sep 1877	22	M	5	2	1	KY	KY	KY							✓	✓	✓				
		" PAULINE	DAU	W	F	JUL 1899	10/12	S				KY	KY	KY													
5	5	MARSHALL, MATISON	HEAD	W	M	JUN 1866	33	M	7			KY	KY	TN				DAY LABORER			✓	✓	✓	O	F	H	
		" MATILDA J.	WIFE	W	F	AUG 1865	34	M	7	1	1	KY	KY	KY							✓	✓	✓				
		FERGUSON, VIRGLE L.	STEP SON	W	M	APR 1888	12	S				KY	KY	KY													
	6	LESTER, EVALINE	HEAD	W	F	JAN 1833	66	S				KY	VA	TN				DAY LABORER			✓	X	✓	R		H	
6	7	MAXEY, LUTHER	HEAD	W	M	Jul 1877	22	M				KY	KY	TN				CLERK- GROCERIES			✓	✓	✓	O	F	H	
		" ELLA R.	WIFE	W	F	Feb 1881	18	M				TN	TN	KY							✓	✓	✓				
		WOOD, EMMA	SISTER-IN-LAW	W	F	Jan 1887	13	S				TN	TN	TN				AT SCHOOL			✓	✓	✓				
7	8	EVANS, ROBERT	HEAD	W	M	MAR 1860	40	M	1			KY	KY	KY				DRY GOODS- MERCHANT			✓	✓	✓	R		H	
		" FLORA B.	WIFE	W	F	AUG 1875	24	M	1			KY	KY	KY							✓	✓	✓				
		EMBERTON, ROXIE M.	SISTER-IN-LAW	W	F	Jul 1877	22	S				KY	KY	KY				MUSIC TEACHER 7			✓	✓	✓				

STATE - KENTUCKY
COUNTY - MONROE
Township or other division — WEST TOMPKINSVILLE
Enumerator MALIA PAGE

Supervisor's Dist. No. 102 Sheet No.
Enumeration Dist. No. 85

No. of Family	No. of Dwelling	NAME	Relation	Color	Sex	DATE OF BIRTH Mon/Yr	Age at last birthday	Marital Status	# Years married	Mother of how many children?	# of these children living	NATIVITY Place of birth (this person)	Father of this person	Mother of this person	CITIZENSHIP	OCCUPATION 10 years +	Months not employed	Attended school in months	Can read	Can write	Speak English	OWNERSHIP Owned or Rent	Owned –no mortage	Farm or house	# of farm schedule
8	9	PEDIGO, WILLIAM F.	HEAD	W	M	May 1823	77	M	48			KY	VA	VA		FARMER			✓	✓	✓	O	F	F	2
		" CAROLINE S.	WIFE	W	F	Mar 1831	69	M	48			KY	VA	KY					✓	✓	✓				
9	10	COPASS, THOMAS	HEAD	W	M	Sep 1862	37	M	13			KY	TN	TN		LAWYER			✓	✓	✓	O	F	H	
		" MANDIE F.	WIFE	W	F	Oct 1869	30	M	13	3	3	KY	KY	KY					✓	✓	✓				
		" WILLIE C.	SON	W	M	Jul 1889	10	S				KY	KY	KY		AT SCHOOL		5	✓	✓	✓				
		" ROBERT C.	SON	W	M	Feb 1893	7	S				KY	KY	KY		AT SCHOOL		5	✓	✓	✓				
		" IONE T.	DAU	W	F	Mar 1899	1	S				KY	KY	KY											
10	11	MOODY, THOMAS B.	HEAD	W	M	Apr 1862	38	M	14			KY	KY	KY		MAIL-CARRIER			✓	✓	✓	O	F	H	
		" BETTIE B.	WIFE	W	F	Apr 1862	38	M	14	3	3	TN	TN	VA					✓	✓	✓				
		" HOWARD Y.	SON	W	M	Dec 1886	13	S				TN	TN	KY		AT SCHOOL		5	✓	✓	✓				
		" CHARLES T.	SON	W	M	Mar 1891	8	S				KY	TN	KY		AT SCHOOL		5	✓	✓	✓				
		" FANNIE M.	DAU	W	F	Nov 1899	9/12	S				KY	TN	KY											
		BROWN, LETHIA	SERVANT	W	F	Jan 1882	18	S				KY	KY	TN		SERVANT			✓	✓	✓				
11	12	EADS, JAMES A.	HEAD	W	M	Jun 1866	33	M	7			KY	TN	KY		BLACKSMITH			X	X	✓	R		H	
		" CATHERINE	WIFE	W	F	Jul 1870	29	M	7	5	4	KY	TN	TN					✓	✓	✓				
		" JAMES W.	SON	W	M	Nov 1887	12	S				ARK	KY	KY		AT SCHOOL		5	✓	✓	✓				
		" MILLARD F.	SON	W	M	May 1894	6	S				KY	KY	KY		AT SCHOOL		5	X	X	✓				
		" WILLIAM H.	SON	W	M	Jul 1897	2	S				KY	KY	KY											
		" JESSIE H.	SON	W	M	Mar 1900	2/12	S				KY	KY	KY											
12	13	JACKSON, GEO. W.	HEAD	W	M	Aug 1843	56	M	32			TN	TN	TN		FARMER			✓	✓	✓	O	F	F	3
		" NANCY J.	WIFE	W	F	Sep 1846	53	M	32			KY	KY	KY					✓	✓	✓				
		14	DAVIS, SAMUEL G.	HEAD	W	M	Feb 1868	32	M	4			KY	KY	TN		BLACKSMITH			K	✓	✓	R		H	
		" LOU C.	WIFE	W	F	Dec 1876	23	M	4	1	1	KY	KY	KY					✓	✓	✓				
		" HERMAN	SON	W	M	Aug 1898	1	S				KY	KY	KY											
13	15	BARTLEY, TURNER	HEAD	W	M	Jan 1837	63	M				KY	KY	KY		FARMER			✓	✓	✓	O	F	F	4
		" MARY A.	WIFE	W	F	Jul 1844	55	M				KY	KY	KY					✓	✓	✓				

STATE - KENTUCKY
COUNTY - MONROE
Township or other division: WEST TOMPKINSVILLE Enumerator: MALIA PAGE

Supervisor's Dist. No. 102 Sheet No. ___
Enumeration Dist. No. 85

No. of Family	No. of Dwelling	NAME	Relation	Color	Sex	Date of Birth Mon/Yr	Age at last birthday	Marital Status	# Years married	Mother of how many children?	# of these children living	Place of birth (this person)	Father of this person	Mother of this person	Year of immigr.	# years in U.S.	Naturalization	Occupation 10 years +	Months not employed	Attended school in months	Can read	Can write	Speak English	Owned or Rent	Owned -no mortgage	Farm or house	# of Farm schedule
		BARTLEY, WALTER F.	Son	W	M	Nov 1882	17	S				KY	KY	KY				FARM LABORER			✓	✓	✓				
		" ARTHUR H.	Son	W	M	Apr 1886	14	S				KY	KY	KY				FARM LABORER			✓	✓	✓				
14	16	KIDWELL, MARTIN D.	Head	W	M	Apr 1858	42	M	16			KY	KY	KY				GEN. MERCHANT			✓	✓	✓	O	F	H	5
		" VIOLA S.	Wife	W	F	Sep 1861	38	M	16	6	6	KY	TN	TN							✓	✓	✓				
		" EVIE L.	Dau	W	F	Sep 1885	14	S				KY	KY	KY				AT SCHOOL		5	✓	✓	✓				
		" ISHAM N.	Son	W	M	May 1887	13	S				KY	KY	KY				AT SCHOOL		5	✓	✓	✓				
		" CECIL T.	Son	W	M	Feb 1889	11	S				KY	KY	KY				AT SCHOOL		5	✓	✓	✓				
		" OLEAN M.	Dau	W	F	Oct 1893	6	S				KY	KY	KY													
		" CARSON R.	Son	W	M	Sep 1897	2	S				KY	KY	KY													
		" HENRY C.	Son	W	M	Sep 1899	8/12	S				KY	KY	KY													
15	17	FORD, CAS T.	Head	W	M	Jun 1875	24	M				KY	KY	KY				CLERK - DRY GOODS			✓	✓	✓	R		H	
		" VIRGIE B.	Wife	W	F	Oct 1868	21	M				KY	KY	KY							✓	✓	✓				
16	18	COPASS, WILLIAM B.	Head	W	M	Jul 1859	40	M	11			KY	TN	TN				CLERK - DRY GOODS			✓	✓	✓	O		H	
		" OLIE F.	Wife	W	F	Sep 1871	28	M	11	2	2	TN	TN	TN							✓	✓	✓				
		" DANA M.	Dau	W	F	Dec 1890	9	S				TN	KY	TN				AT SCHOOL		5	✓	✓	✓				
		" BESSIE	Dau	W	F	Jun 1897	2	S				KY	KY	TN													
17	19	RHOTEN, JOHN	Head	W	M	Apr 1868	32	M	5			KY	KY	KY				—			✓	✓	✓	R		H	
		" CYTHA	Wife	W	F	Apr 1879	21	M	5	3	3	KY	KY	TN							✓	✓	✓				
		" OMA	Dau	W	F	May 1896	4	S				KY	KY	KY													
		" IDA V.	Dau	W	F	Dec 1897	2	S				KY	KY	KY													
		" ARGUS L.	Son	W	M	May 1900	1/12	S				KY	KY	KY													
18	20	EAGLE, EDD M.	Head	W	M	Aug 1864	35	S				KY	TN	KY				DOCTOR			✓	✓	✓	O		H	
19	21	SMITH, JAMES W.	Head	W	M	Jun 1855	44	M	20			TN	TN	KY				EDITOR - PAPER			✓	✓	✓	O		H	
		" NEVADA	Wife	W	F	Aug 1854	45	M	20	7	7	TN	KY	VA							✓	✓	✓				
		" ELLA T.	Dau	W	F	Aug 1880	19	S				KY	TN	TN				COMPOSITOR - PAPER			✓	✓	✓				
		" JOHN C.	Son	W	M	Dec 1884	15	S				KY	TN	TN				PORTER - HOTEL			✓	✓	✓				

STATE - KENTUCKY
COUNTY - MONROE
Township or other division WEST TOMPKINSVILLE Enumerator MALIA PAGE

Supervisor's Dist. No. 102 Sheet No.
Enumeration Dist. No. 85

Location (No. of Family / No. of Dwelling)	NAME	Relation	Color	Sex	DATE OF BIRTH Mon/Yr	Age at last birthday	Marital Status	# Years married	Mother of how many children?	# of these children living	Place of birth (this person)	Father of this person	Mother of this person	Year of immigr.	# years in U.S.	Naturalization	OCCUPATION 10 years +	Months not employed	Attended school in months	Can read	Can write	Speak English	Owned or Rent	Owned-no mortage	Farm or house	# of farm schedule
	SMITH, JULIA M.	DAU	W	F	Jun 1888	11	S				KY	TN	TN				AT SCHOOL		5	✓	✓	✓				
	" BETTIE J.	DAU	W	F	Aug 1891	8	S				KY	TN	TN				AT SCHOOL		5	✓	✓	✓				
	" SARAH A.	DAU	W	F	Jun 1893	6	S				KY	TN	TN				AT SCHOOL		5	✓	✓	✓				
	" JAMES D.	SON	W	M	Oct 1896	3	S				KY	TN	TN													
20 22	COMER, THOMAS P.	HEAD	W	M	Mar 1826	74	M	47			KY	SC	TN				HOTEL MANAGER			✓	✓	✓	O	M	H	
	" JANE A.	WIFE	W	F	Mar 1829	71	M	47	3	1	VA	VA	VA							✓	✓	✓				
	ARMSTRONG, NANNIE	SERVANT	W	F	May 1851	49	M	1	1	1	TN	PA	IND				COOK			✓	✓	✓				
21 23	HESTAND, JOHN B.	HEAD	W	M	Apr 1846	54	M	26			KY	KY	KY				STOCK TRADER			✓	✓	✓	O	F	F	6
	" MARY A.	WIFE	W	F	Jun 1850	49	M	26	1	1	KY	TN	TN				BOARDING HOUSE MANAGER			✓	✓	✓				
	BROWN, MARY	Servant	W	F	Sep 1869	30	S				TN	TN	TN							✓	✓	✓				
	RAILEY, ROLLING G.	Boarder	W	M	Feb 1872	28	S				KY	KY	KY				CIRCUIT CLERK			✓	✓	✓				
	DUNCAN, R. F.	Boarder	W	M	Jun 1863	36	S				TN	TN	TN				DOCTOR			✓	✓	✓				
	WEIR, ALBERT S.	Boarder	W	M	Feb 1856	44	M	20			TN	TN	VA				DENTIST			✓	✓	✓				
22 24	VANCE, TOBIAS E.	HEAD	W	M	Jun 1869	30	S				KY	KY	KY				TELEPHONE OPERATOR			✓	✓	✓	O	F	F	7
	" FLORA	SISTER	W	F	Jul 1865	34	S				KY	KY	KY				PARTNER			✓	✓	✓				
	JONES, WEALTHIE	Boarder	W	F	Dec 1870	29	S				KY	TN	KY				MILLINERY			✓	✓	✓				
23 25	FORD, JARRETTE C.	HEAD	W	M	Aug 1878	21	M	1			KY	KY	KY				DAY LABORER			✓	✓	✓	R		H	
	" JULIA	WIFE	W	F	Aug 1873	25	M	1	1	1	KY	KY	KY							✓	✓	✓				
	" WALTER R.	SON	W	M	Jun 1899	11/12	S				KY	KY	KY													
24 26	PAGE, GEORGE S.	HEAD	W	M	Apr 1859	41	M	14			KY	KY	KY				PROPT'R HOTEL			✓	✓	✓	O	M	H	
	" NANCY K.	WIFE	W	F	Sep 1865	34	M	14	5	5	KY	KY	KY							✓	✓	✓				
	" MOLLIE A.	DAU	W	F	Aug 1886	13	S				KY	KY	KY				AT SCHOOL		5	✓	✓	✓				
	" BRENTS F.	SON	W	M	Nov 1888	11	S				KY	KY	KY				AT SCHOOL		5	✓	✓	✓				
	" CLEO K.	SON	W	M	Jun 1891	8	S				KY	KY	KY				AT SCHOOL		5	✓	✓	✓				
	" GEORGIA	DAU	W	F	Sep 1895	4	S				KY	KY	KY													
	" CLARENCE M.	SON	W	M	Sep 1898	1	S				KY	KY	KY													

STATE - KENTUCKY
COUNTY - MONROE
Township or other division: WEST TOMPKINSVILLE
Enumerator: MALIA PAGE

Supervisor's Dist. No. 102 Sheet No. ___
Enumeration Dist. No. 85

Location (No. of Family / No. of Dwelling)	NAME	Relation	Color	Sex	Date of Birth (Mon/Yr)	Age at last birthday	Marital Status	# Years married	Mother of how many children?	# of these children living	Place of birth (this person)	Father of this person	Mother of this person	Year of immig.	# years in U.S.	Naturalization	Occupation	Months not employed	Attended school in months	Can read	Can write	Speak English	Owned or Rent	Owned - no mortgage	Farm or house	# of farm schedule
	RAY HERSCHEL B.	Boarder	W	M	Sep 1869	30	S				KY	KY	TN				PHYSICIAN			✓	✓	✓				
	KEMP, SAMPSON	Boarder	W	M	Feb 1864	36	M	9			TN	TN	TN				SALESMAN—PIANO			✓	✓	✓				
	" KATE E.	Boarder	W	F	Sep 1865	35	M	9	2	2	TN	TN	TN							✓	✓	✓				
	" STANTON H.	Boarder	W	M	Nov 1891	8	S				TN	TN	TN				AT SCHOOL		5	✓	✓	✓				
	" ANNA L.	Boarder	W	F	Dec 1894	5	S				TEXAS	TN	TN													
	GENTRY, WOLFORD	Servant	B	M	Mar 1865	35	M	15			KY	KY	VA				COOK			✓	X	✓				
	PITCOCK, BONDS	Servant	W	M	Sep 1873	26	S				KY	KY	KY				DAY LABORER			✓	✓	✓				
25 / 27	BARR, MICHAEL	HEAD	W	M	Aug 1851	48	M	24			TN	TN	MISSISSIPPI				PHOTOGRAPHER			✓	✓	✓	O	M	H	
**	" MARTHA L.	WIFE	W	F	Oct 1853	46	M	24	2	2	KY	KY	KY							✓	✓	✓				
	" JESSIE P.	SON	W	M	Dec 1888	11	S				KY	TN	KY				AT SCHOOL		5	✓	✓	✓				
26 / 28	EVANS, THOMAS P.	HEAD	W	M	Oct 1858	41	M	17			KY	KY	KY				DRUGGIST			✓	✓	✓	O	F	H	
	" MARTHA M.	WIFE	W	F	Jul 1861	38	M	17	5	5	KY	KY	KY							✓	✓	✓				
	" CLOE	DAU	W	F	Feb 1884	16	S				KY	KY	KY				AT SCHOOL		5	✓	✓	✓				
	" BUFORD H.	SON	W	M	May 1887	13	S				KY	KY	KY				AT SCHOOL		8	✓	✓	✓				
	" RAYMOND M.	SON	W	M	Nov 1889	10	S				KY	KY	KY				AT SCHOOL		5	✓	✓	✓				
	" JIM T.	SON	W	M	Mar 1892	8	S				KY	KY	KY				AT SCHOOL		3	X	X	✓				
	" DENNIS G.	SON	W	M	Jan 1898	2	S				KY	KY	KY													
27 / 29	GILL, DOSIER C.	HEAD	W	M	Oct 1846	43	M	29			KY	KY	KY				CLERK—DRY GOODS			✓	✓	✓	R		H	
	" NANCY N.	WIFE	W	F	Mar 1852	48	M	29	5	3	KY	KY	KY							✓	✓	✓				
	" THOMAS B.	SON	W	M	Apr 1881	19	S				KY	KY	KY				BARBER	8		✓	✓	✓				
	" CHARLES R.	SON	W	M	Dec 1888	11	S				KY	KY	KY				AT SCHOOL		10	✓	✓	✓				
30	GILL, SAMUEL	HEAD	W	M	Feb 1872	28	M	2			KY	KY	KY				APPRENTICE—CARPENTER			✓	✓	✓	R		H	
	" CHINA F.	WIFE	W	F	Dec 1878	21	M	2	1	1	KY	KY	KY				NURSE			✓	✓	✓				
	" PAUL E.	SON	W	M	Jun 1899	1/12	S				KY	KY	KY													
OMITTED	BARR, WILLIAM L.		W	M	Jul 1877	22	S				KY	TN	KY				CLERK—DRY GOODS			✓	✓	✓				

STATE - KENTUCKY
COUNTY - MONROE
Township or other division **WEST TOMPKINSVILLE** Enumerator **MALIA PAGE**

Supervisor's Dist. No. **102** Sheet No.
Enumeration Dist. No. **85**

No. of Family	No. of Dwelling	NAME	Relation	Color	Sex	DATE OF BIRTH Mon/Yr	Age at last birthday	Marital Status	# Years married	Mother of how many children?	# of these children living	NATIVITY Place of birth	Father of this person	Mother of this person	CITIZENSHIP Year of immigr.	# years in U.S.	Naturalization	OCCUPATION 10 years +	Months not employed	Attended school in months	Can read	Can write	Speak English	OWNERSHIP Owned or Rent	Owned -no mortage	Farm or house	# of farm schedule
28	31	KEFAUVER, AI	HEAD	W	M	OCT 1867	32	M	7			KY	VA	PENN				MERCHANT- GEN MDSE			✓	✓	✓	O		H	
		" ELECTA	WIFE	W	F	Feb 1874	26	M	7			KY	KY	KY							✓	✓	✓				
		" DAVID	BROTHER	W	M	Feb 1858	42	DIVC				KY	VA	PENN				PARTNER			✓	✓	✓				
29	32	MOODY, WILLIAM	HEAD	W	M	MAR 1868	32	M	6			KY	KY	KY				CLERK- DRUG STORE			✓	✓	✓	R		H	
		" SUSAN	WIFE	W	F	APR 1868	32	M	6	1	1	KY	KY	SC				HOTEL MANAGER			✓	✓	✓				
		" JACKEY NED	SON	W	M	DEC 1894	5	S				KY	KY	KY													
		GREEN, CLAUD	HIRED	W	M	DEC 1878	21	S				KY	TN	TN				HOTEL PORTER			✓	✓	✓				
30	33	EVANS, JULIA A.	HEAD	W	F	Sep 1834	65	Wd		1	1	SC	SC	SC							✓	✓	✓	O	F	H	
31	34	SHIRLEY, EDD	HEAD	B	M	DEC 1858	41	M	14			KY	KY	KY				BRICK- LAYER			✓	✓	✓	O	F	H	
		" SISY	WIFE	B	F	Jun 1860	40	M	14	3	3	KY	KY	KY				WASHER- WOMAN			✓	✓	✓				
		" GENEVA K.	DAU	B	F	MAY 1884	16	S				KY	KY	KY				WASHER- GIRL			✓	✓	✓				
		" BELL	DAU	B	F	Feb 1887	13	S				KY	KY	KY				AT SCHOOL		5	✓	✓	✓				
		" NELLIE	DAU	B	F	AUG 1891	8	S				KY	KY	KY				AT SCHOOL		5	X	X	✓				
32	35	RICHARDSON, ROBERT H.	HEAD	W	M	JAN 1824	76	M	58			TN	VA	VA				PRES.- BANK			✓	✓	✓	O		H	
		" MARGARET	WIFE	W	F	MAR 1829	71	M	58	9	9	KY	NC	KY							✓	✓	✓				
33	36	RICHARDSON, JOHN H.	HEAD	W	M	Nov 1851	48	M	11			KY	TN	KY				CASHIER- BANK			✓	✓	✓	O		H	
		" KATE	WIFE	W	F	AUG 1870	29	M	11	6	3	KY	KY	KY							✓	✓	✓				
		" OLIVIA	DAU	W	F	Sep 1890	10	S				KY	KY	KY				AT SCHOOL		10	✓	✓					
		" HENRY	SON	W	M	MAY 1896	4	S				KY	KY	KY													
		" LESLIE	SON	W	M	NOV 1898	1	S				KY	KY	KY													
		SIMPSON, RILLA	SERVANT	W	F	MAY 1870	30	DIVC				KY	KY	KY				NURSE			✓	✓	✓				
34	37	SARTIN, JOHN W.	HEAD	W	M	DEC 1857	42	M	22			KY	KY	KY				JAILOR			✓	✓	✓			H	
		" POLLIE J.	WIFE	W	F	Feb 1861	39	M	22	9	7	KY	KY	KY							✓	✓	✓				
		" HATTIE	DAU	W	F	Sep 1883	16	S				KY	KY	KY				AT SCHOOL		10	✓	✓	✓				
		" AVERY	SON	W	M	DEC 1885	14	S				KY	KY	KY				AT SCHOOL		5	✓	✓	✓				
		" FLOSSIE L.	DAU	W	M	JUL 1888	11	S				KY	KY	KY				AT SCHOOL		10	✓	✓	✓				

STATE - KENTUCKY
COUNTY - MONROE
Township or other division — WEST TOMPKINSVILLE
Enumerator — MALIA PAGE

Supervisor's Dist. No. 102 Sheet No.
Enumeration Dist. No. 85

Location No. of Family	No. of Dwelling	NAME	Relation	Color	Sex	DATE OF BIRTH Mon/Yr	Age at last birthday	Marital Status	# Years married	Mother of how many children?	# of these children living	Place of birth (this person)	Father of this person	Mother of this person	Year of immigr.	# years in U.S.	Naturalization	OCCUPATION 10 years +	Months not employed	Attended school in months	Can read	Can write	Speak English	Owned or Rent	Owned - no mortage	Farm or house	# of farm schedule
		SARTIN, HERBERT	Son	W	M	DEC 1890	9	S				KY	KY	KY				AT SCHOOL		5	✓	✓					
		" BASIL	Son	W	M	APR 1893	7	S				KY	KY	KY													
		COMER	Son	W	M	OCT 1895	4	S				KY	KY	KY													
		STRODE, REUBEN (PRISONER)		W	M	NOV 1850	49	M	13			KY	KY	KY				FARMER			✓	✓		O	F	F	
		JACKSON, JOHN (PRISONER)		W	M	DEC 1876	23	S				KY	KY	KY				FARMER			X	X	✓				
		PROPES, FRANK (PRISONER)		W	M	APR 1879	21	S				KY	KY	KY				DAY LABORER	6								
		GUEST, SYRUS (PRISONER)		B	M	DEC 1854	45	S				KY	KY	KY				DAY LABORER	3		X	X	✓				
85	38	GREEN, BURIEL W.	Head	W	M	MAR 1862	38	M	14			TN	TN	TN				SILVERSMITH			✓	✓	✓	R		H	
		" BARTHENIA A.	Wife	W	F	APR 1855	35	M	14	2	2	TN	TN	TN							✓	✓	✓				
		" WILLIAM R.	Son	W	M	FEB 1887	13	S				TN	TN	TN				AT SCHOOL		5	✓	✓	✓				
		" ALFRED. J.F.	Son	W	M	NOV 1888	11	S				TN	TN	TN				AT SCHOOL		5	✓	✓	✓				
		DAVIS, NANCY E.	Moth-in-law	W	F	DEC 1837	62	Wd		3	3	TN	TN	TN							X	X	✓				
36	39	MAXEY, RADFORD	Head	W	M	JUN 1863	36	M	16			KY	KY	TN				FARMER			✓	✓	✓	O	F	F	8
		" MOLLIE E.	Wife	W	F	FEB 1866	34	M	16	3	3	KY	KY	KY							✓	✓	✓				
		" PRINCETON	Son	W	M	MAY 1885	15	S				KY	KY	KY				AT SCHOOL		5	✓	✓	✓				
		" MAY E.	Dau	W	F	OCT 1887	12	S				KY	KY	KY				AT SCHOOL		5	✓	✓	✓				
		" NORWOOD	Son	W	M	MAR 1894	6	S				KY	KY	KY													
37	40	CHISM, ALONZO H.	Head	W	M	JUL 1841	58	M	31			KY	KY	KY				SILVERSMITH			✓	✓	✓	O	M	H	
		" MARY L.	Wife	W	F	NOV 1848	51	M	31	1	1	KY	KY	KY							✓	✓	✓				
		ELLIS, VERDA	Hired	W	F	JAN 1879	21	S				TN	TN	TN				COOK			✓	✓	✓				
38	41	CHISM, TROTTIE	Head	W	M	DEC 1869	30	M	6			KY	KY	KY				JEWELRY			✓	✓	✓	O	M	H	
		" BETTIE E.	Wife	W	F	APR 1870	30	M	6	4	3	KY	KY	KY				NURSE			✓	✓	✓				
		" MARY T.	Dau	W	F	JAN 1895	5	S				KY	KY	KY													
		" JAMES H.	Son	W	M	APR 1896	4	S				KY	KY	KY													
		" SALLIE R.	Dau	W	F	JAN 1899	1	S				KY	KY	KY													
39	42	EVANS, TABITHIA	Head	W	F	AUG 1836	63	Wd		13	10	KY	KY	KY				CAPITALIST			✓	✓	✓	O	F	H	

STATE - KENTUCKY
COUNTY - MONROE
Township or other division **WEST TOMPKINSVILLE** Enumerator **MALIA PAGE**

Supervisor's Dist. No. **102** Sheet No.
Enumeration Dist. No. **85**

Location		NAME	Relation	Color	Sex	DATE OF BIRTH Mon/Yr	Age at last birthday	Marital Status	# Years married	Mother of how many children	# of these children living	NATIVITY Place of birth [this person]	Father of this person	Mother of this person	CITIZENSHIP Year of immigr.	# years in U.S.	Naturalization	OCCUPATION 10 years +	Months not employed	EDUCATION Attended school in months	Can read	Can write	Speak English	OWNERSHIP Owned or Rent	Owned —no mortage	Farm or house	# of farm schedule
No. of Family	No. of Dwelling																										
		EVANS, NIMROD	Son	W	M	Oct 1877	22	S				KY	KY	KY				CLERK - GROCERIES			✓	✓	✓				
		TURNER, IRA D.	Boarder	W	M	Jan 1877	22	S				KY	KY	KY				CLERK - DRY GOODS			✓	✓	✓				
		ARMSTRONG, RACHAEL	Servant	W	F	Feb 1856	44	S		1	1	TN	PA	IND				HOUSEKEEPER			✓	✓					
		" GENIE	Boarder	W	F	Sep 1881	18	S				KY	TN	KY				A.T. SCHOOL		10	✓	✓	✓				
40	43	MAXEY, EDGAR	HEAD	W	M	Sep 1874	25	S				KY	KY	KY				FARMER			✓	✓	✓	O	M	F	
		EUBANK, MARGIE M.	SISTER	W	F	May 1854	46	Wd		4	2	KY	KY	KY							✓	✓	✓				
		" ADDIE B	NEICE	W	F	Sep 1882	17	S				KY	KY	KY				COMPOSITOR - PAPER			✓	✓	✓				
		" KENT	NEPHEW	W	M	Jan 1876	24	M	2			KY	KY	KY				LAWYER			✓	✓	✓				
		" ABBIGILL	NIECE	W	F	Sep 1876	24	M	2	1	1	KY	KY	KY				NURSE			✓	✓	✓				
41	44	McMILLIN, JOHN	HEAD	W	M	Jan 1827	73	M	53			KY	KY	KY				FARMER			✓	✓	✓	O	F		9
		" ELIZABETH F.	WIFE	W	F	Feb 1828	72	M	53			TN	NC	NC							✓	✓	✓				
42	45	EMMERT, FRANK	HEAD	W	M	May 1852	48	M	26			KY	KY	KY				MGR. LIVERY STABLE			✓	✓	✓	O	F	H	
		" MARY	WIFE	W	F	Dec 1858	41	M	26			KY	KY	KY							✓	✓	✓				
		" HELEN	DAU	W	F	Mar 1890	10	S				KY	KY	KY				AT SCHOOL		5	✓	✓	✓				
43	46	HALL, JEROME	HEAD	W	M	Jan 1877	23	M	7			TN	SC	TN				DAY LABORER			✓	✓	✓	R	H		
		" DEVONIA	WIFE	W	F	Dec 1877	23	M	7	3	3	KY	TN	KY							✓	✓	✓				
		" HESTER	DAU	W	F	May 1894	6	S				KY	TN	KY													
		" LOLA	DAU	W	F	Nov 1897	2	S				KY	TN	KY													
44	47	MAXEY, EMMA	HEAD	W	F	Nov 1863	36	Wd		1	1	TN	TN	TN				DRESS MAKER			✓	✓	✓	O	F	H	
		" BEDFORD	SON	W	M	Mar 1886	14	S				KY	KY	TN				DAY LABORER	5	5	✓	✓	✓				
		WOOD, CAMELLA	HIRED	W	F	Sep 1884	15	S				TN	TN	KY				SHOP GIRL	3	3	✓	✓	✓				
45	48	KIDWELL, ISHAM D.	HEAD	W	M	Jan 1829	71	M	49			KY	VA	KY				CAPITALIST			✓	✓	✓	O	F	H	
		" SARAH A.	WIFE	W	F	Jun 1833	66	M	49	8	6	KY	NC	VA							✓	✓	✓				
		DENHAM, FLORENCE	HIRED	W	F	May 1882	18	S				KY	KY	KY							✓	✓	✓				
		WHITE, CHARLIE P.	Boarder	W	M	May 1868	32	S				KY	KY	KY				LAWYER			✓	✓	✓				
		WHITE, FRANK M.	SON IN-LAW	W	M	Oct 1866	33	M	2			KY	KY	KY				LAWYER			✓	✓	✓				

STATE - KENTUCKY
COUNTY - MONROE
Township or other division — WEST TOMPKINSVILLE — Enumerator MAHA PAGE

Supervisor's Dist. No. _102_ Sheet No. ___
Enumeration Dist. No. _85_

No. of Family	No. of Dwelling	NAME	Relation	Color	Sex	DATE OF BIRTH Mon/Yr	Age at last birthday	Marital Status	# Years married	# Mother of how many children?	# of these children living	Place of birth (this person)	Father of this person	Mother of this person	Year of immigr.	# years in U.S.	Naturalization	OCCUPATION 10 years +	Months not employed	Attended school in months	Can read	Can write	Speak English	Owned or Rent	Owned - no mortage	Farm or house	# of farm schedule	
46	49	HADDOCK, THOMAS	HEAD	W	M	AUG 1863	36	M	16			TN	TN	TN				SEWER FACTORY			✓	X	✓	O	F	H		
		" ELIZA A.	WIFE	W	F	MAR 1856	44	M	16	0	0	TN	NC	NC							✓	X	✓	O	F	H		
		ELLIS, IRVING	Adopted	W	M	AUG 1890	9	S				KY	KY	KY				AT SCHOOL			✓	X	✓					
47	50	GRISSOM, JOE J.	HEAD	W	M	JAN 1858	42	M	7			ILL	TN	VA				MERCHANT - GEN MDSE			✓	✓	✓	O	F	F	10	
		" TABITHA A.	WIFE	W	F	OCT 1860	39	M	7	3	2	KY	TN	KY							✓	✓	✓					
		" EFFIE	DAU	W	F	MAR 1886	14	S				TN	ILL	TN				AT SCHOOL		10	✓	✓	✓					
		" SUE B.	DAU	W	F	DEC 1887	12	S				TN	ILL	TN				AT SCHOOL		10	✓	✓	✓					
		" BOB	SON	W	M	MAY 1895	5	S				KY	ILL	KY														
		MAXEY CREED H.	Stepson	W	M	JAN 1884	16	S				KY	KY	KY				AT SCHOOL		10	✓	✓	✓					
		HUMES, LILLIE H.	Servant	W	F	JUN 1879	20	S				KY	KY	KY				SERVANT - COOK			✓	✓	✓					
		ALLEE, JOHN	Hired	W	M	JAN 1878	22	S				KY	KY	KY				DAY LABORER			✓	✓	✓					
48	51	HARLAN, JAMES W.	HEAD	W	M	APR 1866	34	M	12			KY	KY	KY				APPRENTICE CARPENTER			✓	✓	✓	R		H		
		" ELLA M.	WIFE	W	F	JAN 1867	33	M	12	3	2	KY	KY	KY							✓	✓	✓					
		" FRANK P.	SON	W	M	JUL 1890	9	S				KY	KY	KY				AT SCHOOL		8	✓	✓	✓					
		" JIMMIE H.	SON	W	M	AUG 1895	4	S				KY	KY	KY														
49	52	CARTER, JAMES C.	HEAD	W	M	OCT 1863	36	M	8			KY	KY	KY				LAWYER			✓	✓	✓	O	F	F	11	
		" IDRU I.	WIFE	W	F	JUL 1872	27	M	8	3	3	TN	TN	TN							✓	✓	✓					
		" LIZZIE A.	DAU	W	F	JUL 1893	6	S				KY	KY	TN				AT SCHOOL		5	✓	✓	✓					
		" PEARL E.	DAU	W	F	JAN 1896	4	S				KY	KY	TN														
		" GRACIE M.	DAU	W	F	MAY 1898	2	S				KY	KY	TN														
		HOLLOWAY, MOLLIE	Servant	W	F	APR 1879	21	S				KY	KY	KY				SERVANT			✓	✓	✓					
50	53	MARTIN, POCOHONTAS	Head	W	F	FEB 1845	55	S				KY	NC	KY							✓	✓	✓	O	F	H		
51	54	YOKLEY PALMORE	Head	W	M	AUG 1867	32	Wd				KY	TN	KY				CABINET MAKER			✓	✓	✓	O	F	H		
52	55	WELCH, GEORGE W.	Head	W	M	JUN 1857	42	M	21			KY	KY	KY				BLACKSMITH			✓	✓	✓	O	m	H		
		" NANCY J.	WIFE	W	F	JAN 1861	39	M	21	9	7	KY	KY	KY							✓	✓	✓					
		" BRASKIT	SON	W	M	DEC 1883	16	S				KY	KY	KY				AT SCHOOL		5	✓	✓	✓					

STATE - KENTUCKY
COUNTY - MONROE
Township or other division — WEST TOMPKINSVILLE — Enumerator MALIA PAGE

Supervisor's Dist. No. 102 Sheet No.
Enumeration Dist. No. 85

Location		NAME	Relation	Color	Sex	DATE OF BIRTH Mon/Yr	Age at last birthday	Marital Status	# Years married	Mother of how many children?	# of these children living	NATIVITY Place of birth [this person]	Father of this person	Mother of this person	CITIZENSHIP Year of immigr.	# years in U.S.	Naturalization	OCCUPATION 10 years +	Months not employed	EDUCATION Attended school in months	Can read	Can write	Speak English	OWNERSHIP Owned or Rent	Owned -no mortage	Farm or house	# of farm schedule	
No. of Family	No. of Dwelling																											
		WELCH, NORA	DAU	W	F	DEC 1885	14	S				KY	KY	KY				AT SCHOOL		5	✓	✓						
		" SAMUEL T.	SON	W	M	Sep 1887	12	S				KY	KY	KY				AT SCHOOL		5	✓	✓						
		" CLARENCE L.	SON	W	M	Feb 1884	6	S				KY	KY	KY														
		" ELLA	DAU	W	F	MAR 1897	3	S				KY	KY	KY														
		" WILLIAM H.	SON	W	M	MAR 1898	1	S				KY	KY	KY														
53	56	LESLIE, JOHN	HEAD	W	M	Jun 1849	50	M	4			KY	NC	GA				PREACHER			✓	✓	✓	O		M H		
		" AMERICA	WIFE	W	F	May 1849	51	M	4	0	0	KY	KY	KY							✓	✓	✓					
		" SALLIE	DAU	W	F	Sep 1879	20	S				KY	KY	KY				DRESS MAKING			✓	✓	✓					
		" JOHN R.	SON	W	M	MAR 1888	12	S				KY	KY	KY				AT SCHOOL		10	✓	✓						
		" SUSIE E.	DAU	W	F	OCT 1890	9	S				KY	KY	KY				AT SCHOOL		5	✓	✓						
		" WILLIAM H.	SON	W	M	OCT 1892	7	S				KY	KY	KY				AT SCHOOL		3	X	X	✓					
54	57	THOMPSON, LORENZO D.)	HEAD	W	M	DEC 1844	55	M	33			KY	KY	KY				CAPITALIST	12		✓	✓	✓	O		FH		
		" COATNEY A.	WIFE	W	F	Jul 1848	51	M	33	2	2	KY	TN	MISSISSIPPI							✓	✓						

HERE ENDS THE ENUMERATION OF TOMPKINSVILLE TOWN

— 341 —

STATE - KENTUCKY
COUNTY - MONROE
Township or other division — WEST TOMPKINSVILLE — Enumerator — MALIA PAGE

Supervisor's Dist. No. _102_ Sheet No. ____
Enumeration Dist. No. _85_ ____

No. of Family	No. of Dwelling	NAME	Relation	Color	Sex	Date of Birth (Mon/Yr)	Age at last birthday	Marital Status	# Years married	Mother of how many children?	# of these children living	Place of birth (this person)	Father of this person	Mother of this person	Year of immigr.	# years in U.S.	Naturalization	Occupation 10 years +	Months not employed	Attended school in months	Can read	Can write	Speak English	Owned or Rent	Owned - no mortgage	Farm or house	# of farm schedule
56	58	PAGE, JOHN B.	Head	W	M	Oct 1848	51	M	30			KY	KY	KY				FARMER			✓	✓	✓	O	M	F	12
		" NANCY J.	Wife	W	F	Jun 1850	49	M	30	2	1	KY	KY	KY							✓	✓	✓				
		" MALIA	Dau	W	F	Jul 1875	24	S				KY	KY	KY				SCHOOL TEACHER			✓	✓	✓				
		HAGAN, BURRIS	Niece	W	F	Apr 1888	12	S				KY	KY	KY				AT SCHOOL		5	✓	✓	✓				
56	59	PAGE, SAMUEL	Head	W	M	Nov 1853	46	M	17			KY	KY	KY				FARMER			✓	✓	✓	R		F	13
		" MARY F.	Wife	W	F	Aug 1853	46	M	17	4	4	KY	KY	KY							✓	✓	✓				
		" BETHEL B.	Son	W	M	Mar 1884	16	S				KY	KY	KY				AT SCHOOL		5	✓	✓	✓				
		" SALLIE J.	Dau	W	F	Nov 1885	14	S				KY	KY	KY				AT SCHOOL		5	✓	✓	✓				
		" ETHEL T.	Dau	W	F	Aug 1888	11	S				KY	KY	KY				AT SCHOOL		5	✓	✓	✓				
		" MAUDIE F.	Dau	W	F	Dec 1892	7	S				KY	KY	KY				AT SCHOOL		5	✓	✓	✓				
57	60	PAGE, JAMES	Head	W	M	Dec 1851	48	M	23			KY	KY	KY				CLERK - DRY GOODS	5		✓	✓	✓	R		H	
		" AMERICA	Wife	W	F	Jan 1861	39	M	23	11	9	KY	KY	KY							X	X	✓				
		" JOSIE	Dau	W	F	Mar 1879	21	S				KY	KY	KY							✓	✓	✓				
		" ROSA E.	Dau	W	F	Jul 1884	15	S				KY	KY	KY							✓	✓	✓				
		" SAMUEL	Son	W	M	Oct 1887	12	S				KY	KY	KY				DAY LABORER			✓	✓	✓				
		" LOU B.	Dau	W	F	Dec 1888	11	S				KY	KY	KY							✓	✓					
		" PEARLIE	Dau	W	F	Oct 1892	7	S				KY	KY	KY							X	X	✓				
		" EDDIE	Son	W	M	Sep 1894	5	S				KY	KY	KY													
		" WILLIAM McKINLEY	Son	W	M	Jan 1896	4	S				KY	KY	KY													
		" HOBERT	Son	W	M	Jan 1896	4	S				KY	KY	KY													
		" CLYDE D.	Son	W	M	Apr 1899	1	S				KY	KY	KY													
58	61	PALMORE, WILLIAM	Head	W	M	Mar 1870	30	M	10			KY	KY	KY				FACTORY HAND - HAULER			✓	✓	✓	R		H	
		" MARY S.	Wife	W	F	Nov 1873	26	M	10	4	4	KY	KY	KY							✓	✓	✓				
		" HERBERT L.	Son	W	M	Aug 1890	9	S				KY	KY	KY				AT SCHOOL		5	✓	✓	✓				
		" OSCAR M.	Son	W	M	Jan 1892	8	S				KY	KY	KY				AT SCHOOL		5	✓	✓	✓				
		" BULAH M.	Dau	W	F	Jun 1894	5	S				KY	KY	KY													

STATE - KENTUCKY
COUNTY - MONROE
Township or other division — WEST TOMPKINSVILLE

Enumerator — MALIA PAGE

Supervisor's Dist. No. 102 Sheet No.
Enumeration Dist. No. 85

Location No. of Family / No. of Dwelling	NAME	Relation	Color	Sex	DATE OF BIRTH Mon/Yr	Age at last birthday	Marital Status	# Years married	Mother of how many children?	# of these children living	Place of birth [this person]	Father of this person	Mother of this person	Year of immigr.	# years in U.S.	Naturalization	OCCUPATION 10 years +	Months not employed	Attended school in months	Can read	Can write	Speak English	Owned or Rent	Owned -no mortage	Farm or house	# of farm schedule
	PALMORE, LULA B.	DAU	W	F	Nov 1895	4	S				KY	KY	KY													
59 62	RUNYON, WILSON	HEAD	W	M	Apr 1861	39	M	12			KY	KY	KY				FACTORY - LATHE-MAN			✓	✓	✓	R		H	
	" ABIGAIL I.	WIFE	W	F	Aug 1867	32	M	12	1	1	KY	KY	KY							✓	✓	✓				
	" WILLE A.	SON	W	M	Mar 1892	8	S				KY	KY	KY				AT SCHOOL		5	✓	✓					
60 63	SHANNON, JOE	HEAD	W	M	Apr 1866	34	M	2			KY	KY	MISSOURI				MGR - AXE HANDLE FACTORY			✓	✓	✓	R		H	
	" ADA B	WIFE	W	F	Jan 1879	21	M	2	1	1	KY	KY	KY							✓	✓	✓				
	MARY P.	DAU	W	F	Jul 1899	10/12	S				KY	KY	KY													
61 64	JENKINS, GEORGE W.	HEAD	W	M	Jan 1871	29	M	11			TN	—	—				ENGINEER - FACTORY			✓	✓	✓	R		H	
	" LUCY F.	WIFE	W	F	Jun 1870	30	M	11	2	2	KY	KY	KY							✓	✓	✓				
	" ANNA E.	DAU	W	F	Sep 1891	8	S				KY	TN	KY				AT SCHOOL		5	X	X	✓				
	" ELBERT B.	SON	W	M	Jun 1893	6	S				KY	TN	KY				AT SCHOOL		5	X	X	✓				
62 65	HODGE, JOHN W.	HEAD	W	M	May 1868	32	M	11			TN	TN	TN				FACTORY - LATHE-MAN			✓	✓	✓	R		H	
	" LORETTIE	WIFE	W	F	Feb 1866	34	M	11	4	4	KY	KY	KY							✓	✓	✓				
	" LOUIE W.	SON	W	M	Sep 1889	10	S				TN	TN	KY				AT SCHOOL		4	✓	✓	✓				
	" RAYMOND P.	SON	W	M	Apr 1891	9	S				TN	TN	KY				AT SCHOOL		4	✓	✓	✓				
	" MANNIE B.	DAU	W	F	Jul 1893	6	S				TN	TN	KY				AT SCHOOL		4	✓	✓	✓				
	" IVY P.	DAU	W	F	Jan 1896	4	S				TN	TN	KY													
63 66	HODGE, NEWTON	HEAD	W	M	Mar 1847	53	M	35			TN	VA	VA							✓	✓	✓	R		H	
	" SARAH	WIFE	W	F	Mar 1837	63	M	35	6	5	NC	NC	NC							✓	✓	✓				
	" PHILLIP J.	SON	W	M	Sep 1869	30	Wd				TN	TN	NC				SAWYER - FACTORY	3		✓	✓	✓				
	" CHARLIE B.	SON	W	M	Oct 1878	21	S				TN	TN	NC				LATHE-MAN - FACTORY			✓	✓	✓				
	" PATTIE M.	Gt-Dau	W	F	Nov 1892	7	S				TN	TN	TN				AT SCHOOL		4	✓	✓	✓				
	HURT, ELIC	Boarder	W	M	Jan 1872	28	S				KY	KY	VA				LATHE-MAN - FACTORY			✓	✓	✓				
64 67	SPEAKMAN, CHARLOTTE	HEAD	W	F	Jul 1833	66	Wd		1	1	KY	NC	TN				HOUSEKEEPER			X	X	✓	O		FH	
	" JAMIE	Gt-Dau	W	F	May 1874	26	S		1	0	KY	KY	TN				WASHER-WOMAN			✓	✓	✓				
	" MONTEVILLE	Gt-Son	W	M	Nov 1877	22	S				KY	KY	KY				PAINTER 6			✓	✓	✓				

TWELFTH CENSUS OF THE UNITED STATES 1900

STATE - KENTUCKY
COUNTY - MONROE
Township or other division: **WEST TOMPKINSVILLE** Enumerator: **MALIA PAGE**

Supervisor's Dist. No. **102** Sheet No.
Enumeration Dist. No. **85**

No. Family	No. Dwelling	Name	Relation	Color	Sex	Date of Birth Mon/Yr	Age	Marital Status	Yrs married	Mother of how many children	# living	Place of birth	Father	Mother	Occupation	Months not emp.	School months	Read	Write	Speak Eng	Ownership
		SPEAKMAN, JIM P.	GR-SON	W	M	Dec 1880	19	S				KY	KY	KY	DAY LABORER	5		✓	✓	✓	
65	68	EMBERTON, JOHN	HEAD	W	M	Nov 1840	59	M	7			KY	KY	TN	FARMER			✓	✓	✓	O F F 14
		" MARY	WIFE	W	F	Jul 1841	58	M	7			KY	KY	KY				✓	✓	✓	
66	69	GRAVEN, CHARLES B.	HEAD	W	M	Jan 1862	38	Wd				KY	KY	KY	FARMER			✓	✓	✓	O M F 15
		" HATTIE B.	DAU	W	F	Jan 1884	16	S				KY	KY	KY				✓	✓	✓	
		" JOE S.	SON	W	M	Sep 1884	15	S				KY	KY	KY	FARM LABORER			X	X	✓	
		" BEDFORD	SON	W	M	Sep 1887	12	S				KY	KY	KY	AT SCHOOL		3	X	X	✓	
		" SANFORD T.	SON	W	M	Mar 1892	8	S				KY	KY	KY	AT SCHOOL			X	X	✓	
		" OLLIE M.	DAU	W	F	Nov 1893	6	S				KY	KY	KY							
		" DANIEL B.	SON	W	M	Jul 1898	2	S				KY	KY	KY							
		" TOMMIE	SON	W	M	Dec 1898	1	S				KY	KY	KY							
67	70	EMBERTON, GEORGE H.	HEAD	W	M	Sep 1841	58	Wd				KY	KY	KY	FARMER			✓	✓	✓	O F H 16
		" LUCY	DAU	W	F	Oct 1873	26	S				KY	KY	KY	MILLINERY			✓	✓	✓	
		" ADA	DAU	W	F	Mar 1878	22	S				KY	KY	KY	TEACHER-SCHOOLS			✓	✓	✓	
		" ETTA	DAU	W	F	Feb 1880	20	S				KY	KY	KY	TEACHER-SCHOOLS			✓	✓	✓	
		" HERBIE	DAU	W	F	Dec 1881	18	S				KY	KY	KY	AT SCHOOL		5	✓	✓	✓	
		" IVY	DAU	W	F	Oct 1883	16	S				KY	KY	KY	AT SCHOOL		5	✓	✓	✓	
		" LENA	DAU	W	F	Jan 1886	14	S				KY	KY	KY	AT SCHOOL		5	✓	✓	✓	
68	71	GUINN, ANDY S.	HEAD	W	M	Aug 1844	55	S				TN	TN	TN	FARMER			X	X	X	F
		" SARAH J.	STEP-MOTHER	W	F	Jul 1844	55	Wd				KY	VA	TN				✓	✓	✓	O F H
		BROWN, CORDELIA	SERVANT	W	F	May 1884	16	S				KY	KY	KY	HOUSEKEEPING			✓	✓	✓	
69	72	STRODE, WILY G.	HEAD	W	M	Aug 1872	27	M	5			KY	IND	KY	FARMER			✓	✓	✓	O M F 17
		" KIRKIE	WIFE	W	F	Apr 1877	23	M	5	2	2	KY	TN	TN				✓	✓	✓	
		" WILLIAM C.	SON	W	M	Feb 1896	4	S				KY	KY	KY							
		" NANNIE B.	DAU	W	F	Dec 1898	1	S				KY	KY	KY							
70	73	STRODE, JAMES B.	HEAD	W	M	Dec 1881	18	S				KY	IND	KY	DAY LABORER			✓	✓	✓	O H

STATE - KENTUCKY
COUNTY - MONROE
Township or other division — WEST TOMPKINSVILLE — Enumerator MALIA PAGE

Supervisor's Dist. No. _102_ Sheet No.
Enumeration Dist. No. _85_

No. of Family	No. of Dwelling	NAME	Relation	Color	Sex	DATE OF BIRTH Mon/Yr	Age at last birthday	Marital Status	Years married	Mother of how many children?	# of these children living	Place of birth [this person]	Father of this person	Mother of this person	Year of immigr.	# years in U.S.	Naturalization	OCCUPATION 10 years +	Months not employed	Attended school in months	Can read	Can write	Speak English	Owned or Rent	Owned -no mortgage	Farm or house	# of farm schedule
		STRODE, LIZZIE	Sister	W	F	Feb 1876	24	S				KY	IND	KY							✓	✓	✓				
		" TINA	Sister	W	F	Sep 1884	15	S				KY	IND	KY				AT SCHOOL		5	✓	✓	✓				
71	74	BROWN, THOMAS	HEAD	W	M	Nov 1873	26	M	7			KY	KY	KY				FARMER			✓	✓	✓	O	F	F	18
		" SARAH E.	WIFE	W	F	MAR 1875	25	M	7	2	2	KY	KY	KY							✓	✓	✓				
		" LONNIE M.	SON	W	M	AUG 1894	5	S				KY	KY	KY													
		" VOLA A.	DAU	W	F	Feb 1900	4/12	S				KY	KY	KY													
72	75	STRODE, BENJAMIN	HEAD	W	M	OCT 1832	67	M	3			KY	KY	KY				FARMER			X	X	✓	O	F	F	19
		" MARY A.	WIFE	W	F	AUG 1874	25	M	3	1	1	KY	KY	KY							✓	✓	✓				
		" ALICE	DAU	W	F	OCT 1897	2	S				KY	KY	KY													
73	76	GOAD, WILLIAM	HEAD	W	M	Feb 1868	32	M	9			TN	TN	KY				FARMER			✓	✓	✓	A	F		20
		" SUSAN J.	WIFE	W	F	Jun 1870	29	M	9	0	0	KY	KY	KY							✓	✓	✓				
		FISH, GENETTIE	ADOPTED	W	F	AUG 1886	13	S				KY	KY	KY				AT SCHOOL		2	X	X	✓				
	77	HOOD, JOHN J.	HEAD	W	M	Sep 1824	75	M	30			VA	VA	VA				FARMER			X	X	✓	O	M	F	20
		" ELIZABETH	WIFE	W	F	Jun 1841	58	M	30	1	1	KY	KY	KY							X	X	✓				
		" SOPHIA	GR-DAU	W	F	Jun 1887	12	S				KY	KY	KY				AT SCHOOL		5	✓	✓	✓				
74	78	McWHERTER, BATLEY	HEAD	W	M	Sep 1863	36	M	11			KY	TN	TN				FARMER			✓	✓		O	F	F	21
		" SARAH	WIFE	W	F	Feb 1863	37	M	11	1	1	KY	KY	KY							✓	✓	✓				
		" AMOS L.	SON	W	M	AUG 1889	10	S				KY	TN	TN				AT SCHOOL		5	✓	✓	✓				
		" JOE H.	BROTHER	W	M	Feb 1870	30	Wd				KY	TN	TN				PREACHER			✓	✓	✓				
75	79	EMBERTON, THOMAS M.	HEAD	W	M	OCT 1854	45	M	22			KY	KY	TN				CARPENTER			✓	✓	✓	O	F	F	22
		" AMANDA J.	WIFE	W	F	AUG 1861	38	M	22	8	8	MO	KY	TN							✓	✓	✓				
		" ALVY L.	SON	W	M	AUG 1880	19	S				KY	KY	MO				FARM LABORER			✓	✓	✓				
		" MILTON G.	SON	W	M	APR 1882	18	S				KY	KY	MO				AT SCHOOL		5	✓	✓	✓				
		" JOE E.	SON	W	M	JAN 1884	16	S				KY	KY	KY				AT SCHOOL		5	✓	✓	✓				
		" WILLIE D.	SON	W	M	Sep 1888	11	S				KY	KY	KY				AT SCHOOL		5	✓	✓	✓				
		" ZONA	DAU	W	F	Jun 1890	9	S				KY	KY	KY				AT SCHOOL		5	✓	✓	✓				

STATE - KENTUCKY
COUNTY - MONROE
Township or other division — WEST TOMPKINSVILLE
Enumerator — MALIA PAGE

Supervisor's Dist. No. 102 Sheet No.
Enumeration Dist. No. 85

No. of Family	No. of Dwelling	NAME	Relation	Color	Sex	Date of Birth Mon/Yr	Age at last birthday	Marital Status	# Years married	Mother of how many children?	# of these children living	Place of birth (this person)	Father of this person	Mother of this person	Year of immigr.	# years in U.S.	Naturalization	OCCUPATION 10 years +	Months not employed	Attended school in months	Can read	Can write	Speak English	Owned or Rent	Owned –no mortgage	Farm or house	# of farm schedule
		EMBERTON, EDD S.	Son	W	M	Nov 1892	7	S				KY	KY	KY				AT SCHOOL		2	✓	✓					
		" CLARENCE P.	Son	W	M	Dec 1894	5	S				KY	KY	KY							✓	✓					
		" MADGE	Dau	W	F	Jun 1896	3	S				KY	KY	KY							✓	✓					
76	80	YOKLEY, JOHN W. (JR)	Head	W	M	Apr 1874	26	M	1			KY	TN	KY				FARMER			✓	✓	✓	O	F	F	23
		" DAMARIUS	Wife	W	F	May 1877	23	M	1	1	1	KY	KY	KY							✓	✓					
		" LENORD K.	Son	W	M	Jul 1899	11/12	S				KY	KY	KY													
77	81	BRYANT, JOHN E.	Head	W	M	Oct 1870	29	M	9			KY	TN	TN				FARMER			✓	✓	✓	O	F	F	24
		" CARRIE L.	Wife	W	F	Oct 1878	21	M	9	3	2	KANSAS	KY	OHIO							✓	✓					
		" EMMA N.	Dau	W	F	Feb 1894	6	S				KY	KANS	KY													
		" HOBERT N.	Son	W	M	Jul 1896	3	S				KY	KANS	KY													
78	82	KEFAUVER, MANDY E.	Head	W	F	Mar 1851	49	DIVC.		2	1	KY	KY	KY				CAPITALIST			✓	✓	✓	O	F	H	
		" EVAN D.	Son	W	M	Oct 1879	20	M	2			KY	KY	KY				PHOTOGRAPHER			✓	✓	✓				
		" OLIVE	Dau-in-law	W	F	Dec 1880	19	M	2	0	0	KY	KY	KY							✓	✓	✓				
79	83	GOOLSBY, HENDERSON	Head	W	M	Oct 1867	32	M	6			TN	TN	TN				FARMER			✓	✓	✓	R		F	
		" MATTIE G.	Wife	W	F	Jan 1878	22	M	6	2	2	TN	KY	TN							✓	✓	✓				
		" WILLIE C.	Son	W	M	Aug 1894	5	S				KY	TN	TN													
		" JAMES S.	Son	W	M	Jul 1897	2	S				KY	TN	TN													
80	84	GOOLSBY, MARY L.	Head	W	F	Jun 1849	50	Wd				TN	TN	TN				CAPITALIST			✓	✓	✓	O	M	H	
		" SALLIE	Dau	W	F	Jan 1869	30	S				TN	TN	TN				DRESS MAKER			✓	✓	✓				
		" LON A.	Son	W	M	May 1873	27	S				KY	TN	TN							✓	✓					
		" MARY E.	Dau	W	F	Dec 1875	24	S				TN	TN	TN							✓	✓	✓				
		" NOAH L.	Son	W	M	Nov 1883	16	S				TN	TN	TN				AT SCHOOL		5	✓	✓	✓				
		LOGAN M.	Son	W	M	Dec 1888	11	S				TN	TN	TN				AT SCHOOL		5	✓	✓	✓				
		PILAND, LITTLE B.	Sis-in-law	W	F	Jul 1880	19	M	2			KY	KY	KY				? (HASITLER) LIVERY			✓	✓	✓				
		" ALSIE B.	Dau	W	F	May 1880	20	M	2	1	0	TN	TN	TN							✓	✓	✓				
81	85	COPASS, JOHN B.	Head	W	M	Dec 1855	44	M				KY	KY	KY				DAY LABORER			✓	✓	✓	R		H	

STATE - KENTUCKY
COUNTY - MONROE
Township or other division: WEST TOMPKINSVILLE
Enumerator: MALIA PAGE

Supervisor's Dist. No. 102 Sheet No.
Enumeration Dist. No. 85

No. of Family	No. of Dwelling	NAME	Relation	Color	Sex	Date of Birth Mon/Yr	Age at last birthday	Marital Status	# years married	Mother of how many children?	# of these children living	Place of birth this person	Father of this person	Mother of this person	Year of immigr.	# years in U.S.	Naturalization	Occupation	Months not employed	Attended school in months	Can read	Can write	Speak English	Owned or Rent	Owned - no mortage	Farm or house	# of farm schedule
		COPASS, DEBBIE E	WIFE	W	F	Jun 1844	55	M		8	8	KY	KY	KY							X	X	✓				
		" WILLIAM J.	SON	W	M	Mar 1878	22	S				KY	KY	KY				DAY LABORER			✓	✓	✓				
		" WILY	SON	W	M	Nov 1881	18	S				KY	KY	KY				DAY LABORER			✓	✓	✓				
		JIMMIE H.	SON	W	M	Mar 1888	12	S				KY	KY	KY				AT SCHOOL		5	✓	✓	✓				
		GRIMSLEY, LON F.	Servant	W	F	Jun 1877	22	S				KY	KY	KY				COOK	1		✓	✓	✓				
82	86	MOODY, ARANAN	HEAD	W	M	Feb 1832	68	M	39			KY	VA	KY				FARMER			✓	✓	✓	O	F	F	25
		" ELIZABETH A	WIFE	W	F	Aug 1844	55	M	39	7	3	KY	KY	KY							✓	✓					
		" SMITH E.	SON	W	M	Aug 1879	20	S				KY	KY	KY				TEACHER-SCHOOL		5	✓	✓	✓				
		" INA	DAU	W	F	Sep 1885	14	S				KY	KY	KY				AT SCHOOL		4	✓	✓	✓				
83	87	WALDEN, MARY	HEAD	W	F	Aug 1838	61	Wd		8	4	KY	KY	TN							✓	✓	✓	R		H	
		" EARL E.	GR-SON	W	M	Nov 1893	6	S				KY	KY	KY													
84	88	JOHNSON, CHARLES M.	Head	W	M	Jan 1875	25	M	2			KY	KY	KY				CARPENTER			✓	✓	✓	O		H	
		" SARAH E.	WIFE	W	F	Jun 1873	26	M	2	2	2	KY	KY	KY							✓	✓	✓				
		NELLIE M.	DAU	W	F	Apr 1898	2	S				KY	KY	KY													
85	89	PALMORE, ELIJAH L.	Head	W	M	Mar 1842	58	M	34			KY	KY	KY				FARMER			✓	✓	✓	O	F	F	26
		" ELZADA L.	Wife	W	F	Mar 1841	59	M	34	6	6	KY	KY	KY							X	X	✓				
		" TROY R.	SON	W	M	Apr 1899	21	S				KY	KY	KY				FARM LABORER			✓	✓	✓				
		" EPHRAIM B.	SON	W	M	May 1882	18	S				KY	KY	KY				AT SCHOOL		3	✓	✓	✓				
86	90	BREWINGTON, MARY E.	HEAD	W	F	Jun 1864	35	S		2	2	TN	TN	KY				WASHER-WOMAN	3		✓	✓	✓	R		H	
		" CORA	DAU	W	F	Dec 1884	15	S				KY	KY	TN							✓	✓	✓				
		" WILLIAM H.	SON	W	M	Mar 1890	10	S				KY	KY	TN				AT SCHOOL		5	✓	✓	✓				
87	91	RUNYON, GIDEON	HEAD	W	M	May 1833	67	M	22			KY	KY	KY							✓	✓	✓	O		H	
		" SUSANA	WIFE	W	F	Jul 1844	55	M	22	2	2	KY	KY	KY							✓	✓	✓				
		" MINNIE M	DAU	W	F	May 1882	18	S				KY	KY	KY													
88	92	PETERMAN, JOHN	HEAD	W	M	Mar 1866	34	M	4			KY	TN	KY				FARMER			✓	✓		O	F	F	27
		" NORMIE	WIFE	W	F	Dec 1872	27	M	4	1	1	KY	KY	KY							✓	✓					

TWELFTH CENSUS OF THE UNITED STATES 1900

STATE - KENTUCKY
COUNTY - MONROE

Township or other division: WEST TOMPKINSVILLE

Enumerator: MALIA PAGE

Supervisor's Dist. No. 102 Sheet No. ___
Enumeration Dist. No. 85 ___

Location No. of Family / No. of Dwelling	NAME	Relation	Color	Sex	DATE OF BIRTH Mon/Yr	Age at last birthday	Marital Status	# Years married	Mother of how many children?	# of these children living	Place of birth [this person]	Father of this person	Mother of this person	Year of immigr.	# years in U.S.	Naturalization	OCCUPATION 10 years +	Months not employed	Attended school in months	Can read	Can write	Speak English	Owned or Rent	Owned -no mortage	Farm or house	# of farm schedule
	PETERMAN, MAY	DAU	W	F	MAY 1898	2	S				KY	KY	KY									✓				
89 93	MAINES, PEARL H.	HEAD	W	M	AUG 1878	21	M				KY	KY	KY				FARMER			✓	✓	✓	R		F	28
"	MOLLIE	WIFE	W	F	JUL 1879	20	M				KY	KY	KY							✓	✓	✓				
94	MAINES, SAMUEL E.	HEAD	W	M	AUG 1870	29	M	4			KY	KY	KY				WAGONER	3		✓	✓	✓	R		H	
"	PALVENIA	WIFE	W	F	AUG 1872	27	M	4	1	1	KY	KY	KY								✓	✓				
"	CLEAR M.	SON	W	M	AUG 1896	3	S				KY	KY	KY													
90 95	HARRIS, GILBERT C.	HEAD	B	M	MAR 1832	68	M	4			KY	KY	KY				FARMER			X	X	✓	O		F	F	29
"	MARY J.	WIFE	B	F	MAR 1877	23	M	4			KY	KY	KY													
91 96	BROWN, JAMES	HEAD	W	M	JUN 1851	48	M	26			KY	KY	KY				FARM LABORER			✓	✓	✓	R		H	
"	PARLEE	WIFE	W	F	OCT 1852	47	M	26	10	9	TN	TN	TN								✓	✓				
"	SANFORD M.	SON	W	M	AUG 1876	23	S				KY	KY	TN				FARM LABORER			✓	✓					
"	JOSIAH	SON	W	M	OCT 1878	21	S				KY	KY	TN				FARM LABORER									
"	EMMA J.	DAU	W	F	MAR 1886	13	S				KY	KY	TN							✓	✓	✓				
"	VIRGIE B.	DAU	W	F	JUL 1888	11	S				KY	KY	TN						0	X	X	✓				
"	MONTGOMERY M	SON	W	M	JUL 1891	8	S				KY	KY	TN						5	X	X	✓				
"	HERCHEL A.	SON	W	M	JUN 1893	6	S				KY	KY	TN						0	X	X	✓				
"	JAMES O.	SON	W	M	JUN 1895	4	S				KY	KY	TN													
92 97	DENHAM, JAMES	HEAD	W	M	DEC 1877	22	M	5			KY	TN	KY				HORSE-JOCKEY			✓	✓	✓	O		F	F	30
"	BERNETTE	WIFE	W	F	MAY 1878	22	M	5			KY	KY	KY							✓	✓	✓				
93 98	GENTRY, BERTIE	HEAD	W	M	JUL 1866	33	M	12			KY	KY	KY				FARMER			✓	✓	✓	O		F	F	31
"	FANNIE	WIFE	W	F	AUG 1866	33	M	12	3	3	KY	KY	KY							✓	✓	✓				
"	CLINT	SON	W	M	JAN 1890	10	S				KY	KY	KY				AT SCHOOL		5	✓	✓	✓				
"	CLARANCE	SON	W	M	SEP 1893	6	S				KY	KY	KY				AT SCHOOL		5	✓	✓	✓				
"	CLARA	DAU	W	F	MAR 1897	3	S				KY	KY	KY													
"	GILLIE F.	MOTHER	W	F	APR 1841	59	Wd				KY	NC	KY							✓	✓	✓				
	PAGE, POLLIE	MOTHER-IN-LAW	W	F	MAY 1831	69	Wd				KY	TN	TN							X	X	✓				

STATE - KENTUCKY
COUNTY - MONROE
Township or other division WEST TOMPKINSVILLE   Enumerator MALLA PAGE

Supervisor's Dist. No. 102 Sheet No.
Enumeration Dist. No. 85

No. of Family	No. of Dwelling	NAME	Relation	Color	Sex	Date of Birth Mon/Yr	Age at last birthday	Marital Status	# Years married	Mother of how many children?	# of these children living	Place of birth (this person)	Father of this person	Mother of this person	Occupation	Months not employed	Attended school in months	Can read	Can write	Speak English	Owned or Rent	Owned -no mortage	Farm or house	# of farm schedule
(98)		PILAND, JOE F.	HIRED	W	M	May 1882	18	S				KY	KY	KY				✓	✓	✓				
		LANKFORD, JOHN	HIRED	B	M	Jan 1885	15	S				KY	KY	KY	FARM LABORER			✓	✓	✓				
94	99	HEADRICK, BARLOW	HEAD	W	M	Dec 1848	51	M	27			KY	TN	TN	DAY LABORER			X	X	✓				
		" NANNIE W.	WIFE	W	F	May 1856	44	M	27	4	4	KY	KY	KY	FARMER			✓	✓		O	M	F	32
		" EDIE E.	DAU	W	F	Mar 1879	21	S				KY	KY	KY				✓	✓					
		" FLORA G.	DAU	W	F	Feb 1892	8	S				KY	KY	KY	AT SCHOOL		5	✓	✓					
95	100	HARLAN, WILLIAM H.	HEAD	W	M	Feb 1846	54	M	21			KY	KY	KY	AT SCHOOL		3	✓	✓	✓				
		" MARY	WIFE	W	F	Jul 1860	39	M	21	8	7	KY	KY	KY	FARMER			✓	✓		O	F	F	33
		" JAMES T	SON	W	M	Jun 1882	18	S				KY	KY	KY	AT SCHOOL		5	✓	✓					
		" WILLIAM J.	SON	W	M	May 1885	15	S				KY	KY	KY	AT SCHOOL		5	✓	✓					
		" MARTHA B.	DAU	W	F	Feb 1887	13	S				KY	KY	KY	AT SCHOOL		5	✓	✓					
		" JOHN W.	SON	W	M	May 1888	12	S				KY	KY	KY	AT SCHOOL		5	✓	✓					
		" ROXIE N.	DAU	W	F	Aug 1890	10	S				KY	KY	KY	AT SCHOOL		5	✓	✓					
		" BASSIE J.	DAU	W	F	Dec 1893	7	S				KY	KY	KY										
		" GEORGE W.	SON	W	M	Aug 1896	4	S				KY	KY	KY										
96	101	EVANS, WILLIE A.	HEAD	W	M	Dec 1856	43	Wd	2	1		KY	KY	KY	—			✓	✓		R		H	
		" BASCAL N.	SON	W	M	Aug 1883	16	S				KY	KY	KY	DAY LABORER			✓	✓					
97	102	WALDEN, WILLIAM J.	HEAD	W	M	Mar 1854	46	M	24			KY	KY	KY	DOCTOR			✓	✓		O	F	F	34
		" MARY J.	WIFE	W	F	May 1860	40	M	24	6	3	KY	KY	KY				✓	✓					
		" MINNIE L.	DAU	W	F	Jul 1881	18	S				KY	KY	KY	AT SCHOOL		5	✓	✓					
		" BLISS	SON	W	M	Mar 1884	16	S				KY	KY	KY	AT SCHOOL		2	✓	✓	✓				
		" CLARA	DAU	W	F	Mar 1888	12	S				KY	KY	KY	AT SCHOOL		5	✓	✓	✓				
98	103	JONES, LUCY	HEAD	B	F	Aug 1875	25	S		5	1	KY	KY	KY	WASHER-WOMAN			X	X	✓	O	F	H	
		" HOWARD	SON	B	M	Jan 1894	6	S				KY	KY	KY										
		" CHINA	SISTER	B	F	Jun 1877	23	S				KY	KY	KY	WASH-WOMAN			X	X	✓				
		" ROSE	NIECE	B	F	Apr 1898	2	S				KY	KY	KY										

STATE - KENTUCKY
COUNTY - MONROE
Township or other division WEST TOMPKINSVILLE Enumerator MALIA PAGE

Supervisor's Dist. No. 102 Sheet No.
Enumeration Dist. No. 85

No. of Family	No. of Dwelling	NAME	Relation	Color	Sex	DATE OF BIRTH Mon/Yr	Age at last birthday	Marital Status	# Years married	Mother of how many children?	# of these children living	Place of birth [this person]	Father of this person	Mother of this person	Year of immigr.	# years in U.S.	Naturalization	OCCUPATION 10 years +	Months not employed	Attended school in months	Can read	Can write	Speak English	Owned or Rent	Owned –no mortgage	Farm or house	# of farm schedule
(103)		JONES, VASSIE	NIECE	W	F	MAR 1900	2/12	S				KY	KY	KY													
		" TONY	BROTHER	W	M	NOV 1883	16	S				KY	KY	KY				DAY LABORER			X	X	✓				
99	104	BERNETTE, ANDREW	Head	B	M	AUG 1839	60	M	15			KY	KY	KY				FIREMAN- MILL			X	X	✓	O		F	H
		" MILLIE	Wife	B	F	JUL 1859	40	M	15	8	6	TN	TN	TN				WASH-WOMAN			X	X	✓				
		" BUSTER	SON	B	M	DEC 1880	19	S				KY	KY	TN				DAY LABORER			✓	✓	✓				
		" WALTER	SON	B	M	SEP 1887	12	S				KY	KY	KY				AT SCHOOL		5	✓	✓	✓				
		" LIZZIE	DAU	B	F	NOV 1889	10	S				KY	KY	KY				AT SCHOOL		5	X	X	✓				
		" DULCENY	DAU	B	F	DEC 1892	7	S				KY	KY	TN				AT SCHOOL		5	X	X	✓				
		" EMMA	DAU	B	F	NOV 1893	6	S				KY	KY	TN													
		" WILLIE	SON	B	M	APR 1897	3	S				KY	KY	TN													
		STONE, LEANN	NIECE	B	F	DEC 1874	25	S				KY	KY	TN				WASH WOMAN			✓	✓	✓				
100	105	McMILLIN, GERTRUDE	HEAD	B	F	SEP 1812	27	M	13	1	1	KY	KY	TN				WASH WOMAN			X	X	✓	O		H	
		" ELIC	SON	B	M	AUG 1887	12	S				KY	KY	TN				DAY LABORER		5	✓	✓	✓				
101	106	FRAIM, RACHEL	Head	B	F	NOV 1839	60	S		6	5	KY	KY	TN				COOK			X	X	✓	O		H	
		" THOMAS	SON	B	M	DEC 1878	21	S				KY	KY	TN				DAY LABORER			✓	✓	✓				
		WEAVER, ESAU	Nephew	B	M	JUN 1874	25	S				KY	KY	TN				DAY LABORER			✓	✓	✓				
102	107	EVANS, JANE	Head	B	F	JAN 1840	60	Wd		3	2	KY	KY	TN				WASH-WOMAN			X	X	✓				
		" MILLIE	DAU	B	F	FEB 1870	30	S				KY	KY	TN				HOUSEKEEPER			✓	✓	✓				
		" LUCY	DAU	B	F	MAR 1875	25	S		3	3	KY	KY	TN				WASH-WOMAN			X	X	X				
		" BONNIE	G-SON	B	M	APR 1889	11	S				KY	KY	TN				AT SCHOOL		5	✓	✓	✓				
		" GEORGE	G-SON	B	M	MAY 1891	9	S				KY	KY	TN				AT SCHOOL		5	X	X	✓				
		" EDWARD	G-SON	B	M	JUN 1895	4	S				KY	KY	TN													
103	108	SHIRLEY, ANNA	Head	B	F	MAY 1850	50	Wd		2	2	KY	KY	KY				WASH-WOMAN			X	X	✓	O	M	H	
		" FRANK	SON	B	M	APR 1880	20	S				KY	KY	KY				DAY LABORER	7		✓	✓	✓				
		" MARGIE	DAU	B	F	JAN 1890	10	S				KY	KY	KY				AT SCHOOL		5	X	✓	✓				
104	109	KIRKPATRICK, FRANCES	Head	B	F	JAN 1840	60	Wd		4	3	KY	KY	KY				WASH-WOMAN	2		X	X	✓	O		F	H

STATE - KENTUCKY
COUNTY - MONROE
Township or other division — WEST TOMPKINSVILLE — Enumerator MALIA PAGE

Supervisor's Dist. No. 102 Sheet No. ___
Enumeration Dist. No. 85 ___

No. of Family	No. of Dwelling	NAME	Relation	Color	Sex	DATE OF BIRTH Mon/Yr	Age at last birthday	Marital Status	# Years married	Mother of how many children?	# of these children living	Place of birth (this person)	Father of this person	Mother of this person	Year of immigr.	# years in U.S.	Naturalization	OCCUPATION 10 years +	Months not employed	Attended school in months	Can read	Can write	Speak English	Owned or Rent	Owned-no mortgage	Farm or house	# of farm schedule
		KIRKPATRICK, BOB	SON	B	M	MAY 1870	30	S				KY	KY	KY				DAY LABORER 2			✓	✓	✓				
105	110	" JOE	HEAD	B	M	AUG 1880	20	S				KY	KY	KY				DAY LABORER			✓	✓	✓	O	F	H	
		" LIZZIE	WIFE	B	F	MAY 1879	21	S				KY	KY	KY				WASH-WOMAN			✓	✓	✓				
106	111	SIMS, RUTHA	Head	B	F	Jan 1875	25	M	1	3	3	KY	KY	KY				WASH-WOMAN			X	X	✓	O	F	H	
		" LELA	DAU	B	F	Feb 1891	8	S				KY	KY	KY				AT SCHOOL			✓	✓					
		" LENA	DAU	B	F	AUG 1896	4	S				KY	KY	KY													
		" LESLIE	SON	B	M	APR 1897	3	S				KY	KY	KY													
107	112	KIRKPATRICK, JOE	HEAD	B	M	MAY 1875	25	M	10			KY	TN	TN				DAY LABORER 6			✓	✓	✓	O	F	H	
		" LIZZIE	WIFE	B	F	MAY 1875	25	M	10	5	5	KY	TN	TN				WASH-WOMAN			X	X	✓				
		" TAYLOR	SON	B	M	APR 1891	9	S				KY	TN	TN				AT SCHOOL		5	✓	✓	✓				
		" FLOSSIE	DAU	B	F	MAY 1892	8	S				KY	TN	TN													
		" MOSS	DAU	B	F	Jun 1893	7	S				KY	KY	TN													
		" BERTIE	SON	B	M	Feb 1894	6	S				KY	TN	TN													
		" BEDFORD	SON	B	M	Jan 1896	4	S				KY	TN	TN													
108	113	WALDEN, JOHN	HEAD	B	M	JAN 1871	29	M	12			KY	KY	KY				BARBER			✓	✓	✓	O	F	H	
		" RILDA	WIFE	B	F	Feb 1873	27	M	12	2	2	KY	KY	KY							✓	✓	✓				
		" MARTHA	DAU	B	F	Sep 1894	5	S				KY	KY	KY													
		" HERBERT	SON	B	M	AUG 1890	9	S				KY	KY	KY				AT SCHOOL		5	✓	✓	✓				
109	114	SELBY, JOHN R.	HEAD	W	M	Sep 1860	39	M	4			IND	OHIO	IND				SALESMAN-MACHINERY			✓	✓	✓	O	F	F	35
		" DASIE	WIFE	W	F	Jan 1876	24	M	4	1	1	KY	TN	KY							✓	✓	✓				
		" ROY R.	SON	W	M	Feb 1898	2	S				KY	IN	KY													
110	115	MATHENA, SMITH	HEAD	W	M	MAR 1849	51	M	29			KY	KY	KY				FARMER			X	X	✓	R	F	36	
		" NALVINA L.	WIFE	W	F	MAR 1843	57	M	29	1	1	KY	TN	TN							✓	✓	✓				
		" WALTER	GR-SON	W	M	NOV 1881	18	S				KY	KY	KY				FARM LABORER			X	X	✓				
		ANDERSON, JOSIE	HIRED	W	F	Feb 1867	33	M	15			ALA	TN	TN				SERVANT			✓	✓	✓				
111	116	WOOD, DUDLEY	HEAD	W	M	DEC 1854	45	M	26			TN	NC	TN				FARMER						O	F	37	

STATE - KENTUCKY
COUNTY - MONROE
Township or other division WEST TOMPKINSVILLE   Enumerator MALIA PAGE

Supervisor's Dist. No. 102 Sheet No.
Enumeration Dist. No. 85

Location		NAME	Relation	Color	Sex	DATE OF BIRTH Mon/Yr	Age at last birthday	Marital Status	# Years married	Mother of how many children?	# of these children living	NATIVITY Place of birth	Father of this person	Mother of this person	CITIZENSHIP Year of immigr. / # years in U.S. / Naturalization	OCCUPATION 10 years +	Months not employed	EDUCATION Attended school in months	Can read	Can write	Speak English	OWNERSHIP Owned or Rent / Owned-no mortgage / Farm or house / # of farm schedule
(11a)		WOOD, MARY	WIFE	W	F	May 1857	43	M	26	13	13	TN	TN	TN					✓	✓	✓	
		" THOMAS W.	Son	W	M	Sep 1876	23	S				KY	TN	TN		FARM LABORER						
		" SAMPSON B.	Son	W	M	Mar 1880	20	S				KY	TN	TN		FARM LABORER						
		" ROXIE A.	Dau	W	F	Aug 1882	17	S				KY	TN	TN		AT SCHOOL		4	✓	✓	✓	
		" TILDA A.	Dau	W	F	Jul 1884	15	S				KY	TN	TN		AT SCHOOL		5	✓	✓		
		" LILLIE A.	Dau	W	F	Sep 1886	13	S				KY	TN	TN		AT SCHOOL		5	✓	✓	✓	
		" ETHEL	Dau	W	F	Sep 1888	11	S				KY	TN	TN		AT SCHOOL		5	✓	✓	✓	
		" JOHNATHON	Son	W	M	Sep 1890	9	S				KY	TN	TN		AT SCHOOL		5	✓	✓	✓	
		" WILLIE	Son	W	M	May 1892	7	S				KY	TN	TN		AT SCHOOL		5				
		" BENTON	Son	W	M	Jul 1894	5	S				KY	TN	TN								
		" ROBERT A.	Son	W	M	Jan 1897	3	S				KY	TN	TN								
		" WADE G.	Son	W	M	Jul 1899	10/12	S				KY	TN	TN								
112 117		HAMMER, JAMES F.	Head	W	M	Aug 1863	36	M	12			KY	KY	KY		FARMER			✓	✓		O F F 38
		" LAURA B.	Wife	W	F	Mar 1869	31	M	12	3	3	KY	TN	KY					✓	✓	✓	
		" ALBERT L.	Son	W	M	Jun 1888	11	S				KY	KY	KY		AT SCHOOL		4	✓	✓	✓	
		" BASIL F.	Son	W	M	Sep 1893	6	S				KY	KY	KY		AT SCHOOL		5	✓	✓	✓	
		" JOE L.	Son	W	M	Sep 1896	3	S				KY	KY	KY								
113 118		BECK, BETTIE	HEAD	B	F	Mar 1876	24	S		2	2					WASH-WOMAN 5			✓	✓		R H
		" JOHNIE	Son	B	M	Jul 1893	6	S														
		" FREDDIE	Son	B	M	Jul 1897	2	S														
114 119		MOORE, GEORGE C.	HEAD	W	M	Mar 1844	55	M	32							FARMER			✓	✓	✓	O F F 39
		" ELIZA	WIFE	W	F	Sep 1841	58	M	32	8	8								✓	✓	✓	
		" GEORGE C (JR)	Son	W	M	Dec 1874	25	S								FARM LABORER 2			✓	✓		
		" MARY E.	Dau	W	F	Jan 1873	27	S											✓	✓		
		" LUELLA J.	Dau	W	F	May 1877	23	S											✓	✓		
		" ROXIE B.	Dau	W	F	Apr 1878	22	S											✓	✓	✓	

STATE – KENTUCKY
COUNTY – MONROE
Township or other division — WEST TOMPKINSVILLE
Enumerator — MALIA PAGE

Supervisor's Dist. No. 102 Sheet No.
Enumeration Dist. No. 85

Location No. of Family / No. of Dwelling	NAME	Relation	Color	Sex	DATE OF BIRTH Mon/Yr	Age at last birthday	Marital Status	# Years married	Mother of how many children	# of these children living	Place of birth (this person)	Father of this person	Mother of this person	Year of immigr.	# years in U.S.	Naturalization	OCCUPATION 10 years +	Months not employed	Attended school in months	Can read	Can write	Speak English	Owned or Rent	Owned -no mortgage	Farm or house	# of farm schedule
(119)	MOORE, LORA E.	DAU	W	F	Sep 1878	21	S				KY	KY	TN							✓	✓	✓				
"	SIDNEY B.	SON	W	M	Jun 1879	20	S				KY	KY	TN				FARM LABORER			✓	✓	✓				
"	LAURA M.	DAU	W	F	Sep 1884	15	S				KY	KY	TN							✓	✓	✓				
115/20	McCOY, WILLIAM	HEAD	B	M	June 1852	47	M	7			KY	KY	KY				FARMER			X	X	✓	O		MF	40
"	MARTHA T.	WIFE	B	F	Mar 1878	22	M	7	4	4	KY	KY	KY							X	X	✓				
"	WILLIAM V.	SON	B	M	Sep 1880	19	S				KY	KY	KY				FARM LABORER		4	X	X	✓				
"	LOU E.	DAU	B	F	Feb 1882	18	S				KY	KY	KY							X	X	✓				
"	JULIA M.	DAU	B	F	Mar 1886	14	S				KY	KY	KY							X	X	✓				
"	JOSEPH F.	SON	B	M	Oct 1887	12	S				KY	KY	KY				FARM LABORER			X	X	✓				
"	FANNIE	DAU	B	F	Apr 1892	8	S				KY	KY	KY													
"	JESSIE	SON	B	M	May 1893	7	S				KY	KY	KY													
"	WESLEY	SON	B	M	Mar 1894	6	S				KY	KY	KY													
"	WERT	SON	B	M	May 1895	5	S				KY	KY	KY													
"	NORA	DAU	B	F	Nov 1897	2	S				KY	KY	KY													
116/21	CARNIHAN, PHILIP	Head	W	M	Jul 1868	31	M	7			TN	TN	TN				FARMER			✓	✓	✓	R		FF	41
"	MARY E.	Wife	W	F	Jul 1866	33	M	7			TN	TN	TN							✓	✓	✓				
117/22	CARNIHAN, GENERAL (W)	Head	W	M	Jun 1860	40	M	10			TN	TN	TN				FARMER			✓	✓	✓	R		FF	42
"	JERUSHA B.	Wife	W	F	Jul 1870	29	M	10	2	2	TN	TN	TN							✓	✓	✓				
"	NEVADA D.	DAU	W	F	May 1891	9	S				KY	TN	TN													
"	MALLIE	DAU	W	F	Dec 1894	5	S				KY	TN	TN													
"	ELIZABETH	MOTHER	W	F	Nov 1840	60	Wd		1	1	TN	TN	TN							✓	X	✓				
118/23	COPASS, ELIZABETH	HEAD	W	F	Jan 1865	35	S				KY	KY	KY				DAY LABORER			X	X	✓	R		H	
"	WILLIE	SON	W	M	Nov 1893	6	S				KY	KY	KY													
"	MARY A.	SISTER	W	F	Dec 1883	16	S				KY	KY	KY							✓	✓	✓				
119/24	HALE, JOHNIE	HEAD	W	M	Aug 1877	22	M	5			KY	KY	KY				FARMER			✓	✓	✓	O		FF	43
"	REBECKA	WIFE	W	F	Apr 1878	21	M	5	2	2	KY	KY	KY							✓	✓	✓				

STATE - KENTUCKY
COUNTY - MONROE
Township or other division WEST TOMPKINSVILLE Enumerator MALIA PAGE

Supervisor's Dist. No. 102 Sheet No.
Enumeration Dist. No. 85

Location No. of Family / No. of Dwelling	NAME	Relation	Color	Sex	DATE OF BIRTH Mon/Yr	Age at last birthday	Marital Status	# Years married	Mother of how many children?	# of these children living	Place of birth [this person]	Father of this person	Mother of this person	Year of immigr.	# years in U.S.	Naturalization	OCCUPATION 10 years +	Months not employed	Attended school in months	Can read	Can write	Speak English	Owned or Rent	Owned - no mortgage	Farm or house	# of farm schedule	
(124)	HALE, VERNA M.	Dau	W	F	Oct 1896	3	S				KY	KY	KY														
"	ANNA M.	Dau	W	F	Sep 1899	9/12	S				KY	KY	KY														
120/125	JACKSON, ELIC	Head	W	M	Apr 1870	30	M	4			KY	TN	TN				FARMER			✓	✓	✓	R		F	44	
"	SANTA M.	Wife	W	F	May 1884	16	M	4	?		KY	TN	KY							X	X	✓					
121/126	FORD, BEN W.	Head	W	M	Dec 1869	30	M	9			KY	KY	KY				FARMER			✓	✓	✓	R		F	45	
"	KIZZIE E.	Wife	W	F	Dec 1870	29	M	9	4	4	KY	KY	KY				FARMER			✓	✓	✓					
"	WESLEY	Son	W	M	Jun 1890	9	S				KY	KY	KY				AT SCHOOL		5	✓	✓	✓					
"	OSWALD	Son	W	M	Mar 1892	8	S				KY	KY	KY				AT SCHOOL		5	✓	✓	✓					
"	OLIE B.	Dau	W	F	Jul 1894	5	S				KY	KY	KY														
"	ANDIE	Son	W	M	Oct 1898	1	S				KY	KY	KY														
122/127	CONDRA, KITTIE	Head	W	F	Jun 1849	50	M	1	5	5	KY	KY	KY				WASH-WOMAN			✓	X	✓	R		F	46	
"	CORA E.	Dau	W	F	Jul 1869	30	S				KY	KY	KY				FARM LABORER			✓	✓	✓					
"	WILLIAM J.	Son	W	M	Mar 1883	17	S				KY	KY	KY				FARMER			✓	✓	✓					
"	AVERY T.	Son	W	M	Apr 1887	13	S				KY	KY	KY				FARM LABORER			✓	X	✓					
123/128	BRANUM, HENRY W.	Head	W	M	Jun 1872	27	M	4			KY	KY	KY				FARMER	4		✓	X	✓	R		F	47	
"	SALLIE	Wife	W	F	Sep 1879	20	M	4	3		KY	KY	KY							✓	✓	✓					
"	MARTIN	Son	W	M	Aug 1898	2	S				KY	KY	KY														
"	JASPER	Son	W	M	May 1899	1	S				KY	KY	KY														
124/129	BROWN, WINFIELD S.	Head	W	M	Dec 1853	46	M	8			KY	TN	KY				FARMING			✓	✓	✓	R		F	48	
"	MARY I.	Wife	W	F	Aug 1874	24	M	8	6	4	KY	KY	KY							✓	✓	✓					
"	JULIA C.	Dau	W	F	Aug 1892	7	S				KY	KY	KY							✓	✓	✓					
"	TOMMIE J.	Son	W	M	Mar 1895	5	S				KY	KY	KY														
"	ALVIA	Son	W	M	Dec 1896	4	S				KY	KY	KY														
125/130	MYATT, GEORGE W.	Head	W	M	Jan 1843	57	M	16			TN	TN	TN				FARMING			✓	✓	✓	O	M	F	49	
"	FEDDIE	Wife	W	F	Oct 1855	44	M	16	7	5	TN	TN	TN							✓	✓	✓					
"	ELDRIDGE E.	Son	W	M	Oct 1867	32	M				TN	TN	TN				FARM LABORER			✓	✓	✓					

STATE - KENTUCKY
COUNTY - MONROE
Township or other division

WEST TOMPKINSVILLE   Enumerator   MALIA PAGE

Supervisor's Dist. No. _102_ Sheet No.
Enumeration Dist. No. _85_

Location No. of Family / No. of Dwelling	NAME	Relation	Color	Sex	DATE OF BIRTH Mon/Yr	Age at last birthday	Marital Status	# Years married	Mother of how many children?	# of these children living	NATIVITY Place of birth [this person]	Father of this person	Mother of this person	CITIZENSHIP Year of immigr. / # years in U.S. / Naturalization	OCCUPATION 10 years +	Months not employed	EDUCATION Attended school in months	Can read	Can write	Speak English	OWNERSHIP Owned or Rent	Owned -no mortgage	Farm or house	# of farm schedule
(130)	MYATT, MARGARET C.	DAU	W	F	APR 1877	23	S				TN	TN	TN											
	" WILLIAM H.	SON	W	M	JUL 1881	18	S				TN	TN	TN		FARM LABORER			✓	✓					
	" LEMUEL	SON	W	M	MAR 1886	14	S				TN	TN	TN		AT SCHOOL		5	✓	✓	✓				
	" ALEXANDER J.	SON	W	M	AUG 1888	11	S				TN	TN	TN		AT SCHOOL		5	✓	✓	✓				
	" THADEUS N.	SON	W	M	MAY 1890	10	S				TN	TN	TN		AT SCHOOL		5	✓	✓					
	" PERLIE J.	DAU	W	F	JAN 1895	5	S				TN	TN	TN											
	" ISAAC HOBERT	SON	W	M	MAY 1896	4	S				TN	TN	TN											
126 131	MYATT, ALFRED	HEAD	W	M	JUN 1878	21	M	4			TN	TN	TN		FARMER			✓	✓		R	H		
	" AVO	WIFE	W	F	JAN 1880	20	M	4	1	1	TN	TN	TN					✓	✓					
	" VESTA M.	DAU	W	F	JAN 1899	1	S				TN	TN	TN											
127 132	LEFEVER, JAMES	HEAD	W	M	AUG 1853	46	M	5			TN	TN	TN		TURNER - CROCK FACTORY			✓	✓	✓	R	H		
	" NANCY J.	WIFE	W	F	MAR 1873	27	M	5	3	1	KY	TN	TN					✓	✓	✓				
	" MARTHA J.	DAU	W	F	APR 1899	1	S				KY	TN	KY											
	" AMERICA	Niece	W	F	SEP 1881	18	S				TN	TN	KY		HOUSEKEEPING			✓	✓	✓				
128 133	HALE, VIRGINIA	Head	W	F	AUG 1848	51	Wd				KY	TN	KY		FARMER			X	X	✓	O	F	50	
	BRANUM, MARTIN L.	BRO	W	M	FEB 1853	47	Wd				KY	TN	KY		BLACKSMITH 12			✓	✓	✓				
	HALE, ELIZA E.	DAU	W	F	NOV 1881	18	S				KY	TN	KY		AT SCHOOL		5	✓	✓	✓				
	" SHERMAN	SON	W	M	OCT 1868	31	M	10			KY	TN	KY		BLACKSMITH			✓	✓	✓	R	F	50	
	" LIZZIE S	D-IN-LAW	W	F	JUL 1872	27	M	10	4	4	KY	KY	KY					✓	✓					
	" MARY	GR-DAU	W	F	APR 1892	8	S				KY	KY	KY		AT SCHOOL		5	✓	✓	✓				
	" BESSIE M.	GR-DAU	W	F	AUG 1894	5	S				KY	KY	KY											
	" VIRGINIA H.	GR-DAU	W	F	JAN 1897	3	S				KY	KY	KY											
	" EDWARD W.	GR-SON	W	M	JUN 1899	11/12	S				KY	KY	KY											
129 134	RHOTON, WILLIAM	HEAD	W	M	AUG 1857	42	M	11			KY	TN	TN		MERCHANT - GEN MDSE			✓	✓	✓	O	F	51	
	" GILLIE S.	WIFE	W	F	NOV 1872	27	M	11	8	3	KY	KY	KY					✓	✓	✓				
	" CLAUD	SON	W	M	FEB 1895	5	S				KY	KY	KY											

STATE - KENTUCKY
COUNTY - MONROE
Township or other division — WEST TOMPKINSVILLE — Enumerator MALIA PAGE

Supervisor's Dist. No. 102 Sheet No.
Enumeration Dist. No. 85

No. of Family	No. of Dwelling	NAME	Relation	Color	Sex	Date of Birth Mon/Yr	Age	Marital Status	# Yrs married	Mother how many children	# living	Birthplace	Father	Mother	Occupation	Attended school (mo.)	Read	Write	Speak Eng.	Owned/Rent	Own/no mort.	Farm/house	# farm sched.
(134)		RHOTON, EDD	Son	W	M	Jan 1897	3	S				KY	KY	KY									
		" FRED	Son	W	M	Oct 1898	1	S				KY	KY	KY									
		GREENUP, ADA M.	Sis-in-law	W	F	May 1890	10	S				KY	KY	KY	At School	3½	✓	✓					
130	135	RHOTON, ELIJAH	Head	W	M	Feb 1872	28	M	8			KY	TN	TN	Farmer		✓	✓		O	F	F	52
		" EMMA J.	Wife	W	F	Feb 1873	27	M	8	3	3	KY	KY	KY			✓	✓					
		" DOC (?)	Son	W	M	Jan 1894	6	S				KY	KY	KY	At School	5	✓	✓					
		" E.K.	Son	W	M	May 1896	4	S				KY	KY	KY									
		" CLIDE G.	Son	W	M	Oct 1898	1	S				KY	KY	KY									
131	136	CORNWELL, NEWTON	Head	W	M	Jun 1874	25	M	4			TN	TN	TN	Farmer		X	X ✓		O	F	F	53
		" EVA LENA	Wife	W	F	May 1879	21	M	4	2	2	KY	KY	KY			✓	✓					
		" FLOSSIE	Dau	W	F	Apr 1892	2	S				KY	TN	TN									
		" BETHEL	Son	W	M	May 1899	1	S				KY	TN	KY									
132	137	HALE, MARK W.	Head	W	M	Jul 1872	27	M	8			KY	TN	KY	Farmer		✓	✓		O	F	F	54
		" LIZA E.	Wife	W	F	Oct 1871	28	M	8	3	3	KY	TN	KY									
		" MYRTIE M.	Dau	W	F	Sep 1892	7	S				KY	TN	KY									
		" EDDIE E.	Son	W	M	Dec 1895	4	S				KY	TN	KY									
		" PEARLIE E.	Dau	W	F	Mar 1898	2	S				KY	TN	TN									
133	138	JACKSON, SHERMAN	Head	W	M	Jul 1866	33	M				KY	TN	TN	Farmer		X	X ✓		O	F	F	55
		" MALACY J.	Wife	W	F	Jan 1876	24	M				KY	TN	TN			✓	✓					
		GILLENWATERS, MARGARET	M-in-law	W	F	Oct 1841	58	Wd				KY	TN	TN			X	X ✓					
134	139	SISCO, HERBERT	Head	W	M	Jan 1838	62	M	1			TN	TN	TN	Day Laborer		✓	✓ ✓		R		H	
		" CLARETTE B.	Wife	W	F	Feb 1861	39	M	1	4	4	TN	TN	TN			✓	✓ ✓					
		" JOHN B.	Son	W	M	Oct 1890	10	S				KY	TN	TN	At School	2	✓	✓					
		" WILLIAM L.	Son	W	M	Oct 1894	5	S				KY	TN	TN									
		" LARKIE B.	Dau	W	F	Mar 1896	4	S				KY	TN	TN									
		" ELIZABETH	Dau	W	F	Mar 1899	1	S				KY	TN	TN									

STATE - KENTUCKY
COUNTY - MONROE
Township or other division — WEST TOMPKINSVILLE Enumerator MALIA PAGE

Supervisor's Dist. No. 102 Sheet No.
Enumeration Dist. No. 85

No. of Family	No. of Dwelling	NAME	Relation	Color	Sex	DATE OF BIRTH Mon/Yr	Age at last birthday	Marital Status	# Years married	Mother of how many children?	# of these children living	Place of birth (this person)	Father of this person	Mother of this person	Year of immigr.	# years in U.S.	Naturalization	OCCUPATION 10 years +	Months not employed	Attended school in months	Can read	Can write	Speak English	Owned or Rent	Owned -no mortage	Farm or house	# of farm schedule
135	140	DAVIS, HARRIS(ON?)	HEAD	W	M	Jun 1840	59	Wd				TN	TN	TN				BUILDER-WAGONS			✓	✓		O		F	56
		" ELLEN	DAU	W	F	Jul 1868	31	S				KY	TN	KY							✓	✓					
		" LAWRENCE B.	SON	W	M	Sep 1873	26	S				KY	TN	KY				TEACHER-SCHOOLS 5			✓	✓					
		" FLORENCE	DAU	W	F	Jul 1875	24	S				KY	TN	KY							✓	✓					
		" PEARL E.	DAU	W	F	Jul 1877	22	S				KY	TN	KY							✓	✓					
		" WILLARD G.	SON	W	M	Nov 1880	19	S				KY	TN	KY				FARM LABORER			✓	✓					
136	141	DENHAM, SARAH J.	HEAD	W	F	Jan 1836	64	Wd		3	3	TN	TN	TN				FARMER			X	X	✓	O		F	57
		" LOU R.	DAU	W	F	Sep 1865	34	-				KY	KY	TN							X	X	✓				
		" MARTHA A.	DAU	W	F	Jun 1871	28	-				KY	KY	TN							✓	✓	✓				
	142	DENHAM, ZACHARIAH	HEAD	W	M	Jun 1870	20	M	4			KY	KY	TN							✓	✓	✓	R		F	57
		" LUDIE	WIFE	W	F	May 1877	23	M	4	2	1	KY	KY	KY							✓	✓	✓				
		" MAUDIE E.	DAU	W	F	Feb 1898	1	S				KY	KY	KY													
137	143	CRANFORD, GEORGE	HEAD	W	M	Aug 1869	30	M	6			KY	KY	TN				FARMER 4			✓	✓	✓	R		F	58
		" SARAH	MOTHER	W	F	Sep 1846	53	Wd		3	1	KY	TN	KY							X	X	✓				
138	144	WALLER, HARM	HEAD	W	M	Sep 1834	65	M	32			TN	TN	TN				FARMER			✓	✓	✓	O		F	59
		" CERILDA	WIFE	W	F	Feb 1848	52	M	32	7	6	KY	KY	VA							✓	✓	✓				
		" SALLIE D.	DAU	W	F	May 1880	20	S				KY	TN	KY							✓	✓	✓				
		" LOCKY W.	DAU	W	F	Mar 1884	16	S				KY	TN	KY				AT SCHOOL		5	✓	✓	✓				
		" OLLIE D.	DAU	W	F	Mar 1890	10	S				KY	TN	KY				AT SCHOOL		5	✓	✓	✓				
139	145	FORD, DAVID B.	HEAD	W	M	Dec 1860	39	M	18			KY	KY	KY				FARMER			✓	✓	✓	O		F	60
		" VIRGINIA	WIFE	W	F	Mar 1868	32	M	18	9	1	KY	KY	KY							✓	✓	✓				
		" MAY B.	DAU	W	F	May 1883	17	S				KY	KY	KY				AT SCHOOL		5	✓	✓	✓				
		" EDGAR T.	SON	W	M	Nov 1884	15	S				KY	KY	KY				AT SCHOOL		5	✓	✓	✓				
		" NONA F.	DAU	W	F	Aug 1886	13	S				KY	KY	KY				AT SCHOOL		5	✓	✓	✓				
		" ARNOLD B.	SON	W	M	Feb 1889	11	S				KY	KY	KY				AT SCHOOL		5	✓	✓	✓				
		" MARY E.	DAU	W	F	Nov 1890	9	S				KY	KY	KY				AT SCHOOL		5	✓	✓	✓				

STATE - KENTUCKY
COUNTY - MONROE
Township or other division: WEST TOMPKINSVILLE
Enumerator: MALIA PAGE
- 357 -
Supervisor's Dist. No. 102 Sheet No.
Enumeration Dist. No. 85

No. of Family	No. of Dwelling	NAME	Relation	Color	Sex	DATE OF BIRTH Mon/Yr	Age at last birthday	Marital Status	# Years married	Mother of how many children?	# of these children living	Place of birth [this person]	Father of this person	Mother of this person	Year of immigr.	# years in U.S.	Naturalization	OCCUPATION 10 years +	Months not employed	Attended school in months	Can read	Can write	Speak English	Owned or Rent	Owned - no mortage	Farm or house	# of farm schedule
	(145)	FORD, LUCY E	DAU	W	F	Jan 1895	5	S				KY	KY	KY													
		" CHESTER E.	SON	W	M	Apr 1897	3	S				KY	KY	KY													
		" - BABY -	SON	W	M	Dec 1899	5/12	S				KY	KY	KY													
140	146	HALL, ARNOLD	HEAD	W	M	Mar 1845	55	M	42	?		KY	KY	KY				FARMER			✓	✓	✓	O	FF	61	
		" ELIZABETH H.	WIFE	W	F	Dec 1847	52	M	42	?	1	1	KY	KY	KY							✓	✓	✓				
141	147	FORD, ALONZO	HEAD	W	M	Jul 1872	27	M	7			KY	KY	KY				FARMER			✓	✓	✓	R	F	62	
		" IDA M.	WIFE	W	F	Aug 1871	28	M	7	3	3	KY	KY	KY							✓	✓	✓				
		" JAMES F.	SON	W	M	May 1895	5	S				KY	KY	KY													
		" HILLARD L.	SON	W	M	Mar 1897	3	S				KY	KY	KY													
		" DORA A.	DAU	W	F	Oct 1899	9/12	S				KY	KY	KY													
142	148	PARSLEY, ANTHONY	HEAD	W	M	Mar 1850	50	M	12			KY	KY	KY				FARMER			X	X	✓	O	FF	63	
		" CORA B	WIFE	W	F	Jul 1868	31	M	12	6	6	KY	KY	KY							✓	✓	✓				
		" HARRISON	SON	W	M	Jul 1888	11	S				KY	KY	KY				AT SCHOOL		5	✓	✓	✓				
		" LE OLIE	DAU	W	F	Mar 1890	10	S				KY	KY	KY				AT SCHOOL		5	✓	✓	✓				
		" HACHELL	SON	W	M	Feb 1892	8	S				KY	KY	KY				AT SCHOOL		4	✓	✓	✓				
		" GRACIE	DAU	W	F	Apr 1894	6	S				KY	KY	KY													
		" HEADRICK	SON	W	M	Jun 1896	3	S				KY	KY	KY													
		" AUDA (?)	SON	W	M	Oct 1897	2	S				KY	KY	KY													
143	149	FORD, JOHN T.	HEAD	W	M	Feb 1852	48	M	11			TN	KY	KY				FARMER			✓	X	✓	O	FF	64	
		" MARY E	WIFE	W	F	Oct 1852	47	M	11	5	2	KY	KY	KY							✓	✓	✓				
		FORD, HARLAN	SON	W	M	Dec 1878	21	M				KY	KY	KY							✓	✓	✓				
		" MALISSA C	DAU	W	F	Mar 1881	19	M				KY	KY	KY							✓	✓	✓				
		" ALPHA	DAU	W	F	Jan 1892	6	S				KY	KY	KY				AT SCHOOL		5	✓	✓	✓				
		" FLORA D.	DAU	W	F	Sep 1897	2	S				KY	KY	KY													
144	150	SIMS, JESSE	HEAD	W	M	Oct 1860	40	M	9			KY	KY	KY				FARMER			✓	✓	✓	R	F	65	
		" SARAH A.	WIFE	W	F	Mar 1856	44	M	9	3	1	KY	KY	KY													

TWELFTH CENSUS OF THE UNITED STATES 1900

STATE - KENTUCKY
COUNTY - MONROE
Township or other division — WEST TOMPKINSVILLE — Enumerator MALIA PAGE

Supervisor's Dist. No. 102   Sheet No.
Enumeration Dist. No. 85

Location (No. of Family / No. of Dwelling)	NAME	Relation	Color	Sex	DATE OF BIRTH Mon/Yr	Age at last birthday	Marital Status	# Years married	Mother of how many children?	# of these children living	Place of birth (this person)	Father of this person	Mother of this person	Year of immigr.	# years in U.S.	Naturalization	OCCUPATION 10 years +	Months not employed	Attended school in months	Can read	Can write	Speak English	Owned or Rent	Owned -no mortage	Farm or house	# of farm schedule
(150)	FORD, THOMAS A.	Son-in-law	W	M	Jan 1887	13	S				KY	KY	KY													
	SIMS, JOSEPH	Son	W	M	May 1882	18	S				KY	KY	KY				FARM LABORER		5	✓	✓	✓				
	" BERNER I.	Son	W	M	Aug 1883	16	S				KY	KY	KY				AT SCHOOL		4	✓	✓					
	FLETCHER, ROXIE	Hired	W	F	Jan 1890	10	S				KY	KY	KY				AT SCHOOL		5	✓	✓					
145 151	KINGRY, WILLIAM	HEAD	W	M	Aug 1882	18	M				KY	KY	KY				FARMER			✓	✓	✓	R		F	66
	" MARY	WIFE	W	F	Dec 1880	19	M				KY	KY	KY							✓	✓					
146 152	PARSLEY, JOHN	HEAD	W	M	Jun 1852	47	Wd				TN	TN	TN				FARMER			✓	✓	✓	O	F	F	67
	EAGLE, BETHENIA	MOTHER	W	F	Dec 1824	75	Wd		10	6	TN	TN	TN							X	X	✓				
	PARSLEY, BERNETTE	DAU	W	F	Nov 1880	19	S				TN	TN	KY							✓	✓					
	" ELIDA C.	DAU	W	F	Feb 1884	16	S				KY	TN	KY							✓	✓					
	" ELIJAH J.	SON	W	M	Feb 1884	16	S				KY	TN	KY				MAIL CARRIER			✓	✓					
	" JAMES I.	SON	W	M	Jun 1887?	12	S				KY	TN	KY							✓	✓					
	" JOHNNIE V.	SON	W	M	Dec 1887?	12	S				KY	TN	KY							✓	✓					
147 153	STEEN, JOHN	HEAD	W	M	Mar 1825	75	M	14			KY	KY	KY				RETIRED FARMER			✓	✓	✓	O		H	
	" TABITHA J.	WIFE	W	F	Mar 1842	58	M	14			TN	TN	KY													
	FLETCHER, ROSA	Hired	W	F	May 1888	12	S				KY	KY	KY				AT SCHOOL		5	✓	✓					
148 154	DOWNING, GEORGE	Head	W	M	Mar 1866	34	M	5			KY	KY	KY				FARMER			✓	✓		O	F	F	68
	" SETTIE B.	Wife	W	F	Sep 1874	25	M	5	2	2	KY	KY	KY							✓	✓					
	" WINFRED	Son	W	M	Jan 1896	4	S				KY	KY	KY													
	" INA	Dau	W	F	Jun 1899	11/12	S				KY	KY	KY													
149 155	CROW, BEN	Head	W	M	May 1854	46	M	20			KY	TN	TN				FARMER			✓	✓		O	F	F	69
	" MARTHA E.	Wife	W	F	Nov 1859	40	M	20	6	6	KY	TN	KY							✓	✓					
	" SANFORD	Son	W	M	Mar 1882	18	S				KY	KY	KY				AT SCHOOL		5	✓	✓					
	" LOU VERDIE	Dau	W	F	Nov 1883	16	S				KY	KY	KY				AT SCHOOL		5	✓	✓	✓				
	" WASHINGTON	Son	W	M	Nov 1885	14	S				KY	KY	KY				AT SCHOOL		5	✓	✓	✓				
	" CLINTON	Son	W	M	Jul 1889	10	S				KY	KY	KY				AT SCHOOL		4½	✓	✓	✓				

STATE - KENTUCKY
COUNTY - MONROE
Township or other division WEST TOMPKINSVILLE **Enumerator** MALIA PAGE

Supervisor's Dist. No. 102 Sheet No.
Enumeration Dist. No. 85

No. of Family	No. of Dwelling	NAME	Relation	Color	Sex	DATE OF BIRTH Mon/Yr	Age at last birthday	Marital Status	# Years married	Mother of how many children?	# of these children living	Place of birth (this person)	Father of this person	Mother of this person	Year of immigr.	# years in U.S.	Naturalization	OCCUPATION 10 years +	Months not employed	Attended school in months	Can read	Can write	Speak English	Owned or Rent	Owned -no mortage	Farm or House	# of farm schedule
		CROW, JOHNIE B.	Son	W	M	Aug 1891	8	S				KY	TN	TN				AT SCHOOL		4	X	X	✓				
		" BASIL	Son	W	M	Mar 1900	3/12	S				KY	TN	KY													
150	156	TAYLOR, MARY	Head	W	F	Feb 1833	67	Wd		4	4	KY	KY	KY				FARMER			✓	✓	✓	O	F	F	70
		" JOHN W.	Son	W	M	Feb 1862	38	S				KY	KY	KY				FARM LABORER			✓	✓					
		BARKER, BESSIE	Adopted child	W	F	Jul 1891	8	S				KY	KY	KY													
151	157	TAYLOR, ARASMUS F.	Head	W	M	Jul 1873	26	M	4			KY	KY	KY				FARM LABOR			✓	✓	✓	R	F	70
		" JENNIE B.	Wife	W	F	Jan 1873	27	M	4	1	1	KY	KY	KY							✓	✓	✓			
		" OLLIE B.	Dau	W	F	Jul 1896	3	S				KY	KY	KY												
152	158	STEEN, JAMES E.	Head	W	M	Mar 1861	39	M	20			KY	KY	KY				FARMER			✓	✓	✓	R	F	71
		" DORTHA	Wife	W	F	Feb 1861	39	M	20			KY	TN	TN							✓	✓	✓			
		" BELDIE B.	Dau	W	F	Dec 1883	16	S				KY	KY	KY				AT SCHOOL		5	✓	✓	✓			
		" JAMES S.	Son	W	M	Sep 1885	14	S				TN	KY	KY				AT SCHOOL		5	✓	✓	✓			
		" WILLIAM A.	Son	W	M	Jul 1887	12	S				KY	KY	KY				AT SCHOOL		5	✓	✓	✓			
		" IDA M.	Dau	W	F	Jun 1891	8	S				KY	KY	KY				AT SCHOOL		5	X	X	✓			
		" SARAH E.	Dau	W	F	Feb 1894	6	S				KY	KY	KY				AT SCHOOL		5	X	X				
		" EDGAR	Son	W	M	Jan 1896	4	S				KY	KY	KY												
		" SYLVESTER	Son	W	M	Mar 1900	3/12	S				KY	KY	KY												
153	159	RAY, NEWTON W.	Head	W	M	May 1839	61	M	33			KY	NC	KY				FARMER			✓	✓	✓	O	F	F	72
		" VIRGINIA	Wife	W	F	Dec 1838	61	M	33	4	4	TN	KY	KY							✓	✓	✓			
		" SAMUEL B. D	Son	W	M	Apr 1872	28	S				KY	KY	TN				Prof. School Tchr.			✓	✓	✓			
		" CHARLES S.	Son	W	M	Jun 1878	21	M				KY	KY	TN				FARMER			✓	✓	✓	O	F	73
		" SUSAN A.	Dau-in-law	W	F	Mar 1883	17	M				KY	KY	KY							✓	✓	✓			
154	160	MARTIN, WILLIAM T.	Head	W	M	Dec 1840	59	M	32			KY	NC	KY				FARMER			✓	✓	✓	O	M	F	73
		" ELIZA J.	Wife	W	F	Jul 1850	49	M	32	7	7	KY	KY	KY							✓	✓	✓			
		" WILLIAM T. (JR)	Son	W	M	Aug 1881	18	S				KY	KY	KY				FARM LABORER			✓	✓	✓			
		" JIMMIE T.	Son	W	M	May 1885	15	S				KY	KY	KY				AT SCHOOL		4½	✓	✓	✓			

STATE - KENTUCKY
COUNTY - MONROE
Township or other division — WEST TOMPKINSVILLE
Enumerator — MALIA PAGE
— 360 —

Supervisor's Dist. No. _102_ Sheet No. ___
Enumeration Dist. No. _85_

Location No. of Family / No. of Dwelling	NAME	Relation	Color	Sex	DATE OF BIRTH Mon/Yr	Age at last birthday	Marital Status	# Years married	Mother of how many children?	# of these children living	Place of birth (this person)	Father of this person	Mother of this person	Year of immigr. to U.S.	# years in U.S.	Naturalization	OCCUPATION 10 years +	Months not employed	Attended school in months	Can read	Can write	Speak English	Owned or Rent	Owned-no mortage	Farm or house	# of farm schedule
(160)	MARTIN, EDD H.	Son	W	M	Nov 1887	12	S				KY	KY	KY				AT SCHOOL		5	✓	✓					
"	HARDIE	Son	W	M	Dec 1888	6	S				KY	KY	KY							✓	✓					
155/161	CREEK, YATES	Head	W	M	Dec 1878	21	M	1			KY	KY	KY				DAY LABORER	6		✓	✓	✓	R	H		
"	MARY	Wife	W	F	Dec 1878	21	M	1			KY	KY	KY							✓	✓	✓				
156/162	WILLIAMS, OSCAR W.	Head	W	M	Dec 1871	28	M	4			KY	KY	KY				COUNTY COURT CLERK			✓	✓	✓	O	F	H	
"	FRANCES L.	Wife	W	F	Nov 1871	28	M	4			KY	KY	KY							✓	✓	✓				
157/163	YOUNG, WILLIAM H.	Head	W	M	May 1856	44	M	25			TN	TN	TN				FARMING			✓	X	✓	O	F	F	74
"	SARAH S.	Wife	W	F	Oct 1858	41	M	25	7	7	TN	TN	TN							X	X	✓				
"	LORETTA B.	Dau	W	F	Oct 1887	12	S				TN	TN	TN				AT SCHOOL		5	✓	✓	✓				
"	MARTHA A.	Dau	W	F	Feb 1885	15	S				TN	TN	TN				AT SCHOOL		5	✓	✓	✓				
"	JOHN D.	Son	W	M	Mar 1888	12	S				TN	TN	TN				AT SCHOOL		5	✓	✓	✓				
"	JAMES B.	Son	W	M	Mar 1891	9	S				TN	TN	TN				AT SCHOOL		5	✓	✓	✓				
"	WILLIAM H.	Son	W	M	Mar 1895	5	S				KY	TN	TN													
158/164	CARNIHAN, JOHN H.	Head	W	M	Aug 1875	24	M	1			KY	KY	KY				FARMER			✓	✓	✓	O	F	F	75
"	MARY J.	Wife	W	F	Mar 1884	16	M	1	1	1	KY	KY	KY							✓	✓	✓				
"	MARTHA E.	Dau	W	F	Feb 1900	4/12	S				KY	KY	KY													
159/165	CROW, HARVY C.	Head	W	M	Aug 1871	28	M	4			TN	TN	KY				FARMER	6		✓	✓	✓	O	F	F	76
"	ANNA J.	Wife	W	F	Apr 1875	25	M	4	1	1	KY	TN	KY							✓	✓	✓				
"	ROXIE M.	Dau	W	F	Jan 1896	4	S				KY	TN	KY													
160/166	EMBERTON, MARTHA	Head	W	F	May 1831	69	Wd	9	5		TN	TN	TN				FARMER			✓	X	✓	O	F	F	77
"	CANZADIE A.	Dau	W	F	Feb 1864	36	S				KY	KY	TN							X	X	✓				
161/167	SYMPSON, MONICA?	Head	W	M	Oct 1875	24	M	3			KY	KY	KY				FARMER			✓	✓	✓	R	E	77	
"	MARY J.	Wife	W	F	Aug 1873	26	M	3	2	2	KY	KY	KY							✓	✓	✓				
"	ATLEY V.	Son	W	M	Oct 1897	2	S				KY	KY	KY													
"	OSCAR H.	Son	W	M	Nov 1899	7/12	S				KY	KY	KY													
162/168	EMBERTON, GEORGE	Head	W	M	Aug 1880	19	M				KY	KY	KY				FARM LABOR			✓	✓		R	H		

STATE - KENTUCKY
COUNTY - MONROE
Township or other division   WEST TOMPKINSVILLE   Enumerator MALIA PAGE

Supervisor's Dist. No. _102_ Sheet No.
Enumeration Dist. No. _85_

No. of Family	No. of Dwelling	NAME	Relation	Color	Sex	DATE OF BIRTH Mon/Yr	Age at last birthday	Marital Status	# Years married	Mother of how many children?	# of these children living	Place of birth (this person)	Father of this person	Mother of this person	Year of immigr.	# years in U.S.	Naturalization	OCCUPATION 10 years +	Months not employed	Attended school in months	Can read	Can write	Speak English	Owned or Rent	Owned -no mortgage	Farm or house	# of farm schedule	
(168)		EMBERTON, JULIA	WIFE	W	F	AUG 1879	20	M				KY	KY	KY							✓	✓	✓					
163	169	FORD, BEN T.	HEAD	W	M	AUG 1830	69	M	49			TN	KY	TN				FARMER	7		X	X	✓	O	F	F	78	
		" MARY	WIFE	W	F	APR 1846	54	M	49	13	4	KY	KY	KY							X	X	✓					
		" NEWTON P.	SON	W	M	Jul 1885	14	S				KY	KY	KY							✓	✓	✓					
164	170	COPASS, ANDY	HEAD	W	M	AUG 1873	26	M	2			KY	KY	KY				FARM LABORER			✓	✓	✓	R		H		
		" MARY (E.?)	WIFE	W	F	OCT 1881	18	M	2			KY	KY	KY							✓	✓	✓					
165	171	CROW, JOHN C.	HEAD	W	M	OCT 1847	52	M	32			TN	TN	TN				FARMER			✓	✓	✓	O	F	F	79	
		" NANCY J.	WIFE	W	F	AUG 1845	54	M	32	4	4	KY	KY	KY							✓	✓	✓					
166	172	COFFELT, ISAAC	HEAD	W	M	Sep 1844	55	M	11			TN	NC	KY				FARMER			✓	✓	✓	O	M	F	80	
		" FLORA J.	WIFE	W	F	JAN 1871	29	M	11	7	7	KY	KY	KY						7	✓	✓	✓					
		" ISAAC E.	SON	W	M	MAY 1890	10	S				KY	KY	KY				AT SCHOOL		5	✓	✓	✓					
		" VESSIE	DAU	W	F	JUN 1891	8	S				KY	KY	KY				AT SCHOOL		8								
		" BERLIE H.	DAU	W	F	MAY 1893	7	S				KY	KY	KY				AT SCHOOL		4								
		" KELLIE B.	SON	W	M	FEB 1894	6	S				KY	KY	KY														
		" LENNIE J.	SON	W	M	JAN 1895	5	S				KY	KY	KY														
Twins		" ADUS B.	DAU	W	F	APR 1898	2	S				KY	KY	KY														
		" ADUS C.	DAU	W	F	APR 1898	2	S				KY	KY	KY														
167	173	COPASS, FRANKLIN P.	HEAD	W	M	Jul 1870	29	M	7			KY	KY	KY				FARMER			✓	✓	✓	R		F	80	
		" FEXIS (?) A.	WIFE	W	F	Nov 1875	24	M	7	1	1	KY	KY	KY							✓	✓	✓					
		" OCIA A.	DAU	W	F	JAN 1894	6	S				KY	KY	KY														
168	174	NETHERTON, BARTON	HEAD	W	M	Sep 1865	34	M	15			KY	TN	TN				FARMER			✓	✓	✓	O	F	F	81	
		" MARY	WIFE	W	F	MAR 1865	35	M	15	2	2	MO	TN	TN							X	X	✓					
		" PALO	SON	W	M	JAN 1889	11	S				TN	KY	MO				AT SCHOOL		5	✓	✓	✓					
		" ELLA	DAU	W	F	Feb 1892	8	S				TN	KY	MO				AT SCHOOL		5	✓	✓	✓					
169	175	KINGRY, JOHN H.	HEAD	W	M	JAN 1844	56	M	28			KY	KY	KY				FARMER			X	X	✓	O	M	F	82	
		" SARAH T.	WIFE	W	F	Dec 1855	44	M	28	10	8	TN	TN	TN							✓	X	✓					

STATE - KENTUCKY
COUNTY - MONROE
Township or other division — WEST TOMPKINSVILLE
Enumerator MALIA PAGE

Supervisor's Dist. No. 102 Sheet No.
Enumeration Dist. No. 85

No. of Family	No. of Dwelling	NAME	Relation	Color	Sex	DATE OF BIRTH Mon/Yr	Age at last birthday	Marital Status	# Years married	Mother of how many children?	# of these children living	Place of birth [this person]	Father of this person	Mother of this person	Year of immigr.	# years in U.S.	Naturalization	OCCUPATION 10 years +	Months not employed	Attended school in months	Can read	Can write	Speak English	Owned or Rent	Owned –no mortage	Farm or house	# of farm schedule
		KINGRY, MAGGIE I.	DAU	W	F	Feb 1877	23	S				KY	KY	TN							✓	✓	✓				
		" JAKIE S.	SON	W	M	Dec 1883	16	S				KY	KY	TN				FARM LABORER			✓	✓	✓				
		" SANFORD J.	SON	W	M	Dec 1885	14	S				KY	KY	TN				AT SCHOOL		4½	✓	✓	✓				
		" JOHNIE L.	SON	W	M	Jan 1888	12	S				KY	KY	TN				AT SCHOOL		5	✓	✓	✓				
		" CLORANDY D.	DAU	W	F	Nov 1890	9	S				KY	KY	TN				AT SCHOOL		5	✓	✓					
		" PHOEBE J.	DAU	W	F	Jun 1892	7	S				KY	KY	TN				AT SCHOOL		5	✓	✓					
170	176	PARSLEY, DANIEL W.	HEAD	W	M	Jan 1849	51	M	20			TN	TN	TN				FARMER			X	X	✓	O	F	F	83
		" NANCY P.	WIFE	W	F	Jan 1858	42	M	20	11	8	KY	KY	KY							✓	✓	✓				
		" URA J.	DAU	W	F	Jan 1882	18	S				KY	TN	KY							✓	✓	✓				
		" SMITH	SON	W	M	Oct 1887	12	S				KY	TN	KY				AT SCHOOL		5	✓	✓	✓				
		" RUSSELL	SON	W	M	Dec 1889	10	S				KY	TN	KY				AT SCHOOL		5	✓	✓	✓				
		" HOMER	SON	W	M	Jan 1892	8	S				KY	KY	KY				AT SCHOOL			X	X	✓				
		" LOTTIE P.	DAU	W	F	Nov 1893	6	S				KY	KY	KY													
		" JOHNIE A.	SON	W	M	Jan 1896	4	S				KY	KY	KY													
		" DEWEY	SON	W	M	Oct 1898	1	S				KY	KY	KY													
171	177	MARSHALL, JAMES M.	HEAD	W	M	Feb 1835	65	M	35			MO	KY	KY				FARMER			✓	✓	✓	O	F	F	84
		" NANCY	WIFE	W	F	Dec 1844	55	M	35	1	1	TN	SC	KY							X	X	✓				
		" ETTA M.	DAU	W	F	Feb 1878	22	S				TN	MO	TN							X	X	✓				
172	178	MARSHALL, BEN	HEAD	W	M	Apr 1871	29	M	1			TN	MO	TN				FARMER			✓	✓	✓	R		E	84
		" MATILDA	WIFE	W	F	Mar 1877	23	M	1			TN	TN	TN													
		" WALTER B.	SON	W	M	Mar 1892	8	S				TN	TN	TN				AT SCHOOL		5	X	X	✓				
		" AMOS B.	SON	W	M	May 1896	4	S				KY	TN	TN													
173	179	DECARD, HIRAM	HEAD	W	M	Aug 1862	37	M	20			KY	KY	TN				FARMER			✓	✓	✓	O	F	F	85
		" OCTAVIA	WIFE	W	F	Feb 1864	36	M	20	4	4	KY	KY	TN							✓	✓	✓				
		" SMITH	SON	W	M	Jan 1882	18	S				KY	KY	KY				AT SCHOOL		5	✓	✓	✓				
		" NORA	DAU	W	F	Jun 1884	15	S				KY	KY	KY				AT SCHOOL		5	✓	✓	✓				

STATE - KENTUCKY
COUNTY - MONROE
Township or other division — WEST TOMPKINSVILLE — Enumerator MALIA PAGE

Supervisor's Dist. No. _102_ Sheet No.
Enumeration Dist. No. _85_

No. of Family	No. of Dwelling	NAME	Relation	Color	Sex	DATE OF BIRTH Mon/Yr	Age at last birthday	Marital Status	# Years married	Mother of how many children?	# of these children living	Place of birth (this person)	Father of this person	Mother of this person	Year of immigr.	# years in U.S.	Naturalization	OCCUPATION 10 years +	Months not employed	Attended school in months	Can read	Can write	Speak English	Owned or Rent	Owned -no mortgage	Farm or house	# of farm schedule
		DECARD, WILLIE E.	DAU	W	F	Jan 1886	14	S				KY	KY	KY				AT SCHOOL		5	✓	✓	✓				
		" CLAYTON	SON	W	M	Apr 1888	12	S				KY	KY	KY				AT SCHOOL		5	✓	✓	✓				
174	180	GULLEY, SARAH M.	HEAD	W	F	Dec 1875	24	Wd				KY	TN	KY				FARMER			✓	✓	✓	O	F	F	86
		" ADA B.	DAU	W	F	Feb 1892	8	S				TN	TN	KY				AT SCHOOL		5	✓	✓	✓				
		" HADIE F.	DAU	W	F	Jun 1894	5	S				TN	TN	KY													
		" MARY N.	DAU	W	F	Sep 1897	2	S				TN	TN	KY													
		" IVY E.	DAU	W	F	Nov 1898	1	S				KY	TN	KY													
175	181	SHIELDS, MARTHA	HEAD	W	F	Aug 1818	81	Wd				TN	TN	TN				FARMER			X	X	✓	O	F	F	87
		CHERRY, ELIZA J.	DAU	W	F	Jun 1855	44	M	7	5	1	TN	TN	TN							✓	✓	✓	R		F	87
		" SAMUEL	S-in-LAW	W	M	Feb 1873	27	M	2			TN	TN	TN				FARMER			✓	✓	✓				
		SHIELDS, GEORGE C.	GR-SON	W	M	Jan 1875	25	S				KY	TN	KY				FARM LABORER			✓	✓	✓				
		" (TRESS?) E.	GR-SON	W	M	Aug 1878	21	S				KY	TN	KY				DAY LABORER			✓	✓	✓				
		" OLIE E.	GR-SON	W	M	Feb 1889	11	S				KY	TN	KY				AT SCHOOL		4	✓	✓	✓				
		" HERMAN I.	GR-SON	W	M	Jul 1894	5	S				KY	TN	KY													
176	182	McCOIN, WADE	HEAD	W	M	Aug 1859	40	M	20			TN	TN	TN				DISTILLERY MAN			✓	✓	✓	R		H	
		" CARRIE E.	WIFE	W	F	Oct 1866	33	M	20	7	7	TN	TN	TN							✓	✓	✓				
		" WALTER B.	SON	W	M	Sep 1881	18	S				TN	TN	TN				AT SCHOOL		5	✓	✓	✓				
		" ETTA I.	DAU	W	F	Oct 1884	15	S				TN	TN	TN				AT SCHOOL		5	✓	✓	✓				
		" ALICE L.	DAU	W	F	Jun 1887	12	S				TN	TN	TN				AT SCHOOL		5	✓	✓	✓				
		" ADA M.	DAU	W	F	Apr 1891	9	S				TN	TN	TN				AT SCHOOL		5	✓	✓	✓				
		" BULAH E.	DAU	W	F	Sep 1893	6	S				TN	TN	TN				AT SCHOOL		4	X	X	✓				
		" WILLIAM J.	SON	W	M	Nov 1895	4	S				TN	TN	TN													
		" BENTON M.	SON	W	M	Jul 1898	1	S				TN	TN	TN													
177	183	RHOTON, DANIEL	HEAD	W	M	Mar 1860	40	M	19			KY	KY	TN				FARMER			✓	✓	✓	O	F	F	88
		" MARY E.	DAU	W	F	Oct 1883	17	S				KY	KY	KY													
		" HENRY C.	SON	W	M	Aug 1886	13	S				KY	KY	KY				AT SCHOOL		5							

TWELFTH CENSUS OF THE UNITED STATES 1900

STATE - KENTUCKY
COUNTY - MONROE
Township or other division: WEST TOMPKINSVILLE Enumerator MALIA PAGE

Supervisor's Dist. No. 102 Sheet No.
Enumeration Dist. No. 85

Location (No. of Family / No. of Dwelling)	NAME	Relation	Color	Sex	Date of Birth (Mon/Yr)	Age at last birthday	Marital Status	# Years married	Mother of how many children?	# of these children living	Place of birth (this person)	Father of this person	Mother of this person	Citizenship	Occupation 10 years +	Months not employed	Attended school in months	Can read	Can write	Speak English	Owned or Rent	Owned -so mortage	Farm or house	# of farm schedule
	RHOTON, CYNTHA J.	DAU	W	F	May 1890	10	S				KY	KY	KY		AT SCHOOL		5	✓	✓					
"	ADA A.	DAU	W	F	Jul 1895	4	S				KY	KY	KY											
178 184	RHOTON, ELIJAH	HEAD	W	M	Sep 1823	76	M	45			KY	KY	KY		FARMER			✓	✓	✓	O	F	F	89
"	NANCY E.	WIFE	W	F	Jul 1838	61	M	45	0	0	KY	KY	KY					✓	✓	✓				
	CURTIS, FRANK	HIRED	W	M	Dec 1886	13	S				KY	KY	KY		FARM LABOR									
179 185	HOWARD, JANIA(?)	HEAD	W	F	Jun 1865	34	Wd	3	2		KY	KY	KY		FARMER			✓	✓	✓	O	F	F	90
"	ALVY E.	SON	W	M	Mar 1894	6	S				KY	KY	KY		AT SCHOOL		4	✓	✓					
"	GLADYS E.	DAU	W	F	Mar 1895	5	S				KY	KY	KY											
180 186	FORD, LOYD J.	HEAD	W	M	Nov 1833	66	M	35			TN	TN	TN		FARMER			✓	✓	✓	O	F	F	91
"	PROVIE J.	WIFE	W	F	Jan 1844	56	M	35	12	5	TN	TN	TN					✓	✓	✓				
181 187	FORD, WILLIAM F.	HEAD	W	M	Oct 1858	41	M	16			KY	TN	TN		FARMER			✓	X	✓	O	F	F	92
"	MARY R.	WIFE	W	F	Jan 1867	33	M	16	7	6	KY	TN	TN					✓	✓	✓				
"	WORLY B.	SON	W	M	Dec 1884	15	S				KY	TN	TN		FARM LABORER			✓	✓	✓				
"	VERDIE C.	DAU	W	F	May 1886	14	S				KY	TN	TN		AT SCHOOL		2	✓	✓	✓				
"	OVAL L.	DAU	W	F	Jul 1888	11	S				KY	TN	TN		AT SCHOOL		3	✓	✓	✓				
"	ARLIE E.	SON	W	M	Feb 1891	9	S				KY	TN	TN		AT SCHOOL		5	✓		✓				
"	ALPA N.	DAU	W	F	Nov 1892	7	S				KY	TN	TN		AT SCHOOL		5							
"	ROLUS L.	SON	W	M	Jun 1894	5	S				KY	TN	TN											
182 188	CROW, GEORGE N.	HEAD	W	M	Aug 1868	31	M	5			KY	TN	TN		FARMER			✓	✓	✓	R		F	93
"	MARY J.	WIFE	W	F	Dec 1873	26	M	5	2	2	KY	KY	KY					✓	✓	✓				
"	EDDIE B.	SON	W	M	Jun 1896	4	S				KY	KY	KY											
"	EDLY H.	SON	W	M	Oct 1897	2	S				KY	KY	KY											
183 189	GATEWOOD, HARPER F.	HEAD	W	M	Apr 1848	52	M	20			KY	VA	KY		FARMER			✓	✓	✓	O	F	F	94
"	HENRIETTA	WIFE	W	F	Mar 1859	41	M	20	10	6	KY	KY	KY					✓	✓	✓				
"	MARCUS	SON	W	M	Oct 1886	13	S				KY	KY	KY		AT SCHOOL		5	✓	✓	✓				
"	SARAH J.	DAU	W	F	Sep 1888	11	S				KY	KY	KY		AT SCHOOL		5	✓	✓	✓				

STATE - KENTUCKY
COUNTY - MONROE
Township or other division: WEST TOMPKINSVILLE
Enumerator: MALIA PAGE

— 365 —

Supervisor's Dist. No. 102 Sheet No.
Enumeration Dist. No. 85

No. of Family	No. of Dwelling	NAME	Relation	Color	Sex	Date of Birth Mon/Yr	Age at last birthday	Marital Status	Years married	Mother of how many children?	# of these children living	Place of birth (this person)	Father of this person	Mother of this person	Occupation	Attended school in months	Can read	Can write	Speak English	Owned or Rent	Owned - no mortgage	Farm or house	# of farm schedule
(189)		GATEWOOD, THOMAS H.	Son	W	M	Apr 1891	9	S				KY	KY	KY	At School	5	✓	✓					
		" POLLIE T.	Dau	W	F	Jun 1892	7	S				KY	KY	KY									
		" HARRIET E.	Dau	W	F	Jan 1895	5	S				KY	KY	KY									
		" RILY J.	Son	W	M	Mar 1900	2/12	S				KY	KY	KY									
184	190	SIMPSON, BO B.	Head	W	M	Dec 1841	58	M	11			KY	KY	KY	Farmer		✓	✓	✓	O	F	F	95
		" AMANDA J.	Wife	W	F	Jan 1868	32	M	11	3	3	TN	TN	TN			✓	✓	✓				
		" SALLIE B.	Dau	W	F	Dec 1890	9	S				KY	KY	TN	At School	5	✓	✓	✓				
		" MAUDIE J.	Dau	W	F	Feb 1896	4	S				KY	KY	TN									
		" DONA B	Dau	W	F	Sept 1898	2	S				KY	KY	TN									
185	191	GOAD, JAMES H.	Head	W	M	Nov 1849	50	M	32			KY	TN	TN	Farmer		✓	✓	✓	O	F	F	96
		" MARY A	Wife	W	F	Nov 1845	54	M	32	6	6	TN	TN	TN			X	X	✓				
		" WILLIAM A.	Son	W	M	Oct 1876	23	S				KY	KY	TN	Teacher (School) 2		✓	✓	✓				
		" MARY J.	Dau	W	F	Sep 1881	18	S				KY	KY	TN									
		" LUCY E	Dau	W	F	Apr 1885	15	S				KY	KY	TN			✓	✓	✓				
186	192	HUTCHERSON, JAMES A.	Head	W	M	May 1873	27	M	10			TN	KY	KY	Farmer		X	X	✓	R		F	97
		" AMANDA J.	Wife	W	F	Feb 1875	25	M	10	4	3	KY	KY	KY			✓	✓	✓				
		" WILLIE W.	Son	W	M	Apr 1892	8	S				KY	TN	KY	At School	3							
		" HARRISON	Son	W	M	Feb 1894	6	S				KY	TN	KY									
		" WEALTHY MAY	Dau	W	F	Jun 1899	11/12	S				KY	TN	KY									
187	193	GOAD, POLLIE	Head	W	F	Apr 1830	70	Wd				KY	KY	KY			✓	✓	✓	O	F	H	
		" RACHEL	Sister	W	F	Apr 1828	72	S				KY	KY	KY			✓	✓	✓				
188	194	HOWARD, GUESS	Head	W	M	Aug 1863	36	M	13			KY	KY	KY	Farmer		X	X	✓	R		F	98
		" TILDA E.	Wife	W	F	Sep 1872	27	M	13	4	4	KY	KY	KY			X	X	✓				
		" MYRTLE	Dau	W	F	Jun 1888	11	S				KY	KY	KY			X	X					
		" ANDREW J.	Son	W	M	Mar 1891	9	S				KY	KY	KY			X	X					
		" ROXIE	Dau	W	F	Mar 1894	6	S				KY	KY	KY									

STATE - KENTUCKY
COUNTY - MONROE
Township or other division WEST TOMPKINSVILLE Enumerator MALIA PAGE

Supervisor's Dist. No. _102_ Sheet No.
Enumeration Dist. No. _85_

No. of Family	No. of Dwelling	NAME	Relation	Color	Sex	Date of Birth Mon/Yr	Age at last birthday	Marital Status	# years married	Mother of how many children	# of these children living	Place of birth (this person)	Father of this person	Mother of this person	Year of immigr.	# years in U.S.	Naturalization	Occupation 10 years +	Months not employed	Attended school in months	Can read	Can write	Speak English	Owned or Rent	Owned - no mortgage	Farm or house	# of farm schedule
		HOWARD, JESSIE F.	Son	W	M	Oct 1898	1	S				KY	KY	KY													
199	195	HALE, JOHN	Head	W	M	Nov 1851	48	M	7			KY	TN	TN				BLACKSMITH			✓	✓	✓	O	F	F	99
		" NANCY J.	Wife	W	F	Feb 1861	39	M	7	4	4	KY	KY	KY							✓	✓	✓				
		" FLORA H.	Dau	W	F	Aug 1887	12	S				KY	KY	KY							✓	✓	✓				
		" JAMES H.	Son	W	M	Sep 1893	6	S				KY	KY	KY							X	X	✓				
		" LAURA B.	Dau	W	F	Sep 1896	3	S				KY	KY	KY													
		" DEWEY	Dau	W	F	Aug 1898	1	S				KY	KY	KY													
190	196	EMBERTON, PONATAN(?)	Head	W	M	Aug 1861	38	M	12			KY	KY	KY				CARPENTER			✓	✓	✓	O		H	
		" NANCY E.	Wife	W	F	Jun 1870	29	M	12	6	5	KY	KY	KY							✓	✓	✓				
		" MARTHA F.	Dau	W	F	Apr 1891	9	S				KY	KY	KY				AT SCHOOL		3	✓	✓	✓				
		" IDA S.	Dau	W	F	Sep 1892	7	S				KY	KY	KY				AT SCHOOL		2	X	X	✓				
		" VIOLA	Dau	W	F	Jun 1895	4	S				KY	KY	KY													
		" JOHN R.	Son	W	M	Mar 1897	3	S				KY	KY	KY													
91	197	HOWARD, JAMES	Head	W	M	Mar 1832	68	Wd				VA	VA	VA							✓	✓	✓	R		H	
		WHEAT, TENNESSEE	Dau	W	F	Oct 1876	23	M	7	2	2	KY	VA	VA							X	X	✓				
		" JENNIE B.	Gr-Dau	W	F	Aug 1894	5	S				KY	KY	KY							X	X	✓				
		ALBANY, JAMES B.	Adopted Son	W	M	Oct 1888	11	S				KY	KY	KY				AT SCHOOL		5	X	X	✓				
92	198	CROW, JOHN N.	Head	W	M	Oct 1859	40	M	8			KY	KY	KY				DAY LABORER			X	X	✓	R		H	
		" RILDA	Wife	W	F	May 1880	20	M	8	3	3	KY	KY	KY							X	X	✓				
		" WALTER	Son	W	M	Apr 1893	7	S				KY	KY	KY													
		" ALICE	Dau	W	F	Jan 1896	4	S				KY	KY	KY													
		" L. K.	Son	W	M	Mar 1899	1	S				KY	KY	KY													
93	199	HOWARD, ANTHONY	Head	W	M	Aug 1866	33	M	10			KY	VA	TN				FARMER	7		X	X	✓	R		F	100
		" SIDNEY	Wife	W	F	Aug 1874	25	M	10	4	4	KY	TN	KY							✓	✓					
		" NANCY B.	Dau	W	F	Jul 1892	7	S				KY	KY	KY													
		" LONA J.	Dau	W	F	Feb 1894	6	S				KY	KY	KY													

STATE - KENTUCKY
COUNTY - MONROE
Township or other division — WEST TOMPKINSVILLE
Enumerator — MALIA PAGE
Supervisor's Dist. No. 102   Sheet No. ___
Enumeration Dist. No. 85

Fam.	Dwell.	NAME	Relation	Color	Sex	Date of Birth Mon/Yr	Age	Marital	Yrs marr.	Mother # children	# living	Birthplace	Father	Mother	Occupation	School mo.	Read	Write	Speak Eng.	Own/Rent	Own-no mortg.	Farm/house	# farm sched.
		HOWARD, EDDIE F.	Son	W	M	Oct 1896	3	S				KY	KY	KY									
		" LETHIE B.	Dau	W	F	Apr 1899	1	S				KY	KY	KY									
		" JANIA	Mother	W	F	Jun 1829	70	Wd		1	1	TN	TN	TN			X	X	✓				
194	200	ADAMS, JAMES	Head	W	M	Aug 1834	55	M	27			TN	VA	TN	FARMER		X	X	✓	O	F	F	101
		" MARY L.	Wife	W	F	Jun 1854	45	M	27	1	1	KY	TN	KY			✓	✓					
		" JAMES T.	Son	W	M	Aug 1877	22	S				KY	TN	KY	FARMER		✓	✓	✓	R		F	101
195	201	COULTER, MARIAN	Head	W	M	May 1875	25	M	2			KY	KY	KY	DAY LABORER		X	X	✓	R		F	102
		" NORA	Wife	W	F	Dec 1883	16	M	2	1	0	KY	KY	KY			✓	✓	✓				
196	202	CROW, NELSON	Head	W	M	Nov 1834	65	Wd				TN	VA	TN	FARMER		X	X	✓	O	F	F	103
		JOHN N.	Son	W	M	Jan 1875	25	S				KY	TN	TN	FARMER		✓	✓	✓				
		ENGLAND, HENCIE	Gr-son	W	M	Sep 1887	12	S				KY	KY	KY	AT SCHOOL	5	✓	✓	✓				
197	203	FORD, JAMES T.	Head	W	M	Jan 1870	30	S				KY	KY	KY	FARMER		✓	✓	✓	O	F	F	104
		" LUTHER	Brother	W	M	May 1878	22	S				KY	KY	KY	FARM LABORER		✓	✓	✓				
198	204	" CLAY	Head	W	M	Jan 1872	28	S				KY	KY	KY	FARMER		✓	✓	✓	O	F	F	104
199	205	FORD, JAMES A.	Head	W	M	Sep 1844	55	M	30			TN	TN	TN	FARMER		✓	✓	✓	O	F	F	105
		" KIZZIE A.	Wife	W	F	May 1847	53	M	30	7	7	KY	TN	KY			X	X	✓				
		" THOMAS R.	Son	W	M	Sep 1876	23	S				KY	TN	KY	FARM LABORER		✓	✓	✓				
		" NANCY E.	Dau	W	F	Nov 1882	17	S				KY	TN	KY			✓	✓					
		BRUCE R.	Son	W	M	Aug 1883	16	S				KY	TN	KY	FARM LABORER		✓	✓					
		SAMPSON	Son	W	M	Feb 1887	13	S				KY	TN	KY	AT SCHOOL	5	✓	✓	✓				
		OSCAR W.	Son	W	M	Jun 1889	10	S				KY	TN	KY	AT SCHOOL	5	✓	✓	✓				
		HAMMER, WILLIAM A.	Fath-in-law	W	M	Dec 1812	87	Wd				TN	VA	KY			X	X	✓				
200	206	ADAMS, CELIA	Head	W	F	Aug 1841	58	Wd				TN	KY	TN			✓	X	✓	O	M	H	
		" JERRY T.	Nephew	W	M	Mar 1872	28	S				KY	KY	TN	FARM LABORER		✓	✓	✓				
		BOTTS, DOCIA A.	Hired	W	F	Dec 1882	17	S				KY	KY	KY	HOUSEKEEPER		X	X	✓				
201	207	CURTIS, JOHN	Head	W	M	Jan 1861	39	M	17			KY	TN	KY	FARMER		✓	✓	✓	O	F	F	106

STATE - KENTUCKY
COUNTY - MONROE
Township or other division: WEST TOMPKINSVILLE Enumerator MALIA PAGE

Supervisor's Dist. No. 102 Sheet No.
Enumeration Dist. No. 85

Location (No. of Family / No. of Dwelling)	NAME	Relation	Color	Sex	DATE OF BIRTH Mon/Yr	Age at last birthday	Marital Status	# Years married	Mother of how many children?	# of these children living	Place of birth (this person)	Father of this person	Mother of this person	OCCUPATION 10 years +	Attended school in months	Can read	Can write	Speak English	Owned or Rent	Owned - no mortgage	Farm or house	# of farm schedule
(207)	CURTIS, NANCY J.	WIFE	W	F	OCT 1861	38	M	17	3	2	KY	KY	KY			✓	✓					
"	DUNCAN	SON	W	M	AUG 1887	12	S				KY	KY	KY	AT SCHOOL	5	✓	✓					
"	VESTER	SON	W	M	AUG 1887	12	S				KY	KY	KY	AT SCHOOL	5	✓	✓					
202 208	CURTIS, JARRETTE	HEAD	W	M	Sep 1872	27	M	4			KY	KY	KY	FARMER		✓	✓		O	F	F	107
"	ISABELL	WIFE	W	F	Nov 1877	22	M	4	2	2	KY	KY	KY			✓	✓					
"	MARINDA	DAU	W	F	Jan 1896	4	S				KY	KY	KY									
"	JOHN	SON	W	M	Feb 1899	1	S				KY	KY	KY									
203 209	CURTIS, LON A.	HEAD	W	M	MAR 1882	18	M				KY	KY	KY	FARMER		✓	✓		R		F	108
"	ISABELL	WIFE	W	F	Jan 1882	18	M				KY	KY	KY			✓	✓					
204 210	CURTIS, HARRY P.	HEAD	W	M	Nov 1873	26	M	2			KY	KY	KY	FARMER		✓	✓	✓	R		F	109
"	MINCIE(?)	WIFE	W	F	Jan 1874	26	M	2	1	1	KY	KY	KY			✓	✓					
"	FLOSSIE	DAU	W	F	Jan 1899	1	S				KY	KY	KY									
205 211	EVANS, JAMES B.	HEAD	W	M	Jul 1868	31	M	5			KY	KY	KY	FARMER		✓	✓	✓	R		F	110
"	ALICE C.	WIFE	W	F	Dec 1878	21	M	5	2	2	KY	KY	KY			✓	✓					
"	JULIUS P.	SON	W	M	Jul 1896	3	S				KY	KY	KY									
"	JENNIE E.	DAU	W	F	Jul 1897	2	S				KY	KY	KY									
206 212	KEYS, DOCTOR G.	HEAD	W	M	MAR 1854	46	M	12			KY	KY	KY	FARMER		✓	X	✓	O	F	F	111
"	MARY E.	WIFE	W	F	AUG 1855	44	M	12	7	7	KY	KY	KY			✓	✓					
"	BASCAL	SON	W	M	MAR 1889	11	S				KY	KY	KY	AT SCHOOL	8	✓	✓	✓				
"	CHARLIE	SON	W	M	MAY 1890	10	S				KY	KY	KY	AT SCHOOL	8	✓	✓	✓				
"	OLIE M	DAU	W	F	Sep 1891	8	S				KY	KY	KY									
"	RAYMOND	SON	W	M	Feb 1893	7	S				KY	KY	KY									
"	HARRY	SON	W	M	Jun 1894	5	S				KY	KY	KY									
"	HOBERT	SON	W	M	Jun 1895	4	S				KY	KY	KY									
"	WILLIE	SON	W	M	MAY 1899	1	S				KY	KY	KY									
"	ELIZABETH	MOTHER	W	F	OCT 1819	80	Wd		1	1	KY	KY	KY			X	X	✓				

STATE - KENTUCKY
COUNTY - MONROE
Township or other division — WEST TOMPKINSVILLE — Enumerator MALIA PAGE

Supervisor's Dist. No. 102   Sheet No.
Enumeration Dist. No. 85

No. of Family	No. of Dwelling	NAME	Relation	Color	Sex	DATE OF BIRTH Mon/Yr	Age at last birthday	Marital Status	# Years married	Mother of how many children?	# of these children living	Place of birth (this person)	Father of this person	Mother of this person	Year of immigr.	# years in U.S.	Naturalization	OCCUPATION 10 years +	Months not employed	Attended school in months	Can read	Can write	Speak English	Owned or Rent	Owned-no mortage	Farm or house	# of Farm schedule
207	213	KEYS, JAMES F.	HEAD	W	M	May 1858	42	M	19			KY	KY	KY				FARMER			✓	✓	✓	R		F	112
		" EMMA	WIFE	W	F	Nov 1860	39	M	19	3	3	KY	KY	KY							✓	X	✓				
		" WALTER	SON	W	M	Nov 1881	18	S				KY	KY	KY							X	X	✓				
		" HASKELL	SON	W	M	Oct 1883	16	S				KY	KY	KY				FARM LABORER			✓	✓	✓				
		" FRED	SON	W	M	Apr 1886	14	S				KY	KY	KY				FARM LABORER			✓	✓	✓				
208	214	RUSSELL, JOSIAH	HEAD	W	M	May 1861	39	M	3			KY	KY	KY				FARM LABORER			✓	✓	✓	R		H	
		" MISSOURI A.	WIFE	W	F	Aug 1877	22	M	3			KY	KY	KY							✓	✓	✓				
		" MANERVY S.	DAU	W	F	Apr 1884	16	S				KY	KY	KY							X	X	✓				
		" LOUVENICE	DAU	W	F	Jul 1887	12	S				KY	KY	KY							✓	✓	✓				
209	215	JACKSON, JOSEPH	HEAD	W	M	Mar 1831	69	M	23			TN	TN	TN							X	X	✓	O		H	
		" IBBIE E	WIFE	W	F	Apr 1845	45	M	23	4	4	KY	KY	KY							X	X	✓				
		HALE, NORAH	DAU	W	F	Nov 1881	18	M	2	1	1	KY	TN	KY							O	✓	✓				
		JACKSON, JOHN T.	SON	W	M	Apr 1885	15	S				KY	TN	KY				AT SCHOOL		5	X	X	✓				
		HALE, JOE	GR SON	W	M	Dec 1899	6/12	S				KY	KY	KY													
210	216	HAMMER, ALONZO	HEAD	W	M	Nov 1850	49	M	6			KY	TN	KY				FARMER			✓	✓	✓	O	FF		113
		" ARTIE W.	WIFE	W	F	Oct 1869	30	M	6	2	2	KY	KY	KY							X	X	✓				
		" WILLIAM	SON	W	M	Nov 1877	22	S				KY	KY	KY				DAY LABORER	7		✓	✓	✓				
		" NANCY E.	DAU	W	F	Mar 1882	18	S				KY	KY	KY							✓	✓	✓				
		" MONTEVILLE	SON	W	M	Dec 1886	14	S				KY	KY	KY				AT SCHOOL			✓	✓	✓				
		" IBBIE E.	DAU	W	F	Oct 1895	4	S				KY	KY	KY													
		" BOOSY M.	DAU	W	F	Apr 1899	1	S				KY	KY	KY													
211	217	JACKSON, WILLIAM T.	HEAD	W	M	Nov 1877	22	M	1			KY	TN	KY				FARMER			✓	✓	✓	R		F	113
		" LAURA	WIFE	W	F	Jun 1880	19	M	1	1	1	KY	KY	KY				NURSE			✓	✓	✓				
		" CLINTON	SON	W	M	Dec 1899	4/12	S				KY	KY	KY													
212	218	GOAD, JAMES	HEAD	W	M	Apr 1825	75	M	12			TN	OH	PA				FARMER			✓	✓	✓	O	FF		114
		" SARAH J	WIFE	W	F	Dec 1859	40		12	5	5	KY	KY	KY							✓	✓	✓				

STATE - KENTUCKY
COUNTY - MONROE
Township or other division   WEST TOMPKINSVILLE   Enumerator MALIA PAGE

Supervisor's Dist. No. _102_ Sheet No.
Enumeration Dist. No. _85_

Location (No. of Family / No. of Dwelling)	NAME	Relation	Color	Sex	DATE OF BIRTH (Mon/Yr)	Age at last birthday	Marital Status	# Years married	Mother of how many children?	# of these children living	Place of birth (this person)	Father of this person	Mother of this person	Year of immigr. / # years in U.S. / Naturalization	OCCUPATION 10 years +	Months not employed	Attended school in months	Can read	Can write	Speak English	Owned or Rent	Owned -no mortgage	Farm or house	# of farm schedule
(216)	GOAD, NOLIA M.	DAU	W	F	Feb 1888	12	S				KY	TN	KY		AT SCHOOL		5	✓	X	✓				
"	LOLA GREY	DAU	W	F	Jun 1889	10	S				KY	TN	KY		AT SCHOOL		5	✓	X	✓				
"	TENNESSEE R.	DAU	W	F	Mar 1891	9	S				KY	TN	KY											
"	MILLIE D.	DAU	W	F	Jul 1893	6	S				KY	TN	KY											
"	NELLIE G.	DAU	W	F	Aug 1899	9/12	S				KY	TN	KY											
213 219	WOOD, RAWDOW	HEAD	W	M	May 1843	57	M	18			KY	KY	KY		FARMER			✓	✓	✓	O	F	F	115
"	LIZZIE J.	WIFE	W	F	Apr 1859	41	M	18	7	5	TN	TN	NC					✓	✓	✓				
"	ADA B.	DAU	W	F	Mar 1885	15	S				KY	KY	TN		AT SCHOOL		3	✓	✓	✓				
"	GEDIE A.	DAU	W	F	Jan 1887	13	S				KY	KY	TN		AT SCHOOL		5	✓	✓	✓				
"	VIRGLE	SON	W	M	Jan 1891	9	S				KY	KY	TN											
"	MAGGIE J.	DAU	W	F	Apr 1893	7	S				KY	KY	TN											
"	PEARLIE M.	DAU	W	F	Feb 1896	4	S				KY	KY	TN											
	WILLIAMS, WILLIAM F.	FATHER IN-LAW	W	M	Oct 1824	75	Wd				TN	TN	TN					✓	✓	✓				
214 220	HALE, JOHN W.	HEAD	W	M	Mar 1868	32	M	4			KY	TN	KY		FARMER			✓	✓	✓	R	F	116	
"	ELLEN	WIFE	W	F	Dec 1874	25	M	4			KY	KY	KY					✓	✓	✓				
215 221	HALE, JOHN	HEAD	W	M	Jun 1844	55	M	35			TN	TN	TN		FARMER			✓	✓	✓	O	F	F	117
"	ELIZABETH H.	WIFE	W	F	May 1842	58	M	35	8	7	KY	KY	KY					✓	✓	✓				
"	SMITH W.	SON	W	M	Jun 1876	23	M	2			KY	KY	TN		FARM LABORER			✓	✓	✓				
"	WESLEY M.	SON	W	M	Jul 1879	20	S				KY	KY	TN		FARM LABORER			✓	✓	✓				
"	THOMAS D.	SON	W	M	Jan 1883	17	S				KY	KY	TN					✓	✓	✓				
216 222	COULTER, JOHN	HEAD	W	M	Jul 1878	21	M	3			KY	KY	KY		FARMER			✓	✓	✓	R	F	118	
"	LUCY J.	WIFE	W	F	Sep 1874	25	M	3	1	1	KY	TN	KY					✓	✓					
	BEDFORD	SON	W	M	Mar 1898	2	S				KY	KY	KY											
217 223	CROW, GRANT	HEAD	W	M	Jun 1840	59	M	40			TN	VA	TN		FARMER			✓	✓	✓	O	F	F	119
"	RHODA	WIFE	W	F	Feb 1838	62	M	40	8	6	TN	TN	TN					✓	✓	✓				
"	SALLIE L.	DAU	W	F	Jun 1872	27	S				KY	TN	TN					✓	✓	✓				

STATE - KENTUCKY
COUNTY - MONROE
Township or other division WEST TOMPKINSVILLE Enumerator MALIA PAGE,

Supervisor's Dist. No. 102 Sheet No.
Enumeration Dist. No. 85

No. of Family	No. of Dwelling	NAME	Relation	Color	Sex	DATE OF BIRTH Mon/Yr	Age at last birthday	Marital Status	# Years married	Mother of how many children?	# of these children living	Place of birth (this person)	Father of this person	Mother of this person	Year of immigr.	# years in U.S.	Naturalization	OCCUPATION 10 years +	Months not employed	Attended school in months	Can read	Can write	Speak English	Owned or Rent	Owned -no mortage	Farm or house	# of farm schedule
		CROW, MINNIE B.	DAU	W	F	Sep 1879	20	S				KY	TN	TN							✓	✓	✓				
218	224	BOTS, JANE	HEAD	W	F	Jan 1851	49	M	20	5	5	KY	KY	KY							✓	✓	✓	O	H		
		" SAMUEL J.	SON	W	M	APR 1882	18	S				KY	KY	KY				DAY LABORER			✓	✓	✓				
		" LAURA M.	DAU	W	F	Feb 1886	14	S				KY	KY	KY				A.T. SCHOOL		5	✓	✓	✓				
		" HOMER	SON	W	M	JAN 1890	10	S				KY	KY	KY				A.T. SCHOOL		5	✓	✓	✓				
219	225	PROFFITT, AMANDA J.	HEAD	W	F	Jul 1843	56	Wd		3	3	TN	TN	TN				FARMER			X	X	✓	O	F	F	120
		" MONTEVILLE V.	SON	W	M	Jun 1876	23	S				KY	KY	TN				FARMER			✓	✓	✓	R	F		120
		" DONA	DAU	W	F	Jul 1884	15	S				KY	KY	TN							✓	✓	✓				
220	226	PROFFITT, ANDREW	HEAD	W	M	Jan 1866	34	M	4			KY	KY	TN				FARMER			✓	✓	✓	R	F		120
		" NOVA B	WIFE	W	F	May 1878	22	M	4	2	2	KY	KY	KY							✓		✓				
		" DONA B.	DAU	W	F	Jun 1897	2	S				KY	KY	KY													
		" GEORGE T.	SON	W	M	Jun 1898	1	S				KY	KY	KY													
221	227	CAPSHAW, DANIEL	HEAD	W	M	May 1852	48	M	25			TN	TN	KY				FARMER			✓	✓	✓	O	F	F	121
		" MARY V.	WIFE	W	F	May 1862	38	M	25	6	6	KY	KY	KY							✓	✓	✓				
		" SALLIE J.	DAU	W	F	Jul 1878	21	S				KY	TN	KY							✓	✓	✓				
		" MINNIE E.	DAU	W	F	DEC 1883	16	S				KY	TN	KY				AT SCHOOL		5	✓	✓	✓				
		" LUCY E.	DAU	W	F	Nov 1886	13	S				KY	TN	KY				AT SCHOOL		5	✓	✓	✓				
		" SAMMIE F	SON	W	M	May 1890	10	S				KY	TN	KY				AT SCHOOL		5	✓	✓	✓				
		" MOTA(?) MAY	DAU	W	F	DEC 1891	8	S				KY	TN	KY							✓	✓	✓	R	F		122
222	228	DENHAM, WILLIAM J.	HEAD	W	M	AUG 1878	21	M	2			KY	KY	KY				FARMER			✓	✓	✓	R	F		122
		" JENNIE B.	WIFE	W	F	JAN 1882	18	M	2	1	1	KY	KY	KY				NURSE			✓	✓	✓				
		" IRA D.	SON	W	M	AUG 1898	1	S				KY	KY	KY													
223	229	HALL, SAM T.	HEAD	W	M	MAY 1858	42	M	13			KY	TN	KY				FARMER			✓	✓	✓	O	F	F	123
		" SUTTIE A.	WIFE	W	F	DEC 1868	31	M	13	2	2	KY	TN	KY				NURSE			✓	✓	✓				
		" FRANKLIN T.	SON	W	M	Feb 1888	12	S				KY	KY	KY				AT SCHOOL		5	✓	✓	✓				
		" MARY W.	DAU	W	F	Feb 1898	2	S				KY	KY	KY													

TWELFTH CENSUS OF THE UNITED STATES 1900

STATE - KENTUCKY
COUNTY - MONROE
Township or other division — WEST TOMPKINSVILLE

— 372 —

Enumerator — MALIA PAGE

Supervisor's Dist. No. 102   Sheet No.
Enumeration Dist. No. 85

No. of Family	No. of Dwelling	NAME	Relation	Color	Sex	DATE OF BIRTH Mon/Yr	Age at last birthday	Marital Status	# Years married	Mother of how many children?	# of these children living	Place of birth [this person]	Father of this person	Mother of this person	Year of immigr.	# years in U.S.	Naturalization	OCCUPATION 10 years +	Months not employed	Attended school in months	Can read	Can write	Speak English	Owned or Rent	Owned -no mortgage	Farm or house	# of farm schedule
229	230	TURNER, FELIX	HEAD	W	M	Jan 1854	46	M	26			KY	VA	VA				KEEPER OF THE ALMS HOUSE			✓	✓		R		F	124
		" MALISSA B.	WIFE	W	F	Apr 1857	43	M	26	4	4	KY	KY	KY							✓	✓	✓				
		" BESSIE M.	DAU	W	F	Oct 1897	2	S				KY	KY	KY							✓	✓	✓				
		BOTTS, JOAN	Hired Girl	W	F	Nov 1877	22	S				KY	KY	KY				COOK		X	X	X	✓				
		WOOD, GEORGIAN	Hired Girl	W	F	Oct 1888	11	S				KY	KY	KY						X	X	X	✓				
		RECORD, SALLIE	PAUPER	W	F	Dec 1827	72	Wd		10		KY	KY	KY						X	X	X	X				
		TURNER, STEVE	PAUPER	W	M	Nov 1839	60	Wd				KY	KY	KY						X	X	X	X				
		WILSON, MARGARET	PAUPER	W	F	Oct 1854	45	M	3	2	1	KY	KY	KY						X	X	X	X				
		COULTER, MALISSIE	PAUPER	W	F	Sep 1864	35	S		1	1	KY	KY	KY						✓	X	X	✓				
		KEYS, BETHANY	PAUPER	W	F	May 1864	36	M	13	5	3	KY	VA	VA						X	X	X	✓				
		SPROWLS, MARTHA	PAUPER	W	F	Oct 1864	35	S		3	3	KY	KY	KY						X	X	X	✓				
		" SARAH	PAUPER	W	F	Aug 1852	47	S				KY	KY	KY						X	X	X	✓				
		SWAFORD, SAMUEL	PAUPER	W	M	Dec 1855	44	M	2			KY	KY	KY						X	X	X	✓				
		" NANCY	PAUPER	W	F	Nov 1856	43	M	2	3	1	KY	TX	KY						✓	X	X	✓				
		PEDIGO, RICHARD	PAUPER	W	M	May 1890	10	S				KY	TN	KY						✓	X	X	✓				
		KEY, JAMES H.	PAUPER	W	M	Mar 1896	4	S				KY	TN	KY													
		FORD, GRANT	PAUPER	W	M	Nov 1864	35	M	2			KY	KY	KY						X	X	✓	✓				
		" NANCY M.	PAUPER	W	F	Dec 1859	40	M	2	2	0	TN	VA	TN						X	X	✓					
		SPOWLS, LEE	PAUPER	W	M	Jan 1891	9	S				KY	KY	KY													
		" WALTER	PAUPER	W	M	Oct 1893	6	S				KY	KY	KY													
		WILSON, JOSEPHINE	PAUPER	W	F	Dec 1897	2	S				KY	TN	KY													
		BARTLEY, JAKE	PAUPER	W	M	May 1882	18	S				KY	KY	KY						X	X	✓	✓				
		FORD, MARY E.	PAUPER	W	F	Oct 1854	45	S				TN	TN	KY						✓	X	✓	✓				
		FORD, NANCY J.	PAUPER	W	F	Oct 1859	40	M	3	1	1	KY	TN	KY						✓	✓	✓	✓				
		" ADAVILLE E.	PAUPER	W	F	Jun 1890	9	S				KY	KY	KY						X	X	✓	✓				
		COULTER, CELINA	PAUPER	W	F	May 1836	64	Wd		1	1	KY	VA	KY						X	X	✓	✓				

STATE - KENTUCKY
COUNTY - MONROE
Township or other division: WEST TOMPKINSVILLE
Enumerator: MALIA PAGE

Supervisor's Dist. No. 102 Sheet No.
Enumeration Dist. No. 85

Location No. of Family	No. of Dwelling	NAME	Relation	Color	Sex	DATE OF BIRTH Mon/Yr	Age at last birthday	Marital Status	# Years married	Mother of how many children?	# of these children living	Place of birth (this person)	Father of this person	Mother of this person	Year of immigr.	# years in U.S.	Naturalization	OCCUPATION 10 years +	Months not employed	Attended school in months	Can read	Can write	Speak English	Owned or Rent	Owned - no mortgage	Farm or house	# of farm schedule
		WOODS, WILLIAM	PAUPER	W	M	DEC 1828	71	M	30			KY	KY	KY							X	X	✓				
		" SARAH	PAUPER	W	F	Feb 1851	49	M	30	7	5	TN	KY	TN							X	X	✓				
		" OLIE	PAUPER	W	F	AUG 1892	7	S				KY	KY	TN									✓				
205	231	JENKINS, HENRY W.	HEAD	W	M	Sep 1861	38	M	22			KY	KY	KY				FARMER			X	X	✓	R		F	125
		" NANCY M.	WIFE	W	F	Apr 1861	39	M	22	7	7	KY	TN	TN							✓	X	✓				
		" BERTIE P.	SON	W	M	Nov 1881	18	S				KY	KY	KY				FARM LABORER			✓	✓	✓				
		" BETTIE J.	DAU	W	F	Feb 1884	16	S				KY	KY	KY							✓	✓	✓				
		" BERTHA A.	DAU	W	F	Oct 1896	13	S				KY	KY	KY				AT SCHOOL		5	✓	X	✓				
		" IDA B.	DAU	W	F	Dec 1888	11	S				KY	KY	KY				AT SCHOOL		5	✓	X	✓				
		" WERTIE C.	SON	W	M	Jun 1892	7	S				KY	KY	KY				AT SCHOOL		5	X	X	✓				
		" JENNIE C.	DAU	W	F	APR 1895	5	S				KY	KY	KY													
		" ICEPHENIA	DAU	W	F	MAY 1898	2	S				KY	KY	KY													
226	232	ADAMS, THOMAS	HEAD	W	M	Jul 1842	57	M	33			KY	VA	TN				FARMER			X	X	✓	O		F	126
		" ELVINA	WIFE	W	F	May 1847	53	M	33	3	3	KY	KY	KY							X	X	✓				
		" LILLIE M.	DAU	W	F	May 1877	23	S				KY	KY	KY							✓	✓	✓				
		" JOHN WESLEY	SON	W	M	Aug 1875	24	M				KY	KY	KY							✓	✓	✓	R		F	126
		" PHOEBE	DAU-IN-LAW	W	F	MAY 1886	14	M				KY	KY	KY							✓	✓	✓				
227	233	FORD, THOMAS	HEAD	W	M	Sep 1846	53	Wd				TN	TN	NC				FARMER	5		✓	✓	✓	R		F	127
228	234	ADAMS, JAMES R.	HEAD	W	M	Feb 1852	48	M	19			KY	TN	KY				FARMER			X	X	✓	O		F	128
		" NANCY	WIFE	W	F	Oct 1855	44	M	19	2	2	KY	KY	KY							X	X	✓				
		" JOSEPH	SON	W	M	Jan —	16	S				KY	KY	KY				AT SCHOOL		5	✓	✓	✓				
		" EVERT H.	SON	W	M	Jan —	14	S				KY	KY	KY				AT SCHOOL		5	X	X	✓				
229	235	ADAMS, JOHN	HEAD	W	M	MAY —	65	UNK?				KY	KY	KY							X	X	✓	O		H	
230	236	EVANS, THOMAS B.	HEAD	W	M	Oct 1832	67	M	31			KY	KY	KY				FARMER			✓	✓	✓	O		F	129
		" MARY C.	WIFE	W	F	APR 1848	52	M	31	3	3	KY	KY	TN							✓	✓	✓				
		" WILLIE F.	SON	W	M	Jun 1883	16	S				KY	KY	KY				AT SCHOOL		8	✓	✓	✓				

TWELFTH CENSUS OF THE UNITED STATES 1900

STATE - KENTUCKY
COUNTY - MONROE
Township or other division: WEST TOMPKINSVILLE

Enumerator: MALIA PAGE

-374-

Supervisor's Dist. No. _102_ Sheet No. _____
Enumeration Dist. No. _85_

No. of Family	No. of Dwelling	NAME	Relation	Color	Sex	DATE OF BIRTH Mon/Yr	Age at last birthday	Marital Status	# years married	Mother of how many children?	# of these children living	Place of birth [this person]	Father of this person	Mother of this person	Year of immigr.	# years in U.S.	Naturalization	OCCUPATION 10 years +	Months not employed	Attended school in months	Can read	Can write	Speak English	Owned or Rent	Owned -no mortgage	Farm or house	# of farm schedule
231	237	HUMES, PETER	HEAD	W	M	DEC 1849	50	M	20			KY	KY	KY				FARMER			✓	✓	✓	R		F	130
		" BELLE	WIFE	W	F	NOV 1856	43	M	20	8	8	KY	KY	KY							✓	✓	✓				
		" WILLIE	SON	W	M	SEP 1880	19	S				KY	KY	KY				FARM LABORER			✓	✓	✓				
		" MARY	DAU	W	F	AUG 1882	17	S				KY	KY	KY						6	✓	✓					
		" VADIE	DAU	W	F	JUL 1885	14	S				KY	KY	KY				AT SCHOOL		4	✓	✓	✓				
		" GARFIELD	SON	W	M	AUG 1887	12	S				KY	KY	KY				AT SCHOOL		5	✓	✓	✓				
		" FLORENCE	DAU	W	F	NOV 1889	10	S				KY	KY	KY				AT SCHOOL		5	✓	✓					
		" ARCHIE	SON	W	M	DEC 1891	8	S				KY	KY	KY													
		" ONE	DAU	W	F	SEP 1895	4	S				KY	KY	KY													
		" DEWEY	SON	W	M	JAN 1898	2	S				KY	KY	KY													
232	238	TURNER, WILLIAM B.	HEAD	W	M	APR 1878	22	M	5			KY	KY	KY				FARMER			✓	✓	✓	R		F	131
		" MELVINA	WIFE	W	F	MAY 1878	22	M	5	2	2	KY	KY	KY							✓	✓					
		" IVY	DAU	W	F	OCT 1896	3	S				KY	KY	KY													
		" IDA	DAU	W	F	DEC 1898	1	S				KY	KY	KY													
233	239	HALL, HARVY D.	HEAD	W	M	OCT 1861	38	M	7			KY	KY	KY				FARMER			✓	✓	✓	R		F	132
		" MARY L.	WIFE	W	F	OCT 1874	25	M	7	4	3	TN	TN	TN				NURSE			✓	✓					
		" FOWLER R.	SON	W	M	FEB 1894	6	S				MO	KY	TN													
		" BESSIE B.	DAU	W	F	JUN 1895	4	S				KY	KY	TN													
		" IRA D.	SON	W	M	APR 1899	1	S				KY	KY	TN													
234	240	HALL, HARMON	HEAD	W	M	NOV 1852	47	M	21			KY	TN	TN				MERCHANT -DRY GOODS			✓	✓	✓	O		F	133
		" NANCY E.	WIFE	W	F	DEC 1856	43	M	21	3	2	KY	TN	TN							✓	✓					
		" WALTER P.	SON	W	M	OCT 1881	18	S				KY	KY	KY				AT SCHOOL		2	✓	✓	✓				
		" OSCAR T.	SON	W	M	JAN 1886	14	S				KY	KY	KY				AT SCHOOL		2	✓	✓	✓				
235	241	HALL, JOHN D.	HEAD	W	M	DEC 1833	66	Wd				TN	TN	TN				FARMER			✓	✓	✓	O		F	134
		" JAMES M.	SON	W	M	AUG 1858	41	S				KY	TN	TN				FARMER			✓	✓	✓				
		" PEARL M.	GR-DAU	W	F	JUN 1884	15	S				KY	KY	KY				AT SCHOOL		5	✓	✓	✓				

STATE - KENTUCKY
COUNTY - MONROE
Township or other division: WEST TOMPKINSVILLE

Enumerator: MALIA PAGE

Supervisor's Dist. No. 102   Sheet No.
Enumeration Dist. No. 85

Location (No. of Family / No. of Dwelling)	NAME	Relation	Color	Sex	DATE OF BIRTH (Mon/Yr)	Age at last birthday	Marital Status	# Years married	Mother of how many children?	# of these children living	Place of birth (this person)	Father of this person	Mother of this person	Year of immigr.	# years in U.S.	Naturalization	OCCUPATION 10 years +	Months not employed	Attended school in months	Can read	Can write	Speak English	Owned or Rent	Owned - no mortgage	Farm or house	# of farm schedule
236 242	TURNER, JOHN D.	HEAD	W	M	Jun 1654	45	M	24			KY	KY	TN				FARMER			✓	✓	✓	O	F	F	135
	HENNER E.	WIFE	W	F	Apr 1851	49	M	24	9		KY	TN	TN							✓	✓					
"	SAMUEL P.	SON	W	M	Mar 1879	21	S				KY	KY	KY				FARM LABORER			✓	✓	✓	O	F	F	136
"	LURA C.	DAU	W	F	Aug 1885	14	S				KY	KY	KY				AT SCHOOL		5	✓	✓	✓				
"	HOMER	SON	W	M	Dec 1890	9	S				KY	KY	KY													
"	CECIL R.	SON	W	M	Mar 1895	5	S				KY	KY	KY													
237 243	TURNER, WILLIAM T.	HEAD	W	M	May 1831	69	M	49			KY	VA	KY				FARMER			✓	✓	✓	O	F	F	137
"	ELLEN D.	WIFE	W	F	Dec 1631	68	M	49	1	1	TN	TN	TN							✓	✓					
	THOMAS, EFFIE G.	HIRED	W	F	Sep 1884	15	S				KY	KY	KY				COOK			✓	✓					
	GRAMLIN, JOHN W.	HIRED	W	M	Dec 1877	22	S				KY	KY	KY				FARM LABORER			✓	✓	✓	O	F	F	138
238 244	JACKSON, JOHN H.	HEAD	W	M	Aug 1826	73	M	49			TN	IN	IN				FARMER			✓	✓	✓	O	F	F	139
"	MARY J.	WIFE	W	F	Sep 1829	70	M	49	9	6	TN	TN	TN							✓	✓					
"	ABBIGAL	DAU	W	F	Feb 1856	44	S				KY	TN	TN							✓	✓					
"	JOHN L.	SON	W	M	Aug 1861	38	S				KY	TN	TN				FARMER			✓	✓					139
"	THOMAS N.S.	SON	W	M	Aug 1870	29	S				KY	TN	TN				FISHER			✓	✓					
239 245	JACKSON, ISAAC S.	HEAD	W	M	Dec 1865	34	M	7			KY	TN	TN				FARMER			✓	✓	✓	R	F	139
"	SUSAN A.	WIFE	W	F	Jun 1872	27	M	7	2	2	KY	KY	KY							✓	✓					
"	ZORA A.	DAU	W	F	Feb 1895	5	S				KY	KY	KY													
"	THOMAS B.	SON	W	M	Mar 1897	3	S				KY	KY	KY										R	H		
240 246	KEY, LOYD T.	HEAD	W	M	Dec 1861	38	M				KY	KY	KY				FARM LABORER			✓	✓		R	H		
"	MALINDA A.	WIFE	W	F	Mar 1858	42	M				KY	TN	TN							✓	✓					
241 247	KEY, MARY	HEAD	W	F	Dec 1626	73	Wd		1	1	KY	VA	VA				FARMER			X	X	✓	R	F	140
242 248	BOTTS, WILLIAM H.	HEAD	W	M	Aug 1851	48	M	23			KY	TN	KY				FARMER			✓	✓	✓	R	F	141
"	NANCY A.	WIFE	W	F	May 1851	49	M	23	8	7	KY	VA	VA							X	X	✓				
"	JAMES B.	SON	W	M	May 1879	21	S				KY	KY	KY				FARM LABORER			X	X	✓				
"	NANCY E.	DAU	W	F	May 1882	18	S				KY	KY	KY							X	X	✓				

TWELFTH CENSUS OF THE UNITED STATES 1900

STATE - KENTUCKY
COUNTY - MONROE
Township or other division

WEST TOMPKINSVILLE

— 376 —

Enumerator MALIA PAGE

Supervisor's Dist. No. 102 Sheet No.
Enumeration Dist. No. 85

Location No. of Family	No. of Dwelling	NAME	Relation	Color	Sex	DATE OF BIRTH Mon/Yr	Age at last birthday	Marital Status	# Years married	Mother of how many children?	# of these children living	NATIVITY Place of birth this person	Father of this person	Mother of this person	CITIZENSHIP Year of immigr.	# years in U.S.	Naturalization	OCCUPATION 10 years +	Months not employed	EDUCATION Attended school in months	Can read	Can write	Speak English	OWNERSHIP Owned or Rent	Owned —no mortgage	Farm or house	# of farm schedule
		BOTTS, ADDIE C.	DAU	W	F	APR 1883	17	S				KY	KY	KY							X	X	✓				
		" MARY L.	DAU	W	F	APR 1885	15	S				KY	KY	KY							X	X	✓				
		" DONA G.	DAU	W	F	APR 1888	12	S				KY	KY	KY							X	X	✓				
		" WILLIAM E.	SON	W	M	OCT 1892	7	S				KY	KY	KY							X	X					
243	249	DENHAM, THOMPSON	HEAD	W	M	AUG 1843	56	M	33			TN	TN	TN				FARMER			X	X	✓	R		F	142
		" LIDA J.	WIFE	W	F	JAN 1850	50	M	33	12	6	KY	KY	NC							X	X	✓				
		" IDA I.	DAU	W	F	MAY 1880	20	S				KY	TN	KY							✓	✓	✓				
		" LULA D.	DAU	W	F	SEP 1883	16	S				KY	TN	KY				AT SCHOOL		4	✓	✓	✓				
		" EMILY S.	DAU	W	F	JUL 1886	13	S				KY	TN	KY				AT SCHOOL		5	✓	✓	✓				
		" SAMUEL J.	SON	W	M	JAN 1888	12	S				KY	TN	KY				AT SCHOOL		5	✓	✓					
244	250	PROFFITT, PERRY F.	HEAD	W	M	AUG 1876	23	M	4			KY	KY	KY				FARMER			✓	✓	✓		O M E		143
		" MARTHA E.	WIFE	W	F	MAR 1879	21	M	4	2	2	KY	KY	KY				NURSE			✓	✓					
		" HOMER B.	SON	W	M	FEB 1897	3	S				KY	KY	KY													
		" PEARLIE M.	DAU	W	F	APR 1899	1	S				KY	KY	KY													
245	251	PROFFITT, JAMES T.	HEAD	W	M	MAR 1866	34	M	8			KY	KY	KY				FARMER			✓	✓	✓	R		F	144
		" LEONA	WIFE	W	F	NOV 1869	30	M	8	4	2	KY	KY	KY							✓	✓	✓				
		" CLIDE B.	SON	W	M	AUG 1895	4	S				KY	KY	KY													
		" ORAL T.	SON	W	M	JUN 1899	11/12	S				KY	KY	KY													
		RICHARD, MARY	GR-MOTHER	W	M	FEB 1822	78	Wd		7	4	KY	VA	VA							✓	✓	✓				
246	252	HALL, MARCUS T	HEAD	W	M	JUL 1864	35	M	11			KY	TN	KY				FARMER			✓	✓	✓	O		F F	145
		" JENNIE	WIFE	W	F	MAR 1868	32	M	11	2	2	KY	KY	KY							✓	✓	✓				
		" ROXIE B.	DAU	W	F	JUN 1891	8	S				KY	KY	KY													
		" ETTA B.	DAU	W	F	MAR 1895	5	S				KY	KY	KY													
247	253	PROFFITT, MELVIN	HEAD	W	M	OCT 1878	21	M	4			KY	KY	KY				FARMER			✓	✓	✓	R		F	146
		" LAURA M.	WIFE	W	F	SEP 1879	20	M	4	2	2	KY	KY	KY				NURSE			✓	✓	✓				
		" NORVIA	SON	W	M	SEP 1896	3	S				KY	KY	KY													

STATE - KENTUCKY
COUNTY - MONROE
Township or other division: WEST TOMPKINSVILLE
Enumerator: MALIA PAGE
Supervisor's Dist. No. _102_ Sheet No. _____
Enumeration Dist. No. _85_ _____

No. of Family	No. of Dwelling	NAME	Relation	Color	Sex	DATE OF BIRTH Mon/Yr	Age at last birthday	Marital Status	# Years married	Mother of how many children?	# of these children living	Place of birth [this person]	Father of this person	Mother of this person	Year of immigr.	# years in U.S.	Naturalization	OCCUPATION 10 years +	Months not employed	Attended school in months	Can read	Can write	Speak English	Owned or Rent	Owned -no mortage	Farm or house	# of farm schedule
		PROFFITT, WALTER	SON	W	M	Nov 1899	6/12	S				KY	KY	KY													
248	254	PROFFITT, MILLARD F.	HEAD	W	M	APR 1853	47	M	27			KY	KY	KY				FARMER			✓	✓	✓	O	F F		147
		" LIZA J.	WIFE	W	F	MAY 1854	46	M	27	9	9	TN	TN	TN							✓	✓	✓				
		" ADA B.	DAU	W	F	Jul 1882	17	S				KY	TN	TN				AT SCHOOL		4	✓	✓	✓				
		" ABIJAH	SON	W	M	Jan 1885	15	S				KY	TN	TN				AT SCHOOL		5	✓	✓	✓				
		" GEORGE E.	SON	W	M	Jan 1888	12	S				KY	TN	TN				AT SCHOOL		5	✓	✓	✓				
		" IDA M.	DAU	W	F	Mar 1890	10	S				KY	TN	TN				AT SCHOOL		5	✓	✓	✓				
		" SALLIE M.	DAU	W	F	Aug 1892	7	S				KY	TN	TN													
		" BEDFORD	SON	W	M	Aug 1896	4	S				KY	TN	TN													
249	255	GUINN, JOE	HEAD	W	M	Oct 1866	33	M	15			KY	TN	TN				FARMER			✓	✓	✓	O	F F		148
		" LEE A.	WIFE	W	F	Oct 1866	33	M	15	4	4	TN	TN	TN							✓	✓	✓				
		" ANDREW	SON	W	M	Sep 1886	13	S				KY	KY	TN				AT SCHOOL		8	✓	✓	✓				
		" MARY B.	DAU	W	F	Oct 1889	10	S				KY	KY	TN				AT SCHOOL			✓	✓	✓				
		" YADA C.	DAU	W	F	Jun 1894	5	S				KY	KY	TN													
		" ADA	DAU	W	F	APR 1898	2	S				KY	KY	TN													
250	256	STRODE, JOHN	HEAD	W	M	Jan 1855	45	M	18			KY	KY	KY				FARM LABORER			✓	✓	✓	O	H		
		" SARAH	WIFE	W	F	Jan 1860	40	M	18			KY	KY	KY							X	X	✓				
251	257	MATHENLA, WILLIAM H	HEAD	W	M	Jan 1840	60	M	9			KY	TN	TN				FARMER			X	X	✓	O	M F		149
		" NANCY J.	WIFE	W	F	Aug 1849	50	M	9			KY	KY	KY							✓	✓	✓				
		" WILLIAM H.	SON	W	M	Mar 1890	10	S				KY	KY	KY				AT SCHOOL		5	✓	✓	✓				
252	258	COULTER, MARION	HEAD	W	M	Sep 1842	57	M	31			KY	TN	TN				FARMER			✓	✓	✓	R	F		150
		" MISSOURI	WIFE	W	F	Sep 1844	55	M	31	12	8	TN	VA	KY							X	X	✓				
		" CELIA	DAU	W	F	Aug 1869	30	S		2	2	KY	TN	KY							✓	✓	✓				
		" MATILDA	DAU	W	F	APR 1878	21	S		1	1	KY	TN	KY							✓	✓	✓				
		" CORA E.	GR-DAU	W	F	Aug 1892	7	S				KY	KY	KY													
		" OLLIE M.	GR-DAU	W	F	Aug 1896	3	S				KY	KY	KY													

STATE - KENTUCKY
COUNTY - MONROE
Township or other division WEST TOMPKINSVILLE Enumerator MALIA PAGE

No. of Family	No. of Dwelling	NAME	Relation	Color	Sex	DATE OF BIRTH Mon/Yr	Age at last birthday	Marital Status	# Years married	Mother of how many children?	# of these children living	Place of birth (this person)	Father of this person	Mother of this person	OCCUPATION 10 years +	Months not employed	Attended school in months	Can read	Can write	Speak English	Owned or Rent	Owned - no mortage	Farm or house	# of farm schedule
		COULTER, ROXIE V.	GR-DAU	W	F	Sep 1842						KY	KY	KY										
253	259	BOWMAN, ISAAC D.	HEAD	W	M	Sep 1860	39	M	12			TN	TN	TN	MERCHANT-GROCERIES			✓	✓	✓	O	F	F	151
		" LAURA A.	WIFE	W	F	Sep 1865	34	M	12	7	7	KY	KY	KY	NURSE			✓	✓	✓				
		" NANCY D.	DAU	W	F	Jun 1888	11	S				KY	TN	KY	AT SCHOOL		5	✓	✓	✓				
		" DARRIS	SON	W	M	Oct 1890	9	S				KY	TN	KY	AT SCHOOL		5	✓	✓	✓				
		" ISAAC (F.)(T.)	SON	W	M	Sep 1891	8	S				KY	TN	KY										
		" DAVID V.	SON	W	M	Jun 1893	6	S				KY	TN	KY										
		" WILLIAM E.	SON	W	M	May 1895	5	S				KY	TN	KY										
		" PEARL	DAU	W	F	Mar 1897	3	S				KY	TN	KY										
		" NOVELLA	DAU	W	F	Dec 1899	6/12	S				KY	TN	KY										
254	260	BUTLER, NANNIE	HEAD	W	F	Jun 1854	45	Wd		5	5	KY	VA	VA	FARMER			✓	✓	✓	O	F	F	152
		STRODE, RELLA D.	DAU	W	F	Apr 1875	25	DIVC.		2	2	KY	KY	KY				✓	✓	✓				
		BUTLER, DEDIE	DAU	W	F	Apr 1881	19	S				KY	KY	KY				✓	✓	✓				
		" WILLIAM	SON	W	M	Nov 1883	16	S				KY	KY	KY	FARMER			✓	✓	✓				
		SYMPSON, ELLA M.	GR-DAU	W	F	Feb 1895	5	S				KY	KY	KY										
		" BERTIE M.	GR-DAU	W	F	Oct 1897	3	S				KY	KY	KY										
255	261	PENNINGTON, LUTHER	HEAD	W	M	Feb 1870	30	S				KY	KY	KY	FARMER			✓	✓	✓	O	F	F	153
		ARMSTRONG, JERIAHA	AUNT	W	F	Sep 1846	53	S				KY	KY	KY				✓	✓	✓				
256	262	EMBERTON, SUSAN H.	HEAD	W	F	Jun 1860	39	S				KY	KY	ALA	FARMER			✓	✓	✓	O	F	F	154
		" SHADA	SISTER	W	F	Oct 1863	36	S				KY	KY	ALA				✓	✓	✓				
		MCMURTRY, MALISSA F.	NIECE	W	F	Mar 1877	23	S				KY	KY	KY				✓	✓	✓				
		EMBERTON, DORA	HIRED	W	F	Feb 1888	12	S				KY	KY	KY	AT SCHOOL		5	✓	✓	✓				
257	263	HALE, JOHN M.	HEAD	W	M	Mar 1850	50	M	32			KY	TN	TN	BLACKSMITH			X	X	✓	O	F	F	155
		" MARY A.	WIFE	W	F	Jul 1850	49	M	32	11	10	KY	KY	KY				X	X	✓				
		" GEORGE E.	SON	W	M	Jan 1880	20	S				KY	KY	KY	FARMER			✓	✓	✓				155
		" VIRGINIA C.	DAU	W	F	Apr 1883	17	S				KY	KY	KY	AT SCHOOL		5	✓	✓	✓				

STATE - KENTUCKY
COUNTY - MONROE
Township or other division: WEST TOMPKINSVILLE
Enumerator: MALIA PAGE

Supervisor's Dist. No. 102 Sheet No.
Enumeration Dist. No. 85

No. of Family	No. of Dwelling	NAME	Relation	Color	Sex	DATE OF BIRTH Mon/Yr	Age at last birthday	Marital Status	# Years married	Mother of how many children?	# of these children living	Place of birth (this person)	Father of this person	Mother of this person	Year of immigr.	# years in U.S.	Naturalization	OCCUPATION 10 years +	Months not employed	Attended school in months	Can read	Can write	Speak English	Owned or Rent	Owned -no mortgage	Farm or house	# of farm schedule
		HALE, WOODFORD	SON	W	M	Aug 1885	14	S				KY	KY	KY				AT SCHOOL		2	✓	✓	✓				
		" MARGARET E.	DAU	W	F	Jan 1889	11	S				KY	KY	KY				AT SCHOOL		5	✓	✓					
		" GERTRUDE	DAU	W	F	Mar 1892	8	S				KY	KY	KY													
		" MARY M.	DAU	W	F	Feb 1894	6	S				KY	KY	KY													
258	264	BUTLER, JOHN F.	HEAD	W	M	Oct 1866	33	M	11			KY	KY	KY				FARMER			✓	✓	✓	R		F	156
		" LORETTA	WIFE	W	F	Aug 1872	27	M	11	6	6	KY	KY	KY				NURSE			✓	✓	✓				
		" LUTHER M.	SON	W	M	Feb 1890	10	S				KY	KY	KY				AT SCHOOL		5	✓	✓	✓				
		" BUFORD G.	SON	W	M	Feb 1892	8	S				KY	KY	KY													
		" MARY E.	DAU	W	F	Mar 1893	7	S				KY	KY	KY													
		" WILLIAM H.	SON	W	M	Jan 1895	5	S				KY	KY	KY													
		" JOHN T	SON	W	M	May 1896	4	S				KY	KY	KY													
		" FLORA D.	DAU	W	F	Dec 1898	1	S				KY	KY	KY													
259	265	HALE, SALLIE	HEAD	W	F	Aug 1878	21	Wd	1	1	1	KY	KY	KY				NURSE			✓	✓		R		H	
		" BESSIE E.	DAU	W	F	Oct 1898	1	S				KY	KY	KY													
260	266	STRODE, SAMUEL H.	HEAD	W	M	Feb 1864	46	M	14			KY	KY	KY				PREACHER			✓	✓		O		F	157
		" LON R	WIFE	W	F	Aug 1867	32	M	14	1	1	KY	KY	KY							✓	✓					
		" SALLIE E.	DAU	W	F	Sep 1892	7	S				KY	KY	KY													
		" EWEL H.	SON	W	M	Sep 1878	21	S				KY	KY	KY				FARM LABORER		6	✓	✓					
261	267	EMBERTON, JAMES E.	HEAD	W	M	Jan 1860	40	M	20			KY	KY	KY				FARMER			✓	✓		O		F	158
		" MARY M.	WIFE	W	F	Sep 1863	36	M	20	9	8	KY	KY	KY							✓	✓					
		" LUCY J.	DAU	W	F	Jun 1882	17	S				KY	KY	KY				AT SCHOOL		5	✓	✓	✓				
		" WILLIAM E.	SON	W	M	Mar 1885	15	S				KY	KY	KY				AT SCHOOL		2½	✓	✓	✓				
		" AUDA J.	SON	W	M	May 1887	13	S				KY	KY	KY				AT SCHOOL		2½	✓	✓	✓				
		" JAMES C.	SON	W	M	Mar 1889	11	S				KY	KY	KY				AT SCHOOL		3	✓	✓	✓				
		" PEARLIE M.	DAU	W	F	Oct 1891	8	S				KY	KY	KY													
		" MAUDIE B.	DAU	W	F	May 1897	3	S				KY	KY	KY													

STATE - KENTUCKY
COUNTY - MONROE
Township or other division WEST TOMPKINSVILLE

TWELFTH CENSUS OF THE UNITED STATES 1900
— 380 —
Enumerator MALIA PAGE

Supervisor's Dist. No. 102   Sheet No.
Enumeration Dist. No. 85

No. of Family	No. of Dwelling	NAME	Relation	Color	Sex	DATE OF BIRTH Mon/Yr	Age at last birthday	Marital Status	# Years married	Mother of how many children?	# of these children living	Place of birth [this person]	Father of this person	Mother of this person	Year of immigr.	# years in U.S.	Naturalization	OCCUPATION 10 years +	Months not employed	Attended school in months	Can read	Can write	Speak English	Owned or Rent	Owned - no mortgage	Farm or house	# of farm schedule	
(267)		EMBERTON, WEALTHY C.	DAU	W	F	Feb 1899	1	S				KY	KY	KY														
262	268	STRODE, JAMES F.	HEAD	W	M	Sep 1851	48	M	18			KY	KY	KY				FARMER			X	X	✓	O	F	F	159	
		" MARY E.	WIFE	W	F	Dec 1850	49	M	18	2	1	KY	KY	KY							✓	✓	✓					
		" WILLIAM J.	SON	W	M	Dec 1885	15	S				KY	KY	KY				AT SCHOOL		5	✓	✓	✓					
		UPTERGROVE, BENTON	BRO-IN-LAW	W	M	Apr 1878	22	S				KY	KY	KY				FARM LABORER			✓	✓	✓					
263	269	STRODE, WILLIAM J.	HEAD	W	M	Jan 1849	50	Wd				KY	KY	KY				FARMER			✓	✓	✓	O	F	F	160	
		" CUBA F.	DAU	W	F	Dec 1895	5					KY	KY	KY														
264	270	JONES, SARAH	HEAD	W	F	Dec 1838	61	Wd		2	0	IND	KY	NC				FARMER			✓	✓	✓	O	F	F	161	
265	271	BRANNON, MARGARET	HEAD	W	F	Mar 1836	64	Wd		1	1	KY	TN	NC				FARMER			✓	✓	✓	O	F	F	162	
		" THOMAS W.	SON	W	M	Jun 1878	21	S				KY	KY	KY				FARMER			✓	✓	✓				162	
266	272	BROWN, JAMES O.	HEAD	W	M	Jan 1863	37	M	18			IND	KY	KY				FARMER			✓	✓	✓	O	F	F	163	
		" LETHA F.	WIFE	W	F	Feb 1863	37	M	18	7	7	TN	TN	TN							✓	✓	✓					
		" BENTON M.	SON	W	M	Nov 1883	16	S				TN	IND	TN				AT SCHOOL		5	✓	✓	✓					
		" HATTIE S.	DAU	W	F	May 1886	14	S				TN	IND	TN				AT SCHOOL		5	✓	✓	✓					
		" JULIA D.	DAU	W	F	Sep 1889	10	S				KY	IND	TN				AT SCHOOL		5	✓	✓	✓					
		" LISSIE T.	DAU	W	F	Dec 1892	7	S				KY	IND	TN														
		" OTIA C.	DAU	W	F	Apr 1895	5	S				KY	IND	TN														
		" LORA M.	DAU	W	F	Feb 1897	3	S				KY	IND	TN														
		" EARL F.	SON	W	M	Aug 1899	9/12	S				KY	IND	TN														
267	273	BROWN, SUSAN	HEAD	W	F	Sep 1837	62	Wd		5	3	KY	KY	NC							✓	✓	✓	O		H		
		" EMMA	GR-DAU	W	F	Mar 1886	14	S				KY	KY	KY							X	X	✓					
268	274	SMITH, CORNELIUS	HEAD	W	M	Dec 1832	67	M	39			KY	TN	TN				FARMER			✓	✓	✓	O	F	F	164	
		" ANNA	WIFE	W	F	Mar 1839	61	M	39	4	4	KY	SC	SC							✓	✓	✓					
		" LIZZIE	DAU	W	F	Aug 1866	33	S				KY	KY	KY				SCHOOL TEACHER			✓	✓	✓					
		" HORACE O.	SON	W	M	Dec 1872	27	S				KY	KY	KY				FARMER			—	—	—				164	
		" ANGELINE A.	DAU	W	F	Mar 1876	24	S				KY	KY	KY							✓	✓	✓					

STATE - KENTUCKY
COUNTY - MONROE
Township or other division — WEST TOMPKINSVILLE   Enumerator MALIA PAGE

Supervisor's Dist. No. 102 Sheet No.
Enumeration Dist. No. 85

No. of Family	No. of Dwelling	NAME	Relation	Color	Sex	DATE OF BIRTH Mon/Yr	Age at last birthday	Marital Status	# Years married	Mother of how many children?	# of these children living	Place of birth [this person]	Father of this person	Mother of this person	Year of immigr.	# years in U.S.	Naturalization	OCCUPATION 10 years +	Months not employed	Attended school in months	Can read	Can write	Speak English	Owned or Rent	Owned - no mortgage	Farm or house	# of farm schedule
269	275	ENGLAND, JOSEPH S.	HEAD	W	M	Sep 1837	62	M	30			KY	KY	KY				FARMER			✓	✓	✓	O		F	165
		" ABIGIL	WIFE	W	F	Oct 1838	61	M	30	2	2	KY	TN	TN							✓	✓	✓				
		" WESTERFIELD B.	SON	W	M	Sep 1874	25	S				KY	KY	KY				DOCTOR			✓	✓	✓				
		" LORA	DAU	W	F	Apr 1879	21	S				KY	KY	KY				TELEPHONE OPERATER			✓	✓	✓				
270	276	ROBERTS, TIMOTHY	HEAD	W	M	Oct 1877	22	M	5			KY	KY	KY				FARMER			✓	✓	✓	R		F	166
		" ELLA	WIFE	W	F	Sep 1880	19	M	5	2	2	KY	KY	KY							X	X	✓				
		" CLARENCE	SON	W	M	Mar 1898	2	S				KY	KY	KY													
		" MARVIN	SON	W	M	Dec 1899	5/12	S				KY	KY	KY													
271	277	WHEAT, ARCH	HEAD	W	M	Dec 1866	33	M	11			KY	KY	KY				FARMER			✓	✓	✓	R		F	167
		" BERTHA M.	WIFE	W	F	Dec 1867	32	M	11	5	4	KY	KY	KY							✓	✓	✓				
		" ADA	DAU	W	F	Jul 1891	8	S				KY	KY	KY				AT SCHOOL		8	✓	X	✓				
		" JESSE J.	SON	W	M	Jan 1892	8					KY	KY	KY													
		" LENA S.	DAU	W	F	Jun 1894	5	S				KY	KY	KY													
272	278	ARMSTRONG, SARAH	HEAD	W	F	Jun 1861	38	Wd		1	1	KY	TN	TN				FARMER			✓	✓		O		F	168
		" WILLIE E.	SON	W	M	Apr 1885	15	S				KY	KY	KY				FARMER			✓	✓	✓	R		F	169
273	279	ARMSTRONG, ANDREW B.	HEAD	W	M	Oct 1858	41	M	19			KY	TN	TN				FARMER			✓	✓	✓				
		" MARY E.	WIFE	W	F	Apr 1864	36	M	19	4	4	KY	KY	KY							✓	✓	✓				
		" EUGENE	SON	W	M	Apr 1882	18	S				KY	KY	KY				FARM LABORER			✓	✓	✓				
		" EUCLAS S.	SON	W	M	Feb 1884	16	S				KY	KY	KY				FARM LABORER			✓	✓	✓				
		" EVALENA	DAU	W	F	Jul 1886	13	S				KY	KY	KY				AT SCHOOL		5	✓	✓	✓				
		" IDA M.	DAU	W	F	Mar 1888	12	S				KY	KY	KY				AT SCHOOL		5	✓	✓	✓				
274	280	RUSSELL, JOHN (W?)	HEAD	W	M	Jan 1849	51	M	19			KY	KY	KY				DAY LABORER			X	X	✓	R		H	
		" MARY	WIFE	W	F	Sep 1858	31	M	19	8	6	KY	KY	KY							X	X	✓				
		" SARAH J.	DAU	W	F	Oct 1889	11	S				KY	KY	KY							X	X	✓				
		" JAMES M.	SON	W	M	Sep 1891	8	S				KY	KY	KY													
		" ALICE	DAU	W	F	Jun 1895	5	S				KY	KY	KY													

STATE - KENTUCKY
COUNTY - MONROE
Township or other division: WEST TOMPKINSVILLE
Enumerator: MALIA PAGE

Supervisor's Dist. No. _102_ Sheet No.
Enumeration Dist. No. _85_

No. of Family	No. of Dwelling	NAME	Relation	Color	Sex	DATE OF BIRTH Mon/Yr	Age at last birthday	Marital Status	# Years married	Mother of how many children?	# of these children living	Place of birth [this person]	Father of this person	Mother of this person	Year of immigr.	# years in U.S.	Naturalization	OCCUPATION 10 years +	Months not employed	Attended school in months	Can read	Can write	Speak English	Owned or Rent	Owned -no mortgage	Farm or house	# of farm schedule
		RUSSELL, HERMAN	Son	W	M	Sep 1896	3	S				KY	KY	KY													
		" OSCAR C.	Son	W	M	May 1900	1/12	S				KY	KY	KY													
275	281	JACKSON, MARY G.	Head	W	F	Aug 1841	58	Wd		5	4	KY	TN	KY				FARMER			✓	✓	✓	O	F	170
		" ARTER B.	Son	W	M	Dec 1872	27	S				KY	KY	KY				MAIL CARRIER			✓	✓	✓			170
276	282	GUM, ALFRED M.	Head	W	M	Apr 1867	33	M	4			KY	KY	KY				FARMER			✓	✓	O	F	F	171
		" SALLIE G.	Wife	W	F	Jul 1870	29	M	4	2	1	KY	KY	KY								✓	✓				
		" JIMMIE H.	Son	W	M	Dec 1898	1	S				KY	KY	KY													
		" MARGARET J.	Mother	W	F	Oct 1839	60	Wd		6	5	KY	VA	VA													
277	283	EUBANK, JESSE T.	Head	W	M	Feb 1870	30	M	8			KY	KY	KY				FARMER			✓	✓	✓	R	F	172
		" SARAH A.	Wife	W	F	Jun 1873	26	M	8	4	4	KY	KY	TN								✓	✓				
		" BESSIE	Dau	W	F	Mar 1893	7	S				KY	KY	KY													
		" DENNIS J	Son	W	M	Apr 1895	5	S				KY	KY	KY													
		" FLORA B.	Dau	W	F	Jan 1897	3	S				KY	KY	KY													
		" ESTY	Son	W	M	Aug 1898	1	S				KY	KY	KY													
278	284	JONES, RADFORD A.	Head	W	M	Feb 1868	32	M	14			KY	KY	KY				FARMER			✓	✓	✓	O	F	F	173
		" MARTHA E.	Wife	W	F	Aug 1863	36	M	14	6	6	KY	KY	KY							✓	✓	✓				
		" ADA M.	Dau	W	F	May 1887	13	S				KY	KY	KY				AT SCHOOL		5	✓	✓	✓				
		" ANNA F.	Dau	W	F	May 1889	11	S				KY	KY	KY				AT SCHOOL		5	✓	✓	✓				
		" LILLIE F.	Dau	W	F	Aug 1890	9	S				KY	KY	KY													
		" HUGH B	Son	W	M	Jul 1893	6	S				KY	KY	KY													
		" MAUD ETHEL	Dau	W	F	May 1896	4	S				KY	KY	KY													
		" ROLLIE G.	Son	W	M	Mar 1898	1	S				KY	KY	KY													
279	285	HOOD, WILLIAM W.	Head	W	M	Jun 1872	27	M	6			KY	KY	KY				FARMER			✓	✓	✓	R	F	174
		" MARY L.	Wife	W	F	Jan 1879	21	M	6	8	2	KY	KY	KY							✓	✓	✓				
		" WALTER C.	Son	W	M	Jun 1898	1	S				KY	KY	KY													
		" EFFIE S.	Dau	W	F	May 1899	7/12	S				KY	KY	KY													

STATE - KENTUCKY
COUNTY - MONROE
Township or other division — WEST TOMPKINSVILLE Enumerator MALIA PAGE

Supervisor's Dist. No. 102 Sheet No.
Enumeration Dist. No. 85

Location		NAME	Relation	Color	Sex	DATE OF BIRTH Mon/Yr	Age at last birthday	Marital Status	# Years married	Mother of how many children?	# of these children living	NATIVITY Place of birth (this person)	Father of this person	Mother of this person	CITIZENSHIP Year of immigr. / # years in U.S. / Naturalization	OCCUPATION 10 years +	Months not employed	Attended school in months	Can read	Can write	Speak English	OWNERSHIP Owned or Rent / Owned-no mortage / Farm or house / # of farm schedule
No. of Family	No. of Dwelling																					
(285)		BRADLY, EVIE J	SON-IN LAW	W	F	MAR 1887	13	S				KY	KY	KY					✓	✓	✓	
280	286	BROWN, NATHAN	HEAD	W	M	Nov 1843	56	M	27			KY	KY	KY		GARDENER			✓	✓	✓	R F 175
		" SUSAN J	WIFE	W	F	Feb 1854	46	M	27	5	5	KY	KY	KY					X	X	✓	
		" GILLIE A.	DAU	W	F	JAN 1882	18	S				KY	KY	KY		AT SCHOOL		5	✓	✓	✓	
		" WILY W.	SON	W	M	DEC 1885	14	S				KY	KY	KY		AT SCHOOL		5	✓	✓	✓	
281	287	HEADRICK, HENRY	HEAD	W	M	Aug 1843	56	M	29			TN	TN	TN		FARMER			✓	✓	✓	O F F 176
		" SARAH E.	WIFE	W	F	APR 1845	55	M	29	2	2	KY	VA	VA		FARM LABORER			✓	✓	✓	
		" WILLIAM J.	SON	W	M	Sep 1883	16	S				KY	TN	KY		AT SCHOOL		5	✓	✓	✓	
		" DEBBIE J.	DAU	W	F	JUN 1886	13	S				KY	TN	KY					✓	✓	✓	
282	288	DENHAM, WILLIAM G.	HEAD	W	M	Sep 1872	27	M	11			TN	KY	TN		FARMER			✓	✓	✓	O F F 177
		" LOUISA A.	WIFE	W	F	OCT 1870	29	M	11	5	5	KY	KY	TN					X	X	✓	
		" JOHN A.	SON	W	M	Feb 1890	10	S				KY	TN	KY		AT SCHOOL		3	X	X	✓	
		" BERTHA M.	DAU	W	F	Dec 1891	8	S				KY	TN	KY		AT SCHOOL		4	✓	✓	✓	
		" WALTER J.	SON	W	M	MAY 1894	6	S				KY	TN	KY								
		" FRANK	SON	W	M	APR 1896	4	S				KY	TN	KY								
		" ERNEST	SON	W	M	AUG 1898	1	S				KY	TN	KY								
283	289	DENHAM, MATILDA J.	HEAD	W	F	Jul 1846	54	Wd		8	7	KY	TN	SC					✓	X	✓	O H
		" ANDERSON W.	SON	W	M	APR 1887	13	S				KY	KY	KY		AT SCHOOL		3	✓	✓	✓	
284	290	EMBERTON, SILAS	HEAD	W	M	OCT 1853	46	M	4			KY	KY	KY		FARMER			X	X	✓	O F F 178
		" CATHERINE A.	WIFE	W	F	DEC 1868	31	M	4	2	2	KY	KY	KY					✓	✓	✓	
		" MARTHA E.	DAU	W	F	OCT 1877	22	S				KY	KY	KY					✓	✓	✓	
		" ESTELLA	DAU	W	F	JAN 1897	3	S				KY	KY	KY								
		" SAMUEL O.	SON	W	M	Jul 1898	1	S				KY	KY	KY								
		COULTER, IRVING L.	ADOPTED SON	W	M	Sep 1889	11	S				KY	KY	KY					✓	✓	✓	O F F 179
285	291	PATTERSON, SARAH T.	HEAD	W	F	Sep 1844	55	Wd		2	0	KY	TN	TN		FARMER			✓	✓	✓	
		BUSH, BAXTER	HIRED	W	M	MAY 1881	19	S				KY	KY	KY		AT SCHOOL		4	✓	✓	✓	

STATE - KENTUCKY
COUNTY - MONROE
Township or other division — WEST TOMPKINSVILLE

-384-

Enumerator MALIA PAGE

Supervisor's Dist. No. _102_ Sheet No. _____
Enumeration Dist. No. _85_

No. of Family	No. of Dwelling	NAME	Relation	Color	Sex	DATE OF BIRTH Mon/Yr	Age at last birthday	Marital Status	# Years married	Mother of how many children?	# of these children living	Place of birth [this person]	Father of this person	Mother of this person	Year of immigr.	# years in U.S.	Naturalization	OCCUPATION 10 years +	Months not employed	Attended school in months	Can read	Can write	Speak English	Owned or Rent	Owned -no mortage	Farm or house	# of farm schedule	
286	292	BOWMAN BENJAMIN J.	HEAD	W	M	Jun 1845	54	M	6			TN	KY	KY				FARMER			✓	✓	✓	O	F	F	180	
		HARRIET	WIFE	W	F	Sep 1865	34	M	6	2	2	KY	KY	KY							✓	✓	✓					
		JOSEPH B.	SON	W	M	Sep 1877	22	S				KY	TN	KY				SCHOOL-TEACHER			✓	✓	✓					
		ESTELLA	DAU	W	F	Dec 1883	16	S				KY	TN	KY				AT SCHOOL		5	-	-						
		LAURA F.	DAU	W	F	Nov 1884	15	S				KY	TN	KY				AT SCHOOL		5	-	-						
		FLORENCE A.	DAU	W	F	Sep 1888	11	S				KY	TN	KY				AT SCHOOL		5	-	-						
		EFFIE E.	DAU	W	F	Nov 1890	9	S				KY	TN	KY				AT SCHOOL		5								
		CLAUDIE C.	SON	W	M	Jan 1892	8	S				KY	TN	KY														
		VOLA M.	DAU	W	F	May 1894	6	S				KY	TN	KY														
		ELLA B.	DAU	W	F	Aug 1895	4	S				KY	TN	KY														
287	293	WAX, WILLIAM E.	HEAD	W	M	Jun 1846	54	M	30			TN	TN	TN				FARMER			✓	✓	✓	O	F	F	181	
		MARGARET A.	WIFE	W	F	May 1848	52	M	30	11	10	KY	TN	TN							✓	✓	✓					
		SARAH T.	DAU	W	F	Jan 1880	20	S				KY	TN	KY							✓	✓						
		GEORGE W.	SON	W	M	Feb 1882	18	S				KY	TN	KY				AT SCHOOL		4	✓	✓	✓					
		JOHN E.	SON	W	M	Aug 1884	15	S				KY	TN	KY				AT SCHOOL		5	✓	✓	✓					
		WINNIE A.	DAU	W	F	Jan 1887	13	S				KY	TN	KY				AT SCHOOL		5	✓	✓	✓					
		HENRY A.	SON	W	M	Jan 1889	11	S				KY	TN	KY				AT SCHOOL		5	✓	✓	✓					
		JOSEPH A.	SON	W	M	Feb 1891	9	S				KY	TN	KY				AT SCHOOL		5	✓	✓	✓					
		ELNORA T.	NIECE	W	F	Jan 1887	13	S				KY	TN	KY				AT SCHOOL		5	✓	✓	✓					
		RUFHUS A.	NEPHEW	W	M	Jan 1889	11	S				KY	TN	KY				AT SCHOOL		5	✓	✓	✓					
288	294	ADAMS, JAMES B.	HEAD	W	M	Jan 1870	30	M	8			KY	KY	KY				DAY LABORER	6		✓	✓		O		H		
		MARGARIT A.	WIFE	W	F	Dec 1866	33	M	8	3	3	KY	KY	KY							✓	✓						
		LENA	DAU	W	M	Nov 1892	7	S				KY	KY	KY														
		FRANK	SON	W	M	Sep 1893	6	S				KY	KY	KY														
		BRUCE	SON	W	M	Jul 1895	4	S				KY	KY	KY														
289	295	HIGH, SARAH E.	HEAD	W	F	Nov 1859	40	Wd		10	4	KY	KY	KY				FARMER			✓	✓		O	F	F	182	✓

STATE - KENTUCKY
COUNTY - MONROE
Township or other division — WEST TOMPKINSVILLE — Enumerator MALIA PAGE

Supervisor's Dist. No. 102 Sheet No.
Enumeration Dist. No. 85

No. of Family	No. of Dwelling	NAME	Relation	Color	Sex	Date of Birth Mon/Yr	Age at last birthday	Marital Status	# Years married	Mother of how many children?	# of these children living	Place of birth (this person)	Father of this person	Mother of this person	Year of immigr.	# years in U.S.	Naturalization	Occupation 10 years +	Months not employed	Attended school in months	Can read	Can write	Speak English	Owned or Rent	Owned-no mortgage	Farm or house	# of farm schedule
		HIGH, LORENZO	SON	W	M	Nov 1878	21	S				KY	KY	KY				FARMER			✓	✓		R		F	183
		" LANDO	SON	W	M	Aug 1880	19	S				KY	KY	KY				FARM LABORER			✓	✓					
		" LAMBERT	SON	W	M	Jun 1883	16	S				KY	KY	KY				AT SCHOOL		5	✓	✓					
		" ELORA	DAU	W	F	Aug 1894	5	S				KY	KY	KY													
290	296	BROWN, HULET	HEAD	W	M	May 1844	56	M	30			KY	KY	KY				FARMER			✓	✓		O		F	184
		" ELIZABETH A.	WIFE	W	F	Feb 1850	50	M	30	5	3	KY	TN	TN							✓	✓					
		" GEORGE C.	SON	W	M	Oct 1870	29	S				KY	KY	KY				FARM LABORER			✓	✓					
		" LILLIE	DAU	W	F	Apr 1876	24	S				KY	KY	KY							✓	✓	✓				
		" DONA	DAU	W	F	Dec 1879	20	S				KY	KY	KY							✓	✓	✓				
		EMBERTON, WILLIAM S.	HIRED	W	M	May 1865	35	S				KY	TN	KY				FARM LABORER			✓	✓	✓				
291	297	HAMMER, WILLIAM (T?)	HEAD	W	M	Oct 1842	57	M	11			KY	KY	KY				FARMER			✓	✓	✓	R		F	185
		" NANCY I.	WIFE	W	F	Nov 1871	28	M	11	3	3	KY	KY	KY							✓	✓					
		" SALLIE E.	DAU	W	F	Mar 1890	10	S				KY	KY	KY				AT SCHOOL		5	✓	✓					
		" HESTER A.	DAU	W	F	Jan 1895	5	S				KY	KY	KY													
		" GRACIE T.	DAU	W	F	Jun 1898	1	S				KY	KY	KY													
		BOWMAN, BENJAMIN D.	HIRED	W	M	Mar 1877	23	S				KY	KY	KY				FARM LABORER			✓	4	✓				
292	298	JACKSON, MARTHA	HEAD	W	M	Nov 1833	66	Wd		3	3	KY	KY	TN				FARMER			✓	✓	✓	O		F	186
		CHANDLER, JOHN	Boarder	W	M	Mar 1874	26	S				KY	KY	KY				FARM LABORER			✓	✓	✓	O		F	187
293	299	HEADRICK, JESSE N.	HEAD	W	M	Mar 1851	49	M	23			KY	TN	TN				FARMER			✓	✓	✓				
		" SALLIE I.	WIFE	W	F	Jan 1861	39	M	23	6	3	KY	KY	KY							✓	✓					
		" JOHN W.	SON	W	M	Sep 1879	20	S				KY	KY	KY				FARM LABORER			✓	✓					
		" ARMAD	DAU	W	F	Sep 1888	11	S				KY	KY	KY				AT SCHOOL		5	✓	✓	✓				
		" ALONZO (F.?)	SON	W	M	Dec 1891	8	S				KY	KY	KY				AT SCHOOL		5	✓	✓	✓				
294	300	HARRIS, WILLIAM (?F-T?)	HEAD	W	M	Jan 1828	72	M	46			KY	KY	KY				FARMER			✓	✓	✓	O		F	188
		" MARTHA E.	WIFE	W	F	Jul 1832	68	M	46			KY	KY	KY							✓	✓	✓				
295	301	EMBERTON, NORE M.	HEAD	W	M	May 1861	39	M	21			KY	KY	KY				FARMER			✓	X	✓	R		F	189

STATE - KENTUCKY
COUNTY - MONROE
Township or other division WEST TOMPKINSVILLE Enumerator MALIA PAGE

Supervisor's Dist. No. 102 Sheet No.
Enumeration Dist. No. 85

No. of Family	No. of Dwelling	NAME	Relation	Color	Sex	Date of Birth Mon/Yr	Age at last birthday	Marital Status	# Years married	Mother of how many children	# of these children living	Place of birth (this person)	Father of this person	Mother of this person	Year of immigr.	# years in U.S.	Naturalization	Occupation 10 years +	Months not employed	Attended school in months	Can read	Can write	Speak English	Owned or Rent	Owned -no mortage	Farm or house	# of farm schedule
		EMBERTON, NANCY	WIFE	W	F	AUG 1861	38	M	21	7	6	KY	KY	KY							✓	✓	✓				
		" ELZIE A.	SON	W	M	OCT 1881	18	S				KY	KY	KY				FARM LABORER			✓	✓	✓				
		" HENRY W.	SON	W	M	APR 1884	16	S				KY	KY	KY				FARM LABORER		5	✓	✓	✓				
		" JENNIE O.	DAU	W	F	FEB 1886	14	S				KY	KY	KY				AT SCHOOL		4	✓	✓	✓				
		" SAMUEL M.	SON	W	M	JUN 1888	11	S				KY	KY	KY				AT SCHOOL		3	✓	✓	✓				
		" LOU E.	DAU	W	F	APR 1893	7	S				KY	KY	KY				AT SCHOOL		3							
		" WILLIE S.	SON	W	M	MAR 1896	4	S				KY	KY	KY													
296	302	WALKER, SAMUEL H.	HEAD	W	M	AUG 1845	54	M	34			KY	KY	KY				FARMER			X	X	✓	R	F	190	
		" MARTHA J.	WIFE	W	F	NOV 1848	52	M	34	11	9	KY	KY	KY							✓	X	✓				
		" LINCOY	SON	W	M	JUN 1879	20	S				KY	KY	KY				FARM LABORER			✓	✓	✓				
		" LAURA	DAU	W	F	JUN 1882	17	S				KY	KY	KY				AT SCHOOL		5	✓	✓	✓				
		" BERTHA	DAU	W	F	JAN 1885	15	S				KY	KY	KY				AT SCHOOL		5	✓	✓	✓				
		" MARTHA M.	DAU	W	F	DEC 1887	12	S				KY	KY	KY				AT SCHOOL		5	✓	✓	✓				
		" FLOSSIE M.	DAU	W	F	FEB 1892	8	S				KY	KY	KY				AT SCHOOL		5							
297	303	DICKERSON, JARRET(?)	HEAD	W	M	MAR 1864	36	M	8			KY	KY	KY				FARMER			✓	✓	✓	O	FF	191	
		" BESSIE E.	WIFE	W	F	SEP 1869	30	M	8	3	2	KY	ALA	KY							✓	✓	✓				
		" MAUD E.	DAU	W	F	NOV 1893	6	S				KY	KY	KY													
		" CLIDE	SON	W	M	JUL 1896	3	S				KY	KY	KY													
		" SARAH F.	Mother	W	F	JAN 1836	64	Wd		1	1	KY	KY	KY							✓	✓	✓				
298	304	NANNY, JAMES L.	HEAD	W	M	MAR 1864	36	M	15			KY	KY	KY				FARM LABORER			✓	X	✓	R	H		
		" , FANNY	WIFE	W	F	DEC 1859	40	M	15			KY	KY	KY							✓	X	✓				
299	305	BARTLEY, INGRAM T.	HEAD	W	M	NOV 1880	19	M	2			KY	KY	KY				FARMER			✓	✓	✓	R	F	192	
		" POLLIE J.	WIFE	W	F	OCT 1870	29	M	2	3	2	KY	KY	KY							✓	✓	✓				
		" MARY S.	DAU	W	F	FEB 1900	4/12	S				KY	KY	KY													
300	306	WALDEN, THOMAS B.	HEAD	W	M	SEP 1835	64	M	33			KY	VA	VA				FARMER			✓	✓	✓	O	FF	193	
		" RACHEL	WIFE	W	F	JAN 1849	51	M	33			KY	KY	KY							✓	✓	✓				

TWELFTH CENSUS OF THE UNITED STATES 1900

— 387 —

STATE - KENTUCKY
COUNTY - MONROE
Township or other division WEST TOMPKINSVILLE
Enumerator MALIA PAGE

Supervisor's Dist. No. 102 Sheet No. ___
Enumeration Dist. No. 85 ___

No. of Family	No. of Dwelling	NAME	Relation	Color	Sex	Date of Birth Mon/Yr	Age at last birthday	Marital Status	# Years married	Mother of how many children	# of these children living	Place of birth [this person]	Father of this person	Mother of this person	Year of immigr.	# years in U.S.	Naturalization	Occupation 10 years +	Months not employed	Attended school in months	Can read	Can write	Speak English	Owned or Rent	Owned -no mortage / Farm or house	# of Farm schedule
		WALDEN, WILLIE E.	SON	W	M	Jun 1876	23	S				KY	KY	KY				FARM LABORER			✓	✓				
		" ROBERT B.	SON	W	M	Dec 1882	17	S				KY	KY	KY				FARM LABORER 4		4	✓	✓				
		" JAMES H.	SON	W	M	Aug 1884	15	S				KY	KY	KY				AT SCHOOL		5	✓	✓				
		" JACOB B.	SON	W	M	Feb 1888	12	S				KY	KY	KY				AT SCHOOL		5	✓	✓				
		" BUFORD E.	SON	W	M	Sep 1891	8	S				KY	KY	KY												
301	307	ALVIS, SARAH M.	HEAD	W	F	Jun 1859	40	Wd		4	2	KY	KY	KY				FARMER			X	X	✓	R	F	194
		WELCH, ROBERT	SON	W	M	May 1883	17	S				KY	KY	KY				AT SCHOOL		5	✓	✓	✓			
		BAZIL, WILLIAM L.	Son-in-law	W	M	Aug 1869	30	M	1			MO	TN	KY				FARMER			✓	✓	✓			
		" MARY E.	DAU	W	F	Aug 1879	20	M	1	1	1	KY	KY	TN				NURSE			✓	✓	✓			
		" CLARENCE D.	SON	W	M	Nov 1899	7/12	S				KY	KY	KY												
302	308	HAMMER, JOEL (E?)	HEAD	W	M	Apr 1852	48	M	13			KY	TN	KY				FARMER			✓	✓		O	M F	195
		" RACHEL C.	WIFE	W	F	Feb 1859	41	M	13	1	1	KY	KY	KY							✓	✓				
		" AUBRA	SON	W	M	Dec 1887	12	S				KY	KY	KY				AT SCHOOL		5	✓	✓	✓			
303	309	GRAVEN, WILLIAM	HEAD	W	M	Jan 1853	47	M	11			KY	KY	KY				FARMER			✓	✓		R	F	196
		" ANNA D.	WIFE	W	F	Apr 1870	30	M	11	2	2	KY	KY	KY							✓	✓				
		" WILLIE A.	SON	W	M	Jan 1890	10	S				KY	KY	KY				AT SCHOOL		5	✓	✓	✓			
		" WALTER H.	DAU	W	F	Jul 1897	2	S				KY	KY	KY												
304	310	EMMERT, BANAFORD	HEAD	W	M	Mar 1868	32	M	6			KY	KY	KY				DAY LABORER			✓	✓	✓	R	H	
		" HARRIETTE	WIFE	W	F	Feb 1872	28	M	6	3	3	KY	KY	KY							✓	✓	✓			
		" MINNIE C.	DAU	W	F	Jul 1895	4	S				KY	KY	KY												
		" ZADIE J.	DAU	W	F	Mar 1897	3	S				KY	KY	KY												
		" EVIE D.	DAU	W	F	Mar 1900	2/12	S				KY	KY	KY												
305	311	DICKERSON, ELIZA J.	HEAD	W	F	Sep 1836	63	Wd		4	4	KY	TN	TN				FARMER			✓	✓		R	F	197
		" MARTHA C.	DAU	W	F	Nov 1862	37	S				KY	KY	KY				FARM LABORER			✓	✓				
306	312	EMBERTON, ROSCOE	HEAD	W	M	Jan 1867	33	M	11			KY	KY	KY				FARMER			✓	✓		R	F	198
		" LUELLA P.	WIFE	W	F	Sep 1872	27	M	11	4	3	KY	KY	KY							✓	✓	✓			

STATE - KENTUCKY
COUNTY - MONROE
Township or other division — WEST TOMPKINSVILLE
Enumerator — MALIA PAGE

Supervisor's Dist. No. _102_ Sheet No.
Enumeration Dist. No. _85_

No. of Family	No. of Dwelling	NAME	Relation	Color	Sex	DATE OF BIRTH Mon/Yr	Age at last birthday	Marital Status	Years married	Mother of how many children?	# of these children living	Place of birth (this person)	Father of this person	Mother of this person	Year of immigr.	# years in U.S.	Naturalization	OCCUPATION 10 years +	Months not employed	Attended school in months	Can read	Can write	Speak English	Owned or Rent	Owned -no mortgage	Farm or house	# of farm schedule
		EMBERTON, EFFIE	DAU	W	F	AUG 1892	7	S				KY	KY	KY													
		" EVERT	SON	W	M	Sep 1894	5	S				KY	KY	KY													
		" CHASSY	DAU	W	F	Sep 1898	1	S				KY	KY	KY													
307	313	HAMMER, JOHN	HEAD	W	M	OCT 1844	55	M	27			KY	KY	KY				Farmer			✓	✓	✓	O	F	199	
		" NANNIE J.	WIFE	W	F	APR 1852	48	M	27	5	5	TN	TN	TN							✓	✓	✓				
		" LONA A.	DAU	W	F	DEC 1882	18	S				KY	KY	TN				AT SCHOOL		2	✓	✓	✓				
		" PLEASANT W.	SON	W	M	AUG 1884	15	S				KY	KY	TN				AT SCHOOL		7	✓	✓	✓				
		" WESLEY B.	SON	W	M	DEC 1886	13	S				KY	KY	TN				AT SCHOOL		8	✓	✓					
308	314	BUSHONG, NANCY	HEAD	W	F	NOV 1846	53	Wd				KY	KY	KY				FARMER			✓	✓	✓	O	F	200	
		ARTERBURN, DEBBIE (?)	DAU	W	F	JAN 1869	31	M	1	1	1	KY	KY	KY							✓	✓	✓				
		" MALISSA F.	GR-DAU	W	F	Sep 1898	1	S				KY	KY	KY													
		JACKSON, SAMUEL A.	HIRED	W	M	JAN 1856	44	M	20			KY	TN	TN				FARMER			✓	✓					
309	315	BUSHONG, SAMUEL M.	HEAD	W	M	OCT 1866	33	M	2			KY	KY	KY				FARMER			✓	✓	✓	R	F	200	
		" CATHERINE	WIFE	W	F	DEC 1865	34	M	2	0	0	KY	KY	KY							✓	✓	✓				
		JACKSON, HENRY J.	HEAD	W	M	Sep 1860	39	S				KY	IN	IN				FARMER			✓	✓	✓	R	F	201	
		" MAHALA J.	SISTER	W	F	MAY 1865	35	S				KY	TN	TN							✓	✓	✓				
311	317	PITCOCK, CYRUS M.	HEAD	W	M	MAY 1842	58	M	35			KY	TN	TN				FARMER			✓	✓	✓	O	M	202	
		" ELIZABETH	WIFE	W	F	AUG 1846	53	M	35	12	10	KY	KY	KY							✓	✓	✓				
		" EDIE T.	DAU	W	F	Sep 1881	18	S				KY	KY	KY							✓	✓					
		" HENRY F.	SON	W	M	Sep 1884	15	S				KY	KY	KY				AT SCHOOL		5	✓	✓	✓				
		" EVIE B.	DAU	W	F	Feb 1889	13	S				KY	KY	KY				AT SCHOOL		5	✓	✓	✓				
		McPHERSON, BETTIE	GR-DAU	W	F	Feb 1897	3	S				KY	KY	KY													
312	318	PITCOCK, TOLBERT S.	HEAD	W	M	Sep 1848	51	M	31			KY	TN	TN				FARMER			✓	✓	✓	O	F	203	
		" MARY T.	WIFE	W	F	AUG 1852	47	M	31	5	5	KY	KY	KY							✓	✓	✓				
		" EVIE	DAU	W	F	Feb 1876	24	S				KY	KY	KY							✓	✓	✓				
		" AVERY	SON	W	M	AUG 1883	16	S				KY	KY	KY				AT SCHOOL		4	✓	✓	✓				

STATE - KENTUCKY
COUNTY - MONROE
Township or other division — WEST TOMPKINSVILLE   Enumerator MALIA PAGE

Supervisor's Dist. No. _102_ Sheet No.
Enumeration Dist. No. _85_

Location		NAME	Relation	Color	Sex	DATE OF BIRTH Mon/Yr	Age at last birthday	Marital Status	# Years married	Mother of how many children?	# of these children living	Place of birth [this person]	Father of this person	Mother of this person	Year of immigr.	# years in U.S.	Naturalization	OCCUPATION 10 years +	Months not employed	Attended school in months	Can read	Can write	Speak English	Owned or Rent	Owned -no mortgage	Farm or house	# of farm schedule	
No. of Family	No. of Dwelling																											
		PITCOCK, HUGH	SON	W	M	MAY 1887	13	S				KY	KY	TN				AT SCHOOL		5	✓	✓	✓					
313	319	BIRGE, JESSE S.	HEAD	W	M	JUN 1866	33	M	16			KY	KY	TN				FARMER			✓	✓	✓	O	M	F	204	
		DAMARIS (For T)	WIFE	W	F	DEC 1863	36	M	16	9	7	KY	KY	KY							✓	✓	✓					
		SAMUEL W.	SON	W	M	OCT 1886	13	S				KY	KY	KY				FARM LABORER 5		5	X	X	✓					
		ERASTUS B.	SON	W	M	OCT 1887	12	S				KY	KY	KY				FARM LABORER 5		5	X	X	✓					
		CHARLIE F.	SON	W	M	Sep 1889	10	S				KY	KY	KY				FARM LABORER 5		5	X	X	✓					
		VERA J.	DAU	W	F	Sep 1891	8	S				KY	KY	KY														
		MOLLIE L.	DAU	W	F	AUG 1893	6	S				KY	KY	KY														
		SARAH E.	DAU	W	F	JAN 1896	4	S				KY	KY	KY														
		JAMES T.	SON	W	M	Feb 1900	3/12	S				KY	KY	KY														
314	320	COPASS, JOHN	HEAD	W	M	Sep 1854	45	M	21			KY	TN	KY				FARMER			X	X	✓	O	F	F	205	
		FRANK W.	WIFE	W	F	MAY 1864	36	M	21	12	11	KY	VA	KY							✓	✓						
		NANCY A.	DAU	W	F	MAY 1881	19	S				KY	KY	KY							✓	✓						
		JAMES E.	SON	W	M	APR 1883	17	S				KY	KY	KY				FARM LABORER			✓	✓	✓					
		LERA	DAU	W	F	Feb 1885	15	S				KY	KY	KY				AT SCHOOL		4	✓	✓	✓					
		ALICE	DAU	W	F	MAR 1887	13	S				KY	KY	KY				AT SCHOOL		4	✓	✓	✓					
		GEORGE S.	SON	W	M	OCT 1888	11	S				KY	KY	KY				FARM LABORER			✓	✓	✓					
		PERRY H.	SON	W	M	OCT 1890	9	S				KY	KY	KY				AT SCHOOL		5	✓	✓	✓					
		SALLIE (E or T)	DAU	W	F	AUG 1892	7	S				KY	KY	KY				AT SCHOOL		5	X	X	✓					
		LUCY P.	DAU	W	F	JAN 1894	6	S				KY	KY	KY														
		DAVID F.	SON	W	M	APR 1896	4	S				KY	KY	KY														
		VESTER J.	SON	W	M	APR 1898	2	S				KY	KY	KY														
		BETSY C. (?)	SON	W	M	APR 1898	2	S				KY	KY	KY														
315	321	PAGE, SAMUEL H.	HEAD	W	M	DEC 1837	62	M	13			KY	SC	KY				FARMER			✓	✓	✓	O	E	F	206	
		SARAH F.	WIFE	W	F	DEC 1856	43	M	13	1	1	KY	KY	KY							✓	✓	✓					
		WILLIAM F.	SON	W	M	Feb 1898	2	S				KY	KY	KY														

STATE - KENTUCKY
COUNTY - MONROE
Township or other division: WEST TOMPKINSVILLE

– 390 –

Enumerator: MALIA PAGE

Supervisor's Dist. No. 102 Sheet No.
Enumeration Dist. No. 95

No. of Family	No. of Dwelling	NAME	Relation	Color	Sex	DATE OF BIRTH Mon/Yr	Age at last birthday	Marital Status	# Years married	Mother of how many children?	# of these children living	Place of birth (this person)	Father of this person	Mother of this person	OCCUPATION 10 years +	Months not employed	Attended school in months	Can read	Can write	Speak English	Owned or Rent	Owned –no mortgage	Farm or house	# of farm schedule
316	322	JACKSON, ALEXANDER H.	HEAD	W	M	Jul 1857	42	M	16			KY	TN	TN	FARMER		X	X	✓		R		F	207
		" MARTHA	WIFE	W	F	Feb 1868	32	M	16			MO	TN	TN					✓					
317	323	FORD, WILLIAM S.	HEAD	W	M	May 1870	30	M	7			MO	TN	TN	FARMER			✓	✓	✓	R		F	208
		" AMANDA	WIFE	W	F	Sep 1854	45	M	7	4	4	MO	TN	KY				✓	✓	✓				
		" OVIE B.	DAU	W	F	Jul 1893	6	S				TN	MO	MO										
		MARY E.	DAU	W	F	Aug 1895	4	S				TN	MO	MO										
		WHITE, PATRICK H.	Adopted Son	W	M	Jan 1887	13	S				KY	TN	MO	FARM LABORER			✓	X	✓				
318	324	PAGE, ALBERTUS G.	HEAD	W	M	Jul 1870	29	M				KY	KY	KY	FARMER			✓	✓		R		F	209
		" EVIE D.	WIFE	W	F	Oct 1877	22	M				KY	KY	KY				✓	✓					
319	325	PITCOCK, WESLEY	HEAD	W	M	Feb 1856	44	M	16			KY	KY	KY	FARMER			✓	✓	✓	O		F	210
		" HARRIET	WIFE	W	F	Dec 1859	40	M	16	10	7	KY	KY	KY				✓	✓					
		" MARVIN R.	SON	W	M	May 1887	13	S				KY	KY	KY	AT SCHOOL		5	✓	✓					
		" LINARD E.	SON	W	M	Mar 1891	9	S				KY	KY	KY	AT SCHOOL		4	✓	✓					
		" WESLEY F.	SON	W	M	Apr 1893	7	S				KY	KY	KY	AT SCHOOL		5							
		" VIOLA J.	DAU	W	F	June 1893	6	S				KY	KY	KY	AT SCHOOL		5	X	X	✓				
		" LIZZIE M.	DAU	W	F	May 1896	4	S				KY	KY	KY										
		" BIRDIE V.	DAU	W	F	Aug 1897	2	S				KY	KY	KY										
		" (INFANT)	DAU	W	F	May 1900	1/12	S				KY	KY	KY										
320	326	PITCOCK, JOHN	HEAD	W	M	Dec 1850	49	M				KY	KY	KY	FARMER			✓	✓		O		F	211
		" MARTHA D.	WIFE	W	F	Jan 1861	39	M				KY	KY	KY				✓	✓					
		" ETTIE F.	DAU	W	F	Aug 1879	20	S				KY	KY	KY	SCHOOL TEACHER			✓	✓					
		" JOHN B.	SON	W	M	Apr 1882	18	S				KY	KY	KY	AT SCHOOL		5	✓	✓					
		" NANCY E.	DAU	W	F	Aug 1883	16	S				KY	KY	KY	AT SCHOOL		5	✓	✓					
		" EFFIE J.	DAU	W	F	Feb 1885	15	S				KY	KY	KY	AT SCHOOL		5	✓	✓					
		" JOSEPH D.	SON	W	M	Mar 1886	14	S				KY	KY	KY	AT SCHOOL		5	✓	✓					
		" DONNA ESTHER	DAU	W	F	Sep 1888	11	S				KY	KY	KY	AT SCHOOL		5	✓	✓	✓				

STATE - KENTUCKY
COUNTY - MONROE
Township or other division: WEST TOMPKINSVILLE   Enumerator: MALIA PAGE

Supervisor's Dist. No. 102   Sheet No.
Enumeration Dist. No. 15

No. of Family	No. of Dwelling	NAME	Relation	Color	Sex	DATE OF BIRTH Mon/Yr	Age at last birthday	Marital Status	# Years married	Mother of how many children?	# of these children living	Place of birth [this person]	Father of this person	Mother of this person	Year of immigr.	# years in U.S.	Naturalization	OCCUPATION 10 years +	Months not employed	Attended school in months	Can read	Can write	Speak English	Owned or Rent	Owned -no mortgage	Farm or house	# of farm schedule
		PITCOCK, ONA B.	DAU	W	F	Jan 1890	10	S				KY	KY	KY				AT SCHOOL		5	✓	✓	✓				
		" OSCAR C.	SON	W	M	Jan 1892	8	S				KY	KY	KY				AT SCHOOL		4							
		" OSMAN L.	SON	W	M	Feb 1894	6	S				KY	KY	KY													
321	327	MOORE, MANERVA J.	HEAD	W	F	Aug 1831	68	Wd		5	5	KY	TN	TN				FARMER			✓	✓	✓	O	F	F	212
		" SAMUEL J.	SON	W	M	Feb 1859	41	S				KY	KY	KY				FARMER			✓	✓	✓				212
		" JOHN W.	SON	W	M	Feb 1863	37	S				KY	KY	KY				FARMER			✓	✓	✓				212
322	328	MOORE, LINDSAY E.	HEAD	W	M	Aug 1854	45	M	16			KY	KY	KY				FARMER			✓	✓	✓	O	F	F	213
		" LOUISA	WIFE	W	F	Dec 1864	35	M	16	5	3	KY	KY	KY							✓	✓	✓				
		" NELLIE E.	DAU	W	F	Aug 1887	12	S				KY	KY	KY				AT SCHOOL		5	✓	✓	✓				
		" ELLA M.	DAU	W	F	Sep 1889	10	S				KY	KY	KY				AT SCHOOL		5	✓	✓	✓				
		" ORPHA	DAU	W	F	Jun 1893	6	S				KY	KY	KY				AT SCHOOL		5							
323	329	HAGAN, JAMES R.	HEAD	W	M	Nov 1866	33	M	10			KY	KY	KY				FARMER			✓	✓	✓	O	M	F	214
		" KITTIE E.	WIFE	W	F	Jan 1868	32	M	10	6	4	KY	KY	TN							✓	✓	✓				
		" THOMAS H.	SON	W	M	Oct 1890	9	S				KY	KY	KY				AT SCHOOL		2	X	X	✓				
		" SARAH F.	DAU	W	F	Aug 1892	7	S				KY	KY	KY													
		" EFFIE J.	DAU	W	F	Oct 1897	3	S				KY	KY	KY													
		" BERTHA B.	DAU	W	F	Jan 1900	4/12	S				KY	KY	KY													
324	330	POLAND, HENRY	HEAD	W	M	Jun 1861	38	M	13			KY	TN	KY				FARMER			✓	✓	✓	R		F	215
		" SARAH	WIFE	W	F	Apr 1861	39	M	13	7	6	KY	KY	KY							✓	✓	✓				
		" DOLLIE N.	DAU	W	F	Aug 1887	12	S				KY	KY	KY				AT SCHOOL		5	✓	✓	✓				
		" BETTIE H.	DAU	W	F	Jun 1888	11	S				TN	KY	KY				AT SCHOOL		5	✓	✓	✓				
		" LANDON E.	SON	W	M	Jun 1892	7	S				KY	KY	KY				AT SCHOOL		4	✓	✓	✓				
		" ROY T.	SON	W	M	May 1896	4	S				KY	KY	KY													
		" DEBBIE M.	DAU	W	F	Jan 1897	3	S				KY	KY	KY													
		" MANERVIA L.	DAU	W	F	Jan 1900	5/12	S				KY	KY	KY													
325	331	HAGAN, JONAS M.	HEAD	W	M	Aug 1867	32	M	12			KY	KY	KY				DAY LABORER			✓	✓	✓	R		H	

STATE - KENTUCKY
COUNTY - MONROE
Township or other division — WEST TOMPKINSVILLE   Enumerator MALIA PAGE

Supervisor's Dist. No. 102   Sheet No.
Enumeration Dist. No. 85

No. of Family	No. of Dwelling	NAME	Relation	Color	Sex	DATE OF BIRTH Mon/Yr	Age at last birthday	Marital Status	# Years married	Mother of how many children?	# of these children living	Place of birth [this person]	Father of this person	Mother of this person	Year of immigr.	# years in U.S.	Naturalization	OCCUPATION 10 years +	Months not employed	Attended school in months	Can read	Can write	Speak English	Owned or Rent	Owned -no mortage	Farm or house	# of farm schedule
		HAGAN, SARAH L.	WIFE	W	F	Feb 1868	32	M	12	3	3	KY	KY	KY							✓	✓	✓				
		" ERA T.	Son	W	M	Mar 1889	11	S				KY	KY	KY				AT SCHOOL		5	✓	✓	✓				
		" ONE E.	Dau	W	F	Sep 1892	7	S				KY	KY	KY				AT SCHOOL		5	✓	✓	✓				
		" DONA H.	Dau	W	F	Aug 1894	5	S				KY	KY	KY													
326	332	PAGE, JOHN B. JR.	HEAD	W	M	Aug 1854	45	M	25			KY	KY	KY				FARMER			✓	✓	✓	O	F	F	216
		" AMANDA C.	WIFE	W	F	Aug 1856	43	M	25	12	10	KY	KY	KY							✓	✓	✓				
		" DOCIA T.	DAU	W	F	Jul 1879	20	S				KY	KY	KY							✓	✓	✓				
		" MYRTIE M.	DAU	W	F	Sep 1880	19	S				KY	KY	KY				AT SCHOOL		4	✓	✓	✓				
		" ADA G.	DAU	W	F	Aug 1884	15	S				KY	KY	KY				AT SCHOOL		4	✓	✓	✓				
		" MINNIE T.	DAU	W	F	Oct 1886	13	S				KY	KY	KY				AT SCHOOL		4	✓	✓	✓				
		" EMERSON G.	Son	W	M	Mar 1889	11	S				KY	KY	KY				AT SCHOOL		3	✓	✓	✓				
		" EDWARD E.	Son	W	M	Mar 1891	9	S				KY	KY	KY				AT SCHOOL		5	✓	✓	✓				
		" NORA E.	DAU	W	F	Dec 1892	7	S				KY	KY	KY				AT SCHOOL		5	✓	✓					
		" FRED S.	Son	W	M	May 1898	3	S				KY	KY	KY													
		" ORVAL B.	Son	W	M	May 1900	1/12	S				KY	KY	KY													
327	333	HAGAN, JOSEPH L.	HEAD	W	M	Jan 1875	25	M	7			KY	KY	KY				FARMER			✓	✓	✓	R		F	
		" ANNA B.	WIFE	W	F	Feb 1878	22	M	7	4	3	KY	KY	KY							✓	✓	✓				
		" ISAAC R.	Son	W	M	Jan 1894	6	S				KY	KY	KY													
		" WILLIAM A.	Son	W	M	Jun 1895	4	S				KY	KY	KY													
		" IDA M.	DAU	W	F	Aug 1897	2	S				KY	KY	KY													
328	334	BASIL, LUCINDA	HEAD	W	F	Dec 1854	45	Wd		8	7	KY	KY	KY				FARMER			X	X	✓	O	F	F	217
		" JOHN H.	Son	W	M	Aug 1881	18	S				KY	KY	KY				FARM LABORER			✓	✓	✓				
		" GEORGEANN	DAU	W	F	Sep 1882	17	S				KY	KY	KY				AT SCHOOL		5	✓	✓	✓				
		" LAURA P.	DAU	W	F	Jul 1884	15	S				KY	KY	KY				AT SCHOOL		5	✓	✓	✓				
		" ALICE	DAU	W	F	Aug 1886	13	S				KY	KY	KY				AT SCHOOL		8	✓	✓	✓				
		" CECIL	Son	W	M	Apr 1895	5	S				KY	KY	KY													

TWELFTH CENSUS OF THE UNITED STATES 1900

STATE - KENTUCKY
COUNTY - MONROE
Township or other division: WEST TOMPKINSVILLE
Enumerator: MALIA PAGE
Supervisor's Dist. No. 102   Sheet No.
Enumeration Dist. No. 85

No. of Family	No. of Dwelling	NAME	Relation	Color	Sex	Date of Birth Mon/Yr	Age at last birthday	Marital Status	# Years married	Mother of how many children?	# of these children living	Place of birth (this person)	Father of this person	Mother of this person	Year of immigr.	# years in U.S.	Naturalization	Occupation 10 years +	Months not employed	Attended school in months	Can read	Can write	Speak English	Owned or Rent	Owned – no mortgage	Farm or house	# of farm schedule
329	335	HARRISON, WILLIAM	HEAD	W	M	Feb 1847	53	M	22			KY	KY	KY				FARMER			✓	✓		O	F	F	218
		" MARTHA E.	WIFE	W	F	Mar 1844	56	M	22	3	3	KY	KY	KY							✓	✓	✓				
		" LUCY	DAU	W	F	Jun 1880	19	S				KY	KY	KY				AT SCHOOL		10	✓	✓	✓				
		" LULA	DAU	W	F	Jan 1884	16	S				KY	KY	KY				AT SCHOOL		5	✓	✓	✓				
		" LOLA	DAU	W	F	Oct 1892	7	S				KY	KY	KY													
330	336	TOOLEY, ISHAM	HEAD	W	M	Jul 1821	78	M	53			KY	VA	VA				FARMER			✓	✓		O	F	F	219
		" ELIZABETH	WIFE	W	F	Jul 1823	76	M	53	5	5	KY	VA	VA							✓	✓	✓				
		" WILSON C.	SON	W	M	Nov 1866	33	M				KY	KY	KY				FARMER			✓	✓	✓				219
		" ANDELLA	DAU-IN-LAW	W	F	Dec 1875	24	M				KY	KY	KY							✓	✓					
331	337	DAVIS, JAMES F.	HEAD	W	M	Mar 1874	25	M	6			KY	KY	KY				FARMER			✓	✓		R		F	220
		" NANCY J.	WIFE	W	F	Aug 1875	24	M	6	3	3	KY	KY	KY							✓	✓	✓				
		" LOLA	DAU	W	F	Jul 1895	4	S				KY	KY	KY													
		" LILIAN	DAU	W	F	Jun 1896	3	S				KY	KY	KY													
		" LEO	SON	W	M	Jun 1898	1	S				KY	KY	KY													
332	338	McCREARY, ALBERT M.	HEAD	W	M	Jan 1853	47	M	20			VA	VA	VA				FARMER			✓	✓		O	F	F	221
		" SARAH E.	DAU	W	F	May 1861	39	M	20	10	9	KY	KY	TN				NURSE			✓	✓					
		" GROVER	SON	W	M	May 1881	19	S				TX	VA	KY				AT SCHOOL		3	✓	✓					
		" ARTHUR Z.	SON	W	M	Jul 1882	17	S				KY	VA	KY				AT SCHOOL		3	✓	✓					
		" FANNY A.	DAU	W	F	Oct 1884	15	S				KY	VA	KY				AT SCHOOL		5	✓	✓					
		" JOHN I.	SON	W	M	Dec 1886	13	S				KY	VA	KY				AT SCHOOL		5	✓	✓					
		" ORA N.	DAU	W	F	Oct 1889	10	S				KY	VA	KY				AT SCHOOL		5	✓	✓					
		" BOB H.	SON	W	M	Dec 1891	8	S				KY	VA	KY				AT SCHOOL		5	✓	✓	✓				
		" THOMAS L.	SON	W	M	Oct 1893	6	S				KY	VA	KY				AT SCHOOL		5	✓	✓					
		" WILLIE C.	SON	W	M	Dec 1896	3	S				KY	VA	KY													
		" LUCAS M.	SON	W	M	Jan 1900	4/12	S				KY	VA	KY													
333	339	PITCOCK, ALBERT S.	HEAD	W	M	Oct 1871	28	M	6			KY	KY	KY				FARMER			✓	✓	✓	R		F	222

STATE - KENTUCKY
COUNTY - MONROE
Township or other division — WEST TOMPKINSVILLE
Enumerator — MALIA PAGE

Supervisor's Dist. No. 102   Sheet No.
Enumeration Dist. No. 85

Location No. of Family	No. of Dwelling	NAME	Relation	Color	Sex	DATE OF BIRTH Mon/Yr	Age at last birthday	Marital Status	# Years married	Mother of how many children?	# of these children living	Place of birth [this person]	Father of this person	Mother of this person	Year of immigr.	# years in U.S.	Naturalization	OCCUPATION 10 years +	Months not employed	Attended school in months	Can read	Can write	Speak English	Owned or Rent	Owned -no mortgage	Farm or house	# of farm schedule
		PITCOCK, CORA B.	WIFE	W	F	DEC 1875	24	M	6	3	3	KY	KY	KY							✓	✓	✓				
		" ZELLA	DAU	W	F	JAN 1895	5	S				KY	KY	KY													
		" OLLIE	DAU	W	F	Feb 1897	3	S				KY	KY	KY													
		" OTTUS D.	SON	W	M	Nov 1899	7/12	S				KY	KY	KY													
334	340	UPTERGROVE, GEORGE	HEAD	W	M	JUN 1855	44	M	12			KY	KY	KY				FARMER			X	X	✓	R	F	222
		" MELINDA	WIFE	W	F	May 1870	30	M	13	4	4	KY	KY	KY				NURSE			✓	✓	✓				
		" OSCAR	SON	W	M	APR 1886	14	S				KY	KY	KY				AT SCHOOL		5	✓	✓	✓				
		" NORA J.	DAU	W	F	Dec 1889	10	S				KY	KY	KY				AT SCHOOL		5	✓	✓	✓				
		" MAUDIE F.	DAU	W	F	Jun 1894	5	S				KY	KY	KY													
		" ROBERT K.	SON	W	M	Nov 1895	4	S				KY	KY	KY													
335	341	YOKLEY, JOHN W.	HEAD	W	M	Jul 1838	62	M	33			TN	TN	NC				FARMER			✓	✓	✓	O	F	F	223
		" NANCY A.	WIFE	W	F	Nov 1848	52	M	33	14	14	KY	KY	KY							✓	✓	✓				
		" JAMES T.	SON	W	M	Mar 1882	18	S				KY	TN	KY				FARM LABORER			✓	✓					
		" DOLLY F.	DAU	W	F	May 1884	16	S				KY	TN	KY				AT SCHOOL		5	✓	✓	✓				
		" FLORENCE R.	DAU	W	F	Feb 1886	14	S				KY	TN	KY				AT SCHOOL		3	✓	✓	✓				
		" MAUD	DAU	W	F	Jan 1888	12	S				KY	TN	KY				AT SCHOOL		5	✓	✓	✓				
		" SIDNEY M.	SON	W	M	Mar 1891	9	S				KY	TN	KY				AT SCHOOL		5	✓	✓	✓				
		" NANCY I.	GR-DAU	W	F	Dec 1892	7	S				KY	KY	KY													
		" (F-TON)? S.	GR-SON	W	M	Jul 1896	3	S				KY	KY	KY													
336	342	SEWELL, STEVEN	HEAD	W	M	Feb 1870	30	M	12			KY	KY	KY				FARMER			X	X	✓	O	M	F	224
		" LUCINDA E.	WIFE	W	F	Sep 1871	28	M	12	6	4	KY	KY	KY							X	X	✓				
		" VINCENT	SON	W	M	Jul 1889	10	S				KY	KY	KY				AT SCHOOL		6	✓	✓					
		" LURLIE M.	DAU	W	F	Jul 1891	8	S				KY	KY	KY													
		" ADIE A.	DAU	W	F	Aug 1896	3	S				KY	KY	KY													
		" SALLIE F.	DAU	W	F	Oct 1899	7/12	S				KY	KY	KY													
337	343	HOOD, ELIZABETH	HEAD	W	F	Apr 1848	52	Wd		4	4	KY	KY	KY							X	X	✓	R		H	

STATE - KENTUCKY	WEST	Supervisor's Dist. No. 107 Sheet No.
COUNTY - MONROE	TOMPKINSVILLE	Enumeration Dist. No. 85
Township or other division	Enumerator MALIA PAGE	

| Location | | NAME | Relation | Color | Sex | DATE OF BIRTH Mon/Yr | Age at last birthday | Marital Status | #Years married | Mother of how many children? | # of these children living | NATIVITY | | | CITIZENSHIP | | | OCCUPATION 10 years + | Months not employed | EDUCATION | | | OWNERSHIP | | | |
No. of Family	No. of Dwelling											Place of birth [this person]	Father of this person	Mother of this person	Year of immigr.	# years in U.S.	Naturalization			Attended school in months	Can read	Can write	Speak English	Owned or Rent	Owned -no mortgage	Farm or house	# of farm schedule
		HOOD, WILLIAM J.	SON	W	M	Sep 1884	15	S				KY	KY	KY				AT SCHOOL		2	✓	✓	✓				
		" MARY E.	DAU	W	F	Jul 1885	14	S				KY	KY	KY				AT SCHOOL		5	✓	✓	✓				
		" ISAAC J.	SON	W	M	APR 1888	12	S				KY	KY	KY				AT SCHOOL		3	✓	✓	✓				
		" JOSEPH H	SON	W	M	MAR 1891	9	S				KY	KY	KY													
		" THOMAS M.	SON	W	M	DEC 1893	6	S				KY	KY	KY													
338	344	(PICK ?), HORACE	HEAD	W	M	JAN 1850	50	M	6			KY	KY	KY				DAY LABORER		6	✓	X	✓	R		H	
		" RUTHIE	WIFE	W	F	DEC 1869	30	M	6	3	3	KY	KY	KY							✓	X	✓				
		" ORLEAN W.	DAU	W	F	MAY 1888	12	S				KY	KY	KY				AT SCHOOL		8							
		" WILLIE	SON	W	M	JAN 1892	8	S				KY	KY	KY													
		" SUSAN E.	DAU	W	F	Feb 1899	1	S				KY	KY	KY													
339	345	McCREARY, JACOB	HEAD	W	M	Jul 1863	36	M	17			KY	VA	VA				DOCTOR			✓	✓	✓	R		H	
		" EMMA	WIFE	W	F	MAY 1865	35	M	17	2	2	KY	KY	KY							✓	✓	✓				
		" BEATRICE	DAU	W	F	Jun 1885	15	S				Nebraska	KY	KY				AT SCHOOL		5	✓	✓	✓				
		" ARMMIA B.	DAU	W	F	DEC 1886	13	S				Nebraska	KY	KY				AT SCHOOL		5	✓	✓	✓				
		HAMMER, FRANCIS	Mother	W	F	AUG 1831	68	Wd		1	1	VA	VA	VA							✓	✓	✓				
340	346	DAVIS, JOHN G.	HEAD	W	M	AUG 1852						VA	VA	VA				FARMER			✓	✓	✓	R		F	225
		" SUSAN F.	WIFE	W	F	APR 1850						VA	VA	VA							X	X	✓				
		" DENNIS E.	SON	W	M	Jul 1881						VA	VA	VA				FARM LABORER			✓	✓	✓				
		" WILLIAM F.	SON	W	M	OCT 1884						VA	VA	VA				AT SCHOOL		5	✓	✓	✓				
		" EMMA M.	DAU	W	F	MAY 1886						VA	VA	VA				AT SCHOOL		5	✓	✓	✓				
341	347	ABSHIRE, JACOB	HEAD	W	M	JAN 1837	63	M	40			VA	VA	VA				FARMER			✓	✓	✓	O	M	F	226
		" MARY A.	WIFE	W	F	Jul 1837	62	M	40	4	4	KY	VA	KY							✓	✓	✓				
		FRIAR PLEASANT	GR-SON	W	M	Jun 1880	19	S				KY	TN	KY				AT SCHOOL		3	✓	✓	✓				
342	348	GENTRY, WILLIAM T.	HEAD	W	M	OCT 1843	56	M	28			KY	VA	KY				FARMER			✓	✓	✓	O	F	F	227
		" LAURA B.	WIFE	W	F	Feb 1856	44	M	28	4	2	TN	KY	TN							✓	✓	✓				
		" EVIE E.	DAU	W	F	Jun 1877	22	S				KY	KY	TN				SCHOOL TEACHER			✓	✓	✓				

STATE - KENTUCKY
COUNTY - MONROE
Township or other division: WEST TOMPKINSVILLE

Enumerator: MALIA PAGE

– 396 –

Supervisor's Dist. No. 102 — Sheet No.
Enumeration Dist. No. 85

No. of Family	No. of Dwelling	NAME	Relation	Color	Sex	Date of Birth Mon/Yr	Age at last birthday	Marital Status	# Years married	Mother of how many children?	# of these children living	Place of birth (this person)	Father of this person	Mother of this person	Year of immigr.	Occupation 10 years +	Attended school in months	Can read	Can write	Speak English	Owned or Rent	Owned - no mortage	Farm or house	# of farm schedule
(346)		MARRS, RICHARD F.	F-IN-LAW	W	M	Sep 1823	76	Wd				KY	TN	TN				✓	✓	✓				
343	349	PAGE, JOHN S.	HEAD	W	M	Feb 1853	47	M	28			KY	KY	KY		FARMER		✓	✓	✓	O	F	F	228
"		SARAH E	WIFE	W	F	Apr 1857	43	M	28	9	8	KY	KY	KY				✓	✓	✓				
"		JOHN T.	SON	W	M	Jan 1873	27	S				KY	KY	KY		FARM LABORER		✓	✓					
"		WILLIAM F.	SON	W	M	Apr 1877	23	S				KY	KY	KY		FARM LABORER		✓	✓	✓				
"		GEORGE B.	SON	W	M	Jan 1883	17	S				KY	KY	KY		FARM LABORER		✓	✓	✓				
"		JAMES H.	SON	W	M	Jan 1885	15	S				KY	KY	KY		AT SCHOOL	5	✓	✓	✓				
"		LOU E.	DAU	W	F	Nov 1889	10	S				KY	KY	KY		AT SCHOOL	5	✓	✓	✓				
"		LUTHER B.	SON	W	M	May 1892	8	S				KY	KY	KY		AT SCHOOL	5	✓	✓					
"		IDA M.	DAU	W	F	Oct 1894	5	S				KY	KY	KY										
344	350	BROWN, JOHN B.	HEAD	W	M	May 1863	37	M	16			KY	KY	KY		FARMER		✓	✓	✓	O	F	F	229
"		LEES B.	WIFE	W	F	Aug 1860	39	M	16	6	4	KY	KY	KY				✓	✓	✓				
"		OLIE A.	DAU	W	F	Aug 1887	12	S				KY	KY	KY		AT SCHOOL	4	✓	✓	✓				
"		KATE C.	DAU	W	F	Jan 1891	9	S				KY	KY	KY		AT SCHOOL	4	✓	✓	✓				
"		ADA B.	DAU	W	F	Jan 1895	5	S				KY	KY	KY										
"		BENJAMIN	SON	W	M	May 1898	2	S				KY	KY	KY										
345	351	TOOLEY, JAMES (P?)	HEAD	W	M	Feb 1873	27	M	2			KY	KY	KY		FARMER		✓	✓	✓	R	F	F	229
"		EMMA	WIFE	W	F	Oct 1878	21	M	2	1	1	KY	KY	KY				✓	✓	✓				
"		ORPHA	DAU	W	F	Jul 1899	10/12	S				KY	KY	KY										
346	352	HAGAN, DAVID	HEAD	W	M	Mar 1841	59	M	11			KY	KY	KY		FARMER		✓	✓	✓	O	M	F	230
"		AMANDA C.	WIFE	W	F	May 1856	44	M	11	4	3	KY	ARK	KY				✓	✓	✓				
"		FINLEY D.	SON	W	M	Jun 1890	9	S				KY	KY	KY										
"		GROVER H.	SON	W	M	Sep 1892	7	S				KY	KY	KY										
"		PEARL	DAU	W	F	Jun 1894	5	S				KY	KY	KY										
347	353	HOLLAND, JOHN	HEAD	W	M	Apr 1853	47	M	27			KY	KY	KY		PREACHER		✓	✓	✓	R	F	231	
"		UNUS	WIFE	W	F	Aug 1853	46	M	27	9	7	KY	KY	KY				✓	✓	✓				

TWELFTH CENSUS OF THE UNITED STATES 1900

STATE - KENTUCKY
COUNTY - MONROE
Township or other division: WEST TOMPKINSVILLE
Enumerator: MALIA PAGE

Supervisor's Dist. No. 102 Sheet No.
Enumeration Dist. No. 65

No. of Family	No. of Dwelling	NAME	Relation	Color	Sex	DATE OF BIRTH Mon/Yr	Age at last birthday	Marital Status	# Years married	Mother of how many children?	# of these children living	Place of birth (this person)	Father of this person	Mother of this person	Year of immigr.	# years in U.S.	Naturalization	OCCUPATION 10 years +	Months not employed	Attended school in months	Can read	Can write	Speak English	Owned or Rent	Owned -no mortgage	Farm or house	# of farm schedule
		HOLLAND, MARCUS	Son	W	M	Dec 1885	14	S				KY	KY	KY				AT SCHOOL		5	✓	✓	✓				
		" BERTHA	Dau	W	F	Oct 1887	12	S				KY	KY	KY				AT SCHOOL		4	✓	✓	✓				
		" VERNA	Dau	W	F	Nov 1889	10	S				KY	KY	KY				AT SCHOOL		5	✓	✓	✓				
		" GEORGE S.	Son	W	M	Jan 1892	8	S				KY	KY	KY				AT SCHOOL		4	✓	✓	✓				
		" ETHEL	Dau	W	F	Apr 1894	6	S				KY	KY	KY													
348	354	HAGAN, LEVI S.	HEAD	W	M	Mar 1872	28	M	9			KY	KY	KY				FARMER			✓	✓	✓	R		F	232
		" GEORGIA A.	WIFE	W	F	Sep 1871	28	M	9	5	2	KY	KY	KY													
		" ISAAC T.	SON	W	M	Sep 1891	8	S				KY	KY	KY													
		" BESSIE B.	DAU	W	F	Nov 1899	6/12	S				KY	KY	KY													
349	355	PITCOCK, ISAAC B.	HEAD	W	M	Jun 1832	67	M	43			KY	TN	TN				FARMER			✓	✓		O	M	F	232
		" SARAH A.	WIFE	W	F	Aug 1838	61	M	43	6	6	KY	KY	TN							✓	✓					
		" ISAAC F.	SON	W	M	Nov 1875	24	M	3			KY	KY	KY				FARMER			✓	✓	✓	O	F	F	233
		" MARTHA B.	D-in-Law	W	F	Oct 1876	23	M	3			KY	KY	KY							✓	✓	✓				
		WOODS, SALLIE W.	—	W	F	Sep 1886	13	S				KY	KY	KY				AT SCHOOL		5	✓	✓	✓				
350	356	PITCOCK, AMBROSE? P.	HEAD	W	M	Jun 1842	57	M	37			KY	TN	TN				FARMER			✓	✓	✓	O	F	F	234
		" LOUCETTI	WIFE	W	F	Apr 1844	56	M	37	11	9	KY	KY	KY							✓	✓	✓				
		" FANNY	DAU	W	F	Oct 1869	30	S				KY	KY	KY							✓	✓	✓				
		" JOHN G.	SON	W	M	Feb 1874	26	S				KY	KY	KY				FARM LABORER			✓	✓	✓				
		" LUCY	DAU	W	F	Dec 1885	14	S				KY	KY	KY				AT SCHOOL		4	✓	✓	✓				
351	357	(DAUSY?) JONATHON C.	HEAD	W	M	Jan 1863	37	M	11			KY	KY	KY				FARMER			✓	✓	✓	O	F	F	236
		(DOSSEY?) MARY L.	WIFE	W	F	Aug 1865	34	M	11	2	2	KY	KY	KY							✓	✓	✓				
		" WILLIAM O.	SON	W	M	Jan 1889	11	S				KY	KY	KY				AT SCHOOL		5	✓	✓	✓				
		" JAMES A.	SON	W	M	Sep 1893	6	S				KY	KY	KY				AT SCHOOL		5							
352	358	HAGAN, WILLIAM	HEAD	W	M	Aug 1860	39	M	20			KY	KY	KY				FARMER			✓	✓	✓	O	F	F	237
		" SARAH	WIFE	W	F	July 1850	49	M	20	5	5	KY	TN	VA							✓		✓				
		" DORA B.	DAU	W	F	Sep 1879	20	S				KY	KY	KY							✓		✓				

STATE - KENTUCKY
COUNTY - MONROE
Township or other division WEST TOMPKINSVILLE Enumerator MALIA PAGE

Supervisor's Dist. No. 102 Sheet No.
Enumeration Dist. No. 85

No. of Family	No. of Dwelling	NAME	Relation	Color	Sex	DATE OF BIRTH Mon/Yr	Age at last birthday	Marital Status	# Years married	Mother of how many children?	# of these children living	Place of birth (this person)	Father of this person	Mother of this person	Year of immigr.	# years in U.S.	Naturalization	OCCUPATION 10 years +	Months not employed	Attended school in months	Can read	Can write	Speak English	Owned or Rent	Owned -no mortage	Farm or house	# of farm schedule
		HAGAN, THOMAS J.	Son	W	M	May 1882	18	S				KY	KY	KY				AT SCHOOL		5	✓	✓	✓				
		" LOCKEY F.	Dau	W	F	Mar 1885	15	S				KY	KY	KY				AT SCHOOL		5	✓	✓	✓				
		" PRINTUS E.	Son	W	M	Feb 1888	12	S				KY	KY	KY				AT SCHOOL		4	✓	✓	✓				
		" JOHN W.	Son	W	M	Jan 1891	9	S				KY	KY	KY				AT SCHOOL		4	✓	✓	✓				
		PITCOCK, MARY R.	Sis-in-Law	W	F	Feb 1837	63	S				KY	KY	KY							✓	✓	✓				
353	359	SARTIN, CAROLINE	Head	W	F	Dec 1836	63	Wd	7	6		TN	TN	TN				FARMER			✓	✓	✓	O	F	F	238
		" HANDSEL	Son	W	M	Jan 1882	18	S				KY	TN	TN				AT SCHOOL		5	✓	✓	✓				
354	360	HAMMER, LEE	Head	W	M	Sep 1871	28	M	7			KY	KY	KY				FARMER			X	X	✓	R		F	239
		" LORETTA	Wife	W	F	May 1873	27	M	7	4	3	KY	KY	KY							✓	✓	✓				
		" FRANK	Son	W	M	Mar 1895	5	S				KY	KY	KY													
		" ORA	Dau	W	F	Apr 1897	3	S				KY	KY	KY													
		" PERRY W.	Son	W	M	Feb 1898	1	S				KY	KY	KY													
355	361	GORDON, JESSE	Head	W	M	Nov 1863	36	M	12			KY	KY	VA				FARMER			X	X	✓	R		F	240
		" ELIZABETH E.	Wife	W	F	Oct 1865	34	M	12	6	5	KY	*	TN	*WASHINGTON, D.C.						8	✓	✓	✓				
		" JOHN W.	Son	W	M	Jan 1889	11	S				KY	KY	KY				AT SCHOOL		8	✓	✓	✓				
		" VANDER L.	Son	W	M	May 1891	9	S				KY	KY	KY													
		" FLORY F.	Dau	W	F	Jan 1894	6	S				KY	KY	KY													
		" CHARLEY E.	Son	W	M	Apr 1896	4	S				KY	KY	KY													
356	362	GORDON, WILLIAM	Head	W	M	Sep 1865	34	M	12			KY	KY	KY				FARMER			X	X	✓	R		F	241
		" MARY	Wife	W	F	Dec 1871	28	M	12	7	4	KY	KY	KY							X	X	✓				
		" HENRY B.	Son	W	M	Oct 1891	8	S				KY	KY	KY				AT SCHOOL		4	X	X	✓				
		" MATTIE F.	Dau	W	F	Feb 1894	6	S				KY	KY	KY													
		" SYLVANUS	Son	W	M	Sep 1895	4	S				KY	KY	KY													
		" MARTHA A.	Mother	W	F	Jan 1840	60	Wd		3	3	KY	KY	KY							X	X	✓	R		F	241
357	363	WRIGHT, LENARD	Head	W	M	Nov 1871	28	M	10			IND	IND	IND				FARMER			X	X	✓	R		F	241
		" LYDIA	Wife	W	F	Dec 1869	30	M	10	8	3	KY	KY	KY							X	X	✓				

STATE - KENTUCKY
COUNTY - MONROE
Township or other division — WEST TOMPKINSVILLE — Enumerator MALIA PAGE

Supervisor's Dist. No. 102 Sheet No.
Enumeration Dist. No. 85

No. of Family	No. of Dwelling	NAME	Relation	Color	Sex	Date of Birth Mon/Yr	Age at last birthday	Marital Status	# Years married	Mother of how many children	# of these children living	Place of birth this person	Father of this person	Mother of this person	Occupation 10 years +	Months not employed	Attended school in months	Can read	Can write	Speak English	Owned or Rent	Owned-no mortage	Farm or house	# of farm schedule
		WRIGHT, SYLVESTER	Son	W	M	Mar 1892	8	S				KY	KY	KY										
		" HATTIE E.	Dau	W	F	Jan 1894	6	S				KY	KY	KY										
		" LEWIS V.	Son	W	M	Aug 1897	2	S				KY	KY	KY										
358	364	GENTRY, ELVIRA	Head	W	F	Jun 1855	44	Wd		3	1	KY	KY	NC	Farmer			✓	✓	✓	O	M	F	239
		WHITE, JOHN A.	Son	W	M	Oct 1875	24	S				KY	KY	KY	Farmer			✓	✓	✓	O	M	F	239
		CURTIS, UNA(?)	Hired	W	F	Oct 1880	19	S				KY	KY	KY	Cook			✓	✓	✓				
359	365	PAGE, MATILDA	Head	W	F	Dec 1824	75	Wd				KY	VA	KY	Farmer			✓	✓	✓	O	F	F	242
	366	KIDWELL, AMANDA	Head	W	F	Aug 1844	55	Wd				KY	VA	VA	Farmer			✓	✓	✓	R		F	242
		COOKSIE, MARY J.	Niece	W	F	Mar 1859	41	S				KY	KY	KY				✓	✓	✓				
360	367	PAGE, CHARLES M.	Head	W	M	Nov 1844	55	M	33			KY	KY	KY	Preacher			✓	✓	✓	O	F	F	243
		" MARINDA	Wife	W	F	Oct 1848	57	M	33	9	7	KY	KY	KY				✓	✓	✓				
		" SAMUEL J.	Son	W	M	Apr 1876	24	S				KY	KY	KY	Farm Laborer			✓	✓	✓				
		" EMMA	Dau	W	F	Jan 1881	19	S				KY	KY	KY	At School		5	✓	✓	✓				
		" MARTHA	Dau	W	F	Jan 1883	17	S				KY	KY	KY	At School		5	✓	✓	✓				
		" MAGGIE	Dau	W	F	Sep 1885	14	S				KY	KY	KY	At School		5	✓	✓	✓				
		" CHARLES T.	Son	W	M	Apr 1888	12	S				KY	KY	KY	At School		5	✓	✓					
		" JENNIE	Dau	W	F	Apr 1890	10	S				KY	KY	KY	At School		5	✓	✓	✓				
361	368	PAGE, JAMES T.	Head	W	M	Jul 1852	47	M	20			KY	KY	KY	Farmer			✓	✓	✓	R		F	244
		" JELILA	Wife	W	F	Jan 1856	44	M	20	4	4	KY	KY	KY				✓	✓	✓				
		" JOSEPH	Son	W	M	Sep 1878	21	S				KY	KY	KY	Farm Laborer			✓	✓	✓				
		" PHOEBE	Dau	W	F	Jul 1880	19	S				KY	KY	KY	At School		5	✓	✓	✓				
		" WESLEY	Son	W	M	Jan 1883	17	S				KY	KY	KY	At School		5	✓	✓	✓				
		" (E— Son ?)	Son	W	M	Nov 1886	13	S				KY	KY	KY	At School		4	✓	✓					
		" PHADDIE	Dau	W	F	May 1889	11	S				KY	KY	KY	At School		4	✓	✓					
362	369	PAGE, JOHN T.	Head	W	M	Aug 1821	78	M	8			KY	KY	KY				✓	✓	✓	O		H	
		" NANCY	Wife	W	F	Dec 1851	48	M	8	0	0	KY	KY	KY				✓	✓	✓				

STATE - KENTUCKY
COUNTY - MONROE
Township or other division — WEST TOMPKINSVILLE — Enumerator MALIA PAGE

Supervisor's Dist. No. _102_ Sheet No.
Enumeration Dist. No. _85_

No. of Family / No. of Dwelling	NAME	Relation	Color	Sex	DATE OF BIRTH Mon/Yr	Age at last birthday	Marital Status	# Years married	Mother of how many children?	# of these children living	Place of birth [this person]	Father of this person	Mother of this person	Year of immigr.	# years in U.S.	Naturalization	OCCUPATION 10 years +	Months not employed	Attended school in months	Can read	Can write	Speak English	Owned or Rent	Owned -no mortgage	Farm or house	# of farm schedule
363 370	PAGE, WESLEY	HEAD	W	M	AUG 1875	24	M	6			KY	KY	KY				FARMER			✓	✓	✓	O	F	F	245
	" ELLEN	WIFE	W	F	DEC 1872	27	M	6	2	2	KY	KY	KY							✓	✓	✓				
	" DELLA	DAU	W	F	DEC 1894	5	S				KY	KY	KY													
	" NELLA	DAU	W	F	Sep 1897	2	S				KY	KY	KY													
364 371	TOOLEY, JOHN B.	HEAD	W	M	Sep 1870	29	M	14			KY	KY	KY				FARMER			✓	✓	✓	O	M	F	246
	" DORA L.	WIFE	W	F	MAR 1872	28	M	14	6	6	KY	KY	KY								✓	✓	✓			
	" JAMES W.	SON	W	M	MAR 1887	13	S				KY	KY	KY				AT SCHOOL		5	✓	✓	✓				
	" CLIDE	SON	W	M	JAN 1889	11	S				KY	KY	KY				AT SCHOOL		5	✓	✓	✓				
	" RUTHA T.	DAU	W	F	AUG 1891	8	S				KY	KY	KY				AT SCHOOL		5	✓	✓					
	" SALLIE	DAU	W	F	APR 1894	6	S				KY	KY	KY				AT SCHOOL		4	X	X	✓				
	" FLORA	DAU	W	F	AUG 1896	4	S				KY	KY	KY													
	" MARTHA A.	DAU	W	F	Feb 1899	1	S				KY	KY	KY													
	BROWN, LENA S.	HIRED	W	F	AUG 1884	15	S				KY	KY	KY				COOK			✓	✓	✓				
365 372	GEARLDS, CALVIN	HEAD	B	M	AUG 1859	40	M	11			KY	KY	KY				DAY LABORER			X	X	✓	R		H	
	" LILA	WIFE	B	F	JAN 1867	33	M	11	4	4	KY	KY	KY							X	X	✓				
	" FED	SON	B	M	AUG 1889	10	S				KY	KY	KY				AT SCHOOL		5	✓	✓	✓				
	" MARINDA	DAU	B	F	MAR 1891	9	S				KY	KY	KY				AT SCHOOL		6	✓	✓	✓				
	" OLIE M.	DAU	B	F	Jul 1893	6	S				KY	KY	KY													
	" MANDA B.	DAU	B	F	MAY 1897	3	S				KY	KY	KY													
366 373	GRIDER, WILLIAM	HEAD	W	M	JUN 1863	36	M	10			KY	KY	KY				FARMER			✓	✓	✓	R	F		247
	" MARTHA	DAU	W	F	AUG 1867	32	M	10	2	2	KY	KY	KY							✓	✓	✓				
	" FLOSSIE	DAU	W	F	MAR 1891	9	S				KY	KY	KY				AT SCHOOL		8	X	X	✓				
	" ALLIE	DAU	W	F	MAR 1900	3/12	S				KY	KY	KY													
367 374	BRYANT, JESSE S.	HEAD	W	M	AUG 1835	64	M	3			KY	KY	KY				FARMER			✓	X	✓	R	F		248
	" MISSOURI L.	WIFE	W	F	APR 1878	22	M	3	1	1	KY	KY	KY							✓	✓	✓				
	" ULISSIS L.	SON	W	M	AUG 1867	32	S				KY	KY	KY				DAY LABORER	5		X	X	✓				

STATE - KENTUCKY
COUNTY - MONROE
Township or other division: WEST TOMPKINSVILLE
Enumerator: MALIA PAGE

Supervisor's Dist. No. 102 Sheet No.
Enumeration Dist. No. 85

No. of Family	No. of Dwelling	NAME	Relation	Color	Sex	Date of Birth Mon/Yr	Age at last birthday	Marital Status	# Years married	Mother of how many children?	# of these children living	Place of birth [this person]	Father of this person	Mother of this person	Year of immigr.	# years in U.S.	Naturalization	Occupation 10 years +	Months not employed	Attended school in months	Can read	Can write	Speak English	Owned or Rent	Owned -no mortage	Farm or house	# of farm schedule
		BRYANT, GRANT S.	Son	W	M	Jul 1870	30	S				KY	KY	KY				DAY LABORER 5			X	X	✓				
		" ROSECRAN S.	Son	W	M	Dec 1872	27	S				KY	KY	KY				DAY LABORER 3			X	X	✓				
		" JOHN E.	Son	W	M	Feb 1875	25	S				KY	KY	KY				DAY LABORER 4			X	X	✓				
		" KNEICY J.	Dau	W	F	Nov 1877	22	S				KY	KY	KY							✓	X	✓				
		" JULIA C.	Dau	W	F	Dec 1879	20	S				KY	KY	KY							X	X	✓				
		" SANFORD K.	Son	W	M	Oct 1881	19	S				KY	KY	KY							X	X	✓				
		" ANNA L.	Dau	W	F	Feb 1898	1	S				KY	KY	KY													
368	375	WILSON, JAMES W.	Head	W	M	Aug 1852	47	D/Wd				KY	IN	TN				FARMER			✓	X	✓	O	F	F	249
		" MILLIE	Dau	W	F	Oct 1875	24	S				KY	KY	KY							X	X	✓				
		" GILLIE C.	Dau	W	F	Jul 1885	14	S				KY	KY	KY				AT SCHOOL 8			✓	✓	✓				
369	376	MURLY, MILTON	Head	W	M	Jun 1855	44	M	8			KY	KY	KY				FARMER 4			✓	✓	✓	O	F	F	250
		" MARY	Wife	W	F	Jun 1872	27	M	8	3	2	KY	KY	KY				NURSE			✓	✓	✓				
		" OLIE R.	Dau	W	F	Oct 1885	15	S				KY	KY	KY				AT SCHOOL		1	✓	✓	✓				
		" OMIA	Dau	W	F	Mar 1886	14	S				KY	KY	KY				AT SCHOOL		2	✓	✓	✓				
		" SLOMIA	Dau	W	F	Mar 1886	14	S				KY	KY	KY				AT SCHOOL		3	✓	✓	✓				
		" WILLIAM G.	Son	W	M	Jan 1888	12	S				KY	KY	KY				AT SCHOOL		5	✓	✓	✓				
370	377	PAGE, ALVIN B.	Head	W	M	Oct 1873	26	M	7			KY	KY	KY				FARMER			✓	✓	✓	O	F	F	251
		" SARAH M.	Wife	W	F	Aug 1873	26	M	7	4	4	KY	KY	KY							✓	✓	✓				
		" BEDFORD	Son	W	M	Oct 1894	5	S				KY	KY	KY													
		" EFFIE	Dau	W	F	Apr 1896	4	S				KY	KY	KY													
		" ELLA	Dau	W	F	Dec 1897	2	S				KY	KY	KY													
		" WALTER	Son	W	M	Jul 1899	10/12	S				KY	KY	KY													
371	378	McMURTRY, WILLIAM T.	Head	W	M	Oct 1867	32	M	11			KY	KY	KY				FARMER			✓	✓	✓	O	F	F	252
		" MARTHA E.	Wife	W	F	Oct 1867	32	M	11	2	2	KY	TN	KY							✓	✓					
		" RICHARD F.	Son	W	M	Aug 1889	10	S				KY	KY	KY				AT SCHOOL		5	✓	✓	✓				
		" WORT C.	Son	W	M	Jan 1891	9	S				KY	KY	KY				AT SCHOOL		5	✓	✓	✓				

STATE - KENTUCKY
COUNTY - MONROE
Township or other division WEST TOMPKINSVILLE

— 402 —

Enumerator MALIA PAGE

Supervisor's Dist. No. _102_ Sheet No.
Enumeration Dist. No. _85_

Location		NAME	Relation	Color	Sex	DATE OF BIRTH Mon/Yr	Age at last birthday	Marital Status	# Years married	Mother of how many children?	# of these children living	NATIVITY Place of birth [this person]	Father of this person	Mother of this person	CITIZENSHIP Year of immigr.	# years in U.S.	Naturalization	OCCUPATION 10 years +	Months not employed	EDUCATION Attended school in months	Can read	Can write	Speak English	OWNERSHIP Owned or Rent	Owned -no mortage	Farm or house	# of farm schedule
372	379	ANDERSON, MARK	HEAD	W	M	DEC 1839	60	M	31			TN	TN	TN				DAY LABORER	6		X	X	✓	R		H	
"		JENNIE	WIFE	W	F	Nov 1849	50	M	31	8	8	TN	TN	TN							X	X	✓				
"		CLARK H.	SON	W	M	Sep 1869	30	S				KY	TN	TN				DAY LABORER	4		✓	✓	✓				
"		FRANK	SON	W	M	Nov 1874	25	S				KY	TN	TN				DAY LABORER	5		✓	✓	✓				
"		WOLFORD T.	SON	W	M	OCT 1878	21	S				KY	TN	TN				DAY LABORER	7		✓	✓	✓				
"		THEODORE	SON	W	M	JAN 1882	18	S				KY	TN	TN				DAY LABORER	6		X	X	✓				
"		GERTRUDE	DAU	W	F	DEC 1888	12	S				KY	TN	TN						4	X	X	✓				
"		BESSIE I.	DAU	W	F	JAN 1890	10	S				KY	TN	TN						4	X	X	✓				
"		JOHN F.	SON	W	M	May 1892	8	S				KY	TN	TN													
"		NANCY J.	DAU	W	F	JAN 1898	2	S				KY	TN	TN													
373	380	PITCOCK, WILLIAM S.	HEAD	W	M	MAR 1871	29	M	3			KY	KY	KY				FARMER			✓	✓	✓	O	F	F	253
"		MATILDA J.	WIFE	W	F	Sep 1869	30	M	3			KY	KY	KY							✓	✓	✓				
374	381	RODDY, JOHN H.	HEAD	W	M	MAR 1873	27	M	3			KY	KY	KY				FARMER			✓	✓	✓	O	F	F	254
"		VERNA A.	WIFE	W	F	APR 1877	23	M	3	2	1	KY	KY	KY				NURSE			✓	✓	✓				
"		GLADYS	SON	W	M	Sep 1899	8/12	S				KY	KY	KY													
375	382	SEWELL, VINCENT A.	HEAD	W	M	Feb 1867	33	M	4			KY	KY	KY				FARMER			✓	✓	✓	O	F	F	255
"		EFFIE F.	WIFE	W	F	Jun 1877	22	M	4	3	1	KY	KY	KY							✓	✓	✓				
"		JOSIE B.	DAU	W	F	DEC 1898	1	S				KY	KY	KY													
376	383	MAINES, ISAAC	HEAD	W	M	Sep 1844	55	M	8			KY	KY	KY				FARMER			✓	✓	✓	O	F	F	256
"		MATILDA	WIFE	W	F	Sep 1865	34	M	8	4	4	KY	KY	KY							✓	✓	✓				
"		WILLIAM R.	SON	W	M	Aug 1892	7	S				KY	KY	KY													
"		OSCAR D.	SON	W	M	OCT 1894	5	S				KY	KY	KY													
"		EZRA E.	SON	W	M	OCT 1896	3	S				KY	KY	KY													
"		OTIS M.	SON	W	M	APR 1900	1/12	S				KY	KY	KY													
377	384	HART, HENRY	HEAD	W	M	Feb 1834	66	M	5			KY	KY	KY				FARMER			✓	✓	✓	O	F	F	257
"		MARY J.	WIFE	W	F	OCT 1848	51	M	5	2	2	KY	KY	KY							✓	✓	✓				

STATE - KENTUCKY
COUNTY - MONROE
Township or other division WEST TOMPKINSVILLE Enumerator MALIA PAGE

Supervisor's Dist. No. _102_ Sheet No.
Enumeration Dist. No. _85_

No. of Family	No. of Dwelling	NAME	Relation	Color	Sex	DATE OF BIRTH Mon/Yr	Age at last birthday	Marital Status	# Years married	Mother of how many children?	# of these children living	Place of birth [this person]	Father of this person	Mother of this person	Year of immigr.	# years in U.S.	Naturalization	OCCUPATION 10 years +	Months not employed	Attended school in months	Can read	Can write	Speak English	Owned or Rent	Owned -no mortage	Farm or house	# of farm schedule
378	385	BARBER, JAMES	HEAD	W	M	May 1859	41	M	4				TN	NC	NC				DAY LABORER		X	X	✓		R		H	
		" ALICE P.	WIFE	W	F	Sep 1875	24	M	4	1	1	KY	KY	KY							✓	✓					
		" JOHN V.	SON	W	M	Nov 1897	2	S				KY	KY	KY													
379	386	RAY, WILLIAM D.	HEAD	W	M	Feb 1869	31	M	5			ILL	KY	KY				FRISCO-PAINTER			✓	✓	✓		O	F	258
		" LOTA C.	WIFE	W	F	Sep 1875	25	M	5	2	2	IND	IND	IND							✓	✓	✓				
		" JOHN R.	SON	W	M	Dec 1895	4	S				IND	ILL	IND													
		" EDDIE D.	SON	W	M	Dec 1898	1	S				KY	ILL	IND													
		" JOHN A.	Brother	W	M	Nov 1873	26	S				KY	KY	KY				PAINTER			✓	✓	✓				
		" FRED H.	Brother	W	M	Apr 1885	15	S				KY	KY	KY				A.T. SCHOOL		8	✓	✓	✓				
		" LIZZIE B.	Sister	W	F	May 1889	11	S				KY	KY	KY				A.T. SCHOOL		8	✓	✓	✓				
380	387	BRAY, ISAAC W.	HEAD	W	M	Sep 1866	33	M	4			KY	KY	TN				FARMER			✓	✓	✓		O	F	259
		" ELIZABETH M.	WIFE	W	F	Jan 1866	34	M	4	2	1	KY	TN	KY							✓	✓	✓				
		" CARLIE C.	SON	W	M	Nov 1897	2	S				KY	KY	KY													
381	388	McPHERSON, RUPHUS M.	HEAD	W	M	Mar 1853	47	M	7			KY	KY	KY				FARMER			✓	✓			R	F	260
		" SALLUS	WIFE	W	F	Jun 1866	33	M	7	5	3	KY	KY	KY							✓	✓	✓				
		" NORA	DAU	W	F	May 1877	23	S				KY	KY	KY							✓	✓	✓				
		" LAURA	DAU	W	F	Jun 1879	20	S				KY	KY	KY							✓	✓	✓				
		" LUDA	DAU	W	F	Jun 1879	20	S				KY	KY	KY							✓	✓	✓				
		" OSCAR	SON	W	M	Nov 1881	18	S				KY	KY	KY				FARM LABORER			✓	✓					
		" EDD	SON	W	M	Dec 1893	6	S				KY	KY	KY													
		" ADA	DAU	W	F	Mar 1895	5	S				KY	KY	KY													
		" BRENTS	SON	W	M	Sep 1899	8/12	S				KY	KY	KY													
382	389	GOAD, SMITH	HEAD	W	M	Apr 1859	41	M	13			TN	KY	KY				FARMER			✓	✓			R	F	261
		" ANNA B.	WIFE	W	F	Apr 1869	31	M	13	6	5	TN	TN	TN													
		" WILLIAM H.	SON	W	M	Nov 1887	12	S				TN	TN	TN				AT SCHOOL		4							
		" DOCIA M.	DAU	W	F	Nov 1893	6	S				TN	TN	TN													

STATE - KENTUCKY
COUNTY - MONROE
Township or other division: WEST TOMPKINSVILLE

Enumerator: MALIA PAGE

Supervisor's Dist. No. 102 Sheet No.
Enumeration Dist. No. 85

No. of Family	No. of Dwelling	NAME	Relation	Color	Sex	DATE OF BIRTH Mon/Yr	Age at last birthday	Marital Status	# Years married	Mother of how many children?	# of these children living	Place of birth (this person)	Father of this person	Mother of this person	Year of immigr.	# years in U.S.	Naturalization	OCCUPATION 10 years +	Months not employed	Attended school in months	Can read	Can write	Speak English	Owned or Rent	Owned -no mortage	Farm or house	# of farm schedule
		GOAD, ALICE	DAU	W	F	MAY 1897	3	S				KY	TN	TN													
		" PEARL	DAU	W	F	MAY 1897	3	S				KY	TN	TN													
		" ELNORA	SON	W	M	DEC 1899	5/12	S				KY	TN	TN													
383	390	HIGH, SAMUEL M.	HEAD	W	M	Jul 1863	36	M	13			KY	KY	KY				FARMER			✓	✓	✓	O	F	F	262
		" REBECCA D.	WIFE	W	F	OCT 1865	34	M	13	2	2	KY	TN	KY							✓	✓	✓				
		" EDGAR G.	SON	W	M	AUG 1887	12	S				KY	KY	KY				AT SCHOOL		5	✓	✓	✓				
		" MAY	DAU	W	F	DEC 1889	10	S				KY	KY	KY				AT SCHOOL		5	✓	✓	✓				
		" CATHERINE	Mother	W	F	MAY 1833	67	Wd		11		KY	TN	TN							✓		✓				
384	391	EMBERTON, LINCHFORD A.	HEAD	W	M	APR 1874	26	-				KY	KY	KY				FARMER			✓	✓	✓	O	F	F	263
		" MARY B.	WIFE	W	F	APR 1879	21	-				KY	KY	KY							✓	✓	✓				
385	392	SPEAKMAN, NEWTON	HEAD	W	M	DEC 1851	48	M	13			KY	KY	KY				WELL DIGGER			✓	X	✓	R	F		264
		" SUSAN F.	WIFE	W	F	Jul 1867	32	M	13	1	1	KY	KY	KY							✓	✓	✓				
		" VALONA C.	DAU	W	F	MAY 1893	7	S				KY	KY	KY													
		WOOD, MARY	HIRED	W	F	DEC 1883	16	S				KY	KY	KY				COOK			X	X	✓				
386	393	EMBERTON, WILLIAM J.	HEAD	W	M	Sep 1859	40	S				KY	KY	TN				FARMER			✓	✓	✓	O	F	F	265
		" HARRIETTE	SISTER	W	F	Jul 1856	43	S				KY	KY	TN							✓	✓					
		" SAMUEL D.	BROTHER	W	M	MAY 1858	42	S				KY	KY	TN				FARM LABORER			✓	✓	✓				
		BRADLEY, THOMAS A.	HIRED	W	M	AUG 1882	17	S				KY	KY	KY				FARM LABORER			✓	✓					
387	394	EMBERTON, POLLIE	HEAD	W	F	JUN 1846	53	Wd		1	1	KY	KY	TN							✓	✓	✓				4
388	395	SHIRLEY, SMITH	HEAD	W	M	May 1876	24	M	6			KY	KY	KY				HOSTLER-LIVERY STABLE			✓	✓	✓	R			4
		" JOSIE F.	WIFE	W	F	Feb 1879	21	M	6	1	1	KY	KY	KY							✓	✓	✓				
		" OLA	DAU	W	F	Feb 1895	5	S				KY	KY	KY													
389	396	GRAVEN, MARY	HEAD	W	F	APR 1835	65	Wd		2	2	KY	TN	KY				FARMER	7		X	X	✓	O	F	F	266
		" EMMA	DAU	W	F	MAY 1882	18	S				KY	KY	KY				AT SCHOOL		5	✓	✓	✓				
390	397	HAMMER, JUDGE U.	HEAD	W	M	AUG 1849	50	M	30			KY	KY	KY				FARMER			✓	✓	✓	O	F	F	267
		" NANCY M.	WIFE	W	F	Jul 1850	49	M	30	6	6	KY	KY	KY							✓	✓	✓				

STATE - KENTUCKY
COUNTY - MONROE
Township or other division — NEST TOMPKINSVILLE — Enumerator MALIA PAGE

Supervisor's Dist. No. 102 — Sheet No.
Enumeration Dist. No. 85

No. of Family	No. of Dwelling	NAME	Relation	Color	Sex	DATE OF BIRTH Mon/Yr	Age at last birthday	Marital Status	# Years married	Mother of how many children?	# of these children living	Place of birth (this person)	Father of this person	Mother of this person	Year of immigr.	# years in U.S.	Naturalization	OCCUPATION 10 years +	Months not employed	Attended school in months	Can read	Can write	Speak English	Owned or Rent	Owned –no mortage	Farm or house	# of farm schedule
		HAMMER, ELIJAH	SON	W	M	MAY 1884	16	S				KY	KY	KY				AT SCHOOL		5	✓	✓	✓				
		" BESSIE	DAU	W	F	DEC 1886	13	S				KY	KY	KY				AT SCHOOL		5	✓	✓	✓				
		" EVERT	GR-SON	W	M	NOV 1892	7	S				KY	KY	KY				AT SCHOOL		5	X	X	✓				
391	398	TURNER, WILLIAM B.	HEAD	W	M	APR 1878	22	M	5			KY	KY	KY				FARMER			✓	✓	✓	R		F	268
		" MELVINA	WIFE	W	F	MAY 1878	22	M	5	2	2	KY	KY	KY							✓	✓	✓				
		" IVY	DAU	W	F	OCT 1896	3	S				KY	KY	KY													
		" IDRU	DAU	W	F	DEC 1898	1	S				KY	KY	KY													
		" JOHN P.	COUSIN	W	M	APR 1884	16	S				KY	KY	KY				FARM LABORER			✓	✓	✓				
		DENHAM, JANICE	HIRED	W	F	DEC 1888	11	S				KY	KY	KY				COOK			✓	✓	✓				

HERE ENDS THE ENUMERATION OF WEST TOMPKINSVILLE PRECINCT

TWELFTH CENSUS OF THE UNITED STATES 1900

STATE - KENTUCKY
COUNTY - MONROE

UNION

Township or other division

- 406 -

Enumerator PERRY W. MILLER

Supervisor's Dist. No. 102 Sheet No.
Enumeration Dist. No. 86

No. of Family	No. of Dwelling	NAME	Relation	Color	Sex	DATE OF BIRTH Mon/Yr	Age at last birthday	Marital Status	# Years married	Mother of how many children?	# of these children living	Place of birth (this person)	Father of this person	Mother of this person	Year of immigr.	# years in U.S.	Naturalization	OCCUPATION 10 years +	Months not employed	Attended school in months	Can read	Can write	Speak English	Owned or Rent	Owned -no mortgage	Farm or house	# of farm schedule
1	1	CURTIS, TURNER G.	HEAD	W	M	AUG 1834	65	M	43			KY	KY	TN				FARMER			X	X	✓	O	H	H	1
		" MARY E.	WIFE	W	F	DEC 1841	58	M	43	10	8	KY	KY	KY							✓	✓	✓				
		" ROSCO O.	SON	W	M	FEB 1872	28	S				KY	KY	KY				DRY GOODS MERCHANT			✓	✓	✓				
		" WALTER S.	SON	W	M	MAY 1874	26	S				KY	KY	KY				FARM LABORER			✓	✓	✓				
		" SEDALIE G.	DAU	W	F	DEC 1876	23	S				KY	KY	KY							✓	✓	✓				
		" JOHN S.	GR-SON	W	M	JUL 1885	14	S				KY	KY	KY				AT SCHOOL		5	✓	✓	✓				
2	2	SABANS, JAMES F.	HEAD	W	M	APR 1872	28	M	2			KY	KY	KY				FARMER			✓	✓	✓	R		F	
		" CORDA	WIFE	W	F	JAN 1881	19	M	2	1	1	KY	KY	KY							✓	✓	✓				
		" FRANK	SON	W	M	MAY 1899	1	S				KY	KY	KY													
3	3	GLOVER, GEO. P.	HEAD	W	M	DEC 1857	42	M	18			KY	KY	KY				FARMER			✓	✓	✓	O	F	F	2
		" MARTHA B.	WIFE	W	F	OCT 1860	39	M	18	4	4	KY	KY	TN							✓	✓	✓				
		" KATE	DAU	W	F	AUG 1863	16	S				KY	KY	KY				AT SCHOOL		5	✓	✓	✓				
		" ANNIE	DAU	W	F	MAR 1888	12	S				KY	KY	KY				AT SCHOOL		5	✓	✓	✓				
		" ORRIN	SON	W	M	APR 1890	10	S				KY	KY	KY				AT SCHOOL		5	✓	✓	✓				
		" AVER	SON	W	M	DEC 1892	7	S				KY	KY	KY				AT SCHOOL		5	✓	✓	✓				
4	4	PARKE, JAMES M. B.	HEAD	W	M	MAR 1843	57	M	33			KY	KY	KY				FARMER			✓	✓	✓	R	F		3
		" MARY M.	WIFE	W	F	SEP 1843	56	M	33	4	2	KY	TN	TN							✓	X	✓				
		" MARIAN M.	SON	W	M	MAR 1874	26	S				KY	KY	KY				FARM LABORER			✓	✓	✓				
		" GULIUS G.	SON	W	M	OCT 1881	18	M				KY	KY	KY				FARM LABORER			✓	✓	✓				
		" IDA E.	DAU-IN-LAW	W	F	APR 1875	25	M				KY	KY	KY							✓	✓	✓				
5	5	ARTERBURN, JAMES G.	HEAD	W	M	FEB 1853	47	M	22			KY	KY	KY				FARMER			✓	✓	✓	O	F	F	4
		" MARGET E.	WIFE	W	F	FEB 1859	41	M	22	9	8	KY	KY	TN							✓	✓	✓				
		" MYRTIE C.	DAU	W	F	APR 1879	21	S				KY	KY	KY							✓	✓	✓				
		" LESLIE B.	DAU	W	F	AUG 1882	17	S				KY	KY	KY				AT SCHOOL		4	✓	✓	✓				
		" LILLIE L.	DAU	W	F	JAN 1885	15	S				KY	KY	KY				AT SCHOOL		5	✓	✓	✓				
		" (ELLARD?) J.	SON	W	M	AUG 1887	12	S				KY	KY	KY				AT SCHOOL		5	✓	✓					

STATE - KENTUCKY
COUNTY - MONROE
UNION
— 407 —
Township or other division
Enumerator PERRY W. MILLER

Supervisor's Dist. No. 102 Sheet No.
Enumeration Dist. No. 86

No. of Family	No. of Dwelling	NAME	Relation	Color	Sex	DATE OF BIRTH Mon/Yr	Age at last birthday	Marital Status	# Years married	Mother of how many children?	# of these children living	OCCUPATION 10 years +	Months not employed	Attended school in months	Can read	Can write	Speak English	Owned or Rent	Owned –no mortgage	Farm or house	# of farm schedule
		ARTERBURN, VERGIL E.	SON	W	M	Jul 1890	10	S				AT SCHOOL		5	✓	✓	✓				
		" ADA M.	DAU	W	F	Jun 1892	7	S				AT SCHOOL		5	✓	✓	✓				
		" DELPHI F.	DAU	W	F	Oct 1894	5	S							X	X	✓				
		" THELMA A.	DAU	W	F	Sep 1898	1	S													
6	6	GRAY, FRANCIS M.	HEAD	W	M	Jul 1838	61	M	30			FARMER			✓	✓	✓	O	F	F	5
		" MARY E.	WIFE	W	F	Oct 1845	54	M	30	2	2				✓	✓	✓				
		" WADE H.	SON	W	M	Jan 1878	22	S				SCHOOL TEACHER	5		✓	✓	✓				
		" SHELBY C.	SON	W	M	May 1879	21	S				FARM LABORER	3		✓	✓	✓				
		FISH, VINA	SERVANT	W	F	May 1883	17	S				HOUSE SERVANT	5		✓	✓	✓				
7	7	JONES, PRESTON	HEAD	W	M	Oct 1868	31	S				FARMER			✓	✓	✓	R		F	6
		" JACOB C.	BROTHER	W	M	Apr 1871	29	S				FARMER			✓	✓	✓				
		" ELIZA A.	MOTHER	W	F	Jul 1831	68	Wd		12	8				✓	✓	✓				
		" VIRTIE A.	NIECE	W	F	May 1889	11	S							✓	✓	✓				
8	8	WALKER, JOE D.	HEAD	W	M	Mar 1871	29	M	7			BLACKSMITH			✓	✓	✓	R		H	
		" CORDELIA	WIFE	W	F	Mar 1873	27	M	7	4	4				✓	✓	✓				
		" ANNIE M.	DAU	W	F	Oct 1893	6	S							X	X	✓				
		" (RHNIE?) J.	DAU	W	F	Feb 1895	5	S													
		" FRED A.	SON	W	M	Feb 1897	2	S													
		" LILLIE V.	DAU	W	F	Jan 1899	1	S													
9	9	JONES, BENTON M.	HEAD	W	M	Oct 1868	31	M	1			FARMER			✓	✓	✓	R		F	7
		" BETTIE	WIFE	W	F	Apr 1876	24	M	1						✓	✓	✓				
10	10	PAYNE, KATE	HEAD	W	F	Apr 1864	36	Wd		1	1	FARMER			✓	✓	✓	R		F	8
		" SUSIE	DAU	W	F	May 1890	10	S							✓	✓	✓				
		GIPSON, HUEY T.	SERVANT	W	M	Mar 1880	20	S				FARM LABORER			✓	✓	✓				
11	11	SABENS, WILLIAM W.	HEAD	W	M	Jan 1846	54	M	35			FARMER			✓	✓	✓	O	F	F	9
		" MARY R.	WIFE	W	F	Feb 1848	52	M	35	8	7				✓	✓	✓				

TWELFTH CENSUS OF THE UNITED STATES 1900

STATE - KENTUCKY
COUNTY - MONROE
UNION
Township or other division

-408-

Enumerator PERRY W. MILLER

Supervisor's Dist. No. 102 Sheet No.
Enumeration Dist. No. 86

No. of Family	No. of Dwelling	NAME	Relation	Color	Sex	DATE OF BIRTH Mon/Yr	Age at last birthday	Marital Status	# Years married	Mother of how many children?	# of these children living	Place of birth [this person]	Father of this person	Mother of this person	Year of immigr.	# years in U.S.	Naturalization	OCCUPATION 10 years +	Months not employed	Attended school in months	Can read	Can write	Speak English	Owned or Rent	Owned -no mortgage	Farm or house	# of farm schedule
		SABENS, WILBORN T.	Son	W	M	MAY 1867	33	Wd				KY	KY	KY				FARMER			✓	✓	✓	R			
		" FLOYD R.	Son	W	M	AUG 1878	21	M				KY	KY	KY				FARM LABOR 4			✓	✓	✓				
		" DELA B.	Dau-in-law	W	F	APR 1882	18	M				KY	KY	KY							✓	✓	✓				
		" CORA E.	Dau	W	F	MAR 1883	17	S				KY	KY	KY				AT SCHOOL		5	✓	✓	✓				
		" WILLIE R.	Son	W	M	MAY 1889	11	S				KY	KY	KY				AT SCHOOL		5	✓	✓	✓				
		" IDA M.	Gr-Dau	W	F	Jul 1892	7	S				KY	KY	KY				AT SCHOOL		5							
		" LOYD T.	Gr-Son	W	M	Jul 1894	5	S				ILL	KY	KY													
12	12	ARNOLD, MARGET A.	Head	W	F	DEC 1837	62	M	39	10	7	KY	KY	KY				FARMER			✓	X	✓	R		F	10
		" ANNIE	Dau	W	F	Jul 1873	26	S				KY	KY	KY							✓	✓	✓				
		" IDA	Dau	W	F	Jun 1877	22	S				KY	KY	KY							X	X	✓				
		" CHARLES F.	Son	W	M	Sep 1880	19	S				KY	KY	KY				FARM LABORER			✓	✓	✓				
13	13	MEADOWS, JAMES L.	Head	W	M	Jul 1879	20	S				KY	KY	TN				FARMER			✓	✓	✓	O	FF		11
14	14	MILLER, HIRAM D.	Head	W	M	Nov 1835	64	M	27			KY	KY	TN				FARMER			✓	✓	✓	O	FF		12
		" JOSY F.	Wife	W	F	OCT 1852	47	M	27	2	2	KY	KY	TN							✓	✓	✓				
		" PERRY W.	Son	W	M	AUG 1874	25	S				KY	KY	KY				SCHOOL TEACHER			✓	✓	✓				
		" ELLA G.	Dau	W	F	APR 1878	22	S				KY	KY	KY							✓	✓	✓				
		STEPHENSON, JENNIE	Mother-in-law	W	F	Jul 1818	81	Wd		8	4	TN	TN	TN							✓	X	✓				
15	15	ENGLAND, ROG	Head	B	M	AUG 1848	51	M	24			KY	KY	KY				FARMER			X	X	✓	O	FF		13
		" AMERICA	Wife	B	F	MAY 1847	53	M	24	12	8	KY	KY	KY							X	X	✓				
		" BELLE	Dau	B	F	Jun 1872	27	S		2	2	KY	KY	KY							X	X	✓				
		" SARAH A.	Dau	B	F	MAR 1877	23	S		3	2	KY	KY	KY							X	X	✓				
		" WALTER B.	Son	B	M	MAR 1879	21	S				KY	KY	KY				SCHOOL TEACHER			✓	✓	✓				
		" IDA M.	Dau	B	F	DEC 1885	14	S				KY	KY	KY				AT SCHOOL		4	✓	✓	✓				
		" DELLA J.	Dau	B	F	Jul 1889	10	S				KY	KY	KY				AT SCHOOL		4	✓	✓	✓				
		" JOHN S.	Son	B	M	MAR 1893	7	S				KY	KY	KY				AT SCHOOL		3	✓	✓	✓				
		" TOM E.	Grandson	B	M	Feb 1890	10	S				KY	KY	KY				AT SCHOOL		3	✓	✓	✓				

STATE - KENTUCKY
COUNTY - MONROE   UNION
Township or other division   Enumerator PERRY W. MILLER

Supervisor's Dist. No. 102 Sheet No. ___
Enumeration Dist. No. 86 ___

No. of Family	No. of Dwelling	NAME	Relation	Color	Sex	Date of Birth Mon/Yr	Age at last birthday	Marital Status	#Years married	Mother #how many children	#of these children living	Place of birth (this person)	Father of this person	Mother of this person	Year of immigr.	#years in U.S.	Naturalization	Occupation	Months not employed	Attended school in months	Can read	Can write	Speak English	Owned or Rent	Owned-no mortgage	Farm or house	#of farm schedule
		ENGLAND, ELLA J.	GR-DAU	B	F	MAY 1896	4	S				KY	KY	KY													
		" GEO. D.	GR-SON	B	M	Jul 1898	1	S				KY	KY	KY													
16	16	GENTRY, HENRY	Head	B	M	APR 1865	35	M	5			KY	KY	KY				FARM LABORER			✓	X	✓	R	H	
		" HETTIE	wife	B	F	DEC 1864	35	M	5	1	1	SC	KY	SC							X	X	✓			
		" CLAY	Son	B	M	Jul 1899	10/12	S				KY	KY	SC												
17	17	LYONS, WILLIAM G.	Head	W	M	APR 1865	35	M	18			KY	KY	TN				FARMER			✓	✓		O	F	14
		" MARY A.	Wife	W	F	MAY 1865	35	M	18	4	4	KY	KY	KY							✓	✓	✓			
		" HASCHALL B.	Son	W	M	JAN 1883	17	S				KY	KY	KY				FARM LABORER	2	4	✓	✓				
		" LERICE	Son	W	M	MAY 1884	16	S				KY	KY	KY				FARM LABORER	2	4	✓	✓				
		" LULA M.	DAU	W	F	JAN 1889	11	S				KY	KY	KY				AT SCHOOL		4	✓	✓				
		" ISAAC	Son	W	M	DEC 1890	9	S				KY	KY	KY				AT SCHOOL		5	✓	✓				
18	18	MILLER, JAMES B.	Head	W	M	Jul 1848	51	M				TN	TN	KY				FARMER			✓	✓		O	F	15
		" PATTIE	Wife	W	F	APR 1876	24	M				KY	KY	KY							✓	✓				
		PEDEN, JERRY	Servant	B	M	APR 1874	26	M	4			KY	KY	KY				FARM LABORER	1		X	X	✓			
		" EDIE	Servant	B	F	MAY 1873	27	M	4	1	1	KY	KY	KY				HOUSE SERVANT			X	X	✓			
		FRAZIER, AMANDA	Servant	B	F	JAN 1888	12	S				KY	KY	KY				HOUSE SERVANT			X	X	✓			
19	19	WILLIAMS, HENRY	Head	B	M	AUG 1847	52	M				KY	KY	KY				FARMER			X	X	✓	R	F	16
		" ALICE	wife	B	F	Jul 1874	26	M		4	4	KY	KY	KY							X	X	✓			
		" LEWIS	Son	B	M	Jul 1887	12	S				KY	KY	KY				AT SCHOOL		3	✓	✓	✓			
		" BESSIE	DAU	B	F	OCT 1890	9	S				KY	KY	KY				AT SCHOOL		3	✓	✓	✓			
		" LORA	DAU	B	F	JAN 1893	7	S				KY	KY	KY				AT SCHOOL		3	X	X	✓			
		" GRACIE	DAU	B	F	Jul 1896	3	S				KY	KY	KY												
20	20	MARTIN, SAM	HEAD	B	M	AUG 1826	73	Wd.				KY	KY	KY				FARMER			X	X	✓	R	F	17
		" GUS	SON	B	M	DEC 1879	20	S				KY	KY	KY				FARM LABORER			✓	✓	✓			
		" FRANK	GR-SON	B	M	Feb 1878	22	S				KY	KY	KY				FARM LABORER			✓	✓	✓			
		" FANNIE	GR-DAU	B	F	Jul 1884	15	S				KY	KY	KY												

STATE - KENTUCKY
COUNTY - MONROE
UNION
Township or other division

TWELFTH CENSUS OF THE UNITED STATES 1900
-410-
Enumerator PERRY W. MILLER

Supervisor's Dist. No. 102 Sheet No.
Enumeration Dist. No. 86

No. of Family	No. of Dwelling	NAME	Relation	Color	Sex	DATE OF BIRTH Mon/Yr	Age at last birthday	Marital Status	# Years married	Mother of how many children?	# of these children living	NATIVITY Place of birth [this person]	Father of this person	Mother of this person	CITIZENSHIP Year of immigr.	# years in U.S.	Naturalization	OCCUPATION 10 years +	Months not employed	Attended school in months	Can read	Can write	Speak English	Owned or Rent	Owned -no mortgage	Farm or house	# of farm schedule
		MARTIN, LURACY GR-SON		B	M	Jul 1884	15	S				KY	KY	KY				FARM LABORER		X	X	✓					
21	21	NICKOLDS, ZACHARIAH	Head	W	M	Feb 1859	41	M	3			KY	KY	KY				FARMER			✓	✓	✓	R	F	18	
		" DONA	Wife	W	F	Jun 1881	18	M	3	1	1	KY	KY	KY							✓	✓	✓				
		" DEHAVEN	Son	W	M	Aug 1897	2	S				KY	KY	KY													
22	22	MEADOW, MARTIN	HEAD	W	M	Nov 1837	62	M	33			KY	KY	KY				FARMER			✓	✓	✓	O	F	19	
		" MARY J.	WIFE	W	F	Jan 1842	58	M	33	7	6	KY	KY	KY							✓	✓	✓				
		" LOVIE M.	DAU	W	F	Oct 1875	24	S				KY	KY	KY							✓	✓	✓				
		" BETTIE H.M.	DAU	W	F	Jan 1880	20	S				KY	KY	KY				AT SCHOOL		5	✓	✓	✓				
		" WALTON W.	SON	W	M	Dec 1882	17	S				KY	KY	KY				AT SCHOOL		5	✓	✓	✓				
23	23	JONES, ROBERT E.	Head	W	M	Sep 1866	33	Wd				KY	TN	KY				BLACKSMITH			✓	✓	✓	R	H		
24	24	GEE, JAMES H.	Head	W	M	Dec 1859	40	M	10			KY	KY	KY				DRY GOODS MERCHANT			✓	✓	✓	O	F	20	
		" PRISCILA	Wife	W	F	Dec 1859	40	M	10	6	6	KY	KY	KY							✓	✓	✓				
		MITCHELL, JOHN H.	Step-Son	W	M	Mar 1888	12	S				KY	KY	KY				AT SCHOOL		7	✓	✓	✓				
		GEE, HERSCHEL	Son	W	M	Oct 1890	9	S				KY	KY	KY				AT SCHOOL		7	✓	✓	✓				
		" ADA	DAU	W	F	Sep 1892	7	S				KY	KY	KY				AT SCHOOL		7	✓	✓	✓				
		" ARGUS	SON	W	M	Apr 1895	5	S				KY	KY	KY													
25	25	WILBORN, GEO. W	HEAD	W	M	Dec 1857	42	M	21			KY	KY	KY				FARMER			✓	✓	✓	O	F	21	
		" RETTA	WIFE	W	F	Oct 1860	39	M	21	4	4	KY	KY	KY							✓	✓	✓				
		" YANCIE P.	SON	W	M	Dec 1879	20	S				KY	KY	KY				FARM LABORER			✓	✓	✓				
		" ADA W.	DAU	W	F	Mar 1888	12	S				KY	KY	KY				AT SCHOOL		6	✓	✓	✓				
		" VERDA G.	DAU	W	F	Feb 1892	8	S				KY	KY	KY				AT SCHOOL		6	✓	✓	✓				
		" SAMMIE	DAU	W	F	Jun 1897	2	S				KY	KY	KY													
26	26	WILBORN, GEORGE R.	HEAD	W	M	May 1838	62	M	41			KY	VA	VA				FARMER			✓	✓	✓	O	F	22	
		" MARTHA S.	WIFE	W	F	Mar 1840	60	M	41	2	2	KY	KY	VA							✓	✓	✓				
		" MARY T.	DAU	W	F	Apr 1863	37	S				KY	KY	KY							✓	✓	✓				
		" ALPHA O.	SON	W	M	Apr 1875	25	S				KY	KY	KY				FARM LABORER			✓	✓	✓				

TWELFTH CENSUS OF THE UNITED STATES 1900

— 411 —

STATE - KENTUCKY
COUNTY - MONROE
Township or other division — UNION
Enumerator — PERRY W. MILLER

Supervisor's Dist. No. 102 Sheet No.
Enumeration Dist. No. 86

No. of Family	No. of Dwelling	NAME	Relation	Color	Sex	DATE OF BIRTH Mon/Yr	Age at last birthday	Marital Status	# Years married	Mother of how many children?	# of these children living	Place of birth [this person]	Father of this person	Mother of this person	Year of immigr.	# years in U.S.	Naturalization	OCCUPATION 10 years +	Months not employed	Attended school in months	Can read	Can write	Speak English	Owned or Rent	Owned –no mortage	Farm or house	# of farm schedule
27	27	FLOWERS, SAMUEL L.	HEAD	W	M	Nov 1867	32	M	11			KY	VA	KY				FARMER			✓	✓		R		F	23
		" CHRISTELA	WIFE	W	F	Mar 1866	34	M	11	2	2	KY	KY	KY							✓	✓	✓				
		" LORNA J.	DAU	W	F	Dec 1889	10	S				KY	KY	KY				AT SCHOOL		6	✓	✓					
		WILLIE W.	SON	W	M	May 1899	1	S				KY	KY	KY													
		WILBORN, SARAH A.	M-IN-LAW	W	F	Mar 1839	61	Wd		1	1	KY	KY	KY							X	X					
28	28	McPHERSON, CAM	HEAD	W	M	Mar 1860	40	M	12			KY	KY	TN				FARMER			✓	✓		R		F	24
		" LUCY C.	WIFE	W	F	May 1865	35	M	12	6	4	TN	TN	MISSISSIPPI							✓	✓					
		" BAKER B.	SON	W	M	Mar 1890	10	S				TN	KY	TN				AT SCHOOL		5	✓	✓	✓				
		" CAMBELL W.	SON	W	M	Jun 1892	7	S				KY	KY	TN				AT SCHOOL		5			✓				
		" GEO. D.	SON	W	M	Aug 1894	5	S				KY	KY	TN													
		" WILLIAM C.	SON	W	M	May 1898	2	S				KY	KY	TN													
29	29	McPHERSON, MARGETT	Head	W	F	Feb 1830	70	Wd		4	4	TN	TN	TN				FARMER			✓	✓		O	M	F	25
		" FANNIE	DAU	W	F	May 1871	29	S				KY	KY	TN							✓	✓					
		PAYNE, MARTHA A.	Boarder	W	F	Oct 1828	71	Wd				TN	KY	TN				FARMER			✓	✓		R		F	26
30	30	CARDER, WILLIAM	HEAD	W	M	May 1855	45	M	24			KY	KY	KY				FARMER			X	X	✓	R		F	26
		" NANCY J.	WIFE	W	F	Aug 1851	48	M	24	8	6	KY	KY	KY							X	X	✓				
		" (NIORTA?)	DAU	W	F	May 1883	17	S				KY	KY	KY				AT SCHOOL		4	✓	✓	✓				
		" LOCKIE C.	DAU	W	F	Jan 1886	14	S				KY	KY	KY				AT SCHOOL		4	✓	✓	✓				
		" JESSE G.	SON	W	M	Jun 1888	11	S				KY	KY	KY				AT SCHOOL		4	✓	✓	✓				
		" HESSY T.	SON	W	M	Jul 1890	9	S				KY	KY	KY				AT SCHOOL		9	✓	✓	✓				
31	31	BARNS, GEO. W.	HEAD	B	M	May 1847	53	M	22			KY	KY	KY				FARMER			✓	✓	✓	O	FF		27
		" HENRETTA	WIFE	B	F	Mar 1848	52	M	22	9	6	KY	KY	KY							✓	✓	✓				
		" LOU G.	DAU	B	F	May 1879	21	S				KY	KY	KY				School TEACHER 7			✓	✓	✓				
		" ANNIE A.	DAU	B	F	Dec 1887	12	S				KY	KY	KY				AT SCHOOL		4	✓	✓	✓				
		" STELLA L.	DAU	B	F	Dec 1883	16	S				KY	KY	KY				AT SCHOOL		4	✓	✓	✓				
		MARTIN, ELLA	S-DAU	B	F	May 1873	27	S				KY	KY	KY				SCHOOL TEACHER 7			✓	✓	✓				

STATE - KENTUCKY
COUNTY - MONROE
Township or other division **UNION**
Enumerator **PERRY W. MILLER**

Supervisor's Dist. No. _102_ Sheet No. _____
Enumeration Dist. No. _86_

No. of Family	No. of Dwelling	NAME	Relation	Color	Sex	DATE OF BIRTH Mon/Yr	Age at last birthday	Marital Status	# Years married	Mother of how many children?	# of these children living	Place of birth [this person]	Father of this person	Mother of this person	Year of immigr.	# years in U.S.	Naturalization	OCCUPATION 10 years +	Months not employed	Attended school in month	Can read	Can write	Speak English	Owned or Rent	Owned -no mortage	Farm or house	# of Farm schedule
(31)		PIPKINS, HENRY	Son-in-law	B	M	May 1847	53	M	22			KY	KY	KY				BLACKSMITH	2		✓	✓					
		" LOLA B	Dau-in-law	B	F	Mar 1848	52	M	22	9	6	KY	KY	KY							✓	✓					
		" ROY J.	S-Gr-Son	B	M	May 1879	21	S				KY	KY	KY				AT SCHOOL		4	✓	✓	✓				
		" JIMMIE G.	S-Gr-Son	B	M	Dec 1887	12	S				KY	KY	KY							✓	✓	✓				
		" JOHN M.	S-Gr-Son	B	M	Dec 1883	16	S				KY	KY	KY													
		MAXEY, WALTER	Boarder	B	M	May 1873	27	S				KY	KY	KY				DAY LABORER	4		✓	✓	✓				
32	32	CARDER, MILLARD	HEAD	W	M	May 1881	19	S				KY	KY	KY				FARMER			✓	✓	✓	R		F	28
33	33	FRAZIER, JAMES	HEAD	W	M	Jun 1870	29	M	3			KY	KY	KY				FARMER			X	X	✓	R		F	29
		" BIRCH	WIFE	W	F	May 1878	22	M	3	3	1	KY	KY	KY							X	X	✓				
		" VERGIL	SON	W	M	Aug 1897	2	S				KY	KY	KY													
34	34	COPASS, JAMES K.	HEAD	W	M	Jan 1845	55	M	31			TN	TN	TN				FARMER			✓	X	✓	R		F	30
		" MARY E.	WIFE	W	F	Jun 1851	48	M	31	3	1	KY	KY	KY							✓	X	✓				
35	35	TYREE, JESSE	HEAD	W	M	Dec 1876	23	M	4			KY	KY	KY				FARMER			✓	X	✓	R		F	31
		" BETTIE A.	WIFE	W	F	Feb 1877	23	M	4			KY	KY	KY							✓	✓	✓				
36	36	WOOD, HENRY C.	HEAD	W	M	Mar 1866	34	M	10			KY	KY	KY				FARMER			X	X	✓	R		F	32
		" MARY E	WIFE	W	F	Nov 1871	28	M	10	1	1	KY	KY	KY							X	X	✓				
		" GEO. W.	SON	W	M	Nov 1890	9	S				KY	KY	KY							✓	X	✓				
37	37	ENGLAND, JAMES	HEAD	W	M	Jun 1845	54	M	6			KY	KY	KY				FARMER			✓	✓	✓	R		F	33
		" MARY L.	WIFE	W	F	Apr 1867	33	M	6	2	2	KY	KY	KY							✓	X	✓				
		" ROY (E?)	SON	W	M	Aug 1897	2	S				KY	KY	KY													
		" ANNIE P.	DAU	W	F	Mar 1900	2/12	S				KY	KY	KY													
38	38	(PEDER?) THOMPSON	HEAD	W	M	Dec 1822	77	M	42			KY	KY	KY				FARMER			✓	✓	✓	O	F	F	34
		" SARAH E	WIFE	W	F	Dec 1837	62	M	42	9	5	TN	TN	KY							✓	✓	✓				
		WALLER, MOSES R.	S-SON	W	M	Jun 1872	27	M	6			KY	TN	KY				FARMER			✓	✓	✓	R		F	
		" PERMELIA	S-D-in-law	W	F	Feb 1866	34	M	6	4	4	KY	KY	KY							✓	✓	✓				
		" MYRTLE B.	Step Gr-Dau	W	F	Aug 1895	4	S				KY	KY	KY													

STATE - KENTUCKY
COUNTY - MONROE
Township or other division UNION

Enumerator PERRY W. MILLER

Supervisor's Dist. No. 102 Sheet No.
Enumeration Dist. No. 86

No. of Family	No. of Dwelling	NAME	Relation	Color	Sex	DATE OF BIRTH Mon/Yr	Age at last birthday	Marital Status	# Years married	Mother of how many children?	# of these children living	Place of birth (this person)	Father of this person	Mother of this person	Year of immigr.	# years in U.S.	Naturalization	OCCUPATION 10 years +	Months not employed	Attended school in months	Can read	Can write	Speak English	Owned or Rent	Owned -no mortgage	Farm or house	# of farm schedule
		WALLER, MINNIE E.	STEP GR-DAU	W	F	Nov 1897	2	S				KY	KY	KY													
		" BUFORD T	S-GR-SON	W	M	Mar 1899	1	S				KY	KY	KY													
		" BULA MAY	S-GR-DAU	W	F	May 1900	0/12	S				KY	KY	KY													
39	39	BRAY, WILLIAM C.	HEAD	W	M	May 1869	31	M	6			KY	KY	KY				FARMER			✓	✓		R		F	35
		" MARTHA F.	WIFE	W	F	Dec 1877	22	M	6	2	2	KY	KY	KY							✓	✓					
		" BERTIE L.	SON	W	M	Dec 1895	4	S				KY	KY	KY													
		" WALTER L.	SON	W	M	Mar 1898	2	S				KY	KY	KY													
40	40	PEDEN, JOHNS S.	Head	W	M	Nov 1855	44	M	26			KY	KY	KY				FARMER			✓	✓		O		F	36
		" AMANDA	Wife	W	F	Oct 1852	47	M	26	1	1	KY	KY	KY							✓	✓					
		" ORVAL T	SON	W	M	Jul 1878	21	S				KY	KY	KY				FARMER			✓	✓					
		PAYNE, LENA E.	NIECE	W	F	Oct 1884	15	S				KY	KY	KY				A.T. SCHOOL		4	✓	✓					
41	41	WALLER, SARAH	HEAD	W	F	Feb 1813	87	Wd				KY	KY	KY							✓	✓		O		F	37
		" DAVID	SON	W	M	Jun 1847	52	Wd				KY	KY	KY				FARMER			✓						
		" SARAH L.	GR-DAU	W	F	Jun 1875	24	S				KY	KY	KY							✓						
		" PATTIN R.	GR-SON	W	M	Oct 1876	23	S				KY	KY	KY				FARM LABORER		3	✓	✓					
		" ELIAS L.	GR-SON	W	M	Oct 1878	21	S				KY	KY	KY				FARM LABORER		4	✓	✓					
42	42	HEADRICK, (CES?) T.	HEAD	W	M	Jul 1877	22	M				KY	KY	KY				FARMER			✓	✓	✓	R		F	38
		" PHOEBA	WIFE	W	F	Jun 1880	19	M				KY	KY	KY							✓	✓					
43	43	SMITH, HARMON T.	HEAD	W	M	Nov 1849	50	M	1			KY	KY	KY				FARMER			✓	✓		O		F	39
		" MARY A.	WIFE	W	F	Apr 1853	47	M	1			KY	KY	KY							✓	✓					
		" LIZA P.	DAU	W	F	Aug 1886	13	S				KY	KY	KY				AT SCHOOL		5	✓	✓					
		" GRACIE T.	DAU	W	F	Nov 1888	11	S				KY	KY	KY				AT SCHOOL		5	✓	✓	✓				
		" LINDSA J.	SON	W	M	Oct 1891	8	S				KY	KY	KY				AT SCHOOL		5	✓	✓	✓				
		" ESTA	DAU	W	F	Mar 1894	6	S				KY	KY	KY													
		" HARRISON	SON	W	M	Feb 1897	3	S				KY	KY	KY													
44	44	BOWLES, WILLIAM B.	HEAD	W	M	Apr 1837	63	M	35			KY	TN	VA				FARMER			✓	✓		O		F	40

STATE - KENTUCKY
COUNTY - MONROE
Township or other division UNION   Enumerator PERRY W. MILLER

Supervisor's Dist. No. _102_ Sheet No.
Enumeration Dist. No. _86_____

No. of Family	No. of Dwelling	NAME	Relation	Color	Sex	DATE OF BIRTH Mon/Yr	Age at last birthday	Marital Status	# Years married	Mother of how many children?	# of these children living	Place of birth (this person)	Father of this person	Mother of this person	Year of immigr.	# years in U.S.	Naturalization	OCCUPATION 10 years +	Months not employed	Attended school in months	Can read	Can write	Speak English	Owned or Rent	Owned -no mortage	Farm or house	# of farm schedule	
		BOWLES, IBBY	WIFE	W	F	Jun 1848	52	M	35			KY	TN	TN							✓	✓	✓					
		" PHILIP	SON	W	M	Feb 1882	18	M	35	7	4	KY	KY	TN				FARM LABORER			✓	✓	✓					
		" FRANK	SON	W	M	APR 1892	8	S				KY	KY	TN				AT SCHOOL		5	✓	✓	✓					
		HAZELIP, MARTHA	Boarder	W	F	Nov 1880	19	S				KY	KY	KY							✓	✓	✓					
45	45	PELER LUCINDA	HEAD	W	F	MAR 1816	84	Wd		6	1	KY	KY	KY							X	X	✓	O	F	F	41	
		" JAMES	SON	W	M	APR 1863	37	M	14			KY	KY	KY				FARMER			X	X	✓					
		" MINNIE	GR-DAU	W	F	MAR 1871	29	M	14	6	5	KY	KY	KY							✓	✓	✓					
		" HARRISON	GR-SON	W	M	Jan 1889	11	S				KY	KY	KY				AT SCHOOL		4	✓	✓	✓					
		" NORAH J	GR-DAU	W	F	MAR 1891	9	S				KY	KY	KY				AT SCHOOL		4								
		" JULIA I	GR-DAU	W	F	Jul 1892	7	S				KY	KY	KY				AT SCHOOL		4								
		" JOE W.	GR-SON	W	M	APR 1896	4	S				KY	KY	KY														
		" SARAH A.	GR-DAU	W	F	Jun 1899	4/12	S				KY	KY	KY														
46	46	FISH JESSE	HEAD	W	M	MAR 1878	22	S				KY	KY	KY				FARMER			✓	✓	✓		R	F	42	
47	47	FISH, JOHN	HEAD	W	M	Feb 1874	26	M	7			KY	KY	KY				FARMER			X	X	✓		R	F	43	
		" MALINDA T.	WIFE	W	F	Nov 1874	25	M	7	4	2	KY	KY	KY							X	X	✓		R	F		
		" WILLIAM H.R.	SON	W	M	Nov 1894	5	S				KY	KY	KY														
		" LILLIE V.	DAU	W	F	OCT 1899	7/12	S				KY	KY	KY														
48	48	FRAZIER, ISAAC	HEAD	W	M	AUG 1852	47	M	18			KY	KY	KY				BLACKSMITH			X	X	✓		O	F	F	44	
		" MARY E.	WIFE	W	F	AUG 1862	37	M	18	6	5	KY	KY	KY							X	X	✓					
		" NELIA E.	DAU	W	F	Jul 1883	16	S				KY	KY	KY				AT SCHOOL		3	✓	✓	✓					
		" MATTIE L.	DAU	W	F	Jun 1885	14	S				KY	KY	KY				AT SCHOOL		3½	✓	✓	✓					
		" MYRTIE E.	DAU	W	F	MAY 1887	13	S				KY	KY	KY				AT SCHOOL		3	✓	✓	✓					
		" JENNIE A.	DAU	W	F	Jun 1889	10	S				KY	KY	KY				AT SCHOOL		3	X	X	✓					
		" LEO P.	SON	W	M	Feb 1892	8	S				KY	KY	KY														
		" BERTIE B.	DAU	W	F	Jul 1896	3	S				KY	KY	KY														
49	49	FRAZIER, JANE	HEAD	W	F	MAR 1837	63	Wd		12	9	KY	KY	KY				FARMER			X	X	✓		O	F	F	45	

STATE - KENTUCKY
COUNTY - MONROE
Township or other division UNION

Enumerator PERRY W. MILLER

Supervisor's Dist. No. 102 Sheet No.
Enumeration Dist. No. 86

No. of Family	No. of Dwelling	NAME	Relation	Color	Sex	DATE OF BIRTH Mon/Yr	Age at last birthday	Marital Status	# Years married	Mother of how many children?	# of these children living	Place of birth (this person)	Father of this person	Mother of this person	Year of immigr.	# years in U.S.	Naturalization	OCCUPATION 10 years +	Months not employed	Attended school in months	Can read	Can write	Speak English	Owned or Rent	Owned -no mortgage	Farm or house	# of farm schedule
		FRAZIER, MARY E.	DAU	W	F	MAR 1865	35	S				KY	KY	KY							✓	✓	✓				
		" ELIZABETH	DAU	W	F	Jul 1850	49	S				KY	KY	KY							✓	✓	✓				
		" NELSON B.	SON	W	M	JAN 1871	29	S				KY	KY	KY				FARMER			✓	✓	✓	R			
50	50	FRAZIER, LONZO G.	Head	W	M	JAN 1876	24	M				KY	KY	KY				FARMER			✓	✓	✓	R		F	46
		" MARTHA L.	WIFE	W	F	AUG 1881	18	M				KY	KY	KY							✓	✓	✓				
51	51	JACKSON, WILLIAM	HEAD	W	M	MAY 1856	44	M	16			KY	KY	KY				DAY LABORER 6			X	X	✓	R		H	
		" LIZA	WIFE	W	F	MAR 1865	35	M	16	8	6	KY	KY	KY							X	X	✓				
		" LIZZIE	DAU	W	F	AUG 1884	15	S				KY	KY	KY				AT SCHOOL		3	X	X	✓				
		" WIRT A.	SON	W	M	MAY 1898	2	S				KY	KY	KY													
52	52	BOWLES (BARNT?) F.	HEAD	W	M	MAY 1870	30	M	1			KY	KY	KY				FARMER			✓	✓	✓	O		F	47
		" LUCY M.	WIFE	W	F	AUG 1878	21	M	1	1	1	KY	KY	KY							✓	✓					
		" PAUL	SON	W	M	MAR 1900	2/12	S				KY	KY	KY													
53	53	NANNIE, JOHN	HEAD	W	M	DEC 1816	83	M	59			KY	KY	KY				FARMER			X	X	✓	R		F	48
		" SYNTHAN	WIFE	W	F	NOV 1821	78	M	59			KY	KY	KY							X	X	✓				
54	54	PLOWLES, THOMAS	Head	W	M	MAY 1835	65	M	9			KY	KY	KY				FARMER			✓	✓	✓	R		F	49
		" LUCINDA C.	WIFE	W	F	APR 1847	53	M	9			KY	KY	KY							X	X	✓				
55	55	" WILLIAM C.	HEAD	W	M	Feb 1863	37	M	19			KY	KY	KY				FARMER			✓	✓	✓	O		F	50
		" SARAH	WIFE	W	F	APR 1860	40	M	9	2	2	KY	KY	KY							✓	✓	✓				
		" VINA	DAU	W	F	MAR 1884	16	S				KY	KY	KY				AT SCHOOL		4	✓	✓	✓				
		" FELIN T	SON	W	M	JUN 1893	6	S				KY	KY	KY				AT SCHOOL		5							
		JACKSON, MARTHA BEL	Boarder	W	F	JUN 1887	12	S				KY	KY	KY				AT SCHOOL		4	✓	✓	✓				
56	56	FITZGERALD, JAMES A.	Head	W	M	MAR 1839	61	M	20			TN	VA	TN	VA			FARMER			✓	✓	✓	O		F	51
		" LUCINDA J.	Wife	W	F	AUG 1854	45	M	20			KY	TN	TN							✓	✓	✓				
57	57	RUSSELL, DANIEL	Head	W	M	AUG 1862	37	M	11			KY	KY	KY				FARMER			✓	✓	✓	R		F	52
		" SARAH	Wife	W	F	AUG 1867	32	M	11	5	5	KY	KY	KY							✓	X	✓				
		" MARY L.	DAU	W	F	JAN 1889	11	S				KY	KY	KY				AT SCHOOL		5	✓	✓	✓				

TWELFTH CENSUS OF THE UNITED STATES 1900

-416-

STATE - KENTUCKY
COUNTY - MONROE
Township or other division **UNION**

Enumerator **PERRY W. MILLER**

Supervisor's Dist. No. **102** Sheet No.
Enumeration Dist. No. **86**

No. of Family	No. of Dwelling	NAME	Relation	Color	Sex	DATE OF BIRTH Mon/Yr	Age at last birthday	Marital Status	# Years married	Mother of how many children?	# of these children living	Place of birth [this person]	Father of this person	Mother of this person	Year of immigr.	# years in U.S.	Naturalization	OCCUPATION 10 years +	Months not employed	Attended school in months	Can read	Can write	Speak English	Owned or Rent	Owned - no mortage	Farm or house	# of farm schedule
		RUSSELL, ELORA	DAU	W	F	DEC 1890	9	S				KY	KY	KY				AT SCHOOL		5	✓	✓	✓				
		" LENARD	DAU	W	F	JAN 1893	7	S				KY	KY	KY				AT SCHOOL		5	✓	✓	✓				
		" NORA E.	DAU	W	F	MAR 1895	5	S				KY	KY	KY													
		" CARTER W.	SON	W	M	AUG 1897	2	S				KY	KY	KY													
58	58	GRIMSLEY, JAMES F.	HEAD	W	M	FEB 1829	71	M	56			KY	KY	TN				FARMER			✓	✓	✓	R		F	53
		" FRANCIS P.	WIFE	W	F	APR 1831	69	M	56	12	9	KY	TN	TN							✓	✓	✓				
		" ELIAS	SON	W	M	NOV 1849	50	Wd				KY	TN	TN				BLACKSMITH			X	X	✓				
		" REBECA	DAU	W	F	DEC 1854	46	S				KY	TN	TN							X	X	✓				
		" ALICE V.	DAU	W	F	JUN 1877	22	S				KY	TN	TN							X	X	✓				
		" DAISY D.	GR-DAU	W	F	DEC 1889	10	S				KY	KY	KY				AT SCHOOL		5	✓	✓	✓				
		MILLER, MARGE - W.	DAU	W	F	JUN 1851	48	Wd		2	2	KY	KY	KY							✓	✓	✓				
		" CARLUS W.	GR-SON	W	M	MAY 1890	10	S				KY	KY	KY				AT SCHOOL		5	X	X	✓				
		" BENJAMIN F.	GR-SON	W	M	APR 1892	8	S				KY	KY	KY				AT SCHOOL		4	X	X	✓				
59	59	HOWARD, ROY W.	HEAD	W	M	APR 1869	31	M	4			KY	KY	KY				FARMER			✓	✓	✓	O	F	F	54
		" VIC	WIFE	W	F	FEB 1878	22	M	4	1	1	KY	KY	KY							✓	✓	✓				
		" ANDREW J.	SON	W	M	FEB 1899	1	S				KY	KY	KY													
60	60	COPASS, IRA G.	HEAD	W	M	NOV 1825	74	M	49			TN	TN	TN				FARMER			✓	✓	✓	O	F	F	55
		" JANE	WIFE	W	F	APR 1832	68	M	49	6	5	TN	TN	TN							X	X	✓				
61	61	COPASS, LINDSAY	HEAD	W	M	MAR 1872	28	M	8			KY	TN	TN				FARMER			✓	✓	✓	R		F	56
		" MARY J.	WIFE	W	F	FEB 1874	26	M	8	4	4	KY	KY	KY							✓	✓	✓				
		" ADA E.	DAU	W	F	APR 1894	6	S				KY	KY	KY													
		" ARLY G.	DAU	W	F	JUN 1895	4	S				KY	KY	KY													
		" JARRETT D.	SON	W	M	APR 1897	3	S				KY	KY	KY													
		" NOLIA J.	DAU	W	F	APR 1900	1/12	S				KY	KY	KY													
62	62	EADS, NANCY F.	HEAD	W	F	MAR 1863	37	Wd		3	3	KY	KY	KY							✓	✓	✓	R		H	
		" JAZZY B.	DAU	W	F	FEB 1894	6	S				KY	KY	KY													

STATE - KENTUCKY
COUNTY - MONROE
Township or other division UNION
Enumerator PERRY W. MILLER

Supervisor's Dist. No. 103 Sheet No.
Enumeration Dist. No. 86

Location No. of Family	No. of Dwelling	NAME	Relation	Color	Sex	DATE OF BIRTH Mon/Yr	Age at last birthday	Marital Status	# Years married	Mother of how many children?	# of these children living	NATIVITY Place of birth [this person]	Father of this person	Mother of this person	CITIZENSHIP Year of immigr.	# years in U.S.	Naturalization	OCCUPATION 10 years +	Months not employed	EDUCATION Attended school in months	Can read	Can write	Speak English	OWNERSHIP Owned or Rent	Owned -no mortgage	Farm or house	# of farm schedule
		EADS, WILLIAM B.	Son	W	M	Mar 1895	5	S				KY	KY	KY													
		" JAMES H.	Son	W	M	Oct 1897	2	S				KY	KY	KY													
63	63	SWIGLEY, JOHN H.	Head	B	M	May 1840	60	M	30			KY	KY	KY				FARMER			X	X	✓	O	M	F	57
		" MATILDA	Wife	B	F	Nov 1854	45	M	30	8	3	KY	KY	KY							X	X	✓				
		" LOU B.	Dau	B	F	Jun 1878	21	S				KY	KY	KY				School Teacher 7			✓	✓	✓				
		" VERD	Dau	B	F	Nov 1886	13	S				KY	KY	KY				At School		5	✓	✓	✓				
		LOLA O.	Son	B	M	Jul 1890	9	S				KY	KY	KY				At School		5	✓	✓	✓				
		KIRK, IVA	Niece	B	F	Sep 1882	17	S				KY	KY	KY				At School		4	✓	✓	✓				
64	64	MAXEY, STEVE	Head	B	M	Aug 1865	34	M	16			KY	KY	KY				FARMER			✓	✓	✓	O	F	F	58
		" MAXEY	Wife	B	F	May 1863	37	M	16	4	4	KY	KY	KY							X	X	✓				
		" FLOYD	Son	B	M	Oct 1886	13	S				KY	KY	KY				At School		4	✓	✓	✓				
		" MOSSIE	Dau	B	F	Oct 1886	13	S				KY	KY	KY				At School		4	✓	✓	✓				
		" SIMMON	Son	B	M	Oct 1888	11	S				KY	KY	KY				At School		4	✓	✓	✓				
		" AUSBURN	Son	B	M	Apr 1890	10	S				KY	KY	KY				At School		4							
65	65	HAWK, WILLIAM S.	Head	W	M	Jul 1867	32	M	11			OHIO	OHIO	VA				CIVIL ENGINEER 3			✓	✓	✓	R	H		
		" MATTIE E.	Wife	W	F	Jun 1869	30	M	11	5	5	KY	TN	TN							✓	✓	✓				
		" MYRTIE J.	Dau	W	F	Jul 1889	10	S				KY	OHIO	KY				At School		5	✓	✓	✓				
		" LIBRAND D.	Son	W	M	Oct 1892	7	S				OHIO	OHIO	KY				At School		5	✓	✓	✓				
		" LOUIE L.	Son	W	M	Oct 1895	4	S				OHIO	OHIO	KY				At School		5							
		" PRUNIA R.	Dau	W	F	Apr 1898	2	S				KY	OHIO	KY													
		" ADA R.	Dau	W	F	Nov 1899	6/12	S				KY	OHIO	KY													
66	66	COPASS, MARLIN	Head	W	M	Jan 1838	62	M	32			TN	TN	TN				FARMER			✓	X	✓	O	F	F	59
		" MARY E.	Wife	W	F	Sep 1845	54	M	32	2	1	KY	KY	KY							✓	✓	✓				
		SMITH, WILLIAM A.	Head	W	M	Jan 1878	22	M				KY	KY	KY				FARMER			X	X	✓	R	F	40	
		" MARTHA J.	Wife	W	F	Apr 1873	27	M				KY	KY	KY							✓	✓	✓				
		WHITE, MARY F.	Boarder	W	F	May 1888	12	S				KY	KY	KY				At School		3	✓	✓	✓				

TWELFTH CENSUS OF THE UNITED STATES 1900

STATE - KENTUCKY
COUNTY - MONROE
Township or other division: UNION

Enumerator: PERRY W. MILLER

— 418 —

Supervisor's Dist. No. 102   Sheet No.
Enumeration Dist. No. 86

No. of Family	No. of Dwelling	NAME	Relation	Color	Sex	Date of Birth Mon/Yr	Age at last birthday	Marital Status	# Years married	Mother of how many children	# of these children living	Place of birth (this person)	Father of this person	Mother of this person	Year of immigr.	# years in U.S.	Naturalization	OCCUPATION 10 years +	Months not employed	Attended school in months	Can read	Can write	Speak English	Owned or Rent	Owned - no mortage	Farm or house	# of farm schedule
		JOBE, JESSE	Boarder	W	M	Aug 1824	75	Wd				KY	TN	KY						X	X	✓					
68	68	CARDER, CLIFTON	Head	W	M	Feb 1853	47	M	25			KY	TN	KY				FARMER		X	X	✓		O	M	F	61
		" SMITH I.	Wife	W	F	Apr 1850	50	M	25	8	8	KY	KY	VA						X	X	✓					
		" JESSE H.	Son	W	M	Mar 1879	21	S				KY	KY	KY				FARM LABORER			✓	✓	✓				
		" ARBAH N.	Dau	W	F	Apr 1882	18	S				KY	KY	KY							✓	✓	✓				
		" MARY T.	Dau	W	F	Mar 1886	14	S				KY	KY	KY				AT SCHOOL		4	✓	✓	✓				
		" JAMES R.	Son	W	M	Mar 1888	12	S				KY	KY	KY				AT SCHOOL		4	✓	✓	✓				
		" WILLIE J.	Son	W	M	Feb 1892	8	S				KY	KY	KY				AT SCHOOL		4	✓	✓	✓				
		" GILBERT	Son	W	M	May 1896	4	S				KY	KY	KY													
69	69	WHEAT, JESSE W.	Head	W	M	May 1873	27	M	4			KY	KY	KY				FARMER			✓	✓	✓		R	F	62
		" LUCY J.	Wife	W	F	Jun 1875	24	M	4	2	2	KY	KY	KY							✓	✓	✓				
		" MARVIN B.	Son	W	M	Mar 1898	2	S				KY	KY	KY													
		" MINA	Dau	W	F	Apr 1900	2/12	S				KY	KY	KY													
70	70	SHERLEY, SHERMAN R.	Head	W	M	Sep 1875	24	M	1			KY	KY	KY				FARMER			✓	✓	✓		O	F	63
		" SUVILA	Wife	W	F	Sep 1878	21	M	1	1	1	KY	KY	KY							✓	✓	✓				
		" HERSCHELL T.	Son	N	M	Sep 1899	8/12	S				KY	KY	KY													
		" BETSY	Cousin	W	F	Jan 1828	72	Wd				KY	KY	KY						X	X	✓					
71	71	THOMAS, SAMUEL H.	Head	W	M	Aug 1862	37	M	11			KY	KY	KY				FARMER			✓	✓	✓		O	F	64
		" MELVINA	Wife	W	F	Dec 1863	36	M	11	4	4	KY	KY	KY							✓	✓	✓				
		" JOHN F.	Son	W	M	Jan 1890	10	S				KY	KY	KY				AT SCHOOL		5	✓	✓	✓				
		" DEWEY E.	Son	W	M	Jul 1892	7	S				KY	KY	KY				AT SCHOOL		5	✓	✓	✓				
		" AUDIA J.	Son	W	M	Mar 1894	6	S				KY	KY	KY													
		" ADA M.	Dau	W	F	Feb 1898	2	S				KY	KY	KY													
72	72	PAYNE, ABSALOM	Head	W	M	Sep 1835	64	M	14			TN	TN	TN				FARMER			✓	✓	✓		O	F	65
		" NANCY G.	Wife	W	F	Jan 1843	57	M	14			KY	KY	KY							✓	X	✓				
73	73	SPEAR, HIRAM B.	Head	W	M	Jul 1861	38	M	18			KY	KY	KY				FARMER			✓	✓	✓		R	F	66

STATE - KENTUCKY
COUNTY - MONROE
Township or other division UNION Enumerator PERRY W. MILLER

Supervisor's Dist. No. 102 Sheet No.
Enumeration Dist. No. 86

No. of Family	No. of Dwelling	NAME	Relation	Color	Sex	DATE OF BIRTH Mon/Yr	Age at last birthday	Marital Status	# Years married	Mother of how many children?	# of these children living	Place of birth (this person)	Father of this person	Mother of this person	Year of immigr.	# years in U.S.	Naturalization	OCCUPATION 10 years +	Months not employed	Attended school in months	Can read	Can write	Speak English	Owned or Rent	Owned -no mortage	Farm or house	# of farm schedule
		SPEAR, REBECA E.	WIFE	W	F	Jan 1862	36	M	18	8	8	KY	KY	KY							✓	✓	✓				
		" HUEY E.	SON	W	M	Jun 1883	16	S				KY	KY	KY				AT SCHOOL		4	✓	✓	✓				
		" DEWEY M.	SON	W	M	Aug 1885	14	S				KY	KY	KY				AT SCHOOL		4	✓	✓	✓				
		" OLIE B.	DAU	W	F	Aug 1887	12	S				KY	KY	KY				AT SCHOOL		3	✓	✓	✓				
		" ORA E.	DAU	W	F	Sep 1889	10	S				KY	KY	KY				AT SCHOOL		3	✓	✓	✓				
		" LEOH C.	SON	W	M	Nov 1891	8	S				KY	KY	KY				AT SCHOOL		4							
		" ODAS S.	SON	W	M	Dec 1893	6	S				KY	KY	KY													
		" DALLAS E.	SON	W	M	May 1896	4	S				KY	KY	KY													
		" VALLIE H.	DAU	W	F	Dec 1898	1	S				KY	KY	KY													
74	74	DENHAM, RICHARD	HEAD	W	M	Oct 1847	52	M	25			KY	KY	KY				FARMER			✓	✓	✓	R		F	67
		" MARY E.	WIFE	W	F	Jun 1857	42	M	25	1	1	KY	KY	KY							✓	✓	✓				
		" MOTTEN C.	SON	W	M	Mar 1876	24	S				KY	KY	KY				FARM LABORER			✓	✓	✓				
75	75	JACKSON, WILLIAM L.	HEAD	W	M	Mar 1865	35	M	14			KY	KY	KY				FARMER			✓	✓	✓	O		FF	68
		" MARY I.	WIFE	W	F	Jul 1849	50	M	14	8	7	KY	TN	KY							✓	✓	✓				
		MARTIN, POCA	S-DAU	W	F	Jan 1881	19	S				KY	KY	KY				AT SCHOOL		2	✓	✓	✓				
		" HULET	S-SON	W	M	Jan 1883	17	S				TX	KY	KY				AT SCHOOL		2	✓	✓	✓				
		" LOLIE B.	S-DAU	W	F	Dec 1885	14	S				KY	KY	KY				AT SCHOOL		4	✓	✓	✓				
76	76	JACKSON, JOHN C.	HEAD	W	M	Nov 1869	30	M	12			KY	KY	KY				FARMER			✓	✓	✓	O		F	69
		" ELNORA	WIFE	W	F	Aug 1873	26	M	12	5	5	KY	KY	KY							✓	✓	✓				
		" MYRTIE M.	DAU	W	F	Oct 1889	10	S				KY	KY	KY				AT SCHOOL		5	✓	✓	✓				
		" RADFORD D.	SON	W	M	Apr 1893	7	S				KY	KY	KY				AT SCHOOL		4	✓	✓	✓				
		" BARRY B.	SON	W	M	Jul 1895	4	S				KY	KY	KY				AT SCHOOL		5							
		" (HOVEY ?)	SON	W	M	Feb 1897	3	S				KY	KY	KY													
		" BAZ	SON	W	M	Jul 1899	10/12	S				KY	KY	KY													
77	77	BROWN, JAMES J.	HEAD	W	M	Dec 1845	54	M	30			KY	KY	KY				FARMER			✓	X	✓	O		FF	70
		" SARAH F.	WIFE	W	F	Dec 1848	51	M	30	?	?	KY	KY	KY							✓	✓	✓				

STATE - KENTUCKY
COUNTY - MONROE
Township or other division UNION
Enumerator PERRY W. MILLER

Supervisor's Dist. No. 102 Sheet No.
Enumeration Dist. No. 86

No. of Family	No. of Dwelling	NAME	Relation	Color	Sex	DATE OF BIRTH Mon/Yr	Age at last birthday	Marital Status	# Years married	Mother of how many children?	# of these children living	Place of birth [this person]	Father of this person	Mother of this person	Year of immigr.	# years in U.S.	Naturalization	OCCUPATION 10 years +	Months not employed	Attended school in months	Can read	Can write	Speak English	Owned or Rent	Owned -no mortage	Farm or house	# of farm schedule
		BROWN, JOHNIE G.	BRO	W	M	Nov 1852	47	S				KY	KY	KY				DAY LABORER 4			✓	✓	✓				
		MURPHY, GROVIE D.	Boarder	W	F	Dec 1890	9	S				KY	KY	KY				AT SCHOOL		4	✓	✓	✓				
78	78	HOOD, WILLIAM T.	HEAD	W	M	Nov 1849	50	M	31			KY	KY	KY				FARMER			✓	✓	✓	O	F	F	71
		" MARTHA G.	WIFE	W	F	Jun 1854	45	M	31	8	7	KY	KY	KY						5	X	X	✓				
		" SAMUEL J.	SON	W	M	Dec 1880	19	S				KY	KY	KY				FARM LABORER 2			✓	✓	✓				
		" WILLIAM W.	SON	W	M	Dec 1883	16	S				KY	KY	KY				FARM LABORER			✓	✓	✓				
		" JAMES T.	SON	W	M	Mar 1886	14	S				KY	KY	KY				AT SCHOOL		4	✓	✓	✓				
		" ANNIE B.	DAU	W	F	Mar 1888	12	S				KY	KY	KY				AT SCHOOL		4	✓	✓	✓				
		" AVRY J.	SON	W	M	Aug 1890	9	S				KY	KY	KY				AT SCHOOL		4	✓	✓	✓				
		" HUBY B.	SON	W	M	Dec 1895	4	S				KY	KY	KY													
79	79	BROWN, SAM J.	HEAD	W	M	Jun 1873	26	M	6			KY	KY	KY				FARMER			✓	✓	✓	R		F	72
		" MARY L.	WIFE	W	F	Aug 1880	19	M	6	1	1	KY	KY	KY							✓	✓	✓				
		" TOMMY W.	SON	W	M	Nov 1899	6/12	S				KY	KY	KY													
80	80	HALL, IRVAN R.	HEAD	W	M	Mar 1864	36	M	12			TN	SC	TN				FARMER			✓	✓	✓	R		F	73
		" BELL	WIFE	W	F	Jan 1868	32	M	12	4	2	TN	KY	KY							✓	✓	✓				
		" IRVA	SON	W	M	Jan 1890	10	S				TN	TN	TN				AT SCHOOL		4	✓	✓					
		" OVA	DAU	W	F	Dec 1898	1	S				KY	TN	TN													
		GRACE, LINDSAY	Boarder	W	M	Mar 1876	24	S				KY	KY	TN				DAY LABORER 4			✓	✓	✓	R		F	74
81	81	NICKOLDS, WILLIAM M.	Head	W	M	Feb 1867	33	M	4			KY	KY	KY				FARMER			✓	✓	✓				
		" SUSAN	WIFE	W	F	Aug 1877	22	M	4			KY	KY	KY							✓	✓	✓				
82	82	SHIRLEY, WILLIAMS	HEAD	W	M	Mar 1870	30	M	12			KY	KY	KY				FARMER			✓	✓	✓	O	F	F	75
		" Bettie J.	WIFE	W	F	Jul 1872	27	M	12	7	5	KY	KY	KY							✓	✓	✓				
		" ELLA	DAU	W	F	Dec 1889	10	S				KY	KY	KY				AT SCHOOL		5	✓	✓	✓				
		" CLAY	SON	W	M	Sep 1891	8	S				KY	KY	KY				AT SCHOOL		5	✓	✓	✓				
		" HESSY	SON	W	M	Feb 1893	7	S				KY	KY	KY				AT SCHOOL		4	✓	✓	✓				
		" SMITHIE	SON	W	M	Feb 1898	2	S				KY	KY	KY													

STATE - KENTUCKY
COUNTY - MONROE
Township or other division   UNION

Enumerator   PERRY W. MILLER

Supervisor's Dist. No. _102_ Sheet No.
Enumeration Dist. No. _86_

No. of Family	No. of Dwelling	NAME	Relation	Color	Sex	Date of Birth Mon/Yr	Age at last birthday	Marital Status	# Years married	Mother of how many children?	# of these children living	Place of birth (this person)	Father of this person	Mother of this person	Year of immigr.	# years in U.S.	Naturalization	OCCUPATION 10 years +	Months not employed	Attended school in months	Can read	Can write	Speak English	Owned or Rent	Owned -no mortgage	Farm or house	# of farm schedule
		SHIRLEY, EVERT	Son	W	M	Apr 1900	1/12	S				KY	KY	KY													
83	83	KINGERY, JOSHUA	Head	W	M	May 1857	43	M	10			KY	KY	KY				FARMER			✓	X	✓	O	F	F	76
		" ELIZABETH	Wife	W	F	Jul 1863	36	M	10	4	4	KY	KY	KY							✓	✓	✓				
		" LAURA J.	Dau	W	F	Sep 1890	9	S				KY	KY	KY				AT SCHOOL		5							
		" EMMA (D?)	Dau	W	F	Aug 1894	5	S				KY	KY	KY													
		" DORA F.	Dau	W	F	Sep 1895	4	S				KY	KY	KY													
		" DULCIA B.	Dau	W	F	- 1899	1	S				KY	KY	KY													
84	84	WHEAT, ALLEN B.	Head	W	M	Feb 1878	22	M	2			KY	KY	KY				FARMER			✓	✓	✓	R		F	77
		" JENNIE S.	Wife	W	F	Jan 1880	20	M	2	1	1	KY	KY	KY							✓	✓	✓				
		" LECTA G.	Dau	W	F	Jan 1900	4/12	S				KY	KY	KY													
85	85	KINGERY, JACOB	Head	W	M	May 1865	35	M	15			KY	KY	KY				FARMER			✓	✓	✓	R		F	78
		" ELLA	Wife	W	M	Apr 1865	35	M	15	2	2	KY	KY	KY							✓	✓	✓				
		" WILLIE A.	Son	W	M	Aug 1884	15	S				KY	KY	KY				AT SCHOOL		5	✓	✓					
		" SARAH T.	Dau	W	F	Nov 1888	11	S				KY	KY	KY				AT SCHOOL		4	✓	✓	✓				
86	86	KINGERY, PETER	Head	W	M	Sep 1855	44	M	20			KY	KY	KY				FARMER			X	X	✓	R		F	79
		" MARY A.	Wife	W	F	May 1851	49	M	20			KY	KY	KY							✓	✓					
		BROWN, JAMES G.	Boarder	W	M	Sep 1877	22	S				KY	KY	KY				DAY LABORER	3		✓	✓					
87	87	CARTER, JOE B.	Head	W	M	Oct 1856	43	M	21			KY	KY	KY				FARMER			✓	✓	✓				
		" DELCENIA	Wife	W	F	Sep 1862	37	M	21	9	9	KY	KY	KY							✓	✓	✓				
		" MARY B.	Dau	W	F	Sep 1879	20	S				KY	KY	KY							✓	✓	✓				
		" FRANCIS K.	Dau	W	F	May 1881	19	S				KY	KY	KY				AT SCHOOL		4	✓	✓	✓				
		" BETHEL S.	Son	W	M	Oct 1884	15	S				KY	KY	KY				AT SCHOOL		4½	✓	✓	✓				
		" EDGAR A.	Son	W	M	Jul 1887	12	S				KY	KY	KY				AT SCHOOL		5	✓	✓	✓				
		" ANNIE B.	Dau	W	F	Oct 1889	10	S				KY	KY	KY				AT SCHOOL		4	✓	✓	✓				
		" JENNIE E.	Dau	W	F	Dec 1891	8	S				KY	KY	KY				AT SCHOOL		4	✓	✓	✓				
		" MINTIA A.	Dau	W	F	May 1894	6	S				KY	KY	KY													

TWELFTH CENSUS OF THE UNITED STATES 1900

STATE - KENTUCKY
COUNTY - MONROE
Township or other division UNION

- 422 -

Enumerator PERRY W. MILLER

Supervisor's Dist. No. 102 Sheet No.
Enumeration Dist. No. 86

No. of Family	No. of Dwelling	NAME	Relation	Color	Sex	Date of Birth Mon/Yr	Age at last birthday	Marital Status	# Years married	Mother of how many children	# of these children living	Place of birth (this person)	Father of this person	Mother of this person	Year of immigr.	# years in U.S.	Naturalization	OCCUPATION 10 years +	Months not employed	Attended school in months	Can read	Can write	Speak English	Owned or Rent	Owned-no mortgage	Farm or house	# of farm schedule
		CARTER, HATTIE T.	DAU	W	F	Aug 1896	3	S				KY	KY	KY													
		" CALEB E.	SON	W	M	Sep 1898	1	S				KY	KY	KY													
88	88	WAX, WILLIAM P.	HEAD	W	M	Nov 1873	26	M	3			KY	KY	KY				FARMER			✓	✓	✓	O	F	F	81
		" JENNIE M.	WIFE	W	F	Sep 1878	21	M	3	1	1	KY	KY	KY							✓	✓	✓				
		" ELVA J.	DAU	W	F	Dec 1900	5/12	S				KY	KY	KY													
89	89	GUM, WILLIAM J.	HEAD	W	M	Jan 1870	30	M	12			KY	KY	KY				FARMER			✓	✓	✓	O	F	F	82
		" DORA B.	WIFE	W	F	Aug 1870	29	M	12	2	2	KY	KY	KY							✓	✓	✓				
		" AUDIE D.	SON	W	M	Aug 1891	8	S				KY	KY	KY				AT SCHOOL		5							
		" RULE M.	DAU	W	F	Aug 1893	6	S				KY	KY	KY				AT SCHOOL		5							
90	90	WOOD, BENNIE	HEAD	W	M	Apr 1878	22	M	1			KY	KY	KY				FARMER			✓	✓	✓	O	F	F	83
		" ROXIE R.	WIFE	W	F	May 1873	27	M	1			KY	KY	KY							✓	✓	✓				
91	91	HEADRICK, JAMES	HEAD	W	M	Apr 1830	70	M	21			KY	KY	KY				MILLER			✓	✓	✓	R		H	
		" SARAH E.	WIFE	W	F	Aug 1846	53	M	21			KY	KY	KY							✓	✓	✓				
92	92	BOWLES, RACHEL	HEAD	W	F	Aug 1850	49	Wd		4	4	KY	KY	KY				FARMER			✓	✓	✓	O	F	F	84
		" HUBBY	SON	W	M	Sep 1875	24	S				KY	KY	KY				SCHOOL TEACHER 7)			✓	✓	✓				
		" LENA	DAU	W	F	Nov 1878	21	S				KY	KY	KY				SCHOOL TEACHER 7)			✓	✓	✓				
		" HASCAL	SON	W	M	May 1883	17	S				KY	KY	KY				FARM LABOR			✓	✓	✓				
		HUGHES, HUBERT	Nephew	W	M	May 1887	13	S				KY	KY	KY				AT SCHOOL		5	✓	✓					
		" GRANVILLE	Nephew	W	M	Jul 1889	10	S				KY	KY	KY				AT SCHOOL		5	✓	✓					
93	93	HEADRICK, ISAAC V.	Head	W	M	Apr 1841	59	M	2			TN	TN	TN				FARMER			✓	✓	✓	O	F	F	85
		" MARY J.	WIFE	W	F	Mar 1868	32	M	2	1	1	KY	KY	KY							✓	✓	✓				
		" JOHN F.	SON	W	M	Oct 1872	27	S				KY	TN	KY				FARM LABOR			✓	✓	✓				
		" JOE C.	SON	W	M	Oct 1876	23	S				KY	TN	KY				SCHOOL TEACHER			✓	✓	✓				
		" (?) DURASTUS	SON	W	M	Aug 1882	17	S				KY	TN	KY				AT SCHOOL		5	✓	✓	✓				
		" FRED	SON	W	M	Sep 1898	1	S				KY	KY	KY													
94	94	BARTLEY, JESSE G.	HEAD	W	M	Oct 1859	40	M	20			KY	KY	KY				FARMER			✓	✓	✓	O	F	F	86

STATE - KENTUCKY
COUNTY - MONROE
Township or other division UNION Enumerator PERRY W. MILLER

Supervisor's Dist. No. 102 Sheet No.
Enumeration Dist. No. 86

No. of Family	No. of Dwelling	NAME	Relation	Color	Sex	DATE OF BIRTH Mon/Yr	Age at last birthday	Marital Status	# Years married	Mother of how many children?	# of these children living	Place of birth (this person)	Father of this person	Mother of this person	OCCUPATION 10 years +	Attended school in months	Can read	Can write	Speak English	Owned or Rent	Owned -no mortgage	Farm or house	# of farm schedule
		BARTLEY, SUSAN A.	WIFE	W	F	Sep 1836	63	M	20	4	4	TN	TN	TN			X	X	✓				
95	95	NANNIE, CHARLES	HEAD	W	M	Mar 1850	50	M	20			TN	TN	TN	FARMER		X	X	✓	R		F	87
	"	SARAH	WIFE	W	F	Jul 1841	58	M	20	1	1	KY	KY	TN			X	X	✓				
96	96	NANNIE, JANE	HEAD	W	F	Mar 1840	60	Wd	?	4	2	KY	KY	KY	WASH WOMAN 4		X	X	✓	R		H	
	"	SARAH	DAU	W	F	Feb 1880	20	S				KY	KY	KY			X	X	✓				
	"	SAM	GR-SON	B	M	Apr 1883	17	S				KY	KY	KY	DAY LABORER 4		X	X	✓				
	"	JOE C.	GR-SON	B	M	May 1898	2	S				KY	KY	KY			X	X	✓				
		MAXEY, MARTHA	DAU	B	F	Jan 1870	30	(Wd?)				KY	KY	KY			X	X	✓				
97	97	MARTIN, TOM	HEAD	B	M	May 1860	40	Wd				KY	KY	KY	DAY LABORER 5		X	X	✓	R		H	
	"	TINKER	SON	B	M	Apr 1888	12	S				KY	KY	KY	AT SCHOOL	2	X	X	✓				
98	98	BRAY, SARAH T.	HEAD	W	F	Mar 1838	62	Wd				KY	KY	KY	FARMER		✓	✓	✓	O	FF		88
	"	JOSEPH P.	SON	W	M	Apr 1875	25	S				KY	KY	KY	FARMER		✓	✓	✓				
		INGRUM W.	SON	W	M	Aug 1881	18	S				KY	KY	KY	FARM LABORER	2	✓	✓	✓				
		JONES, ADA J.	GR-DAU	W	F	Jan 1897	3	S				KY	KY	KY						R		F	89
99	99	HARLAN, JOHN M.	HEAD	W	M	May 1862	38	M	17			KY	KY	KY	FARMER		✓	✓	✓				
		JOSIPHINE E.	WIFE	W	F	Jun 1857	42	M	17	2	1	KY	KY	KY			✓	✓	✓				
	"	ROBERT V.	SON	W	M	Oct 1886	13	S				KY	KY	KY	AT SCHOOL	5	✓	✓	✓				
100	100	HOSS, GEO. W.	HEAD	W	M	Feb 1848	52	M	19			KY	KY	KY	FARMER		✓	✓	✓	O	FF		90
	"	MARY L.	WIFE	W	F	May 1856	44	M	19			KY	KY	KY			✓	✓	✓				
	"	LULA M.	NIECE	W	F	Feb 1894	6	S				KY	KY	KY									
101	101	BOWLES, HIRAM P.	Head	W	M	Jun 1865	34	M	5			KY	KY	KY	FARMOR		✓	✓	✓	R		F	91
	"	MARY L.	WIFE	W	F	Apr 1875	25	M	5	2	2	KY	KY	KY			✓	✓	✓				
	"	ADIE L.	DAU	W	F	May 1896	4	S				KY	KY	KY									
	"	LOREN D.	SON	W	M	Mar 1898	2	S				KY	KY	KY	FARMER					O	FF		92
102	102	SHIRLEY, FRANK S.	HEAD	W	M	Nov 1862	37	M	11			KY	KY	KY	FARMER		✓	✓	✓				
	"	BETTIE A.	WIFE	W	F	Jun 1869	30	M	11	5	5	KY	TN	KY			✓	✓	✓				

STATE - KENTUCKY
COUNTY - MONROE
Township or other division   UNION   Enumerator PERRY W. MILLER

Supervisor's Dist. No. 102   Sheet No.
Enumeration Dist. No. 86

Location		NAME	Relation	Color	Sex	DATE OF BIRTH Mon/Yr	Age at last birthday	Marital Status	# Years married	Mother of how many children?	# of these children living	NATIVITY			CITIZENSHIP			OCCUPATION 10 years +	Months not employed	EDUCATION				OWNERSHIP			
No. of Family	No. of Dwelling											Place of birth (this person)	Father of this person	Mother of this person	Year of immigr.	# years in U.S.	Naturalization			Attended school in months	Can read	Can write	Speak English	Owned or Rent	Owned -no mortgage	Farm or house	# of farm schedule
		SHIRLEY, ZACK T.	Son	W	M	Oct 1890	9	S				KY	KY	KY				AT SCHOOL		5	✓	✓	✓				
		" HIRAM Z.	Son	W	M	Aug 1892	7	S				KY	KY	KY				AT SCHOOL		5	✓	✓	✓				
		" LOU E.	Dau	W	F	Oct 1894	5	S				KY	KY	KY													
		" JESSE S. R.	Son	W	M	May 1897	3	S				KY	KY	KY													
		" EARL D.	Son	W	M	Oct 1899	7/12	S				KY	KY	KY													
103	103	LYONS, JENNIE	Head	W	F	Jan 1864	36	Wd		4	4	KY	KY	KY				FARMER			✓	✓	✓	O	F	F	93
		" RINDA	Dau	W	F	Sep 1886	13	S				KY	KY	KY				AT SCHOOL		4	✓	✓	✓				
		" HADE	Son	W	M	Oct 1889	10	S				KY	KY	KY				AT SCHOOL		4	✓	✓	✓				
		" KATE	Dau	W	F	Jul 1891	8	S				KY	KY	KY				AT SCHOOL		4	✓	✓	✓				
		" LECTIE(?)	Dau	W	F	Apr 1896	4	S				KY	KY	KY													
104	104	BUSHONG, PERRY	Head	W	M	Dec 1840	59	M	39			KY	KY	KY				FARMER			✓	✓	✓	O	F	F	94
		" MARY E.	Wife	W	F	Jul 1846	53	M	39	12	11	KY	KY	KY							✓	✓	✓				
		" JOHN M.	Son	W	M	May 1873	27	S				KY	KY	KY				FARM LABORER			✓	✓	✓				
		" JACOB	Son	W	M	Jan 1878	22	S				KY	KY	KY				FARM LABORER			✓	✓	✓				
		" NANNIE	Dau	W	F	May 1880	20	S				KY	KY	KY				AT SCHOOL		5	✓	✓	✓				
		" ELSA	Dau	W	F	Aug 1882	17	S				KY	KY	KY				AT SCHOOL		5	✓	✓					
		" NONNA	Dau	W	F	Apr 1885	15	S				KY	KY	KY				AT SCHOOL		4	✓	✓	✓				
		" ETTIE	Dau	W	F	Jul 1888	11	S				KY	KY	KY				AT SCHOOL		4	✓	✓	✓				
105	105	LYONS, JOHN E.	Head	W	M	Aug 1853	46	Wd				KY	KY	KY				FARMER			✓	✓	✓	O	F	F	95
		" LEWIS	Son	W	M	May 1877	22	S				KY	KY	KY				FARM LABORER			✓	✓	✓				
		" EDDIE	Son	W	M	Jul 1879	20	S				KY	KY	KY				FARM LABORER			✓	✓					
		" SAMUEL	Son	W	M	Oct 1882	17	S				KY	KY	KY				AT SCHOOL		4	✓	✓	✓				
		" DOLLIE B.	Dau	W	F	Jun 1886	13	S				KY	KY	KY				AT SCHOOL		5	✓	✓	✓				
		" SARAH	Dau	W	F	Oct 1891	8	S				KY	KY	KY				AT SCHOOL		4							
		" LENA	Dau	W	F	Mar 1893	7	S				KY	KY	KY				AT SCHOOL		4							
106	106	KINGERY, WILLIAM	Head	W	M	Aug 1844	55	M	34			KY	KY	KY				MILLER			X	X	✓	O	F	F	96

STATE - KENTUCKY
COUNTY - MONROE
Township or other division UNION
Enumerator PERRY W. MILLER

Supervisor's Dist. No. 102 Sheet No.
Enumeration Dist. No. 86

No. of Family	No. of Dwelling	NAME	Relation	Color	Sex	Date of Birth Mon/Yr	Age at last birthday	Marital Status	# Years married	Mother of how many children?	# of these children living	Place of birth [this person]	Father of this person	Mother of this person	Year of immigr.	# years in U.S.	Naturalization	Occupation 10 years +	Months not employed	Attended school in months	Can read	Can write	Speak English	Owned or Rent	Owned-no mortgage	Farm or house	# of farm schedule
		KINGERY, JAMES C.	SON	W	M	MAR 1871	29	M	4			KY	KY	KY				FARMER			✓	✓	✓				
		" IBA S.	DAU-LAW	W	F	OCT 1876	23	M	4	2	2	KY	KY	KY							✓	✓	✓				
		" HORACE	GR-SON	W	M	MAY 1897	3	S				KY	KY	KY													
		" WILLIAM	GR-SON	W	M	JAN 1899	1	S				KY	KY	KY													
07	107	HAYES, SARAH W.	HEAD	W	F	DEC 1853	46	Wd				KY	KY	KY							✓	✓	✓	O	F	F	97
		" ROY G.	SON	W	M	APR 1877	23	S				KY	KY	KY				FARMER			✓	✓	✓				
08	108	HOWARD, ELIZABETH	HEAD	W	F	OCT 1826	73	Wd		15	14	KY	KY	KY							✓	✓	✓	O	F	F	98
		" CORA M.	DAU	W	F	JAN 1850	50	S				KY	KY	KY							✓	✓					
		" LOUISA J.	DAU	W	F	APR 1852	48	S				KY	KY	KY							✓	✓					
		" LUCY M.	DAU	W	F	OCT 1857	42	S				KY	KY	KY							✓	✓					
		" JOHN B.	SON	W	F	JUN 1864	35	Wd				KY	KY	KY				FARMER			✓	✓					
		" WILLIE G.	SON	W	M	SEP 1870	29	Wd				KY	KY	KY				FARMER			✓	✓					
		" WILLIAM C.	GR-SON	W	M	AUG 1889	10	S				KY	KY	KY				AT SCHOOL		5	✓	✓					
		" CARL P.	GR-SON	W	M	JAN 1892	8	S				KY	KY	KY				AT SCHOOL		5							
		" EARNEST J.	GR-SON	W	M	DEC 1894	5	S				KY	KY	KY													
		" ARGIE J.	GR-SON	W	M	MAR 1899	1	S				KY	KY	KY													
09	109	THOMAS, JOSEPH M.	HEAD	W	M	JUL 1836	63	M	29			KY	VA	VA				FARMER			✓	✓	✓	O	F	F	99
		" MARTHA L.	WIFE	W	F	JUL 1844	55	M	29	8	8	IN	IN	IN							✓	✓	✓				
		" SARAH E.	DAU	W	F	JAN 1873	27	S				KY	KY	TN							✓	✓	✓				
		" SMITH R.	SON	W	M	APR 1874	26	S				KY	KY	TN				FARM LABORER 2			✓	✓					
		" JOE A.	DAU	W	F	AUG 1878	21	S				KY	KY	KY							✓	✓					
		" WILLIE J.	SON	W	M	DEC 1879	20	S				KY	KY	KY				FARM LABORER			✓	✓	✓				
		" GEO. G.	SON	W	M	MAR 1882	18	S				KY	KY	KY				FARM LABORER 3			✓	✓	✓				
		" LUCAS B.	DAU	W	F	DEC 1884	15	S				KY	KY	KY				AT SCHOOL		4	✓	✓	✓				
		" MARY F.	DAU	W	F	AUG 1887	12	S				KY	KY	KY				AT SCHOOL		5	✓	✓	✓				
10	110	WEBB, LIZZIE E.	HEAD	W	F	JAN 1863	47	Wd		5	5	KY	KY	KY				FARMER			✓	✓	✓	O	F	F	100

STATE - KENTUCKY
COUNTY - MONROE
Township or other division **UNION**
Enumerator **PERRY W. MILLER**

Supervisor's Dist. No. *102* Sheet No.
Enumeration Dist. No. *86*

No. of Family	No. of Dwelling	NAME	Relation	Color	Sex	Date of Birth Mon/Yr	Age at last birthday	Marital Status	# Years married	Mother of how many children?	# of these children living	Place of birth (this person)	Father of this person	Mother of this person	Year of immigr.	# years in U.S.	Naturalization	OCCUPATION 10 years +	Months not employed	Attended school in months	Can read	Can write	Speak English	Owned or Rent	Owned -no mortage	Farm or house	# of farm schedule
		WEBB, JAMES H.	SON	W	M	Jul 1880	19	S				KY	KY	KY				FARM LABORER			✓	✓					
		" BETTIE S.	DAU	W	F	Dec 1887	12	S				KY	KY	KY				AT SCHOOL		5	✓	✓					
11	11	NICKOLDS, JAMES F.	HEAD	W	M	Jan 1861	39	M	14			KY	KY	KY				FARMER			✓	✓		R		F	101
		" REBECCA	WIFE	W	F	Aug 1871	28	M	14	5	5	KY	KY	KY							✓	✓					
		" BETTIE A.	DAU	W	F	Jan 1888	12	S				KY	KY	KY				AT SCHOOL		4	✓	✓					
		" WILLIAM J.	SON	W	M	Jan 1890	10	S				KY	KY	KY				AT SCHOOL		4	✓	✓					
		" WALTER D.	SON	W	M	Dec 1892	7	S				KY	KY	KY				AT SCHOOL		4							
		" MARTHA S.	DAU	W	F	Apr 1894	6	S				KY	KY	KY													
		" NELSON	SON	W	M	Oct 1898	1	S				KY	KY	KY													
12	112	JACKSON, ISAAC R.	HEAD	W	M	Apr 1848	52	M	26			KY	KY	KY				FARMER			✓	✓		O		F	102
		" SARAH E.	WIFE	W	F	Sep 1847	52	M	26	3	3	KY	KY	KY							✓	✓					
		" JOHN R.	SON	W	M	Jul 1880	19	S				KY	KY	KY				FARM LABORER			✓	✓					
		" NANNIE	DAU	W	F	Mar 1883	17	S				KY	KY	KY				AT SCHOOL		4	✓	✓					
		" JOE	BROTHER	W	M	May 1854	46	S				KY	KY	KY				FARM LABORER			✓	✓					
13	113	EMBERTON, FANNIE	HEAD	W	F	Feb 1824	76	Wd				KY	KY	KY							✓	✓		O		F	103
		" ALLEN J.	SON	W	M	Oct 1847	52					KY	KY	KY				FARMER			X	X	✓				
14	14	SMIRES, JOHN K.	HEAD	W	M	Mar 1867	33	M	11			TN	PA	TN				FARMER			✓	✓	✓	R		F	104
		" MINNIE	WIFE	W	F	Apr 1868	32	M	11	3	3	TN	TN	TN							✓	✓					
		" HARRISON	SON	W	M	Apr 1890	10	S				TN	TN	TN				AT SCHOOL		5	✓	✓					
		" HERSCHELL	SON	W	M	Mar 1892	8	S				TN	TN	TN				AT SCHOOL		4							
		" DOVIE	SON	W	M	Apr 1894	6	S				TN	TN	TN													
15	15	RAILEY, ANTHONY J.	HEAD	W	M	Sep 1843	56	M	34			KY	KY	KY				FARMER			✓	✓	✓	O		F	105
		" ADELADE G.	WIFE	W	F	Feb 1849	50	M	34	8	8	KY	KY	KY							✓	✓	✓				
		" ROLAN G.	SON	W	M	Feb 1868	32	S				KY	KY	KY				CIRCUIT COURT CLERK			✓	✓					
		" DONNIE A.	DAU	W	F	Aug 1874	25	S				KY	KY	KY							✓	✓	✓				
		" PEARL E.	DAU	W	F	Oct 1878	21	S				KY	KY	KY							✓	✓	✓				

TWELFTH CENSUS OF THE UNITED STATES 1900

STATE - KENTUCKY
COUNTY - MONROE
Township or other division: UNION
Enumerator: PERRY W. MILLER

Supervisor's Dist. No. 102 Sheet No.
Enumeration Dist. No. 86

No. of Family	No. of Dwelling	NAME	Relation	Color	Sex	DATE OF BIRTH Mon/Yr	Age at last birthday	Marital Status	# Years married	Mother of how many children?	# of these children living	Place of birth [this person]	Father of this person	Mother of this person	Year of immigr.	# years in U.S.	Naturalization	OCCUPATION 10 years +	Months not employed	Attended school in months	Can read	Can write	Speak English	Owned or Rent	Owned –no mortgage	Farm or house	# of farm schedule
		RAILEY, OLLIE L.	Son	W	M	Feb 1882	18	S				KY	KY	KY				AT SCHOOL		5	✓	✓	✓				
		" GROVER T.	Son	W	M	Nov 1884	15	S				KY	KY	KY				AT SCHOOL		5	✓	✓	✓				
116	116	HUMES, MALINDA	Head	W	F	Feb 1850	50	S				KY	KY	KY							X	X	✓	R		H	
		" POLLY	Cousin	W	F	May 1850	50	S				KY	KY	KY							X	X	✓				
117	117	DENHAM, RUFUS	Head	W	M	Aug 1871	28	M	8			KY	KY	KY				FARMER			✓	✓	✓	O	F	F	106
		" ALICE	Wife	W	F	Feb 1871	29	M	8	2	2	KY	KY	KY							✓	✓	✓				
		" HERSCHALL	Son	W	M	Feb 1893	7	S				KY	KY	KY				AT SCHOOL		5							
		" PEARL	Dau	W	F	Feb 1897	3	S				KY	KY	KY													
118	118	SHIRLEY, JAMES	Head	W	M	Mar 1860	40	M	4			KY	KY	KY				FARMER			X	X	✓	R		F	107
		" MILLIE	Wife	W	F	Apr 1875	25	M	4	2	2	KY	KY	KY							X	X	✓				
		" PHOEBA	Dau	W	F	Jan 1898	2	S				KY	KY	KY													
		" SARAH	Dau	W	F	Feb 1900	3/12	S				KY	KY	KY													
119	119	DENHAM, JOHN W.	Head	W	M	May 1869	36	M	8			KY	KY	KY				FARMER			✓	✓	✓	O	F	F	108
		" BETTIE	Wife	W	F	Feb 1873	27	M	8			KY	KY	KY							✓	✓	✓	O	F	F	109
120	120	DENHAM, JOHN H.	Head	W	M	Nov 1845	64	M	29			TN	TN	TN				FARMER			✓	✓	✓				
		" SUSAN M.	Wife	W	F	Mar 1854	46	M	29	2	2	TN	PA	TN							✓	✓	✓				
		" JAMES W.	Son	W	M	Oct 1872	27	S				KY	TN	TN				SCHOOL TEACHER	7		✓	✓	✓				
		" HENRY H.	Son	W	M	Jun 1875	24	S				KY	TN	TN				SCHOOL TEACHER	7		✓	X	✓	R		H	
121	121	STRODE, ELIZABETH	Head	W	F	Sep 1857	42	WD	5	3		KY	KY	KY							X	X	✓				
		" ALBETIE	Son	W	M	Mar 1881	19	S				KY	KY	KY				DAY LABORER	3		X	X	✓				
		" ARLANDO	Son	W	M	Mar 1882	18	S				KY	KY	KY				DAY LABORER	4		X	X	✓				
		" WILLIAM F.	Son	W	M	Jn 1893	6	S				KY	KY	KY				SAWYER						R		H	
122	122	CABAL, WILLIAM A.	Head	W	M	May 1838	62	M	39			KY	KY	KY							✓	✓	✓	R		H	
		" MARY E.	Wife	W	F	Dec 1842	57	M	39	9	4	KY	KY	KY							✓	✓	✓				
		" LUCY	Dau	W	F	Oct 1872	27	S				KY	KY	KY							✓	✓	✓				
		" MAGGIE	Dau	W	F	May 1876	24	S				KY	KY	KY							✓	✓	✓				

STATE - KENTUCKY
COUNTY - MONROE
Township or other division **UNION**
Enumerator **PERRY W. MILLER**

Supervisor's Dist. No. **102** Sheet No.
Enumeration Dist. No. **86**

Location		NAME	Relation	Color	Sex	DATE OF BIRTH Mon/Yr	Age at last birthday	Marital Status	#Years married	Mother of how many children?	# of these children living	NATIVITY Place of birth [this person]	Father of this person	Mother of this person	CITIZENSHIP Year of immigr.	# years in U.S.	Naturalization	OCCUPATION 10 years +	Months not employed	Attended school in months	Can read	Can write	Speak English	OWNERSHIP Owned or Rent	Owned -no mortage	Farm or house	# of farm schedule
No. of Family	No. of Dwelling																										
		CABAL, EDWIN	Son	W	M	Aug 1879	20	S				KY	KY	KY				DAY LABORER	3		✓	✓	✓				
		" EMERSON L.	Son	W	M	Mar 1881	19	S				KY	KY	KY				DAY LABORER	2		✓	✓	✓				
		" WILLIAM A.	Son	W	M	Feb 1886	14	S				KY	KY	KY				AT SCHOOL		5	✓	✓	✓				
		" EDIE J.	GR-SON	W	M	Feb 1897	3	S				KY	KY	KY													
123	123	ROBERTS, LIZA	HEAD	W	F	May 1862	38	WD	4	4		KY	ILL	TN							X	X	✓	R		H	
		" MINNIE	DAU	W	F	Jun 1889	10	S				TN	KY	KY				AT SCHOOL		5	✓	✓	✓				
124	124	OWENS, ROBERT B.	HEAD	W	M	Feb 1868	32	M	1			TN	VA	TN				FARMER			✓	✓	✓	R		F	110
		" CARRY	WIFE	W	F	Oct 1882	17	M	1	1	1	KY	KY	KY							✓	✓					
		" BUFORD R.	Son	W	M	May 1900	9/12	S				KY	KY	KY													
125	125	BUSHONG, HARMON S.	HEAD	W	M	Aug 1857	42	M	21			KY	MISSIPPI	KY				FARMER			✓	✓	✓	O		F	111
		" LAURA A.	WIFE	W	F	Aug 1857	42	M	21	1	1	ILL	KY	KY							✓	✓	✓				
		" WALTER B.	Son	W	M	Mar 1881	19	S				KY	KY	IL				AT SCHOOL		5	✓	✓	✓				
		" MARTHA J.H.	Mother	W	F	Feb 1833	67	WD		1	1	KY	KY	KY							✓	✓	✓				
126	126	MARTIN, WILLIAM	Head	W	M	Apr 1843	57	M	35			KY	KY	VA				FARMER			✓	✓	✓	O		F	112
		" BETHIA F.	Wife	W	F	Feb 1846	54	M	35	11	9	KY	KY	KY							✓	✓	✓				
		" JAMES A.	Son	W	M	Nov 1869	30	WD				KY	KY	KY				FARMER			✓	✓	✓				
		" GEO. P.	Son	W	M	Mar 1872	28	S				KY	KY	KY				FARMER			✓	✓	✓				
		" JOHN S.	Son	W	M	Jul 1874	25	S				KY	KY	KY				FARM LABORER			✓	✓	✓				
		" JESSE E.	Son	W	M	Nov 1876	23	S				KY	KY	KY				SCHOOL TEACHER		4½	✓	✓	✓				
		" ED H.	Son	W	M	Feb 1882	18	S				KY	KY	KY				AT SCHOOL		6	✓	✓	✓				
		" LONNIE E.	DAU	W	F	Apr 1884	16	S				KY	KY	KY				AT SCHOOL		3	✓	✓	✓				
		" WILLIE F.	Son	W	M	Oct 1887	12	S				KY	KY	KY				AT SCHOOL		5	✓	✓	✓				
		" LOU V.	DAU	W	F	Mar 1892	8	S				KY	KY	KY				AT SCHOOL		5	✓	✓	✓				
		" ZADIE E.	GR-DAU	W	F	Feb 1895	5	S				KY	KY	KY													
		" MAUDEY S.	GR-DAU	W	F	Dec 1897	2	S				KY	KY	KY													
127	127	BIRGE, SAM	HEAD	W	M	Feb 1879	21	M	2			KY	KY	TN				FARMER			✓	✓	✓	R		F	113

STATE - KENTUCKY
COUNTY - MONROE
Township or other division — UNION

Enumerator PERRY W. MILLER

Supervisor's Dist. No. _102_ Sheet No.
Enumeration Dist. No. _86_

No. of Family	No. of Dwelling	NAME	Relation	Color	Sex	DATE OF BIRTH Mon/Yr	Age at last birthday	Marital Status	# Years married	Mother of how many children?	# of these children living	Place of birth [this person]	Father of this person	Mother of this person	Year of immigr.	# years in U.S.	Naturalization	OCCUPATION 10 years +	Months not employed	Attended school in months	Can read	Can write	Speak English	Owned or Rent	Owned -no mortgage	Farm or house	# of farm schedule
		BIRGE, STORIA	WIFE	W	F	Nov 1879	20	M	2	1	1	KY	KY	KY							✓	✓	✓				
		" ELIJAH	SON	W	M	Jun 1899	11/12	S				KY	KY	KY							✓	✓	✓				
128	128	ARTURBURN, LORANZO D	Head	W	M	Feb 1856	44	M	15			KY	KY	KY				FARMER			✓	✓	✓	O	F	F	114
		" BETTIE	Wife	W	F	Aug 1858	41	M	15	12	5	KY	KY	KY							✓	✓	✓				
		" MARY A.	Dau	W	F	Sep 1887	12	S				KY	KY	KY				AT SCHOOL		4	✓	✓	✓				
		" JOHN L.	Son	W	M	Aug 1888	11	S				KY	KY	KY				AT SCHOOL		3	✓	✓	✓				
		" AMBRUS C.	Son	W	M	Aug 1890	9	S				KY	KY	KY				AT SCHOOL		4	✓	✓	✓				
		" LORANZO C.	Son	W	M	Aug 1896	3	S				KY	KY	KY													
		" NOAH T.	Son	W	M	Dec 1899	5/12	S				KY	KY	KY													
129	129	BIRGE, MARGET	HEAD	W	F	Jul 1636	63	WD	14	12		KY	KY	KY							X	X	✓	O		H	
130	130	BILLINGSLEY, ELIZABETH	HEAD	W	F	Jan 1840	60	WD		5	5	KY	KY	KY							✓	✓	✓	O	F	F	115
		WALKER, MARTHA	DAU	W	F	May 1873	27	WD		6	4	KY	KY	KY							✓	X	✓				
		" LOLA P.	GR-DAU	W	F	Aug 1889	10	S				KY	KY	KY							✓	✓					
		" FRANK H.	GR-SON	W	M	Apr 1891	9	S				KY	KY	KY													
		" DEWEY P.	GR-SON	W	M	Feb 1896	4	S				KY	KY	KY													
		" PEARLIE J.	GR-DAU	W	F	Jun 1898	1	S				KY	KY	KY													
131	131	BILLINGSLEY, JESSE S.	HEAD	W	M	Dec 1861	38	M	13			KY	KY	KY				FARMER			✓	✓	✓	R	F		116
		" MARTHA E.	WIFE	W	F	Jun 1861	38	M	13	6	6	KY	KY	KY							✓	X	✓				
		" BEVERLY R.	Son	W	M	Feb 1886	14	S				KY	KY	KY				AT		4	✓	✓	✓				
		" JAMES F.	Son	W	M	Mar 1889	11	S				KY	KY	KY				AT		4	✓	✓	✓				
		" JOSEPH F.	Son	W	M	May 1890	10	S				KY	KY	KY				AT		3	✓	✓	✓				
		" JOHNIE M.	Son	W	M	Oct 1891	8	S				KY	KY	KY				AT		3							
		" ADA S.	DAU	W	F	Jul 1893	6	S				KY	KY	KY													
		" WILLIAM S.	SON	W	M	Mar 1896	4	S				KY	KY	KY							✓	✓	✓				
132	132	HODGES, JOHN M.	HEAD	W	M	May 1864	36	WD				KY	TN	KY				DAY LABORER 5			✓	✓	✓	R		H	
133	133	BRAY, GEO. B.	HEAD	W	M	Jul 1875	24	M	1			KY	KY	KY				FARMER			✓	✓	✓	O	F	F	117

STATE - KENTUCKY
COUNTY - MONROE
Township or other division — UNION

— 430 —

Enumerator — PERRY W. MILLER

Supervisor's Dist. No. 102 Sheet No.
Enumeration Dist. No. 86

No. of Family / No. of Dwelling	NAME	Relation	Color	Sex	DATE OF BIRTH Mon/Yr	Age at last birthday	Marital Status	# Years married	Mother of how many children?	# of these children living	NATIVITY Place of birth [this person]	Father of this person	Mother of this person	CITIZENSHIP Year of immigr.	# years in U.S.	Naturalization	OCCUPATION 10 years +	Months not employed	Attended school in months	Can read	Can write	Speak English	Owned or Rent	Owned –no mortgage	Farm or house	# of farm schedule
	BRAY, MARY T.	WIFE	W	F	OCT 1877	22	M	1	1	1	KY	KY	KY							✓	✓	✓				
	" NOAH F.	SON	W	M	May 1900	0/12	S				KY	KY	KY													
134/134	BIRGE, THOMAS P.	HEAD	W	M	NOV 1875	24	M	8			KY	KY	KY				FARMER			✓	✓	✓	O	F	F	118
	" MARY T.	WIFE	W	F	May 1877	23	M	8	5	4	KY	KY	KY							✓	✓	✓				
	" VIRGIL O.	SON	W	M	APR. 1893	7	S				KY	KY	KY				AT SCHOOL		4							
	" BARLY	SON	W	M	Jan. 1895	5	S				KY	KY	KY													
	" ADA	DAU	W	F	May 1897	3	S				KY	KY	KY													
	" WALTER F.	SON	W	M	MAR 1900	2/12	S				KY	KY	KY													
135/135	BRAY, HENRY F.	HEAD	W	M	Jan 1859	41	M	0			KY	KY	KY				FARMER			✓	✓	✓	O	F	F	119
	" DORA A.	WIFE	W	F	APR 1876	24	M	0	0	0	KY	KY	KY							✓	✓	✓				
	" ALONZO T.	SON	W	M	OCT 1888	11	S				KY	KY	KY				AT SCHOOL		4	✓	✓	✓				
	" FLORENCE P.	DAU	W	F	Feb 1891	9	S				KY	KY	KY				AT SCHOOL		4	✓	✓	✓				
	" WILLIAM P.	SON	W	M	DEC 1892	7	S				KY	KY	KY													
136/136	McWHERTER, JOHN	HEAD	W	M	MAY 1866	34	M	12			KY	TN	TN				BLACKSMITH			✓	✓	✓	O	F	F	120
	" SARADA	WIFE	W	F	Jan 1862	38	M	12	3	3	KY	KY	KY							✓	✓	✓				
	" ZONIE P.	DAU	W	F	Jan 1889	11	S				KY	KY	KY				AT SCHOOL		5	✓	✓	✓				
	" SALLIE M.	DAU	W	F	OCT 1891	8	S				KY	KY	KY				AT SCHOOL		5	✓	✓	✓				
	" PEARLIE	DAU	W	F	AUG 1894	5	S				KY	KY	KY													
	JONES, GRACIE T.	NIECE	W	F	Sep 1891	8	S				KY	KY	KY				AT SCHOOL		5							
137/137	WHITE, JAMES S.	HEAD	W	M	Jul 1859	40	WD				KY	KY	KY				FARMER			✓	✓	✓	R		F	121
	" VESTA	SON	W	M	Jul 1879	20	S				KY	KY	KY							✓	✓	✓				
	" ELLA B.	DAU	W	F	Feb 1881	19	S				KY	KY	KY							X	X	✓				
	" VIRGIA	DAU	W	F	Feb 1884	16	S				KY	KY	KY				AT SCHOOL		3	✓	✓	✓				
	" LOY T.	SON	W	M	Jul 1889	10	S				KY	KY	KY				AT SCHOOL		4	✓	✓	✓				
	" OTTO	SON	W	M	OCT 1892	7	S				KY	KY	KY				AT SCHOOL		3							
	" CLYDE B.	SON	W	M	OCT 1893	6	S				KY	KY	KY													

— 431 —

STATE - KENTUCKY
COUNTY - MONROE
Township or other division: UNION
Enumerator: PERRY W. MILLER

Supervisor's Dist. No. 102   Sheet No.
Enumeration Dist. No. 86

No. of Family	No. of Dwelling	NAME	Relation	Color	Sex	Date of Birth Mon/Yr	Age at last birthday	Marital Status	# Years married	Mother of how many children?	# of these children living	Place of birth (this person)	Father of this person	Mother of this person	Year of immigr. / # years in U.S. / Naturalization	Occupation	Months not employed	Attended school in months	Can read	Can write	Speak English	Owned or Rent	Owned – no mortgage	Farm or house	# of farm schedule
138	138	BRAY, PASCHAL B.	HEAD	W	M	DEC 1835	64	M	39			KY	KY	KY		FARMER			✓	✓	✓	O		F F	122
		" HETTIE T.	WIFE	W	F	AUG 1834	65	M	39	8	6	KY	KY	KY					✓	✓	✓				
139	139	MEADOWS, ERASTES H.	Head	W	M	OCT 1844	55	M	29			KY	VA	VA		FARMER			✓	✓	✓	O		F F	123
		" EDDIE	Wife	W	F	Feb 1846	54	M	29	0	0	KY	TN	TN					✓	✓	✓				
140	140	BARTLEY, SATERFIELD	Head	W	M	APR 1859	41	M	22			KY	KY	VA		FARMER			✓	✓	✓	O		M F	124
		" EDDIE	WIFE	W	F	APR 1859	41	M	22	5	4	KY	TN	TN					X	X	✓				
		" EMMA	DAU	W	F	MAR 1890	10	S				KY	KY	KY		AT SCHOOL		4	✓	✓	✓				
		" LAURA	DAU	W	F	Feb 1892	8	S				KY	KY	KY		AT SCHOOL		4							
		" JOHN F.	SON	W	M	DEC 1896	3	S				KY	KY	KY											
41	141	BACON, JOHN O.	HEAD	W	M	Sep 1839?	40	M	22			KY	TN	VA		FARMER			X	X	✓	O		F F	125
		" MARY E.	WIFE	W	F	Jun 1839?	40	M	22	7	7	KY	TN	KY					✓	✓	✓				
		" OLLIE G.	SON	W	M	APR 1880	20	S				KY	KY	KY		FARM LABORER			✓	✓	✓				
(*See below)		" RENA T.	DAU	W	F	OCT 1881	18	S				KY	KY	KY		AT SCHOOL		4	✓	✓	✓				
		" → JIMMIE D.	SON	W	M	JAN 1889	11	S				KY	KY	KY		AT SCHOOL		5	✓	✓	✓				
		" WILLIE J.	SON	W	M	JUN 1891	8	S				KY	KY	KY		AT SCHOOL		5	✓	✓					
		" EDDIE A.	DAU	W	F	OCT 1894	5	S				KY	KY	KY											
42	142	HAMILTON, ROBERT W.	HEAD	W	M	APR 1828	72	WD				TN	TN	TN		FARMER			X	X	✓	O		F F	126
43	143	SMITH, ANDREW	HEAD	W	M	Nov 1846	53	M	32			TN	TN	TN		FARMER			✓	✓	✓	O		F F	127
		" MARY J.	WIFE	W	F	AUG 1844	55	M	32	8	6	TN	TN	TN					✓	✓	✓				
		" ALLEN G.	SON	W	M	MAY 1887	13	S				KY	TN	IN		AT SCHOOL		5	✓	✓	✓				
		" JOHN H.	SON	W	M	MAR 1891	9	S				KY	TN	TN		AT SCHOOL		5	✓	✓	✓				
144	144	HAMILTON, JAMES T.	HEAD	W	M	AUG 1863	36	M	12			KY	KY	KY		FARMER			✓	X	✓	R		F	128
		" EVA	WIFE	W	F	DEC 1871	28	M	12	5	5	KY	KY	KY					✓	✓	✓				
		" JULIA	DAU	W	F	Feb 1882	18	S				KY	KY	KY		AT SCHOOL		4	✓	✓	✓				
		" TANNER	DAU	W	F	MAY 1889	11	S				KY	KY	KY		AT SCHOOL		3	✓	✓	✓				
		" LAURA E.	DAU	W	F	JAN 1891	9	S				KY	KY	KY		AT SCHOOL		4	✓	✓	✓				
*		BACON, JENNIE	DAU	W	F	OCT 1884	15	S				KY	KY	KY		AT SCHOOL		5	✓	✓	✓				

STATE - KENTUCKY
COUNTY - MONROE
Township or other division UNION

– 432 –

Enumerator PERRY W. MILLER

Supervisor's Dist. No. 102 Sheet No.
Enumeration Dist. No. 86

No. of Family	No. of Dwelling	NAME	Relation	Color	Sex	Date of Birth Mon/Yr	Age at last birthday	Marital Status	# Years married	Mother of how many children?	# of these children living	Place of birth (this person)	Father of this person	Mother of this person	Year of immigr.	# years in U.S.	Naturalization	Occupation 10 years +	Months not employed	Attended school in months	Can read	Can write	Speak English	Owned or Rent	Owned -no mortage	Farm or house	# of farm schedule
		HAMILTON, ETHEL	DAU	W	F	AUG 1893	6	S				KY	KY	KY				AT SCHOOL		3	✓	✓					
		" BOB	SON	W	M	Feb 1896	4	S				KY	KY	KY													
		" MAT	SON	W	M	OCT 1899	7/10	S				KY	KY	KY													
145	145	LAYNE, JOE C.	HEAD	W	M	MAR 1840	60	M	19			KY	KY	KY				FARMER			✓	✓	✓	O	F	F	129
		" SARAH –?	WIFE	W	F	JAN 1857	43	M	19	9	9	KY	KY	KY							✓	✓	✓				
		" ETTIE S.	DAU	W	F	May 1883	17	S				KY	KY	KY				AT SCHOOL		5	✓	✓	✓				
		" PHOEBA F.	DAU	W	F	Sep 1884	15	S				KY	KY	KY				AT SCHOOL		5	✓	✓	✓				
		" ALICE	DAU	W	F	Nov 1885	14	S				KY	KY	KY				AT SCHOOL		5	✓	✓	✓				
		" OSCAR T.	SON	W	M	May 1887	13	S				KY	KY	KY				AT SCHOOL		5	✓	✓	✓				
		" LIZZIE H.	DAU	W	F	JAN 1889	11	S				KY	KY	KY				AT SCHOOL		5	✓	✓	✓				
		" VEDA B.	DAU	W	F	Sep 1890	9	S				KY	KY	KY				AT SCHOOL		5	✓	✓	✓				
		" PEARLIE M.	DAU	W	F	JAN 1893	7	S				KY	KY	KY				AT SCHOOL		5							
		" LOU V.	DAU	W	F	JUN 1895	4	S				KY	KY	KY													
146	146	HEADRICK, HENRY A.	HEAD	W	M	JAN 1838	62	M	39			TN	TN	TN				FARMER			✓	✓	✓	O	F	F	130
		" SARAH B.	WIFE	W	F	OCT 1842	57	M	39	6	4	KY	KY	KY							✓	✓	✓				
		" BULA D.	DAU	W	F	JUN 1882	17	S				KY	KY	KY						4							
		BRAY, LULA M.	DAU	W	F	MAY 1880	20	WD				KY	KY	KY							✓	✓	✓				
147	147	BARTLEY, HIRAM H.	Head	W	M	Jul 1863	36	M	15			KY	KY	KY				FARMER			✓	✓	✓	O	F	F	131
		" EVA E.	Wife	W	F	Jul 1869	30	M	15	3	3	KY	KY	KY							✓	✓	✓				
		" BERTHA	DAU	W	F	AUG 1890	9	S				KY	KY	KY				AT SCHOOL		5	✓	✓	✓				
		" FLOYD	SON	W	M	JAN 1893	7	S				KY	KY	KY				AT SCHOOL		4							
		THOMAS C.	SON	W	M	Sep 1896	3	S				KY	KY	KY													
148	148	FISH, ROBERT M.	Head	W	M	APR 1875	25	S				KY	KY	KY				DAY LABORER	5		X	X	✓	R		H	
149	149	BRAY, HENRY T.	Head	W	M	Feb 1862	38	M	8			KY	KY	KY				FARMER			✓	✓	✓	R		F	132
		" ABIGIL	Wife	W	F	DEC 1854	45	M	8	1	1	KY	KY	KY							✓	✓	✓				
		" BEATHA A.	DAU	W	F	APR 1888	12	S				KY	KY	KY				AT SCHOOL		5	✓	✓	✓				

STATE - KENTUCKY
COUNTY - MONROE
Township or other division UNION
Enumerator PERRY W. MILLER

No. of Family	No. of Dwelling	NAME	Relation	Color	Sex	DATE OF BIRTH Mon/Yr	Age at last birthday	Marital Status	# Years married	Mother of how many children?	# of these children living	Place of birth [this person]	Father of this person	Mother of this person	Year of immigr.	# years in U.S.	Naturalization	OCCUPATION 10 years +	Months not employed	Attended school in month	Can read	Can write	Speak English	Owned or Rent	Owned - no mortgage	Farm or house	# of farm schedule
		BRAY, RALPH	Son	W	M	Dec 1893	6	S				KY	KY	KY													
150	150	HAYS, AMLET G.	Head	W	M	Mar 1872	28	M	6			KY	KY	KY				FARMER			✓	✓	✓	R		F	133
		" EMMA A.	Wife	W	F	Oct 1875	24	M	6	2	2	KY	TN	KY							✓	✓	✓				
		" KATHLEEN	Dau	W	F	Dec 1894	5	S				KY	KY	KY													
		" JAMES W.	Son	W	M	Sep 1898	1	S				KY	KY	KY													
151	151	HAYS, JAMES A.	Head	W	M	Oct 1836	63	M	45			KY	TN	TN				FARMER			✓	✓	✓	O		F	F 134
		" JULIA A.	Wife	W	F	Dec 1838	61	M	45	11	8	KY	KY	KY							✓	✓	✓				
		" SMITH H.	Son	W	M	Oct 1877	22	S				KY	KY	KY				FARMER			✓	✓	✓				
		FISH, MARY A.	Boarder	W	F	Feb 1881	19	S				KY	KY	KY							✓	✓	✓				
152	152	MITCHELL, WILLIAM T.	Head	W	M	Oct 1861	38	M	19			KY	KY	KY				FARM LABORER			✓	✓	✓	R		H	
		" LAURA L.	Wife	W	F	Dec 1861	38	M	19	8	6	KY	KY	KY							✓	✓	✓				
		" MATTIE M.	Dau	W	F	Aug 1883	16	S				KY	KY	KY				AT SCHOOL		4	✓	✓	✓				
		" NELLIE M.	Dau	W	F	Sep 1885	14	S				KANSAS	KY	KY				AT SCHOOL		4	✓	✓	✓				
		" ANNIE M.	Dau	W	F	May 1887	13	S				KANSAS	KY	KY				AT SCHOOL		4	✓	✓	✓				
		" RAY	Son	W	M	Jul 1890	9	S				IND	KY	KY				AT SCHOOL		5							
		" MARY E.	Dau	W	F	Mar 1893	7	S				IND	KY	KY				AT SCHOOL		4							
153	153	COMER, JOSEPH	Head	W	M	Aug 1872	27	M	1			KY	TN	KY				DEALER IN MDSE			✓	✓		O		F H	
		" MAUDE R.	Wife	W	F	Jan 1876	24	M	1			KY	KY	KY							✓	✓	✓				
		" LIDIE	Dau	W	F	Nov 1899	6/12	S				KY	KY	KY													
154	154	KINGERY, PETER	Head	W	M	Aug 1846	53	M	25			KY	KY	KY				FARMER			✓	✓	✓	O		F	F 135
		" LOUVI A. J.	Wife	W	F	Jun 1859	40	M	25	8	8	KY	KY	KY							✓	✓	✓				
		" MARTHA R.	Dau	W	F	Jun 1880	19	S				KY	KY	KY							✓	✓	✓				
		" MARGET H.	Dau	W	F	May 1882	18	S				KY	KY	KY							✓	✓	✓				
		" FELIX O.	Son	W	M	Mar 1884	16	S				KY	KY	KY				AT SCHOOL		5	✓	✓	✓				
		" BETTIE	Dau	W	F	Apr 1886	14	S				KY	KY	KY				AT SCHOOL		5	✓	✓	✓				
		" FREDRICK	Son	W	M	Jul 1889	10	S				KY	KY	KY				AT SCHOOL		5	✓	✓	✓				

STATE - KENTUCKY
COUNTY - MONROE
Township or other division **UNION**   Enumerator **PERRY W. MILLER**

Supervisor's Dist. No. **102** Sheet No.
Enumeration Dist. No. **86**

No. of Family	No. of Dwelling	NAME	Relation	Color	Sex	DATE OF BIRTH Mon/Yr	Age at last birthday	Marital Status	# Years married	Mother of how many children?	# of these children living	Place of birth (this person)	Father of this person	Mother of this person	Year of immigr.	# years in U.S.	Naturalization	OCCUPATION 10 years +	Months not employed	Attended school in months	Can read	Can write	Speak English	Owned or Rent	Owned -no mortage	Farm or house	# of farm schedule
		KINGERY, CLARENCE	Son	W	M	Mar 1894	6	S				KY	KY	KY													
		" VIRGIL C.	Son	W	M	Jun 1896	3	S				KY	KY	KY													
155	155	HOPE, JAMES M.	Head	W	M	Dec 1860	39	M	18			KY	TN	KY				FARMER			✓	✓	✓	O	F	F	136
		" MARTHA P.	Wife	W	F	Aug 1863	36	M	18	5	5	KY	KY	KY							✓	✓	✓				
		" MYRTIE M.	Dau	W	F	Apr 1884	16	S				KY	KY	KY				AT SCHOOL		3	✓	✓	✓				
		" EISAPHENIA B.	Dau	W	F	Feb 1891	9	S				KY	KY	KY				AT SCHOOL		4	✓	✓					
		" MASON A.	Son	W	M	Jul 1893	6	S				KY	KY	KY				AT SCHOOL		4							
		" JAMES H.	Son	W	M	Oct 1895	4	S				KY	KY	KY													
		" ELSA L.	Dau	W	F	Sep 1897	2	S				KY	KY	KY													
156	156	KINGERY, ELIJAH H.	Head	W	M	Jul 1850	49	M	31			KY	KY	KY				BLACKSMITH			✓	✓	✓	O	F	F	137
		" SARAH E.	Wife	W	F	Feb 1856	44	M	31	13	12	KY	KY	KY							✓	✓	✓				
		" ALONZO	Son	W	M	Oct 1878	21	S				KY	KY	KY				FARM LABORER 2			✓	✓					
		" TOM B.	Son	W	M	Aug 1881	18	S				KY	KY	KY				FARM LABORER 3			✓	✓	✓				
		" NELIA A.	Dau	W	F	Feb 1880	20	S				KY	KY	KY				AT SCHOOL		4	✓	✓	✓				
		" QUINTILLA	Dau	W	F	Apr 1884	16	S				KY	KY	KY				AT SCHOOL		5	✓	✓	✓				
		" FLOID	Son	W	M	May 1890	10	S				KY	KY	KY				AT SCHOOL		5	✓	✓	✓				
		" LENA	Dau	W	F	May 1894	6	S				KY	KY	KY													
		" SARAH L.	Dau	W	F	Mar 1896	4	S				KY	KY	KY													
157	157	CARDER, GEO. F.	Head	W	M	Mar 1878	22	M	3			KY	KY	KY				FARMER			✓	✓	✓	R	F	138	
		" MARY B.	Wife	W	F	Apr 1878	22	M	3	1	1	KY	KY	KY							✓	✓					
		" ADA B.	Dau	W	F	Oct 1899	7/12	S				KY	KY	KY													
158	158	HOPE, THOMAS M.	Head	W	M	Feb 1870	30	M	8			KY	TN	KY				FARMER			✓	✓	✓	O	F	F	139
		" ALICE	Wife	W	F	Jul 1873	26	M	8	4	4	KY	TN	VA							✓	✓					
		" ZELPHIA J.	Dau	W	F	Jul 1892	7	S				KY	KY	KY				AT SCHOOL		5							
		" ISAAC H.	Son	W	M	Nov 1894	5	S				KY	KY	KY													
		" LINDSAY F.	Son	W	M	Mar 1897	3	S				KY	KY	KY													

STATE - KENTUCKY
COUNTY - MONROE
Township or other division UNION Enumerator PERRY W. MILLER

Supervisor's Dist. No. *102* Sheet No.
Enumeration Dist. No. *86*

No. of Family	No. of Dwelling	NAME	Relation	Color	Sex	Date of Birth Mon/Yr	Age at last birthday	Marital Status	# Years married	Mother of how many children	# of these children living	Place of birth [this person]	Father of this person	Mother of this person	Occupation	Can read	Can write	Speak English	Attended school (months)	Owned or Rent	Owned -no mortage	Farm or house	# of farm schedule
		HOPE, AMANDA E.	DAU	W	F	Sep 1899	8/12	S				KY	KY	KY									
159	159	HOPE, JOHN G.	HEAD	W	M	Nov 1831	68	M	45			TN	TN	KY	FARMER	✓	✓			O	F	F	140
"		AMANDA	WIFE	W	F	Dec 1837	62	M	45	12	8	KY	KY	TN		✓	✓	✓					
"		ISAAC D.	SON	W	M	Apr 1875	25	M	2			KY	TN	KY	FARMER	✓	✓	✓					
"		SARAH L.	D-IN-LAW	W	F	Mar 1876	24	M	2	1	1	KY	KY	KY		✓	✓						
"		EDWIN G.	GR-SON	W	M	Oct 1899	7/12	S				KY	KY	KY									
160	160	NANNIE, SAM	HEAD	W	M	Aug 1842	58	M	20			KY	KY	KY	FARMER	X	X	✓		O	F	F	141
"		ELIZABETH	WIFE	W	F	Sep 1855	44	M	20	1	1	TN	KY	KY		✓	✓	✓					
"		INGRAM A.T.	SON	W	M	Oct 1884	15	S				KY	KY	KY	AT SCHOOL	✓	✓	✓	4				
161	161	KINGERY, JAMES	HEAD	W	M	Dec 1875	24	M	6			KY	KY	KY	FARMER	✓	X	✓		R		F	142
"		IZZA	WIFE	W	F	Apr 1870	30	M	6	1	1	KY	KY	KY		✓	✓	✓					
"		MELVIN	SON	W	M	Mar 1895	5	S				KY	KY	KY									
162	162	KINGERY, WILLIAM	HEAD	W	M	Feb 1825	75	M	56			KY	VA	VA	FARMER	✓	✓	✓		O	F	F	143
"		REBECA	WIFE	W	F	Oct 1824	75	M	56	2	1	KY	TN	TN		X	X	✓					
"		POMP	GR-SON	W	M	Sep 1878	21	S				KY	KY	KY	FARM LABOAER	X	X	✓					
"		NELLA	GR-DAU	W	F	Nov 1883	16	S				KY	KY	KY	FARMER	X	X	✓		R		F	144
163	163	GRIMSLEY, JESSE S.	HEAD	W	M	Apr 1863	37	M	14			KY	KY	KY		✓	✓	✓					
"		MARY S.	WIFE	W	F	Sep 1868	31	M	14	6	6	KY	KY	KY		✓	✓	✓					
"		DONNIA E.	DAU	W	F	Apr 1888	12	S				KY	KY	KY	AT SCHOOL	✓	✓	✓	5				
"		HARRISON T.	SON	W	M	Aug 1889	10	S				KY	KY	KY	AT SCHOOL	✓	✓	✓	5				
"		BESSIE	DAU	W	F	Mar 1891	9	S				KY	KY	KY	AT SCHOOL				4				
"		JOHNIE M.	SON	W	M	Aug 1892	7	S				KY	KY	KY	AT SCHOOL				4				
"		MELVIN	SON	W	M	Aug 1893	6	S				KY	KY	KY									
"		MINNIE B.	DAU	W	F	Dec 1899	5/12	S				KY	KY	KY									
164	164	FISH, RENIA J.	HEAD	W	F	Apr 1857	43	M	11	11	11	KY	KY	KY		✓	X	✓		O	F	F	
		KINGERY, HATTIE	DAU	W	F	Oct 1886	13	S				KY	KY	KY		X	X	✓					

STATE - KENTUCKY
COUNTY - MONROE
Township or other division UNION
Enumerator PERRY W. MILLER

Supervisor's Dist. No. 102 Sheet No.
Enumeration Dist. No. 86

Location No. of Family	No. of Dwelling	NAME	Relation	Color	Sex	DATE OF BIRTH Mon/Yr	Age at last birthday	Marital Status	# Years married	Mother of how many children?	# of these children living	NATIVITY Place of birth (this person)	Father of this person	Mother of this person	CITIZENSHIP Year of immigr.	# years in U.S.	Naturalization	OCCUPATION 10 years +	Months not employed	EDUCATION Attended school in months	Can read	Can write	Speak English	OWNERSHIP Owned or Rent	Owned - no mortgage	Farm or house	# of farm schedule
		KINGERY, DORA	DAU	W	F	Oct 1886	13	S				KY	KY	KY						X	X	✓				
		" BUSTER	SON	W	M	Jun 1888	11	S				KY	KY	KY						X	X	✓				
		" LOUVISA J.	DAU	W	F	Feb 1890	10	S				KY	KY	KY												
		FISH, ANNIE B.	DAU	W	F	Mar 1895	5	S				KY	KY	KY												
165	165	KINGERY, WILLIAM E.	HEAD	W	M	Sep 1873	26	M	9			KY	KY	KY				FARMER			✓	✓	✓	R	F	145
		" SARAH	WIFE	W	F	Jul 1873	26	M	9	0	0	KY	KY	KY							✓	✓	✓			
		WEBB, VINA	Boarder	W	F	Apr 1846	54	S				KY	KY	KY							✓	✓	✓			
		" ELIZABETH	Boarder	W	F	Mar 1883	17	S				KY	KY	KY							✓	✓	✓			
166	166	DAVIS, SAMP	HEAD	W	M	Apr 1870	30	M	7			KY	KY	KY				FARMER			✓	✓	✓	R	F	146
		" FANNY	WIFE	W	F	Sep 1876	23	M	7	3	3	KY	KY	KY							✓	✓	✓			
		" WILLIAM F.	SON	W	M	May 1894	6	S				KY	KY	KY								✓	✓			
		" MARY	DAU	W	F	Feb 1896	4	S				KY	KY	KY												
		" LENA	DAU	W	F	Sep 1898	1	S				KY	KY	KY												
167	167	BACON, JESSE	HEAD	W	M	Apr 1850	50	M	25			KY	KY	KY				FARMER			X	X	✓	O	F	147
		" SARAH B.	WIFE	W	F	Mar 1854	46	M	25	6	5	KY	KY	KY							✓	✓	✓			
		" ISAAC D.	SON	W	M	Oct 1877	22	S				KY	KY	KY				FARM LABORER			✓	✓	✓			
		" JOHN M.	SON	W	M	Jul 1879	20	S				KY	KY	KY				FARM LABORER			✓	✓	✓			
		" RINIA M.	DAU	W	F	Feb 1889	11	S				KY	KY	KY				AT SCHOOL		5	✓	✓	✓			
		" LUCY S.	DAU	W	F	Jul 1891	8	S				KY	KY	KY				AT SCHOOL		5	✓	✓	✓			
168	168	WILBORN, JOHN R.	HEAD	W	M	Jul 1862	37	M	14			KY	KY	KY				FARMER			✓	✓	✓	O	F	148
		" BETTIE C.	WIFE	W	F	Jun 1864	35	M	14	2	2	KY	KY	KY							✓	✓	✓			
		" FLORA M.	DAU	W	F	Apr 1889	11	S				KY	KY	KY				AT SCHOOL		5	✓	✓	✓			
		" STELLA F.	DAU	W	F	Aug 1892	7	S				KY	KY	KY				AT SCHOOL		5	✓	✓	✓			
		" MALINDA	Mother	W	F	May 1824	76	WD				KY	KY	KY							✓	✓	✓			
169	169	HAYS, JOE M.	HEAD	W	M	Oct 1874	25	M	5			KY	KY	KY				FARMER			✓	✓	✓	R	F	149
		" BROCKIE	WIFE	W	F	Mar 1879	21	M	5	3	1	KY	KY	KY							✓	✓	✓			

STATE - KENTUCKY
COUNTY - MONROE
Township or other division: UNION
Enumerator: PERRY W. MILLER

Supervisor's Dist. No. 102 Sheet No.
Enumeration Dist. No. 86

No. of Family	No. of Dwelling	NAME	Relation	Color	Sex	DATE OF BIRTH Mon/Yr	Age at last birthday	Marital Status	# Years married	Mother of how many children?	# of these children living	Place of birth [this person]	Father of this person	Mother of this person	Year of immigr.	# years in U.S.	Naturalization	OCCUPATION 10 years +	Months not employed	Attended school in months	Can read	Can write	Speak English	Owned or Rent	Owned - no mortgage	Farm or house	# of farm schedule
		HAYS, IDA M.	DAU	W	F	OCT 1898	1	S				KY	KY	KY													
170	170	GEARLDS, ASBERRY W.	HEAD	W	M	APR 1865	35	M	12			KY	KY	KY				FARMER			✓	✓	✓	O	F	F	150
		" BRITTIE M.	WIFE	W	F	DEC 1866	33	M	12	3	3	KY	KY	KY													
		" ORA G.	SON	W	M	AUG 1891	8	S				KY	KY	KY				AT SCHOOL		5							
		" OCIE	DAU	W	F	JUL 1892	7	S				KY	KY	KY				AT SCHOOL		5							
		" ROSNY J.	SON	W	M	MAR 1894	6	S				KY	KY	KY													
		ARTERBURN, MARY L.	AUNT	W	F	FEB 1833	67	WD				TN	TN	TN							X	X	✓				
		WALKER, ZABRA A.	AUNT	W	F	SEP 1823	76	WD				TN	TN	TN							X	X	✓				
171	171	FISH, WILLIAM H.	HEAD	W	M	JUL 1874	26	M	6			KY	KY	KY				FARMER			✓	✓	✓	R		F	151
		" MARGET	WIFE	W	F	OCT 1878	21	M	6	2	2	KY	KY	KY							✓	✓	✓				
		" BIRTTIE M.	DAU	W	F	MAR 1896	4	S				KY	KY	KY													
		" HASCHALL	SON	W	M	JUN 1898	1	S				KY	KY	KY													
172	172	GENTRY, WOLFORD	HEAD	B	M	MAR 1865	35	M	16			KY	KY	KY				FARMER			✓	✓	✓	O	F	F	152
		" BELLE	WIFE	B	F	MAR 1863	37	M	14	1	1	KY	KY	KY							X	X	✓				
		" WARNNIE	DAU	B	F	APR 1893	7	S				KY	KY	KY													
		PAYNE, JANE	SIS-IN-LAW	B	F	MAR 1861	39	S				KY	KY	KY							X	X	✓				
173	173	CARTER, HIRAM K.	HEAD	W	M	APR 1832	68	WD				KY	VA	SC				FARMER			X	X	✓	O	F	F	153
		" TABITHA E.	DAU	W	F	JUL 1869	30	WD				KY	KY	KY							✓	X	✓				
		" LOU B.	GR-DAU	W	F	FEB 1888	12	S				KY	KY	KY				AT SCHOOL		5	✓	✓					
		" HERBERT	GR-SON	W	M	JUN 1891	8	S				KY	KY	KY				AT SCHOOL		5							
		" MARGIA	GR-DAU	W	F	JUN 1894	5	S				KY	KY	KY				AT SCHOOL		5							
174	174	BARTLEY, MARY	HEAD	W	F	NOV 1831	68	WD		9	5	VA	VA	VA							X	X	✓				
		" GEO. W.	SON	W	M	AUG 1868	31	M	12			KY	KY	KY				FARMER			✓	✓	✓	O	F	F	154
		" IBBIE	DAU-IN-LAW	W	F	MAR 1872	28	M	12	5	5	KY	KY	KY				AT SCHOOL		5	✓	✓	✓				
		" ELZA H.	GR-SON	W	M	APR 1889	11	S				KY	KY	KY				AT SCHOOL		4	✓	✓	✓				
		" BIRTIE A.	GR-ANN (?)	W	F	SEP 1890	9	S				KY	KY	KY				AT SCHOOL		4							

STATE - KENTUCKY
COUNTY - MONROE
Township or other division **UNION**
Enumerator **PERRY W. MILLER**
Supervisor's Dist. No. **102** Sheet No.
Enumeration Dist. No. **86**

No. of Family	No. of Dwelling	NAME	Relation	Color	Sex	Date of Birth Mon/Yr	Age at last birthday	Marital Status	# Years married	Mother of how many children?	# of these children living	Place of birth (this person)	Father of this person	Mother of this person	Year of immigr.	# years in U.S.	Naturalization	Occupation 10 years +	Months not employed	Attended school in months	Can read	Can write	Speak English	Owned or Rent	Owned - no mortage	Farm or house	# of farm schedule
		BARTLEY, SAMMIE V.	GR-DAU	W	F	Dec 1892	7	S				KY	KY	KY													
		" ELLA F.	GR-DAU	W	F	Jan 1896	4	S				KY	KY	KY													
		" NORAH E.	GR-DAU	W	F	Aug 1897	2	S				KY	KY	KY													
175	175	BIBY, WILLIAM C.	HEAD	W	M	May 1869	31	M	11			KY	KY	KY				FARMER			✓	✓	✓	O	F	F	155
		" ANN T.	WIFE	W	F	Aug 1873	26	M	11	6	6	KY	KY	KY							✓	✓	✓				
		" LUTHER H.	SON	W	M	Nov 1889	10	S				KY	KY	KY				AT SCHOOL		5	✓	✓	✓				
		" SARAH G.	DAU	W	F	Feb 1891	9	S				KY	KY	KY				AT SCHOOL		4							
		" OVIL T.	SON	W	M	Jan 1893	7	S				KY	KY	KY				AT SCHOOL		4							
		" OSCAR G.	SON	W	M	Aug 1895	4	S				KY	KY	KY													
		" JOHNIE P.	SON	W	M	Mar 1898	2	S				KY	KY	KY													
		" WILLIE D.	SON	W	M	Feb 1900	3/12	S				KY	KY	KY													
176	176	ROBINSON, JOHN	HEAD	W	M	May 1878	22	M	2			KY	KY	KY				FARMER			✓	✓	✓	R		F	156
		" MINNIE	WIFE	W	F	Feb 1877	23	M	2			KY	KY	KY							✓	✓	✓				
177	177	HOWARD, JESSE	HEAD	W	M	Mar 1852	48	M	30			KY	KY	KY				FARMER			✓	✓	✓	R		F	157
		" BETTIE	WIFE	W	F	Jan 1853	47	M	30	6	3	KY	KY	KY							✓	✓	✓				
		" ALONZO	SON	W	M	Jul 1880	19	S				KY	KY	KY				FARM LABORER			✓	✓	✓				
		" LILLIE M.	DAU	W	F	May 1889	11	S				KY	KY	KY				AT SCHOOL		5	✓	✓	✓				
178	178	HOWARD, MARY F.	HEAD	W	F	Jun 1852	47	WD				KY	KY	KY				FARMER			✓	✓		O	F	F	158
		" ANN L.	DAU	W	F	Apr 1881	19	S				KY	KY	KY				AT SCHOOL		5	✓	✓	✓				
		" JOE B.	SON	W	M	Dec 1886	13	S				KY	KY	KY				AT SCHOOL		3	✓	✓	✓				
		" BETHIE	DAU	W	F	Mar 1890	10	S				KY	KY	KY				AT SCHOOL		5	✓	✓	✓				
		" CARLISLE	SON	W	M	May 1893	7	S				KY	KY	KY							✓	✓					
179	179	KINGERY, GEO. W.	HEAD	W	M	May 1870	30	M	2			KY	KY	KY				FARMER			✓	✓	✓	R		F	159
		" MARY	WIFE	W	F	Apr 1880	20	M	2	2	2	KY	KY	KY							✓	✓	✓				
		" ETTA	DAU	W	F	Jan 1897	3	S				KY	KY	KY													
		" HERMAN	SON	W	M	Feb 1899	1	S				KY	KY	KY													

STATE - KENTUCKY
COUNTY - MONROE
Township or other division   UNION   Enumerator PERRY W. MILLER

Supervisor's Dist. No. _102_ Sheet No.
Enumeration Dist. No. _86_

No. of Family	No. of Dwelling	NAME	Relation	Color	Sex	DATE OF BIRTH Mon/Yr	Age at last birthday	Marital Status	# Years married	Mother of how many children?	# of these children living	Place of birth [this person]	Father of this person	Mother of this person	OCCUPATION 10 years +	Attended school in months	Can read	Can write	Speak English	Owned or Rent	Owned -no mortgage	Farm or house	# of farm schedule
180	180	HOWARD, BINE	HEAD	W	F	APR 1859	41	WD				KY	KY	KY	FARMER		✓	✓	✓	O	F	F	160
		" CLEMMY	SON	W	M	MAY 1882	18	S				KY	KY	KY	FARM LABORER		✓	✓					
		" THOMAS C.	SON	W	M	OCT 1884	15	S				KY	KY	KY	AT SCHOOL	5	✓	✓	✓				
		" ANNIE B.	DAU	W	F	NOV 1886	13	S				KY	KY	KY	AT SCHOOL	5	✓	✓	✓				
181	181	HIGH, JOE C.	HEAD	W	M	AUG 1874	25	M	4			KY	KY	KY	FARM LABORER		X	X	✓	R		H	
		" BETTIE J.	WIFE	W	F	DEC 1879	20	M	4	2	2	KY	KY	KY			✓	✓	✓				
		" CLYDE E.	SON	W	M	JUN 1898	1	S				KY	KY	KY									
		" CLEMMY	SON	W	M	MAR 1900	7/12	S				KY	KY	KY									
182	182	DUNCAN, SAM	HEAD	W	M	MAY 1863	37	M	9			IOWA	IND	IND	FARMER		✓	✓	✓	R		F	161
		" KITTIE E.	WIFE	W	F	FEB 1874	26	M	9	3	3	KY	KY	KY			✓	✓	✓				
		" HELLEN E.	DAU	W	F	JAN 1893	7	S				KY	KY	KY									
		" WILLIE H.	SON	W	M	JAN 1895	5	S				KY	KY	KY									
		" FREDIE E.	SON	W	M	APR 1897	3	S				KY	KY	KY									
183	183	BUSHONS, JOHN L.	HEAD	W	M	JAN 1866	34	M	6			KY	KY	KY	FARMER		✓	✓	✓	O	F	F	162
		" VICTORIA	WIFE	W	F	OCT 1873	27	M	6			KY	KY	KY			✓	✓	✓				
		" NANCY T.	MOTHER	W	F	MAR 1824	76	WD				KY	KY	KY			X	X	✓				
184	184	WHITE, WILLIAM F.	HEAD	W	M	FEB 1868	32	M	7			KY	KY	KY	FARMER		✓	✓	✓	O	F	F	163
		" ELIZA J.	WIFE	W	F	SEP 1876	24	M	7	4	2	KY	KY	KY			✓	✓	✓				
		" LINARD	DAU	W	F	OCT 1895	4	S				KY	KY	KY									
		" ACIE	DAU	W	F	NOV 1898	1	S				KY	KY	KY									
185	185	GENTRY, TURNER G.	HEAD	W	M	MAY 1850	50	M	23			KY	KY	KY	FARMER		✓	✓	✓	O	F	F	164
		" LOU	WIFE	W	F	APR 1854	46	M	23	2	2	KY	KY	KY			✓	✓	✓				
		" ARKIE G.	SON	W	M	JAN 1889	11	S				KY	KY	KY	AT SCHOOL	5	✓	✓	✓				
186	186	WHITE, HARMON H.	HEAD	W	M	OCT 1864	35	M	15			KY	KY	KY	FARMER		✓	✓	✓	O	F	F	165
		" SUSAN M.	WIFE	W	F	APR 1864	36	M	15	6	6	KY	KY	KY			✓	✓	✓				
		" ESTER	SON	W	M	JUN 1886	13	S				KY	KY	KY	AT SCHOOL	5	✓	✓	✓				

STATE - KENTUCKY
COUNTY - MONROE
Township or other division UNION
Enumerator PERRY W. MILLER

Supervisor's Dist. No. 102 Sheet No.
Enumeration Dist. No. 86

No. of Family	No. of Dwelling	NAME	Relation	Color	Sex	DATE OF BIRTH Mon/Yr	Age at last birthday	Marital Status	# Years married	Mother of how many children?	# of these children living	NATIVITY Place of birth (this person)	Father of this person	Mother of this person	CITIZENSHIP Year of immigr.	# years in U.S.	Naturalization	OCCUPATION 10 years +	Months not employed	EDUCATION Attended school in months	Can read	Can write	Speak English	OWNERSHIP Owned or Rent	Owned -no mortage	Farm or house	# of farm schedule
		WHITE, ETHEL	DAU	W	F	Jan 1888	12	S				KY	KY	KY				AT SCHOOL		5	✓	✓	✓				
		" ELVIE G.	DAU	W	F	Dec 1889	10	S				KY	KY	KY				AT SCHOOL		5	✓	✓	✓				
		" LANIE S.	DAU	W	F	Dec 1891	8	S				KY	KY	KY													
		" JANIE	DAU	W	F	Mar 1898	2	S				KY	KY	KY													
		" MAGGIE M.	DAU	W	F	Feb 1900	3/12	S				KY	KY	KY													
187	187	CLEMMONS, MARION F.	HEAD	W	M	Feb 1841	59	M	34			KY	KY	KY				FARMER			✓	✓	✓	O	F	F	166
		" MARGET E.	WIFE	W	F	Jul 1846	53	M	34	8	8	KY	KY	KY							✓	✓	✓				
		" SARAH	DAU	W	F	Oct 1867	32	S				KY	KY	KY							✓	✓	✓				
		" MAUDE	DAU	W	F	Sep 1875	24	S				KY	KY	KY							✓	✓	✓				
		" ROXIE	DAU	W	F	Feb 1878	22	S				KY	KY	KY							✓	✓	✓				
		" PERRY A.	SON	W	M	Aug 1880	19	S				KY	KY	KY							✓	✓	✓				
		" LUCY S.	DAU	W	F	Jun 1883	16	S				KY	KY	KY				AT SCHOOL		5	✓	✓	✓				
		" JOHN F.	SON	W	M	Aug 1886	13	S				KY	KY	KY				AT SCHOOL		5	✓	✓	✓				
188	188	MILLER, LINDSAY N.	HEAD	W	M	May 1876	24	M				KY	KY	KY				FARMER			✓	✓	✓	O	F	F	167
		" ETHEL	WIFE	W	F	Dec 1881	18	M				KY	KY	KY				FARMER			✓	✓	✓				
189	189	MILLER, RUBEN F.	HEAD	W	M	Sep 1873	26	M	4			KY	KY	KY				FARMER			✓	✓	✓	O	F	F	168
		" ANNIE B.	WIFE	W	F	May 1876	24	M	4	2	2	KY	KY	KY							✓	✓					
		" WILLIAM A.	SON	W	M	Jul 1897	2	S				KY	KY	KY													
		" IBBIA T.	SISTER	W	F	Sep 1881	18	S				KY	KY	KY				AT SCHOOL		9	✓	✓					
190	190	HAMILTON, JAMES H.	HEAD	W	M	Apr 1862	38	M	18			KY	KY	KY				FARMER			✓	✓	✓	O	F	F	169
		" MARY S.	WIFE	W	F	Mar 1869	31	M	18	8	6	KY	KY	KY							✓	✓					
		" EFFIE C.	DAU	W	F	Dec 1884	15	S				KY	KY	KY				AT SCHOOL		4	✓	✓	✓				
		" JOHN W.	SON	W	M	Mar 1887	13	S				KY	KY	KY				AT SCHOOL		4	✓	✓	✓				
		" IDA B.	DAU	W	F	Apr 1889	11	S				KY	KY	KY				AT SCHOOL		4	✓	✓	✓				
		" ELZAD M.	DAU	W	F	May 1891	9	S				KY	KY	KY				AT SCHOOL		4	✓	✓					
		" ADA T.	DAU	W	F	Oct 1894	5	S				KY	KY	KY													

STATE - KENTUCKY
COUNTY - MONROE
Township or other division: UNION
Enumerator: PERRY R. MILLER
Supervisor's Dist. No. 102 Sheet No.
Enumeration Dist. No. 86

No. of Family	No. of Dwelling	NAME	Relation	Color	Sex	Date of Birth Mon/Yr	Age at last birthday	Marital Status	# Years married	Mother of how many children?	# of these children living	Place of birth (this person)	Father of this person	Mother of this person	Year of immigr.	# years in U.S.	Naturalization	Occupation	Months not employed	Attended school in months	Can read	Can write	Speak English	Owned or Rent	Owned -no mortage	Farm or house	# of farm schedule
		HAMILTON, ISAAC J.	Son	W	M	Oct 1898	1	S				KY	KY	KY													
191	191	STEPENSON, SARAH C.	Head	W	F	Nov 1852	47	WD		1	1	KY	KY	KY							✓	✓	✓	R		H	
	"	GEORGE A.	Son	W	M	Aug 1890	9	S				KY	KY	KY				At School		5	✓	✓	✓				
192	192	WHITLOW, LEWIS V.	Head	W	M	May 1874	26	M	6			KY	KY	KY				Farmer			✓	✓	✓	R		F	170
	"	ELLA	Wife	W	F	Mar 1875	25	M	6	3	3	KY	KY	KY							✓	✓	✓				
	"	ERNIE	Dau	W	F	Jun 1895	4	S				KY	KY	KY													
	"	HUBERT	Son	W	M	Oct 1897	2	S				KY	KY	KY													
	"	ADDIE	Dau	W	F	Nov 1899	6/12	S				KY	KY	KY													
		HAMILTON, CATHERINE A.	M-in-Law	W	F	Jan 1835	65	WD		4	4	KY	KY	KY							X	X	✓				
193	193	McPHERSON, JAMES B.	Head	W	M	Nov 1863	36	M	11			KY	KY	KY				Farmer			✓	✓	✓	O		F	171
	"	BERCHA	Wife	W	F	Oct 1871	28	M	11	6	6	KY	KY	KY							✓	✓	✓				
	"	CECIL	Son	W	M	Oct 1889	10	S				KY	KY	KY				At School		5	✓	✓	✓				
	"	DONNIA	Dau	W	F	Oct 1891	8	S				KY	KY	KY													
	"	ACIE	Son	W	M	Mar 1895	5	S				KY	KY	KY													
	"	HOMER	Son	W	M	May 1897	3	S				KY	KY	KY													
	"	LEE	Son	W	M	Feb 1899	1	S				KY	KY	KY													
	"	NEIVER	Dau	W	F	Feb 1900	3/12	S				KY	KY	KY													
194	194	GENTRY, EDWARD B.	Head	W	M	Oct 1839	60	WD				KY	KY	KY				Farmer			✓	✓	✓	O		F	172
	"	AMBROSIA	Dau	W	F	Oct 1869	30	S				KY	KY	KY							✓	✓	✓				
	"	ODAS B.	Son	W	M	Oct 1880	19	S				KY	KY	KY				At School		9	✓	✓	✓				
	"	EDDIE O.	Son	W	M	Sep 1883	16	S				KY	KY	KY				At School		4	✓	✓	✓				
195	195	GENTRY, JOSEPH G.	Head	W	M	Jul 1871	28	M	2			KY	KY	KY				Farmer			✓	✓	✓	R		E	173
	"	BETTIE E.	Wife	W	F	Aug 1878	21	M	2	2	2	KY	KY	KY							✓	✓	✓				
		HARLEY H.	Son	W	M	Aug 1897	2	S				KY	KY	KY													
		HERMON	Son	W	M	Feb 1899	1	S				KY	KY	KY													
196	196	BOWLES, WILBORN F.	Head	W	M	Jan 1861	39	M	5			KY	KY	KY				Farmer			✓	✓	✓	O		F	174

STATE - KENTUCKY
COUNTY - MONROE
Township or other division UNION

Enumerator PERRY W. MILLER

Supervisor's Dist. No. _102_ Sheet No.
Enumeration Dist. No. _86_

No. of Family	No. of Dwelling	NAME	Relation	Color	Sex	Date of Birth Mon/Yr	Age at last birthday	Marital Status	# Years married	Mother of how many children	# of these children living	Place of birth (this person)	Father of this person	Mother of this person	Year of immigr.	# years in U.S.	Naturalization	OCCUPATION 10 years +	Months not employed	Attended school in month	Can read	Can write	Speak English	Owned or Rent	Owned -no mortgage	Farm or house	# of farm schedule
		BOWLES, L. JENNIE	WIFE	W	F	Jan 1881	19	M	5	2	2	KY	KY	KY							✓	✓	✓				
		" MERIDA V.	SON	W	M	Jul 1895	4	S				KY	KY	KY													
		" WILLIAM H.	SON	W	M	Apr 1900	1/12	S				KY	KY	KY													
		" BIRTIE	DAU	W	F	Oct 1884	15	S				KY	KY	KY				AT SCHOOL		4	✓	✓	✓				
197	197	MOSIER, JOHN H.	HEAD	W	M	Dec 1869	30	M	10			KY	KY	KY				FARMER			X	X	✓	O	F	F	175
		" BETTIE H.	WIFE	W	F	Jul 1866	33	M	10	4	4	KY	KY	KY							✓	✓	✓				
		" ETHER	DAU	W	F	Mar 1891	9	S				KY	KY	KY				AT SCHOOL		9	✓	✓	✓				
		" BENTON	SON	W	M	Mar 1893	7	S				KY	KY	KY				AT SCHOOL		9							
		" CECIL	SON	W	M	Aug 1896	3	S				KY	KY	KY													
		" LELA	DAU	W	F	Apr 1899	1	S				KY	KY	KY													
198	198	WADE, CHARLES G.	HEAD	W	M	Apr 1859	41	M	2			KY	KY	KY				FARMER			✓	✓	✓	O	F	F	176
		" HENRIETTA	WIFE	W	F	Mar 1875	25	M	2	0	0	KY	KY	KY							✓	✓	✓				
		" JABEZ	SON	W	M	Mar 1885	15	S				KY	KY	KY				AT SCHOOL		4	✓	✓	✓				
199	199	JOBE, CHASE	HEAD	W	M	Oct 1839	60	M	17			TN	TN	TN				FARMER			✓	✓	✓	O	F	F	177
		" ELIZABETH	WIFE	W	F	Jul 1846	53	M	17	1	1	TN	TN	TN							X	X	✓				
		" JOHN B.C.	SON	W	M	Apr 1884	16	S				KY	TN	TN				AT SCHOOL		5	✓	✓					
200	200	HODGES, GEO. W.	HEAD	W	M	Oct 1871	28	M				KY	TN	TN				FARMER			✓	✓	✓	O	F	F	178
		" RINDA	WIFE	W	F	Apr 1878	22	M				KY	KY	KY							✓	✓	✓				
		" HARRET	SISTER	W	F	Dec 1854	45	S				KY	TN	TN							✓	✓	✓				
201	201	HAMILTON, LIZZY J.	HEAD	W	F	Nov 1822	77	WD		8	6	KY	KY	KY							✓	X	✓	O	F	F	179
		" GEO. W	SON	W	M	Aug 1866	33	S				KY	KY	KY				FARMER			✓	✓	✓				
202	202	BRYANT, WILLIAM A.	HEAD	W	M	Jul 1833	66	M	7			KY	VA	KY				FARMER			✓	✓	✓	O	F	F	180
		" RETTA	WIFE	W	F	Jan 1862	38	M	7	2	2	KY	KY	TN							✓	✓	✓				
		" VIRGIA	DAU	W	F	Feb 1896	4	S				KY	KY	KY													
		" HARLEY C.	SON	W	M	Oct 1899	1/12	S				KY	KY	KY													
203	203	ARTERBURN, WILLIAM	HEAD	W	M	Jul 1865	34	M	14			KY	KY	KY				FARMER			✓	✓	✓	O	F	F	181

STATE - KENTUCKY
COUNTY - MONROE
Township or other division: UNION
Enumerator: PERRY W. MILLER

Supervisor's Dist. No. _102_ Sheet No.
Enumeration Dist. No. _86_

No. of Family	No. of Dwelling	NAME	Relation	Color	Sex	Date of Birth Mon/Yr	Age at last birthday	Marital Status	# Years married	Mother of how many children?	# of these children living	Place of birth (this person)	Father of this person	Mother of this person	Occupation 10 years +	Attended school in months	Can read	Can write	Speak English	Owned or Rent	Owned –no mortage	Farm or house	# of Farm schedule
		ARTERBURN, ELLEN	Wife	W	F	Apr·1869	31	M	14	2	2	KY	KY	KY			✓	✓	✓				
		" ARTHUR	Son	W	M	Feb·1887	13	S				KY	KY	KY	At School	4	✓	✓	✓				
		" TOMMIE	Son	W	M	Feb·1890	10	S				KY	KY	KY	At School	4	✓	✓	✓				
		CARDER, FILMORE	Servant	W	M	Jan·1880	20	S				KY	KY	KY	Farm Laborer	3	X	X	✓				
		HAMILTON, DOVIE	Servant	W	F	May·1882	18	S				KY	KY	KY			✓	✓	✓				
204	204	BRYANT, SANFORD R.	Head	W	M	Jan·1841	59	M	0			KY	VA	KY	Farmer		✓	✓	✓	O	F	F	182
		" MANURVA	Wife	W	F	Sep·1858	41	M	0	1	1	KY	KY	TN			✓	✓	✓				
		TUDOR, RONNIE C.	S.Son	W	M	Dec·1882	17	S				KY	KY	KY	At School	5	✓	✓	✓				
205	205	BYBEE, SARAH E.	Head	W	F	Oct·1844	55	WD		4	4	KY	TN	KY			✓	✓	✓	O	F	F	
		WEBB, LENA	Servant	W	F	Jun·1884	16	S				KY	KY	KY			✓	✓	✓				
		BYBEE, PEARLIE	Gr-Son	W	M	Aug·1894	5	S				KY	KY	KY									
206	206	BYBEE, LONNIE G.	Head	W	M	Oct·1873	26	M	5			KY	KY	KY	Farmer		✓	✓	✓	R		F	183
		" MINNIE	Wife	W	F	Mar·1879	21	M	5	2	2	KY	KY	KY			✓	✓	✓				
		" ADA M.	Dau	W	F	May·1898	2	S				KY	KY	KY									
		" RAMY P.	Son	W	M	Aug·1899	9/12	S				KY	KY	KY	Farmer		X	X	✓	R		F	184
207	207	BIRGE, JOHN	Head	W	M	Apr·1880	20	M	3			KY	KY	KY	Farmer		X	X	✓	R		F	184
		" BELLE	Wife	W	F	Feb·1882	18	M	3	1	1	KY	KY	KY			✓	✓	✓				
		" MINNIE M.	Dau	W	F	Feb·1900	3/12	S				KY	KY	KY									
208	208	TERRY, ELIJAH	Head	W	M	Apr·1850	50	M	25			TN	TN	TN	Farmer		X	X	✓	O	F	F	185
		" CANZADA	Wife	W	F	Jan·1851	49	M	25	0	0	KY	KY	KY			X	X	✓				
209	209	VANCE, JAMES E.D.	Head	W	M	Oct·1857	42	M	13			KY	KY	KY	Farmer		X	X	✓	O	F	F	186
		" NANCY E.	Wife	W	F	Feb·1868	32	M	13	0	0	KY	KY	KY			✓	✓	✓				
		MILLER, OLIE	Boarder	W	M	Dec·1893	6	S				KY	KY	KY									
210	210	JACKSON, LEW	Head	W	M	Mar·1863	37	M	1			KY	KY	KY	Farmer		X	X	✓	R		F	187
		" BECA	Wife	W	F	Apr·1860	40	M	1			KY	KY	KY			X	X	✓				
		CRABTREE, WALTER	Boarder	W	M	Sep·1876	23	S				KY	KY	KY	Farmer					O	F	F	188

—444—

STATE - KENTUCKY
COUNTY - MONROE
Township or other division **UNION**

Enumerator **PERRY W. MILLER**

Supervisor's Dist. No. **102** Sheet No.
Enumeration Dist. No. **86**

No. of Family	No. of Dwelling	NAME	Relation	Color	Sex	Date of Birth Mon/Yr	Age at last birthday	Marital Status	# Years married	Mother of how many children?	# of these children living	Place of birth this person	Father of this person	Mother of this person	Year of immigr.	# years in U.S.	Naturalization	Occupation 10 years +	Months not employed	Attended school in months	Can read	Can write	Speak English	Owned or Rent	Owned - no mortage	Farm or house	# of farm schedule
211	211	CRABTREE, JAMES	Head	W	M	Apr·1840	60	M	43			KY	KY	KY				FARMER			✓	✓	✓	O	F	F	188
		" AMANDA	Wife	W	F	May·1842	58	M	43	11	10	KY	KY	KY							X	X	✓				
		" CHARLES	Son	W	M	Sep·1881	18	S				KY	KY	KY				AT SCHOOL		4	✓	✓	✓				
212	212	BUTTON, WILLIAM S.	Head	W	M	Jan·1838	62	WD				KY	KY	KY				FARMER			✓	✓	✓	O	F	F	189
		OBANION, WILLIAM E.	Son-n-law	W	M	Apr·1855	45	M	7			KY	KY	KY				FARMER			✓	✓	✓				
		" ELLA G.	Dau	W	F	Jun·1868	31	M	7	2	2	KY	KY	KY							✓	✓	✓				
		" MONA(?) G.	Gr-Dau	W	F	Mar·1895	5	S				KY	KY	KY													
		" LENACE M.	Gr-Dau	W	F	May·1896	4	S				KY	KY	KY													
213	213	ROBINSON, JAMES S.	Head	W	M	Apr·1845	55	M	4			KY	KY	KY				FARMER			✓	✓	✓	O	F	F	190
		" ABBIE	Wife	W	F	May·1858	42	M	4			KY	KY	KY							✓	✓	✓				
		" ARK G.	Son	W	M	Jun·—	18	S				KY	KY	KY				FARM LABORER 2			✓	✓	✓				
214	214	WHITE, JAMES H.	Head	W	M	Jul·1842	57	M	7			KY	KY	KY				FARMER			✓	✓	✓	O	F	F	191
		" ELIZEBETH J.	Wife	W	F	Apr·1847	53	M	7	3	2	KY	KY	KY							✓	✓	✓				
		" THOMAS F.	Son	W	M	Aug·1881	18	S				KY	KY	KY				FARM LABORER			✓	✓	✓				
		" ELIZEBETH J.	Dau	W	F	Oct·1885	14	S				KY	KY	KY				AT SCHOOL		4	✓	✓	✓				
		" BERLY W.	Gr-Son	W	M	Nov·1891	8	S				KY	KY	KY				AT SCHOOL		4	✓	✓	✓				
215	215	HAMILTON, JOHN L.	Head	W	M	Feb·1850	50	M	26			KY	KY	KY				FARMER	0		✓	✓	✓	O	F	F	192
		" SAMATHY P.	Wife	W	F	Dec·1855	44	M	26	5	4	KY	KY	KY							X	X	✓				
		" FANNY B.	Dau	W	F	Jun·1881	18	S				KY	KY	KY							✓	✓	✓				
		" ROLLIE C.	Son	W	M	Jul·1892	7	S				KY	KY	KY													
216	216	HAMILTON, OLLIE M.	Head	W	M	Oct·1877	22	M	0			KY	KY	KY				FARMER			✓	✓	✓	R		F	193
		" MELVINA	Wife	W	F	Mar·1881	19	M	0			KY	KY	KY							✓	✓	✓				
217	217	WHITE, CLAYTON G.	Head	W	M	Nov·1869	30	M	3			KY	KY	KY				FARMER			✓	✓	✓	O	F	F	194
		" BERTIE	Wife	W	F	May·1874	26	M	3	0	0	KY	KY	KY							✓	✓	✓				
		PAYNE, EDGAR	Servant	W	M	Apr·1885	15	S				KY	KY	KY				FARM LABORER			✓	✓	✓				
218	218	HODGES, BIRT	Head	W	M	Sep·1858	41	M	20			KY	KY	KY				FARMER			✓	✓	✓	R		F	195

STATE - KENTUCKY
COUNTY - MONROE
Township or other division — UNION
Enumerator — PERRY W. MILLER

Supervisor's Dist. No. 102   Sheet No. ___
Enumeration Dist. No. 86 ___

No. of Family	No. of Dwelling	NAME	Relation	Color	Sex	DATE OF BIRTH Mon/Yr	Age at last birthday	Marital Status	# Years married	Mother of how many children?	# of these children living	Place of birth (this person)	Father of this person	Mother of this person	Year of immigr.	# years in U.S.	Naturalization	OCCUPATION 10 years +	Months not employed	Attended school in months	Can read	Can write	Speak English	Owned or Rent	Owned - no mortage	Farm or house	# of farm schedule
		HODGES, CASSIA	WIFE	W	F	Mar·1860	40	M	20	4	4	KY	KY	KY							✓	✓	✓				
		" GROVER C.	SON	W	M	Sep·1883	16	S				KY	KY	KY				AT SCHOOL		4	✓	✓	✓				
		" CHANNIA	SON	W	M	Feb·1885	15	S				KY	KY	KY				AT SCHOOL		5	✓	✓	✓				
219	219	KINGERY, JOHN	HEAD	W	M	Mar·1868	32	M	10			KY	KY	KY				FARMER			X	X	✓	R		F	196
		" CHRIS E	WIFE	W	F	Apr·1867	33	M	10	3	3	KY	KY	KY													
		" MARY	DAU	W	F	Jan·1891	9	S				KY	KY	KY				AT SCHOOL		4							
		" FRANK	SON	W	M	May·1896	4	S				KY	KY	KY													
		" FRED	SON	W	M	May·1896	4	S				KY	KY	KY				FARMER			✓	✓	✓	O		F	197
220	220	WHITE, ASBERRY	HEAD	W	M	Dec·1827	72	M	34			KY	KY	KY													
		" PERMELIA S.	WIFE	W	F	Dec·1844	55	M	34	3	3	KY	KY	KY													
		" ERCY	Boarder	W	M	Feb·1886	14	S				KY	KY	KY				AT SCHOOL		4							
221	221	HAYS, HARMON (H? K?)	Head	W	M	Feb·1861	39	M	19			KY	KY	KY				FARMER			✓	✓	✓	O		F	198
		" LOU D.	WIFE	W	F	Jan·1862	38	M	19	7	6	KY	KY	KY							✓	✓	✓				
		" HAMPTON	SON	W	M	Mar·1882	18	S				KY	KY	KY				AT SCHOOL		4	✓	✓	✓				
		" JAMES W.	SON	W	M	Mar·1884	16	S				KY	KY	KY				AT SCHOOL		4	✓	✓	✓				
		" JULIA I.	DAU	W	F	Nov·1886	13	S				KY	KY	KY				AT SCHOOL		5	✓	✓	✓				
		" HOWARD	SON	W	M	Oct·1889	10	S				KY	KY	KY				AT SCHOOL		5	✓	✓	✓				
		" ANNIE	DAU	W	F	May·1892	8	S				KY	KY	KY				AT SCHOOL		9							
		" NED	SON	W	M	Nov·1896	3	S				KY	KY	KY							X	X	✓	O		F	199
222	222	ARTERBURN, WILLIAM D.	HEAD	W	M	Mar·1826	74	WD				TN	VA	TN													
		" ED	SON	W	M	Dec·1865	34	M	5			KY	TN	KY				FARMER			✓	✓	✓				
		" MARTHA	D-in-LAW	W	F	Feb·1876	24	M	5			KY	KY	KY							✓	✓	✓				
		" JOHN E.	GR-SON	W	M	Feb·1887	13	S				KY	KY	KY				AT SCHOOL		5	✓	✓	✓				
		" NETTIE M.	GR-DAU	W	F	Oct·1889	10	S				KY	KY	KY				AT SCHOOL		5	✓	✓	✓				
		STROUD, JOHNNIE M.	GR-SON	W	M	Sep·1889	10	S				KY	KY	KY				AT SCHOOL		5	✓	✓	✓				
		BACON, LOU T.	DAU	W	F	Jan·1856	44	M		2	2	KY	KY	KY							✓	✓	✓				

STATE - KENTUCKY
COUNTY - MONROE
Township or other division UNION

Enumerator PERRY W. MILLER

Supervisor's Dist. No. 102 Sheet No. _____
Enumeration Dist. No. 86 _____

No. of Family	No. of Dwelling	NAME	Relation	Color	Sex	DATE OF BIRTH Mon/Yr	Age at last birthday	Marital Status	# Years married	Mother of how many children?	# of these children living	NATIVITY Place of birth [this person]	Father of this person	Mother of this person	CITIZENSHIP Year of immigr.	# years in U.S.	Naturalization	OCCUPATION 10 years +	Months not employed	Attended school in months	Can read	Can write	Speak English	Owned or Rent	Owned – no mortage	Farm or house	# of farm schedule
(222)		BACON, CHARLIE D	GR-SON	W	M	Jul 1888	11	S				KY	KY	KY				AT SCHOOL		5	✓	✓	✓				
		" VERNA	GR-DAU	W	F	Oct 1891	8	S				KY	KY	KY				AT SCHOOL			✓	✓	✓				
		WATT, LIZA	Servant	W	F	Mar 1855	45	S				KY	KY	KY							X	X	✓				
223	223	JOHNS, JAMES G.	HEAD	W	M	Jan 1865	35	M	10			TN	TN	TN				FARMER			✓	✓	✓	O	F	F	200
		" LAURA E.	WIFE	W	F	Oct 1871	28	M	10	1	1	KY	KY	KY							✓	✓	✓				
		" ADA M.	DAU	W	F	Feb 1892	8	S				KY	KN	KY				AT SCHOOL		4							
224	224	WILBORN, JOE F.	HEAD	W	M	Oct 1856	43	M	13			KY	KY	KY				FARMER			✓	✓	✓	O	F	F	201
		" PRISCILLA	WIFE	W	F	Dec 1864	35	M	13	1	1	KY	KY	KY							✓	✓					
		" BEULAH	DAU	W	F	Jan 1888	12	S				KY	KY	KY				AT SCHOOL		5	✓	✓	✓				
225	225	JOHNS, JOHN	HEAD	W	M	Apr 1814	86	M	41			KY	KY	KY				FARMER			X	X	✓	O	F	F	202
		" LOUCINDA	WIFE	W	F	May 1834	66	M	41	2	2	KY	KY	KY							✓	✓	✓				
226	226	WHITLOW, JOE	HEAD	W	M	Apr 1876	24	M	5			KY	KY	KY				FARMER			X	✓	✓	R		F	203
		" LIZZIE	WIFE	W	F	Dec 1874	25	M	5	4	4	KY	KY	KY							X	X	✓				
		" MOSS	SON	W	M	Mar 1888	12	S				KY	KY	KY				AT SCHOOL		4	X	X	✓				
		" NORA D.	DAU	W	F	Apr 1895	5	S				KY	KY	KY													
		" DELLA	DAU	W	F	Sep 1897	2	S				KY	KY	KY													
		" LAWRENCE	SON	W	M	May 1899	1	S				KY	KY	KY													
227	227	MILLER, SAM	HEAD	W	M	Jul 1872	27	M	10			KY	KY	KY				FARMER			X	X	✓	R		F	204
		" CRESIA	WIFE	W	F	Apr 1876	24	M	10	4	4	KY	KY	KY							X	X	✓				
		" VERGIL	SON	W	M	Sep 1891	8	S				KY	KY	KY				AT SCHOOL		4							
		" ELAW	DAU	W	F	Jul 1893	6	S				KY	KY	KY													
		" ANNA	DAU	W	F	Feb 1898	2	S				KY	KY	KY													
		" FRANK	SON	W	M	Jul 1899 10/12		S				KY	KY	KY													
228	228	HOWARD, SMITH B.	HEAD	W	M	Mar 1847	53	M	21			KY	KY	KY				FARMER			✓	✓	✓	O		F	205
		" KATE	WIFE	W	F	Apr 1855	45	M	21	6	4	KY	KY	KY							✓	✓	✓				
		" CAM	SON	W	M	Dec 1881	18	S				KY	KY	KY				AT SCHOOL			✓	✓	✓				

STATE - KENTUCKY
COUNTY - MONROE
Township or other division UNION Enumerator PERRY W. MILLER

Supervisor's Dist. No. 102 Sheet No.
Enumeration Dist. No. 86

No. of Family	No. of Dwelling	NAME	Relation	Color	Sex	Date of Birth Mon/Yr	Age at last birthday	Marital Status	# Years married	Mother of how many children?	# of these children living	Place of birth [this person]	Father of this person	Mother of this person	Year of immigr.	# years in U.S.	Naturalization	Occupation 10 years +	Months not employed	Attended school in months	Can read	Can write	Speak English	Owned or Rent	Owned –no mortage	Farm or house	# of farm schedule
		HOWARD, FRANK	Son	W	M	Feb 1884	16	S				KY	KY	KY				AT SCHOOL		5	✓	✓	✓				
		" NELLIE M.	Dau	W	F	May 1886	14	S				KY	KY	KY				AT SCHOOL		5	✓	✓	✓				
		" ANNIE B.	Dau	W	F	May 1893	7	S				KY	KY	KY													
229	229	WILBORN, JAMES W.	Head	W	M	Jan 1855	45	M	22			KY	KY	KY				FARMER			✓	✓	✓	O	F	F	206
		" ROXANA	Wife	W	F	Sep 1861	38	M	22	1	1	KY	KY	KY							✓	✓	✓				
		" MELVIN M.	Son	W	M	Jun 1879	20	S				KY	KY	KY				FARMER			✓	✓	✓				
230	230	CRABTREE, GEORGE (H.?)	Head	W	M	Sep 1865	34	M	14			KY	KY	KY				FARMER			✓	✓	✓	O	F	F	207
		" MARTHA E.	Wife	W	F	Nov 1867	32	M	14	4	4	KY	KY	KY							✓	✓	✓				
		" LINNA B.	Son	W	M	Mar 1887	13	S				KY	KY	KY				AT SCHOOL		4	✓	✓	✓				
		" GEORGE H.	Son	W	M	Jan 1889	11	S				KY	KY	KY				AT SCHOOL		4	✓	✓	✓				
		" MYRTIE O.	Dau	W	F	Feb 1891	9	S				KY	KY	KY				AT SCHOOL		5	✓	✓					
		" FANNY G.	Dau	W	F	Sep 1893	6	S				KY	KY	KY													
231	231	ROBINSON, JOHN L.	Head	W	M	Apr 1872	28	M	6			KY	KY	KY				FARMER			✓	✓	✓	R		F	208
		" ALICE	Wife	W	F	May 1876	24	M	6	2	2	KY	KY	KY							✓	✓					
		" LINDSAY	Son	W	M	Apr 1895	5	S				KY	KY	KY													
		" IVA L.	Dau	W	F	May 1898	2	S				KY	KY	KY													
232	232	CRABTREE, WILLIAM	Head	W	M	Apr 1863	37	M	18			KY	KY	KY				FARMER			✓	✓	✓	O	F	F	209
		" DARCUS	Wife	W	F	Oct 1855	44	M	18	10	9	KY	KY	KY							X	X	✓				
		" MINNIE	Dau	W	F	Apr 1884	16	S				KY	KY	KY				AT SCHOOL		3	✓	✓	✓				
		" CLEO	Son	W	M	Jul 1885	14	S				KY	KY	KY				AT SCHOOL		3	✓	✓	✓				
		" REN	Son	W	M	Sep 1886	13	S				KY	KY	KY				AT SCHOOL		3	✓	✓					
		" WILLIAM H.	Son	W	M	Apr 1888	12	S				KY	KY	KY				AT SCHOOL		3	✓	✓	✓				
		" DONNIE	Dau	W	F	Dec 1889	10	S				KY	KY	KY				AT SCHOOL		3	✓	✓	✓				
		" GEO. H.	Son	W	M	Sep 1891	8	S				KY	KY	KY				AT SCHOOL		4	✓	✓	✓				
		" TILDA M.	Dau	W	F	Aug 1894	5	S				KY	KY	KY													
		" LELA S.	Dau	W	F	Sep 1896	3	S				KY	KY	KY													

TWELFTH CENSUS OF THE UNITED STATES 1900

STATE - KENTUCKY
COUNTY - MONROE
Township or other division — UNION

Enumerator — PERRY W. MILLER

Supervisor's Dist. No. 102 Sheet No.
Enumeration Dist. No. 86

No. of Family	No. of Dwelling	NAME	Relation	Color	Sex	DATE OF BIRTH Mon/Yr	Age at last birthday	Marital Status	# Years married	Mother of how many children?	# of these children living	Place of birth (this person)	Father of this person	Mother of this person	Year of immigr.	# years in U.S.	Naturalization	OCCUPATION 10 years +	Months not employed	Attended school in months	Can read	Can write	Speak English	Owned or Rent	Owned - no mortage	Farm or house	# of farm schedule
		CRABTREE, JACK	Son	W	M	Jan. 1899	1	S				KY	KY	KY													
233	233	MOORE, WILLIAM H.	Head	W	M	Mar. 1867	38	M	6			KY	KY	KY				FARMER			✓	✓	✓	O	F	F	210
		" EVIE B.	Wife	W	F	Mar. 1873	27	M	6	1	0	KY	KY	KY							✓	✓	✓				
234	234	WILBORN, ROBERT E.	Head	W	M	Feb. 1871	29	M	8			KY	KY	KY				FARMER			✓	✓	✓	R		F	211
		" ELLEN	Wife	W	F	Jan. 1870	30	M	8	1	1	KY	KY	KY							✓	✓	✓				
		" CULLUS	Son	W	M	Jun. 1895	4	S				KY	KY	KY													
235	235	SARTIN, JOE	Head	B	M	May. 1870	30	M				KY	KY	KY				DAY LABORER 2			X	X	✓	O	E	H	
236	236	DAVIS, GEO. C.	Head	W	M	Apr. 1837	63	WD				KY	KY	KY				FARMER			✓	✓	✓	O	F	F	212
		" JAMES S.	Son	W	M	Jul. 1863	37	M	0			KY	KY	KY				FARMER			✓	✓	✓				
		" ANNIE B.	Dau-in-law	W	F	Mar. 1882	18	M	0			KY	KY	KY							✓	✓	✓				
		" FANNY	Dau-in-law	W	F	Jan. 1853	45	WD		2	2	KY	KY	KY							✓	✓	✓				
		" FLOSSIE G.	Gr-Dau	W	M	Oct. 1887	12	S				KY	KY	KY				AT SCHOOL			✓	✓	✓				
		" JAMES	Gr-Son	W	M	Jun. 1891	8	S				KY	KY	KY				AT SCHOOL			✓	✓	✓				

STATE - KENTUCKY
COUNTY - MONROE
Township or other division **GAMALIEL**
Enumerator **ISAAC N. RENEAU**
— 449 —

No. of Family	No. of Dwelling	NAME	Relation	Color	Sex	DATE OF BIRTH Mon/Yr	Age at last birthday	Marital Status	# Years married	Mother of how many children?	# of these children living	Place of birth [this person]	Father of this person	Mother of this person	Year of immigr.	# years in U.S.	Naturalization	OCCUPATION 10 years +	Months not employed	Attended school in months	Can read	Can write	Speak English	Owned or Rent	Owned -no mortgage	Farm or house	# of farm schedule
1	1	VAUGHN, SMITH B.	HEAD	W	M	DEC-1851	48	M	14			TN	TN	TN				DISTILLER			✓	✓	✓	O	M	H	1
		" IRENA P.	WIFE	W	F	JUN-1869	30	M	14	7	6	TN	MO	TN							✓	✓	✓				
		" ORVILLE R.	SON	W	M	DEC-1886	13	S				TN	TN	TN				AT SCHOOL		8½	✓	✓	✓				
		" ALVIS R.	SON	W	M	FEB-1888	12	S				KY	TN	TN				AT SCHOOL		5	✓	✓	✓				
		" MIRTLE A.	DAU	W	F	MAR-1892	8	S				KY	TN	TN				AT SCHOOL		5							
		" HENRY S.	SON	W	M	FEB-1894	6	S				KY	TN	TN													
		" MAMIE E.	DAU	W	F	JUN-1897	2	S				TN	TN	TN													
		" ALTIE M.	DAU	W	F	MAY-1900	9/12	S				KY	TN	TN													
		" DERINDA	Mother	W	F	JAN-1821	79	WD				TN	TN	SC							X	X	✓				
2	2	McPEAK, JORDAN I.	HEAD	W	M	JUN-1846	54	M	24			KY	NC	NC				FARMER			✓	✓	✓	R		F	2
		" FRANCES	WIFE	W	F	APR-1858	42	M	24	1	1	TN	NC	NC							✓	✓	✓				
		" VIRGINIA	DAU.	W	F	OCT-1879	20	S				KY	KY	TN							✓	✓	✓				
		" JOHN J.	SON	W	M	JUL-1882	17	S				KY	KY	TN				FARM LABORER		4	✓	✓					
		" CAROLINA B.	DAU	W	F	APR-1885	15	S				KY	KY	TN				AT SCHOOL		5	✓	✓					
		" GEORGE W.	SON	W	M	JUL-1887	12	S				KY	KY	TN				AT SCHOOL		5	✓	✓					
		" WILLIAM S.	SON	W	M	JUN-1890	9	S				KY	KY	TN				AT SCHOOL									
		" LORETTA E.	DAU	W	F	JUN-1893	6	S				KY	KY	TN													
3	3	POWELL, JOHN M.	HEAD	W	M	MAY-1862	38	M	17			KY	TN	TN				FARMER			✓	✓	R		F	3	
		" CARMINTA C.	WIFE	W	F	MAR-1858	42	M	17	4	3	TN	TN	TN							X	X	✓				
		" MAC G.	SON	W	M	MAR-1883	17	S				KY	KY	TN				AT SCHOOL		5	✓	✓	✓				
		" ELZIE E.	SON	W	M	JUN-1887	12	S				KY	KY	TN				AT SCHOOL		5	✓	✓	✓				
		" DAVID H.	SON	W	M	SEP-1894	5	S				KY	KY	TN													
4	4	PERIGO, JOHN (B?)	HEAD	W	M	DEC-1854	45	M	19			KY	TN	TN				FARMER			X	X	✓	R		F	
		" MINTA C.	WIFE	W	F	MAR-1865	35	M	19	6	6	KY	TN	TN							✓	✓	✓				
		" MARTHA N.	DAU	W	F	DEC-1883	16	S				KY	KY	KY							✓	✓	✓				
		" DONA C.	DAU	W	F	JAN-1886	14	S				KY	KY	KY				AT SCHOOL		2	✓	✓	✓				

STATE - KENTUCKY
COUNTY - MONROE
Township or other division GAMALIEL

Enumerator ISAAC N. RENEAU

Supervisor's Dist. No. 102 Sheet No.
Enumeration Dist. No. 87

No. of Family	No. of Dwelling	NAME	Relation	Color	Sex	Date of Birth Mon/Yr	Age at last birthday	Marital Status	# Year married	Mother of how many children	# of these children living	Place of birth (this person)	Father of this person	Mother of this person	Year of immigr. / # years in US / Naturalization	Occupation 10 years +	Months not employed	Attended school in months	Can read	Can write	Speak English	Owned or Rent	Owned -no mortage	Farm or house	# of farm schedule
		PERIGO, ABSALOM P.	Son	W	M	Mar-1890	10	S				KY	KY	KY		At School		2	✓	✓	✓				
		" RUPHUS C.	Son	W	M	Apr-1893	7	S				KY	KY	KY		At School		2							
		" CORA E.	Dau	W	F	Feb-1898	2	S				KY	KY	KY											
5	5	PERIGO, ABSALOM B.	Head	W	M	May-1825	75	M	48			TN	VA	VA		Farmer			X	X	✓	O	F	F	4
		" CHARLOTTY	Wife	W	F	Oct-1830	69	M	48	8	6	TN	VA	VA					X	X	✓				
6	6	RODDY, ROBERT	Head	W	M	Aug-1846	53	M	28			TN	TN	TN		Laborer - Sawmill			✓	✓	✓	O	F	F	5
		" MARY	Wife	W	F	Jan-1849	51	M	28	5	5	TN	TN	TN					✓	✓	✓				
		" JONES	Son	W	M	Jun-1878	21	S				TN	TN	TN						✓	✓				
		" LONA	Dau	W	F	Jan-1883	17	S				TN	TN	TN					X	X	✓				
		" JAMES	Son	W	M	Jun-1887	12	S				TN	TN	TN		At School			✓	✓	✓				
7	7	PERDUE, LUCINDA	Head	W	F	Feb-1828	72	WD				TN	TN	TN		Farmer			✓	X	✓	O	F	F	6
8	8	EAKLE, JOHN	Head	W	M	Nov-1854	45	M	21			TN	TN	TN		Farmer			✓	X	✓			F	
		" MARGET	Wife	W	F	Mar-1856	44	M	21	5	5	KY	KY	TN					✓	✓	✓				
		" JOSEPH	Son	W	M	Mar-1880	20	S				KY	TN	KY		Farm Laborer			✓	X	✓				
		" CHRISTOPHER	Son	W	M	Apr-1888	12	S				KY	TN	KY		At School		5	✓	X	✓				
		" ONIE	Dau	W	F	Apr-1891	9	S				KY	TN	KY		At School		5	✓	✓	✓				
		" CLARENCE	Son	W	M	Aug-1896	3	S				KY	TN	KY											
		" LILLIE M	Dau	W	F	Apr-1900	1/12	S				KY	TN	KY											
9	9	DIXON, WILLIAM L.	Head	W	M	Feb-1862	38	M	7			TN	TN	TN		Farmer			✓	✓	✓	O	M	E	7
		" LOU E.	Wife	W	F	Nov-1874	25	M	7	4	4	TN	TN	TN					✓	✓	✓				
		" VIRGIE	Dau	W	F	Feb-1894	6	S				KY	TN	TN											
		" BERTHA	Dau	W	F	Nov-1895	4	S				KY	TN	TN											
		" TESSIE	Son	W	M	Jan-1898	2	S				KY	TN	TN											
		" EDNA	Dau	W	F	Jan-1900	5/12	S				KY	TN	TN											
10	10	DYRE, JAMES	Head	W	M	Oct-1866	33	WD				TN	TN	TN		Farmer			✓	X	✓	R	F	F	9
		" FANNIE	Dau	W	F	May-1986	14	S				KY	TN	TN					✓	✓	✓				

TWELFTH CENSUS OF THE UNITED STATES 1900

STATE - KENTUCKY
COUNTY - MONROE
Township or other division GAMALIEL
Enumerator ISAAC N. RENEAU
Supervisor's Dist. No. 102 Sheet No.
Enumeration Dist. No. 87

No. of Family	No. of Dwelling	NAME	Relation	Color	Sex	DATE OF BIRTH Mon/Yr	Age at last birthday	Marital Status	# Years married	Mother of how many children?	# of these children living	Place of birth [this person]	Father of this person	Mother of this person	Year of immigr.	# years in U.S.	Naturalization	OCCUPATION 10 years +	Months not employed	Attended school in months	Can read	Can write	Speak English	Owned or Rent	Owned -no mortage	Farm or house	# of farm schedule	
		DYRE, CHARLOTTIE L.	DAU	W	F	Aug.1887	12	S				TN	TN	TN				AT SCHOOL		2½	✓	X	✓					
		" MARY L.	DAU	W	F	Aug.1887	12	S				TN	TN	TN				AT SCHOOL		2½	✓	X	✓					
		" ADELINE	DAU	W	F	Mar.1890	10	S				TN	TN	TN				AT SCHOOL		2½	✓	X	✓					
		" SARAH A.	DAU	W	F	Apr.1891	9	S				TN	TN	TN				AT SCHOOL		3								
		" DOLLIE A.	DAU	W	F	Jun.1893	6	S				TN	TN	TN														
		" JAMES A.	SON	W	M	Sep.1894	5	S				TN	TN	TN														
		" HATTIE E.	DAU	W	F	Oct.1896	3	S				TN	TN	TN														
		" ISAAC R.	SON	W	M	Apr.1898	2	S				TN	TN	TN														
11	11	PERIGO, ISAAC N.	HEAD	W	M	Aug.1858	41	M	20			KY	TN	TN				FARMER			✓	X	✓	O	F	F	10	
		" ADELINE	WIFE	W	F	Nov.1862	37	M	20	5	5	KY	KY	KY							✓		✓					
		" WASHINGTON	SON	W	M	Jan.1882	18	S				KY	KY	KY				FARM LABORER 6			✓		✓					
		" CORRONA D.	DAU	W	F	Jul.1884	15	S				KY	KY	KY							✓		✓					
		" JOHN J.	SON	W	M	Jun.1881	13	S				KY	KY	KY				FARM LABORER 6			✓	X	✓					
		" FRONY B.	DAU	W	F	Jan.1892	8	S				KY	KY	KY				AT SCHOOL		2								
		" ALLIE M.	DAU	W	F	Nov.1899	6/12	S				KY	KY	KY														
12	12	WHEELER, THOMAS B.	HEAD	W	M	Feb.1855	45	M	24			KY	KY	KY				FARMER			✓	✓	✓	R	F	11	
		" MARY	WIFE	W	F	Aug.1859	40	M	24	10	9	TN	KY	TN							✓	✓	✓					
		" WILLIAM	SON	W	M	Apr.1877	23	S				KY	KY	TN				FARM LABORER 6			✓	✓	✓					
		" THOMAS H.	SON	W	M	Dec.1878	21	S				KY	KY	TN				FARM LABORER 4			✓	✓	✓					
		" HERSHAL	SON	W	M	Nov.1881	18	S				KY	KY	TN				FARM LABORER 2			✓	✓	✓					
		" JAMES Y.	SON	W	M	Apr.1885	15	S				KY	KY	TN				AT SCHOOL		4	✓	✓	✓					
		" LUCY C.	DAU	W	F	Feb.1887	13	S				KY	KY	TN				AT SCHOOL		5	✓	✓	✓					
		" BERT B.	SON	W	M	Oct.1890	9	S				KY	KY	TN				AT SCHOOL		5								
		" BESSIE E.	DAU	W	F	Jan.1895	5	S				KY	KY	TN														
		" MALLIE B.	DAU	W	F	Aug.1897	2	S				KY	KY	TN														
13	13	MORRISON, JOHN O.	HEAD	W	M	Nov.1822	77	M	21			KY	VA	KY				FARMER			✓	✓	✓	O	F	F	12	

STATE - KENTUCKY
COUNTY - MONROE
Township or other division: GAMALIEL
Enumerator: ISAAC N. RENEAU

Supervisor's Dist. No. 102 Sheet No.
Enumeration Dist. No. 87

No. of Family	No. of Dwelling	NAME	Relation	Color	Sex	DATE OF BIRTH Mon/Yr	Age at last birthday	Marital Status	# Years married	Mother of how many children	# of these children living	Place of birth (this person)	Father of this person	Mother of this person	Year of immigr.	# years in U.S.	Naturalization	OCCUPATION 10 years +	Months not employed	Attended school in month	Can read	Can write	Speak English	Owned or Rent	Owned -no mortgage	Farm or house	# of farm schedule
		MORRISON, PARIE J.	WIFE	W	F	Nov 1858	41	M	21	6	6	KY	TN	TN							✓	✓	✓				
		" JOSEPH C	Son	W	M	Apr 1885	15	S				KY	KY	KY				FARM LABORER			✓	✓	✓				
		" ALMARINDA	Dau	W	F	Jul 1886	13	S				KY	KY	KY				AT SCHOOL		3	✓	✓	✓				
		" PARIE M. C.	Dau	W	F	Apr 1889	11	S				KY	KY	KY				AT SCHOOL		3	✓	✓	✓				
		" FRANCIS W.	Son	W	M	Aug 1891	8	S				KY	KY	KY				AT SCHOOL		3							
		" MARY A. —?	Dau	W	F	Nov 1893	6	S				KY	KY	KY													
		" IRA W. B.	Son	W	M	Dec 1845	4	S				KY	KY	KY													
14	14	TURNER, WILLIAM J.	Head	W	M	Jun 1868	31	M	11			KY	KY	TN				FARMER			X	X	✓	O	F	F	13
		" LEVESTA	Wife	W	F	Jan 1865	35	M	11	5	4	KY	KY	IND							✓	✓	✓				
		" ARDA M.	Dau	W	F	Jan 1891	9	S				KY	KY	KY				AT SCHOOL		5							
		" ROSA Z.	Dau	W	F	Mar 1894	6	S				KY	KY	KY													
		" EDGAR E.	Son	W	M	Apr 1896	6	S				KY	KY	KY													
		" RADFORD H.	Son	W	M	Jul 1898	1	S				KY	KY	KY													
		GENTRY, MARTHA A.	M-IN-L	W	F	Jan 1820	70	WD				IND	IND	IND							✓	X	✓				
15	15	MOORE, JOHN	HEAD	W	M	Mar 1861	39	M	2			MO	KY	KY				FARMER			X	X	✓	R	F	14	
		" MARGET	Wife	W	F	Feb 1861	39	M	2	6	4	TN	TN	KY							X	X	✓				
16	16	YORK, MARY J.	Head	W	F	Jul 1838	61	S		6	6	TN	TN	TN				FARMER			✓	✓	✓	O	F	F	15
		" SUSAN	Dau	W	F	Nov 1870	29	S				KY	TN	TN							✓	✓	✓				
		" NEWTON D.	Son	W	M	Mar 1876	24	S				KY	KY	TN				FARM LABORER			✓	✓	✓				
		" MOLLIE B.	GR-DAU	W	F	Oct 1887	12	S				KY	KY	KY				AT SCHOOL		2	✓	X	✓				
		" DORA J.	GR-DAU	W	F	Mar 1891	9	S				KY	KY	KY				AT SCHOOL		2							
		" JAMES C.	GR-SON	W	M	Aug 1894	5	S				KY	KY	KY													
17	17	YORK, IRA S. F.	HEAD	W	M	Apr 1867	33	M	8			KY	TN	KY				FARMER			✓	✓	✓	O	M	F	16
		" ELISIBETH	Wife	W	F	Feb 1880	20	M	8	2	2	KY	KY	KY							X	X	✓				
		" PEARL J	Dau	W	F	May 1896	4	S				KY	KY	KY													
		" JEAMS A. G.	Son	W	M	Jul 1899 10/12		S				KY	KY	KY													

STATE - KENTUCKY
COUNTY - MONROE
Township or other division GAMALIEL
Enumerator ISAAC N. RENEAU
Supervisor's Dist. No. 102 Sheet No.
Enumeration Dist. No. 87

Location (No. of Family / No. of Dwelling)	NAME	Relation	Color	Sex	Date of Birth Mon/Yr	Age at last birthday	Marital Status	# Years married	Mother — how many children	# of these children living	Place of birth (this person)	Father of this person	Mother of this person	Citizenship	Occupation 10 years +	Months not employed	Attended school in months	Can read	Can write	Speak English	Owned or Rent	Owned no mortage	Farm or house	# of farm schedule
18 18	McPEAK, DEMARCY	HEAD	W	F	DEC-1841	58	Wd		4	2	KY	TN	TN		FARMER			✓	X	✓	O		F	17
	DISMAN, NANNY J.	DAU	W	F	Sep-1866	33	Wd		6	6	TN	TN	KY		FARM LABORER			X	X	✓				
"	JEAMS A.	GR-SON	W	M	Dec-1884	15	S				KY	TN	TN		FARM LABORER			X	X	✓				
"	WILLIAM L.	GR-SON	W	M	Dec-1887	12	S				KY	KY	KY		FARM LABORER			✓	X	✓				
"	DORA E.	GR-DAU	W	F	Jan-1890	10	S				KY	KY	KY		AT SCHOOL		1	✓	X	✓				
"	CHRISTENA A.	GR-DAU	W	F	Sep-1893	6	S				KY	KY	KY		AT SCHOOL		1							
"	ANDREW C.	GR-SON	W	M	APR-1897	3	S				KY	KY	KY											
"	RADFORD D.	GR-SON	W	M	APR-1900	2/12	S				KY	KY	KY											
19 19	PERIGO, BENJAMIN	HEAD	W	M	OCT-1857	42	M	20			KY	KY	VA		FARMER			✓	✓		O		F	18
"	MARY E.	WIFE	W	F	MAY-1862	38	M	20	9	6	KY	KY	TN					X	X	✓				
"	WILLIAM J.	SON	W	M	Jul-1883	16	S				KY	KY	KY		FARM LABORER			X	X	✓				
"	NANNIE D.	DAU	W	F	MAR-1888	12	S				KY	KY	KY		AT SCHOOL									
"	BETTIE E.	DAU	W	F	APR-1892	8	S				KY	KY	KY		AT SCHOOL									
"	JOHN W.	SON	W	M	Jan-1894	6	S				KY	KY	KY											
"	MARTHA H.	DAU	W	F	Jun-1897	2	S				KY	KY	KY		FARMER			X	X	✓	R		F	19
20 20	YORK, WILLIAM M.	HEAD	W	M	MAY-1874	26	M	6			KY	KY	TN		FARMER			X	X	✓	R		F	19
"	NANSY	WIFE	W	F	Jul-1869	30	M	6	3	2	KY	TN	TN					✓	✓	✓				
"	ALBERT H.	SON	W	M	Nov-1894	5	S				KY	KY	KY											
"	NINNIE S.	DAU	W	F	Aug-1899	9/12	S				KY	KY	KY											
21 21	YORK, ARRY	HEAD	W	F	Jan-1844	56	S				TN	TN	TN		FARMER			X	X	✓			F	
"	OLLIE	DAU	W	F	Jul-1886	13	S				KY	KY	TN		AT SCHOOL		1	✓	X	✓				
22 22	RENEAU, JOHN W.	HEAD	W	M	APR-1846	54	M	32			TN	TN	TN		FARMER			✓	✓	✓	O		F	20
"	MARY T.	WIFE	W	F	Jan-1841	59	M	32	7	6	TN	TN	KY					✓	✓	✓				
"	ISAAC N.	SON	W	M	Jun-1872	27	S				KY	TN	TN		TEACHER (SCHOOL)		7	✓	✓	✓				
"	THOMAS M.	SON	W	M	Sep-1880	19	S				KY	TN	TN		FARM LABORER			✓	✓	✓				
23 23	KING, ZACHERIA	HEAD	W	M	AUG-1848	51	M	24			KY	KY	KY		FURNITURE MAKER			X	X	✓	R		H	

TWELFTH CENSUS OF THE UNITED STATES 1900
-454-

STATE - KENTUCKY
COUNTY - MONROE
Township or other division: GAMALIEL
Enumerator: ISAAC N. RENEAU

Supervisor's Dist. No. 102 Sheet No.
Enumeration Dist. No. 87

No. Family	No. Dwelling	Name	Relation	Color	Sex	Date of Birth Mon/Yr	Age	Marital	Yrs mar	Mother of #	# living	Birthplace	Father	Mother	Occupation 10 yrs+	Months not empl	School (mo)	Read	Write	Speak Eng	Own/Rent	Farm/house	# farm sched
(23)		KING, LOUIZA	Wife	W	F	Aug 1856	43	M	24	8	8	TN	TN	TN				X	X	✓			
		ISAAC B.	Son	W	M	Dec 1876	23	S				KY	KY	TN	DAY LABORER			X	X	✓			
		HENRY A.	Son	W	M	Apr 1880	20	S				TN	KY	TN	DAY LABORER			X	X	✓			
		JOHN R.	Son	W	M	Feb 1881	19	S				TN	KY	TN	DAY LABORER			X	X	✓			
		LONIE P.	Dau	W	F	Oct 1888	11	S				KY	KY	TN	AT SCHOOL		2	X	X	✓			
		BURTIE D.	Son	W	M	Jun 1890	9	S				TN	KY	TN	AT SCHOOL		2	X	X	✓			
		ARRENA P.	Dau	W	F	Aug 1893	6	S				TN	KY	TN									
		MARY E.	Dau	W	F	Jun 1895	4	S				TN	KY	TN									
		WILLIAM M.	Son	W	M	Oct 1897	2	S				TN	KY	TN									
24	24	EAKLE, CHRISTOPHER	Head	W	M	Jan 1860	40	M	12			MO	TN	TN	FARMER			X	X	✓	R	F	21
		MARY E.	Wife	W	F	Sep 1856	43	M	12	6	5	KY	KY	KY				✓	✓	✓			
		JORDAN S.	Son	W	M	Feb 1889	11	S				KY	MO	KY	AT SCHOOL		5	✓	✓	✓			
		VICTORIA	Dau	W	F	May 1894	6	S				KY	MO	KY									
		DANIELS, ELZIE	Lodger	W	M	Sep 1892	7	S				KY	KY	KY	AT SCHOOL		2½	✓	X	✓			
25	25	MCPEAK, ANNIE	Head	W	F	Nov 1835	64	Wd		6	5	TN	TN	TN				✓	X	✓	R	F	22
		LORETTA	Dau	W	F	Apr 1859	42	S				KY	TN	TN	FARMER			✓	✓	✓			
		DANIELS, BIRDIE B.	Gr-Dau	W	F	Nov 1889	10	S				KY	KY	KY	AT SCHOOL		5	✓	✓	✓			
		ROSA	Gr-Dau	W	F	Jul 1898	5	S				KY	KY	KY									
26	26	FORD, GREEN B.	Head	W	M	Dec 1859	40	M	19			KY	TN	KY	FARMER			✓	✓	✓	R	F	23
		SINTHY J.	Wife	W	F	Sep 1865	34	M	19			KY	KY	KY				X	X	✓			
		JOE	Son	W	M	Dec 1882	17	S				KY	KY	KY	FARM LABORER			X	X	✓			
		WILLIE L.	Son	W	M	Aug 1887	12	S				KY	KY	KY	FARM LABORER			X	X	✓			
		MELLIE F.	Dau	W	F	Mar 1888	11	S				TN	KY	KY				X	X	✓			
		NINNIE L.	Dau	W	F	Dec 1894	5	S				TN	KY	KY									
		ARTHUR A.	Son	W	M	Aug 1897	2	S				TN	KY	KY									
		NORA N.	Dau	W	F	Nov 1899	6/12	S				TN	KY	KY									

TWELFTH CENSUS OF THE UNITED STATES 1900

STATE - KENTUCKY
COUNTY - MONROE
Township or other division **GAMALIEL**

Enumerator **ISAAC N. RENEAU**

Supervisor's Dist. No. **102** Sheet No.
Enumeration Dist. No. **87**

No. of Family	No. of Dwelling	NAME	Relation	Color	Sex	DATE OF BIRTH Mon/Yr	Age at last birthday	Marital Status	# Years married	Mother of how many children?	# of these children living	Place of birth [this person]	Father of this person	Mother of this person	Year of immigr.	# years in U.S.	Naturalization	OCCUPATION 10 years +	Months not employed	Attended school in months	Can read	Can write	Speak English	Owned or Rent	Owned –no mortgage	Farm or house	# of farm schedule
27	27	FORD, JOSEPH C.	HEAD	W	M	Oct. 1861	38	M	18			KY	TN	KY				FARMER			✓	✓	✓	R		F	24
		" SARAH J.	WIFE	W	F	Dec. 1861	38	M	18	4	3	KY	KY	KY							X	X	✓				
		" MINNIE B.	DAU	W	F	Sep. 1882	17	S				KY	KY	KY							✓	✓	✓				
		" ELZIE P.	SON	W	M	Oct. 1889	10	S				TN	KY	KY													
		" ROSE E.	DAU	W	F	Oct. 1893	6	S				TN	KY	KY													
28	24	FORD, BENJAMIN	HEAD	W	M	Nov. 1820	79	M	49			TN	TN	TN				FARMER			X	X	✓	R		F	
		" MILLIE	WIFE	W	F	Mar. 1831	69	M	49	5	5	TN	NC	VA							X	X	✓				
29	29	TEMPLE, MARION	HEAD	W	M	Jan. 1869	31	M	8			KY	KY	KY				FARMER			X	X	✓	R		F	25
		" NORA N.	WIFE	W	F	May 1875	25	M	8	4	3	TN	TN	TN							✓	✓	✓				
		" ELLER L.	DAU	W	F	Feb. 1894	6	S				TN	KY	TN													
		" SARAH J.	DAU	W	F	Oct. 1896	3	S				KY	KY	TN													
		" CAMMIE L.	DAU	W	F	Jun. 1898		S				TN	KY	TN													
30	30	REAGAN, WILLIAM W.	HEAD	W	M	Nov. 1861	38	M				KY	VA	TN				FARMER			✓	✓	✓	O		F	26
		" ORIE M	WIFE	W	F	Aug. 1878	21	M	0	0		TN	KY	KY							✓	✓	✓				
		" RADFORD B.	SON	W	M	Jan. 1886	14	S				KY	KY	TN				AT SCHOOL		2	✓	✓	✓				
		" WILLIAM S.	SON	W	M	Nov. 1888	11	S				KY	KY	TN				AT SCHOOL		4½	✓	✓	✓				
		" JAMES O.	SON	W	M	Dec. 1891	8	S				KY	KY	TN				AT SCHOOL		5							
		" VIRGIL C.	SON	W	M	Dec. 1897	2	S				KY	KY	TN													
31	31	FORD, GEORGE W.	HEAD	W	M	Sep. 1858	41	M	4			KY	TN	VA				FARMER			X	X	✓	R		F	27
		" MARTHY L.	WIFE	W	F	Oct. 1872	27	M	4	2	2	KY	VA	VA							✓	X	✓				
		" ARRY	DAU	W	F	Mar. 1883	17	S				KY	KY	KY							✓	✓	✓				
		" ALLIE J.	SON	W	M	Mar. 1885	15	S				KY	KY	KY				FARM LABORER			X	X	✓				
		" ALFORD C.	SON	W	M	Sep. 1886	13	S				TN	KY	KY				FARM LABORER			X	X	✓				
		" MAGNOLIA	DAU	W	F	May 1888	12	S				TN	KY	KY							X	X	✓				
		" JAMES M.	SON	W	M	Feb. 1891	9	S				TN	KY	KY													
		" WILLIAM R.	SON	W	M	Apr. 1897	3	S				TN	KY	KY													

STATE - KENTUCKY
COUNTY - MONROE
Township or other division — GAMALIEL — Enumerator ISAAC N. RENEAU

Supervisor's Dist. No. *102* Sheet No.
Enumeration Dist. No. *87*

Location No. of Family / No. of Dwelling	NAME	Relation	Color	Sex	DATE OF BIRTH Mon/Yr	Age at last birthday	Marital Status	# Years married	Mother of how many children?	# of these children living	Place of birth (this person)	Father of this person	Mother of this person	Year of immigr.	# years in U.S.	Naturalization	OCCUPATION 10 years +	Months not employed	Attended school in months	Can read	Can write	Speak English	Owned or Rent	Owned - no mortgage	Farm or house	# of farm schedule
(31)	FORD, MINNIE B	DAU	W	F	APR·1844	1	S				TN	KY	KY													
32 32	JENKINS, CHRISTOPHER	HEAD	W	M	OCT·1875	24	M	3			KY	KY	KY				FARMER			✓	✓	✓	O	FF	28
"	SARAH F.	WIFE	W	F	DEC·1882	17	M	3	1	1	TN	TN	TN							✓	✓	✓			
"	BESSIE	DAU	W	F	DEC·1898	1	S				KY	KY	TN												
	ROARK, BERTON	Lodger	W	M	AUG·1882	17	S				TN	TN	TN				FARM LABORER			X	X	✓			
33 33	McCOY, ROBERT	HEAD	W	M	JAN·1869	31	M	7			KY	KY	KY				FARMER			✓	X	✓	R	F	29
"	BANNIE	WIFE	W	F	DEC·1870	29	M	7	3	3	KY	KY	KY							✓	✓	✓			
"	WILLIE	SON	W	M	AUG·1894	5	S				KY	KY	KY												
"	SAMUEL	SON	W	M	AUG·1896	3	S				KY	KY	KY												
"	RADFORD	SON	W	M	JUL·1899	10/12	S				KY	KY	KY												
34 34	FERGUSON, PAGAN	HEAD	W	M	MAR·1862	38	M	16			TN	TN	TN				FARMER			✓	X	✓	O	FF	30
"	FANNY M.	WIFE	W	F	DEC·1868	31	M	16	7	7	KY	TN	TN							✓	✓	✓			
"	MOLLIE E.	DAU	W	F	OCT·1885	14	S				KY	TN	KY				AT SCHOOL		4	✓	✓	✓			
"	LORETTIE E.	DAU	W	F	NOV·1887	12	S				KY	TN	KY				AT SCHOOL		4	✓	✓	✓			
"	THOMAS	SON	W	M	OCT·1889	10	S				KY	TN	KY				AT SCHOOL		3	✓	✓	✓			
"	WILLIAM C.	SON	W	M	MAR·1892	8	S				KY	TN	KY				AT SCHOOL		5						
"	JOSEPH W.	SON	W	M	SEP·1893	6	S				KY	TN	KY				AT SCHOOL		5						
"	WIRT H.	SON	W	M	OCT·1895	4	S				KY	TN	KY												
"	CLAY M.	SON	W	M	SEP·1898	1	S				KY	TN	KY												
35 35	YORK, POLLY A.	HEAD	W	F	OCT·1848	51	Wd		7	6	TN	VA	TN				FARMER			✓	X	✓	R	F	31
"	ALICE	DAU	W	F	NOV·1878	21	S				KY	TN	TN							✓	✓	✓			
"	FRANCES	DAU	W	F	JAN·1882	18	S				TN	TN	TN				AT SCHOOL		1	✓	✓	✓			
"	JOHN	SON	W	M	JUN·1885	14	S				TN	TN	TN				AT SCHOOL		1	✓	✓	✓			
"	MARY S.	DAU	W	F	SEP·1888	11	S				KY	TN	TN				AT SCHOOL		1	✓	✓	✓			
36 36	FERGUSON, (WAADE?)	HEAD	W	M	JUN·1869	30	M	9			KY	TN	TN				FARMER			✓	✓	✓	O	FF	32
"	SINTHA	WIFE	W	F	OCT·1875	24	M	9	4	4	TN	TN	TN							✓	✓	✓			

STATE - KENTUCKY
COUNTY - MONROE
Township or other division: GAMALIEL
Enumerator: ISAAC N. RENEAU
Supervisor's Dist. No. 102   Sheet No.
Enumeration Dist. No. 87

No. of Family	No. of Dwelling	NAME	Relation	Color	Sex	DATE OF BIRTH Mon/Yr	Age at last birthday	Marital Status	# Years married	Mother of how many children?	# of these children living	Place of birth (this person)	Father of this person	Mother of this person	Occupation	Attended school in months	Can read	Can write	Speak English	Owned or Rent	Owned -no mortgage	Farm or house	# of farm schedule
		FERGUSON, WILLIAM A.	Son	W	M	Jul.1892	7	S				KY	KY	TN	AT SCHOOL	3							
		" JAMES E.	Son	W	M	Jan.1895	5	S				KY	KY	TN									
		" VIRGIL C.	Son	W	M	Mar.1897	3	S				KY	KY	TN									
		" JOHN M.	Son	W	M	Mar.1899	1	S				KY	KY	TN									
		" SARAH E.	Mother	W	F	Oct.1839	60	Wd		5	3	TN	TN	TN			✓	✓	✓				
37	37	EAGLE, WILSON F.	Head	W	M	Aug.1865	34	M	13			KY	TN	KY	FARMER		✓	✓	✓	O	F	F	33
		" EVELINE	Wife	W	F	Sep.1862	37	M	13	7	6	TN	TN	TN			✓	✓	✓				
		" VINA E.	Dau	W	F	Mar.1888	12	S				KY	KY	TN	AT SCHOOL	3	✓	✓	✓				
		" JAMES T.	Son	W	M	May.1889	11	S				KY	KY	TN	AT SCHOOL	3							
		" HENRY A.	Son	W	M	Sep.1893	6	S				KY	KY	TN	AT SCHOOL	3							
		" LOU V.	Dau	W	F	Dec.1894	5	S				KY	KY	TN									
		" HERBERT	Son	W	M	Jan.1897	3	S				KY	KY	TN									
		" OSCAR	Son	W	M	Oct.1899	7/12	S				KY	KY	TN									
38	38	GENTRY, LEVESTY	Head	W	M	Jun.1841	58	Divc.		2	1	KY	NC	SC	FARMER		✓	✓	✓	O	F	F	34
		McCOY, CANZADY	Dau	W	F	Jul.1867	32	Divc.		1	1	KY	KY	KY			✓	X	✓				
		" AMON	Gr.Son	W	M	Jan.1890	10	S				KY	KY	KY	AT SCHOOL								
39	39	HALCOMB, BENJAMIN	Head	W	M	Oct.1842	57	M	34			KY	NC	SC	FARMER		✓	✓	✓	O	F	F	35
		" SARAH A.	Wife	W	F	Mar.1851	49	M	34	6	5	TN	TN	TN			✓	✓	✓				
		" JOHN P.	Son	W	M	Aug.1880	19	S				KY	KY	TN	FARM LABORER								
		" FRANK	Son	W	M	Mar.1886	14	S				KY	KY	TN	FARM LABORER		✓	✓	✓				
40	40	BEALS, ISAAC T.R.	Head	W	M	Sep.1855	44	M	22			KY	TN	TN	FARMER		✓	✓	✓	O	F	F	36
		" MARY J.	Wife	W	F	Jan.1861	39	M	22	4	4	KY	IN	KY			✓	✓	✓				
		" LILLIE G.	Dau	W	F	Apr.1879	21	S				KY	KY	KY	AT SCHOOL	8	✓	✓	✓				
		" FLORENCE G.	Dau	W	F	Feb.1882	18	S				KY	KY	KY	AT SCHOOL	5	✓	✓	✓				
		" DAVIE L.	Son	W	M	Nov.1883	16	S				KY	KY	KY	FARM LABORER	5	✓	✓	✓				
		" MARY M.	Dau	W	F	May.1899	1	S				KY	KY	KY									

STATE - KENTUCKY
COUNTY - MONROE
Township or other division GAMALIEL

Enumerator ISAAC N. RENEAU

— 458 —

Supervisor's Dist. No. 102 Sheet No.
Enumeration Dist. No. 87

Location		NAME	Relation	Color	Sex	DATE OF BIRTH Mon/Yr	Age at last birthday	Marital Status	# Years married	Mother of how many children?	# of these children living	NATIVITY Place of birth [this person]	Father of this person	Mother of this person	CITIZENSHIP Year of immigr.	# years in U.S.	Naturalization	OCCUPATION 10 years +	Months not employed	EDUCATION Attended school in months	Can read	Can write	Speak English	OWNERSHIP Owned or Rent	Owned –no mortgage	Farm or house	# of farm schedule	
41	41	BRANDON, ALEXANDER	Head	W	M	Feb. 1856	44	M	16			KY	KY	KY				FARMER		X	X	✓		R		F	37	
		" LUCY A.	Wife	W	F	Aug. 1862	37	M	16	7	7	KY	TN	KY							✓	✓	✓					
		" LAWRENCE	Son	W	M	Sep. 1885	14	S				TN	KY	KY				FARM LABORER			✓	✓	✓					
		" ALTIE	Dau	W	F	Apr. 1887	3	S				TN	KY	KY				AT SCHOOL		5	✓	✓	✓					
		" OBIE	Son	W	M	Jun. 1888	11	S				TN	KY	KY				AT SCHOOL		5	✓	✓	✓					
		" JODIE	Son	W	M	Apr. 1891	9	S				TN	KY	KY				AT SCHOOL										
		" ELLER	Dau	W	F	Feb. 1894	6	S				KY	KY	KY				AT SCHOOL		1	✓							
		" PEARL	Dau	W	F	Dec. 1895	4	S				KY	KY	KY														
		" HERMAN	Son	W	M	Nov. 1898	1	S				KY	KY	KY														
42	42	TAYLOR, JEFF	Head	W	M	Nov. 1851	48	M	16			TN	VA	TN				FARMER			✓	✓	✓		O		MF	38	
		" DOSSE	Wife	W	F	Oct. 1858	41	M	16	7	7	TN	TN	TN							✓	✓	✓					
		" CLOE E.	Dau	W	F	Jan. 1884	16	S				TN	TN	TN				AT SCHOOL		6	✓	✓	✓					
		" JACK H.	Son	W	M	Apr. 1886	14	S				TN	TN	TN				AT SCHOOL		4	✓	✓	✓					
		" HERSHAL J.	Son	W	M	Aug. 1887	12	S				TN	TN	TN				AT SCHOOL		4	✓	✓	✓					
		" LILLIARD T.	Son	W	M	Apr. 1889	11	S				TN	TN	TN				AT SCHOOL		5	✓	✓	✓					
		" HOMER E.	Son	W	M	Oct. 1891	8	S				TN	TN	TN				AT SCHOOL		5								
		" OCIE E.	Dau	W	F	Aug. 1893	6	S				TN	TN	TN														
		" DAISY	Dau	W	F	Apr. 1895	5	S				TN	TN	TN														
43	43	GOODE, EBENEZER	Head	W	M	Feb. 1832	68	M	13			KY	NC	KY				FARMER			✓	✓	✓		R		F	39	
		" SCIOTA	Wife	W	F	Oct. 1843	56	M	13	0	0	KY	KY	KY							✓	✓	✓					
44	44	HALCOMB, CRITTENTON	Head	W	M	Aug. 1876	23	M	4			KY	KY	TN				FARMER			✓	✓	✓		R		F	40	
		" HAILY	Wife	W	F	Jan. 1881	19	M	4	2	1	TN	TN	TN							✓	✓	✓					
		" WILLIAM B.	Son	W	M	Feb. 1898	2	S				KY	KY	TN														
45	45	FOWLER, ABBIE G.	Head	W	F	Feb. 1848	52	Wd		7	5	TN	TN	TN				FARMER			✓	✓	✓		O		MF	41	
		" LARY E.	Dau	W	F	Apr. 1876	24	S				KY	KY	KY							✓	✓	✓					
		" JAMES N.	Son	W	M	Oct. 1877	22	S				KY	KY	KY				FARMER			✓	✓	✓					

TWELFTH CENSUS OF THE UNITED STATES 1900

— 459 —

STATE - KENTUCKY
COUNTY - MONROE
Township or other division: GAMALIEL

Enumerator: ISAAC N. RENEAU

Supervisor's Dist. No. 102 Sheet No.
Enumeration Dist. No. 87

No. of Family	No. of Dwelling	NAME	Relation	Color	Sex	Date of Birth Mon/Yr	Age at last birthday	Marital Status	#Years married	Mother of how many children	# of these children living	Place of birth (this person)	Father of this person	Mother of this person	Year of immigr.	#years in U.S.	Naturalization	Occupation	Months not employed	Attended school in months	Can read	Can write	Speak English	Owned or Rent	Owned-no mortgage	Farm or house	# of farm schedule
		FOWLER, VICTORIA C.	DAU	W	F	DEC. 1880	19	S				KY	KY	KY				AT SCHOOL		2	✓	✓					
46	46	HAYES, JASPER	HEAD	W	M	MAR. 1838	62	M	22			KY	KY	TN				FARMER			✓	✓	✓	O	F	F	42
		" VIRGINIA	WIFE	W	F	NOV. 1850	49	M	22	6	6	TN	TN	TN							✓	✓					
		" IDA B.	DAU	W	F	SEP. 1872	27	S				KY	KY	TN							✓	✓					
		" VANAS	SON	W	M	OCT. 1878	21	S				KY	KY	TN				FARM LABORER			✓	✓	✓				
		" HOWARD	SON	W	M	JUN. 1880	19	S				KY	KY	TN				FARM LABORER			✓	✓					
		" NORA	DAU	W	F	DEC. 1881	18	S				KY	KY	TN				AT SCHOOL		4	✓	✓	✓				
		" NANNIE	DAU	W	F	FEB. 1884	16	S				KY	KY	TN				AT SCHOOL		9	✓	✓					
		" FRED N.	SON	W	M	OCT. 1886	13	S				KY	KY	TN				AT SCHOOL		7	✓	✓					
		" GLEN	SON	W	M	AUG. 1888	11	S				KY	KY	TN				AT SCHOOL		6	✓	✓					
		RUSSELL, ISBIL	SISTER	W	F	OCT. 1831	68	Wd		4	3	KY	KY	TN							✓	✓					
47	47	THOMERSON, HENRY J.	HEAD	W	M	SEP. 1853	46	M	17			KY	VA	KY				FARMER			✓	✓		O	F	F	43
		" MARY E.	WIFE	W	F	MAY 1877	33	M	17	3	1	TN	TN	TN							✓	✓					
		" JOHNY P.	SON	W	M	OCT. 1884	15	S				KY	KY	TN				AT SCHOOL		9	✓	✓					
48	48	PAGE, WILLIAM W.	HEAD	W	M	MAR. 1856	44	S				KY	KY	KY				MERCHANT-DRY GOODS			✓	✓		R		H	
		COMER, WIRT	PARTNER	W	M	APR. 1869	31	S				KY	TN	KY				MERCHANT-DRY GOODS			✓	✓					
49	49	SILVEY, HIRAM J.	HEAD	W	M	NOV. 1864	35	M	9			KY	NC	TN				SALESMAN-DRY GOODS			✓	✓		O		H	
		" SALLIE J.	WIFE	W	F	OCT. 1863	36	M	9	4	4	KY	KY	TN							✓	✓					
		" PAUL	SON	W	M	AUG. 1892	7	S				KY	KY	KY				AT SCHOOL		5							
		" TRIGG	SON	W	M	OCT. 1894	5	S				KY	KY	KY													
		" NANNIE L.	DAU	W	F	JAN. 1897	3	S				KY	KY	KY													
		" ERMINE	DAU	W	F	MAY 1899	1	S				KY	KY	KY													
50	50	ALLEN, JOHN G.	HEAD	W	M	JUN. 1869	30	M	10			KY	KY	KY				FARMER			X	X	✓	O	F	F	44
		" MARTHY J.	WIFE	W	F	JUL. 1872	27	M	10	6	5	KY	KY	KY							✓	✓	✓				
		" WILLIS	SON	W	M	DEC. 1890	9	S				KY	KY	KY				AT SCHOOL		5							
		" THOMAS	SON	W	M	MAR. 1892	8	S				TN	KY	KY				AT SCHOOL		5							

STATE - KENTUCKY
COUNTY - MONROE
Township or other division GAMALIEL Enumerator ISAAC N. RENEAU

Supervisor's Dist. No. _102_ Sheet No.
Enumeration Dist. No. _87_

Location No. of Family	No. of Dwelling	NAME	Relation	Color	Sex	DATE OF BIRTH Mon/Yr	Age at last birthday	Marital Status	# Years married	Mother of how many children?	# of these children living	Place of birth (this person)	Father of this person	Mother of this person	Year of immigr.	# years in U.S.	Naturalization	OCCUPATION 10 years +	Months not employed	Attended school in months	Can read	Can write	Speak English	Owned or Rent	Owned –no mortgage	Farm or house	# of farm schedule
(50)		ALLEN, LONA F.	DAU	W	F	DEC. 1894	5	S				KY	KY	KY													
		" GEORGE	SON	W	M	DEC. 1897	2	S				KY	KY	KY													
		" SAMUEL	SON	W	M	Feb. 1900	4/12	S				KY	KY	KY													
51	51	MOORE, LUTHER	HEAD	W	M	MAY. 1867	33	M	7			TN	TN	KY				SCHOOL TEACHER			✓	✓	✓	O	F	F	45
		" LORA	WIFE	W	F	SEP. 1869	30	M	7	3	2	KY	TN	KY							✓	✓	✓				
		" OLIVE M.	DAU	W	F	MAY. 1896	4	S				TN	TN	KY													
		" BESSY F.	DAU	W	F	DEC. 1897	2	S				TN	TN	KY													
		SANDERS, NORA	Lodger	W	F	SEP. 1874	15	S				TN	TN	TN				AT SCHOOL		6	✓	✓					
52	52	JENKINS, DAVID W.	HEAD	W	M	MAY. 1872	28	M	6			KY	KY	KY				FARMER			✓	✓	✓	R	F	46	
		" MARGET	WIFE	W	F	AUG. 1872	27	M	6	3	3	KY	KY	KY							✓	✓					
		" OLLIE M.	DAU	W	F	JUN. 1894	5	S				KY	KY	KY													
		" LEXIE J.	DAU	W	F	OCT. 1896	3	S				KY	KY	KY													
		" BUSSIE F.	DAU	W	F	DEC. 1898	1	S				KY	KY	KY													
53	53	HARLAN, SAMUEL D.	HEAD	W	M	MAR. 1852	48	M	7			TN	KY	KY				MERCHANT (DRUGS)			✓	✓	✓	O		H	
		" MARTHA	WIFE	W	F	FEB. 1862	38	M	7			TN	TN	TN							✓	✓	✓				
		BROOKS, LILLIAN	Lodger	W	F	APR. 1890	10	S				KY	KY	KY				AT SCHOOL		7½	✓	✓					
54	54	JENKINS, ERNEST	HEAD	W	M	SEP. 1877	22	M				KY	KY	KY				SALESMAN (DRUGS)			✓	✓	✓	R		H	
		" CRITTIE	WIFE	W	F	JAN. 1879	21	M				TN	TN	TN							✓	✓	✓				
55	55	TURNER, PRICE	HEAD	W	M	FEB. 1867	33	M	14			TN	KY	VA				FARMER			✓	✓	✓	O	F	F	47
		" BETTIE	WIFE	W	F	SEP. 1862	37	M	14	7	7	KY	TN	KY							✓	✓	✓				
		" PEARL	DAU	W	F	DEC. 1887	12	S				TN	TN	KY				AT SCHOOL		6	✓	✓	✓				
		" SAMUEL	SON	W	M	JUN. 1889	10	S				TN	TN	KY				AT SCHOOL		6	✓	✓	✓				
		" RUPHUS	SON	W	M	JAN. 1891	9	S				TN	TN	KY				AT SCHOOL		6	✓	✓	✓				
		" MAMIE	DAU	W	F	OCT. 1892	7	S				TN	TN	KY				AT SCHOOL		6	✓	✓	✓				
		" HERSHAL	SON	W	M	NOV. 1894	5	S				TN	TN	KY													
		" PERRY	SON	W	M	JAN. 1897	3	S				KY	TN	KY													

STATE - KENTUCKY
COUNTY - MONROE
Township or other division: GAMALIEL
Enumerator: ISAAC N. RENEAU
Supervisor's Dist. No. 102 Sheet No.
Enumeration Dist. No. 87

No. of Family	No. of Dwelling	NAME	Relation	Color	Sex	DATE OF BIRTH Mon/Yr	Age at last birthday	Marital Status	# Years married	Mother of how many children?	# of these children living	Place of birth (this person)	Father of this person	Mother of this person	OCCUPATION 10 years +	Attended school in months	Can read	Can write	Speak English	Owned or Rent	Owned -no mortgage	Farm or house	# of farm schedule
		TURNER, MATILDA	DAU	W	F	APR 1899	1	S				KY	TN	KY									
56	56	McCORGAH, EUGENE P.	HEAD	W	M	Sep 1866	33	M	5			TEX	TN	KY	FARMER		✓	✓	✓	O	M	F	48
		" MAY E.	WIFE	W	F	Jul 1869	30	M	5	2	2	MO	TN	KY			✓	✓					
		" LORETTA A.	DAU	W	F	DEC 1895	4	S				TN	TEX	MO									
		" THEOCLARA	DAU	W	F	Nov 1897	2	S				TN	TEX	MO									
		GRISAM, ELIZA A.	M-IN-LAW	W	F	Jun 1829	60	Wd		6	5	KY	KY	KY			✓	✓	✓				
57	57	GRISHAM, RUPHAS E.	Head	W	M	Nov 1860	39	M	14			KY	KY	KY	FARMER		✓	✓	✓	O	M	F	49
		" MELISSA	Wife	W	F	May 1870	30	M	14	6	6	KY	KY	KY			✓	✓	✓				
		" GRACE	DAU	W	F	Dec 1887	12	S				KY	KY	KY	AT SCHOOL	4½	✓	✓	✓				
		" FRED	SON	W	M	Jun 1890	9	S				KY	KY	KY	AT SCHOOL	4	✓						
		" ETHEL	DAU	W	F	Feb 1892	8	S				TN	KY	KY	AT SCHOOL								
		" ANNIE	DAU	W	F	Jan 1894	6	S				TN	KY	KY									
		" ESTER	DAU	W	F	Feb 1896	4	S				TN	KY	KY									
		" CECIL M.	DAU	W	F	Aug 1898	1	S				KY	KY	KY									
58	58	EMBERTON, JAMES E.	HEAD	W	M	Sep 1873	26	M	3			KY	KY	KY	SALESMAN (DRY GOODS)		✓	✓	✓	R		H	
		" GUSTIE J.	WIFE	W	F	Feb 1874	26	M	3			KY	KY	KY			✓	✓	✓				
59	59	PLUMLEE, LAYTON	HEAD	W	M	Nov 1858	41	M	14			TN	TN	TN	MERCHANT (DRY GOODS)		✓	✓	✓	O		H	
		" DONA	WIFE	W	F	May 1872	28	M	14	1	1	TN	TN	TN			✓	✓	✓				
		" HERMAN	SON	W	M	Nov 1887	12	S				TN	TN	TN	AT SCHOOL	7	✓	✓	✓				
60	60	COMER, THOMAS W.	Head	W	M	Feb 1848	52	Wd				KY	TN	KY	FARMER		✓	✓	✓	O	F	F	50
		" ELLA C.	DAU	W	F	Jan 1877	23	S				KY	KY	KY			✓	✓	✓				
		" ADRIENNE	DAU	W	F	Sep 1878	21	S				KY	KY	KY			✓	✓	✓				
		" HARRY	SON	W	M	APR 1881	19	S				IN	KY	KY	AT SCHOOL	6	✓	✓	✓				
		" FRED	SON	W	M	JAN 1887	13	S				KY	KY	KY	AT SCHOOL	6	✓	✓	✓				
61	61	DONOHO, JOHN P.	HEAD	W	M	Mar 1841	59	M	37			TN	TN	NC	HOTEL KEEPER		✓	✓	✓	O		H	
		" MARY J.	WIFE	W	F	Oct 1842	57	M	37			KY	KY	KY			✓	✓	✓				

STATE - KENTUCKY
COUNTY - MONROE
Township or other division **GAMALIEL**   Enumerator **ISAAC N. RENEAU**

Supervisor's Dist. No. **102** Sheet No.
Enumeration Dist. No. **87**

No. of Family	No. of Dwelling	NAME	Relation	Color	Sex	DATE OF BIRTH Mon/Yr	Age at last birthday	Marital Status	# Years married	Mother of how many children?	# of these children living	Place of birth [this person]	Father of this person	Mother of this person	Year of immigr.	# years in U.S.	Naturalization	OCCUPATION 10 years +	Months not employed	Attended school in months	Can read	Can write	Speak English	Owned or Rent	Owned - no mortage	Farm or house	# of farm schedule
62	62	HARLAN, CICERO	HEAD	W	M	FEB. 1873	27	M	8			TN	TN	TN				FARMER			✓	✓	✓	R		F	51
		" EMLIE	WIFE	W	F	MAY. 1872	28	M	8	3	2	KY	KY	KY							✓	✓	✓				
		" NANNIE M.	DAU	W	F	APR. 1894	6	S				KY	TN	KY							✓	✓					
		" JESSIE S.	SON	W	M	DEC. 1895	4	S				KY	TN	KY													
63	63	MAXEY, CHARLEY	HEAD	B	M	FEB. 1873	27	M	1			TN	TN	TN				FARMER			X	X	✓	R		F	
		" ARCHIE	WIFE	B	F	APR. 1882	18	M	1	1	1	KY	KY	KY							✓	✓	✓				
		" HARRET	DAU	B	F	MAR. 1900	3/12	S				KY	TN	KY													
64	64	GOAD, HANEY	HEAD	W	M	JUN. 1878	26	M				KY	KY	KY				FARMER			✓	✓	✓	R		F	52
		" BELL	WIFE	W	F	OCT. 1882	17	M				TN	TN	TN							X	✓	✓				
65	65	HAMILTON, OLIVER P.	HEAD	W	M	AUG. 1864	35	M	8			TN	TN	TN				PHYSICIAN			✓	✓	✓	O		H	
		" NAVADA	WIFE	W	F	NOV. 1869	30	M	8	0	0	KY	KY	KY							✓	✓	✓				
		WARD, BASSIE	LODGER	W	F	AUG. 1890	9	S				KY	KY	KY				AT SCHOOL		5							
66	66	STEEN, WILLIAM F.	HEAD	W	M	JUN. 1836	63	M	40			KY	VA	SC				FARMER			✓	✓	✓	O		F	
		" SARAH	WIFE	W	F	MAY. 1840	60	M	40	7	6	KY	TN	TN							✓	✓	✓				
67	67	EMBERTON, JASPER	HEAD	W	M	JUN. 1851	48	M	28			KY	KY	TN				FARMER			✓	✓	✓	R		F	
		" MARGET	WIFE	W	F	NOV. 1850	49	M	28	1	1	KY	KY	KY							✓	✓	✓				
68	68	HALE, ALEXANDER	HEAD	W	M	OCT. 1854	45	M	24			KY	TN	TN				FARMER			✓	✓	✓	O		F	53
		" SARAH J.	WIFE	W	F	OCT. 1855	44	M	24	10	8	KY	TN	TN							✓	X	✓				
		" VIRGIL	SON	W	M	MAR. 1880	20	S				KY	KY	KY				FARM LABORER			✓	✓	✓				
		" WALTER	SON	W	M	JUN. 1882	17	S				KY	KY	KY				FARM LABORER			✓	✓	✓				
		" ALICE	DAU	W	F	FEB. 1889	11	S				KY	KY	KY				AT SCHOOL		3½	✓	✓					
		" MAUD	DAU	W	F	DEC. 1890	9	S				KY	KY	KY				AT SCHOOL		3½							
		" FRED	SON	W	M	OCT. 1893	6	S				KY	KY	KY													
		" ADER	DAU	W	F	SEP. 1896	3	S				KY	KY	KY													
		" HERMAN	SON	W	M	NOV. 1898	1	S				KY	KY	KY													
69	69	BALES, JAMES C.	HEAD	W	M	DEC. 1860	39	Wd				KY	TN	TN				CARPENTER			✓	✓	✓	R		H	

STATE - KENTUCKY
COUNTY - MONROE
Township or other division — GAMALIEL   Enumerator ISAAC N. RENEAU

Supervisor's Dist. No. 102 Sheet No.
Enumeration Dist. No. 87

No. of Family	No. of Dwelling	NAME	Relation	Color	Sex	DATE OF BIRTH Mon/Yr	Age at last birthday	Marital Status	# Years married	Mother of how many children?	# of these children living	Place of birth [this person]	Father of this person	Mother of this person	Year of immigr.	# years in U.S.	Naturalization	OCCUPATION 10 years +	Months not employed	Attended school in months	Can read	Can write	Speak English	Owned or Rent	Owned - no mortage	Farm or house	# of farm schedule
		BALES, LOLA F.	DAU	W	F	OCT.1885	14	S				KY	KY	KY				AT SCHOOL		9	✓	✓	✓				
		" MARY	MOTHER	W	F	DEC.1828	71	Wd		9	8	TN	TN	TN							✓	✓	✓				
70	70	ALLEN, ROY	HEAD	W	M	SEP.1870	29	M	10			KY	KY	KY				DAY LABORER 4			X	X	✓	R	H		
		" TABITHIA E.	WIFE	W	F	OCT.1872	27	M	10	5	4	KY	TN	KY							✓	✓	✓				
		" CARLOS C.	SON	W	M	MAR.1894	6	S				KY	KY	KY													
		" COMER J.	SON	W	M	JUL.1896	3	S				KY	KY	KY													
		" ESSIE F.	DAU	W	F	FEB.1898	2	S				TN	KY	KY													
		" CLIDIE	SON	W	M	MAY.1900	1/12	S				KY	KY	KY													
91	71	CRABTREE, FRANK	HEAD	W	M	APR.1858	42	M	20			TN	TN	TN				PHYSICIAN			✓	✓	✓	O	F F		54
		" TEXIE	WIFE	W	F	JUL.1858	41	M	20	10	10	KY	KY	KY							✓	✓	✓				
		" IVA	DAU	W	F	SEP.1880	19	S				TN	TN	KY				MUSIC TEACHER 4			✓	✓	✓				
		" ORA	DAU	W	F	JUL.1881	18	S				TN	TN	KY				SCHOOL TEACHER 4			✓	✓	✓				
		" VERDA	DAU	W	F	MAR.1884	16	S				TN	TN	KY				AT SCHOOL		6	✓	✓	✓				
		" ESSIE	DAU	W	F	JAN.1886	14	S				TN	TN	KY				AT SCHOOL		5	✓	✓	✓				
		" VERA	DAU	W	F	JAN.1888	12	S				KY	KY	KY				AT SCHOOL		5	✓	✓					
		" LURA	DAU	W	F	DEC.1889	10	S				KY	TN	KY				AT SCHOOL		5	✓						
		" GROVER	SON	W	M	DEC.1891	8	S				KY	TN	KY				AT SCHOOL		5							
		" EMMONS	SON	W	M	AUG.1893	6	S				KY	TN	KY				AT SCHOOL		5							
		" MAMIE	DAU	W	F	APR.1896	4	S				KY	TN	KY													
		" SANFORD	SON	W	M	OCT.1898	1	S				KY	TN	KY													
72	72	PITCOCK, JAMES F.	HEAD	W	M	MAY.1860	40	M	14			KY	KY	KY				FARMER			✓	✓		O	F F		55
		" NANSIE E.	WIFE	W	F	JUL.1860	39	M	14	6	5	KY	GA	TN							✓	✓					
		" DELLIE A.	DAU	W	F	MAY.1880	20	S				TN	KY	KY							X	X	X				
		" VARRY	DAU	W	F	APR.1891	9	S				KY	KY	KY				AT SCHOOL		5							
		" MANDICA	SON	W	M	NOV.1892	7	S				KY	KY	KY				AT SCHOOL		5							
		" RICHARD	SON	W	M	OCT.1894	5	S				KY	KY	KY													

TWELFTH CENSUS OF THE UNITED STATES 1900

STATE - KENTUCKY
COUNTY - MONROE
Township or other division GAMALIEL   Enumerator ISAAC N. RENEAU

Supervisor's Dist. No. 102 Sheet No.
Enumeration Dist. No. 87

Location No. of Family	No. of Dwelling	NAME	Relation	Color	Sex	DATE OF BIRTH Mon/Yr	Age at last birthday	Marital Status	# Years married	Mother of how many children?	# of these children living	Place of birth (this person)	Father of this person	Mother of this person	Year of immigr.	# years in U.S.	Naturalization	OCCUPATION 10 years +	Months not employed	Attended school in months	Can read	Can write	Speak English	Owned or Rent	Owned -no mortgage	Farm or house	# of farm schedule
		PITCOCK, WOLFORD	SON	W	M	Jul. 1897	2	S				KY	KY	KY													
73	73	ENGLAND, SAMUEL	HEAD	W	M	Jan. 1860	40	M	19			KY	KY	KY				FARMER			✓	✓	✓	O	F	F	56
		" ETTA B.	WIFE	W	F	Oct. 1863	36	M	19	5	4	KY	KY	KY							✓	✓	✓				
		" JOHN (G.?)	SON	W	M	Nov. 1882	17	S				KY	KY	KY				At School		4	✓	✓	✓				
		" ESTELLA M.	DAU	W	F	Jan. 1884	14	S				KY	KY	KY				At School		4	✓	✓	✓				
		" HARLAN E.	SON	W	M	Mar. 1887	13	S				KY	KY	KY				At School		4	✓	✓	✓				
		" KATIE	DAU	W	F	Jan. 1890	10	S				KY	KY	KY				At School		4	✓	✓	✓				
74	74	PIPKIN, KIT E.	HEAD	B	M	Mar. 1872	28	M	8			KY	KY	TN				FARMER			✓	✓	✓	R	F	57	
		" DELLA	WIFE	B	F	Dec. 1876	23	M	8	4	4	KY	VA	KY							✓	✓	✓				
		" RUTHA	DAU	B	F	Feb. 1895	5	S				KY	KY	KY													
		" LILLIE	DAU	B	F	Aug. 1896	3	S				KY	KY	KY													
		" BESSIE	DAU	B	F	Sep. 1898	1	S				KY	KY	KY													
		" OMIE	DAU	B	F	Apr. 1900 2/12		S				KY	KY	KY													
75	75	POLLIS, GEORGE A.	HEAD	W	M	Jan. 1860	40	M	20			KY	VA	KY				FARMER			X	X	✓	O	F	F	58
		" NANSY	WIFE	W	F	Oct. 1856	43	M	20	4	4	KY	KY	KY							✓	✓	✓				
		" COMER	SON	W	M	Mar. 1884	16	S				KY	KY	KY				At School		5	✓	✓	✓				
		" VERDA	DAU	W	F	Sep. 1889	10	S				KY	KY	KY				At School		5	✓	✓	✓				
76	76	BRADLEY, WILLIAM H.	Head	B	M	Nov. 1854	45	M	3			TN	TN	TN							X	X	✓	C	F	F	59
		" AR'DEL	WIFE	B	F	Feb. 1852	48	M	3	0	0	KY	KY	KY							✓	✓	✓				
		" TAYLOR C.	SON	B	M	May 1882	18	S				TN	TN	TN				FARM LABORER		8	✓	✓	✓				
77	77	BROOKS, JACK M.	HEAD	W	M	Oct. 1870	29	Wd				KY	KY	KY				FARMER			✓	✓	✓	R		F	60
		" JANIE	WIFE	W	F	Dec. 1871	28	M	0	0	0	KY	KY	KY							✓	✓	✓				
		" TENNIE M.	SON	W	M	Jul. 1897	2	S				KY	KY	KY													
78	78	PITCOCK, PERLINA E.	HEAD	W	F	Oct. 1830	69	Wd				KY	KY	KY							✓	✓	✓	O	F	H	
		" MARY E.	DAU-IN-LAW	W	F	Mar. 1867	33	Wd		1	1	KY	KY	TN							✓	✓	✓				
		" WALTER N.	GR-SON	W	M	Jan. 1888	12	S				KY	KY	KY				At School		7	✓	✓	✓				

STATE - KENTUCKY
COUNTY - MONROE
Township or other division **GAMALIEL**   Enumerator **ISAAC N. RENEAU**

Supervisor's Dist. No. **102** Sheet No.
Enumeration Dist. No. **87**

No. of Family	No. of Dwelling	NAME	Relation	Color	Sex	DATE OF BIRTH Mon/Yr	Age at last birthday	Marital Status	# Years married	Mother of how many children	# of these children living	Place of birth [this person]	Father of this person	Mother of this person	Year of immigr.	# years in U.S.	Naturalization	OCCUPATION 10 years +	Months not employed	Attended school in months	Can read	Can write	Speak English	Owned or Rent	Owned -no mortage	Farm or house	# of farm schedule
79	79	CRAWFORD, BIRTIE	HEAD	W	M	Nov.1868	31	M	7			KY	KY	KY				BLACKSMITH			✓	✓		O		F	61
		" LAURA R	WIFE	W	F	Apr.1878	22	M	7	3	3	KY	KY	KY							✓	✓	✓				
		" BESSIE	DAU	W	F	Oct.1894	5	S				KY	KY	KY													
		" JOHN L.	SON	W	M	Nov.1897	2	S				KY	KY	KY													
		" MABEL	DAU	W	F	Nov.1899	7/12	S				KY	KY	KY													
80	80	CRAWFORD, SAMUEL	HEAD	W	M	Jul.1848	51	WD				KY	KY	KY				BLACKSMITH			✓	✓		O		H	
		" MARY Q.	DAU	W	F	Nov.1873	26	S				KY	KY	KY				TELEPHONE OPERATOR			✓	✓	✓				
		" LAURA	DAU	W	F	Jan.1877	23	S				KY	KY	KY				SCHOOL TEACHER 7			✓	✓	✓				
		" ESTELLA	DAU	W	F	Sep.1879	20	S				KY	KY	KY				AT SCHOOL		5	✓	✓	✓				
		" ANNIE	DAU	W	F	Feb.1882	18	S				KY	KY	KY				AT SCHOOL		5	✓	✓	✓				
		" BETTIE	DAU	W	F	Nov.1884	15	S				KY	KY	KY				AT SCHOOL		5	✓	✓	✓				
		" BLANCH	DAU	W	F	May.1892	8	S				KY	KY	KY				AT SCHOOL		5						R	
81	81	JACKSON, GEO. W	HEAD	W	M	Mar.1872	28	M	8			KY	IN	TN				DAY LABORER 2			✓	✓	✓	R		H	
		" MINNIE	WIFE	W	F	Jan.1877	23	M	8	4	3	KY	TN	TN							✓	✓					
		" ALTIE P.	DAU	W	F	Jul.1894	5	S				KY	KY	KY													
		" DENNIS M.	SON	W	M	Jan.1897	3	S				KY	KY	KY													
		" BETHEL O.	SON	W	M	Oct.1898	1	S				KY	KY	KY										R		F	62
82	82	FORD, JOHN H.	HEAD	W	M	May.1878	22	S				KY	IN	IN				FARMER			✓	✓	✓	O		H	
83	83	COMER, SARAH T.	HEAD	W	F	Nov.1851	48	WD				KY	KY	KY							✓	✓	✓				
		" MAY C.	DAU	W	F	Aug.1880	19	S				KY	KY	KY							✓	✓	✓	R		H	
	84	GREEN, SIDNEY M.	HEAD	W	M	May.1868	32	M	8			TN	KY	KY				DRUMMER 0			✓	✓	✓				
		" LODI	WIFE	W	F	Oct.1875	24	M	8	1	1	KY	KY	KY							✓	✓	✓				
		" EDWARD	SON	W	M	Feb.1895	5	S				KY	TN	KY										R		H	
84	85	TAYLOR, OSCAR W.	HEAD	W	M	Mar.1870	30	M	9			KY	TN	TN				DAY LABORER			✓	✓	✓				
		" LILLIE M.	WIFE	W	F	Jan.1870	30	M	9	6	4	MO	TN	KY							✓	✓		R		H	
		" ROLLIE	SON	W	M	Dec.1891	8	S				TN	KY	MO				AT SCHOOL		4½							

TWELFTH CENSUS OF THE UNITED STATES 1900

STATE - KENTUCKY
COUNTY - MONROE
Township or other division **GAMALIEL**

Enumerator **ISAAC N. RENEAU**

Supervisor's Dist. No. **102** Sheet No.
Enumeration Dist. No. **87**

No. of Family	No. of Dwelling	NAME	Relation	Color	Sex	Date of Birth Mon/Yr	Age at last birthday	Marital Status	# Years married	Mother of how many children?	# of these children living	Place of birth (this person)	Father of this person	Mother of this person	Year of immigr.	# years in U.S.	Naturalization	Occupation 10 years +	Months not employed	Attended school in months	Can read	Can write	Speak English	Owned or Rent	Owned - no mortage	Farm or house	# of Farm schedule
		TAYLOR, LUCY	DAU	W	F	Jun.1893	6	S				TN	KY	MO													
		" EVA	DAU	W	F	Dec.1896	3	S				KY	KY	MO													
		" DAISY	DAU	W	F	Sep.1898	9/12	S				KY	KY	MO													
85	86	HOLLAND, BETHIE E	Head	W	F	Oct.1869	30	WD				KY	KY	KY							✓	X ✓	✓	R		H	
		" MARY L.	DAU	W	F	Apr.1887	13	S				TN	TN	KY				AT SCHOOL		2	✓	X ✓					
		" DOLLIE A.	DAU	W	F	May.1890	10	S				TN	TN	KY				AT School		2	✓	X ✓					
		" LIZZIE J.	DAU	W	F	Dec.1896	3	S				KY	TN	KY													
86	87	CLARK, WILLIAM H.	Head	W	M	Mar.1861	39	M	6			KY	TN	TN				FARMER			✓	✓	✓	O	F	F	63
		" ANNIE L.	WIFE	W	F	Jan.1872	28	M	6	3	2	KY	KY	KY							✓	✓	✓				
		" ROXIE	DAU	W	F	Nov.1894	5	S				KY	KY	KY													
		" DAVIE	SON	W	M	Feb.1900	4/12	S				KY	KY	KY													
87	88	CLARK, SAMUEL H.	Head	W	M	Mar.1866	34	M	14			KY	KY	KY				FARMER			✓	✓	✓	O	F	F	
		" LIZZIE	WIFE	W	F	Dec.1866	33	M	14	7	7	KY	KY	KY							✓	✓	✓				
		" ZORA	DAU	W	F	Feb.1887	13	S				KY	KY	KY				AT SCHOOL		5	✓	✓	✓				
		" OMER	SON	W	M	Mar.1889	11	S				KY	KY	KY				AT School		2	✓	X	✓				
		" VERDIE	DAU	W	F	Jul.1891	8	S				KY	KY	KY				AT School		5							
		" ALTIE	DAU	W	F	Oct.1893	1	S				KY	KY	KY													
		" TAN	SON	W	M	Dec.1895	4	S				KY	KY	KY													
		" MAUD	DAU	W	F	Apr.1898	2	S				KY	KY	KY													
		" ANNIE	DAU	W	F	Feb.1900	3/12	S				KY	KY	KY													
88	89	SUTTON, JOHN W.	HEAD	W	M	Mar.1870	30	M	11			TN	TN	TN				FARMER			✓	✓	✓	R		F	64
		" BELL	WIFE	W	F	Dec.1862	37	M	11	1	1	KY	TN	TN							X	✓	✓				
		" PERRY F.	SON	W	M	May.1882	18	S				TN	TN	TN				FARM LABORER			✓	✓	✓				
89	90	RUSSELL, KINCHEN W.	Head	W	M	Jan.1862	38	WD				KY	KY	KY				FARMER			X	X	✓	O	F	F	65
		" WILLIE E.	SON	W	M	Oct.1881	18	S				KY	KY	KY				FARM LABORER			X	X	✓				
		" LONNA E.	SON	W	M	Nov.1883	16	S				KY	KY	KY				FARM LABORER			X	X	✓				

STATE - KENTUCKY
COUNTY - MONROE
Township or other division GAMALIEL   Enumerator ISAAC N. RENEAU

Supervisor's Dist. No. _102_ Sheet No.
Enumeration Dist. No. _87_

No. of Family	No. of Dwelling	NAME	Relation	Color	Sex	DATE OF BIRTH Mon/Yr	Age at last birthday	Marital Status	# Years married	Mother of how many children?	# of these children living	Place of birth (this person)	Father of this person	Mother of this person	Year of immigr.	# years in U.S.	Naturalization	OCCUPATION 10 years +	Months not employed	Attended school in months	Can read	Can write	Speak English	Owned or Rent	Owned –no mortage	Farm or house	# of farm schedule
		RUSSELL, DOCTOR J.	Son	W	M	Jul.1886	13	S				KY	KY	KY				FARM LABORER			X	X	✓				
		" KITTIE A.D.	Dau	W	F	Mar.1889	11	S				KY	KY	KY				AT SCHOOL		2	X	X	✓				
		" WILLIAM F.D.	Son	W	M	Aug.189	8	S				KY	KY	KY				AT SCHOOL		2							
		" JOHN E.B.	Son	W	M	Nov.1892	7	S				KY	KY	KY				AT SCHOOL		2							
		" DUDLIE	Son	W	M	May.1896	4	S				KY	KY	KY													
		" SIDNEY F	Son	W	M	Jun.1897	2	S				KY	KY	KY													
		KERBY, LAURA Z.	Lodger	W	F	Jun.1866	34	S		2	2	IND	TN	ALA							✓	✓					
		" ALLIE B.	—	W	F	Jan.1892	8	S				TN	TN	IND				AT SCHOOL		2½							
90	91	TURNER, JEFFERSON	HEAD	W	M	Aug.1867	32	M	3			KY	KY	KY				FARMER			X	X	✓	R	F	66	
		" ELIZABETH	WIFE	W	F	Jul.1876	23	M	3	1	1	KY	TN	TN							X	X	✓				
		" VINA B.	DAU	W	F	Nov.1897	2	S				KY	KY	KY													
91	92	DISMAN, HENDERSON	HEAD	W	M	Sep.1844	55	M	36			TN	TN	TN				FARMER			✓	✓	✓	O	F	F	67
		" CALEY	WIFE	W	F	Mar.1852	48	M	36	6	3	TN	TX	TN							X	X	✓				
		" JOHN	Son	W	M	Apr.1882	18	S				KY	TN	TN				FARM LABORER			✓	✓	✓				
92	93	HUMPHREY, JOHN W.	HEAD	W	M	Apr.1850	29	M	29			KY	KY	KY				FARMER			✓	✓	✓	R	E	68	
		" MARY J.	WIFE	W	F	Feb.1853	29	M	29	12	4	TN	TN	KY							✓	✓	✓				
		" WILLIAM	Son	W	M	Dec.1875	24	S				IN	KY	IN				DAY LABORER	9		✓	✓	✓				
		" NOLIA B.	DAU	W	F	May.1886	14	S				IN	KY	TN				AT SCHOOL		4½	✓	✓	✓				
		" JOHN E.	Son	W	M	Feb.1888	12	S				TN	KY	TN				AT SCHOOL		4½	✓	✓	✓				
		" MARTHY J.	DAU	W	F	Mar.1892	8	S				KY	KY	IN				AT SCHOOL		3							
93	94	GWYNNE, JOE H.	HEAD	W	M	Sep.1863	36	M	8			TN	TN	TN							✓	✓		O	M	E	69
		" MARTHA	WIFE	W	F	Jul.1869	30	M	8	5	5	TN	TN	TN							X	X	✓				
		" ARDIE M.	DAU	W	F	Oct.1883	16	S				TN	TN	TN							✓	X	✓				
		" ROBERT E.	Son	W	M	Nov.1892	7	S				TN	TN	TN				AT SCHOOL		5							
		" JEAMS H.	Son	W	M	May.1894	6	S				TN	TN	TN													
		" BONNIE M.	DAU	W	F	Dec.1895	4	S				TN	TN	TN													

STATE - KENTUCKY
COUNTY - MONROE
Township or other division **GAMALIEL**   Enumerator **ISAAC N. RENEAU**

Supervisor's Dist. No. **102** Sheet No.
Enumeration Dist. No. **87**

No. of Family	No. of Dwelling	NAME	Relation	Color	Sex	DATE OF BIRTH Mon/Yr	Age at last birthday	Marital Status	# Years married	Mother of how many children?	# of these children living	Place of birth this person	Father of this person	Mother of this person	Year of immigr.	# years in U.S.	Naturalization	OCCUPATION 10 years +	Months not employed	Attended school in months	Can read	Can write	Speak English	Owned or Rent	Owned -no mortage	Farm or house	# of farm schedule	
		GWYNNE, MARY C.	DAU	W	F	MAR 1898	2	S				KY	TN	TN														
		" REGGIE	SON	W	M	JAN 1900	5/12	S				KY	TN	TN														
94	95	BLANKINSHIP, E/ABEL	HEAD	W	F	AUG 1866	33	WD		6	5	KY	KY	TN							✓	✓		R	H			
		" BERTIE C.	SON	W	M	AUG 1887	12	S				KY	TN	KY				AT SCHOOL		1	✓	X	✓					
		" HERBERT W.	SON	W	M	JUL 1889	10	S				KY	TN	KY				AT SCHOOL		1	✓	X	✓					
		" RUTHA J.	DAU	W	F	AUG 1892	7	S				KY	TN	KY														
		" WALTER T.	SON	W	M	FEB 1893	7	S				KY	TN	KY				AT SCHOOL		1								
		" LILLIE B	DAU	W	F	JUL 1898	1	S				KY	TN	KY														
95	96	RYHERD, SARAH J.	HEAD	W	F	AUG 1845	54	WD		9	7	TN	TN	TN				FARMER			✓	✓		O	FF	70		
		" CLAY	SON	W	M	SEP 1867	32	S				KY	KY	TN				FARMER			✓	✓						
		" VALENTINE	SON	W	M	DEC 1877	22	S				KY	KY	TN				FARMER			✓	✓						
		" SARAH	DAU	W	F	JUN 1880	19	S				KY	KY	TN							✓	X	✓					
		" BETTIE T.	DAU	W	F	JAN 1884	16	S				KY	KY	TN							✓	✓						
96	97	TURNER, HAYDON	HEAD	W	M	OCT 1841	58	M	1			KY	VA	TN				FARMER			✓	✓	✓	O	FF	71		
		" ESPASIA	WIFE	W	F	FEB 1856	44	M	1	0	0	KY	TN	KY							✓	✓	✓					
		" WILLIAM S.	SON	W	M	AUG 1875	24	S				KY	KY	KY				FARMER			✓	✓	✓					
		" CASIL C.	SON	W	M	JUL 1883	16	S				KY	KY	TN				FARM LABORER			✓	✓	✓					
97	98	OGDEN, NANCY J.	HEAD	W	F	JUL 1863	36	WD		6	6	TN	KY	TN							✓	X	✓	R	H			
		" HILLY H.	SON	W	M	APR 1886	14	S				TN	KY	TN				FARM LABORER	7		X	X	✓					
		" NORA T.	DAU	W	F	AUG 1888	11	S				KY	KY	TN							✓	X	✓					
		" JAMES E.	SON	W	M	MAR 1892	8	S				TN	KY	TN														
		" BERNICE A.	DAU	W	F	MAY 1895	5	S				KY	KY	TN														
		" GEORGIAN	DAU	W	F	JAN 1898	1	S				KY	KY	TN														
98	99	WOODCOCK, THOMAS	HEAD	W	M	AUG 1844	55	M	32			TN	TN	TN				FARMER			✓	✓	✓	O	FF	72		
		" SUSAN	WIFE	W	F	JAN 1855	55	M	32	7	5	TN	TN	TN							X	X	✓					
		" LIZZIE	DAU	W	F	AUG 1872	27	S				KY	TN	TN							✓	✓	✓					

STATE - KENTUCKY
COUNTY - MONROE
Township or other division GAMALIEL   Enumerator ISAAC N. RENEAU

Supervisor's Dist. No. 102 Sheet No.
Enumeration Dist. No. 87

No. of Family	No. of Dwelling	NAME	Relation	Color	Sex	DATE OF BIRTH Mon/Yr	Age at last birthday	Marital Status	# Years married	Mother of how many children?	# of these children living	Place of birth (this person)	Father of this person	Mother of this person	Year of immigr.	# years in U.S.	Naturalization	OCCUPATION 10 years +	Months not employed	Attended school in months	Can read	Can write	Speak English	Owned or Rent	Owned -no mortage	Farm or house	# of farm schedule
		WOODCOCK, JAMIE	DAU	W	F	Nov. 1874	25	S				KY	TN	TN							✓	✓	✓				
		" MAMIE T.	DAU	W	F	Jul. 1884	15	S				KY	TN	TN							✓	✓	✓				
		RYHERD, MALLEY	DAU	W	F	Jun. 1877	22	WD				KY	KY	TN							✓	✓	✓				
99	100	JINKENS, CYRUS A.	HEAD	W	M	Jan. 1841	59	M	33			KY	TN	TN				FARMER			✓	✓	✓	O	F	F	73
		" ROSEANN	WIFE	W	F	May. 1846	54	M	33	6	6	KY	VA	KY							✓	✓	✓				
		" FRANK B.	SON	W	M	Jul. 1879	20	S				KY	KY	KY				FARM LABORER			✓	✓	✓				
		" MAUD J.	DAU	W	F	May. 1883	17	S				KY	KY	KY				AT SCHOOL		2	✓	✓	✓				
		" THOMAS J.	SON	W	M	Sep. 1886	13	S				KY	KY	KY				AT SCHOOL		3	✓	✓	✓				
100	101	JINKENS, THOMAS	HEAD	W	M	Aug. 1849	50	M	23			KY	KY	KY				FARMER			✓	✓	✓	O	F	F	74
		" SERILDA J.	WIFE	W	F	Jun. 1858	41	M	23	9	9	KY	KY	TN							✓	✓	✓				
		" JOHN P.	SON	W	M	Dec. 1879	20	S				KY	KY	KY				FARM LABORER			✓	✓	✓				
		" JAMES A.	SON	W	M	Dec. 1881	18	S				KY	KY	KY				FARM LABORER		4	✓	✓	✓				
		" ANNIE	DAU	W	F	Dec. 1885	14	S				KY	KY	KY				AT SCHOOL		5	✓	✓	✓				
		" SAMMIE	SON	W	M	Dec. 1885	14	S				KY	KY	KY				AT SCHOOL		4	✓	✓	✓				
		" ELLIE	DAU	W	F	Jul. 1888	11	S				KY	KY	KY				AT SCHOOL		5	✓	✓	✓				
		" ROXIE	DAU	W	F	Sep. 1890	9	S				KY	KY	KY				AT SCHOOL		6	✓	✓	✓				
		" BETTIE	DAU	W	F	Mar. 1894	6	S				KY	KY	KY				AT SCHOOL		5							
		" HATTIE	DAU	W	F	Sep. 1896	3	S				KY	KY	KY													
		" STANLEY	SON	W	M	Oct. 1900 7/12		S				KY	KY	KY													
101	102	MEADOR, ELZIE M.	HEAD	W	M	Jun. 1859	40	M	12			TN	TN	TN				PHYSICIAN			✓	✓	✓	O	F	F	75
		" CAMILA C.	WIFE	W	F	Dec. 1868	31	M	12	3	3	TN	TN	TN							✓	✓	✓				
		" HUBERT S.	SON	W	M	May. 1889	11	S				TN	TN	TN				AT SCHOOL		2	X	X	✓				
		" MALLIE E.	DAU	W	F	Nov. 1893	6	S				TN	TN	TN				AT SCHOOL		1							
		" ELZIE A.	SON	W	M	Aug. 1898	1	S				TN	TN	TN													
102	103	CRAG, JOHN T.	HEAD	W	M	Aug. 1867	32	M	8			TN	TN	TN				FARM LABORER			X	X	✓	R		H	
		" IDER A.	WIFE	W	F	Dec. 1875	24	M	8	3	3	KY	KY	KY							✓	✓	✓				

STATE - KENTUCKY
COUNTY - MONROE
Township or other division **GAMALIEL**

Enumerator **ISAAC N. RENEAU**

Supervisor's Dist. No. _102_ Sheet No.
Enumeration Dist. No. _87_

No. of Family	No. of Dwelling	NAME	Relation	Color	Sex	DATE OF BIRTH Mon/Yr	Age at last birthday	Marital Status	# Years married	Mother of how many children?	# of these children living	NATIVITY Place of birth [this person]	Father of this person	Mother of this person	CITIZENSHIP Year of immigr.	# years in U.S.	Naturalization	OCCUPATION 10 years +	Months not employed	EDUCATION Attended school in months	Can read	Can write	Speak English	OWNERSHIP Owned or Rent	Owned -no mortage	Farm or house	# of farm schedule
		CRAG, CAMIE M.	DAU	W	F	JAN. 1893	7	S				TN	TN	KY				AT SCHOOL		4½							
		" DEWITT	SON	W	M	DEC. 1894	5	S				TN	TN	KY													
		" HORACE G.	SON	W	M	AUG. 1899	10/12	S				TN	TN	KY													
103	104	DYRE, ROBERT	HEAD	W	M	OCT. 1855	44	M	24			KY	TN	TN				FARMER			✓	✓	✓	O	F	F	76
		" SARAH S.	WIFE	W	F	AUG. 1851	48	M	24	2	2	KY	KY	KY							✓	✓					
		" CICERO	SON	W	M	MAR. 1892	8	S				KY	KY	KY				AT SCHOOL		4							
105		DYRE, LEN C.	HEAD	W	M	AUG. 1878	21	M	0			TN	KY	KY				FARMER			✓	✓		R		F	77
		" ELLEN	WIFE	W	F	FEB. 1874	16	M	0	0	0	TN	TN	TN							✓	✓					
104	106	CREEK, GEORGE B.	HEAD	W	M	OCT. 1861	38	M	3			KY	KY	KY				FARMER			✓	✓		R		F	78
		" SELA	WIFE	W	F	MAY 1876	24	M	3	3	3	TN	TN	TN							✓	✓					
		" LUCY	DAU	W	F	MAY 1888	12	S				KY	KY	TN				AT SCHOOL		2½	X	X	✓				
		" GEORGE	SON	W	M	OCT. 1898	1	S				KY	KY	KY													
		GREEN, GILLMORE	S-SON	W	M	JUL. 1891	8	S				KY	KY	KY				AT SCHOOL		5							
		" ELIJAH	S-SON	W	M	JUL. 1893	6	S				KY	KY	KY				AT SCHOOL		5							
105	107	GUM, SAMUEL	HEAD	W	M	JUN. 1851	48	M	20			KY	KY	KY				FARMER			✓	✓	✓	O	F	F	79
		" ALLEN	WIFE	W	F	JUL. 1852	47	M	20	6	4	TN	TN	TN							✓	✓	✓				
		" ROSELL	DAU	W	F	AUG. 1883	16	S				KY	KY	TN							✓	✓	✓				
		" BERTIE	SON	W	M	JAN. 1885	15	S				KY	KY	TN				AT SCHOOL		5	✓	✓	✓				
		" LOIS	DAU	W	F	JAN. 1889	11	S				KY	KY	TN				AT SCHOOL		4½	✓	✓	✓				
		" POSIE D.	SON	W	M	JUL. 1894	5	S				KY	KY	TN													
106	108	DUNCAN, WILLIAM H.	HEAD	W	M	MAY 1862	38	M	5			TN	TN	VA				FARMER			✓	✓	✓	O	F	F	80
		" ELLA	WIFE	W	F	FEB. 1867	33	M	5	4	1	KY	TN	KY							✓	✓	✓				
		" WINFORD	SON	W	M	APR. 1898	2	S				KY	TN	KY													
		" NANCY	MOTHER	W	F	APR. 1835	65	WD		13	9	VA	VA	VA							✓	✓	✓				
		" EDGAR E.	BROTHER	W	M	FEB. 1871	29	S				KY	TN	VA							✓	✓	✓				
107	109	EMBERTON, JASPER	HEAD	W	M	OCT. 1848	51	M	25			KY	KY	TN				FARMER			✓	✓	✓	O	F	F	81

—471—

STATE - KENTUCKY
COUNTY - MONROE
Township or other division **GAMALIEL** Enumerator **ISAAC N. RENEAU**

Supervisor's Dist. No. _102_ Sheet No.
Enumeration Dist. No. _87_

No. of Family	No. of Dwelling	NAME	Relation	Color	Sex	DATE OF BIRTH Mon/Yr	Age at last birthday	Marital Status	# Years married	Mother of how many children?	# of these children living	Place of birth [this person]	Father of this person	Mother of this person	Year of immigr.	# years in U.S.	Naturalization	OCCUPATION 10 years +	Months not employed	Attended school in months	Can read	Can write	Speak English	Owned or Rent	Owned -no mortage	Farm or house	# of farm schedule
		EMBERTON, LOIS M.	WIFE	W	F	APR. 1858	42	M	25	5	5	KY	KY	TN							✓	✓	✓				
		" ROXIE	DAU	W	F	JUL. 1877	22	S				KY	KY	KY				MUSIC TEACHER 4			✓	✓	✓				
		" PEARL	DAU	W	F	JUL. 1879	20	S				KY	KY	KY							✓	✓	✓				
		" ALTIE	DAU	W	F	JUN. 1881	18	S				KY	KY	KY				AT SCHOOL		5	✓	✓	✓				
		" HAYES	SON	W	M	FEB. 1887	13	S				KY	KY	KY				AT SCHOOL		5	✓	✓	✓				
108	110	PIPKIN, EDGAR A.	HEAD	B	M	JUN. 1873	26	M	1			KY	TN	KY				FARMER			✓	✓	✓	R		F	82
		" LOLLIE L.	WIFE	B	F	AUG. 1880	19	M	1	1	1	TN	KY	TN													
		" EDNA M.	DAU	B	F	FEB. 1900	4/12	S				KY	KY	TN													
109	111	TAYLOR, JOHN	HEAD	W	M	JUL. 1861	38	M	10			TN	TN	TN				MILLER			XX	✓	R		H		
		" SARAH	WIFE	W	F	AUG. 1870	29	M	10	7	6	TN	TN	TN							XX	✓					
		" CHARLEY	SON	W	M	MAR. 1886	14	S				TN	TN	TN				AT SCHOOL		1	✓	X	✓				
		" BERTHA	DAU	W	F	AUG. 1889	10	S				TN	TN	TN				AT SCHOOL		1	XX	✓					
		" FLOYD	SON	W	M	JUL. 1892	7	S				TN	TN	TN													
		" BELL	DAU	W	F	JAN. 1894	6	S				TN	TN	TN													
		" RUDAH	SON	W	M	MAY. 1898	2	S				KY	TN	TN													
		" LILLIE	DAU	W	F	JAN. 1900	5/12	S				KY	TN	TN													
110	112	THOMPSON, JAMES B.	HEAD	W	M	JAN. 1851	49	M	26			KY	VA	KY				FARMER			XX	✓	R		F	83	
		" LUCY A.	WIFE	W	F	JAN. 1859	41	M	26	10	7	KY	KY	KY							✓	✓	✓				
		" WILLIAM J.	SON	W	M	JAN. 1876	24	S				KY	KY	KY				FARM LABORER			✓	X	✓				
		" GEORGE R.	SON	W	M	OCT. 1883	16	S				KY	KY	KY				FARM LABORER			✓	X	✓				
		" MILLIE C.	DAU	W	F	APR. 1886	14	S				KY	KY	KY							✓	✓	✓				
		" RACHEL E.	DAU	W	F	JAN. 1889	11	S				KY	KY	KY				AT SCHOOL		5	✓	✓	✓				
		" LORA S.	DAU	W	F	NOV. 1895	4	S				KY	KY	KY													
		" BETTIE E.	DAU	W	F	SEP. 1898	1	S				KY	KY	KY													
111	113	CRAWFORD, JAMES B.	HEAD	W	M	OCT. 1850	49	M	9			KY	KY	KY				FARMER			✓	✓	✓	O		F	84
		" ANNIE	WIFE	W	F	JUL. 1850	49	M	9	0	0	KY	KY	KY							✓	✓	✓				

STATE - KENTUCKY
COUNTY - MONROE
Township or other division — GAMALIEL

Enumerator — ISAAC N. RENEAU

Supervisor's Dist. No. 102 Sheet No.
Enumeration Dist. No. 87

No. of Family	No. of Dwelling	NAME	Relation	Color	Sex	DATE OF BIRTH Mon/Yr	Age at last birthday	Marital Status	# Years married	Mother of how many children?	# of these children living	NATIVITY Place of birth (this person)	NATIVITY Father of this person	NATIVITY Mother of this person	CITIZENSHIP	OCCUPATION 10 years +	Months not employed	Attended school in months	Can read	Can write	Speak English	OWNERSHIP
		CRAWFORD, FLORA	DAU	W	F	Jun. 1880	19	S				KY	KY	KY		AT SCHOOL		5	✓	✓	✓	
		" JOSEPH E	SON	W	M	Feb. 1883	17	S				KY	KY	KY		AT SCHOOL		6	✓	✓	✓	
		" GENNIE P.	DAU	W	F	Sep. 1887	12	S				KY	KY	KY		AT SCHOOL		6	✓	✓	✓	
112	114	CROPPER, HENRY (S?)	HEAD	W	M	Aug. 1860	39	M	12			KY	TN	TN		FARMER			✓	✓	✓	O F F 85
		" FANNIE	WIFE	W	F	Jul. 1864	35	M	12	5	4	TN	TN	TN					✓	✓	✓	
		" WILLIAM T.	SON	W	M	Sep. 1888	11	S				KY	KY	TN		AT SCHOOL		4	✓	✓	✓	
		" SARAH M.	DAU	W	F	Sep. 1890	9	S				KY	KY	TN		AT SCHOOL		4				
		" JAMES E.	SON	W	M	Nov. 1892	7	S				KY	KY	TN		AT SCHOOL		3				
		" JOHN L.	SON	W	M	Jun. 1896	4	S				KY	KY	TN								
		" ELISABETH	Mother	W	F	Apr. 1820	80	WD		1	1	TN	NC	VA					✓	✓	✓	
113	115	CROPPER, SAMUEL	HEAD	W	M	Oct. 1857	42	M	20			TN	TN	TN		FARMER			✓	✓	✓	O F F 86
		" MARTHA A.	WIFE	W	F	Nov. 1862	37	M	20	6	6	TN	TN	TN					✓	✓	✓	
		" BRUCE A.	SON	W	M	Sep. 1884	15	S				KY	TN	TN		FARM LABORER		2	✓	✓	✓	
		" RETHA	DAU	W	F	Nov. 1887	12	S				KY	TN	TN		AT SCHOOL		1	✓	✓	✓	
		" CHARLEY	SON	W	M	Sep. 1890	9	S				KY	TN	TN		AT SCHOOL		2				
		" ARDIE	DAU	W	F	Feb. 1894	6	S				KY	TN	TN								
		" FRED	SON	W	M	Mar. 1897	3	S				KY	TN	TN								
		" DEVLAS H.	SON	W	M	Mar. 1881	19	M	0			KY	TN	TN		FARMER			✓	✓	✓	
		" SARAH A.	D-LAW	W	F	Aug. 1882	17	M	0	0	0	KY	TN	TN					✓	✓	✓	
114	116	TAYLOR, JOHN B.	HEAD	W	M	Nov. 1873	26	M	7			KY	KY	KY		FARMER			✓	✓	✓	O F F 87
		" CORA	WIFE	W	F	Oct. 1870	29	M	7	3	3	KY	KY	TN					✓	✓	✓	
		" EDWARD	SON	W	M	May 1894	6	S				TN	KY	KY								
		" LASKA	DAU	W	F	Apr. 1896	4	S				TN	KY	KY								
		" HERSHAL	SON	W	M	Nov. 1898	1	S				KY	KY	KY								
115	117	DECKARD, CRISTOPHER	HEAD	W	M	Oct. 1869	30	M	7			KY	KY	KY		FARMER			✓	✓	✓	O M F 88
		" SARAH	WIFE	W	F	Jul. 1866	33	M	7	4	4	KY	TN	KY					✓	✓	✓	

TWELFTH CENSUS OF THE UNITED STATES 1900

STATE - KENTUCKY
COUNTY - MONROE
Township or other division   GAMALIEL   Enumerator   ISAAC N. RENEAU

Supervisor's Dist. No. _102_ Sheet No.
Enumeration Dist. No. _87_

No. of Family	No. of Dwelling	NAME	Relation	Color	Sex	DATE OF BIRTH Mon/Yr	Age at last birthday	Marital Status	# Years married	Mother of how many children?	# of these children living	Place of birth (this person)	Father of this person	Mother of this person	Year of immigr.	# years in U.S.	Naturalization	OCCUPATION 10 years +	Months not employed	Attended school in months	Can read	Can write	Speak English	Owned or Rent	Owned -no mortage	Farm or house	# of farm schedule	
		DECKARD, OTIS L.	Son	W	M	Sep. 1893	6	S				KY	KY	KY														
		" OCIE M.	Dau	W	F	May 1895	5	S				KY	KY	KY														
		" ARTHUR C.	Son	W	M	Jul. 1897	2	S				KY	KY	KY														
		" OLIE B.	Dau	W	F	Dec. 1898 6/12		S	(1899?)			KY	KY	KY														
116	118	DECKARD, ALLEN S.	Head	W	M	Mar. 1857	43	M	24			KY	TN	IL				FARMER			✓	✓	✓	O	F	F	89	
		" MILLIE C.	Wife	W	F	Mar. 1859	41	M	24	5	4	KY	KY	KY							✓	✓	✓					
		" CISERO	Son	W	M	Jan. 1880	20	S				TN	KY	KY				FARM LABORER			✓	✓	✓					
		" LUCRETIA G.	Dau	W	F	Dec. 1881	18	S				KY	KY	KY							✓	✓	✓					
		" EUBERT W.	Son	W	M	Feb. 1885	15	S				KY	KY	KY				AT SCHOOL			✓	✓	✓					
117	119	FORD, JAMES T.	Head	W	M	Oct. 1870	29	M	10			KY	TN	TN				FARMER			✓	X	✓	R		F	90	
		" ESTELLER	Wife	W	F	Oct. 1872	27	M	10	4	4	KY	TN	KY							✓	✓	✓					
		" BULAH	Dau	W	F	Sep. 1890	9	S				KY	KY	KY				AT SCHOOL		5								
		" JOHN T.	Son	W	M	Aug. 1894	5	S				KY	KY	KY														
		" HOMER	Son	W	M	Jun. 1896	3	S				KY	KY	KY														
		" BESSIE	Dau	W	F	Sep. 1898	1	S				KY	KY	KY														
118	120	RIGGS, CESIL C.	Head	W	M	Jan. 1839	61	M	16			TN	TN	TN				PHYSICIAN			✓	✓	✓	O	F	F	91	
		" SARAH L.	Wife	W	F	Jul. 1860	39	M	16	6	2	TN	TN	TN							✓	✓	✓					
		" MAGNAS	Son	W	M	Feb. 1885	15	S				KY	TN	TN				AT SCHOOL		4	✓	✓	✓					
		" THOMAS T.	Son	W	M	May 1886	14	S				KY	TN	TN				AT SCHOOL		3½	✓	✓	✓					
		McCRACKIN, SARAH J.	Lodger	W	F	Nov. 1844	55	S				TN	TN	TN				HOUSEKEEPER			X	X	✓					
		DUNCAN, MARY	Lodger	W	F	Oct. 1841	58	WD				TN	TN	KY							✓	✓	✓					
		BROOKS, WILLIAM M.	Hired	W	M	Jul. 1879	20	S				KY	TN	KY				FARM LABORER			✓	✓	✓					
119	121	RYHERD, ULYSSES G.	Head	W	M	Nov. 1867	32	M	7			KY	KY	KY				FARM LABORER			✓	✓	✓	R		H		
		" MARY L.	Wife	W	F	Dec. 1862	37	M	7	5	5	KY	TN	KY							✓	✓	✓					
		" BRANSFORD	Son	W	M	Jan. 1887	13	S				KY	KY	KY							X	X	✓					
		" DEHAVEN	Son	W	M	Aug. 1894	5	S				KY	KY	KY														

STATE - KENTUCKY
COUNTY - MONROE
Township or other division **GAMALIEL**   Enumerator **ISAAC N. RENEAU**

Supervisor's Dist. No. _102_   Sheet No. ____
Enumeration Dist. No. _87_ _____

No. of Family	No. of Dwelling	NAME	Relation	Color	Sex	DATE OF BIRTH Mon/Yr	Age at last birthday	Marital Status	#Years married	Mother of how many children?	# of these children living	Place of birth (this person)	Father of this person	Mother of this person	Year of immigr.	# years in U.S.	Naturalization	OCCUPATION 10 years +	Months not employed	Attended school in months	Can read	Can write	Speak English	Owned or Rent	Owned –no mortgage	Farm or house	# of farm schedule
		RYHERD, BENNIE E.	SON	W	M	SEP.1896	3	S				KY	KY	KY													
		" NANSIE	DAU	W	F	OCT. 1898	1	S				KY	KY	KY													
120	122	JENKINS, ISAAC A.	HEAD	W	M	FEB.1860	40	M	20			KY	KY	KY				FARMER			✓	✓	✓	O	F	F	92
		" SARAH J.	WIFE	W	F	DEC.1848	51	M	20			KY	TN	TN							✓	✓	✓				
121	123	JENKINS, WILLIS F.	HEAD	W	M	JAN.1877	28	M	8			KY	KY	KY				FARMER			✓	✓	✓	O	F	F	93
		" NETTIE	WIFE	W	F	JAN.1876	24	M	8	3	2	KY	KY	KY							✓	✓	✓				
		" ALTIE V.	DAU	W	F	MAY.1896	4	S				KY	KY	KY													
		" DAISY A.	DAU	W	F	OCT.1899	8/12	S				KY	KY	KY													
		" THOMAS A.	COUSIN	W	M	NOV.1889	10	S				(TEXAS) TX	KY	KY				A.T. SCHOOL		4½	✓	✓					
122	124	JENKINS, THOMAS	HEAD	W	M	MAY.1836	64	WD				KY	VA	VA				FARMER			✓		✓	O	F	F	94
		" GEORGE	GR-SON	W	M	JUN.1892	7	S				KY	KY	KY				A.T. SCHOOL		5							
123	125	JENKINS, SAMUEL	HEAD	W	M	JAN.1877	23	M	2			KY	KY	KY				FARMER			✓	✓	✓	O	F	F	95
		" FLAUDA	WIFE	W	F	JUL.1881	18	M	2	1	1	KY	KY	KY							✓	✓	✓				
		" CLARA E.	DAU	W	F	NOV.1898	1	S				KY	KY	KY													
124	126	ENGLAND, BARTON	HEAD	W	M	APR.1820	80	M	18			KY	VA	KY				FARMER			X	X	✓	O	F	F	96
		" SARAH E.	WIFE	W	F	JUN.1834	65	M	18			TN	TN	NC							✓	✓	✓				
125	127	CREEK, JAMES S.	HEAD	W	M	DEC.1837	62	M	35			KY	KY	KY				FARMER			✓	✓	✓	O	F	F	97
		" ELISABETH	WIFE	W	F	JUL.1841	58	M	35	12	9	KY	TN	TN							✓	✓	✓				
		" JASPER P.	SON	W	M	SEP.1877	22	S				KY	KY	KY				FARM LABORER			✓	✓	✓				
		" THOMAS D.	SON	W	M	SEP.1879	20	S				KY	KY	KY				FARM LABORER		3½	✓	✓	✓				
		" ROSA E.	DAU	W	F	AUG.1883	16	S				KY	KY	KY				A.T. SCHOOL		4	✓	✓	✓				
		" SAMUEL H.	SON	W	M	JUL.1885	14	S				KY	KY	KY				A.T. SCHOOL		5	✓	✓	✓				
		" BOB C.	SON	W	M	NOV.1888	11	S				KY	KY	KY				A.T. SCHOOL		5	✓	✓	✓				
126	128	TURNER, ROSS	HEAD	W	M	AUG.1848	51	M	1			KY	VA	KY				FARMER			✓	✓	✓	O	F	F	98
		" MATTIE	WIFE	W	F	OCT.1863	36	M	1	0	0	TN	TN	TN							✓	✓	✓				
		" GEORGE P.	SON	W	M	APR.1880	20	S				KY	KY	KY				FARM LABORER		4½	✓	✓	✓				

STATE - KENTUCKY
COUNTY - MONROE
Township or other division GAMALIEL   Enumerator ISAAC N. RENEAU

Supervisor's Dist. No. 102 Sheet No.
Enumeration Dist. No. 87

No. of Family	No. of Dwelling	NAME	Relation	Color	Sex	Date of Birth Mon/Yr	Age at last birthday	Marital Status	#Years married	Mother of how many children?	# of these children living	Place of birth [this person]	Father of this person	Mother of this person	Year of immigr.	#years in U.S.	Naturalization	Occupation	Months not employed	Attended school in months	Can read	Can write	Speak English	Owned or Rent	Owned-no mortage	Farm or house	# of farm schedule
		TURNER, SUSAN B.	DAU	W	F	Jul.1883	16	S				KY	KY	KY				AT SCHOOL		4½	✓	✓					
		" WILLIAM A.	SON	W	M	Dec.1886	13	S				KY	KY	KY				AT SCHOOL		4½	✓	✓					
27	29	YORK, JAMES J.C.	HEAD	W	M	Jun.1872	27	M	0			KY	KY	TN				FARMER			✓	✓	✓	R		F	99
		" DORA	WIFE	W	F	Mar.1881	19	M	0	1	1	TN	KY	TN							X	X	✓				
		CRAYTON	DAU	W	F	Apr.1900	2/12	S				KY	KY	KY													
28	30	BROWN, NANCY E.	HEAD	W	F	Sep.1855	44	WD		3	2	TN	TN	TN				FARMER			X	X	✓	O		F	100
		" ODIE O.	SON	W	M	Aug.1891	8	S				KY	TN	TN													
		" OLIE D.	DAU	W	F	Aug.1892	7	S				KY	TN	TN													
		RIGGS, SINTHY	Mother	W	F	Jun.1837	62	WD		9	6	TN	TN	TN							✓	X	✓				
		" BELL	Sister	W	F	Nov.1877	22	S				KY	TN	TN							✓	✓	✓				
29	31	ENGLAND, HARLIN	HEAD	W	M	Aug.1850	49	M	8			KY	KY	KY				FARMER			✓	✓	✓	O		F	101
		" MARTHA	WIFE	W	F	Jan.1866	34	M	8	4	4	KY	KY	KY							✓	✓	✓				
		" DELA	DAU	W	F	Jan.1877	23	S				KY	KY	KY							✓	✓	✓				
		" ROMA E.	DAU	W	F	Nov.1881	18	S				KY	KY	KY							✓	✓	✓				
		" ROLLIE	DAU	W	F	Oct.1882	17	S				KY	KY	KY				AT		5	✓	✓	✓				
		" ADER	DAU	W	F	Oct.1884	15	S				KY	KY	KY				AT		2½	✓	✓	✓				
		" HERBERT	SON	W	M	Feb.1887	13	S				KY	KY	KY				AT		2½	✓	✓	✓				
		" NOLIE	DAU	W	F	Aug.1889	10	S				KY	KY	KY				AT		5	✓	✓	✓				
		" ROXIE	DAU	W	F	Jul.1892	7	S				KY	KY	KY				AT		5							
		" HARVIE	SON	W	M	Aug.1893	6	S				KY	KY	KY				AT		2½							
		" HARRISON	SON	W	M	Jul.1895	4	S				KY	KY	KY													
		" BARTON	SON	W	M	Jan.1898	2	S				KY	KY	KY													
30	32	CREEK, WILLIAM	HEAD	W	M	Sep.1866	34	M	7			KY	KY	KY				FARMER			✓	✓	✓	O		F	102
		" TRUDY E.	WIFE	W	F	Jun.1872	27	M	7	3	3	KY	KY	KY							✓	✓	✓				
		" DUEY	SON	W	M	Aug.1893	6	S				KY	KY	KY				AT SCHOOL		5							
		" MARY T.	DAU	W	F	Jul.1895	4	S				KY	KY	KY													

STATE - KENTUCKY
COUNTY - MONROE
Township or other division: GAMALIEL   Enumerator: ISAAC N. RENEAU

Supervisor's Dist. No. 102   Sheet No.
Enumeration Dist. No. 87

Location (Fam/Dwel)	Name	Relation	Color	Sex	Date of Birth Mon/Yr	Age	Marital Status	Yrs married	Mother # children	# living	Birthplace / Father / Mother	Occupation	Months not employed	Attended school	Can read	Can write	Speak English	Ownership
	CREEK, ELISABETH	DAU	W	F	APR 1900	2/12	S				KY KY KY							
	JENKINS, NOLIE	NIECE	W	F	SEP 1891	8	S				KY							
131/133	KIRKPATRICK, NILES	HEAD	B	M	MAY 1842	58	M	5			KY	FARM LABORER		X	X	✓		R H
	" ARTIE	WIFE	B	F	Jul 1874	25	M	5	2	1	KY			X	X	✓		
	" MILLY M	DAU	B	F	Jun 1897	2	S				KY							
	EVANS, OLLIE	NIECE	B	F	Jan 1891	9	S				KY							
132/134	REAGAN, SILAS S.	HEAD	W	M	MAR 1836	64	M	40			TN VA VA	FARMER			✓	✓	✓	O M F 103
	" ADLAD	WIFE	W	F	DEC 1839	60	M	40	9	5	TN VA VA				✓	✓	✓	
	" ENOC G.	SON	W	M	MAR 1875	25	S				KY TN TN	FARM LABORER			✓	✓	✓	
	" JOSEPH C.	SON	W	M	Nov 1881	18	S				TN TN TN	FARM LABORER			✓	✓	✓	
	HARGIS, SAMUEL	GR-SON	W	M	AUG 1885	14	S				KY TN KY	FARM LABORER	2½		✓	✓	✓	
	" VIRGIE	GR-DAU	W	F	DEC 1887	12	S				TN TN KY	AT SCHOOL	3		✓	✓		
	" MANDA J.	GR-DAU	W	F	FEB 1890	10	S				KY TN KY	AT SCHOOL	3		✓	✓	✓	
133/135	RIGGS, SAMUEL H.	HEAD	W	M	JUN 1862	37	M	16			KY TN TN	FARMER			✓	✓	✓	O FF 104
	" FANNIE	WIFE	W	F	Jul 1863	36	M	16	6	6	KY KY KY				✓	✓		
	" LEXIE	DAU	W	F	OCT 1884	15	S				KY KY KY	AT SCHOOL	5		✓	✓	✓	
	" ARLOE C.	SON	W	M	JAN 1886	14	S				KY KY KY	AT SCHOOL	4		✓	✓	✓	
	" NELLIE	DAU	W	F	APR 1888	12	S				KY KY KY	AT SCHOOL	4		✓	✓	✓	
	" CLAY H.	SON	W	M	APR 1894	6	S				KY KY KY							
	" DIVIE R.	SON	W	M	APR 1894	6	S				KY KY KY							
	" ESSIE	DAU	W	F	JUN 1897	2	S				KY KY KY							
134/136	BURGESS, JESSIE	HEAD	W	M	SEP 1854	45	M	26			MO VA TN	FARMER		X	X	✓		R F 105
	" CANZADY	WIFE	W	F	Jan 1853	47	M	26	6	6	KY TN KY			X	X	✓		
	" HILLER C.	SON	W	M	SEP 1875	24	S				KY MO KY	FARM LABORER			✓	✓	✓	
	" AUSTIN	SON	W	M	JUN 1878	21	S				KY MO KY	FARM LABORER			✓	✓	✓	
	" CHARLES S.	SON	W	M	JUN 1881	18	S				KY MO KY	FARM LABORER	4		✓	✓	✓	

STATE - KENTUCKY
COUNTY - MONROE
Township or other division GAMALIEL   Enumerator ISAAC N. RENEAU

Supervisor's Dist. No. 102   Sheet No.
Enumeration Dist. No. 87

No. of Family	No. of Dwelling	NAME	Relation	Color	Sex	DATE OF BIRTH Mon/Yr	Age at last birthday	Marital Status	# Years married	Mother of how many children	# of these children living	Place of birth [this person]	Father of this person	Mother of this person	Year of immigr.	# years in U.S.	Naturalization	OCCUPATION 10 years +	Months not employed	Attended school in months	Can read	Can write	Speak English	Owned or Rent	Owned -no mortgage	Farm or house	# of farm schedule
(136)		BURGESS, LELER B.	DAU	W	F	Jan. 1886	14	S				KY	MO	KY				AT SCHOOL		5	✓	✓	✓				
		" VEONIA	DAU	W	F	May. 1889	11	S				KY	MO	KY				AT SCHOOL		3½	X	X	✓				
		" ELIZABETH	MOTHER	W	F	May. 1814	86	WD		5	4	TN	TN	TN							X	X	✓				
135	137	FULSE, JARAT J.	HEAD	W	M	Jan. 1858	42	M	14			KY	TN	TN				FARMER			✓	✓	✓	O	F	F	106
		" LUCY A.	WIFE	W	F	Aug. 1863	36	M	14	5	5	KY	TN	KY							✓	✓	✓				
		" NEUMORS	SON	W	M	Mar. 1887	13	S				KY	KY	KY				AT SCHOOL		4½	✓	✓	✓				
		" ALTIE M.	DAU	W	F	Oct. 1889	10	S				KY	KY	KY				AT SCHOOL		4½	✓	✓	✓				
		" TOMMIE	SON	W	M	Jul. 1892	7	S				KY	KY	KY				AT SCHOOL		3							
		" ADER	DAU	W	F	Aug. 1898	1	S				KY	KY	KY													
		" MAMIE Z.	DAU	W	F	May. 1900	1/12	S				KY	KY	KY													
		BRYANT, WILLIAM J.	FATHER IN LAW	W	M	Mar. 1837	63	WD				TN	TN	VA				FARMER			✓	✓	✓			F	
136	138	FULSE, BURLIE J.	HEAD	W	M	Nov. 1877	22	M	4			KY	KY	KY				FARMER			✓	✓	✓	R		F	107
		" PATTIE F.	WIFE	W	F	Mar. 1879	21	M	4	4	2	KY	KY	KY							✓	✓	✓				
		" BESSIE M.	DAU	W	F	Mar. 1898	2	S				KY	KY	KY													
		" JAMES H.	SON	W	M	Mar. 1900	2/12	S				KY	KY	KY													
137	139	BURNETTE, ABRAHAM	HEAD	W	M	Sep. 1866	33	M	14			KY	KY	KY				FARMER			X	X	✓	R		F	108
		" MARY L.	WIFE	W	F	Mar. 1867	33	M	14	5	5	KY	KY	KY							✓	✓	✓				
		" WILLIAM	SON	W	M	Dec. 1886	13	S				KY	KY	KY				AT SCHOOL		4	✓	✓	✓				
		" BERTHA A.	DAU	W	F	Feb. 1890	10	S				KY	KY	KY				AT SCHOOL		5	✓	✓	✓				
		" MATTIE	DAU	W	F	May. 1892	8	S				KY	KY	KY				AT SCHOOL		5	✓	✓	✓				
		" MARY E.	DAU	W	F	Jan. 1894	6	S				KY	KY	KY													
		" ISAAC	SON	W	M	Jul. 1898	11/12	S				KY	KY	KY													
138	140	COLLY, WILLIAM J.	HEAD	W	M	Mar. 1873	27	S				TN	TN	TN				MERCHANT			✓	✓	✓	R		H	
139	141	ENGLAND, WOLFORD J.	HEAD	W	M	Oct. 1863	36	M	5			KY	KY	TN				FARMER			✓	✓	✓	O	F	H	109
		" MANDA	WIFE	W	F	Mar. 1864	36	M	5	1	1	KY	KY	KY							X	X	✓				
		" ZELLER	DAU	W	F	Jan. 1884	16	S				KY	KY	KY							✓	✓	✓				

STATE - KENTUCKY
COUNTY - MONROE
Township or other division **GAMALIEL** Enumerator **ISAAC N. RENEAU**

Supervisor's Dist. No. **102** Sheet No.
Enumeration Dist. No. **87**

No. of Family	No. of Dwelling	NAME	Relation	Color	Sex	Date of Birth Mon/Yr	Age at last birthday	Marital Status	# Years married	Mother of how many children?	# of these children living	Place of birth (this person)	Father of this person	Mother of this person	Year of immigr.	# years in U.S.	Naturalization	Occupation 10 years +	Months not employed	Attended school in months	Can read	Can write	Speak English	Owned or Rent	Owned -no mortage	Farm or house	# of farm schedule
		ENGLAND, JESSEY	Son	W	M	Jan. 1887	13	S				KY	KY	KY				AT SCHOOL		5	✓	✓	✓				
		" ALTIE	Dau	W	F	Sep. 1869	10	S				KY	KY	KY				AT SCHOOL		5	✓	✓					
		" ICIE	Dau	W	F	Mar. 1898	2	S				KY	KY	KY													
140	142	DECKARD, JEFFERSON	Head	W	M	Sep. 1859	40	M	16			KY	TN	KY				FARMER			✓	X	✓	O	F	F	110
		" MARY E.	Wife	W	F	Jan. 1869	31	M	16	7	7	KY	TN	KY							✓	X	✓				
		" NETTIE J.	Dau	W	F	May. 1885	15	S				KY	KY	KY				AT SCHOOL		3	✓	✓	✓				
		" DONNIE M.	Dau	W	F	Jan. 1886	14	S				KY	KY	KY				AT SCHOOL		3	✓	✓	✓				
		" FLARDIE B.	Dau	W	F	Feb. 1888	12	S				KY	KY	KY				AT SCHOOL		3	✓	✓	✓				
		" HIGHRAM	Son	W	M	Feb. 1890	10	S				KY	KY	KY				AT SCHOOL		3	✓	X	✓				
		" FRANK C.	Son	W	M	Dec. 1892	7	S				KY	KY	KY				AT SCHOOL		1							
		" FRED	Son	W	M	Apr. 1895	5	S				KY	KY	KY													
		SAMUEL A.	Son	W	M	Sep. 1898	1	S				KY	KY	KY													
141	143	REAGAN, SILAS P.	Head	W	M	Apr. 1871	29	M	1			KY	KY	TN				FARMER			X	X	✓	R		F	111
		" IDA B.	Wife	W	F	Jan. 1877	23	M	1	1	1	KY	TN	TN							✓	✓	✓				
		" GENA A.	Son	W	M	Aug. 1899	10/12	S				KY	KY	KY													
142	144	GUM, JAMES	Head	W	M	Mar. 1837	63	M	18			KY	KY	KY				FARMER			X	X	✓	O	F	F	112
		" RILDA	Wife	W	F	Nov. 1839	60	M	18	0	0	TN	VA	TN							✓	✓	✓				
		ROBINSON, LAZARUS	Cousin	W	F?	Feb. 1891	9	S				KY	KY	KY				AT SCHOOL		4½							
		WILSON, WILLIE	Sis-in-Law	W	F	May. 1845	55	WD		6	6	TN	VA	TN							✓	✓	✓				
143	145	CRUISE, ELLIS	Head	W	M	Oct. 1866	33	M	1			KY	TN	KY				FARMER			✓	✓	✓	R		F	113
		" MATILDA	Wife	W	F	Mar. 1869	40	M	1			KY	KY	KY							✓	✓	✓				
		" BURTIE	Brother	W	M	May. 1878	22	S				KY	TN	KY							✓	✓	✓				
144	146	BELCHER, MADISON N.	Head	W	M	Mar. 1862	38	M	14			KY	KY	TN				FARMER			✓	✓	✓	O	M	F	114
		" MISSOURI A.	Wife	W	F	Sep. 1856	43	M	14	3	3	ALA	NC	NC							✓	✓	✓				
		" VIRGIL A.	Son	W	M	Oct. 1886	13	S				KY	KY	ALA				AT SCHOOL		4	✓	✓	✓				
		" HALLIE P.	Dau	W	F	Oct. 1890	9	S				KY	KY	ALA						0							

STATE - KENTUCKY
COUNTY - MONROE
Township or other division GAMALIEL Enumerator ISAAC N. RENEAU

Supervisor's Dist. No. *102* Sheet No.
Enumeration Dist. No. *87*

No. of Family	No. of Dwelling	NAME	Relation	Color	Sex	Date of Birth Mon/Yr	Age at last birthday	Marital Status	# Years married	Mother of how many children	# of these children living	Place of birth (this person)	Father of this person	Mother of this person	Year of immigr.	# years in U.S.	Naturalization	Occupation 10 years +	Months not employed	Attended school in months	Can read	Can write	Speak English	Owned or Rent	Owned -no mortgage	Farm or house	# of farm schedule
(146)		BELCHER, JAMES H.	SON	W	M	Jun. 1894	5	S				KY	KY	ALA													
145	147	WADE, JOHN S.	HEAD	W	M	Dec. 1820	79	WD				NC	VA	NC				FARMER			✓	✓	✓	O	F	F	115
146	148	WADE, JOHN B.	HEAD	W	M	Jan. 1848	52	M	20			GA	NC	NC				FARMER			✓	✓	✓	O	F	F	116
		" MARY E.	WIFE	W	F	May 1855	45	M	20	5	5	KY	TN	TN							✓	✓					
		" MINNIE B.	DAU	W	F	Dec. 1879	20	S				KY	GA	KY							✓	✓					
		" ARLIE D.	SON	W	M	Dec. 1886	15	S				KY	GA	KY				AT SCHOOL		2	✓	✓					
		" EMMIE E.	DAU	W	F	Jan. 1888	12	S				KY	GA	KY				AT SCHOOL		5	✓						
		" AUSVILLE S.	SON	W	M	Sep. 1890	9	S				KY	GA	KY				AT SCHOOL		5							
		" OSCHAR J.	SON	W	M	Aug. 1891	8	S				KY	GA	KY				AT SCHOOL		5							
147	149	EMBERTON, MARY B.	HEAD	W	F	Mar. 1866	34	WD		9	6	KY	KY	KY				FARMER			✓	✓	✓	R		F	117
		" AVERY B.	SON	W	M	Oct. 1884	15	S				KY	KY	KY				FARM LABORER		4	✓	✓	✓				
		" OVEY T.	DAU	W	F	Aug. 1888	11	S				KY	KY	KY				AT SCHOOL		5	✓	✓					
		" ALFRED	SON	W	M	Jan. 1890	10	S				KY	KY	KY				AT SCHOOL		4	✓	X	✓				
		" ORIE N.	DAU	W	F	Aug. 1891	8	S				KY	KY	KY				AT SCHOOL		4							
		" GARVON	SON	W	M	Feb. 1895	5	S				KY	KY	KY													
		" EVIE	DAU	W	F	Apr. 1897	3	S				KY	KY	KY													
148	150	DICKERSON, WILLIAM S.	HEAD	W	M	Nov. 1865	34	M	13			KY	KY	KY				FARMER			✓	✓	✓	O	F	F	118
		" MARTHY J.	WIFE	W	F	May 1869	31	M	13	6	6	KY	KY	KY													
		" MARGIE M.	DAU	W	F	Mar. 1888	12	S				KY	KY	KY				AT SCHOOL		5	✓	✓					
		" LOTTIE B.	DAU	W	F	Mar. 1890	10	S				KY	KY	KY				AT SCHOOL		5	✓	✓	✓				
		" GUSTAVA	DAU	W	F	May 1892	8	S				KY	KY	KY				AT SCHOOL		5							
		" ISAAC S.	SON	W	M	Feb. 1895	5	S				KY	KY	KY													
		" EARLY V.	SON	W	M	Sep. 1897	2	S				KY	KY	KY													
		" JAMES H.	SON	W	M	May 1900	0/12	S				KY	TN	TN													
149	151	DICKERSON, JOHN W.	HEAD	W	M	Nov. 1834	65	M	35			KY	TN	TN				FARMER			✓	✓	✓	O	F	F	119
		" ANGIE	WIFE	W	F	Oct. 1842	57	M	35	12	11	KY	VA	VA							✓	✓	✓				

STATE - KENTUCKY
COUNTY - MONROE
Township or other division: GAMALIEL
Enumerator: ISAAC N. RENEAU

Supervisor's Dist. No. 102 Sheet No.
Enumeration Dist. No. 87

No. of Family	No. of Dwelling	NAME	Relation	Color	Sex	Date of Birth Mon/Yr	Age at last birthday	Marital Status	# Years married	Mother of how many children	# of these children living	Place of birth (this person)	Father of this person	Mother of this person	Year of immigr.	# years in U.S.	Naturalization	Occupation	Months not employed	Attended school in months	Can read	Can write	Speak English	Owned or Rent	Owned - no mortgage	Farm or house	# of farm schedule
		DICKERSON, ISAAC	SON	W	M	APR. 1875	25	S				KY	KY	KY				FARMER			✓	✓	✓				
		" SELISTA D.	DAU	W	F	MAR. 1880	20	S				KY	KY	KY							✓	✓	✓				
		" AUTHOR F.	SON	W	M	NOV. 1882	17	S				KY	KY	KY				FARM LABORER			✓	✓	✓				
		" HARVIE	SON	W	M	AUG. 1884	15	S				KY	KY	KY				FARM LABORER		3	✓	✓	✓				
		" ISAAC	FATHER	W	M	DEC. 1807	92	WD				TN	*	TN	*TURKEY						✓	✓	✓				
150	152	DICKERSON, ULISSUS	HEAD	W	M	DEC. 1872	27	M	3			KY	KY	KY				FARMER			✓	✓	✓	R		F	120
		" JADIE	WIFE	W	F	APR. 1879	21	M	3	2	1	KY	KY	KY							✓	✓	✓				
		" DAVIE	SON	W	M	FEB. 1899	1	S				KY	KY	KY													
151	153	PROFITT, LONZO C.	HEAD	W	M	SEP. 1876	23	M	1			KY	TN	TN				FARMER			✓	✓	✓	R		F	121
		" MARY	WIFE	W	F	AUG. 1876	23	M	1			KY	KY	TN							✓	✓	✓				
152	154	DICKERSON, TOLLEY V.	HEAD	W	M	SEP. 1869	30	M	12			KY	KY	KY				PAINTER	4		✓	✓	✓	O		FH	
		" LIDDA R.	WIFE	W	F	MAY. 1871	29	M	12	4	3	KY	KY	TN							✓	✓	✓				
		" ORIE E.	DAU	W	F	Jul. 1891	8	S				KY	KY	KY				AT SCHOOL		5							
		" LEVIE P.	SON	W	M	Sep. 1893	6	S				KY	KY	KY													
		" ROXIE B.	DAU	W	F	Jun. 1896	3	S				KY	KY	KY													
153	155	DICKERSON, WILLIAM	HEAD	W	M	SEP. 1839	60	M	32			KY	KY	KY				FARMER			✓	✓	✓	O		F	123
		" LUCY C.	WIFE	W	F	NOV. 1848	51	M	32	8	7	KY	VA	VA							X	X	✓				
		" JASPER	SON	W	M	NOV. 1879	20	S				KY	KY	KY				FARM LABORER			✓	✓	✓				
		" FRONA B.	DAU	W	F	NOV. 1884	15	S				KY	KY	KY				AT SCHOOL		4	✓	✓	✓				
154	156	FULSE, JOHN S.	HEAD	W	M	AUG. 1851	48	M	24			KY	KY	KY				FARMER			✓	✓	✓	O		F	124
		" NELCENA	WIFE	W	F	MAR. 1860	40	M	24	11	9	KY	KY	KY							X	X	✓				
		" VERNA M.	DAU	W	F	MAY 1885	15	S				KY	KY	KY				AT SCHOOL		5	✓	✓	✓				
		" GARLAND C.	SON	W	M	NOV. 1888	11	S				KY	KY	KY				AT SCHOOL		4	✓	✓	✓				
		" HOMER B.	SON	W	M	Jul. 1890	9	S				KY	KY	KY				AT SCHOOL		5							
		" GUSTAVIE	DAU	W	F	Jan. 1893	7	S				KY	KY	KY				AT SCHOOL		5							
		" JOCEPHAS	SON	W	M	Jan. 1896	4	S				KY	KY	KY													

STATE - KENTUCKY
COUNTY - MONROE
Township or other division: GAMALIEL   Enumerator: ISAAC N. RENEAU

Supervisor's Dist. No. 102 Sheet No.
Enumeration Dist. No. 87

No. of Family	No. of Dwelling	NAME	Relation	Color	Sex	Date of Birth Mon/Yr	Age at last birthday	Marital Status	# Years married	Mother of how many children?	# of these children living	Place of birth [this person]	Father of this person	Mother of this person	Occupation 10 years +	Attended school in months	Can read	Can write	Speak English	Owned or Rent	Owned –no mortgage	Farm or house	# of farm schedule
		FULSE, NOVIE D.	DAU	W	F	SEP.1898	1	S				KY	KY	KY									
155	157	GOODE, CHARLEY	HEAD	W	M	SEP.1872	27	M	6			KY	TN	KY	FARMER		✓	✓	✓	R		F	125
		" CASSEY	WIFE	W	F	JUN.1876	23	M	6	2	2	KY	KY	KY			✓	✓	✓				
		" CARNEY C.	SON	W	M	JUN.1895	4	S				KY	KY	KY									
		" INA J.	DAU	W	F	MAR.1897	3	S				KY	KY	KY									
156	158	GOODE, JOHN A.W.	HEAD	W	M	JAN.1839	61	M	38			TN	VA	TN	FARMER		✓	✓		O	F	F	126
		" ELIZABETH M.	WIFE	W	F	JUN.1843	56	M	38	8	6	KY	TN	TN			✓	✓	✓				
		" CORTEZ	SON	W	M	JUN.1883	16	S			2	KY	KY	KY	AT SCHOOL	2	✓	X	✓				
		" CUSTER A.	SON	W	M	JUN.1883	16	S			1	KY	TN	KY	AT SCHOOL	2	✓	✓	✓				
		" NOLA	DAU	W	F	APR.1886	14	S				KY	TN	KY	AT SCHOOL	4	✓	✓	✓				
157	159	PROFFITT, NEWTON R.	HEAD	W	M	JAN.1866	34	M	10			KY	TN	TN	FARMER		✓	✓	✓	R		F	127
		" OMIE	WIFE	W	F	APR.1872	28	M	10	3	3	KY	KY	KY			✓	✓	✓				
		" BUENA	DAU	W	F	MAY.1891	9	S				KY	KY	KY	AT SCHOOL	5							
		" GAZETIE	DAU	W	F	SEP.1894	5	S				KY	KY	KY									
		" HUIE T	SON	W	M	NOV.1898	7/12	S				KY	KY	KY									
		TURNER, SALLEE	MOTH-IN-LAW	W	F	MAY.1844	56	WD		3	2	KY	VA	TN			✓	✓	✓				
158	160	GRAMLIN, HENRY H.	HEAD	W	M	OCT.1855	44	M	22			MO	TN	TN	FARMER		✓	✓	✓	R		F	128
		" MELISA A.	WIFE	W	F	MAR.1859	41	M	22	8	7	KY	KY	TN			✓	✓	✓				
		" WALTER	SON	W	M	SEP.1880	19	S				KY	MO	KY	FARM LABORER		✓	✓	✓				
		" ADA	DAU	W	F	JAN.1885	15	S				KY	MO	KY	AT SCHOOL	2½	✓	✓	✓				
		" LEVI	SON	W	M	FEB.1889	11	S				KY	MO	KY	AT SCHOOL	2½	✓	X	✓				
		" ELLA E.	DAU	W	F	SEP.1891	8	S				KY	MO	KY	AT SCHOOL	3							
		" CORA	DAU	W	F	JAN.1894	6	S				KY	MO	KY									
159	161	LANGFORD, GRIGG	HEAD	B	M	FEB.1861	39	M	0			KY	KY	KY	FARMER		X	X	✓	R		F	129
		" ELSIE	WIFE	B	F	NOV.1862	37	M	0	2	2	KY	KY	VA			✓	✓	✓				
160	162	ENGLAND, JESSEY S.	HEAD	W	M	FEB.1857	43	M	23			KY	KY	TN	FARMER		✓	✓	✓	O	F	F	130

STATE - KENTUCKY
COUNTY - MONROE
Township or other division GAMALIEL Enumerator ISAAC N. RENEAU

Supervisor's Dist. No. 102 Sheet No.
Enumeration Dist. No. 87

No. of Family	No. of Dwelling	NAME	Relation	Color	Sex	DATE OF BIRTH Mon/Yr	Age at last birthday	Marital Status	# Years married	Mother of how many children?	# of these children living	Place of birth [this person]	Father of this person	Mother of this person	Year of immigr.	# years in U.S.	Naturalization	OCCUPATION 10 years +	Months not employed	Attended school in months	Can read	Can write	Speak English	Owned or Rent	Owned - no mortgage	Farm or house	# of farm schedule	
		ENGLAND, MARY E.	WIFE	W	F	SEP. 1862	37	M	23	10	9	ILL	KY	KY							✓	X	✓					
		" TIPTON	SON	W	M	SEP. 1881	18	S				KY	KY	ILL				FARM LABORER			✓	✓	✓					
		" JOHN	SON	W	M	JAN. 1884	16	S				KY	KY	ILL				FARM LABORER		1½	✓	✓	✓					
		" SARAH E.	DAU	W	F	JUL. 1886	13	S				KY	KY	ILL				AT SCHOOL		5	✓	✓	✓					
		" WILLIAM S.	SON	W	M	JUL. 1888	11	S				KY	KY	ILL				AT SCHOOL		3	✓	X	✓					
		" MABEL	DAU	W	F	MAY 1890	10	S				KY	KY	ILL				AT SCHOOL		4	✓	✓	✓					
		" CHARLEY E.	SON	W	M	NOV. 1893	6	S				KY	KY	ILL						0								
		" LEONA A.	DAU	W	F	AUG. 1894	3	S				KY	KY	ILL														
		" DEWEY	SON	W	M	OCT. 1898	1	S				KY	KY	ILL														
161	163	EAKLE, HENRY	HEAD	W	M	MAY 1869	31	M	3			KY	TN	TN				FARMER			X	X	✓	R		F	131	
		" BERTHA	WIFE	W	F	MAR. 1882	18	M	3	1	1	KY	KY	KY							✓	✓	✓					
		" EMLEY	DAU	W	F	APR. 1900	4/12	S				KY	KY	KY														
162	164	POTTER, ARCHIBLE N.	HEAD	W	M	DEC. 1832	67	M	7			TN	TN	TN				PHYSICIAN			✓	✓	✓	O		F	32	
		" MALISSA J.	WIFE	W	F	JAN. 1864	36	M	7	4		KY	TN	KY							X	X	✓					
		" CARLAS J.	SON	W	M	SEP. 1894	5	S				KY	TN	KY														
		" TRUDA E.	DAU	W	F	APR. 1896	4	S				KY	TN	KY														
		" OMIE B.	DAU	W	F	MAR. 1899	1	S				KY	TN	KY														
		GRAMLIN, MARY V.	GR-DAU	W	F	MAR. 1889	11	S				KY	KY	TN				AT SCHOOL		5	✓	✓	✓					
163	165	FORD, BENJAMIN	HEAD	W	M	OCT. 1832	67	WD				TN	TN	MD							✓	X	✓	O		H		
164	166	PROFFITT, JOHN W.	HEAD	W	M	AUG. 1860	39	M	18			KY	TN	TN				FARMER			✓	✓	✓	O		F	133	
		" MARY	WIFE	W	F	JUL. 1865	34	M	18	7	7	KY	KY	KY							✓	X	✓					
		" OSCAR	SON	W	M	OCT. 1883	16	S				KY	KY	KY				FARM LABORER		5	✓	✓	✓					
		" LORA	DAU	W	F	NOV. 1886	13	S				KY	KY	KY				AT SCHOOL		5	✓	✓	✓					
		" OVA	DAU	W	F	OCT. 1888	11	S				KY	KY	KY				AT SCHOOL		5	✓	✓	✓					
		" BETTIE	DAU	W	F	NOV. 1890	9	S				KY	KY	KY				AT SCHOOL		5								
		" LUCIE	DAU	W	F	NOV. 1892	7	S				KY	KY	KY				AT SCHOOL		5								

STATE - KENTUCKY
COUNTY - MONROE
Township or other division **GAMALIEL**
Enumerator **ISAAC N. RENEAU**

Supervisor's Dist. No. _102_ Sheet No.
Enumeration Dist. No. _87_

No. of Family	No. of Dwelling	NAME	Relation	Color	Sex	Date of Birth Mon/Yr	Age at last birthday	Marital Status	#Years married	Mother of how many children	# of these children living	Place of birth (this person)	Father of this person	Mother of this person	Year of immigr.	# years in U.S.	Naturalization	Occupation	Months not employed	Attended school in months	Can read	Can write	Speak English	Owned or Rent	Owned -no mortgage	Farm or house	# of farm schedule
		PROFFITT, AUDIE	SON	W	M	AUG. 1896	3	S				KY	KY	KY													
		" IVA	DAU	W	F	DEC. 1898	1	S				KY	KY	KY													
165	167	BURNETTE, SUSAN	HEAD	W	F	MAR. 1818	82	WD		6	3	TN	VA	TN							X	X	✓	O		H	
166	168	CROW, JOHN H.	HEAD	W	M	SEP. 1848	51	M	21			TN	VA	TN				FARMER			X	X	✓	O	F	F	134
		" HENRETTA	WIFE	W	F	DEC. 1861	38	M	21	8	7	KY	KY	KY							X	X	✓				
		" VIRINDA	DAU	W	F	FEB. 1881	19	S				KY	TN	KY								✓	✓				
		" THOMAS	SON	W	M	MAY. 1882	18	S				KY	TN	KY				FARM LABORER		2	X	✓	✓				
		" LUCY J.	DAU	W	F	APR. 1884	16	S				KY	TN	KY				AT SCHOOL		4	✓	✓	✓				
		" EVA	DAU	W	F	SEP. 1886	13	S				KY	TN	KY				AT SCHOOL		4	✓	✓					
		" JOHN D.	SON	W	M	OCT. 1892	7	S				KY	TN	KY				AT SCHOOL		3							
		" MAYGO	SON	W	M	MAY. 1897	3	S				KY	TN	KY													
		" CALLEY C.	SON	W	M	MAY. 1900	1/12	S				KY	TN	KY													
		" GEMIMNA	SISTER	W	F	JUN. 1843	56	S				TN	VA	TN							X	X	✓				
		" LIZA	SISTER	W	F	OCT. 1861	38	S				TN	VA	TN							X	X	✓				
167	169	BURNETTE, JOHN P.	HEAD	W	M	SEP. 1849	50	M	27			KY	TN	TN				FARMER			✓	✓	✓	O	F	F	135
		" NACKEY	WIFE	W	F	NOV. 1850	49	M	27	8	6	KY	TN	KY							X	X	✓				
		" JOCIE E.	DAU	W	F	AUG. 1876	23	S				KY	KY	KY							X	X	✓				
		" MINNIE	DAU	W	F	DEC. 1883	16	S				KY	KY	KY				AT SCHOOL		1	✓	✓	✓				
		" TURNER	SON	W	M	JUL. 1887	12	S				KY	KY	KY				AT SCHOOL		3	✓	✓	✓				
		" ROXIE	DAU	W	F	SEP. 1893	6	S				KY	KY	KY													
168	170	ENGLAND, JAMES M.	HEAD	W	M	DEC. 1867	32	M	10			KY	KY	KY				FARMER			X	X	✓	R	F		136
		" KITTIE A.	WIFE	W	F	SEP. 1866	30	M	10	4	4	KY	TN	KY							X	X	✓				
		" ESSIE	DAU	W	F	MAY. 1891	9	S				KY	KY	KY				AT SCHOOL		5							
		" OCIE	DAU	W	F	JUN. 1893	6	S				KY	KY	KY				AT SCHOOL		5							
		" IDER	DAU	W	F	JUN. 1896	3	S				KY	KY	KY													
		" PEARL	DAU	W	F	APR. 1899	1	S				KY	KY	KY													

STATE - KENTUCKY
COUNTY - MONROE
Township or other division **GAMALIEL**

Enumerator **ISAAC N. RENEAU**

Supervisor's Dist. No. **102** Sheet No.
Enumeration Dist. No. **87**

No. of Family	No. of Dwelling	NAME	Relation	Color	Sex	DATE OF BIRTH Mon/Yr	Age at last birthday	Marital Status	# Years married	Mother of how many children?	# of these children living	Place of birth (this person)	Father of this person	Mother of this person	Year of immigr.	# years in U.S.	Naturalization	OCCUPATION 10 years +	Months not employed	Attended school in months	Can read	Can write	Speak English	Owned or Rent	Owned –no mortgage	Farm or house	# of farm schedule	
		ENGLAND, WILLIAM	Father	W	M	Oct. 1827	72	WD				KY	VA	SC				FARMER			X	X	✓			F		
169	171	CROW, SHERMAN	Head	W	M	Feb. 1866	34	M	15			KY	TN	TN				FARMER			X	X	✓	O	F	F	137	
"		MARY J.	Wife	W	F	Mar. 1866	34	M	15	7	5	KY	KY	TN							✓	✓	✓					
"		ROSE O.	Dau	W	F	Jan. 1891	9	S				KY	KY	KY				AT SCHOOL		4								
"		OVIE J.	Dau	W	F	Jul. 1893	6	S				KY	KY	KY														
"		SHANNON	Son	W	M	Feb. 1895	5	S				KY	KY	KY														
"		ROXIE M.	Dau	W	F	Sep. 1896	3	S				KY	KY	KY														
"		INAS	Dau	W	F	Apr. 1899	1	S				KY	KY	KY														
170	172	McCOY, SAMUEL	Head	W	M	May. 1874	26	M	3			KY	KY	KY				FARMER			✓	✓	✓	O	M	F	138	
"		MINTIE	Wife	W	F	Dec. 1875	24	M	3	2	2	KY	KY	KY							✓	✓	✓					
"		SADIE	Dau	W	F	Dec. 1897	2	S				TN	KY	KY														
"		RAY	Son	W	M	Jun. 1899	11/12	S				TN	KY	KY														
"		TOLLIE	Brother	W	M	Aug. 1880	19	S				KY	KY	KY				FARM LABORER			✓	✓	✓					
171	173	ELDRIDGE, GEORGE	Head	B	M	Sep. 1855	44	M	18			TN	VA	TN				FARMER			✓	X	✓	L		F	139	LEASE ?
"		ETHEL	Wife	B	F	Apr. 1861	39	M	18	7	7	KY	KY	TN							X	X	✓					
"		NELIA	Dau	B	F	Nov. 1884	15	S				KY	TN	KY							X	X	✓					
"		MELIA	Dau	B	F	Nov. 1884	15	S				KY	TN	KY				AT SCHOOL		2½	✓	✓	✓					
"		SAMUEL D.	Son	B	M	Jul. 1887	12	S				KY	TN	KY				AT SCHOOL		3	✓	✓	✓					
"		JAMES U.	Son	B	M	Oct. 1890	9	S				KY	TN	KY				AT SCHOOL		3								
"		JOHN T.	Son	B	M	Sep. 1893	6	S				KY	TN	KY														
"		GEORGE P.	Son	B	M	Dec. 1895	4	S				KY	TN	KY														
"		BETTIE M.	Dau	B	F	Dec. 1895	4	S				KY	TN	KY														
172	174	JENKINS, WILLIAM A.	Head	W	M	Sep. 1869	30	M	6			KY	KY	KY				FARMER			✓	✓	✓	O	F	F	140	
"		NETTIE F.	Wife	W	F	Mar. 1877	23	M	6	3	3	KY	KY	KY							✓	✓	✓					
"		WALTER H.	Son	W	M	Dec. 1894	5	S				KY	KY	KY														
"		FRED	Son	W	M	Nov. 1896	3	S				KY	KY	KY														

TWELFTH CENSUS OF THE UNITED STATES 1900

-485-

STATE - KENTUCKY
COUNTY - MONROE
Township or other division **GAMALIEL** Enumerator **ISAAC N. RENEAU**

Supervisor's Dist. No. *102* Sheet No. ___
Enumeration Dist. No. *87*

No. of Family	No. of Dwelling	NAME	Relation	Color	Sex	Date of Birth Mon/Yr	Age at last birthday	Marital Status	# Years married	Mother of how many children?	# of these children living	Birthplace (this person)	Father	Mother	Occupation	Attended school (months)	Can read	Can write	Speak English	Owned or Rent	Farm or house	# of farm schedule
		JENKINS, GENIE P.	DAU	W	F	Nov.1898	1	S				KY	KY	KY								
173	175	CREASY, JOHN W.	HEAD	W	M	Nov.1861	38	M	17			TN	TN	TN	FARMER		✓	✓	✓	O	F	141
		" MARTHA A.	WIFE	W	F	May.1866	34	M	17	6	4	KY	TN	TN			✓	✓	✓			
		" JAMES A.	SON	W	M	Mar.1884	16	S				TN	TN	KY	FARM LABORER	2	✓	✓	✓			
		" RADFORD D.	SON	W	M	Nov.1892	7	S				KY	TN	KY	FARM LABORER	1						
		" LEONA	DAU	W	F	Apr.1895	5	S				KY	TN	KY								
		" ORIE A.	DAU	W	F	Apr.1898	2	S				KY	TN	KY								
174	176	HALE, GEORGE W.	HEAD	W	M	May.1857	43	M	22			KY	TN	TN	FARMER		✓	✓	✓	O	F	142
		" VICTORIA	WIFE	W	F	Oct.1855	44	M	22	10	6	KY	TN	KY								
		" LUNCEFORD	SON	W	M	Apr.1879	21	S				KY	KY	KY	FARM LABORER		✓	✓	✓			
		" CLAUD	SON	W	M	Sep.1880	19	S				ARK	KY	KY	FARM LABORER	3	✓	✓	✓			
		" FRANCES	DAU	W	F	Oct.1883	16	S				KY	KY	KY			✓	✓	✓			
		" SHERMAN	SON	W	M	Feb.1884	16	S				KY	KY	KY	FARM LABORER	1	✓	✓	✓			
		" WILLIAM C.	SON	W	M	Mar.1887	13	S				KY	KY	KY								
		" MAGGIE	DAU	W	F	Feb.1899	1	S				KY	KY	KY	FARMER		✓	✓	✓	O	F	143
175	177	ENGLAND, SAMUEL A.	HEAD	W	M	Mar.1859	41	M	21			KY	KY	TN			X	X	✓			
		" FRANCES	WIFE	W	F	Jan.1864	36	M	21	9	7	TN	TN	TN			✓	✓	✓			
		" MADISON	SON	W	M	Jul.1879	20	S				KY	KY	TN	FARM LABORER		✓	✓	✓			
		" CLAY	SON	W	M	May.1882	18	S				KY	KY	TN	FARM LABORER	4	✓	✓	✓			
		" LEE	SON	W	M	Sep.1886	13	S				KY	KY	TN	FARM LABORER	5	✓	✓	✓			
		" EVIE	DAU	W	F	May.1891	9	S				KY	KY	TN	AT SCHOOL	5	✓	✓				
		" CLARA	DAU	W	F	Sep.1894	5	S				KY	KY	TN								
		" HILLAS	SON	W	M	Jul.1897	2	S				KY	KY	TN								
		" HUBERT	SON	W	M	Feb.1899	1	S				KY	TN	KY			X	X	✓		H	
176	178	QUINN, LIDDIA M.	HEAD	W	F	Apr.1848	52	S				KY	TN	KY						R	H	
177	179	JENKINS, GEORGE F.	HEAD	W	M	Dec.1870	29	M	7			KY	KY	KY	FARMER		✓	✓		R	H	

STATE - KENTUCKY
COUNTY - MONROE
Township or other division **GAMALIEL**   Enumerator **ISAAC N. RENEAU**

Supervisor's Dist. No. **102** Sheet No. ___
Enumeration Dist. No. **87** ___

No. Family	No. Dwelling	Name	Relation	Color	Sex	Date of Birth Mon/Yr	Age	Marital Status	Yrs married	Mother of how many	# living	Birthplace	Father	Mother	Occupation	School mos.	Can read	Can write	Speak Eng.	Own/Rent	Owned/Farm	Farm sched.
		JENKINS, MARGET A.	WIFE	W	F	Aug-1871	28	M	7	2	2	KY	KY	KY			✓	✓				
		" NORA	DAU	W	F	Jan-1895	5	S				KY	KY	KY								
		" LAURA	DAU	W	F	Jan-1897	3	S				KY	KY	KY								
178	180	JENKINS, JOHN W.	HEAD	W	M	Mar-1833	67	M	44			KY	KY	KY	FARMER		✓	✓	✓	O	F F	144
		" ELIZABETH	WIFE	W	F	Jan-1836	64	M	44	13	8	KY	KY	KY			✓	✓	✓			
		" FLORENCE	DAU	W	F	Mar-1877	23	S				KY	KY	KY			✓	✓				
179	181	RYHERD, ABRAM D.	HEAD	W	M	Jul-1837	62	M	41			KY	TN	TN	FARMER		✓	✓	✓	O	F F	145
		" TABITHA J.	WIFE	W	F	Sep-1834	65	M	41	9	5	KY	KY	KY			✓	X	✓			
		" GEORGE L.	SON	W	M	Sep-1864	35	WD				KY	KY	KY	FARMER		✓	✓	✓	R	F	146
		" MARY C.	DAU	W	F	Nov-1866	33	S				KY	KY	KY			✓	✓	✓			
		HALE, GEORGE	Lodger	W	M	Apr-1880	20	S				KY	KY	KY	FARM LABORER							
180	182	RYHERD, JOHN T.	HEAD	W	M	Aug-1862	37	M	7			KY	KY	KY	FARMER		✓	✓	✓	O	F F	147
		" MARY L.	WIFE	W	F	Jul-1873	26	M	7	4	4	KY	KY	KY			✓	✓	✓			
		" EDGAR L.	SON	W	M	Oct-1892	7	S				KY	KY	KY	AT SCHOOL	2						
		" CLIDE	DAU	W	F	Aug-1894	5	S				KY	KY	KY								
		" LAURA M.	DAU	W	F	Jun-1896	3	S				KY	KY	KY								
		" ANNIE B.	DAU	W	F	Jun-1898	1	S				KY	KY	KY								
181	183	BURNETTE, JAMES W.	HEAD	W	M	Mar-1849	57	M	16			KY	KY	KY	FARMER		X	X	✓	O	F F	148
		" SARAH	WIFE	W	F	May-1862	38	M	16	1	1	KY	KY	KY			X	X	✓			
		" BURTON	SON	W	M	Feb-1882	18	S				KY	KY	KY	FARM LABORER	3	✓	✓	✓			
182	184	ARTIBURN, MILBOURN G.	HEAD	W	M	Jan-1878	22	M	6			KY	KY	KY	FARMER		X	X	✓	O	F F	149
		" VERNER	WIFE	W	F	Mar-1879	21	M	6	4	3	KY	KY	KY			✓	✓	✓			
		" McKINLEY	SON	W	M	Nov-1896	3	S				KY	KY	KY								
		" SOLLIE	SON	W	M	Aug-1898	1	S				KY	KY	KY								
		" BETTIE	DAU	W	F	Feb-1900	3/12	S				KY	KY	KY								
183	185	BURNETTE, JOHN	HEAD	W	M	Jul-1864	35	M	18			KY	KY	KY	FARMER		X	X	✓	O	F F	150

TWELFTH CENSUS OF THE UNITED STATES 1900

−487−

STATE - KENTUCKY
COUNTY - MONROE
Township or other division: GAMALIEL
Enumerator: ISAAC N. RENEAU

Supervisor's Dist. No. 102   Sheet No.
Enumeration Dist. No. 87

No. of Family	No. of Dwelling	NAME	Relation	Color	Sex	DATE OF BIRTH Mon/Yr	Age at last birthday	Marital Status	# Years married	Mother of how many children?	# of these children living	Place of birth (this person)	Father of this person	Mother of this person	Year of immigr.	# years in U.S.	Naturalization	OCCUPATION 10 years +	Months not employed	Attended school in months	Can read	Can write	Speak English	Owned or Rent	Owned -no mortgage	Farm or house	# of farm schedule
		BURNETTE, MANDA J.	WIFE	W	F	JAN.1868	32	M	18			KY	KY	KY							X	X	✓		O	F F	151
184	186	EMBERTON, JACOB W.	HEAD	W	M	JUN.1862	37	M	1			KY	VA	VA				FARMER			✓	✓	✓	O	F F		
		" ALICE J.	WIFE	W	F	JUN.1872	27	M	1	1	1	KY	TN	KY							✓	✓	✓				
		" RADFORD B.	SON	W	M	SEP.1884	15	S				KY	KY	KY				FARM LABORER		5	✓	✓	✓				
		" VIRGIE C.	DAU	W	F	OCT.1886	13	S				KY	KY	KY				AT SCHOOL		5	✓	✓	✓				
		" DONNIE J.	DAU	W	F	FEB.1889	11	S				KY	KY	KY				AT SCHOOL		5	✓	✓	✓				
		" MAUDY G.	DAU	W	F	APR.1891	9	S				KY	KY	KY				AT SCHOOL		5							
		" IVA P.	DAU	W	F	AUG.1893	6	S				KY	KY	KY													
		" HUBERT	SON	W	M	MAY.1899	1	S				KY	KY	KY													
		BROOKS, BURLEY D.	LODGER	W	M	OCT.1885	14	S				KY	TN	KY				AT SCHOOL		4	✓	✓	✓				
185	187	JENKINS, JOHN N.	HEAD	W	M	JAN.1875	25	M	2			KY	KY	KY				FARMER			✓	✓	✓	O	F F	152	
		" BERTHA M.	WIFE	W	F	APR.1875	25	M	2	1	1	KY	KY	KY							✓	✓	✓				
		" IVA M.	DAU	W	F	SEP.1898	1	S				KY	KY	KY													
186	188	HOWARD, PRESTON	HEAD	B	M	MAY.1858	42	M	19			KY	KY	VA				FARMER			X	X	✓	R	F		
		" POLLEY	WIFE	B	F	FEB.1863	37	M	19	9	8	KY	KY	VA							✓	✓	✓				
		" WILLIAM	SON	B	M	MAR.1883	17	S				KY	KY	KY				FARM LABORER		4	✓	X	✓				
		" MARY F.	DAU	B	F	SEP.1884	15	S				KY	KY	KY				AT SCHOOL		2	X	X	✓				
		" NANNIE	DAU	B	F	MAR.1887	13	S				KY	KY	KY				AT SCHOOL		5	✓	✓	✓				
		" JOHN	SON	B	M	DEC.1889	10	S				KY	KY	KY				AT SCHOOL		2	✓	✓	✓				
		" LULA	DAU	B	F	JUL.1891	8	S				KY	KY	KY													
		" ELZIE	SON	B	M	NOV.1893	6	S				KY	KY	KY													
		" HOMER	SON	B	M	JUL.1897	2	S				KY	KY	KY													
187	189	PIPKIN, GEORGE	HEAD	B	M	MAR.1842	58	M	34			TN	TN	TN				FARMER			X	X	✓	O	F F	153	
		" LIZZIE	WIFE	B	F	JAN.1842	58	M	34	8	7	TN	VA	VA							X	X	✓				
		" ROSCO	SON	B	M	AUG.1875	24	S				KY	TN	TN				SCHOOL TEACHER			✓	✓	✓				
		" SISCO	DAU	B	F	APR.1878	22	S				KY	TN	TN							✓	✓	✓				

STATE - KENTUCKY
COUNTY - MONROE
Township or other division GAMALIEL

Enumerator ISAAC N. RENEAU

Supervisor's Dist. No. 102 Sheet No.
Enumeration Dist. No. 87

No. of Family	No. of Dwelling	NAME	Relation	Color	Sex	DATE OF BIRTH Mon/Yr	Age at last birthday	Marital Status	# Years married	Mother of how many children?	# of these children living	Place of birth [this person]	Father of this person	Mother of this person	Year of immigr.	# years in U.S.	Naturalization	OCCUPATION 10 years +	Months not employed	Attended school in months	Can read	Can write	Speak English	Owned or Rent	Owned - no mortage	Farm or house	# of farm schedule
		PIPKIN, KATE E.	DAU	B	F	OCT.1883	16	S				KY	TN	TN				AT SCHOOL		3	✓	✓	✓				
		" VEOLIA	SON	B	M	OCT.1886	13	S				KY	TN	TN				AT SCHOOL		4	✓	✓	✓				
188	90	BOTTS, JAMES W.	HEAD	W	M	JUN.1863	36	M	13			KY	TN	KY				FARMER			✓	✓	✓	O	F	F	154
		" JULIA	WIFE	W	F	SEP.1865	34	M	13	8	6	KY	KY	KY							✓	✓	✓				
		" FRED	SON	W	M	NOV.1888	11	S				KY	KY	KY				FARM LABORER		3	✓	✓	✓				
		" CEPHUS	SON	W	M	MAR.1891	9	S				KY	KY	KY				AT SCHOOL		3							
		" BERTHA J.	DAU	N	F	AUG.1893	6	S				KY	KY	KY													
		" LONA P.	DAU	W	F	OCT.1895	4	S				KY	KY	KY													
		" LESSIE M.	DAU	W	F	JAN.1898	2	S				KY	KY	KY													
		" J. DOUGLAS	SON	W	M	OCT.1899	7/12	S				KY	KY	KY													
189	91	HARLAN, WILLIAM C.	HEAD	W	M	FEB.1852	48	M	26			TN	TN	TN				FARMER			✓	✓	✓	O	F	F	165
		" ELIZABETH H.	WIFE	W	F	MAR.1854	46	M	26	9	8	TN	TN	TN							✓	✓	✓				
		" BETHEL M.	SON	W	M	OCT.1879	20	S				TN	TN	TN				FARM LABORER			✓	✓	✓				
		" ROXIE B.	DAU	W	F	APR.1877	23	S				TN	TN	TN							✓	✓	✓				
		" MAGGIE E.	DAU	W	F	SEP.1881	18	S				KY	TN	TN				AT SCHOOL		4	✓	✓	✓				
		" JESSIE J.	SON	W	M	FEB.1884	16	S				KY	TN	TN				AT SCHOOL		4	✓	✓	✓				
		" SAMUEL A.	SON	W	M	NOV.1885	14	S				KY	TN	TN				AT SCHOOL		4	✓	✓	✓				
		" BENTON R.	SON	W	M	MAY.1890	10	S				KY	TN	TN				AT SCHOOL		4½	✓	✓	✓				
		" (L)TEXIE M.	DAU	W	F	FEB.1894	6	S				KY	TN	TN													
		" KANSAS C.	SON	W	M	SEP.1898	1	S				KY	TN	TN													
190	92	HOWARD, ALBERT J.	HEAD	B	M	MAY.1850	50	M	23			KY	TN	VA				FARMER	4		✓	✓	✓	O	F	F	156
		" FRANCES	WIFE	B	F	MAY.1858	42	M	23	10	7	KY	KY	VA							X	X	✓				
		" MINNIE	DAU	B	F	JUL.1877	22	S				KY	KY	KY							✓	✓	✓				
		" THOMAS	SON	B	M	OCT.1879	20	S				KY	KY	KY				FARM LABORER	6		✓	✓	✓				
		" VIRGIL	SON	B	M	JUN.1886	13	S				KY	KY	KY				FARM LABORER	4	3	✓	✓	✓				
		" EVIE A.	DAU	B	F	AUG.1890	9	S				KY	KY	KY				AT SCHOOL		5							

STATE - KENTUCKY
COUNTY - MONROE
Township or other division GAMALIEL   Enumerator ISAAC N. RENEAU

Supervisor's Dist. No. 102 Sheet No.
Enumeration Dist. No. 87

No. of Family	No. of Dwelling	NAME	Relation	Color	Sex	Date of Birth Mon/Yr	Age at last birthday	Marital Status	#Years married	Mother of how many children?	# of these children living	Place of birth (this person)	Father of this person	Mother of this person	Year of immigr.	# years in U.S.	Naturalization	Occupation 10 years +	Months not employed	Attended school in months	Can read	Can write	Speak English	Owned or Rent	Owned - no mortage	Farm or house	# of farm schedule
		HOWARD, KENSIE	Son	B	M	Feb. 1896	4	S				KY	KY	KY													
		" HERMAN	Son	B	M	Aug. 1899	8/12	S				KY	KY	KY													
191	193	HOWARD, BENJAMIN	Head	B	M	May. 1867	33	M	20			KY	KY	KY				FARMER			✓	✓		O	F	F	157
		" ELLEN	Wife	B	F	Feb. 1868	32	M	20	1	1	KY	KY	KY							X	X	✓				
		RIGGS, MONTIE W.	Gr-Son	B	M	Apr. 1889	11	S				KY	KY	KY				AT SCHOOL		5	✓	✓	✓				
		" MOSSIE L.	Gr-Son	B	M	Jul. 1892	7	S				KY	KY	KY				AT SCHOOL		5							
192	194	BAILEY, JANE	Head	B	F	Jan. 1835	65	WD		7	1	KY	KY	KY							X	X	✓	O		H	
		RICHISON, GILLIE	Niece	B	F	Sep. 1871	28	S		3	2	KY	KY	KY							✓	✓	✓				
		" PEARL	Niece	B	F	Mar. 1893	7	S				KY	KY	KY													
		" JOHN	Nephew	B	M	Jan. 1897	3	S				KY	KY	KY													
		" BASIL	Nephew	B	M	Mar. 1899	1	S				KY	KY	KY													
193	195	RIGGS, JOHN	Head	B	M	Jan. 1870	30	M	9			KY	KY	KY				FARM LABORER	6		X	X	✓	R		H	
		" NANNIE	Wife	B	F	Nov. 1875	24	M	9	6	3	KY	KY	KY							X	X	✓				
		" JOHN D.	Son	B	M	May. 1894	6	S				KY	KY	KY													
		" ELLER	Dau	B	F	Jun. 1899	11/12	S				KY	KY	KY													
194	196	WEST, NANCY	Head	B	F	Jul. 1873	26	S		4	4	TN	TN	TN							X	X	✓	O		H	
		" CORA B.	Dau	B	F	Mar. 1890	10	S				KY	KY	TN				AT SCHOOL		3	✓	X	✓				
		" CLARANCE P.	Son	B	M	Jul. 1892	7	S				KY	KY	TN				AT SCHOOL		1							
		" ROBERT R.	Son	B	M	Nov. 1895	4	S				KY	KY	TN													
		" JOHN	Son	B	M	Jul. 1899	10/12	S				KY	KY	TN													
195	197	WEST, PETER	Head	B	M	Mar. 1837	63	M	23			VA	VA	VA				FARMER			✓	✓	✓	O	F	F	158
		" GEORGIAN	Wife	B	F	May. 1844	56	M	23	7	4	KY	KY	KY							X	X	✓				
		" HETTIE	Dau	B	F	May. 1889	11	S				KY	VA	KY				AT SCHOOL		5	✓	✓	✓				
196	198	HOWARD, WILLIAM	Head	B	M	Dec. 1873	26	M	7			KY	TN	TN				FARMER	4		✓	✓	✓	O	F	F	159
		" CORA	Wife	B	F	Nov. 1880	19	M	7	2	2	KY	KY	KY							X	X	✓				
		" MARY B.	Dau	B	F	Aug. 1894	5	S				KY	KY	KY													

TWELFTH CENSUS OF THE UNITED STATES 1900

STATE - KENTUCKY
COUNTY - MONROE
Township or other division **GAMALIEL**　Enumerator **ISAAC N. RENEAU**

Supervisor's Dist. No. **102**　Sheet No.
Enumeration Dist. No. **87**

No. of Family	No. of Dwelling	NAME	Relation	Color	Sex	DATE OF BIRTH Mon/Yr	Age at last birthday	Marital Status	# Years married	Mother of how many children?	# of these children living	Place of birth [this person]	Father of this person	Mother of this person	Year of immigr.	# years in U.S.	Naturalization	OCCUPATION 10 years +	Months not employed	Attended school in months	Can read	Can write	Speak English	Owned or Rent	Owned - no mortgage	Farm or house	# of farm schedule
		HOWARD, ULER T.	DAU	B	F	Jul. 1897	2	S				KY	KY	KY													
197	199	HOWARD, ALBERT S.	Head	B	M	Jan. 1825	75	S				KY	VA	SC				FARM LABORER 6			X	X	✓	O		F	H
198	200	CROW, THOMAS	HEAD	W	M	Jun. 1861	38	M	19			KY	TN	KY				FARMER			X	8	✓	R		F	160
		" MARY C.	WIFE	W	F	Apr. 1866	34	M	19	9	8	KY	TN	KY							X	X	✓				
		" WILLIAM S.	SON	W	M	Jul. 1882	17	S				KY	KY	KY				FARM LABORER			X	X	✓				
		" GRANT	SON	W	M	Jan. 1884	16	S				KY	KY	KY				FARM LABORER		1	✓	X	✓				
		" NELSON	SON	W	M	Feb. 1886	14	S				KY	KY	KY				AT SCHOOL		1	X	X	✓				
		" SAMUEL	SON	W	M	Mar. 1888	12	S				KY	KY	KY				AT SCHOOL		1	X	X	✓				
		" ICIE B.	DAU	W	F	Feb. 1892	8	S				KY	KY	KY				AT SCHOOL		1							
		" SARAH L.	DAU	W	F	Apr. 1894	6	S				KY	KY	KY													
		" MANDA J.	DAU	W	F	Jul. 1895	4	S				KY	KY	KY													
		" HOMER	SON	W	M	Oct. 1898	1	S				KY	KY	KY													
199	201	PEDIGO, ROBERT	HEAD	W	M	Mar. 1849	51	M	24			TN	TN	TN				FARMER			✓	✓	✓	O		F	161
		" MATILDA C.	WIFE	W	F	Jul. 1857	42	M	24	8	7	KY	KY	TN							✓	✓	✓				
		" SARAH E.	DAU	W	F	Apr. 1878	22	S				KY	KY	KY							✓	✓	✓				
		" IDA B.	DAU	W	F	Feb. 1880	20	S				KY	TN	KY							✓	✓	✓				
		" MARGARET E.	DAU	W	F	Sep. 1884	15	S				KY	TN	KY				AT SCHOOL		4½	✓	✓	✓				
		" WILLIAM T.	SON	W	M	Jul. 1887	12	S				KY	TN	KY				AT SCHOOL		4½	✓	✓	✓				
		" JAMES G.	SON	W	M	Apr. 1890	10	S				KY	TN	KY				AT SCHOOL		4½	✓	✓	✓				
		" BASSIE P.	DAU	W	F	Sep. 1893	6	S				KY	TN	KY													
		" IVAN F.	SON	W	M	Nov. 1895	4	S				KY	TN	KY													
		WEBB, EDGAR S.	HIRED	W	M	Jan. 1884	16	S				KY	KY	KY				FARM LABORER 6			✓	X	✓				
200	202	WEBB, WILLIAM G.	HEAD	W	M	Feb. 1878	22	M	5			KY	KY	KY				FARMER			✓	✓	✓	R		F	162
		" LYDIA S.	WIFE	W	F	Nov. 1879	20	M	5	3	3	KY	KY	KY							✓	X	✓				
		" HENRY J.	SON	W	M	Mar. 1896	4	S				KY	KY	KY													
		" WILLIAM F.	SON	W	M	May 1898	2	S				KY	KY	KY													

STATE - KENTUCKY
COUNTY - MONROE
Township or other division: GAMALIEL   Enumerator: ISAAC N. RENEAU

Supervisor's Dist. No. 102 Sheet No.
Enumeration Dist. No. 87

Fam	Dwel	Name	Relation	Color	Sex	Date of Birth Mon/Yr	Age	Marital	Yrs mar	# chn	# living	Birthplace	Father	Mother	Occupation	Education	Ownership
		WEBB, TILDA E.	DAU	W	F	DEC 1899 6/12		S				KY	KY	KY			
		SUSAN J.	SISTER	W	F	DEC 1880	19	S				KY	KY	KY		✓✓✓	
		JAMES P.	BROTHER	W	M	SEP 1887	12	S				KY	KY	KY	FARM LABORER	X X ✓	
		SAMUEL N.	BROTHER	W	M	APR 1891	9	S				KY	KY	KY			
		MARY E.	SISTER	W	F	FEB 1893	7	S				KY	KY	KY			
201	203	BELCHER, JOHN W.	HEAD	W	M	SEP 1848	51	M	7			KY	KY	KY	FARMER	✓ X ✓	O F F 163
		ELIZABETH	WIFE	W	F	DEC 1849	50	M	7	0	0	TN	VA	TN		X X ✓	
		ALVIE G.	SON	W	M	MAY 1875	25	M	0			KY	KY	KY	FARMER	✓ X ✓	R F 164
		LOLA M.	D-IN-LAW	W	F	JUN 1883	16	M	0	0	0	KY	KY	KY		✓ ✓ ✓	
		ROSA O.	DAU	W	F	SEP 1886	13	S				KY	KY	KY	AT SCHOOL	1 ✓ ✓ ✓	
202	204	FULKS, THOMAS	HEAD	W	M	APR 1828	72	M	54			KY	TN	TN	FARMER	✓ ✓ ✓	O F F 165
		CHARITY	WIFE	W	F	JAN 1825	75	M	54	1	1	KY	NC	VA		X X ✓	
		LOTTIE	GR-DAU	W	F	MAR 1884	16	S				TEXAS	KY	KY		2 ✓ ✓ ✓	
		CLONA D.	GR-SON	W	M	MAR 1886	14	S				TEXAS	KY	KY	FARM LABORER	2 ✓ ✓ ✓	
203	205	ENGLAND, SAMUEL D.	HEAD	W	M	FEB 1876	24	M	2			KY	KY	KY	FARMER	✓ ✓ ✓	O F F 166
		ROENA L.	WIFE	W	F	MAR 1877	23	M	2	1	1	KY	KY	KY		✓ ✓ ✓	
		CLAYTON C.	SON	W	M	JAN 1899	1	S				KY	KY	KY			
204	206	FOX, DANIEL	HEAD	W	M	NOV 1842	57	M	37			TN	VA	TN	FARMER	✓ X ✓	O F F 167
		MARY J.	WIFE	W	F	JUN 1846	54	M	37	12	9	KY	KY	KY		X X ✓	
		JARAT B.	SON	W	M	AUG 1884	15	S				KY	KY	KY	FARM LABORER	✓ ✓ ✓	
		SAMUEL P.	SON	W	M	JAN 1887	13	S				KY	TN	KY	FARM LABORER	✓ ✓ ✓	
205	207	FOX, CLAYBOURN B.	HEAD	W	M	JUL 1882	17	M				KY	TN	KY	FARMER	✓ ✓ ✓	R F 168
		MARY E.	WIFE	W	F	JAN 1884	16	M	0	0	0	KY	KY	KY		✓ ✓ ✓	
206	208	FOX, JAMES E.	HEAD	W	M	OCT 1874	25	M	5			KY	TN	KY	FARMER	✓ ✓ ✓	R F 169
		LUCY	WIFE	W	F	SEP 1878	21	M	5	2	2	KY	KY	KY		✓ ✓ ✓	
		LUVIE G.	SON	W	M	MAY 1896	4	S				KY	KY	KY			

STATE - KENTUCKY
COUNTY - MONROE
Township or other division GAMALIEL

TWELFTH CENSUS OF THE UNITED STATES 1900
— 492 —
Enumerator ISAAC N. RENEAU

Supervisor's Dist. No. 102 Sheet No.
Enumeration Dist. No. 87

Location No. of Family	No. of Dwelling	NAME	Relation	Color	Sex	DATE OF BIRTH Mon/Yr	Age at last birthday	Marital Status	# Years married	Mother of how many children?	# of these children living	Place of birth [this person]	Father of this person	Mother of this person	Year of immigr.	# years in U.S.	Naturalization	OCCUPATION 10 years +	Months not employed	Attended school in months	Can read	Can write	Speak English	Owned or Rent	Owned -no mortgage	Farm or house	# of farm schedule
		FOX, ADA C.	DAU	W	F	SEP·1898	1	S				KY	KY	KY													
207	209	COMER, GILLIE S.	HEAD	W	F	APR·1853	47	WD		7	6	KY	KY	KY				FARMER			X	X	✓	O	F	F	170
		" LUCIE B.	DAU	W	F	MAR·1875	25	S				KY	KY	KY							✓	✓	✓				
		" BURFORD C.	SON	W	M	MAY·1881	19	S				KY	KY	KY				FARM LABORER			X	X	✓				
		" VIRGIL D.	SON	W	M	JUL·1884	15	S				KY	KY	KY				FARM LABORER			X	X	✓				
		" ELLIE B.	DAU	W	F	MAR·1889	11	S				KY	KY	KY							X	X	✓				
208	210	BURK, L. CAINEY	HEAD	W	M	NOV·1861	38	M	13			KY	KY	KY				FARMER			X	X	✓	O	F	F	171
		" MILLEY P.	WIFE	W	F	DEC·1865	34	M	13	4	4	KY	TN	KY							✓	✓	✓				
		" JOHN S.	SON	W	M	MAR·1888	12	S				KY	KY	KY				AT SCHOOL		5	✓	✓	✓				
		" JAMES S.	SON	W	M	OCT·1889	10	S				KY	KY	KY				AT SCHOOL		5	✓	✓	✓				
		" ENRICK A.	SON	W	M	NOV·1891	8	S				KY	KY	KY				AT SCHOOL		5	✓	✓	✓				
		" DOCIE I.	DAU	W	F	FEB·1895	5	S				KY	KY	KY													
209	211	BELCHER, ISAAC N.	HEAD	W	M	AUG·1868	31	M	9			KY	KY	TN				FARMER			✓	✓	✓	R		F	172
		" ELIZA J.	WIFE	W	F	AUG·1870	29	M	9	3	3	KY	KY	KY							✓	✓	✓				
		" CARLA J.	SON	W	M	FEB·1892	8	S				KY	KY	KY				AT SCHOOL		5							
		" GENORA	DAU	W	F	APR·1895	5	S				KY	KY	KY													
		" CALLIE C.	SON	W	M	MAY·1898	1	S				KY	KY	KY													
210	212	BELCHER, SARAH M.	HEAD	W	F	OCT·1836	63	WD		10	6	TN	TN	TN				FARMER			✓	✓	✓	O	F	F	173
		" PALO P.	SON	W	M	SEP·1878	21	S				KY	KY	TN				FARMER			✓	✓	✓				
		" HATLIE O.	SON	W	M	APR·1881	19	S				KY	KY	TN				FARM LABORER			✓	✓	✓				
211	213	PROFFITT, ISAAC F.	HEAD	W	M	JAN·1871	29	M	6			KY	TN	TN				FARMER			✓	✓	✓	O	F	F	174
		" SARAH	WIFE	W	F	AUG·1872	27	M	6	3	3	KY	KY	KY							✓	✓	✓				
		" GUY	SON	W	M	DEC·1895	5	S				KY	KY	KY													
		" WIRT	SON	W	M	JAN·1898	2	S				KY	KY	KY													
		" UREY	SON	W	M	NOV·1899	7/12	S				KY	KY	KY													
		GEARLS, ADA	SIS-IN-LAW	W	F	MAR·1870	30	S				KY	KY	KY				SCHOOL TEACHER 4			✓	✓	✓				

TWELFTH CENSUS OF THE UNITED STATES 1900

— 493 —

STATE - KENTUCKY
COUNTY - MONROE
Township or other division GAMALIEL
Enumerator ISAAC N. RENEAU

Supervisor's Dist. No. 102 Sheet No.
Enumeration Dist. No. 87

No. of Family	No. of Dwelling	NAME	Relation	Color	Sex	DATE OF BIRTH Mon/Yr	Age at last birthday	Marital Status	# Years married	Mother of how many children?	# of these children living	Place of birth [this person]	Father of this person	Mother of this person	Year of immigr.	# years in U.S.	Naturalization	OCCUPATION 10 years +	Months not employed	Attended school in months	Can read	Can write	Speak English	Owned or Rent	Owned -no mortage	Farm or house	# of farm schedule
		GEARLS, EARNEST	NEPHEW	W	M	SEP. 1888	11	S				KY	KY	KY				AT SCHOOL		6	✓	✓	✓				
212	214	PROFFITT, GEORGE P.	HEAD	W	M	SEP. 1867	32	M	11			KY	KY	KY				FARMER			✓	✓	✓	O	F	F	175
		" MAHALEY J.	WIFE	W	F	NOV. 1868	31	M	11	5	5	KY	KY	KY							✓	✓	✓				
		" VINNIE	DAU	W	F	MAR. 1890	10	S				KY	KY	KY				AT SCHOOL		5	✓	✓	✓				
		" ODIS	SON	W	M	APR. 1892	8	S				KY	KY	KY				AT SCHOOL		5							
		" VADA	DAU	W	F	AUG. 1894	5	S				KY	KY	KY													
		" GRACIE	DAU	W	F	NOV. 1896	3	S				KY	KY	KY													
		" MARGET	DAU	W	F	JUN. 1899	1	S				KY	KY	KY													
213	215	BUSH, WILLIAM S.	HEAD	W	M	MAR. 1852	48	M	23			KY	KY	TN				FARMER			✓	✓	✓	O	F	F	176
		" MARY B.	WIFE	W	F	FEB. 1860	40	M	23	8	8	KY	TN	TN							✓	✓	✓				
		" SOFA D.	DAU	W	F	OCT. 1878	21	S				KY	KY	KY							✓	✓					
		" EMMA D.	DAU	W	F	MAY. 1884	16	S				KY	KY	KY				AT SCHOOL		3	✓	✓					
		" CRITTIE R.	DAU	W	F	APR. 1887	13	S				KY	KY	KY				AT SCHOOL		2½	✓	✓					
		" TANDY E.	SON	W	M	FEB. 1890	10	S				KY	KY	KY				AT SCHOOL		4	✓	✓	✓				
		" JENNIE M.	DAU	W	F	APR. 1892	8	S				KY	KY	KY				AT SCHOOL		4							
		" AUBREY S.	SON	W	M	SEP. 1895	4	S				KY	KY	KY													
		" ALMA B.	DAU	W	F	JUN. 1898	1	S				KY	KY	KY													
214	216	PROFFITT, THOMAS W.	HEAD	W	M	NOV. 1833	66	M	45			TN	TN	TN				FARMER			✓	✓	✓	O	F	F	177
		" MARGET	WIFE	W	F	SEP. 1834	65	M	45	11	10	TN	TN	TN							✓	X	✓				
		" VIRGIL C.	SON	W	M	MAY. 1880	20	S				KY	TN	TN				FARM LABORER		5	✓	✓	✓				
		GRAMLIN, JOHN M.	LODGER	W	M	OCT. 1883	16	S				KY	KY	KY				FARM LABORER		5	✓	✓	✓				
		" ROBERT M.	LODGER	W	M	MAY. 1886	14	S				KY	KY	KY				FARM LABORER		4	✓	✓	✓				
		PROFFITT, MATILDA	SISTER	W	F	NOV. 1831	68	S				TN	TN	TN							✓	✓	✓				
215	217	APOLIS, LECK	HEAD	W	M	MAR. 1877	23	M	4			KY	KY	KY				FARMER			✓	✓	✓	R		F	178
		" LIZZIE	WIFE	W	F	JUL. 1878	21	M	4	2	2	KY	KY	KY							✓	✓	✓				
		" HOMER	SON	W	M	JUL. 1897	2	S				KY	KY	KY													

STATE - KENTUCKY
COUNTY - MONROE
Township or other division: GAMALIEL
Enumerator: ISAAC N. RENEAU
Supervisor's Dist. No. 102   Sheet No. ___
Enumeration Dist. No. 87

No. of Family	No. of Dwelling	NAME	Relation	Color	Sex	Date of Birth Mon/Yr	Age at last birthday	Marital Status	# Years married	Mother of how many children	# of these children living	Place of birth (this person)	Father of this person	Mother of this person	Occupation	Attended school in months	Can read	Can write	Speak English	Owned or Rent	Farm or house	# of farm schedule
		APOLIS, OLIE	DAU	W	F	May-1899	1	S				KY	KY	KY								
216	218	HAYES, HARLIN	HEAD	W	M	Nov-1854	45	M	22			KY	KY	TN	FARMER		✓	✓	✓	O	F F	179
		" KATE C	WIFE	W	F	Apr-1857	43	M	22	3	3	KY	KY	KY			✓	✓	✓			
		" JOHN H	SON	W	M	Jan-1890	10	S				KY	KY	KY	AT SCHOOL		✓	✓				
		" NANNIE M	DAU	W	F	May-1896	4	S				KY	KY	KY		4	✓	✓				
217	219	TAYLOR, ESIBEL J	HEAD	W	F	Apr-1850	50	WD	11	9		KY	KY	KY	FARMER		✓	✓	✓	O	F F	180
		" HERBERT H	SON	W	M	Sep-1876	23	S				KY	KY	KY	FARM LABORER		✓	✓	✓			
		" ORIE J	DAU	W	F	Nov-1879	20	S				KY	KY	KY	SCHOOL TEACHER 7		✓	✓	✓			
		" GEORGE C	SON	W	M	Apr-1882	18	S				KY	KY	KY	FARM LABORER	4	✓	✓	✓			
		" BERDIE K	DAU	W	F	Jan-1887	13	S				KY	KY	KY		5	✓	✓	✓			
		" JAMES O	SON	W	M	Apr-1890	10	S				KY	KY	KY		5	✓	✓	✓			
218	220	COMER, ROBERT F	HEAD	W	M	Apr-1847	53	M	34			KY	TN	KY	FARMER		✓	✓	✓	O	E E	181
		" MARY F	WIFE	W	F	Aug-1846	53	M	34	12	10	KY	KY	KY			✓	✓	✓			
		" HATTIE	DAU	W	F	Oct-1876	23	S				KY	KY	KY	SCHOOL TEACHER 4		✓	✓	✓			
		" MAUD	DAU	W	F	Dec-1877	22	S				KY	KY	KY			✓	✓	✓			
		" JEFFERSON J	SON	W	M	May-1880	20	S				KY	KY	KY	FARM LABORER	7	✓	✓	✓			
		" RUBY	DAU	W	F	Feb-1884	16	S				KY	KY	KY	AT							
		" JAMES H	SON	W	M	Jun-1886	13	S				KY	KY	KY	AT							
		" ORAL L	SON	W	M	Jan-1888	12	S				KY	KY	KY	AT							
		" WILLIAM B	SON	W	M	Jan-1890	10	S				KY	KY	KY	AT							
219	221	WEST, JOHN	HEAD	B	M	May-1875	25	M	3			TN	TN	TN	FARMER		✓	X	✓	R	F	182
		" EFFIE	WIFE	B	F	Jan-1862	18	M	3	1	1	KY	KY	KY			✓	✓	✓			
		" RADFORD	SON	B	M	Jun-1899	11/12	S				KY	KY	KY								
220	222	CROW, JAMES	HEAD	W	M	Oct-1858	41	M	14			KY	TN	TN	FARMER		X	X	✓	R	F	183
		" SARAH	WIFE	W	F	Feb-1866	34	M	14	7	7	KY	KY	KY			✓	✓	✓			
		" JESSEY	SON	W	M	Nov-1886	13	S				KY	KY	KY	FARM LABORER	4	✓	✓	✓			

STATE - KENTUCKY
COUNTY - MONROE
Township or other division GAMAHEL

Enumerator ISAAC N. RENEAU

Supervisor's Dist. No. 102 Sheet No.
Enumeration Dist. No. 87

No. of Family	No. of Dwelling	NAME	Relation	Color	Sex	DATE OF BIRTH Mon/Yr	Age at last birthday	Marital Status	# Years married	Mother of how many children?	# of these children living	Place of birth (this person)	Father of this person	Mother of this person	Year of immigr.	# years in U.S.	Naturalization	OCCUPATION 10 years +	Months not employed	Attended school in months	Can read	Can write	Speak English	Owned or Rent	Owned –no mortage	Farm or house	# of farm schedule
		CROW, VANUS	Son	W	M	Oct. 1888	11	S					KY	KY	KY				FARM LABORER	4		✓	✓	✓				
		" CLAUD	Son	W	M	Aug. 1890	9	S					KY	KY	KY				AT SCHOOL	4								
		" THOMAS	Son	W	M	Aug. 1892	7	S					KY	KY	KY				AT SCHOOL	4								
		" CLARA	Dau	W	F	Aug. 1894	5	S					KY	KY	KY													
		" BURLEY	Son	W	M	Jan. 1897	3	S					KY	KY	KY													
		" HUBERT	Son	W	M	Apr. 1899	1	S					KY	KY	KY													
221	223	NEWMAN, JOHN J.	Head	W	M	Dec. 1833	66	WD				TN	NC	KY				FARMER			✓	✓		O	F	F	184
		BAILEY, SARAH E.	Lodger	W	F	Jul. 1877	22	S				KY	KY	KY				HOUSEKEEPER			✓	✓	✓				
		" J. DOUGLAS	Lodger	W	M	Feb. 1894	6	S				KY	TN	KY													
		" OFFEY B.	Lodger	W	M	Jan. 1896	4	S				KY	TN	KY													
222	224	ENGLAND, LEE R.	Head	W	M	Dec. 1857	42	M	6			KY	KY	TN				FARMER			✓	✓	✓	O	F	F	185
		" MARY J.	Wife	W	F	Sep. 1876	23	M	6	3	3	KY	TN	TN							✓	✓	✓				
		" FRANK	Son	W	M	Jul. 1894	5	S				KY	KY	KY													
		" WILLIAM H.	Son	W	M	Jan. 1897	3	S				KY	KY	KY													
		" ULA C.	Dau	W	F	Feb. 1899	1	S				KY	KY	KY													
223	225	ADAMS, WILLIAM	Head	W	M	Jul. 1845	54	M	14			TN	VA	TN				FARMER			✓	✓	✓	O	F	F	186
		" MARY E.	Wife	W	F	Jul. 1859	40	M	14	9	5	KY	TN	TN							X	X	X				
		" JERRY F.	Son	W	M	May. 1878	22	S				KY	TN	KY				FARMER			✓	✓	✓				
		" AVERY	Son	W	M	Nov. 1885	14	S				KY	KY	KY				FARM LABORER	2½		✓	✓	✓				
		" ONIE	Dau	W	F	Jan. 1889	11	S				KY	TN	KY				AT SCHOOL		5	✓	✓	✓				
		" NELSON	Son	W	M	Jul. 1892	7	S				KY	TN	KY				AT SCHOOL		5							
		" BETTIE	Dau	W	F	Jan. 1895	5	S				KY	TN	KY													
		" ANDREW	Son	W	M	Dec. 1898	1	S				KY	TN	KY													
224	226	MOORE, LANDON D	Head	W	M	Apr. 1857	43	M	18			TN	TN	KY				FARMER			✓	✓	✓	O	F	F	187
		" LUCETTIE	Wife	W	F	Jul. 1862	37	M	18	4	4	TN	TN	TN							✓	✓	✓				
		" OSCAR	Son	W	M	Dec. 1882	17	S				TN	TN	TN				FARM LABORER	5		✓	✓	✓				

STATE - KENTUCKY
COUNTY - MONROE
Township or other division **GAMALIEL**

Enumerator **ISAAC N. RENEAU**

Supervisor's Dist. No. _102_ Sheet No.
Enumeration Dist. No. _87_

No. of Family	No. of Dwelling	NAME	Relation	Color	Sex	Date of Birth Mon/Yr	Age at last birthday	Marital Status	# Years married	Mother of how many children?	# of these children living	Place of birth (this person)	Father of this person	Mother of this person	Year of immigr.	# years in U.S.	Naturalization	OCCUPATION 10 years +	Months not employed	Attended school in months	Can read	Can write	Speak English	Owned or Rent	Owned -no mortgage	Farm or house	# of farm schedule
		MOORE, OVIE	DAU	W	F	SEP. 1886	13	S				TN	TN	TN				AT SCHOOL		5	✓	✓					
		" ULAR	DAU	W	F	JUL. 1889	10	S				KY	TN	TN				AT SCHOOL		4	✓	✓					
		" IVA B.	DAU	W	F	DEC. 1895	4	S				KY	TN	TN													
225	227	MARSHALL, GEORGE W.	HEAD	W	M	OCT. 1861	38	M	19			TN	MO	TN				FARMER			✓	✓	✓	O	M	F	188
		" MARY E.	WIFE	W	F	FEB. 1861	39	M	19	4	4	KY	TN	TN							✓	✓					
		" HASCHAL	SON	W	M	DEC. 1881	18	S				TN	TN	KY				FARM LABORER		6	✓	✓					
		" CLAUD J.	SON	W	M	JAN. 1884	16	S				KY	TN	KY				FARM LABORER		6	✓	✓					
		" PEARL	DAU	W	F	JUL. 1887	12	S				KY	TN	KY				AT SCHOOL		5	✓	✓					
		" HOMER	SON	W	M	OCT. 1890	9	S				KY	TN	KY				AT SCHOOL		5	✓	✓					
		SILVEY, WILLIAM	BRO-IN-LAW	W	M	NOV. 1870	29	S				KY	KY	TN							X	X					
226	228	COMPTON, HIRAM	HEAD	W	M	MAY 1848	52	M	20			KY	TN	TN				FARMER			✓	✓	✓	O	F	F	189
		" PARZETTIE	WIFE	W	F	APR. 1861	39	M	20	7	7	KY	KY	TN							✓	✓					
		" LONA A.	DAU	W	F	SEP. 1881	18	S				KY	KY	KY							✓	✓					
		" PALO	SON	W	M	JAN. 1883	17	S				KY	KY	KY				FARM LABORER			✓	✓					
		" FLORA	DAU	W	F	FEB. 1885	15	S				KY	KY	KY				AT SCHOOL		3½	✓	✓					
		" EDGAR	SON	W	M	MAR. 1887	13	S				KY	KY	KY				AT SCHOOL		3½	✓	✓					
		" ULAR C.	DAU	W	F	AUG. 1893	6	S				KY	KY	KY							✓	✓					
		" ESSIE B.	DAU	W	F	OCT. 1895	4	S				KY	KY	KY							✓	✓					
		" BESSIE	DAU	W	F	MAR. 1898	2	S				KY	KY	KY							✓	✓					
227	229	CROW, NELSON	HEAD	W	M	APR. 1858	42	M	14			KY	TN	TN				FARMER			✓	✓	✓	O	F	F	190
		" PARZETTI	WIFE	W	F	DEC. 1863	36	M	14	5	5	KY	KY	KY							✓	✓					
		" BERTHIE B.	DAU	W	F	SEP. 1888	11	S				KY	KY	KY				AT SCHOOL		5	✓	✓					
		" FATE	SON	W	M	AUG. 1890	9	S				KY	KY	KY				AT SCHOOL		4							
		" DILLIE A.	DAU	W	F	APR. 1892	8	S				KY	KY	KY				AT SCHOOL		4							
		" SARAH J.	DAU	W	F	SEP. 1893	6	S				KY	KY	KY													
		" VADIE	DAU	W	F	FEB. 1898	2	S				KY	KY	KY													

STATE - KENTUCKY
COUNTY - MONROE
Township or other division GAMALIEL
Enumerator ISAAC N. RENEAU

Supervisor's Dist. No. 102 Sheet No.
Enumeration Dist. No. 87

Location No. of Family	No. of Dwelling	NAME	Relation	Color	Sex	DATE OF BIRTH Mon/Yr	Age at last birthday	Marital Status	# Years married	Mother of how many children?	# of these children living	Place of birth [this person]	Father of this person	Mother of this person	CITIZENSHIP	OCCUPATION 10 years +	Months not employed	Attended school in months	Can read	Can write	Speak English	Owned or Rent	Owned - no mortgage	Farm or house	# of farm schedule
228	270	STEEN, JOHN W.	Head	W	M	Nov. 1877	22	M	3			KY	KY	KY		FARMER			✓	✓	✓	R		F	191
		" SOFLONIE B.	Wife	W	F	May. 1879	21	M	3	0	0	KY	KY	KY					✓	✓	✓				
	231	STEEN, WILLIAM S.	Head	W	M	Sep. 1865	34	M	4			KY	KY	KY		FARMER			✓	✓	✓	O	M	F	192
		" SUSAN	Wife	W	F	Feb. 1849	51	M	4	0	0	TN	TN	TN					X	X	✓				
		" ALICE	Dau	W	F	Sep. 1888	11	S				KY	KY	KY		AT SCHOOL		4	✓	✓	✓				
		" THOMAS	Son	W	M	Aug. 1890	9	S				KY	KY	KY		AT SCHOOL		5		✓	✓				
		" MIRTLE	Dau	W	F	Jun. 1893	6	S				KY	KY	KY		AT SCHOOL		3							
229	232	POWELL, RUPHAS C.	Head	W	M	May. 1831	69	M	9			TN	NC	TN		FARMER			✓	✓	✓	R		F	193
		" MANERVA	Wife	W	F	Jan. 1874	26	M	9	6	5	KY	TN	KY					✓	✓					
		" LADY B.	Dau	W	F	Mar. 1894	6	S				KY	TN	KY											
		" DONNY M.	Dau	W	F	May. 1895	5	S				KY	TN	KY											
		" RUPHAS C. JR	Son	W	M	Jan. 1897	3	S				KY	TN	KY											
		" WILLIAM M.	Son	W	M	Oct. 1898	1	S				KY	TN	KY											
		" EDMON T.	Son	W	M	Apr. 1900	2/12	S				KY	TN	KY		FARMER			✓	✓	✓	O	E	F	194
230	233	BRAY, GEORGE	Head	W	M	Mar. 1853	47	M	20			TN	KY	KY					✓	✓	✓				
		" SALETIE A.	Wife	W	F	Dec. 1859	40	M	20	7	4	TN	KY	TN					✓	✓	✓				
		" WILMER	Son	W	M	Oct. 1881	18	S				KY	TN	TN		FARM LABORER		3	✓	✓	✓				
		" EMMER	Dau	W	F	Mar. 1883	17	S				KY	TN	TN					✓	✓	✓				
		" LONNIE	Son	W	M	Feb. 1890	10	S				KY	TN	TN		AT SCHOOL		4	✓	✓	✓				
		" CARLIS	Son	W	M	Oct. 1892	7	S				KY	TN	TN		AT SCHOOL		3½							
231	234	STEWART, JOSEPH W.	Head	W	M	Jan. 1843	57	M	22			TN	MISS	PA	MISSISSIPPI	FARMER			X	X	✓	R		F	195
		" MATILDA E.	Wife	W	F	May. 1862	38	M	22	11	6	TN	TN	TN		FARMER			X	X	✓				
		" JOHN W.	Son	W	M	Jul. 1882	17	S				KY	TN	TN		FARMER			✓	✓	✓				
		" ELLEN	Dau	W	F	Mar. 1885	15	S				KY	TN	TN		AT SCHOOL		2	✓	✓	✓				
		" DORA E.	Dau	W	F	May. 1889	11	S				KY	TN	TN		AT SCHOOL		2	X	X	✓				
		" DONA	Dau	W	F	Oct. 1891	8	S				KY	TN	TN		AT SCHOOL		1							

STATE - KENTUCKY
COUNTY - MONROE
Township or other division GAMALIEL   Enumerator ISAAC N. RENEAU

Supervisor's Dist. No. _102_ Sheet No.
Enumeration Dist. No. _57_

No. of Family	No. of Dwelling	NAME	Relation	Color	Sex	DATE OF BIRTH Mon/Yr	Age at last birthday	Marital Status	# Years married	Mother of how many children?	# of these children living	Place of birth [this person]	Father of this person	Mother of this person	Year of immigr.	# years in U.S.	Naturalization	OCCUPATION 10 years +	Months not employed	Attended school in months	Can read	Can write	Speak English	Owned or Rent	Owned -no mortage	Farm or house	# of farm schedule
		STEWART, ISAM K.	SON	W	M	AUG·1895	4	S				KY	TN	TN													
		" HERSHAL R.	SON	W	M	OCT·1899 8/12		S				KY	TN	TN													
232	235	COUNTS, ISAAC N.	HEAD	W	M	NOV·1865	34	M	5			KY	TN	KY				FARMER			✓	✓		R		F	196
		" BURNETTIE	WIFE	W	F	APR·1873	27	M	5	3	3	KY	KY	KY							✓	✓					
		" MARY L.	DAU	W	F	NOV·1894	5	S				KY	KY	KY													
		" HENRY J.	SON	W	M	FEB·1896	4	S				KY	KY	KY													
		" ADOLPHAS	SON	W	M	AUG·1897	2	S				KY	KY	KY													
233	236	SISCO, ELISHA	HEAD	W	M	JUL·1842	57	M	36			TN	TN	TN				FARMER			X	X	✓	O		F	197
		" EMILINE	WIFE	W	F	MAY·1843	57	M	36	7	4	TN	TN	VA							✓	✓	✓				
		" ELLEN	DAU	W	F	MAY·1868	32	S				TN	TN	TN							✓	✓	✓				
		" THOMAS	SON	W	M	OCT·1873	26	S				TN	TN	TN				FARM LABORER			✓	✓	✓				
234	237	SISCO, WILLIAM	HEAD	W	M	APR·1875	25	M	5			TN	TN	TN				FARMER			✓	✓	✓	R		F	198
		" ADER	WIFE	W	F	JUL·1876	23	M	5	2	2	KY	KY	TN							✓	✓	✓				
		" ALTIE	DAU	W	F	FEB·1897	3	S				KY	TN	KY													
		" ELISHA, JR	SON	W	M	JUL·1899 10/12		S				KY	TN	KY													
235	238	APPLE, LUKE G.	HEAD	W	M	DEC·1865	34	M	15			TN	TN	TN				LABORER (SAW MILL)			✓	✓	✓	R		F	199
		" MARTHY A.	WIFE	W	F	NOV·1867	32	M	15	6	4	TN	TN	TN							✓	✓	✓				
		" ALTIE M.	DAU	W	F	DEC·1888	11	S				TN	TN	TN				AT SCHOOL		5	✓	✓	✓				
		" ORIE L.	DAU	W	F	JUN·1892	7	S				TN	TN	TN				AT SCHOOL		5							
		" EVIE E.	DAU	W	F	NOV·1895	4	S				TN	TN	TN													
		" NEVADA M.	DAU	W	F	JUL·1898	1	S				KY	TN	TN													
		" ZEKLE	BROTHER	W	M	FEB·1882	18	S				TN	TN	TN				LABORER (SAW MILL)			✓	✓	✓				
236	239	DECKARD, JAMES H.	HEAD	W	M	MAR·1837	63	M	39			TN	TN	TN				FARMER			✓	✓	✓	O		F	200
		" DORCAS	WIFE	W	F	JAN·1838	62	M	39	9	9	TN	TN	TN							X	X	✓				
		" CASIL	SON	W	M	FEB·1876	24	S				KY	TN	TN				FARM LABORER			✓	✓	✓				
		" NOLIA	DAU	W	F	APR·1883	17	S				KY	TN	TN				AT SCHOOL		2	✓	✓	✓				

STATE - KENTUCKY
COUNTY - MONROE
Township or other division GAMALIEL Enumerator ISAAC N. RENEAU

Supervisor's Dist. No. 102 Sheet No.
Enumeration Dist. No. 87

Location (No. Family / No. Dwelling)	NAME	Relation	Color	Sex	Date of Birth Mon/Yr	Age at last birthday	Marital Status	# Years married	Mother of how many children	# of these children living	Place of birth (this person)	Father	Mother	Occupation	Attended school in months	Can read	Can write	Speak English	Owned or Rent	Farm or house	# of farm schedule
237 240	DECKARD, CANCEL	HEAD	W	M	DEC. 1879	20	M	2			KY	TN	TN	FARMER		✓	✓	✓	R	F	201
"	LENA	WIFE	W	F	NOV. 1881	18	M	2	0	0	KY	KY	KY			✓	✓	✓			
238 241	DECKARD, JAMES W.	HEAD	W	M	FEB. 1868	32	M	9			KY	TN	TN	FARMER		✓	✓	✓	R	F	202
"	FLORENCE	WIFE	W	F	OCT. 1875	24	M	9	4	4	KY	KY	KY			✓	✓	✓			
"	BECCA	DAU	W	F	APR. 1893	7	S				KY	KY	KY	AT SCHOOL	4						
"	ONIE	DAU	W	F	JAN. 1894	6	S				KY	KY	KY								
"	FRANK	SON	W	M	JUN. 1896	3	S				KY	KY	KY								
"	OCIE	DAU	W	F	MAY 1898	2	S				KY	KY	KY								
239 242	FORD, BENJAMIN	HEAD	W	M	AUG. 1836	63	M	35			TN	TN	TN	FARMER		X	X	✓	O	F	203
"	CATHERINE	WIFE	W	F	JAN. 1842	58	M	35	8	7	TN	TN	TN			X	X	✓			
"	NERVA	DAU	W	F	OCT. 1874	25	S				TN	TN	TN			✓	✓	✓			
"	WALTER J.	SON	W	M	MAY 1883	17	S				KY	TN	TN	FARM LABORER		✓	✓	✓			
"	HARRISON	GR-SON	W	M	NOV. 1890	9	S				KY	KY	KY	AT SCHOOL	5						
"	CHARLEY	GR-SON	W	M	JAN. 1893	7	S				KY	KY	KY	AT SCHOOL	3						
240 243	SMITH, AARON Y.	HEAD	W	M	MAY 1839	61	M	5			TN	TN	TN	FARMER		✓	✓	✓	O	F	204
"	LETHA B.	WIFE	W	F	NOV. 1860	39	M	5	2	2	TN	TN	TN			✓	✓	✓			
"	MOSIER M.	SON	W	M	OCT. 1876	23	S				TN	TN	KY	SCHOOL TEACHER		✓	✓	✓			
"	ELLIE M.	DAU	W	F	JAN. 1882	18	S				TN	TN	KY	AT SCHOOL	3	✓	✓	✓			
"	AARON I.	SON	W	M	FEB. 1885	15	S				TN	TN	KY	FARM LABORER	5	✓	✓				
"	EDNA H.	DAU	W	F	DEC. 1887	12	S				TN	TN	KY	AT SCHOOL	4 5	✓	✓	✓			
"	GLADICE W.	DAU	W	F	MAY 1895	5	S				TN	TN	TN								
"	AZEL C.	SON	W	M	OCT. 1897	2	S				TN	TN	TN								
241 244	McALPIN, MARTHA	HEAD	W	F	NOV. [1878?] 22		WD		5	5	TN	TN	KY			✓	✓	✓	R	H	
"	LAROO	SON	W	F	JUL. 1898	11					TN	TN	TN	AT SCHOOL	5	✓	✓	✓			
"	HESPER	DAU	W	F	DEC. 1891	8	S				TN	TN	TN	AT SCHOOL	5						
"	ANNIE	DAU	W	F	OCT. 1893	6	S				TN	TN	TN								

STATE - KENTUCKY
COUNTY - MONROE
Township or other division **GAMALIEL**   Enumerator **ISAAC N. RENEAU**

Supervisor's Dist. No. **102** Sheet No.
Enumeration Dist. No. **87**

No. of Family	No. of Dwelling	NAME	Relation	Color	Sex	DATE OF BIRTH Mon/Yr	Age at last birthday	Marital Status	# Years married	Mother of how many children?	# of these children living	Place of birth (this person)	Father of this person	Mother of this person	Year of immigr.	# years in U.S.	Naturalization	OCCUPATION (10 years +)	Months not employed	Attended school in months	Can read	Can write	Speak English	Owned or Rent	Owned –no mortg.	Farm or house	# of farm schedule	
(283)		RAY, SIDNEY C.	SON	W	M	Nov. 1885	14	S				TN	TN	TN				AT SCHOOL		2½	✓	✓	✓					
	"	MARY T.	DAU	W	F	Oct. 1888	11	S				TN	TN	TN							✓	✓	✓					
	"	EARNEST T.	SON	W	M	Feb. 1892	8	S				TN	TN	TN				AT SCHOOL		5		✓	✓					
	"	FRED B.	SON	W	M	Aug. 1896	3	S				TN	TN	TN														
	"	HERMAN T.	SON	W	M	Aug. 1899	9/10	S				TN	TN	TN														

HERE ENDS GAMALIEL

Unreadable Surnames
P. 185-186 -195-201-218-395 Check here
to see if it might be one of your family!

ABSHIRE 395
ADAMS 62-65-367-373-384-495
ADISON 96
ADWELL 97
AGERS 1-61-121
ALBANY 366
ALLEE 94-339
ALLEN 61-222-459-460-463-502-503-
506-507
ALONZO 234
ALVIS 387
AMYX 173
ANDERS 231-232
ANDERSON 194-196-255-350-402
ANDREWS 221-222
APPLE 498
APOLIS 493-494
ARMS 212
ARMSTRONG 331-334-338-378-381
ARNETT 289-304
ARNOLD 408
ARTERBERRY 187-188
ARTERBURN 10-19-82-107-116-388-
406-407-429-442-443-
437-445
ARTIBURN 486-487
ASHLOCK 190
ATCHLEY 203-213-295

AUSTIN 31-36-40
AUTRY 249

BACHELDER 68
BACON 119-431-436-445-446
BAILEY 128-189-192-217-272
292-293-295-296-297
489-495
BAILY 507
BALARD 249
BALES 462-463
BALL 243
BARBER 403
BARKER 359
BARKESELL 205-207
BARLOW 28-95-97-109-130
BARNES 272
BARNS 411
BARR 335
BARTLEY 91-106-108-109-134
135-149-151-156-158-165
275-276-332-333-372-386
422-423-431-432-437-438
BASIL See BAZZLE
BASKET, BASKETT 193-215-217
264
BASS 39
BAXTER 262-263-330
BAYSE 241

BAZZLE 134-146-154-169-387-392
BE-? 218

BEALS 14-457
BEATON 65
BECK 171-351
BECKHAN 75-76
BEDFORD 152-153-220-221-222-223
255
BEDWELL 288
BELCHER 119-124-131-136-153-177
178-180-478-479-491-492
BERNETTE 349 see also BURNETT
BIBY 438 see also BYBEE
BIGGERS 179
BIGGERSTAFF 215-216-223-238-239
243-259-277-280-323
BIGHT 247
BILLINGSLEY 146-163-429
BIRCH 144-147
BIRDWELL 319
BIRG 89
BIRGE 389-428-429-430-443
BISHOP 44-46-302
BLACK 81-297
BLAIR 231-232 see also BLARE
BLAND 279
BLANKENSHIP 468
BLARE 189 see also BLAIR
BLYSE 39
BOCKMAN 167
BOLES 120-191 see also BOWLES,
BOWLS
BOLTON 242
BOON 185-190-191-198-200-278-299

CLEMMONS 440
COBY 1
CLOID 248
CLOYD 239-278-327
COCHRAN 93-94COE
198-203-204-205-207-214-215-242-243
COFFEE 294
COFFELT 361
COLEY 477
COLLEY 24
COLLINS 6-7-17
COLMAN 239
COLTER 310 see also COULTER
COMBS 60-88-90-91-92-264-301
COMER 37-305-334-433-459-461-465
      492-494
COMPTON 309-317-329-496-506
CONDRA 321-324-353
CONKIN 257-258-324-327-328
COOK 34-35-36-37-47-58-105-106
COOKSIE 399
COPAS-COPASS 139-161-221-253
      264-265-274-332-333-345
      346-352-361-389-412-416
COPASS cont. 417-501-502-507
CORNWELL 319-355
CORRO 236-237
COSBY 66
COULTER 328-329-367-370-372-377
      378-383 see also COLTER
COUNTS 55-78-260-498-500
COX 311-503-504

CRABTREE   55-187-443-444-447
      448-463
CRAFFORD   213-234-235-242-243
      259-260 see also
      CRAWFORD
CRAIGHEAD 305
CRAG 469-470
CRANE 290
CRANFORD 356
CRANTZ 37
CRAW FORD 45-465-471-472 see
      Also CRAFFORD
CREASY 485
CREEK 2-16-61-62-63-76-123-360
      470-474-475-476
CREWS 160-170 see also CRUISE,
      CRUSE, CRUZE
CROFFORD 289-319 see also
      CRAWFORD
CROPPER 472
CROSS 21-24
CROW 76-236-358-359-360-361-364
      366-367-370-371-483
CROW, cont. 484-490-494-495-496
CROWBOX 310
CRUISE 478 see also CREWS, CRUSE,
      CRUZE
CRUSE 140
CRUZE 154
CULLENS 258
CURTIS 154-155-168-310-327-364
      367-368-399-406

DANIEL 71
DANIELS 454
DARVY 286
DAUSY 397 see also DOSSEY
DAVIS 7-61-172-173-190-260-267
      290-296-308-321-322-331
      332-337-356-393-395
      436-448
DAWSON 52
DECARD 362-363 see also DECKARD
DECK 202
DECKARD 472-473-478-498-499-500
      504-505-506
DEMPSY 42-43
DENHAM 11-93-94-95-113-158-165
      197-322-338-347-356-371
      376-383-405-419-427
DEWEESE 9-76-77
DIAL 48-104-112
DICKEN 191-293
DICKENS 185-255
DICKERSON 10-177-386-387-479-480
DIRE 193-218 see also DYER-DYRE
DISMAN 6-467-453
DISHMAN 263
DIXION 260
DIXON 143-450
DOCKRY 167
DODSON 211-215-221-235-330
DOLLIN 12
DONOHO 461

GEE 17-202-203-214-223-281-325-410

GENTRY 36-37-41-75-78-103-110-111
125-241-242-250-320-335-347
395-399-409-437-439-440-441
452-457

GERALD 115

GETTINGS 227

GHINT 50

GIBBS 37-41

GIDONS 245

GILL 335

GILLAM 43

GILLENWATERS 7-8-12-13-14-15-28
30-51-106-282-321-355

GIPSON 407

GIT 197

GLAZEBROOK 258

GLOVER 406

GLURES 53

GOAD 21-23-26-29-35-36-38-42-298
302-344-365-369-370-403-462

GOLDEN 92 see also GAULDEN

GOODALL 111-121

GOODE 458-481

GOODMAN 36-39-40-41-42-45-46-49
112

GOOLSBEY 113-187-197-345

GORDON 398

GOSNELL 118

GRACE 282-297-300-304-305-420

GRAMLIN 375-481-482-493

GRAVEN 343-387-404

GRAVENS 271

GRAVES 17-214-222-231-260-283

GRAVIN 257-258

GRAY 196-201-233-234-237-407

GREEN 1-5-7-9-336-337465-470

GREENE 258

GREENUP 355

GREGORY 45-48

GRIDER 168-177-232-400

GRIMESLY 142-177-218-265-288
346-416-435

GRINESTAFF 303-307-

GRISAM 461

GRISHAM 461

GRISSOM 183-283-296-297-298
299-339

GROGAN 200

GROOM[S] 27-39

GUEST 337

GUFFEY 500

GUINN 343-377

GULLEY 244-363

GUM 28-29-60-65-382-422-470-478

GWYNNE 467-468

HADDOCK 339

HAGAN 23-33-34-40-53-135-141-145
146-147-153-156-157-165-168
174-251-259-272-273-341-391
392-396-397-398

HALCOMB 63-457-458

HALE 10-60-111-156-175-196-309
310-322-352-353-354-355-366
369-370-378-379-462-485-486

HALL 77-203-244-245-295-304-338
357-358-371-374-376-420

HALLCELL 197-198-201-202-204
209-210-236

HALSELL 277

HAME 129

HAMILTON 431-432-440-441-442
443-444-462

HAMMER 232-233-267-268-289-314
315-316-325-329-330-351
367-369-385-387-388-395
398-404-405-503

HAMMETT 96

HAMPTON 200

HANNER 324

HARDEN 223

HARDIN 143-144-159

HARGIS 476

HARIS 219-236-243 see also HARRIS

HARLAN 96-141-142-157-158-160-167
170-171-172-174-179-258
264-322-331-339-348-423
460-462-488

HARLIN 37-38-93-267

HARP 31-32

HARPER 172

HARRIS 36-47-178-347-385

HARRISON 393

HART 402

KELLEY 294
KELS 233
KELSO 121
KEMP 335
KERBY 467
KEY 4-16-48-49-68-372-375
KEYS 102-368-369-372
KIDWELL 233-249-283-284-333
     338-399
KING 4-453-454
KINGERY 86-164-421-424-425-433
     434-435-436-438-445
KINGRY 358-361-362
KINSLOW 8
KIRBY 21-112-116-122
KIRK 220-239-240-258-417
KIRKPATRICK 120-220-225-226-227
     230-349-350-476
KITTER 101
KNIGHT 119
KNUCKLES 171
KUR [KERR?] 214

LANCASTER 5-6
LANDERS 323
LANDRUM 19
LANE see also LAYNE 38-43-101-102
     128-129
LANEY 239
LANGFORD 481
LANKFORD 348

LARANCE 118
LAUHERN 201
LAWRENCE 26
LAWSON 110-295
LAYNE see also LANE 47-53-432
LEASTER 171-172
LEE 5-27-55-72-92-93-102-103-125-323
LEFEVER 354
LEMONS 168
LESLIE 259-324-325-340
LESTER 331
LEVI 260
LEWIS 5-29-57-502
LIGHTFOOT 17
LIKESTON 209
LOGAN 236
LOLLAR 212
LONG 207-208-215
LOUIS 260
LOVELADY 111
LOYD 19-20-83-107-111-123
LUIS 254
LYNES 128
LYON 279-280
LYONS 96-409-424

McALPIN 499-500
McCLERRAN 183
McCOIN 363
McCORGAH 461
McCOY 238-352-456-457-484-504
McCRACKIN 473

McCREARY
McCUE 21-22-100-116-127
McDONALD 173
McGUIRE 163-164
McMILAND 211
McMILLAND 221-235
McMILLEN 121
McMILLIN 286-338-349
McMURTRY 378-401
McNEICE 320
McPEAK 5-250-251-449-453-454
McPHERSON 388-403-404-411-441
McWERTER 15
McWHERTER 137-325-344-430

MACUNE 100
MAHANY 67
MAINES 347-402
MANES 259
MARCUM 9-128
MARRS 86-396
MARS 268
MARSH 4
MARSHAL 264-268
MARSHALL 331-362-496
MARTAIN 97-100-104-115-119-120
MARTIN 67-273-339-359-360-409-410
     411-419-423-428-502-507
MASON 100-101
MATHENA 350
MATHENIA 377
MATHEWS 287

TREVITT 74
TRIVETT 79
TUDOR 443
TURNER 6-15-37-49-72-73-74-75-76-77
78-84-85-86-87-90-92-98-99
104-113-115-120-225-252-260
338-372-374-375-405-452-460
461-467-468-474-475-481
TYREE 79-80-412

UPTERGROVE 380-394

VAN 290
VANCE 10-220-274-334-443
VANEVER 234
VAUGHN 2-204-449
VAUTER 135
VAWTER 142
VEACH 99-100
VIBBERT 250
VIBERT 180-236

WADE 442-479
WALBERT 34-35
WALDEN 137-141-150-170-346-348
350-386-387
WALDON 232
WALKER 90-145-160-161-177-386-407
429-437
WALLER 33-44-97-98-301-356-412-413
WALLING 151

WARD 20-23-27-117-118-462
WARDE 104
WASHAM 159
WATSON 183-184-185-186-234
WATT 446
WAX 74-114-384-422
WEAVER 349
WEBB 125-126-425-426-436-443
490-491
WEIR 334
WELBORN 91
WELCH 58-107-108-339-340-387
WEST 489-494
WHEAT 52-53-70-71-174-320-321-324
366-381-418-421
WHEELER 18-451
WHITE 152-153-157-173-174-185-215
216-225-238-239-257-263-264
303-317-328-338-390-399-417
430-439-444-445
WHITEHEAD 83-84-103-118-128
WHITESIDES 197-222
WHITLOW 441-446
WHITNEY 24-27
WILBORN 95-410-411-436-446-447-448
WILEY 162
WILKERSON 23
WILLIAMS 6-38-44-109-120-129-145
147-148-182-200-203-210-211
216-233-234-235-236-248-268
276-280-281-282-294-360-370
409

WILLIAMSON 41
WILLMORE 503
WILLSON 60-249
WILSON 57-163-172-248-249-372
401-478
WISDOM 127
WOLF 167
WOOD 27-184-264-266-295-306-307
308-309-318-319-321-323-326
331-338-350-351-370-372-397
404-412-422
WOODCOCK 66-468-469
WOODS 26-28-373
WRICH 73   see also RICH
WRIGHT 148-149-155-156-249-283
294-398-399

YATES 193
YOKELY-YOKLEY 17-18-262-268-269
270-272-327-331-339-345-394
YONG 122
YORK 56-452-453-456-475
YOUNG 27-50-204-218-272-360